Lecture Notes in Computer Science 8134

Commenced Publication in 1973
Founding and Former Series Editors:
Gerhard Goos, Juris Hartmanis, and Jan van Leeuwen

Lecture Notes in Computer Science 8143

Commenced Publication in 1973
Founding and Former Series Editors:
Gerhard Goos, Juris Hartmanis, and Jan van Leeuwen

Editorial Board

David Hutchison
Lancaster University, UK
Takeo Kanade
Carnegie Mellon University, Pittsburgh, PA, USA
Josef Kittler
University of Surrey, Guildford, UK
Jon M. Kleinberg
Cornell University, Ithaca, NY, USA
Alfred Kobsa
University of California, Irvine, CA, USA
Friedemann Mattern
ETH Zurich, Switzerland
John C. Mitchell
Stanford University, CA, USA
Moni Naor
Weizmann Institute of Science, Rehovot, Israel
Oscar Nierstrasz
University of Bern, Switzerland
C. Pandu Rangan
Indian Institute of Technology, Madras, India
Bernhard Steffen
TU Dortmund University, Germany
Madhu Sudan
Microsoft Research, Cambridge, MA, USA
Demetri Terzopoulos
University of California, Los Angeles, CA, USA
Doug Tygar
University of California, Berkeley, CA, USA
Gerhard Weikum
Max Planck Institute for Informatics, Saarbruecken, Germany

Jason Crampton   Sushil Jajodia
Keith Mayes (Eds.)

Computer Security – ESORICS 2013

18th European Symposium
on Research in Computer Security
Egham, UK, September 9-13, 2013
Proceedings

 Springer

Volume Editors

Jason Crampton
Royal Holloway, University of London
Information Security Group
Egham Hill, Egham, TW20 0EX, UK
E-mail: jason.crampton@rhul.ac.uk

Sushil Jajodia
George Mason University
Center for Secure Information Systems
4400 University Drive, Fairfax, VA 22030-4422, USA
E-mail: jajodia@gmu.edu

Keith Mayes
Royal Holloway, University of London
Information Security Group
Egham Hill, Egham, TW20 0EX, UK
E-mail: keith.mayes@rhul.ac.uk

ISSN 0302-9743   e-ISSN 1611-3349
ISBN 978-3-642-40202-9   e-ISBN 978-3-642-40203-6
DOI 10.1007/978-3-642-40203-6
Springer Heidelberg Dordrecht London New York

Library of Congress Control Number: 2013944563

CR Subject Classification (1998): K.6.5, E.3, D.4.6, K.4.4, C.2.0, J.1, H.2.7

LNCS Sublibrary: SL 4 – Security and Cryptology

Typesetting: Camera-ready by author, data conversion by Scientific Publishing Services, Chennai, India

Printed on acid-free paper

Springer is part of Springer Science+Business Media (www.springer.com)

Preface

This volume contains the papers selected for presentation at the 18th European Symposium on Research in Computer Security (ESORICS 2013), held during September 9–13, 2013, in Egham, UK.

In response to the symposium's call for papers, 242 papers were submitted to the conference from 38 countries. These papers were evaluated on the basis of their significance, novelty, technical quality, as well as on their practical impact and/or their level of advancement of the field's foundations.

The Program Committee's work was carried out electronically, yielding intensive discussions over a period of a few weeks. Of the papers submitted, 43 were selected for presentation at the conference (resulting in an acceptance rate of 18%). We note that many top-quality submissions were not selected for presentation because of the high technical level of the overall submissions, and we are certain that many of these submissions will, nevertheless, be published at other competitive forums in the future.

An event like ESORICS 2013 depends on the volunteering efforts of a host of individuals and the support of numerous institutes. There is a long list of people who volunteered their time and energy to put together and organize the conference, and who deserve special thanks. Thanks to all the members of the Program Committee and the external reviewers for all their hard work in evaluating the papers. We are also very grateful to all the people whose work ensured a smooth organization process: the ESORICS Steering Committee, and its Chair Pierangela Samarati in particular, for their support; Giovanni Livraga, for taking care of publicity; Sheila Cobourne, for maintaining the website; and the Local Organizing Committee, for helping with organization and taking care of local arrangements. We would also like to express our appreciation to everyone who organized the workshops (CATACRYPT, Cryptoforma, DPM, EUROPKI, QASA, SETOP, STM, Trustworthy Clouds) co-located with ESORICS. A number of organizations also deserve special thanks, including Royal Holloway University of London for acting as host, and the ESORICS sponsors: CESG, Transport for London, ISG Smart Card Centre, Crisp Telecom Limited, and NESSoS.

Last, but certainly not least, our thanks go to all the authors who submitted papers and all the symposium's attendees. We hope you find the proceedings of ESORICS 2013 stimulating and a source of inspiration for your future research and education programs.

September 2013

Jason Crampton
Sushil Jajodia
Keith Mayes

Organization

General Chair

Keith Mayes   Royal Holloway, University of London, UK

Program Chairs

Jason Crampton   Royal Holloway, University of London, UK
Sushil Jajodia   George Mason University, USA

ESORICS Steering Committee

Michael Backes   Saarland University, Germany
Joachim Biskup   University of Dortmund, Germany
Frédéric Cuppens   Télécom Bretagne, France
Sabrina De Capitani di
    Vimercati   Università degli Studi di Milano, Italy
Yves Deswarte   LAAS, France
Dieter Gollmann   TU Hamburg-Harburg, Germany
Sokratis Katsikas   University of Piraeus, Greece
Miroslaw Kutylowski   Wroclaw University of Technology, Poland
Javier Lopez   University of Malaga, Spain
Jean-Jacques Quisquater   UCL Crypto Group, Belgium
Peter Ryan   University of Luxembourg, Luxembourg
Pierangela Samarati (Chair)   Università degli Studi di Milano, Italy
Einar Snekkenes   Gjøvik University College, Norway
Michael Waidner   TU Darmstadt, Germany

Publicity Chair

Giovanni Livraga   Università degli Studi di Milano, Italy

Local Organizing Committee

Geraint Price   Royal Holloway, University of London, UK
Gerhard Hancke   Royal Holloway, University of London, UK
Kostas Markantonakis   Royal Holloway, University of London, UK
Lorenzo Cavallaro   Royal Holloway, University of London, UK
Sheila Cobourne   Royal Holloway, University of London, UK

Emma Mosley   Royal Holloway, University of London, UK
Jenny Lee   Royal Holloway, University of London, UK

Program Committee

Gail-Joon Ahn   Arizona State University, USA
Massimiliano Albanese   George Mason University, USA
Claudio Agostino Ardagna   Università degli Studi di Milano, Italy
Alessandro Armando   University of Genova, Italy
Michael Backes   Saarland University and Max Planck Institute
                              for Software Systems, Germany
David Basin   ETH Zurich, Switzerland
Kevin Bauer   MIT Lincoln Laboratory, USA
Lujo Bauer   Carnegie Mellon University, USA
Konstantin Beznosov   UBC, Canada
Marina Blanton   University of Notre Dame, USA
Carlo Blundo   Università di Salerno, Italy
Kevin Butler   University of Oregon, USA
Srdjan Capkun   ETH Zurich, Switzerland
Liqun Chen   Hewlett-Packard Laboratories, UK
Sherman S.M. Chow   Chinese University of Hong Kong, SAR China
Marco Cova   University of Birmingham, UK
Jason Crampton   Royal Holloway, University of London, UK
Frédéric Cuppens   TELECOM Bretagne, France
Sabrina De Capitani
   Di Vimercati   Università degli Studi di Milano, Italy
Roberto Di Pietro   Università di Roma Tre, Italy
Claudia Diaz   K.U. Leuven, Belgium
Josep Domingo-Ferrer   Rovira i Virgili University, Spain
Wenliang Du   Syracuse University, USA
Riccardo Focardi   Università Ca' Foscari di Venezia, Italy
Simon Foley   University College Cork, Ireland
Sara Foresti   Università degli Studi di Milano, Italy
Cedric Fournet   Microsoft, UK
Keith Frikken   Miami University, USA
Dieter Gollmann   Hamburg University of Technology, Germany
Dimitris Gritzalis   Athens University of Economics and Business,
                              Greece
Gerhard Hancke   Royal Holloway, University of London, UK
Amir Herzberg   Bar Ilan University, Israel
Michael Huth   Imperial College London, UK
Sushil Jajodia   George Mason University, USA
Aaron Johnson   Naval Research Laboratory, USA
Jonathan Katz   University of Maryland, USA
Stefan Katzenbeisser   TU Darmstadt, Germany
Engin Kirda   Northeastern University, USA

Markulf Kohlweiss	Microsoft Research Cambridge, UK
Steve Kremer	INRIA Nancy - Grand Est, France
Miroslaw Kutylowski	Wroclaw University of Technology, Poland
Adam J. Lee	University of Pittsburgh, USA
Wenke Lee	Georgia Institute of Technology, USA
Yingjiu Li	Singapore Management University, Singapore
Benoit Libert	Technicolor, France
Javier Lopez	University of Malaga, Spain
Wenjing Lou	Virginia Polytechnic Institute and State University, USA
Pratyusa K Manadhata	HP Labs, USA
Luigi Mancini	Università di Roma La Sapienza, Italy
Fabio Martinelli	IIT-CNR, Italy
Sjouke Mauw	University of Luxembourg, Luxembourg
Atsuko Miyaji	Japan Advanced Institute of Science and Technology, Japan
Gregory Neven	IBM Zurich Research Laboratory, Switzerland
Stefano Paraboschi	Università di Bergamo, Italy
Kenneth Paterson	Royal Holloway, University of London, UK
Dusko Pavlovic	Royal Holloway, University of London, UK
Günther Pernul	Universität Regensburg, Germany
Frank Piessens	Katholieke Universiteit Leuven, Belgium
Michalis Polychronakis	Columbia University, USA
Alexander Pretschner	Technische Universität München, Germany
Kui Ren	State University of New York at Buffalo, USA
Mark Ryan	University of Birmingham, UK
P.Y.A. Ryan	University of Luxembourg, Luxembourg
Andrei Sabelfeld	Chalmers University of Technology, Sweden
Ahmad-Reza Sadeghi	TU Darmstadt, Germany
Rei Safavi-Naini	University of Calgary, Canada
Pierangela Samarati	Università degli Studi di Milano, Italy
Radu Sion	Stony Brook University, USA
Nigel Smart	University of Bristol, UK
Einar Snekkenes	Gjvik University College, Norway
Vipin Swarup	The MITRE Corporation, USA
Roberto Tamassia	Brown University, USA
Carmela Troncoso	IBBT-K.U.Leuven, ESAT/COSIC, Belgium
Yevgeniy Vahlis	University of Toronto, Canada
Jaideep Vaidya	Rutgers University, USA
Vijay Varadharajan	Macquarie University, Australia
Venkat Venkatakrishnan	University of Illinois at Chicago, USA
Luca Viganò	University of Verona, Italy
Michael Waidner	Fraunhofer SIT, Germany
Bogdan Warinschi	University of Bristol, USA
Ting Yu	North Carolina State University, USA
Moti Yung	Google and Columbia University, USA

Additional Reviewers

Ahmadi, Ahmad
Alfardan, Nadhem
Aliasgari, Mehrdad
Alimomeni, Mohsen
Androulaki, Elli
Arriaga, Afonso
Asharov, Gilad
Balsa, Ero
Banescu, Sebastian
Basu, Anirban
Batten, Ian
Baum, Carsten
Beato, Filipe
Ben Hamouda, Fabrice
Bertolissi, Clara
Bkakria, Anis
Blaskiewicz, Przemyslaw
Boyd, Colin
Bozzato, Claudio
Broser, Christian
Brzuska, Christina
Cachin, Christian
Calvi, Alberto
Calzavara, Stefano
Carbone, Roberto
Catalano, Dario
Chandran, Nishanth
Chen, Jiageng
Chen, Ling
Chen, Si
Chen, Xihui
Cheval, Vincent
Choo, Euijin
Collberg, Christian
Cremers, Cas
Cuppens-Boulahia, Nora
Datta, Anupam
De Benedictis, Alessandra
De Caro, Angelo
De Groef, Willem
De Ryck, Philippe
Del Tedesco, Filippo
Delaune, Stéphanie

Devriese, Dominique
Du, Changlai
Durgin, Nancy
Epasto, Alessandro
Farnan, Nicholas
Farràs, Oriol
Ferdman, Mike
Fernandez-Gago, Carmen
Fitzgerald, William Michael
Frank, Mario
Fromm, Alexander
Fuchs, Andreas
Fuchs, Ludwig
Futa, Yuichi
Gajek, Sebastian
Galbraith, Steven
Galindo, David
Garrison, William
Gasti, Paolo
Gelernter, Nethanel
George, Wesley
Ghiglieri, Marco
Gilad, Yossi
Giustolisi, Rosario
Gjomemo, Rigel
Goberman, Michael
Grewal, Gurchetan S.
Hadi Ahmadi, Ashish Kisti
Hajian, Sara
Hanzlik, Lucjan
Hedin, Daniel
Herfert, Michael
Herrmann, Michael
Heuser, Stephan
Hoens, T. Ryan
Holzer, Andreas
Hosek, Petr
Idrees, Sabir
Jansen, Rob
Jhawar, Mahavir
Jia, Limin
Joaquim, Rui
Jonker, Hugo

Jorgensen, Zachery
Joye, Marc
Kalabis, Lukas
Kamara, Seny
Keppler, David
Khader, Dalia
Klaedtke, Felix
Kluczniak, Kamil
Komanduri, Saranga
Konidala, Divyan
Kordy, Barbara
Kostiainen, Kari
Krzywiecki, Lukasz
Kubiak, Przemysław
Kumari, Prachi
Kywe, Su Mon
Künnemann, Robert
Lancrenon, Jean
Li, Jin
Li, Yan
Liu, Jia
Livraga, Giovanni
Lochbihler, Andreas
Loftus, Jake
Lombardi, Flavio
Lovat, Enrico
Ma, Di
Magazinius, Jonas
Majcher, Krzysztof
Malacaria, Pasquale
Malisa, Luka
Manulis, Mark
Marinovic, Srdjan
Mathur, Suhas
Maurice, Clementine
Mazurek, Michelle
Meadows, Catherine
Meier, Stefan
Min, Byungho
Mitrou, Lilian
Moataz, Tarik
Molinaro, Cristian
Mood, Benjamin
Moyano, Francisco
Muehlberg, Jan Tobias

Mutti, Simone
Mylonas, Alexis
Netter, Michael
Nikiforakis, Nick
Nojoimian, Mehrdad
Nuñez, David
Oligeri, Gabriele
Omote, Kazumasa
Orlandi, Claudio
Oswald, Elisabeth
Oya, Simon
Palazzi, Bernardo
Pang, Jun
Paterson, Maura
Paul, Giura
Peacock, Thea
Peeters, Roel
Peroli, Michele
Peters, Thomas
Petit, Jonathan
Phillips, Joshua
Pieczul, Olgierd
Pinto, Alexandre
Poettering, Bertram
Pujol, Marta
Qin, Zhan
Radomirovic, Sasa
Rafnsson, Willard
Ranganathan, Aanjhan
Ranise, Silvio
Reisser, Andreas
Rial, Alfredo
Riesner, Moritz
Rijmen, Vincent
Riva, Ben
Roman, Rodrigo
Saracino, Andrea
Sayaf, Rula
Scerri, Guillaume
Schneider, Thomas
Schuldt, Jacob
Schulz, Steffen
Schunter, Matthias
Sepehrdad, Pouyan
Sgandurra, Daniele

Shafiq, Basit
Shakarian, Paulo
Shen, Entong
Shi, Jie
Shirazi, Fatemeh
Shulman, Haya
Simo, Hervais
Smans, Jan
Smith, Geoffrey
Soria Comas, Jordi
Soriente, Claudio
Soupionis, Yannis
Squarcina, Marco
Stebila, Douglas
Stefanov, Emil
Stopczynski, Martin
Struminski, Tomasz
Sun, Wenhai
Syverson, Paul
Tews, Erik
Theoharidou, Marianthi
Torabi Dashti, Mohammad
Toz, Deniz
Tsoumas, Bill
Tuerpe, Sven
Tupakula, Uday

Van Acker, Steven
Verde, Nino Vincenzo
Villani, Antonio
Virvilis, Nick
Vitali, Domenico
Wachsmann, Christian
Wang, Bing
Wang, Lusha
Watson, Gaven J.
Weber, Michael
Wei, Wei
Wüchner, Tobias
Yan, Qiben
Yautsiukhin, Artsiom
Yu, Jiangshan
Zagorski, Filip
Zanella-Béguelin, Santiago
Zhang, Bingsheng
Zhang, Liang Feng
Zhang, Ning
Zhang, Tao
Zhang, Xifan
Zhang, Yihua
Zhou, Lan
Zugenmaier, Alf

Table of Contents

Cryptography and Computation

Measurement and Evaluation

Applications of Cryptography

Code Analysis

Network Security

Formal Models and Methods

Protocol Analysis

Privacy Enhancing Models and Technologies

E-voting and Privacy

Malware Detection

Access Control

Attacks

Language-Based Protection

Practical Covertly Secure MPC for Dishonest Majority – Or: Breaking the SPDZ Limits

Ivan Damgård[1], Marcel Keller[2], Enrique Larraia[2], Valerio Pastro[1], Peter Scholl[2], and Nigel P. Smart[2]

[1] Department of Computer Science, Aarhus University
[2] Department of Computer Science, University of Bristol

Abstract. SPDZ (pronounced "Speedz") is the nickname of the MPC protocol of Damgård et al. from Crypto 2012. In this paper we both resolve a number of open problems with SPDZ; and present several theoretical and practical improvements to the protocol. In detail, we start by designing and implementing a covertly secure key generation protocol for obtaining a BGV public key and a shared associated secret key. We then construct both a covertly and actively secure preprocessing phase, both of which compare favourably with previous work in terms of efficiency and provable security.

We also build a new online phase, which solves a major problem of the SPDZ protocol: namely prior to this work preprocessed data could be used for only one function evaluation and then had to be recomputed from scratch for the next evaluation, while our online phase can support reactive functionalities. This improvement comes mainly from the fact that our construction does not require players to reveal the MAC keys to check correctness of MAC'd values.

1 Introduction

For many decades multi-party computation (MPC) had been a predominantly theoretic endeavour in cryptography, but in recent years interest has arisen on the practical side. This has resulted in various implementation improvements and such protocols are becoming more applicable to practical situations. A key part in this transformation from theory to practice is in adapting theoretical protocols and applying implementation techniques so as to significantly improve performance, whilst not sacrificing the level of security required by real world applications. This paper follows this modern, more practical, trend.

Early applied work on MPC focused on the case of protocols secure against passive adversaries, both in the case of two-party protocols based on Yao circuits [18] and that of many-party protocols, based on secret sharing techniques [5,9,22]. Only in recent years work has shifted to achieve active security [16,17,21], which appears to come at vastly increased cost when dealing with more than two players. On the other hand, in the real applications active security may be more stringent than one would actually require. In [2,3] Aumann and Lindell introduced the notion of covert security; in this security model an adversary who deviates from the protocol is detected with high (but not necessarily overwhelming) probability, say 90%, which still translates into an incentive on the adversary to behave in an honest manner. In contrast active security achieves the

J. Crampton, S. Jajodia, and K. Mayes (Eds.): ESORICS 2013, LNCS 8134, pp. 1–18, 2013.
© Springer-Verlag Berlin Heidelberg 2013

same effect, but the adversary can only succeed with cheating with negligible probability. There is a strong case to be made, see [2,3], that covert security is a "good enough" security level for practical application; thus in this work we focus on covert security, but we also provide solutions with active security.

As our starting point we take the protocol of [13] (dubbed SPDZ, and pronounced Speedz). In [13] this protocol is secure against active static adversaries in the standard model, is actively secure, and tolerates corruption of $n - 1$ of the n parties. The SPDZ protocol follows the preprocessing model: in an offline phase some shared randomness is generated, but neither the function to be computed nor the inputs need be known; in an online phase the actual secure computation is performed. One of the main advantages of the SPDZ protocol is that the performance of the online phase scales linearly with the number of players, and the basic operations are almost as cheap as those used in the passively secure protocols based on Shamir secret sharing. Thus, it offers the possibility of being both more flexible and secure than Shamir based protocols, while still maintaining low computational cost.

In [11] the authors present an implementation report on an adaption of the SPDZ protocol in the random oracle model, and show performance figures for both the offline and online phases for both an actively secure variant and a covertly secure variant. The implementation is over a finite field of characteristic two, since the focus is on providing a benchmark for evaluation of the AES circuit (a common benchmark application in MPC [21,10]).

Our Contributions: In this work we present a number of contributions which extend even further the ability the SPDZ protocol to deal with the type of application one is likely to see in practice. All our theorems are proved in the UC model, and in most cases, the protocols make use of some predefined ideal functionalities. We give protocols implementing most of these functionalities, the only exception being the functionality that provides access to a random oracle. This is implemented using a hash functions, and so the actual protocol is only secure in the Random Oracle Model. We back up these improvements with an implementation which we report on.

Our contributions come in two flavours. In the first flavour we present a number of improvements and extensions to the basic underlying SPDZ protocol. These protocol improvements are supported with associated security models and proofs. Our second flavour of improvements are at the implementation layer, and they bring in standard techniques from applied cryptography to bear onto MPC.

In more detail our protocol enhancements, in what are the descending order of importance, are as follows:

1. In the online phase of the original SPDZ protocol the parties are required to reveal their shares of a global MAC key in order to verify that the computation has been performed correctly. This is a major problem in practical applications since it means that secret-shared data we did not reveal cannot be re-used in later applications. Our protocol adopts a method to accomplish the same task, without needing to open the underlying MAC key. This means we can now go on computing on any secret-shared data we have, so we can support general reactive computation rather than just secure function evaluation. A further advantage of this technique is that some

of the verification we need (the so-called "sacrificing" step) can be moved into the offline phase, providing additional performance improvements in the online phase.

2. In the original SPDZ protocol [11,13] the authors assume a "magic" key generation phase for the production of the distributed Somewhat Homomorphic Encryption (SHE) scheme public/private keys required by the offline phase. The authors claim this can be accomplished using standard generic MPC techniques, which are of course expensive. In this work we present a key generation protocol for the BGV [6] SHE scheme, which is secure against covert adversaries. In addition we generate a "full" BGV key which supports the modulus switching and key switching used in [15]. This new sub-protocol may be of independent interest in other applications which require distributed decryption in an SHE/FHE scheme.

3. In [11] the modification to covert security was essentially ad-hoc, and resulted in a very weak form of covert security. In addition no security proofs or model were given to justify the claimed security. In this work we present a completely different approach to achieving covert security, we provide an extensive security model and provide full proofs for the modified offline phase (and the key generation protocol mentioned above).

4. We introduce a new approach to obtain full active security in the offline phase. In [13] active security was obtained via the use of specially designed ZKPoKs. In this work we present a different technique, based on a method used in [20]. This method has running time similar to the ZKPoK approach utilized in [13], but it allows us to give much stronger guarantees on the ciphertexts produced by corrupt players: the gap between the size of "noise" honest players put into ciphertexts and what we can force corrupt players to use was exponential in the security parameter in [13], and is essentially linear in our solution. This allows us to choose smaller parameters for the underlying cryptosystem and so makes other parts of the protocol more efficient.

It is important to understand that by combining these contributions in different ways, we can obtain two different general MPC protocols: First, since our new online phase still has full active security, it can be combined with our new approach to active security in the offline phase. This results in a protocol that is "syntactically similar" to the one from [13]: it has full active security assuming access to a functionality for key generation. However, it has enhanced functionality and performance, compared to [13], in that it can securely compute reactive functionalities. Second, we can combine our covertly secure protocols for key generation and the offline phase with the online phase to get a protocol that has covert security throughout and does not assume that key generation is given for free.

Our covert solutions all make use of the same technique to move from passive to covert security, while avoiding the computational cost of performing zero-knowledge proofs. In [11] covert security is obtained by only checking a fraction of the resulting proofs, which results in a weak notion of covert security (the probability of a cheater being detected cannot be made too large). In this work we adopt a different approach, akin to the cut-and-choose paradigm. We require parties to commit to random seeds for a number of runs of a given sub-protocol, then all the runs are executed in parallel, finally all bar one of the runs are "opened" by the players revealing their random seeds.

If all opened runs are shown to have been performed correctly then the players assume that the single un-opened run is also correctly executed.

A pleasing side-effect of the replacement of zero-knowledge proofs with our custom mechanism to obtain covert security is that the offline phase can be run in much smaller "batches". In [11,13] the need to amortize the cost of the expensive zero-knowledge proofs meant that the players on each iteration of the offline protocol executed a large computation, which produced a large number of multiplication triples [4] (in the millions). With our new technique we no longer need to amortize executions as much, and so short runs of the offline phase can be executed if so desired; producing only a few thousand triples per run.

Our second flavour of improvements at the implementation layer are more mundane; being mainly of an implementation nature. This extended abstract presents the main ideas behind our improvements and details of our implementation. For a full description including details of the associated sub-procedures, security models and associated full security proofs please see the full version of this paper at [12].

2   SPDZ Overview

We now present the main components of the SPDZ protocol; in this section unless otherwise specified we are simply recapping on prior work. Throughout the paper we assume the computation to be performed by n players over a fixed finite field $\mathbb{F}_p$ of characteristic p. The high level idea of the online phase is to compute a function represented as a circuit, where privacy is obtained by additively secret sharing the inputs and outputs of each gate, and correctness is guaranteed by adding additive secret sharings of MACs on the inputs and outputs of each gate. In more detail, each player P_i has a uniform share $\alpha_i \in \mathbb{F}_p$ of a secret value $\alpha = \alpha_1 + \cdots + \alpha_n$, thought of as a fixed MAC key. We say that a data item $a \in \mathbb{F}_p$ is $\langle \cdot \rangle$-shared if P_i holds a tuple $(a_i, \gamma(a)_i)$, where a_i is an additive secret sharing of a, i.e. $a = a_1 + \cdots + a_n$, and $\gamma(a)_i$ is an additive secret sharing of $\gamma(a) := \alpha \cdot a$, i.e. $\gamma(a) = \gamma(a)_1 + \cdots + \gamma(a)_n$.

For the readers familiar with [13], this is a simpler MAC definition. In particular we have dropped δ_a from the MAC definition; this value was only used to add or subtract public data to or from shares. In our case δ_a becomes superfluous, since there is a straightforward way of computing a MAC of a public value a by defining $\gamma(a)_i \leftarrow a \cdot \alpha_i$.

During the protocol various values which are $\langle \cdot \rangle$-shared are "partially opened", i.e. the associated values a_i are revealed, but not the associated shares of the MAC. Note that linear operations (addition and scalar multiplication) can be performed on the $\langle \cdot \rangle$-sharings with no interaction required. Computing multiplications, however, is not straightforward, as we describe below.

The goal of the offline phase is to produce a set of "multiplication triples", which allow players to compute products. These are a list of sets of three $\langle \cdot \rangle$-sharings $\{\langle a \rangle, \langle b \rangle, \langle c \rangle\}$ such that $c = a \cdot b$. In this paper we extend the offline phase to also produce "square pairs" i.e. a list of pairs of $\langle \cdot \rangle$-sharings $\{\langle a \rangle, \langle b \rangle\}$ such that $b = a^2$, and "shared bits" i.e. a list of single shares $\langle a \rangle$ such that $a \in \{0, 1\}$.

In the online phase these lists are consumed as MPC operations are performed. In particular to multiply two $\langle \cdot \rangle$-sharings $\langle x \rangle$ and $\langle y \rangle$ we take a multiplication triple

$\{\langle a \rangle, \langle b \rangle, \langle c \rangle\}$ and partially open $\langle x \rangle - \langle a \rangle$ to obtain ϵ and $\langle y \rangle - \langle b \rangle$ to obtain δ. The sharing of $z = x \cdot y$ is computed from $\langle z \rangle \leftarrow \langle c \rangle + \epsilon \cdot \langle b \rangle + \delta \cdot \langle a \rangle + \epsilon \cdot \delta$.

The reason for us introducing square pairs is that squaring a value can then be computed more efficiently as follows: To square the sharing $\langle x \rangle$ we take a square pair $\{\langle a \rangle, \langle b \rangle\}$ and partially open $\langle x \rangle - \langle a \rangle$ to obtain ϵ. We then compute the sharing of $z = x^2$ from $\langle z \rangle \leftarrow \langle b \rangle + 2 \cdot \epsilon \cdot \langle x \rangle - \epsilon^2$. Finally, the "shared bits" are useful in computing high level operation such as comparison, bit-decomposition, fixed and floating point operations as in [1,7,8].

The offline phase produces the triples in the following way. We make use of a Somewhat Homomorphic Encryption (SHE) scheme, which encrypts messages in $\mathbb{F}_p$, supports distributed decryption, and allows computation of circuits of multiplicative depth one on encrypted data. To generate a multiplication triple each player P_i generates encryptions of random values a_i and b_i (their shares of a and b). Using the multiplicative property of the SHE scheme an encryption of $c = (a_1 + \cdots + a_n) \cdot (b_1 + \cdots + b_n)$ is produced. The players then use the distributed decryption protocol to obtain sharings of c. The shares of the MACs on a, b and c needed to complete the $\langle \cdot \rangle$-sharing are produced in much the same manner. Similar operations are performed to produce square pairs and shared bits. Clearly the above (vague) outline needs to be fleshed out to ensure the required covert security level. Moreover, in practice we generate many triples/pairs/shared-bits at once using the SIMD nature of the BGV SHE scheme.

3 BGV

We now present an overview of the BGV scheme as required by our offline phase. This is only sketched, the reader is referred to [6,14,15] for more details; our goal is to present enough detail to explain the key generation protocol later.

3.1 Preliminaries

Underlying Algebra: We fix the ring $R_q = (\mathbb{Z}/q\mathbb{Z})[X]/\Phi_m(X)$ for some cyclotomic polynomial $\Phi_m(X)$, where m is an parameter which can be thought of as a function of the underlying security parameter. Note that q may not necessarily be prime. Let $R = \mathbb{Z}[X]/\Phi_m(X)$, and $\phi(m)$ denote the degree of R over $\mathbb{Z}$, i.e. Euler's ϕ function. The message space of our scheme will be R_p for a prime p of approximately 32, 64 or 128-bits in length, whilst ciphertexts will lie in either $R_{q_0}^2$ or $R_{q_1}^2$, for one of two moduli q_0 and q_1. We select $R = \mathbb{Z}[X]/(X^{m/2} + 1)$ for m a power of two, and $p = 1 \pmod{m}$. By picking m and p this way we have that the message space R_p offers $m/2$-fold SIMD parallelism, i.e. $R_p \cong \mathbb{F}_p^{m/2}$. In addition this also implies that the ring constant c_m from [13,15] is equal to one.

We wish to generate a public key for a leveled BGV scheme for which n players each hold a share, which is itself a "standard" BGV secret key. As we are working with circuits of multiplicative depth at most one we only need two levels in the moduli chain $q_0 = p_0$ and $q_1 = p_0 \cdot p_1$. The modulus p_1 will also play the role of P in [15] for the

SwitchKey operation. The value p_1 must be chosen so that $p_1 \equiv 1 \pmod{p}$, with the value of p_0 set to ensure valid distributed decryption.

Random Values: Each player is assumed to have a secure entropy source. In practice we take this to be /dev/urandom, which is a non-blocking entropy source found on Unix like operating systems. This is not a "true" entropy source, being non-blocking, but provides a practical balance between entropy production and performance for our purposes. In what follows we model this source via a procedure $s \leftarrow$ Seed(), which generates a new seed from this source of entropy. Calling this function sets the players global variable cnt to zero. Then every time a player generates a new random value in a protocol this is constructed by calling $\mathrm{PRF}_s(\mathrm{cnt})$, for some pseudo-random function PRF, and then incrementing cnt. In practice we use AES under the key s with message cnt to implement PRF.

   The point of this method for generating random values is that the said values can then be verified to have been generated honestly by revealing s in the future and recomputing all the randomness used by a player, and verifying his output is consistent with this value of s.

   From the basic PRF we define the following "induced" pseudo-random number generators, which generate elements according to the following distributions but seeded by the seed s:

- $\mathcal{HWT}_s(h, n)$: This generates a vector of length n with elements chosen at random from $\{-1, 0, 1\}$ subject to the condition that the number of non-zero elements is equal to h.
- $\mathcal{ZO}_s(0.5, n)$: This generates a vector of length n with elements chosen from $\{-1, 0, 1\}$ such that the probability of coefficient is $p_{-1} = 1/4$, $p_0 = 1/2$ and $p_1 = 1/4$.
- $\mathcal{DG}_s(\sigma^2, n)$: This generates a vector of length n with elements chosen according to the discrete Gaussian distribution with variance σ^2.
- $\mathcal{RC}_s(0.5, \sigma^2, n)$: This generates a triple of elements (v, e_0, e_1) where v is sampled from $\mathcal{ZO}_s(0.5, n)$ and e_0 and e_1 are sampled from $\mathcal{DG}_s(\sigma^2, n)$.
- $\mathcal{U}_s(q, n)$: This generates a vector of length n with elements generated uniformly modulo q.

If any random values are used which **do not** depend on a seed then these should be assumed to be drawn using a secure entropy source (again in practice assumed to be /dev/urandom). If we pull from one of the above distributions where we do not care about the specific seed being used then we will drop the subscript s from the notation.

Broadcast: When broadcasting data we assume two different models. In the online phase during partial opening we utilize the method described in [13]; in that players send their data to a nominated player who then broadcasts the reconstructed value back to the remaining players. For other applications of broadcast we assume each party broadcasts their values to all other parties directly. In all instances players maintain a running hash of all values sent and received in a broadcast (with a suitable modification for the variant used for partial opening). At the end of a protocol run these running hashes are compared in a pair-wise fashion. This final comparison ensures that in the case of at least two honest parties the adversary must have been consistent in what was sent to the honest parties.

3.2 Key Generation

The key generation algorithm generates a public/private key pair such that the public key is given by $\mathfrak{pk} = (a, b)$, where a is generated from $\mathcal{U}(q_1, \phi(m))$ (i.e. a is uniform in R_{q_1}), and $b = a \cdot \mathfrak{s} + p \cdot \epsilon$ where ϵ is a "small" error term, and $\mathfrak{s}$ is the secret key such that $\mathfrak{s} = \mathfrak{s}_1 + \cdots + \mathfrak{s}_n$, where player P_i holds the share $\mathfrak{s}_i$. Recall since m is a power of 2 we have $\phi(m) = m/2$.

The public key is also augmented to an extended public key $\mathfrak{epk}$ by addition of a "quasi-encryption" of the message $-p_1 \cdot \mathfrak{s}^2$, i.e. $\mathfrak{epk}$ contains a pair $\mathfrak{enc} = (b_{\mathfrak{s},\mathfrak{s}^2}, a_{\mathfrak{s},\mathfrak{s}^2})$ such that $b_{\mathfrak{s},\mathfrak{s}^2} = a_{\mathfrak{s},\mathfrak{s}^2} \cdot \mathfrak{s} + p \cdot \epsilon_{\mathfrak{s},\mathfrak{s}^2} - p_1 \cdot \mathfrak{s}^2$, where $a_{\mathfrak{s},\mathfrak{s}^2} \leftarrow \mathcal{U}(q_1, \phi(m))$ and $\epsilon_{\mathfrak{s},\mathfrak{s}^2}$ is a "small" error term. The precise distributions of all these values will be determined when we discuss the exact key generation protocol we use.

3.3 Encryption and Decryption

$\mathsf{Enc}_{\mathfrak{pk}}(\mathbf{m})$: To encrypt an element $m \in R_p$, using the modulus q_1, we choose one "small polynomial" (with $0, \pm 1$ coefficients) and two Gaussian polynomials (with variance σ^2), via $(v, e_0, e_1) \leftarrow \mathcal{RC}_s(0.5, \sigma^2, \phi(m))$. Then we set $c_0 = b \cdot v + p \cdot e_0 + m$, $c_1 = a \cdot v + p \cdot e_1$, and set the initial ciphertext as $\mathfrak{c}' = (c_0, c_1, 1)$.

$\mathsf{SwitchModulus}((c_0, c_1), \ell)$: The operation $\mathsf{SwitchModulus}(\mathfrak{c})$ takes the ciphertext $\mathfrak{c} = ((c_0, c_1), \ell)$ defined modulo q_ℓ and produces a ciphertext $\mathfrak{c}' = ((c_0', c_1'), \ell - 1)$ defined modulo $q_{\ell-1}$, such that $[c_0 - \mathfrak{s} \cdot c_1]_{q_\ell} \equiv [c_0' - \mathfrak{s} \cdot c_1']_{q_{\ell-1}} \pmod{p}$. This is done by setting $c_i' = \mathsf{Scale}(c_i, q_\ell, q_{\ell-1})$ where Scale is the function defined in [15]; note we need the more complex function of Appendix E of the full version of [15] if working in dCRT representation as we need to fix the scaling modulo p as opposed to modulo two which was done in the main body of [15]. As we are only working with two levels this function can only be called when $\ell = 1$.

$\mathsf{Dec}_{\mathfrak{s}}(\mathfrak{c})$: Note, that this operation is never actually performed, since no-one knows the shared secret key $\mathfrak{s}$, but presenting it will be instructive: Decryption of a ciphertext (c_0, c_1, ℓ) at level ℓ is performed by setting $m' = [c_0 - \mathfrak{s} \cdot c_1]_{q_\ell}$, then converting m' to coefficient representation and outputting $m' \bmod p$.

$\mathsf{DistDec}_{\mathfrak{s}_i}(\mathfrak{c})$: We actually decrypt using a simplification of the distributed decryption procedure described in [13], since our final ciphertexts consist of only two elements as opposed to three in [13]. For input ciphertext (c_0, c_1, ℓ), player P_1 computes $\mathbf{v}_1 = c_0 - \mathfrak{s}_i \cdot c_1$ and each other player P_i computes $\mathbf{v}_i = -\mathfrak{s}_i \cdot c_1$. Each party P_i then sets $\mathbf{t}_i = \mathbf{v}_i + p \cdot \mathbf{r}_i$ for some random element $\mathbf{r}_i \in R$ with infinity norm bounded by $2^{\mathsf{sec}} \cdot B/(n \cdot p)$, for some statistical security parameter sec, and the values $\mathbf{t}_i$ are broadcast; the precise value B being determined in the full version of this abstract [12]. Then the message is recovered as $\mathbf{t}_1 + \cdots + \mathbf{t}_n \pmod{p}$.

3.4 Operations on Encrypted Data

Homomorphic addition follows trivially from the methods of [6,15]. So the main remaining task is to deal with multiplication. We first define a $\mathsf{SwitchKey}$ operation.

SwitchKey(d_0, d_1, d_2): This procedure takes as input an extended ciphertext $\mathfrak{c} = (d_0, d_1, d_2)$ defined modulo q_1; this is a ciphertext which is decrypted via the equation

$$[d_0 - \mathfrak{s} \cdot d_1 - \mathfrak{s}^2 \cdot d_2]_{q_1}.$$

The SwitchKey operation also takes the key-switching data $\mathfrak{enc} = (b_{\mathfrak{s},\mathfrak{s}^2}, a_{\mathfrak{s},\mathfrak{s}^2})$ above and produces a standard two element ciphertext which encrypts the same message but modulo q_0.

- $c_0' \leftarrow p_1 \cdot d_0 + b_{\mathfrak{s},\mathfrak{s}^2} \cdot d_2 \pmod{q_1}$, $c_1' \leftarrow p_1 \cdot d_1 + a_{\mathfrak{s},\mathfrak{s}^2} \cdot d_2 \pmod{q_1}$.
- $c_0'' \leftarrow \mathsf{Scale}(c_0', q_1, q_0)$, $c_1'' \leftarrow \mathsf{Scale}(c_1', q_1, q_0)$.
- Output $((c_0'', c_1''), 0)$.

Notice we have the following equality modulo q_1:

$$c_0' - \mathfrak{s} \cdot c_1' = (p_1 \cdot d_0) + d_2 \cdot b_{\mathfrak{s},\mathfrak{s}^2} - \mathfrak{s} \cdot \left((p \cdot d_1) - d_2 \cdot a_{\mathfrak{s},\mathfrak{s}^2}\right)$$
$$= p_1 \cdot (d_0 - \mathfrak{s} \cdot d_1 - \mathfrak{s}^2 d_2) - p \cdot d_2 \cdot \epsilon_{\mathfrak{s},\mathfrak{s}^2},$$

The requirement on $p_1 \equiv 1 \pmod{p}$ is from the above equation as we want this to produce the same value as $d_0 - \mathfrak{s} \cdot d_1 - \mathfrak{s}^2 d_2 \mod q_1$ on reduction modulo p.

Mult($\mathfrak{c}, \mathfrak{c}'$): We only need to execute multiplication on two ciphertexts at level one, thus $\mathfrak{c} = ((c_0, c_1), 1)$ and $\mathfrak{c}' = ((c_0', c_1'), 1)$. The output will be a ciphertext $\mathfrak{c}''$ at level zero, obtained via the following steps:

- $\mathfrak{c} \leftarrow \mathsf{SwitchModulus}(\mathfrak{c})$, $\mathfrak{c}' \leftarrow \mathsf{SwitchModulus}(\mathfrak{c}')$.
- $(d_0, d_1, d_2) \leftarrow (c_0 \cdot c_0', c_1 \cdot c_0' + c_0 \cdot c_1', -c_1 \cdot c_1')$.
- $\mathfrak{c}'' \leftarrow \mathsf{SwitchKey}(d_0, d_1, d_2)$.

4   Protocols Associated to the SHE Scheme

In this section we present two sub-protocols associated with the SHE scheme; namely our distributed key generation and a protocol for proving that a committed ciphertext is well formed.

4.1   Distributed Key Generation Protocol for BGV

The protocol for distributed key generation protocol is given in Figure 1. It makes use of an abstract functionality $\mathcal{F}_{\mathrm{COMMIT}}$ which implements a commitment functionality. In practice this functionality is implemented in the random oracle model via hash functions, see the full version for details [12]. Here we present a high level overview.

As remarked in the introduction, the authors of [13] assumed a "magic" set up which produces not only a distributed sharing of the main BGV secret key, but also a distributed sharing of the square of the secret key. That was assumed to be done via some other unspecified MPC protocol. The effect of requiring a sharing of the square of the secret key was that they did not need to perform KeySwitching, but ciphertexts were 50% bigger than one would otherwise expect. Here we take a very different approach:

The protocol Π_{KEYGEN}

Initialize:

1. Every player P_i samples a uniform $e_i \leftarrow \{1, \ldots, c\}$ and asks $\mathcal{F}_{\text{COMMIT}}$ to broadcast the handle $\tau_i^e \leftarrow \mathsf{Commit}(e_i)$ for a commitment to e_i.
2. Every player P_i samples a seed $s_{i,j}$ and asks $\mathcal{F}_{\text{COMMIT}}$ to broadcast $\tau_{i,j}^s \leftarrow \mathsf{Commit}(s_{i,j})$.
3. Every player P_i computes and broadcasts $a_{i,j} \leftarrow \mathcal{U}_{s_{i,j}}(q_1, \phi(m))$.

Stage 1:

4. All the players compute $a_j \leftarrow a_{1,j} + \cdots + a_{n,j}$.
5. Every player P_i computes $\mathfrak{s}_{i,j} \leftarrow \mathcal{HWT}_{s_{i,j}}(h, \phi(m))$ and $\epsilon_{i,j} \leftarrow \mathcal{DG}_{s_{i,j}}(\sigma^2, \phi(m))$,
   and broadcasts $b_{i,j} \leftarrow [a_j \cdot \mathfrak{s}_{i,j} + p \cdot \epsilon_{i,j}]_{q_1}$.

Stage 2:

6. All the players compute $b_j \leftarrow b_{1,j} + \cdots + b_{n,j}$ and set $\mathfrak{pk}_j \leftarrow (a_j, b_j)$..
7. Every player P_i computes and broadcasts $\mathfrak{enc}_{i,j}' \leftarrow \mathsf{Enc}_{\mathfrak{pk}_j}(-p_1 \cdot \mathfrak{s}_{i,j}, \mathcal{RC}_{s_{i,j}}(0.5, \sigma^2, \phi(m)))$.

Stage 3:

8. All the players compute $\mathfrak{enc}_j' \leftarrow \mathfrak{enc}_{1,j}' + \cdots + \mathfrak{enc}_{n,j}'$.
9. Every player P_i computes $\mathfrak{zero}_{i,j} \leftarrow \mathsf{Enc}_{\mathfrak{pk}_j}(0, \mathcal{RC}_{s_{i,j}}(0.5, \sigma^2, \phi(m)))$.
10. Every player P_i computes and broadcasts $\mathfrak{enc}_{i,j} \leftarrow (\mathfrak{s}_{i,j} \cdot \mathfrak{enc}_j') + \mathfrak{zero}_{i,j}$.

Output:

11. All the players compute $\mathfrak{enc}_j \leftarrow \mathfrak{enc}_{1,j} + \cdots + \mathfrak{enc}_{n,j}$ and set $\mathfrak{epk}_j \leftarrow (\mathfrak{pk}_j, \mathfrak{enc}_j)$.
12. Every player P_i calls $\mathcal{F}_{\text{COMMIT}}$ with $\mathsf{Open}(\tau_i^e)$. If any opening failed, the players output the numbers of the respective players, and the protocol aborts.
13. All players compute the challenge $\mathsf{chall} \leftarrow 1 + \left(\left(\sum_{i=1}^n e_i \right) \bmod c \right)$.
14. Every player P_i calls $\mathcal{F}_{\text{COMMIT}}$ with $\mathsf{Open}(\tau_{i,j}^s)$ for $j \neq \mathsf{chall}$. If any opening failed, the players output the numbers of the respective players, and the protocol aborts.
15. All players obtain the values committed, compute all the derived values and check that they are correct.
16. If any of the checks fail, the players output the numbers of the respective players, and the protocol aborts. Otherwise, every player P_i sets
    - $\mathfrak{s}_i \leftarrow \mathfrak{s}_{i,\mathsf{chall}}$,
    - $\mathfrak{pk} \leftarrow (a_{\mathsf{chall}}, b_{\mathsf{chall}})$, $\mathfrak{epk} \leftarrow (\mathfrak{pk}, \mathfrak{enc}_{\mathsf{chall}})$.

Fig. 1. The protocol for key generation.

we augment the public key with the keyswitching data from [15] and provide an explicit covertly secure key generation protocol.

Our protocol will be covertly secure in the sense that the probability that an adversary can deviate without being detected will be bounded by $1/c$, for a positive integer c. Our basic idea behind achieving covert security is as follows: Each player runs c instances of the basic protocol, each with different random seeds, then at the end of the main protocol all bar a random one basic protocol runs are opened, along with the respective random seeds. All parties then check that the opened runs were performed honestly and, if any party finds an inconsistency, the protocol aborts. If no problem is detected, the parties assume that the single unopened run is correct. Thus intuitively the adversary can cheat with probability at most $1/c$.

We start by discussing the generation of the main public key $\mathfrak{pk}_j$ in execution j where $j \in \{1, \ldots, c\}$. To start with the players generate a uniformly random value $a_j \in R_{q_1}$. They then each execute the standard BGV key generation procedure, except that this is done with respect to the global element a_j. Player i chooses a low-weight secret key and then generates an LWE instance relative to that secret key. Following [15], we choose

$$\mathfrak{s}_{i,j} \leftarrow \mathcal{HWT}_s(h, \phi(m)) \text{ and } \epsilon_{i,j} \leftarrow \mathcal{DG}_s(\sigma^2, \phi(m)).$$

Then the player sets the secret key as $\mathfrak{s}_{i,j}$ and their "local" public key as $(a_j, b_{i,j})$ where $b_{i,j} = [a_j \cdot \mathfrak{s}_{i,j} + p \cdot \epsilon_{i,j}]_{q_1}$.

Note, by a hybrid argument, obtaining n ring-LWE instances for n different secret keys but the same value of a_j is secure assuming obtaining one ring-LWE instance is secure. In the LWE literature this is called "amortization". Also note in what follows that a key modulo q_1 can be also treated as a key modulo q_0 since q_0 divides q_1 and $\mathfrak{s}_{i,j}$ has coefficients in $\{-1, 0, 1\}$.

The global public and private key are then set to be $\mathfrak{pk}_j = (a_j, b_j)$ and $\mathfrak{s}_j = \mathfrak{s}_{1,j} + \cdots + \mathfrak{s}_{n,j}$, where $b_j = [b_{1,j} + \cdots + b_{n,j}]_{q_1}$. This is essentially another BGV key pair, since if we set $\epsilon_j = \epsilon_{1,j} + \cdots + \epsilon_{n,j}$ then we have

$$b_j = \sum_{i=1}^{n} (a_j \cdot \mathfrak{s}_{i,j} + p \cdot \epsilon_{i,j}) = a_j \cdot \mathfrak{s}_j + p \cdot \epsilon_j,$$

but generated with different distributions for $\mathfrak{s}_j$ and ϵ_j compared to the individual key pairs above.

We next augment the above basic key generation to enable the construction of the KeySwitching data. Given a public key $\mathfrak{pk}_j$ and a share of the secret key $\mathfrak{s}_{i,j}$ our method for producing the extended public key is to produce in turn (see Figure 1 for the details on how we create these elements in our protocol).

- $\mathfrak{enc}'_{i,j} \leftarrow \mathsf{Enc}_{\mathfrak{pk}_j}(-p_1 \cdot \mathfrak{s}_{i,j})$
- $\mathfrak{enc}'_j \leftarrow \mathfrak{enc}'_{1,j} + \cdots + \mathfrak{enc}'_{n,j}$.
- $\mathfrak{zero}_{i,j} \leftarrow \mathsf{Enc}_{\mathfrak{pk}_j}(0)$
- $\mathfrak{enc}_{i,j} \leftarrow (\mathfrak{s}_{i,j} \cdot \mathfrak{enc}'_j) + \mathfrak{zero}_{i,j} \in R_{q_1}^2$.
- $\mathfrak{enc}_j \leftarrow \mathfrak{enc}_{1,j} + \cdots + \mathfrak{enc}_{n,j}$.
- $\mathfrak{epk}_j \leftarrow (\mathfrak{pk}_j, \mathfrak{enc}_j)$.

Note, that $\mathfrak{enc}'_{i,j}$ is not a valid encryption of $-p_1 \cdot \mathfrak{s}_{i,j}$, since $-p_1 \cdot \mathfrak{s}_{i,j}$ does not lie in the message space of the encryption scheme. However, because of the dependence on the secret key shares here, we need to assume a form of circular security; the precise assumption needed is stated in the full version [12]. The encryption of zero, $\mathfrak{zero}_{i,j}$, is added on by each player to re-randomize the ciphertext, preventing an adversary from recovering $\mathfrak{s}_{i,j}$ from $\mathfrak{enc}_{i,j}/\mathfrak{enc}'_j$. We call the resulting $\mathfrak{epk}_j$ the *extended public key*. In [15] the keyswitching data $\mathfrak{enc}_j$ is computed directly from $\mathfrak{s}_j^2$; however, we need to use the above round-about way since $\mathfrak{s}_j^2$ is not available to the parties.

Finally we open all bar one of the c executions and check they have been executed correctly. If all checks pass then the final extended public key $\mathfrak{epk}$ is output and the players keep hold of their associated secret key share $\mathfrak{s}_i$. See Figure 1 for full details of the protocol.

Theorem 1. *In the $\mathcal{F}_{\text{COMMIT}}$-hybrid model, the protocol Π_{KEYGEN} implements $\mathcal{F}_{\text{KEYGEN}}$ with computational security against any static adversary corrupting at most $n - 1$ parties.*

$\mathcal{F}_{\text{KEYGEN}}$ simply generates a key pair with a distribution matching what we sketched above, and then sends the values $a_i, b_i, \mathfrak{enc}_i', \mathfrak{enc}_i$ for every i to all parties and shares of the secret key to the honest players. Like most functionalities in the following, it allows the adversary to try to cheat and will allow this with a certain probability $1/c$. This is how we model covert security. See the full version for a complete technical discription of $\mathcal{F}_{\text{KEYGEN}}$.

The BGV cryptosystem resulting from $\mathcal{F}_{\text{KEYGEN}}$ is proven semantically secure by the following theorem from the full version of this paper [12].

Theorem 2. *If the functionality $\mathcal{F}_{\text{KEYGEN}}$ is used to produce a public key $\mathfrak{epk}$ and secret keys $\mathfrak{s}_i$ for $i = 0, \ldots, n-1$ then the resulting cryptosystem is semantically secure based on the hardness of $\text{RLWE}_{q_1, \sigma^2, h}$ and the circular security assumption mentioned earlier.*

4.2   EncCommit

We use a sub-protocol $\Pi_{\text{ENCCOMMIT}}$ to replace the Π_{ZKPoPK} protocol from [13]. In this section we consider a covertly secure variant rather than active security; this means that players controlled by a malicious adversary succeed in deviating from the protocol with a probability bounded by $1/c$. In our experiments we pick $c = 5$, 10 and 20. In the full version of this paper we present an actively secure variant of this protocol.

Our new sub-protocol assumes that players have agreed on the key material for the encryption scheme, i.e. $\Pi_{\text{ENCCOMMIT}}$ runs in the $\mathcal{F}_{\text{KEYGEN}}$-hybrid model. The protocol ensures that a party outputs a validly created ciphertext containing an encryption of some pseudo-random message m, where the message m is drawn from a distribution satisfying condition cond. This is done by committing to seeds and using the cut-and-choose technique, similarly to the key generation protocol. The condition cond in our application could either be uniformly pseudo-randomly generated from R_p, or uniformly pseudo-randomly generated from $\mathbb{F}_p$ (i.e. a "diagonal" element in the SIMD representation).

The protocol $\Pi_{\text{ENCCOMMIT}}$ is presented in Figure 2. A proof of the following theorem, and a description of the associated ideal functionality, are given in the full version of this paper [12].

Theorem 3. *In the $(\mathcal{F}_{\text{COMMIT}}, \mathcal{F}_{\text{KEYGEN}})$-hybrid model, the protocol $\Pi_{\text{ENCCOMMIT}}$ implements $\mathcal{F}_{\text{SHE}}$ with computational security against any static adversary corrupting at most $n - 1$ parties.*

$\mathcal{F}_{\text{SHE}}$ offers the same functionality as $\mathcal{F}_{\text{KEYGEN}}$ but can in addition generate correctly formed ciphertexts where the plaintext satisfies a condition cond as explained above, and where the plaintext is known to a particular player (even if he is corrupt). Of course, if we use the actively secure version of $\Pi_{\text{ENCCOMMIT}}$ from the full version, we would get a version of $\mathcal{F}_{\text{SHE}}$ where the adversary is not allowed to attempt cheating.

Protocol $\Pi_{\text{ENCCOMMIT}}$

Usage: The specific distribution of the message is defined by the input parameter cond. The output is a single message $\mathbf{m}_i$ private to each player, and a public ciphertext $\mathfrak{c}_i$ from player i. The protocol runs in two phases; a commitment phase and an opening phase.

KeyGen: The players execute Π_{KEYGEN} to obtain $\mathfrak{s}_i$, $\mathfrak{pt}$, and $\mathfrak{ept}$.

Commitment Phase:

1. Every player P_i samples a uniform $e_i \leftarrow \{1, \ldots, c\}$, and queries $\text{Commit}(e_i)$ to $\mathcal{F}_{\text{COMMIT}}$, which broadcasts a handle τ_i^e.

2. For $j = 1, \ldots, c$
   (a) Every player P_i samples a seed $s_{i,j}$ and queries $\text{Commit}(s_{i,j})$ to $\mathcal{F}_{\text{COMMIT}}$, which broadcasts a handle $\tau_{i,j}^s$.
   (b) Every player P_i generates $\mathbf{m}_{i,j}$ according to cond using $\text{PRF}_{s_{i,j}}$.
   (c) Every player P_i computes and broadcasts $\mathfrak{c}_{i,j} \leftarrow \text{Enc}_{\mathfrak{pt}}(\mathbf{m}_{i,j})$ using $\text{PRF}_{s_{i,j}}$ to generate the randomness.

3. Every player P_i calls $\mathcal{F}_{\text{COMMIT}}$ with $\text{Open}(\tau_i^e)$. All players get e_i. If any opening failed, the players output the numbers of the respective players, and the protocol aborts.

4. All players compute chall $\leftarrow 1 + \left(\left(\sum_{i=1}^n e_i \right) \bmod c \right)$.

Opening Phase:

5. Every player P_i calls $\mathcal{F}_{\text{COMMIT}}$ with $\text{Open}(\tau_{i,j}^s)$ for all $j \neq$ chall so that all players obtain the value $s_{i,j}$ for $j \neq$ chall. If any opening fails, the players output the numbers of the respective players, and the protocol aborts.

6. For all $j \neq$ chall and all $i' \leq n$, the players check whether $\mathfrak{c}_{i',j}$ was generated correctly using $s_{i',j}$. If not, they output the numbers of the respective players i', and the protocol aborts.

7. Otherwise, every player P_i stores $\{\mathfrak{c}_{i',\text{chall}}\}_{i' \leq n}$ and $m_{i,\text{chall}}$.

Fig. 2. Protocol that allows ciphertext to be used as commitments for plaintexts

5   The Offline Phase

The offline phase produces pre-processed data for the online phase (where the secure computation is performed). To ensure security against active adversaries the MAC values of any partially opened value need to be verified. We suggest a new method for this that overcomes some limitations of the corresponding method from [13]. Since it will be used both in the offline and the online phase, we explain it here, before discussing the offline phase.

5.1   MAC Checking

We assume some value a has been $\langle \cdot \rangle$-shared and partially opened, which means that players have revealed shares of the a but not of the associated MAC value γ, this is still additively shared. Since there is no guarantee that the a are correct, we need to check it holds that $\gamma = \alpha a$ where α is the global MAC key that is also additively shared. In [13], this was done by having players commit to the shares of the MAC. then open α and check everything in the clear. But this means that other shared values become useless because the MAC key is now public, and the adversary could manipulate them as he desires.

So we want to avoid opening α, and observe that since a is public, the value $\gamma - \alpha a$ is a linear function of shared values γ, α, so players can compute shares in this value locally and we can then check if it is 0 without revealing information on α. As in [13], we can optimize the cost of this by checking many MACs in one go: we take a random linear combination of a and γ-values and check only the results of this. The full protocol is given in Figure 3; it is not intended to implement any functionality – it is just a procedure that can be called in both the offline and online phases.

Protocol MACCheck

Usage: Each player has input α_i and $(\gamma(a_j)_i)$ for $j = 1, \ldots, t$. All players have a public set of opened values $\{a_1, \ldots, a_t\}$; the protocol either succeeds or outputs failure if an inconsistent MAC value is found.

MACCheck($\{a_1, \ldots, a_t\}$):

1. Every player P_i samples a seed s_i and asks $\mathcal{F}_{\text{COMMIT}}$ to broadcast $\tau_i^s \leftarrow$ Commit(s_i).
2. Every player P_i calls $\mathcal{F}_{\text{COMMIT}}$ with Open(τ_i^s) and all players obtain s_j for all j.
3. Set $s \leftarrow s_1 \oplus \cdots \oplus s_n$.
4. Players sample a random vector $\mathbf{r} = \mathcal{U}_s(p, t)$; note all players obtain the same vector as they have agreed on the seed s.
5. Each player computes the public value $a \leftarrow \sum_{j=1}^t r_j \cdot a_j$.
6. Player i computes $\gamma_i \leftarrow \sum_{j=1}^t r_j \cdot \gamma(a_j)_i$, and $\sigma_i \leftarrow \gamma_i - \alpha_i \cdot a$.
7. Player i asks $\mathcal{F}_{\text{COMMIT}}$ to broadcast $\tau_i^\sigma \leftarrow$ Commit(σ_i).
8. Every player calls $\mathcal{F}_{\text{COMMIT}}$ with Open(τ_i^σ), and all players obtain σ_j for all j.
9. If $\sigma_1 + \cdots + \sigma_n \neq 0$, the players output $\varnothing$ and abort.

Fig. 3. Method to Check MACs on Partially Opened Values

MACCheck has the following important properties.

Lemma 1. *The protocol* MACCheck *is correct, i.e. it accepts if all the values a_j and the corresponding MACs are correctly computed. Moreover, it is* sound, *i.e. it rejects except with probability $2/p$ in case at least one value or MAC is not correctly computed.*

The proof of Lemma 1 is given in the full version of this paper.

5.2 Offline Protocol

The offline phase itself runs two distinct sub-phases, each of which we now describe. To start with we assume a BGV key has been distributed according to the key generation procedure described earlier, as well as the shares of a secret MAC key and an encryption $\mathfrak{c}_\alpha$ of the MAC key as above. We assume that the output of the offline phase will be a total of at least n_I input tuples, n_m multiplication triples, n_s squaring tuples and n_b shared bits.

In the first sub-phase, which we call the tuple-production sub-phase, we over-produce the various multiplication and squaring tuples, plus the shared bits. These are then "sacrificed" in the tuple-checking phase so as to create at least n_m multiplication triples, n_s squaring tuples and n_b shared bits. In particular in the tuple-production phase we produce (at least) $2 \cdot n_m$ multiplication triples, $2 \cdot n_s + n_b$ squaring tuples, and n_b shared bits. Tuple-production is performed by a variant of the method from [13] (precise details are in the full version of this paper). The two key differences between our protocol and that of [13], is that

1. The expensive ZKPoKs, used to verify that ciphertexts encrypting random values are correctly produced, are replaced with our protocol $\Pi_{\text{EncCommit}}$.
2. We generate squaring tuples and shared bits, as well as multiplication triples.

The tuple production protocol can be run repeatedly, alongside the tuple-checking sub-phase and the online phase.

The second sub-phase of the offline phase is to check whether the resulting material from the prior phase has been produced correctly. This check is needed, because the distributed decryption procedure needed to produce the tuples and the MACs could allow the adversary to induce errors. We solve this problem via a sacrificing technique, as in [13], however, we also need to adapt it to the case of squaring tuples and bit-sharings. Moreover, this sacrificing is performed in the offline phase as opposed to the online phase (as in [13]); and the resulting partially opened values are checked in the offline phase (again as opposed to the online phase). This is made possible by our protocol MACCheck which allows to verify the MACs are correct without revealing the MAC key α. The tuple-checking protocol is presented in the full version of this paper [12].

We show that the resulting protocol Π_{PREP}, securely implements the functionality $\mathcal{F}_{\text{PREP}}$, which models the offline phase. The functionality $\mathcal{F}_{\text{PREP}}$ outputs some desired number of multiplication triples, squaring tuples and shared bits. Full details of $\mathcal{F}_{\text{PREP}}$ and Π_{PREP} are given in the full version, along with a proof of the following theorem.

Theorem 4. *In the $(\mathcal{F}_{\text{SHE}}, \mathcal{F}_{\text{COMMIT}})$-hybrid model, the protocol Π_{PREP} implements $\mathcal{F}_{\text{PREP}}$ with computational security against any static adversary corrupting at most $n-1$ parties if p is exponential in the security parameter.*

The security flavour of Π_{PREP} follows the security of EncCommit, i.e. if one uses the covert (resp. active) version of EncCommit, one gets covert (resp. active) security for Π_{PREP}.

6   Online Phase

We design a protocol Π_{ONLINE} which performs the secure computation of the desired function, decomposed as a circuit over $\mathbb{F}_p$. Our online protocol makes use of the pre-processed data coming from $\mathcal{F}_{\text{PREP}}$ in order to input, add, multiply or square values. Our protocol is similar to the one described in [13]; however, it brings a series of improvements, in the sense that we could push the "sacrificing" to the preprocessing phase, we have specialised procedure for squaring etc, and we make use of a different MAC-checking method in the output phase. Our method for checking the MACs is simply the MACCheck protocol on all partially opened values; note that such a method has a lower soundness error than the method proposed in [13], since the linear combination of partially opened values is truly random in our case, while it has lower entropy in [13].

In the full version of the paper we present the protocol Π_{ONLINE}, which is the obvious adaption of the equivalent protocol from [13]. In addition we present an ideal functionality $\mathcal{F}_{\text{ONLINE}}$ and prove the following theorem.

Theorem 5. *In the $\mathcal{F}_{\text{PREP}}$-hybrid model, the protocol Π_{ONLINE} implements $\mathcal{F}_{\text{ONLINE}}$ with computational security against any static adversary corrupting at most $n - 1$ parties if p is exponential in the security parameter.*

7   Experimental Results

7.1   KeyGen and Offline Protocols

To present performance numbers for our key generation and new variant of the offline phase for SPDZ we first need to define secure parameter sizes for the underlying BGV scheme (and in particular how it is used in our protocols). This is done in the full version for various choices of n (the number of players) and p (the field size).

We then implemented the preceding protocols in C++ on top of the MPIR library for multi-precision arithmetic. Modular arithmetic was implemented with bespoke code using Montgomery arithmetic [19] and calls to the underlying mpn_ functions in MPIR. The offline phase was implemented in a multi-threaded manner, with four cores producing initial multiplication triples, square pairs, shared bits and input preparation mask values. Then two cores performed the sacrificing for the multiplication triples, square pairs and shared bits.

In Table 1 we present execution times (in wall time measured in seconds) for key generation and for an offline phase which produces 100000 each of the multiplication tuples, square pairs, shared bits and 1000 input sharings. We also present the average time to produce a multiplication triple for an offline phase running on one core and producing 100000 multiplication triples only. The run-times are given for various values of n, p and c, and all timings were obtained on 2.80 GHz Intel Core i7 machines with 4 GB RAM, with machines running on a local network.

We compare the results to that obtained in [11], since no other protocol can provide malicious/covert security for $t < n$ corrupted parties. In the case of covert security the authors of [11] report figures of 0.002 seconds per (un-checked) 64-bit multiplication triple for both two and three players; however the probability of cheating being detected was lower bounded by $1/2$ for two players, and $1/4$ for three players; as opposed to our probabilities of $4/5$, $9/10$ and $19/20$. Since the triples in [11] were unchecked we need to scale their run-times by a factor of two; to obtain 0.004 seconds per multiplication triple. Thus for covert security we see that our protocol for checked tuples are superior both in terms error probabilities, for a comparable run-time.

When using our active security variant we aimed for a cheating probability of 2^{-40}; so as to be able to compare with prior run times obtained in [11], which used the method

Table 1. Execution Times For Key Gen and Offline Phase (Covert Security)

n	$p \approx$	c	Run Times KeyGen	Run Times Offline	Time per Triple (sec)	n	$p \approx$	c	Run Times KeyGen	Run Times Offline	Time per Triple(sec)
2	2^{32}	5	2.4	156	0.00140	3	2^{32}	5	3.0	292	0.00204
2	2^{32}	10	5.1	277	0.00256	3	2^{32}	10	6.4	413	0.00380
2	2^{32}	20	10.4	512	0.00483	3	2^{32}	20	13.3	790	0.00731
2	2^{64}	5	5.9	202	0.00194	3	2^{64}	5	7.7	292	0.00267
2	2^{64}	10	12.5	377	0.00333	3	2^{64}	10	16.3	568	0.00497
2	2^{64}	20	25.6	682	0.00634	3	2^{64}	20	33.7	1108	0.01004
2	2^{128}	5	16.2	307	0.00271	3	2^{128}	5	21.0	462	0.00402
2	2^{128}	10	33.6	561	0.00489	3	2^{128}	10	44.4	889	0.00759
2	2^{128}	20	74.5	1114	0.00937	3	2^{128}	20	99.4	2030	0.01487

from [13]. Again we performed two experiments one where four cores produced 100000 multiplication triples, squaring pairs and shared bits, plus 1000 input sharings; and one experiment where one core produced just 100000 multiplication triples (so as to produce the average cost for a triple). The results are in Table 2.

Table 2. Execution Times for Offline Phase (Active Security)

$p \approx$	$n = 2$ Offline	$n = 2$ Time per Triple	$n = 3$ Offline	$n = 3$ Time per Triple
2^{32}	2366	0.01955	3668	0.02868
2^{64}	3751	0.02749	5495	0.04107
2^{128}	6302	0.04252	10063	0.06317

By way of comparison for a prime of 64 bits the authors of [11] report on an implementation which takes 0.006 seconds to produce an (un-checked) multiplication triple for the case of two parties and equivalent active security; and 0.008 per second for the case of three parties and active security. As we produce checked triples, the cost per triple for the results in [11] need to be (at least) doubled; to produce a total of 0.012 and 0.016 seconds respectively.

Thus, in this test, our new active protocol has running time about twice that of the previous active protocol from [13] based on ZKPoKs. From the analysis of the protocols, we do expect that the new method will be faster, but only if we produce the output in large enough batches. Due to memory constraints we were so far unable to do this, but we can extrapolate from these results: In the test we generated 12 ciphertexts in one go, and if we were able to increase this by a factor of about 10, then we would get results better than those of [13,11], all other things being equal. More information can be found in the full version [12].

7.2 Online

For the new online phase we have developed a purpose-built bytecode interpreter, which reads and executes pre-generated sequences of instructions in a multi-threaded manner. Our runtime supports parallelism on two different levels: independent rounds of communication can be merged together to reduce network overhead, and multiple threads can be executed at once to allow for optimal usage of modern multi-core processors.

In Table 3 we present timings (again in elapsed wall time for a player) for multiplying two secret shared values. Results are given for three different varieties of multiplication, reflecting the possibilities available: purely sequential multiplications; parallel multiplications with communication merged into one round (50 per round); and parallel multiplications running in 4 independent threads (50 per round, per thread). The experiments were carried out on the same machines as the offline phase, running over a local network with a ping of around 0.27ms. For comparison, the original implementation of the online phase in [13] gave an amortized time of 20000 multiplications per second over a 64-bit prime field, with three players.

Table 3. Online Times

		Multiplications/sec		
		Sequential	50 in Parallel	
n	$p \approx$	Single Thread	Single Thread	Four Threads
2	2^{32}	7500	134000	398000
2	2^{64}	7500	130000	395000
2	2^{128}	7500	120000	358000
3	2^{32}	4700	100000	292000
3	2^{64}	4700	98000	287000
3	2^{128}	4600	90000	260000

Acknowledgements. The first and fourth author acknowledge partial support from the Danish National Research Foundation and The National Science Foundation of China (under the grant 61061130540) for the Sino-Danish Center for the Theory of Interactive Computation, and from the CFEM research center (supported by the Danish Strategic Research Council). The second, third, fifth and sixth authors were supported by EPSRC via grant COED–EP/I03126X. The sixth author was also supported by the European Commission via an ERC Advanced Grant ERC-2010-AdG-267188-CRIPTO, the Defense Advanced Research Projects Agency and the Air Force Research Laboratory under agreement number FA8750-11-2-0079[1] , and by a Royal Society Wolfson Merit Award.

References

1. Aliasgari, M., Blanton, M., Zhang, Y., Steele, A.: Secure computation on floating point numbers. In: Network and Distributed System Security Symposium, NDSS 2013. Internet Society (2013)
2. Aumann, Y., Lindell, Y.: Security against covert adversaries: Efficient protocols for realistic adversaries. In: Vadhan, S.P. (ed.) TCC 2007. LNCS, vol. 4392, pp. 137–156. Springer, Heidelberg (2007)
3. Aumann, Y., Lindell, Y.: Security against covert adversaries: Efficient protocols for realistic adversaries. J. Cryptology 23(2), 281–343 (2010)
4. Beaver, D.: Efficient multiparty protocols using circuit randomization. In: Feigenbaum, J. (ed.) CRYPTO 1991. LNCS, vol. 576, pp. 420–432. Springer, Heidelberg (1992)

[1] The US Government is authorized to reproduce and distribute reprints for Government purposes notwithstanding any copyright notation hereon. The views and conclusions contained herein are those of the authors and should not be interpreted as necessarily representing the official policies or endorsements, either expressed or implied, of DARPA, AFRL, or the U.S. Government.

5. Bogdanov, D., Laur, S., Willemson, J.: Sharemind: A framework for fast privacy-preserving computations. In: Jajodia, S., Lopez, J. (eds.) ESORICS 2008. LNCS, vol. 5283, pp. 192–206. Springer, Heidelberg (2008)

6. Brakerski, Z., Gentry, C., Vaikuntanathan, V.: (leveled) fully homomorphic encryption without bootstrapping. In: ITCS, pp. 309–325. ACM (2012)

7. Catrina, O., Saxena, A.: Secure computation with fixed-point numbers. In: Sion, R. (ed.) FC 2010. LNCS, vol. 6052, pp. 35–50. Springer, Heidelberg (2010)

8. Damgård, I., Fitzi, M., Kiltz, E., Nielsen, J.B., Toft, T.: Unconditionally secure constant-rounds multi-party computation for equality, comparison, bits and exponentiation. In: Halevi, S., Rabin, T. (eds.) TCC 2006. LNCS, vol. 3876, pp. 285–304. Springer, Heidelberg (2006)

9. Damgård, I., Geisler, M., Krøigaard, M., Nielsen, J.B.: Asynchronous multiparty computation: Theory and implementation. In: Jarecki, S., Tsudik, G. (eds.) PKC 2009. LNCS, vol. 5443, pp. 160–179. Springer, Heidelberg (2009)

10. Damgård, I., Keller, M.: Secure multiparty AES. In: Sion, R. (ed.) FC 2010. LNCS, vol. 6052, pp. 367–374. Springer, Heidelberg (2010)

11. Damgård, I., Keller, M., Larraia, E., Miles, C., Smart, N.P.: Implementing AES via an actively/covertly secure dishonest-majority MPC protocol. In: Visconti, I., De Prisco, R. (eds.) SCN 2012. LNCS, vol. 7485, pp. 241–263. Springer, Heidelberg (2012)

12. Damgård, I., Keller, M., Larraia, E., Pastro, V., Scholl, P., Smart, N.P.: Practical covertly secure MPC for dishonest majority – or: Breaking the SPDZ limits (2012)

13. Damgård, I., Pastro, V., Smart, N.P., Zakarias, S.: Multiparty computation from somewhat homomorphic encryption. In: Safavi-Naini, R., Canetti, R. (eds.) CRYPTO 2012. LNCS, vol. 7417, pp. 643–662. Springer, Heidelberg (2012)

14. Gentry, C., Halevi, S., Smart, N.P.: Fully homomorphic encryption with polylog overhead. In: Pointcheval, D., Johansson, T. (eds.) EUROCRYPT 2012. LNCS, vol. 7237, pp. 465–482. Springer, Heidelberg (2012)

15. Gentry, C., Halevi, S., Smart, N.P.: Homomorphic evaluation of the AES circuit. In: Safavi-Naini, R., Canetti, R. (eds.) CRYPTO 2012. LNCS, vol. 7417, pp. 850–867. Springer, Heidelberg (2012)

16. Kreuter, B., Shelat, A., Shen, C.-H.: Towards billion-gate secure computation with malicious adversaries. In: USENIX Security Symposium 2012, pp. 285–300 (2012)

17. Lindell, Y., Pinkas, B., Smart, N.P.: Implementing two-party computation efficiently with security against malicious adversaries. In: Ostrovsky, R., De Prisco, R., Visconti, I. (eds.) SCN 2008. LNCS, vol. 5229, pp. 2–20. Springer, Heidelberg (2008)

18. Malkhi, D., Nisan, N., Pinkas, B., Sella, Y.: Fairplay - Secure two-party computation system. In: USENIX Security Symposium 2004, pp. 287–302 (2004)

19. Montgomery, P.L.: Modular multiplication without trial division. Math. Comp. 44, 519–521 (1985)

20. Nielsen, J.B., Nordholt, P.S., Orlandi, C., Burra, S.S.: A new approach to practical active-secure two-party computation. In: Safavi-Naini, R., Canetti, R. (eds.) CRYPTO 2012. LNCS, vol. 7417, pp. 681–700. Springer, Heidelberg (2012)

21. Pinkas, B., Schneider, T., Smart, N.P., Williams, S.C.: Secure two-party computation is practical. In: Matsui, M. (ed.) ASIACRYPT 2009. LNCS, vol. 5912, pp. 250–267. Springer, Heidelberg (2009)

22. SIMAP Project. SIMAP: Secure information management and processing, http://alexandra.dk/uk/Projects/Pages/SIMAP.aspx

Practical and Employable Protocols
for UC-Secure Circuit Evaluation over $\mathbb{Z}_n$

Jan Camenisch[1], Robert R. Enderlein[1,2], and Victor Shoup[3]

[1] IBM Research – Zurich, Säumerstrasse 4, 8803 Rüschlikon, Switzerland
[2] Department of Computer Science, ETH Zürich, 8092 Zürich, Switzerland
[3] New York University, Courant Institute, NY 10012 New York, United States

Abstract. We present a set of new, efficient, universally composable two-party protocols for evaluating reactive arithmetic circuits modulo n, where n is a safe RSA modulus of unknown factorization. Our protocols are based on a homomorphic encryption scheme with message space $\mathbb{Z}_n$, zero-knowledge proofs of existence, and a novel "mixed" trapdoor commitment scheme. Our protocols are proven secure against *adaptive corruptions* (assuming secure *erasures*) under standard assumptions in the CRS model (without random oracles). Our protocols appear to be the most efficient ones that satisfy these security requirements. In contrast to prior protocols, we provide facilities that allow for the use of our protocols as building blocks of higher-level protocols.

Keywords: Two-party computation, Practical Protocols, UC-Security.

1 Introduction

Designing and proving secure large and complex cryptographic protocols is very challenging. Today, the security proofs of most practical protocols consider only a single instance of the protocol and therefore all security guarantees are lost if such a protocol is run concurrently with other protocols or with itself, in other words, when used in practice. Better security guarantees can be obtained when using composability frameworks—Canetti's Universal Composability (UC) [8], the similar GNUC [22] by Hofheinz and Shoup, or other frameworks [36,28,31]—which ensure that protocols proved secure in the framework remain secure under arbitrary composition. This also simplifies the design of protocols: high-level protocols can be composed from building block protocols and the security proofs of the high-level protocols can be based on the security of the building blocks and so become modular and easier.

Unfortunately, protocols proven secure in such composability frameworks are typically an order of magnitude less efficient than their traditional counterparts with "single-instance" security. Moreover, most UC-secure schemes and protocols found in the literature can not be used as building blocks for higher-level protocols because they do not offer the proper interfaces. That is, unless one considers only multi-party protocols with honest majority, it is typically not possible to ensure that a party's output of one building block is used as the party's input to another building block. We note that the situation for two-party protocols is different from UC-secure multi-party protocols with an honest majority where it is possible to secret-share all input and output values and then, by the virtue of the majority's honesty, it is ensured that the right outputs are used as inputs to the next building block.

J. Crampton, S. Jajodia, and K. Mayes (Eds.): ESORICS 2013, LNCS 8134, pp. 19–37, 2013.
© Springer-Verlag Berlin Heidelberg 2013

In this paper we are therefore interested in practically useful UC-secure building block protocols that provide interfaces so that parties in higher-level protocols can prove to each other that their inputs to one building block protocol correspond to the outputs of another building block protocol. More precisely, we provide a set of two-party protocols for evaluating an arithmetic circuit with reactive inputs and outputs. The protocols accept as (additional) inputs and provide as (additional) outputs tailored commitment values which, in conjunction with UC zero-knowledge proofs, make them a useful building block for higher-level protocols. In Section 8 of the full version of this paper [4], we we demonstrate the usefulness of our protocols by providing as example application an oblivious pseudorandom function evaluation. Additionally, we point out that our protocols can be used to implement the subprotocols required by Camenisch et al.'s credential authenticated identification and key-exchange protocols [3] (see Section 6.3 of their paper).

Apart from being the only protocols that allow for their use as building blocks, ours are also more efficient than existing UC-secure two-party reactive circuit evaluation protocols [18,24,19,2] which were designed to be used as standalone protocols.

Our contribution. Our main contribution is twofold: *1)* we provide a mechanism for protocol designers to easily integrate our arithmetic circuit functionality in their higher-level protocol in a practical yet secure manner; and *2)* we provide a concrete construction of the circuit evaluation protocol that is in itself more efficient than prior work. We achieve the latter by using cryptographic primitives that work very well together. Additionally, the tools we use in our construction—especially our novel mixed trapdoor commitment scheme—may be of independant interest.

Our protocols evaluate an arithmetic circuit modulo a composite number n, where n is a product of two large safe primes that is assumed to be generated by a trusted third party, and whose factorization remains otherwise unknown. We believe that in many practical cases, this is a natural assumption.

Our protocols are *universally composable* and proven secure under standard assumptions in a setting where parties can be *corrupted at any time*. It additionally assumes that *secure erasures* are possible and that parties can agree on a *common reference string* (CRS). We do not require random oracles. We strongly believe that achieving security against adaptive corruptions is crucial in order to achieve any meaningful sense of security in the "real world", where computers are compromised on a regular basis. The assumption of secure erasures is a pragmatic compromise: without it, obtaining a practical protocol seems unlikely; moreover, this assumption does not seem that unrealistic. Likewise, as it is impossible to achieve universal composability without some kind of setup assumption [11], a CRS seems like a reasonable, pragmatic compromise.

Our ideal functionality. We denote our basic ideal functionality for verifiably evaluating arithmetic circuits modulo n by $\mathcal{F}_{ABB}$ (our functionality is similar to Nielsen's arithmetic black box [32], hence the name). Parties compute the circuit step-by-step in a reactive manner by sending identical instructions with identical common input to $\mathcal{F}_{ABB}$. (For some instructions, one party must additionally provide private input to $\mathcal{F}_{ABB}$.) We assume that a higher-level protocol orchestrates the steps the parties take.

$\mathcal{F}_{\text{ABB}}$ processes instructions from the two parties of the following types: *Input:* a party inserts a value in $\mathbb{Z}_n$ into the circuit; *Linear Combination:* a linear combination of values in the circuit is computed; *Multiplication:* the product of two values in the circuit is computed; *Output:* a value in the circuit is output to a party; *Proof:* a party can prove an arbitrary statement to the other party in zero-knowledge involving values that she input in the circuit, values she got as an output, and values external to the circuit.

A party can use the *Proof* instruction to prove that the value inside a commitment used in the higher-level protocol is the same as a value in the circuit. This instruction thus makes it easy and practical to compose $\mathcal{F}_{\text{ABB}}$ with a higher-level protocol. To input a committed value from a higher-level protocol into the circuit, $\mathcal{P}$ would first use the *Input* instruction to set the value in the circuit, and then use the *Proof* instruction to convince $\mathcal{Q}$ that the new value corresponds to what was in the commitment. Similarly to transfer a value from the circuit to the higher-level protocol, $\mathcal{P}$ would first get the value with the *Output* instruction, generate a commitment in the higher-level protocol, and then use the *Proof* instruction to convince $\mathcal{Q}$ that the commitment contains the value that was output by the circuit.

All of our results are presented in the GNUC framework [22]. This has two advantages. First, the GNUC framework is mathematically consistent, and so our results have a clear mathematical meaning. Second, the GNUC framework supports the notion of a *system parameter*, which is how we wish to model the modulus n (a system parameter is formally modeled as an "ideal functionality", to which all parties—including the environment—have direct access).

Additional features. In Section 5 of the full version [4], we extend our framework with some features, such as generating random values and computing multiplicative inverses modulo n, using standard techniques. Other features require an extension of our ideal functionality. In particular we extend our ideal functionality with an *Exponentiated Output* instruction, which allows us to directly implement Jarecki and Liu's two-party protocol for computing an oblivious pseudorandom function (OPRF) [25].

Efficiency. Our protocols are quite practical; in particular, they do not require any expensive "cut and choose" techniques. The complexity of our protocols can be summarized as follows: if the circuits involved have t gates, the communication complexity is $O(t)$ elements of $\mathbb{Z}_{n^2}$ (and groups of similar or smaller order) and the computational complexity is $O(t)$ exponentiations in $\mathbb{Z}_{n^2}$ (and groups of similar or smaller order). We report on an experimental comparison of our protocols with relevant prior work in Section 6.1. We show that our protocols are practical, and that small circuits can be run in a few seconds—for example our implementation of Jarecki and Liu's OPRF (see [4]) would run in 0.84 seconds (for a 1248-bit modulus) on the authors' laptop computers.

Roadmap. In Section 2 we introduce the notation used in this paper, recapitulate some fundamental theory, and present our new mixed trapdoor commitment scheme. We describe our ideal functionality $\mathcal{F}_{\text{ABB}}$ for circuit evaluation in Section 3, and construct a concrete protocol in Section 4. We discuss the main ideas of our security proof in Section 5. In Section 6 we disucss related work, and compare the efficiency of our protocol with relevant related work.

2   Preliminaries

In this section we will introduce the notation used throughout this paper and provide some background on the UC model, zero-knowledge proofs of existence, and homomorphic encryption. Finally we provide a new construction of a commitment scheme, which might be of independant interest.

2.1   Notation

By $\mathbb{N}_i$ we denote the set of all natural numbers between 0 and $(i-1)$, by $\mathbb{Z}_i$ we denote the ring of integers modulo i. We use $\mathbb{N}_i^*$ and $\mathbb{Z}_i^*$ to denote $\mathbb{N}_i \setminus \{0\}$ and $\mathbb{Z}_i \setminus \{0\}$, respectively. If $\mathbb{A}$ is a set, then $a \xleftarrow{\$} \mathbb{A}$ means we set a to a random element of that set. If A is a Probabilistic Polynomial-Time (PPT) algorithm, then $y \xleftarrow{\$} \mathsf{A}(x)$ means we assign y to the output of $\mathsf{A}(x)$ when run with fresh random coins on input x.

Let Σ denote a fixed, finite alphabet of symbols (for example Unicode codepoints). Throughout this text we will use monospace fonts to denote characters in Σ, e.g.: P or Q. By Σ^* we denote the set of strings over Σ. We use the list-encoding function $\langle \cdot \rangle$ like in the GNUC paper [22]: If $a_1, \ldots, a_n \in \Sigma^*$, then $\langle a_1, \ldots, a_n \rangle$ is a string over Σ that encodes the list $(a_1, \ldots, a_n)$ in some canonical way.

If AP is a set, $AP \leftarrow k$ is a shorthand notation for inserting k into it: $AP \leftarrow AP \cup k$.

If V is an associative array, then $V[k] \leftarrow v$ denotes the insertion of the value v into the array under the identifier k. By $v' \leftarrow V[k]$, we denote the retrieval of the value associated with identifier k, and storing that retieved value in the variable v'. In this paper, we will never insert the same identifier twice in any array, and we will always use identifiers that were previously input into the array when retrieving a value.

$\mathcal{P}$ and $\mathcal{Q}$ denote the two parties in an interactive protocol, and $\mathcal{A}$ the adversary.

2.2   UC and GNUC Models

Protocols constructed for and proven secure in a composability framework can be securely composed in arbitrary ways. To date, there are five such frameworks: Universal Composability (UC) by Canetti [8], the similar GNUC framework by Hofheinz and Shoup [22], Reactive Simulatability by Pfitzmann and Waidner [36], IITMs by Küsters [28], and Abstract Cryptography by Maurer and Renner [31]. Even though the UC and GNUC frameworks differ in their mathematical formalism, they are essentially the same [22]. To understand this paper, it is sufficient to be familiar with either.

In the UC/GNUC framework, an abstract specification—often called the ideal functionality—describing the input and output behaviour of the protocol is given. A cryptographic protocol is then said to securely implement this ideal functionality, if an external adversary cannot distinguish between a run of the actual protocol and a run where the ideal functionality is performed by a trusted third party receiving the inputs and generating the ouputs for all parties. The protocol can now be used instead of the ideal functionality in any arbitrary complex system.

In this paper we make use of standard ideal functionalities: authenticated channels ($\mathcal{F}_{\mathrm{ach}}$), secure channels ($\mathcal{F}_{\mathrm{sch}}$), and zero-knowledge proofs ($\mathcal{F}_{\mathrm{ZK}}$) as described in Section 12.1 of the GNUC paper [22]. The first two functionalities are essentially the same as Canetti's [8]. The $\mathcal{F}_{\mathrm{ZK}}$ functionality of GNUC differs from Canetti's definition in that the instance of the predicate to be proven is a private input of the prover, and is delivered to the verifier only in the last message of the protocol: this enables the prover to securely erase her witnesses before revealing the statement to be proven.

We follow the formalism of GNUC to model common reference strings and system parameters—see Section 10 of the GNUC paper [22].

2.3 Zero-Knowledge Proofs of Existence

In the UC model, all proofs are necessarily proofs of *knowledge*. By embracing the extension to the UC model proposed by Camenisch, Krenn, and Shoup [5], it becomes possible to perform proofs of *existence* in addition to proofs of *knowledge*. The former are computationally significantly less expensive. To that effect, the paper introduced the *gullible* zero-knowledge functionality $\mathcal{F}_{gZK}$. Roughly speaking, $\mathcal{F}_{gZK}$ is similar to the well-known zero-knowledge proof functionality $\mathcal{F}_{ZK}$, except that not all the witnesses can be extracted. $\mathcal{F}_{gZK}$ is not an ideal functionality in the UC/GNUC sense, but abstracts a concrete zero-knowledge proof protocol using secure channels $\mathcal{F}_{sch}$ and a CRS.

When specifying the predicate to be proven, we will use the notation introduced by Camenisch, Krenn, and Shoup [5] (which is very similar to the Camenisch-Stadler notation [7]); for example: $\maltese\alpha \; \exists\beta \; : \; y = g^\beta \wedge z = g^\alpha h^\beta$ is used for proving the existence of the discrete logarithm of y to the base g, and of a representation of z to the bases g and h such that the h-part of this representation is equal to the discrete logarithm of y to the base g. Furthermore, knowledge of the g-part of the representation (discrete logarithm of the Elgamal plaintext) is proven. Variables quantified by $\maltese$ can be extracted by the simulator in the security proof, while variables quantified by $\exists$ cannot.

In this paper, we will be proving statements involving encryptions and commitments, all of which can be easily translated into predicates of the form considered in Camenisch et al.'s paper [5]. For predicates of this type, $\mathcal{F}_{gZK}$ can be efficiently realized in the CRS model.

Ideal functionality $\mathcal{F}_{gZK}$. In Camenisch et al's paper, the $\mathcal{F}_{gZK}$ ideal functionality was formally defined for the UC model, but one can easily port it to the GNUC model. We provide here only an informal description of $\mathcal{F}_{gZK}$, and refer their paper for details.

In the following we let R be a binary predicate that maps a triple (x, w_k, w_e) to 0 or 1, where x is called the *instance* and the pair (w_k, w_e) the *witness*. $\mathcal{F}_{gZK}$ is parametrized by R and a leakage function ℓ (which for example reports the length of its input). The functionality also expects an arbitrary label to distinguish different proof instances.

The common input to $\mathcal{F}_{gZK}$ is an arbitrary label. The prover's input is (x, w_k, w_e) where $R(x, w_k, w_e) = 1$. Next, $\mathcal{F}_{gZK}$ leaks the length of the instance and witness $\ell(x, w_k)$ to the adversary $\mathcal{A}$. After an acknowledgement by $\mathcal{A}$, $\mathcal{F}_{gZK}$ delivers the instance x to the verifier, while simultaneously erasing the witness (w_k, w_e). In the security proof, the simulator can extract w_k, but not w_e. Per convention, $\mathcal{F}_{gZK}$ rejects malformed messages and messages with duplicate labels.

2.4 Homomorphic Semantically Secure Encryption

Definition. We define the key generation function $(\mathsf{pk}, \mathsf{sk}) \xleftarrow{\$} \mathsf{KeyGen}(\mathsf{n})$, where n is a safe RSA modulus of unknown factorization. We define the encryption function

$E \leftarrow Enc(v, pk, r)$ that takes as input a plaintext v, a public key pk and some random-ness r, and outputs a ciphertext E. We will also use the shorthand notation $(E, r) \xleftarrow{\$} Enc(v, pk)$ in which the randomness r is chosen inside the Enc function. The corre-sponding decryption function $v' \leftarrow Dec(E, sk)$ takes as input the ciphertext and se-cret key, and outputs the plaintext. We assume that the encryption is homomorphic with respect to addition over $\mathbb{Z}_n$: $\forall v_1, v_2 \in \mathbb{Z}_n, r_1, r_2 : (pk, sk) \in KeyGen(n) \implies Dec(Enc(v_1, pk, r_1) * Enc(v_2, pk, r_2), sk) = v_1 + v_2$.

We require that correctness of encryption and decryption be efficiently provable with $\mathcal{F}_{gZK}$, and that it is possible to efficiently prove knowledge of sk given pk with $\mathcal{F}_{gZK}$. We will use a shorthand notation to denote such proofs, e.g.: $\exists sk, v : (pk, sk) \in KeyGen(n) \wedge v = Dec(E, sk)$.

Camenisch-Shoup encryption. An example of such an encryption scheme is the simpli-fied version of Camenisch-Shoup encryption [6,14] with a short private key and short randomness, described by Jarecki and Shmatikov [26]. The key generation function is: $x \xleftarrow{\$} \mathbb{Z}_{\lfloor\sqrt{n}\rfloor}, g' \xleftarrow{\$} \mathbb{Z}_{n^2}^*, g \leftarrow g'^{2n}, y \leftarrow g^x$; the secret key sk is x, and the public key pk is (g, y). To encrypt the message $v \in \mathbb{Z}_n$: $r \xleftarrow{\$} \mathbb{Z}_{\lfloor\sqrt{n}\rfloor}, u \leftarrow g^r, e \leftarrow y^r(n+1)^v \pmod{n^2}$; the ciphertext E is (u, e). To decrypt: $v''' \leftarrow (e/u^x)^2, v'' \leftarrow \frac{v'''-1}{n}$ (over the integers), $v' \leftarrow v'' \cdot 2^{-1} \pmod{n}$; output v'. This scheme is semantically secure if Paillier's Decision Composite Residuosity Assumption [35] holds.

2.5 Mixed Trapdoor Commitment Scheme

We now construct a commitment scheme which we will use instead of traditional UC commitment schemes [9] in our circuit evaluation protocol. Our commitment scheme works well with proofs of *existence* using $\mathcal{F}_{gZK}$, resulting in an efficiency gain in the overall protocol.[1] To the best of our knowledge, this is a novel scheme.

We define a mixed trapdoor commitment scheme to be a commitment scheme that is either: perfectly hiding and equivocable; or statistically binding, depending on the dis-tribution of the CRS. Mixed trapdoor commitments are similar to UC commitments [9] in that *1)* the simulator can equivocate commitments in the security proof without being caught, even if he has to provide all randomness used to generate the commitment to the adversary; and *2)* the simulator can use an adversary who equivocates commitments to solve a hard cryptographic problem. However unlike UC commitments, in mixed trapdoor commitments *3)* the simulator *does not need to extract the openings or the committed values* from $\mathcal{F}_{gZK}$.

Definition. Let $\mathfrak{cp}_i \xleftarrow{\$} ComGen_i(n)$ for $i \in \{0, 1\}$ be functions that generate param-eters for a commitment scheme. If $i = 0$, the commitment scheme is perfectly hid-ing (computationally binding), and if $i = 1$, the commitment scheme is statistically binding (computationally hiding). For the perfect-hiding setting, we define the function $(\mathfrak{cp}'_0, t) \xleftarrow{\$} ComGen'_0(n)$ that additionally outputs a trapdoor t. We further require that $\mathfrak{cp}_0, \mathfrak{cp}'_0$, and $\mathfrak{cp}_1$ are pairwise computationally indistinguishable.

---

[1] The efficiency gain due to using proofs of existence instead of proofs of knowledge outweighs the efficiency loss due to the more complex commitment scheme.

We define the function $(\mathfrak{C}, \mathfrak{x}) \xleftarrow{\$} \mathsf{Com}_{\mathfrak{cp}_i}(v)$ that takes as input a value $v \in \mathbb{Z}_n$ to be committed, and outputs a commitment $\mathfrak{C}$ and an opening $\mathfrak{x}$ to the commitment. We will also use the notation $\mathfrak{C} \leftarrow \mathsf{Com}_{\mathfrak{cp}_i}(v, \mathfrak{x})$, where the opening is chosen outside of the function. Conversely, we define the verification function $\mathsf{ComVfy}_{\mathfrak{cp}_i}(\mathfrak{C}, \mathfrak{x}, v)$ that checks whether the tuple $(\mathfrak{C}, \mathfrak{x})$ is one of the possible values generated by $\mathsf{Com}_{\mathfrak{cp}_i}(v)$. The commitments are homomorphic with respect to addition over $\mathbb{Z}_n$: $\mathsf{ComVfy}_{\mathfrak{cp}_i}(\mathfrak{C}_1, \mathfrak{x}_1, v_1) \wedge \mathsf{ComVfy}_{\mathfrak{cp}_i}(\mathfrak{C}_2, \mathfrak{x}_2, v_2) \implies \mathsf{ComVfy}_{\mathfrak{cp}_i}(\mathfrak{C}_1 * \mathfrak{C}_2, \mathfrak{x}_1 + \mathfrak{x}_2, v_1 + v_2)$. With a trapdoor t it is possible to efficiently equivocate commitments in the perfect-hiding setting: $\forall v' \in \mathbb{Z}_n$; $\mathfrak{x}' \leftarrow \mathsf{Trapdoor}_{\mathfrak{cp}'_0}(t, \mathfrak{C}, \mathfrak{x}, v, v')$: $\mathsf{ComVfy}_{\mathfrak{cp}'_0}(\mathfrak{C}, \mathfrak{x}, v) \implies \mathsf{ComVfy}_{\mathfrak{cp}'_0}(\mathfrak{C}, \mathfrak{x}', v')$.

We require that verifying a commitment be efficient with $\mathcal{F}_{\mathsf{gZK}}$.

In the sequel, we drop the subscript $\mathfrak{cp}_i$ if it clear which parameters need to be used.

Construction based on Elgamal. We now provide the construction of a mixed trapdoor commitment scheme based on Elgamal encryption. We construct ComGen_1 as follows: *1)* find the first prime $\mathfrak{p}$ such that $\mathfrak{p} = k \cdot n + 1$ for some $k \in \mathbb{N}$— according to a heuristic[2] by Wagstaff [38]: $\mathfrak{p} < n \cdot (\log n)^2$; *2)* find a generator $\mathfrak{g}$ of a subgroup of $\mathbb{Z}_\mathfrak{p}$ of order n; *3)* select $\mathfrak{a}, t, m$ at random from $\mathbb{Z}_n$; *4)* compute $\mathfrak{h} \leftarrow \mathfrak{g}^\mathfrak{a}$, $\mathfrak{y} \leftarrow \mathfrak{g}^m \mathfrak{h}^t$, $\mathfrak{u} \leftarrow \mathfrak{g}^t$, i.e., $(\mathfrak{y}, \mathfrak{u})$ is the Elgamal encryption of $\mathfrak{g}^m$ with the public key $(\mathfrak{g}, \mathfrak{h})$; *5)* output $\mathfrak{cp}_1 \leftarrow (\mathfrak{p}, \mathfrak{g}, \mathfrak{h}, \mathfrak{y}, \mathfrak{u})$. In practice, where we want to select a random common reference string $\mathfrak{cp}_1$, it is also possible to randomly sample $\mathfrak{h}, \mathfrak{y}$, and $\mathfrak{u}$ from the subgroup generated by $\mathfrak{g}$. With high probability, we have that $\gcd(\mathfrak{a}, n) = \gcd(m, n) = \gcd(t, n) = 1$, which means that $\mathfrak{h}, \mathfrak{y}, \mathfrak{u}$ are all of order n. We construct ComGen_0 similarly, except that in step 3, we set $m \leftarrow 0$. The function ComGen'_0 additionally outputs t.

To commit to $v \in \mathbb{Z}_n$, one sets $\mathfrak{x} \xleftarrow{\$} \mathbb{Z}_n$; $\mathfrak{C}_1 \leftarrow \mathfrak{y}^v \mathfrak{h}^\mathfrak{x}$; $\mathfrak{C}_2 \leftarrow \mathfrak{u}^v \mathfrak{g}^\mathfrak{x}$; and $\mathfrak{C} \leftarrow (\mathfrak{C}_1, \mathfrak{C}_2)$. The latter is a re-randomized encryption of $\mathfrak{g}^{m \cdot v}$. Verification is trivial. Finally, if $m = 0$ and one knows the trapdoor information t, one can open the commitment $\mathfrak{C}$ to a different value $v' \in \mathbb{Z}_n$ by setting $\mathfrak{x}' \leftarrow (v - v') \cdot t + \mathfrak{x}$.

3   Our Ideal Functionality $\mathcal{F}_{\mathsf{ABB}}$

In this section, we will give a short informal definition of the ideal functionality $\mathcal{F}_{\mathsf{ABB}}$ (arithmetic black box) for doing computation over $\mathbb{Z}_n$. We give the formal definition in the full version [4].

The functionality $\mathcal{F}_{\mathsf{ABB}}$ reacts to a set of instructions. Per convention, both parties must agree on the instruction and the shared input before $\mathcal{F}_{\mathsf{ABB}}$ executes it. An instruction may require $\mathcal{P}$ and $\mathcal{Q}$ to send multiple messages to $\mathcal{F}_{\mathsf{ABB}}$ in a specific order, however $\mathcal{F}_{\mathsf{ABB}}$ may run other instructions concurrently while waiting for the next message. More precisely $\mathcal{P}$ and $\mathcal{Q}$ can: provide inputs to $\mathcal{F}_{\mathsf{ABB}}$; ask it do to a linear combination or multiplication of previous inputs or intermediate results; ask it to output a value to one of them; and do an arbitrary zero-knowledge proof involving inputs/outputs to/from the circuit and external witnesses. These instructions can be arbitrarily interleaved, intermediate results output and new inputs be provided. The input values provided by $\mathcal{P}$ and $\mathcal{Q}$ may depend on output values obtained. Following the GNUC formalism, each message sent to $\mathcal{F}_{\mathsf{ABB}}$ is prefixed with a label which contains, among others, the name

---

[2] We confirmed this experimentally for 250 randomly generated 1248-bit safe RSA moduli.

of the instruction to execute, the current step in the instruction this message refers to, and the shared input φ; the private inputs are always part of the message body.

State. The ideal functionality $\mathcal{F}_{\text{ABB}}$ is stateful. It maintains an associative array V, mapping identifiers (in $\Sigma^\star$) to integer values (in $\mathbb{Z}_n$).

Instructions. These are the instructions supported by $\mathcal{F}_{\text{ABB}}$:

- *Input from $\mathcal{P}$:* $\mathcal{P}$'s private input is the value v. $\mathcal{F}_{\text{ABB}}$ parses the shared input φ as $\langle k \rangle$, where k will be the identifier associated to the value v, and sets $V[k] \leftarrow v$.
- *Input from $\mathcal{Q}$:* $\mathcal{Q}$'s private input is v. $\mathcal{F}_{\text{ABB}}$ parses φ as $\langle k \rangle$, and sets $V[k] \leftarrow v$.
- *Linear combination:* $\mathcal{F}_{\text{ABB}}$ parses φ as $\langle m, k_0, v_0, \langle k_1, v_1 \rangle, \ldots, \langle k_{m-1}, v_{m-1} \rangle \rangle$ and sets: $V[k_0] \leftarrow v_0 + \sum_{i=1}^{m-1} V[k_i] \cdot v_i$.
- *Multiplication:* $\mathcal{F}_{\text{ABB}}$ parses φ as $\langle k_0, k_1, k_2 \rangle$ and sets: $V[k_0] \leftarrow V[k_1] \cdot V[k_2]$.
- *Output to $\mathcal{P}$:* $\mathcal{F}_{\text{ABB}}$ parses φ as $\langle k \rangle$, and sends $V[k]$ (as a *delayed output*) to $\mathcal{P}$.
- *Output to $\mathcal{Q}$:* $\mathcal{F}_{\text{ABB}}$ parses φ as $\langle k \rangle$, and sends $V[k]$ (as a *delayed output*) to $\mathcal{Q}$.
- *Proof by $\mathcal{P}$:* This instruction can be used to prove a statement about values that were input/output to/from from the circuit ($\mathcal{F}_{\text{ABB}}$) and witnesses from a higher-level protocol. $\mathcal{P}$'s private input is $\langle x, w_k \rangle$. $\mathcal{F}_{\text{ABB}}$ parses φ as $\langle m, \langle k_0, \ldots, k_{m-1} \rangle, R \rangle$, where is R is a binary predicate that is compatible with $\mathcal{F}_{\text{gZK}}$ and which can involve *1)* values that were input by $\mathcal{P}$ to $\mathcal{F}_{\text{ABB}}$, *2)* values that were output to $\mathcal{P}$ from $\mathcal{F}_{\text{ABB}}$, and *3)* witnesses external to $\mathcal{F}_{\text{ABB}}$; x is an instance for R; w_k is a list of witnesses that are external to the circuit whose knowledge are proven; and $k_0, \ldots, k_{m-1}$ are identifiers of values in the circuit that were input by $\mathcal{P}$ or output to $\mathcal{P}$. $\mathcal{F}_{\text{ABB}}$ checks if the predicate holds, i.e., if $R\big(x, \ w_k \cup (V[k_0], \ldots, V[k_{m-1}])\big) = 1$; and sends $\langle x \rangle$ (as a *delayed output*) to $\mathcal{Q}$. In the full version [4], we define an extention of $\mathcal{F}_{\text{ABB}}$ denoted $\mathcal{F}_{\text{gABB}}$ which also allows for proofs of *existence* inside this functionality.
- *Proof by $\mathcal{Q}$:* Similar to *Proof by $\mathcal{P}$* , with the roles of $\mathcal{P}$ and $\mathcal{Q}$ reversed.
- *Dynamic corruption:* $\mathcal{F}_{\text{ABB}}$ accepts a special corrupt message from $\mathcal{P}$ or $\mathcal{Q}$. From then on, all input and output of the corrupted party is redirected to the adversary $\mathcal{A}$, and $\mathcal{A}$ may recover all of the corrupted party's input (by asking $\mathcal{F}_{\text{ABB}}$ for it).

Treatment of invalid input. In case $\mathcal{F}_{\text{ABB}}$ receives a message it does not expect, a message that it cannot parse, or a message with a label it has seen previously from the same party, it simply ignores the message.

Comments. The value of n is not an input to $\mathcal{F}_{\text{ABB}}$, nor is it modeled as a CRS. Rather, it is modeled in the GNUC framework as a *system parameter*. Roughly speaking, this is a special type of ideal functionality to which all parties, including the environment, have common access. The value of n is generated by a trusted party, and no other party learns its factorization. Furthermore, the modulus n can be re-used across different protocol instances. In the setting of credential-authenticated identification [3] this is completely natural, as one can use a modulus generated by the credential issuer. In a different context, we can also imagine using the modulus n of a well-known and respected certificate authority (e.g., the modulus in Verisign's root certificate).

Our ideal functionality $\mathcal{F}_{\text{ABB}}$ shares some similarity with Nielsen's arithmetic black box (ABB) [32], and Damgård and Orlandi's $\mathcal{F}_{\text{AMPC}}$ [19]. The major difference is that our $\mathcal{F}_{\text{ABB}}$ includes the *Proof* instruction, allowing values from higher-level protocols to be input and output securely. This instruction is crucial as it allows meaningful composition with other protocols (see Introduction). Unlike $\mathcal{F}_{\text{AMPC}}$, we do not support random number generation in the vanilla $\mathcal{F}_{\text{ABB}}$ for simplicity; see Section 5 of the full version [4] for an algorithm generating these that uses only our core set of instructions.

4   Construction

We now show how to construct a protocol Π_{ABB} for circuit evaluation modulo n. Our protocol uses two ideal functionalities: $\mathcal{F}_{\text{ach}}$ (authenticated channels) and $\mathcal{F}_{\text{gZK}}$ (zero-knowledge proofs). Additionally, we make use of a system parameter, the modulus n of unknown factorization; and a CRS, consisting of the output of ComGen_1 (statistically-binding commitment).

High-level idea. The high-level idea of our construction is that $\mathcal{P}$ and $\mathcal{Q}$ generate additive shares of all the values (inputs and intermediate results) in the circuit. Identifiers are used to keep track of the values and the cryptographic objects associated with them. Like for $\mathcal{F}_{\text{ABB}}$, parties agree on the instruction to be performed by sending a message containing an identical instruction name and identical common input to the protocol Π_{ABB}. The instructions of Π_{ABB} are implemented as follows: *Input* is achieved by one party setting her share to the input, and generating a commitment to that share; the other party sets his share to zero. *Output* is achieved by one party sending her share to the other party. For the *Linear combination* instruction, each party does a linear combination of their shares locally. For the *Multiplication* instruction, we make use of two instances of a 2-party subroutine Π_{mul}: on $\mathcal{P}$'s input a, and $\mathcal{Q}$'s input b, Π_{mul} outputs u to $\mathcal{P}$ and v to $\mathcal{Q}$ such that $u + v = a \cdot b$. The *Proof* instruction can be done with the help of a zero-knowledge proof functionality $\mathcal{F}_{\text{gZK}}$. To ensure security against malicious adversaries, both parties update the commitments to the shares in each instruction, and prove in zero-knowledge that all their computations were done honestly.

The Π_{mul} subroutine makes use of a homomorphic (modulo n), semantically secure, public-key encryption scheme, along with our mixed trapdoor commitment scheme. To achieve security against adaptive corruptions, new encryption/decryption keys need to be generated for every multiplication. To do this in a practical way, we use the semantically secure version of Camenisch-Shoup encryption [6,14,26] with a short private key and short randomness, as described in Section 2.4. One key feature of this scheme is that key generation is fast: just a single exponentiation modulo n^2. Another key feature is that many encryption/decryption keys can be used in conjunction with the same n, which is crucial. Our commitment scheme is also used extensively in the overall protocol. We use the construction presented in Section 2.5 and work in the group of integers modulo a prime of the form $k \cdot n + 1$. The homomorphic properties of the commitment scheme makes this choice of prime particularly useful and practical. Another tool we make heavy use of is UC zero-knowledge. Because of the proposed implementations of encryption and commitment schemes, these proof systems can all be implemented using the approach proposed by Camenisch et al. [5]. Because the encryption and commitment schemes are both homomorphic modulo n, all of our cryptographic tools work very well together, and yield quite practical protocols. We also stress that our protocols are designed in a modular way: they only make use of these abstract primitives, and not of *ad hoc* algebraic constructions.

$\mathcal{P}$ **proceeds as follows:**	$\mathcal{Q}$ **proceeds as follows:**
$\mathcal{P}$'s input is $\langle \varphi, v \rangle$ with $v \in \mathbb{Z}_n$.	$\mathcal{Q}$'s input is $\langle \varphi \rangle$.
Parse φ as $\langle k \rangle$ with $k \in \Sigma^*$. Abort if $k \in AP$.	Parse φ as $\langle k \rangle$ with $k \in \Sigma^*$. Abort if $k \in AQ$.
Mark the identifier as assigned: $AP \leftarrow k$.	Mark the identifier as assigned: $AQ \leftarrow k$.
Set shares: $SP[k] \leftarrow v$ and $SQ[k] \leftarrow 0$.	Set own share: $SQ[k] \leftarrow 0$.
Commit to share: $(CP[k], XP[k]) \xleftarrow{\$} \mathsf{Com}(v)$.	Commit: $CQ[k] \leftarrow \mathsf{Com}(0,0)$; $XQ[k] \leftarrow 0$.
$\mathcal{P}$ proves the following to $\mathcal{Q}$ using $\mathcal{F}_{\mathrm{gZK}}$ with label $\langle \mathtt{ip}, \varphi \rangle$: $$\maltese v \ \exists XP[k] : \mathsf{ComVfy}(CP[k], XP[k], v) \ .$$ The value $CP[k]$ is delivered to $\mathcal{Q}$ via $\mathcal{F}_{\mathrm{gZK}}$.	
Set other's commitment: $CQ[k] \leftarrow \mathsf{Com}(0,0)$.	
Mark value as ready: $RP \leftarrow k$.	Mark value as ready: $RQ \leftarrow k$.
Mark it as known: $KP \leftarrow k$.	Mark it as known by $\mathcal{P}$: $KP \leftarrow k$.

Fig. 1. Input from $\mathcal{P}$

4.1 Realizing Π_{ABB}

$\mathcal{P}$ and $\mathcal{Q}$ each maintain the following global state: several associative arrays mapping the identifier of a value in the circuit (in Σ^*) to a variety of cryptographic objects: SP and SQ map to the shares of $\mathcal{P}$ and $\mathcal{Q}$ of the values in the circuit (in $\mathbb{Z}_n$), respectively; CP and CQ map to the commitment of the corresponding shares; XP (maintained by $\mathcal{P}$ only) and XQ ($\mathcal{Q}$ only) map to the opening of the commitments. For the *Proof* functionality, both parties maintain lists of identifiers corresponding to values that are known to $\mathcal{P}$ and $\mathcal{Q}$: KP and KQ, respectively. Additionally, to ensure "thread-safety", they also maintain: lists of assigned identifiers AP ($\mathcal{P}$ only) and AQ ($\mathcal{Q}$ only) to avoid assigning the same identifier to several variables; and lists of identifiers RP ($\mathcal{P}$ only) and RQ ($\mathcal{Q}$ only) corresponding to values that are ready to be used in other instructions. The array that one would obtain by summing the entries of SP and SQ corresponding to values that are ready (i.e., $\{(k, v) | k \in RP \cap RQ \wedge v = SP[k] + SQ[k]\}$), corresponds to the array V of the ideal functionality, that maps identifiers to values in the circuit.

All other variables that we will introduce are local to one instance of a instruction or an instance of the Π_{mul} subroutine. Several instructions may be active at the same time, however we assume (following the GNUC model) that all operations performed during an activation (the time interval between starting to process a new input message and sending a message to another functionality) happen atomically.

Input from $\mathcal{P}$. In this instruction, $\mathcal{P}$ inputs a value v into the circuit and associates it with the identifier k: $\mathcal{P}$ sets her own share to v, and $\mathcal{Q}$ sets his share to 0. Then $\mathcal{P}$ generates a commitment to her share, which she sends (along with proof) to $\mathcal{Q}$. See Figure 1 for the construction.

Input from $\mathcal{Q}$. Similar to the previous instruction, with the roles of $\mathcal{P}$ and $\mathcal{Q}$ reversed.

Output to $\mathcal{Q}$. In this instruction, $\mathcal{Q}$ retrieves the value identified by k from the circuit: $\mathcal{P}$ sends her share to $\mathcal{Q}$ together with a proof of correctness. See Figure 2.

Output to $\mathcal{P}$. Similar to the previous instruction, with the roles of $\mathcal{P}$ and $\mathcal{Q}$ reversed.

Linear combination. In this instruction, a linear combination of values in the circuit (plus an optional constant) is computed: $V[k_0] \leftarrow v_0 + \sum_{i=1}^{m-1} V[k_i] \cdot v_i$. Concretely, both

$\mathcal{P}$ proceeds as follows:	$\mathcal{Q}$ proceeds as follows:
Both parties' input is $\langle\varphi\rangle$. It is parsed as $\varphi = \langle k\rangle$ with $k \in \Sigma^\star$.	
Wait until $k \in RP$.	Wait until $k \in RQ$.
$\mathcal{P}$ proves the following to $\mathcal{Q}$ using $\mathcal{F}_{\mathrm{gZK}}$ with label $\langle\mathrm{oq},\varphi\rangle$: $\exists XP[k] : \mathrm{ComVfy}(CP[k], XP[k], SP[k])$. The value $SP[k]$ is delivered to $\mathcal{Q}$ via $\mathcal{F}_{\mathrm{gZK}}$.	
Mark value as known to $\mathcal{Q}$: $KQ \leftarrow k$.	Save $SP[k]$, and mark as known: $KQ \leftarrow k$. $\mathcal{Q}$ returns $(SP[k] + SQ[k])$.

Fig. 2. Output to $\mathcal{Q}$

$\mathcal{P}$ proceeds as follows:	$\mathcal{Q}$ proceeds as follows:
Both parties' input is $\langle\varphi\rangle$. It is parsed as $\varphi = \langle m, k_0, v_0, \langle k_1, v_1\rangle, \ldots, \langle k_{m-1}, v_{m-1}\rangle\rangle$ with $m \in \mathbb{N}^*, \forall i \in \mathbb{N}_m : k_i \in \Sigma^*$ and $\forall i \in \mathbb{N}_m : v_i \in \mathbb{Z}_n$.	
Abort if $k_0 \in AP$. Mark identifier: $AP \leftarrow k_0$. Wait until $\forall i \in \mathbb{N}_m : k_i \in RP$. Update own share: $SP[k_0] \leftarrow v_0 + \sum_{i=1}^{m-1} SP[k_i] \cdot v_i$; com.: $CP[k_0] \leftarrow \mathrm{Com}(v_0, 0) * \prod_{i=1}^{m-1} CP[k_i]^{v_i}$; opening: $XP[k_0] \leftarrow \sum_{i=1}^{m-1} XP[k_i] \cdot v_i$; $\mathcal{Q}$'s commitment: $CQ[k_0] \leftarrow \prod_{i=1}^{m-1} CQ[k_i]^{v_i}$.	Abort if $k_0 \in AQ$. Mark identifier: $AQ \leftarrow k_0$. Wait until $\forall i \in \mathbb{N}_m : k_i \in RQ$. Update own share: $SQ[k_0] \leftarrow \sum_{i=1}^{m-1} SQ[k_i] \cdot v_i$; commitment: $CQ[k_0] \leftarrow \prod_{i=1}^{m-1} CQ[k_i]^{v_i}$; opening: $XQ[k_0] \leftarrow \sum_{i=1}^{m-1} XQ[k_i] \cdot v_i$; $\mathcal{P}$'s c.: $CP[k_0] \leftarrow \mathrm{Com}(v_0, 0) * \prod_{i=1}^{m-1} CP[k_i]^{v_i}$.
$\mathcal{P}$ sends the empty string to $\mathcal{Q}$ using $\mathcal{F}_{\mathrm{ach}}$ with label $\langle 1,\varphi\rangle$ to ensure that they agree on φ.	
Mark value as ready: $RP \leftarrow k_0$.	Mark value as ready: $RQ \leftarrow k_0$.

Fig. 3. Linear combination

parties perform local operations on their shares. Additionally, $\mathcal{P}$ sends an empty message to $\mathcal{Q}$ to ensure that both parties agree on the shared input φ. See Figure 3.

Multiplication. In this instruction, the product of two values in the circuit is computed: $V[k_0] \leftarrow V[k_1] \cdot V[k_2]$. We can rewrite this as:

$$SP[k_0] + SQ[k_0] \leftarrow \underbrace{SP[k_1]{\cdot}SP[k_2]}_{\hat{p}} + \underbrace{SP[k_1]{\cdot}SQ[k_2]}_{(\tilde{u}+\tilde{v})} + \underbrace{SQ[k_1]{\cdot}SP[k_2]}_{(u+v)} + \underbrace{SQ[k_1]{\cdot}SQ[k_2]}_{\hat{q}}$$

where we introduce $\hat{p}, \hat{q}, \tilde{u}, \tilde{v}, u, v$ to simplify the discussion. The idea of this protocol is for $\mathcal{P}$ and $\mathcal{Q}$ to compute $\hat{p}$ and $\hat{q}$, respectively, using their private shares. They then jointly compute $\tilde{u}$ and $\tilde{v}$ using the Π_{mul} subroutine, which we introduce for clarity and which we describe in Section 4.2. Afterwards, u and v are computed using a second instantiation of Π_{mul}. Finally, $\mathcal{P}$ sets $SP[k_0] \leftarrow \hat{p}+\tilde{u}+u$ and $\mathcal{Q}$ sets $SQ[k_0] \leftarrow \hat{q}+\tilde{v}+v$. See Figure 4 for the construction.

One can optimize the protocol in Figure 4 by using the same homomorphic encryption key for both instances of Π_{mul} and merging the proofs inside and outside of Π_{mul} whenever possible.[3] We can thus save one proof of correctess for the encryption key, and save on some overhead in $\mathcal{F}_{\mathrm{gZK}}$.

---

[3] Concretely, one would merge the proofs with the following labels: *1)* $\langle\mathrm{m5},\varphi\rangle$, $\langle\mathrm{cm1},\langle\mathrm{m7},\varphi\rangle\rangle$ and $\langle\mathrm{cm1},\langle\mathrm{m8},\varphi\rangle\rangle$; *2)* $\langle\mathrm{m6},\varphi\rangle$, $\langle\mathrm{cm2},\langle\mathrm{m7},\varphi\rangle\rangle$, and $\langle\mathrm{cm2},\langle\mathrm{m8},\varphi\rangle\rangle$; *3)* $\langle\mathrm{cm3},\langle\mathrm{m7},\varphi\rangle\rangle$ and $\langle\mathrm{cm3},\langle\mathrm{m8},\varphi\rangle\rangle$; *4)* $\langle\mathrm{cm4},\langle\mathrm{m7},\varphi\rangle\rangle$ and $\langle\mathrm{cm4},\langle\mathrm{m8},\varphi\rangle\rangle$.

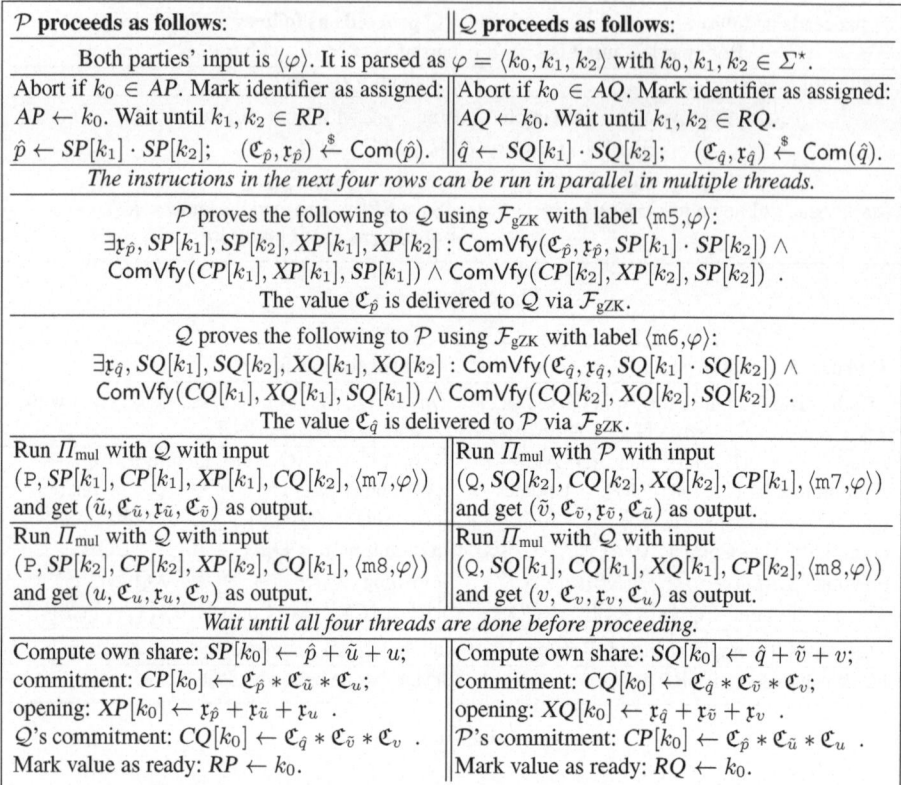

$\mathcal{P}$ **proceeds as follows:**	$\mathcal{Q}$ **proceeds as follows:**
Both parties' input is $\langle\varphi\rangle$. It is parsed as $\varphi = \langle k_0, k_1, k_2\rangle$ with $k_0, k_1, k_2 \in \Sigma^\star$.	
Abort if $k_0 \in AP$. Mark identifier as assigned:	Abort if $k_0 \in AQ$. Mark identifier as assigned:
$AP \leftarrow k_0$. Wait until $k_1, k_2 \in RP$.	$AQ \leftarrow k_0$. Wait until $k_1, k_2 \in RQ$.
$\hat{p} \leftarrow SP[k_1] \cdot SP[k_2]$; $\quad(\mathfrak{C}_{\hat{p}}, \mathfrak{r}_{\hat{p}}) \overset{\$}{\leftarrow} \mathsf{Com}(\hat{p})$.	$\hat{q} \leftarrow SQ[k_1] \cdot SQ[k_2]$; $\quad(\mathfrak{C}_{\hat{q}}, \mathfrak{r}_{\hat{q}}) \overset{\$}{\leftarrow} \mathsf{Com}(\hat{q})$.

The instructions in the next four rows can be run in parallel in multiple threads.

$\mathcal{P}$ proves the following to $\mathcal{Q}$ using $\mathcal{F}_{\mathrm{gZK}}$ with label $\langle\mathrm{m5},\varphi\rangle$:
$$\exists \mathfrak{r}_{\hat{p}}, SP[k_1], SP[k_2], XP[k_1], XP[k_2] : \mathsf{ComVfy}(\mathfrak{C}_{\hat{p}}, \mathfrak{r}_{\hat{p}}, SP[k_1] \cdot SP[k_2]) \wedge$$
$$\mathsf{ComVfy}(CP[k_1], XP[k_1], SP[k_1]) \wedge \mathsf{ComVfy}(CP[k_2], XP[k_2], SP[k_2]) .$$
The value $\mathfrak{C}_{\hat{p}}$ is delivered to $\mathcal{Q}$ via $\mathcal{F}_{\mathrm{gZK}}$.

$\mathcal{Q}$ proves the following to $\mathcal{P}$ using $\mathcal{F}_{\mathrm{gZK}}$ with label $\langle\mathrm{m6},\varphi\rangle$:
$$\exists \mathfrak{r}_{\hat{q}}, SQ[k_1], SQ[k_2], XQ[k_1], XQ[k_2] : \mathsf{ComVfy}(\mathfrak{C}_{\hat{q}}, \mathfrak{r}_{\hat{q}}, SQ[k_1] \cdot SQ[k_2]) \wedge$$
$$\mathsf{ComVfy}(CQ[k_1], XQ[k_1], SQ[k_1]) \wedge \mathsf{ComVfy}(CQ[k_2], XQ[k_2], SQ[k_2]) .$$
The value $\mathfrak{C}_{\hat{q}}$ is delivered to $\mathcal{P}$ via $\mathcal{F}_{\mathrm{gZK}}$.

Run Π_{mul} with $\mathcal{Q}$ with input	Run Π_{mul} with $\mathcal{P}$ with input
$(\mathrm{P}, SP[k_1], CP[k_1], XP[k_1], CQ[k_2], \langle\mathrm{m7},\varphi\rangle)$	$(\mathrm{Q}, SQ[k_2], CQ[k_2], XQ[k_2], CP[k_1], \langle\mathrm{m7},\varphi\rangle)$
and get $(\tilde{u}, \mathfrak{C}_{\tilde{u}}, \mathfrak{r}_{\tilde{u}}, \mathfrak{C}_{\tilde{v}})$ as output.	and get $(\tilde{v}, \mathfrak{C}_{\tilde{v}}, \mathfrak{r}_{\tilde{v}}, \mathfrak{C}_{\tilde{u}})$ as output.
Run Π_{mul} with $\mathcal{Q}$ with input	Run Π_{mul} with $\mathcal{Q}$ with input
$(\mathrm{P}, SP[k_2], CP[k_2], XP[k_2], CQ[k_1], \langle\mathrm{m8},\varphi\rangle)$	$(\mathrm{Q}, SQ[k_1], CQ[k_1], XQ[k_1], CP[k_2], \langle\mathrm{m8},\varphi\rangle)$
and get $(u, \mathfrak{C}_u, \mathfrak{r}_u, \mathfrak{C}_v)$ as output.	and get $(v, \mathfrak{C}_v, \mathfrak{r}_v, \mathfrak{C}_u)$ as output.

Wait until all four threads are done before proceeding.

Compute own share: $SP[k_0] \leftarrow \hat{p} + \tilde{u} + u$;	Compute own share: $SQ[k_0] \leftarrow \hat{q} + \tilde{v} + v$;
commitment: $CP[k_0] \leftarrow \mathfrak{C}_{\hat{p}} * \mathfrak{C}_{\tilde{u}} * \mathfrak{C}_u$;	commitment: $CQ[k_0] \leftarrow \mathfrak{C}_{\hat{q}} * \mathfrak{C}_{\tilde{v}} * \mathfrak{C}_v$;
opening: $XP[k_0] \leftarrow \mathfrak{r}_{\hat{p}} + \mathfrak{r}_{\tilde{u}} + \mathfrak{r}_u$;	opening: $XQ[k_0] \leftarrow \mathfrak{r}_{\hat{q}} + \mathfrak{r}_{\tilde{v}} + \mathfrak{r}_v$;
$\mathcal{Q}$'s commitment: $CQ[k_0] \leftarrow \mathfrak{C}_{\hat{q}} * \mathfrak{C}_{\tilde{v}} * \mathfrak{C}_v$.	$\mathcal{P}$'s commitment: $CP[k_0] \leftarrow \mathfrak{C}_{\hat{p}} * \mathfrak{C}_{\tilde{u}} * \mathfrak{C}_u$.
Mark value as ready: $RP \leftarrow k_0$.	Mark value as ready: $RQ \leftarrow k_0$.

Fig. 4. Multiplication. The subroutine Π_{mul} is defined in Section 4.2 and Figure 6

$\mathcal{P}$ **proceeds as follows:**	$\mathcal{Q}$ **proceeds as follows:**
$\mathcal{P}$'s input is $\langle\varphi, x, \tilde{m}, w_k\rangle$.	$\mathcal{Q}$'s input is $\langle\varphi\rangle$, where
She parses φ like $\mathcal{Q}$; x is an instance for R;	$\varphi = \langle m, \langle k_0, \ldots, k_{m-1}\rangle, R\rangle$;
$\tilde{m} \in \mathbb{N}$; $w_k = \langle w_{k,0}, \ldots, w_{k,\tilde{m}-1}\rangle$ is a list of	R is a predicate that is compatible with $\mathcal{F}_{\mathrm{gZK}}$;
witnesses.	$m \in \mathbb{N}$; and $\forall i \in \mathbb{N}_m : k_i \in \Sigma^\star$.
Wait until $\forall i \in \mathbb{N}_m : k_i \in KP$.	Wait until $\forall i \in \mathbb{N}_m : k_i \in KP$.

$\mathcal{P}$ proves the following to $\mathcal{Q}$ using $\mathcal{F}_{\mathrm{gZK}}$ parametrized with R and with label $\langle\mathrm{pp},\varphi\rangle$:
$$\maltese w_{k,0}, \ldots, w_{k,\tilde{m}-1} \, \exists V[k_0], \ldots, V[k_{m-1}], XP[k_0], \ldots, XP[k_{m-1}] :$$
$$\bigwedge_{i=0}^{m-1} \mathsf{ComVfy}(CP[k_i], XP[k_i], V[k_i] - SQ[k_i]) \wedge$$
$$R\big(x, (w_{k,0}, \ldots, w_{k,\tilde{m}-1}) \cup (V[k_i], \ldots, V[k_{m-1}])\big) = 1 .$$
The instance of the statement to be proven, x, is delivered to $\mathcal{Q}$ via $\mathcal{F}_{\mathrm{gZK}}$.

	$\mathcal{Q}$ **returns** x.

Fig. 5. Proof by $\mathcal{P}$

Proof by $\mathcal{P}$. In this instruction, $\mathcal{P}$ proves to $\mathcal{Q}$ in zero-knowledge some statement involving *1)* witnesses outside of the circuit, *2)* values that $\mathcal{P}$ input into the circuit, and *3)* values that $\mathcal{P}$ got as an output from the circuit. See Figure 5 for the construction.

Proof by $\mathcal{Q}$. Similar to the previous instruction, with the roles of $\mathcal{P}$ and $\mathcal{Q}$ reversed.

$\mathcal{P}$ **proceeds as follows:**	$\mathcal{Q}$ **proceeds as follows:**
$\mathcal{P}$'s input is $(\mathrm{P}, a, \mathfrak{C}_a, \mathfrak{r}_a, \mathfrak{C}_b, \lambda)$.	$\mathcal{Q}$'s input is $(\mathrm{Q}, b, \mathfrak{C}_b, \mathfrak{r}_b, \mathfrak{C}_a, \lambda)$.
$(\mathsf{pk}, \mathsf{sk}) \xleftarrow{\$} \mathsf{KeyGen}(n); \quad w \xleftarrow{\$} \mathbb{Z}_n;$	$s \xleftarrow{\$} \mathbb{Z}_n; \quad t \xleftarrow{\$} \mathbb{Z}_n;$
$(\mathsf{E}_w, \mathsf{r}_w) \xleftarrow{\$} \mathsf{Enc}(w, \mathsf{pk})$.	$(\mathfrak{C}_s, \mathfrak{r}_s) \xleftarrow{\$} \mathsf{Com}(s); \quad (\mathfrak{C}_t, \mathfrak{r}_t) \xleftarrow{\$} \mathsf{Com}(t)$.
$\mathcal{P}$ proves the following to $\mathcal{Q}$ using $\mathcal{F}_{\mathsf{gZK}}$ with label $\langle \mathsf{cm1}, \lambda \rangle$:	
$\lambda w \; \exists \mathsf{sk} : (\mathsf{pk}, \mathsf{sk}) \in \mathsf{KeyGen}(n) \wedge w = \mathsf{Dec}(\mathsf{E}_w, \mathsf{sk})$.	
The values $\mathsf{E}_w, \mathsf{pk}$ are delivered to $\mathcal{Q}$ via $\mathcal{F}_{\mathsf{gZK}}$ after $\mathcal{P}$ securely erases r_w.	
$\sigma \leftarrow a - w$.	$(\mathsf{E}_t, \mathsf{r}_t) \xleftarrow{\$} \mathsf{Enc}(t, \mathsf{pk}); \quad \mathsf{E}_y \leftarrow (\mathsf{E}_w)^s * \mathsf{E}_t$.
$\mathcal{Q}$ proves the following to $\mathcal{P}$ using $\mathcal{F}_{\mathsf{gZK}}$ with label $\langle \mathsf{cm2}, \lambda \rangle$:	
$\lambda s \; \exists t, \mathfrak{r}_s, \mathfrak{r}_t, \mathsf{r}_t : \mathsf{ComVfy}(\mathfrak{C}_s, \mathfrak{r}_s, s) \wedge \mathsf{ComVfy}(\mathfrak{C}_t, \mathfrak{r}_t, t) \wedge \mathsf{E}_y = (\mathsf{E}_w)^s * \mathsf{Enc}(t, \mathsf{pk}, \mathsf{r}_t)$.	
The values $\mathfrak{C}_s, \mathfrak{C}_t$ and E_y are delivered to $\mathcal{P}$ via $\mathcal{F}_{\mathsf{gZK}}$ after $\mathcal{Q}$ securely erases r_t.	
$y \leftarrow \mathsf{Dec}(\mathsf{E}_y, \mathsf{sk}); \quad (\mathfrak{C}_y, \mathfrak{r}_y) \xleftarrow{\$} \mathsf{Com}(y)$.	$\delta \leftarrow b - s; \quad \mathfrak{r}_\delta \leftarrow \mathfrak{r}_b - \mathfrak{r}_s$.
$\mathcal{P}$ proves the following to $\mathcal{Q}$ using $\mathcal{F}_{\mathsf{gZK}}$ with label $\langle \mathsf{cm3}, \lambda \rangle$:	
$\exists y, w, \mathfrak{r}_y, \mathfrak{r}_a, \mathsf{sk} : \mathsf{ComVfy}(\mathfrak{C}_y, \mathfrak{r}_y, y) \wedge y = \mathsf{Dec}(\mathsf{E}_y, \mathsf{sk}) \wedge w = \mathsf{Dec}(\mathsf{E}_w, \mathsf{sk}) \wedge$	
$(\mathsf{pk}, \mathsf{sk}) \in \mathsf{KeyGen}(n) \wedge \mathsf{ComVfy}(\mathfrak{C}_a, \mathfrak{r}_a, w + \sigma)$.	
The values $\mathfrak{C}_y, \sigma$ are delivered to $\mathcal{Q}$ via $\mathcal{F}_{\mathsf{gZK}}$ after $\mathcal{P}$ securely erases sk.	
$\mathcal{Q}$ proves the following to $\mathcal{P}$ using $\mathcal{F}_{\mathsf{gZK}}$ with label $\langle \mathsf{cm4}, \lambda \rangle$:	
$\exists \mathfrak{r}_\delta : \mathsf{ComVfy}(\mathfrak{C}_b * (\mathfrak{C}_s)^{-1}, \mathfrak{r}_\delta, \delta)$.	
The value δ is delivered to $\mathcal{P}$ via $\mathcal{F}_{\mathsf{gZK}}$.	
Compute own share: $u \leftarrow \delta \cdot a + y$;	Compute own share: $v \leftarrow \sigma \cdot s - t$;
opening: $\mathfrak{r}_u \leftarrow \mathfrak{r}_a \cdot \delta + \mathfrak{r}_y$;	opening: $\mathfrak{r}_v \leftarrow \mathfrak{r}_s \cdot \sigma - \mathfrak{r}_t$;
and commitment: $\mathfrak{C}_u \leftarrow (\mathfrak{C}_a)^\delta * \mathfrak{C}_y$.	and commitment: $\mathfrak{C}_v \leftarrow (\mathfrak{C}_s)^\sigma * (\mathfrak{C}_t)^{-1}$.
Compute $\mathcal{Q}$'s commitment: $\mathfrak{C}_v \leftarrow (\mathfrak{C}_s)^\sigma * (\mathfrak{C}_t)^{-1}$.	Compute $\mathcal{P}$'s commitment: $\mathfrak{C}_u \leftarrow (\mathfrak{C}_a)^\delta * \mathfrak{C}_y$.
$\mathcal{P}$ **returns** $(u, \mathfrak{C}_u, \mathfrak{r}_u, \mathfrak{C}_v)$.	$\mathcal{Q}$ **returns** $(v, \mathfrak{C}_v, \mathfrak{r}_v, \mathfrak{C}_u)$.

Fig. 6. The Π_{mul} protocol

4.2 The Π_{mul} Subroutine for Multiplication of Committed Inputs

We now give the construction of the 2-party $\mathcal{F}_{\mathsf{gZK}}$-hybrid protocol Π_{mul} for multiplication of committed inputs, which we use as a subroutine in Π_{ABB} in the multiplication instruction. In a nutshell: on $\mathcal{P}$'s private input a and $\mathcal{Q}$'s private input b, Π_{mul} outputs shares to the product: u to $\mathcal{P}$ and v to $\mathcal{Q}$, such that $u + v = a \cdot b$.

The protocol draws on ideas from Ishai et al's $\tilde{\pi}^{\mathsf{OT}}$ protocol—defined in Appendix A.2 of the full version of their paper [23]—and uses a similar approach as many two-party computation protocols (e.g., Damgård and Orlandi's π_{mul} protocol [20]). We fleshed out the details of Ishai et al.'s protocol to make it secure against *active* adversaries, improve its efficiency, and integrate it into our overall protocol.

The basic idea of the protocol is for $\mathcal{P}$ and $\mathcal{Q}$ to first obtain shares y and $(-t)$ on the product of two *random* values w and s, respectively: $y - t = w \cdot s$; second to erase all intermediate state used in the previous step; third to exchange the values $\sigma = (a - w)$ and $\delta = (b - s)$; and finally to obtain shares on the product of the actual input values a and b by outputting $u = \delta \cdot a + y$ and $v = \sigma \cdot b - t$, respectively. Commitments and relevant proofs are used during all steps. We refer to Figure 6 for the construction.

The erasure in Step 2 is needed to ensure security against *adaptive* adversaries: since the encryption scheme used in our protocol is not receiver–non-committing [10], the simulator cannot produce a convincing view of the first step for any other value of w. In fact, there are no known practical receiver–non-committing schemes that satisfy our requirements. By erasing state in Step 2, the simulator is dispensed with producing that view in Step 3.

4.3   Efficiency Considerations for the Zero-Knowledge Proofs in Π_{ABB}

Careful design enables us to achieve a very efficient and practical construction. In particular, we minimize the amount of computation required inside the realization π of the zero-knowledge proof functionality $\mathcal{F}_{gZK}$, which accounts for the majority of the runtime of our protocol, as follows.

1) Instead of using the Paillier encryption scheme as in Camenisch et al. [5] to verifiably encrypt the witnesses whose *knowledge* is proven in π, we use the Camenisch-Shoup encryption scheme with short keys, short randomness, and with modulus n^2. Paillier encryption implies the use of a different modulus, since the simulator needs to know its factorization to extract the witnesses.

2) We use homomorphic commitment and encryption schemes that work with groups of the same order n. Most of the witnesses used in $\mathcal{F}_{gZK}$ therefore live in a group of known order n, and most operations inside π stay inside groups of order n. We therefore do not need to encrypt values larger than n in π, and can avoid expensive integer commitments in π [5].

3) We use the cheaper proofs of *existence* [5] instead of proofs of *knowledge* wherever possible. This reduces the number of verifiable encryptions needed inside π.

4) Finally, we use an encryption scheme in Π_{mul} where the proof of correctness of key generation is cheap. (For Camenisch-Shoup encryption with full key length and Paillier encryption, this proof is very expensive.)

5   Security Proof (Main Ideas)

For reasons of space, we provide the security proof in the full version [4] and explain only the main ideas here.

We use the standard approach for proving the security of protocols in the UC or GNUC models: we construct a straight-line simulator S such that for all polynomial-time–bounded environments $\mathcal{Z}$ and all polynomial-time–bounded adversaries $\mathcal{A}$, the environment $\mathcal{Z}$ cannot distinguish a protocol execution with $\mathcal{A}$ and Π_{ABB} in the $(\mathcal{F}_{ach}, \mathcal{F}_{gZK})$-hybrid "real" world from a protocol execution with S and $\mathcal{F}_{ABB}$ in the "ideal" world. We prove that $\mathcal{Z}$ cannot distinguish these two worlds by defining a sequence of intermediate "hybrid" worlds (the first one being the real world and the last one the ideal world) and showing that $\mathcal{Z}$ cannot distinguish between any two consecutive hybrid worlds in that sequence. We follow the formalism of the GNUC framework to deal with CRS's and system parameters (see Section 10 of the GNUC paper [22]).

The main difficulties in constructing the simulator S are as follows: *1)* S has to extract the inputs of all corrupted parties; *2)* S has to compute and send commitments and ciphertexts on behalf of the honest parties without knowing their inputs, i.e., S cannot commit and encrypt the right values; *3)* when an honest party gets corrupted mid-protocol, S has to provide to $\mathcal{A}$ the full *non-erased* intermediate state of the party, in particular the opening of the commitments and the randomness of the encryptions.

To address the first difficulty, recall that the parties are required to perform a proof of *knowledge* of all new inputs to the circuit. The simulator $\mathcal{S}$ can therefore recover the input of all corrupted parties with the help of $\mathcal{F}_{gZK}$. In the first few hybrid worlds, the statistically binding commitments ensure that the values in the circuit stay consistent with the inputs. In the subsequent hybrid worlds, the computational indistinguishability of the two types of CRS ensure that the adversary cannot equivocate commitments even when $\mathcal{S}$ uses the perfectly-hiding CRS with trapdoor.

We now address the second and third difficulty. Upon corruption of a party, $\mathcal{S}$ is allowed to recover the original input of that party from $\mathcal{F}_{ABB}$. By using the perfectly-hiding CRS with trapdoor, $\mathcal{S}$ can equivocate all commitments it made so far to ensure that the committed values are consistent with the view of the adversary. By construction, $\mathcal{S}$ never needs to reveal the randomness used for an encryption for which it does not know the plaintext. Recall that in Π_{mul}, the parties first encrypt a random offset, then erase the decryption key and the randomness used to encrypt, and only then deliver the encryption of the offset plus party's input to the adversary (recall that $\mathcal{F}_{gZK}$ allows the erasure of witnesses *before* delivering the statement to be proven to the other party). The simulator $\mathcal{S}$ can adjust the offset so that the view delivered to the adversary is consistent. See also Appendix A.2 of Ishai et al.'s paper [23].

The rest of the security proof is now straightforward.

6 Related Work and Comparison

There is an extensive literature on the subject of multi-party computation (MPC); however, most of these settings consider only the case of an honest majority, which is not helpful for the two-party case.

Canetti et al. [12] present the first MPC protocols for general functionalities that are secure with dishonest majority in the UC framework; however, these protocols are rather a proof of concept, i.e., they are not at all practical, as they rely on generic zero-knowledge proofs.

More efficient MPC protocols for evaluating *boolean* circuits, secure with dishonest majority, have been designed [29,30,34,37]. Impressive results have been obtained in particular for the evaluation of the AES block cipher [37,15,16,27,33]. While such protocols could be used to evaluate arithmetic circuits modulo n, a heavy price would have to be paid: each gate in the arithmetic circuit would "blow up" into many boolean gates, resulting in an impractical protocol.

The first practical protocols for evaluating arithmetic circuits modulo n were presented by Cramer et al. [13] (CDN-protocol) and Damgård and Nielsen [18] (DN-protocol). While both protocols assume an honest majority, they can be shown to be secure in the two-party case (as noted by Ishai et al. [24,23]) if one relaxes the requirement for fair delivery of messages (fair delivery is impossible in the two-party case). Both protocols have stronger set-up assumptions than ours: they assume the existence of a trusted third party that distributes shares of the secret key to all parties. The CDN-protocol is only *statically* secure and is not UC-secure, and we therefore exclude it from our comparison. The DN-protocol is *adaptively* secure (with erasures) in the UC model (secure *without erasures* only in the honest majority case), and is slightly (about 30%) slower than ours.

Ishai et al. [23,24] present protocols for evaluating arithmetic circuits in several algebraic rings, including one for the ring $\mathbb{Z}_n$ for a composite n. These protocols achieve security with a dishonest majority, and are secure with respect to *adaptive* corruptions (assuming erasures), but only against *honest-but-curious* adversaries. They note that standard techniques can be used to make their protocols secure also for *malicious* adversaries, however it is not clear if the resulting construction will be practical. Our protocol draws on ideas from their construction, however we are able to achieve a significant speed-up compared to a naive implementation using "standard techniques" by ensuring that all commitments live in $\mathbb{Z}_n$ and by using the short-key variant of the homomorphic encryption scheme.

Damgård and Orlandi [19] (DO-protocol), as well as Bendlin et al. [2] (BDOZ-protocol), give protocols for evaluating arithmetic circuits modulo a prime p. Damgård et al. [21] (SPDZ-protocol) later improved upon the BDOZ-protocol. These protocols divide the workload into a computationally intensive *pre-processing* phase and a much lighter *on-line* phase. The pre-processing phase is statically secure, however the on-line phase can be made adaptively secure (in the UC-model) [19,2,21]. These papers optimize the runtime of the on-line phase (the BDOZ- and SPDZ-protocols make use of local additions and multiplications only). In the pre-processing phase of these protocols, it is necessary to prepare for many multiplications gates (about 80 in the BDOZ-, several hundred in the DO-, and tens of thousands in the SPDZ-protocol) making these protocols impractical for small circuits. This pre-processing phase takes several minutes even for reasonable security parameters. Our protocol is better suited for small circuits.

Even for large circuits, the computational complexity of our protocol is about 3.3 times lower than that of the BDOZ- and DO-protocols. It must be noted that the BDOZ- and DO-protocols have slightly weaker setup assumptions than ours: they only require a *random string* as the CRS, while we also need an *RSA modulus with unknown factorization* as a system parameter. (This is not a huge drawback of our protocol, see Section 3.)

The SPDZ-protocol is about an order of magnitude faster than our protocol, however, unlike the BDOZ-, DO-, and our protocols, it cannot evaluate reactive circuits, severely limiting its applicability in the real world. It also requires a trusted key setup, which is a stronger setup assumption than ours. (Concurrently to our work, Damgård et al. [17] lifted the restriction on reactive circuits, but only in the *random oracle model*. They also lifted the restriction on the trusted key setup but only for *covert* security.)

None of the UC-secure protocols discussed have an equivalent to the *Proof* instruction in their ideal functionality. This makes it hard to compose them with other protocols because of the issue with non-committed inputs in a 2-party setting, as dicussed in the introduction, thus negating some of the advantages of working in the UC model.

6.1 Efficiency Comparison

Table 1 summarizes the amortized runtimes per multiplication gate of our protocol, the DN- (when run as a 2-party protocol), the DO-, and the BDOZ-protocols. We assume that the runtime of an exponentiation with a fixed modulus length scales linearly with the size of the exponent. Let exp.n denote the runtime per bit in the exponent of an exponentiation modulo n or modulo p,[4] and similarily exp.n^2 for exponentiations modulo

---

[4] In practice, exponentiations modulo p are only a few percent slower than modulo n.

Table 1. Estimated amortized runtime per multiplication in various protocols. The numbers in the last column are for $s = 80$, $lb\,n = 1248$, $exp.n = 1.3\,\mu s$, and $exp.n^2 = 4.8\,\mu s$. Results for our work use the *optimized* variant of our *Multiplication* instruction. Results for the DO-protocol and the BDOZ-protocol are for circuits having a multiple of $4.8 \cdot s$ and s multiplication gates, respectively; the performance of these protocols degrades dramatically for smaller circuits. For the DO-protocol we used parameters $\lambda = 0.25$ and $B = 3.6 \cdot s$.

	Amortized runtime per multiplication gate	with $s=80$
This work	$(90 \cdot s + 200 \cdot lb\,n)\,exp.n + (\ 66 \cdot s + 40.5 \cdot lb\,n)\,exp.n^2$	**602 ms**
2-party DN [18]	$(216 \cdot s + 130\ \cdot lb\,n)\,exp.n^2$	862 ms
DO-protocol [19]	$(2004 \cdot s + 151 \cdot s^2)\,exp.n + (\ 84 \cdot s + 88\ \cdot lb\,n)\,exp.n^2$	2025 ms
BDOZ-protocol [2]	$(256 \cdot s + 368\ \cdot lb\,n)\,exp.n^2$	2303 ms

n^2. Let $lb\,n$ be equal to $\log_2(n)$. Let s be the security parameter. For each protocol, we counted the number of exponentiations with an exponent of at least s bits. Faster operations, in particular multiplications and divisions, are ignored. We also ignored the time needed for secure channel setup, did not consider multi-exponentiations, and ignored network delay. We provide an estimate of the runtime when run with the "smallest general purpose" security level of the Ecrypt-II recommendations [1] ($s = 80$, $lb\,n = 1248$) on a standard laptop with a 64-bit operating system.[5]

For a fair comparison, we replace all Paillier encryptions [35] in the protocols we compare with by Paillier encryptions *with short randomness*. The encryption function is thus changed as follows: $r \xleftarrow{\$} \mathbb{Z}_{\lfloor\sqrt{n}\rfloor}$, $c \leftarrow (1 + n)^m g^r \pmod{n^2}$; output c. (Where $g = (g')^n$ is pre-computed and part of the public key.)

Acknowledgements. We are grateful to Stephan Krenn and to the anonymous reviewers for their comments. This work was supported by the European Community through the Seventh Framework Programme (FP7), under grant agreements n°257782 for the project ABC4Trust and n°321310 for the project PERCY.

References

1. Babbage, S., Catalano, D., Cid, C., de Weger, B., Dunkelman, O., Gehrmann, C., Granboulan, L., Güneysu, T., Hermans, J., Lange, T., Lenstra, A., Mitchell, C., Näslund, M., Nguyen, P., Paar, C., Paterson, K., Pelzl, J., Pornin, T., Preneel, B., Rechberger, C., Rijmen, V., Robshaw, M., Rupp, A., Schläffer, M., Vaudenay, S., Vercauteren, F., Ward, M.: ECRYPT II Yearly Report on Algorithms and Keysizes (2011)
2. Bendlin, R., Damgård, I., Orlandi, C., Zakarias, S.: Semi-homomorphic Encryption and Multiparty Computation. In: Paterson, K.G. (ed.) EUROCRYPT 2011. LNCS, vol. 6632, pp. 169–188. Springer, Heidelberg (2011)
3. Camenisch, J., Casati, N., Gross, T., Shoup, V.: Credential Authenticated Identification and Key Exchange. In: Rabin, T. (ed.) CRYPTO 2010. LNCS, vol. 6223, pp. 255–276. Springer, Heidelberg (2010)

---

[5] The computer used for the benchmarks had an Intel i7 Q820 processor clocked at 1.73 GHz. We used version 5.0.2 of the GNU Multiple Precision Arithmetic Library.

4. Camenisch, J., Enderlein, R.R., Shoup, V.: Practical Universally Composable Circuit Evaluation over Z_n. IACR Cryptology ePrint Archive, 2013:205 (2013)
5. Camenisch, J., Krenn, S., Shoup, V.: A Framework for Practical Universally Composable Zero-Knowledge Protocols. In: Lee, D.H., Wang, X. (eds.) ASIACRYPT 2011. LNCS, vol. 7073, pp. 449–467. Springer, Heidelberg (2011)
6. Camenisch, J., Shoup, V.: Practical Verifiable Encryption and Decryption of Discrete Logarithms. In: Boneh, D. (ed.) CRYPTO 2003. LNCS, vol. 2729, pp. 126–144. Springer, Heidelberg (2003)
7. Camenisch, J., Stadler, M.: Proof Systems for General Statements about Discrete Logarithms. Institute for Theoretical Computer Science, ETH Zürich, Tech. Rep., 260 (1997)
8. Canetti, R.: Universally Composable Security: A New Paradigm for Cryptographic Protocols. IACR Cryptology ePrint Archive, 2000:67 (2000)
9. Canetti, R., Fischlin, M.: Universally Composable Commitments. In: Kilian, J. (ed.) CRYPTO 2001. LNCS, vol. 2139, pp. 19–40. Springer, Heidelberg (2001)
10. Canetti, R., Halevi, S., Katz, J.: Adaptively-Secure, Non-interactive Public-Key Encryption. In: Kilian, J. (ed.) TCC 2005. LNCS, vol. 3378, pp. 150–168. Springer, Heidelberg (2005)
11. Canetti, R., Kushilevitz, E., Lindell, Y.: On the Limitations of Universally Composable Two-Party Computation Without Set-Up Assumptions. J. Cryptology 19(2), 135–167 (2006)
12. Canetti, R., Lindell, Y., Ostrovsky, R., Sahai, A.: Universally Composable Two-Party and Multi-Party Secure Computation. In: STOC, pp. 494–503 (2002)
13. Cramer, R., Damgård, I., Nielsen, J.B.: Multiparty Computation from Threshold Homomorphic Encryption. In: Pfitzmann, B. (ed.) EUROCRYPT 2001. LNCS, vol. 2045, pp. 280–299. Springer, Heidelberg (2001)
14. Damgård, I., Jurik, M.: A Length-Flexible Threshold Cryptosystem with Applications. In: Safavi-Naini, R., Seberry, J. (eds.) ACISP 2003. LNCS, vol. 2727, pp. 350–364. Springer, Heidelberg (2003)
15. Damgård, I., Keller, M.: Secure Multiparty AES. In: Sion, R. (ed.) FC 2010. LNCS, vol. 6052, pp. 367–374. Springer, Heidelberg (2010)
16. Damgård, I., Keller, M., Larraia, E., Miles, C., Smart, N.P.: Implementing AES via an Actively/Covertly Secure Dishonest-Majority MPC Protocol. In: Visconti, I., De Prisco, R. (eds.) SCN 2012. LNCS, vol. 7485, pp. 241–263. Springer, Heidelberg (2012)
17. Damgård, I., Keller, M., Larraia, E., Pastro, V., Scholl, P., Smart, N.P.: Practical Covertly Secure MPC for Dishonest Majority – Or: Breaking the SPDZ Limits. In: Crampton, J., Jajodia, S., Mayes, K. (eds.) ESORICS 2013. LNCS, vol. 8134, pp. 1–18. Springer, Heidelberg (2013)
18. Damgård, I., Nielsen, J.B.: Universally Composable Efficient Multiparty Computation from Threshold Homomorphic Encryption. In: Boneh, D. (ed.) CRYPTO 2003. LNCS, vol. 2729, pp. 247–264. Springer, Heidelberg (2003)
19. Damgård, I., Orlandi, C.: Multiparty Computation for Dishonest Majority: From Passive to Active Security at Low Cost. In: Rabin, T. (ed.) CRYPTO 2010. LNCS, vol. 6223, pp. 558–576. Springer, Heidelberg (2010)
20. Damgård, I., Orlandi, C.: Multiparty Computation for Dishonest Majority: from Passive to Active Security at Low Cost. IACR Cryptology ePrint Archive, 2010:318 (2010)
21. Damgård, I., Pastro, V., Smart, N.P., Zakarias, S.: Multiparty Computation from Somewhat Homomorphic Encryption. In: Safavi-Naini, R., Canetti, R. (eds.) CRYPTO 2012. LNCS, vol. 7417, pp. 643–662. Springer, Heidelberg (2012)
22. Hofheinz, D., Shoup, V.: GNUC: A New Universal Composability Framework. IACR Cryptology ePrint Archive, 2011:303 (2011)
23. Ishai, Y., Prabhakaran, M., Sahai, A.: Secure Arithmetic Computation with No Honest Majority. IACR Cryptology ePrint Archive, 2008:465 (2008)

24. Ishai, Y., Prabhakaran, M., Sahai, A.: Secure Arithmetic Computation with No Honest Majority. In: Reingold, O. (ed.) TCC 2009. LNCS, vol. 5444, pp. 294–314. Springer, Heidelberg (2009)
25. Jarecki, S., Liu, X.: Efficient Oblivious Pseudorandom Function with Applications to Adaptive OT and Secure Computation of Set Intersection. In: Reingold, O. (ed.) TCC 2009. LNCS, vol. 5444, pp. 577–594. Springer, Heidelberg (2009)
26. Jarecki, S., Shmatikov, V.: Efficient Two-Party Secure Computation on Committed Inputs. In: Naor, M. (ed.) EUROCRYPT 2007. LNCS, vol. 4515, pp. 97–114. Springer, Heidelberg (2007)
27. Kreuter, B., Shelat, A., Shen, C.: Towards Billion-Gate Secure Computation with Malicious Adversaries. IACR Cryptology ePrint Archive, 2012:179 (2012)
28. Küsters, R.: Simulation-Based Security with Inexhaustible Interactive Turing Machines. In: IEEE Computer Security Foundations Workshop, pp. 309–320 (2006)
29. Lindell, Y., Pinkas, B.: An Efficient Protocol for Secure Two-Party Computation in the Presence of Malicious Adversaries. In: Naor, M. (ed.) EUROCRYPT 2007. LNCS, vol. 4515, pp. 52–78. Springer, Heidelberg (2007)
30. Lindell, Y., Pinkas, B., Smart, N.P.: Implementing Two-Party Computation Efficiently with Security Against Malicious Adversaries. In: Ostrovsky, R., De Prisco, R., Visconti, I. (eds.) SCN 2008. LNCS, vol. 5229, pp. 2–20. Springer, Heidelberg (2008)
31. Maurer, U., Renner, R.: Abstract Cryptography. In: ICS, pp. 1–21 (2011)
32. Nielsen, J.B.: On Protocol Security in the Cryptographic Model. PhD thesis, BRICS, Computer Science Department, University of Aarhus (2003)
33. Nielsen, J.B., Nordholt, P.S., Orlandi, C., Burra, S.S.: A New Approach to Practical Active-Secure Two-Party Computation. In: Safavi-Naini, R., Canetti, R. (eds.) CRYPTO 2012. LNCS, vol. 7417, pp. 681–700. Springer, Heidelberg (2012)
34. Nielsen, J.B., Orlandi, C.: LEGO for Two-Party Secure Computation. In: Reingold, O. (ed.) TCC 2009. LNCS, vol. 5444, pp. 368–386. Springer, Heidelberg (2009)
35. Paillier, P.: Public-Key Cryptosystems Based on Composite Degree Residuosity Classes. In: Stern, J. (ed.) EUROCRYPT 1999. LNCS, vol. 1592, pp. 223–238. Springer, Heidelberg (1999)
36. Pfitzmann, B., Waidner, M.: A Model for Asynchronous Reactive Systems and its Application to Secure Message Transmission. In: IEEE Security & Privacy, pp. 184–200 (2001)
37. Pinkas, B., Schneider, T., Smart, N.P., Williams, S.C.: Secure Two-Party Computation Is Practical. In: Matsui, M. (ed.) ASIACRYPT 2009. LNCS, vol. 5912, pp. 250–267. Springer, Heidelberg (2009)
38. Wagstaff Jr., S.S.: Greatest of the Least Primes in Arithmetic Progressions Having a Given Modulus. Mathematics of Computation 33(147), 1073–1080 (1979)

Privacy-Preserving Accountable Computation

Michael Backes[1,2], Dario Fiore[1], and Esfandiar Mohammadi[2]

[1] Max-Planck Insitute for Software Systems, Saarbrücken, Germany
fiore@mpi-sws.org
[2] Saarland University, Saarbrücken, Germany
{backes,mohammadi}@cs.uni-saarland.de

Abstract. Accountability of distributed systems aims to ensure that whenever a malicious behavior is observed, it can be irrefutably linked to a malicious node and that every honest node can disprove false accusations. Recent work, such as PeerReview and its extensions, shows how to achieve accountability in both deterministic and randomized systems. The basic idea is to generate tamper-evident logs of the performed computations such that an external auditor can check the system's actions by mere recomputation. For randomized computations it is more challenging: revealing the seed of the pseudo-random generator in the logs would break the unpredictability of future values. This problem has been addressed in a previous work, CSAR, which formalizes a notion of accountable randomness and presents a realization. Although all these techniques have been proven practical, they dramatically (and inevitably) expose a party's private data, e.g., secret keys. In many scenarios, such a privacy leak would clearly be unaccepable and thus prevent a successful deployment of accountability systems.

In this work, we study a notion of privacy-preserving accountability for randomized systems. While for deterministic computations zero-knowledge proofs offer a solution (which is even efficient for some computations), for randomized computations we argue that efficient solutions are less trivial. In particular, we show that zero-knowledge proofs are incompatible with the notion of accountable randomness considered in CSAR if we aim at efficient solutions. Therefore, we propose an alternative definition of accountable randomness, and we use it as a building block to develop the new notion of privacy-preserving accountable randomized computation. We present efficient instantiations for interesting classes of computations, in particular for digital signature schemes as the arguably most important cryptographic primitive.

1 Introduction

In distributed systems, checking whether a node's operation is correct or faulty is a major concern. Indeed, faulty actions can occur for many reasons: a node can be affected by a hardware or software failure, a node can be compromised

J. Crampton, S. Jajodia, and K. Mayes (Eds.): ESORICS 2013, LNCS 8134, pp. 38–56, 2013.
© Springer-Verlag Berlin Heidelberg 2013

by an attacker, or a node's operator can deliberately tamper with its software. Detecting such faulty nodes is often very difficult, in particular for large-scale systems.

Recent work proposed *accountability* as a paradigm to ensure that whenever an incorrect behavior is observed, it can be linked to a malicious node. At the same time, honest nodes gain the ability to disprove any false accusations. Examples of these accountability systems include PeerReview [15] and its extension [2]. The basic idea of PeerReview is that every user generates a tamper-evident log which contains a complete trace of the performed computations. Later, an auditor (in PeerReview any other node in the distributed system) can check the correctness of the user's operations by inspecting the logs, replaying the execution of the user using a reference implementation, and finally comparing its result. The above approach is however restricted to deterministic systems. Indeed, in order to enable the replay of a randomized computation one should publish the seed of the pseudo-random generator in the logs. Clearly, this would completely destroy the unpredictability of future pseudo-random values. This issue was addressed by CSAR, an extension of PeerReview [2]. More specifically, the main contribution in [2] is to formalize a notion of accountable randomness, called *strong accountable randomness*, and to present the construction of a pseudo-random generator satisfying this property. Informally, strong accountable randomness consists of the following requirements: (i) the pseudo-random generator generates values that look random, even to the party who computes them; (ii) it is possible to verify that the values were computed correctly; (iii) the unpredictability of future values (i.e., those for which a proof was not yet issued) does not get compromised; and (iv) the above properties are fulfilled even if a malicious party is involved in the seed generation.

While the approach of PeerReview and CSAR is very general and has been proven practical, these techniques have an inherent drawback: they inevitably expose a party's private data. In many scenarios such a privacy leak is unacceptable and might thus discourage the adoption of accountability systems. For instance, consider a company that runs its business using a specific software. There are many cases in which companies' tasks have to comply with legal regulations, and having a system which allows an auditor to check this compliance in a reliable way would be highly desirable. On the other hand, companies have a lot of data that they want to keep secret. This data might include, for instance, business secrets such as internal financial information, or secret keys for digital signatures or encryption schemes.[1]

In spite of its utter importance, the idea of providing accountability while preserving the privacy of the party's data has not been yet properly explored in previous work.

---

[1] While in principle such a problem can be solved by using generic secure multi-party computation techniques (SMPC) [10], all known SMPC protocols require the verifier to participate in the computation, which is infeasible in practice, whereas in our setting the verifier only participates in the verification by checking the tamper-resistant log, which is much better suited for practice.

1.1 Our Contribution

We address this important open problem in the area of accountability providing three main contributions:

- We formalize a notion of privacy-preserving accountability for randomized systems. At a high level, our notion requires that a user is able to produce a log that convinces an auditor of the correctness of (1) the outcome of a computation (e.g., that $y = P(x)$), and (2) the generated randomness. At the same time, the contents of the log neither compromise the secrecy of specific inputs of the computation nor the unpredictability of the randomness generated in the future. Our notion is defined in the UC framework, and thus allows for arbitrary composability.[2]
- We focus on efficient realizations of privacy-preserving accountability for randomized systems. We show that a construction can be obtained by using the non-interactive proof system by Groth and Sahai [13] which supports statements in the language of pairing-product equations, and a pseudorandom function, due to Dodis and Yampolskiy [9], which works in bilinear groups and is thus compatible with this language. With the above proof system we can characterize a variety of computations: efficient solutions exist for the case of algebraic computations with equations of degree up to 2, but also arbitrary circuits can be supported [12].
- We show interesting applications of privacy-preserving accountability for randomized systems to digital signatures. We present a signature scheme in which the signer can show that the secret key and the signatures are generated "correctly", i.e., by using accountable randomness. This essentially ensures that a signature has been created using a specific algorithm.

Our Contribution in Detail. In this section we give a high level explanation of the technical ideas and the approaches used in this paper.

OUR NOTION AND ITS RELATION WITH STRONG RANDOMNESS. In the case of deterministic computations the notion of privacy-preserving accountability would essentially fall into the well-known application area of zero-knowledge proofs [11]. However, we model randomized computations: consequently we want that even the randomness is accountable, i.e., correctly generated. While such a notion, called strong accountable randomness, has already been introduced in [2], we show that it is *not* realizable without random oracles (see Section 3.1).

Recall that strong accountable randomness requires that the pseudo-randomness of the generated values must hold even against the party who knows the seed. Clearly, this is a very strong property. A random oracle helps its realization as it essentially destroys any algebraic properties or relations that one may recognize in such values. But without the help of this "magic" tool, it is clear that the party computing the values knows *at least* how they were computed.

---

[2] We are aware that the UC framework has flaws. Our results, however, can be straightforwardly migrated to other simulation-based composability frameworks [23,18,16].

Our impossibility result left us with two opportunities: (1) either define privacy-preserving accountability for randomized computations in the strongest possible way (i.e., so as to imply strong randomness) but be aware that it would be realizable only using random oracles, or (2) define a slightly weaker version of accountable randomness. Although the first option would be preferable, a careful analysis revealed that its efficient realization is very unlikely. Indeed, any meaningful notion of privacy-preserving accountable computation fulfilling the properties we have in mind will need zero-knowledge proofs in order to be realized. At the same time, these proofs would have to involve a pseudo-random generator that satisfies strong randomness by using a hash function modeled as a random oracle. We are not aware of any hash function that allows for efficient zero-knowledge proofs and whose actual implementation maintains unpredictability properties close to the ideal ones of a random oracle (i.e., its use in a scheme does not fall prey to trivial attacks). This is why we decided to follow the second approach.

ON REALIZING ACCOUNTABLE SIGNATURES. While focusing on more specific applications of our accountability system, we asked how to efficiently prove statements that involve the randomness generated by our system. For instance, many cryptographic protocols rely on correctly distributed randomness, but such randomness usually cannot be revealed (thus CSAR is not a solution). In particular, this property is very interesting for digital signatures as it would allow for the accountability of this primitive, namely the signer could show that the secret key and the signatures are generated correctly (i.e., by using accountable randomness) and at the same time the signer does not leak such confidential data to the auditor.

Towards this goal, the technical challenge is that for the combination of Groth-Sahai proofs and our specific pseudo-random generator random values that need to be hidden can only be group elements.[3] We are not aware of any signature scheme, from the literature, in which *all* random values (e.g., the secret key and the randomness) can be computed using our pseudo-random generator. In this work we propose the construction of such a signature scheme which thus satisfies our notion of accountability.

2   Preliminary: The UC Framework

In this work, we formulate and prove our results in a composable, simulation-based model, in which the security of a protocol is obtained by comparison with an idealized setting where a trusted machine is available. More specifically, we use the UC framework [6]. Our results also apply to other simulation-based composability frameworks, such as IITM [18], RSIM [23], or GNUC [16].

We consider attackers that are global, static and active, i.e., an attacker that controls some parties and that controls the entire network. Such attackers are typically modelled in the UC framework by only considering protocols parties that have a designated communication tape for directly passing messages to

---

[3] In particular, every known pseudo-random function compatible with Groth-Sahai outputs group elements.

the attacker. Since the attacker controls the network, it can decide whether, in which order, and to whom network message are passed. Additionally every protocol party has a communication tape for directly passing messages to the so-called *environment*, a PPT machine that represents any user of the protocol, such as the web-browser or an operating system.

The security of a protocol is defined by comparing the execution of the protocol, i.e., of all protocol parties, with an idealized setting, called *ideal world*. The ideal world is defined just as the real world except for the existence of designated, incorruptible machines, called *ideal functionalities*. These ideal functionalities represent a scenario in which the same functionality is executed using a trusted machine to whom all parties have direct access. Formally, an ideal functionality directly communicates with the environment via so-called *dummy parties*, which forward all messages as instructed. This ideal functionality characterizes the leakage of the protocol and the possibilities of the attacker to influence the outcome of the protocol.

The security of a protocol π is defined by comparison with its corresponding ideal functionality $\mathcal{F}$ as follows: a protocol π *UC-realizes* an ideal functionality $\mathcal{F}$ if for all probabilistic polynomial-time (PPT) attackers $\mathcal{A}$ (against the protocol) there is a PPT attacker S (against the ideal functionality) such that no PPT machine (the environment $\mathcal{E}$) can distinguish an interaction with π and $\mathcal{A}$ from an interaction with $\mathcal{F}$ and S. A protocol π is considered UC-secure if it UC-realizes the corresponding ideal functionality.

For modeling setups, such as a PKI or a CRS, often ideal functionalities, such as $\mathcal{F}_{\mathrm{CRS}}$, are used in description of the protocol. A setting in which both ideal functionalities and protocols occur is called a *hybrid world*. These ideal functionalities directly communicate with the protocol parties, since (formally) the protocol parties are part of the environment from the perspective of these ideal functionalities. These hybrid world can also be used to abstract away from cryptographic subprotocols, such as authenticated channels.

3   Defining Accountable Computation

In this section, we introduce a rigorous definition of accountable computation. As discussed in the introduction, this notion has to work for randomized systems, and thus have to guarantee accountable randomness. Towards this goal, we will first show that the previous notion of accountable randomness considered in [2] cannot be realized in the standard model. Then we will introduce our relaxed definition, for which we discuss efficient realizations in Section 4.

We consider a setting with a party VE, called the auditor, that performs the audit and a computation party that performs the computation and, upon request, produces proofs that the computation has been correctly performed. Assuming an evaluation function EVAL for computing results, an accountable computation scheme is a collection of three algorithms: SETUP is run to generate the system's parameters that are distributed to every party and to the verifier; PROV is run by the party to prove statements about a computation and it produces a log; V is run by the verifier on input the log to check its correctness.

On (init) from $\mathcal{E}$ for honest P
 draw random values
  $r_1, \ldots, r_n \leftarrow \{0,1\}^n$
 store $(\mathsf{rand}_1, \ldots, \mathsf{rand}_n) :=$
  $(r_1, \ldots, r_n)$
 send (init) to $\mathcal{A}$
 output (initd) to $\mathcal{E}$

On (getrand, i) from $\mathcal{A}$
 send rand_i to $\mathcal{A}$

On (comp, i, sid) from $\mathcal{E}$ for honest P
 set $\mathsf{re} := (\mathsf{rand}_i)$
 store $\mathsf{proofs}(sid, i) := (\mathsf{re}, 1)$
 send (re, i, sid) to $\mathcal{A}$ and $\mathcal{E}$

On (comp, i, sid) from $\mathcal{E}$ for malicious P
 send (comp, i, sid) to $\mathcal{A}$
 wait for a response $(output, \mathsf{re}, b, sid')$
 from $\mathcal{A}$
 store $\mathsf{proofs}(sid', i) := (\mathsf{re}, b)$
 output $(output)$ to $\mathcal{E}$

On (vr, i, sid) from $\mathcal{E}$ for honest Ve
 let $(\mathsf{re}, b) := \mathsf{proofs}(sid, i)$
 if $b = 1$
 then output $(\mathsf{rand}_i, i, 1)$ to $\mathcal{E}$
 else output $(\mathsf{re}, i, 0)$ to $\mathcal{E}$

On (vr, i, sid) from $\mathcal{E}$ for malicious Ve
 send (vr, i, sid) to $\mathcal{A}$
 wait for a response m from $\mathcal{A}$
 output m to $\mathcal{E}$

Fig. 1. The ideal functionality $\mathcal{F}_{\mathrm{SR}}$ for strong randomness generation

For deterministic computations and for proofs that should not hide any secrets (e.g., decryption keys) previous work offers efficient solutions [15,14]. In the case of randomized computations, however, the computing party additionally needs to prove that the randomness has been honestly generated, e.g., in order to prove that signature key does not intentionally leave a trapdoor for malicious third parties. Therefore, randomized accountable computation needs a fourth algorithm INIT, that is run in a trusted set-up phase and in which the computing party gets a secret seed and the auditor a corresponding public seed.

Backes, Druschel, Haeberlen, and Unruh studied the problem of accountable randomness and introduced the notion of strong randomness [2]. The authors even presented an efficient construction that satisfies this property; however, their realization guarantees strong randomness only in the random oracle model. In the next section, we show that realizing their notion in the standard model is *impossible*.

NOTATION. In the description of the ideal functionalities and the protocol template, we use for persistently stored variables the font variable and for values the font *value*.

3.1 Strong Randomness Is Not Realizable

Backes, Druschel, Haeberlen, and Unruh define strong randomness by means of an ideal functionality $\mathcal{F}_{\mathrm{SR}}$. This ideal functionality (formally explained in Figure

1) basically offers an interface for a computing party P to send commands to compute a pseudo-random generator, and $\mathcal{F}_{SR}$ offers an interface for auditors V_E to verify that these (pseudo-)random values are correctly distributed and unpredictably for the party that computes them. In addition, $\mathcal{F}_{SR}$ has an initialization phase, in which random values rand_i are drawn uniformly at random, and $\mathcal{F}_{SR}$ offers the attacker $\mathcal{A}$ a randomness oracle: upon a query $(\mathtt{getrand}, i)$, $\mathcal{F}_{SR}$ responds with rand_i.

The Ideal Functionality $\mathcal{F}_{sr}$. Beside an initialization phase (via the command init), $\mathcal{F}_{SR}$ offers two commands comp and vr. If a party is malicious, $\mathcal{F}_{SR}$ allows the attacker to determine the behavior for these commands. For honest parties, upon $(\mathtt{comp}, i, sid)$ the pseudo-random element with the index i is generated (and internally stored in $\mathsf{proofs}(sid, i)$). For honest parties, the flag b in $\mathsf{proofs}(sid, i)$ is set to 1 and for malicious parties, the flag is set to 0. Upon $(\mathtt{vr}, i, sid)$, $\mathcal{F}_{SR}$ reads $\mathsf{proofs}(sid, i)$ and if $b = 1$ then it outputs the real random element and otherwise the stored element re.

For any (reasonable) two-party protocol Π, we show how the environment $\mathcal{E}$ can, in the standard model, easily distinguish whether it is communicating with Π and the real attacker $\mathcal{A}$ or $\mathcal{F}_{SR}$ and a simulator. Assume that the computing party P is compromised. Recall that $\mathcal{E}$ knows all secrets of P, in particular, any secret information used to compute the pseudorandom generator. We assume $\mathcal{A}$ to be the dummy attacker that simply forwards everything. $\mathcal{E}$ performs the following steps:

1. Send the command $(\mathtt{comp}, i, sid)$ to P.
2. Since P is compromised, $\mathcal{A}$ has to answer for P. Since $\mathcal{A}$ is the dummy attacker, $\mathcal{A}$ forwards this duty to $\mathcal{E}$.
3. $\mathcal{E}$ computes the honest output (re, i) of that party P on its own, typically the output of a pseudo-random function on some seed and input i.
4. $\mathcal{E}$ sends the honestly computed output (re, i) as a response to $\mathcal{A}$.
5. $\mathcal{A}$ dutifully forwards the output (re, i) to the compromised P.
6. P sends the honestly computed output (re, i) over the network, i.e., to $\mathcal{A}$.
7. $\mathcal{A}$ simply delivers the message to V_E.
8. $\mathcal{E}$ sends $(\mathtt{vr}, i, sid)$ to V_E and waits for a response $((\mathsf{re}', i'), b)$
9. $\mathcal{E}$ outputs 1 if $(\mathsf{re}, i) = (\mathsf{re}', i')$ and $b = 1$; otherwise output 0

In the ideal setting, the attacker $\mathcal{A}$ will actually be the simulator. Now, if the simulator behaves differently from the attacker in steps 2, 5 or 7 (i.e., it does not let $\mathcal{E}$ compute the answer for P, does not forward the output (re, i) to the compromised P, or it does not deliver the message in step 7), then $\mathcal{E}$ can use this unexpected behavior to distinguish the two settings. Thus, the simulator has to act towards $\mathcal{E}$ as the dummy attacker (see step 5). At this point we have two possible cases for the answer of $\mathcal{F}_{SR}$ to the environment upon the command $(\mathtt{vr}, i, sid)$: (i) either $b = 0$, or (ii) $b = 1$. In the case when $b = 0$, the environment will output 0 regardless of the value re'. If $b = 1$, recall that $\mathcal{F}_{SR}$ outputs $(\mathsf{re}', i') = (\mathsf{rand}_i, i)$, where rand_i is uniformly chosen. Namely, $\mathcal{F}_{SR}$ replaces the value re sent by the simulator. Since rand_i is uniformly chosen, with overwhelming probability we have that $\mathsf{rand}_i \neq re$. Hence, in the ideal setting $\mathcal{E}$ will output 0 with overwhelming probability. In contrast, in the real setting the environment always outputs 1 if $b = 1$ and 0 if $b = 0$.

We stress that in the random oracle model, this argument does not go through. Indeed, to compute re in step 3, $\mathcal{E}$ might have to query the RO. At that point the simulator could program the output of the RO such that it coincides with the uniformly chosen rand_i[4]. The main problem with this notion of strong randomness is realizing it against such a strong distinguisher (i.e., the environment) in UC. Since the seed of a pseudo-random function cannot be hidden from the environment, the latter can easily distinguish random values from the output of the pseudorandom function. We remark that the ideal functionality given in [2] is presented in a simplified setting where prover and verifier are the same machine. This can be done by assuming that the verifier is always honest (as verification is a public procedure). It is not hard to see that our counter-example works for this simplified setting as well. Indeed, we are not making any assumption on the honesty of the verifier.

3.2 Our Notion of Accountable Computation

In the standard model, it is not possible to realize strong randomness (see Section 3.1). The main problem is that the output of the pseudo-random generator has to be unpredictable even to the party that performs the computation. Unsurprisingly, such a result cannot hold in the standard model. Therefore, we weaken the definition of strong randomness in order to adapt it and make it realizable in the standard model. To do so, intuitively we require that the outputs of the pseudo-random generator be indistinguishable from random as long as the seed remains hidden. However, since our main goal is to provide accountability for the computations performed by the system, we directly integrate this (weaker) definition of strong randomness into a fully-fledged definition of accountable randomized computation.

Protocol Template for Real Accountable Computation. The core of an accountable computation scheme are four algorithms (SETUP, INIT, PROV, V) that will be used by the parties P and VE in a canonical protocol.

This protocol template assumes authenticated channels between party P and auditor VE. This assumption corresponds to the common assumption that accountable systems have to maintain a tamper-evident record that provides non-repudiable evidence of all the actions that are sent via these authenticated channels. This authenticated channel is abstracted as an ideal functionality $\mathcal{F}_{\mathrm{AUTH}}$ that guarantees that the network attacker cannot send messages on behalf of P. Typically, such an authenticated channel is realized using a PKI and by attaching a digital signature to every message[5]. Moreover, we introduce two set-up functionalities. The first set-up is a standard CRS functionality $\mathcal{F}_{\mathrm{CRS}}$ that is needed

---

[4] Roughly speaking, this is the approach taken by the proof in [2].

[5] The functionality $\mathcal{F}_{\mathrm{AUTH}}$ is standard, we do not present its definition here. We refer the interested reader to previous work [6].

for creating non-interactive zero-knowledge proofs. Technically, $\mathcal{F}_{\text{CRS}}$ runs the SETUP algorithm and distributes its output to all parties. The second set-up assumption models the initial trusted phase in which P receives a seed, for generating pseudorandom values, and VE receives a corresponding public information, which will enable VE to later check whether the pseudorandom values are generated correctly. This set-up assumption is modeled as a functionality $\mathcal{F}_{\text{PKIF}}$ that internally runs the INIT algorithm and accordingly distributes the result, i.e., the seed to P and the public information to VE. The goal of having $\mathcal{F}_{\text{PKIF}}$ is to ensure that the seed is generated truly randomly, even at a malicious party P. In practice this assumption can be realized in several ways, e.g., P and VE run a parallel coin tossing protocol, INIT is executed in a trusted hardware or in a phase of the protocol where P is guaranteed to behave honestly, or INIT is externally executed by a trusted entity who securely distributes the output. We stress that, even if not very efficient, this phase has to be run only once.

The computing party P is initialized before its first run (via init), and then it can be invoked (via comp) as a subroutine for computing programs (storing proofs about the execution) and publicly announcing the results. Moreover, P reacts to network requests (via vr) to prove statement about its announced results. The auditor VE is invoked by $\mathcal{F}_{\text{PKIF}}$ for the initialization of P (via init), and then can be invoked (via vr) as a subroutine to verify publicly announced results. Last, VE reacts to network announcements of P (via cp) that a result has been computed. The computing party P, upon init, queries both set-up functionalities $\mathcal{F}_{\text{CRS}}$ and $\mathcal{F}_{\text{PKIF}}$ in order to receive the public parameters and the seed for the pseudo-random generator. Upon an invocation (comp, p, s, sid) with a program p and secret inputs s, P computes the program, adds a proof to the log and publicly announces the result. Upon a network message (vr, re, p, sid) from the authenticated channel with VE, P outputs the corresponding proof, or an error message if such a proof does not exist.

The auditor VE, upon being called by an initialization message (init) from the seed generation, queries in turn $\mathcal{F}_{\text{CRS}}$ for the CRS and then stores all values. Upon a network message $(\text{prf}, re, p, cnt, sid)$ over the authenticated channel $\mathcal{F}_{\text{AUTH}}$ with P, VE stores the message and notifies the environement. Upon an invocation $(\text{vr}, re, p, cnt, sid)$, the auditor first asks via $\mathcal{F}_{\text{AUTH}}$ the computing party P for a proof, and then verifies this proof and outputs the result to the environment.

Ideal Functionality for Accountable Computation. The desired security properties for accountable randomized computation are captured by the ideal functionality described in Figure 2. The functionality offers the same interface to the environment as the protocol template and represents the "ideal" behavior of the protocol. In addition, however, the functionality explicitly allows the attacker to intercept messages, and it internally maintains a randomness function RA_{se} for modeling pseudorandomness.

The ideal functionality has interfaces to both the channel from the environment to P and the channel from the environment to VE. Therefore, we distinguish

On (init) **from** $\mathcal{E}$
for honest P
  $se \xleftarrow{\$} \{0,1\}^{\eta}$
  se := se; cnt := 0
  send (init) to $\mathcal{A}$
  output (initd, cnt)
  to $\mathcal{E}$ from P

On (comp, p, s, sid)
from $\mathcal{E}$ **for honest P**
  if $p \in L_{\mathcal{R}}$ **then**
    store tc := cnt
    run re := $\mathrm{EVAL}^{\mathrm{RA_{se}}}(p, \mathsf{cnt}, s)$
    sta(sid) := (re, p, cnt)
    wit(re, p, cnt, sid) := s
    pe(sid) := (prf, re, p, tc, sid)
    cnt := cnt + 1
    send (prf, re, p, tc, sid) to $\mathcal{A}$
    P outputs (re, p, tc, sid) to $\mathcal{E}$

On (deli, sid) **from** $\mathcal{A}$
  let (prf, re, p, cnt, sid) := pe(sid)
  store sta(sid) := (re, p, cnt)
  VE outputs (cp, re, p, cnt, sid) to $\mathcal{E}$

$\mathbf{Ra_{se}}$: **When called on** (cnt)
  if P is honest **then**
    $r \xleftarrow{\$} Rg(\mathrm{F})$; output r
  else
    $r := \mathrm{EVAL}(\mathrm{F}, cnt, \mathsf{se})$; output r

On (vr, re, p, cnt, sid) **from** $\mathcal{E}$ **for honest Ve**
  if (re, p, cnt) = sta(sid) **then**
    send (vr, re, p, cnt, sid) to $\mathcal{A}$
    wait for a response (deli, s', sid)
    if P is honest
      then secr := wit(re, p, cnt, sid)
      else secr := s'
    if (re, pg) = (re, p) $\wedge$ re = $\mathrm{EVAL}^{\mathrm{RA_{se}}}(p, \mathsf{tc}, \mathsf{secr}, \mathsf{se})$
      then output (re, p, 1) to $\mathcal{E}$
      else output (re, pg, 0) to $\mathcal{E}$

Fig. 2. The ideal functionality for accountable computation

from which of these channels an environment message comes and to which we output messages. Moreover, the functionality maintains internal (shared) data-structures, such as sta and wit which are used for verification, and se which is used for pseudo-random values.

Upon (init) for P, the functionality honestly draws a random seed and notifies the attacker that it has been initialized. Upon (comp, p, s, sid), the ideal functionality computes the program on the inputs, stores the secret inputs for later verification, and publicly announces the result. Upon a message (deli, sid) by the attacker, the statement is registered in pg and the environment is notified. Upon (vr, re, p, cnt, sid), the functionality recomputes the result with the stored witness. We stress that for malicious parties the attacker is allowed to give the witnesses for the statement in the deli message. Otherwise, the simulator does not work, because the real protocol does not reveal the proof earlier.

In contrast to the real protocol, for honest P the functionality returns truly random values as a result of $\mathrm{RA_{se}}$, instead of the result of the pseudorandom function. This basically models that the pseudo-random generation should satisfy the usual notion of pseudorandomness, in which the challenger is always honest.

We stress that for dishonest parties P (and honest VE) our ideal functionality still guarantees that the PRF has been honestly computed. Malicious parties in the ideal model are canonically modeled by merely forwarding the input to the attacker and storing its results in the internal data-structures, such as sta.

4   Instantiations of Accountable Computation Schemes

Now that we have a clear definition of accountable randomized computation, we will show how it can be realized by means of suitable cryptographic tools. First, we describe below a generic paradigm to achieve this notion. However, since in the most generic case this generic construction may lead to rather inefficient instantiations, we will then show how to realize *efficient* accountable randomized computation for a significant class of computations.

A GENERIC CONSTRUCTION. The basic idea is to use UC-secure protocols for non-interactive zero-knowledge proofs, a perfectly binding commitment, and a pseudorandom function. Moreover, we assume the availability of ideal functionalities for the generation of the common reference string, the random sampling of a seed for the PRF, and for implementing authenticated channels (e.g., using signatures). At a high level, the generic scheme works as follows. In the setup phase, the parties ask for the common reference string for the NIZK proof system. Next, to initialize the system, every user invokes the ideal functionality in order to obtain a random seed se of a pseudorandom function F_{se}. It also samples random coins $open_{se}$, and computes a commitment $C = \text{COM}(se; open_{se})$, which is published in the authenticated log. The pair $se, open_{se}$ is instead maintained by the party. Later, whenever a party is asked to compute a function p on inputs s, it will compute $re = p(s)$ and will create a proof π using the NIZK proof system for the NP statement "$\exists s : output = p(s)$". To prove correctness of randomness generation, i.e., that $r = F_{se}(cnt)$, the user can use the same approach and generate a proof for the statement "$\exists (se, open_{se}) : r = F_{se}(cnt) \wedge C = Com(se; open_{se})$". The proof $\Pi = (p, re, \pi, cnt)$ is published in the log. Finally, the auditor can verify proofs by running the verification procedure of the NIZK proof system.

4.1   Useful Tools and Definitions

Before describing our efficient instantiation, here we introduce the algebraic tools and the cryptographic primitives that will be useful in our construction.

BILINEAR GROUPS. Let $\mathcal{G}(1^k)$ be an algorithm that on input the security parameter 1^k outputs a tuple $\text{pp}_{BM} = (p, \mathbb{G}_1, \mathbb{G}_2, \mathbb{G}_T, e)$ such that: p is a prime of at least k bits, $\mathbb{G}_1, \mathbb{G}_2, \mathbb{G}_T$ are groups of order p, and $e : \mathbb{G}_1 \times \mathbb{G}_2 \rightarrow \mathbb{G}_T$ is an efficiently computable and non-degenerate bilinear map.

The q-Decisional Diffie-Hellman Inversion (q-DDHI, for short) problem in $\mathbb{G}_1$ (same definition would hold in $\mathbb{G}_2$) is defined as follows.

Definition 1 (q-DDHI). *Let* $(p, \mathbb{G}_1, \mathbb{G}_2, \mathbb{G}_T, e) \xleftarrow{\$} \mathcal{G}(1^k)$, $g_1 \in \mathbb{G}_1$ *be a generator, and* $x \xleftarrow{\$} \mathbb{Z}_p$ *be chosen at random. Let* T *be the tuple* $(g_1, g_1^x, g_1^{x^2}, \ldots, g_1^{x^q})$, *and* Z *be a randomly chosen element of* $\mathbb{G}_1$. *We define the advantage of an* *adversary* $\mathcal{A}$ *in solving the* q-Decisional Diffie-Hellman Inversion *problem as* $\mathbf{Adv}_{\mathcal{A}}^{qDDHI}(k) = \left| \Pr[\mathcal{A}(p, T, g^{1/x}) = 1] - \Pr[\mathcal{A}(p, T, Z) = 1] \right|$, *where the probability is taken over the random choices of* $\mathcal{G}, x, Z$ *and the random coins of* $\mathcal{A}$. *We say that the* q-DDHI Assumption *holds in* $\mathbb{G}_1$ *if for every PPT algorithm* $\mathcal{A}$, *and for any* q *polynomial in* k, *the advantage* $\mathbf{Adv}_{\mathcal{A}}^{qDDHI}(k)$ *is negligible.*

GROTH-SAHAI PROOF SYSTEM. Groth and Sahai [13] describes a way to generate efficient, non-interactive, witness-indistinguishable proofs for statements in the language $\mathcal{L}_{\mathsf{GS}}$ of so-called *"pairing product equations"*. If $\{\mathcal{X}_i\}_{i=1}^{m} \in \mathbb{G}_1$ and $\{\mathcal{Y}_i\}_{i=1}^{n} \in \mathbb{G}_2$ are variables, and $\{\mathcal{A}_i\}_{i=1}^{n} \in \mathbb{G}_1$, $\{\mathcal{B}_i\}_{i=1}^{m} \in \mathbb{G}_2$, $a_{i,j} \in \mathbb{Z}_p$ and $t_T \in \mathbb{G}_T$ are constants, $\mathcal{L}_{\mathsf{GS}}$ is the language of equations of the following form:

$$\prod_{i=1}^{n} e(\mathcal{A}_i, \mathcal{Y}_i) \prod_{i=i}^{m} e(\mathcal{X}_i, \mathcal{B}_i) \prod_{i=1}^{m} \prod_{j=1}^{n} e(\mathcal{X}_i, \mathcal{Y}_j) = t_T$$

The Groth-Sahai proof system can be instantiated in prime order groups by assuming its security based on either the SXDH or Decision Linear assumptions.

The main technique behind Groth-Sahai proofs is the use of specific commitment schemes that allow to commit to elements in $\mathbb{G}_1$ or $\mathbb{G}_2$. In particular, the proof system generates a common reference string which can be of two different and indistinguishable forms. When the CRS is instantiated for perfect soundness, the commitment is perfectly binding, whereas in the witness-indistinguishability setting the CRS leads to a perfectly hiding commitment. More importantly, the two modes of generation are computationally indistinguishable under the SXDH (resp. DLin) assumption, and both modes allow trapdoors that work as follows. In the perfectly binding setting, commitments have the form of ElGamal (resp. Boneh-Boyen-Shacham) ciphertexts, and the trapdoor is the decryption key, which thus allows to make the commitments *extractable*. In the perfectly hiding setting, instead, the trapdoor allows to equivocate the commitments, i.e., to create a commitment to some (random) value g_1^r, and to later open it to a different value g_1^x. These trapdoors are usually referred to as the extraction and simulation trapdoor respectively.

For lack of space, we refer the interested reader to [13] for a detailed and formal description of the Groth-Sahai proof system. Here we recall that such a scheme is defined by three algorithms (GS.SETUP, GS.PROVE, GS.VER) that allow to, respectively, generate the parameters, create proofs and verify proofs. Moreover, for security, the system is also equipped with "extraction" and "simulation" algorithms (GS.EXTRACTSETUP, GS.EXTRACT, GS.SIMSETUP, GS.SIMPROVE). In its basic instantiation, the Groth-Sahai scheme provides witness-indistinguishable proofs. However, Groth and Sahai interestingly show that for certain cases these techniques can be used to achieve zero-knowledge [13]. A significant case is the one in which all the equations being simultaneously satisfied have the constant value $t_T = 1$, the identity element in $\mathbb{G}_T$. Other statements have been shown to be modifiable in order to obtain zero-knowledge-friendly statements. We refer the interested reader to [13] for more details. For the sake of our work, we denote this subset of $\mathcal{L}_{\mathsf{GS}}$ that allows for zero-knowledge proofs as $\mathcal{L}_{\mathsf{GS-ZK}}$.

THE PSEUDORANDOM NUMBER GENERATION. As a tool for generating the randomness in our accountable computation we use the following pseudorandom function $F_s(c) = g_1^{\frac{1}{s+c}}$, which is also known as Boneh-Boyen weak signature [5], and Dodis-Yampolskiy PRF [9]. The function is proven pseudo-random under the q-DDHI assumption in $\mathbb{G}_1$, and for a domain D of size q where q is polynomial in the security parameter. We observe that the restriction on the domain's size is not a severe limitation in our setting as we will use the function in a stateful way to generate a sequence of values $F_s(1), F_s(2), \ldots$. The number of values is bounded by the the system's running time which is polynomial in the security parameter. More importantly for our application, the function is known to allow for efficient Groth-Sahai proofs. The idea of using zero-knowledge proofs to show the correctness of the outputs of a pseudorandom function is somewhat similar to the notion of simulatable verifiable random functions [7], with the only exception that in the latter case proofs do not need to be fully zero-knowledge. Belenkiy, Chase, Kohlweiss, and Lysyanskaya point this out [3] and propose a construction based on Groth-Sahai proofs.

4.2   An Efficient Instantiation of Accountable Computation

In this section we show how to realize accountable randomized computation for the language $\mathcal{L}_{\text{GS-ZK}}$ of pairing product equations with zero-knowledge statements. It is worth noting that using $\mathcal{L}_{\text{GS-ZK}}$ one can prove the simultaneous satisfiability of multiple algebraic equations whose degree is up to 2. In the description of our scheme we give an explicit description of the algorithms F and F.PROVE for the generation and the verification of the generated pseudorandom values. These algorithms are however a specific case of computations and proofs.

- SETUP(1^k): generate the description of bilinear groups $\text{pp}_{BM} = (p, \mathbb{G}_1, \mathbb{G}_2, \mathbb{G}_T, g_1, g_2, e)$ and the parameters $\text{pp}_{GS} \xleftarrow{\$} \text{GS.SETUP}(\text{pp}_{BM})$ of the Groth-Sahai proof system. Return $\text{pp} = (\text{pp}_{BM}, \text{pp}_{GS})$.
- INIT(pp): as a seed, sample a random value $s \xleftarrow{\$} \mathbb{Z}_p$ and random opening $open_s$. The party keeps a secret key $fsk = (s, open_s)$ while a public verification key is $fpk = \text{COM}(g_2^s; open_s)$ is published to the log.
- PROV(pp, fsk, p, s): compute $re = p(s)$, run $\pi \xleftarrow{\$} \text{GS.PROVE}(\text{pp}_{GS}, St, w)$ where the statement St is created from the program p and the result re, whereas the witness is the secret input s. Output $\Pi = (p, re, \pi, cnt)$.
- F(pp, fsk, cnt): increment the counter $cnt \leftarrow cnt + 1$, and output $y = g_1^{\frac{1}{s+cnt}}$.
- F.PROVE(pp, fsk, cnt): proving the correctness of a pseudorandom value $y = $ F(pp, fsk, cnt) basically consists in creating a composable NIZK proof π for the language $\mathcal{L}_{PRF} = \{fpk, cnt, y : \exists s, open_s : fpk = \text{COM}(g_2^s; open_s) \wedge y = g_1^{\frac{1}{s+cnt}}\}$[6]. Output $\Pi = (F, y, \pi, cnt)$.
- V(pp, fpk, Π): parse Π as (p, re, π, cnt). Use the verification algorithm of Groth-Sahai to verify the proof π with respect to (public) values fpk, p, re, cnt.

---

[6] Belenkiy et al. show in [3] how to create such a proof using Groth-Sahai.

In terms of performances, the efficiency of the above instantiation heavily depends on the efficiency of the Groth-Sahai scheme. It is worth noting that although at the end our solution is not as efficient as CSAR, it is though the first providing such a strong privacy guarantee.

To prove the security of our accountable computation we will show that it realizes the ideal functionality of accountable randomized computation. In using the above instantiation in our protocol template we require the generation of different GS parameters pp_{GS} for every prover party. Generating different GS parameters, i.e., a different CRS, for every party avoids the need of being able to extract and simulate with the same CRS, which in turn allows us to use more efficient GS constructions. We stress that it is possible to use a strengthened GS proof system that allows for simultaneous simulation and extraction with the same CRS, and then to use only one CRS for all parties. However, since in our scenario we anyway assume the distribution of a public key for every prover, our restriction of using many CRS would not significantly weaken the set-up model.

Theorem 1. *Let Π be our protocol's template instantiated with the algorithms from Section 4.2, and let $\mathcal{F}$ be the ideal functionality from Figure 2. If the q-DDHI assumption holds in $\mathbb{G}_1$ and Groth-Sahai is secure, then Π securely UC-realizes $\mathcal{F}$.*

For lack of space, the proof of this theorem appears in the full version.

5   Using Verifiable Randomness Privately: Signatures

The previous section describes an accountable randomized computation for the language $\mathcal{L}_{GS-ZK}$ of pairing product equations (of a certain form), and for a specific pseudorandom function $F_s(x)$. It is worth noting that the generated (pseudo)randomness have a specific structure: the values are elements of the group $\mathbb{G}_1$. While in general one can use a suitable hash function in order to generate, e.g., binary strings out of group elements, such an arbitrary use of the randomness does not always allow for efficient zero-knowledge proofs. To be more concrete, if one wants to prove the correctness of a certain computation in which a value R generated using $F_s(cnt)$ is one of the secret inputs, then R must be a variable in the language $\mathcal{L}_{GS-ZK}$, i.e., R must be in $\mathbb{G}_1$.

Such a situation leaves us with an open question about the uses of the accountable randomness generated by our protocol. In this section, we address this problem and we propose an application to an important cryptographic primitive: digital signatures. In digital signatures, randomness is usually used to: (1) generate the secret signing key, (2) create the signature. If the randomness source is bad, the signature might be forgeable. Our scheme assumes a good randomness seed and given that seed proves that all signatures use "good" randomness.

5.1   An Accountable Signature Scheme

In this section, we tackle this problem and we propose a signature scheme that fits the setting of our accountable randomized computation, i.e., that of bilinear pairings. To achieve this goal, the faced technical challenge is that virtually all existing constructions use either secret keys or random values that are "in the exponent". We solved this problem by proposing a new scheme which has the desired property, namely both the secret key and the randomness used in the signing algorithm are group elements. The proposed construction works within the accountable computation system. In particular, it uses the same pseudorandom generator and shares the same state.

The Security Model. Our signature scheme is stateful, in the sense that every message is signed with respect to a counter which gets incremented every time (in particular, the same counter is never re-used), and the signature is verified against the counter. For security, we consider the standard notion of *unforgeability under chosen message attack* in the stateful setting. This model considers an adversary that has access to a signing oracle and whose goal is to produce a forgery that either verifies against a "new" counter (i.e., a counter greater than the one in the system after the last query), or it verifies for an "old" counter (i.e., one for which a signature was obtained from the oracle) but for a message that is different from the one asked to the oracle.

Since our signature scheme is part of the accountability system (i.e., it shares the same parameters) we have to model the fact that an adversary may obtain additional information. For instance, it might ask for proofs about arbitrary statements. For this reason, we consider an extension of the unforgeability game, in which the adversary is granted access to an additional oracle $\mathcal{O}(\cdot)$ which can be either one of the algorithms $\text{PROV}(\mathsf{pp}, \mathit{fsk}, \cdot, s)$, $\text{F}(\mathsf{pp}, \mathit{fsk}, \mathit{cnt})$, $\text{F.PROVE}(\mathsf{pp}, \mathit{fsk}, \mathit{cnt})$. We assume that F and F.PROVE are computed on the next counter, whereas PROV is evaluated on a program p chosen by the adversary. For lack of space, a formal definition of our unforgeability experiment will appear only in the full version.

Our Construction. Before describing our construction, we give a high level description of our techniques. Our starting point is an idea, earlier proposed by Bellare and Goldwasser, for building signature schemes from zero-knowledge proofs [4]. Roughly speaking, Bellare-Goldwasser's scheme works as follows. The key generation consists of generating the seed s of a PRF and publishing its commitment C as the public verification key. Next, to sign a message m one computes the PRF on the message, $y = f_s(m)$, and proves in zero-knowledge that $y = f_s(m)$ and s is the same value in the commitment C.

In our case, the pseudorandom function is computed on a state, the counter, and thus we cannot apply it to an arbitrary message m. To solve this issue we create a signature on m by using the randomness $R = \text{F}_s(\mathit{cnt}) \in \mathbb{G}_1$ and computing a value $\sigma = h^m \cdot R$, where h is also random value that is kept as the secret key. The actual signature is σ together with a zero-knowledge proof that σ is indeed created as $h^m \cdot \text{F}_s(\mathit{cnt})$. The security relies on the soundness and zero-knowledge properties of the proof system, and the observation is that such value σ is essentially an information theoretic one-time MAC on m (if one assumes that h is random and so is every R).

More in detail, our construction works as follows. Let pp be the public parameters of the system consisting of a tuple $\mathsf{pp} = (p, \mathbb{G}_1, \mathbb{G}_2, \mathbb{G}_T, g_1, g_2, e, \mathsf{pp}_{GS})$ where pp_{GS} are the parameters of a NIZK Groth-Sahai proof system.

- SIGKEYGEN(pp): use the pseudorandom function to generate $h \leftarrow F(\mathsf{pp}, fsk, \mathsf{cnt}) \in \mathbb{G}_1$. Next, commit to h using random coins $open_h$, set $vk = \mathrm{COM}(h, open_h)$ and $sk = (h, open_h)$.
- SIGN(pp, fsk, sk, m). Let $m \in \mathbb{Z}_p \setminus \{0\}$ be the message, and let cnt be the system's counter for randomness generation. A signature on m is generated as follows. First, use the pseudorandom function to generate randomness $R \leftarrow F(\mathsf{pp}, fsk, \mathsf{cnt})$. Next, compute $\sigma \leftarrow h^m \cdot R$, $C'_h = \mathrm{COM}(h; open'_h)$ $C_R = \mathrm{COM}(R; open_R)$, $C'_R = \mathrm{COM}(R, open'_R)$, a composable NIZK proof π_1 for the statement $\exists(h, open'_h, R, open'_R) : \sigma = h^m \cdot R \wedge C'_h = \mathrm{COM}(h, open'_h) \wedge C'_R = \mathrm{COM}(R; open'_R)$, a composable NIZK proof π_2 that $\exists(g_2^s, open_s, R, open'_r) : C_R = \mathrm{COM}(R; open_R) \wedge R = F_s(\mathsf{cnt})$, and composable NIZK proofs π_R and π_h proving that C_R and C'_R, and vk and C'_h commit to the same values. Output $\Sigma = (\sigma, C_R, C'_R, C'_h, \pi_1, \pi_2, \pi_h, \pi_R)$.
- SIGVER(pp, vk, m, cnt, Σ): use the verification algorithm of Groth-Sahai to verify proofs $\pi_1, \pi_2, \pi_R, \pi_h$.

Theorem 2. *If the Groth-Sahai proof system is secure, and the function $F_s(x)$ is pseudorandom, then the signature scheme is unforgeable.*

For lack of space, the proof appears only in the full version.

6   Related Work

Previous work proposed the use of accountability for several goals, such as to achieve real-world security [19], to incentivize cooperative behavior [8], to foster innovation and competition in the Internet [20,1], and to design dependable networked systems [24]. Systems have been built to provide accountability for both deterministic and randomized systems. In the previous section we already mentioned PeerReview [15] and its extension, CSAR [2]. Another example is CATS [25], a network storage service with strong accountability properties. The basic idea of CATS is to use a trusted publishing medium for publishing the logs and to ensure their integrity. The logs are then checked against a set of rules that describe the expected behavior of a node. Another system, repeat and compare [22], uses the accountability approach to guarantee content integrity in a peer-to-peer content distribution network built over untrusted nodes. Its basic idea is to use a set of trusted nodes that locally reproduce a random sample of the generated content and compare it to the one published by the untrusted nodes. Recently, another system, NetReview [14], successfully built upon the idea of PeerReview to enable the detection of faults caused by ISPs in the Border Gateway Protocol (BGP).

On the definitional side, Küsters, Truderung, and Vogt introduced a definition of accountability and compared it to the notion of verifiability [17]. They show that verifiability is weaker than accountability as the former does not require that a malicious party is always detectable. We notice that our definition implicitly assumes authenticated channels. Hence, it does not only capture verifiable computation, but also accountable computation.

The idea of generating accountable randomness is closely related to the notion of verifiable random functions (VRFs) [21], and simulatable VRFs [7]. In a nutshell, VRFs are pseudo-random functions that allow for publicly verifiable proofs about the correctness of the function's outputs. Moreover, all values for which a proof has not been issued are guaranteed to remain pseudorandom. Although this is intuitively the same requirement as in our case, there are a couple of differences due to some technical details. The difference mainly deals with the fact that our notion is simulation-based in a composability framework, and should not reveal any information about the seed, a property which is not necessarily captured by (simulatable) VRFs. To this extent, our techniques are related to the extension of simulatable VRFs proposed by Belenkiy, Chase, Kohlweiss, and Lysyanskaya [3], from which we borrow some of the technical ideas.

7   Conclusion and Future Work

In this paper we have investigated the notion of accountability for systems that execute randomized computations and want to keep the inputs of these computations private. We formalized a rigorous definition that models all the essential security properties, and we showed an efficient instantiation for interesting classes of computations based on techniques of the Groth-Sahai proof system. Furthermore, we proposed a digital signature scheme that enjoys the accountability properties of our system: the signer can convince an auditor that the secret signing key and the signatures are correctly generated (i.e., by using good randomness), and the auditor neither learns the signature key nor the randomness used for the signatures. For future work, it would be interesting to explore extensions of our scheme to provide accountability for other important cryptographic primitives, such as encryption, as well as to investigate efficient instantiations for richer classes of computations.

References

1. Argyraki, K., Maniatis, P., Irzak, O., Ashish, S., Shenker, S.: Loss and delay accountability for the internet. In: IEEE International Conference on Network Protocols, ICNP 2007, pp. 194–205 (October 2007)
2. Backes, M., Druschel, P., Haeberlen, A., Unruh, D.: Csar: A practical and provable technique to make randomized systems accountable. In: Proceedings of the Network and Distributed System Security Symposium, NDSS 2009 (2009)

3. Belenkiy, M., Chase, M., Kohlweiss, M., Lysyanskaya, A.: Compact e-cash and simulatable VRFs revisited. In: Shacham, H., Waters, B. (eds.) Pairing 2009. LNCS, vol. 5671, pp. 114–131. Springer, Heidelberg (2009)
4. Bellare, M., Goldwasser, S.: New paradigms for digital signatures and message authentication based on non-interactive zero knowledge proofs. In: Brassard, G. (ed.) CRYPTO 1989. LNCS, vol. 435, pp. 194–211. Springer, Heidelberg (1990)
5. Boneh, D., Boyen, X.: Short signatures without random oracles and the sdh assumption in bilinear groups. Journal of Cryptology 21, 149–177 (2008)
6. Canetti, R.: Universally composable security: A new paradigm for cryptographic protocols. IACR Cryptology ePrint Archive, 2000:67 (2000)
7. Chase, M., Lysyanskaya, A.: Simulatable VRFs with applications to multi-theorem NIZK. In: Menezes, A. (ed.) CRYPTO 2007. LNCS, vol. 4622, pp. 303–322. Springer, Heidelberg (2007)
8. Dingledine, R., Freedman, M.J., Molnar, D.: Accountability. In: Peer-to-Peer: Harnessing the Power of Disruptive Technologies. O'Reilly and Associates (2001)
9. Dodis, Y., Yampolskiy, A.: A verifiable random function with short proofs and keys. In: Vaudenay, S. (ed.) PKC 2005. LNCS, vol. 3386, pp. 416–431. Springer, Heidelberg (2005)
10. Goldreich, O., Micali, S., Wigderson, A.: How to play any mental game. In: Proceedings of the 19th Annual ACM Symposium on Theory of Computing, STOC 1987, pp. 218–229. ACM (1987)
11. Goldwasser, S., Micali, S., Rackoff, C.: The knowledge complexity of interactive proof systems. SIAM J. Comput. 18(1), 186–208 (1989)
12. Groth, J.: Short pairing-based non-interactive zero-knowledge arguments. In: Abe, M. (ed.) ASIACRYPT 2010. LNCS, vol. 6477, pp. 321–340. Springer, Heidelberg (2010)
13. Groth, J., Sahai, A.: Efficient noninteractive proof systems for bilinear groups. SIAM Journal on Computing 41(5), 1193–1232 (2012)
14. Haeberlen, A., Avramopoulos, I., Rexford, J., Druschel, P.: NetReview: Detecting when interdomain routing goes wrong. In: Proceedings of the 6th Symposium on Networked Systems Design and Implementation, NSDI 2009 (2009)
15. Haeberlen, A., Kuznetsov, P., Druschel, P.: PeerReview: Practical accountability for distributed systems. In: Proceedings of the 21st ACM Symposium on Operating Systems Principles, SOSP 2007 (2007)
16. Hofheinz, D., Shoup, V.: Gnuc: A new universal composability framework. IACR Cryptology ePrint Archive, p. 303 (2011)
17. Küsters, R., Truderung, T., Vogt, A.: Accountability: definition and relationship to verifiability. In: Proceedings of the 17th ACM Conference on Computer and Communications Security, CCS 2010, pp. 526–535 (2010)
18. Küsters, R.: Simulation-based security with inexhaustible interactive turing machines. In: Proc. 19th IEEE Computer Security Foundations Workshop, pp. 309–320 (2006)
19. Lampson, B.W.: Computer security in the real world. In: Proc. Annual Computer Security Applications Conference (December 2000)
20. Laskowski, P., Chuang, J.: Network monitors and contracting systems: competition and innovation. In: Proceedings of the 2006 Conference on Applications, Technologies, Architectures, and Protocols for Computer Communications, SIGCOMM 2006, New York, NY, USA, pp. 183–194 (2006)

21. Micali, S., Rabin, M.O., Vadhan, S.P.: Verifiable random functions. In: 40th FOCS, New York, New York, USA, October 17-19, pp. 120–130 (1999)
22. Michalakis, N., Soulé, R., Grimm, R.: Ensuring content integrity for untrusted peer-to-peer content distribution networks. In: Proceedings of the 4th USENIX Conference on Networked Systems Design & Implementation, NSDI 2007, p. 11 (2007)
23. Pfitzmann, B., Waidner, M.: A model for asynchronous reactive systems and its application to secure message transmission. IEEE Symposium on Security and Privacy, p. 0184 (2001)
24. Yumerefendi, A.R., Chase, J.S.: Trust but verify: accountability for network services. In: Proceedings of the 11th Workshop on ACM SIGOPS European Workshop, EW 11, New York, NY, USA (2004)
25. Yumerefendi, A.R., Chase, J.S.: Strong accountability for network storage. In: 5th USENIX Conference on File and Storage Technologies (2007)

Verifying Web Browser Extensions' Compliance with Private-Browsing Mode*

Benjamin S. Lerner, Liam Elberty, Neal Poole, and Shriram Krishnamurthi

Brown University

Abstract. Modern web browsers implement a *private browsing mode* that is intended to leave behind no traces of a user's browsing activity on their computer. This feature is in direct tension with support for *extensions*, which can silently void this guarantee.

We create a static type system to analyze JavaScript extensions for observation of private browsing mode. Using this type system, extension authors and app stores can convince themselves of an extension's safety for private browsing mode. In addition, some extensions intentionally violate the private browsing guarantee; our type system accommodates this with a small annotation overhead, proportional to the degree of violation. These annotations let code auditors narrow their focus to a small fraction of the extension's codebase.

We have retrofitted type annotations to Firefox's APIs and to a sample of actively used Firefox extensions. We used the type system to verify several extensions as safe, find actual bugs in several others (most of which have been confirmed by their authors), and find dubious behavior in the rest. Firefox 20, released April 2, 2013, implements a finer-grained private browsing mode; we sketch both the new challenges in this implementation and how our approach can handle them.

1 Introduction

Modern web browsers are feature-rich systems, providing a highly customizable environment for browsing, running web apps, and downloading content. People use browsers for a wide variety of reasons, and now routinely conduct sensitive transactions with them. Accordingly, recent browsers have added support for so-called *private browsing mode*, in which the browser effectively keeps no record of the user's activities: no history or cache is preserved, no cookies are retained, etc. The precise guarantee provided by private browsing mode is, however, rather more subtle, since a strict policy of retaining absolutely no record would preclude standard browsing activities such as downloading any files.

Ensuring the correctness of private browsing mode is therefore challenging on its own, but the situation is trickier still. Most browsers support *extensions*,[1] written in JavaScript (JS), that allow users to customize the browser with third-party code—which run with the browser's full privileges and can hence also save

---

* This work is partially supported by the US National Science Foundation.
[1] These are distinct from *plugins* such as Flash or Java; we exclude plugins here.

J. Crampton, S. Jajodia, and K. Mayes (Eds.): ESORICS 2013, LNCS 8134, pp. 57–74, 2013.

files or other traces of the user's activity. In short, the presence of extensions can completely undermine the browser's privacy efforts.

The extension community is vibrant, with over 60 million daily extension users, and billions of total installations [16]. The potential privacy harm from faulty extensions is correspondingly huge. Unfortunately, all three involved parties—browser authors, extension authors, and end-users—have difficulty properly protecting end-users from these problems. For browser authors, there is no universally safe default: running extensions automatically is clearly unsafe, but disabling them by default would also disable extensions such as AdBlock, which serve to enhance the overall privacy of the browser! Moreover, users currently have no way to make an informed decision about which extensions to re-enable. And worse still, even extension authors do not fully understand what private browsing mode entails: in the course of this work, for instance, one extension author we contacted replied, "when I wrote [the extension], the private browsing stuff didn't exist (to be honest, I'm only peripherally aware of it now)."

To date, browser vendors—primarily Mozilla and Google, whose browsers feature the most sophisticated extension support—provide extension authors with only rather vague guidelines on proper behavior when in private browsing mode. Mozilla enforces its guidelines via manual code audits on all the extensions uploaded to their site. Unfortunately, these audits are a bottleneck in the otherwise-automated process of publishing an extension [34, 35]. It is also possible for violations—sometimes flagrant ones [23]—to slip through, and *our work finds more violations, even in extensions that have passed review and been given a security check*. Moreover, if policies ever changed, Mozilla would face the daunting task of re-auditing thousands of extensions.

Contributions

We propose a new mechanism for verifying that extensions behave properly in private browsing mode. Our approach uses a lightweight type system for JS that exposes all potentially privacy-violating actions as type errors: the lack of type errors proves the extension is privacy-preserving. Authors can tell the type-checker precisely which errors to ignore, and only these annotations must then be audited in a security review. This paper makes the following contributions:

- We design a type system that segregates "potentially unsafe" code from "provably safe" code. Our system is *lightweight*—we typecheck *only* the code that may run in private browsing mode, and extension authors must only annotate code that is not provably safe. Most utility code is easily safe and requires no annotation. (Section 4)
- We implement our approach for the extension APIs found in Mozilla Firefox. Ascribing types to Firefox's APIs is non-trivial; the types must match their quirky idioms with high fidelity in order to be useful. (Section 5)
- We evaluate our system by retrofitting type annotations onto 12 real-world extensions. Relatively few annotations are needed. We verify six extensions as safe, finding private-browsing (but not necessarily privacy) violations in the rest; three were confirmed by their authors as bugs. (Section 6)

Due to page limits, we necessarily elide detailed examples of our approach; full details can be found in the companion technical report [20].

2 Background: Extensions and Privacy

Browser extensions define both UI and behavior, the former written in markup that varies between browsers and the latter written in JavaScript. Though interesting in its own right [18], the UI code is essentially inert markup and therefore largely irrelevant for our security concerns here. We present a brief overview of how extensions are written in Firefox and Chrome.

2.1 Classic Firefox Extension Model

Firefox extensions define their functionality in JS, and trigger it via event handlers in the markup of their UI. These event handlers can use the same DOM methods as typical web pages, but in addition, they are given a suite of APIs providing low-level platform features such as file-system access and process management, as well as access to history and preferences, and many other functions. These APIs are obtained via a factory; for example, the following constructs a file object:

```
var file = Components
          .classes["@mozilla.org/file/local;1"]
          .createInstance(Components.interfaces.nsILocalFile);
```

The `Components.classes` array contains "contract IDs" naming various available object types, mapped to factories for constructing instances. As of version 13, Firefox defines 847 contract IDs and 1465 interfaces: a huge API surface.

One of these APIs, `Components.interfaces.nsIPrivateBrowsingService`, allows code to check if it is running in private-browsing mode, and to cause the browser to enter or exit private-browsing mode. The former check is essential for writing privacy-aware code; the latter methods are particularly troublesome (see Section 5).

2.2 Chrome and Jetpack Extension Model

The traditional security response to such a situation is to lock down and narrow the API surface area. Chrome's architecture has done so. The back-end of a Chrome extension is written against a much smaller API: a mere 26 objects to access bookmarks, cookies, tabs, etc [11]. Though there are no APIs to access the filesystem directly, there are experimental APIs for local storage, and extensions have unrestricted access to cross-origin XHR: extensions can still persist state. This relatively spartan API means Chrome extensions are inherently less capable than Firefox ones, and despite that they can still violate incognito-mode guarantees. In particular, an extension can create an implicit channel that leaks sensitive data from an incognito tab to a concurrent public one; from there the data can easily be saved to disk. See Section 3.2 for further discussion.

In a similar vein, Firefox has been working on a new extension model, known as "jetpacks" or "SDK addons". These extensions are a hybrid: they have access to a small API similar to Chrome's, but if necessary can get access to the Components object and access the rest of the platform. Such access is discouraged, in favor of enhancing the SDK APIs to obviate the need.

3   Subtleties of Private Browsing Mode

The intuitive goals of the various private browsing mode implementations are easy to state, but their precise guarantees are subtly different. In particular, the security versus usability trade-offs of private browsing mode are particularly important, and impact the design.

3.1   Usability Trade-Offs in Specifying Private Browsing Mode

Private browsing mode is often described as the browser "not remembering anything" about the current session. One implementation approach might be to prohibit all disk writes altogether. Indeed, the initial planning for Firefox's private browsing mode [22] states, "The bullet-proof solution is to not write anything to disk. This will give users maximum confidence and will remove any possible criticism of the feature from security experts."[2]

However, the high-level intent of private-browsing mode is a statement about the state of users' computers *after* their sessions have terminated; it says nothing about what happens *during* their sessions. In particular, a user might reasonably expect the browser to "work like normal" while browsing, and "forget" everything about the session afterward. Such a private-browsing implementation might well handle many forms of persistent state during the session on behalf of the user, such as history, cookies, or cache. Additionally, a user can ask the browser explicitly to take certain stateful actions, such as downloading a file or updating bookmarks. Therefore, simply turning off persistence APIs is not an option.

3.2   Mode Concurrency and Switching

How isolated is private browsing? Chrome (and now Firefox; see Section 8) allows users to have both "normal" and "incognito" windows open concurrently; can this concurrency be exploited to leak data from private browsing? Similarly, can an extension hoard data in private browsing mode, and then release it when the window switches to normal mode?

The mitigation for this attack differs in its details between the two browsers, but amounts to isolating extensions' state to within a single window, which is then the unit of normal or private modes. In particular, all the scripts that implement the behavior of Firefox windows run in the context of each window.[3] When

---

[2]   Even these precautions may not suffice: virtual memory might swap private browsing mode information to persistent storage [3].

[3]   The Firefox expert might know about "backstage pass" contexts, which can persist. Such contexts are internal to Gecko and to our knowledge cannot be intentionally accessed by script. Even if they could, we can reflect this in our typed APIs.

earlier versions of Firefox transition between modes, they close all currently-open private windows and re-open the public ones from the prior session. Crucially, this means extensions' state is effectively destroyed and re-initialized as these windows are opened, so extensions cannot passively hoard data and have it automatically leak into public mode. Instead, they must actively use APIs to persist their data, and we detect and flag such uses.

In Chrome, extensions are partitioned into two pieces: a background task running in a standalone context, and content scripts running in the context of individual pages. The background task can execute privileged operations, but cannot obtain data about the user's open pages directly. Instead, the content script must send such data to the background task over a well-specified API, and again we can detect and flag such uses.

In short, browsers are engineered such that there is no implicit communications channel between private-mode windows and public ones. Persisting any data from one to the other requires explicitly using an API to do so, and our system is specifically designed to raise warnings about just those APIs. Accordingly, for the remainder of this paper, we can safely assume that the presence or absence of private mode is effectively *constant* while analyzing an extension, because it *is* constant for the duration of any given JS context. (We describe how our approach may adapt to Firefox's new design in Section 8.)

4   Our Approach: Type-Based Extension Verification

We assume that the browser vendor has correctly implemented private-browsing mode and focus on whether extensions violate it. We perform this analysis through a *type system* for JS. In particular, any accesses to potentially harmful APIs must be syntactically marked in the code, making the reviewers' job a simple search, rather than a reading of the entire extension. Furthermore, we define an *affirmative privacy burden*: rather than require all developers to annotate all code, we require annotations only where code might violate private browsing expectations. Our type system is based on TeJaS, a type system for JS [14], with several variations.

4.1   Informal Description

Type systems are program analyses that determine whether a semantic property holds of a given program, based on that program's syntactic structure. A type system is comprised of three parts: a type *language* for describing the types of expressions in the program, a type *environment* assigning types to the predefined APIs, and a type *checker* that takes as input a program to be checked and the type environment, and then attempts to validate the program against a set of rules; programs that pass the typechecker possess the desired semantic property.

Our particular type language defines a type, @Unsafe, which our environment assigns to the potentially-unsafe APIs (e.g., file.create) to prevent them from being called, and to the potentially-unsafe objects (e.g., localStorage) to prevent their properties from being accessed. This can be quite refined: objects may contain a mix of safe and unsafe methods. For example, in our system, it is perfectly fine to open and read from existing files, but it is unsafe to create them; therefore, only the first line below causes an error:

```
file.create(NORMAL_FILE_TYPE, 0x644);
var w = file.isWritable();
```

The type checker will complain:

```
Cannot dereference an @Unsafe value at 1:0-11 (i.e., file.create).
```

In response, the programmer can: 1) rewrite the code to eliminate the call to file.create, or 2) prove to the type checker that the code is never called in private browsing mode, or 3) "cheat" and insert a typecast, which will eliminate the error report but effectively flag the use for audit. Often, very simple changes will suffice as proof:

```
if (WeAreNotInPrivateBrowsingMode()) {
  file.create(NORMAL_FILE_TYPE, 0x644);
}
var w = file.isWritable();
```

(We show in Section 4.4 how to implement WeAreNotInPrivateBrowsingMode().)

4.2   The Type System Guarantee

Extensions that have been annotated with types and pass the typechecker enjoy a crucial safety guarantee. This guarantee is a direct consequence of TeJaS's own type-safety theorem [14], the soundness of Progressive Types [29], and the correctness of our type environment:

> **If an extension typechecks successfully, using arbitrary type annotations (including @Unsafe), and if an auditor confirms that any "cheating" is in fact safe, then it does not violate the private-browsing mode invariants. Moreover, the auditor must check *only* the "cheating" code; all other code is statically safe.**

In the following subsections, we explain how the typechecker recognizes the example above as safe, and make precise what "cheating" is and why it is sometimes necessary.

4.3   Type System Ergonomics

A well-engineered type system should be capable of proving the desired properties about source code and be flexible enough to prove others, with a minimum of invasive changes to the code. Typically, these properties are phrased as *preservation* and *progress* guarantees: respectively, well-typed programs preserve their types at each step of execution, and can make progress without runtime error. Our goal here is a relatively weak progress guarantee: we only prevent extensions from calling @Unsafe APIs; other runtime errors may still occur, but such errors cannot cause private-browsing violations.

As a strawman, one inadequate approach to proving privacy-safety might be to maintain a list of "banned words"—the names of the unsafe APIs—and ensure that the program does not mention them or include any expressions that might evaluate to them. Such an approach inflexiblly prohibits developers from naming their functions with these banned words. It also proscribes much of JS's expressiveness, such as using objects as dictionaries (lest some subexpression evaluate to a banned word which is then used as a field name).

Another approach might graft checks for @Unsafe calls onto a more traditional, stronger progress guarantee. This is costly: for example, consider the information needed to ensure the (safe) expression 1+o.m("x") makes progress. The type system must know that o is an object with a field m that is a safe function that accepts string arguments and returns something that can be added to 1. Conveying such detailed information to the type system often requires substantial annotation[4]. But this is overkill in our setting: if any of the facts about the expression above were false, it would likely cause a runtime error, but *still would not call anything @Unsafe* .

Instead, we design a type system that *can* support such precise types, but that does not *force* them upon the developer. We provide a default type in our system that can type everything except the unsafe APIs: code that never calls anything unsafe does not need any annotation. Using such a type relaxes the progress guarantee to the weaker one above: nonsensical expressions may now typecheck, but still will never call @Unsafe APIs. Developers that *want* the stronger progress guarantee can add precise type annotations *gradually* to their code. The next subsection explains how our type system achieves this flexibility.

4.4   The Private-Browsing Type System

Preliminaries. Our type system contains primitive types for numeric, null and undefined values, variadic function types with distinguished receiver parameters (the type of this within the function), regular expressions, and immutable records with presence annotations on fields. It also contains type-level functions, equi-recursive types, and reference cells. On top of this, we add support for (unordered) union and (ordered) intersection types. In particular, the type Bool is the union of singleton types (True + False).

Safe Types. We define a (slightly-simplified) *extension type* that includes all possible JS values [31]:

```
type Ext = rec e . Num + Bool + Undef + Str + Null + Ref {
    __proto__ :! Src { },
    __code__ :? [e] e ... => e,
    * :? e
}
```

---
[4] Type *inference* for objects is of little help, as it is often undecidable [25].

In words, values of type Ext may be null, boolean, or other base types, or mutable objects whose fields, if present, are also of this type. The __proto__ field is a read-only object (about whose fields we know nothing), while __code__ (when present) models JS functions, which are objects with an internal code pointer.

Ext is the default type for all expressions, and any Ext-typed code need not be annotated, justifying our "lightweight" claims. As Section 4.3 mentioned, developers are free to add more precise types to their code gradually. Any such types will be subtypes of Ext, meaning that richly-typed code will successfully interoperate with Ext-typed code without having to modify the Ext-typed code further.

Marking APIs with the @Unsafe Type. We define a new primitive type @Unsafe that is ascribed in our initial type environment to all potentially-harmful APIs. This type is unrelated by subtyping to any other types besides Top, Bot or intersections or unions that already contain it. Accordingly, any attempts to use values of this type will cause type errors: because it is distinct from function types it cannot be applied; because it is distinct from object types it cannot be dereferenced, etc. @Unsafe values can be assigned to variables or fields, provided they have also been annotated as @Unsafe.

Checking for Private-Browsing Mode. Our efforts to segregate @Unsafe values from safe Ext code are overzealous: we do not need to prevent *all* usages of @Unsafe values. Recall the revised example from Section 4.1: code that has checked that it is *not* in private-browsing mode may use @Unsafe values.

To capture this intuition, we define the typechecking rules for if statements as follows:

IF-TRUE
$$\frac{\Gamma \vdash c : \mathtt{True} \qquad \Gamma \vdash t : \tau}{\Gamma \vdash \mathtt{if}\ c\ t\ f : \tau}$$

IF-FALSE
$$\frac{\Gamma \vdash c : \mathtt{False} \qquad \Gamma \vdash f : \tau}{\Gamma \vdash \mathtt{if}\ c\ t\ f : \tau}$$

IF-OTHER
$$\frac{\Gamma \vdash c : \mathtt{Bool} \qquad \Gamma \vdash t : \tau \qquad \Gamma \vdash f : \tau}{\Gamma \vdash \mathtt{if}\ c\ t\ f : \tau}$$

For conditionals where we statically know whether the condition is True or False, we only typecheck the relevant branch: the other branch is statically known to be dead code. Otherwise, we must typecheck both branches. Under these rules the dead code could be arbitrarily broken; nevertheless it will never run. Note that here, "dead code" really means "not live in private-browsing mode".

This leads to our key encoding of the nsIPrivateBrowsingService API's privateBrowsingEnabled flag. Normally, this flag would have type Bool. But we only care when it is *true*; when it is false, it is fine to use @Unsafe values. We therefore give it the type True. IF-TRUE then permits the example in Section 4.1 to typecheck without error.

"Cheating". As pointed out in Section 3.1, we may want to allow extensions to use @Unsafe APIs even in private-browsing mode, to preserve "normal operations". This may be because they do not store "sensitive" information, or because they are run only in response to explicit user action. Statically determining whether information is sensitive is an information-flow problem, a thorny (and orthogonal) one we deliberately avoid. Moreover, the control flow of browsers is quite complex [19], making it challenging to link code to the event that triggered it. We are not aware of any successful efforts to apply static information flow to real-world JS, and certainly none that also apply to the browser's control flow. Instead, we require extension authors to annotate all those uses of @Unsafe values that cannot statically be shown to be dead code. To do this, we introduce one last type annotation: cheat τ. When applied to an expression, it asserts the expression has type τ and does not actually check its type.

Obviously, cheating will let even unsafe extensions typecheck. Therefore all cheat typecasts must either be manually audited by a human to confirm their safety, or verified by more sophisticated (perhaps expensive) runtime systems. For now we assume a human auditor; by having these annotations we let future researchers focus on the remaining problems of fully-automated audit.

5 Theory to Practice in Firefox

We have laid out our technique that developers would ideally use from the outset as they develop new extensions, and the theorem in Section 4.1 ensures that their efforts would be worthwhile. In this section, we explain the details of instantiating our system for Firefox's APIs. The companion technical report [20] contains additional details and worked examples.

5.1 Translating Typed Interfaces

Most of Mozilla's APIs are defined in typed interface files (written in a variant of WebIDL[5]), which we parse into our type language. The translation begins smoothly: each interface is translated as a read-only reference to an object type; this ensures that extensions cannot attempt to delete or redefine built-in methods. Functions and attributes on interfaces are then translated as fields of the appropriate type on the translated object types.

However, these IDL files have three problems: they can be overspecific, underspecific, or incomplete. For example, a function declared to expect a string argument can in fact be given any JS value, as the glue code that marshals JS values into C++ will implicitly call toString on the value. By contrast, functions such as getElementsByClassName return an nsIDOMNodeList, whereas the semantics of the method ensure that all the nodes in that list are in fact of the more specific type nsIDOMElement. Finally, the contents of the Components object are not specified in any interface, but rather dynamically constructed in C++ code; similarly, some XUL elements are defined entirely dynamically by XBL code. We need a mechanism to address each of these difficulties.

Rather than hard-code a list of corrections, we can exploit two existing IDL features for a flexible resolution. First, IDL permits "partial" interfaces, which

---

[5] http://www.w3.org/TR/WebIDL/

are simply inlined into the primary definition at compilation time. Second, IDL syntax includes "extended attributes" on interface members, functions and their parameters, which may affect the translation to types: for instance, [noscript] members are not included in the JS environment, and [array] parameters are of type Array<τ> rather than τ. For missing types, we create a "type-overrides" file and add new type definitions there. For over- and under-specific types, we define a new extended attribute [UseType(τ)] to replace the type specified by the IDL, and in the type-overrides file define partial interfaces whose sole purpose is to revise the shortcomings of the input IDL. For example, we define a "DOM-ElementList" type, and override getElementsByClassName to return it instead.

5.2   Encoding @Unsafe Values and the Flag for Private Browsing Mode

We define two more IDL attributes, [Unsafe] and [PrivateBrowsingCheck], and use them to annotate the relevant properties in the Mozilla environment. Per Section 4, these are translated to the types @Unsafe and True, respectively.

As mentioned in Section 2.1, the nsIPrivateBrowsingService object also allows extensions to switch Firefox into and out of private browsing mode. Even though Firefox does not wholly restart, it does effectively recreate all JS contexts. Nevertheless, we consider exiting private-browsing mode to be poor behavior for extensions, so we mark these APIs as @Unsafe as well. Any benign uses of this API must now be cheated, and their use justified in a security review.

5.3   Encoding the Components Object

All of Mozilla's APIs are accessed via roughly this idiom:

```
Components.classes[cID].createInstance(Components.interfaces.interfaceName)
```

An accurate but imprecise type for this function would simply be nsIJSIID -> nsISupports: the argument type is an "interface ID", and the result is the root type of all the Mozilla interfaces. But this function can return over 1400 different types of objects, some (but not all) of which are relevant to private-browsing mode. We therefore need a more precise return type, and since this function is used ubiquitously by extension code, we must avoid requiring developer annotations. The key observation is that the set of possible return types is known *a priori*, and the specific return type is selected by the provided interface ID argument. This is known as "finitary overloading" [26], and is encoded in our system with intersection types.[6]

6   Case Study: Verifying Firefox Extensions

To evaluate the utility and flexibility of our type system, two of the authors (both undergraduates with no experience with engineering type systems) retrofitted

---

[6] Firefox 3's new API, Component.utils.import("script.js", [obj]), is not amenable to similar static encoding and consequently requires manual audits.

Extension	Size	Violates PBM?	Confirmed by author?	Violates privacy?
The Middle Mouse Button v1.0	51	No		
Print v0.3.4	59	No		
Rapidfire v0.5	119	No		
Commandrun v0.10.0	147	Yes	Yes	Yes
Open As Webfolder v0.28	153	Yes	No	No
CheckFox v0.9.2	188	No		
The Tracktor Amazon Price Tracker v1.0.7	232	No		
Fireclam v0.6.7	437	Yes	No	No
Cert Viewer Plus v1.7	974	Yes	No	Yes
Textarea Cache v0.8.5	1103	No		
ProCon Latte Content Filter v3.3	2015	Yes	Yes	Yes
It's All Text v1.6.3	2623	Yes	Yes	Yes
Total	8101	6	3	4

Fig. 1. Extensions analyzed for private-browsing violations: note that not all private-browsing violations are actual privacy violations. The technical report [20] has more details on the extensions and annotations, and provides more excerpts.

type annotations onto 12 existing Firefox extensions, chosen from a snapshot of Firefox extensions as of November 2011. Some were selected because we expected them to have non-trivial correctness guarantees; the rest based on their brevity and whether they mentioned unsafe APIs. All extensions had passed Mozilla's security review: ostensibly they should all comply with private-browsing mode. We had no prior knowledge of the behavior or complexity of the extensions chosen beyond their description.

The results are summarized in Fig. 1. We analyzed 6.8K non-comment lines of code (8.1KLOC including comments and our type definitions), and found private-browsing violations in 6 of the 12 extensions—of which only 4 truly violate privacy. Below, we highlight interesting excerpts from some of these extensions.

6.1 Accommodating Real-World Extension Code

Our type system is designed to be used during the development process rather than after, but existing extensions were not written with our type system in mind. We therefore permitted ourselves some local, minimal code refactorings to make the code more amenable to the type checker. These changes let us avoid many typecasts, and (arguably) make the code clearer as well; we recommend them as best practices for writing new code with our type system.

First, we ensured that all variables were declared and that functions were defined before subsequent uses. Additionally, developers frequently used placeholder values of the wrong type—null instead of -1, or undefined instead of null—that we corrected where obvious.

Second, our type system infers the type of variables from the type of their initializer, for which it infers the strictest type it can. For instance, initializers of

false, "foo" and null yield types False, /foo/ (the regular expression matching the literal string), and Null respectively—rather than Bool, String, and
whichever particular object type is eventually used. This can be useful: distinguishing True from False values lets us elide dead branches of code and thereby
check for private browsing mode, and similarly, distinguishing string literals from
each other enables support for JS objects' first-class field names [28]. Sometimes,
however, this is overly-specific. For instance, a truly boolean-valued variable
might be initialized to true and later modified to false; if its type was inferred
as True, the subsequent assignment would result in a type error! In such cases,
we therefore manually annotate the initializers with their more general types.

Third, we replaced the idiomatic field-existence check if (!foo.bar) with if
(!("bar" in foo)), as the typechecker will complain when the field does not
exist in the former, whereas the latter has the same dynamic effect but does
not impose any type constraints. (When the field name is known to exist, this
idiom also checks whether the field's value is not null, zero or false; we did not
rewrite such usages.)

Additionally, we permitted ourselves two other refactorings to accommodate
weaknesses in our current prototype system. First, our system does not model
the marshaling layer of Mozilla's API bindings; for instance, passing a non-string
value where a string parameter is expected will yield a type error. We therefore
added (""+) to expressions to ensure that they had type Str.

Second, Mozilla APIs include QueryInterface methods that convert the provided value from one interface to another. Code using these functions effectively
changes the type of a variable during the course of execution. Our type system
cannot support that; we refactored such code to use auxiliary variables that
each are of a single type.

6.2   Example Extensions

In the process of making these extensions pass the type checker, we were forced
to cheat 38 call-sites to @Unsafe functions as innocuous. Those 38 call sites are
potential privacy violations appearing in five extensions, of which we think four
truly violate private browsing mode (the other uses @Unsafe functions to setup
initial preferences to constant—and therefore not privacy-sensitive—values). We
have contacted the authors of these extensions, and two have responded, both
confirming our assessment. A sixth extension uses cheats slightly differently, and
the process of typechecking it revealed a large security hole that we reported: it
was confirmed by its author and by Mozilla, and was promptly fixed. We highlight three of these extensions—one (almost) safe and two not—to highlight how
subtle detecting privacy violations can be. The companion technical report [20,
section VI] contains full details of the necessary annotations.

Almost Safe: Textarea Cache [32]. This extension maintains backups of
the text entered by users into textareas on web pages, to prevent inadvertently
losing the data. Such behavior falls squarely afoul of Mozilla's prohibition against

recording data "relating to" web pages in private browsing mode. The developer was aware of this, and included a check for private-browsing mode in one of the extension's core functions:

```
textareaCache.inPrivateBrowsing = function () {
  if (this._PBS) return this._PBS.privateBrowsingEnabled;
  else return true; // N.B.: used to be false
};
textareaCache.beforeWrite = function(node) {
  if (this.inPrivateBrowsing()) return;
  ...
  this.writeToPref(node);
};
```

Our system recognizes that inPrivateBrowsing has type () -> True, and therefore determines the @Unsafe call on line 9 is dead code. (Note that this is strictly more expressive than checking for the literal presence of the private-browsing flag at the call-site of the @Unsafe function: the flag has been wrapped in a helper function that is defined arbitrarily far from the beforeWrite function, yet beforeWrite is itself correctly typechecked as safe.) Several other unguarded code paths, however, result in writing data to disk, and these are all flagged as type errors by our system. Tracing carefully through these calls reveals that they are all writing only pre-existing data, and not recording anything from the private session.

An interesting subtlety arises in this code due to backward-compatibility: This extension is intended to be compatible with old versions of Firefox that predate private browsing mode, and in such versions, clearly inPrivateBrowsing is false. Accordingly, the default on line 4 used to be false, which prevents the function from having the desired return type. Annotating and typechecking this code directly revealed this mismatch; once changed to true, the modified code validates as safe.

A cleaner, alternate solution exists if we allow ourselves to refactor the extension slightly. As written, the _PBS field is initialized lazily, and so must have type nsIPrivateBrowsingService + Undef. That Undef prevents the type system from realizing the return false is dead code. If we rewrite the initializer to be eager, then _PBS has type nsIPrivateBrowsingService, which is never undefined, and again the function typechecks with the desired return type.

Unsafe: ProCon Latte Content Filter [24]. This "featured" (i.e., nominated as top-quality[7]) extension maintains keyword-based white- and black-lists of sites. A user can add URLs to these lists that persist into subsequent browsing sessions; this persistence is achieved by APIs that store preferences in the user's profile. These APIs all are flagged by the typechecker as @Unsafe—and as we annotated this extension, we determined that these APIs were reachable from within private browsing mode. In other words, the type checker helped

---

[7] https://addons.mozilla.org/en-us/developers/docs/policies/recommended

determine that URLs could be added to these lists even while in private browsing mode, a clear (or possibly deliberate) policy violation. The extension author confirmed that this behavior is a bug: URLs were not intended to persist past private browsing mode.

Unsafe: Commandrun [1]. It is obvious that the Commandrun extension must be unsafe for private browsing. In fact, it is egregiously unsafe, as it allows an arbitrary website to spawn a process (from a whitelist configured by the user) and pass it arbitrary data. (Even worse, the version of this extension we analyzed had a further flaw that would allow websites to bypass the whitelist checking.) Yet counterintuitively, this extension produces no errors about *calling* @Unsafe functions: no such calls are present in the source of the extension! Instead, the extension creates an object that will launch the process, and then injects that object into untrusted web content (edited for brevity):

```
CommandRunHandler = function() {
  this.run = /*:cheat @Unsafe*/function(command, args){ ... };
  this.isCommandAllowed = function(command, args){ ... };
};
CommandRun = {
  onPageLoad: function(event) {
    var win = event.originalTarget.defaultView.wrappedJSObject;
    win.CommandRun = new CommandRunHandler();
} };
```

The `CommandRunHandler.run` function (line 2) is annotated as @Unsafe, but it is never directly called from within this extension, so it does not directly cause any further type errors.

The true flaw in this extension occurs where the object is leaked to web content on lines 7 and 8, and our type system *does* raise an error here. Gecko, by default, surrounds all web-content objects in security wrappers to prevent inadvertent tampering with them, but exposes the actual objects via a `wrappedJSObject` field on the wrappers. Our type environment asserts that such wrapped objects must only contain fields of type `Ext`, but the `CommandRunHandler` object has an @Unsafe field, and therefore the assignment on line 8 causes a type error. The only way to make this code type-check is to cheat either the reference to `wrappedJSObject` or to the `CommandRunHandler`, thereby exposing this flaw to any auditor. We contacted the author of this extension, who promptly confirmed and fixed the bugs.

7   Related Work

Our work clearly builds upon a rich area of security research and a growing body of work analyzing JS. We consider each in turn.

7.1   Security-Related Efforts

Many recent projects relate to extension security, authoring, or analysis. Several entail pervasive changes within the browser [5, 8–10]; we focus on techniques that do not need such support, and briefly describe the most relevant such projects. None of them handle our present use cases.

ADsafety. The closest relative of our work is ADsafety [27], which uses TeJaS [14] to verify the correctness of ADsafe [2]. That work focused primarily on verifying the ADsafe sandbox itself, and then used a type similar to our Ext to typecheck "widgets" running within that sandbox. Unlike extensions here, the environment available to widgets is entirely Ext-typed; indeed, the whole purpose of a sandbox is to eliminate *all* references to unsafe values! The extension-safety problem here is more refined, and permits such unsafe values in non-private execution.

IBEX. Guha et al. [13] develop Fine, a secure-by-construction language for writing extensions. Fine is pure, dependently-typed, and bears no resemblance to idiomatic JS. Extensions must be (re-)written entirely in it in order to be verified. Accordingly, the barrier to entry in their system is quite high, and they explicitly do not attempt to model the browser APIs available besides the DOM.

VEX. Bandhakavi et al. [4] design a system that statically attempts to discover unsafe information flows in extension code, for instance from unsanitized strings to calls to eval. By their own admission, their system is neither sound nor complete: they explicitly check only for five flow patterns in extensions and so miss any other potential errors, and any errors they raise may still be false positives. This provides no reliable guarantee for browser vendors. Additionally, they do not address the conditional safety of API usage which is the hallmark of the private-browsing mode problem.

Beacon. Karim et al. [17] design an analysis for Mozilla Jetpack extensions (see Section 2.2) to detect capability leaks, where privileged objects (such as unmediated filesystem objects) are exposed to arbitrary extension code. While laudable, this approach does not work for detecting private-browsing violations: filesystem capabilities are entirely permitted in public mode. Additionally, their tool is unsound, as it does not model reflective property accesses.

7.2   Language-Level Analyses

Progressive Types. As mentioned, our type system is based on that of Guha et al. [14], with enhancements that simplify reasoning about our relaxed progress guarantees. These enhancements are a form of *progressive typing* [29], in which the programmers using a type system can choose whether to defer some static type checks until runtime, in exchange for a easier-to-satisfy type checker.

Type Systems for JS. TeJaS is one of a handful of type disciplines for JS. The two most fully-featured are the Closure compiler [12] and Dependent JS [7]. The former is informally defined, and makes no claims that its type system entails a soundness guarantee. Further, the type language it uses is too coarse to help with the problem examined here. Dependent JS, by contrast, uses dependent types to capture challenging idioms in JS, such as the punning between arrays and dictionaries, and strong updates that change variables' types. However, the largest example the authors checked using Dependent JS is barely larger than the third-smallest extension we examine. Moreover, their language imposes huge annotation overheads: the type annotations are comparable in length to the original program! In short, while powerful, such a system is impractical and overkill for our purposes, and we can achieve our desired guarantee without the proof obligations entailed by dependent type systems.

Language-Based Security. Schneider et al. [30] survey the broad area of language-based security mechanisms. Cappos et al. [6] build a language-based sandbox for Python, such that even privileged scripts cannot access resources they should not. And other sandboxes exist for JS along the lines of ADsafe [2, 21, 33] to try to corral web programs. But none of these approaches explicitly address the modal nature of enforcement that we need for private-browsing guarantees.

Certified Browsers. Jang et al. [15] present an implementation of a browser kernel implemented in Coq, which allows them to formalize desirable security properties of the browser kernel such as non-interference between separate tabs, and the absence of cookie leakages between sites. Their current development is for a fixed-function browser; enhancing it to support extensions and private-browsing mode are intriguing avenues of future work.

8   Breaking News: It Gets Worse!

Firefox 20—released on April 2, 2013—has adopted per-window private browsing granularity (à la Chrome). Unfortunately, existing Firefox APIs enable extensions to access *all* windows, which now include both public and private ones; we have confirmed that this allows sensitive data to leak. Moreover, one such API is used over 6,400 times in our corpus: we expect that extensions using this API—even those using it *safely* in earlier Firefox versions—may now inadvertently violate privacy. We have contacted Mozilla, who indicate that closing this leak (and others) may not be technically feasible.

However, we believe our approach still works. Instead of ignoring non-private-browing code, we must analyze it. We can define another type environment in which inPrivateBrowsing is now False and a different set of APIs (e.g., window enumeration) are marked either as @Unsafe or as returning potentially-@Unsafe data. Running the type checker in this environment will then flag potential leakage of private data to public scope.

References

[1] Abeling, A.: Commandrun:: Add-ons for Firefox (November 2011),
    https://addons.mozilla.org/en-us/firefox/addon/commandrun/ (retrieved)
[2] ADsafe (November 2009), http://www.adsafe.org/ (retrieved)
[3] Aggrawal, G., Bursztein, E., Jackson, C., Boneh, D.: An analysis of private brows-
    ing modes in modern browsers. In: USENIX Security Symposium. USENIX Asso-
    ciation, Berkeley (2010)
[4] Bandhakavi, S., King, S.T., Madhusudan, P., Winslett, M.: VEX: vetting browser
    extensions for security vulnerabilities. In: USENIX Security Symposium, p. 22.
    USENIX Association, Berkeley (2010)
[5] Barth, A., Felt, A.P., Saxena, P., Boodman, A.: Protecting browsers from ex-
    tension vulnerabilities. In: Network and Distributed System Security Symposium
    (NDSS) (March 2010)
[6] Cappos, J., Dadgar, A., Rasley, J., Samuel, J., Beschastnikh, I., Barsan, C., Kr-
    ishnamurthy, A., Anderson, T.: Retaining sandbox containment despite bugs in
    privileged memory-safe code. In: ACM Conference on Computer and Communi-
    cations Security, CCS, pp. 212–223. ACM, New York (2010)
[7] Chugh, R., Herman, D., Jhala, R.: Dependent types for JavaScript. In: ACM SIG-
    PLAN Conference on Object-Oriented Programming, Systems, Languages, and
    Applications, OOPSLA, pp. 587–606. ACM, New York (2012)
[8] Dhawan, M., Ganapathy, V.: Analyzing information flow in JavaScript-based
    browser extensions. In: Annual Computer Security Applications Conference, AC-
    SAC, pp. 382–391. IEEE Computer Society, Washington, DC (2009)
[9] Djeric, V., Goel, A.: Securing script-based extensibility in web browsers. In:
    USENIX Security Symposium. USENIX Association, Berkeley (2010)
[10] Fredrikson, M., Livshits, B.: RePriv: Re-envisioning in-browser privacy. Tech. rep.,
    Microsoft Research (August 2010)
[11] Google. chrome.* APIs – Google Chrome extensions (April 2012),
    http://code.google.com/chrome/extensions/api_index.html (retrieved)
[12] Google. Closure tools — Google developers (November 2012),
    https://developers.google.com/closure/compiler/ (retrieved)
[13] Guha, A., Fredrikson, M., Livshits, B., Swamy, N.: Verified security for browser
    extensions. In: IEEE Symposium on Security and Privacy (Oakland), pp. 115–130.
    IEEE Computer Society, Washington, DC (2011)
[14] Guha, A., Saftoiu, C., Krishnamurthi, S.: Typing local control and state using flow
    analysis. In: Barthe, G. (ed.) ESOP 2011. LNCS, vol. 6602, pp. 256–275. Springer,
    Heidelberg (2011)
[15] Jang, D., Tatlock, Z., Lerner, S.: Establishing browser security guarantees through
    formal shim verification. In: USENIX Security Symposium. USENIX Association,
    Berkeley (2012)
[16] Jostedt, E.: Firefox add-ons cross more than 3 billion downloads! Written (July
    2012), https://blog.mozilla.org/blog/2012/07/26/
    firefox-add-ons-cross-more-than-3-billion-downloads/
[17] Karim, R., Dhawan, M., Ganapathy, V., Shan, C.-C.: An analysis of the Mozilla
    Jetpack extension framework. In: Noble, J. (ed.) ECOOP 2012. LNCS, vol. 7313,
    pp. 333–355. Springer, Heidelberg (2012)
[18] Lerner, B.S.: Designing for Extensibility and Planning for Conflict: Experiments
    in Web-Browser Design. Ph.D. thesis, University of Washington Computer Science
    & Engineering (August 2011)

[19] Lerner, B.S., Carroll, M.J., Kimmel, D.P., de la Vallee, H.Q., Krishnamurthi, S.: Modeling and reasoning about DOM events. In: USENIX Conference on Web Application Development, WebApps. USENIX Association, Berkeley (2012)

[20] Lerner, B.S., Elberty, L., Poole, N., Krishnamurthi, S.: Verifying web browser extensions' compliance with private-browsing mode. Tech. Rep. CS-13-02, Brown University (March 2013)

[21] Miller, M.S., Samuel, M., Laurie, B., Awad, I., Stay, M.: Caja: Safe active content in sanitized JavaScript. Tech. rep., Google Inc. (2008)

[22] Mozilla. PrivateBrowsing – MozillaWiki (April 2012),
https://wiki.mozilla.org/PrivateBrowsing (retrieved)

[23] Newton, S.: Ant video downloader firefox addon tracking my browsing (May 2011),
http://iwtf.net/2011/05/10/ant-video-downloader-firefox
-addon-tracking-my-browsing/ (written)

[24] Paolini, H.: ProCon latte content filter :: Add-ons for Firefox (November 2011),
https://addons.mozilla.org/en-us/firefox/addon/procon-latte/ (retrieved)

[25] Pierce, B.C.: Bounded quantification is undecidable. In: ACM SIGPLAN-SIGACT Symposium on Principles of Programming Languages, POPL, pp. 305–315. ACM Press, New York (1992)

[26] Pierce, B.C.: Types and Programming Languages. The MIT Press (2002)

[27] Politz, J.G., Eliopoulos, S.A., Guha, A., Krishnamurthi, S.: ADsafety: type-based verification of JavaScript sandboxing. In: USENIX Security Symposium, p. 12. USENIX Association, Berkeley (2011)

[28] Politz, J.G., Guha, A., Krishnamurthi, S.: Semantics and types for objects with first-class member names. In: Workshop on Foundations of Object-Oriented Languages, FOOL (2012)

[29] Politz, J.G., de la Vallee, H.Q., Krishnamurthi, S.: Progressive types. In: ACM International Symposium on New Ideas, New Paradigms, and Reflections on Programming and Software, Onward! 2012, pp. 55–66. ACM, New York (2012)

[30] Schneider, F.B., Morrisett, G., Harper, R.: A language-based approach to security. In: Wilhelm, R. (ed.) Informatics: 10 Years Back, 10 Years Ahead. LNCS, vol. 2000, pp. 86–101. Springer, Heidelberg (2001)

[31] Scott, D.: Lambda calculus: Some models, some philosophy. In: The Kleene Symposium, pp. 223–265 (1980)

[32] Sun, H.: Textarea cache :: Add-ons for Firefox (November 2011),
https://addons.mozilla.org/en-us/firefox/addon/textarea-cache/
(retrieved)

[33] The Caja Team. Caja (November 2009), http://code.google.com/p/google-caja/
(written)

[34] Villalobos, J.: The add-on review process (February 2010),
http://blog.mozilla.org/addons/2010/02/15/
the-add-on-review-process-and-you (written)

[35] Villalobos, J.: Queue weekly status 2012-04-20 (April 2012),
https://forums.mozilla.org/addons/viewtopic.php?f=21&t=8719 (written)

A Quantitative Evaluation of Privilege Separation in Web Browser Designs

Xinshu Dong, Hong Hu, Prateek Saxena, and Zhenkai Liang

Department of Computer Science, National University of Singapore
{xdong,huhong,prateeks,liangzk}@comp.nus.edu.sg

Abstract. Privilege separation is a fundamental security concept that has been used in designing many secure systems. A number of recent works propose re-designing web browsers with greater privilege separation for better security. In practice, however, privilege-separated designs require a fine balance between security benefits and other competing concerns, such as performance. In fact, performance overhead has been a main cause that prevents many privilege separation proposals from being adopted in real systems. In this paper, we develop a new measurement-driven methodology that *quantifies* security benefits and performance costs for a given privilege-separated browser design. Our measurements on a large corpus of web sites provide key insights on the security and performance implications of partitioning dimensions proposed in 9 recent browser designs. Our results also provide empirical guidelines to resolve several design decisions being debated in recent browser re-design efforts.

Keywords: Privilege separation, browser design, measurement.

1 Introduction

Privilege separation is a fundamental concept for designing secure systems. It was first proposed by Saltzer et al. [31] and has been widely used in re-designing a large number of security-critical applications [9, 12, 28]. In contrast to a monolithic design, where a single flaw can expose all critical resources of a privileged authority, a privilege-separated design groups the components of a system into *partitions* isolated from each other. According to the principle of least privilege, each partition is assigned the minimum privileges it needs for its operation at run-time. Intuitively, this reduces the risk of compromising the whole system, because the attacker only gains a small subset of privileges afforded by the compromised component. Common intuition suggests that the more we isolate components, the better. We question this intuition from a pragmatic standpoint, and systematically measure the security benefits and costs of privilege-separating large-scale systems (such as a web browser) retroactively. Our empirical data suggests that "the more the better" premise is *not* categorically true. Instead, we advocate that practical designs may need to balance several trade-offs in retrofitting least privilege to web browsers.

Web browsers are the underlying execution platform shared between web applications. Given their importance in defeating threats from the web, web browsers have been a prime area where privilege separation is being applied. For instance, numerous

J. Crampton, S. Jajodia, and K. Mayes (Eds.): ESORICS 2013, LNCS 8134, pp. 75–93, 2013.
© Springer-Verlag Berlin Heidelberg 2013

clean-slate browser proposals [9,18,20,21,23,24,33,35] and commercial browsers like Bromium [2] and Invincea [3] are customizing privilege separation boundaries in web browsers. However, excessive isolation between code components also incurs performance cost. Ideally, a practical browser design should balance security gains and the additional performance costs incurred by a new design. In browser design proposals, many important design dimensions are actively being debated. Should browsers put each web origin in its own partition? Should browsers host sub-resources (such as images, SVG, PDF, iframes) of a web page in separate partitions? Should sub-resources belonging to one origin be clubbed into the same partition? Should two code units (say, the JavaScript engine and the Document Object Model (DOM)) be assigned to different partitions? A systematic methodology to understand the empirical benefits and costs achieved by a partitioning strategy is important, but has not been investigated in depth.

Our Study. In this work, we study security and performance implications of choosing one or more of these partitioning dimensions in browser designs. To do this, we first extract a conceptual "blueprint" of the web browser that captures the logical components of a typical web browser. Then, we empirically measure a variety of parameters that measure security gains and performance costs of separating these logical components. This measurement is performed on a real web browser (Mozilla Firefox) using a large-scale test harness of the Alexa Top 100 web sites. Our measurements enable us to estimate the security benefits gained against the performance costs that arise when choosing a partitioning strategy.

Based on empirical data, we draw several inferences about the benefits and costs of design dimensions proposed in 9 recent browser design proposals. Our measurements lend pragmatic insights into some of the crucial design questions on how to partition web browsers. For example, we find that using separate OS processes to load cross-origin sub-resources requires 51 OS processes per web site, while giving marginal improvement in security for the increased performance cost. As another example, we find that isolating the JavaScript engine and the DOM creates a performance bottleneck, but also affords significant security gains. Many such empirical results are quantified in Section 5. Our measurements identify key performance bottlenecks in the browser designs we study, and we find that several of the bottlenecks identified correlate well with browser implementation efforts for design proposals that have public implementations. We hope our results and methodology serve as a baseline for further research on the problem, and are instructive in identifying early bottlenecks in upcoming browser designs.

Methodology. Browsers are examples of large-scale systems, with millions of lines-of-code. For example, the browser we choose as the blueprint in this work (Firefox) has a development history of 8 years and comprises of over 3 million lines of code. If a security architect is tasked with privilege-separating an existing browser (like Firefox), how does she estimate security gains and performance bottlenecks of any particular privilege-partitioning configuration? In this paper, we take a step towards quantitatively studying this question with empirical data measurements. In previous research on privilege-separated browsers, performance measurements have been "after-the-fact", *i.e.*, after a chosen partitioning configuration has been implemented. In this work, we develop and report on a more rigorous measurement-based methodology that estimates the security benefits and performance costs, without requiring a time-intensive implementation. Our methodology precisely formulates back-of-the-envelope calculations that security architects often use, and thereby systematizes a typical security argument with empirical rigor. Most prior works on browser re-design report performance on a small scale (typically on 5-10 sites). Our data-driven methodology leads to design decisions that are backed by a large-scale dataset.

Our methodology only aims to estimate weak upper bounds on the performance incurred by a proposed browser partitioning scheme. We recognize that these estimates can, of course, be reduced in actual implementations with careful optimizations and engineering tricks. However, our methodology lets us identify the likely bottlenecks where significant engineering effort needs to be invested. The metrics we evaluate in this work are *not* new and, in fact, we only systematize the measurement of quantities that prior works base their security arguments on. For instance, most prior works (somewhat informally) argue security based on two artifacts: (a) the reduction in size of the trusted computing base (TCB), and (b) the reduction in number of known vulnerabilities affecting the TCB after the re-design. To unify the security arguments previously proposed, we systematically measure these quantities using real-world data — 3 million lines of Firefox code and its corresponding bug database (comprising 8 years of Firefox development history).

Contributions. Our goal in this paper is not to suggest new browser designs, or to undermine the importance of clean-slate designs and measurement methodologies proposed in prior work. On the contrary, without extensive prior work in applying privilege separation of real systems, the questions we ask in the paper would not be relevant. However, we argue to "quantify" the trade-offs of a privilege-separated design and enable a more systematic foundation for comparing designs.

In summary, we make the following contributions in this paper:

- We propose a systematic methodology to quantify security and performance parameters in privilege-separated designs, without requiring an implementation of the design.
- We perform a large-scale study on Firefox (>3 million LOC) on the Alexa Top 100 web sites.
- We draw inferences on the likely benefits and costs incurred by various partitioning choices proposed in 9 recent browser designs proposals, giving empirical data-driven insights on these actively debated questions.

2   Overview

In this section, we introduce the concept of privilege separation, and then discuss privilege-separated designs in web browsers, including their goals and various design dimensions.

2.1   Privilege Separation in Concept

Privilege separation aims to determine how to minimize the attacker's chances of obtaining unintended access to other part of the program. We consider each running instruction of a software program belongs to a *code unit* and a run-time *authority*. A code unit is a logical unit of program code, such as a software component, a function or a group of statements. The run-time *authority* can be a user ID or a web session, etc. Specifically, let p_i be the probability for any code unit or authority other than i to get unintended access to resources r_i belonging to i. From a purely security perspective, the goal is to minimize the attacker's advantage. We can model this advantage using a variety of mathematical functions. For instance, an attacker's worst-case advantage from compromising a single vulnerability may be defined as $max(p_i)$; a privilege-separated design is good if it yields a large value of $(1 - max(p_i))$ [1]. However, as we argue in this paper, a practical privilege-separated design often departs significantly from this conceptual formulation. We argue that this purely security-focused viewpoint ignores the implicit performance costs associated with partitioning. Rather than focusing on mathematical modeling, we focus on the key methodology to quantify the benefits of a privilege partitioning scheme in this work.

2.2   Privilege Separation in Browsers

Blueprint. To discuss trade-offs in partitioning, we use a conceptual blueprint that shows the various code units in a typical browser. We have manually extracted this from Mozilla Firefox, a popular web browser, and we show it in Figure 1[2]. We have confirmed that this conceptual blueprint is also consistent with WebKit-based browsers and models sufficient details for comparing prior works on browser re-design. This blueprint intuitively explains the processing of web pages by various browser components. A web page is first received by the Network module that prepares content to be parsed by the HTML parser. The HTML parser creates a DOM, which can then invoke other execution engines such as the JavaScript engine, CSS, and so on. The legitimate flow of processed content between components is illustrated by arrows in Figure 1; for brevity, we skip explaining the details. In a single-process browser, all these components execute in the same partition. Web browser designs utilize privilege separation to isolate the resources owned by different authorities, which are defined next.

Isolating Authorities. Web browsers abstractly manage resources owned by one of the following authorities: *web origins*, the *system authority*, and the *user authority*. Web origins correspond to origins [4] of HTML pages, sourced scripts, CSS and so on. The system authority denotes the privilege of the browser core, also referred to as the chrome privilege. It has access to sensitive OS resources, such as the file system, network, display, etc. We associate the user authority to UI elements of the browser, which convey necessary security indicators to allow them to make sensible security decisions, such as security prompts, certificate warnings, access to preferences and settings [30].

---

[1] Alternative definitions of attacker's advantage are easy to consider—for example, considering the average case with avg rather than max. We can assign additional weights to the resources r_i via a severity function $\mathcal{S}(j, r_i)$ if failure protect r_i from j has more severity than other resources, etc.

[2] Security analysts can pick different blueprints in their design; our methodology is largely agnostic to the blueprint used.

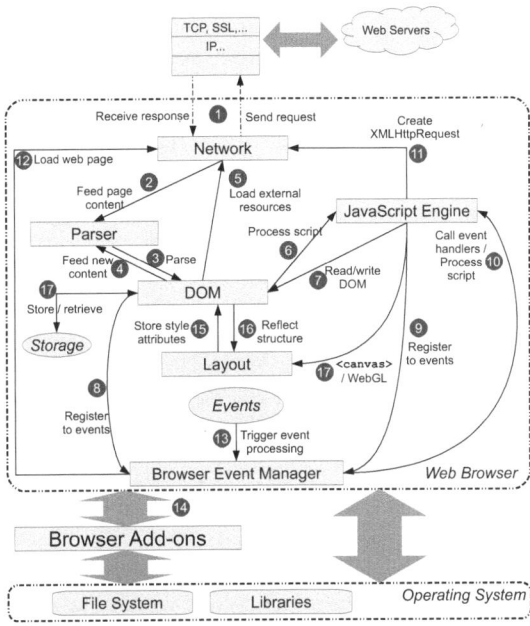

Fig. 1. Browser Blueprint. *It shows typical interactions between browser components in processing a web page.*

Security Threats. Security vulnerabilities can result in one authority gaining unintended access to resources of another. In web browsers, we can classify threats based on which authority gains privileges of which other authority.

- *CROSS-ORIGIN: Cross-Origin Data & Privilege Leakage*, due to vulnerabilities such as missing security checks for access to JavaScript objects or XMLHttpRequest status, and capability leaks [11].
- *WEB-TO-SYS: Web-to-System Privilege Escalation*, via vulnerable JavaScript APIs exposed by the browser components or plugins.
- *WEB-TO-COMP: Web-to-Component Privilege Escalation*, allowing attackers to run arbitrary code in vulnerable browser components, consisting of different memory corruption errors in the browser code.

There are also other categories of browser vulnerabilities. For completeness, we list them below. However, these are beyond the scope of the same-origin policy and we do not measure the security benefits of applying privilege separation to mitigate them.

- *USER: Confusion of User Authority*. These vulnerabilities may allow attackers to manipulate user interfaces to confuse, annoy, or trick users, hijacking their abilities in making reasonable security decisions. Recent incidents of mistakenly accepting bogus or compromised certificates [36] also belong to this category.

Table 1. Privilege Separation in Browsers *The table explains different partitioning dimensions in browser designs. For the right part of the table, same symbols denote the corresponding components are in the same partition.*

Browser	Isolation Primitive	Partitioning Dimension	Plugins	JS	HTML Parser	DOM	Layout	Network	Storage
Firefox	Process	Nil	Separate	⊕	⊕	⊕	⊕	⊕	⊕
Chrome	Process	By Origin, By Component	With Hosting Page or Separate	⊕	⊕	⊕	⊕	○	○
Tahoma	VMs	By Origin	With Hosting Page	⊕	⊕	⊕	⊕	⊕	⊕
Gazelle	Process	By Origin, By Sub-resource, By Component	Separate Per Origin	⊕	⊕	⊕	⊕	○	○
OP	Process	By Origin, By Component	Separate Per Origin & Plugin	⊕	○	○	○⊘	◇	⊙
OP2	Process	By Origin, By Sub-resource, By Component	Separate Per Origin	⊕	⊕	⊕	⊕	◇	⊙
IE8/9	Process	Per Tab	With Hosting Page (ActiveX)	⊕	⊕	⊕	⊕	⊕	⊕
IBOS	Process	By Origin, By Sub-resource, By Component	Separate	⊕	⊕	⊕	⊕	○	⊘
WebShield	Host	Nil	With Hosting Page	⊕	⊕	○	○	⊕○	⊕

- *INTRA-ORIGIN: Intra-Web-Origin Data & Privilege Leakage.* This category of browser vulnerabilities results in running code within the authority of a web origin. These include bugs in parsing malformed HTML content, identifying charsets, providing HTTP semantics and so on. They can introduce popular forms of web attacks, such as XSS, CSRF and so on.

Partitioning Dimensions. 9 recent browser designs propose several ways of partitioning to mitigate the aforementioned threats. In this paper, we apply systematic methodology to study the security and performance trade-offs in these partitioning dimensions. Table 1 summarizes the design dimensions considered in each browser design, and we explain these dimensions below.

- *By origin*: Each origin has a separate partition. This mitigates CROSS-ORIGIN vulnerabilities between web pages. For example, IBOS [33], Gazelle [35], Google Chrome [9], OP [20] and OP2 [21] all isolate primarily on origins [3]. In Chrome's default setting, web pages from different origins but belonging to the same "site instance"[4] are exceptions to this isolation rule.
- *By sub-resource*: When an origin is loaded as a sub-resource in another origin, say as an iframe or as an image, web browsers can isolate the sub-resources. This provides additional isolation between cross-origin resources, especially in mashups that integrate contents from various origins, and prevents CROSS-ORIGIN vulnerabilities from sub-sources explicitly included by an origin. For example, Gazelle [35] allocates a separate process for each destination origin of the resource and IBOS [33] uses a separate process for each unique pair of requester-destination origins; Chrome does not isolate sub-resources.

---

[3] OP and OP2 propose isolating web pages within the same origin, but the same-origin policy does not recognize such intra-origin boundaries and permits arbitrary access between web pages of the same origin. From a security analysis perspective, we treat them as the same.

[4] Connected web pages from the domains and subdomains with the same scheme. [17].

- *By component*: Different components are isolated in different partitions. Web browsers have proposed isolating individual components that are inadvertently exposed across origins, but do not need the full privileges of the system authority. For example, the OP browser [20] isolates the HTML parser and the JavaScript engine in different partitions. This prevents exploits of a WEB-TO-COMP vulnerabilities. Browsers also isolate components that need heavy access to resources of the system authority (such as the file system, network) from components that need only access to web origin resources. For example, Google Chrome [9] and Gazelle [35] separate components into web components (renderers) and system components (browser kernels). Partitioning along this dimension prevents WEB-TO-SYS vulnerabilities in the codebase of renderer partitions.

3   Quantifying Trade-Offs with Empirical Measurements

How do we systematically evaluate the security and performance trade-offs of a given partitioning configuration? To answer this question, we measure several security and performance parameters. Our methodology places arguments made previously on a more systematic foundation backed by empirical data.

3.1   Security Parameters

The goal of measuring security improvements is to estimate the reduction in the likelihood of an attacker obtaining access to certain privileged resources, which we introduced as probabilities p_i in Section 2.1. Estimating the resilience of software to unforeseen future has been an open problem [22, 25, 29]. In this work, our goal is not to investigate new metrics or compare with existing ones; instead, we aim to systematize measurements of metrics that have already been proposed in works on privilege separation. Security analysts argue improvements in security using two metrics: (a) reduction in TCB, i.e., the size of code that needs to be trusted to protect resource r_i, and (b) reduction in impact of previously known security vulnerabilities [5]. Next we explain the intuitive rationale behind the parameters we adopt in our evaluation. We leave details on how we measure them to Section 5.

S1: Known Vulnerabilities in Code Units. One intuitive argument is that if a component A has more vulnerabilities historically than B, then A is less secure than B. Therefore, for a given partitioning scheme, we can compute the total number of vulnerabilities for code units in one partition as the vulnerability count for that partition. The smaller the count, the less is the remaining possibility of exploiting that partition to gain unintended access to its resources.

S2: Severity Weightage. It is important to characterize the impact or severity of vulnerabilities. As we discuss in Section 2.2, different vulnerabilities give access to different resources. For instance, WEB-TO-SYS vulnerabilities give web attackers full access to system resources (including all other origins), so they are strictly more severe than

---

[5] Note that these metrics are instances of *reactive* security measurement, which have been debated to have both advantages [10] and disadvantages [29].

CROSS-ORIGIN vulnerability. To measure this, we categorize security vulnerabilities according to their severity.

S3: TCB Reduction. An intuitive argument is that if the code size of a trusted partition is small, it is more amenable to rigorous formal analysis or security analysis by human experts. If a resource r_i, such as the raw network access, is granted legitimate access to one component, then the size of the partition containing that component is the attack surface for accessing r_i. In security arguments, this partition is called the trusted computing base (TCB). By measuring the total code size of each partition, we can measure the relative complexity of various partitions and compute the size of TCB for different resources[6].

3.2 Performance Parameters

The precise performance costs of a privilege-separated design configuration can be precisely determined only after it has been implemented, because various engineering tricks can be used to eliminate or mitigate performance bottlenecks. However, implementing large re-designs has a substantial financial cost in practice. We propose a systematic methodology to calculate upper bounds on the performance costs of implementing a given partitioning configuration. These bounds are weak because they are calculated assuming a straightforward implementation strategy of isolating code units in separate containers (OS processes or VMs), tunneling all communications over inter-process calls as proposed in numerous previous works on browser re-design. This strategy does not discuss any engineering trick that can be used in the final implementation. We argue that such a baseline is still useful and worthy of systematic investigation. For instance, it lets the security analyst identify parts of the complex system that are going to be obvious performance bottlenecks. Our methodology is fairly intuitive and, in fact, often utilized by security architects in back-of-the-envelope calculations to estimate bottlenecks. We explain the performance cost parameters **C1-C7** we are able to quantitatively measure below. Mechanisms for measuring these parameters and the inference from combining them are discussed in Section 5.

C1: Number of Calls between Code Units. If two code units are placed in separate partitions, calls between them need to be tunneled over inter-partition communication channels such as UNIX domain sockets, pipes, or network sockets. Depending on the number of such calls, the cost of communication at runtime can be prohibitive in a naive design. If a partitioning configuration places tightly coupled components in separate partitions, the performance penalty can be high. To estimate such bottlenecks, we measure the number of calls between all code units and between authorities when the web browser executes the full test harness.

C2: Size of Data Exchanged between Code Units. If two code units are placed in separate partitions, read/write operations to data shared between them need to be mirrored into each partition. If the size of such data read or written is high, it may create

---

[6] We do not argue whether code size is the right metric as compared to its alternatives [15,26]; of course, these alternatives can be considered in the future. We merely point out that it has been widely used in previous systems design practice and in prior research on privilege separation.

a performance bottleneck. Two common engineering tricks can be used to reduce these bottlenecks: (a) using shared memory or (b) by re-designing the logic to minimize data sharing. Shared memory does not incur performance overhead, but has trades-off security to an extent. First, as multiple parties may write to the shared memory regions, it is subject to the time-of-check-to-time-of-use (TOCTTOU) attack [37]; second, complex data structures with deep levels of pointers are easily (sometimes carelessly) shared across partitions that makes sanitization of shared data error-prone and difficult to implement correctly. To estimate the size of inter-partition data exchange, we measure the size of data that are exchanged between different code units. This measurement identifies partition boundaries with light data exchange, where Unix domain sockets or pipes are applicable, as well as boundaries with heavy data exchange where performance bottlenecks need to be resolved with careful engineering.

C3: Number of Cross-Origin Calls. Client-side web applications can make cross-origin calls, such as `postMessage`, and via cross-window object properties, such as `window.location`, `window.top`, and functions `location.replace`, `window.close()`, and so on. We measure such calls to estimate the inter-partition calls if different origins are separated into different partitions.

C4: Size of Data Exchanged in Cross-Origin Calls. Similar to **C2**, we also measure the size of data exchanged between origins to estimate the size of memory that may need to be mirrored in origin-based isolation.

C5: Number & Size of Cross-Origin Network Sub-resources. One web origin can load sub-resources from other origins via network interfaces. If the requester is separated in a different partition than the resource loader, inter-partition calls will occur. We measure these number and size of sub-resources loading to evaluate the number of partitions and size of memory required for cross-origin sub-resource isolation.

C6: Cost of an Inter-partition Call under Different Isolation Primitives. Partitioning the web browser into more than one container requires using different isolation primitives, such as processes and VMs. These mechanisms have different performance implications when they are applied to privilege separation. We measure the inter-partition communication costs of 3 isolation primitives in this work: Linux OS processes, LAN-connected hosts, and VMs; other primitives such as software-based isolation (heap isolation [8], SFI [34]) and hardware-based methods (using segmentation) can be calculated similarly.

C7: Size of Memory Consumption for a Partition under Different Isolation Primitives With different isolation primitives, memory overhead differs when we create additional partitions in privilege separation. This is also an important aspect of performance costs dependent on design choices.

4   Measurement Methodology

To measure the outlined parameters above, we take the following as inputs: *1)* an executable *binary* of a web browser with debug information, *2)* a blueprint of the browser, including a set of code units and authorities for partitioning, and *3)* a large test harness under which the web browser is subject to dynamic analysis.

We focus our measurements on the main browser components and we presently exclude measurements on browser add-ons and plugins. Our measurements are computed from data measured during the execution of the test harness dynamically, since computing these counts precisely using static analysis is difficult and does not account for runtime frequencies. Based on measurement data, we compare with partitioning choices in recent browser design proposals, and evaluate the security benefits and performance costs in those design dimensions.

In this work, we perform the measurement on a debug build of Firefox, a blueprint manually abstracted from Firefox and WebKit designs, historical Firefox vulnerabilities retrieved from Mozilla Security Advisories [27], and Alexa Top 100 web sites.

Since the engineering effort required to conduct such a large-scale study is nontrivial, we develop an assistance tool to automate our measurement and analysis to a large extent. Especially for the measurement of inter-partition function calls and data exchange sizes, we develop an Intel Pin tool. It applies dynamic instrumentation on the Firefox browser to intercept function calls and memory access. By maintaining a simulated call stack structure, we capture the caller-callee relationships during browser execution over test harness web pages. Before our experiments, we register accounts for the Alexa Top 100 web sites, when applicable, and log into these web sites using a vanilla Firefox browser under a test Firefox profile. Then we manually run Firefox instrumented by the Pin tool to browse the front pages of the web sites under the same test profile, so that contents requiring authentication are also rendered. As Firefox is slowed down by the Pin tool, it took one of the authors around 10 days to finish the browsing of the 100 web sites.

5   Experimental Evaluation

We conduct empirical measurements to obtain the data for evaluating browser designs. Our measurements are mainly conducted on a Dell™ server running Ubuntu 10.04 64bit, with 2 Xeon® 4-core E5640 2.67GHz CPUs and 48GB RAM. For the measurement of inter-partition communication overhead, we connected two Dell™ desktop machines with a dual-core i5-650 3.2GHz CPU and 4GB RAM via a 100 Mbps link.

5.1   Measurement Goals

Our measurements aim to measure the following:

Goal 1. Security benefits of isolating a browser component with regard to the number of historical security vulnerabilities that can be mitigated by privilege separation.

Goal 2. Worst-case estimation of additional inter-partition calls and data exchange that would be incurred by isolating a component, and by isolating an authority (web origin).

Goal 3. Memory and communication overhead incurred by different isolation primitives.

Table 2. Kilo-lines of Source Code in Firefox Components. *In our experiments, we consider the following components: 0. NETWORK, 1. JS, 2. PARSER, 3. DOM, 4. BROWSER, 5. CHROME, 6. DB, 7. DOCSHELL, 8. EDITOR, 9. LAYOUT, 10. MEMORY, 11. MODULES, 12. SECURITY, 13. STORAGE, 14. TOOLKIT, 15. URILOADER, 16. WIDGET, 17. GFX, 18. SPELLCHECKER, 19. NSPR, 20. XPCONNECT, and 21. OTHERS.*

Comp#	0	1	2	3	4	5	6	7	8	9	10	11	12	13	14	15	16	17	18	19	20
LOC	136	367	74	155	32	3	131	21	77	366	10	269	763	17	223	24	137	478	24	188	53

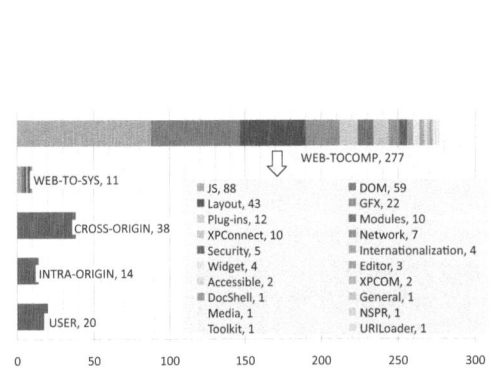

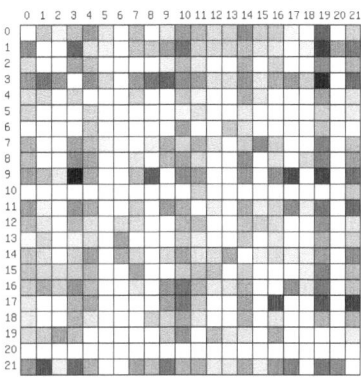

(a) Number of Historical Security Vulnerabilities in Firefox, Categorized by Severity and Firefox Components

(b) Gray-scaled Chart of Call Counts across Code Units. *Components are numbered as with Table 2.* Each cell at (i, j) denote the number of calls from Component i to Component j.

Fig. 2. Summary of Vulnerability Study and Performance Measurement

5.2   Measurement over Alexa Top 100 Web Sites

Next, we explain how we measure these metrics and present their results.

For *Goal 1*: Security Benefits. We measure the number of historical security vulnerabilities in each Firefox component according to each severity category (Security Parameters **S1, S2**) and the size of source code in Firefox components (Security Parameter **S3**).

We implement a Perl utility with 95 lines of code to crawl and fetch Firefox bug reports online [27]. According to the blueprint of browser components, and our classification of vulnerability severity, we count the 362 vulnerabilities[7] we have access to, by *1) browser component*, and *2) severity category*. Figure 2(a) depicts the number of Firefox vulnerabilities with our categorization outlined in Section 2.2. We can see that 76.5% of the security vulnerabilities are WEB-TO-COMP vulnerabilities (277), which can lead to code execution. There is also a large amount of CROSS-ORIGIN vulnerabilities (38), whereas the number of other categories is much smaller. Among browser components, the JavaScript engine has the largest number of vulnerabilities (88). The Layout module (43) and DOM (59) also have large amount of vulnerabilities. These are

---

[7] 2 of them are uncategorized due to insufficient information.

all major components consisting of complex browser logic. On the other hand, more peripheral components have less vulnerabilities. For example, the Editor has only 3 WEB-TO-COMP vulnerabilities. Such results are in line with our intuition that more complex and critical components tend to have more vulnerabilities discovered.

We use the wc utility to measure the lines of source code for all .h, .c and .cpp files in Firefox components. Table 2 lists the lines of source code we measure for different components in Firefox. Components such as JavaScript, Layout and Security, etc. have large size code size. These data reflect the (relative) complexity of different browser components (See **S3**).

For *Goal 2*: Performance Costs. We dynamically measure performance costs corresponding to Performance Parameters **C1-C5**, respectively.

Inter-code-unit Call Overhead. For Performance Parameters **C1** and **C2**, we apply our Pin tool on Firefox to browse Alexa Top 100 web sites, counting the number of function calls whose caller and callee belong to two different components, and the size of data exchanged during the function calls. We briefly discuss the results below, and the detailed measurement data can be found online at [1].

The numbers of inter-code-unit function calls (in 1000s) between different browser components are illustrated in Figure 2(b). These calls may become inter-partition calls after privilege separation. Thus, the larger the number is between the two components, the higher is the communication cost if they are isolated into different partitions. We find that there are 4,270,599,380 times of calls between the Layout engine and the DOM during our measurements, 369,305,460 times between the GFX rendering engine and the Layout engine, and 133,374,520 times between the JavaScript engine and the DOM. Heavy calls between these components correspond to tight interactions during run time, such as DOM scripting and sending layout data for rendering.

We also measure data exchange sizes between components. For example, the DOM and the Layout engine have larger data exchange than other components: 172,206.36 Kilobytes over the 100 web sites.

Cross-Origin Call Overhead. Similarly, for calls and data exchange between different web origins (Performance Parameters **C3** and **C4**), we intercept the calls to client-side communication channels in Firefox, retrieve the caller and callee origins, and record the size of data passed in postMessage calls. For Performance Parameter **C5**, we intercept all network responses to Firefox, and identify whose requester and destination origins are different. We record such cases with the size of data passed in the HTTP response body. Table 3 summarizes the number of client-side calls to access other origins and the size of data exchanged in such calls.

More Results on Sub-resource Loading To evaluate in more detail the performance implications in using separate partitions for sub-resource loading, we measure the number of cross-origin sub-resources for each of the Alexa Top 100 web sites. Figure 3(a) illustrates the significant differences in the number of different origins of network subresource requests for each web page we measured. In our measurement, the largest number is 51, with www.sina.com.cn. Figure 3(b) shows that the reoccurrence rate of unique pairs of different requester and destination origins is very small. More than

Table 3. Cross-Origin Calls & Sub-Resource Loading

Cross-Origin Access		Number of Calls	Data Size Exchanged in Calls (KB)
Browser Side	`postMessage`	4,031	587
	`location`	9	-
	`window.parent`	24	-
	`window.frames`	3,330	-
Network sub-resource	Images, CSS, etc.	10,745	131,920

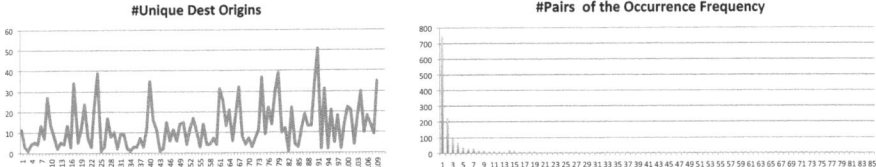

(a) Number of Different Destination Origins of Cross-Origin Resource Requests *The largest number of different destination origins from one site is 51, while the smallest number is 1.*

(b) Occurrence Frequencies of Unique Pairs of Different Requestor-Destination Origins *746 unique pairs only occur once, while only 164 unique pairs occur more than 15 times.*

Fig. 3. Sub-resource Loading Measurements

746 pairs occur only once. In fact, there are in total 1,515 such unique pairs, averaged to 1,515 / 100 = 15 pairs for each page.

For *Goal 3*: Isolation Primitive Overhead. We measure the performance overhead under different isolation primitives, in communication cost for Performance Parameter **C6**, and in memory consumption for Performance Parameter **C7**.

We use a simple client-server communication program to measure the inter-partition call costs between Unix domain sockets, between hosts connected via LAN, and between virtual machines on the same VM host. We average over 10,000 rounds of each primitive with message lengths varying from 50 to 8K bytes. Table 4 summarizes our measurements on round trip times for inter-partition communications with the three isolation primitives. Unix domain sockets are 6-10 times more efficient than cross-VM communications.

Table 4. Round-Trip Time (RTT) of Unix Domain Socket, Network and Cross-VM Communications, *in nanoseconds*, Averaged over 10,000 Runs Each

Size of MSG (in bytes)	Average RTT for Unix Domain Socket	Average RTT for Network Comm	Average RTT for Cross-VM Comm
50	4673	87642	252008
500	5045	176160	288276
1000	5145	276841	252107
2K	5821	367356	251605
4K	6838	449262	269845
8K	9986	638598	336999

By checking the size of an empty process on different hosts, we estimate that the memory used by an almost-empty process is about 120k-140K. As this number stays very stable across different runs, we take this as the memory consumption of creating processes. For the Ubuntu guest OS we create, the writeable/private memory used by VirtualBox is about 25M bytes and the memory used by guest OS running in VirtualBox is about 90M bytes. We take 90M as the size of memory cost with a VM partition or a single host, and 25M as the memory overhead from a VM daemon in our quantification. Therefore, a Linux process incurs 90M / 130K = 709 times lower memory overhead than a VM.

5.3 Inference from Measurement Data

In this section, we summarize the high-level findings from our detailed measurements. Specifically, we revisit the partitioning dimensions outlined earlier and evaluate their security-performance trade-offs. We also summarize the performance bottlenecks that our measurements highlight.

Table 5. Security Benefits and Performance Costs of Partitioning Dimensions *Performance costs are per page, averaged over Alexa Top 100 web sites*

Partitioning Dimension	#Vulnerabilities Migitated	Lines of Code Partitioned	Comm Cost	Data Exchanges Cost	Memory Cost
Single Process	0	N.A.	0	0	0.13K
One Process per Origin (w/o Cross-Origin Sub-Resource Isolation)	0	N.A.	0	0	130K
One Process per Origin (with Cross-Origin Sub-Resource Isolation)	38	N.A.	0.37ms	5.87MB	1.4MB
One Process per Pair of Requester-Destination of Sub-Resource	38	N.A.	0.91ms	7.19MB	2.1MB
Renderer/Browser Division	81	1,863K	2.59min	3.54MB	130KB
JS/DOM Separation (Process)	147	JS:367K DOM:155K	6.67s	572.6KB	130KB
JS/DOM Separation (Network)	147	JS:367K DOM:155K	3.78min	572.6KB	90MB
Layout/Window Manager (GFX+Widget) Separation	69	Layout:367K GFX+Widget:615K	19.15s	739.3KB	130KB
DOM/Layout Separation	102	DOM:155K Layout:367K	3.56min	1.68MB	130KB

Table 5 summarizes the estimated security benefits and performance costs for each design point along the dimensions being debated in present designs. The values in the table for performance costs are per web page, if applicable, averaged over the Top 100 Alexa pages.

Origin-Based isolation. One process per origin without separating cross-origin sub-resources have no security benefits. If contents from another origin hosted as sub-resources (such as PDF) can be processed in the same partition, security vulnerabilities can still permit unintended escalation of privileges. This is consistent with the observations made by several browser designs that propose hosting sub-resources in separate containers. Doing so, mitigates the CROSS-ORIGIN vulnerabilities (38 out of 362).

Sub-resource Isolation. Several browsers propose isolating each pair of requester-destination of sub-resources to be further isolated in separate partitions. Our data suggests that (a) this has no further security benefit in our model, and (b) it has a large performance cost. For instance, the memory cost of creating several partitions (using processes) is large and will be a performance bottleneck. In our measurement, one web page can include up to 51 third-party sub-resources. If all these cross-origin sub-resources are to be isolated by different processes, and consider a typical browser process need 20 Megabytes [5], then around 1 Gigabyte memory overhead will be incurred just for loading third-party resources for this single web page. Therefore, although sub-resource isolation can mitigate 38 CROSS-ORIGIN vulnerabilities, browsers may need to optimize memory usage for processes that load sub-resources before they can practically adopt this proposal.

It is interesting to compare our identified bottlenecks to choices made by today's web browsers. For instance, Google Chrome does not suffer from this performance bottleneck by making a security-performance trade-off. It adopts a different strategy by grouping resources according to a site-instance of the hosting page, which significantly reduces the number of processes created [17]. We leave the detailed definition and discussion of this strategy out of scope; however, we believe that our methodology does identify realistic practical constraints.

Component-Based Isolation. Isolation by components mitigates WEB-TO-COMP vulnerabilities. For example, the JavaScript engine and the DOM have 147 such vulnerabilities. At the same time, the 367K of source code (TCB) in the JavaScript engine can be isolated, which is 10% of the entire browser. Nevertheless, since they have frequent interactions, such isolation costs prohibitively high communication and memory overhead. Hence, although beneficial for security, such a partitioning dimension is less practical for adoption. For instance, designers of OP redacted the decision to isolate JavaScript engine and the HTML parser within one web page instance in OP2; our measurement identifies this high overhead as a bottleneck.

Renderer/Browser Kernel Isolation. We also take a popular architecture of renderer/browser kernel division for evaluation. We evaluate our methodology on the Google Chrome design model to measure the security benefits and performance costs. Such a partitioning dimension would prevent WEB-TO-COMP vulnerabilities in the renderer process, and WEB-TO-SYS vulnerabilities. If we apply the Firefox code size to this design, the size of TCB in the kernel process would be around 1,863K, i.e., 53.5% of the browser codebase. Note that this is just a rough estimation based on our blueprint of coarse-grained components. Further dividing components can reduce the necessary code size that needs to be put into the browser kernel process.

Our measurements identify potential performance bottlenecks that correlate with actual browser implementations. Specifically, we find that isolation between components in the renderer processes and the browser kernel process, as in Chrome, would incur very high performance overhead, such as between the GFX and the Layout engine. However, such performance bottlenecks do not appear in Chrome. Over the past few years, a substantial amount of efforts [7] have been spent on improving and securing the inter-partition communications in the Chrome browser. Besides, Chrome also uses GPU command buffers and other engineering tricks to improve performance of rendering and communication [16]. This verifies our observation that potential performance bottlenecks need to be re-engineered to reduce their overhead.

Component Partitioning with High Security Benefits. We identify a few browser components that have high security benefits to be isolated from other components. For example, the JavaScript engine is a fairly complex component with 367K lines of source code, has 88, i.e., 31.8% of, WEB-TO-COMP vulnerabilities. Isolating it from other browser components will mitigate a large faction of vulnerabilities. Other typical example components include the Layout engine with 367K lines of source code and 43 (15.5%) WEB-TO-COMP vulnerabilities, as well as GFX, the rendering component for Firefox, with 478K lines of source code and 22 (7.9%) WEB-TO-COMP vulnerabilities.

Component Partitioning with High Performance Costs. We identify the main browser components that have tight interactions with other browser components. Thus, isolating them from others would incur high performance costs. For example, our measurements find 133,374,520 function calls between the JavaScript engine and the DOM, and 369,305,460 calls between the GFX rendering engine and the Layout engine. To show why they can become performance bottlenecks, here is a simple calculation. Suppose they are separated by processes, a single RTT with Unix domain sockets would cost a delay of around 5000 nanoseconds. If there is no additional optimization is in place, these numbers correspond to 133,374,520 * 5000 nanoseconds / 100 pages = 6.67 seconds/page and 18.47 seconds/page, respectively. Such performance overhead is prohibitively high. Security architects should either avoid such partitioning, or take further measures to optimize these performance bottlenecks.

6   Related Work

Privilege Separation. The concept of privilege separation in computer systems was proposed by Saltzer et al. [31]. Since then it has been used in the re-design of several legacy OS applications [12, 28] (including web browsers) and even web applications [5, 8, 19]. Similar to our goals in this work, several automated techniques have been developed to aid analysts to partition existing applications, such as PrivTrans [14], Jif/Split [38], and Wedge [13]. Most of these works have focused on the problem of privilege minimization, i.e., inferring partitions where maximum code executes in partitions with minimum or no privileges, while performance is measured "after-the-fact". Our work, in contrast, aims to quantify performance overhead with privilege-separated designs with only a blueprint without the actual implementations. Our work also differs with them by performing measurements on binary code, rather than source code.

Privilege Separation in Browsers. Our work is closely related to the re-design of web browsers, which has been an active area of research [9, 18, 20, 21, 23, 24, 33, 35]. Our work is motivated by the design decisions that arise in partitioning web browsers, which performs a complex task of isolating users, origins and the system. Among them, IE uses tab-based isolation, Google Chrome [9] isolates web origins into different renderer processes, while Gazelle [35] further isolates sub-resources and plugins. Our measurements have shown that some web pages may include 51 sub-resources of different destination origins. Our data quantifies the number of partitions that may be created in such designs as well as in further partitioned browsers, such as OP [20] and OP2 [21]. In addition, our measurements also evaluate the performance costs in VM-based isolation, such as Tahoma [18], and memory consumption from separate network processes for sub-resources in IBOS [33] design. Our work advocates privilege-separated browsers for better security, and identifies potential performance bottlenecks that need to be optimized to trim their performance costs.

Evaluation Metrics. Estimation of security benefits using bug counts is one way of quantifying security. Riscorla et al. discuss potential drawbacks of such reactive measurement [29]. Other methods have been proposed, but are more heavy-weight and require detailed analysis of source code [22, 25, 32]. Performance measurement metrics such as inter-partition calls and data exchange have been identified in the design of isolation primitives such as SFI [34]. We provide an in-depth empirical analysis of these metrics in a widely used web browser (Mozilla Firefox).

7 Conclusion

In this paper, we propose a measurement-based methodology to quantify security benefits and performance costs of privilege-partitioned browser designs. With an assistance tool, we perform a large-scale study of 9 browser designs over Alexa Top 100 web sites. Our results provide empirical data on security and performance implications of various partitioning dimensions adopted by recent browser designs. Our methodology will help evaluate performance overhead in designing future security mechanisms in browsers. We hope this will enable more privilege-separated browser designs to be adopted in practice.

Acknowledgments. We thank anonymous reviewers for their valuable feedback. This research is partially supported by the research grant R-252-000-519-112 from Ministry of Education, Singapore.

References

1. Additional tables on performance evaluation,
   `http://compsec.comp.nus.edu.sg/bci/additional-tables.pdf`
2. Bromium, `http://www.bromium.com/`
3. Invincea, `http://www.invincea.com/`
4. Akhawe, D., Barth, A., Lam, P.E., Mitchell, J., Song, D.: Towards a formal foundation of web security. In: Proceedings of the 23rd IEEE Computer Security Foundations Symposium, CSF 2010 (2010)
5. Akhawe, D., Saxena, P., Song, D.: Privilege separation in html5 applications. In: Proceedings of the 21st USENIX Security Symposium (2012)
6. Alexa: Top sites (2012), `http://www.alexa.com/topsites` (retrieved)
7. Azimuth Security: The chrome sandbox part 2 of 3: The IPC framework,
   `http://blog.azimuthsecurity.com/2010/08/`
   `chrome-sandbox-part-2-of-3-ipc.html`
8. Barth, A., Felt, A.P., Saxena, P., Boodman, A.: Protecting browsers from extension vulnerabilities. In: Proceedings of the 17th Annual Network and Distributed System Security Symposium, NDSS 2010 (2010)

9. Barth, A., Jackson, C., Reis, C.: The Google Chrome Team: The security architecture of the chromium browser. Tech. rep. (2008)
10. Barth, A., Rubinstein, B.I.P., Sundararajan, M., Mitchell, J.C., Song, D., Bartlett, P.L.: A learning-based approach to reactive security. In: Sion, R. (ed.) FC 2010. LNCS, vol. 6052, pp. 192–206. Springer, Heidelberg (2010)
11. Barth, A., Weinberger, J., Song, D.: Cross-origin javascript capability leaks: detection, exploitation, and defense. In: Proceedings of the 18th USENIX Security Symposium (2009)
12. Bernstein, D.J.: Some thoughts on security after ten years of qmail 1.0. In: Proceedings of the 2007 ACM Workshop on Computer Security Architecture, CSAW 2007 (2007)
13. Bittau, A., Marchenko, P., Handley, M., Karp, B.: Wedge: splitting applications into reduced-privilege compartments. In: Proceedings of the 5th USENIX Symposium on Networked Systems Design and Implementation, NSDI 2008 (2008)
14. Brumley, D., Song, D.: Privtrans: automatically partitioning programs for privilege separation. In: Proceedings of the 13th USENIX Security Symposium (2004)
15. Certification Authorities Software Team (CAST): What is a "decision" in application of modified condition/decision coverage (mc/dc) and decision coverage (dc)?,
    http://www.faa.gov/aircraft/air_cert/design_approvals/
    air_software/cast/cast_papers/media/cast-10.pdf
16. Chromium: GPU command buffer, http://www.chromium.org/
    developers/design-documents/gpu-command-buffer
17. Chromium: Process models — process-per-site-instance,
    http://www.chromium.org/developers/design-documents/
    process-models#1_Process_per_Site_Instance
18. Cox, R.S., Gribble, S.D., Levy, H.M., Hansen, J.G.: A safety-oriented platform for web applications. In: Proceedings of the 2006 IEEE Symposium on Security and Privacy (2006)
19. Felt, A.P., Finifter, M., Weinberger, J., Wagner, D.: Diesel: applying privilege separation to database access. In: Proceedings of the 6th ACM Symposium on Information, Computer and Communications Security, ASIACCS 2011 (2011)
20. Grier, C., Tang, S., King, S.T.: Secure web browsing with the op web browser. In: Proceedings of the 2008 IEEE Symposium on Security and Privacy (2008)
21. Grier, C., Tang, S., King, S.T.: Designing and implementing the op and op2 web browsers. ACM Transactions on the Web (2011)
22. Hart, T.E., Chechik, M., Lie, D.: Security benchmarking using partial verification. In: Proceedings of the 3rd USENIX Workshop on Hot Topics in Security, HotSec 2008 (2008)
23. IEBlog: Tab isolation, http://blogs.msdn.com/b/ie/archive/
    2010/03/04/tab-isolation.aspx
24. Li, Z., Tang, Y., Cao, Y., Rastogi, V., Chen, Y., Liu, B., Sbisa, C.: Webshield: Enabling various web defense techniques without client side modifications. In: Proceedings of the Network and Distributed System Security Symposium, NDSS 2011 (2011)
25. Lie, D., Satyanarayanan, M.: Quantifying the strength of security systems. In: Proceedings of the 2nd USENIX Workshop on Hot Topics in Security, HotSec 2007 (2007)
26. McCabe, T.J.: A complexity measure. In: Proceedings of the 2nd International Conference on Software Engineering, ICSE 1976 (1976)
27. Mozilla Foundation: Mozilla foundation security advisories,
    http://www.mozilla.org/security/announce/
28. Provos, N., Friedl, M., Honeyman, P.: Preventing privilege escalation. In: Proceedings of the 12th USENIX Security Symposium (2003)
29. Rescorla, E.: Is finding security holes a good idea? IEEE Security and Privacy 3(1), 14–19 (2005)

30. Roesner, F., Kohno, T., Moshchuk, A., Parno, B., Wang, H.J., Cowan, C.: User-driven access control: Rethinking permission granting in modern operating systems. In: Proceedings of the 2012 IEEE Symposium of Security and Privacy (2012)
31. Saltzer, J.H., Schroeder, M.D.: The protection of information in computer systems. Proceedings of the IEEE (1975)
32. Ta-Min, R., Litty, L., Lie, D.: Splitting interfaces: Making trust between applications and operating systems. In: Proceedings of the 7th USENIX Symposium on Operating Systems Design and Implementation, OSDI 2006 (2006)
33. Tang, S., Mai, H., King, S.T.: Trust and protection in the illinois browser operating system. In: Proceedings of the 9th USENIX Conference on Operating Systems Design and Implementation, OSDI 2010 (2010)
34. Wahbe, R., Lucco, S., Anderson, T.E., Graham, S.L.: Efficient software-based fault isolation. ACM SIGOPS Operating Systems Review 27(5), 203–216 (1993)
35. Wang, H.J., Grier, C., Moshchuk, A., King, S.T., Choudhury, P., Venter, H.: The multi-principal os construction of the gazelle web browser. In: Proceedings of the 18th USENIX Security Symposium (2009)
36. Wikipedia: DigiNotar, http://en.wikipedia.org/wiki/DigiNotar
37. Wikipedia: Time of check to time of use, http://en.wikipedia.org/wiki/Time_of_check_to_time_of_use
38. Zdancewic, S.A.: Programming languages for information security. Ph.D. thesis, Cornell University (2002)

Estimating Asset Sensitivity by Profiling Users

Youngja Park[1], Christopher Gates[2], and Stephen C. Gates[1]

[1] IBM T.J. Watson Research Center, Yorktown Heights, NY 10598, USA
[2] Purdue University, Indiana, USA
{young_park,scgates}@us.ibm.com, gates2@purdue.edu

Abstract. We introduce algorithms to automatically score and rank information technology (IT) assets in an enterprise, such as computer systems or data files, by their business value and criticality to the organization. Typically, information assets are manually assigned classification labels with respect to the confidentiality, integrity and availability. In this paper, we propose semi-automatic machine learning algorithms to automatically estimate the sensitivity of assets by profiling the users. Our methods do not require direct access to the target assets or privileged knowledge about the assets, resulting in a more efficient, scalable and privacy-preserving approach compared with existing data security solutions relying on data content classification. Instead, we rely on external information such as the attributes of the users, their access patterns and other published data content by the users. Validation with a set of 8,500 computers collected from a large company show that all our algorithms perform significantly better than two baseline methods.

Keywords: Asset Sensitivity, Criticality, Data Security, Information Security.

1 Introduction

Recently, a growing number of advanced persistent threats (APTs) [7] and insider threats [18] have demonstrated the capability of attacking specific highly sensitive entities in a government or company. The computer security community has recognized that not all IT assets have the same value or importance to the company, and, therefore, they require different levels of protection corresponding to their sensitivity and value. By prioritizing the security efforts and budget to better protect highly sensitive assets, organizations can reduce the security risk. Further, quantitative measurement of the sensitivity of IT assets enables other important applications such as intelligent file backup and business continuity planning.

To achieve this vision, all assets in an organization need to be assigned a sensitivity value that properly indicates the business value and criticality to the organisation. Currently, the asset classification is primarily done manually by the system administrators with respect to the confidentiality, integrity and availability of the assets. However, there are critical limitations in the manual approach. First, it is very hard for a large organization to assign appropriate labels to all the assets in the organization. The number of assets in a large organization can grow huge, and, often, the assets are created and managed independently in different departments, so it is extremely hard to catalog and centrally manage all the assets. Second, most of the guidelines are descriptive and can

J. Crampton, S. Jajodia, and K. Mayes (Eds.): ESORICS 2013, LNCS 8134, pp. 94–110, 2013.

be interpreted subjectively. Therefore, the classification of assets can differ significantly by different human judges. Third, they typically measure the sensitivity using a coarse-grained (3 to 5-scale) rating as in the Bell-LaPadula model [5] ranging from the most sensitive (e.g., *Top Secret*) to the least sensitive (e.g, *Un-classified*).

In this paper, we explore methods for semi-automatically scoring various assets within an enterprise using information about the users. To our knowledge, there has been little effort to automatically quantify the sensitivity of IT assets. Previous studies mostly focus on a specific type of assets, e.g., data files [4,12,13] or network assets [3], or propose a ranking method using a small number of manually generated features [10]. We propose a new method for determining asset values using automatically extracted features that are generic to various asset types including data and network assets. We use only information about the users of the target asset including attributes of the users, their access patterns and externally published data by the users such as personal and project webpages and files shared by the users. Note that this information can be easily extracted and does not require direct access to the target asset or detailed knowledge about the asset, such as the owner of the asset and the sensitivity of the data in the asset.

Further, we note that there are many different aspects for an asset being considered sensitive, and the criterion can change over time. For instance, a computer is considered very sensitive because it stores sensitive data (i.e., confidentiality), or it hosts important applications for the business (i.e., availability). Based on these observations, we apply *instance-based learning* approaches, making the system domain independent and easy to adapt to new sensitive asset types. Given a small set of *known* sensitive assets, we learn their characteristics and score other sensitive assets using the models. In this work, we explore a kNN (Nearest Neighbor)-based method, a clustering-based method and the kNN-based method with distance metric learning techniques. We validate the algorithms using a real-world data set comprising about 8,500 computers. Our experiments show that all our algorithms perform significantly better than the baseline cases, and the kNN-based method with distance metric learning techniques outperform the other algorithms. The main contributions of this paper are as follows.

- Previous studies presented solutions for a specific IT asset type such as data, servers or computer networks, forcing companies to manage multiple heterogenous approaches. Our methods rely on meta-level information that can be extracted from most IT assets in the same way. This domain-independent set of features makes our methods applicable to many different IT asset types.
- Further, extraction of the meta-level features does not require direct access to the target assets or privileged knowledge about the assets, and, thus, our method is very efficient and can be easily scalable to a large set of heterogeneous assets.
- Our system assigns a quantitative value to each asset rather than a coarse-grained set of labels, allowing companies to adopt more fine-grained security measures.
- A major obstacle in applying machine learning methods to computer security problems is the lack of labeled data. In this work, we propose new semi-supervised machine learning methods that learn the characteristics of sensitive assets from a small number of examples.
- We validate our approaches with a large set of real data. Experimental results confirm that the proposed algorithms can retrieve sensitive assets with high ranks producing higher precision and recall than baseline methods.

2   Meta-level Features of Assets

As discussed in the introduction, a main goal of this study is to identify a set of features that can be uniformly used for different asset types and be extracted without having to access the target asset or privileged knowledge about the asset. This set of features may not be as accurate as a small set of features carefully produced by domain experts, but it makes the system very efficient and scalable and can provide a good estimate for *potentially* sensitive assets.

In this study, we investigate 72 features from three kinds of knowledge — who accesses the asset (user features), how they access the asset (usage features) and what kinds of tasks or projects the users work on (external content features). Table 1 describes the high-level feature categories used in this study.

Table 1. Features for estimating the sensitivity of IT assets

Feature Categories	Feature Definition
User Features	
Manager vs. NonManager	Is the user a manager or a non-manager employee
Job Roles	Job roles in the organization such as *S/W Developer* and *Finance*
Rank in the organizational hierarchy	The distance from the highest-ranked employee to the user in the organization hierarchy
Usage Features	
Access Frequency	the total number of accesses by a user (heavy or light)
Access Pattern	the patterns of the accesses (e.g., regular, semi-regular, irregular)
External Content Features	
External Data Content	Topics discovered from the externally published data content such as papers, patent and webpages of the users

2.1   User Features

User attributes such as job roles and the rank in the organization may affect the sensitivity of the asset. For instance, an asset used primarily by executives would elevate the sensitivity of the asset. In this work, we leverage these types of user attributes for sensitivity estimation.

To extract the attributes of the users, we first need to identify the users of the asset in the access logs. Some access logs, such as logs for a file repository or a system log-on, typically contain the user accounts, thus, identifying the users is straightforward for these assets. For computer network assets, user accounts are generally not available in the logs (e.g., DNS logs). Instead, the logs contain the IP address from which the lookup was requested. The process of determining which user is performing a DNS lookup is not a trivial task. In most situations, we first need to find the most likely candidate user who is assigned to a specific IP address during a specific time period. The resolution of an IP address to a user, while easy in a simple system, becomes more challenging in a dynamic system with many different ways to access the network and with a large set of users. Users can log into the network over WiFi or using an ethernet cable, or from remote locations via VPN (virtual private network).

For computers in a network, we perform the IP to user mapping using various sources including media access control (MAC) addresses, application (e.g., internal web portals) logs, and WiFi logs. If the MAC address is present, then, during a DHCP session setup, we can correlate the MAC address used for that session to the IP address that is assigned, which, in turn, can give us an IP to user mapping. However, the MAC addresses are not reliable for users using OS X and are often unavailable when new devices are introduced. To alleviate the limitations, we also use application and WiFi logs for the user mapping. The application level logs can correlate the act of a user logging into an application (such as an internal web portal) to an IP address. The WiFi logs can correlate a user establishing a connection to the WiFi with the authentication credentials that are used to log in to the system. Since the user to IP mapping is not perfect, we discard all DNS lookups for which we are unable to identify the user and all logs that are resolved to more than one user (i.e., ambiguous logs) for our study.

After obtaining the set of users of an asset, we extract various user attributes that can indicate the users' job roles and the sensitivity of the data they generate. The high-level categories of the user attributes used in this work are shown in Table 1. We extract 26 user attributes in total including *Manager, NonManager, Rank-High, Rank-Middle, Rank-Low*, and 21 different job roles defined in the company such as *IT Specialist, Human Resources* and *Finance*. Note that these attributes can be extracted from most companies' employee directory. The feature value of each feature is the number of users who possess the attribute. For instance, if 100 managers, 500 non-manager employees and 1 high-rank employee accessed the asset, the asset is represented *Manager*=100, *NonManager*=500 and *Rank-High*=1.

2.2   Usage Features

The access patterns of the users add additional insights on the sensitivity of an asset. For instance, a user who occasionally uses the asset will have less impact than a user who uses the asset frequently. On the other hand, if a user's access pattern is very regular (e.g., every day at 5am), that may indicate that the user is running an automated job (e.g., file backup), so the accesses should not affect much on the asset's sensitivity. Figure 1 shows typical daily DNS lookup activities.

In this work, we analyze access logs with the timestamps to discover the frequency of a user's access and the patterns of the accesses. We first group the logs by each pair of a user and an asset, and record the number of log entries as the access frequency of the user to the asset. We categorize the access frequency into *Heavy* or *Light* using a pre-defined threshold. Further, we determine if a connection to the asset is done through an automated access or a manual access (i.e., access pattern). We observe that automated accesses tend to be regular, for instance, once a day at 4am or once every hour, while human accesses are more sporadic. In other words, automated accesses are more predictable while human accesses are more uncertain. Based on this observation, we apply

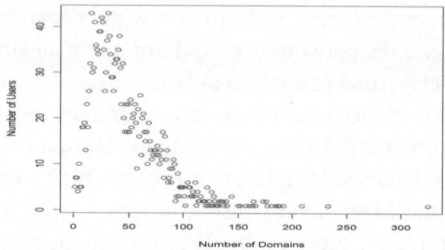

Fig. 1. Number of unique domains accessed per user in a single day. The data show that most users access 20 to 30 different domains in a day, while a few users connect to over 200 different domains.

the Shannon entropy, $H(X)$, which measures the uncertainty in a random variable [16] to determine the access patterns.

$$H(X) = -\sum_i p(x_i) \log(p(x_i))$$

Now, we explain in detail how we measure the entropy of user accesses. First, for each user and asset pair, we split all the accesses over each hour of the day (i.e., grouping accesses into 24 time slots). For instance, we count how many accesses a user initiated at the 9am–9:59am period in the logs collected over a long period time. Figure 2 shows two sets of access patterns over the 24 time slots. Figure 2(a) illustrates cases where the accesses were made at the same time periods repeatedly, while Figure 2(b) shows cases where the accesses spread across many different time slots. After obtaining a

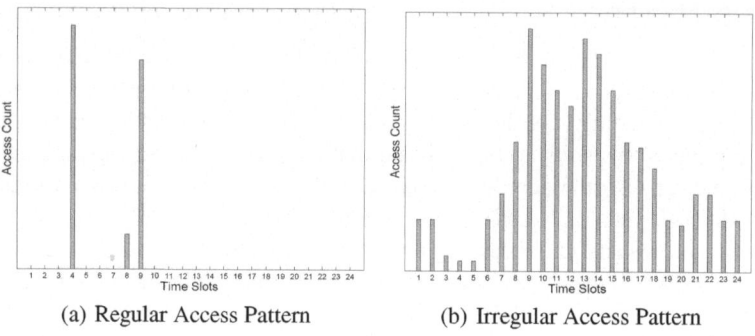

(a) Regular Access Pattern   (b) Irregular Access Pattern

Fig. 2. Access Patterns

24-dimensional count vector for a user-asset pair, we then normalize the counts into probability distributions and compute the entropy. If an access distribution produces a low entropy, then the accesses are regarded as automated accesses. We divide access patterns into three categories–*Regular*, *SemiRegular* and *Irregular*–based on the entropy values (i.e., high, medium and low respectively).

By combining the access frequency and the access pattern features, we generate 6 usage features: *RegularHeavy*, *RegularLight*, *Semi-regularHeavy*, *Semi-regularLight*, *IrregularHeavy* and *IrregularLight*. If the accesses by a user to an asset exhibit a regular pattern (i.e., low entropy), and the user has a large number of accesses, it is considered as *RegularHeavy*. On the other hand, if the access pattern is irregular (i.e., high entropy) and the access count is low, then it is considered as *IrregularLight*. Similarly to the user features, the number of users that exhibit a certain access pattern is the feature value for the asset, i.e., how many users access the asset using *RegularHeavy* or *RegularLight* pattern.

2.3 External Content Features

The sensitivity of an asset is dependent largely on how sensitive the data in the asset are, and, thus, the topics of data in the assets can be good indicators of the asset sensitivity. When content inspection can be performed, the sensitivity can be measured by the techniques presented in [12,13]. When direct content inspection is not feasible, we propose to use external data contents generated by the users as a substitute. External contents of a user can include any documents or data sources the user produced outside the target asset, such as papers, patents, and project webpages. These external contents are used to conjure the user's job responsibilities and the tasks the user is working on. Note that we only extract the contents that can be accessed without an access permission to the host system. Some examples of external data content include:

- Published documents such as patents and papers
- Titles of files the user has shared in a file-sharing site
- Wiki or project websites where the user is a member of
- Personal webpages
- Blogs created by the user
- Tags the users added on webpages

Document of a User: We combine all the external data published by a user and generate a document for the user using the *bag-of-word* representation. We then remove *stop words* [1] and count the occurrences of each word in the user document. The basic assumption is that more frequently used words indicate the topics of the user more strongly than less frequently used words.

Document of an Asset: We then generate a hypothetical document for an asset by combining the documents of its users. Furthermore, we assume that the users who access the asset more frequently influence the content of the asset more than the users who uses it occasionally. We scale the frequency of words in the user documents based on the frequency of the user's access, which is defined as the number of days the user accessed the asset. Figure 3 depicts the high level process of generating documents for assets, and Definition 1 provides a formal description.

---

[1] Stop words are very commonly used words in most documents such as prepositions (e.g., "to", "in") and pronouns (e.g., "I", "this").

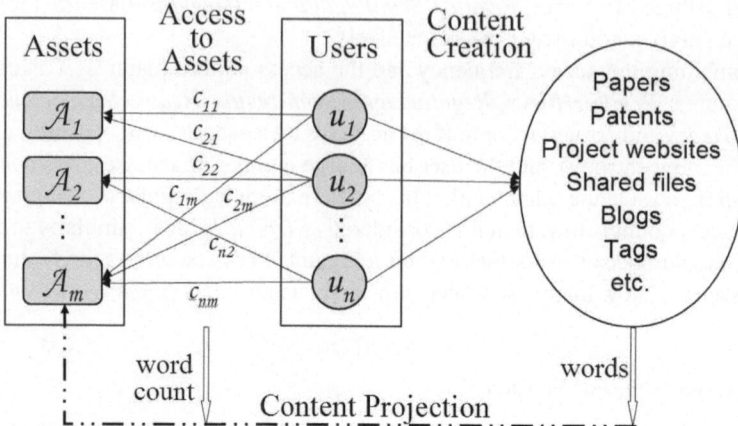

Fig. 3. High level description of content generation for assets using external user contents and the users's access counts to the assets. The words in an asset document come from external contents generated by the asset users, and the counts of the word occurrences in the document are determined based on both the word counts in the user documents and the users' access counts for the asset.

Definition 1. *Let asset $\mathcal{A}$ have n users, $\mathcal{U} = \{u_1, \cdots, u_n\}$, and the document of a user u_i be $\mathcal{D}(u_i)$. Then, the document of asset $\mathcal{A}$, $\mathcal{D}(\mathcal{A})$, is defined as $\mathcal{D}(\mathcal{A}) = \bigcup_{u_i \in \mathcal{U}} \bigcup_{w_j \in \mathcal{D}(u_i)} w_j$. Further, the count of a word in $\mathcal{D}(\mathcal{A})$, $c(w_j)$, is computed as*

$$c(w_j) = \sum_{i=1}^{n} \delta_i \cdot c(w_{ji})$$

$c(w_{ji})$ is the count of word w_j in $\mathcal{D}(u_i)$, and δ_i is the weight of user u_i for the asset $\mathcal{A}$ and defined as $\log(\#days(u_i, \mathcal{A}))$.

Topic Discovery: Once we generate a document representation of an asset, a set of assets can be considered as a collection of documents. The document collection for all assets in an organization typically contain a large number of words. Treating individual words as features will result in a very high dimensional feature space and data sparseness issues. Instead, we can group the words into topics and use the topics as the content features. Each asset can then be represented as the probability distributions over the discovered topics.

In this work, we apply Latent Dirichlet Allocation (LDA) [6], a generative topic modeling technique, to discover the topics from a collection of documents. LDA is a probabilistic generative model for collections of discrete data such as text collections. Each document in a corpus is modeled as a finite mixture over underlying set of topics, and each topic is, in turn, modeled as a distribution over words. LDA allows for multiple topic assignments to a document (i.e., probabilistic clustering) and, thus, better explains the underlying topic distributions in the given corpus.

LDA assumes the following generative process for creating a document d in a collection of document $\mathcal{D}$:

1. For each document $d \in \mathcal{D}$, a distribution over topics is sampled from a Dirichlet distribution, $\theta \sim Dir(\alpha)$.
2. For each word w in a document, select a topic, z, according to the distribution, *Multinomial*(θ).
3. Finally, a word is chosen from a multinomial probability conditioned on the topic, $p(w|z, \beta)$. β is a matrix of word probabilities over topics which is to be estimated from the training data.

LDA requires the number of topics to be discovered as an input parameter. In this work, we run LDA with 40 topics, and, therefore, each asset is represented as a probability distribution over the 40 topics. Table 2 shows three sample topics discovered from our data set.

Table 2. Sample topics discovered from document representations of computer servers. Topic5 indicates *Speech Recognition*, Topic28 is related to related to *Analytics and Business Intelligence*. *BAMS* stands for business analytics and management. Topic37 is related to *Computer Security*.

Topics	Most Relevant Words
Topic5	speech, recognition, system, using, models, language, translation, based, detection, arabic, transcription, model, speaker
Topic28	business, community, management, analytics, method, system, supply, project, *BAMS*, data, performance, applications, research
Topic37	system, computing, virtual, security, community, secure, method, research, data, trusted, applications, operating

2.4 Feature Normalization

The selection of features is critical for machine learning methods, as the data are represented as points in a multi-dimensional feature space, where a feature corresponds to an axes. Another important consideration is the range of feature values. Most data mining and machine learning algorithms rely on a metric or a distance function to evaluate how similar two data points are in the feature space. When there is a large difference in the range of the feature values along different axes, these metrics implicitly assign higher weights to features with larger ranges. To mitigate the effect, a feature normalization technique is often applied and converts all features into an equal range.

In this study, the values of the user and usage features are the counts of the features in the target asset, while the content topic features are the probabilities in range of [0, 1]. The raw count values, especially for the usage features, can grow very large when the data set is collected over a long time period. We normalize the user and usage features using the cumulative distribution function (CDF) following the findings by Aksoy and Haralick [1] [2]. CDF-based feature normalization is performed as follows. Given a

---

[2] We experimented with other feature normalization techniques such as linear scaling, unit range normalization and rank normalization, and the CDF normalization performed best for our data.

random variable $x \in \mathbb{R}$ with cumulative distribution function $F_x(x)$, the normalized feature value, $\tilde{x}$, of x is defined as $\tilde{x} = F_x(x)$ which is uniformly distributed in $[0, 1]$.

3   Sensitivity Estimation Algorithms

In this section, we present our algorithms for estimating the sensitivity of assets. As noted earlier, there are many different aspects that make an asset sensitive to the organization. For instance, an asset is considered sensitive because it contains sensitive business data, or it hosts important applications. Based on these observations, we apply *instance-based learning* approaches, in which we learn the characteristics of sensitive assets from a small number of *known* sensitive assets. Therefore, our methods do not require any prior knowledge about the domain or the target assets, making the algorithms very flexible and easy to adapt to new domains. In this work, we explore three semi-supervised machine learning approaches: a kNN-based method, a clustering-based method, and the kNN method with distance metric learning techniques.

3.1 kNN-Based Method

The k-nearest neighbor classification is a type of *instance-based learning* which assigns a new data point to the majority class among its k nearest neighbors from the training data set [8]. The kNN approach is extremely flexible and non-parametric, and no assumption is made about the probability distribution of the features. The similarity is computed based on the distances between feature vectors in the feature space.

More formally, let $X = \{x_1, \ldots, x_n\}$ be the training data set, and $Y = \{y_1, \ldots, y_C\}$ be the set of classes. In the basic kNN classification, the class for a new data point x is defined as $\arg\max_{1 \leq i \leq C} \sum_{j=1}^{k} 1(y_i, y_j)$, where y_j is the class of the j-th neighbor, and $1(y_i, y_j)$ is an indicator function that returns 1 if $y_i = y_j$ and 0 otherwise. In many applications, the vote is weighted by the distance between the new point and a neighbor, and the decision is influenced more by closer neighbors.

$$\arg\max_{1 \leq i \leq C} \sum_{j=1}^{k} \omega(d(x, x_j)) \cdot 1(y_i, y_j)$$

where $\omega(d(x, x_j))$ is a weight function that is inversely related to the distance $d(x, x_j)$.

In this work, we extend the weighted kNN approach and compute the sensitivity of a new asset based on the distance to its kNN assets in the training data and the sensitivity scores of the kNN assets. When the sensitivity scores are not provided for the training data, we can assign the same value to all the training data. The sensitivity of a new asset $\mathcal{A}$, $\mathcal{V}(\mathcal{A})$, is then defined as a weighted average score of its k-nearest neighbors among the *known* sensitive assets, $\{\mathcal{S}_1, \ldots, \mathcal{S}_k\}$.

$$\mathcal{V}(\mathcal{A}) = \sum_{i=1}^{k} e^{-d(\mathcal{A}, \mathcal{S}_i)} \cdot \mathcal{V}(\mathcal{S}_i) \tag{1}$$

$\mathcal{V}(\mathcal{S}_i)$ is the sensitivity value of $\mathcal{S}_i$, and $e^{-d(\mathcal{A}, \mathcal{S}_i)}$ is the weight function where $d(\mathcal{A}, \mathcal{S}_i)$ is the Euclidean distance of the two assets. The kNN-based sensitivity estimation is described in Algorithm 1.

Algorithm 1. Sensitivity Estimation based on k-Nearest Neighbors

---

1: **Input:** Unlabeled assets $\mathcal{A} = \{\mathcal{A}_1, \ldots, \mathcal{A}_n\}$, a set of *known* sensitive assets $\mathcal{S} = \{\mathcal{S}_1, \ldots, \mathcal{S}_m\}$, and, *optionally*, the sensitivity scores of $\mathcal{S}$, $\mathcal{V} = \{\mathcal{V}(\mathcal{S}_1), \ldots, \mathcal{V}(\mathcal{S}_m)\}$
2: **Output:** Ordered list of assets $\mathcal{A}' = \{\mathcal{A}'_1, \ldots, \mathcal{A}'_n\}$, where $\mathcal{V}(\mathcal{A}'_i) \geq \mathcal{V}(\mathcal{A}'_{i+1})$
3: **for** $\mathcal{A}_i \in \mathcal{A}$ **do**
4:     $kNN(\mathcal{A}_i) \leftarrow \{\mathcal{S}_i, \ldots, \mathcal{S}_k\}$, k assets from $\mathcal{S}$ that are closest to $\mathcal{A}_i$
5:     Compute the sensitivity of $\mathcal{A}_i$, $\mathcal{V}(\mathcal{A}_i)$ using Equation (1)
6: Sort $\mathcal{A}$ in descending order of $\mathcal{V}(\mathcal{A}_i)$

3.2 Clustering-Based Method

The clustering-based method considers that the assets are from many different business units such as product development groups, HR or Finance department, and, therefore, they will naturally form distinct groups. Suppose only one sensitive asset from the HR department is included in the training data. With the kNN method with $k > 1$, the sensitivity of assets from the HR department will be measured with assets from other departments. By taking into account the subgroups in the dataset, we can determine the sensitivity level of an asset using the sensitive assets from the same subgroup.

First, a clustering technique is used to discover these underlying subgroups in the data set. We then generate the centroid of the sensitive assets in each cluster, which is the the mean of the sensitive assets in the cluster. Similarly to the kNN-based method, we measure the sensitivity of an asset $\mathcal{A}$ as the weighted average score of the k-nearest centroids as described in Algorithm 2. The difference of the kNN-based approach and the clustering-based approach is illustrated in Figure 4.

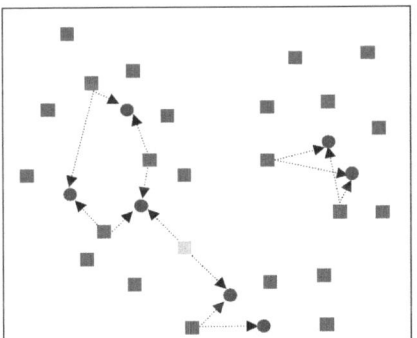

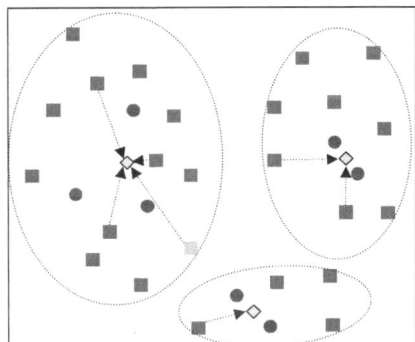

(a) kNN-based method where k=2   (b) Nearest centroid-based method

Fig. 4. Illustrations of the kNN and Clustering-based methods for sensitivity estimation. The circle symbols denote known sensitive assets and the square symbols denote unlabeled assets. The diamond symbols in 4(b) represent the centroid of the sensitive assets in each cluster. Note that the sensitivity of the light-colored (yellow) square is measured with a sensitive asset from a different cluster in Figure 4(a).

Algorithm 2. Sensitivity Estimation based on k-Nearest Centroids

1: **Input:** Unlabeled assets $\mathcal{A} = \{\mathcal{A}_1, \ldots, \mathcal{A}_n\}$, a set of *known* sensitive assets $\mathcal{S} = \{\mathcal{S}_1, \ldots, \mathcal{S}_m\}$, and, *optionally*, the sensitivity scores of $\mathcal{S}$, $\mathcal{V} = \{\mathcal{V}(\mathcal{S}_1), \ldots, \mathcal{V}(\mathcal{S}_m)\}$

2: **Output:** Ordered list of assets $\mathcal{A}' = \{\mathcal{A}'_1, \ldots, \mathcal{A}'_n\}$, where $V(\mathcal{A}'_i) \geq V(\mathcal{A}'_{i+1})$

3: Cluster all assets, $\mathcal{A} \cup \mathcal{S}$, into K subgroups, $\mathcal{C} = \{\mathcal{C}_1, \ldots, \mathcal{C}_K\}$.

4: **for** $\mathcal{C}_i \in C$ **do**

5:     $\mathcal{S}^i \leftarrow \mathcal{C}_i \cap \mathcal{S}$ // the set of sensitive assets in $\mathcal{C}_i$

6:     $\bar{C}_i \leftarrow$ the centroid of $\mathcal{S}^i$

7:     $\mathcal{V}(\bar{C}_i) \leftarrow$ the mean sensitivity value of $\mathcal{S}^i$

8: **for** $\mathcal{A}_i \in \mathcal{A}$ **do**

9:     Let $\bar{C} = \{\bar{C}_1, \ldots, \bar{C}_k\}$ be the k nearest centroids from $\mathcal{A}_i$

10:     $\mathcal{V}(\mathcal{A}_i) \leftarrow \sum_{i=1}^{k} e^{-d(\mathcal{A}, \bar{C}_i)} \cdot \mathcal{V}(\bar{C}_i)$

11: Sort $\mathcal{A}$ in descending order of $\mathcal{V}(\mathcal{A}_i)$

3.3 kNN Method with Distance Metric Learning

The accuracy of many machine learning algorithms including both *k*NN classification and clustering is heavily dependant on the distance (or similarity) metric used for the input data. However, when the data are in a high-dimensional space, the selection of an optimal distance metric is not intuitive. Distance metric learning is a machine learning technique that aims to automatically learn a distance metric for the input data from a given set of labeled data points. The basic idea is to learn a distance metric that puts instances from a same class closer to each other and instances from different classes far apart. Recently, many studies have demonstrated that an automatically learned distance metric significantly improves the accuracy of classification, clustering and retrieval tasks [17,14,20].

Distance metric learning algorithms are further divided into global distance metric learning and local distance metric learning. Global distance metric learning algorithms learn a distance metric that satisfy all the pairwise constraints, i.e., keep all the data points within the same classes close, while separating all the data points from different classes. Local distance metric learning algorithms, on the other hand, learn a distance metric satisfying local constraints, and has been shown to be more effective than global distance learning for multi-modal data.

In this study, we apply a global distance learning algorithm and a local distance metric learning algorithm to transform the feature space. For global learning, we apply Relevant Component Analysis (RCA) [17] to learn a distance metric as proposed in [2]. The RCA-based distant metric learning algorithm learns a Mahalanobis distance metric using only equivalence constraints (i.e., instances in the same class) and finds a new feature space with the most relevant features from the constraints. It maximizes the similarity between the original data set X and the new representation Y constrained by the mutual information $I(X, Y)$. By projecting X into the new space through feature transformation, two data objects from the same class have a smaller distance in Y than in X. For local distance metric learning, we apply the Large Margin Nearest Neighbor (LMNN) distance learning algorithm [14]. The LMNN algorithm also learns a Mahalanobis distance metric, but it identifies k-nearest neighbors, determined by Euclidean distance, that share the same label and enforces the k-nearest neighbors belong to the same class while instances from different classes are separated by a large margin.

After the feature space projection using the distance metric learning algorithms, we apply the kNN-based sensitivity estimation method described in section 3.1.

4   Experimental Results and Evaluation

To validate the algorithms, we conducted experiments with a real life data set comprising about 8,500 computers. In this section, we describe in detail the experimental settings and evaluation results. Henceforth, we denote the kNN-based method using the original feature space as kNN, the centroid-based method as $Centroid$, the kNN method with the LMNN distance metric learning as $LMNN$, and the kNN method with the RCA distance metric learning as RCA.

4.1   Data

The computers used in the experiments were extracted from DNS logs collected in the authors' organization over 3.5 months from April, 1, 2012 to July, 15, 2012. We extracted 12,521 unique computers for which we were able to identify the user but discarded the computers with only one user or fewer than three look-up requests, resulting in 8,472 computers. We use the 8,472 computers for training and evaluation of our models–80% of the computers for training and 20% for evaluation respectively. Using the mapping of IP address to user described in section 2.1, we identified 2,804 unique users for the 8,472 computers.

In a separate effort, the company had attempted to manually compile a list of servers, for the purpose of disaster recovery and business continuity, that host important applications of the company. The list provides the server names and their business criticality value (BCV) assigned manually by domain experts. Each computer is assigned with a BCV from five BCV categories–BCV1 to BCV5–and each BCV category is associated with a numeric value from 10 (BCV1) to 50 (BCV5). We found 253 servers from this list in our collected data set, and, thus, use the 253 servers as the labeled (i.e., ground truth) data for this study. The ground truth data account for about 3% of the experimental data, and we use the data set for both training and evaluation of the algorithms. Table 5 and Figure 6 show the size of the experimental data, the size of the ground truth set, and the distribution of the ground truth data over the five BCV categories.

4.2   Evaluation Metrics

We observe that the problem of identifying sensitive assets can be cast as an information retrieval (IR) problem — finding relevant (sensitive) assets in a large collection of assets and ranking them according to their relevance. This allows us to apply the evaluation metrics developed for IR such as recall, precision and discounted cumulative gain (DCG) [19,11,9] to validate the performance of our algorithms.

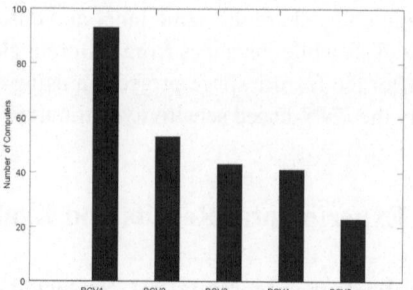

No. of computers	8,472
No. of unique users	2,804
No. of known sensitive computers	253

Fig. 5. Experimental data set

Fig. 6. Distribution of the ground truth data across the business criticality values

Precision and Recall: Precision and recall are widely used metrics for binary decision problems including information retrieval and pattern recognition. In a binary decision problem, a system labels data samples either positive or negative. Precision measures the fraction of samples classified as positive that are truly positive, and recall measures the fraction of positive samples that are correctly classified.

$$Precision = \frac{|\{\text{true positives in the result}\}|}{|\{\text{all samples in the result}\}|} \quad Recall = \frac{|\{\text{true positives in the result}\}|}{|\{\text{all positive samples}\}|}$$

In a ranked retrieval context as in our study and in most web search engines, precision and recall are typically measured at the top n results. Further, when the class distribution is skewed, Precision-Recall (PR) curves are often used. A PR curve is generated by plotting the precision at different levels of recall rates, and provides a more comprehensive view on the system's performance.

Discounted Cumulative Gain (DCG): In addition to ranking the results, when the relevance of an instance is measured using a multi-scale rating (e.g., from *completely relevant* to *completely irrelevant*), the quality of the results can be more precisely measured using a graded relevance scale of the results. For instance, two search engines can produce the same precision and recall, but the search engine that retrieves documents with a higher relevance scale at the top of the results is more useful.

DCG measures the usefulness (or gain) of a search result based on its position in a search result list. The gain of each result is discounted logarithmically proportional to its position in the ranked list, and the DCG of a system is defined as the accumulated gain from the top of the result list to the bottom [9].

$$DCG = REL_1 + \sum_{r=2}^{n} \frac{REL_r}{\log_2(r)}$$

where REL_r is the relevance score of the result at rank r, and n is the number of instances in the result.

For IR systems, the relevance of a search result is typically judged using a 5-scale rating from 0 (completely irrelevant) to 4 (completely relevant). For our study, we use the five BCVs as the relevance scores of computer assets by mapping the BCVs of [10, 50] into [1, 5], and by assigning 0 to all other computer assets.

4.3   Baseline Methods

We designed two hypothetical baseline methods to compare our algorithms with. The first baseline produces a random ordering of the assets (hereafter denoted as *Random*). The second baseline is based on the assumption that assets used by high-rank employees are more sensitive than those used by low-rank employees. This method (denoted as *OrgRank*) produces a ranking of the assets by sorting the assets in descending order by *Rank-High*, *Rank-Middle*, and *Rank-Low* (the *Rank* features described in Table 1).

4.4   Experimental Results

In the experiments, each algorithm produces a ranked list of the computer assets, and we compare the six algorithms based on precision, recall and DCG. We set k to 3 for all kNN-based methods, and, for the clustering-based method, we generated 150 clusters for the data and $k = 1$ for similarity estimation. The evaluation is conducted using 5-fold cross validation methods. In a 5-fold cross validation, the ground truth data is randomly divided into 5 equally sized subgroups, and each of the subgroups is used for evaluation. At i-th validation ($1 \leq i \leq 5$), the i-th subgroup (i.e., 20% of the data) is withheld to evaluate the model's performance, and the remaining four subgroups (i.e., 80% of the data) are used to train the model. Since cross validation does random splitting of the ground truth data, we conducted 5-fold cross validation 10 times, and all the results reported here are the average performance of the 10 runs. The results of the *Random* baseline system is also the average performance from 10 random orderings.

Precision and Recall: First, we show the precision-recall curves of the algorithms. The precisions are measured at 20 different recall rates ranging from 0.05 to 1 as shown in Figure 7(a). All four algorithms yield significantly higher precision up to $recall=0.2$ than the baseline systems, with *LMNN* outperforming the others. We notice that the precision drops rapidly as the recall increases. This is mainly due to the high skew in the class distribution in our data set (only 0.6% of samples are positive).

Next, we examine recall in more detail, as high recall is more desirable for the applications with highly imbalanced data. Figure 7(b) shows the recall levels measured at the top n% ($5\% \leq n \leq 30\%$) of the most sensitive assets in the ranked lists. As we can see, our algorithms produce much higher recall than the baseline systems, and the distance metric learning methods outperform the other algorithms across all levels of n. For instance, *RCA* achieves about 300% and 57% higher recall than *Random* at top 5% and top 30% respectively. Interestingly, *OrgRank* performs very poorly and produces much lower precision and recall than *Random*.

Discounted Cumulative Gain: Figure 8 shows the DCG values at each rank in the ranked list of the data. As noted, DCG is a better metric for applications where the relevance is judged in multi-scales. The comparison of DCG clearly show that our

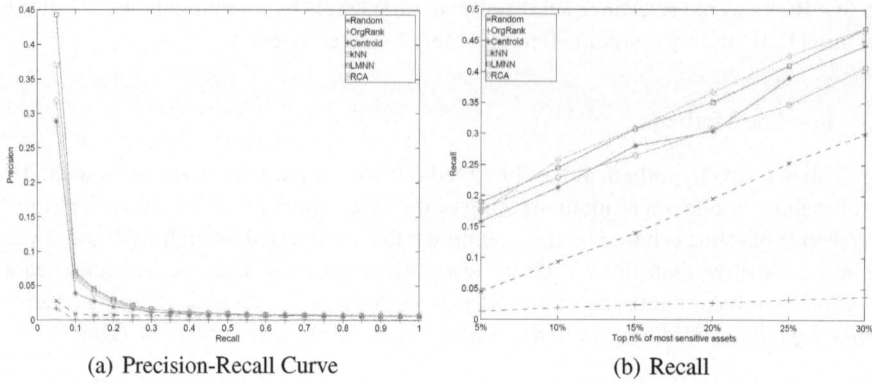

(a) Precision-Recall Curve   (b) Recall

Fig. 7. Comparison of the precision and recall. Figure 7(a) shows the precision at different recall levels. Figure 7(b) shows the recall measured at top $n\%$ of the ranked data.

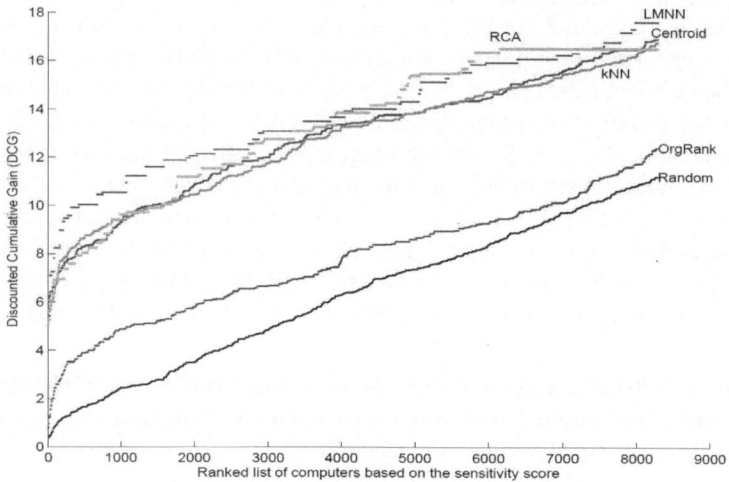

Fig. 8. The discounted cumulative gains of different algorithms. The x-axis represents the ranks of the data in descending order, i.e., x=1 represents the most sensitive computer ranked by each algorithm.

algorithms perform significantly better than the baseline methods, and *LMNN* performs slightly better than the other algorithms. Further, our algorithms converge much more quickly achieving high DCGs early in the ranked list. This shows that our algorithms are able to assign high ranks to highly sensitive assets. We also notice that the *OrgRank* method performs better than *Random* when measured by DCG.

5   Related Work

There have been little work on automatically measuring the sensitivity (or criticality) of IT assets. A related body of work has been studied by [3,10,12,13,15]. Park *et al.* [12,13]

and Beaver *et al.* [4] proposed methods for scoring the value of the information stored in host computers using text processing and classification. While these methods are very useful for data security, they can not be applied to other types of IT assets. Further, these methods require direct access to the assets to crawl the data, thus, they are harder to apply to a large scale heterogenous environment. Beaudoin and Eng presented a method for computing the values of network assets based on the network topology, systemic dependencies among the network assets and the interfaces between the network [3]. They manually assign the initial values to some of the sources called "user services", and percolate the values from the user services back to the supporting assets using a graph mining algorithm. Sawilla and Ou presented *AssetRank*, a generalization of the PageRank algorithm, which calculates the importance of an asset to an attacker [15]. Their approach uses the dependency relationships in the attack graph and the vulnerability attributes to compute the relative importance of attacker assets rather than the importance of the asset itself. Kim and Kang [10] described a method for scoring and ranking cyber assets using a small number of hand-crafted features. They utilize three types of features – static factors (e.g., the criticality of application on the asset and value of data on the asset), static value-sensitive factors (e.g., who owns the machine) and dynamic value-sensitive factors (e.g., who is currently logged onto the machine). Crucially, their features are hard to extract automatically, and, thus, they extract the feature values in five-point scale from domain experts using a user survey.

6 Discussion and Conclusions

In this paper, we proposed algorithms for automatically scoring IT assets with a minimum of human intervention. Our algorithms provide several technical advantages that make our system more efficient, scalable, and privacy preserving than other existing methods. First, our methods do not require access to the assets or any detailed knowledge about the targets. Second, the features are very domain-independent and can be mostly extracted from access logs. Third, we apply semi-supervised machine learning approaches to minimize human efforts.

We confirmed through experiments that our algorithms perform much better than a random ordering or a simple hypothesis-based approach. Further, the performance improvement was larger when the multi-scale sensitivity values were taken into account. This indicates that our algorithms were able to retrieve assets with higher scores at higher ranks. The experiments also demonstrated that distance metric learning techniques improves the accuracy of the algorithms.

The system envisions to provide fine-grained security on high-value enterprise assets and help large enterprises manage the security risks associated with these assets. Firstly, the fine grained estimation of sensitivity values can be used to define access control policies based on the sensitivity levels. For instance, we can define access control policies granting access to assets with sensitivity levels up to a defined threshold. Another application of the dynamic computation of sensitivity values is in risk-based security methods. These methods typically rely on bounding the worst case damage caused by incorrect access control decisions. The ability to dynamically estimate the sensitivity values would make risk based methods effective and applicable in practice.

References

1. Aksoy, S., Haralick, R.M.: Feature normalization and likelihood-based similarity measures for image retrieval. Pattern Recognition Letters 22(5), 563–582 (2001)
2. Bar-Hillel, A., Hertz, T., Shental, N., Weinshall, D.: Learning distance functions using equivalence relations. In: Proceedings of International Conference on Machine Learning, ICML, pp. 11–18 (2003)
3. Beaudoin, L., Eng, P.: Asset valuation technique for network management and security. In: Proceedings of the Sixth IEEE International Conference on Data Mining Workshops, ICDMW 2006, pp. 718–721. IEEE Computer Society (2006)
4. Beaver, J.M., Patton, R.M., Potok, T.E.: An approach to the automated determination of host information value. In: IEEE Symposium on Computational Intelligence in Cyber Security, CICS, pp. 92–99. IEEE (2011)
5. Bell, D.E., LaPadula, L.J.: Secure computer systems: Mathematical foundations. MITRE Corporation, 1 (1973)
6. Blei, D., Ng, A., Jordan, M.: Latent dirichlet allocation. Journal of Machine Learning Research 3, 993–1022 (2003)
7. Cole, E.: Advanced Persistent Threat: Understanding the Danger and How to Protect Your Organization. Syngress (2012)
8. Cover, T., Hart, P.: Nearest neighbor pattern classification. IEEE Transactions on Information Theory 13(1), 21–27 (1967)
9. Jarvelin, K., Kekalainen, J.: Cumulated gain-based evaluation of ir techniques. ACM Transactions on Information Systems (4), 422–446 (2002)
10. Kim, A., Kang, M.H.: Determining asset criticality for cyber defense. Technical Report NRL/MR/5540–11-9350, NAVAL RESEARCH LAB WASHINGTON (2011)
11. Manning, C.D., Raghavan, P., Schütze, H.: Introduction to Information Retrieval. Cambridge University Press (2008)
12. Park, Y., Gates, S.C., Teiken, W., Chari, S.N.: System for automatic estimation of data sensitivity with applications to access control and other applications. In: Proceedings of The ACM Symposium on Access Control Models and Technologies, SACMAT (2011)
13. Park, Y., Gates, S.C., Teiken, W., Cheng, P.-C.: An experimental study on the measurement of data sensitivitys. In: Proceedings of Workshop on Building Analysis Datasets and Gathering Experience Returns for Security, BADGERS, pp. 68–75 (2011)
14. Weinberger, K.Q., Blitzer, J., Saul, L.K.: Distance metriclearning for large margin nearest neighbor classification. In: Proceedings of the Neural Information Processing Systems Conference, NIPS (2005)
15. Sawilla, R.E., Ou, X.: Identifying critical attack assets in dependency attack graphs. In: Jajodia, S., Lopez, J. (eds.) ESORICS 2008. LNCS, vol. 5283, pp. 18–34. Springer, Heidelberg (2008)
16. Shannon, C.E.: A Mathematical Theory of Communication. Bell System Technical Journal (1948)
17. Shental, N., Hertz, T., Weinshall, D., Pavel, M.: Adjustment learning and relevant component analysis. In: Heyden, A., Sparr, G., Nielsen, M., Johansen, P. (eds.) ECCV 2002, Part IV. LNCS, vol. 2353, pp. 776–790. Springer, Heidelberg (2002)
18. Stamati-Koromina, V., Ilioudis, C., Overill, R., Georgiadis, C.K., Stamatis, D.: Insider threats in corporate environments: a case study for data leakage prevention. In: Proceedings of the Fifth Balkan Conference in Informatics, BCI 2012, pp. 271–274 (2012)
19. Voorhees, E.M.: Variations in relevance judgments and the measurement of retrieval effectiveness. In: Proceedings of the 21 st Annual International ACM SIGIR Conference on Research and Development in Information Retrieval, vol. 24, pp. 315–323 (1998)
20. Yang, L.: Distance metric learning: A comprehensive survey (2006)

Practical Secure Logging:
Seekable Sequential Key Generators

Giorgia Azzurra Marson[1] and Bertram Poettering[2]

[1] CASED & TU Darmstadt
[2] Information Security Group at Royal Holloway, University of London

Abstract. In computer forensics, log files are indispensable resources that support auditors in identifying and understanding system threats and security breaches. If such logs are recorded locally, i.e., stored on the monitored machine itself, the problem of *log authentication* arises: if a system intrusion takes place, the intruder might be able to manipulate the log entries and cover her traces. Mechanisms that cryptographically protect collected log messages from manipulation should ideally have two properties: they should be *forward-secure* (the adversary gets no advantage from learning current keys when aiming at forging past log entries), and they should be *seekable* (the auditor can verify the integrity of log entries in any order, at virtually no computational cost).

We propose a new cryptographic primitive, a *seekable sequential key generator* (SSKG), that combines these two properties and has direct application in secure logging. We rigorously formalize the required security properties and give a provably-secure construction based on the integer factorization problem. We further optimize the scheme in various ways, preparing it for real-world deployment. As a byproduct, we develop the notion of a *shortcut one-way permutation* (SCP), which might be of independent interest.

Our work is highly relevant in practice. Indeed, our SSKG implementation has become part of the logging service of the *systemd* system manager, a core component of many modern commercial Linux-based operating systems.

1 Introduction

Pseudorandom generators. A pseudorandom generator (PRG) is an unkeyed cryptographic primitive that deterministically expands a fixed-length random seed to a longer random-looking string [18]. Most often, PRGs find application in environments where truly random bits are a scarce resource; for instance, once a system managed to harvest an initial seed of, say, 128 uniformly distributed bits from a suitable (possibly physical) entropy source, a PRG can securely stretch this seed to a much larger number of bits. While such mechanisms are indispensable for constrained devices like smartcards, (variants of) PRGs are also long-serving components of modern PC operating systems. A well-known example is the /dev/urandom device available in virtually all current Linux/UNIX derivates.

J. Crampton, S. Jajodia, and K. Mayes (Eds.): ESORICS 2013, LNCS 8134, pp. 111–128, 2013.
© Springer-Verlag Berlin Heidelberg 2013

Other applications exploit the feature that the output of PRGs can be *re-generated*: as PRGs are deterministic primitives, the entire output sequence can be reconstructed from the initial seed, whenever needed. This directly allows employment of PRGs for symmetric encryption (formally, one could view stream ciphers like RC4[1] or AES-CTR as PRGs with practically infinite output length), but also in distributed systems, where locally separate agents can synchronously generate identical sequences of (pseudo-)random bits.

For PRGs with very large output length (e.g., stream ciphers) we introduce the notion of seekability; a PRG is *seekable* if, for a fixed seed, 'random access' to the output sequence is possible. For example, the PRG obtained by operating a block cipher in counter mode is seekable: one can quickly jump to any part of the output string by setting the counter value to the right 'address'. In contrast, RC4 is not known to be seekable: presumably, in order to jump to position k in the output string, one has to iterate the cipher k times.

Forward security. The concept of forward security (FS), best-known from the context of cryptographic key establishment (KE), expresses the inability of an adversary to gain advantage from the 'corruption' of entities. For example, consider an instance of a two-party public key-authenticated KE protocol. We say that the established session key enjoys *forward security*[2] if an adversary cannot obtain any useful information about that key, even if participants, after completing the protocol instance, surrender their respective secret keys. In key exchange, forward security is recognized as one of the most fundamental security goals [30,8].

Although less commonly seen, the notion of forward security extends to other cryptographic settings and primitives. For instance, in *forward-secure public key encryption* (FS-PKE, [7]), time is subdivided into a discrete number of epochs $t_0, t_1, \ldots$, and messages are encrypted in respect to a combination (pk, t_k) of public key and time epoch. Recipients, starting in epoch t_0 with an initial key sk_0, use an update procedure $sk_{i+1} \leftarrow f(sk_i)$ to *evolve* the decryption key from epoch to epoch. An FS-PKE is *correct* if a recipient holding key sk_k can decrypt all ciphertexts addressed to corresponding epoch t_k; it is *forward-secure* if secrecy of all messages addressed to 'past' epochs $t_j, j < k$, is preserved even if the adversary obtains a copy of sk_k. Clearly, FS-PKE only offers a security advantage over plain public key encryption if users securely erase 'expired' decryption keys.

Similarly to FS-PKE, also *forward-secure signature schemes* [2] work with time epochs and evolving keys; briefly speaking, their security properties ensure that an adversary holding an epoch's signing key sk_k cannot forge signatures for prior epochs $t_j, j < k$ (i.e., 'old' signatures remain secure).

Secure logging. Computer log files, whether manually or mechanically evaluated, are among the most essential resources that support system administrators in

---

[1] In fact, practical distinguishing attacks against RC4 are known [11]; RC4 is hence a PRG only 'syntax-wise'.

[2] in the context of key establishment also known as 'forward secrecy'

their day-to-day business. Such files are generated on hosts and communication systems, and record a large variety of system events, including users logging on or off, network requests, memory resources reaching their capacity, malfunctioning of disk drives, and crashing software.

While regular analysis of system logs allows administrators to maintain systems' health and long uptimes, log files are also indispensable in computer forensics, for the identification and comprehension of system intrusions and other security breaches. However, if logs are recorded locally (i.e., on the monitored machine itself) the problem of *log authentication* arises: if a system intrusion takes place, the intruder might be able to manipulate the log entries and cover her traces. So-called 'log sanitizers' aim at frustrating computer forensics and are known to be a standard tool in hackers' arsenal.

Two approaches to avert the threat of adversarial modification of audit logs seem promising. One such option is the deployment of *online logging*. Here, log messages are transferred over a network connection to a remote log sink immediately after their creation, in the expectancy that entries caused by system intrusions have reached their destination before they can be tampered with. As a side effect, online logging might also ease security auditing by the fact that log entries are concentrated at a single point. However, as every local buffering of log records increases the risk of their suppression by the intruder, full-time availability of the log sink is an absolute security requirement in this setting. But observe that the intruder might be able provoke downtimes at the sink (e.g., by running a DOS attack against it) or might disrupt the network connection to it (e.g., by injecting reset packets into TCP connections, jamming wireless connections, etc.). An independent problem comes from the difficulty to select an appropriate level of granularity for the events to be logged. For instance, log files created for forensic analysis might ideally contain verbose information like an individual entry for every file opened, every subprocess started, and so on. Network connections and log sinks might quickly reach their capacities if events are routinely reported in such a high resolution. This holds in particular if log sinks serve multiple monitored hosts simultaneously.

Storing high volume log data is less an issue in *secured local logging* where a networked log sink is not assumed. In such a setting, log messages are protected from adversarial tampering by cryptographic means. It cannot be expected that standard integrity-protecting primitives like message authentication codes (MAC) or signature schemes on their own will suffice to solve the problem of log authentication: a skilled intruder will likely manage to extract corresponding secret keys from corrupted system's memory. Instead, forward-secure signatures and forward-secure message authentication schemes have been proposed for secure logging [29,24,34]. Clearly, local logging can never prevent the intruder from deleting stored entries. However, cryptographic components might ensure that such manipulations are guaranteed to be indicated to the log auditor.

1.1   Contributions, Organization, Applications

The key contribution of this paper is the development of a new cryptographic primitive: a *seekable sequential key generator* (SSKG). Briefly, a *sequential key generator* (SKG) is a stateful PRG that outputs a sequence of fixed-length strings — one per invocation. The essential security property is indistinguishability of these strings from uniformly random. For SSKG, we additionally require seekability, i.e., the existence of an efficient algorithm that allows to jump to any position in the output sequence. For both, SKG and SSKG, we demand that indistinguishability hold with forward security.

This paper is organized as follows. We start in Sections 2 and 3 by formalizing the functionality and security properties of SKG and SSKG. We show that a related primitive by Bellare and Yee securely instantiates an SKG; however, it is not seekable. Aiming at constructing an SSKG, we introduce in Section 4 an auxiliary primitive, a *shortcut one-way permutation* (SCP), that we instantiate in the factoring-based setting. In Section 5 we expose our SSKG; it is particularly efficient, taking only one modular squaring operation per invocation. We conclude in Section 6 by proposing further optimizations that substantially increase efficiency of our SSKG, making it ready for deployment in practice.

We argue that a (seekable) SKG is the ideal primitive to implement a secured local logging system, as described above. The construction is immediate: the strings output by the SKG are used as keys for a MAC which is applied to all log messages. After each authentication tag has been computed and appended to the particular log message, the SKG is evolved to the next state, making the described authentication forward-secure. The log auditor, starting with a copy of the SKG's original seed, can recover all MAC keys and verify authenticity of all log entries. Typically, log auditors will require random access to these MAC keys — SSKGs provide exactly this functionality.

Further applications for SKGs and SSKGs. Potential applications of SKG and SSKG are given not only by secure logging, but also by digital cameras, voice recorders and backup systems [29]. In more detail, digital cameras could be equipped with an authentication mechanism that individually authenticates every photo taken. Such cameras could support modern journalism that, when reporting from armed conflict zones, is more and more reliant on amateurs for the documentation of events; in such settings, where post-incidental (digital) manipulation inherently has to be anticipated, cryptographic SKG-like techniques could support the verification of authenticity of reported images.

1.2   Related Work

Secured local logging. An early proposal to use forward-secure cryptography to protect locally-stored audit logs is by Kelsey and Schneier [20,21,29]. The core of their scheme is an (evolving) 'authentication key': for each time epoch t_i there is a corresponding authentication key A_i. This key is used for multiple purposes: as a MAC key to authenticate all log messages occurring in epoch t_i, for deriving an epoch-specific encryption key K_i by computing $K_i \leftarrow H_0(A_i)$, and for computing next epoch's authentication key via iteration $A_{i+1} \leftarrow H_1(A_i)$ (where H_0, H_1 are hash functions). An implementation of [29] in tamper-resistant hardware is reported by Chong, Peng and Hartel [9]. Unfortunately, the scheme by Kelsey and Schneier lacks a formal security analysis.[3]

The first rigorous analysis of forward-secure secret key cryptography was given by Bellare and Yee [3]. They propose constructions of forward-secure variants of PRGs, symmetric encryption schemes, and message authentication codes, and analyze them in respect to formal security models. We anticipate here that our security definitions are strictly stronger than those from [3], capturing a larger class of application scenarios.

The work of Holt [14] can be seen as an extension of [29]. With *logcrypt*, the author proposes a symmetric scheme and an asymmetric scheme for secure logging. While the former is similar to [29] (but apparently offers provable security), the latter bases on the forward-secure signature scheme by Bellare and Miner [2]. Holt also discusses the efficiency penalties experienced in the asymmetric variant. We finally note that [14] suggests to store regular *metronome entries* in log files in order to thwart truncation attacks where adversary cuts off the most recent set of log entries.

Ma and Tsudik propose deployment of *forward-secure sequential aggregate signatures* for integrity-protected logging [23,24]. Their provably-secure construction builds on compact constant-size authenticators with all-or-nothing security (i.e., if any single log message is suppressed by the adversary, this will be noticed). Such aggregate signatures naturally defend against truncation attacks, making Holt's metronome entries disposable.

Waters *et al.* [32] identify searchable audit logs as an application of identity-based encryption. Here, in order to increase users' privacy, log entries are not only authenticated but also encrypted. This encryption is done in respect to a set of keywords; records encrypted towards such keywords are identifiable and decryptable by agents who hold keyword-dependent private keys.

Another interesting approach towards forward-secure logging was proposed by Yavuz and Ning [33], and Yavuz, Ning, and Reiter [34]. In their scheme, the key evolving procedure and the computation of (aggregatable) authentication tags take not more than a few hash function evaluations and finite field multiplications each; these steps are hence implementable on sensors and other devices with constrained computing power. However, the required workload on verifier's side is much higher: one exponentiation per log entry.

An IETF-standardized secure logging scheme is *signed syslog messages* by Kelsey, Callas, and Clemm [19]. The authors describe an extension to the standard UNIX *syslog* facility that authenticates log entries via a regular signature scheme (e.g., DSA). The scheme, however, does not provide forward security.

We conclude by recommending Itkis' excellent survey on methods in forward-secure cryptography [16].

---

[3] It is, in fact, not difficult to see that the scheme is *generically* insecure (i.e., a security proof cannot exist).

Seekable PRGs. We are not aware of any work so far that focuses on the seekability of PRGs. The observation that block ciphers operated in counter mode can be seen as seekable PRGs, in contrast to most other stream ciphers, is certainly folklore. We point out that the famous Blum-Blum-Shub PRG [4,5] is forward-secure. Moreover, its underlying number-theoretic structure seems to allow for seekability. Unfortunately it is not efficient: the computation of each individual output bit requires one modular squaring.

2   Sequential Key Generators

We introduce *sequential key generators* (SKG) and their security properties. Note that a similar primitive, *stateful generator*, was proposed by Bellare and Yee [3]. However, our syntax is more versatile and our security models are stronger, as we will see. We extend SKGs to (seekable) SSKGs in Section 3.

2.1   Functionality and Syntax

An SKG consists of four algorithms: GenSKG generates a set par of public parameters, GenState0 takes par and outputs an initial state st_0, update procedure Evolve maps each state st_i to a successor state st_{i+1}, and GetKey algorithm derives from any state st_i a corresponding (symmetric) key K_i. Keys $K_0, K_1, \ldots$ are supposed to be used in higher level protocols, for example as keys for symmetric encryption or message authentication schemes.

Typically, SKG instances are not run in a single copy; rather, after distributing 'clones' of initial state st_0 to a given set of parties, several copies of the same SKG instance are run concurrently and independently, potentially on different host systems, not necessarily in synchronization. If Evolve and GetKey algorithms are deterministic, respective sequences $K_0, K_1, \ldots$ of computed symmetric keys will be identical for all copies. This setting is illustrated in Figure 1 and formalized as follows.

Definition 1 (Syntax of SKG). *A sequential key generator is a tuple* SKG = {GenSKG, GenState0, Evolve, GetKey} *of efficient algorithms as follows:*

- GenSKG(1^λ). *On input of security parameter* 1^λ, *this algorithm outputs a set* par *of public parameters.*
- GenState0(par). *On input of public parameters* par, *this algorithm outputs an initial state* st_0.
- Evolve(st_i). *On input of state* st_i, *this deterministic algorithm outputs 'next' state* st_{i+1}. *For convenience, for any* $m \in \mathbb{N}$, *by* Evolve^m *we denote the m-fold composition of* Evolve, *i.e.,* Evolve$^m(\mathsf{st}_i) = \mathsf{st}_{i+m}$.
- GetKey(st_i). *On input of state* st_i, *this deterministic algorithm outputs key* $K_i \in \{0,1\}^{\ell(\lambda)}$, *for a fixed polynomial* ℓ. *For convenience, for any* $m \in \mathbb{N}$, *we write* GetKey$^m(\mathsf{st}_i)$ *for* GetKey(Evolve$^m(\mathsf{st}_i)$).

We also pose the informal requirement on Evolve algorithm that it securely erase state st_i after deriving state st_{i+1} from it. Note that secure erasure is generally considered difficult to achieve and requires special care [12].

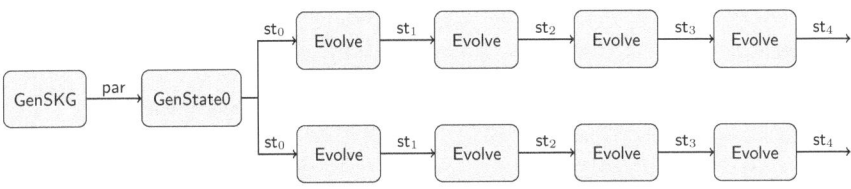

Fig. 1. Interplay of GenSKG, GenState0, and Evolve algorithms of an SKG. The figure shows two copies of the same SKG instance running in parallel. GetKey algorithm can be applied to each intermediate state st_i to derive key K_i.

2.2 Security Requirements

The fundamental security property of SKGs is the indistinguishability of keys K_i from random strings of the same length. Intuitively, for any n of adversary $\mathcal{A}$'s choosing, target key K_n is required to be indistinguishable from random even if $\mathcal{A}$ has access to all other keys K_i, $i \neq n$. This feature ensures generic composability of SKGs with applications that rely on uniformly and independently distributed keys K_i. In addition to the indistinguishability requirement, forward security demands that an 'old' key K_n remain secure even when $\mathcal{A}$ learns state st_m, for any $m > n$ (e.g., by means of a computer break-in).

We give two game-based definitions of these indistinguishability notions: one with and one without forward security.

Definition 2 (IND and IND-FS Security of SKG). *A sequential key generator* SKG *is* indistinguishable against adaptive adversaries (IND) *if for all efficient adversaries* $\mathcal{A} = (\mathcal{A}_1, \mathcal{A}_2)$ *that interact in experiments* $\mathrm{Expt}^{\mathrm{IND},b}$ *from Figure 2 the following advantage function is negligible, where the probabilities are taken over the random coins of the experiment (including over $\mathcal{A}$'s randomness):*

$$\mathrm{Adv}^{\mathrm{IND}}_{\mathrm{SKG},\mathcal{A}}(\lambda) = \left| \Pr\left[\mathrm{Expt}^{\mathrm{IND},1}_{\mathrm{SKG},\mathcal{A}}(1^\lambda) = 1 \right] - \Pr\left[\mathrm{Expt}^{\mathrm{IND},0}_{\mathrm{SKG},\mathcal{A}}(1^\lambda) = 1 \right] \right| \ .$$

The SKG is indistinguishable with forward security against adaptive adversaries (IND-FS) *if analogously defined advantage function* $\mathrm{Adv}^{\mathrm{IND\text{-}FS}}_{\mathrm{SKG},\mathcal{A}}(\lambda)$ *is negligible.*

It is not difficult to see that the IND-FS notion is strictly stronger than the IND notion. The proof of Lemma 1 appears in the full version [25, Appendix A].

Lemma 1 (IND-FS $\Rightarrow$ IND). *Any sequential key generator* SKG *that is indistinguishable with forward security against adaptive adversaries is also indistinguishable against adaptive adversaries.*

2.3 Comparison with Stateful Generators

Stateful generators, first described by Bellare and Yee [3, Section 2.2], aim at similar applications as SKGs. Syntactically, the two primitives are essentially

$\text{Expt}_{\text{SKG},\mathcal{A}}^{\text{IND},b}(1^\lambda)$:
  (a) $\text{KList} \leftarrow \emptyset$
  (b) $\text{par} \leftarrow_R \text{GenSKG}(1^\lambda)$
  (c) $\text{st}_0 \leftarrow_R \text{GenState0}(\text{par})$
  (d) $(state, n) \leftarrow_R \mathcal{A}_1^{\mathcal{O}_{\text{Key}}}(\text{par})$
    $-$ If $\mathcal{A}$ queries $\mathcal{O}_{\text{Key}}(i)$:
      (a) $\text{KList} \leftarrow \text{KList} \cup \{i\}$
      (b) $K_i \leftarrow \text{GetKey}^i(\text{st}_0)$
      (c) Answer $\mathcal{A}$ with K_i
  (e) $K_n^0 \leftarrow_R \{0,1\}^{\ell(\lambda)}$
  (f) $K_n^1 \leftarrow \text{GetKey}^n(\text{st}_0)$
  (g) $b' \leftarrow_R \mathcal{A}_2^{\mathcal{O}_{\text{Key}}}(state, K_n^b)$
    $-$ Answer $\mathcal{O}_{\text{Key}}$ queries as above
  (h) Return 0 if $n \in \text{KList}$
  (i) Return b'

$\text{Expt}_{\text{SKG},\mathcal{A}}^{\text{IND-FS},b}(1^\lambda)$:
  (a) $\text{KList} \leftarrow \emptyset$
  (b) $\text{par} \leftarrow_R \text{GenSKG}(1^\lambda)$
  (c) $\text{st}_0 \leftarrow_R \text{GenState0}(\text{par})$
  (d) $(state, n, m) \leftarrow_R \mathcal{A}_1^{\mathcal{O}_{\text{Key}}}(\text{par})$
    $-$ Answer $\mathcal{O}_{\text{Key}}$ queries as in Expt^{IND}
  (e) $K_n^0 \leftarrow_R \{0,1\}^{\ell(\lambda)}$
  (f) $K_n^1 \leftarrow \text{GetKey}^n(\text{st}_0)$
  (g) $\text{st}_m \leftarrow \text{Evolve}^m(\text{st}_0)$
  (h) $b' \leftarrow_R \mathcal{A}_2^{\mathcal{O}_{\text{Key}}}(state, \text{st}_m, K_n^b)$
    $-$ Answer $\mathcal{O}_{\text{Key}}$ queries as in Expt^{IND}
  (i) Return 0 if $n \in \text{KList}$ or $m \leq n$
  (j) Return b'

Fig. 2. Security experiments for SKG without and with forward security

identical. However, the security definition of stateful generators is weaker and less versatile than the one of SKGs. Concretely, in the (game-based) security definition for stateful generators, after having incremental access to a sequence $k_0, k_1, \ldots$ of keys that are either all real (i.e., $k_i = K_i \,\forall i$) or all random (i.e., $k_i \in_R \{0,1\}^{\ell(\lambda)} \,\forall i$), the adversary eventually requests to see the 'current' state st_m and, based upon the result, outputs a guess on whether keys $k_0, \ldots, k_{m-1}$ were actually real or random. Important here is the observation that an adversary that corrupts a state st_m *cannot* request access to keys K_i, $i > m$, before making this corruption (in contrast to our model). This is a severe limitation in contexts where multiple parties evolve states of the same SKG instance independently of each other and in an asynchronous manner; for instance, in the secure logging scenario, the adversary might *first* observe the log auditor verifying MAC tags on 'current' time epochs and *then* decide to corrupt a monitored host that is out of synchronization, e.g., because it is powered down and hence didn't evolve its state. As such concurrent and asynchronous conditions are not considered in the model by Bellare and Yee, in some practically relevant settings the security of the constructions from [3] should not be assumed.

2.4 A Simple Construction

It does not seem difficult to construct SKGs from standard cryptographic primitives. Indeed, many of the stateful generators proposed in [3], constructed from PRGs and PRFs, are in fact IND-FS-secure SKGs. For concreteness, we reproduce a simple PRG-based design. Its security is analysed in [3, Theorem 1].

Construction 1 (PRG-based SKG [3]) *Let* $G : \{0,1\}^\lambda \to \{0,1\}^{\lambda+\ell(\lambda)}$ *be a PRG, where for each* $x \in \{0,1\}^\lambda$ *we write* $G(x)$ *as* $G(x) = G_L(x) \| G_R(x)$ *with* $G_L(x) \in \{0,1\}^\lambda$ *and* $G_R(x) \in \{0,1\}^{\ell(\lambda)}$. *Let then* GenSKG *output the empty string,* GenState0 *sample* $\text{st}_0 \leftarrow_R \{0,1\}^\lambda$, $\text{Evolve}(\text{st}_i)$ *output* $G_L(\text{st}_i)$, *and* $\text{GetKey}(\text{st}_i)$ *output* $G_R(\text{st}_i)$.

3   Seekable Sequential Key Generators

We have seen that secure SKGs exist and are not too difficult to construct. Moreover, the scheme from Construction 1 is efficient. Indeed, if it is instantiated with a hash function-based PRG, invocations of Evolve and GetKey algorithms take only a small (constant) number of hash function evaluations. However, this assessment of efficiency is adequate only if SKG's keys K_i are used (and computed) in sequential order. We argue that in many potential fields of application such access structures are not given; instead, random access to the keys is required, likely implying a considerable efficiency penalty if keys need to be computed iteratively via $K_i \leftarrow \mathsf{GetKey}^i(\mathsf{st}_0)$. The following examples illustrate that random access patterns do not intrinsically contradict the envisioned sequential nature of SKGs.

Consider a host that uses SKG's keys K_i to authenticate continuously incurring log messages. A second copy of the same SKG instance would be run by the log auditor. From time to time the latter might want to check the integrity of an arbitrary selection of these messages[4]. Observe that this scenario does not really correspond to the setting from Figure 1: While the upper SKG copy might represent the host that evolves keys in the expected linear order $K_i \rightarrow K_{i+1}$, the auditor (running the independent second copy) would actually need non-sequential access to SKG's keys.

For a second example in secure logging, assume SKG's epochs are coupled to absolute time intervals (e.g., one epoch per second). If a host is powered up after a long down-time, in order to resynchronize its SKG state, it is required to do a 'fast-forward' over a large number of epochs. Ideally, an SKG would support the option to skip an arbitrary number of Evolve steps in short time[5].

A variant of SKG that explicitly offers random access capabilities is introduced in this section. We claim that many practical applications can widely benefit from the extended functionality. Observe that the advantage of SSKGs over SKGs is purely efficiency-wise; in particular, the definition of SSKG's security will be (almost) identical to the one for SKGs.

3.1   Functionality and Syntax

When comparing to regular SKGs, the distinguishing property of *seekable sequential key generators* (SSKG) is that keys K_i can be computed *directly* from initial state st_0 and index i, i.e., without executing the Evolve procedure i times. The corresponding new algorithm, Seek, and its relation to the other SKG algorithms is visualized in Figure 3. For reasons that will become clear later, when extending SKG's syntax towards SSKG, in addition to introducing the Seek algorithm we also had to slightly adapt the signature of the GenSKG algorithm:

---

[4] For example, after a zero-day vulnerability in a software product run on the monitored host becomes public, the log auditor might want to retrospectively look for specific irregularities in log entries related to that vulnerability.

[5] Clearly, a (fast-)forward algorithm with execution time linear in the number δ of skipped epochs is trivially achievable. The question is: can we do better than $O(\delta)$?

Definition 3 (Syntax of SSKG). *A* seekable sequential key generator *is a tuple* SSKG = {GenSSKG, GenState0, Evolve, Seek, GetKey} *of efficient algorithms as follows:*

- GenSSKG(1^λ). *On input of security parameter* 1^λ, *this algorithm outputs a set* par *of public parameters and a seeking key* sk.
- GenState0, Evolve, GetKey *as for SKGs (cf. Definition 1).*
- Seek(sk, st_0, m). *On input of seeking key* sk, *initial state* st_0, *and* $m \in \mathbb{N}$, *this deterministic algorithm returns a state* st_m.

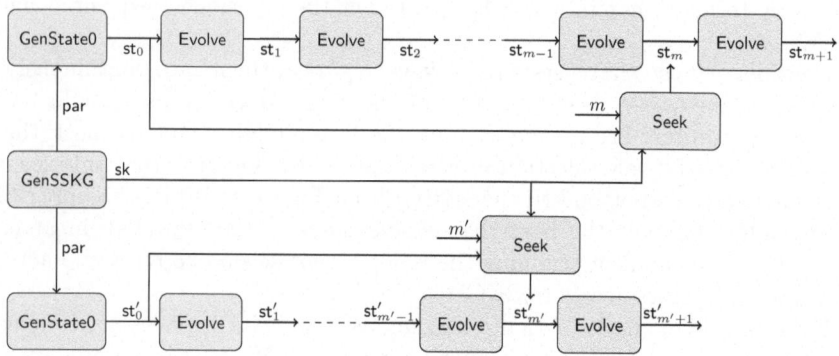

Fig. 3. Interplay of the different SSKG algorithms. The figure shows two independent SSKG instances running in parallel. Given seeking key sk and respective instance's initial state st_0, one can seek directly to any arbitrary state st_m. As in SKGs, GetKey algorithm can be applied to any intermediate state st_i to derive key K_i.

In contrast to SKGs, for SSKGs we need to explicitly require consistency of keys computed with Seek and Evolve algorithms:

Definition 4 (Correctness of SSKG). *A* seekable sequential key generator SSKG *is* correct *if, for all* $\lambda \in \mathbb{N}$, *all* (par, sk) $\leftarrow_R$ GenSSKG(1^λ), *and all* $\mathsf{st}_0 \leftarrow_R$ GenState0(par), *we have that* Seek(sk, st_0, m) = Evolve^m(st_0) *for all* $m \in \mathbb{N}$.

Remark 1 (Security notions IND *and* IND-FS *for SSKG).* Indistinguishability of SSKGs is defined in exactly the same way as for regular SKGs, with one purely syntactical exception: As the new GenSSKG algorithm outputs the auxiliary seeking key, the experiments in Figure 2 need to be adapted such that the par $\leftarrow_R$ GenSKG(1^λ) line is replaced by (par, sk) $\leftarrow_R$ GenSSKG(1^λ). However, seeking key sk is irrelevant for the rest of the experiment.

Example 1 (Practical SSKG setting). We describe a practical setting of secured local logging with multiple monitored hosts. The system administrator first runs GenSSKG algorithm to establish system-wide parameters; each host then runs GenState0 algorithm to create its individual initial state st_0, serving as a basis for specific sequences $(\mathsf{st}_i)_{i \in \mathbb{N}}$ and $(K_i)_{i \in \mathbb{N}}$. The log auditor, having access to seeking key sk and to initial states st_0 of all hosts, can reproduce all corresponding keys K_i without restriction. Observe that, as the SSKG instances run on different hosts are independent of each other, authenticated log messages from one host cannot be 'replayed' on other hosts.

In practice, it might be difficult to find 'the right' frequency with which keys should be evolved. Recall that, even if forward-secure log authentication is in place, an intruder cannot be prevented from manipulating the log entries of the epoch in which he got access to a system. This suggests that keys should be updated at least every few seconds — and even more often to obtain protection against fully-automated attack tools. On battery-powered mobile devices, however, too frequent wakeups from system's sleep mode with the only purpose of evolving keys will noticeably contribute to draining devices' energy reserves.

Remark 2 (On the necessity of seeking trapdoors). For standard SKGs, the secret material managed by users is restricted to one 'current' state st_i. In contrast, for SSKGs, we introduced additional secret information, sk, required to perform the seek operation. One might ask whether this step was really necessary. We fixed the syntax of SSKGs as given in Definition 3 for a technical reason: the SSKG construction we present in Section 5 is factoring-based and its Seek algorithm requires knowledge of modulus' factorization $n = pq$. However, as knowledge of p and q thwarts the one-wayness of designated Evolve operation, we had to formally separate the entities that can and cannot perform the Seek operation. While this property slightly narrows the applicability of SSKGs, it is irrelevant for the intended secure logging scenario as described in Example 1.

4 Shortcut Permutations

We introduce a novel primitive, *shortcut one-way permutation* (SCP), as a building block for our SSKG construction in Section 5. Consider a finite set $\mathcal{D}$ together with an efficient permutation $\pi : \mathcal{D} \to \mathcal{D}$. Clearly, for any $x \in \mathcal{D}$ and $m \in \mathbb{N}$, it is easy to compute the m-fold composition $\pi^m(x) = \pi \circ \cdots \circ \pi(x)$ in linear time $O(m)$, by evaluating the permutation m times. In shortcut permutations, we have the efficiency requirement that the value $\pi^m(x)$ can be computed more efficiently than that, using a dedicated algorithm. In addition, we require one-wayness of π: given $y \in \mathcal{D}$, it should be impossible to compute $\pi^{-1}(y)$.

While we will rigorously specify the one-wayness requirement of SCPs, we do not give a precise definition of what 'more efficiently' means for the computation of π^m. The reason is that we aim at practicality of our construction, and, in general, practical efficiency strongly depends on the concrete parameter sizes and computing platforms in use. However, we anticipate that the SCPs that we construct in Section 4.1 have algorithms that compute $\pi^m(x)$ in constant time.

We next formalize the syntax and functionality of SCPs. For technical reasons, the definition slightly deviates from the above intuition in that the algorithm which efficiently computes π^m also requires an auxiliary input, the *shortcut information*.

Definition 5 (Syntax of SCP). *A shortcut permutation is a triple* SCP = {GenSCP, Eval, Express} *of efficient algorithms as follows:*

- GenSCP(1^λ). *This probabilistic algorithm, on input of security parameter 1^λ, outputs public parameters* pp *and a corresponding shortcut information* sc. *We assume that each specific value* pp *implicitly defines a finite domain $\mathcal{D} = \mathcal{D}(\text{pp})$. We further assume that elements from $\mathcal{D}$ can be efficiently sampled with uniform distribution.*
- Eval(pp, x). *This deterministic algorithm, given public parameters* pp *and a value $x \in \mathcal{D}$, outputs a value $y \in \mathcal{D}$.*
- Express(sc, x, m). *This deterministic algorithm takes shortcut information* sc, *an element $x \in \mathcal{D}$, and a non-negative integer m, and returns a value $y \in \mathcal{D}$.*

A shortcut permutation SCP *is* correct *if, for all $\lambda \in \mathbb{N}$ and all* (pp, sc) $\leftarrow_R$ GenSCP(1^λ), *we have that (a)* Eval(pp, $\cdot$) *implements a bijection $\pi : \mathcal{D} \to \mathcal{D}$, and (b)* Express(sc, x, m) = $\pi^m(x)$, *for all $x \in \mathcal{D}$ and $m \in \mathbb{N}$.*

As the newly introduced shortcut property is solely an efficiency feature, it does not appear in our specification of one-way security. In fact, the one-wayness definitions of SCPs and of regular one-way permutations [18] are essentially the same. Observe that we model one-wayness only for the case that the adversary does not have access to shortcut information sc.

Definition 6 (One-wayness of SCP). *We say that a shortcut permutation* SCP *is* one-way *if the probability*

$$\Pr\big[(\text{pp}, \text{sc}) \leftarrow_R \text{GenSCP}(1^\lambda); y \leftarrow_R \mathcal{D}(\text{pp}); x \leftarrow_R \mathcal{B}(\text{pp}, y) : \text{Eval}(\text{pp}, x) = y\big]$$

is negligible in λ, for all efficient adversaries $\mathcal{B}$.

Remark 3 (Comparison of SCPs and TDPs). The syntax of (one-way) SCPs is, to some extent, close to that of trapdoor permutations (TDPs, [18]). However, observe the significant difference between the notions of *trapdoor* and *shortcut*. While a TDP's trapdoor allows efficient *inversion* of the permutation (i.e., computation of π^{-1}), a shortcut in our newly defined primitive allows *acceleration* of the computation of π^m, for arbitrary m. In particular, for SCPs, there might be no way to invert π even if the shortcut information is available. We admit, though, that in our number-theory-based constructions from Section 4.1 one-wayness does not hold for adversaries that obtain the shortcut information: any party knowing the shortcut can also efficiently invert the permutation.

4.1   Constructions Based on Number Theory

We propose an efficient number-theoretic SCP construction: FACT-SCP.

Let N be a Blum integer, i.e., $N = pq$ for primes p, q such that $p \equiv q \equiv 3 \bmod 4$. Let $QR_N = \{x^2 : x \in \mathbb{Z}_N^\times\}$ denote the set of *quadratic residues* modulo N. It is well-known [26] that the squaring operation $x \mapsto x^2 \bmod N$ is a permutation on QR_N. Moreover, computing square roots in QR_N, i.e., inverting this permutation, is as hard as factoring N. This intuition is the basis of the following hardness assumption.

Definition 7 (SQRT assumption). *For probabilistic algorithms* GenSQRT *that take as input security parameter* 1^λ *and output tuples* (N, p, q, φ) *such that* $N = pq$, *factors* p *and* q *are prime and satisfy* $p \equiv q \equiv 3 \bmod 4$, *and* $\varphi = \varphi(N) = |\mathbb{Z}_N^\times|$, *the* SQRT *problem is said to be* hard *if for all efficient adversaries* $\mathcal{A}$ *the success probability*

$$\Pr\left[(N, p, q, \varphi) \leftarrow_R \mathsf{GenSQRT}(1^\lambda); y \leftarrow_R QR_N; x \leftarrow_R \mathcal{A}(N, y) : x^2 \equiv y \bmod N\right]$$

is negligible in λ, *where the probability is taken over the random coins of the experiment (including* $\mathcal{A}$'s *randomness). The* SQRT *assumption states that there exists an efficient algorithm* GenSQRT *for which the* SQRT *problem is hard.*

The construction of an SCP based on the SQRT assumption is now straightforward:

Construction 2 (FACT-SCP) *Construct* SQRT-*based SCP as follows: Let* GenSCP(1^λ) *run* GenSQRT(1^λ) *and output* pp $= N$ *and* sc $= \varphi$, *let* $\mathcal{D} = QR_N$, *let* Eval(N, x) *output* $x^2 \bmod N$, *and let* Express(φ, x, m) *output* $x^{(2^m \bmod \varphi)} \bmod N$.

Remark 4 (Correctness and security of FACT-SCP*).* Observe that the specified domain $\mathcal{D}$ is efficiently samplable (take $x \leftarrow_R \mathbb{Z}_N^\times$ and square it), that correctness of the SCP follows from standard number-theoretic results (in particular [26, Fact 2.160] and [26, Fact 2.126]), and that every Express operation takes about one exponentiation modulo N. Further, comparing the experiments in Definitions 6 and 7 makes evident that FACT-SCP is one-way if the SQRT problem is hard for GenSQRT, i.e., if integer factorization is hard [26, Fact 3.46].

Similarly to FACT-SCP, in the full version [25, Appendix C] we define the RSA-based RSA-SCP. Observe that both constructions rely on different, though related, number-theoretic assumptions. In fact, while the security of FACT-SCP can be shown to be equivalent to the hardness of integer factorization, RSA-SCP can be reduced 'only' to the RSA assumption. Although equivalence of the RSA problem and integer factorization is widely believed, a proof has not been found yet. Hence, in some sense, SQRT-based schemes are more secure than RSA-based schemes. In addition to that, our SQRT-based scheme has a (slight) performance advantage over our RSA-based scheme (squaring is more efficient than raising to the power of e). The only situation we are aware of in which RSA-SCP might have an advantage over FACT-SCP is when the most often executed operation is Express, and deployment of multiprime RSA is acceptable (e.g., $N = pqr$). Briefly, in the multiprime RSA setting [17,13], private key operations can be implemented particularly efficiently, based on the Chinese Remainder Theorem (CRT). Observe that Definition 8 in [25, Appendix C] is general enough to cover the multiprime setting.

5 Seekable Sequential Key Generators from Shortcut Permutations

We construct an SSKG from a generic SCP. Briefly, the Evolve operation corresponds to the Eval algorithm, the Seek algorithm is implemented via SCP's

Express procedure, and keys K_i are computed by applying a hash function (modeled as a random oracle in the security analysis) to the corresponding state st_i.

Construction 3 (SCP-SSKG) *Let* SCP = {GenSCP, Eval, Express} *be a shortcut permutation, and let* $H : \{0,1\}^* \rightarrow \{0,1\}^{\ell(\lambda)}$ *be a hash function, for a polynomial* ℓ. *Then the algorithms of our seekable sequential key generator* SCP-SSKG *are specified in Figure 4.*

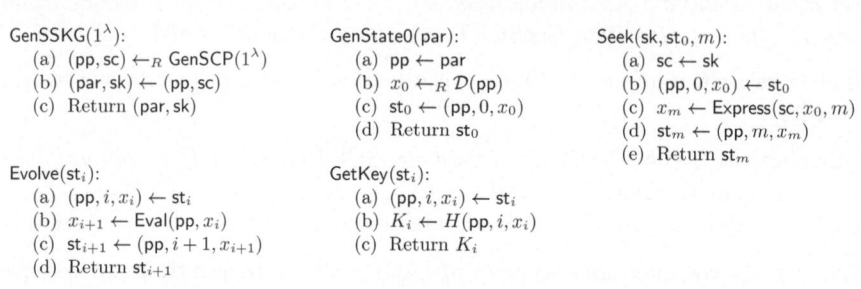

Fig. 4. SCP-based SSKG construction SCP-SSKG

Correctness of Construction 3 follows by inspection. We state IND-FS security of SCP-SSKG in Theorem 1; the corresponding proof appears in the full version [25, Appendix D]. Recall that IND security follows by Lemma 1.

Theorem 1 (Security of SCP-SSKG). *The SSKG from Construction 3 offers* IND-FS *security if* SCP *is a one-way shortcut permutation, in the random oracle model.*

6   Implementing Seekable Sequential Key Generators

Let FACT-SSKG denote the factorization-based SSKG obtained by combining Constructions 2 and 3. Some implementational details that increase the efficiency and versatility of this construction are discussed next.

We first propose a small tweak to the scheme that affects the storage size of the initial state. Recall that, in foreseen applications of SSKGs, the initial state st_0 is first created by (randomized) GenState0 algorithm and then copied to other parties (cf. discussion in Section 2.1). In FACT-SSKG, between 1024 to 4096 bits would have to be copied, depending on the desired level of security [1], just counting the size of $x_0 \in QR_N$. However, in the specific application we are aiming at, described in detail in Section 6.1, that much bandwidth is not available. We hence propose to make GenState0 algorithm deterministic, now providing it with an explicit random seed of short length (e.g., 80–128 bits); all randomness required by the original GenState0 algorithm is deterministically extracted from that seed via a PRG, and only 128 bits (or less) have to be shared with other parties. We implement this new feature by introducing an auxiliary algorithm, RndQR, that deterministically maps seed $\in \{0,1\}^{\ell(\lambda)}$ to an element in QR_N such that the distribution of RndQR(N, seed) with random seed is negligibly close to the uniform distribution on QR_N. The new GenState0 and RndQR algorithms are shown in Figure 5. The admissibility of proposed RndQR construction is confirmed by [10] and [27, §B.5.1.3], in the random oracle model.

The second modification of FACT-SSKG improves the efficiency of the Seek operation. A standard trick [17,6] to speed up private operations in factoring-based schemes is via the Chinese Remainder Theorem (CRT). For instance, if an exponentiation $y \leftarrow x^k \bmod N$ is to be computed and the factorization $N = pq$ is known, then y can be obtained by CRT-decomposing x into $x_p \leftarrow x \bmod p$ and $x_q \leftarrow x \bmod q$, by computing $y_p \leftarrow x_p^{k \bmod \varphi(p)} \bmod p$ and $y_q \leftarrow x_q^{k \bmod \varphi(q)} \bmod q$ independently of each other, and by mapping (y_p, y_q) back to $\mathbb{Z}_N$ (by applying the CRT a second time). The described method to compute x^k is approximately four times faster than evaluating the term directly, without the CRT [26, Note 14.75]. The correspondingly modified Seek algorithm is shown in Figure 5.

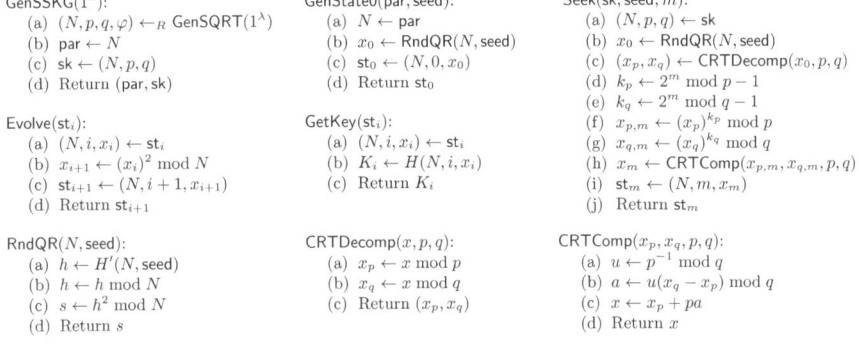

Fig. 5. Algorithms of optimized FACT-SSKG, together with auxiliary RndQR, CRTDecomp, and CRTComp algorithms. In the specification of RndQR we assume a hash function $H' : \{0,1\}^* \rightarrow \{0,\ldots,2^t - 1\}$, where $t = \lceil \log_2 N \rceil + 128$.

We combine Remark 4, Theorem 1, and Lemma 1 to obtain:

Corollary 1 (Security of FACT-SSKG). *Under the assumption that integer factorization is hard, our seekable sequential key generator FACT-SSKG offers both IND and IND-FS security, in the random oracle model.*

6.1 Deployment in Practice

We implemented FACT-SSKG (incorporating the tweaks described above) [28]. In fact, the code is part of the *journald* logging component of the *systemd* system and service manager, the core piece of many modern commercial Linux-based operating systems [31]. The SSKG is used as described in the introduction: it is combined with a cryptographic MAC in order to implement secured local logging, called *Forward-Secure Sealing* in journald. Generation of initial state st_0 takes place on the system whose logs are to be protected. The corresponding seed is shown on screen only (hence the restriction on seed's size), both in text and as QR code [15]; the latter may be scanned off the screen with devices such as mobile phones. The separation between on-disk storage of public parameters and on-screen display of the seed is done in order to ensure the latter will not remain on the system. Each time the SKG state is evolved, a MAC tag protecting the data written since the previous MAC operation is appended to the log file. An offline verification tool that checks the MAC tag sequence of log files taken from a system is provided. If a log file is corrupted, the verification tool will determine the time range where the integrity of the log file is intact. When the SKG state is evolved, particular care is taken to ensure the previous state is securely deleted from the file system and underlying physical storage, which includes techniques to ensure secure removal even on modern copy-on-write file systems.

On the technical side, our implementation supports modulus sizes of 512–16384 bits (1536 bits is recommended), uses SHA256 for key derivation, and relies on HMAC-SHA256 for integrity protection. The code links against the *gcrypt* library [22] for large integer arithmetic and the SHA256 hash function, and is licensed under an Open Source license (LGPL 2.1).

Conclusion

We review different cryptographic schemes for log file protection and point out that they all lack an important usability feature: *seekability*. In short, seekability allows users of sequential key generators to jump to any position in the otherwise forward-secure keystream, in negligible time. We introduce a new primitive, *seekable sequential key generator* (SSKG), and give two provably-secure factorization-based constructions. As a side product, we introduce the concept of *shortcut one-way permutations* (SCP), which may find independent application.

Acknowledgments. The authors thank the anonymous reviewers of ESORICS 2013 for their valuable comments. Giorgia Azzurra Marson was supported by CASED and Bertram Poettering by EPSRC Leadership Fellowship EP/H005455/1.

References

1. Babbage, S., Catalano, D., Cid, C., de Weger, B., Dunkelman, O., Gehrmann, C., Granboulan, L., Güneysu, T., Hermans, J., Lange, T., Lenstra, A., Mitchell, C., Näslund, M., Nguyen, P., Paar, C., Paterson, K., Pelzl, J., Pornin, T., Preneel, B., Rechberger, C., Rijmen, V., Robshaw, M., Rupp, A., Schläffer, M., Vaudenay, S., Vercauteren, F., Ward, M.: ECRYPT yearly report on algorithms and keysizes (September 2012), http://www.ecrypt.eu.org/documents/D.SPA.20.pdf

2. Bellare, M., Miner, S.K.: A forward-secure digital signature scheme. In: Wiener, M. (ed.) CRYPTO 1999. LNCS, vol. 1666, pp. 431–448. Springer, Heidelberg (1999)
3. Bellare, M., Yee, B.S.: Forward-security in private-key cryptography. In: Joye, M. (ed.) CT-RSA 2003. LNCS, vol. 2612, pp. 1–18. Springer, Heidelberg (2003)
4. Blum, L., Blum, M., Shub, M.: Comparison of two pseudo-random number generators. In: Chaum, D., Rivest, R.L., Sherman, A.T. (eds.) CRYPTO 1982, Santa Barbara, CA, USA, pp. 61–78. Plenum Press, New York (1983)
5. Blum, L., Blum, M., Shub, M.: A simple unpredictable pseudo-random number generator. SIAM Journal on Computing 15(2), 364–383 (1986)
6. Boneh, D., Shacham, H.: Fast variants of RSA. RSA Cryptobytes 5(1), 1–9 (2002)
7. Canetti, R., Halevi, S., Katz, J.: A forward-secure public-key encryption scheme. Journal of Cryptology 20(3), 265–294 (2007)
8. Canetti, R., Krawczyk, H.: Analysis of key-exchange protocols and their use for building secure channels. In: Pfitzmann, B. (ed.) EUROCRYPT 2001. LNCS, vol. 2045, pp. 453–474. Springer, Heidelberg (2001)
9. Chong, C.N., Peng, Z., Hartel, P.H.: Secure audit logging with tamper-resistant hardware. In: Gritzalis, D., di Vimercati, S.D.C., Samarati, P., Katsikas, S.K. (eds.) SEC. IFIP Conference Proceedings, vol. 250, pp. 73–84. Kluwer (2003)
10. Desmedt, Y.: Securing traceability of ciphertexts – towards a secure software key escrow system (extended abstract). In: Guillou, L.C., Quisquater, J.-J. (eds.) EUROCRYPT 1995. LNCS, vol. 921, pp. 147–157. Springer, Heidelberg (1995)
11. Fluhrer, S.R., Mantin, I., Shamir, A.: Weaknesses in the key scheduling algorithm of RC4. In: Vaudenay, S., Youssef, A.M. (eds.) SAC 2001. LNCS, vol. 2259, pp. 1–24. Springer, Heidelberg (2001)
12. Gutmann, P.: Secure deletion of data from magnetic and solid-state memory. In: Proceedings of the Sixth USENIX Security Symposium, San Jose, CA, vol. 14 (1996)
13. Hinek, M.J., Low, M.K., Teske, E.: On some attacks on multi-prime RSA. In: Nyberg, K., Heys, H.M. (eds.) SAC 2002. LNCS, vol. 2595, pp. 385–404. Springer, Heidelberg (2003)
14. Holt, J.E.: Logcrypt: forward security and public verification for secure audit logs. In: Buyya, R., Ma, T., Safavi-Naini, R., Steketee, C., Susilo, W. (eds.) ACSW Frontiers. CRPIT, vol. 54, pp. 203–211. Australian Computer Society (2006)
15. International Organization for Standardization (ISO). Information Technology – Automatic identification and data capture techniques – QR Code 2005 bar code symbology specification. ISO/IEC 18004:2006 (2006)
16. Itkis, G.: Forward security, adaptive cryptography: Time evolution (2004)
17. Jonsson, J., Kaliski, B.: Public-Key Cryptography Standards (PKCS) #1: RSA Cryptography Specifications Version 2.1. RFC 3447 (Informational) (February 2003)
18. Katz, J., Lindell, Y.: Introduction to Modern Cryptography. Chapman and Hall/CRC Press (2007)
19. Kelsey, J., Callas, J., Clemm, A.: Signed Syslog Messages. RFC 5848 (Proposed Standard) (May 2010)
20. Kelsey, J., Schneier, B.: Cryptographic support for secure logs on untrusted machines. In: Proceedings of the 7th USENIX Security Symposium (1998)
21. Kelsey, J., Schneier, B.: Minimizing bandwidth for remote access to cryptographically protected audit logs. In: Recent Advances in Intrusion Detection (1999)
22. Koch, W.: GNU Privacy Guard – gcrypt library, http://www.gnupg.org/

23. Ma, D., Tsudik, G.: Extended abstract: Forward-secure sequential aggregate authentication. In: 2007 IEEE Symposium on Security and Privacy, Oakland, California, USA, May 20-23, pp. 86–91. IEEE Computer Society Press (2007)
24. Ma, D., Tsudik, G.: A new approach to secure logging. Trans. Storage 5(1), 2:1–2:21 (2009)
25. Marson, G.A., Poettering, B.: Practical secure logging: Seekable sequential key generators. Cryptology ePrint Archive, Report 2013/397 (2013), http://eprint.iacr.org/2013/397
26. Menezes, A.J., van Oorschot, P.C., Vanstone, S.A.: Handbook of Applied Cryptography. The CRC Press series on discrete mathematics and its applications. CRC Press (2000); N.W. Corporate Blvd., Boca Raton, FL 33431-9868, USA (1997)
27. National Institute of Standards and Technology (NIST). Recommendation for random number generation using deterministic random bit generators (revised) (March 2007), NIST Special Publication 800-90
28. Poettering, B.: fsprg – seekable forward-secure pseudorandom generator, http://cgit.freedesktop.org/systemd/systemd/tree/src/journal/fsprg.c
29. Schneier, B., Kelsey, J.: Secure audit logs to support computer forensics. ACM Trans. Inf. Syst. Secur. 2(2), 159–176 (1999)
30. Shoup, V.: On formal models for secure key exchange. Technical Report RZ 3120, IBM (1999)
31. systemd. System and service manager, http://www.freedesktop.org/wiki/Software/systemd/
32. Waters, B.R., Balfanz, D., Durfee, G., Smetters, D.K.: Building an encrypted and searchable audit log. In: NDSS 2004, San Diego, California, USA, February 4-6. The Internet Society (2004)
33. Yavuz, A.A., Ning, P.: BAF: An efficient publicly verifiable secure audit logging scheme for distributed systems. In: ACSAC, pp. 219–228. IEEE Computer Society (2009)
34. Yavuz, A.A., Ning, P., Reiter, M.K.: BAF and FI-BAF: Efficient and publicly verifiable cryptographic schemes for secure logging in resource-constrained systems. ACM Trans. Inf. Syst. Secur. 15(2), 9 (2012)

Request-Based Comparable Encryption

Jun Furukawa

NEC Corporation, Kanagawa 211-8666, Japan
j-furukawa@ay.jp.nec.co.jp

Abstract. An order-preserving encryption (OPE) scheme preserves the numerical order of numbers under encryption while hiding their original values in a some extent. However, if all the numbers in a certain domain are encrypted by an OPE, the original numbers can be restored from their order. We introduce a notion of novel encryption scheme "request-based comparable encryption" that provides a certain level of security even when OPEs cannot. A request-based comparable encryption hides original values, but it enables any pair of encrypted values to be compared each other when and only when one of them is accompanied by a "token". We also consider its weaker notion and a concrete construction satisfying it. We consider a request-based comparable encryption complements OPEs and can be an essential security primitive.

Keywords: order-preserving encryption, request-based, database encryption, range query.

1 Introduction

1.1 Background and Motivation

A database (DB) is a system that stores a large amount of data and passes its portions when requested. It has been an indispensable platform for variety of services through the network. Since many DBs store sensitive information, they are potentially vulnerable to abuse, leakage, and theft. Hence, it is important to unfailingly protect confidentiality of their data. An access control is a fairly effective approach for it, but it is helpless if the DB is compromised. Hence, it is desirable to enforce DBs by such an encrypting mechanism that the keys for decryption are kept by only data owners (not DB). This strategy is considered to be especially effective for the database-as-service, and can indeed be found in [12,20,21].

Although encrypting data in a DB can be effective in protecting data, it tends to spoil the availability of the DB since the DB can handle data only in limited manner. This may require users to retrieve all data in the DB, decrypt them, find necessary data among them, and process them all by himself. This imposes a large amount of computation, communication, and the memory on the user.

A searchable encryption [2,5,17,19] enables DBs to search necessary data without decrypting them, and an order-preserving encryption (OPE) [1,8,9] enables DBs to recognize the numerical order of data without decrypting them.

J. Crampton, S. Jajodia, and K. Mayes (Eds.): ESORICS 2013, LNCS 8134, pp. 129–146, 2013.

These ability recovers the availability of DBs by enabling them to return only the ciphertexts of data that are required by the users.

A relational database (RDB) [16], which is the most widely-used database nowadays, frequently selects data in a certain range from a table. This task can be done by an OPE even if data are encrypted. Since such selection of data drastically reduces the amount of computation and communication of the users, OPE is considered to be one of pivotal primitives for RDB with encrypted data. This is why the proposal of an OPE [8] immediately received attention from the applied community [18,25,26,29,31,34]. An OPE as well as a searchable encryption plays an important role for CryptDB [29], an encrypted RDB, to mark practical efficiency in TPC-C [32] measure.

Boldyreva et al. proposed an OPE [8] and studied the security of OPEs [9] for its practical use. Their positive result shows that OPEs enjoy reasonable security as long as the number of ciphertexts is sufficiently small compared to the square root of size of the domain of relevant numbers. But nothing is guaranteed in the case the number of ciphertexts is larger than that. Indeed, it is clear, as in the following example, that OPEs fail to hide anything about encrypted numbers in some cases. Consider a set of numbers that includes the all numbers in a domain D and every elements of this set are encrypted by an OPE. If all of these encrypted numbers are given to an adversary, the adversary is able to decrypt all the ciphertexts simply by sorting all of them.

That an OPE has a limitation in its secure use causes a serious concern for encrypted DBs since the OPE is a pivotal primitive for them. Several stronger primitives such as the committed efficiently-orderable encryption (CEOE) [9] that exploits a monotone minimal perfect hash function [3], range query methods in a public key setting [30,11], and searchable encryptions in a public key setting [5,6,10] have been proposed, but these are not sufficient for salvaging the benefit of DBs in the case described above. An order-preserving encryption with additional interactions [28] can enhance the security, but most applications assume that an RDB handles a thread of instructions without such additional interactions. It is now clear that we definitely need a novel cryptographic primitive so as an encrypted DB to function with practical efficiency and security.

1.2   Request-Based Comparable Encryption

In this paper, we propose a novel notion of cryptographic primitive called "request-based comparable encryption (comparable encryption for short)" that complements OPEs. The comparable encryption overcomes the limitation of OPEs just as the searchable encryption in [17,13,22] does the limitation of deterministic encryptions. It is a symmetric key encryption with such an additional mechanism that enables one to compare an encrypted number to other encrypted numbers if and only if the one is given a token associated to this number. Searches in [11] are also triggered by tokens.

Let us consider applying a comparable encryption to an encrypted DB. The DB stores encrypted numbers only and, upon a range query, it receives tokens for the edges of the range. Then, the DB is able to compare these stored encrypted values with the edge values without interacting with the user[1]. Thus, the DB is able to select out the data which the user required via the query. We emphasize that encrypted values themselves cannot be compared each other unless either of them is an edge unlike the case of OPE. Although the token does leak some numerical orders of the data to the DB, what is leaked to the DB is what the DB needs for processing data with practical efficiency. A protocol such as "private information retrieval" introduced in [14,15,23] leaks less data to DB, but such an approach inevitably requires heavy computational and communicational cost for DBs. This is not practical for realistic DBs and we thus dismiss such an approach.

If a user makes a huge number of range queries to a database and this database accumulates all tokens in these range queries, the database may acquire enough knowledge to decrypt all ciphertexts in some cases. Our approach is no longer effective in such an extreme case as OPE is no longer so. However, real users rarely deposit their data to totally untrusted DBs. The real concerns are that DBs leak their data because of careless system managers, viruses, via unpatched vulnerability of the system, design error, or configuration fault. As long as an intrusion of an adversary is temporal, it succeeds to seize only those tokens that are in insertion or selection queries which are made at the time of the intrusion. An example of temporal intrusion is a leakage of the memory data with respect a query. Such a temporal intrusion only enables the adversary to compare the each element in the stored data with the encrypted numbers in the query. Since such a comparison is already delegated to the DB in the query corrupted, leakage of this result can be considered as the minimum, unavoidable, and acceptable as long as efficiency is required.

1.3   A Weaker Property and Our Comparable Encryption

The introduced comparable encryption is a very promising primitive for practical encrypted DBs. However, we have not completely succeeded to propose an ideal comparable encryption with practical efficiency. We find no definite reason that it is inherently impossible but we have not. As the DB cannot be practical unless with practical efficiency literally, we propose a comparable encryption that has a weaker property than ideal one, but has a stronger security property than OPE and has practical efficiency. In particular, our comparable encryption is such that its tokens leak knowledge more than ideally allowed.

To evaluate the difference of security properties between the ideal one and ours, we first formalized the ideal security requirement and its weaker variant as well. Then, as a measure of the security level of this weaker variant, we evaluate the expected ratio between the number of occasions when a token of an ideal scheme leaks and the number of occasions when a token of a weaker scheme

---

[1] Since DB receives a sequence of requests at one time to avoid heavy communication and incoherent transaction, DB needs to process requests without interacting with the user.

leaks, which we show to be only at most "2.8". Suppose a temporal intrusion leaked a token as well as encrypted numbers. Then, the probability that this token helps to distinguish any of two encrypted numbers is 2.8 times larger in our scheme than in an ideal scheme.

Our comparable encryption is proved to satisfies this weaker property in the standard model but is sufficiently fast. The length of ciphertext is proportional to the bit length of the maximum number. The size of database shall increase severely if all data are encrypted with our comparable encryption. However, if the encryption is limitedly applied to only highly confidential data that require comparison, the database can remain in moderate size. Such limitation is common when a current product for database encryption such as [27] is used. Hence, although to reduce ciphertext length is highly desirable, our comparable encryption as it is still has practical value. The dominant cost for encryption, generation of token, and comparison are the cost for computing hash values in these processes, whose number of computation is again proportional to the bit length of the maximum number [2], which cost is very light. Considering the merit of efficiency that our scheme enjoys, we consider the weakness of our scheme is not so serious.

1.4   Organization:

The paper is organized as follows: Section 2 introduces the model of comparable encryption and describes its basic functionality. Section 3 presents a concrete scheme of comparable encryption and compares complexity of our scheme with that of OPE. Section 4 introduces the security requirement of ideal comparable encryptions and its weaker variant. Then it evaluates the difference between the two security requirements. Section 5 concludes the paper and poses an open problem.

2   Model

We introduce the model of comparable encryption and a basic property. Comparable encryption is composed of four algorithms, Gen, Enc, Der, and Cmp.

Gen: A probabilistic algorithm that, given a security parameter $\kappa \in \mathbb{N}$ and a range parameter $n \in \mathbb{N}$, outputs a parameter $param$ and a master key $mkey$. n is included in $param$.

$$(param, mkey) = \mathsf{Gen}(\kappa, n)$$

Enc: A probabilistic algorithm that, given a parameter $param$, a master key $mkey$, and a number $0 \leq num < 2^n$, outputs a ciphertext $ciph$.

$$ciph = \mathsf{Enc}(param, mkey, num)$$

---
[2] The cost for the decryption is constant if we provide this functionality.

Der: A possibly probabilistic algorithm that, given a parameter *param*, a master
key *mkey*, and a number $0 \leq num < 2^n$, outputs a token *token*.

$$token = \mathsf{Der}(param, mkey, num)$$

Cmp: An algorithm that, given a parameter *param*, two ciphertexts *ciph* and
ciph', and a token *token*, outputs $-1, 1$, or 0.

$$\mathsf{Cmp}(param, ciph, ciph', token) \in \{-1, 1, 0\}$$

Although we call the scheme *encryption*, it provides no **decryption** algorithm.
But such a functionality can be easily provided by appending an ordinary ci-
phertext $\widetilde{ciph}$ to each comparable encryption ciphertext *ciph* as $ciph|\widetilde{ciph}$ and
preparing an ordinary decryption algorithm for it. Then, decryption is straightforward. Although we consider the decryption algorithm is necessary in practice,
we omit it in our model for the simplicity of the presentation.

We assume *ciph* and *token* input to Cmp are related so that they satisfy
$ciph = \mathsf{Enc}(param, mkey, num)$ and $token = \mathsf{Der}(param, mkey, num)$ for the
same $param, mkey$, and num. The output of Cmp is $-1, 1$, or 0, respectively,
when $num < num', num > num'$, or $num = num'$. This requirement is formalized in the following property of completeness.

Definition 1. *We say a comparable encryption is* **complete** *if, for every $\kappa \in \mathbb{N}$,
$n \in \mathbb{N}$, and $0 \leq num, num' < 2^n$, there exist* $param, mkey, token, ciph$, *and* $ciph'$
such that

$$(param, mkey) = \mathsf{Gen}(\kappa, n) \quad , \quad token = \mathsf{Der}(param, mkey, num)$$
$$ciph = \mathsf{Enc}(param, mkey, num) \quad , \quad ciph' = \mathsf{Enc}(param, mkey, num')$$
$$\mathsf{Cmp}(param, ciph, ciph', token) = \begin{cases} -1 & if & num < num' \\ 1 & if & num > num' \\ 0 & if & num = num' \end{cases}$$

*hold with overwhelming probability. Where probability is taken over the distribu-
tion of random tapes input to* Gen, Enc, *and* Der.

3   Proposed Scheme

3.1   Preliminaries and Overview of Our Scheme

Our construction of comparable encryption exploits prefix-preserving encryption
(PPE) [35,4,24]. PPE considers each message as a sequence of blocks. If two
messages have the same sequence of n blocks as their prefixes, the encryptions
of these messages also have the same sequence of n blocks as their prefixes. But
the rest of blocks are different. Thus, a PPE preserves the equivalence of prefix
blocks. A PPE as-is does not meet the purpose of our comparable encryption
since it enables neither to hide the similarity of two numbers nor to recognize
the numerical order of two numbers from their ciphertexts. Our comparable

encryption is similar to PPE in that it also considers numbers as a sequence of blocks, where each block is a bit".

We list here some of the terms necessary in the rest of the paper. Suppose that n is a given fixed number such that $num = \sum_{i=0}^{n-1} b_i 2^i$ and $num' = \sum_{i=0}^{n-1} b_i' 2^i$ with $b_i, b_i' \in \{0, 1\}$ for all $0 \le i \le n - 1$. We let $(b_0, \ldots, b_{n-1})$ and $(b_0', \ldots, b_{n-1}')$, respectively, represent num and num'. We say the most significant prefix $(n - \ell - 1)$ bits of num is $(b_{\ell+1}, \ldots, b_{n-1})$. We let $\mathsf{MSPBs}(num, \ell) = (b_{\ell+1}, \ldots, b_{n-1})$ denotes this relation.

Our comparable encryption uses PPE ciphertext of a number num as the token of num ($token = \mathsf{Der}(param, mkey, num)$). Note that, if tokens of num and num' are, respectively, $token = \mathsf{Der}(param, mkey, num)$ and $token' = \mathsf{Der}(param, mkey, num')$ and if $\mathsf{MSPBs}(num, \ell) = \mathsf{MSPBs}(num', \ell)$, then $\mathsf{MSPBs}(token, \ell) = \mathsf{MSPBs}(token', \ell)$ holds. Let $token = (d_0, \ldots, d_{n-1})$. If each ℓ'-th bit of num, i.e. $b_{\ell'}$, is probabilistically encrypted by $d_{\ell'}$, then one can check whether or not $\mathsf{MSPBs}(num, \ell) = \mathsf{MSPBs}(num', \ell)$ holds for given ℓ (e.g., by decrypting them) using either $token$ or $token'$. But, whether $\mathsf{MSPBs}(num, \ell) = \mathsf{MSPBs}(num', \ell)$ or not is hidden if the both $token$ and $token'$ are kept hidden. This mechanism enables to compare the similarity of encrypted two numbers only when either of their tokens is given.

When $\mathsf{MSPBs}(num, \ell) = \mathsf{MSPBs}(num', \ell)$ but $\mathsf{MSPBs}(num, \ell - 1) \ne \mathsf{MSPBs}(num', \ell - 1)$, Cmp compares num and num' by comparing ℓ-th bits of num and num'(b_ℓ and b_ℓ' respectively). For this comparison, $e_\ell = b_\ell + mask_\ell \bmod 3$ is generated with a random looking mask $mask_\ell$, and encryption of e_ℓ is included in the ciphertext of num. Let $mask_\ell'$ and e_ℓ' be also generated in the same manner for num' here. Suppose that $mask_\ell$ and $mask_\ell'$ depend on only on $\mathsf{MSPBs}(num, \ell)$ and $\mathsf{MSPBs}(num', \ell)$ respectively (as well as on the master key), then $mask_\ell = mask_\ell'$ if $\mathsf{MSPBs}(num, \ell) = \mathsf{MSPBs}(num', \ell)$. Then b_ℓ and b_ℓ' are revealed from e_ℓ and e_ℓ' if b_ℓ and b_ℓ' are different (i.e.,$\mathsf{MSPBs}(num, \ell - 1) \ne \mathsf{MSPBs}(num', \ell - 1)$), since $e_\ell - e_\ell' = b_\ell - b_\ell' = 1 \bmod 3$ if $b_\ell = 1$ but $e_\ell - e_\ell' = 2 \bmod 3$ if $b_\ell = 0$. But b_ℓ and b_ℓ' are hidden if b_ℓ and b_ℓ' are the same (i.e., $\mathsf{MSPBs}(num, \ell - 1) = \mathsf{MSPBs}(num', \ell - 1)$), since $e_\ell - e_\ell' = b_\ell - b_\ell' = 0 \bmod 3$ does not depend on b_ℓ. b_i and b_i' for $i < \ell$ are hidden if $\mathsf{MSPBs}(num, \ell - 1) \ne \mathsf{MSPBs}(num', \ell - 1)$, since $e_i - e_i' \bmod 3$ depends on $mask_i - mask_i' \bmod 3$ which is pseudo-random. If $token$ is designed to reveals e_ℓ and e_ℓ', one can decide which number (num or num') is greater from their ciphertexts. Note that b_i and b_i' for none of $i \ne \ell$ is revealed.

The above construction of comparable encryption from PPE provides satisfactory functionality of comparable encryption. However, its tokens leak knowledge more than the numerical order of numbers. Suppose that $ciph$ and $ciph'$ are, respectively ciphertexts of two numbers num and num'. From $ciph$, $ciph'$, and the token $token$ of num, one can recognize not only the numerical order of num and num' but also the most significant bit at which num and num' differ. This is not a scheme with an ideal security property, but this is the best we can provide at this moment. And we analyze the negative impact of this leakage later.

3.2   Construction

Now we present the specific construction of our comparable encryption below.

Gen: Suppose a security parameter $\kappa \in \mathbb{N}$ and the number of digit n. Gen first randomly chooses a hash function $\mathsf{Hash} : \{0,1\}^\kappa \times \{0,1\}^{4+\kappa+1} \to \{0,1\}^\kappa$ and assigns $param = (n, \mathsf{Hash})$. Next, Gen uniformly and randomly chooses a master key $mkey \in \{0,1\}^\kappa$. Gen outputs $param = (n, \mathsf{Hash})$ and $mkey$.

Der: Suppose that $param = (n, \mathsf{Hash})$, $mkey$, and a number $num = (b_0, b_1, \ldots, b_{n-1}) := \sum_{0 \le i \le n-1} b_i 2^i$ are given. Der generates

$$d_n = \mathsf{Hash}(mkey, (0, 0^\kappa, 0))$$
$$d_i = \mathsf{Hash}(mkey, (1, d_{i+1}, b_i)) \qquad \text{for} \quad i = n-1, \ldots, 0$$

Der outputs the token $token = (d_0, d_1, \ldots, d_n)$.

Enc: Suppose that $param = (n, \mathsf{Hash})$, $mkey$, and a number $num = (b_0, b_1, \ldots, b_{n-1})$ are given. Enc first generates $(d_0, d_1, \ldots, d_n) = \mathsf{Der}(param, mkey, num)$ and then randomly chooses random number $I \in \{0,1\}^\kappa$. Next, Enc generates

$$c_i = \mathsf{Hash}(d_i, (2, I, 0))$$
$$e_i = \mathsf{Hash}(mkey, (4, d_{i+1}, 0)) + b_i \bmod 3$$
$$f_i = \mathsf{Hash}(d_{i+1}, (5, I, 0)) + e_i \bmod 3$$

for $i = n-1, \ldots, 0$. Enc finally outputs ciphertext $ciph = (I, (c_0, \ldots, c_{n-1}), (f_0, \ldots, f_{n-1}))$.

Cmp: Suppose that $param = (n, \mathsf{Hash})$, a pair of ciphertexts $ciph = (I, (c_0, \ldots, c_{n-1}), (f_0, \ldots, f_{n-1}))$ and $ciph' = (I', (c'_0, \ldots, c'_{n-1}), (f'_0, \ldots, f'_{n-1}))$, and a token $token = (d_0, d_1, \ldots, d_n)$ are given.

1. Cmp searches and find j such that

$$(0 \le j \le n-1) \quad \wedge$$
$$\left(\forall k \text{ s.t. } j < k < n, \ c'_k = \mathsf{Hash}(d_k, (2, I', 0)) \right) \wedge \left(c'_j \ne \mathsf{Hash}(d_j, (2, I', 0)) \right)$$

In case

$$\forall k \text{ s.t. } 0 \le k < n, \ c'_k = \mathsf{Hash}(d_k, (2, I', 0))$$

hold, Cmp outputs 0 and stops.

2. Cmp generates

$$e_j = f_j - \mathsf{Hash}(d_{j+1}, (5, I, 0)) \bmod 3$$
$$e'_j = f'_j - \mathsf{Hash}(d_{j+1}, (5, I', 0)) \bmod 3$$

3. Cmp outputs

$$\begin{array}{rll} 1 & \text{if} & e_j - e'_j = 1 \bmod 3 \\ -1 & \text{if} & e_j - e'_j = 2 \bmod 3 \end{array}$$

Here, input $(c_1, \ldots, c_n)$ are unnecessary. But we include them in the input only for the simplicity of the description.

3.3   Completeness of Our Comparable Encryption

The theorem 1 below guarantees that our scheme successfully compares encrypted numbers.

Definition 2. *We say a function* Hash $: \{0,1\}^\kappa \times \{0,1\}^\ell \to \{0,1\}^L$ *is a pseudorandom function if every poly-time distinguisher D has an advantage in distinguishing whether it is accessing* Hash$(K, \cdot)$ *with randomly chosen key $K \in \{0,1\}^\kappa$ or it is accessing a random function $R : \{0,1\}^\ell \to \{0,1\}^L$ with at most negligible probability in κ.*

Theorem 1. *The proposed comparable encryption is complete as long as* Hash *is a pseudorandom function.*

Proof. Let $num = \sum_{i=0}^{n-1} b_i 2^i$, $num' = \sum_{i=0}^{n-1} b_i' 2^i$, ℓ be the largest ℓ' such that MSPBs(num, ℓ') = MSPBs(num', ℓ') holds, $(d_0, \ldots, d_n)$ = Der$(param, mkey, num)$, $(d_0', \ldots, d_n')$ = Der$(param, mkey, num')$, $(I, (c_0, \ldots, c_{n-1}), (f_0, \ldots, f_{n-1}))$ = Enc$(param, mkey, num)$, and $(I', (c_0', \ldots, c_{n-1}'), (f_0', \ldots, f_{n-1}'))$ = Enc$(param, mkey, num')$. Since d_i and d_i' depend only on $\{b_j\}_{j=i+1,\ldots,n-1}$ and $\{b_j'\}_{j=i+1,\ldots,n-1}$ respectively and on $mkey$, that $b_i = b_i'$ holds for $i = \ell+1, \ldots, n-1$ implies that $d_i = d_i'$ holds for $i = \ell+1, \ldots, n-1$. Hence, Hash$(d_k', (2, I', 0)) = c_k' =$ Hash$(d_k, (2, I', 0))$ for $i = \ell+1, \ldots, n-1$.

If $num = num'$, Hash$(d_k', (2, I', 0)) = c_k' =$ Hash$(d_k, (2, I', 0))$ holds for $i = 0, \ldots, n-1$. Hence, the output of Cmp is 0 if $num = num'$. If $num \neq num'$, then $d_\ell = d_\ell'$ holds with negligible probability. This is because, if collision occurs with non-negligible probability for a function whose output length is κ, such a function can be distinguished from the random function by using collisions. Hence, Hash$(d_\ell', (2, I', 0)) = c_\ell' \neq$ Hash$(d_\ell, (2, I', 0))$ with overwhelming probability. For this ℓ,

$$
\begin{aligned}
e_\ell - e_\ell' &:= (f_\ell - \mathsf{Hash}(d_{\ell+1}, (5, I, 0))) - (f_\ell' - \mathsf{Hash}(d_{\ell+1}, (5, I', 0))) \bmod 3 \\
&= (\mathsf{Hash}(mkey, (4, d_{\ell+1}, 0)) + b_\ell) - (\mathsf{Hash}(mkey, (4, d_{\ell+1}', 0)) + b_\ell') \bmod 3 \\
&= (\mathsf{Hash}(mkey, (4, d_{\ell+1}, 0)) + b_\ell) - (\mathsf{Hash}(mkey, (4, d_{\ell+1}, 0)) + b_\ell') \bmod 3 \\
&= b_\ell - b_\ell' \bmod 3
\end{aligned}
$$

Since that $num > num'$ if $b_\ell = 1 > 0 = b_\ell'$ and that $num < num'$ if $b_\ell = 0 < 1 = b_\ell'$, the output of Cmp is 1 if $num > num'$ and is -1 if $num < num'$.

3.4   Efficiency

We compare complexity measures of our scheme with those of OPE. We list them when numbers num are chosen as $0 \leq num < 2^n$ in the Table 1. The dominant cost of computation is computation of hash functions in our scheme. Hence, we evaluate the computational complexity of our scheme by the number of hash function Hash. Encryption in OPE [8] requires sampling from negative hypergeometric distribution, which cost is denoted by "sampling". This requires rather high cost.

Table 1. Comparison

	Our Scheme	OPE[8]
ciphertext(text) length (bits)	$(n+1)\kappa + 2n$	$n + \text{constant}$
token length (bits)	$(n+1)\kappa$	-
encryption cost	$(4n+1) \cdot \mathsf{Hash}$	$n \cdot \mathsf{sampling}$
token generation cost	$(n+1) \cdot \mathsf{Hash}$	-
comparison cost	$(n-B+2) \cdot \mathsf{Hash}$	$(n-B) \cdot \text{bit-comparison}$

"bit-comparison" is very light computation and n bit-comparison operations is usually executed in one operation. B is the largest ℓ such that $\mathsf{MSPBs}(num, \ell) = \mathsf{MSPBs}(num', \ell)$ holds.

From the table, we see that OPE is more efficient except for generating ciphertexts. However, we consider that the cost our comparable encryption requires is still acceptable for most applications, and a comparable encryption is essential for data to which OPE cannot be applied securely.

4   Security Analysis

We analyze the security of our scheme. As our scheme is not ideal comparable encryption, we introduce a weaker security requirement of comparable encryption as well as the ideal one.

We require comparable encryption to be semantically secure under chosen plaintext attacks as long as no token is generated. When a token *token* is generated with respect to a number *num*, it is best if *token* only enables to compare this *num* with other encrypted numbers. To capture such a requirement, we start from defining a distinguishing game of comparable encryption. In this game, the adversary may send the challenger either of two types of test query, that is, type I and type II. This type indicates whether or not ciphertext in the test query is accompanied with the corresponding token. Then we define two notions of resolved games followed by two related definitions of indistinguishability of comparable encryption. The first notion captures ideal comparable encryption but the latter captures comparable encryption with an extra leakage of knowledge.

We chose game-based definition rather than simulation-based definitions (in [17,13,22]) because what each token leaks depends on all issued ciphertexts, which bothers ideal functionality to check all of them every time a token is issued. However, game-based definition requires to check if issued tokens have leaked something crucial only once at the end of the game.

4.1   Ideal Indistinguishability

Definition 3. *The* **distinguishing game** *is played between challenger C and adversary A^* as in the following. It begins when C receives a security parameter $\kappa \in \mathbb{N}$ and a range parameter $n \in \mathbb{N}$, runs $(\text{param}, \text{mkey}) \leftarrow \mathsf{KeyGen}(\kappa, n)$, and gives param to A^*. C responds to queries from A^* in the game as follows;*

- *Whenever C receives* (encrypt, num) *for any* $0 \le num < 2^n$, *it returns* ciph $=$ Enc(param, mkey, num).
- *Whenever C receives* (cmprkey, num) *for any* $0 \le num < 2^n$, *it returns* token $=$ Der(param, mkey, num).
- *C receives* (test, type, num_0^*, num_1^*) *such that* $0 \le num_0^*, num_1^* < 2^n$, $num_0^* \le num_1^*$, *and type* $\in \{I, II\}$ *only once in the game. On receiving this message, C randomly chooses* $b \in \{0, 1\}$ *and generates* ciph* $=$ Enc(param, mkey, num_b^*) *and* token* $=$ Der(param, mkey, num_b^*). *Then C returns*

$$
\begin{array}{ll}
ciph^* & if \quad type = I \\
token^*, ciph^* & if \quad type = II.
\end{array}
$$

At the end of the game, A sends $b' \in \{0, 1\}$ to C. The result of the game $\mathsf{Exp}_{C,A}^{\kappa}$ *is 1 if $b = b'$; otherwise 0.*

Type I tests indistinguishability of the encryption of num_b^*. Type II tests indistinguishability of the token with respect to num_b^*. We do not consider chosen-ciphertext attacks here since encrypt-then-MAC [7] generic construction can easily make the scheme resistant for them when an ordinary ciphertext is concatenated to each ciphertext so as to be decryptable.

The distinguishing game challenges the adversary's ability to distinguish ciphertexts. However, if a certain set of queries is sent to the challenger, it is inevitable to prevent rational adversaries from distinguishing these ciphertexts. This is because that tokens enable to compare encrypted numbers inevitably leaks their orders. Hence, the cases and only the cases when such a leakage trivially helps distinguishing ciphertexts/tokens need to be excluded from the games to measures the strength of the scheme. For this purpose we introduce the notion of resolved games.

Definition 4. *We say a distinguishing game is* **resolved** *if A^* queries such* (command, num) *that the following relation holds during the game, where* command *is* cmprkey *if type* $= I$ *but* command *is either* cmprkey *or* encrypt *if type* $= II$.

$$
(num_0^* \le num \le num_1^*) \wedge (num_0^* \ne num_1^*), \tag{1}
$$

which relation can be equivalently expressed as

$$
((num_0^* < num) \wedge (num_1^* \not< num)) \vee ((num \not< num_0^*) \wedge (num < num_1^*)).
$$

The first form of the relation in Def. 4 represents that num is between num_0^* and num_1^* but the case $num_0^* = num = num_1^*$ is excluded. It is crystal clear that two test messages can be distinguishable if a token that can distinguish them is queried (type I). And it is also clear that two test tokens can be distinguishable if an message that these tokens decide in different way is encrypted (type II).

The second form of the relation in Def. 4 represents that num_0^* and num_1^* are related to num in different way via the relation "$<$". The first and the second forms are equivalent but the second form has more affinity with distinguishability, and we use the second type of form for Def. 6.

Definition 5. *We say that a comparable encryption is **indistinguishable (Ind)** if, for every polynomial time adversary A^*, $\mathsf{Adv}^{\kappa}_{C,A^*} := |\Pr[\mathsf{Exp}^{\kappa}_{C,A^*} = 0] - \Pr[\mathsf{Exp}^{\kappa}_{C,A^*} = 1]|$ is negligible with respect to κ in the game which is not resolved.*

We emphasize that num^*_0 and num^*_1 are always distinguishable in resolved games as long as the comparable encryption is complete. In other words, adversaries are not considered to be successful in distinguishing ciphertexts if and only if distinguishing them is trivially possible due to the functionality of the scheme.

4.2 Weak Indistinguishability

The indistinguishability in Def. 5 is ideal but the scheme we devised does not satisfy this property. However, the scheme partially achieves this property. Hence, we need to estimate what and how much it achieves. A token for *num* in our scheme leaks one bit for each ciphertext addition to that in an ideal scheme leaks. As we want estimate the relative impact of this leakage compared to the impact of what an ideal scheme leaks, we introduce a security notion that include this leakage in term of indistinguishability. For this purpose, we introduce weak indistinguishability.

We say $num <_\ell num'$ if $num < num'$, $\mathsf{MSPBs}(num, \ell) = \mathsf{MSPBs}(num', \ell)$, and $b_\ell \neq b'_\ell$ all hold. Note that "$num \not<_\ell num'$" (the negation of $num <_\ell num'$) holds for some ℓ even if $num < num'$. We will see how this notion works.

Suppose that $num < num' < num^{\ddagger}$ and $\mathsf{MSPBs}(num, \ell) = \mathsf{MSPBs}(num', \ell)$ and $\mathsf{MSPBs}(num', \ell') = \mathsf{MSPBs}(num^{\ddagger}, \ell')$ for $\ell < \ell'$. It is trivial that $token^{\dagger} = \mathsf{Der}(param, mkey, num^{\dagger})$ and $ciph^{\dagger} = \mathsf{Enc}(param, mkey, num^{\dagger})$ enable to distinguish $ciph = \mathsf{Enc}(param, mkey, num)$ and $ciph' = \mathsf{Enc}(param, mkey, num')$ if $num < num^{\dagger} < num'$. In our scheme, $token^{\ddagger} = \mathsf{Der}(param, mkey, num^{\ddagger})$ and $ciph^{\ddagger} = \mathsf{Enc}(param, mkey, num^{\ddagger})$ also enable to distinguish $ciph$ and $ciph'$. This is because as follows. $ciph$, $ciph^{\ddagger}$, and $token^d dagger$ reveal that ℓ-th bit of num and $num^{\ddagger}$ are different. $ciph'$, $ciph^{\ddagger}$, and $token^d dagger$ reveal that ℓ-th bit of num' and $num^{\ddagger}$ are the same. The notion "$<_\ell$" captures this property by $num <_\ell num^{\ddagger}$ and $num' \not<_\ell num^{\ddagger}$.

Definition 6. *We say a distinguishing game is **weakly resolved** if A^* queries such (command, num) that the following relation holds during the game, where command is cmprkey if type $= I$ but command is either cmprkey or encrypt if type $= II$.*

$$\exists \ell (0 \leq \ell < n) \ s.t.$$
$$((num^*_0 <_\ell num) \wedge (num^*_1 \not<_\ell num)) \vee ((num \not<_\ell num^*_0) \wedge (num <_\ell num^*_1)) . (2)$$

Here, n is the range parameter given to C at the beginning of the game.

Note that Def. 4 and Def. 6 are different only in that "$\exists \ell$" is added and that $<$ is replaced with $<_\ell$. The Fig. 1 illustrates this difference between Def. 4 and Def. 6 in the case $num^*_0 = 9$ and $num^*_1 = 13$. The figure consists of nodes of a tree expressed by dots. The leftmost dot is the root and rightmost dots are

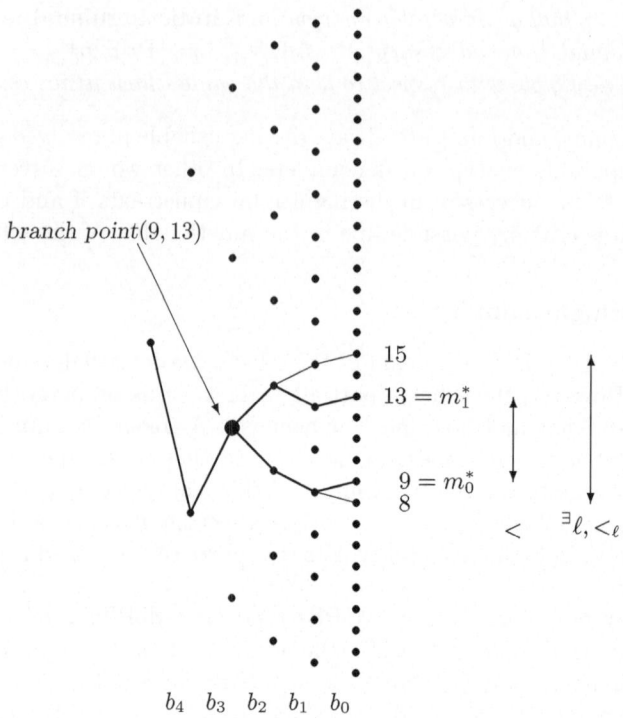

branch point(9, 13)

15
$13 = m_1^*$

$9 = m_0^*$
8

$<$ $\exists \ell, <_\ell$

b_4 b_3 b_2 b_1 b_0

Fig. 1. Tree Representations of 9 and 13, and the ranges specified by "$<$" and "$\exists \ell, <_\ell$"

leaves. Other dots are internal nodes. Each path from the root to a leaf expresses a number in $[0, 2^5)$. Each path consists of five edge and each edge represents a bit. An upward edge represents 1 and downward one represents 0. Hence 13, which is $(b_4, b_3, b_2, b_1, b_0) = (0, 1, 1, 0, 1)$, is expressed as a path that advances from the root to a leaf by choosing directions (down,up,up,down,up) at nodes on the path.

In the case of Fig. 1, the game is resolved if (command, num) for $m_0^* = 9 \leq num \leq 13 = m_1^*$ is queried but the game is weakly resolved if (command, num) for $8 \leq num \leq 15$ is queried. Note that these numbers $8, 9, 13, 15$ share the same node pointed indicated by "branch point(9, 13)" in the figure. Here, 8 and 15 are the minimum and the maximum number that share the node where 9 and 13 branch away. Def. 6 forbids numbers in wider range to be queried so as the game to be not resolved than Def. 4 forbids. We consider how much this range is widened is how much schemes get weaker. In this example, the range $13 - 9 + 1 = 5$ is widened to $15 - 8 + 1 = 8$ by the ratio of $8/5 = 1.6$. We later argue that the expected value of this ratio is 2.8.

Definition 7. *We say that a comparable encryption is* **weakly indistinguishable (wInd-secure)** *if, for every polynomial time adversary* A^*, $\mathrm{Adv}_{C, A^*}^\kappa :=$

$|\Pr[\mathsf{Exp}^{\kappa}_{C,A^*} = 0] - \Pr[\mathsf{Exp}^{\kappa}_{C,A^*} = 1]|$ *is negligible with respect to κ in the game which is not weakly resolved.*

Since Def. 7 considers that the game is resolved under wider class of queries than Def. 5 does, it provides weaker security. But we consider this difference is in moderate extent. The impact of difference between Def. 7 and Def. 5 is analyzed in Subsection 4.3.

Theorem 2. *The proposed comparable encryption is* **weakly indistinguishable** *as long as* Hash *is a pseudorandom function.*

Proof. The proof is straightforward. We replace some of outputs of hash functions with random variable and then simply prove indistinguishability of them. The proof is given in Appendix A.

4.3   Comparison of Two Indistinguishability Notions

Although a comparable encryption that are only wInd-secure leaks more knowledge than ideal ones, ciphertexts in it reveal no knowledge without tokens. Hence, such a comparable encryption is still effective, unlike OPEs, even when encrypting numbers that are densely distributed in a table. But, as there is a chance for an adversary to obtain tokens, it is now essential to evaluate the amount of knowledge that these tokens leak.

From a simple observation, each token with respect to num leaks where num and num' branch away for each encryption of num'. This is a great amount of information if we insist on semantic security. But it is not clear in the context of such an encryption schemes that comparisons are already possible. Hence, we evaluate the how knowledge of these branching bits gives an impact in distinguishing numbers compared to the ideal comparable encryption. We do not consider ours is the only way to evaluate the impact and consider a lot of discussion is necessary. We hope our evaluation opens the problem.

Suppose that $0 \le num^*_0, num^*_1 < 2^n$ are given. Let $D(num^*_0, num^*_1)$ be the number of num that satisfies Eq. (1) and let $N(num^*_0, num^*_1)$ be the number of num that satisfies Eq. (2). Then $R(num^*_0, num^*_1) = N(num^*_0, num^*_1)/D(num^*_0, num^*_1)$ is the ratio of "the number of occasions when tokens of a weaker scheme leaks" to "the number of occasions when tokens of an ideal scheme leaks", which represents how much wInd-secure comparable encryption is weak compared to ideal comparable encryption. When the ratio is one, a wInd-secure comparable encryption has no worse than ideal comparable encryptions. But the ratio that is larger than one signifies the weakness of wInd-secure comparable encryption.

Since the ratio $R(num^*_0, num^*_1)$ varies over the choice of pair (num^*_0, num^*_1), the ratio at a single point cannot represents the total security of wInd-secure comparable encryptions. Hence, we evaluate its expected value over uniformly and randomly chosen (num^*_0, num^*_1) and consider it as a measure of the weakness of wInd-secure comparable encryptions. Although imposing uniform distribution is rather crude, we have no reasonable alternative choice.

Let $\ell(x,y)$ be largest ℓ such that $\mathsf{MSPBs}(x,\ell) = \mathsf{MSPBs}(y,\ell)$ holds. Then, the expected value of $R(num_0^*, num_1^*)$ is,

$$\frac{2}{2^n(2^n-1)} \sum_{0 \le x < y < 2^n} R(x,y) = \frac{2}{2^n(2^n-1)} \sum_{0 \le x < y < 2^n} \frac{2^{\ell(x,y)}-1}{y-x}$$

$$= \frac{2}{2^n(2^n-1)} \sum_{\ell=0}^{n-1} \sum_{\{x,y \mid \ell(x,y)=\ell\}} \frac{2^{\ell}-1}{y-x}$$

$$= \frac{2}{2^n(2^n-1)} \sum_{\ell=0}^{n-1} 2^{n-1-\ell} \sum_{0 \le a,b < 2^{\ell-1}} \frac{2^{\ell}-1}{a+b+1}$$

$$\lesssim \frac{2}{2^n(2^n-1)} \sum_{\ell=0}^{n-1} 2^{n+1+\ell} \frac{1}{2^{2(\ell-1)}} \int_{a=1}^{2^{\ell-1}} \int_{b=1}^{2^{\ell-1}} \frac{2^{\ell}}{a+b} db\, da$$

$$\lesssim \frac{2}{2^n(2^n-1)} \sum_{\ell=0}^{n-1} 2^{n+1+\ell} \cdot 2\ln 2 = 4\ln 2 \lesssim 2.8$$

Therefore, we may conclude that, in average, the number of values that helps adversary distinguish num_0^* and num_1^* in wInd-secure comparable encryption is at most 2.8 times as large as that of values in ideal comparable encryptions. We consider this is not a considerable sacrifice for achieving practically efficiency of comparable encryption in most applications. This measure is based on rather crude assumption of the distribution but note that tokens are always deleted after their use.

As well as the expected ratio $N(num_0^*, num_1^*)/D(num_0^*, num_1^*)$, we give two more measures of comparison in Table 2. The expected value of $D(num_0^*, num_1^*)/N(num_0^*, num_1^*)$ is almost $1/2$. The expected value of $N(num_0^*, num_1^*)$ divided by the expected value of $D(num_0^*, num_1^*)$ is at most 2. Although the interpretations of these measures are not as natural as that of the expected value of ratio $N(num_0^*, num_1^*)/D(num_0^*, num_1^*)$, they measures the security of wInd-secure schemes in some extent. Both measures indicate better security as they get closer to 1.

Table 2. Various comparison measures

Measures	value
Expected Value of "$N(num_0^*, num_1^*)/D(num_0^*, num_1^*)$"	≤ 2.8
Expected Value of "$D(num_0^*, num_1^*)/N(num_0^*, num_1^*)$"	≤ 2
"E.V. of $N(num_0^*, num_1^*)$"/ "E. V. of $D(num_0^*, num_1^*)$"	$\ge 1/2$

5   Summary and Open Problem

We introduced a novel type of encryption scheme called comparable encryption, which enables one to compare the numerical order of two encrypted numbers only when either of numbers is accompanied by a token. We presented an ideal property and a weaker but reasonably nice property of comparable encryption. We also constructed a comparable encryption that satisfies only the weaker property but is practically efficient. We consider a comparable encryption is a useful primitive for encrypted DBs and consider proposing an efficient comparable encryption with the ideal property is a remaining important challenge. Our construction can be its starting point. By comparing efficiency of OPE and comparable encryption, we suggest to use an OPE in encrypted DBs when its positive result (shown by [9]) holds but suggest to use a comparable encryption when that positive result no longer holds.

References

1. Agrawal, R., Kiernan, J., Srikant, R., Xu, Y.: Order-preserving encryption for numeric data. In: Weikum, G., König, A.C., Deßloch, S. (eds.) SIGMOD Conference, pp. 563–574. ACM (2004)
2. Amanatidis, G., Boldyreva, A., O'Neill, A.: Provably-secure schemes for basic query support in outsourced databases. In: Barker, S., Ahn, G.-J. (eds.) Data and Applications Security 2007. LNCS, vol. 4602, pp. 14–30. Springer, Heidelberg (2007)
3. Belazzougui, D., Boldi, P., Pagh, R., Vigna, S.: Monotone minimal perfect hashing: searching a sorted table with $o(1)$ accesses. In: Mathieu, C. (ed.) SODA, pp. 785–794. SIAM (2009)
4. Bellare, M., Boldyreva, A., Knudsen, L.R., Namprempre, C.: Online ciphers and the hash-CBC construction. In: Kilian, J. (ed.) CRYPTO 2001. LNCS, vol. 2139, pp. 292–309. Springer, Heidelberg (2001)
5. Bellare, M., Boldyreva, A., O'Neill, A.: Deterministic and efficiently searchable encryption. In: Menezes, A. (ed.) CRYPTO 2007. LNCS, vol. 4622, pp. 535–552. Springer, Heidelberg (2007)
6. Bellare, M., Fischlin, M., O'Neill, A., Ristenpart, T.: Deterministic encryption: Definitional equivalences and constructions without random oracles. In: Wagner (ed.) [33], pp. 360–378
7. Bellare, M., Namprempre, C.: Authenticated encryption: Relations among notions and analysis of the generic composition paradigm. In: Okamoto, T. (ed.) ASIACRYPT 2000. LNCS, vol. 1976, pp. 531–545. Springer, Heidelberg (2000)
8. Boldyreva, A., Chenette, N., Lee, Y., O'Neill, A.: Order-preserving symmetric encryption. In: Joux, A. (ed.) EUROCRYPT 2009. LNCS, vol. 5479, pp. 224–241. Springer, Heidelberg (2009)
9. Boldyreva, A., Chenette, N., O'Neill, A.: Order-preserving encryption revisited: Improved security analysis and alternative solutions. In: Rogaway, P. (ed.) CRYPTO 2011. LNCS, vol. 6841, pp. 578–595. Springer, Heidelberg (2011)
10. Boldyreva, A., Fehr, S., O'Neill, A.: On notions of security for deterministic encryption, and efficient constructions without random oracles. In: Wagner (ed.) [33], pp. 335–359
11. Boneh, D., Waters, B.: Conjunctive, subset, and range queries on encrypted data. In: Vadhan, S.P. (ed.) TCC 2007. LNCS, vol. 4392, pp. 535–554. Springer, Heidelberg (2007)
12. Ceselli, A., Damiani, E., di Vimercati, S.D.C., Jajodia, S., Paraboschi, S., Samarati, P.: Modeling and assessing inference exposure in encrypted databases. ACM Trans. Inf. Syst. Secur. 8(1), 119–152 (2005)

13. Chase, M., Kamara, S.: Structured encryption and controlled disclosure. IACR Cryptology ePrint Archive, 2011:10 (2011)
14. Chor, B., Goldreich, O., Kushilevitz, E., Sudan, M.: Private information retrieval. In: FOCS, pp. 41–50 (1995)
15. Chor, B., Kushilevitz, E., Goldreich, O., Sudan, M.: Private information retrieval. J. ACM 45(6), 965–981 (1998)
16. Codd, E.F.: A relational model of data for large shared data banks. Commun. ACM 13(6), 377–387 (1970)
17. Curtmola, R., Garay, J.A., Kamara, S., Ostrovsky, R.: Searchable symmetric encryption: improved definitions and efficient constructions. In: Juels, A., Wright, R.N., di Vimercati, S.D.C. (eds.) ACM Conference on Computer and Communications Security, pp. 79–88. ACM (2006)
18. Ding, Y., Klein, K.: Model-driven application-level encryption for the privacy of e-health data. In: ARES, pp. 341–346. IEEE Computer Society (2010)
19. Goh, E.-J.: Secure indexes. Cryptology ePrint Archive, Report 2003/216 (2003), http://eprint.iacr.org/
20. Hacigümüs, H., Iyer, B.R., Li, C., Mehrotra, S.: Executing sql over encrypted data in the database-service-provider model. In: Franklin, M.J., Moon, B., Ailamaki, A. (eds.) SIGMOD Conference, pp. 216–227. ACM (2002)
21. Hacigümüs, H., Mehrotra, S., Iyer, B.R.: Providing database as a service. In: ICDE, pp. 21–38. IEEE Computer Society (2002)
22. Kamara, S., Papamanthou, C., Roeder, T.: Dynamic searchable symmetric encryption. In: Yu, T., Danezis, G., Gligor, V.D. (eds.) ACM Conference on Computer and Communications Security, pp. 965–976. ACM (2012)
23. Kushilevitz, E., Ostrovsky, R.: Replication is not needed: Single database, computationally-private information retrieval. In: FOCS, pp. 364–373 (1997)
24. Li, J., Omiecinski, E.R.: Efficiency and security trade-off in supporting range queries on encrypted databases. In: Jajodia, S., Wijesekera, D. (eds.) Data and Applications Security 2005. LNCS, vol. 3654, pp. 69–83. Springer, Heidelberg (2005)
25. Liu, H., Wang, H., Chen, Y.: Ensuring data storage security against frequency-based attacks in wireless networks. In: Rajaraman, R., Moscibroda, T., Dunkels, A., Scaglione, A. (eds.) DCOSS 2010. LNCS, vol. 6131, pp. 201–215. Springer, Heidelberg (2010)
26. Lu, W., Varna, A.L., Wu, M.: Security analysis for privacy preserving search of multimedia. In: ICIP, pp. 2093–2096. IEEE (2010)
27. Oracle. Oracle database 11g, oracle advanced security, http://www.oracle.com/technology/global/jp/products/security/db_security/htdocs/aso.html
28. Popa, R.A., Li, F.H., Zeldovich, N.: An ideal-security protocol for order-preserving encoding. Cryptology ePrint Archive, Report 2013/129 (2013), http://eprint.iacr.org/
29. Popa, R.A., Redfield, C.M.S., Zeldovich, N., Balakrishnan, H.: Cryptdb: protecting confidentiality with encrypted query processing. In: Wobber, T., Druschel, P. (eds.) SOSP, pp. 85–100. ACM (2011)
30. Shi, E., Bethencourt, J., Chan, H.T.-H., Song, D.X., Perrig, A.: Multi-dimensional range query over encrypted data. In: IEEE Symposium on Security and Privacy, pp. 350–364. IEEE Computer Society (2007)
31. Tang, Q.: Privacy preserving mapping schemes supporting comparison (2010)
32. TPC-C. Transaction processing performance council, http://www.tpc.org/tpcc/
33. Wagner, D. (ed.): CRYPTO 2008. LNCS, vol. 5157. Springer, Heidelberg (2008)

34. Wang, C., Cao, N., Li, J., Ren, K., Lou, W.: Secure ranked keyword search over encrypted cloud data. In: ICDCS, pp. 253–262. IEEE Computer Society (2010)
35. Xu, J., Fan, J., Ammar, M.H., Moon, S.B.: Prefix-preserving ip address anonymization: Measurement-based security evaluation and a new cryptography-based scheme. In: ICNP, pp. 280–289. IEEE Computer Society (2002)

A Proof of Theorem 2

The proof is by contraposition. Suppose that there exists an adversary A^* such that $\mathsf{Adv}^{\kappa}_{C,A^*}$ is not negligible with respect to κ in the game which is not weakly resolved. Then, we show that Hash is distinguishable from the random function, which is against the assumption that they are pseudorandom function. In particular, we consider a sequence of games by challengers C, C_1, and C_2 and then prove the theorem by the hybrid argument. We let $\mathsf{Branch}(num, num')$ denote the largest ℓ such that $\mathsf{MSPBs}(num, \ell) = \mathsf{MSPBs}(num', \ell)$ holds.

Proof. From two lemmas 1 and 2 and the hybrid argument, $|\mathsf{Adv}^{\kappa}_{C,A^*} - \mathsf{Adv}^{\kappa}_{C_2,A^*}|$ is negligible in κ as long as Hash is a pseudorandom function. Since $\mathsf{Adv}^{\kappa}_{C_2,A^*} = 0$ from Lemma 3, $\mathsf{Adv}^{\kappa}_{C,A^*}$ is negligible in κ. Hence, the theorem is proved.

Definition 8. *Challenger C_1 is the same as the challenger C in Definition 3 except the following:*

- *At the beginning of the game, C_1 discards mkey.*
- *C_1 prepares a table and simulate hash function $\mathsf{Hash}(\text{mkey}, \cdot)$. That is, whenever C_1 generates $\text{output} = \mathsf{Hash}(\text{mkey}, \text{input})$ for some input, C_1 let output be output' if an entry $(\text{input}, \text{output}')$ is in the table. Otherwise, C_1 randomly chooses $\text{output} \in \{0,1\}^{\kappa}$ and writes $(\text{input}, \text{output})$ into the table.*

Note that $(d_i)_{i=0,\dots,n}$ and $(e_i)_{i=0,\dots,n}$ that C_1 outputs for every num is completely random.

Lemma 1. *Assume that Hash is a pseudorandom function. For every polynomial time A^*, $|\mathsf{Adv}^{\kappa}_{C_1,A^*} - \mathsf{Adv}^{\kappa}_{C,A^*}|$ is negligible in κ.*

Proof. Since mkey is used for only input to hash functions and is never revealed to A^*, the lemma follows from the indistinguishability of pseudorandom function.

Definition 9. *Challenger C_2 is the same as the challenger C_1 except the following:*

- *Let $(\bar{d}_0, \dots, \bar{d}_n)$ and $(\hat{d}_0, \dots, \hat{d}_n)$ be*

$$(\bar{d}_0, \dots, \bar{d}_n) = \mathsf{Der}(\text{param}, \text{mkey}, num^*_0)$$
$$(\hat{d}_0, \dots, \hat{d}_n) = \mathsf{Der}(\text{param}, \text{mkey}, num^*_1).$$

Note that $\bar{d}_i = \hat{d}_i$ for all i such that $\mathsf{Branch}(num^*_0, num^*_1) < i \le n$
C_2 prepares a table and simulate hash function $\mathsf{Hash}(\bar{d}_i, \cdot)$ and $\mathsf{Hash}(\hat{d}_i, \cdot)$ for all i such that $0 \le i \le \mathsf{Branch}(num^*_0, num^*_1)$. The simulation is as is the before.

Lemma 2. *Assume that* Hash *is a pseudorandom function. For every polynomial time* A^*, $|\mathsf{Adv}^{\kappa}_{C_2,A^*} - \mathsf{Adv}^{\kappa}_{C_1,A^*}|$ *is negligible in* κ.

Proof. Let $num_0^* = (\bar{b}_0, \ldots, \bar{b}_{n-1})$, $num_1^* = (\hat{b}_0, \ldots, \hat{b}_{n-1})$, and $B = \mathsf{Branch}(num_0^*, num_1^*)$. Then $\bar{b}_i = \hat{b}_i$ for all i such that $B < i \leq n$. Suppose that the adversary queries (command, num) for $num := (b_0, \ldots, b_{n-1})$. If $b_i = \bar{b}_i$ for all i such that $B < i < n$, then $\mathsf{Branch}(num_1^*, num) \leq B$. This implies that the distinguishing game is weakly resolved. Therefore, there exists i such that $b_i \neq \bar{b}_i$ and that $B < i < n$, as long as the distinguishing game is not weakly resolved.

- In the case when $type = I$, none of $\bar{d}_0, \ldots, \bar{d}_B, \hat{d}_0, \ldots, \hat{d}_B$ is revealed to the adversary. For such data to be revealed, all $\bar{d}_{B+1}, \ldots, \bar{d}_B$ needs to be revealed. But the existence of i such that $b_i \neq \bar{b}_i$ and that $B < i < n$ prevents it. Since, the values $\bar{d}_0, \ldots, \bar{d}_B, \hat{d}_0, \ldots, \hat{d}_B$ are randomly chosen and unrevealed, the hardness of distinguishing random values with outputs of $\mathsf{Hash}(\bar{d}_i, \cdot)$ and $\mathsf{Hash}(\hat{d}_i, \cdot)$ for all i such that $0 \leq i \leq \mathsf{Branch}(num_0^*, num_1^*) = B$ follows from the indistinguishability of pseudorandom function. This proves the lemma in the case $type = I$.
- In case when $type = II$, one of tuples $(\bar{d}_0, \ldots, \bar{d}_B)$ and $(\hat{d}_0, \ldots, \hat{d}_B)$ is given to the adversary depending on the value of b unlike the case when $type = I$. We assume $b = 0$ in the following without lose of generality. Then, $\bar{d}_0, \ldots, \bar{d}_B$ are given to A^* in this case. Unlike the case when $type = I$, $\mathsf{Hash}(mkey, (4, \bar{d}_{i+1}, 0))$ is used only for generating $\bar{e}_i := \mathsf{Hash}(mkey, (4, \bar{d}_{i+1}, 0)) + \bar{b}_i \bmod 3$ for $i = 0, \ldots, B-1$ in $ciph^*$. Hence, replacing $\mathsf{Hash}(\bar{d}_{i+1}, (5, I, 0))$ in $\bar{f}_i := \mathsf{Hash}(\bar{d}_{i+1}, (5, I, 0)) + \mathsf{Hash}(mkey, (4, \bar{d}_{i+1}, 0)) + \bar{b}_i \bmod 3$ with a random value for $i = 1, \ldots, B$ does not affect the distribution of $\bar{f}_i$. This is because the distribution of $\bar{f}_i$ for $i = 0, \ldots, B-1$ are already random. This proves the lemma in the case $type = II$.

Lemma 3. *For every polynomial time* A^*, $\mathsf{Adv}^{\kappa}_{C_2,A^*} = 0$.

Proof. The lemma follows from the fact that $ciph^*$ does not depend on b, which can be shown as follows. The difference in $ciph^*$ between num_0^* and num_1^* may occur only in (c_i, f_i) for $i = 0, \ldots, B$. Since each $\mathsf{Hash}(\bar{d}_i, \cdot)$ (we assume $b = 0$ w.l.g.) for $i = 0, \ldots, B$ is randomly chosen, every c_i for $i = 0, \ldots, B$ does not depend on b. Since each $\mathsf{Hash}(\bar{d}_i, \cdot)$ for $i = 0, \ldots, B$ is randomly chosen, every f_i for $i = 0, \ldots, B$ does not depend on b. Therefore, the lemma is proved.

Ensuring File Authenticity in Private DFA Evaluation on Encrypted Files in the Cloud

Lei Wei and Michael K. Reiter

Department of Computer Science
University of North Carolina at Chapel Hill
{lwei,reiter}@cs.unc.edu

Abstract. Cloud storage, and more specifically the encryption of file contents to protect them in the cloud, can interfere with access to these files by partially trusted third-party service providers and customers. To support such access for pattern-matching applications (e.g., malware scanning), we present a protocol that enables a client authorized by the data owner to evaluate a deterministic finite automaton (DFA) on a file stored at a server (the cloud), even though the file is encrypted by the data owner for protection from the server. Our protocol contributes over previous work by enabling the client to detect any misbehavior of the server; in particular, the client can verify that the result of its DFA evaluation is based on the file stored there by the data owner, and in this sense the file and protocol result are authenticated to the client. Our protocol also protects the privacy of the file and the DFA from the server, and the privacy of the file (except the result of evaluating the DFA on it) from the client. A special case of our protocol solves private DFA evaluation on a private and authenticated file in the traditional two-party model, in which the file contents are known to the server. Our protocol provably achieves these properties for an arbitrarily malicious server and an honest-but-curious client, in the random oracle model.

1 Introduction

Outsourcing file storage to clouds is a dominant trend today that appears likely to continue for the foreseeable future. However, cloud storage comes with increased risks of data manipulation, since the data is stored outside the administrative control of the data owner. Numerous techniques have thus been developed to enable third parties who search on the data to confirm that the cloud service faithfully serves requests using the data owner's intended data (e.g., [26,25,21]).

Such techniques, however, typically do not account for the privacy of searches and the data itself. To protect cloud-resident files from disclosure, it is not uncommon for the data owner to encrypt her files before storing them. Specialized cryptographic protocols are then needed to permit third parties to perform searches on that data. For example, a data owner may wish to enable an antivirus vendor to perform malware scanning on her cloud-resident files without decrypting the files in the cloud. Similarly, owners of a genome database may

J. Crampton, S. Jajodia, and K. Mayes (Eds.): ESORICS 2013, LNCS 8134, pp. 147–163, 2013.
© Springer-Verlag Berlin Heidelberg 2013

wish to enable qualified researchers to perform searches on the data (e.g., [1,2]), again without decrypting the files in the cloud. These applications are especially challenging if the third parties should be given only limited access to the data (versus disclosing all of it to them) and because the searches themselves may be sensitive: malware signatures can be used to develop malware to evade them [18,32] and searches on genome datasets may reflect proprietary research directions.

Protocols for a third-party client to perform private searches on encrypted data in the cloud, while revealing nothing to the cloud server and nothing but the search result to the client, do exist for some types of searches (e.g., [27,11,30]). To our knowledge, however, none also enforces that the cloud server employs the data that the data owner stored at the cloud server. Indeed, the traditional notion that a protocol is secure against arbitrarily malicious adversaries provides no guarantees on what *input* a malicious party may use in the protocol.

In this paper, we provide a protocol that enables a client to evaluate a deterministic finite automaton (DFA) on a file encrypted at the cloud server so that the authenticity of the file input by the server and the integrity of the computation result are both enforced. At the same time, the protocol provably protects the file contents (except for the result of the computation) from an honest-but-curious client (and heuristically from even a malicious client) and provably protects both the file contents and DFA from an arbitrarily malicious server. To our knowledge, our protocol is the first example of performing secure DFA computation on both encrypted *and authenticated* data.

Traditionally, one needs to know the file content and the signature to verify the authenticity of a file, and so the main technical difficulty in our case is to ensure computation on authenticated (signed) data without disclosing the plaintext to either party. The most common approach one might first consider to solve this problem is to leverage zero-knowledge proof techniques. By asking the data owner to publish commitments of the file character signatures, the server might then prove that his input used in the protocol is consistent with the published commitments. In the ways we see to instantiate this intuition, however, it would require much higher computation and communication costs than our protocol. Instead, we introduce a new technique to enforce correct server behavior and the authenticity of the input on which it is allowed to operate, without relying on zero-knowledge proofs at all. At a high level, the protocol takes advantage of the verifiability of the computation result to check the correctness of the server behavior. The protocol is designed so that that legitimate outputs are encoded in a small space only known to the client, and any malicious behavior by the server will result in the final output lying outside this space, which is then easily detected by the client. We prove this property (in the random oracle model) and the privacy of both the file and the DFA against an arbitrarily malicious server. We also prove the privacy of the file (except for the result of the DFA evaluation) against an honest-but-curious client.

The rest of this paper is structured as follows. We discuss related work in Section 2 and review our goals in Section 3. We detail our protocol and summarize its security proof in Section 4. We discuss the impact of file updates in Section 5. We discuss extensions in Section 6 and conclude in Section 7.

2   Related Work

The topic on which we focus in this paper falls into the general paradigm of two-party secure computation [31,15]. The specific problem of private DFA evaluation was first studied by Troncoso-Pastoriza et al. [29] who presented a protocol for honest-but-curious adversaries in which one party can evaluate its private DFA on a string held by another party, without either party leaking any information about its input beyond what is implied by the outcome of the evaluation. Since then, the problem has been extensively studied. Frikken [13] presented a protocol that improved on the round complexity and computational costs. Gennaro et al. [14] proposed a protocol that is secure against malicious adversaries. Mohassel et al. [23] presented a protocol that significantly improves on the computational costs of both participants. Blanton and Aliasgari [4] proposed protocols that outsource the computation to two computational servers by secret sharing the DFA and data between them (with extension to multiple servers). The work by Wei and Reiter [30] is the most relevant to ours. They introduced new protocols in the cloud outsourcing scenario where a client can evaluate a DFA on the encrypted data stored on a cloud server, once authorized to do so by the data owner. However, the protocol does not guarantee the authenticity of the data input by the cloud server. The related problem of secure pattern matching has also attracted attention [16,17,19], though again without treatment of data authenticity as we consider here.

Secure computation on authenticated input was previously considered in the context of private set intersection. Several works [7,10,9,28] studied private intersection of certified sets, in which the set elements of each party must be certified by a trusted third party for use in performing the intersection. However, none considered the scenario where the data input to one party is only in ciphertext form and must remain hidden to it. In addition, to our knowledge we are the first to consider secure computation on authenticated data in the context of private DFA evaluation.

One of our protocol extensions (Section 6) secret-shares the file decryption key between the server and client in order to perform DFA evaluation on the encrypted data. In this respect, the protocols of Choi et al. [8] are related. They developed protocols based on a garbled circuit technique that enable two parties to compute any functionality after a secret decryption key is shared between them. This work, however, did not enforce authenticity of the protocol inputs.

3   Goals

A deterministic finite automaton M is a tuple $\langle Q, \Sigma, \delta, q_{init} \rangle$ where Q is a set of $|Q| = n$ *states*; Σ is a set (*alphabet*) of $|\Sigma| = m$ *symbols*; $\delta : Q \times \Sigma \to Q$ is a transition function; and q_{init} is the initial state. (A DFA can also specify a set $F \subseteq Q$ of accepting states; we ignore this here to save space, though our protocols can easily be adapted to accommodate it, similar to the techniques suggested in previous work [30].) Our goal is to enable a client holding a DFA M to interact with a server holding a file ciphertext to evaluate M on the file plaintext. More specifically, the client should output the final state to which the file plaintext drives the DFA; i.e., if the plaintext file is a sequence $\langle \sigma_k \rangle_{k \in [\ell]}$ where $[\ell]$ denotes the set $\{0, 1, \ldots, \ell - 1\}$ and where each $\sigma_k \in \Sigma$, then the client should output $\delta(\ldots \delta(\delta(q_{\mathrm{init}}, \sigma_0), \sigma_1), \ldots, \sigma_{\ell-1})$. We also permit the client to learn the file length ℓ and the server to learn the number of states n in the client's DFA. (Indeed, because the DFA output leaks $\log n$ bits about the file to the client, the server should know n to measure the leakage to the client and to limit the number of DFA queries the client is allowed, accordingly.) However, the client should learn nothing else about the file; the server should learn nothing else about the client's DFA and nothing about the file plaintext.

An additional goal of our protocols — and their main contribution over prior work — is to ensure that the client detects if the server deviates from the protocol. More specifically, we presume that a data owner stores the file ciphertext at the server, together with accompanying authentication data. We require that the client return the result of evaluating its DFA on the file stored by the data owner or else that the client detect the misbehavior of the server. In this paper we do not explicitly concern ourselves with misbehavior of the client, owing to the use cases outlined in Section 1 that involve a partially trusted third-party customer or service provider (e.g., antivirus vendor). That said, we believe our protocol to be heuristically secure against an arbitrarily malicious client.

4   Private DFA Evaluation on Signed and Encrypted Data

In this section we present a protocol meeting the goals described in Section 3: the client learns only the length of the file and the output of his DFA evaluation on the file stored at the server; the server learns only the number of states in the client's DFA and the length of the file; and the client detects any misbehavior by the server that would cause him to return an incorrect result. Again, we do not consider misbehavior of the client here; the client is honest-but-curious only. In this section we consider the file as static. The impact of file updates will be discussed in Section 5.

4.1   Preliminaries

Let "$\leftarrow$" denote assignment and "$s \xleftarrow{\$} S$" denote the assignment to s of a randomly chosen element of set S. Let κ be a security parameter. Let ParamGen be an algorithm that, on input 1^κ, produces $(p, G_1, G_2, g, e) \leftarrow \mathsf{ParamGen}(1^\kappa)$ where p is a prime; G_1 and G_2 are multiplicative groups of order p; g is a generator of G_1; and $e : G_1 \times G_1 \to G_2$ is an efficiently computable bilinear map such that $e(P^u, Q^v) = e(P, Q)^{uv}$ for any $P, Q \in G_1$ and any $u, v \in \mathbb{Z}_p^*$.

BLS Signatures. Our protocol makes use of the Boneh-Lynn-Shacham (BLS) signature scheme [6]. Suppose $(p, G_1, G_2, g, e) \leftarrow \mathsf{ParamGen}(1^\kappa)$ and let H_1 be a hash function $\mathsf{H}_1 : \{0,1\}^* \rightarrow G_1$. The BLS scheme consists of a triple of algorithms $(\mathsf{BLSKeyGen}, \mathsf{BLSSign}, \mathsf{BLSVerify})$, defined as follows.

$\underline{\mathsf{BLSKeyGen}(p, G_1, G_2, g, e)}$: Select $x \stackrel{\$}{\leftarrow} \mathbb{Z}_p^*$. Return private signing key $\langle G_1, x \rangle$ and public verification key $\langle p, G_1, G_2, g, e, h \rangle$ where $h \leftarrow g^x$.

$\underline{\mathsf{BLSSign}_{\langle G_1, x \rangle}(m)}$: Return the signature $\mathsf{H}_1(m)^x$.

$\underline{\mathsf{BLSVerify}_{\langle p, G_1, G_2, g, e, h \rangle}(m, s)}$: Return true if $e(\mathsf{H}_1(m), h) = e(s, g)$ and false otherwise.

Paillier encryption. Our scheme is built using the additively homomorphic encryption scheme due to Paillier [24]. This cryptosystem has a plaintext space $\mathbb{R}$ where $\langle \mathbb{R}, +_{\mathbb{R}}, \cdot_{\mathbb{R}} \rangle$ denotes a commutative ring. Specifically, this encryption scheme includes algorithms PGen, PEnc, and PDec where: PGen is a randomized algorithm that on input 1^κ outputs a public-key/private-key pair $(pek, pdk) \leftarrow \mathsf{PGen}(1^\kappa)$; PEnc is a randomized algorithm that on input public key pek and plaintext $m \in \mathbb{R}$ (where $\mathbb{R}$ can be determined as a function of pek) produces a ciphertext $c \leftarrow \mathsf{PEnc}_{pek}(m)$, where $c \in C_{pek}$ and C_{pek} is the ciphertext space determined by pek; and PDec is a deterministic algorithm that on input a private key pdk and ciphertext $c \in C_{pek}$ produces a plaintext $m \leftarrow \mathsf{PDec}_{pdk}(c)$ where $m \in \mathbb{R}$. In addition, $\mathcal{E}$ supports an operation $+_{pek}$ on ciphertexts such that for any public-key/private-key pair (pek, pdk), $\mathsf{PDec}_{pdk}(\mathsf{PEnc}_{pek}(m_1) +_{pek} \mathsf{PEnc}_{pek}(m_2)) = m_1 +_{\mathbb{R}} m_2$. Using $+_{pek}$, it is possible to implement $\cdot_{pek}$ for which $\mathsf{PDec}_{pdk}(m_2 \cdot_{pek} \mathsf{PEnc}_{pek}(m_1)) = m_1 \cdot_{\mathbb{R}} m_2$.

In Paillier encryption, the ring $\mathbb{R}$ is $\mathbb{Z}_N$, the ciphertext space $C_{\langle N, g \rangle}$ is $\mathbb{Z}_{N^2}^*$, and the relevant algorithms are as follows.

$\underline{\mathsf{PGen}(1^\kappa)}$: Choose random $\kappa/2$-bit strong primes p_1, p_2; set $N \leftarrow p_1 p_2$; choose $g \in \mathbb{Z}_{N^2}^*$ with order a multiple of N; and return the public key $\langle N, g \rangle$ and private key $\langle N, g, \lambda(N) \rangle$ where $\lambda(N)$ is the Carmichael function of N.

$\underline{\mathsf{PEnc}_{\langle N, g \rangle}(m)}$: Select $r \stackrel{\$}{\leftarrow} \mathbb{Z}_N^*$ and return $g^m r^N \mod N^2$.

$\underline{\mathsf{PDec}_{\langle N, g, \lambda(N) \rangle}(c)}$: Return $m = \dfrac{L(c^{\lambda(N)} \mod N^2)}{L(g^{\lambda(N)} \mod N^2)} \mod N$, where L is a function that takes input elements from the set $\{u < N^2 \mid u \equiv 1 \mod N\}$ and returns $L(u) = \frac{u-1}{N}$.

$\underline{c_1 +_{\langle N, g \rangle} c_2}$: Return $c_1 c_2 \mod N^2$.

$\underline{m \cdot_{\langle N, g \rangle} c}$: Return $c^m \mod N^2$.

We use $\sum_{pek}$ to denote summation using $+_{pek}$; $\sum_{\mathbb{R}}$ to denote summation using $+_{\mathbb{R}}$; and $\prod_{\mathbb{R}}$ to denote the product using $\cdot_{\mathbb{R}}$ of a sequence.

4.2   Initial Construction without File Encryption

We denote the file stored at the server as consisting of characters $\sigma_0, \ldots, \sigma_{\ell-1}$, where each $\sigma_k \in \Sigma$. Prior to storing this file at the server, however, the data owner uses its private BLS signing key $\langle G_1, x \rangle$ to produce $s_k \leftarrow \mathsf{BLSSign}_{\langle G_1, x \rangle}(\sigma_k \| k)$ for each $k \in [\ell]$ — i.e., a per-file-character signature that incorporates the position of the character in the file[1] — and stores these signed characters at the **server**, instead. (Here, "$\|$" denotes concatenation.) Note that since $s_k = \mathsf{H}_1(\sigma_k \| k)^x$, anyone knowing the corresponding verification key $\langle p, G_1, G_2, g, e, h \rangle$ cannot only verify s_k but can also extract σ_k and k, by simply testing for each $\sigma \in \Sigma$ and $k \in [\ell]$ whether $e(\mathsf{H}_1(\sigma \| k), h) = e(s_k, g)$. As such, while in our initial protocol description, the data owner stores $s_0, \ldots, s_{\ell-1}$ at the **server**, this implicitly conveys $\sigma_0, \ldots, \sigma_{\ell-1}$, as well.

The basic structure of the protocol, which is borrowed from previous work [30], involves the **client** encoding its DFA transition function δ as a bivariate polynomial $f(x, y)$ over $\mathbb{R}$ where x is the variable representing a DFA state and y is the variable representing an input symbol. In our protocol, the **client** and **server** then evaluate this polynomial together, using a single round of interaction per state transition (i.e., per file character), in such a way that the **client** observes only ciphertexts of states and file characters and the **server** observes only a randomly blinded state. More specifically, in our protocol, if the current DFA state is q, then the **server** observes only $\pi(q) +_\mathbb{R} \varphi$ for $\varphi \xleftarrow{\$} \mathbb{R}$ chosen by the **client** and where $\pi : Q \to \mathbb{R}$ maps DFA states to distinct ring elements. The **client**, with knowledge of π and φ, can calculate $f(x, y)$ so that $f(\pi(q) +_\mathbb{R} \varphi, \sigma) = \pi(\delta(q, \sigma))$ for each $q \in Q$ and $\sigma \in \Sigma$. Then, starting with a ciphertext of $\pi(q)$ for the DFA state q resulting from processing file characters $\sigma_0, \ldots, \sigma_{k-1}$, the **client** can interact with the **server** to obtain a ciphertext of $f(\pi(q) +_\mathbb{R} \varphi, \sigma_k)$ [30].

The central innovation in our protocol is a technique by which the **client**, without knowing s_k, can compute an encoding of the file character σ_k that the **server** must use in round k of the evaluation. If the **server** does not, it "throws off" the evaluation in a way that the **server** cannot predict. As a result, if the **server** deviates from the protocol, the end result of the evaluation will be an unpredictable element of the ring $\mathbb{R}$, which will not correspond to *any* state of the DFA with overwhelming probability. To accomplish this, the **client** defines the encoding of character $\sigma \in \Sigma$ and position $k \in [\ell]$ to be $\tau(\sigma, k, \psi_k) = \mathsf{H}_2(e(\mathsf{H}_1(\sigma \| k)^{\psi_k}, h))$, where H_2 is a hash function $\mathsf{H}_2 : G_2 \to \mathbb{R}$ (modeled as a random oracle) and where $\psi_k \xleftarrow{\$} \mathbb{Z}_p^*$ is selected by the **client** in the round for the k-th character. If the **client** sends $\Psi_k \leftarrow g^{\psi_k}$ to the **server** in the round for the k-th character, then the **server** can compute $\tau(\sigma_k, k, \psi_k)$ for the file character σ_k as $\tau(\sigma_k, k, \psi_k) = \mathsf{H}_2(e(s_k, \Psi_k))$. However, without ψ_k the **server** will be unable to compute the encoding $\tau(\sigma, k, \psi_k)$ for any $\sigma \neq \sigma_k$.

The final difficulty to overcome lies in the fact that the **client**, by altering the encoding of each character $\sigma \in \Sigma$ per round k, must also recompute $f(x, y)$ to account for this new encoding. As such, the **client** recomputes $f(x, y)$ to satisfy $f(\pi(q) +_\mathbb{R} \varphi_k, \tau(\sigma, k, \psi_k)) = \pi(\delta(q, \sigma))$ per round k, for every $q \in Q$ and

---

[1] The file name or other identifier could be included along with the character position, to detect the exchange of characters between files. Similarly, the length ℓ can be included to detect file truncation. These issues are discussed further in Section 5.

$\sigma \in \Sigma$. In our algorithm, we encapsulate this calculation as $\langle a_{ij} \rangle_{i \in [n], j \in [m]} \leftarrow$ ToPoly$(Q, \Sigma, \delta, \pi, k, \varphi_k, \beta_k, \psi_k)$ where $\langle a_{ij} \rangle_{i \in [n], j \in [m]}$ are the coefficients forming f, i.e., so that $f(x, y) = \sum_{\mathbb{R} i=0}^{n-1} \sum_{\mathbb{R} j=0}^{m-1} a_{ij} \cdot_{\mathbb{R}} x^i \cdot_{\mathbb{R}} y^j$. (The value β_k will become relevant in Section 4.3 and can be ignored for now.)

This protocol is shown in Figure 1. The protocol is written with the steps performed by the client listed on the left (lines c101–c120), with those performed by the server on the right (lines s101–s113), and with the messages exchanged between them in the middle (lines m101–m106). The client takes as input the data owner's public verification key $\langle p, G_1, G_2, g, e, h \rangle$, a public encryption key ek', and its DFA $\langle Q, \Sigma, \delta, q_{\text{init}} \rangle$. (For the moment, ignore the additional input dk, which will be discussed in Section 4.3.) The server takes as input $\langle p, G_1, G_2, g, e, h \rangle$, the DFA alphabet Σ, and the signed file characters s_0, ..., $s_{\ell-1}$, i.e., signed with the data owner's private key $\langle G_1, x \rangle$ corresponding to $\langle p, G_1, G_2, g, e, h \rangle$. (Again, please ignore the b_k values for now. These will be discussed in Section 4.3.) Note that neither the client nor the server receives any information about the private key dk', and so values encrypted under ek' (θ in line c104, and ρ in line c109) are never decrypted or otherwise used in the protocol. These values are included in the protocol only to simplify its proof and need not be included in a real implementation of the protocol.

At the beginning of the protocol, the server generates the public/private key pair (pek, pdk) (line s102) that defines the ring $\mathbb{R}$ for the protocol run. The server conveys pek and the file length ℓ to the client (m101). Upon receiving this message, the client selects an injection $\pi : Q \to \mathbb{R}$ at random from the set of all such injections, denoted $\text{Injs}(Q \to \mathbb{R})$ (c103). The client sends the number n of states in his DFA in message m102. (To simplify our proofs, the client also sends the chosen injection π encrypted under ek' to server, denoted by θ. We will not discuss this further here.)

The heart of the protocol is the loop represented by lines c106–c117 for the client and lines s104–s112 for the server. The client begins each iteration of this loop with a ciphertext α of the current DFA state, which it blinds with the blinding term φ_k (c107) using the additive homomorphic property of Paillier encryption (c108). The client also selects ψ_k (c110) and creates Ψ_k (c111) as described above, and sends the now-blinded ciphertext α and Ψ_k to the server (m103). After decrypting the blinded state γ (s105) and using Ψ_k and s_k to create the encoding $\eta = \tau(\sigma, k, \psi_k)$ for the character σ_k being processed in this loop iteration (s106), the server creates the encryption of $\gamma^i \cdot_{\mathbb{R}} \eta^j$ for each $i \in [n]$ and $j \in [m]$ (s107–s111). After the server sends these values back to the client (m104), the client uses them together with the coefficients of f that it computed as described above (c113) to assemble a ciphertext of the new DFA state (c116).

After this loop iterates ℓ times, the client sends the state ciphertext to the server (m105). The server decrypts the (random) state (s113) and returns it (m106). The client checks to be sure that the result represents a valid state (c118) and, if so, returns the corresponding state as the result (c120).

client($\langle p, G_1, G_2, g, e, h\rangle$, $dk, ek', \langle Q, \Sigma, \delta, q_{\text{init}}\rangle$)	server($\langle p, G_1, G_2, g, e, h\rangle$, $\Sigma, \langle s_k, b_k\rangle_{k\in[\ell]}$)

c101. $n \leftarrow |Q|, m \leftarrow |\Sigma|$

s101. $m \leftarrow |\Sigma|$
s102. $(pek, pdk) \leftarrow \mathsf{PGen}(1^\kappa)$

m101. $\xleftarrow{\quad pek,\ell \quad}$

c102. $\langle N, g\rangle \leftarrow pek, \ \mathbb{R} \leftarrow \mathbb{Z}_N$

s103. $\langle N, g\rangle \leftarrow pek, \ \mathbb{R} \leftarrow \mathbb{Z}_N$

c103. $\pi \xleftarrow{\$} \mathsf{Injs}(Q \rightarrow \mathbb{R})$
c104. $\theta \leftarrow \mathsf{Enc}_{ek'}(\pi)$

m102. $\xrightarrow{\quad n,\theta \quad}$

c105. $\alpha \leftarrow \mathsf{PEnc}_{pek}(\pi(q_{\text{init}}))$
c106. $\mathbf{for}\ k \leftarrow 0 \ldots \ell - 1$

s104. $\mathbf{for}\ k \leftarrow 0 \ldots \ell - 1$

c107. $\varphi_k \xleftarrow{\$} \mathbb{R}$
c108. $\alpha \leftarrow \alpha +_{pek} \mathsf{PEnc}_{pek}(\varphi_k)$
c109. $\rho \leftarrow \mathsf{Enc}_{ek'}(\varphi_k)$
c110. $\psi_k \xleftarrow{\$} \mathbb{Z}_p^*$
c111. $\Psi_k \leftarrow g^{\psi_k}$

m103. $\xrightarrow{\quad \alpha,\rho,\Psi_k \quad}$

s105. $\gamma \leftarrow \mathsf{PDec}_{pdk}(\alpha)$
s106. $\eta \leftarrow \mathsf{H}_2(e(s_k, \Psi_k))$
s107. $\mathbf{for}\ i \in [n]$
s108. $\mathbf{for}\ j \in [m]$
s109. $\mu_{ij} \leftarrow \mathsf{PEnc}_{pek}(\gamma^i \cdot_{\mathbb{R}} \eta^j)$
s110. $\mathbf{endfor}$
s111. $\mathbf{endfor}$

m104. $\xleftarrow{\langle\mu_{ij}\rangle_{i\in[n],j\in[m]},b_k}$

c112. $\beta_k \leftarrow \mathsf{Dec}_{dk}(b_k)$
c113. $\langle a_{ij}\rangle_{i\in[n],j\in[m]}$
          $\leftarrow \mathsf{ToPoly}(Q, \Sigma, \delta, \pi, k, \varphi_k, \beta_k, \psi_k)$
c114. $\mathbf{if}\ \exists i, j : a_{ij} \neq 0 \wedge \gcd(a_{ij}, N) > 1$
c115. $\mathbf{then\ abort}$
c116. $\alpha \leftarrow \sum_{i=0}^{n-1}{}_{pek} \sum_{j=0}^{m-1}{}_{pek}\ a_{ij} \cdot_{pek} \mu_{ij}$
c117. $\mathbf{endfor}$

s112. $\mathbf{endfor}$

m105. $\xrightarrow{\quad \alpha \quad}$

s113. $\gamma^* \leftarrow \mathsf{PDec}_{pdk}(\alpha)$

m106. $\xleftarrow{\quad \gamma^* \quad}$

c118. $\mathbf{if}\ \gamma^* \notin \{\pi(q)\}_{q\in Q}$
c119. $\mathbf{then\ abort}$
c120. $\mathbf{else\ return}\ \pi^{-1}(\gamma^*)$

Fig. 1. Protocol Π, described in Section 4

4.3   Adding File Encryption

As presented so far, our protocol guarantees the integrity of the DFA evaluation against a malicious server. However, the confidentiality of the file content is not protected from the server because the signatures of the file characters are known to the server. With cloud outsourcing becoming increasingly popular, there is need to enable a data owner to outsource her file to the cloud while protecting its privacy, as well, against a potentially untrusted cloud provider. So, in this section, we refine our protocol so that it provides the same guarantees while also protecting the confidentiality of the file content from the server.

As we described our protocol so far, the server holds the BLS signature $s_k = H_1(\sigma_k||k)^x$, which enables him to learn σ_k by testing for each $\sigma \in \Sigma$ whether $e(H_1(\sigma||k), h) = e(s_k, g)$. So, to hide σ_k from the server, it is necessary to change the signature s_k to prevent the server from confirming a guess at the value of σ_k.

To do so, in our full protocol the data owner randomizes the signature by raising it to a random power, i.e., $s_k \leftarrow H_1(\sigma||k)^{x \cdot \beta_k}$ where $\beta_k \overset{\$}{\leftarrow} \mathbb{Z}_p^*$. s_k then does not leak information about σ_k to the server because it is randomly distributed in G_1. However, this randomization also introduces new difficulties for the server and client to perform the DFA evaluation, since both of them need to be able to compute the same encoding for each σ_k despite s_k being randomized in this way.

To facilitate this evaluation, the data owner encrypts β_k under a public key ek of an encryption scheme whose plaintext space includes $\mathbb{Z}_p^*$ and provides its ciphertext, denoted b_k, along with s_k to the server; see the input arguments to server in Figure 1. Of course, the server should not be able to decrypt b_k, since this would again enable him to reconstruct σ_k. As such, the data owner provides the corresponding private decryption key dk only to the client; see the input arguments to the client. Analogous to previous protocols [30], conveying dk can serve as a step by which the data owner authorizes a client to perform DFA queries on its file stored at the server. (In Section 6, we summarize an alternative approach that does not disclose dk or $\langle \beta_k \rangle_{k \in [\ell]}$ to the client.)

Given this setup, the full protocol Π thus executes the following additional steps. First, the client defines the encoding of character $\sigma \in \Sigma$ and position $k \in [\ell]$ to be $\tau(\sigma, k, \beta_k, \psi_k) = H_2(e(H_1(\sigma||k)^{\beta_k \psi_k}, h))$, where again H_2 is a hash function $H_2 : G_2 \to \mathbb{R}$ (modeled as a random oracle) and where $\psi_k \overset{\$}{\leftarrow} \mathbb{Z}_p^*$ is selected by the client in the round for character k. Note that the client needs to know β_k to compute $\tau(\sigma, k, \beta_k, \psi_k)$, and recall that the client needs to know $\tau(\sigma, k, \beta_k, \psi_k)$ for each $\sigma \in \Sigma$ in order to compute $f(x, y)$ to satisfy $f(\pi(q) +_{\mathbb{R}} \varphi_k, \tau(\sigma, k, \beta_k, \psi_k)) = \pi(\delta(q, \sigma))$ for every $q \in Q$ and $\sigma \in \Sigma$. Therefore, it is necessary for the client to include β_k as an argument to the ToPoly call (i.e., ToPoly$(Q, \Sigma, \delta, \pi, k, \varphi_k, \beta_k, \psi_k)$ in c113) and to delay that call until after receiving b_k in m104 and using it to obtain β_k (c112).

4.4   Communication and Storage

Protocol Π has a communication complexity of $O(\ell mn\kappa)$ bits, dominated by message m104 consisting of mn elements of $\mathbb{Z}_{N^2}^*$ sent by the server in each of ℓ rounds, where $pek = \langle N, g \rangle$ and N is κ bits in length. The storage cost on the server is dominated by the size of $\langle s_k, b_k \rangle_{k \in [\ell]}$. Now letting κ denote the maximum of the security parameters for the BLS signatures (i.e., the s_k values) and the ciphertexts (i.e., the b_k values), and assuming that the bit length of each value type is linear in its security parameter (which is the case for BLS signatures and, say, Paillier ciphertexts), the storage cost is $O(\kappa \ell)$ bits.

4.5   Security

For brevity, we defer a full proof of security for Π to a forthcoming technical report. In this section we simply highlight the central insights and lemmas needed to complete that proof.

Privacy against server *adversaries.* The insight needed for arguing file and DFA privacy against server adversaries is to notice that, aside from $\langle b_k \rangle_{k \in [\ell]}$ provided as input to the server and the encrypted function θ sent by the client (m102), the values observed by the server are independent of the file contents or the DFA state. That is, each $s_k = \mathsf{H}_1(\sigma \| k)^{x \cdot \beta_k}$ is distributed independently of σ because $\beta_k \xleftarrow{\$} \mathbb{Z}_p^*$, and the values $\gamma \leftarrow \mathsf{PDec}_{pdk}(\alpha)$ that the server recovers in line s105 are independent of the current DFA state and the file contents, owing to its blinding by the client (c107–c108). Similarly, γ^* is independent of the DFA and file contents because it is simply a random ring element determined by the random selection of π in line c103, and no other output from π is ever disclosed to the server. Also note that ρ and Ψ_k sent to the server (m103) are independent of the file characters or DFA states. Consequently, any information leakage about the file or DFA to the server must originate in a leakage either from the ciphertexts $\langle b_k \rangle_{k \in [\ell]}$ or from the ciphertext θ, for which the server holds neither decryption key. Consequently, it is possible to reduce the DFA and file privacy against server adversaries to the IND-CPA security [3] of encryption under ek or ek', respectively.

Privacy against honest-but-curious client *adversaries.* The final state γ^* of the DFA evaluation is revealed to the client in line m106, but aside from this value, the only other values sent to the client are a Paillier public key pek (m101), ciphertexts $\langle \mu_{ij} \rangle_{i \in [n], j \in [m]}$ encrypted under that public key, and the ciphertext b_k. The plaintext β_k of b_k is independent of the file content, and so its disclosure to the client (c112) does not reveal additional information about the file. Consequently, any leakage about the file (beyond the final state γ^* to which the file pushed the DFA) must originate from the ciphertexts $\langle \mu_{ij} \rangle_{i \in [n], j \in [m]}$ and so can be used to attack the IND-CPA security [3] of the Paillier encryption scheme.

This reasoning pertains equally well to malicious client-compromising adversaries and so we believe our protocol is heuristically secure against malicious client adversaries, as well. However, the simulation for the client adversary uses the plaintexts of the values θ (m102) and ρ (m103) sent by the client, which are correct only if the client is honest-but-curious. We could *force* the correctness of these values against an arbitrarily malicious client through the addition of zero-knowledge proofs, but we do not pursue that here.

Detection of server misbehavior. There are essentially two avenues by which a server might attempt to misbehave while escaping detection. The first is to create $\tau(\sigma, k, \beta_k, \psi_k) = \mathsf{H}_2(e(\mathsf{H}_1(\sigma\|k)^{\beta_k \psi_k}, h))$ for some $\sigma \neq \sigma_k$, and to use $\tau(\sigma, k, \beta_k, \psi_k)$ as η in the protocol. The second is to cause the client to execute a state transition into an erroneous state in Q without computing $\tau(\sigma, k, \beta_k, \psi_k)$ for some $\sigma \neq \sigma_k$. We first show that the former implies the ability to break the *bilinear computational Diffie-Hellman assumption* [6]:

Assumption 1. *For any probabilistic polynomial-time adversary $\mathcal{A}$,*

$$\mathbb{P}\left(v = e(g, g)^{z_1 z_2 z_3} \;\middle|\; \begin{array}{l} (p, G_1, G_2, g, e) \leftarrow \mathsf{ParamGen}(1^\kappa); \\ z_1, z_2, z_3 \xleftarrow{\$} \mathbb{Z}_p^*; v \leftarrow \mathcal{A}(p, G_1, G_2, g, e, g^{z_1}, g^{z_2}, g^{z_3}) \end{array} \right)$$

is negligible as a function of κ.[2]

Lemma 1. *Let H_1 and H_2 be random oracles. Under Assumption 1, there is no probabilistic polynomial time server-compromising adversary $\mathcal{S}$ that computes $\tau(\sigma, k, \beta_k, \psi_k)$ for some $k \in [\ell]$ and $\sigma \neq \sigma_k$ with non-negligible probability, after interacting with the client in protocol Π.*

Proof. Suppose such a server adversary $\mathcal{S}$ exists. We build an adversary $\mathcal{A}$ that takes in a challenge $(p, G_1, G_2, g, e, g^{z_1}, g^{z_2}, g^{z_3})$ as input, interacts with $\mathcal{S}$, and outputs $e(g, g)^{z_1 z_2 z_3}$ with non-negligible probability, violating Assumption 1. $\mathcal{A}$ is defined as follows, where $Z_1 = g^{z_1}$, $Z_2 = g^{z_2}$ and $Z_3 = g^{z_3}$:

- **Setup:** $\mathcal{A}$ generates a public/private key pair (ek, dk) for an encryption scheme, a file length $\ell > 0$, an alphabet Σ such that $|\Sigma| > 1$, and a sequence of plaintext file characters $\langle \sigma_k \rangle_{k \in [\ell]}$, $\sigma_k \in \Sigma$. $\mathcal{A}$ sets $\mathsf{H}_1(\sigma_k\|k) \leftarrow g^u$ where $u \xleftarrow{\$} \mathbb{Z}_p^*$ and then computes the encrypted file sequence $\langle s_k, b_k \rangle_{k \in [\ell]}$ such that $s_k \leftarrow Z_1^{u\beta_k}$ for $\beta_k \xleftarrow{\$} \mathbb{Z}_p^*$ and $b_k \leftarrow \mathsf{Enc}_{ek}(\beta_k)$. $\mathcal{A}$ invokes $\mathcal{S}(\langle p, G_1, G_2, g, e, Z_1 \rangle, \Sigma, \langle s_k, b_k \rangle_{k \in [\ell]})$. Note that the file ciphertext $\langle s_k, b_k \rangle_{k \in [\ell]}$ is well formed because $e(s_k, g) = e(Z_1^{u\beta_k}, g) = e(g^{z_1 u\beta_k}, g) = e(g, g)^{z_1 u\beta_k} = e(g^u, g^{z_1})^{\beta_k} = e(\mathsf{H}_1(\sigma_k\|k), Z_1)^{\beta_k}$, as in the real protocol. Finally, $\mathcal{A}$ chooses $k^* \xleftarrow{\$} [\ell]$ and $\sigma^* \xleftarrow{\$} \Sigma \setminus \{\sigma_{k^*}\}$.
- **Simulation for $\mathcal{S}$:** After receiving pek and ℓ from $\mathcal{S}$ (m101), $\mathcal{A}$ chooses $n > 0$ arbitrarily and computes θ exactly as in the real protocol, using an encryption key ek' of its own choosing. $\mathcal{A}$ sends n and θ to $\mathcal{S}$ (m102).

---

[2] A function μ is *negligible as a function of κ* if for every positive polynomial p, there is some κ_0 such that $\mu(\kappa) < 1/p(\kappa)$ for all $\kappa > \kappa_0$.

In round $k \in [\ell]$, $\mathcal{A}$ computes α to be the ciphertext of random element of $\mathbb{R}$. If $k \neq k^*$, then $\mathcal{A}$ generates the random challenge Ψ_k exactly as specified in c110–c111. If $k = k^*$, then $\mathcal{A}$ sets $\Psi_k \leftarrow Z_3$. In either case, $\mathcal{A}$ then sends α and Ψ_k to $\mathcal{S}$ (m103).

After ℓ such rounds, $\mathcal{A}$ computes α to be the ciphertext of a random element of $\mathbb{R}$, and sends it to $\mathcal{S}$ (m105).

- **Hash queries to H_1:** For any query that was previously posed to H_1, $\mathcal{A}$ returns the value returned to that previous query, and for new queries, $\mathcal{A}$ generates a return value as follows. If the query is $\sigma^* \| k^*$, then $\mathcal{A}$ returns Z_2. For all other queries, $\mathcal{A}$ picks $u \overset{\$}{\leftarrow} \mathbb{Z}_p^*$ and returns g^u.
- **Hash queries to H_2:** For any query that was previously posed to H_2, $\mathcal{A}$ returns the value returned to that previous query. For new queries, $\mathcal{A}$ picks $r \overset{\$}{\leftarrow} \mathbb{Z}_N$ and returns r to $\mathcal{S}$.

The view that $\mathcal{A}$ simulates for $\mathcal{S}$ is indistinguishable from a real protocol execution. If $\mathcal{S}$ computes

$$
\begin{aligned}
\tau(\sigma^*, k^*, \beta_{k^*}, \psi_k) &= H_2(e(H_1(\sigma^* \| k^*)^{\beta_{k^*} \psi_k}, Z_1)) \\
&= H_2(e(Z_2^{\beta_{k^*} z_3}, Z_1)) \\
&= H_2(e(g,g)^{z_1 z_2 z_3 \beta_{k^*}})
\end{aligned}
$$

then $\mathcal{A}$ can output $e(g,g)^{z_1 z_2 z_3}$ with non-negligible probability by selecting a random query χ that $\mathcal{S}$ made of H_2 and returning $\chi^{\beta_{k^*}^{-1} \bmod p}$. The probability that $\mathcal{A}$ outputs $e(g,g)^{z_1 z_2 z_3}$ is then $\frac{1}{(m-1) \cdot \ell \cdot \#(H_2)}$ times the probability that $\mathcal{S}$ produces $\tau(\sigma, k, \beta_k, \psi_k)$ for some $k \in [\ell]$ and $\sigma \neq \sigma_k$, where $\#(H_2)$ is the number of queries that $\mathcal{S}$ poses to H_2. If the latter probability is non-negligible, then the former is, too. $\qquad \square$

We now consider the second possibility, i.e., that the **server** causes the **client** to execute a state transition into an erroneous state in Q without computing $\tau(\sigma, k, \beta_k, \psi_k)$ for some $\sigma \neq \sigma_k$. To prove that this happens with negligible probability, we leverage properties specific to the Paillier cryptosystem.

Lemma 2. *Let H_2 be a random oracle, and let $\mathcal{S}$ be a **server**-compromising adversary. If in no round k does $\mathcal{S}$ compute $\tau(\sigma, k, \beta_k, \psi_k)$ for some $\sigma \neq \sigma_k$, then the **client** outputs an incorrect state $q \in Q$ with probability at most negligibly more than $\frac{n-1}{N}$.*

Proof. In round k, the **client** transitions to the next DFA state by encoding the DFA transition function using a polynomial f satisfying $f(\pi(q) +_\mathbb{R} \varphi_k, \tau(\sigma, k, \beta_k, \psi_k)) = \pi(\delta(q, \sigma))$ for every $q \in Q$ and $\sigma \in \Sigma$; let $f(x,y) = \sum_{i=0}^{n-1} \sum_{j=0}^{m-1} a_{ij} \cdot_\mathbb{R} x^i \cdot_\mathbb{R} y^j$. To cause a state transition to an erroneous state $q' \in Q$, a **server** adversary must therefore produce ciphertexts $\langle \mu_{ij} \rangle_{i \in [n], j \in [m]}$ with corresponding plaintexts $\langle \nu_{ij} \rangle_{i \in [n], j \in [m]}$ so that

$$
\pi(q') = \sum_{i=0}^{n-1} \sum_{j=0}^{m-1} a_{ij} \cdot_\mathbb{R} \nu_{ij} \tag{1}
$$

without having any information about $\tau(\sigma, k, \beta_k, \psi_k)$ for any $\sigma \neq \sigma_k$ (since H_2 is a random oracle). Note that the distribution of $\langle a_{ij} \rangle_{i \in [n], j \in [m]}$ is *not* independent of the DFA transition function δ and the injection π. That is, once π is fixed, only certain values for $\langle a_{ij} \rangle_{i \in [n], j \in [m]}$ are possible.

We argue the result under the conservative assumption that δ and π *uniquely determine* $\langle a_{ij} \rangle_{i \in [n], j \in [m]}$ (which in general they do not). Even then, for any $i' \in [n]$ and $j' \in [m]$ such that $a_{i'j'} \neq 0$ and $\gcd(a_{i'j'}, N) = 1$ (lines c114–c115 abort the protocol if $\gcd(a_{ij}, N) > 1$ for some $a_{ij} \neq 0$), and for any choices of $\langle \nu_{ij} \rangle_{i \in [n], j \in [m]}$ excepting $\nu_{i'j'}$, there is exactly one value for $\nu_{i'j'}$ in $\mathbb{Z}_N$ that satisfies (1). Moreover, prior to the last message sent by the client (m105), the server receives no information about π. So, the probability $\mathcal{S}$ succeeds in selecting $\langle \nu_{ij} \rangle_{i \in [n], j \in [m]}$ to satisfy (1) is $\frac{1}{N}$, and since there are $n - 1$ possible erroneous states q', the probability $\mathcal{S}$ succeeds in causing an erroneous state transition to any $q' \in Q$ is at most $\frac{n-1}{N}$.

Finally, while the server learns $\pi(q)$ for one $q \in Q$ in the last client-to-server message (m105) — if it behaved thus far — it does so only for the correct state q at this point. Again, it can then guess $\pi(q')$ for an incorrect $q' \in Q$ to return as γ^* with probability only $\frac{n-1}{N}$. □

5   On File Updates

Protocol Π is presented for a static file, and so in this section we consider the impact of file updates. As we discuss below, these impacts are nontrivial, and so our protocol is arguably most useful for static files.

To enable protocol Π, the data owner signs the file position k along with σ_k when producing s_k to detect the server reordering file characters, i.e., $s_k \leftarrow H_1(\sigma \| k)^{x \cdot \beta_k}$ where $\beta_k \overset{\$}{\leftarrow} \mathbb{Z}_p^*$. Such a representation would require any character insertion or deletion at position k to further require updating the signature $s_{k'}$ for all $k' > k$. If the total file length ℓ is also included as an input to H_1 to detect file truncation, then insertions and deletions may require updating the signatures $s_{k'}$ for all $k' < k$, as well. This latter cost can be eliminated by not including ℓ as an input to H_1 but rather to have the data owner sign ℓ and the server to forward this signature along with ℓ to the client in message m101. The former cost can be mitigated somewhat by breaking each file into blocks (essentially smaller files) so that insertions and deletions require only the affected blocks to be rewritten. In this case, the block index within the file should presumably also be included as an input to H_1 to detect block reorderings by the server.

Even with these modifications, there remain other complexities in handling file updates, in that a server could simply use a stale version of the file when performing protocol Π with the client, ignoring any earlier updates to the file by the data owner. Detecting a server that selectively suppresses updates seems to require additional interaction between the data owner and the client and has been the subject of much study (for file stores subject to reads and updates only) under the banner of *fork consistency* [22]. We leave as future work the integration of our DFA evaluation techniques with these ideas, i.e., so that DFA evaluations performed against stale files are efficiently detected when the client subsequently interacts with the data owner.

6 Extensions

The protocol Π can be extended in various ways that may be of interest and that we will discuss here. The first "extension" is simply the removal of the file encryption step described in Section 4.3, which is suitable for the standard two-party model where the server's input need not be kept secret from the server himself. This simplification eliminates the dk, β_k and b_k values from the protocol, implicitly setting $\beta_k = 1$.

A more interesting variant of the protocol addresses the concern that the protocol as stated in Figure 1 discloses the decryption key dk and the values $\langle \beta_k \rangle_{k \in [\ell]}$ to the client, either of which can be used to decrypt the file from its ciphertext $\langle s_k, b_k \rangle_{k \in [\ell]}$. While this file ciphertext is not disclosed to the client during the protocol, it seems unnecessarily permissive to disclose its decryption key to every client that performs a DFA evaluation on the file: if the file ciphertext were ever unintentionally disclosed, then any such client could decrypt the file if it retained the key. In the rest of this section we discuss an extension to the protocol in Figure 1 to avoid disclosing dk and the values $\langle \beta_k \rangle_{k \in [\ell]}$ to the client.

In order to avoid disclosing dk to the client, one alternative is for the data owner to provide shares of dk to both the client and the server, so as to enable a two-party decryption of each b_k. Then, rather than sending only b_k to the client in message m104, the server can also send its contribution to the decryption of b_k, enabling the client to complete the decryption of b_k without learning dk itself.

Still, however, this alternative would disclose β_k to the client, which would enable it to determine σ_k if s_k were ever disclosed. To avoid disclosing β_k, one strategy is for the server to first blind β_k with another random value t_k, i.e., to execute the protocol with $\beta_k t_k$ in place of just β_k. Of course, this factor t_k would also then need to be reflected in k-th file character used in the protocol, i.e., so the server would use $s_k^{t_k} = H_1(\sigma_k \| k)^{x \beta_k t_k}$ in place of s_k in the protocol. Because the server does not have access to β_k but rather has access only to its ciphertext b_k, it is necessary that the encryption scheme used to construct b_k enable the computation of a ciphertext $\hat{b}_k$ from b_k and t_k such that $\mathsf{Dec}_{dk}(\hat{b}_k) = \beta_k t_k \bmod N'$ for some value N' such that $p \mid N'$. In this case, selecting $t_k \xleftarrow{\$} \mathbb{Z}_{N'}$ suffices to ensure that $\beta_k t_k \bmod N'$ is distributed independently of β_k and so hides β_k from the client when it learns $\beta_k t_k \bmod N'$.

An encryption scheme meeting our requirements (supporting two-party decryption and homomorphism on ciphertexts) is ElGamal encryption [12] in a subgroup of $\mathbb{Z}_{N'}^*$. However, note that setting $N' = p$ is inefficient: the security parameter κ and so the size of p required for security is an order of magnitude less for BLS signing than it would be for ElGamal encryption in a subgroup of $\mathbb{Z}_p^*$ [20], and so setting $N' = p$ would add considerable expense to the protocol.

As such, a more efficient construction would be to choose $N' = pp'$ for another prime p'. ElGamal encryption is believed to be secure with a composite modulus even if its factorization is known [5].

7 Conclusion

We presented a protocol by which a data owner can outsource storage of a file to an untrusted cloud server while still enabling partially trusted third-party clients (e.g., customers and service providers) to evaluate DFAs on that data. Our protocol is novel in provably enabling the client to detect the server's misbehavior — including the use of a file other than the data owner's in the protocol — in the random oracle model, while simultaneously protecting the privacy of the file and of the DFA from an arbitrarily malicious server. Moreover, our protocol provably protects the privacy of the file (except for the DFA evaluation result) from an honest-but-curious client (and heuristically does so from an arbitrarily malicious one). We accomplish these goals without the use of zero-knowledge proofs, yielding a protocol that is more efficient than alternatives of which we are aware. We believe that our protocol has applications to malware scanning or genome analysis on encrypted, cloud-resident data, and we plan to explore these applications in ongoing work.

Acknowledgments. This work was supported in part by NSF grant 0910483.

References

1. GenBank, http://www.ncbi.nlm.nih.gov/genbank/
2. United Kingdom National DNA Database,
   http://www.npia.police.uk/en/8934.htm
3. Bellare, M., Desai, A., Pointcheval, D., Rogaway, P.: Relations among notions of security for public-key encryption schemes. In: Krawczyk, H. (ed.) CRYPTO 1998. LNCS, vol. 1462, pp. 26–45. Springer, Heidelberg (1998)
4. Blanton, M., Aliasgari, M.: Secure outsourcing of DNA searching via finite automata. In: Foresti, S., Jajodia, S. (eds.) Data and Applications Security and Privacy XXIV. LNCS, vol. 6166, pp. 49–64. Springer, Heidelberg (2010)
5. Boneh, D.: The decision Diffie-Hellman problem. In: Buhler, J.P. (ed.) ANTS 1998. LNCS, vol. 1423, pp. 48–63. Springer, Heidelberg (1998)
6. Boneh, D., Lynn, B., Shacham, H.: Short signatures from the weil pairing. In: Boyd, C. (ed.) ASIACRYPT 2001. LNCS, vol. 2248, pp. 514–532. Springer, Heidelberg (2001)
7. Camenisch, J., Zaverucha, G.M.: Private intersection of certified sets. In: Dingledine, R., Golle, P. (eds.) FC 2009. LNCS, vol. 5628, pp. 108–127. Springer, Heidelberg (2009)
8. Choi, S.G., Elbaz, A., Juels, A., Malkin, T., Yung, M.: Two-party computing with encrypted data. In: Kurosawa, K. (ed.) ASIACRYPT 2007. LNCS, vol. 4833, pp. 298–314. Springer, Heidelberg (2007)
9. De Cristofaro, E., Kim, J., Tsudik, G.: Linear-complexity private set intersection protocols secure in malicious model. In: Abe, M. (ed.) ASIACRYPT 2010. LNCS, vol. 6477, pp. 213–231. Springer, Heidelberg (2010)

10. De Cristofaro, E., Tsudik, G.: Practical private set intersection protocols with linear complexity. In: Sion, R. (ed.) FC 2010. LNCS, vol. 6052, pp. 143–159. Springer, Heidelberg (2010)

11. Curtmola, R., Garay, J., Kamara, S., Ostrovsky, R.: Searchable symmetric encryption: Improved definitions and efficient constructions. In: 13th ACM Conference on Computer and Communications Security, pp. 79–88 (2006)

12. ElGamal, T.: A public key cryptosystem and a signature scheme based on discrete logarithms. IEEE Transactions on Information Theory 31(4), 469–472 (1985)

13. Frikken, K.B.: Practical private DNA string searching and matching through efficient oblivious automata evaluation. In: Gudes, E., Vaidya, J. (eds.) Data and Applications Security XXIII. LNCS, vol. 5645, pp. 81–94. Springer, Heidelberg (2009)

14. Gennaro, R., Hazay, C., Sorensen, J.S.: Text search protocols with simulation based security. In: Nguyen, P.Q., Pointcheval, D. (eds.) PKC 2010. LNCS, vol. 6056, pp. 332–350. Springer, Heidelberg (2010)

15. Goldreich, O., Micali, S., Wigderson, A.: How to play any mental game. In: 19th ACM Symposium on Theory of Computing, pp. 218–229 (1987)

16. Hazay, C., Lindell, Y.: Efficient protocols for set intersection and pattern matching with security against malicious and covert adversaries. Journal of Cryptology 23(3), 422–456 (2010)

17. Hazay, C., Toft, T.: Computationally secure pattern matching in the presence of malicious adversaries. In: Abe, M. (ed.) ASIACRYPT 2010. LNCS, vol. 6477, pp. 195–212. Springer, Heidelberg (2010)

18. Higgins, K.J.: Black hat: How to hack IPS signatures (2007),
    http://www.darkreading.com/security/perimeter-security/
    208804656/black-hat-how-to-hack-ips-signatures.html

19. Katz, J., Malka, L.: Secure text processing with applications to private DNA matching. In: 17th ACM Conference on Computer and Communications Security, pp. 485–492 (2010)

20. Lenstra, A.K., Verheul, E.R.: Selecting cryptographic key sizes. Journal of Cryptology 14(4), 255–293 (2001)

21. Li, F., Hadjieleftheriou, M., Kollios, G., Reyzin, L.: Authenticated index structures for aggregation queries. ACM Transactions on Information and System Security 13(4) (December 2010)

22. Mazières, D., Shasha, D.: Building secure file systems out of Byzantine storage. In: 21st Symposium on Principles of Distributed Computing, pp. 108–117 (July 2002)

23. Mohassel, P., Niksefat, S., Sadeghian, S., Sadeghiyan, B.: An efficient protocol for oblivious DFA evaluation and applications. In: Dunkelman, O. (ed.) CT-RSA 2012. LNCS, vol. 7178, pp. 398–415. Springer, Heidelberg (2012)

24. Paillier, P.: Public-key cryptosystems based on composite degree residuosity classes. In: Stern, J. (ed.) EUROCRYPT 1999. LNCS, vol. 1592, pp. 223–238. Springer, Heidelberg (1999)

25. Pang, H., Zhang, J., Mouratidis, K.: Scalable verification for outsourced dynamic databases. In: 35th International Conference on Very Large Databases, pp. 802–813 (2009)

26. Papamanthou, C., Tamassia, R., Triandopoulos, R.: Authenticated hash tables. In: 15th ACM Conference on Computer and Communications Security, pp. 437–448 (2008)

27. Song, D.X., Wagner, D., Perrig, A.: Practical techniques for searches on encrypted data. In: 2000 IEEE Symposium on Security and Privacy (2000)

28. Stefanov, E., Shi, E., Song, D.: Policy-enhanced private set intersection: sharing information while enforcing privacy policies. In: Fischlin, M., Buchmann, J., Manulis, M. (eds.) PKC 2012. LNCS, vol. 7293, pp. 413–430. Springer, Heidelberg (2012)
29. Troncoso-Pastoriza, J.R., Katzenbeisser, S., Celik, M.: Privacy preserving error resilient DNA searching through oblivious automata. In: 14th ACM Conference on Computer and Communications Security, pp. 519–528 (2007)
30. Wei, L., Reiter, M.K.: Third-party private DFA evaluation on encrypted files in the cloud. In: Foresti, S., Yung, M., Martinelli, F. (eds.) ESORICS 2012. LNCS, vol. 7459, pp. 523–540. Springer, Heidelberg (2012)
31. Yao, A.C.: Protocols for secure computations. In: 23rd IEEE Symposium on Foundations of Computer Science, pp. 160–164 (1982)
32. Zhuge, J., Holz, T., Song, C., Guo, J., Han, X., Zou, W.: Studying malicious websites and the underground economy on the Chinese web. In: Workshop on the Economics of Information Security (June 2008)

HI-CFG: Construction by Binary Analysis and Application to Attack Polymorphism

Dan Caselden[1], Alex Bazhanyuk[2], Mathias Payer[3],
Stephen McCamant[4], and Dawn Song[3]

[1] FireEye, Inc.
[2] Intel Corporation
[3] University of California, Berkeley[**]
[4] University of Minnesota

Abstract. Security analysis often requires understanding both the control and data-flow structure of a binary. We introduce a new program representation, a hybrid information- and control-flow graph (HI-CFG), and give algorithms to infer it from an instruction-level trace. As an application, we consider the task of generalizing an attack against a program whose inputs undergo complex transformations before reaching a vulnerability. We apply the HI-CFG to find the parts of the program that implement each transformation, and then generate new attack inputs under a user-specified combination of transformations. Structural knowledge allows our approach to scale to applications that are infeasible with monolithic symbolic execution. Such attack polymorphism shows the insufficiency of any filter that does not support all the same transformations as the vulnerable application. In case studies, we show this attack capability against a PDF viewer and a word processor.

1 Introduction

In security analysis it is often necessary to understand both the information-flow and control-flow structure of a large code base. Disassemblers concentrate on recovering control-flow structure, and some research systems [18,26,17] reverse engineer data structures. But there is insufficient automated support for understanding the flow of information between data structures, and the relationship between data structures and code. We propose new techniques that combine information-flow analysis with control-flow graph recovery to scale precise binary analysis to large software systems, and apply them to generating polymorphic attacks against programs that support complex input transformations.

Applications are getting larger and more complex due to increasing functionality, a more sophisticated software stack, and new abstractions and concepts that simplify development. These applications are hard to debug and vulnerabilities are becoming more and more complex, e.g., a vulnerable program location might only be reached after a specific input is passed through several buffers and

---

[**] The authors were all at UC Berkeley while performing the primary research.

J. Crampton, S. Jajodia, and K. Mayes (Eds.): ESORICS 2013, LNCS 8134, pp. 164–181, 2013.
© Springer-Verlag Berlin Heidelberg 2013

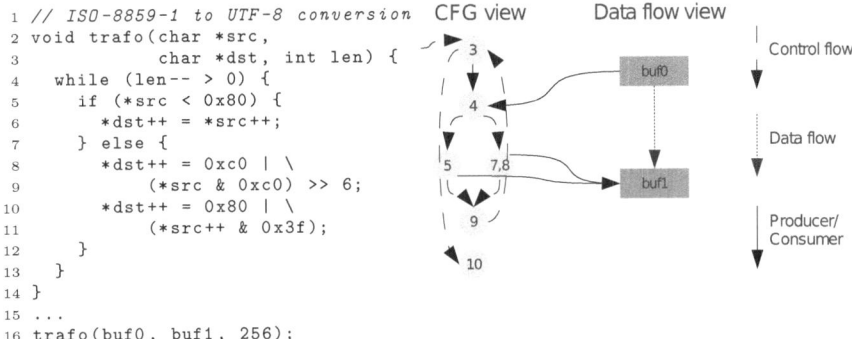

```
 1  // ISO-8859-1 to UTF-8 conversion
 2  void trafo(char *src,
 3             char *dst, int len) {
 4    while (len-- > 0) {
 5      if (*src < 0x80) {
 6        *dst++ = *src++;
 7      } else {
 8        *dst++ = 0xc0 | \
 9               (*src & 0xc0) >> 6;
10        *dst++ = 0x80 | \
11               (*src++ & 0x3f);
12      }
13    }
14  }
15  ...
16  trafo(buf0, buf1, 256);
```

Fig. 1. This example shows both (a) simple transformation and (b) the corresponding HI-CFG

functions whereas the data can be modified by each function. Symbolic execution is a great tool to analyze security properties of an application given a potentially vulnerable program location. Unfortunately, symbolic execution does not scale well to large contexts and long-running programs with multiple input transformations, due to the explosion of the number of possible paths that have to be evaluated and the state that has to be tracked. A simple alternative to symbolic execution is (concrete) fuzzing or fuzz testing. Fuzz testing uses templates to probabilistically generate input data that tries to trigger a program crash. A security analyst then analyzes the crash logs to locate vulnerabilities. Due to the probabilistic input generation fuzz testing is unlikely to reach a vulnerability that is guarded by complex, low-probability conditions.

This paper introduces a new program representation, a Hybrid Information- and Control-Flow Graph (HI-CFG), that captures both the information-flow graph and the control-flow graph of a program. The HI-CFG shows the data structures within a program as well as the code that generates and uses these data structures, inferring an explicit connection of producer and consumer edges between data-flow nodes and blocks in the control-flow graph. Figure 1(a) shows a simple example of a transformation and the corresponding HI-CFG graph. The transformation that copies data from buffer buf0 to buf1. Figure 1(b) shows the HI-CFG that contains the control flow graph as well as the data flow graph and the producer/consumer edges between the two graphs.

Using the information in the HI-CFG about individual data structures (i.e., buffers) and transformations enables an iterative, step-by-step analysis of these buffer transformations. Instead of using monolithic symbolic execution that reverses all transformations in a single (but potentially exponentially large) step, iterative symbolic execution starts from a potentially vulnerable program location and reverses each transformation individually. Figure 2 shows a vulnerability hidden behind several transformations that can be reversed using iterative symbolic execution.

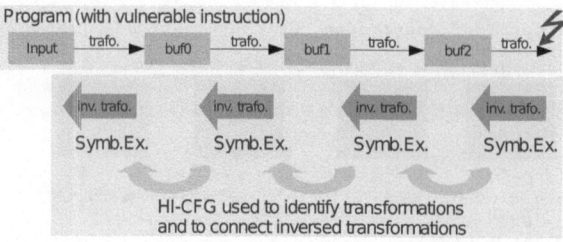

Fig. 2. Iteratively reversing a set of data transformations based on information from the HI-CFG

One possible way to build a HI-CFG is using source-based program analysis. Unfortunately, in the context of security analysis, the source-code of a program is usually not available and the program itself might be stripped. This paper presents an algorithm to build a HI-CFG for a given binary-only program based on the analysis of an execution trace for a benign input that executes the buffer transformations but does not necessarily trigger the vulnerability. Prerequisites for the algorithm are only the (stripped) binary and a benign input that executes the buffer transformations.

Another advantage of the HI-CFG from an attacker's perspective is that given one vulnerability the symbolic execution engine can be used to generate many different exploit paths, leveraging different encodings or different transformations. Often transformations are many-to-one (e.g., many different deflate compressed streams decode to the same original data) and the symbolic execution engine can be used to produce different encodings for a specific target string. Also, many file formats allow a specific program location to be reached by different chains of transformations. With file formats that allow recursive objects, an attacker can choose from an infinite amount of transformations. Such attacks can only be detected if the analysis tool has deep knowledge of the file format and implements all transformations as well.

We evaluate the feasibility of HI-CFG construction using only a stripped binary for two case studies: a PDF viewer, and a word processor. For both programs, we describe the construction of the HI-CFG as well as how symbolic execution can be used to generate different attacks by inverting transformations along the HI-CFG buffer chains.

The contributions of this paper are:

1. we introduce a new program representation, a *Hybrid Information- and Control-Flow Graph (HI-CFG)*, which combines control-flow and data-flow information by inferring producer/consumer edges;
2. we give algorithms for building a HI-CFG given only a stripped binary program and a benign input to that program;
3. we evaluate the security capabilities of the HI-CFG using two case studies for large, real-world programs: Poppler and AbiWord.

Our symbolic execution approach for attack generation is not a contribution here; it is described in more detail in a technical report [21]. Further information about the project is available on the BitBlaze web site [12].

2   The Hybrid Information- and Control-Flow Graph

For the central program representation used in our approach we propose what we call a Hybrid Information- and Control-Flow Graph ("HI-CFG" for short, pronounced "high-C-F-G"). The HI-CFG combines information about code, data, and the relationships between them. Because data structures represent the interface between code modules, a HI-CFG is a suitable representation for many tasks that require decomposing a large binary program into components.

We start by describing the kinds of nodes and edges found in a HI-CFG (Section 2.1). Then we mention potential variations of the concept and applications for which they would be suitable (Section 2.2).

2.1   Nodes and Edges

A HI-CFG is a graph with two kinds of nodes: ones representing the program's data structures, and ones representing its code blocks. Data structure nodes are connected with *information-flow* edges showing how information is transferred from one data structure to another. Code block nodes are connected with *control-flow* edges indicating the order in which code executes. Finally, data nodes and code nodes are connected by *producer-consumer* edges, showing which information is created and used by which code: a producer edge connects a code block to a data structure it generates, while a consumer edge connects a data structure to a code block that uses it. A more detailed example HI-CFG is shown in Figure 3.

The subgraph of a HI-CFG consisting of code blocks and control-flow edges is similar to a control-flow graph or call graph, and the subgraph consisting of data structure nodes and information-flow edges is similar to a data-flow graph. However, the HI-CFG is more powerful than a simple combination of a

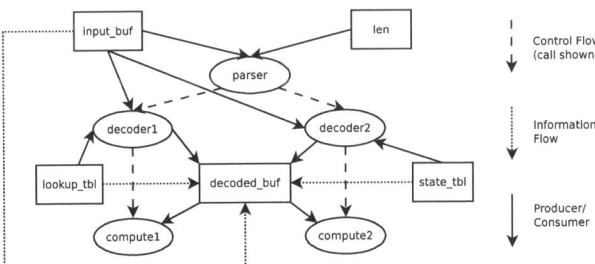

Fig. 3. A detailed example of a coarse-grained HI-CFG for a program which parses two kinds of commands from its input, decodes those commands using lookup tables, and then performs an appropriate computation for each command.

control-flow graph and a data-flow graph, because the producer-consumer edges additionally allow an analysis to find the code that is relevant to data or the data that is relevant to part of the code.

2.2 Generality and Uses

We can create a HI-CFG with differing levels of granularity for code and data. A fine-grained code representation has one code block per basic block, while a coarse-grained representation has one code block per function. Analogously, a fine-grained data representation has a data structure node for each atomic value (like an integer), while a coarse-grained data representation has one data structure node per allocated memory region. To record information about finer-grained structure, we can augment a coarse-grained data structure node with an inferred type that describes its internal structure.

When an analysis can recover only part of the information about a program's structure, such as when combining static and dynamic approaches, we can also annotate each HI-CFG edge with a *confidence* value between 0 and 1. A confidence value of 1 represents a relationship that our system knows definitively to hold, whereas a fractional value indicates an uncertain relationship.

Component Identification. One application of a HI-CFG would be to identify functional components within a binary. The hierarchical, modular structure of a program is important at the source level for both developer understanding and separate compilation, but this structure is lost after a compiler produces a binary. Below the level of a dynamically linked library, a text segment is an undifferentiated sequence of instructions. However we would often like to determine which parts of a binary implement a certain functionality, such as to extract and reuse that functionality in another application. Caballero et al. [5] demonstrate the security applications of such a capability for single functions, but many larger functional components would also be valuable to extract.

An insight that motivates the use of a HI-CFG for this problem is that the connection between different areas of functionality in code are data structures. A data structure that is written by one part of the code and read by another represents the interface between them. Thus locating these data structures and dividing the code between them is the key to finding functional components. Given a HI-CFG, the functional structure of the program is just a hierarchical decomposition of the HI-CFG into connected subgraphs. Data structures connected to multiple areas represent the interfaces of those components.

Information-Flow Isolation. A different kind of decomposition would be valuable for programs that operate on sensitive data. In a monolithic binary program, a vulnerability anywhere might allow an attacker to access any information in the program's address space. But often only a small part of an application needs to access sensitive information directly. Just as automatic privilege separation [4] partitions a program to minimize the portion that requires operating system privileges, we would like to partition a program to minimize the portion that requires access to sensitive information. This problem can again be seen as finding a structure within the HI-CFG, but for information-flow isolation we wish to find a partition into exactly two components, where there is information flow from the non-sensitive component to the sensitive one but not vice-versa.

Attack Generation. For this paper, our application of the HI-CFG is to find the structure of a program's buffer usage to facilitate efficient attack generation. For this, we use a relatively coarse-grained HI-CFG. We represent code at the level of functions, so control-flow edges correspond to function calls and returns. To represent data structures, we use a level of granularity intermediate between atomic values and memory allocations: our tool detects buffers consisting of adjacent memory locations that are accessed in a uniform way, for instance an array. Our current prototype implementation detects only one level of buffers, so we do not infer types to represent their internal structure.

Because our HI-CFG construction algorithm, as described in Section 3, is based on dynamic analysis, each edge in the HI-CFG represents a relationship that was observed on a real program execution. Thus all edges effectively have confidence 1.0. The converse feature of this dynamic approach is that relationships that did not occur in the observed execution do not appear in the HI-CFG. However this is acceptable for our purposes because we base the HI-CFG, and thus the search for an attack, on an analyst-chosen benign execution. If desired the analyst can repeat the search with a benign input that exercises different parts of the program functionality.

3   Dynamic HI-CFG Construction

In this section, we describe our approach to HI-CFG construction: first some infrastructure details, then techniques for collecting control-flow information from dynamic traces, categorizing memory accesses into an active memory model, grouping data accesses into buffers, tracking information flow via targeted taint analysis, and merging significantly similar buffers.

3.1   Infrastructure

To construct a HI-CFG via dynamic analysis, we take a trace-based approach. We use the BitBlaze Tracecap tool to record instruction traces. Tracecap also records statistics about loaded executables and libraries, and produces a log of function calls including arguments and return values that we later use to track standard memory allocation routines.

Our modular trace analysis system interfaces with Intel's XED2 [15] library (for instruction decoding). It includes an offline taint propagation module that allows for a virtually unlimited number of taint marks, and a configurable number of taint marks per byte in memory and registers. The implementation of the trace collection and trace analysis focuses on x86 while the techniques for HI-CFG construction apply to general architectures.

3.2 Control Flow

The HI-CFG construction module primarily identifies functions by observing call and ret in the instruction trace. At a call instruction, the module updates the call stack for the current thread and creates a control-flow edge from the caller to the callee. (This includes indirect call instructions such as those used for C++ virtual methods.) At a ret, the module finds the matching entry in the call stack and marks any missed call stack entries as invalidated.

In addition to literal call instructions, our system also recognizes optimized tail-calls by noticing execution at addresses that have previously been call targets. A limitation of this approach is that tail-called functions will never be recognized if not normally called. This limitation of the current implementation could be addressed by adding a static analysis step to the HI-CFG construction process, but it has not been a problem so far.

3.3 Memory Hierarchy

The HI-CFG construction records memory accesses in a hierarchical model of memory which follows the lattice shown in Figure 4. space types at the top of the lattice represent an entire process address space. At the bottom of the lattice, primitives represent memory accesses observed in the instruction trace. The categorization of a memory access corresponds to a path from the top of the lattice to the bottom. Existing entries in the memory model add their own types as additional requirements in the path. For example, a memory access under an existing dynamically allocated memory region will at least have the path space, dynamic region, dynamic allocation, primitive. The memory model will then insert the memory access and create or adjust layers according to the types in the path.

Memory structures such as dynamic allocations and stack frames are added to the memory model as they are identified by one of several indicators. Dynamic

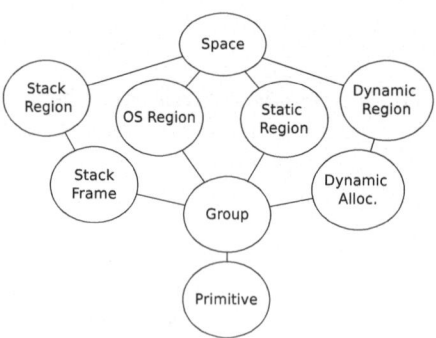

Fig. 4. The hierarchy of types in the model of memory used in our HI-CFG construction algorithm

allocations are added to the memory model by tracking standard memory allocation routines such as `malloc` and `free`. Stack frames are created by tracking `esp`
during `call` instructions and claiming all memory accesses between the base of
the stack frame and the end of the stack region during matched `ret` instructions.

Memory structures such as stack and dynamic regions are based on memory
pages. The "region" type classification relies on the intuition that most programs
tend to use each page for a single purpose such as for stacks, dynamic allocations, memory-mapped executables, or operating system structures. Additional
constraints prohibit stack frames and dynamic allocations from appearing in the
memory model without their respective regions.

3.4   Grouping Buffers

Instruction traces contain every individual load and store instruction performed
by the traced program, but for the HI-CFG we wish to group these accesses into
buffers to better understand their structure. We identify buffers as groups of
adjacent memory locations between which the program expresses commonality.

We experimented with several heuristics for identifying buffers and currently
use a combination of two approaches. Our first system recognizes instructions
that calculate memory access addresses by adding an index to a base pointer. The
system searches the operands involved in the address calculation for a suitable
base pointer (which must point to an active page of memory). Upon finding a
suitable base pointer, the system submits a candidate buffer consisting of an address equal to the value of the base pointer and a size that extends the buffer from
the base pointer to the end of the observed memory access. For example, analyzing a one-byte memory access of address 0x800000ff by the instruction "`movzbl
(%esi,%edx,1), %eax`" where the base pointer `esi` is 0x80000000 would yield
a 0x100-byte candidate buffer from 0x80000000 to 0x800000ff.

The first system often detects both arrays consisting of homogeneous data
types and structures consisting of heterogeneous data types. However, it fails
when the address of the memory access is constructed by pointer arithmetic
across multiple instructions. Our second system addresses this weakness by recognizing spatially adjacent memory accesses. To reduce the false positive rate of
buffer detections, our second system also tracks the order of memory accesses
within each function. Upon observing a return instruction and updating the call
stack, or freeing a chunk of dynamically allocated memory, the second system
uses the accesses from the returned function or freed memory as starting points
to search through the active memory model for linear access patterns. Specifically, our system numbers the accesses sequentially and then sorts them by their
address. A long enough run of adjacent accesses (currently 6) form a group if for
each pair of adjacent accesses, the distances between them, both in the sequential order and in address, match. A pseudocode description of this algorithm,
simplified to omit the treatment of nested functions and some optimizations, is
in Figure 5. An example of the algorithm applied to `strcpy` can be found in a
companion technical report [8]. Similar access patterns across multiple calls to
the same function, such as by functions that access one byte of a buffer per call,

are also recognized by this system. In addition, access patterns are stored within buffers so that they may grow with subsequent accesses. If found, the system will submit the candidate buffer for further processing described next.

```
const MIN_SIZE = 6
for insn in trace
  match insn.type of
    case CALL: opcount := 0; accesses := []
    case LOAD(addr) or STORE(addr):
      append(accesses, (addr, opcount++))
    case RETURN:
      a := sort(accesses, by(addr))
      for indexes i in a
        group := [ a[i] ]
        old_stride := None
        for indexes j=i, j+1 in a
          new_stride := (a[j+1].addr − a[j].addr, a[j+1].opcount − a[j].opcount)
          if (old_stride == None) old_stride := new_stride
          if (old_stride ≠ new_stride) break
          append(group, a[j+1])
        if (group.length ≥ MIN_SIZE) make_group(group)
```

Fig. 5. Pseudocode for identifying linear access patterns in a trace

Once the two systems have submitted their candidate buffers, the HI-CFG module combines the sets of discovered buffers (keeping all non-overlapping buffers, and preferring larger buffers in the case of overlap) and commits them to the active memory model. Adding a buffer to the active memory model merges the grouped memory accesses with the new buffer, which summarizes relational information such as producer and consumer relationships with functions and information flow to other buffers, which are described in the next subsection. Our system merges a subsequent buffer with an existing one if the starting or ending addressing of the new buffer matches either the starting or ending address of the old one, or if either buffer is completely contained within the other.

3.5 Information Flow

To trace the information flow between buffers, our system primarily uses a specialized form of dynamic taint analysis [23,24]. We introduce a fresh taint mark for each buffer as a possible source for information flow. We then propagate these taint marks forward through execution as the data values are copied into registers and memory locations, or used in arithmetic or bitwise operations. When a value with a taint mark is stored into another buffer distinct from the source buffer, we record an information flow from the source to that target. Like most techniques based on dynamic taint analysis, this technique will not in general account for all possible implicit flows. Therefore, we supplement it with an upper-bound technique that constructs a low-confidence information-flow edge whenever the temporal sequence of buffers consumed and produced by a function would allow an information flow. (In other words, if a function first reads from buffer A, and then later writes to buffer B, we create a low-confidence information flow edge from A to B.)

3.6   Buffer Summarization

Buffers in the active memory model are moved into the historical memory model when they or their hierarchical parents are deactivated. Primarily, this occurs for stack allocated buffers (when functions return) and dynamically allocated buffers (when the allocated chunk is freed). The remaining entries in the active memory model are deactivated when the HI-CFG construction module analyzes the last instruction in the trace.

Passthrough buffers, through which information flows without being acted upon by multiple functions, are not added to the historical memory model after deactivation. The motivations for this choice are twofold: first, passthrough buffers are generally less interesting for our analysis and their removal is a slight optimization; second, passthrough buffers will connect legitimately separate sections of the HI-CFG with information flow. Removing passthrough buffers improves the precision of the HI-CFG by eliminating cases that would indicate spurious information flow: for instance, if memcpy copied through an internal buffer that were not removed, every source of a copy would appear information-flow connected to every target.

We define passthrough buffers as those that satisfy the following criteria:

- The buffer is not a source of information flow (i.e., it has at least one incoming information flow edge).
- The buffer is not a sink of information flow (i.e., it has at least one outgoing information flow edge).
- The buffer is produced and/or consumed by exactly one function.

If all of the criteria are met, the passthrough buffer is removed from the graph, and new information flow edges connect buffers that were connected by the passthrough buffer. When deactivated buffers do not meet the criteria for passthrough buffers, they are moved into the historical memory model and *summarized*, as we describe next.

The summarization process finds buffers that are related (intuitively, multiple instances of the "same" buffer), and merges them along with their relational information. We define when two buffers should be merged by giving each buffer a value we call a *key*. Two buffers should be merged if they have both the same parent and the same key. In the current implementation we store an MD5 hash of the key material to save space. The key includes an identifier for the type of an object, and by default it also contains the object's offset within its parent.

The keys for dynamic allocations and stack frames contain different information in addition to a type identifier. Dynamic allocations use the calling context of the allocation site, up to a configurable depth (currently set to 10 calls), similar to a probabilistic calling context [3]. Stack frames use the address of the function. As a result, our system is able to identify two local variables or dynamic allocations as the same across multiple calls to a function and in the presence of custom memory allocation wrappers.

We use a disjoint-set union-find data structure [13] to manage the identities of buffers as they are summarized. The merging of buffers corresponds to a *union* operation, and we use a *find* operation with path compression to maintain a canonical representative, associated for instance with a taint mark. This allows the tool to efficiently maintain information-flow from historical buffers even after they are deactivated.

4   Application: Attack Polymorphism

As our primary example of a security application of a HI-CFG, we describe how to use the transformation structure represented in the HI-CFG to efficiently produce new attacks that differ in the transformations applied to the input before reaching a vulnerability. We first describe the technique and how it uses the HI-CFG, then describe experiments applying the technique to two vulnerable document-processing applications.

4.1   Transformation-Aware Attack Generation with a HI-CFG

In a large application, an input value will typically undergo a number of trans- formations before being used in a vulnerable function. Moreover, the sequence of transformations that apply may vary depending on the input structure. For instance portions of a document might appear in one of several encoding for- mats, or they might be compressed. This flexibility is potentially powerful for an attacker, because it allows for polymorphism: the same underlying attack can be carried out using a wide variety of input files which look superficially dissimilar.

We show that using the transformation structure available in the HI-CFG, along with symbolic execution, an attacker can easily generate transformed at- tack inputs, without a need to understand the transformations. We treat the generation of transformed inputs as a search problem, and we use the struc- ture of transformations to guide the search. Symbolic execution does not scale to generate complete inputs to a large program. But using the transformation structure, we can apply symbolic execution to search for a pre-image of a single transformation at a time.

Specifically, our approach generates a HI-CFG from an execution of the vul- nerable program on a benign input which does not contain an attack, but does exercise the desired transformations. We also presume that the attacker has enough knowledge to trigger the attack in the vulnerable function (perhaps also by symbolic execution); in general this is not enough to directly give a program input that triggers the vulnerability. Our system uses the transformation struc- ture from the HI-CFG to determine the relevant transformations performed on

Table 1. Set-up of the different test cases. All values are in bytes

	Test 1	Test 2	Test 3	Test 4	Test 5
Hex encoded	10	16	55	125	250
RLE encoded	5	8	25	60	120
Object data	12	10	29	57	114

the program input to produce the buffer contents used by the vulnerable function. It then uses repeated searches based on symbolic execution, working backward from the vulnerable function's input buffer. For each transformation, it computes a pre-image: buffer contents for a previous buffer, which when passed through the transformation, yield the contents for the next buffer in the transformation sequence. This process is shown graphically in Figure 2.

A sequence of transformations leading to the function containing a potential vulnerability will appear in the HI-CFG as a path. The first node in the path is a buffer representing the program input. The remaining nodes in the path before the last are additional buffers internal to the program, connected by information-flow edges. Finally, the path ends with a consumer edge leading to the function containing the potential vulnerability. There may be multiple such paths, such as if there are buffers containing both primary data and meta-data. Among all the paths of the form described above, we choose the path for which the size of the smallest buffer on the path is maximized, to prefer primary data buffers.

Given the sequence of buffers, the HI-CFG also contains information about which functions implement each transformation. Specifically, each function that implements part of the transformation will have a consumer edge from the earlier buffer and a producer edge to the later buffer. In the case where the transformation is spread across multiple functions, the nearest call-graph ancestor that dominates all of the functions connected to both buffers will generally be a function whose execution performs the transformation.

4.2 Performance Comparison between Iterative and Monolithic Symbolic Execution

This section empirically evaluates the proposition that iteratively reversing individual transformation is faster than reversing all transformations in one single (but more complex) step.

Our test program sets up a chain of two transformations. The input is first hex decoded (pairs of ASCII characters in the ranges 0–9, a–f, or A–F map into data bytes, skipping whitespace). The data bytes are then decompressed according to a byte-level run length encoding (RLE), in which compressed bytes indicate either a repeat count for a single byte, or a run of bytes to be copied verbatim. Both encoding schemes are supported for objects in PDF files: in sequence they encode data that is compressed but still printable.

For our performance evaluation we use three different configurations of the same application with different input data. See Table 1 for the different test

Table 2. Scalability of iterative symbolic execution compared to monolithic symbolic execution. All numbers are in seconds, the timeout was set to 12 hours.

	Test 1 [s]	Test 2 [s]	Test 3 [s]	Test 4 [s]	Test 5 [s]
Iterative SE	20	183	77	816	37635
Monolithic SE	599	14042	35972	Timeout	Timeout

configurations of the data that is used for the two transformations. We then evaluate both iterative and monolithic symbolic execution. Monolithic symbolic execution uses the object data as its target and directly recovers the hex encoded input data. Iterative symbolic execution leverages the HI-CFG representation to split up the large transformation into two transformations and recovers the RLE encoded data first and uses the result from the first step as input for the second step where the RLE encoded data is reversed to hex encoded data.

The experiments use our binary symbolic execution tool FuzzBALL [2,20], which builds in turn on the Vine library from the BitBlaze framework [27]. To further improve its performance on generating transformation pre-images, FuzzBALL includes support for pruning unproductive paths, prioritizing paths by the prefix length they produce, and handling loads and stores to tables with single large formulas. These are described in detail in a technical report [21], and the implementation is available from the BitBlaze web site. To isolate the benefit of the HI-CFG, we enable these other optimizations for monolithic symbolic execution as well.

Table 2 shows the different performance for iterative and monolithic symbolic execution. Even for very short input sequences with only few bytes as object data iterative symbolic execution clearly outperforms monolithic symbolic execution by 30x (for Test 1). For larger test cases iterative symbolic execution outperforms monolithic symbolic execution by up to 78x (Test 2) or 467x (Test 3).

4.3 Case Studies

As case studies, we apply our attack polymorphism to two vulnerable document-processing systems: the PDF parsing library Poppler and the word processor AbiWord. These programs are open-source, and we use the source code to verify our results, but the system does not use the source code or source-level information such as debugging symbols.

Poppler. Poppler is a PDF processing library used in applications such as Evince. The vulnerability for which we generate attacks is cataloged as CVE-2010-3704 [22]. The vulnerability is an integer overflow in a Type 1 font character index, which can trigger an arbitrary memory write. The "stream" that contains an embedded font within a PDF document is typically compressed to save space; it can also be encrypted if the document uses access control, or transformed using other filters. By applying our system with benign documents that use various filters, we can create PDF files where the exploit is transformed in various ways.

We can also apply symbolic execution to create the malicious font itself; details are in a previous technical report [8]. We used a separate benign input and generated a separate HI-CFG for each sequence of transformations. For space reasons we give a detailed description of the first; the others were similar.

The most common PDF compression format is FlateDecode, using the Deflate algorithm of RFC 1951 [10]. As a benign input, we use a PDF file generated by pdftex applied to a small TEX file, which contains a FlateDecode-compressed font. The execution trace from the benign execution contains 13,560,478 instructions, and constructing the HI-CFG took about 1.2 hours (4217 s) on a Xeon X5670. The HI-CFG contains 1283 functions and 1590 groups.

An excerpt of the relevant portion of the HI-CFG generated by our tool is shown in Figure 6. Input passes through a sequence of four buffers before the vulnerable code is triggered, so given contents for the final buffer which trigger a vulnerability in the font parser, our system compute three levels of preimages. However, two of the transformations are direct copies for which preimage computation is trivial. Between the second and third buffers our system computes a preimage under the FlateDecode transformation: a compressed font that decompresses to the attack font. One average this requires searching through 111 execution paths, and takes a little less than two hours (6598.69 s over ten runs dropping the fastest and slowest, on an Intel Core 2 Duo E8400).

Another commonly-used transformation of streams in PDF files is RC4 encryption. It is relatively easy for our symbolic execution system to re-encrypt modified data by constructing pre-images because RC4 is a stream cipher, and the key is fixed. We applied our technique to a version of the previously described sample document with RC4 and an owner password. There is one symbolic path, and the running time is 20 seconds, mostly devoted to program startup.

Two further transformations supported by Poppler include run-length encoding and a hexadecimal encoding of binary data, as described in Section 4.2. We test inverting these two transformations with a PDF file that again contains the benign Type 1 font, but run-length encoded and then hex-encoded. As seen with the implementation in Section 4.2, these transformations are relatively easy to invert; the preimage computation requires 143 seconds and 315 symbolic paths.

AbiWord. AbiWord is a word-processing application that supports a number of file formats. In particular we examined its processing of documents in Office

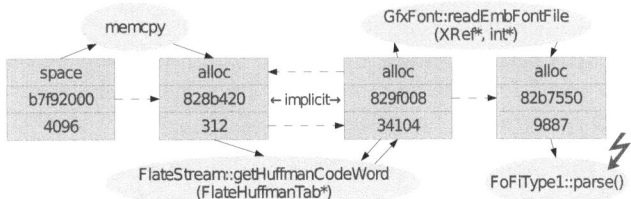

Fig. 6. An excerpt of the HI-CFG for our Poppler case study showing the buffer sequence. The input travels from left to right and FoFiType1::parse contains the vulnerability.

Open XML format (used with the extension .docx) from Microsoft Word. An Office Open XML document is structured as a compressed Zip file containing multiple XML documents representing the document contents and metadata.

Recent versions of AbiWord (we used 2.8.2) suffer from a crash in XML processing that is triggered when a shading tag occurs outside of a paragraph tag; we have not determined whether this bug is exploitable. The execution trace collected from the benign execution contains 69,503,117 instructions, and constructing the HI-CFG took about 5.8 hours (20910 s). The generated HI-CFG contains 5379 functions and 5838 groups. Looking at the sequence of buffers in the HI-CFG, the document data starts in a standard-IO input buffer, and is then decompressed by the `inflate` function. The decompressed buffer is then copied via `memmove` into a structure called the parser context, which is used by `xmlParseDocument`; the function containing the vulnerability is a callback from this parser. An XML document triggering the crash could be found using a schema-aware random testing tool, or the details of the attack can also be completed using symbolic execution of the parser [8].

Given the crash-inducing XML text, our tool finishes the task of producing an attack .docx file by finding a preimage for the compression used for the XML text in the .docx file's Zip encapsulation. In fact, Zip files use the same DEFLATE algorithm mentioned earlier in the Poppler case study, though an independent implementation. On average (across 10 runs dropping the fastest and slowest), the search requires 237 seconds and 92 symbolic paths.

4.4   Discussion

Next we discuss in more detail some of the limitations and implications of the attack polymorphism capability.

Invertible Transformations. Our approach for computing inverse images via symbolic execution depends on several features of a transformation implementation in order to find an inverse efficiently. While common, these features are not universal. First, our tool is designed for transformations whose input and output come via contiguous data structures such as arrays that are accessed sequentially. With additional data-structure inference, the approach could be extended to more complex linked and nested structures. However it must be clear when the transformation has committed to an output value: our current approach works when each output location is written exactly once. Second, pruning is most effective if the transformation's input and output are closely interleaved, so that unproductive paths can be pruned early. One example of a class of transformations that do not satisfy these features, and cannot generally be inverted by our approach, are cryptographic hash functions.

Implications for Attack Filters. Our results show that it is easy for an attacker to create variants of an attack that are camouflaged using transformations supported by an input format, such as the various filters supported in PDF documents. The consequence for the designers of defenses such as network sensors and anti-virus systems is that in order to recognize all the variants of an attack, these systems would have to duplicate all of the transformations implemented in the system they protect. For instance to recognize all possible variants of an attack PDF, a defense system would need to include decoders for all the stream formats supported by Adobe Reader.

5 Related Work

Our techniques for determining which memory accesses constitute a buffer are most similar to the array detection algorithms of Howard [26,25], a tool which infers data-structure definitions from binary executions. Our algorithms are somewhat simpler because we do not currently attempt, for instance, to detect multidimensional arrays. Other systems that perform type inference from binaries include REWARDS [18] which has been used to guide a search for vulnerabilities, and TIE [17] which can be either a static or dynamic analysis. Similar algorithms have also been used for inferring the structure of network protocols [7]. By contrast, our HI-CFG also contains information about code and the relationships between code and data, which are needed for our application.

Perhaps the most similar end-to-end approach to attack generation is the decomposition and restitching of Caballero et al. [6]. They also tackle the problem of vulnerability conditions which are difficult to trigger because of other transformations the input undergoes, in their case studies decryption. Though they use symbolic exploration to find vulnerabilities, they use a different technique, based on searching for an inverse function in the same binary, to generate preimages. The decomposition and restitching technique can also recompute checksums, which is a key capability of TaintScope [28]. TaintScope uses taint-directed fuzzing to search for vulnerabilities, and a checksum can typically be recomputed using simple concrete execution. However TaintScope uses symbolic execution, including lookup tables identified by IDAPro, to find preimages for simple transformations of the checksum value in a file, such as endian conversions or decimal/binary translation.

The AEG [1] and MAYHEM [9] systems also generate attack inputs using symbolic execution. AEG automates some additional aspects of exploit generation not covered in this paper, such as generating some common kinds of jumps to shellcode. However, these projects do not describe any vulnerabilities as involving transformation of the input prior to the vulnerable code, which is the key challenge we address.

The kinds of program information contained in the HI-CFG are available separately using existing techniques; the focus of our contribution is the extra value that comes from combining them in a single representation. For instance, having both information-flow and producer-consumer edges allows our approach to characterize a transformation in terms of both the data structures it operates on and the code that implements it. The program dependence graph (PDG) [11,14] also has edges representing both control and data flow, but it is unsuitable for our application as it has no nodes representing data structures.

Our problem of computing preimages for transformations is similar to the "gadget inversion" performed by Inspector Gadget [16], which also applies to functionality automatically discovered within a binary. Inspector Gadget's search for inverses uses only concrete executions, but it keeps track of which output bytes depend on which input bytes. Symbolic execution can be seen as a generalization in that symbolic expressions indicate not just which input values an output value depends on, but the functional form of that dependence. This often allows symbolic execution to compute a preimage using many fewer executions.

Our technique is based on searching backwards through the program execution to see if a vulnerability can be triggered by the input. A similar intuition has been applied to the control flow of a program (as opposed to information flow as we consider); examples include the static analysis tool ARCHER [29] and the call-chain-backward symbolic execution approach of Ma et al. [19].

6   Conclusion

In this paper we introduce a new data structure, the Hybrid Information- and Control-Flow Graph (HI-CFG), and give algorithms for constructing a HI-CFG from binary-level traces. The HI-CFG captures the structure of buffers and transformations that a program uses for processing its input. This structure lets us generate transformed attack inputs efficiently, because understanding the structure of transformations allows our system to find preimages for them one-by-one. We show the feasibility and applicability of our approach in two case studies of the Poppler PDF library and the AbiWord word processor. This demonstrated ease of constructing attacks using complex transformation sequences implies that the problem of filtering such attacks is very difficult.

Acknowledgments. We thank László Szekeres and Lenx Tao Wei for suggestions and help related to the experiments and previous papers. This work was supported by NSF awards CCF-0424422, 0842695, and 0831501; MURI awards N000140911081 (ONR) and FA9550-09-1-0539 (AFOSR), and DARPA award HR0011-12-2-005. However the findings and conclusions are those of the authors and do not necessarily reflect the views of the NSF or other supporters.

References

1. Avgerinos, T., Cha, S.K., Hao, B.L.T., Brumley, D.: AEG: Automatic exploit generation. In: NDSS 2011 (2011)
2. Babić, D., Martignoni, L., McCamant, S., Song, D.: Statically-directed dynamic automated test generation. In: ISSTA 2011 (2011)
3. Bond, M.D., McKinley, K.S.: Probabilistic calling context. In: OOPLSA 2007 (2007)
4. Brumley, D., Song, D.: Privtrans: automatically partitioning programs for privilege separation. In: USENIX Security 2004 (2004)
5. Caballero, J., Johnson, N.M., McCamant, S., Song, D.: Binary code extraction and interface identification for security applications. In: NDSS 2010 (2010)
6. Caballero, J., Poosankam, P., McCamant, S., Babic, D., Song, D.: Input generation via decomposition and re-stitching: Finding bugs in malware. In: CCS 2010 (2010)

7. Caballero, J., Yin, H., Liang, Z., Song, D.: Polyglot: Automatic extraction of protocol message format using dynamic binary analysis. In: CCS 2007 (2007)
8. Caselden, D., Bazhanyuk, A., Payer, M., Szekeres, L., McCamant, S., Song, D.: Transformation-aware exploit generation using a HI-CFG. Tech. Rep. UCB/EECS-2013-85, University of California, Berkeley (May 2013)
9. Cha, S.K., Avgerinos, T., Rebert, A., Brumley, D.: Unleashing MAYHEM on binary code. In: IEEE S&P 2012 (2012)
10. Deutsch, P.: DEFLATE compressed data format specification. IETF RFC 1951 (May 1996)
11. Ferrante, J., Ottenstein, K.J., Warren, J.D.: The program dependence graph and its use in optimization. TOPLAS 9(3) (1987)
12. HI-CFG project information page, http://bitblaze.cs.berkeley.edu/hicfg/
13. Hopcroft, J.E., Ullman, J.D.: Set merging algorithms. SIAM J. Comput. 2(4) (1973)
14. Horwitz, S., Reps, T.W., Binkley, D.: Interprocedural slicing using dependence graphs. TOPLAS 12(1) (1990)
15. Intel: Pin website (November 2012), http://www.pintool.org/
16. Kolbitsch, C., Holz, T., Kruegel, C., Kirda, E.: Inspector Gadget: Automated extraction of proprietary gadgets from malware binaries. In: IEEE S&P 2010 (2010)
17. Lee, J., Avgerinos, T., Brumley, D.: TIE: Principled reverse engineering of types in binary programs. In: NDSS 2011 (2011)
18. Lin, Z., Zhang, X., Xu, D.: Automatic reverse engineering of data structures from binary execution. In: NDSS 2010 (2010)
19. Ma, K.-K., Yit Phang, K., Foster, J.S., Hicks, M.: Directed symbolic execution. In: Yahav, E. (ed.) SAS 2011. LNCS, vol. 6887, pp. 95–111. Springer, Heidelberg (2011)
20. Martignoni, L., McCamant, S., Poosankam, P., Song, D., Maniatis, P.: Path-exploration lifting: Hi-fi tests for lo-fi emulators. In: ASPLOS 2012 (2012)
21. McCamant, S., Payer, M., Caselden, D., Bazhanyuk, A., Song, D.: Transformation-aware symbolic execution for system test generation. Tech. Rep. UCB/EECS-2013-125, University of California, Berkeley (June 2013)
22. MITRE: CVE-2010-3704: Memory corruption in FoFiType1::parse (October 2010) http://cve.mitre.org/cgi-bin/cvename.cgi?name=CVE-2010-3704
23. Newsome, J., Song, D.: Dynamic taint analysis: Automatic detection, analysis, and signature generation of exploit attacks on commodity software. In: NDSS 2005 (2005)
24. Schwartz, E.J., Avgerinos, T., Brumley, D.: All you ever wanted to know about dynamic taint analysis and forward symbolic execution (but might have been afraid to ask). In: IEEE S&P 2010 (2010)
25. Slowinska, A., Stancescu, T., Bos, H.: Body armor for binaries: preventing buffer overflows without recompilation. In: USENIX ATC 2012 (2012)
26. Slowinska, A., Stancescu, T., Bos, H.: Howard: a dynamic excavator for reverse engineering data structures. In: NDSS 2011 (2011)
27. Song, D., Brumley, D., Yin, H., Caballero, J., Jager, I., Kang, M.G., Liang, Z., Newsome, J., Poosankam, P., Saxena, P.: BitBlaze: A new approach to computer security via binary analysis. In: ICISS 2008 (2008) (keynote invited paper)
28. Wang, T., Wei, T., Gu, G., Zou, W.: TaintScope: A checksum-aware directed fuzzing tool for automatic software vulnerability detection. In: IEEE S&P 2010 (2010)
29. Xie, Y., Chou, A., Engler, D.R.: ARCHER: using symbolic, path-sensitive analysis to detect memory access errors. In: ESEC/FSE 2003 (2003)

AnDarwin: Scalable Detection of Semantically Similar Android Applications

Jonathan Crussell, Clint Gibler, and Hao Chen

University of California, Davis
{jcrussell,cdgibler,chen}@ucdavis.edu

Abstract. The popularity and utility of smartphones rely on their vibrant application markets; however, plagiarism threatens the long-term health of these markets. We present a scalable approach to detecting similar Android apps based on their semantic information. We implement our approach in a tool called AnDarwin and evaluate it on 265,359 apps collected from 17 markets including Google Play and numerous third-party markets. In contrast to earlier approaches, AnDarwin has four advantages: it avoids comparing apps pairwise, thus greatly improving its scalability; it analyzes only the app code and does not rely on other information — such as the app's market, signature, or description — thus greatly increasing its reliability; it can detect both full and partial app similarity; and it can automatically detect library code and remove it from the similarity analysis. We present two use cases for AnDarwin: finding similar apps by different developers ("clones") and similar apps from the same developer ("rebranded"). In ten hours, AnDarwin detected at least 4,295 apps that have been the victims of cloning and 36,106 apps that are rebranded. By analyzing the clusters found by AnDarwin, we found 88 new variants of malware and identified 169 malicious apps based on differences in the requested permissions. Our evaluation demonstrates AnDarwin's ability to accurately detect similar apps on a large scale.

1 Introduction

As of March 2012, Android has a majority smart phone marketshare in the United States [15]. The Android operating system provides the core smart phone experience, but much of the user experience relies on third-party apps. To this end, Android has an official market and numerous third-party markets where users can download apps for social networking, games, and more. In order to incentivize developers to continue creating apps, it is important to maintain a healthy market ecosystem.

One important aspect of a healthy market ecosystem is that developers are financially compensated for their work. Developers can charge directly for their apps, but many choose instead to offer free apps that are ad-supported or contain in-app billing for additional content. There are several ways developers may lose potential revenue: a paid app may be "cracked" and released for free or a free app may be copied, or "cloned", and re-released with changes to the ad libraries

J. Crampton, S. Jajodia, and K. Mayes (Eds.): ESORICS 2013, LNCS 8134, pp. 182–199, 2013.

that cause ad revenue to go to the plagiarist [20]. App cloning has been widely reported by developers, smart phone security companies and the academic community [8,10,11,16,21,33,32]. Unfortunately, the openness of Android markets and the ease of repackaging apps contribute to the ability of plagiarists to clone apps and resubmit them to markets.

Another aspect of a healthy market ecosystem is the absence of low-quality spam apps which may pollute search results, detracting from hard-working developers. Of the 569,000 apps available on the official Android market, 23% are low-quality [7]. Oftentimes, spammers will submit the same app with minor changes as many different apps using one or more developer accounts.

To improve the health of the market ecosystem, a scalable approach is needed to detect similar app for use in finding clones and potential spam. As of November, 2012, there are over 569,000 Android apps on the official Android market. Including third-party markets and allowing for future growth, there are too many apps to be analyzed using existing tools.

To this end, we develop an approach for detecting similar apps on a unprecedented scale and implement it in a tool called AnDarwin. Unlike previous approaches that compare apps pair-wise, our approach uses multiple clusterings to handle large numbers of apps efficiently. Our efficiency allows us to avoid the need to pre-select potentially similar apps based on their market, name, or description, thus greatly increasing the detection reliability. Additionally, we can use the app clusters produced by AnDarwin to detect when apps have had similar code injected (e.g. the insertion of malware). We investigate two applications of AnDarwin: finding similar apps by different developers (cloned apps) and groups of apps by the same developer with high code reuse (rebranded apps). We demonstrate the utility of AnDarwin, including the detection of new variants of known malware and the detection of new malware.

2 Background

2.1 Android

Android users have access to many markets where they can download apps such as the official Android market – Google Play [2], and other, third-party markets such as GoApk [1] and SlideME [3].

Developers must sign an app with their developer key before uploading it to a market. Most markets are designed to self-regulate through ratings and have no vetting process which has allowed numerous malicious apps onto the markets [34]. Google Play has developed a Bouncer service [26] to automatically analyze new apps. However, its effectiveness for finding similar apps, such as spam and clones, which may not be malicious, has not been studied.

2.2 Program Dependence Graphs

A Program Dependence Graph (PDG) represents a method in a program, where each node is a statement and each edge shows a dependency between statements.

There are two types of dependencies: data and control. A data dependency edge between statements s_1 and s_2 exists if there is a variable in s_2 whose value depends on s_1. For example, if s_1 is an assignment statement and s_2 references the variable assigned in s_1 then s_2 is data dependent on s_1. A control dependency between two statements exists if the truth value of the first statement controls whether the second statement executes.

2.3   Code Clones and Reuse Detection

Many approaches have been developed over the years to detect code clones [19,22,24,25]. A code clone is two or more segments of code that have the same semantics but come from different sources. Finding and eliminating code clones has many software engineering benefits such as increasing maintainability and improving security, as vulnerabilities in clones only need to be found and patched once. Plagiarism and code clone detection share the same common goal: detecting reused code. However, code clone detection is largely focused on intra-app reuse, while plagiarism detection focuses on inter-app reuse, where the apps have separate code bases and have been identified as having different authors.

Tools that detect code clones generally fall into one of four categories: string-based, token-based, tree-based and semantics-based with semantics-based detection being potentially the most robust and often the most time consuming. Early approaches considered code as a collection of strings, usually based on lines, and reported code clones based on identical lines [9]. More recently, DECKARD [22] and its successor [19] use the abstract syntax tree of a code base to create vectors which are then clustered to find similar subtrees.

3   Threat Model

Our goal is to find Android apps that share a nontrivial amount of code, published by either the same or different developers. We determine similarity based on code alone and do not use meta data such as market, developer, package or description for any purpose other than analyzing the results of AnDarwin's clusters of similar apps. We consider only similarities between the DEX code of apps. We choose to leave native code to future work as only a small percentage (7%) of the 265,359 apps we analyzed include native code.

4   Methodology

AnDarwin consists of four stages as depicted in Figure 1. First, it represents each app as a set of vectors computed over the app's Program Dependence Graphs (Section 4.1). Second, it finds similar code segments by clustering all the vectors of all apps (Section 4.2). Third, it eliminates library code based on the frequency of the clusters (Section 4.3). Finally, it detects apps that are similar, considering both full and partial app similarity (Section 4.4).

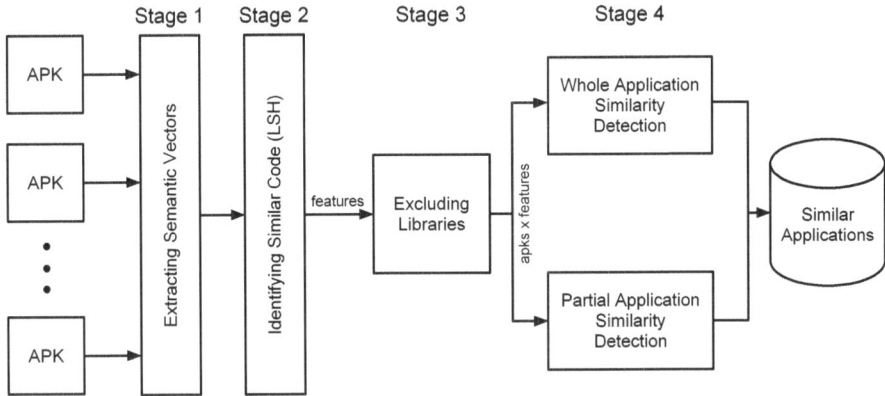

Fig. 1. Overview of AnDarwin

We base the first two stages of AnDarwin on the approaches of Jiang et al. [22] and Gabel et al. [19] to find code clones in a scalable manner. AnDarwin uses these results to detect library code and, ultimately, to detect similar apps.

4.1 Extracting Semantic Vectors

The first stage of AnDarwin represents each app as a set of semantic vectors as follows. First, AnDarwin computes an undirected PDG of each method in the app using only data dependencies for the edges (as control dependencies edges may be easier to modify). Each PDG is then split into connected components as multiple data-independent computations may occur within the same method. We call these connected components *semantic blocks* since each captures a building block of the method and represents semantic information stored in the PDG. Finally, AnDarwin computes a *semantic vector* to represent each semantic block. Each node in the semantic block represents a statement in the method and has a type corresponding to that statement. For example, a node representing an *add* might have the type *binary operation*. To capture this information, semantic vectors are calculated by counting the frequency of nodes of each type in the semantic block. Continuing the above example, a semantic block with just x adds would have an x in the dimension corresponding to binary operations. AnDarwin uses a total of 20 node types, however, we could easily use more node information such as which binary operation is being performed to increase the precision of our vectors without dramatically increasing the complexity (Section 4.5). Semantic blocks with fewer than 10 nodes are discarded because they usually represent trivial and uncharacteristic code.

4.2   Identifying Similar Code

When two semantic blocks are code clones, they share the majority of their nodes and, thus, their semantic vectors will be similar. Therefore, we can identify code clones by finding near-neighbors of semantic vectors. While not all near-neighbors will be code clones, this technique works well in practice (Section 5).

To determine all the near-neighbors, we could attempt to compute similarity pairwise between all the semantic vectors. However, this approach is quadratic in the number of vectors which is computationally prohibitive given that there can easily be millions of vectors. Instead, we leverage Locality Sensitive Hashing (LSH), which is an algorithm to efficiently find approximate near-neighbors in a large number of vectors [5]. LSH achieves this by hashing vectors using many hash functions from a special family that have a high probability of collision if the vectors are similar. To identify near-neighbors, LSH first hashes all the vectors with the special hash functions and then looks for near-neighbors among the hash collisions. This allows LSH to identify approximate clusters of similar vectors (code clones) which AnDarwin will use to detect similar apps.

Since semantic blocks of vastly different sizes are unlikely to be code clones, we can improve the scalability further by grouping the vectors based on their magnitudes [22]. To ensure that code clones near the group boundaries are not missed, we compute groups such that they overlap slightly. LSH can then cluster each group quickly as each individual group is much smaller than the set of all vectors. Moreover, each LSH computation is independent which allows all the groups to be run in parallel. This also has the added benefit that we can tailor the clustering radius for each group to the magnitude of the vectors within the group — potentially allowing us to detect more code clones.

4.3   Excluding Library Code

A library is a collection of code that is designed to be shared between many apps. In Android, libraries are embedded in apps which makes it difficult to distinguish app code from library code. This is problematic because app similarity detection tools should not consider library code when analyzing apps for similarity. Prior approaches [16,32] identified libraries using white lists and manual efforts; however, these approaches are inherently not scalable and prone to omission. In contrast, AnDarwin automatically detects libraries by leveraging the results of its clustering of similar code (Section 4.2).

A library consists of many semantic blocks which are mapped to semantic vectors by AnDarwin. When an app includes a library it inherits all the semantic vectors derived from library code. Therefore, when the semantic vectors are clustered and AnDarwin maps features to apps, features from library code will appear in many more apps. This is also the case for boilerplate code and any common compiler constructs which tend to occur in many apps. To exclude these uncharacteristic features, AnDarwin ignores any feature that appears in more than a threshold number of apps.

4.4   Detecting Similar Apps

The previous sections describe how AnDarwin creates features by clustering semantic vectors and how characteristic features are selected. AnDarwin determines app similarity based on these characteristic features using two approaches, one for full app similarity and the other for partial app similarity.

Full App Similarity Detection. For full app similarity detection, AnDarwin represents each app as a set of features. In the simplest case, two very similar apps will have mostly or completely overlapping feature sets. Dissimilar apps' feature sets, on the other hand, should have little to no overlap. This is captured in the Jaccard Index of their two feature sets F_A and F_B, which reduces the problem of finding similar app to that of finding similar sets.

$$J(A, B) = \frac{|F_A \cap F_B|}{|F_A \cup F_B|} \tag{1}$$

Partial App Similarity Detection. The above approach successfully finds apps that share most of their code but it is not robust enough to find clones that share only a part of their code. For example, consider an app and a copy of it that has added many methods and also removed many original methods to maintain a similar size. Although the app feature sets of these two apps agree on many features, their Jaccard Index may be low. To detect partial similarity, for each feature not excluded in the previous section, AnDarwin computes the set of apps that contain the feature. If two features have similar app sets, as determined by the Jaccard Index, these two features are shared by the same set of apps. If enough features share the same set of apps, AnDarwin has discovered a non-trivial amount of code sharing of non-library code. Therefore, by creating clusters of features based on their app sets, AnDarwin can detect partial app similarity by finding similar sets.

Finding Similar Sets. Both full and partial app similarity detection require finding similar sets. As in Section 4.2, we could attempt to compute similarity pairwise between all the sets, however, this is again computationally prohibitive. Fortunately, this can be approximated efficiently using MinHash [12,13].

MinHash was originally developed at Alta Vista to detect similar websites when represented as a set of features. To understand how MinHash works, first consider the binary matrix representation of the sets for full app similarity detection where columns are apps and rows are features. Let $h(A)$ be the MinHash of an app, A, and let it be defined as the first row of the matrix (going top-to-bottom) that is a one for the column corresponding to A. Then, if we were to create a random permutation of the rows of the binary matrix, for two apps, A and B, the probability that $h(A) = h(B)$ is the same as the Jaccard Index of the two app feature sets [29]. Rather than using just one permutation which may not find that two similar sets have the same MinHash value, many permutations and MinHash values can be calculated — creating a MinHash signature vector. These signature vectors are calculated for each app and can be clustered using

LSH (see Section 4.2). Therefore, MinHash allows AnDarwin to efficiently detect both full and partial app similarity.

The output of MinHash is a list of pairs of sets that are similar which we combine to create clusters of similar sets. To do so, we initialize a union-find data structure, which enables fast cluster merging and element lookup, with each set in a cluster by itself. We then process each pair, (X, Y) and merge the two clusters that contain X and Y if they are not already in the same cluster. By merging clusters in this way, the average similarity of sets within each cluster is decreasing with each pair processed. For example A may be similar to B, B to C, and C to D but this does not mean that A must be similar to D. We believe this is an acceptable trade off and leave alternative approaches to future work.

4.5   Time Complexity

In this section, we examine the total time complexity of AnDarwin. Let N be the number of apps analyzed. Then, the complexity of extracting semantic vectors is trivially $O(N * m)$, where m is the average number of methods per app (m is independent of N). The complexity of identifying similar code with LSH is: $O(d \sum_{g \in G} |g|^\rho \log |g|)$ [22]. Where d is the dimension of the semantic vectors (20), G is the set of vector groups, $|g|$ is the size of the vector group ($|g| <= N * m$) and $0 < \rho < 1$. This produces at most $O(N * m)$ clusters when there are no code clones at all. Finally, the complexity of MinHash is: $O(n \log n)$ where n is the number of sets. For full app similarity detection where there is one set per app, $n = N$, and for partial app similarity detection where there is one set per code clone, $n <= N * m$. Therefore, the total time complexity of AnDarwin is linearithmic, $O(N \log N)$, in the number of apps analyzed.

5   Evaluation

We have implemented our approach in a tool called AnDarwin. AnDarwin uses dex2jar [28] version 0.9.8 to convert DEX byte code to Java byte code. To build the PDGs required to represent apps as a set of semantic vectors, AnDarwin uses the T. J. Watson Libraries for Analysis (WALA) [14]. WALA supports building PDGs from Java byte code, eliminating the need for decompilation. Once AnDarwin has converted all the apps and represented them as sets of semantic vectors, AnDarwin uses the LSH code from [5] to cluster the semantic vectors to create features. These clustering results are then used to create the feature sets and app sets described in Section 4.4. Finally, to detect full and partial app similarity, AnDarwin uses MinHash, which we implemented based on [29].

We crawled 265,359 apps from 17 Android markets including the official market and numerous third-party markets (Table 1).

Table 1. Market origins of the apps analyzed by AnDarwin. Since some apps appear on multiple markets, the total apps in the table is slightly more than the total 265,359 apps analyzed.

Market	Apps	Market	Apps	Market	Apps
Google Play	224,108	SlideME	16,479	m360	15,248
Brothersoft	14,749	Android Online	10,381	1Mobile	9,777
Gfan	7,229	Eoemarket	5,515	GoApk	3,243
Freeware Lovers	1,428	AndAppStore	1,301	SoftPortal	1,017
Androidsoft	613	AppChina	404	ProAndroid	370
AndroidDownloadz	245	PocketGear	227		

5.1 Semantic Vectors

There are a total of 87,386,000 methods included in the 265,359 apps. These methods produced a total of 90,144,000 semantic vectors, meaning that on average a method has 1.03 connected components. Among the 90,144,000 semantic vectors, there are 4,825,000 distinct vectors. The average size of these 4,825,000 vectors is 77.87 nodes. The largest has 17,116 nodes. When we manually investigated the largest method, we found that the app builds a massive 5-dimensional array using hard coded values depending on different flags. Although perhaps not the best coding style, this large semantic vector does represent valid code that could be copied.

5.2 Code Features

In total, AnDarwin found 87,386,000 methods included in the 265,359 apps that are clustered into 3,085,998 distinct features by LSH. 133,753 (4.3%) of these features are present in more than 250 apps and thus are not used in either full or partial app similarity detection. We selected this threshold based on the following insight: only features from library code tend to map to methods that share the same method signatures. Therefore, if the ratio of the number of apps a feature appears in to the number of distinct method signatures for that feature is large, it is highly likely that the feature represents library code. To select a library code threshold, we select a value and then count the number of excluded features for which this ratio is large and evaluate whether the threshold is acceptable. Using a ratio of four, we selected the threshold such that at least 50% of the excluded features exhibit this trait. We note that this threshold may be easily tweaked depending on false positive and false negative requirements.

5.3 App Complexity

Overall, AnDarwin found that a large number of apps are not very complex. Figure 2a shows the number of features per apps for the 265,359 apps before

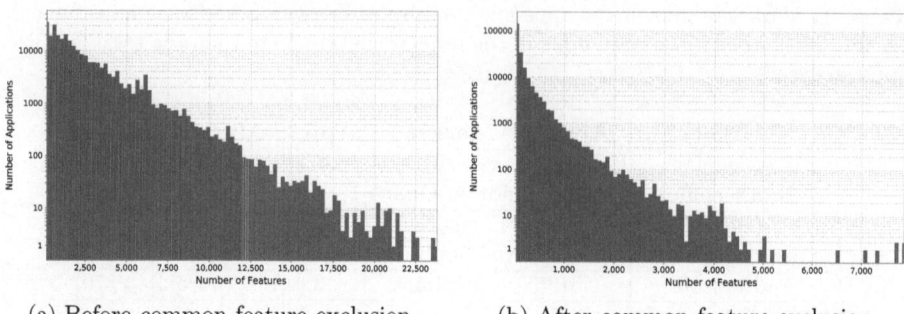

(a) Before common feature exclusion   (b) After common feature exclusion

Fig. 2. Distribution of the number of features per app on logarithnic scale

common feature exclusion. On average, apps have 2,045 features and the largest app has 23,918 features. Once libraries are excluded, the number of apps with at least one feature drops to 231,184. Figure 2b shows that the average complexity drops dramatically once common features are excluded. The average number of features for these apps is 148, with the largest app having 7,908 features.

This is interesting from a software development point of view because it suggests that through libraries and good API design, most Android apps don't have to be very complex in order to perform their function.

5.4   Full App Similarity Detection

Using full app similarity detection (Section 4.4), AnDarwin found 28,495 clusters consisting of a total of 150,846 distinct apps. Figure 3a shows the sizes of the clusters. As expected, the majority of clusters consist of just two apps. Surprisingly, some clusters are much larger, the largest of which consists of 281 apps. We will investigate these clusters in Section 6.2.

To evaluate the quality of the clusters, we compute intra-cluster app similarity based on the average Jaccard Index (Equation 1) between each pair of apps. For each cluster C, we compute the similarity score, $Sim(C)$, as:

$$Sim(C) = avg\{(A, B) \in C : J(A, B)\} \qquad (2)$$

The similarity scores are between 0 and 1, where a score close to 1 indicates that all apps in the cluster have almost identical feature sets. Figure 3b shows the cumulative distribution of the similarity scores of the 28,495 clusters. It shows that almost no clusters have similarity scores below 0.5, and more than half of the clusters have similarity scores of over 0.80. This demonstrates the effectiveness of AnDarwin in clustering highly similar apps.

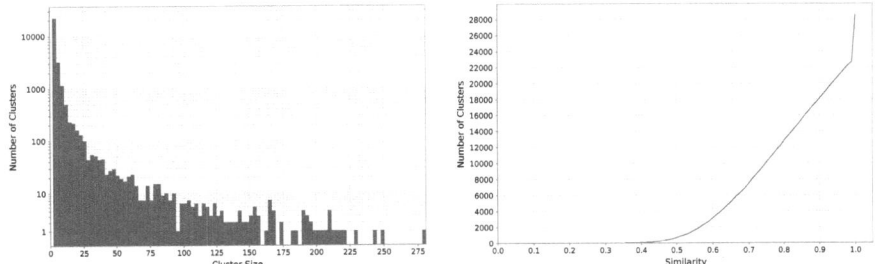

(a) Histogram of the cluster sizes on loga- (b) Cumulative distribution function of
rithmic scale $Sim(C)$

Fig. 3. Full App Similarity Detection

5.5 Partial App Similarity Detection

Using partial app similarity detection, AnDarwin found 11,848 clusters consisting of 88,464 distinct apps. Figures 4a and 4b show the sizes and similarity of
these clusters, respectively. As partial app similarity is designed to detect app
pairs that share only a portion of their code, we cannot measure them with
Equation 1. Consider the scenario where an attacker copies an app but adds
an arbitrarily large amount of code. In this case, Equation 1 will be small even
though the original and clone share all of the original app's features. Therefore,
for each cluster C, we compute the similarity score, $Sim_p(C)$, as:

$$Sim_p(C) = avg\{(A, B) \in C : \frac{|F_A \cap F_B|}{\min(|F_A|, |F_B|)}\} \tag{3}$$

Figure 4b shows the cumulative distribution function of $Sim_p(C)$ for the
partial app similarity detection clusters. Comparing Figure 3b to Figure 4b,
we observe that some clusters based on partial app similarity have low intra-
cluster similarity scores while almost no cluster based on full app similarity has
similarity scores below 0.5. On the surface, this might suggest that partial app
similarity produces lower quality clusters. However, this in fact shows the power
of partial app similarity. When a cluster has a low similarity score, it indicates
that the common features among the apps in this cluster are relatively small
compared to the app sizes, so full app similarity detection cannot identify these
common features.

5.6 Performance

We evaluated AnDarwin's performance on a server with quad Intel Xeon E7-
4850 CPUs (80 logical cores with hyper threading) and 256GB DDR3 memory.
Using 75 threads, it took 4.47 days to extract semantic vectors (Stage 1) from all
265,359 apps (only 109 seconds per thread to process each app). We note that

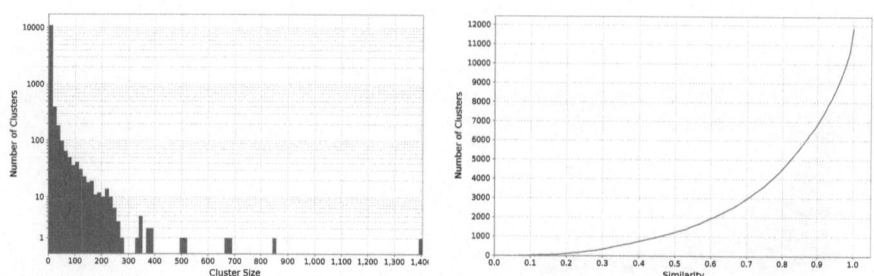

(a) Histogram of the cluster sizes on loga- (b) Cumulative distribution function of
rithmic scale $Sim_p(C)$

Fig. 4. Partial App Similarity Detection

this stage only occurs once for each app, regardless of changes to subsequent
stages and can be parallelized to any number of servers to reduce the total time.

The next most expensive stages are the LSH clustering in Stage 2 (Section 4.2)
and the two MinHash-based clusterings in Stage 4 (Section 4.4). LSH clusters all
4,825,000 distinct vectors in just over 49 minutes. This time could be reduced to
seven minutes if we were to run all the groups in parallel, rather than serially (as
done in our current implementation). Full app similarity detection runs in just
over 35 minutes. In total, it takes under ten hours to complete full app similarity
detection including all the database operations and data transformations. On its
own, partial app similarity detection took seven hours but this is expected as it
clusters 2,952,245 sets whereas full app similarity detection only clusters 265,359.
Interestingly, this time estimates how long it would take to run MinHash for
full app similarity detection on 2,952,245 apps. Both MinHash times could be
improved by using more than our single server.

5.7   Accuracy

Full App Similarity Detection. To measure the false positive rate of An-
Darwin's full app similarity detection, we leverage DNADroid [16], a tool that
robustly compares Android apps pairwise for code reuse. DNADroid uses subgraph isomorphism to detect similarity between the PDGs of two apps. In the
author's evaluation of DNADroid, it had an experimental false positive rate of
0%, making it an ideal tool for evaluating AnDarwin's accuracy.

Unfortunately, DNADroid is too computationally expensive to apply to all
the pairs of apps AnDarwin found. Instead, we randomly selected 6,000 of the
28,495 clusters and then randomly selected one app from each cluster to compare
against all other apps in the cluster. This resulted in a total of 25,434 pairs which
it took DNADroid 83 hours to analyze.

DNADroid assigns each app in a pair a coverage value which indicates how
much of the app's PDG nodes appear in the other app. To assess AnDarwin, we
use the maximum of these two coverage values for each pair. DNADroid found
that 96.28% of the clusters had 70% of the max coverage values over 50%(equal

to the Jaccard Index used by AnDarwin) and 95.50% of the clusters had 90% of them over the threshold. Using the 70% criteria, this gives full app similarity detection a false positive rate of just 3.72% at the cluster level.

We do not attempt to measure the false negative rate of AnDarwin as there is no feasible way to find ground truth, e.g., all the similar apps in our collection of 265,359 apps.

Partial App Similarity Detection. Unfortunately, DNADroid and its coverage values are inappropriate for evaluating the accuracy of partial app similarity detection. DNADroid considers apps as a whole and calculates similarity based on the matched portion to the size of the whole app. If DNADroid were used to verifying partial app similarity detection, we would incorrectly report a false positive in the case where two apps share a part of their code but not a significant (over the DNADroid coverage threshold of 50%) amount of their total code. Again, due to the lack of ground truth, we do not attempt to measure the false positive or false negative rate of partial app similarity detection.

6   Findings

6.1   Clone Victims

One use case of AnDarwin is finding clones on a large scale. Clones are different apps (not different versions of the same app) that are highly similar but have different owners. We determine ownership using two identifiers associated with each app we crawl: 1) the developer account name plus the market name and 2) the public key fingerprint of the private key that digitally signed the app. Assuming that a developer's account and her private key are not compromised, no two apps with different owners can share both of these identifiers. Therefore, we assume apps have different owners if they do not share either identifier.

Definitively counting the number of clones is non-trivial as it requires knowing which apps are the originals. Instead, we estimate the number of apps that are the victims of cloning. Each app belongs to at most one cluster and each app in a cluster is similar to at least one other app in the cluster. Therefore, each cluster is a family of similar apps which must have a victim app, the original app, even if we have not crawled the victim app. Then, the number of victims is at least equal to the number of clusters where there is more than one owner, as determined by the two identifiers above. Using just the full app similarity clusters, which were vetted in Section 5.7, AnDarwin found that at least 4,295 apps have been the victims of cloning.

6.2   Rebranded Apps

Using full app similarity detection, AnDarwin found 764 clusters containing more than 25 apps. Our investigation of these large clusters found a trend that some developers rebrand their apps to cater to different markets. The idea of rebranding is not a new concept – it has been widely used on the web (e.g. WordPress blogs). For example, one cluster consists of weather apps each targeting a different city. Similarly, we found clusters for news, trivia, books, radio stations, wallpapers, puzzles, product updates and even mobile banking apps. Some of these rebrandings are as trivial as just swapping the embedded images.

To estimate the number of rebranded apps, we use the owner identifiers described in Section 6.1 to map each app to an owner. If at least 25 apps in a cluster have the same owner, we consider those apps to be rebranded. Using this metric, 599 of the 764 clusters with at least 25 apps include rebranded apps. In total, we found 36,106 rebranded apps.

A surprising example of app rebranding is a cluster of mobile banking apps. This cluster contains 109 distinct apps that share a common package name prefix. Searching by this prefix, we found 175 apps on the Google Play Store, which includes 80 of the 109 apps present in our clusters. Interestingly, several of the apps were available on both 1Mobile and Play, and two of the apps are signed by a different key than the other 107 apps.

6.3   New Variants of Known Malware

Once malware has been discovered, it is important to use this knowledge to identify variants of the malware in an automated way. We hypothesize that by analyzing the clusters produced by AnDarwin containing known malware we may automatically discover new variants of those malware. Using the malware dataset from [34], we found 333 apps were clustered with known malware and were not included in the malware dataset.

We uploaded these 333 apps to VirusTotal [4], a website for running a suite of anti-virus software on files. It recognized 136 as malware, with 88 never having been uploaded to VirusTotal before. Among the 136 malware, approximately 20 are variants of the DroidKungFu family [23]. Approximately another 20 are identified as belonging to various malware families described in [34]. The remaining apps are identified as adware that contains either AirPush or AdWo. These advertising libraries show ads even when the app is not running [30] and have been known to have misleading ad campaigns [31]. These results demonstrate AnDarwin's utility for discovering new variants of malware.

6.4   New Malware Detection in Clones

Zhou et al. [34] found that 86.0% of their malware samples were repackaged versions of legitimate apps with additional malicious code, aiming to increase their chances of being installed by providing useful functionality. Since malware often requires many more permissions than regular apps, we hypothesize that we may detect new malware by searching for apps that require more permissions than the others in the same cluster. Intuitively, apps that are clustered together have similar code and for some to require more permissions is suspicious. To investigate this hypothesis, we searched for apps that require excessive permissions as follows (using clusters from both full and partial app similarity detection). First, for each cluster, we compute the union of the permissions required by all its apps. Then, we identify apps that require at least 85% of the permission union. Finally, if the apps identified in the previous step are fewer than 15% of the total apps in the cluster, we mark these apps as suspicious. Using this criterion, we found 608 suspicious apps. 16 of these apps overlap with the malware dataset from [34] and 1 overlaps with the previous section.

As before, we uploaded these apps to VirusTotal and it identified 243 as malware. Furthermore, 169 of these had never been seen before. This represents a lower bound on the actual number of malware in the suspicious apps as we did not investigate the suspicious apps for new malware which may not be identified by VirusTotal. The identified malware is from known families such as DroidKungFu [23], BaseBridge [18] and Geinimi [27]. By searching for apps with excessive permissions, AnDarwin identified known malware as suspicious without prior knowledge of their existence. This result demonstrates that AnDarwin is an effective tool for identifying suspicious apps for more detailed analysis.

7   Discussion

7.1   Adversarial Response

A specific use case of AnDarwin is to find plagiarized apps in a scalable manner. Based on our implementation details, plagiarists may attempt to evade detection using obfuscation. Some of these obfuscation techniques are effective against AnDarwin, however, they are difficult to perform automatically.

Futile Obfuscations. AnDarwin is robust against all transformations that do not alter methods' PDGs, which is the basis for our similarity detection. This includes, but is not limited to, (1) syntactical changes such as renaming packages, classes, methods and variables, (2) refactoring changes such as combining or splitting classes and moving methods between classes, and (3) method restructuring such as splitting methods with multiple connected components into separate methods and reordering code segments within a method that are data and control independent.

AnDarwin is also robust against code addition. A plagiarist may add a few methods or a new library to their plagiarized app. Since the original and the plagiarized app still share a core of similar code, AnDarwin would still detect them using partial app similarity detection.

Potentially Effective Obfuscations. AnDarwin is less robust against obfuscations that dramatically alter methods' PDGs. For example, plagiarists may be able to alter app methods to mimic the semantic vectors of library code or use PDG node splitting to increase the distance between the original semantic vector and the plagiarized one. Additionally, plagiarists could artificially join connected components within methods using dead code to increase the distance between the semantic vectors or split each connected component into a set of very small methods that are too small to be considered by AnDarwin. Ultimately, plagiarists could reimplement the original app.

The subversions listed above are difficult for most similarity detection tools to detect, including AnDarwin. Fortunately, all these subversions require substantial effort on the part of the plagiarists as it would be difficult for tools to do this automatically. Further, such a tool would require intimate knowledge of the targeted app to ensure that the plagiarized app still functions correctly.

7.2 Probability of a False Positive

In this section, we examine the probability that two dissimilar apps are clustered together by full app similarity detection. Consider two similar apps that share n features. Assuming that features are independent, which is the case when library code is excluded, then:

$$Pr[\text{share n features}] = Pr[\text{share feature}]^n = Pr[\text{share close SV}]^n \qquad (4)$$

Where "close SV" means two semantic vectors that will be clustered together by LSH or are identical. Now, consider the case where two apps are not similar, but are clustered together anyway. This means they must still agree on n features, where each of these n agreements is a false positive which we shall refer to as a *feature collision*. Feature collisions can occur in two ways: (1) semantic vector collision and (2) non-code clone semantic blocks generating "close" semantic vectors. Fortunately, even if the probability of a feature collision is very high, there has to be n feature collisions in order to have a false positive. We have found that, on average, apps contain 148 features after excluding common features. Therefore, in order for two unrelated apps to have a Jaccard Index above our threshold of 50%, there must be approximately 100 feature collisions. Even if the probability of a feature collision was 95%, the probability of a false positive with this many features would be less than one percent.

8 Related Work

There have been several approaches proposed recently to find similar Android apps. Closest to AnDarwin is [33]. They use a heuristic based on how tightly classes within the app are coupled (using its call graph) to split apps into primary and rider sections. Then, they represent the primary section as vectors which they cluster in linearithmic time. This heuristic allows [33] to detect some partial app similarity, however, it would be easy for a plagiarist to circumvent these heuristics by adding dead code to the call graph to artificially couple unrelated classes. In contrast, AnDarwin's partial app similarity does not rely on heuristics. Additionally, while AnDarwin's features represent the functionality of methods of an app and are thus difficult to change, [33]'s features include the app's permissions, the Android API calls used and several other features, all of which may be easily changed. [33] can also detect commonly injected code by clustering the rider sections, however, they use the same features and heuristics which are easily changed and circumvented, respectively. All other related work described below compares applications pairwise, yielding significant scalability problems. Additionally, neither [33] nor any other related work provides the ability to robustly find partial app similarity, as AnDarwin does.

Androguard [6] currently supports two methods of similarity detection: comparing apps using the SHA256 hashes of methods and basic blocks and using the normal compression distance of pairs of methods between apps. DEXCD [17] detects Android clones by comparing similarities in streams of tokens from Android DEX files. DroidMOSS [32] computes a series of fingerprints for each app based on the fuzzy hashes of consecutive opcodes, ignoring operands. Apps are then compared pairwise for repackaging by calculating the edit distance between the overall fingerprint of each app. DNADroid [16] compares apps based on the PDGs of their methods. Juxtapp [21] disassembles each app and creates k-grams over the opcodes inside the app's methods. Next it hashes the k-grams to create features which are used to represent each app and then computes similarity by comparing sets of these features between pairs of apps. All of these approaches except DNADroid are vulnerable to plagiarism that involves moderate amounts of adding or modifying statements, though DNADroid's comparison is computationally expensive.

9   Conclusion

We present AnDarwin, a tool for finding apps with similar code on a large scale. In contrast with earlier approaches, AnDarwin does not compare apps pairwise, drastically increasing its scalability. AnDarwin accomplishes this using two stages of clustering: LSH to group semantic vectors into features and Min-Hash to detect apps with similar feature sets (full app) and features that often occur together (partial app). We evaluated AnDarwin on 265,359 apps crawled from 17 markets. AnDarwin identified at least 4,295 apps that have been cloned and an additional 36,106 apps that are rebranded. From the clusters discovered by AnDarwin, we found 88 new variants of malware and could have discovered 169 new malware. We also presented a cluster post-processing methodology for finding apps that have had similar code injected. AnDarwin has a low false positive rate — only 3.72% for full app similarity detection. Our findings indicate that AnDarwin is an effective tool to identify rebranded and cloned apps and thus could be used to improve the health of the market ecosystem.

Acknowledgements. We would like to thank the anonymous reviewers for their insightful feedback as well as Liang Cai, Dennis Xu, Ben Sanders, Justin Horton, and Jon Vronsky for their assistance in obtaining Android applications. This paper is based upon work supported by the National Science Foundation under Grant No. 1018964. Any opinions, findings, and conclusions or recommendations expressed in this material are those of the author and do not necessarily reflect the views of the National Science Foundation.

References

1. Goapk market (April 2012), http://market.goapk.com
2. Google play (April 2012), https://play.google.com/store/apps
3. Slideme: Android community and application marketplace (April 2012), http://slideme.org/
4. Virus total (June 2012), https://www.virustotal.com
5. Andoni, A., Indyk, P.: Near-optimal hashing algorithms for approximate nearest neighbor in high dimensions. In: 47th Annual IEEE Symposium on Foundations of Computer Science, FOCS 2006, pp. 459–468. IEEE (2006)
6. Androguard. Androguard: Manipulation and protection of android apps and more... (April 2012), http://code.google.com/p/androguard/
7. AppBrain. Number of available android applications (November 2012), http://www.appbrain.com/stats/number-of-android-apps
8. BajaBob. Smalihook.java found on my hacked application (May 2012), http://stackoverflow.com/questions/5600143/android-game-keeps-getting-hacked
9. Baker, B.S.: On finding duplication and near-duplication in large software systems. In: Proceedings of 2nd Working Conference on Reverse Engineering 1995, pp. 86–95. IEEE (1995)
10. Scott Beard. Market shocker! iron soldiers xda beta published by alleged thief (May 2012), http://androidheadlines.com/2011/01/market-shocker-iron-soldiers-xda-beta-published-by-alleged-thief.html
11. The Lookout Blog. Security alert: Gamex trojan hides in root-required apps - tricking users into downloads (April 2012), http://blog.mylookout.com/blog/2012/04/27/security-alert-gamex-trojans-hides-in-root-required-apps-tricking-users-into-downloads/
12. Broder, A.Z.: On the resemblance and containment of documents. In: Proceedings of the Compression and Complexity of Sequences 1997, pp. 21–29. IEEE (1997)
13. Broder, A.Z., Charikar, M., Frieze, A.M., Mitzenmacher, M.: Min-wise independent permutations. In: Proceedings of the Thirtieth Annual ACM Symposium on Theory of Computing, pp. 327–336. ACM (1998)
14. IBM T.J. Watson Research Center. T.j. watson libraries for analysis (wala) (April 2012), http://wala.sourceforge.net
15. comScore. comscore reports march 2012 u.s. mobile subscriber market share (May 2012), http://www.comscore.com/Press_Events/Press_Releases/2012/4/comScore_Reports_March_2012_U.S._Mobile_Subscriber_Market_Share
16. Crussell, J., Gibler, C., Chen, H.: Attack of the clones: Detecting cloned applications on android markets. In: Foresti, S., Yung, M., Martinelli, F. (eds.) ESORICS 2012. LNCS, vol. 7459, pp. 37–54. Springer, Heidelberg (2012)
17. Davis, I.: Dexcd (April 2012), http://www.swag.uwaterloo.ca/dexcd/index.html
18. Doherty, S., Krysiuk, P.: Android.basebridge (November 2012), http://www.symantec.com/security_response/writeup.jsp?docid=2011-060915-4938-99
19. Gabel, M., Jiang, L., Su, Z.: Scalable detection of semantic clones. In: ACM/IEEE 30th International Conference on Software Engineering, ICSE 2008, pp. 321–330. IEEE (2008)
20. Gibler, C., Stevens, R., Crussell, J., Chen, H., Zang, H., Choi, H.: Adrob: Examining the landscape and impact of android application plagiarism. To Appear in the Proceedings of 11th International Conference on Mobile Systems, Applications and Services (2013)

21. Hanna, S., Huang, L., Wu, E., Li, S., Chen, C., Song, D.: Juxtapp: A scalable system for detecting code reuse among android applications. In: Flegel, U., Markatos, E., Robertson, W. (eds.) DIMVA 2012. LNCS, vol. 7591, pp. 62–81. Springer, Heidelberg (2013)
22. Jiang, L., Misherghi, G., Su, Z., Glondu, S.: Deckard: Scalable and accurate tree-based detection of code clones. In: Proceedings of the 29th International Conference on Software Engineering, pp. 96–105. IEEE Computer Society (2007)
23. Jiang, X.: Droidkungfu (November 2012),
    http://www.csc.ncsu.edu/faculty/jiang/DroidKungFu.html
24. Komondoor, R., Horwitz, S.: Using slicing to identify duplication in source code. In: Cousot, P. (ed.) SAS 2001. LNCS, vol. 2126, pp. 40–56. Springer, Heidelberg (2001)
25. Li, Z., Lu, S., Myagmar, S., Zhou, Y.: Cp-miner: Finding copy-paste and related bugs in large-scale software code. IEEE Transactions on Software Engineering 32(3), 176–192 (2006)
26. Lockheimer, H.: Android and security (April 2012),
    http://googlemobile.blogspot.com/2012/02/android-and-security.html
27. OGorman, G., Honda, H.: Android.geinimi (November 2012),
    http://www.symantec.com/security_response/
    writeup.jsp?docid=2011-010111-5403-99
28. pxb1988. dex2jar: A tool for converting android's .dex format to java's .class format (April 2012), https://code.google.com/p/dex2jar/
29. Rajaraman, A., Leskovec, J., Ullman, J.: Mining of massive datasets (2012),
    http://infolab.stanford.edu/~ullman/mmds/book.pdf
30. Spring, T.: Sneaky mobile ads invade android phones (June 2012),
    http://www.pcworld.com/article/245305/
    sneaky_mobile_ads_invade_android_phones.html
31. Android Threats. Android/adwo (February 2013),
    http://android-threats.org/androidadwo/
32. Zhou, W., Zhou, Y., Jiang, X., Ning, P.: Detecting repackaged smartphone applications in third-party android marketplaces. In: Proceedings of 2nd ACM Conference on Data and Application Security and Privacy, CODASPY 2012 (2012)
33. Zhou, W., Zhou, Y., Grace, M., Jiang, X., Zou, S.: Fast, scalable detection of piggybacked mobile applications. In: Proceedings of the Third ACM Conference on Data and Application Security and Privacy, pp. 185–196. ACM (2013)
34. Zhou, Y., Jiang, X.: Dissecting android malware: Characterization and evolution. In: Proceedings of 33rd Symposium on Security and Privacy. IEEE (2012)

BISTRO: Binary Component Extraction
and Embedding for Software Security Applications

Zhui Deng, Xiangyu Zhang, and Dongyan Xu

Department of Computer Science and CERIAS, Purdue University, West Lafayette, IN 47907
{deng14,xyzhang,dxu}@cs.purdue.edu

Abstract. In software security and malware analysis, researchers often need to
directly manipulate binary program – benign or malicious – without source code.
A useful pair of binary manipulation primitives are binary functional component
extraction and *embedding*, for extracting a functional component from a binary
program and for embedding a functional component in a binary program, respectively. Such primitives are applicable to a wide range of security scenarios such as
legacy program hardening, binary semantic patching, and malware function analysis. Unfortunately, existing binary rewriting techniques are inadequate to support binary function carving and embedding. In this paper, we present BISTRO, a
system that supports these primitives *without* symbolic information, relocation information, or compiler support. BISTRO preserves functional correctness of both
the extracted functional component and the stretched binary program (with the
component embedded) by patching them in a systematic fashion. We have implemented an IDA Pro-based prototype of BISTRO and evaluated it using real-
world Windows software. Our results show the effectiveness of BISTRO, with
each stretched binary incurring low time and space overhead. Furthermore, we
demonstrate BISTRO's capabilities in various security applications.

1 Introduction

In software security and malware analysis, researchers often need to manipulate binary
code – benign or malicious – without source code and symbolic information. One pair
of complementary binary manipulation primitives is to (1) extract a re-usable functional
component from a binary program and (2) embed a value-added functional component
in an existing binary program. We call these primitives *binary component extraction*
and *embedding*. The primitives are useful in a wide range of software security scenarios. In *security hardening of legacy binaries*, binary component embedding enables the
retrofitting of legacy or close-source software with a third-party functional component
that performs a value-added security function such as access control. In *binary semantic patching*, binary programs from different vendors may leverage the same functional
component. Suppose one vendor identifies a vulnerability in such a component and releases a patched version for its own program; whereas other vendors are not aware of
the vulnerability or have not patched their products. We can apply binary component
extraction to carve out the patched component from a patched program and replace the
vulnerable version of the same component in an un-patched program using binary component embedding. In *malware analysis*, binary component extraction and embedding

J. Crampton, S. Jajodia, and K. Mayes (Eds.): ESORICS 2013, LNCS 8134, pp. 200–218, 2013.

supports "plug and play" of malicious functions extracted from malware captured in the wild. One can even "stitch" multiple extracted malware functions to compose a new piece of malware – a capability that might help enable strategic cyber defence.

Binary component extraction and embedding poses significant challenges. Brute force extraction and insertion of binary functions will most likely fail. Instead, both the extracted component and the target binary program need to be carefully transformed. For example, instructions in the target binary need to be shifted to create space for the embedded function; when a function is extracted from its origin binary, the instructions in it need to be re-positioned and re-packaged; accesses to global variables need to be re-positioned; function pointers need to be properly handled; and indirect jumps/calls need to have their target addresses recalculated. These problems are especially challenging when the binary component or the target binary program is *not relocatable*, which is often the case when dealing with legacy or malware binaries.

Despite advances in binary instrumentation and rewriting, existing techniques are inadequate to address the binary component extraction and embedding challenges. Dynamic binary instrumentation tools such as PIN, Valgrind, DynamoRIO [2] and QEMU perform instrumentation only when a binary program is executed on their infrastructures. They do not generate an instrumented, stand-alone binary for production runs. Static binary rewriting tools such as Diablo [4], Alto [5], Vulcan [30], and Atom [7] can generate instrumented, stand-alone binaries. However, they require symbolic information or that the binaries be generated by special compilers.

More lightweight techniques exist that do not require symbolic information or special compilers [8–13]. Among them, some create *trampolines* at the end of a target binary in which instrumentation is placed and then use control flow *detours* to access the trampolines [8–10]. The others duplicate the body of a target binary program in its virtual memory space and only the replica is instrumented. The original binary body is retained in its original position to provide a kind of control flow forwarding mechanism [11–13]. However, none of these techniques supports extraction of binary component or implanting an extracted component in another binary. Many of them cause substantial space/performance overhead. To the best of our knowledge, none of them has been successfully applied to large-scale Windows applications or kernel code. A more detailed comparison is presented in our technical report [1].

Recently, researchers proposed approaches that focus on identification, extraction and reuse of components from binaries. Inspector Gadget [29] performs dynamic slicing to identify and extract components from malware. The extracted component might have incomplete code path coverage due to the limitation of dynamic analysis. BCR [16] adopts a combination of static and dynamic approach to extract a function from a binary. However, it uses labels to represent jump/call targets, thus does not preserve the semantic of indirect jumps/calls. ROC [23] uses dynamic slicing to identify reusable functional components in a binary but does not extract them. These approaches do not aim to reuse extracted components for enhancing legacy binaries. Moreover, they cannot extract components from non-executable binaries (e.g., malware corpse) due to the use of dynamic analysis.

In this paper, we present BISTRO, a systematic approach to binary functional component extraction and embedding. BISTRO automatically performs the following:

(1) extracting a functional component, with its instructions and data section entries non-contiguously located in the virtual address space, from an original binary and (2) embedding a binary component of any size at any user-specified location in a target binary, without requiring symbolic information, relocation information, or compiler support. For both extraction and embedding, BISTRO preserves the functionalities of the target binary program and the extracted component by accurately patching them. BISTRO performs extraction and embedding efficiently and the "stretched" target binary after embedding only incurs small time and space overhead.

We have developed a prototype of BISTRO as an IDA-Pro [21] plugin. We have conducted extensive evaluation and case studies using real-world Windows applications (e.g., Firefox and Adobe Reader), kernel drivers, and malware. Our evaluation (Section 6) indicates BISTRO's efficiency and precision in patching extracted components and target binaries. Moreover, the stretched target binary incurs small performance overhead (1.9% on average) and space overhead (10.9% on average). We have applied BISTRO to the following usage cases: (1) We carve out patched components from a binary and use them to replace their vulnerable versions in other applications, achieving binary semantic patching (Section 6.2); (2) We stitch malicious functions from an un-executable Conficker worm [14] sample and compose a new, executable malware (Section 6.3); and (3) We demonstrate the realistic threat of *trojan-ed* kernel drivers with malicious rootkit functions embedded in benign driver – using real-world drivers and rootkits[1].

2   Overview and Assumptions

An overview of BISTRO is shown in Figure 1. BISTRO has two key components: *binary extractor* and *binary stretcher*.

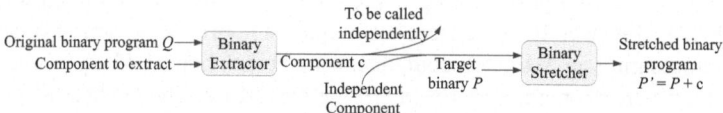

Fig. 1. Overview of BISTRO

The binary extractor is responsible for extracting a designated functional component c from an original binary Q. c includes both code and data of the functional component. The extractor does so by removing the unwanted code and data from Q and then collapsing the remaining data and code into a re-usable component c that occupies a contiguous virtual address region. More importantly, the instructions in c are properly patched for repositioning. We note that c can either be called as a library function or be embedded directly in another binary program.

The binary stretcher is responsible for stretching the target binary P to make "room" (holes in its address space) to embed a function component. As shown in Figure 1, the stretcher takes the target binary P and the to-be-embedded component c as input; stretches P, and patches the code in P to allow the embedding of c. The output of the stretcher is a "stretched" binary $P' = P + c$ ready for execution.

---

[1] Due to lack of space, Case (3) is presented in our technical report [1].

Summary of Enabling Techniques. Both the binary extractor and stretcher are based on the same binary stretching algorithm (Section 3). The overarching idea is to shift instructions for creating space (stretcher) or squeezing out unwanted space (extractor). The algorithm focuses on patching the control transfer and global data reference instructions by precisely computing the adjusted offsets. For instance, if a component with size $|c| = n$ is inserted, all the original instructions following the insertion point will be shifted by n bytes, and control transfers to any of the shifted instructions need to be incremented by n.

To address the challenge of handling indirect calls and call back functions invoked by external libraries, we develop another algorithm (Section 4.1) that stretches a subject binary at the original entries of functions that are potential targets of indirect calls, creating small holes (usually a few bytes) to hold a long jump instruction to forward any calls to those functions to their shifted locations. These holes must not be shifted by any stretching/shrinking operations. They always stay in their original positions and thus are called "*anchors*". Our algorithm precisely takes into account these anchors when performing stretching/shrinking. To handle indirect jumps, we leverage an efficient perfect hashing scheme to translate jump targets dynamically. These techniques are used to patch indirect jumps/calls in both extracted components and target binaries.

Assumptions. We make the following assumptions (hence stating the *non-goals* of BISTRO): (1) The user, not BISTRO, will predetermine the semantic appropriateness of embedding component c in target program P. Furthermore, he/she will decide the specific location to insert c. This can be practically done by performing reverse engineering on P. For example, to harden P with some security policy enforcement mechanism based on control flow [6], the user can reconstruct the control flow graph of P, collect its dominance and post-dominance information, and decide proper locations to insert c. (2) The identification of c in the original binary Q is done a priori through manual or automated techniques, such as Inspector Gadget [29], binary slicing [15], binary differencing [31], and BCR [16]. While we will present our experience with functional component identification in our case studies (Section 6), the identification technique itself is *outside* the scope of this paper. (3) Binaries can be properly disassembled (e.g., by IDA-Pro) *before* being passed to BISTRO. This assumption is supported by the large number of real-world, off-the-shelf binaries in our experiments. Although we currently do not handle obfuscated or self-modifying binaries, we note that, in addition to IDA-Pro, other conservative disassembling [13, 35] and unpacking [34] tools can also be used as the pre-processor of BISTRO to handle more sophisticated binaries.

3   Basic Algorithm for Binary Extraction/Stretching

In this section, we present the basic algorithm (Algorithm 1) executed by both the binary extractor and stretcher of BISTRO. For the time being, we assume (1) there is no indirect control transfer and (2) global data is directly referenced in an instruction using its address. The algorithm takes the subject binary and a list of virtual address intervals called *snippets* representing (1) the holes to be created in the binary in the case of stretching *or* (2) the unwanted instruction/data blocks in the case of shrinking (extraction). First, for each byte in the binary, the algorithm computes a mapping between its original index in the binary and its corresponding index after the snippets are inserted/removed. After that, the algorithm patches address operands in control transfer and global data reference instructions, and copy each byte to its mapped location according to the mapping.

Practical Challenges. To make BISTRO work for real-world large-scale software, we still need to overcome a number of practical challenges *not* addressed by Algorithm 1. Solutions to these challenges will be presented in the next few sections.

- The target of an indirect control transfer instruction (e.g., `call eax`) is computed during execution and takes different values depending on the execution path. Such an instruction cannot be patched by Algorithm 1.

Algorithm 1. Basic binary stretching/shrinking algorithm

Input:	P – the subject binary; it has $size$ and $base\_addr$ fields to represent its size when loaded into memory and base loading address, respectively.
	M – a list of address intervals represent code/data to be inserted/removed, sorted increasingly by their location; each interval has $addr$, len and $type$ fields, denoting the location, size and type respectively. Type "INSERT" means inserting right before $addr$; "REMOVE" means the block starting at $addr$ is to be removed.
Output:	P' – the stretched/shrunk binary.

```
 1: function BASICSTRETCHING(P, M)              25:     if map[i] ≠ ⊥ then
 2:    map ← ComputeMapping(P, M)               26:       if P[i] is instruction then
 3:    P' ← PatchTarget(P, map)                 27:         ins ← P[i]
 4: end function                                28:         for each data address operand op in ins do
                                                 29:           target ← op.addr − P.base_addr
 5: function COMPUTEMAPPING(P, M)               30:           off ← map[target] − target
 6:    offset ← 0                               31:           op.addr ← op.addr + off
 7:    m ← M.begin()                            32:         end for
 8:    for i ← 0 to P.size do                   33:         if ins is near call/jump then
 9:      if m.addr == P.base_addr + i then      34:           target ← i + ins.len + ins.target
10:        if m.type == INSERT then             35:           off ← map[target] − target
11:          offset ← offset + m.len            36:           off' ← map[i + ins.len] − (i + ins.len)
12:        else if m.type == REMOVE then        37:           ins.target ← ins.target + off − off'
13:          offset ← offset − m.len            38:         else if ins is far call/jump then
14:          i ← i + m.len                      39:           target ← ins.target − P.base_addr
15:        end if                               40:           off ← map[target] − target
16:        m ← M.next()                         41:           ins.target ← ins.target + off
17:      end if                                 42:         end if
18:      map[i] ← i + offset                    43:         P'[map[i]] ← ins
19:    end for                                  44:       else if P[i] is data then
20:    return map                               45:         P'[map[i]] ← P[i]
21: end function                                46:       end if
                                                47:     end if
22: function PATCHTARGET(P, map)                48:   end for
23:    P' ← {nop, nop, ..., nop}                49:   return P'
24:    for i ← 0 to P.size do                   50: end function
```

- Function pointers may be present in data or in an instruction as an immediate operand. These function pointers might be passed as parameters to external libraries as callback functions. If a function is relocated due to stretching, the external library will call back to a wrong address. All these have to be properly handled to ensure correctness of binary stretching/shrinking.
- Accesses to global data may be via data pointers (e.g., `mov ebx, ptr_data;` `mov eax, [ebx+4]`). The addresses of data are not known until runtime. These instructions cannot be patched using Algorithm 1 either.

4   Handling Indirect Control Transfer

Handling indirect jumps and calls is one of the key challenges in the design of BISTRO. The difficulty is that the jump/call target cannot be known statically and thus is hard to patch. To understand the challenge, consider the example in Figure 2. On the left, there are three objects that are connected via pointers, with two of type B and one of type A. On the right, part of function foo() is presented. The function takes two parameters stored in eax and ebx denoting pointer values. These two pointers may be aliased to each other. If so, ecx at 0x4302B2 gets the value 0x400340 defined at 0x4302A0, and then eventually the call instruction at 0x4302BD acquires the function pointer 0x444142. However, if the two pointer parameters are not aliased, the call instruction may get a completely different target, making statically patching it difficult.

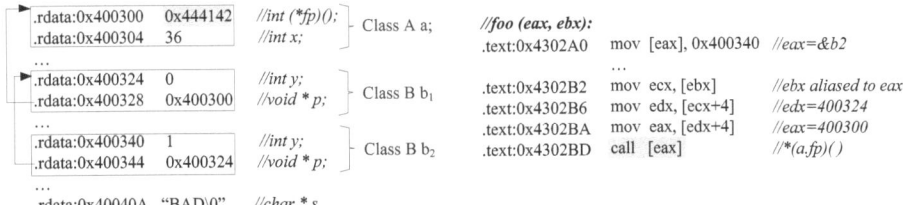

Fig. 2. An example showing indirect call handling in binary stretching/extraction.

A naive solution is to identify and patch any constant value in the binary that appears to be a jump/call target. But this is not safe as such values may not be jump/call targets. Notice in the example, there is a null-terminated string "BAD" at address 0x40040A. With the little endian representation in x86, this string has the same binary value as the function pointer at 0x400300. Without type information, it is impossible to know whether the value is a string or function pointer. Failure to identify and patch a function pointer leads to broken control-flow, changing the semantics of the target binary. Misclassifying a string as a function pointer leads to undesirable changes to data. While it is plausible to leverage recent advances in binary type inference to type constants in a binary [17–20], the involvement of aliasing as in the example makes such analysis very difficult. In fact, IDA-Pro [21] failed to recognize the function pointer for this case.

If a binary has a relocation table and it does not perform any address space layout self-management such as through a packer, the relocation table will provide the positions of all constant values that are jump/call targets for BISTRO to patch them, thus lead to a sound and complete solution to binary stretching/shrinking. However, relocation table may be absent or contain bogus entries in legacy and malware binaries. Hence, for the rest of the paper, *we do not assume the presence of relocation tables in our design and evaluation*. Next, we describe how to handle indirect calls in Section 4.1 and indirect jumps in Section 4.2.

4.1   Handling Indirect Calls

Indirect calls are very common in modern binaries to leverage the flexibility of function pointers. We have discussed the difficulty of handling function pointers at the beginning of Section 4. In fact, there is a more challenging situation, in which a binary may pass its function addresses to external library functions which call back the provided functions (e.g., a user function *cmp()* is provided as a parameter to an external library function *qsort()*). In this case, if a function entry has changed due to stretching or shrinking, its invocation sites are outside the body of the binary and thus beyond our control. It is difficult to patch call back function pointer parameters before they are passed on to libraries for two reasons. First, a function pointer might not directly appear as a parameter. It could be a member of a structure passed to an external library. It may even require several layers of pointer indirection to access its value. Patching that is challenging. Second, for many external library functions, we cannot assume the availability of their prototype definitions, it is hence difficult to know their parameter types.

To handle indirect calls including call back functions, we propose to stretch the target binary to make small holes at the entry point of each function that may be an indirect call target. These holes are called *anchors*; they should not be moved during stretching/shrinking. Inside an anchor, we place a jump instruction that jumps to its mapped new address in the stretched/shrunk binary, which is the new entry of the function. As such, we do not need to identify or patch any function pointers in the binary.

Since an anchor must be placed at a fixed address in the stretched binary, it could coincide with instructions that.get shifted to that address. To ensure correctness, we put a jump right before an anchor to jump over it. We call the jump the *prefix* of an anchor.

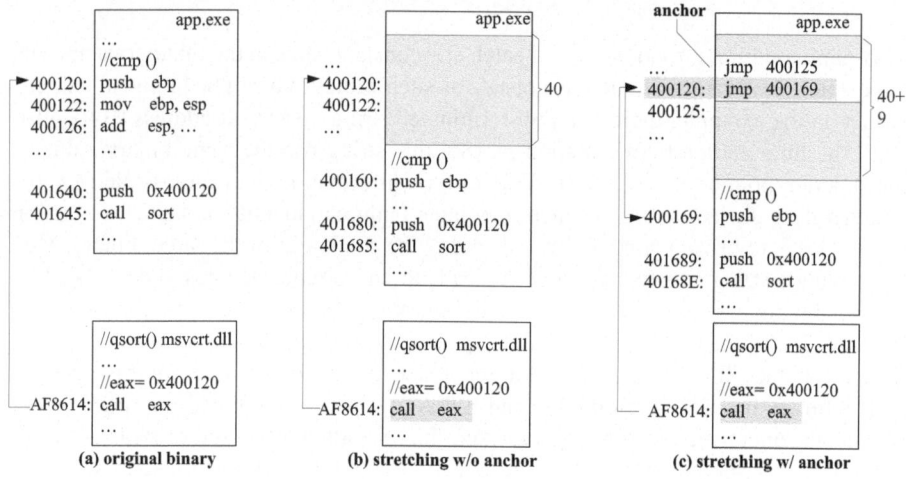

Fig. 3. Stretching with Anchors. The shaded area in (b) is the 40-byte snippet inserted.

Consider the example in Figure 3(a). The call-back function *cmp()* is invoked inside *qsort()*. The entry address of function *cmp()* in the original binary is 0x400120. When we stretch without anchors (Figure 3(b)) in function *qsort()*, the indirect call to *cmp()* at 0xAF8614 will incorrectly go to 0x400120 in the shaded area. When we stretch with anchors (Figure 3(c)), an anchor containing the jump instruction will be placed at 0x400120. Any indirect call that goes to the original entry address of *cmp()*,

0x400120, will be redirected to the actual function body at the new entry address. The jump instruction preceding 0x400120 is its prefix.

Anchor-Based Algorithm. With the presence of anchors, fixing control flow transfer instructions becomes more challenging than in Algorithm 1. We hence devise a new algorithm (Algorithm 2). The idea is to divide the stretching/shrinking operation into two phases. In phase one, the subject binary program is stretched/shrunk using Algorithm 1 to create space for the inserted snippets or removed blocks. Then the stretched/shrunk binary is further stretched to insert anchors using a similar procedure. Separating the two phases substantially simplifies the interference of anchors.

Algorithm 2. Anchor-based stretching algorithm.

Input:	P – the subject binary; it has $size$ and $base\_addr$ fields to represent its size when loaded into memory and base loading address, respectively.
	M – a list of code/data snippets to be inserted/removed, sorted increasingly by their location; each snippet has $addr$, len and $type$ fields, denoting the location, size and type respectively.
	A – a list of anchors to be placed, sorted increasingly by their location; each anchor has $addr$ and len fields, denoting the location and the content size, respectively.
Output:	$anchor\_map$ – the mapping between the indices after placing snippets and their corresponding indices after anchors are placed.
	$prefixlen[a]$ – the prefix length of an anchor a.

```
 1: function STRECHINGWITHANCHOR(P, M, A)        15:        if P[prefix] is not the start of an instruction then
 2:    map ← ComputeMapping(P, M)                16:           prefix ← start of instruction before prefix
 3:    Pt ← PatchTarget(P, map)                  17:        end if
 4:    anchor_map ← ComputeAcMapping(Pt, A)      18:        prefixlen[ac] ← i − prefix
 5:    P' ← PatchTarget(Pt, anchor_map)          19:        i ← prefix
 6: end function                                 20:        offset ← offset + ac.len + prefixlen[ac]
                                                  21:        ac ← A.next()
 7: function COMPUTEACMAPPING(P, A)              22:     else
 8:    offset ← 0                                23:        anchor_map[i] ← i + offset
 9:    ac ← A.begin()                            24:        i ← i + 1
10:    i ← 0                                     25:     end if
11:    while i < P.size do                       26:  end while
12:       curaddr ← P.base_addr + i + offset     27:  return anchor_map
13:       if ac.addr == curaddr then             28: end function
14:          prefix ← i − SIZEOF(JMP)
```

Pruning Anchors. Potentially, we can create anchors for all function entries to guarantee that we never miss any necessary function call forwarding. However, this is not efficient. In fact, we only need to create anchors for the subset of functions that could be the possible target of some indirect call. Assuming a 32-bit machine, we construct the subset with the following criterion: *Any four-byte data value or any four-byte immediate operand in an instruction is considered a possible indirect call target, if it is equal to one of the function entries.* We obtain this subset by sequentially scanning data and code sections. Our pruning heuristic is very effective in practice. For example, the code section size of *gcc* in SPEC CPU 2000 benchmark suite is over 1MB, with over 2000 functions; after pruning, there are only 271 functions left that need anchors.

Embedding a Component with Anchors. If an extracted component contains a function that may be invoked by an indirect call in the component, BISTRO will create an anchor *in the target binary* at exactly the same address of the function entry in *the component's original binary* to allow proper forwarding. If the anchor conflicts with some existing anchor in the target binary, BISTRO will integrate the two overlapping anchors into an arbitration function and redirect control flow to the function instead. The function further determines which real target it should forward the call to. The calls from the target binary and those from the to-be-embedded component are distinguished by setting a flag. The arbitration function uses the flag to decide the real forwarding target.

In some rare cases, the space between two function entries might not be enough to hold the anchors. In such cases, instead of using the jump instruction for redirection, we use a software interrupt instruction, which takes only one byte. When an indirect call reaches the old function entry, a software exception will be generated and intercepted by our exception handler, which will redirect the control flow to the new function entry.

4.2   Handling Indirect Jumps

Indirect jumps are different from indirect calls as the jump targets may not be function entries, but rather anywhere in the binary. If we adopt the anchor approach, there would be too many anchors needed. One might leverage some heuristics such as that indirect jumps usually receive their targets from jump tables and thus simply patch the jump table entries. However, this is unsafe because of the difficulty of determining jump table boundaries. A jump table may not be distinguishable from regular data. Hence, we propose a different approach. Specifically, we insert a code snippet right before each indirect jump to translate the jump target to its mapped address in the stretched binary at runtime, as shown in the example below.

```
jmp eax        mov eax, mapping[eax - old_base]
        ⟶     add eax, new_base
               jmp eax
```

Note that the example is just for illustration. In our implementation, we use perfect hashing for address lookup, which will be explained later, and preserve the flag register during translation. Since a complete byte-to-byte mapping is computed in Algorithm 1, any indirect jump target could be properly translated and handled by this method. Observe that additional instructions need to be added to perform translation. We can easily handle this by stretching the subject binary to accommodate those instructions.

Branch Target Set Pruning. Although the translation using a complete mapping guarantees safety, it also introduces significant memory overhead. Each byte in the original binary requires 4 bytes to represent its mapped address. In fact, we only need a subset of the mapping: the stretched/shrunk binary will be safe as long as the mapping contains translation for every possible indirect jump target.

We construct the set with the following criterion: *any four-byte data value or any four-byte immediate operand in an instruction is considered a possible indirect jump target, if the value falls in the range of some code section.* We further prune the set by removing the values that point to the middle of an existing instruction. Note that the strategy is safe for long/set jumps as their jump targets are acquired at runtime. This pruning strategy is very effective in practice. For example, the code section size of Adobe Reader X (AcroRd32.exe) is over 800KB, with over 260K instructions; after pruning, there are only 3635 possible branch targets left.

Perfect Hash Translator. The remaining challenge is to achieve fast translation. Note that after pruning, the jump target set becomes a sparse set in the address space. As a compromise between memory consumption and runtime overhead, we choose to use perfect hashing for translation. A perfect hash function maps a set of keys to another set of integer values without any collision. It guarantees $O(1)$ translation time. We use gperf [22] to generate the perfect hash function for the jump target set and compile it into a linkable .obj file that can be embedded in the target binary through BISTRO.

A perfect hash function may require more space than the N keys to achieve $O(1)$ translation time. In practice, we find the size of generated perfect hash functions acceptable. For example, for the 3635 branch targets of Adobe Reader, the generated hash function is about 152KB, which is about 11% of the size of the Adobe Reader binary.

5   Handling Data References

Binary extraction/stretching may cause relocation of data entries, so we need to ensure the correctness of instructions referencing those data. We discuss how to address this problem from the perspectives of the target binary and the component to be embedded.

Compared to the component, the target binary is usually more complex and involves a lot of global data references. To handle this problem efficiently, we group data in the binary as continuous data blocks. If a data block might be indirectly accessed, we will make sure the block is not re-located to avoid patching data accesses, by wrapping the block in an anchor. Note that the number of data access instructions is much larger than the number of indirect jumps/calls. Otherwise, if the data block is only directly accessed, we allow it to be relocated (by Algorithm 1). We use the following criterion: *if the value of any four-byte data, or any four-byte immediate operand (in an instruction) that is not directly used as an address falls in the range of a data block, then this block might be indirectly accessed using data pointers and hence should not be re-located.*

In contrast, data entries extracted as part of the to-be-embedded component are most likely to be relocated. For example, if they are sparsely distributed in the address space, the BISTRO extractor (Section 2) will collapse them into a contiguous block, causing relocation. We adopt a method similar to the dynamic jump target translation scheme to translate data reference addresses. We add a comparison before translation to avoid translating stack or heap accesses. According to our experience, only 2% of dynamic memory references need to be translated. We further use offline static peephole scanning to identify references that surely access stack and avoid instrumenting them completely.

6   Evaluation

We have implemented BISTRO for Win32 PE binaries as an IDA-Pro plug-in. We have addressed a variety of engineering challenges such as virtual space layout re-arrangement with a large embedded component, patching PE header, import and export tables, and re-generating relocation table. We omit the details due to space limitation.

6.1   Performance: Efficiency and Overhead

We first evaluate the performance of BISTRO by stretching (1) real-world Windows-based applications and (2) SPEC CPU 2000 binaries. Our experiments are done on a

Table 1. Performance results of stretching Windows software and SPEC CPU 2000 binaries

Binary	Instr. Count	Indirect Jumps	Indirect Calls	Call/Jump Targets: Anchors(%)	Data Blocks: Data Anchors(%)	File Size (KB) Orig: Stch'ed	growth(%)	Initial Mem. Image Size (KB) Orig: Stch'ed	growth(%)	Run Time (s) Orig: Stch'ed	overhead(%)	Stretching Time (s)
SPEC CPU 2000 benchmarks												
164.gzip	19825	19	103	98: 23 (23.47%)	163: 1 (0.61%)	86.5: 98.5	13.87%	424: 440	3.77%	83.2: 84.6	1.68%	0.752
175.vpr	54595	53	106	229: 31 (13.54%)	404: 1 (0.25%)	232: 248.5	7.11%	248: 268	8.06%	64.5: 64.6	0.16%	0.755
176.gcc	337033	456	260	3855: 271 (7.03%)	2580: 14 (0.54%)	1264: 1393	10.21%	1348: 1480	9.79%	33.3: 33.9	1.8%	1.420
181.mcf	20566	36	103	144: 25 (17.36%)	100: 2 (2.00%)	76.5: 85.5	11.76%	100: 108	8%	40.2: 40.4	0.5%	0.685
186.crafty	65375	56	130	312: 29 (9.29%)	247: 1 (0.40%)	283: 298.5	5.48%	1344: 1360	1.19%	38.2: 38.9	1.83%	0.935
197.parser	44554	36	112	155: 27 (17.42%)	463: 1 (0.22%)	164: 173.5	5.79%	352: 360	2.27%	83.1: 83.5	0.48%	0.754
252.eon	114249	50	441	1659: 1253 (75.53%)	1455: 1 (0.07%)	499: 575	15.23%	592: 668	12.84%	42.7: 44.7	4.68%	0.950
253.perlbmk	164093	148	211	2166: 499 (23.04%)	1293: 6 (0.46%)	626: 743	18.69%	648: 764	17.9%	63.3: 67.9	7.27%	1.118
254.gap	129464	35	1357	816: 625 (76.59%)	1142: 1 (0.09%)	452.5: 492	8.73%	896: 936	4.46%	35.4: 37.2	5.08%	1.001
255.vortex	132034	66	145	446: 71 (15.92%)	738: 1 (0.14%)	561: 585	4.28%	588: 612	4.08%	50.6: 51.1	0.99%	1.050
256.bzip2	21360	36	101	145: 25 (17.24%)	150: 1 (0.67%)	87.5: 99	13.14%	172: 184	6.98%	73.4: 74.6	1.63%	0.714
300.twolf	64669	41	106	193: 30 (15.54%)	391: 2 (0.51%)	253: 263	3.95%	296: 304	2.7%	93.2: 93.6	0.43%	0.809
177.mesa	143679	211	552	2675: 473 (17.68%)	942: 5 (0.53%)	549.5: 652.5	18.74%	568: 672	18.31%	64.9: 65.6	1.08%	0.990
179.art	23353	38	103	149: 26 (17.45%)	103: 2 (1.94%)	85.5: 94.5	10.53%	104: 112	7.69%	32: 32.3	0.94%	0.690
183.equake	21824	38	101	146: 27 (18.49%)	116: 1 (0.86%)	88.5: 97	9.6%	104: 112	7.69%	26.1: 26.1	0%	0.720
188.ammp	61214	39	128	224: 70 (31.25%)	279: 1 (0.36%)	235.5: 245.5	4.25%	252: 264	4.76%	88.7: 88.3	1.92%	0.780
Average	-	-	-	- (24.80%)	- (0.60%)	-	10.09%	-	7.53%	-	1.90%	-
Real-world Windows-based Software												
putty	107220	57	662	942: 291 (30.89%)	93: 1 (1.08%)	444: 496	11.71%	472: 524	11.02%	-	-	0.865
gvim	561626	294	5111	3893: 1004 (25.79%)	5081: 22 (0.43%)	1950.5: 2150	10.23%	2008: 2212	10.16%	-	-	2.121
notepad++	272434	159	4302	4897: 2695 (55.03%)	3394: 7 (0.21%)	1584: 1864	17.68%	1660: 1940	16.87%	-	-	1.480
Adobe Reader	273710	146	2543	3635: 2160 (59.42%)	3037: 11 (0.36%)	1445.9: 1702.4	17.74%	1472: 1728	17.39%	-	-	1.556
Chrome	230234	82	1280	1842: 933 (50.65%)	930: 6 (0.65%)	1211: 1338	10.49%	1240: 1368	10.32%	-	-	1.391
Average	-	-	-	- (44.36%)	- (0.55%)	-	13.57%	-	13.15%	-	-	-

Dell Inspiron 15R laptop with Intel(R) Core(TM) i5-2410M 2.30GHz CPU and 4GB memory, running Windows 7 SP1. For the SPEC CPU 2000 benchmark suite, we use the "win32-x86-vc7" config file which includes all integer benchmark binaries and four floating-point benchmark binaries. We compile the benchmark suite using Visual Studio 2010, with full optimizations. To test BISTRO on non-relocatable binaries, we set "/DYNAMICBASE:NO" switch for the compiler to prevent it from generating relocatable binaries. The application binaries are readily available and we do not know about their compilers. Although the binaries of Adobe Reader and Chrome web browser carry relocation tables, we ignore them for testing our solutions for non-relocatable binaries.

We measure the following performance metrics: (1) space overhead – for both binary file and initial memory image – of a stretched binary compared with its original version, (2) runtime overhead of the stretched binary, and (3) time for BISTRO to stretch the binary. In particular, we are interested in the overhead incurred *by* BISTRO *itself*, not by the execution of the embedded components. As such, we embed a minimal component (a one-byte snippet) into each subject binary in our experiments. To create a "worst-case" scenario, we insert it at the beginning of each binary so that every byte in the binary gets shifted, which entails *all* indirect control transfer targets in the binary to be redirected. The measured overhead is hence the upper bound of overhead.

For each SPEC 2000 binary, we run both its original and stretched versions, and compare their execution time and file/initial image size. We do not measure the execution time of the Windows applications because they are all interactive. We experience no perceivable overhead when using their stretched versions.

The results are shown in Table 1. From the *Indirect Jumps* and *Indirect Calls* [2] columns, we observe that indirect calls are very common in application binaries, indicating that they might be C++ programs. Further investigation confirms our speculation, indicating BISTRO's effectiveness for binaries compiled from C++ programs.

---

[2] We exclude indirect calls to external library functions through import address table (IAT), as these external targets are not handled by our redirection mechanisms.

Moreover, there are much less indirect jumps than indirect calls, indicating they are likely to have less impact on runtime overhead. Note that a small number of indirect jumps does not imply an equally small number of potential indirect jump targets. In fact, due to the difficulty of identifying jump table boundaries, we conservatively consider any constant in a binary that appears to be an instruction address as a potential jump target. The large number of potential jump targets and the low impact on performance justify our design choice of using the slightly more expensive but more flexible dynamic target translation scheme (Section 4.2), compared to the anchor scheme (Section 4.1).

The *Call/Jump Targets: Anchors* column shows the number of potential indirect call/jump targets, the number of anchors generated, and their comparison. Observe that the number of anchors created is small, compared to the size of the potential set. For binaries from C++ programs, due to the heavy use of virtual methods, it is not a surprise to see many anchors created. The *Data Blocks: Data Anchors* column shows that only less than 1% of all data blocks need to be preserved at their original locations using anchors. From the *File Size* columns, we can see BISTRO only increases the file size by 10.1% on average for SPEC programs, and 13.6% for application binaries. The overhead is dominated by the perfect hash tables. The *Initial Mem. Image Size* columns show the initial memory consumption when the binary is loaded into memory, which increases by only 7.5% on average for SPEC programs and 13.2% for application programs. Note that BISTRO does not cause any additional memory overhead during execution. The *Run Time* columns present the runtime overhead, which is only 1.9% on average. Except *eon*, *perlbmk* and *gap*, all SPEC binaries have less than 2% overhead. The last column *Stretching Time* shows the stretching time of BISTRO. The time is consistently short, implying that BISTRO can stretch a binary at runtime when it is loaded.

6.2   Case Study I: Binary-Level Semantic Patching Using BISTRO

Code reuse is a common practice in software development. One popular approach is to directly compile and statically link a piece of re-usable code with the target software – either directly in the executable or in some private library – to make the software self-contained, avoid compatibility problems, and improve performance. Indeed, developers of many popular programs (e.g., *chrome* and *firefox*) reuse code this way. The consequence is that programs reusing the same code may have the code placed at different locations in their address spaces. The reused code may not even have the same instructions if compiled by different compilers.

Table 2. Results of binary semantic patching using BISTRO

Vulnerability	Patch Extracted From	Vulnerable Application Patched	Original File Size (KB)	Patched File Size (KB) w. / w.o. Reloc	Semantic Patch Available	Vendor Patch Available
CVE-2010-1205	libpng 1.2.43 → 1.2.44 (rpng2-win.exe)	Firefox 3.6.6 (xul.dll)	11747.5	12371.5 / 13005	6/25/2010	7/20/2010
CVE-2011-3026	libpng 1.4.8 → 1.4.9 (rpng2-win.exe)	Zoner Photo Studio 15 (Zxl.dll)	8225.1	8502.1 / 9181.6	2/18/2012	N/A
SA47322 / CVE-2012-0025	IrfanView 4.30 → 4.32 (Fpx.dll)	XnView 1.99.5 (Xfpx.dll)	356	368 / 400	12/20/2011	N/A
		LeadTools 17.5 (ltkdku.dll)	138.5	143 / 151	12/20/2011	N/A
SA47388	XnView 1.98.5 → 1.98.8 (Xfpx.dll)	IrfanView 4.35 (Fpx.dll)	432	448 / 508	3/12/2012	N/A
		LeadTools 17.5 (ltkdku.dll)	372.5	428.5 / 493.5	3/12/2012	N/A
SA48772 / CVE-2012-0278	IrfanView 4.33 → 4.34 (Fpx.dll)	XnView 1.99.5 (Xfpx.dll)	356	368 / 400	4/13/2012	N/A
		LeadTools 17.5 (ltkdku.dll)	138.5	142.5 / 150.5	4/13/2012	N/A
SA49091	XnView 1.98.8 → 1.99 (Xfpx.dll)	LeadTools 17.5 (ltkdku.dll)	372.5	428.5 / 488.5	6/15/2012	N/A

However, code reuse via static linking introduces a security liability: When a piece of re-usable code contains a vulnerability, all programs that reuse the code will suffer from the same vulnerability. If these programs have been shipped in binary forms, the only way to fix the vulnerability is to release multiple binary patches – one for each program and by the corresponding vendor. However, not all vendors react to a vulnerability with equal timeliness and some may not even be aware of the vulnerability not in their own code. Thus it may be desirable for customers, who do *not* have source code access, to patch these programs without vendors' involvement. Binary *syntactic patching*, which directly applies a patch for software A to software B sharing the same (vulnerable) code, will hardly work, because of the different locations of the code and the syntactic differences between the two code copies (due to different compilers used or different call/jump targets inside the copies).

In our first case study, we show that BISTRO can enable *binary semantic patching*. Assume that software A and B share a function f and the vendor of A has released a binary patch of f for a vulnerability. Let the patched program and the patched function be A' and f', respectively. We will use BISTRO to extract f' from A' and embed it to B to replace the vulnerable version. Note that BISTRO is critical in ensuring the extracted f' is properly patched and the target binary B is properly stretched to contain f'.

We acquire a group of application binaries that leverage the same vulnerable component using public, vendor-provided information (e.g., which libraries are used in the software) or by finding similar binary snippets using the binary comparison tool *bindiff* [31]. Suppose at least one binary in the group, say A, has a patched version A'. Our goal is to extract a *semantic* patch out of A' and transplant it to patch the other vulnerable binaries $\{B_1, ..., B_n\}$.

We collect 6 real-world vulnerabilities, with their CVE or Secunia IDs shown in Column 1 of Table 2. For each vulnerability, the vulnerable program(s) that has been patched by its vendor is shown in Column 2. The file names in braces represent the files that are patched. Column 3 shows a list of other un-patched programs with the same vulnerabilities. Column 6 shows the patch release date for the application in Column 2, i.e. the earliest date we can extract the semantic patch. Column 7 shows the date when the vendors for the software in Column 3 release their patches (N/A means no vendor patch is available yet). Most of the applications used in this case study are close-source (except *libpng* and *firefox*). Observe that most of the applications in Column 3 do not have vendor patches so far. For *firefox*, the new version (3.6.7) which patched the vulnerability was released – but with a one-month latency. With BISTRO, we can fix all these vulnerable applications as soon as one vendor releases the corresponding patch.

Failure of Syntactic Patching. We first verify that simple syntactic patching does not work – that is, using an existing binary differencing tool that generates and applies patches (e.g., *xdelta, bsdiff, bspatch*, etc.) will not properly patch $B_{1...n}$. For each vulnerability in Table 2, we use *bsdiff* to extract the syntactic difference between the pair of shared functions (f and f') in the versions in Column 2 as a patch, and use *bspatch* to apply it to the corresponding vulnerable applications in Column 3. None of the resultant binaries works. Further inspection shows that syntactic patches cannot properly fix the call/jump targets that are different among copies of the same reused code.

Patch Transplanting. We have developed a binary semantic patching tool based on BISTRO and *bindiff*. The identification of the vulnerable function f in A and $B_{1...n}$ and the patched function f' in A' is omitted here since it is not the main focus of this paper. Details are presented in our technical report [1]. We use BISTRO to extract f' from A' as the semantic patch for f. For each vulnerable binary B, we use BISTRO to cut out f and then stretch the resulting binary to implant f' at the same starting address of f. BISTRO ensures the correctness of both f' and the patched binary B' by properly stretching and patching control transfer instructions and data references. Our patching tool tries to avoid extracting dependent functions or global data entries of f' (i.e., functions being called and global data accessed by f') as much as possible by redirecting them to their counterparts in the target binary B. Since f' is a patched version of f, they likely share the same dependencies. For example, for each function invocation to function g' inside f', if *bindiff* is able to identify the matching function g in B, our tool will automatically redirect the invocation in the extracted patch to g, without extracting g'. To be conservative, g and g' must be fully matched. Otherwise, g' will be extracted as part of the semantic patch.

We evaluate our patching tool on the subjects in Table 2. We apply our tool in two different ways to stress-test the robustness of BISTRO: first, we use the relocation information when it is present in the binary; second, we do not use relocation information at all. In both runs, the patching is successful: the patched applications work well and no longer suffer from the corresponding vulnerabilities. Columns 4 and 5 show the file size changes. We note that the patches are not large, each consisting of tens to hundreds of instructions. However, it is not straightforward to generate them independently because of the nature of the vulnerabilities being patched.

The first two vulnerabilities are in *libpng*, which is widely used in various software to read, write and render PNG images. The two vulnerable applications in Column 3 have *libpng* statically linked in their private DLLs (*xul.dll* and *Zxl.dll*). To patch these DLLs, we extract the semantic patch from *rpng2-win.exe*, a sample application in the *libpng* package. The remaining four vulnerabilities lie in *libfpx*, a library to handle the Flashpix (.fpx) image format. For the four vulnerabilities, only the first one was patched by the maintainer of *libfpx*; the other three were patched by individual developers who use *libfpx*. However, as shown in the table, individual developers only care about patching the *libfpx* code in their *own* applications. Using our binary semantic patching tool, users of the un-patched applications can transplant the patches and eliminate the vulnerabilities without the help of application developers.

6.3 Case Study II: Malware Stitching Using BISTRO

In the second case study, we demonstrate how BISTRO helps in the study of cyber attacks and counter-attacks. Specifically, we use BISTRO to compose a new, *executable* malware by stitching 3 separate functional components extracted from a *non-executable* sample of the Conficker worm [14]. It is an *unpacked* version without relocation information. Based on the published technical report of Conficker [14] and manual code inspection, we identify the code and data associated with the following 3 components:

- **DNS API hijacking.** This component prevent DNS query of the web sites in a blacklist by hijacking the functions *Query_Main*, *DNSQuery_A*, *DNSQuery_W* and

DNSQuery_UTF8 in *dnsapi.dll*. The result is that those web sites will no longer be accessible using their domain names.

- **Code injection.** To hijack the functions in *dnsapi.dll* used by a process (e.g., Internet Explorer), the malware must inject itself into the address space of the process. This component performs the injection. It takes the process identifier (PID) of the target process and the path of the malware as parameters.
- **Process identification.** This component gets a process' PID using its process name and provide the PID to the code injection component.

It takes us 60 minutes to manually identify the three components above. After that we use BISTRO to extract the components from the Conficker sample. We then create a dummy DLL to serve as the container of those components. Next, we use BISTRO to embed the 3 components into the empty DLL, right before the *DllMain()* function. After that, we add instructions to function *DllMain()* to invoke the inserted components. The invocation code first checks if the current process is the target process. If so, it will invoke the DNS API hijacking component to hijack the DNS query. If not, it will call the process identification component to find the PID of the target process, and then call the DLL injection component to inject itself into the target process for DNS API hijacking. The whole composition process takes us about 30 minutes.

To verify the functionality of the newly composed malware, we select two applications as our targets (in two experiment runs): Internet Explorer and FlashFXP (an FTP client). After being loaded, the malware injects itself into the target processes. Then, in the target application, we try to access web site *avast.com*, which is blacklisted by Conficker [14]. Interestingly, the access was not blocked at first (namely, the malware did not succeed). After debugging, we found that it was due to a bug in Conficker's original code: the hijacked *DNSQuery_W()* has one unnecessary instruction which sets a wrong return value. We point out that *we would not have spotted the problem, had we not made these components executable and observed their runtime behavior.* After removing this instruction using BISTRO, both IE and FlashFXP are successfully compromised: they can no longer access *avast.com* due to a DNS query error.

7   Discussion

BISTRO cannot work on self-modifying, self-checking or obfuscated binaries. Self-modifying binaries generate instructions dynamically during runtime, which could not be statically patched using BISTRO. Self-checking binaries use checksum or other integrity checks to detect changes made to their code by BISTRO. Obfuscated binaries in many cases cannot be properly disassembled. However, we note that all other static binary rewriting/instrumentation techniques face the same challenge.

Our anchor and branch target set pruning criteria assume the constants in a binary represent a superset of all possible indirect control transfer targets. This assumption should hold for binaries generated by common compilers. One exception is position independent code (PIC), which obtains addresses at runtime and uses them to compute indirect control transfer targets. All PIC we encountered has the form of making a call and then obtaining the return address from the stack (e.g., *call $+5; pop eax*), which is the address of the instruction right after the call. We identify all such instructions and insert snippets to adjust the addresses to their mapped addresses. Also, special compilers or hand-written binaries might violate our assumption. For example, in the instruction sequence *mov eax, Target; add eax, 5; jmp eax*, the actual target is *Target* +5 instead of the constant *Target*; our pruning heuristic will miss the actual target. For such binaries, we can choose not to prune the anchor set or the branch target set.

Currently, BISTRO only supports Win32 PE binaries. However, the design is general, without relying on specific features of Win32 PE.

8 Related Work

The most related work is discussed in Section 1 (with details in [1].) In this section, we discuss other related work in the general area of binary manipulation. They fall into three categories: (1) static binary rewriting, (2) dynamic binary rewriting, and (3) binary component identification, extraction and reuse.

Static Binary Rewriting. Static binary rewriting is widely applied to many scenarios, such as in-lined reference monitors [33], software fault isolation [24, 25, 6, 26], binary instrumentation [10, 9, 11, 5, 7, 4], binary obfuscation [36, 37] and retrofitting security in legacy binaries [27, 12]. Most of these rewriters require the binary to be compiled by specific compilers, or contains symbolic information.

PEBIL [11], REINS [33], STIR [13] and SecondWrite [12] are recently developed rewriters targeting stripped binaries. However, they all aim at rewriting a single binary, so they all keep the original code and data sections in place. In contrast, BISTRO supports "transplanting" binary components from one or more binaries to a target binary, which requires rewriting and combining multiple binaries. Keeping original code and data sections in place may result in address space conflicts and hence is not an option for BISTRO. Detour-based techniques [10, 8, 9] are lightweight and can work on stripped binaries. However, they cannot patch non-trivial jumps/calls that are repositioned.

Dynamic Binary Rewriting. Dynamic binary rewriters [2, 3, 28] are generally more robust as they do not require specific compilers or symbolic information. It is possible to apply them to conduct binary stretching and transplanting. However, we choose to use a static approach mainly because of the following two reasons: (1) Dynamic binary rewriters usually have much higher run time overhead than static ones. (2) It is more difficult to deploy a instrumented binary using dynamic approaches, as the rewriter itself must be deployed along with the binary.

Binary Component Identification, Extraction and Reuse. Recently, researchers proposed to identify, extract and reuse components from binaries for security applications [29, 16, 23]. Kolbitsch et al. proposed Inspector Gadget [29], which performs dynamic slicing on a malware binary to identify and extract the slice pertinent to a specific malicious functionality, and wrap the slice into a stand-alone binary that could be reused later to execute the malicious functionality. Inspector Gadget is able to extract component from self-modifying code, which is not supported by BISTRO due to the limitation of static binary manipulation. Using dynamic slicing, Inspector Gadget also avoids the problem of handling indirect calls/jumps in BISTRO as all call/jump targets are directly known in the slice. However, the slice may not cover all possible code paths, which could result in incorrect execution when the user provides an input that would lead to a code path which is not included in the slice. Compared to Inspector Gadget, BISTRO statically extracts the component from the binary, which involves handling of indirect calls/jumps but provides better code path coverage.

Caballero et al. proposed BCR [16] to identify and extract a function from a binary using a combination of static and dynamic analysis. The extracted function, in the format of disassembly, is wrapped in a C file to be reused. BCR statically disassembles the designated function starting at its entry point; when encountering indirect call/jumps, BCR utilizes dynamic execution trace to find the call/jump targets. During the extraction, BCR rewrites all calls/jumps to use labels. Using labels implies that indirect call/jump can only have one target, which may not always hold in practice. Although BCR specially handles indirect jumps that use jump tables, there are other forms of multiple-target indirect calls/jumps such as function pointers and vtables. Compared to BCR, BISTRO preserves the original semantic of indirect calls/jumps when performing component extraction, hence does not suffer from this problem.

Neither Inspector Gadget nor BCR could extract components from non-executable binaries (as in Section 6.3) because they are based on dynamic analysis. This is a very common case in malware analysis, where a given malware sample may not run due to various reasons (e.g., missing dependent libraries, missing inputs). In such a case, BISTRO can still perform component extraction statically. Moreover, neither Inspector Gadget nor BCR supports reusing extractedcomponents to enhance legacy binaries (as in Section 6.2), as they lack the capability of embedding instructions that invoke the components into the target binary. BISTRO is able to handle such a scenario by performing both binary component extraction and embedding.

Lin et al. proposed ROC [23] which uses dynamic slicing to identify reusable functional components in a binary. Different from BISTRO, ROC only invokes the identified components from the *same* binary; it does not support extracting a component for reuse in a *different* binary.

9   Conclusions

We have developed a new pair of binary program manipulation primitives called BISTRO for extracting and re-packaging a functional component from a binary program; and for embedding a functional component in a target binary program, respectively. We address the challenges of patching control transfer instructions and data references to preserve the semantics of both the extracted component and the stretched binary program, especially indirect calls and jumps. BISTRO incurs low runtime overhead (1.9% on average) and small space overhead (11% on average). The extraction and embedding operations are highly efficient, with less than 1.5s for most cases. We have applied BISTRO to two security application scenarios, demonstrating its efficiency, precision, and versatility.

Acknowledgements. We thank the anonymous reviewers and our shepherd, Pratyusa Manadhata, for their insightful comments. This research has been supported by DARPA under Contract 12011593. Any opinions, findings, and conclusions in this paper are those of the authors only and do not necessarily reflect the views of DARPA.

References

1. Deng, Z., Zhang, X., Xu, D.: BISTRO: Binary Component Extraction and Embedding for Software Security Applications. CERIAS Technical Report TR 2013-3, Purdue University (June 2013)
2. Bruening, D.: Efficient, transparent, and comprehensive runtime code manipulation. Ph.D. dissertation. MIT (2004)
3. Bellard, F.: Qemu, a fast and portable dynamic translator. In: USENIX ATC 2005 (2005)
4. De Sutter, B., De Bus, B., De Bosschere, K.: Link-time binary rewriting techniques for program compaction. In: TOPLAS 2005 (2005)
5. Muth, R., Debray, S., Watterson, S., De Bosschere, K.: Alto: a link-time optimizer for the compaq alpha. In: SPE 2001 (2001)
6. Abadi, M., Budiu, M., Erlingsson, U., Ligatti, J.: Control-flow integrity principles, implementations, and applications. In: TISSEC 2009 (2009)
7. Eustace, A., Srivastava, A.: Atom: A flexible interface for building high performance program analysis tools. In: USENIX ATC 1995 (1995)
8. Buck, B., Hollingsworth, J.K.: An api for runtime code patching. In: IJHPCA 2000 (2000)
9. Romer, T., Voelker, G., Lee, D., Wolman, A., Wong, W., Levy, H., Bershad, B., Chen, B.: Instrumentation and optimization of win32/intel executables using etch. In: USENIX Windows NT Workshop (1997)
10. Hunt, G., Brubacher, D.: Detours: Binary interception of win32 functions. In: USENIX Windows NT Symposium (1999)
11. Laurenzano, M., Tikir, M., Carrington, L., Snavely, A.: Pebil: Efficient static binary instrumentation for linux. In: ISPASS 2010 (2010)
12. O'Sullivan, P., Anand, K., Kotha, A., Smithson, M., Barua, R., Keromytis, A.D.: Retrofitting security in COTS software with binary rewriting. In: Camenisch, J., Fischer-Hübner, S., Murayama, Y., Portmann, A., Rieder, C. (eds.) SEC 2011. IFIP AICT, vol. 354, pp. 154–172. Springer, Heidelberg (2011)
13. Wartell, R., Mohan, V., Hamlen, K., Lin, Z.: Binary stirring: Self-randomizing instruction addresses of legacy x86 binary code. In: CCS 2012 (2012)
14. Porras, P., Saidi, H., Yegneswaran, V.: Conficker c analysis. SRI International (2009)
15. Johnson, N., Caballero, J., Chen, K., McCamant, S., Poosankam, P., Reynaud, D., Song, D.: Differential slicing: Identifying causal execution differences for security applications. In: IEEE S&P 2011 (2011)
16. Caballero, J., Johnson, N., Mccamant, S., Song, D.: Binary code extraction and interface identification for security applications. In: NDSS 2010 (2010)
17. Balakrishnan, G., Reps, T.: Analyzing memory accesses in x86 executables. In: Duesterwald, E. (ed.) CC 2004. LNCS, vol. 2985, pp. 5–23. Springer, Heidelberg (2004)
18. Slowinska, A., Stancescu, T., Bos, H.: Howard: A dynamic excavator for reverse engineering data structures. In: NDSS 2011 (2011)
19. Lee, J., Avgerinos, T., Brumley, D.: Tie: Principled reverse engineering of types in binary programs. In: NDSS 2011 (2011)
20. Lin, Z., Zhang, X., Xu, D.: Automatic reverse engineering of data structures from binary execution. In: NDSS 2010 (2010)
21. Hex-Rays, Ida pro disassembler,
    http://www.hex-rays.com/products/ida/index.shtml
22. Schmidt, D.: Gperf: a perfect hash function generator. More C++ gems (2000)
23. Lin, Z., Zhang, X., Xu, D.: Reuse-oriented camouflaging trojan: Vulnerability detection and attack construction. In: DSN 2010 (2010)

24. Wahbe, R., Lucco, S., Anderson, T., Graham, S.: Efficient software-based fault isolation. OS Review (1994)
25. McCamant, S., Morrisett, G.: Evaluating sfi for a cisc architecture. In: USENIX Security 2006 (2006)
26. Erlingsson, Ú., Abadi, M., Vrable, M., Budiu, M., Necula, G.: Xfi: Software guards for system address spaces. In: OSDI 2006(2006)
27. Prasad, M., Chiueh, T.: A binary rewriting defense against stack based buffer overflow attacks. In: USENIX ATC 2003 (2003)
28. Scott, K., Kumar, N., Velusamy, S., Childers, B., Davidson, J., Soffa, M.: Retargetable and reconfigurable software dynamic translation. In: CGO 2003 (2003)
29. Kolbitsch, C., Holz, T., Kruegel, C., Kirda, E.: Inspector gadget: Automated extraction of proprietary gadgets from malware binaries. In: IEEE S&P 2010 (2010)
30. Srivastava, A., Edwards, A., Vo, H.: Vulcan: Binary transformation in a distributed environment. Tech. Rep., Microsoft Research (2001)
31. Flake, H.: Structural comparison of executable objects. In: DIMVA 2004 (2004)
32. Falliere, N., Murchu, L., Chien, E.: W32. stuxnet dossier. White paper, Symantec Corp., Security Response (2011)
33. Wartell, R., Mohan, V., Hamlen, K., Lin, Z.: Securing untrusted code via compiler-agnostic binary rewriting. In: ACSAC 2012 (2012)
34. Dinaburg, A., Royal, P., Sharif, M., Lee, W.: Ether: malware analysis via hardware virtualization extensions. In: CCS 2008 (2008)
35. Nanda, S., Li, W., Lam, L., Chiueh, T.: BIRD: binary interpretation using runtime disassembly. In: CGO 2006 (2006)
36. Moser, A., Kruegel, C., Kirda, E.: Limits of static analysis for malware detection. In: ACSAC 2007 (2007)
37. Popov, I., Debray, S., Andrews, G.: Binary obfuscation using signals. In: USENIX Security 2007 (2007)

Vulnerable Delegation of DNS Resolution

Amir Herzberg[1] and Haya Shulman[2,*]

[1] Computer Science Department,
Bar Ilan University, Ramat Gan, Israel
[2] Fachbereich Informatik,
Technische Universität Darmstadt/EC-SPRIDE, Darmstadt, Germany
{amir.herzberg,haya.shulman}@gmail.com

Abstract. A growing number of networks delegate their DNS resolution to trusted upstream resolvers. The communication to and from the upstream resolver is invisible to off-path attackers. Hence, such delegation is considered to *improve* the resilience of the resolvers to cache-poisoning and DoS attacks, and also to provide other security, performance, reliability and management advantages.

We show that, merely relying on an upstream resolver for security may in fact result in vulnerability to DNS poisoning and DoS attacks. The attack proceeds in modular steps: detecting delegation of DNS resolution, discovering the IP address of the internal (proxy) resolver, discovering the source port used for the (victim) DNS request and then completing the attack. The steps of the attack can be of independent use, e.g., proxy resolver can be exposed to denial of service attacks once its IP address is discovered.

We provide recommendations for securing the DNS service delegation, to avoid these vulnerabilities.

Keywords: network security, DNS cache poisoning, port randomization.

1 Introduction

Increasingly, organisations delegate sensitive network-operation functions to trusted providers ('clouds'). The motivations are diverse, and include cost-savings, efficiency, reliability, and even security, i.e., the trusted (cloud) provider is deemed to be able to provide good or even better security. In this work, we study a particularly important type of such delegation: the use of *upstream DNS resolver*, e.g., OpenDNS[1]. An *upstream resolver* is a DNS resolver operated by a trusted provider, outside of the customer's network, and used directly by the customer's *DNS proxy* (local resolver) [2].

---

[*] This work was carried out while the second author was in the Department of Computer Science, Bar Ilan University.

[1] Many upstream resolvers are *open/public*, i.e., provide resolution service to any Internet client address, e.g., OpenDNS and Google-public-DNS.

[2] Some authors use the term 'forwarder' for upstream resolver, while others use this term for DNS proxy (local) resolver. To avoid confusion, we use the 'upstream' and 'proxy' resolver terms throughout this work.

J. Crampton, S. Jajodia, and K. Mayes (Eds.): ESORICS 2013, LNCS 8134, pp. 219–236, 2013.
© Springer-Verlag Berlin Heidelberg 2013

Since DNS services are critical and often attacked, upstream DNS resolvers are increasingly adopted by many networks, and recommended by leading experts and vendors, e.g., Google, OpenDNS, Comodo and Akamai. For example, Akamai describe their upstream DNS service, dubbed *eDNS*, as follows [1]:

'Using eDNS, a customer's primary DNS servers are not directly exposed to end users, so the risks of cache-poisoning and denial-of-service attacks are mitigated.'

In this work, we show that typical use of upstream DNS resolvers, can actually result in *illusion of security* exposing to *DNS cache poisoning and DoS vulnerabilities*.

To understand the potential *loss* of security due to the use of upstream DNS resolvers, we next briefly discuss a simple case: *DNSSEC validation*. DNSSEC, [RFC4033-4035], is a standard for signing DNS records, allowing resolvers to validate DNS responses, and hence ensuring security against man-in-the-middle (MitM) attackers. So far, DNSSEC is not widely deployed, both at the zones as well as at the resolvers. For example, Google reports that less than 1% of the DNS records it retrieves are signed; and [2] tested queries to org and found that 0.8% of the resolvers were validating. Clearly, the deployment of DNSSEC is still very limited; we hope that our results will encourage wider adoption.

Some upstream DNS resolvers, e.g., Google's public DNS, perform DNSSEC validation. How does that effect the security of their customers? Clearly, since these upstream resolvers validate responses, this prevents attacks where false responses are sent to the upstream resolver. However, the proxy resolver may be vulnerable to an attacker sending forged responses directly to the proxy resolver, unless the the proxy resolver will also perform validation. In this way, the use of upstream resolver may cause reduction of security, due to illusion of security (by the upstream resolver).

The use of upstream resolvers was recommended by Kaminsky and other experts, e.g., [3], as a defense against his off-path attack [4]. Indeed this configuration is believed to defend against cache-poisoning attacks [5], and as a result many proxies (that use upstream resolvers) are not patched. Furthermore, DNS checker services, e.g., [6,7,8], designed to check if resolution services are secure, are oblivious to the proxy-behind-upstream resolver scenario, and do not report a problem, even when the proxy is using fixed a source port. Although many studies report that resolvers adopted port randomisation, recommended in [RFC5452], those statistics do not apply to proxies-behind-upstream resolvers, most of which use fixed or predictable ports; we confirmed this using CAIDA's data traces [9]), see Section 4.

We show that, in contrast to folklore belief, customers whose proxy resolver uses (a secure) upstream resolver for DNS services, with or without DNSSEC validation, may actually be susceptible not only to a MitM attacker, but even to an off-path attacker. Namely, such customers may fall victim to *illusion of security*.

Attacker Model. We assume an *off-path attacker* on the Internet that can send packets with a spoofed source IP address. The attacker also controls a weak, 'puppet' (sandboxed client) [10], such as a client running scripts or presenting Flash content.

Related Work. Cache poisoning poses one of the significant threats to DNS and to Internet infrastructure. DNS poisoning can facilitate many other attacks, e.g., injection of malware, phishing, website hijacking/defacing, circumventing same origin policy. The main technique for DNS poisoning (by the common *off-path* attackers) is by generating spoofed responses to DNS requests which were sent by resolvers. The best defense against DNS cache poisoning is cryptographic authentication of the responses, using DNSSEC [RFC4033-4035]. In addition to preventing attacks by off-path attackers, DNSSEC also defends against MitM attackers. Unfortunately, DNSSEC is not widely deployed and most resolvers use challenge-response mechanisms as a defense against off-path attackers, i.e., resolvers validate that the response echoes some unpredictable (random) values sent within the request, such as the DNS transaction ID (TXID) field and the source port, see [RFC5452] for more details; firewall-based defenses were also proposed against poisoning [11].

Significant research effort was dedicated to identifying vulnerabilities allowing off-path attacks, and improving defenses. We next review the main results.

Klein [12] showed that some implementations use weak TXID values which can be predicted. Indeed, as pointed out by Vixie [13] already in 1995, the TXID field alone is simply too short (16 bits) to provide sufficient defense against a determined *off-path* attacker, who can foil it by sending multiple spoofed responses. Bernstein [14] suggested to improve the defense against spoofed responses by sending DNS requests from *random ports*, which can add a significant amount of entropy. To prevent the *birthday attack*, where attacker causes resolver to issue multiple requests for the same domain in order to increase the probability of a match with one of the spoofed responses, Bernstein [14] and others suggest to limit the maximal number of concurrent requests for the same resource record.

Many implementations did not integrate support for these suggestions till the Kaminsky attack, [4], which showed that DNS cache poisoning was a practical threat, by leveraging the known birthday weakness and the fact that TXID is too short, in tandem with an innovative method allowing to repeat the attack without the cache limitation (rather than waiting for the cached record to expire). As a result, it became obvious that changes were needed to prevent DNS poisoning. Indeed, most DNS resolvers were either patched or configured to use a patched upstream resolver. The most basic patches are source port randomisation and birthday protection, [RFC5452]. Recently we showed, [15], that NAT devices that support port randomisation recommended in [RFC6056] are vulnerable to port derandomisation attacks, and expose resolvers to cache poisoning; we also presented techniques, [16,17], allowing to circumvent other patches.

In this work we show that the recommendation to (merely) rely on (a patched and secure) upstream resolver may also fail to ensure security and such proxy resolvers may yet be vulnerable to (off-path) poisoning. In particular, we show how off-path attackers may find the IP address of the proxy resolver, as a first step in a poisoning attack or for denial-of service attacks. This is in spite of the fact that upstream resolver are hidden from attackers, since their IP address is not visible; we show how off-path attacker can find the IP address of the proxy and abuse it, e.g., for denial-of service attacks.

Our contributions and observations. This work has the following contributions:
▶ We present technique that allows to detect the use of upstream resolvers (Section 2).
▶ We show how an off-path attacker can find the IP address of a proxy resolver, contradicting the belief that the use of an upstream resolver hides the address of the proxy (e.g., to defend against DoS attacks[3]); see Section 3.
▶ In Section 4, we present efficient and practical techniques that allow an off-path attacker to find the source port of a proxy resolver. Our attacks apply to proxies that are configured to use an upstream resolver, and are effective for the common case when the proxy supports either a fixed or sequentially incrementing source ports. We also show how to extend our attacks, so that they apply to resolvers connected directly (without upstream resolver), for the common case of *per-destination incrementing* source ports, recommended in [RFC6056].
▶ We conducted measurements on CAIDA data traces [9], and found that *multiple* proxies use fixed or sequential source ports, and are thus vulnerable; see Section 4. Since many name servers, that collect statistics on DNS requests, report that random ports are widely deployed, our statistics also imply that fixed (or sequentially incrementing) ports, well known to be vulnerable, are more commonly used for proxies (using upstream resolvers) than for resolvers making direct requests to name servers.
▶ The best defense against DNS poisoning is to use DNSSEC validation (on the clients), and we hope that this paper will help advance adoption of DNSSEC. However, since DNSSEC adoption is not trivial and may take a long time, and since DNSSEC does *not* prevent the DoS attack (when the proxy's IP address is exposed), we present several efficient defenses against all of the vulnerabilities in this work, in the full version of this manuscript [18].

2   Detecting an Upstream Resolver

In this section we show that it is possible to detect whether DNS resolution on a client's network is done using an upstream resolver, using a puppet (e.g., sandboxed script) running on the client. This allows an attacker to detect if the network is vulnerable to our attacks. The detection can be used for benign purposes, e.g., collecting statistics, however we focus on its use as part of an attack; in this case, the measurements are done by an attacker generating requests from a client (e.g., using puppet), to a name server operated by the attacker. The detection exploits the fact that when using an upstream resolver, the (round trip) delay Δ_R for a complete DNS resolution, from client to attacker's name

---

[3] One of the advantages of using upstream resolvers is that proxies have limited bandwidth. Therefore, launching denial of service against proxies is often significantly easier.

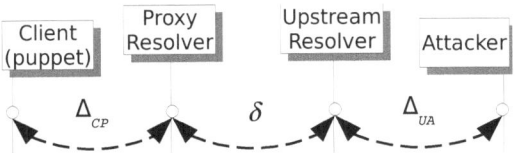

Fig. 1. The latencies between a client, an off-path attacker and a resolver

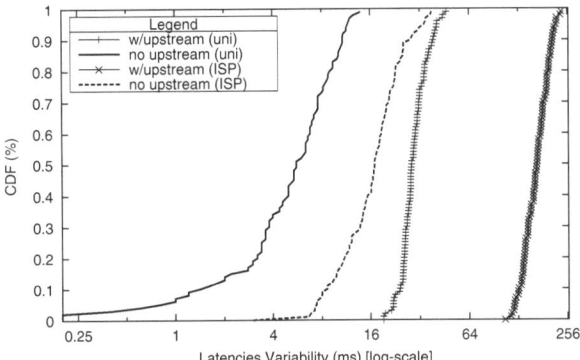

Fig. 2. Distribution of 100 measurements of δ values, with and without upstream resolver, for the two configurations: university proxy (with or without Google's upstream resolver), and an ADSL-connected proxy in an ISP (with or without the ISP's upstream resolver)

server (via both proxy and upstream resolver), can be broken down to three components, as shown in Figure 1: $\Delta_R = \Delta_{CP} + \delta + \Delta_{UA}$ (Δ_{CP} is the delay from client to proxy, δ is the delay from proxy to upstream resolver, and Δ_{UA} is the delay from the upstream resolver to the attacker's name server). We chose a different notation for δ since this is not a measured value, but computed using measurements of the other values: $\delta = \Delta_R - \Delta_{CP} - \Delta_{UA}$. Furthermore, δ is exactly the indicator for the use of an upstream resolver; when an upstream resolver is used, $\delta >> 0$, while when an upstream resolver is not used, $\delta \approx 0$. See our experimental results in Fig. 2. The detection exploits the fact, that we can easily measure Δ_R, Δ_{CP} and Δ_{UA}, and then test if δ is significant, indicating existence of an upstream resolver; see [18] for details and techniques to sample the Δ_R, Δ_{CP} and Δ_{UA} parameters.

Evaluation Results. We tested our proxy detection method via active measurements which we collected on two different network topologies: (1) puppet and local DNS resolver were set up on our university's wired 100Gb/s Ethernet network, and Google-Public-DNS (at IP 8.8.8.8) was used as an upstream resolver, and (2) puppet and the DNS resolver were set up on an ADSL network of a commercial ISP, and the upstream resolver was set up on a different network segment in the same wireless network of the ISP. We ran two tests in each topology (total of four tests): *without* an upstream resolver and *with* an upstream resolver. During each of the four tests we collected 100 samples (of latency) for each of the following parameters: Δ_{CA}, Δ_{CP}, and Δ_{UA} (in milliseconds). Based on these values we then calculated 100 values of δ for each of the four sequences of test (plotted in Figure 2), as follows: Repeat for $i = 1...100$: (1) calculate average of $j = 5$ samples[4] selected at random from a 100 samples from (each of) Δ_{CA}, Δ_{UA} and Δ_{CP} respectively, and (2) then calculate the latencies difference:

$$\delta_i = \frac{1}{j} \cdot \sum_{k=0}^{j} \left(\Delta_{CA} - \Delta_{UA} - \Delta_{CP} \right)$$

As can be seen from the measurements, Figure 2, the latency differences between configurations, with and without an upstream resolver, are significant.

3   Proxy DNS Resolver IP Address Discovery

In this section we show techniques to discover the address of the proxy, allowing denial of service as well as for cache poisoning attacks on proxy resolvers.

The idea is: (1) to find the network address block of the puppet, and then (2) to traverse the address block, until the resolver is found. To traverse the network block we apply IP defragmentation-cache poisoning. We present defragmentation-cache poisoning of a single host in Section 3.1. Then, Section 3.2, we show how to apply defragmentation-cache poisoning for resolver's IP discovery.

Network Address Block. The attacker runs a `whois.net` tool[5] on the IP address of the client (on which the puppet is running) to find out the network address block allocated to that network. One of the IP addresses on that network block is the IP address of the victim proxy resolver (that the attacker wishes to attack). The IPs range is typically not large; we ran a `whois` tool on 100,000 top domains according to Alexa, and found, that 70% of the networks have less than 2^{15} IP addresses, see Figure 3.

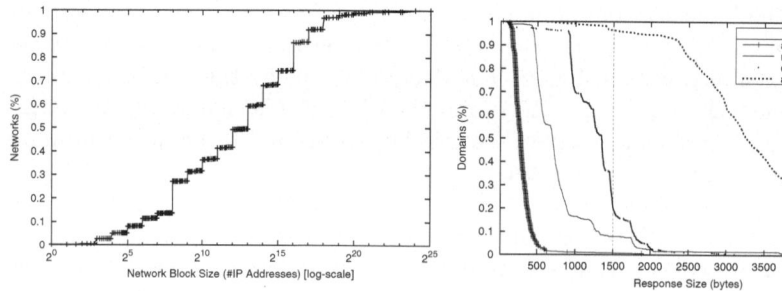

Fig. 3. The size of network blocks of 100,000 top domains from Alexa

Fig. 4. Length of ANY, regular and NX-DOMAIN responses of gov domains

---

[4] Other values of j could be used $(0 < j < 100)$, but $j = 5$ provided sufficiently good results.

[5] http://www.whois.net/ip-address-lookup/

IP Fragmentation. The basic requirement of our IP address discovery technique is fragmentation: the attacker should (1) trigger a DNS request to a domain which responses exceed the MTU (maximal transmission unit), e.g., responses from domains that adopted DNSSEC typically exceed the MTU (see Fig. 4), and then (2) replace the authentic second fragment, of a fragmented DNS response, with a spoofed second fragment. The resulting packet is discarded by the resolver, and resolver retransmits the DNS request. If the packet arrives at host other than the resolver, no packet loss occurs. We use this timing channel to detect the IP address of the resolver.

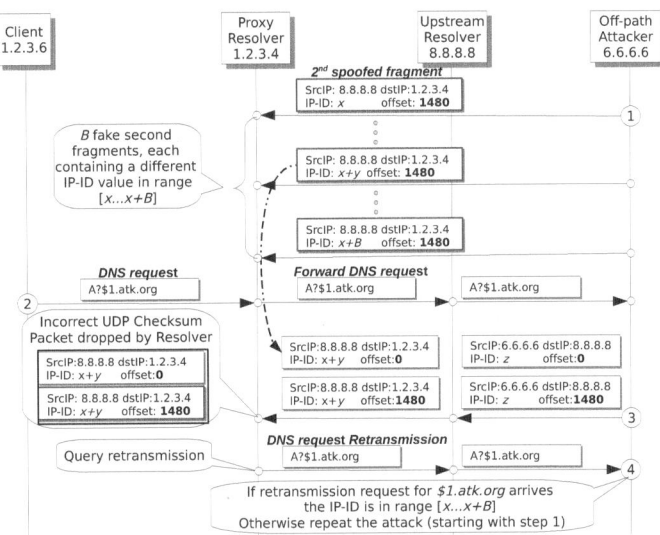

Fig. 5. Defragmentation-cache poisoning via a spoofed second fragment

3.1 Defragmentation-Cache Poisoning via Second Fragment

Defragmentation-cache poisoning is caching of spoofed fragments, in IP defragmentation cache, which get reassembled with the authentic fragments. The number of fragments that the recipient host can cache is limited[6]. We use B to denote the number of spoofed fragments sent by the attacker. The defragmentation-cache poisoning attack, illustrated in Figure 5, begins when the attacker sends B spoofed second fragments (step 1), which are stored at the defragmentation cache of the destination (for 30 seconds by default), and triggers (via a puppet) a DNS request, for its own domain, e.g., `atk.org` (step 2). When the authentic first fragment (of the DNS response) arrives, it is reassembled with the (cached) spoofed second fragment (step 3); the resulting IP packet has incorrect checksum, and is discarded by

---

[6] Typical defragmentation cache size allows several thousands of fragments; operating systems often impose a limit on the number of cached fragments per each (source, destination, protocol) triple. For example, in recent versions of the Linux kernel, the default value is 64 (and it is kept via the variable *ipfrag_max_dist*; see [19]).

the IP layer at the proxy (after defragmentation). Hence, the proxy retransmits the request after a timeout.

The probability that the IP-ID of a legitimate (fragmented) response matches the IP-ID of one of the (up to B) spoofed second fragments, which the attacker sent, depends on the IP-ID assignment method. We next analyse efficiency of defragmentation-cache poisoning for common IP-ID allocation methods: *incrementing* (supported by more than 70% of name servers) and *random* (supported by less than 1% of name servers); statistics are based on the IP-ID allocation methods supported by name servers of top level domains.

Random IP-ID. In a random IP-ID allocation the name server selects the IP-ID values in each response uniformly. Let n be the number of DNS requests triggered by the attacker and B the number of spoofed second fragments sent by the attacker. Note that defragmentation-cache poisoning allows to circumvent the *birthday protection*, thus enabling the attacker to trigger concurrent requests; see [18]. The probability for successful poisoning is:

$$\Pr[success] \cong 1 - \left(1 - \frac{B}{2^{16}}\right)^n \tag{1}$$

See graph representing defragmentation cache-poisoning success probability, based on Eq. (1), in Figure 6; results of the experimental evaluation appear in the full paper version [18].

Incrementing IP-ID. Incrementing IP-ID can be either global (i.e., a single counter to all destinations) or per-destination (i.e., first IP-ID to some destination is selected at random and subsequent packets are allocated sequentially incrementing values). If the upstream resolver uses separate interfaces for communication to the Internet and for communication to the proxy, then the procedure for discovering the global and the per-destination IP-ID is similar. If the same network interface is used for communication to the Internet and to the proxy, then the IP-ID discovery, in case of a global counter, is simple: the attacker can trigger a query to a host that it controls and sample the IP-ID value. The attacker can efficiently hit the correct IP-ID by using a *meet-in-the-middle* strategy. The attacker triggers $\frac{2^{16}}{B}$ DNS requests and plants B spoofed second fragments in the defragmentation-cache of the recipient, each fragment i contains IP-ID value of $\{i \cdot \frac{2^{16}}{B}\}_{i=1}^{B}$.

3.2 Discovering Resolver's IP via Defragmentation-Cache Poisoning

The idea behind our IP discovery technique is the following: the attacker applies defragmentation-cache poisoning, via a second spoofed fragment, that is sent to each IP in the IP address block allocated to the victim network. The second fragment with the IP of the proxy poisons the defragmentation cache and ruins the DNS response sent by the upstream resolver to the proxy. The attacker then inspects the subsequent DNS requests from the upstream resolver to learn

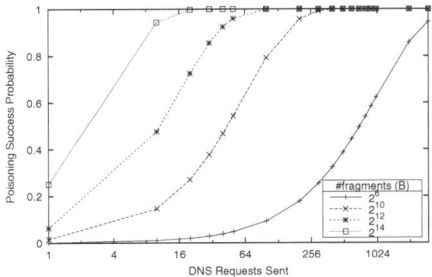
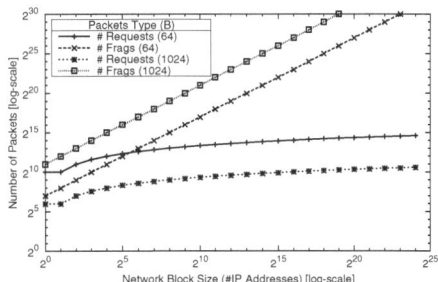

Fig. 6. Defragmentation-cache poisoning success probability per attempt, by analysis (Eq. (1)), for $B \in \{64, 1024, 4096, 16384\}$ (number of fake second fragments in cache) and different numbers of DNS requests, for random IP-ID assignment

Fig. 7. Number of spoofed second fragments and DNS requests, for different network blocks ($2^0 - 2^{24}$), and for $B \in \{64, 1024\}$ (number of fake second fragments in cache), assuming per-dest IP-ID assignment

information about the reaction of the proxy. The reaction from the proxy is used as a side-channel, and allows to determine if the address of the proxy is found. Application of defragmentation cache poisoning for attacks is not new, and was mainly used for denial of service attacks, see [RFC6274] and [20,21]. The first application of fragmentation for attacks on DNS was in [15,16] for name server pinning and for cache-poisoning, respectively. Let B be the maximal number of fragments that can be cached at the defragmentation cache of the resolver, then $\frac{2^{16}}{B}$ is the maximal number of requests required in order to find the correct IP-ID for a single recipient, assuming a sequentially incrementing IP-ID is supported. Let $/x$ denote the CIDR subnet mask of the address block, returned from the whois.net query on the IP address of the puppet, and set $y = 32 - x$. Then 2^y is the number of IP addresses in a network block defined by the network part $/x$. We use binary search for proxy resolver IP address discovery, and since there are 2^y addresses, the procedure has to be repeated $\log 2^y = y$ times.

IP Address Discovery. For each $0 \leq i \leq y$, repeat:

(1) During attempt i the attacker triggers $\frac{2^{16}}{B}$ DNS requests (via the puppet) for records in its own domain, and sends $B\frac{2^y}{2^i} = B \cdot 2^{y-i}$ spoofed second fragments to a set of $\frac{2^y}{2^i}$ IP addresses (from the network address block); each fragment has a source IP address of the upstream resolver, destination IP addresses are from the network block (which the attacker traverses), and offset value of 1480. These fragments are stored at the defragmentation cache of the recipients, and then discarded if not reassembled (after 30 seconds by default).

(2) The upstream resolver receives the requests from the proxy and forwards them to attacker's name server. The responses to those requests result in (fragmented) referrals to subdomains of attacker's domain. The attacker inspects the subsequent requests from the upstream resolver to learn the reaction of the proxy resolver, and uses it as side-channel, to determine if the IP of the proxy was among the set of $\frac{2^y}{2^i}$ IP addresses that it sent the spoofed fragments to, in step (1).

(3) If the attacker sent the fragments to the correct IP address of the proxy, then when the authentic first fragment, sent by the upstream resolver, arrives, real first fragment and fake second fragment will be defragmented. Prior to accepting and caching responses, the resolver validates a number of fields, e.g., UDP port and checksum, DNS TXID. The reassembled response has incorrect checksum and is hence discarded by the proxy. If there is a pending DNS request, which the proxy resolver sent earlier to the upstream resolver, it times-out and the proxy retransmits its DNS request. The upstream resolver forwards[7] it to attacker's name server.

If the attacker receives a retransmitted DNS request - it knows that the IP of the proxy is in the set of $\frac{2^y}{2^i}$ tested IP addresses. In contrast, if the response arrives correctly to the resolver - there is no timeout, and the attacker receives a referral request (it responded with that referral to the request from upstream resolver in step 2). In this case, the attacker knows that the IP was not among the set of the IPs sampled in the current attempt, and repeats the attack with the next set of IPs.

Analysis and Experimental Evaluation. In our experimental evaluation the upstream resolver ran on a Linux OS, which implements a per-destination incrementing IP-ID allocation method, and our analysis and evaluation are adapted to this case; globally incrementing IP-ID can be sampled directly.

During the ith iteration the attacker sends $\frac{2^{16}}{B}$ DNS requests and $B\frac{2^y}{2^i} = B \cdot 2^{y-i}$ spoofed second fragments ($0 \leq i \leq y$). The number of *spoofed second fragments* that the attacker has to send in the worst case, can be expressed via geometric series:

$$B \cdot 2^y \sum_{i=0}^{y} \frac{1}{2^i} = B \cdot 2^y \cdot \left(1 + \frac{1}{1 - \frac{1}{2^y}}\right) = B \cdot 2^y \cdot 2 = B \cdot 2^{y+1}$$

Notice that $\frac{1}{1-\frac{1}{2^y}} \approx 1$ since $\frac{1}{2^y} \approx 0$. The number of *DNS requests* that the puppet has to trigger in the worst case is: $\log 2^y \cdot \frac{2^{16}}{B} = y \cdot \frac{2^{16}}{B}$. The number of packets (requests and spoofed fragments) can be expressed as (see analysis in Fig. 7): $\left(\frac{2^{16}}{B} + B\frac{2^y}{2^0}\right) + ... + \left(\frac{2^{16}}{B} + B\frac{2^y}{2^y}\right) = y \cdot \frac{2^{16}}{B} + B \cdot 2^{y+1}$

Resolvers Behind NAT Devices. If the puppet and the proxy resolver are behind a many-to-one (network address translation) NAT device, then they share the same IP address. To take this possibility into account the attacker should start the search with the IP of the puppet, and extend its search at each iteration (following the binary search technique). We ran statistics on two CAIDA datasets from 2012 [9], that were collected on equinix-chicago and equinix-sanjose monitors on high-speed Internet backbone links. Both traces contained packets sent from distinct 89750 source IP addresses, collected over two minutes interval.

---

[7] To ensure that the upstream resolver does not respond to the proxy from the cache, the attacker sets a low TTL (time-to-live), e.g., TTL=0, on the requested record.

We ran the following test to check for DNS resolvers behind NAT devices: (1) we collected all DNS requests, i.e., packets sent to port 53; (2) we created a set of IP addresses that sent at least one DNS request per second (to ensure that we do not mistakenly interpret a host for a resolver behind a NAT; (3) we ran over the traces to check if those IP addresses also sent packets to other ports, including port 80, and 443. We then concluded with high probability that those resolvers were behind NAT devices. We came up with a total of 3492, out of 89750, resolvers behind NAT devices.

Restricted Rate. The attacker may be restricted to transmit at a low rate, e.g., to launch a stealth attack in order to evade detection in networks that are known to be well-monitored, or if the attacker does not have sufficient resources and its transmission rate is limited. We next calculate the number of IPs that the attacker can try at each attempt, when it is restricted by a rate of R Bytes/sec. Let τ seconds be the maximal time that fragments are stored in the defragmentation-cache; typical (default) value of τ is 30 seconds. Let f be the size (in bytes) of the second fragment; the second fragment can be of minimal size, e.g., 8 bytes and the 20 byte IP header. Then, the maximal number of IPs that the attacker can sample during a single attempt is $x < \frac{\tau \cdot R}{B \cdot f}$. With a modest rate of $50,000$ Bytes/sec (50 KB/sec), and $B = 64$ (fragments per host IP), the attacker can sample 781 IP addresses in a single iteration, and with 50MB/sec the attacker can sample at most $78,125$ IP addresses each time, i.e., more than the size of many network blocks. Most network blocks are not too large, and can be traversed efficiently (see Section 3.2 and Figure 3).

IP-ID Discovery. Once the attacker completes the IP discovery, it knows the that the IP-ID is in range of $\frac{2^{16}}{B}$ potential values. The attacker can also find the precise value of the IP-ID of the upstream resolver (in its communication to the victim proxy resolver); the knowledge of the IP-ID value is useful for UDP port discovery (see Section 4). The attacker again applies a binary search on the range of $\frac{2^{16}}{B}$ potential IP-ID values. This requires $\log \frac{2^{16}}{B}$ attempts in the worst-case. Since during each attempt the attacker sends $\frac{2^{16}}{B}/2^i = \frac{2^{16}}{B \cdot 2^i}$ spoofed second fragments, in the worst-case the attacker will send a total of $\frac{2^{17}}{B}$ spoofed second fragments:

$$\frac{2^{16}}{B} \sum_{i=0}^{\frac{2^{16}}{B}} \frac{1}{2^i} = \frac{2^{16}}{B} \cdot \left(1 + \frac{1}{1 - \frac{1}{\frac{2^{16}}{B}}}\right) \cong \frac{2^{17}}{B}$$

4   UDP Port Discovery and DNS-Cache Poisoning

The next step towards a successful cache poisoning is to find the port that the proxy resolver assigns to the request which the attacker wishes to poison.

We collected statistics from two CAIDA datasets from 2012 [9] and found that many proxies, which delegate DNS resolution to upstream resolvers, support the following popular port allocations: *fixed port*, *globally incrementing* and *per-destination incrementing*[8]. We used the traces to collect all the DNS requests (destination port 53) over UDP, and then filtered out IP addresses with a single DNS request, and collected only the sources that sent two or more requests. This allowed us to infer information about the source port allocation of the remaining DNS requests. We found that 30% of the requests were sent from some fixed port and 54% of the requests were sent from incrementing ports. Notice that the packets' traces are collected by CAIDA on (several) *backbone (OC192) links*, therefore, most DNS requests, appearing in those traces, are probably sent from proxies to upstream resolvers, since local DNS (proxy) resolvers are located on LANs; this premise is also coherent with the standard, [RFC5625] that states: 'proxy resolvers receive DNS requests from clients on the LAN side, forward those verbatim to one of the known upstream recursive resolvers on the WAN'.

The use of a fixed client port was shown to be vulnerable by Kaminsky [4]: the attacker triggers a DNS request to a name server under its control and learns the port the resolver uses for DNS requests. Security experts also identified the globally incrementing port assignment as vulnerable: the attacker can use a sampling procedure similar to [4], to obtain the current port value and then extrapolate the port that will be assigned by the (victim) resolver to the subsequent DNS request which the attacker wishes to poison. A per-destination incrementing port is believed to be secure, and is a recommended standard [RFC6056], since different ports' sequences are assigned by the resolver to different destinations; in particular learning the port value to one destination does not leak the port value to some other destination. We checked the *predictability rate* assigned by the popular DNS checker service provided by the OARC [7], to resolvers that send DNS requests with per-destination incrementing port. The tool reported (the highest) GREAT score to a *per-destination fixed* port (i.e., a different *fixed* port is assigned to each destination) and to a *per-destination incrementing* port (i.e., *sequentially* incrementing to each destination), indicating that both port allocation methods are believed to be secure by the DNS experts. However, our results (within) show otherwise.

In this section we present techniques that allow to predict the ports efficiently for each of the three popular allocation methods (above), contrary to folklore belief that, when a resolver does not send queries to the Internet directly, but only via an upstream resolver, it is secure. Our techniques do not rely on sampling the port, since in our setting this is not possible: the attacker *does not receive DNS requests from the proxy-resolver directly*, but only via an upstream DNS resolver. Furthermore, our results show that sequential allocation, whether per-destination or global, *surprisingly* allows for a more efficient port prediction, than a fixed port allocation; see comparison in [18].

During the port discovery the attacker triggers queries to a domain that it controls. This allows the attacker to control, not only the time at which the

---

[8] The effect of globally incrementing and per-destination incrementing ports' assignment methods is identical when proxies delegate DNS resolution to an upstream resolver.

request is triggered but also the *time at which the response is sent*; furthermore, if the attacker does not respond at all, this will result in a timeout at the resolver and in a retransmission of the DNS request. The attacker then traverses the port range until a correct port is found. Notice that often not all ports are used[9] and the supported ports ranges are significantly smaller than 2^{16}, e.g., it is considered safe to use ports in the range $(1024 - 49152)$, [RFC5452]. Therefore, some ports are more probable than others.

The attacker succeeds in a poisoning attack (of its own domain) when a correct port is found. As a result the attacker receives a subsequent request to the IP that was returned in the *poisoned record*, instead of a retransmission request.

However, prior to accepting and caching a DNS response resolvers validate a number of fields (recommended in [RFC5452]), e.g., IP addresses, UDP port, DNS TXID. The attacker knows the IP addresses: the address of the proxy-resolver was found using techniques in Section 3, and the address of the upstream is known since it sends the DNS requests to the name servers. The attacker has to find the correct UDP port and DNS TXID. A naive strategy is to apply the Kaminsky attack [4], however, this requires sending 2^{32} packets in the worst case in *each poisoning attempt* and is thus not feasible.

We devise a new approach for port discovery (explained next) which we dub the *Midway Rendezvous*. We show that this approach allows to significantly reduce the complexity of port discovery. We then propose to apply the midway rendezvous with two different strategies for port discovery: (1) an *optimised exhaustive search* and (2) *search via defragmentation-cache poisoning*; we compare the efficiency and complexity of both strategies in [18].

Midway Rendezvous. The idea is to traverse the ports range in a direction opposite to port incrementation, supported by the resolver. At each iteration i the attacker sends spoofed DNS responses, to p ports, each time decreasing the port number; p can be arbitrary, e.g., $p = 1$, and typically depends on attacker's bandwidth. Thus the attacker *walks* the port range towards the *direction* in which the resolver *walks*. In the worst case, they meet after $\frac{2^{16}}{2p}$ attempts, where p is the number of ports tried during each attempt. The value of p depends on port assignment method supported by the resolver. When incrementing ports are used, $1 \leq p \leq 15$; if the attacker samples a single port each time, i.e., $p = 1$, the attacker has to traverse half the ports range (assuming maximal ports range of 2^{16}). When a *fixed port* assignment is supported, $p = 0$, the attacker has to repeat the attack till it meets the fixed port (used by the resolver), and has to traverse in the worst case, $2^{16} - 1$ ports.

When next show how to apply this strategy using two different techniques *optimised exhaustive search* and *search via defragmentation-cache poisoning*, and compare efficiency.

---

[9] DNS running on Windows server 2008 uses ports range $(49152 - 65535)$ and Windows 2000/XP/server 2003 use ports from range $(1025 - 5000)$. Older Bind versions use fixed ports.

4.1   Optimised Exhaustive Port Search

The attacker applies the *midway rendezvous* to discover the port and proceeds as follows (Figure 8): For $i = 1...15$ or till 'port is found', repeat: (1) attacker triggers a DNS request to a record in a domain under its control, and (2) sends $p \cdot 2^{16}$ DNS responses to p (decreasing) ports' values starting with the highest port, e.g., 65535, for each possible TXID value (this is required to be able to detect when the correct port is hit, otherwise the response is discarded by the proxy resolver); in the worst case, the attacker sends $p \cdot 2^{16}$ responses. If the port is not one of the p ports tested at the current iteration, then increment i and update the port for next iteration.   Although practical, this technique has a disadvantage: in order to hit the correct UDP port the attacker has to also guess the TXID. In the next section we show that the attacker can apply first-fragment defragmentation-cache poisoning to *split* the distribution of TXID and port to two separate distributions of size (at most) 2^{16} each (assuming all maximal number of ports is used).

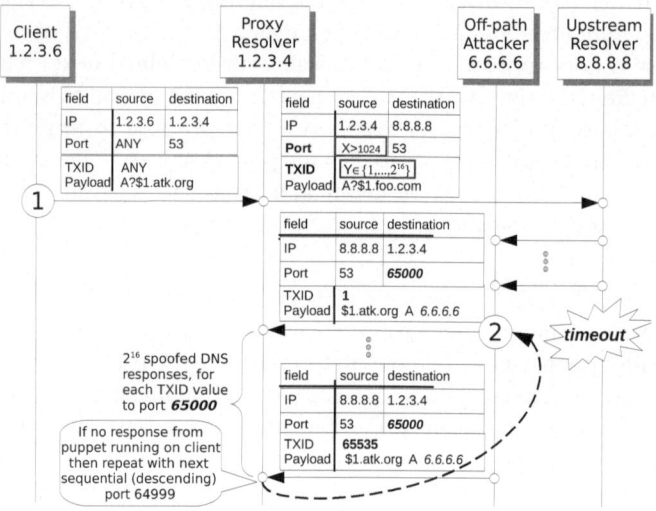

Fig. 8. DNS request port discovery: in step 1, the puppet triggers a DNS request to a resource within the attacker's domain. The off-path attacker, in step 2, at IP 6.6.6.6, sends 2^{16} fake responses (each containing a different TXID value) to each port of the DNS resolver. If failure - repeat the attack from step 2. When timeout, repeat the attack from step 1.

4.2   Port Discovery via First Fragment Defragmentation-Poisoning

The attacker can often improve the efficiency of port discovery, and in what follows we present port discovery which uses a technique we dub first-fragment defragmentation-cache poisoning. The steps of the attack are illustrated in Figure 9. We assume that the attacker knows the IP-ID value, e.g., it ran earlier the IP discovery phase, which also exposes the current IP-ID value (details in Section 3).

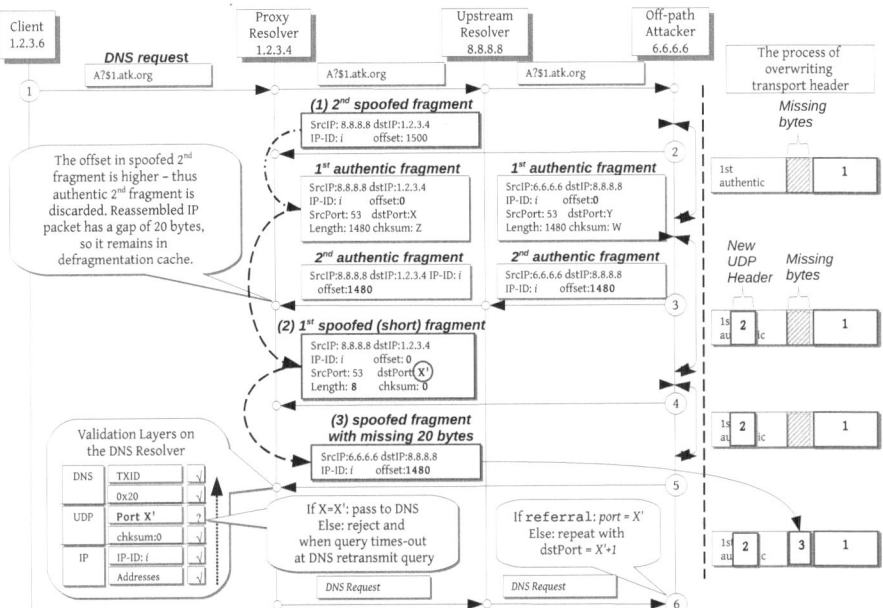

Fig. 9. DNS port discovery: in step 1, the puppet triggers a DNS request to a resource within the attacker's domain. The off-path attacker, in step 2, at IP 6.6.6.6, plants a spoofed first fragment (with UDP length 8 bytes, and checksum 0) into the defragmentation cache of the resolver. The first authentic fragment is reassembled with the spoofed fragment, and then with the authentic second fragment. If the port is correct, the attacker will receive a referral, otherwise timeout and retransmission of the previous request.

The idea is to use fragmentation to overwrite the transport layer header of the fragmented IP packet sent by the upstream resolver to the proxy. In each such attempt the attacker sends a spoofed fragment with a source IP of the upstream resolver and includes a guess for a port. If the guess is correct - the response is accepted and cached by the resolver. Otherwise, if the port in the spoofed fragment is incorrect - the proxy rejects the response, and retransmits the request. This allows the attacker to distinguish the two events.

The goal of this step is to craft a spoofed first fragment, with a new port, and to overwrite only the transport layer header in the authentic first fragment. However, if two fragments contain identical offsets, then the last arriving fragment overwrites the first. Therefore, in order for the spoofed fragment to overwrite the transport header of the authentic fragment, it must arrive at the resolver *after* the first authentic fragment, and *before* the IP packet is reassembled, when the authentic second fragment arrives. Let $f = f_1 \| f_2$ be the IP packet consisting of two fragments f_1 starts at offset 0 and is of length $|f_1|$ and f_2 starts at offset $|f_1|$ and is of length $|f_2|$. The steps of the attack are described next.

(1) attacker sends a spoofed second fragment f_2', starting at offset $(|f_1| + \epsilon)$, where ϵ is some number of bytes.

(2) attacker triggers a DNS request (whose response is fragmented). When the first authentic fragment f_1 arrives it is reassembled with the spoofed second fragment f'_2 that is already in the defragmentation cache; when the authentic second fragment f_2 arrives, it is discarded since a spoofed fragment starts and ends at a higher offset ($|f_1| + \epsilon$). However, the reassembled IP packet does not leave the defragmentation cache since there is a gap of ϵ bytes that are still missing.

(3) The attacker sends a short fragment that overwrites *only* the UDP header in the original first fragment. This fragment overlaps with first 8 bytes (the UDP header) with the authentic first fragment; the fragment contains checksum 0, which indicates that checksum validation is disabled[10], more fragments is set to 1 (mf=1), and offset is 0. When initiating the attack, the attacker sets the UDP port in this spoofed first fragment to 2^{16}, and decrements its value during each subsequent iteration, following the *midway rendezvous* strategy.

(4) Then the attacker sends a fragment that starts at offset $|f_1|$ and is of size ϵ to fill the gap.

4.3   Analysis and Experimental Evaluation

Let r be a DNS response size in bytes; for simplicity we round to 100 bytes (also in our experimental evaluation). Let R bytes/sec be the transmission rate of the attacker. Let t seconds be a limit on the timeout for a DNS request (i.e., including all retransmitted requests for that query) and let q be a number of times a pending query is retransmitted until it is terminated and SERVERFAIL is returned. Resolvers implement retransmission policy based on round trip time estimates of the name servers, [RFC1536], and support timeout management with exponential backoff. When a timeout occurs resolver enters an exponential backoff phase, i.e., the timeout is doubled, and query is retransmitted. Resolvers implement variable timeout and retransmission values, typically up to 45 seconds (which is also a recommended ceiling for total timeout for a query [RFC1536]), and attempt up to 15 retransmissions. For instance, Unbound*1.4.19* sets t to a maximal value of 40 seconds and Bind*9.8.1* sets $t \leq 30$ seconds and $q \leq 10$, i.e., supports up to 10 retransmissions before terminating a query.

In each retransmission the resolver advances the port (in case an incrementing allocation is supported). This allows the attacker to sample a number of ports in a single iteration (since with each retransmission there is a new pending request).

Optimised Exhaustive Port Search. The number of iterations i that the attacker has to repeat (or the number of queries that the puppet triggers) in the worst case, assuming that in a single iteration the resolver triggers q retransmissions (before terminating a DNS request) and the attacker samples p ports, is: (1) $i \leq \frac{2^{15}}{(p+q)}$ for incrementing port, and (2) $i \leq \frac{2^{16}}{p}$ for some (unknown) fixed port.

The maximal number of ports p that the attacker can test in a single iteration is $p \leq \frac{t \cdot R}{r \cdot 2^{16}}$; assuming that 2^{16} is the number of possible values of TXID.

---

[10] UDP checksum validation is optional, and it can be disabled by name servers by setting it to 0 (0000 in hexadecimal). When the checksum is disabled it is not validated by the resolvers.

The analysis vs evaluation results are in technical report [18]. Once the port is known the attacker launches a DNS cache poisoning attack, i.e., sends 2^{16} spoofed DNS responses, for some victim domain, such that each response contains a different TXID value.

Port Discovery via Defragmentation-Cache Poisoning. The number of iterations required to hit the correct port in the worst case is: $\frac{2^{16}}{(q+1)}$ for a fixed port and $\frac{2^{15}}{(q+1)}$ for incrementing port assignment; during each iteration the attacker matches the original query and up to q retransmissions. Since the attacker does not need to match the TXID, at each iteration only 3 fragments are sent (more fragments will not improve the efficiency of the attack); this significantly reduces the complexity of the attack. However, note that, the attacker cannot sample more than a single port, for each DNS request, since the payload is taken only from the last fragment, therefore, $p = 1$.

The worst-case number of requests required to guess the port is $\frac{2^{15}}{(q+1)}$ for incrementing allocation and $\frac{2^{15}}{(q+1)}$ for a fixed allocation. During each iteration $3(q+1)$ fragments are sent, thus the worst case number of fragments is $3(q+1) \cdot \frac{2^{15}}{(q+1)} = 3 \cdot 2^{15}$ for incrementing allocation and $3(q+1) \cdot \frac{2^{16}}{(q+1)} = 3 \cdot 2^{16}$ for a fixed port.

5   Conclusions

We presented DNS poisoning attacks on proxy DNS resolvers, i.e., resolvers which use an upstream resolver. This attack is significant, since a large and growing number of networks use upstream resolvers (and hence are vulnerable), and prior to this work, a common belief was that this setting protects the proxy resolvers from poisoning and DoS attacks. This belief is also partially due to the fact that DNS resolver-testing services, report this DNS configuration as secure. It is therefore imperative that networks, operating proxies, adopt appropriate corrective defenses, as described in [18].

Acknowledgements. We thank the anonymous referees for their comments on the earlier version of this work. This research was supported by grant 1354/11 from the Israeli Science Foundation (ISF), and by the Ministry of Science and Technology, Israel. We are grateful for support for CAIDA's Internet Traces [9] that is provided by the National Science Foundation, the US Department of Homeland Security, and CAIDA Members.

References

1. Akamai: Enchanced DNS (eDNS) (April 2013),
   http://www.akamai.com/html/solutions/enhanced_dns.html
2. Gudmundsson, O., Crocker, S.D.: Observing DNSSEC Validation in the Wild. In: SATIN (March 2011)

3. Kaminsky, D.: Dan Kaminsky's Blog, http://dankaminsky.com/2008/07/21/130/
4. Kaminsky, D.: It's the End of the Cache As We Know It. In: Black Hat Conference (August 2008), http://www.blackhat.com/presentations/bh-jp-08/bh-jp-08-Kaminsky/BlackHat-Japan-08-Kaminsky-DNS08-BlackOps.pdf
5. Dagon, D., Provos, N., Lee, C.P., Lee, W.: Corrupted DNS resolution paths: The rise of a malicious resolution authority. In: NDSS. The Internet Society (2008)
6. Gibson Research Corporation: DNS Nameserver Spoofability Test (2012), https://www.grc.com/dns/dns.htm
7. DNS-OARC: Domain Name System Operations Analysis and Research Center (2008), https://www.dns-oarc.net/oarc/services/porttest
8. Provos, N.: DNS Testing Image (July 2008), http://www.provos.org/index.php?/archives/43-DNS-Testing-Image.html
9. CAIDA: Anonymized Internet Traces 2012 Dataset (2012), http://www.caida.org/data/passive/passive_2012_dataset.xml
10. Antonatos, S., Akritidis, P., Lam, V.T., Anagnostakis, K.G.: Puppetnets: Misusing Web Browsers as a Distributed Attack Infrastructure. ACM Transactions on Information and System Security 12(2), 12:1–12:15 (2008)
11. Herzberg, A., Shulman, H.: Unilateral Antidotes to DNS Cache Poisoning. In: Rajarajan, M., Piper, F., Wang, H., Kesidis, G. (eds.) SecureComm 2011. LNICST, vol. 96, pp. 319–336. Springer, Heidelberg (2012)
12. Klein, A.: BIND 9 DNS cache poisoning. Report, Trusteer, Ltd., Israel (2007)
13. Vixie, P.: DNS and BIND security issues. In: Proceedings of the 5th Symposium on UNIX Security, pp. 209–216. USENIX Association, Berkeley (1995)
14. Bernstein, D.J.: DNS Forgery (November 2002), Internet publication at http://cr.yp.to/djbdns/forgery.html
15. Herzberg, A., Shulman, H.: Security of Patched DNS. In: Foresti, S., Yung, M., Martinelli, F. (eds.) ESORICS 2012. LNCS, vol. 7459, pp. 271–288. Springer, Heidelberg (2012)
16. Herzberg, A., Shulman, H.: Fragmentation Considered Poisonous: or one-domain-to-rule-them-all.org. In: IEEE CNS 2013, The Conference on Communications and Network Security (2013)
17. Herzberg, A., Shulman, H.: Antidotes for DNS Poisoning by Off-Path Adversaries. In: International Conference on Availability, Reliability and Security (ARES), pp. 262–267. IEEE, IEEE Computer Society (2012)
18. Herzberg, A., Shulman, H.: Vulnerable Delegation of DNS Resolution. Technical Report 13-05, Bar Ilan University, Network security group (April 2013)
19. Kernel.org: Linux Kernel Documentation (2011), http://www.kernel.org/doc/Documentation/networking/ip-sysctl.txt
20. Gilad, Y., Herzberg, A.: Fragmentation Considered Vulnerable: Blindly Intercepting and Discarding Fragments. In: Proc. USENIX Workshop on Offensive Technologies (August 2011)
21. Gont, F.: Security Implications of Predictable Fragment Identification Values. Internet-Draft of the IETF IPv6 maintenance Working Group (6man) (March 2012) (Expires September 30, 2012)

Formal Approach for Route Agility against Persistent Attackers

Jafar Haadi Jafarian, Ehab Al-Shaer, and Qi Duan

Department of Software and Information Systems
University of North Carolina at Charlotte
Charlotte, NC, USA
{jjafaria,ealshaer,qduan}@uncc.edu

Abstract. To proactively defend against denial of service attacks, we propose an agile multipath routing approach called random route mutation (RRM) which combines game theory and constraint satisfaction optimization to determine the optimal strategy for attack deterrence while satisfying security, performance and QoS requirements of the network. Our contribution in this paper is fourfold: (1) we model the interaction between RRM defender and DoS attacker as a game in order to determine the parameters by which the defender can maximize her benefit, (2) we model route selection as a constraint satisfaction optimization and formalize it using Satisfiability Modulo Theories (SMT) to identify efficient practical routes, (3) we provide algorithms for sound and smooth deployment of RRM on conventional as well as software-defined networks, and (4) we develop analytical and experimental models to investigate the effectiveness and limitation of RRM under different network and adversarial parameters. Our analysis and preliminary implementation show that RRM can protect up to 90% of flow packets from being attacked against persistent attackers, as compared with single-path routing schemes. Moreover, our implementation shows that RRM can be efficiently deployed on networks without causing any disruption for flows.

1 Introduction

The tragic effect of DoS attacks on networks are significantly aggravated by adoption of conventional least-cost single-path routing schemes. While such route selection simplifies reachability and manageability, it gives adversaries significant advantages to gradually learn network routes and plan DoS flooding attacks accurately. For instance, intruders can disrupt the data session simply by attacking one of the intermediate nodes along the associated route. Such a DoS attack is feasible since only one single predictable route is chosen, and this singularity enables intruders to readily discover the route and devote their resources to attacking it.

In this paper we present a random multi-route approach, called random route mutation (RRM), which protects designated flows by routing them via an optimal number of randomly-chosen routes such that each route satisfies security,

J. Crampton, S. Jajodia, and K. Mayes (Eds.): ESORICS 2013, LNCS 8134, pp. 237–254, 2013.
© Springer-Verlag Berlin Heidelberg 2013

capacity, overlap and QoS constraints of the network. RRM significantly raises the bar for attackers because to completely compromise the flow, intruders must subvert all the routes and thus require more resources than those needed for attacking a single route. Also, nondeterministic route selection disrupts reconnaissance for attack planning and wastes attacker resources by forcing her to blindly disperse her resources across network routes. Moreover, although routes are chosen randomly, constraint-satisfying route selection guarantees that each route has the desired security and performance-related properties.

We assume a persistent adversarial model where attacker is RRM-aware and aims to defeat RRM by frequent hopping between network routes. The number of hopping (mutation) between routes determines attacker's strategy because the more routes the adversary attacks, the higher the probability of hitting the random routes which are chosen by RRM.

The first challenge of RRM is to determine the optimal number of routes for flow transmission such that the defender's benefit is maximized while making her indifferent to the attacker's strategy. We refer to this problem as *optimal strategy selection* and model it as a static game of complete information between attacker and defender, where players' strategies are defined in terms of number of mutations and their payoffs are defined based on the tradeoff between the benefit and cost of mutation.

Knowing the number of routes, the next challenge is to determine a set of qualified routes such that each route satisfies security and performance constraints of the network. In this paper, we consider the following constraints, but other constraints can be added as well:

- *Capacity constraint*: the routes should not include those nodes that are already overloaded (based on node capacity) or those nodes that do not fulfil the bandwidth requirement of the flow.
- *Overlap constraint*: to increase unpredictability and achieve fair load balancing, the overlap between the routes should be less than the tolerable overlap threshold.
- *Security constraint*: the routes should preserve security enforcement by access control policies such as firewalls; *e.g.*, if a flow must pass through a firewall, the firewall must be included in all the routes.
- *QoS constraint*: the routes should maintain the required quality, such as bounded delays or number of hops.

We refer to this problem as *optimal route selection* and model it as a constraint satisfaction problem using generalized Boolean/arithmetic format of Satisfiability Modulo Theory (SMT). We use SMT solvers to discover a random set of constraint-satisfying routes.

Knowing the set of routes, the final challenge is to design a sound mechanism for route installation and revocation such that mutating from one route to another does not cause any transient or permanent unreachability and the flow is transmitted soundly and without any packet loss. We refer to this problem as *route mutation planning*. We provide a formal algorithm for this problem and prove that it guarantees reachability throughout flow transmission.

While deployment of RRM on conventional network layer architectures is challenging, more recent application-layer architectures such as overlay networks (*e.g.*, RON [2], SOS [4], and VNET/P [17]) and emerging software-defined networking (*e.g.*, OpenFlow [11]) provide promising platforms for RRM. We implemented RRM algorithms in POX [10], a network SDN controller written in Python that communicates with OpenFlow 1.0 switches. In our implementation on SDN, mutation from one route to another is accomplished via a series of flow table updates in all the switches both along the old and new routes.

To evaluate RRM effectiveness, we introduce an analytical metric called MPE (Mutation Protection Effectiveness) which measures average effectiveness of RRM against attackers by taking into account the attacker's strategy and capability. Moreover, we used our implemented framework for extensive evaluation of RRM effectiveness in real-world scenarios. Our analytical and experimental evaluation shows that RRM is significantly effective against DoS attackers.

Previous works on multipath routing in wireless networks such as [16] propose using random forwarding to avoid jamming and blackhole attacks. These works are far from being practical for wired networks because of many topological, QoS and security constraints. Moreover, unlike previous works [16], we do not use random walk heuristic-based algorithms to identify random routes because it is infeasible to design a random walk algorithm to satisfy multiple constraints simultaneously.

The rest of the paper is organized as follows: Section 2 discusses our basic methodology. Section 3 presents implementation details of RRM. Section 4 shows the evaluation results. Section 5 presents related work. Section 6 concludes the paper.

2   Technical Approach

2.1   Adversarial Modeling

RRM effectiveness against static attackers (attackers that do not move) is obviously high. However, to accurately evaluate effectiveness for realistic scenarios, we assume a generalized *persistent* RRM-aware adversarial model. In this model, the attacker is characterized by two parameters: her capability and the number of routes she attacks. Attacker's capability, denoted as r, is defined in terms of the number of nodes that are known to the attacker. Attacker's mutation intervals, denoted as M_a, defines the attacker's strategy in the network. More specifically, at each mutation interval, the attacker uniformly chooses a route and attacks it. If the adversary by chance attacks a route that is being used by RRM, she would stay on the route for as long as RRM continues using the route; that is, until the expiration of defender's mutation interval.

The objective of RRM is to protect a flow f that is being transmitted from a source S to a destination D, such that the portion of the flow that evades the attack is maximized. To distance our model from security through obscurity, we assume that the attacker knows the flow properties including its source and destination, its size and duration, as well as the starting time of its transmission.

2.2   Overview

RRM responsibilities in a network are performed by a RRM controller with privileged accesses to network routers/switches. Alg. 1 defines the main algorithm of this controller. After each mutation interval (T seconds), the algorithm uses *ChangeRoute* to revoke the route r_k and install r_{k+1}. Note that for each route, its reverse route must also be installed. r_k^{-1} denotes the reverse route of r_k. The *ChangeRoute* algorithm is described in Section 2.5.

Algorithm 1. RRM Controller algorithm for route mutation of a flow from S to D

---

determine optimal defender strategy (M_d^*) by finding NE of the game   ▷ Sec. 2.3
determine qualified routes $r_1, \ldots, r_{M_d^*}$ using SMT solver   ▷ Sec. 2.4
upon expiration of kth defender mutation interval
    $ChangeRoute(r_k \rightarrow r_{k+1})$ ▷ Sec. 2.5
    $ChangeRoute(r_k^{-1} \rightarrow r_{k+1}^{-1})$

2.3   Optimal Strategy Selection

Of fundamental significance is the problem of determining the number of routes that are used for transmitting a flow. Although it is intuitive that using more routes provides higher benefit for the defender on average, it also increases the cost associated with the routing. Therefore, choosing the optimal mutation strategy for the defender partly depends on the benefit-cost tradeoff of the mutation.

In addition to this tradeoff, the defender benefit also depends on the mutation strategy of the attacker. If the defender's mutation rate is slower than that of the attacker's, it is straightforward to see that RRM will be less effective. However, although faster hopping between routes increases the probability of hitting a flow route for the attacker, it also increases detectability of the attacker and her resources. Therefore, the defender and attacker mutation strategies can be defined as a static game of complete information, where each player aims to determine her Nash equilibrium strategy by considering other players' strategies and the cost associated with her own strategy.

The game is defined as $\Gamma = \langle I, S, U \rangle$, where $I = \{a, d\}$ is the set of players, $S = \{M_a, M_d\}$ denotes the set of strategies for the attacker and defender, and $U = \{u_a, u_d\}$ defines the payoff function for each player. Note that the attacker's strategy is defined in terms of the number of routes, M_a, that she attacks during flow transmission. Defender's strategy is defined in terms of number of routes, M_d, that are used for flow transmission.

To evaluate RRM effectiveness against attackers, we define *mutation protection effectiveness* metric (MPE) as the average percentage of the flow that is transmitted without being compromised. Suppose the defender aims to transmit a flow f between a given source and destination and the network consists of n nodes. The flow is transmitted during M_d mutation intervals such that $1/M_d$ portion of f is transmitted during each interval.

To calculate MPE, we first need to calculate node compromise probability, x:

$$x = \frac{r}{n}$$

The probability that a route is compromised is equal to the probability that *at least* one node in the route is compromised by the attacker. Assume L denotes the maximum length of routes in terms of nodes, and p_i denotes the percentage of routes with length i. Assuming *disjointness* between routes (no node is shared between routes), the route expected compromise probability, denoted as X, is:

$$X = \sum_{i=1}^{L} p_i (1 - (1-x)^i) \tag{1}$$

If $M_a \leq M_d$, the attacker may hit the flow at each interval with probability X. Since route compromise probabilities are disjoint, the number of routes hit by the attacker follows binomial distribution $\sim B(M_a, X)$. Therefore, the average number of routes hit by the attacker is $X \cdot M_a$, and each hit compromises one $1/M_d$ portion of the flow. For this case, MPE is:

$$MPE(M_a, M_d) = 1 - \frac{M_a}{M_d} X$$

For scenarios where $M_a > M_d$, the number of routes hit by the attacker follows binomial distribution $\sim B(M_d, X)$. The average number of routes hit by the attacker is $X \cdot M_d$. However, the exact percentage of the flow hit by the attacker is more complex because the attacker is mutating faster than the defender and she may hit one defender interval (route) after a portion of the flow has been transmitted. Suppose $z = \lceil M_a/M_d \rceil$; *i.e.*, for each defender mutation, the attacker mutates z times (defender is stationary to attacker during these intervals). Based on the adversary model, if the attacker hits a route that is being used, she will remain there until the defender's mutation interval expires. During the ith defender interval, the attacker mutates z times. If the attacker hits the defender's route during the first mutation with probability X, then the whole flow is compromised. The probability that the attacker does not hit the flow during the first mutation, but during the second mutation is $(1 - X)X$ (geometric distribution), and the portion of the flow that is compromised is $\frac{(z-1)/z}{M_d}$. Generally, when $M_a > M_d$ the average percentage of the flow which is compromised during one defender interval is:

$$\sum_{k=1}^{z} (1 - X)^{k-1} \cdot X \cdot (z - k + 1)/z \cdot 1/M_d$$

Therefore, for this scenario MPE is:

$$MPE(M_a, M_d) = 1 - M_d \cdot \left(\sum_{k=1}^{z} (1 - X)^{k-1} \cdot X \cdot (z - k + 1)/z \cdot 1/M_d \right)$$

We can combine both cases into the following formula:

$$MPE(M_a, M_d) = 1 - \min(M_a, M_d) \cdot \left(\sum_{k=1}^{z} (1-X)^{k-1} \cdot X \cdot (z-k+1)/z \cdot 1/M_d \right)$$

$$(2)$$

where $z = \lceil M_a/M_d \rceil$. For example, for static attackers where $M_a = 1$:

$$MPE(1, M_d) = 1 - \frac{X}{M_d}$$

If both attacker and defender mutate with the same speed M:

$$MPE(M, M) = 1 - X$$

The defender's utility is defined based on the benefit from protecting the flow in terms of MPE and the cost of M_d mutations. Mutation cost emanates from updating routing tables and installing new routes in routers/switches of the network. On the other hand, the attacker's utility is defined based on the benefit from compromise (1 - MPE) and the cost of M_a mutations. The attacker mutation cost originates from the fact that as the attacker increases the number of attacked routes, her detection probability increases. Note that these benefit and cost functions are application-dependent and differ based on the properties of the flow and network. Eq. 3 and 4 denote *generic* utility functions for defender and attacker respectively, where Π denotes the benefit function, Θ denotes the cost function, and N denotes the number of disjoint routes.

$$u_d(M_a, M_d) = \Pi_d(MPE(M_a, M_d)) - \Theta_d(M_d) \qquad (3)$$
$$u_a(M_a, M_d) = \Pi_a(1 - MPE(M_a, M_d)) - \Theta_a(M_a) \qquad (4)$$
$$M_a, M_d \in (0, N]$$

Since the route compromise probabilities are disjoint, N is the upper bound for both players' strategies. The objective of the game is to determine the Nash equilibrium (NE) strategy profile (M_a^*, M_d^*). Note that if the cost of mutation is 0, both players tend to maximize their mutation. For such scenarios, (N, N) is the Nash equilibrium of the game. Otherwise, both players can deviate by increasing their mutation and achieving higher payoffs (Fig. 3). However, if mutation cost functions are nonzero, then the players' payoffs depend on the trade-off between benefit and cost of mutations. Numerical analysis of the game to determine the pure Nash equilibrium requires $\theta(N^2)$ payoff calculations. If no pure strategy NE exists, we either determine the mixed Nash equilibrium of the game and then randomly choose a strategy according to the distribution, or we assume that the attacker plays $M_a = N$ and determine the M_d that maximizes defender's payoff.

To determine the defender mutation interval, we simply divide flow duration T_f by M_d^*; i.e., $T = T_f/M_d^*$. Flow duration is either provided as input or determined based on flow size and network bandwidth.

2.4   Optimal Route Selection

Route selection is accomplished by formalizing RRM constraints and using off-the-shelf SMT solvers to determine M_d^* qualified routes between the designated source and destination. However, for large M_d^*, the computational complexity, as well as topological limitations, does not allow SMT solvers to determine all the routes at once. Instead, we relax the problem by defining a relatively small window size w such that at each iteration, SMT solver determines w new routes until all M_d^* routes are generated. While computational limitations of SMT solvers necessitate smaller window sizes, overhead resulting from multiple model solving necessitates larger windows. In our approach, we set $w = 10$.

We can model the network as a directed graph $G = (V, E)$, where V is the set of hosts and E is the set of links. Suppose there is a flow with source S and destination D ($S, D \in V$). Also assume the network contains n nodes $v_1, \dots, v_n$ and m edges $e_1, \dots, e_m$. The capacity of node v_i is denoted as $C(v_i)$. Moreover, the Boolean variable b_i^k denotes inclusion of node v_i in the kth route: if $b_i^k = 1$, then node v_i is used for the flow; otherwise v_i is not used for the flow. Our objective is to use a SMT solver to find a satisfiable assignment to all the variables b_i^k. The following formalization models the problem of discovering w qualified routes between S and D:

$$b_S^k = 1, b_D^k = 1, 1 \le k \le w \tag{5}$$

$$b_i^k = 1 \Rightarrow \sum_{v_j \in \chi(v_i)} b_j^k = 2, \ \forall v_j \text{ except } S \text{ and } D, 1 \le k \le w \tag{6}$$

$$\sum_{v_j \in \chi(y)} b_j^k = 1, \ y \in \{S, D\}, 1 \le k \le w \tag{7}$$

$$\sum_{1 \le i \le n} b_i^k \le L, \ 1 \le k \le w \tag{8}$$

$$b_i^k = 1, \ \forall v_i \text{ contains } \mathbb{A}, 1 \le k \le w \tag{9}$$

$$b_i^k = 0, \ \forall C(v_i) \le B_f, 1 \le k \le w \tag{10}$$

$$((b_i^k = 1) \wedge (b_i^l = 1)) \Leftrightarrow \zeta_i^{k,l} = 1), \ \forall i, 1 \le k, l \le w, k \ne l \tag{11}$$

$$\eta_{k,l} = \sum_{1 \le i \le n} \zeta_i^{k,l}, \ 1 \le k, l \le w, k \ne l \tag{12}$$

$$\eta_{k,l} \le L_p, \ 1 \le k, l \le w, k \ne l \tag{13}$$

$$b_i^k, \zeta_i^{k,l} \in \{0, 1\}, \ \forall i, k, l \tag{14}$$

Eq. 5 guarantees that the source and destination of each route are S and D. Eq. 6 guarantees that each intermediate node of each route is adjacent to exactly two nodes in the route. This also disallows inclusion of cycles in the routes. Moreover, Eq. 7 states that S and D are only adjacent to only one node in each route.

Eq. 8 (*QoS constraint*) guarantees that the length of the route does not exceed L. Note that we assume a uniform delay for each network link.

Eq. 9 (*Security constraint*) guarantees that the route must pass through the nodes that contain required access control devices (such as firewalls), which are denoted as $\mathbb{A}$.

Eq. 10 (*Capacity constraint*) guarantees that the route should avoid the nodes that do not have the capacity that is required by the flow (denoted as B_f).

Eq. 11, Eq. 12 and Eq. 13 (*Overlap constraint*) guarantee that any two routes in the w intervals will have the maximum number of overlapping nodes L_p. More specifically, Eq. 11 defines parameter $\zeta_i^{k,l}$ such that $\zeta_i^{k,l} = 1$ if node v_i is shared between kth and lth routes. Eq. 12 counts the number of overlapping nodes between the two routes and denotes it as $\eta_{k,l}$. Finally, Eq. 13 guarantees that the number of overlapping routes does not exceed the threshold L_p; *i.e.*, $\eta_{k,l} \leq L_p$. Eq. 14 specifies the value range of the variables.

If SMT solver fails to find any satisfiable assignment, we will relax the constraints (*e.g.*, increase L_p in Eq. 13, or decrease w) and solve the model again. Note that in this paper, we only consider RRM for a single flow. However, RRM for multiple flows can be defined similarly. In this case one needs to find the routes for every flow and there may be additional constraints that are related to the priority of the flows.

2.5   Route Mutation Planning

Given M_d^* routes, the objective of route mutation planning is to ensure end-to-end reachability throughout flow transmission. To achieve this objective, we must ensure that at any point during transmission all routers know how to forward the incoming flow packets toward the destination. More specifically, we must ensure that any mutation from the old route r_o to the new route r_n does not cause unreachability. Alg. 2 describes a route management algorithm that guarantees end-to-end reachability.

Theorem 1. *Alg. 2 guarantees sound and lossless flow transmission.*

Proof. Assume Alg. 2 does not guarantee lossless flow transmission. This implies that there exists a router rt that fails to forward the flow packets at some point. All network routers can be categorized into four classes based on their inclusion or exclusion in r_o and r_n.

– $rt \notin r_n \wedge rt \notin r_o$: such routers will never receive any flow packets, because no router will ever have any rule to forward flow packets to them.
– $rt \in r_n \wedge rt \notin r_o$: the router will not receive any packet before r_n entries are added because no router in r_o will forward any flow packet to them. Afterwards, the router will forward the flow packets soundly.
– $rt \in r_n \wedge rt \in r_o$: the router will forward packets soundly, either based on r_o or r_n entries.

– $rt \notin r_n \wedge rt \in r_o$: the latest time that rt may receive a packet after r_n is activated will less than the round-trip time between the source and destination. Before this time, rt will forward the packets soundly. Afterwards, the router will not receive any flow packets.

Therefore, none of the routers will fail to forward the flow packets, resulting in a contradiction.

Algorithm 2. route mutation planning algorithm

---
function CHANGEROUTE($r_o \rightarrow r_n$)

    add entries for all routers rt s.t. $rt \in r_n \wedge rt \notin r_o$

    modify entries for all routers rt s.t. $rt \in r_n \wedge rt \in r_o$

    wait for one RTT

    delete entries for all routers rt s.t. $rt \in r_o \wedge rt \notin r_n$

---

3 Implementation

Implementation of RRM on conventional networks can be done by installing static route entries in the routing tables of the corresponding routers. For example, to configure static routes in the Cisco routers, the administrator can specify the exact routing entry by using the command "ip route". The administrator can also define the priority of the static entry (also called administrative distance) to override the dynamic route entries. Route selection and mutation planning will be performed by the central controller which has privileged access to all routers in the network. Flow and network attributes are provided as input parameters to the controller via a designated interface. The controller (1) determines M_d^* and T by determining the game equilibrium, (2) uses a SMT solver such as Z3 [12] to determine the set of routes, and (4) uses its privileged access to update the routing entries for each mutation interval according to Alg. 2.

Thorough evaluation of RRM effectiveness and overhead requires its deployment in large-scale networks with random topologies. To this aim, we deployed RRM on a software-defined network (SDN). In SDN, the network controller monitors and controls the entire network from a central vantage point via an interface, such as OpenFlow [11]. Due to flexibility and programmability of network switches in software-defined networks, mutation from one route to another can be accomplished as a series of flow table updates in all the switches both along the old and new routes.

We used Mininet [5] python libraries to develop a random topology generator that constitutes large-scale software-defined networks with various edge distribution models. The network is managed by a python POX [10] controller. The POX controller acts as the central authority to manage route mutation in switches. Optimal route selection is performed using Z3 [12] binding to Python. Our prototype implementation shows that route mutation in SDN can be deployed soundly and without packet loss.

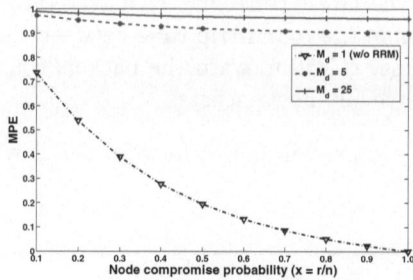

Fig. 1. MPE for static attackers for various r and M_d

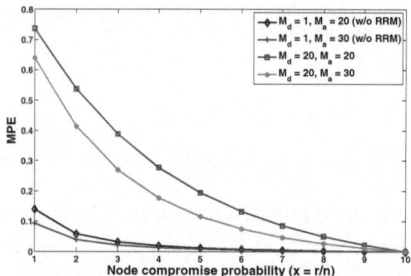

Fig. 2. MPE for static defenders (no RRM) for various r, M_a, and M_d

4   Evaluation

We evaluate effectiveness and overhead of RRM through theoretical and experimental analysis.

4.1   Effectiveness

Expected Theoretical Effectiveness. In Section 2.3 we define our analytical evaluation metric, called MPE that denotes the average theoretical effectiveness of RRM against persistent attackers in terms of the average percentage of the flow that is transmitted without being compromised. Although analytical MPE is defined based on the assumption that routes are disjoint ($L_p = 0$ in Eq. 13), it provides an accurate approximation of RRM effectiveness in random topologies.

Fig. 1 shows effectiveness of RRM against static attackers with different capabilities. Note that (1) RRM is significantly effective against static attackers, and (2) increasing M_d (the defender mutation speed) slightly improves RRM effectiveness against static attackers.

Fig. 2 compares effectiveness of RRM against persistent attackers in the non-RRM network. Non-RRM network is a network where $M_d = 1$; $i.e.$, the defender is not mutating. Note that (1) persistent attacks on non-RRM networks are very

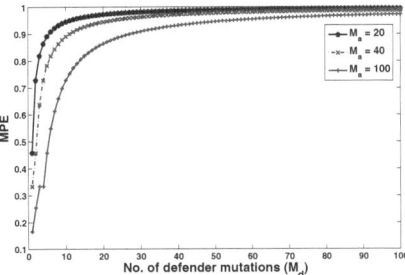

Fig. 3. MPE for various M_d and M_a

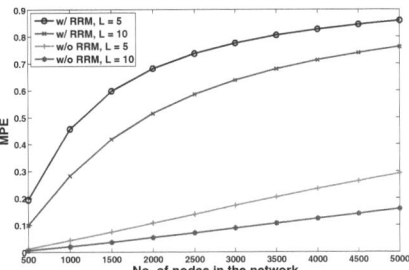

Fig. 4. MPE for various n and L

disruptive, and (2) as the number of defender's mutation intervals approaches that of attacker's, RRM effectiveness is improved.

Fig. 3 compares RRM effectiveness for various attacker and defender mutation interval lengths. Note that as the ratio of M_d over M_a increases, MPE approaches 1. However, both M_d and M_a cannot theoretically exceed the number of node-disjoint routes, which is limited for practical networks [18].

Fig. 4 compares the effect of network size (n), and the route length L on MPE in non-RRM and RRM ($M_d = M_a$) networks with the fixed attacker capability $r = 250$. Note that as the network size increases, the node compromise probability decreases which improves MPE. Also the advantage of RRM over non-RRM gradually decreases with the increase of n. This is because for large non-RRM networks, the attacker needs longer time to hit the route.

Theoretical Effectiveness for Threshold-Critical Flows. Certain classes of flows such as Shamir's threshold k-out-of-n secret sharing scheme [15] require threshold-critical effectiveness; *i.e.*, the flow transmission is successful as long as less than a certain percentage of flow packets are compromised.

For a flow that can tolerate up to l route (*i.e.*, interval) compromises, MPE^l denotes the probability that *at most l* intervals are compromised by the attacker. Note that l is an application-dependent input parameter, which is determined based on sensitivity and criticality of the flow. If each route is compromised

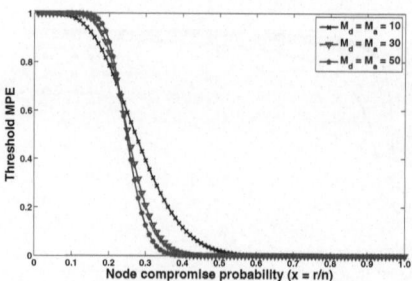

Fig. 5. Threshold MPE ($l = M_d/4$) for various r

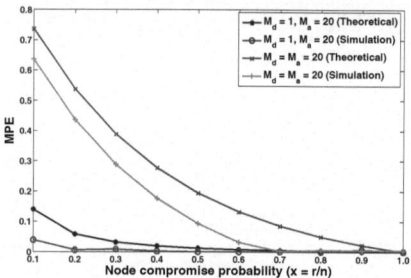

Fig. 6. Comparison of analytical and experimental MPE for various r and M_d

independently of other routes (routes are disjoint) and both players are mutating with the same rate (*i.e.*, $M_a = M_d$), the probability that exactly i mutation intervals are hit is denoted as the random variable Z and follows binomial distribution $Z \sim B(M_d, X)$ [16]. Accordingly, MPE^l can be defined as:

$$MPE^l = P(Z \leq l) = \sum_{i=0}^{l} \binom{M_d}{i} \cdot (X)^i \cdot (1 - X)^{M_d - i} \tag{15}$$

Also, it is straightforward to show that $E(MPE^l) = 1 - X$:

$$E(MPE^l) = \frac{1}{M_d} \sum_{i=0}^{M_d} P(Z \leq i) =$$

$$= \frac{1}{M_d} (M_d - P(Z = 1) - \dots iP(Z = i) - \dots - M_d P(Z = M_d))$$

$$= \frac{1}{M_d} (M_d - E(Z)) =$$

$$= 1 - X \tag{16}$$

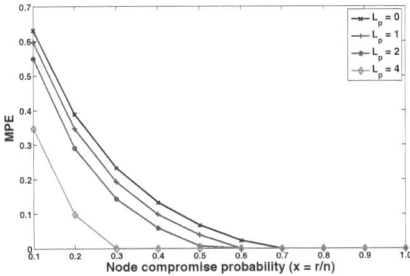

Fig. 7. Experimental MPE for various L_p and r

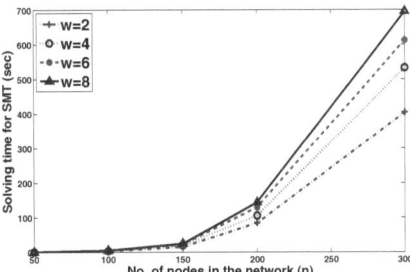

Fig. 8. SMT solving time for different w

which is consistent with Eq. 2. Fig. 5 shows the effect of mutation intervals on threshold MPE. Note that all lines intersect at the point where $l/M = X$; *i.e.*, where the route compromise probability is equal to the tolerable threshold. Moreover, contrary to the average MPE, in cases where $l/M > X$, increasing M_d has a negative effect on the threshold MPE.

Experimental Effectiveness. In practical networks, very few node-disjoint routes can be found for a fixed source and destination [18]. For overlapping routes, the assumption that the compromise probabilities of routes are independent is not valid. Therefore, for random topologies we calculate MPE via experimentation. In order to generate required topologies we developed a random topology generator for Mininet that allows generation of random Mininet networks with n switches and average node degree d according to one of the Erdos-Rnyi (random graph), Barabsi-Albert (scale-free), or Watts and Strogatz (small-world) models.

To generate the ith simulation scenario, n and d are provided to the generator. The generator creates a network by uniformly choosing one of the random graph, scale-free or small-world models. This ensures that the calculated MPE demonstrates the average effectiveness of RRM for various real-world network models. Then, given r the controller determines M_d^* and uses the SMT solver

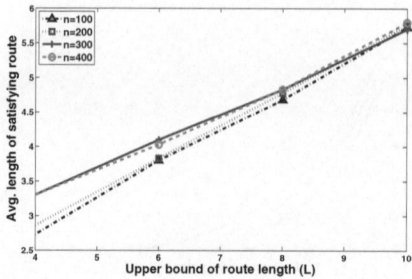

Fig. 9. Average route length for different L and n

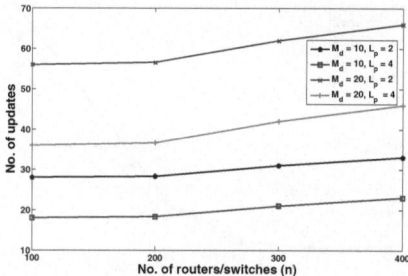

Fig. 10. Average no. of routing table updates for various M_d and L_p

to determine the set of routes. Next, at each mutation interval the controller uses one of these routes for flow transmission. The attacker is simulated in the following way: given r, for each simulation we randomly choose r nodes as the set of nodes known to the attacker. We also assume that the attacker is rational and plays her best strategy M_a^*. At each interval, the attacker uniformly selects one node and attacks it. If this node belongs to any route that is currently being used by RRM, we mark the portion as compromised.

To approximate expected MPE with acceptable accuracy, we use the Monte Carlo method [14]. Suppose random variable Y_i denotes MPE of the ith simulation for $i = 1, \ldots, l$ as iid sequence of samples of MPE. Using the law of large numbers, the approximation of expected MPE is:

$$\widehat{E}(MPE) = \frac{1}{l} \sum_{i=1}^{l} Y_i$$

The estimated magnitude of error for $\widehat{E}(MPE)$ is of order $\sigma_{\widehat{MPE}}$. For each simulation scenario, the expected MPE is approximated by repeating the simulation until the error falls below the threshold.

Fig. 6 compares analytical and experimental MPE for random networks with $n = 1000$, $d = 5$ and $L = 5$. Note that analytical MPE serves as an upper bound for RRM effectiveness. Also note that expected MPE of the flow approaches 0 when node compromise probability approaches 1. This means that if an adversary is highly persistent and highly capable, RRM will lose its effectiveness.

Fig. 7 compares the experimental MPEs for various overlap constraints. Note that for $L_p = 0$, the experimental MPE is consistent with analytical MPE. Moreover, as L_p increases, MPE decreases significantly. This is because as the overlap between the routes increases, attack on a node has higher probability of compromising more than one route.

4.2   Overhead Evaluation and Limitations

Alg. 1 describes the general outline of the RRM controller algorithm. The complexity and computational overhead of each step is as follows:

- Optimal strategy selection: numerical calculation of pure Nash equilibrium requires at most $\theta(N^2)$ steps.
- Optimal route selection: Satisfiability problem is NP-complete in general. However, recent advances in SMT solvers have made them scalable to satisfiability problems with thousands of variables. Fig. 8 shows the time of SMT solving for optimal route mutation on a machine with Quad Core processor (3.3GHz, 6M cache) and 4 GB DDR3 RAM. We can see that the SMT solving time increases with the network size n, especially when the number of switches/routers in the network reaches 300. This is also because the number of possible routes increases exponentially with the size of the network. This has a negative effect on scalability of RRM. However, (1) RRM is used to protect the designated flows, and normal traffic is routed via conventional protocols, and (2) instead of using one centralized controller, the RRM responsibilities can be distributed among several cooperating controllers.
- Route mutation planning: the *RouteChange* algorithm installs a new route in $O(n)$. The upper bound for the number of routing table updates is $O(M_d^*L)$. However, the accurate number of updates depends on the average route lengths and the average number of overlaps between routes. Fig. 9 shows the average length of the route found by the SMT formalization for random networks with different sizes and different length upper bounds. We can see that the average route length of the RRM algorithm converges to some value with the increase of network size. Fig. 10 shows the experimentation results for the average number of routing table updates (flow entries in SDN) in networks with different number of mutation intervals and different overlap upper bounds. In this figure, $L = 6$. Note that (1) higher mutation speeds requires higher number of updates, (2) higher overlaps between routes reduces the number of updates, and (3) although the number of updates increases linearly with the network size, but since route lengths are upper bounded the linear line has a mild upward slope.

5   Related Works

Applying multipath routing in computer networks had been proposed as early as 1970s, but the original purpose is mainly for load balancing. The protocols such as Split Multiple Routing (SMR) [1], multipath DSR [3], AOMDV [8], and AODVM [18] try to find disjoint paths in routing. However, in practical networks, the number of disjoint paths is usually very small [18].

Other protocols try to improve security through multipath routing such as SPREAD [7], SRP [13], SecMR [9], DSM [6]. The route selection in these protocols is deterministic. This means if the attacker knows the algorithm, the routes can be predicted.

The multipath algorithm in [16] generates randomized multipath routes that are also highly dispersive and energy efficient in wireless sensor networks. The algorithm is also based on random walk and its variants and the generated multipath routes are highly resilient to black hole attacks.

Unlike previous approaches, our work provides an automated, nondeterministic, and optimal approach to route mutation problem by formalizing the strategy selection based on game-theoretic concepts, and formalizing route selection as a constraint satisfaction problem with various operational, QoS and security constraints. Moreover, in our approach the route selection is random and designed to counter persistent and informed adversaries.

6   Conclusion

In this paper, we present RRM as a proactive defense strategy against DoS attackers. To the best of our knowledge, RRM is the first proposed technique that offers an efficient practical random route mutation which considers flow, network and security constraints as well as attacker's capabilities and strategies. Our analysis and preliminary implementation show that RRM is feasible and flexible, guarantees end-to-end reachability and can decrease the percentage of disrupted packets to less than 10% of the case without RRM.

One drawback of RRM is its limited scalability due to the centralized control as well as the overhead raised from solving the SMT model for large networks. For future work, we plan to investigate how several controllers can interact to improve the scalability of RRM. Solutions include separating the route selection and the route planning, or dividing the network into several segments each managed by a separate controller.

References

1. Lee, S.-J., Gerla, M.: Split multipath routing with maximally disjoint paths in ad hoc networks. In: IEEE International Conference on Communications, ICC 2001, vol. 10, pp. 3201–3205 (2001)
2. Andersen, D., Balakrishnan, H., Kaashoek, F., Morris, R.: Resilient overlay networks. In: Proceedings of the Eighteenth ACM Symposium on Operating Systems Principles, SOSP 2001, pp. 131–145. ACM, New York (2001)

3. Johnson, D.B., Maltz, D.A., Broch, J.: DSR: the dynamic source routing proto-col for multihop wireless ad hoc networks. In: Ad Hoc Networking, pp. 139–172. Addison-Wesley, Boston (2001)
4. Keromytis, A.D., Misra, V., Rubenstein, D.: SOS: an architecture for mitigating ddos attacks. IEEE Journal on Selected Areas in Communications 22(1), 176–188 (2004)
5. Lantz, B., Heller, B., McKeown, N.: A network in a laptop: rapid prototyping for software-defined networks. In: Proceedings of the Ninth ACM SIGCOMM Work-shop on Hot Topics in Networks, Hotnets 2010, pp. 19:1–19:6. ACM, New York (2010)
6. Lee, P., Misra, V., Rubenstein, D.: Distributed algorithms for secure multi-path routing in attack-resistant networks. IEEE/ACM Transactions on Network-ing 15(6), 1490–1501 (2007)
7. Lou, W., Liu, W., Fang, Y.: SPREAD: enhancing data confidentiality in mobile ad hoc networks. In: IEEE INFOCOM, pp. 2404–2413 (2004)
8. Marina, M., Das, S.: On-demand multipath distance vector routing in ad hoc net-works. In: Proceedings of IEEE International Conference on Network Protocols, ICNP, pp. 14–23 (2001)
9. Mavropodi, R., Kotzanikolaou, P., Douligeris, C.: SecMR - a secure multipath routing protocol for ad hoc networks. Ad Hoc Networks 5(1), 87–99 (2007)
10. OpenFlow group at Stanford University: POX Wiki (2013), https://openflow.stanford.edu/display/ONL/POX+Wiki
11. McKeown, N., Anderson, T., Balakrishnan, H., Parulkar, G., Peterson, L., Rexford, J., Shenker, S., Turner, J.: Openflow: enabling innovation in campus networks. ACM SIGCOMM Computer Communication Review 38(2), 69–74 (2008)
12. Microsoft: Z3: An Efficient Theorem Prover (2012), http://research.microsoft.com/en-us/um/redmond/projects/z3/
13. Papadimitratos, P., Haas, Z.J.: Secure routing for mobile ad hoc networks. In: SCS Communication Networks and Distributed Systems Modeling and Simulation Conference, San Antonio, TX, USA, pp. 193–204 (2002)
14. Robert, C.P., Casella, G.: Monte Carlo Statistical Methods, 1st edn. Springer (1999)
15. Shamir, A.: How to share a secret. Commun. ACM 22(11), 612–613 (1979)
16. Shu, T., Krunz, M., Liu, S.: Secure data collection in wireless sensor networks using randomized dispersive routes. IEEE Transactions on Mobile Computing 9(7), 941–954 (2010)
17. Xia, L., Cui, Z., Lange, J.R., Tang, Y., Dinda, P.A., Bridges, P.G.: VNET/P: bridg-ing the cloud and high performance computing through fast overlay networking. In: Proceedings of the 21st international symposium on High-Performance Parallel and Distributed Computing, pp. 259–270. ACM Press, New York (2012)
18. Ye, Z., Krishnamurthy, S.V., Tripathi, S.K.: A framework for reliable routing in mobile ad hoc networks. In: IEEE INFOCOM, pp. 270–280 (2003)

Appendix: Table of Parameters

Table 1. Description of main parameters

B_f	capacity required by the flow
b_i^k	variable denoting whether node v_i belongs to the kth route
$C(v_i)$	capacity of the node i
f	flow
L	maximum route length
L_p	upper bound for number of overlapping nodes between the routes
M_a	attacker strategy: no. of attacker's mutations
M_d	defender strategy: no. of defender's mutations
N	average no. of routes between a given source and destination
n	no. of nodes in the network
r	no. of network nodes known to attacker
S	source or sender of the flow
D	destination or receiver of the flow
p_i	percentage of routes with length i
T_f	duration of the flow f
x	node compromise probability ($x = r/n$)
X	route compromise probability
z	ratio of attacker to defender mutations $z = \lceil M_a/M_d \rceil$
v_i	network node
u_a	attacker's payoff function
u_d	defender's payoff function
$\eta_{k,l}$	variable denoting number of shared nodes between kth and lth routes
$\mathbb{A}$	nodes that include access control devices
$\chi(v_i)$	the set of neighbors of node v_i
Π	the benefit function
Θ	the cost function

Plug-and-Play IP Security
Anonymity Infrastructure instead of PKI

Yossi Gilad and Amir Herzberg

Department of Computer Science, Bar Ilan University
mail@yossigilad.com, amir.herzberg@gmail.com

Abstract. We present the *Plug-and-Play IP Security (PnP-IPsec)* protocol. PnP-IPsec automatically establishes IPsec security associations between gateways, avoiding the need for manual administration and coordination between gateways, and the dependency on IPsec public key certificates - the two problems which are widely believed to have limited the use of IPsec mostly to intra-organization communication.

PnP-IPsec builds on *Self-validated Public Data Distribution (SvPDD)*, a protocol that we present to establish secure connections between remote peers/networks, without depending on pre-distributed keys or certification infrastructure. Instead, SvPDD uses available anonymous communication infrastructures such as Tor, which we show to allow detection of MitM attacker interfering with communication. SvPDD may also be used in other scenarios lacking secure public key distribution, such as the initial connection to an SSH server.

We provide an open-source implementation of PnP-IPsec and SvPDD, and show that the resulting system is practical and secure.

1 Introduction

Consider two Internet users, Alice and Bob. Alice wants to communicate securely, and possibly anonymously, with Bob. For anonymity, Alice may use an anonymity service, such as the *Tor* network of relays [5]. However, Alice also wants to encrypt her messages to Bob; how can she obtain securely Bob's public key?

The standard answer is that Alice will send a request to Bob and receive back his public key, certified by a trusted *Certificate Authority (CA)* [12], like in normal use of SSL/TLS, e.g., by browsers; if anonymity is desired, all communication would be via the anonymity service, e.g., Tor. However, this does not apply to the IP-security protocol (IPsec) [15], where traditional certificates are less appropriate, and which requires configuration (of security policies, network blocks, etc.). Furthermore, users may prefer complementary or alternative mechanisms to trusting a CA, e.g., due to several incidents where CAs authentication mechanisms were broken and false certificates were issued: CAs have been compromised, e.g., [4], and used insecure cryptographic primitives [22]. Can Alice securely receive Bob's public key, without depending on a trusted CA for authentication? Can she take advantage of IPsec, if supported by Bob?

J. Crampton, S. Jajodia, and K. Mayes (Eds.): ESORICS 2013, LNCS 8134, pp. 255–272, 2013.
© Springer-Verlag Berlin Heidelberg 2013

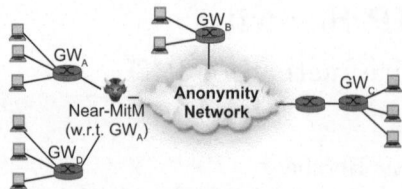 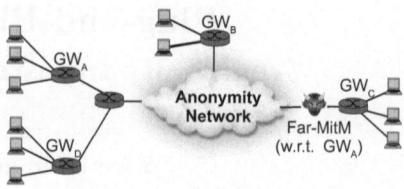

(a) Near-MitM Attacker. Communication between GW$_A$ and *all* other peers
routes via the attacker.

(b) Far-MitM Attacker. Only communication between GW$_A$ and GW$_C$ routes
via the attacker.

Fig. 1. Types of MitM attackers with respect to GW$_A$.

In this work we show that this is possible. We first present Self-validated
Public Data Distribution (SvPDD), which provides public key distribution using
an anonymity service, instead of relying on authentication and certification of
Bob by a trusted CA. SvPDD can use an existing anonymity service such as Tor,
the largest public anonymity network, as we do in our prototype implementation.

The basic idea of SvPDD is simple: Bob will periodically *self-validate* that
communication to and from himself is not tampered with, by sending *to himself*
anonymized requests for his public key, and validating that his responses arrive
correctly (with correct public key) and in timely fashion. Any tampering by
a MitM attacker with the response (public key) would be detected by Bob.
Similarly, Alice will use the anonymity network to send self-addressed 'requests';
a MitM trying to block Alice's communication will not be able to distinguish
between this 'self-test' communication and 'real' communication between Alice
and Bob, and hence Alice will detect any tampering.

SvPDD detects when a MitM attacker disrupts communication as well as
points-out the attacker's *location*. We classify MitM attackers with respect to a
particular party $\mathcal{P}$ to either of two types, illustrated in Figure 1:

Near-MitM who can manipulate communication between $\mathcal{P}$ and a significant
  portion the network. This attacker will usually be en-route between $\mathcal{P}$ to
  the anonymity network.
Far-MitM who can manipulate communication between $\mathcal{P}$ and few remote
  peers. This attacker will usually be 'near' with respect to those peers.

This property is significant; a system administrator cannot do much about a
'far' MitM attacker disrupting communication with some peer and may ignore
such warning, but an alert about a 'near' MitM attacker is likely to result in
immediate corrective actions (such as changing ISP or scanning for malware).

SvPDD seems especially beneficial to facilitate adoption and deployment of
IPsec, the standard protocol for cryptographically-protecting IP traffic. IPsec is
a mature, well-validated protocol providing strong security guarantees. In particular, IPsec provides defenses against Denial of Service (DoS) attacks, while
the main alternatives, SSL and TLS, run over TCP, and hence are vulnerable to
TCP's DoS attacks such as SYN flooding [6] and Ack-Storm [1] (although note

that IPsec should also be implemented correctly to avoid DoS vulnerabilities, see [11]). IPsec is implemented in most operating systems and in many devices (it is even part of IPv6 specification). However, actual use of IPsec is very limited; the main reason seems to be the difficulty in establishing IPsec connections, which normally require manual establishment of keys. SvPDD provides an alternative, allowing secure and completely-automated establishment of IPsec keys between peers, without requiring (rarely-available) IP-address based certificates.

There is another challenge to the deployment of IPsec: the need to coordinate its use among peers. Even if all IPsec peers had appropriate public-key certificates from a trusted CA, in order for IPsec to be deployed between two peers, each peer must be aware of the deployment at the other end, by an appropriate security-policy rule setup by the administrator. Coordination is even more challenging to support IPsec's *tunnel mode*, where an IPsec gateway machine protects an entire network; here, the security-policy rule must specify the network block(s) connected via the given peer (network gateway).

To completely address the IPsec deployment challenges, we present the *Plug-and-Play IP Security (PnP-IPsec)* protocol, built on top of SvPDD. PnP-IPsec automatically establishes IPsec security associations between networks (and/or hosts); see the layering of PnP-IPsec and SvPDD in Figure 2. PnP-IPsec adds two functions to SvPDD: (1) automated detection of remote peers, including handling of scenarios where there are multiple PnP-IPsec gateways en route to the destination; and (2) validation of the address block protected by the remote gateway. In order to establish a secure IPsec connection between two networks, all that is required is for each of the networks to independently run PnP-IPsec; all the rest is done automatically by PnP-IPsec.

1.1   Our Contribution

We present two protocols, SvPDD and PnP-IPsec. SvPDD uses an available anonymization service such as Tor to establish secure public keys between peers, without requiring off-path key distribution or certification authorities. This provides alternative means for validation of public keys, for protocols and systems where appropriate public-key certificates are unavailable.

PnP-IPsec, built on top of SvPDD, allows automated IPsec tunnel establishment, without requiring coordinated administration or key distribution infrastructure. PnP-IPsec automatically detects the existence of a remote PnP-IPsec gateway, obtains its public key and network block, and validates that the remote gateway indeed controls that network block.

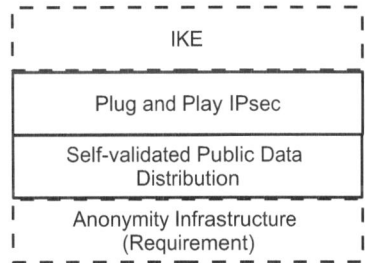

Fig. 2. The layering of our protocols (boxed with solid lines) and related protocols (boxed with dashed lines).

SvPDD and PnP-IPsec provide the following defense against MitM attackers:

- A far MitM attacker w.r.t. both peers cannot interfere with the protocol.
- A near-MitM with respect to one of the peers may interfere with the protocol, but in this case it will be detected by the administrator of that peer.

We provide an open-source implementation for our protocols (see Section 7) and hope that this will increase deployment of IPsec.

SvPDD is not limited to IPsec, and our implementation may be integrated into other protocols, such as SSH, in order to cope with a MitM attacker during the initial setup (when the user learns the server's unauthenticated public key), or even TLS/SSL, to provide additional means to obtain and validate the public key (protect users against CA authentication failures).

Lastly, this paper has the conceptual contribution of showing how anonymity infrastructure can be used in lieu of PKI, to establish security between arbitrary peers, without common administration, pre-shared keys or CAs.

1.2   Related Work

Ishai et al. [13] presented a theoretical study of how two parties may use a shared anonymous broadcast medium, to establish a shared secret key between them; the two parties work in coordinated manner, which in practice implies, they could have also established keys while coordinating, hence their work is not of much practical impact. However, their work does provide some of the concepts used and extended in our work, where we establish keys between arbitrary parties, without assuming any coordination between them in advance. Hence, our work extends their conceptual contribution, and shows that the basic idea of using anonymity to establish security can also have practical implications.

There have been multiple efforts to simplify deployment of cryptographic protocols by automating their setup, without certification authorities or coordinated management; we discuss these efforts below.

Several protocols, such as SSH [26] and BTNS [23,25], are based on the *Leap of Faith (LoF)* approach (also called 'Trust On First Use'). In LoF, public keys are exchanged without any validation during the first connection, and later used (assuming the initially-exchanged public keys were correct); SSH applications also display the public key to the users, allowing users to use off-path validation of the public key (but few do). LoF protocols assume a handicap of the MitM attacker, i.e., that he does not impersonate during the initial handshake; in contrast to these works, SvPDD and PnP-IPsec do not assume this limitation.

A notable effort for mitigating the need for coordinate deployment of IPsec is by the FreeS/WAN project [9], who attempted ([21]) to create an *opportunistic* version of IKE, as documented in [18,19]. The specification requires the network administrator to place a reverse DNS record mapping to the network's gateway and public key. The initiator retrieves the DNS record and uses the fetched configuration (gateway address and public key) to start the IKE negotiation. However, using [19] requires configuration of the reverse DNS tree, which is complex, and furthermore allows only one level of gateways - typically, by an ISP or a large organization; it does not allow multiple gateways, or protection of small networks and individual hosts (who do not control the reverse-DNS records).

Perspectives [24] and Convergence [16] are proposals for web-server public key validation mechanisms, to replace or complement the existing certificates (issued by CAs trusted by the browsers). Both rely on the use of a set of trusted 'notary' servers, which collect (and potentially cache) the public keys for the users. The idea is that a MitM near the client is not en route between most of the notaries and the server, allowing the client to learn the keys from the notaries (according to their majority). SvPDD performs a similar function to these proposals, with two advantages: (1) SvPDD does not require establishment and maintenance of a new infrastructure of notaries, and instead leverages an existing, general-purpose, anonymity infrastructure (Tor), which has many users and handles high traffic rates, compared to which the traffic generated by our protocols is negligible (see [17]); and (2) SvPDD provides better security to the users by not requiring them to trust new entities for authentication, and only to trust the anonymity network to anonymize their requests.

Double-Check [2] shows how one can validate self-signed certificates by accessing the server from various locations, suggesting Tor as an available proxy infrastructure. Double-Check helps against a MitM attacker that controls some of the routes to the server, but fails if attacker controls all (or most) of the routes *from the client* or *to the server*. In contrast, SvPDD utilizes anonymity, and suggests the concept of self-validation. SvPDD provides the same benefits as Double-Check, and in addition, using self-validation, SvPDD detects and provides a clear indication when an attacker controls all (or most) of the routes near the client or near the server.

PnP-IPsec shares some aspects with a previous work of ours, LOT [7], an opportunistic tunneling protocol for establishing credentials between two arbitrary networks in order to detect and block spoofed packets. However, there are substantial differences. First, LOT was designed to secure against off-path (non-eavesdropping) rather than MitM attackers. Second, LOT creates hop-by-hop tunnels, decapsulating and re-encapsulating information at every node on the path; this property is avoided in PnP-IPsec, which establishes gateway-to-gateway IPsec tunnels.

2   SvPDD: Model and Security Requirements

SvPDD runs on two peers, a querier and a responder, without coordinated management or common public key infrastructure. The basic goal is that the querier will learn the responder's response for his query; however, clearly if there is a MitM connecting one of the peers to the network, then the MitM can prevent satisfying this goal simply by blocking all communication between the peers. This section describes the model and security requirements of the SvPDD protocol.

Anonymity Infrastructure. We assume the availability of an anonymity network. Peers can send messages via the anonymity network, hiding the intended recipient; and receive messages from the network, while the sender remains hidden.

Furthermore, we assume that the querier has the public key of the anonymity network, i.e., can send authenticated and encrypted messages to it; this property holds for many anonymity networks, such as Tor [5] and Mix-Nets [20], where the client has a hard-coded copy of the network's public key.

Notice that while the querier sends and receives authenticated content from the anonymity network, he *does not* trust the network to authenticate other peers (in contrast to CAs in the public key infrastructure).

Attacker Model. We consider two types of MitM attackers, defined according to the near-MitM threshold, denoted by δ: a *near-MitM* attacker with respect to a peer $\mathcal{P}$ obtains a message that $\mathcal{P}$ sends or receives from the anonymity network with probability greater than δ; otherwise, the attacker is considered a *far-MitM* with respect to $\mathcal{P}$. If attacker $\mathcal{A}$ *obtains* a message, then he can block it or modify its content (MitM capabilities). We assume that the attacker is either near the querier or responder (but not both), or far with respect to both peers.

Based on the analysis that we present in Section 4, we require that $0 < \delta \leq \frac{1}{8}$; the exact value of δ is a local configuration provided by the system administrator, who essentially sets the threshold for a MitM-alert: the lower that δ is, the more attackers will be classified as 'near-MitM' (in our implementation the default configuration is $\delta = \frac{1}{10}$).

Communication Model. When a peer $\mathcal{P}$ *sends* a message to the anonymity network: if the MitM attacker $\mathcal{A}$ is near $\mathcal{P}$ then he obtains the message, as well as the identity of the sender; otherwise, $\mathcal{A}$ obtains the message and sender's identity with probability δ.

Similarly, when a peer $\mathcal{P}$ *receives* a message from the anonymity network: if $\mathcal{A}$ is near $\mathcal{P}$, then he obtains the message as well as the identity of the recipient; otherwise, $\mathcal{A}$ obtains the message and identity of the recipient with probability δ.

Notice that our communication model is the 'worst-case' scenario, where a near-MitM obtains a message from or to $\mathcal{P}$ with probability 1 (i.e., obtains all such messages), and a far-MitM obtains such a message with probability δ.

Security Requirements. A public data distribution protocol with security parameter n is secure if the following properties hold, except with negligible probability in n:

No False Alert: if $\mathcal{A}$ is far with respect to $\mathcal{P}$, then $\mathcal{P}$ does not alert for MitM.
Authenticity: if neither peer alerts for MitM, then the querier learns the correct response for his query, exactly as sent by the responder.

From these properties follows the *availability* property: if $\mathcal{A}$ is far with respect to both peers, then the querier learns the correct response for his query.

3   SvPDD: Protocol

In this section we present Self-validated Public Data Distribution (SvPDD), a protocol that allows a querier to retrieve and validate content from a responder and satisfies the security requirements in Section 2.

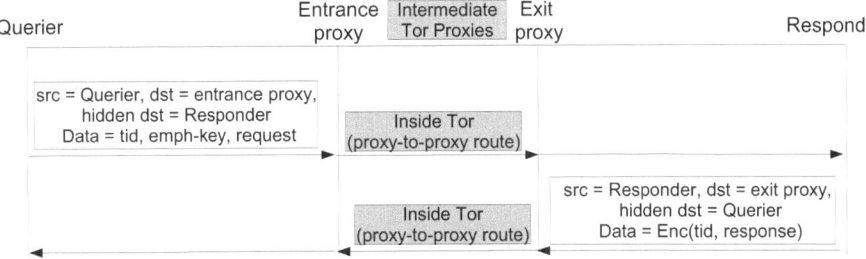

Fig. 3. A Query-Response Transaction over the Tor Anonymity Network.

3.1   The Query-Response Transaction

In an SvPDD *transaction* the querier sends a query for which the responder sends a response, both messages are transmitted via the anonymity network; see illustration in Figure 3. Each transaction belongs to one of two classes:

Peer-to-Peer (p2p). The querier attempts to learn the responder's response.
Self. A 'dummy' transaction, the peer is both the querier and the responder.

Each transaction has a random identifier, denoted by *tid*, which is chosen by the querier and attached to the transaction messages. We refer to a message that belongs to a p2p/self-transaction as a p2p/self-message (respectively).

A peer *can validate* that self-transaction messages were not modified or blocked by a MitM since the peer is both the sender and recipient of messages: he knows 'what he sends' and compares it with 'what he receives'. In order to keep track of self transactions, each peer keeps a global *self-table* that maps the identifiers of self-transactions to their corresponding messages as sent and received (to allow validation), as well as each message's transmission time.

Message Indistinguishability. An important property of SvPDD messages is that two messages of the same type (query or response), but of different classes (p2p and self), are *indistinguishable*. Namely, a MitM attacker who observes the message (that routes via the anonymity network) usually cannot learn the identities of both the sender and recipient, and detect whether they are different (a p2p-message) or the same (a self-message).

The following describes the content of query and response messages:

Query Message. The querier initiates the transaction by sending a query message to the responder. The message specifies a random ephemeral public key that the querier generates[1] and the request from the responder (see Figure 3).

In our model (described in Section 2), the querier has the public key of the anonymity network, and therefore queries are authenticated and encrypted until they leave the anonymity network (to reach their destination). However, a MitM

---

[1] The ElGamal encryption scheme, for example, allows to efficiently generate private and public key-pairs.

near the responder can observe the clear-text query; in order to satisfy the desired message indistinguishability property, we require that the query is either constant (e.g., all SSH clients specify the same query, for the server's public key) or chosen according to a *fixed* distribution that is independent of the querier's identity or message history.

Response Message. When a responder receives a query message, he replies with a response message. The response specifies the requested data encrypted with the querier's ephemeral key (see Figure 3). Note that we rely on the indistinguishability property of the (probabilistic) encryption scheme [10], hence, a MitM attacker who observes the response cannot learn according to its content whether it is a response for a self or p2p query (unless the MitM modifies the encryption key in the query, risking that the query was 'self').

Transaction Completion. A transaction is *complete* if one of the following conditions is true: either (1) a response was received in context of this transaction, or (2) the query is stale (decided according to its transmission time). In the latter case, we say that the transaction is expired.

3.2   The Query-Response Session

In order to retrieve data from the responder, the querier starts an SvPDD-*session* which is composed of n p2p-transactions (where n is a security parameter). In each transaction in the session, the querier sends the same request (but with a different transaction identifier and ephemeral public key) to the responder. The querier saves a per-session *p2p-table* which maps the transaction identifier (*tid*) to the corresponding query and response (if received).

The querier and responder perform self-transactions in the background, in parallel to ongoing query-response sessions (see details in Section 3.3).

Message Validation. When a peer receives a message, it first checks whether its *tid* field indicates a self-transaction; if yes, then the message is assigned the class 'self' and otherwise the class 'p2p'. The validation process is different for each message class.

If the received message (query or response) is a self-message, then the peer validates that the message was not modified while it was in-transit. If the self-message was modified, then its transaction is marked as 'failed'.

In contrast to self-messages, the recipient peer cannot validate the content of p2p-messages. The recipient only validates, in case of a p2p-response, that it belongs to an uncompleted transaction in some session (otherwise the response is discarded).

MitM Detection. Each self-transaction is associated with a result that is either success or failure. The result of a self-transaction is failure if: (1) it expired (see 'transaction completion' in Section 3.1); or (2) the transaction was marked as 'failed' during the message validation process (above). When a self-transaction completes, its result is enqueued in a cyclic, n entry long, history queue (where n is the number of transactions in each session).

If there are at least $3\delta n$ 'failure' results in the party's history queue, where $0 < \delta \leq \frac{1}{8}$ is the near-MitM threshold (see Section 2), then SvPDD *alerts* the local administrator of a near-MitM.

Session Completion. An SvPDD-session completes when all its transactions have completed. The session is then associated with a success or failure result, depending on the responses that were received for the queries in its context: If more than $\frac{1}{2}n$ (i.e., a majority) transactions of that session received an identical response, then the session result is success and that response is returned. Otherwise, the session's result is failure and no response is returned.

Notice that the threshold for a near-MitM alert ($3\delta n$) is lower than that of completing a session in success ($\frac{1}{2}n > 3\delta n$, since $\delta \leq \frac{1}{8}$). In the following section we present a security analysis and show that this property ensures the desired security requirements, defined in Section 2.

3.3   Protocol Execution

In order to retrieve authenticated data from the responder, the querier starts an SvPDD-session. Additionally, SvPDD runs in the background, on both the querier and responder, and initiates self-transactions. SvPDD monitors the results of the n recent self-transactions, and alerts for a MitM in case that $3\delta n$ of them are assigned the 'failure' result.

Self-Transactions Instantiation. SvPDD approximates the rate of p2p-messages and sends self-messages at roughly the same rate. The reasoning is that if the peers send only few self-messages, then a MitM can change arbitrary messages, which are likely to be p2p; in contrast, if the peers send many self-messages, then SvPDD's overhead grows large.

A peer $\mathcal{P}$ instantiates approximately one self-transaction for every p2p-transaction. This is achieved by measuring $r(t)$, the number of new p2p-transactions that $\mathcal{P}$ participates-in during time period t (each period has the same length). During period $t + 1$, $\mathcal{P}$ instantiates $r(t) + c$ new self-transactions; where $c \geq 1$ is a constant value, such that even if the rate of new p2p-messages increases during period $t + 1$, it is still likely to be less than the number of new self-transactions.

3.4   Instantiation over Tor

One of the advantages of SvPDD is that suitable anonymity infrastructures are already available. In particular, it is possible to instantiate SvPDD over Tor [5], the largest publicly available and well-studied anonymity network. Using Tor, queries and responses route via a *Tor circuit*, which is a chain of proxies (chosen by the querier), see Figure 3. Each transaction is relayed over a different random

Tor circuit, such that transactions of the same session cannot be associated together by a MitM observer.

The querier (running the Tor-client software) has the public keys of the Tor proxies, which are used to authenticate and encrypt query messages until they leave the network to reach the responder. This satisfies our assumption on the anonymity network from Section 2.

In an online technical report [8] we describe the Tor network and SvPDD instantiation over it in greater detail.

4   SvPDD: Analysis

In this section we show that SvPDD satisfies the security requirements presented in Section 2.

No False Alert Requirement. A far MitM with respect to a peer $\mathcal{P}$ obtains a message (sent to or from $\mathcal{P}$) with probability δ. Since in every transaction there are two messages (request and response), the probability that the far MitM attacker obtains at least one message of a transaction is no more than 2δ (in this case the attacker can modify or block the message, i.e., corrupt the transaction).

Let the random variable η denote the number of self-transactions, out of the recent n self-transactions, where the far MitM obtains at least one message. The expected value of η is $E[\eta] \leq 2\delta n$. However, the attacker must modify or block at least $3\delta n$ messages of the n recent self-transactions in order to cause a false alert for near-MitM (see SvPDD definition in Section 3.2).

Hoeffding's inequality allows to bound the probability that $\eta \geq 3\delta n$; i.e., that η deviates from its expected value by at least δn, see Equation 1:

$$\Pr[\eta \geq 3\delta n] \leq e^{-2(\delta n)^2} \tag{1}$$

This bound shows that the probability that the far-MitM attacker succeeds in causing a false alert is a negligible function in n. In an online technical report [8] we further explain the mathematical analysis behind the result in Equation 1.

Authenticity Requirement. The SvPDD protocol sends roughly the same amount of self and p2p-messages. A message of one class is indistinguishable from that of the other; therefore, an attacker that modifies a protocol message, modifies with probability $\frac{1}{2}$ a p2p-message and with probability $\frac{1}{2}$ a self-message.

Assume that the total number of messages that near-MitM attacker modifies is *less than* $7\delta n$. Let ξ denote the number of p2p-messages that he modifies. Since each message that the attacker modifies has probability $\frac{1}{2}$ to be 'p2p', the expected value of ξ is $E[\xi] < \frac{7}{2}\delta n$. However, in order to provide a false response, the attacker must modify messages of more than $\frac{1}{2}n \geq 4\delta n$ p2p-transactions of a particular SvPDD-session (since $0 < \delta \leq \frac{1}{8}$).

Hoeffding's inequality allows to bound the probability that $\xi \geq 4\delta n$ (and therefore, bound the probability that $\xi > \frac{1}{2}n$); i.e., that ξ deviates from its expected value by at least $\frac{1}{2}\delta n$, see Equation 2:

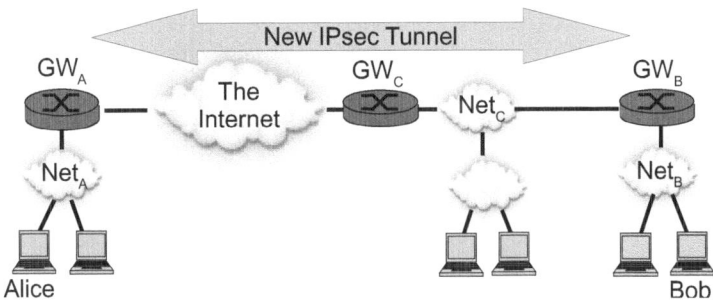

Fig. 4. PnP-IPsec Deployment Topology. Alice and Bob are communicating hosts; PnP-IPsec is deployed on GW_A and GW_B and establishes an IPsec tunnel between them.

$$\Pr\left[\xi \geq 4\delta n\right] \leq e^{-2(\frac{1}{2}\delta n)^2} = e^{-\frac{1}{2}(\delta n)^2} \tag{2}$$

Complementary, assume that the total number of messages that the near-MitM attacker modifies is *at least* $7\delta n$. Let ξ' denote the number of self-messages that he modifies. Since each message that the attacker modifies has probability $\frac{1}{2}$ to be 'self', the expected value of ξ' is $E\left[\xi'\right] \geq \frac{7}{2}\delta n$. However, in order to avoid a MitM alert, the attacker must modify less than $3\delta n$ self-messages.

Hoeffding's inequality allows to bound the probability that $\xi' < 3\delta n$; i.e., that ξ' deviates from its expected value by at least $\frac{1}{2}\delta n$, see Equation 3:

$$\Pr\left[\xi' < 3\delta n\right] \leq e^{-2(\frac{1}{2}\delta n)^2} = e^{-\frac{1}{2}(\delta n)^2} \tag{3}$$

The bounds in Equations 2 and 3 show that the probability that the attacker succeeds in violating the authenticity property is a negligible function in n. In an online technical report [8] we further explain the mathematical analysis behind the results in Equations 2 and 3.

5   Plug-and-Play IP Security

This section presents Plug-and-Play IP Security (PnP-IPsec), a protocol that establishes an IPsec tunnel [15] between two network gateways without coordinated administration and without relaying on a public key infrastructure.

Figure 4 illustrates a typical deployment topology for PnP-IPsec. The protocol's goal is that if there are two communicating hosts, Alice and Bob, behind two PnP-IPsec gateways, then the gateways will *automatically* establish an IPsec tunnel to secure all communication between their networks. In this section we assume that there are no intermediate PnP-IPsec gateways (such as GW_C in Figure 4), Section 6 extends the protocol to handle this scenario.

PnP-IPsec builds on SvPDD; namely, each gateway uses SvPDD to retrieve and validate the IPsec configuration from its peer. Figure 5 illustrates the three phases that compose PnP-IPsec, which we describe in the following three subsections. In the fourth subsection we describe the protocol's security properties.

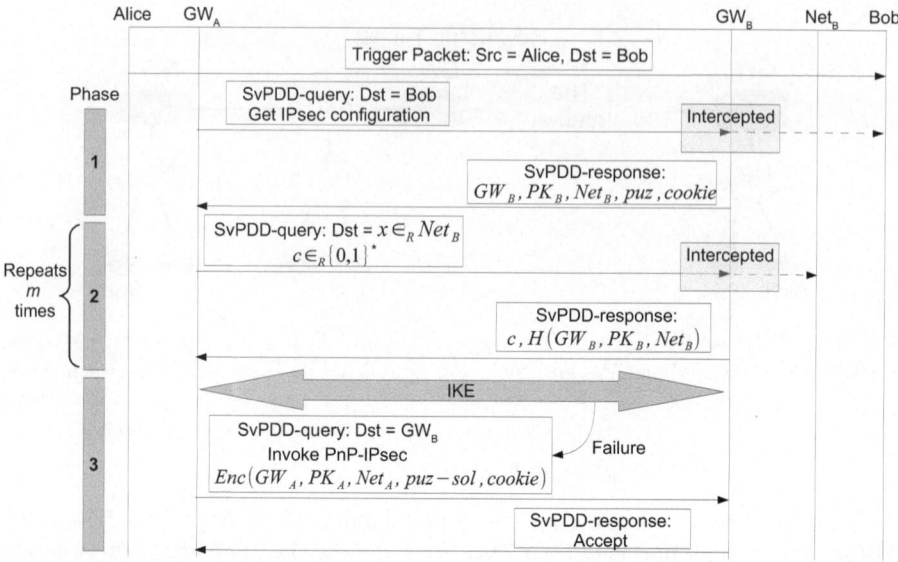

Fig. 5. PnP-IPsec Diagram. Dashed arrows mark destinations of intercepted packets.

5.1   Initiation Phase

PnP-IPsec is initiated by a gateway, GW_A, when it forwards a packet from Alice to Bob. This is the *trigger* packet illustrated in Figure 5. The initiation is probabilistic: a trigger packet initiates the handshake with a (configurable) probability $p > 0$; the lower p is, the lower PnP-IPsec overhead and the more time is required to establish a tunnel.

GW_A begins the PnP-IPsec handshake by initiating an SvPDD-session to retrieve the IPsec configuration of the gateway closest to Bob. The response configuration includes the following three elements, which in 'classic setup' of IPsec are manually configured by the network administrator at both gateways.

1. The gateway's (responder) IP address; which is the encapsulation end-point for tunneled traffic.
2. The gateway's public key; used to secure IPsec messages.
3. The network address block behind the gateway; traffic to this network block will be encapsulated.

Additionally, the response includes a client puzzle [3] and a cookie that allows the responder to re-generate the puzzle (without keeping state). The initiator solves this puzzle in order to request the responder to initiate a PnP-IPsec handshake in the opposite direction; as we describe in the last phase of the handshake. The use of a client-puzzle protects the responder from a denial of service (DoS) attack that persuades him to initiate PnP-IPsec handshakes with arbitrary peers (see security discussion in Subsection 5.4).

Since GW$_A$ does not know the address of Bob's gateway, SvPDD-queries (i.e., IPsec configuration requests) are sent to Bob's address. The queries traverse the route from the anonymity network to Bob, allowing Bob's gateway, GW$_B$, to intercept the queries and respond. See phase 1 in Figure 5.

The responder (GW$_B$) only handles the queries if it is unaware of another PnP-IPsec gateway 'behind it' that is also a gateway of Bob. The reason is that PnP-IPsec should establish IPsec tunnels between the closest gateways to Alice and Bob (the communicating hosts) in order to protect their communication from intermediate malicious nodes (MitM attackers). In Section 6 we show how gateways automatically learn which of their subnets have a 'closer' gateway.

5.2 Validation Phase

In this phase the initiator validates that the responder controls the claimed network address block (provided in the Initiation phase). This phase is similar to the network block validation process that we presented in [7], except that the messages here are sent over SvPDD in order to cope with a MitM attacker (see analysis in Section 5.4); we briefly present the network block validation protocol.

Network block validation is composed of m parallel SvPDD-sessions (m is a security parameter), where in each session the initiator (GW$_A$) picks a *random address* in the responder's (GW$_B$) claimed network block and sends a challenge to it (each session is associated with a different address). If GW$_B$ is indeed the gateway of that address, then it can intercept the challenge and respond; see phase 2 in Figure 5. If *all* challenges receive correct responses, then GW$_B$ is validated to control the network block that it claimed.

The following describes the challenge and response messages.

Challenge. The challenge is an SvPDD-query for a random string, denoted by c.

Response. The response is the tuple $< c, H(\mathsf{GW_B}, \mathsf{pk_B}, \mathsf{net_B}) >$, where c is an echo of the challenge and $< \mathsf{GW_B}, \mathsf{pk_B}, \mathsf{net_B} >$ is GW$_B$'s IPsec configuration; H is a cryptographic hash function.

When GW$_A$ receives the response (returned by SvPDD after a challenge-response session completes), it verifies that the value c is correct. GW$_A$ also verifies that the hash value matches that of GW$_B$, pk$_B$ and net$_B$ which were received in the Initiation phase, in order to ensure that the responder does not change.

5.3 Invocation Phase

In the last phase, GW$_A$ invokes IKE [14] and attempts to bootstrap IPsec (phase 3 in Figure 5), using the remote configuration $< \mathsf{GW_B}, \mathsf{pk_B}, \mathsf{net_B} >$.

If GW$_B$ has the corresponding configuration of GW$_A$ ($< \mathsf{GW_A}, \mathsf{pk_A}, \mathsf{net_A} >$), then IKE will establish an IPsec tunnel between the two gateways[2]. Otherwise, IKE aborts; in this case, GW$_A$ requests GW$_B$ to initiate a PnP-IPsec handshake

---

[2] Since the gateways run PnP-IPsec without coordination, it is likely that GW$_B$ had already received GW$_A$'s public IPsec configuration.

in the opposite direction (see Figure 5). The request is an SvPDD-query which specifies GW_A's public IPsec configuration configuration, $< GW_A, pk_A, net_A >$, as well as the solution to the client puzzle (i.e., proof of work) and cookie that GW_B sent in the Initiation phase. This request is encrypted using GW_B's public key; therefore, it does not leak the identity of the initiator (GW_A), which is required in order to anonymize queries and use SvPDD (see Section 3.1).

When GW_B receives this request, it re-generates the puzzle using the cookie and verifies the solution of the puzzle. If the solution is correct, then GW_B may accept the request, if it is interested in setting up a tunnel with GW_A (e.g., this may depend on the Initiator's network, net_A); otherwise GW_B rejects the request. If GW_B accepts, then it continues to the handshake's Validation phase.

In the Invocation phase of this second handshake both gateways will have each other's configurations (IKE can bootstrap IPsec). However, if IKE initiation does not succeed (on the second time), then a MitM is assumed to block IKE (preventing establishment of IPsec), and the gateways block the (clear-text) traffic between their networks.

5.4   Security Discussion

In this subsection we motivate the security properties of PnP-IPsec.

Discovery: PnP-IPsec gateways of communicating hosts quickly detect each other.

Assume that Alice sends packets to Bob. For every such packet, the probability that GW_A (Alice's gateway) initiates the PnP-IPsec handshake is p; namely, the probability that the handshake *does not initiate* after k packets is $(1 - p)^k$, i.e., exponentially decreasing (since $p > 0$). When GW_A completes the PnP-IPsec handshake, i.e., retrieves and validates GW_B's public IPsec configuration, it triggers the handshake in the opposite direction. Namely, only a few packets travel between Alice and Bob before the gateways discover each other.

Authentication: a PnP-IPsec gateway learns the IPsec configuration from the correct responder, rather than a MitM attacker.

This property of PnP-IPsec follows from the authenticity property of SvPDD, since the configuration is obtained over an SvPDD-session (in the Initiation phase).

Correctness: a gateway only learns a correct configuration from its peer.

The gateway learns the configuration from the correct peer (the authenticity property). It is left to show that this configuration is also correct; namely, that a malicious responder cannot persuade the initiator that it controls a false network block. We now motivate why such malicious responder will not pass the Validation phase, i.e., the responder will not be able to provide a correct response for at least one challenge; we refer to [7] for further details.

Assume that the responder controls net_1, but advertises $net_2 \neq net_1$; namely, $\frac{|net_1 \cap net_2|}{|net_2|} = \alpha < 1$. The probability that the responder receives all challenges is α^{-m}, where m is the number of challenge-response sessions (and number of different challenge destination addresses); i.e., the probability that a gateway does not control the entire network block that it claims, but passes the Validation phase, is negligible in m. In practice the ratio is often $\alpha \ll 1$, because ISPs use CIDR address allocation; we refer to [7] for further analysis of the network block validation technique.

Resilience to DoS: PnP-IPsec does not open a new denial of service attack vector on the responder.

We show that: first, PnP-IPsec has low communication and computational requirements from the responder; and second, the responder does not keep any state during the handshake.

First, in terms of communication load, the responder only sends one message (response) for every message (query) that the initiator sends. In terms of computation, the responder generates a client puzzle in the Initiation phase, which is very efficient (client puzzles [3] are means to mitigate DoS attacks). An initiator can cause the responder to initiate a handshake, however this requires solving the responder's puzzle, which has significant computational overhead.

Second, in terms of memory, the responder does not keep state per-peer or between requests: (1) the responder provides its (single, global) public IPsec configuration during the Initiation phase; (2) the responder only requires the challenge-field specified in the challenge packet in order to generate the corresponding response during the Validation phase; (3) the responder re-generates, rather than saves, the client puzzle (using the cookie) when it receives a request to initiate a PnP-IPsec handshake in the Invocation phase.

6   Extending PnP-IPsec for Multiple Gateways

PnP-IPsec should establish an IPsec tunnel between the gateways that are 'closest' to the communicating hosts; these are GW_A and GW_B in the example network topology that is illustrated in Figure 4. However, an intermediate *non-malicious* gateway, such as GW_C, who is unaware of the existence of a gateway behind it (i.e., GW_B) may unintentionally 'hijack' the PnP-IPsec handshake by responding to the Initiation-phase message that GW_A sends to Bob (see Figure 5). This section describes the discovery process for lower-tier gateways, where GW_C learns that net_B is, in-fact, under control of GW_B[3].

6.1   Proactive Gateway Discovery

In order to detect higher-tier gateways, a PnP-IPsec gateway sends a discovery message to a random address outside of its network block. This message specifies a random identifier, the gateway's public key and its network block.

If a gateway, say GW_B (see Figure 4), connects to the Internet via another PnP-IPsec gateway, GW_C, then GW_C will intercept the discovery message and

---

[3] A malicious GW_C may not follow the protocol described in this section and hijack connections to net_B, in this case GW_B will identify GW_C as a near MitM (since PnP-IPsec builds over SvPDD).

initiate a network block validation process with GW_B. Network block validation is similar to that described in Section 5.2 except that it does not run over SvPDD; i.e., the challenges and responses are transmitted directly to their destinations (and not via the anonymity network). The reason that we do not employ SvPDD is that, in this case, protection against MitM attackers is not required: if there is a MitM attacker between GW_C and GW_B who hijacks the PnP-IPsec handshake, then he will be detected since PnP-IPsec runs over SvPDD (our goal in this section is only to detect intermediate non-malicious PnP-IPsec gateways).

If the network block validation completes successfully, then GW_C learns that net_B is in-fact under control of GW_B. In this case, GW_C will not respond to future PnP-IPsec messages sent to or from net_B (see network illustration in Figure 4), which will allow GW_A and GW_B to use PnP-IPsec and establish a tunnel.

Dynamic Network Topologies. New PnP-IPsec gateways can unexpectedly set-up while others can suddenly shut-down. Therefore, PnP-IPsec gateways periodically send discovery messages, in order to allow new higher-tier gateways to detect their presence (and network block ownership).

Additionally, gateways (such as GW_C in Figure 4) periodically send challenges to their subnets (such as net_B) that are marked as controlled by lower-tier gateways (i.e., GW_B) in order to ensure that the lower-tier gateways are still available and control their subnets.

Finally, when a PnP-IPsec gateway (such as GW_B) gracefully shuts down, it sends a prune message to its higher-tier gateway (GW_C) in order to revoke ownership over the subnet (net_B) immediately.

7   Implementation and Deployment

We implemented PnP-IPsec as well as the underlying SvPDD protocol, as an open-source application for Linux gateways; our implementation is available at http://pnpipsec.sourceforge.net/.

In order to deploy PnP-IPsec, the network administrator only needs to install our application on the local gateway and provide it with the gateway's private/public key pair (since the keys are not signed, e.g., by a CA, they may also be automatically generated at install time). PnP-IPsec learns the reminder of the local IPsec configuration, i.e., gateway's IP address and the network address block behind it, by reading the routing table. The configuration also includes the near-MitM threshold (δ), the probability to initiate a PnP-IPsec handshake (p), and security parameters (n, m), which have default values that may be modified by the administrator. The following is an example of a deployment command:

```
PnpIPsec.py private-key-file public-key-file
```

In terms of efficiency, our implementation establishes an IPsec tunnel between two gateways, whose networks communicate at the rate 1mbps, in approximately two minutes; each gateway sends less than 3MB of PnP-IPsec traffic. This measurement is by using the default parameters: $\delta = \frac{1}{10}, p = \frac{1}{100}, n = 40, m! = 20$.

8   Conclusions and Future Work

Our main conclusion from this work is that while 'conservative' key infrastructures such as key distribution centers and certification authorities may be inconvenient for deployment of some protocols, other infrastructures may be suitable. In particular, we showed how available anonymity networks can be utilized to allow convenient and secure deployment of IPsec.

We presented SvPDD, a query-response protocol that utilizes an anonymity infrastructure to cope with the man-in-the-middle threat model. We built PnP-IPsec over SvPDD, which allows automatic establishment of IPsec tunnels. We provided an open-source implementation of PnP-IPsec and hope that this work will increase the deployment of the IPsec defense.

Future Work. The model considered in this paper, of using an available anonymity infrastructure in order to authenticate public keys and data, is practical. It is therefore desirable to formally define this model which may benefit other scenarios and protocols.

Furthermore, we believe that our protocols could further be improved. In terms of efficiency, the use of anonymity networks to relay messages usually comes at the price of encapsulation overhead. Can we improve the performance of SvPDD without jeopardizing its security requirements? In terms of functionality, can we extend PnP-IPsec to support setup of multicast IPsec tunnels?

Acknowledgements. We would like to thank Adrian Perrig and the anonymous referees for their helpful comments and suggestions. This research was supported by grant 1354/11 from the Israeli Science Foundation (ISF), and a grant from the Ministry of Science and Technology, Israel.

References

1. Abramov, R., Herzberg, A.: TCP Ack Storm DoS Attacks. Computers & Security 33, 12–27 (2013)
2. Alicherry, M., Keromytis, A.D.: DoubleCheck: Multi-Path Verification against Man-in-the-Middle Attacks. In: ISCC, pp. 557–563. IEEE (2009)
3. Aura, T., Nikander, P., Leiwo, J.: DoS-Resistant Authentication with Client Puzzles. In: Christianson, B., Crispo, B., Malcolm, J.A., Roe, M. (eds.) Security Protocols. LNCS, vol. 2133, pp. 170–177. Springer, Heidelberg (2001)
4. Comodo^{TM}. Incident Report (March 2011), Published online
   http://www.comodo.com/Comodo-Fraud-Incident-2011-03-23.html
5. Dingledine, R., Mathewson, N., Syverson, P.F.: Tor: The Second-Generation Onion Router. In: USENIX Security Symposium, pp. 303–320. USENIX (2004)
6. Eddy, W.: TCP SYN Flooding Attacks and Common Mitigations. RFC 4987 (Informational) (August 2007)
7. Gilad, Y., Herzberg, A.: LOT: A Defense Against IP Spoofing and Flooding Attacks. ACM Transactions on Information and System Security 15(2), 6:1–6:30 (2012)

8. Gilad, Y., Herzberg, A.: Plug-and-Play IP Security: Anonymity Infrastructure Instead of PKI. Technical report, Bar Ilan University, Dept. of Computer Science, Network Security Lab, (June 2013), Published online http://eprint.iacr.org/2013/410

9. Gilmore, J.: FreeS/WAN, Published online www.freeswan.org

10. Goldwasser, S., Micali, S.: Probabilistic Encryption. Journal of Computer and System Sciences 28(2), 270–299 (1984)

11. Herzberg, A., Shulman, H.: Stealth DoS Attacks on Secure Channels. In: Proceedings of Network and Distributed Systems Security (NDSS). Internet Society (February 2010)

12. Housley, R., Ford, W., Polk, W., Solo, D.: Internet X.509 Public Key Infrastructure Certificate and CRL Profile. RFC 2459 (Proposed Standard) (January 1999); Obsoleted by RFC 3280

13. Ishai, Y., Kushilevitz, E., Ostrovsky, R., Sahai, A.: Cryptography from Anonymity. In: IEEE Symposium on Foundations of Computer Science, FOCS, pp. 239–248 (2006)

14. Kaufman, C., Hoffman, P., Nir, Y., Eronen, P.: Internet Key Exchange Protocol Version 2 (IKEv2). RFC 5996 (Proposed Standard) (September 2010); Updated by RFC 5998

15. Kent, S., Seo, K.: Security Architecture for the Internet Protocol. RFC 4301 (Proposed Standard) (December 2005); Updated by RFC 6040

16. Marlinspike, M.: Convergence (2011), Published online http://convergence.io

17. The Tor Project. Tor Metrics Portal (April 2013), Published online https://metrics.torproject.org/graphs.html

18. Richardson, M.: A Method for Storing IPsec Keying Material in DNS. RFC 4025 (Proposed Standard) (March 2005)

19. Richardson, M., Redelmeier, D.H.: Opportunistic Encryption using the Internet Key Exchange (IKE). RFC 4322 (Informational) (December 2005)

20. Sampigethaya, K., Poovendran, R.: A Survey on Mix Networks and Their Secure Applications. Proceedings of the IEEE 94(12), 2142–2181 (2006)

21. Schmeing, C.: FreeS/WAN Announcement (2004), Published online http://www.freeswan.org/ending_letter.html

22. Stevens, M., Sotirov, A., Appelbaum, J., Lenstra, A., Molnar, D., Osvik, D.A., de Weger, B.: Short Chosen-Prefix Collisions for MD5 and the Creation of a Rogue CA Certificate. In: Halevi, S. (ed.) CRYPTO 2009. LNCS, vol. 5677, pp. 55–69. Springer, Heidelberg (2009)

23. Touch, J., Black, D., Wang, Y.: Problem and Applicability Statement for Better-Than-Nothing Security (BTNS). RFC 5387 (Informational) (November 2008)

24. Wendlandt, D., Andersen, D.G., Perrig, A.: Perspectives: Improving SSH-style Host Authentication with Multi-Path Probing. In: Isaacs, R., Zhou, Y. (eds.) USENIX Annual Technical Conference, pp. 321–334. USENIX Association (2008)

25. Williams, N., Richardson, M.: Better-Than-Nothing Security: An Unauthenticated Mode of IPsec. RFC 5386 (Proposed Standard) (November 2008)

26. Ylonen, T., Lonvick, C.: The Secure Shell (SSH) Protocol Architecture. RFC 4251 (Proposed Standard) (January 2006)

Managing the Weakest Link

A Game-Theoretic Approach for the Mitigation of Insider Threats

Aron Laszka[1,2], Benjamin Johnson[1,3], Pascal Schöttle[1,4],
Jens Grossklags[1], and Rainer Böhme[4]

[1] College of Information Sciences and Technology,
Pennsylvania State University, USA
[2] Department of Networked Systems and Services,
Budapest University of Technology and Economics, Hungary
[3] Department of Mathematics, University of California, Berkeley, USA
[4] Department of Information Systems, University of Münster, Germany

Abstract. We introduce a two-player stochastic game for modeling secure team selection to add resilience against insider threats. A project manager, Alice, has a secret she wants to protect but must share with a team of individuals selected from within her organization; while an adversary, Eve, wants to learn this secret by bribing one potential team member. Eve does not know which individuals will be chosen by Alice, but both players have information about the bribeability of each potential team member. Specifically, the amount required to successfully bribe each such individual is given by a random variable with a known distribution but an unknown realization.

We characterize best-response strategies for both players, and give necessary conditions for determining the game's equilibria. We find that Alice's best strategy involves minimizing the information available to Eve about the team composition. In particular, she should select each potential team member with a non-zero probability, unless she has a perfectly secure strategy. In the special case where the bribeability of each employee is given by a uniformly-distributed random variable, the equilibria can be divided into two outcomes – either Alice is perfectly secure, or her protection is based only on the randomness of her selection.

Keywords: Insider Threats, Cyberespionage, Game Theory, Computer Security, Access Control.

1 Introduction

Providing effective access control in organizations has been refered to as the "traditional center of gravity of computer security" since it is a melting pot for human factors, systems engineering and formal computer science approaches [1]. Over the last decades, a large number of important contributions have been made to address various technical challenges to the problem of access control for important systems and sensitive data [18,19].

J. Crampton, S. Jajodia, and K. Mayes (Eds.): ESORICS 2013, LNCS 8134, pp. 273–290, 2013.

This body of research is motivated in equal parts by the threat of malicious attackers from the outside and potential abuse by legitimate system users. Anderson further distinguishes between those situations in which insiders exploit technical vulnerabilities of a system in opportunistic ways, and other situations in which employees abuse the trust placed in them [1]. In our work, we address the latter dimension of the problem space.

Data theft by trusted employees covers a significant share of insider attacks. For example, a CERT investigation of 23 attacks showed that "in 78% of the incidents, the insiders were authorized users with active computer accounts at the time of the incident. In 43% of the cases, the insider used his or her own username and password to carry out the incident" [16].

These attacks are occasionally attributed to disgruntled employees and are said to be primarily destructive in nature. However, the steady rise of cyber-espionage activities strongly motivates the threat scenario of employees stealing information for monetary rewards. A recent article summarized publicly-known United States legal data from the past four years and stated that "nearly 100 individual or corporate defendants have been charged by the Justice Department with stealing trade secrets or classified information" [10]. The article just considered theft benefiting one particular foreign nation. Therefore, it is reasonable to assume that the data merely represents the tip of the proverbial iceberg.

Turning a trusted employee into a spy provides a number of benefits for an outside attacker. First, a security compromise by an insider might not be discoverable in comparison to external network-based attacks that might leave traces identifiable for expert forensics teams. The result is that a corporation cannot adequately plan and respond to evidence of a stolen trade secret. Second, an insider can point the attacker towards particularly valuable secrets by identifying the so-to-speak needle in the haystack. Given the accelerating data growth within corporations it makes sense to assume that attackers are also suffering from information overload as a result of their successful but unguided network penetrations. Third, an insider can help the attacker interpret the stolen data through complementary communications that do not have to take place at the work location. Lastly, having an insider conduct the attack might be the only feasibly way for an attacker to circumvent the defenses of particularly well-defended targets such as military and intelligence services, i.e., the attacker makes use of the human as the weakest link.

In this paper, we develop a formal model in which an attacker sidesteps technical security mechanisms by offering a bribe to one member of a project team who works with sensitive data or business secrets. By applying game-theoretic tools, we derive optimal strategies for the defender and attacker, respectively, and provide numerical results to illustrate and explain our findings.

With our work, we intend to start a discussion about considering the composition of project teams as a formal and critical dimension of a comprehensive corporate security policy.

The remainder of the paper is structured as follows: Section 2 provides the background for our research and considers related work. In Section 3, we define the basic properties of our model. The conditions for Nash equilibria are given in Section 4. Section 5 instantiates our model with explicit distributions, and numerical illustrations of the derived solutions are given in Section 6. We discuss our results and provide concluding remarks in Section 7.

2   Background and Related Work

2.1   Studies on Insider Threats and Cyber-espionage

Over the last several years, much research has been published in the area of insider threats, using different models and loss figures. For example, Carnegie Mellon University's CERT has published several reports concerning the field of insider threats, and industrial and economic espionage. Their 2011 report identifies two different models of espionage [13]. Motivating for our scenario is the so-called *Ambitious Leader Model*, where a leader (either from the inside or the outside of the organization), tries to convince (other) employees to follow her and to divulge secrets. In an earlier work, the institute identified several indicators that preceded either industrial espionage or sabotage, and thus could give hints if an employee might be vulnerable to being bribed [3]. In our research, we do not explicitly model behavioral and motivational factors that influence the trustworthiness of an employee. Instead, we assume that the defender has an indicator available to measure the *level of trustworthiness*.

The awareness of this threat is represented, for example, by a brochure published by the Federal Bureau of Investigation (FBI) [8], that lists:

> "A domestic or foreign business competitor or foreign government intent on illegally acquiring a company's proprietary information and trade secrets may wish to place a spy into a company in order to gain access to non-public information. *Alternatively, they may try to recruit an existing employee to do the same thing.*"

Additionally, the FBI "estimates that every year billions of U.S. dollars are lost to foreign and domestic competitors who deliberately target economic intelligence in flourishing U.S. industries and technologies [9]." The FBI further lists the following recommended activities for organizations: "Implement a proactive plan for safeguarding trade secrets, and confine intellectual knowledge on a need-to-know basis [9]."

Another example from Germany includes a 2012 report which identifies the loss for the German industry caused by industrial espionage to be around 4.2 billion € [6]. In this study, over 70% of these losses were caused by members of their own organization, through a combination of giving away intellectual property (47.8%) and failing to disclose their knowledge due to social factors (22.7%). Note that these numbers might be unreliable and interest-driven, as highlighted in [2].

2.2   Related Work

This paper touches several different research areas. The struggle between hiders of information and seekers of information is ubiquitous in the study of steganography, the field from which our idea originated [11]. This inspiration arose from exploring the plight of a steganographer who wishes to hide k bits in a binary cover sequence of length n, and a steganalyst who wishes to detect whether the sequence has been modified. That model differs significantly from our model here, as the authors assume an equal a priori probability of modified and unmodified sequences, and the function that measures the predictability of sequence positions is part of the model as a parameter.

Another area that is directly connected to the situation we model is the organization of firms under weak intellectual property rights. For example, in [17], the author considers a situation in which a monopolist may distribute intellectual property across two employees. There is also a competitor who might hire one of these two to gain access to the intellectual property. The author models this situation as a leader–follower game, and derives equilibria.

There are many additional research directions covering the subject of insider threats, including deterrence theory [7], game theory [12] and trust models [5], which are all tangent to our model. But, to the best of our knowledge, none of the published models gives directions for a project manager on how to staff a team, that has to know a specific intellectual property, while being aware that an attacker might try to bribe one of his personnel.

3   Model Definition

In this section, we describe a two-player, non-zero-sum, non-deterministic game which models the team composition scenario. First, we describe the general context and environment of the game. Next, we introduce the game's players. Then we define these players' pure strategies, and the payoffs resulting from these simple choices. Finally, we introduce notation to represent mixed strategies and express the players' expected payoffs in terms of this notation.

3.1   Environment

In our model, an organization with a secret of high value has N employees who are qualified to operate on projects that require knowing the secret. The organization must share the secret with at least k employees in order to operate. The employees have varying levels of trustworthiness. For a given employee i, this trustworthiness level is given by a random variable T_i whose distribution $\mathcal{T}_i$ is known. We explicitly disregard other constraints on team building and assume that all aspects of the trustworthiness of an employee can be captured by the random variable T_i. If $T_i = t_i$, then employee i will reveal her known secrets whenever she is bribed by an amount at least t_i, but she will not reveal the secret if she is bribed by an amount less than t_i. We use the standard notation

$$F_{T_i}(b) = \Pr[T_i \leq b] \tag{1}$$

to denote the probability that the trustworthiness level of employee i is at most b.

3.2 Players

The players in our game are Alice and Eve. Alice is an organization's project manager who is responsible for selecting a team of qualified employees to work on a confidential project. The project requires each team member to know a secret of the organization, and this secret has a value S. Alice needs to share this secret with k of her N qualified employees. Eve is a spy from either inside or outside of the organization. Eve wants to know the secret and has the resources to bribe or eavesdrop on one of Alice's employees. If Eve eavesdrops, the trustworthiness level of an employee can be interpreted as a measure of difficulty for Eve to eavesdrop on that employee. Note that Eve does not know which employees are on the team.

3.3 Strategy Sets

Alice's pure strategy choice is to select a subset of her N employees with whom to share the secret. Formally, she chooses a size-k subset I of $\{1, \ldots, N\}$.

Eve's pure strategy choice is to select one employee and an amount to bribe. Formally, she chooses a pair (i, b) consisting of an index $i \in \{1, \ldots, N\}$ and a bribe value $b \in \mathbb{R}_{\geq 0}$.

3.4 Payoffs

Suppose that Alice plays a pure strategy I, and Eve plays a pure strategy (i, b). If $i \in I$ and $T_i \leq b$, then Eve wins the value of the secret minus the amount of the bribe, and Alice loses the value of the secret. In all other cases, Eve loses the amount of the bribe, and Alice loses nothing.

Table 1. Payoffs for Alice and Eve for the strategy profile $I, (i, b)$

Strategy profile and outcome	Payoff for Alice	Eve
$i \in I$ and $T_i \leq b$	$-S$	$S - b$
$i \notin I$ or $T_i > b$	0	$-b$

3.5 Representation of Mixed Strategies

A mixed strategy is a distribution over pure strategies. For Alice, the canonical representation of her mixed strategy space is a finite probability distribution on the set of size-k subsets of $\{1, \ldots, N\}$. For Eve, the canonical representation of her mixed strategy space is a continuous probability distribution over the set $\{1, \ldots, N\} \times \mathbb{R}_{\geq 0}$. Because of the structure of the game, the payoff for both players is determined by simpler representations of the strategy spaces than the canonical ones, and we proceed to describe these representations next.

Mixed Strategy for Alice. In the canonical representation of Alice's mixed strategy, we would let a_I denote the probability that she recruits the members of the size-k set I into the project team. However, since Eve can bribe only one employee, the payoff for any mixed strategy depends only on the probabilities of sharing the secret with each employee. Since several different mixed strategies might induce the same projection onto employee probabilities, we gain simplicity by restricting our attention to these projections.

By overloading notation, for each $i = 1, \ldots, N$, we let a_i denote the probability that Alice shares the secret with employee i. Formally,

$$a_i = \sum_{I : i \in I} a_I. \tag{2}$$

The requirement that Alice has to share the secret with k employees induces the notational constraint

$$\sum_{i=1}^{N} a_i = k. \tag{3}$$

Furthermore, it can be shown easily that, for any sequence $\langle a_i \rangle$ of N probabilities whose sum is k, there exists a mixed strategy for Alice whose projection is $\langle a_i \rangle$. Consequently, we will represent Alice's mixed strategies by such sequences for the remainder of this paper.

Mixed Strategy for Eve. To represent Eve's mixed strategies, which are distributions over the set $\{1, \ldots, N\} \times \mathbb{R}_{\geq 0}$, we introduce two random variables, Y and B. Random variable Y takes values in $\{1, \ldots, N\}$, and it represents which employee Eve has chosen to bribe. Random variable B takes values in $\mathbb{R}_{\geq 0}$, and represents the amount of the bribe.

Overloading notation in a way that is similar to what we did for Alice, for each $i = 1, \ldots, N$, we define e_i to be the probability that Eve bribes employee i, so that we have

$$e_i = \Pr[Y = i]. \tag{4}$$

Since Eve always chooses exactly one employee, we have

$$\sum_{i=1}^{N} e_i = 1. \tag{5}$$

To describe a distribution over bribes, we sometimes use the notation

$$F_B(b) = \Pr[B \leq b], \tag{6}$$

which gives the probability that the value of the bribe chosen by Eve is at most b. It is also useful to describe the conditional distributions over bribes focused on a particular employee i. For each $i = 1, \ldots, N$, let B_i be the random variable whose range is the set of all possible bribes to player i, and whose distribution $\mathcal{B}_i$ is defined by

$$F_{B_i}(b) = \Pr[B_i \leq b] = \Pr[B \leq b | Y = i]. \tag{7}$$

In what follows, we will represent Eve's mixed strategies as pairs $(\langle e_i \rangle, \langle \mathcal{B}_i \rangle)$, where each e_i is the probability that Eve bribes the employee i, and each $\mathcal{B}_i$ is a distribution over bribe values, conditioned on the assumption that Eve chooses to bribe employee i.

3.6   Payoffs for Mixed Strategies

In order to use the simplified mixed-strategy representation defined above, we have to express the players' expected payoffs in terms of these representations. If Alice plays a mixed strategy represented by $\langle a_i \rangle$ and Eve plays a mixed strategy represented by $(\langle e_i \rangle, \langle \mathcal{B}_i \rangle)$, then the expected payoff for Alice is

$$-S \cdot \sum_{i=1}^{N} a_i \cdot e_i \cdot \Pr[T_i \leq B_i] \tag{8}$$

and the expected payoff for Eve is

$$S \cdot \sum_{i=1}^{N} (a_i \cdot e_i \cdot \Pr[T_i \leq B_i]) - \sum_{i=1}^{N} e_i \cdot E[B_i], \tag{9}$$

where $E[B_i]$ denotes the expected value of B_i under the distribution $\mathcal{B}_i$.

4   Analytical Results

Our goal in this section is to derive analytical results on the structure of the Nash equilibria of the game. We begin by characterizing Alice's and Eve's best-response strategies. Then, we use these characterizations to constrain Alice's and Eve's strategies in an equilibrium. Finally, based on these constraints, we formulate an algorithm for computing an equilibrium.

4.1   Best-Response Strategies

Alice's Best Response. For a fixed strategy of Eve, Alice's best response minimizes the probability of the secret being compromised. Since the probability of employee i being targeted and successfully bribed is $e_i \cdot \Pr[T_i < B_i]$, Alice has to choose a set I of k employees to minimize $\sum_{i \in I} e_i \cdot \Pr[T_i \leq B_i]$. However, as the set of k employees minimizing the probability of the secret being disclosed can be non-unique, Alice's best response can be a mixed strategy $\langle a_i \rangle$ whose support consists of more than k employees. This notion is formalized by the following lemma:

Lemma 1. *Given Eve's mixed strategy $(\langle e_i \rangle, \langle \mathcal{B}_i \rangle)$, Alice's best response can be characterized as follows:*

- *For any employee i, if there are at least $N - k$ employees whose probabilities of being targeted and successfully bribed are strictly greater than that of i, then $a_i = 1$.*

– *For any employee i, if there are at least k employees whose probabilities of being targeted and successfully bribed are strictly less than that of i, then $a_i = 0$.*

Proof. First, for any employee i, if there are at least $N - k$ employees whose probabilities of sharing the secret are strictly greater than that of i, then i is a member of every size-k subset of employees that minimizes the probability of the secret being disclosed. Thus, in any best response, Alice always shares the secret with this employee i.

Second, for any employee i, if there are at least k employees whose probabilities of sharing he secret are strictly less than that of i, then i cannot be a member of any k-subset that minimizes the probability of the secret being disclosed. Thus, i cannot be in the support of any mixed strategy that is a best response for Alice.   □

Eve's Best Response. Suppose that Alice is playing a mixed strategy where a_i is the probability that she shares the secret with employee i. We define $\mathrm{MaxUE}(\mathcal{T}_i, a_i)$ to be the maximum payoff that Eve can attain from targeting employee i. Formally,

$$\mathrm{MaxUE}(\mathcal{T}_i, a_i) = \max_{b \in \mathbb{R}_{\geq 0}} \left(a_i \cdot S \cdot \Pr[T_i \leq b] - b \right). \tag{10}$$

Lemma 2. *For any employee i and trustworthiness distribution $\mathcal{T}_i$, Eve's maximum payoff $\mathrm{MaxUE}(\mathcal{T}_i, a_i)$ as a function of Alice's secret-sharing probability a_i has the following properties:*

1. $\mathrm{MaxUE}(\mathcal{T}_i, 0) = 0$,
2. $\mathrm{MaxUE}(\mathcal{T}_i, x)$ is increasing in x,
3. $\mathrm{MaxUE}(\mathcal{T}_i, x)$ is uniformly continuous in x.

Proof.

1. First, it is clear that the maximum of $\max_{b \in \mathbb{R}_{\geq 0}}(-b)$ is attained at $b = 0$.
2. To show that the function is increasing in x, let $x, y \in [0, 1]$ with $x < y$. Let b_x be a bribe value at which the maximum payoff is attained for secret-sharing probability x, that is, $\mathrm{MaxUE}(\mathcal{T}_i, x) = x \cdot S \cdot \Pr[T_i \leq b_x] - b_x$. Then, we have

$$\mathrm{MaxUE}(\mathcal{T}_i, y) \geq y \cdot S \cdot \Pr[T_i \leq b_x] - b_x$$
$$\geq x \cdot S \cdot \Pr[T_i \leq b_x] - b_x$$
$$= \mathrm{MaxUE}(\mathcal{T}_i, x).$$

3. Finally, to show uniform continuity, let $x, y \in [0, 1]$ with $x < y$, and let b_y be a bribe value at which the maximum payoff is attained for secret-sharing probability y, that is, $\mathrm{MaxUE}(\mathcal{T}_i, y) = y \cdot S \cdot \Pr[T_i \leq b_y] - b_y$. Using the previous result that $\mathrm{MaxUE}(\mathcal{T}_i, y)$ is increasing, we have

$$0 < \mathrm{MaxUE}(\mathcal{T}_i, y) - \mathrm{MaxUE}(\mathcal{T}_i, x)$$
$$\leq (y \cdot S \cdot \Pr[T_i \leq b_y] - b_y) - (x \cdot S \cdot \Pr[T_i \leq b_y] - b_y)$$
$$= (y - x) \cdot S \cdot \Pr[T_i \leq b_y]$$
$$\leq (y - x) \cdot S.$$

So $\mathrm{MaxUE}(\mathcal{T}_i, x)$ satisfies a Lipschitz condition in the variable x with Lipschitz constant S; and hence, it is uniformly continuous. $\square$

For a given employee, it is possible for more than one bribe value to give Eve the maximal payoff. We define $\mathrm{ArgMaxBE}(\mathcal{T}_i, x)$ to be the set of bribes that give Eve her maximum payoff for employee i, which is a function of the employee's trustworthiness level distribution and the probability of receiving the secret from Alice. Formally,

$$\mathrm{ArgMaxBE}(\mathcal{T}_i, a_i) = \underset{b \in \mathbb{R}_{\geq 0}}{\mathrm{argmax}}\, (a_i \cdot S \cdot \Pr[T_i \leq b] - b). \tag{11}$$

Using this notation, we may define constraints on Eve's best response strategy as follows.

Lemma 3. *Given any strategy $\langle a_i \rangle$ for Alice, Eve's best response selects an employee i with the largest $\mathrm{MaxUE}(\mathcal{T}_i, a_i)$ over all $i \in \{1, \ldots, N\}$, and then chooses a bribe value b from $\mathrm{ArgMaxBE}(\mathcal{T}_i, a_i)$. If there are multiple pairs (i, b) satisfying these constraints, then Eve may choose any distribution whose support is a subset of these payoff-maximizing pure strategies.*

Proof. Follows readily from Equations (9), (10), and (11). $\square$

4.2   Nash Equilibria

Above, we introduced constraints on best-response strategies. In the following subsection, we introduce additional constraints on equilibrium strategies.

Alice's Strategy in an Equilibrium. It is generally in Alice's interest to minimize the maximum attainable payoff for Eve, as this generally (but, since the game is non-zero sum, not necessarily) minimizes her loss. We know that Eve's best response is always to choose an employee (or a set of employees) which will maximize $\mathrm{MaxUE}(\mathcal{T}_i, a_i)$ over i. Therefore, in an equilibrium, Alice's strategy should try to equalize these quantities, subject to the constraints that her sharing probabilities cannot exceed 1 and that they sum to k.

This notion is made formal in the following theorem:

Theorem 1. *In any Nash equilibrium,*

1. *if $a_i, a_j < 1$, then $\mathrm{MaxUE}(\mathcal{T}_i, a_i) = \mathrm{MaxUE}(\mathcal{T}_j, a_j)$, and*
2. *if $a_j < a_i = 1$, then $\mathrm{MaxUE}(\mathcal{T}_i, a_i) \leq \mathrm{MaxUE}(\mathcal{T}_j, a_j)$.*

Proof. Let $\langle a_i \rangle, (\langle e_i \rangle, \langle \mathcal{B}_i \rangle)$ be Alice's and Eve's mixed strategies and assume that this strategy profile is a Nash equilibrium.

1. For the sake of contradiction, suppose that $a_i, a_j < 1$ and it holds that $\mathrm{MaxUE}(\mathcal{T}_i, a_i) \neq \mathrm{MaxUE}(\mathcal{T}_j, a_j)$. We can assume without loss of generality that $\mathrm{MaxUE}(\mathcal{T}_i, a_i) < \mathrm{MaxUE}(\mathcal{T}_j, a_j)$. Then, $\mathrm{MaxUE}(\mathcal{T}_j, a_j) > 0$, which (from Lemma 2.1) implies that $a_j > 0$. From Lemma 3, we have that the support of Eve's best-response mixed strategy does not include i. Thus, Alice may strictly increase a_i towards 1, and strictly decrease every other non-zero component of her strategy for employees other than i, while still satisfying the constraint $\sum_m a_m = k$. By decreasing her secret-sharing probability on every employee that Eve might bribe, Alice necessarily decreases the total probability of Eve learning the secret. Therefore, Alice can improve her expected payoff by changing her strategy, which contradicts the equilibrium condition.
2. For the sake of contradiction, suppose that $a_j < a_i = 1$ and that $\mathrm{MaxUE}(\mathcal{T}_i, a_i) > \mathrm{MaxUE}(\mathcal{T}_j, a_j)$. Then, $\mathrm{MaxUE}(\mathcal{T}_i, a_i) > 0$, which (based on Lemma 2) implies that $a_i > 0$. Consequently, we have (from Lemma 3) that the support of Eve's mixed strategy does not include employee j. So Alice may simultaneously increase a_j towards 1 and decrease her non-zero secret-sharing probabilities for employees other than j, all while satisfying the constraint $\sum_m a_m = k$. Again, by decreasing her secret-sharing probability on every employee that Eve might bribe, Alice necessarily decreases the total probability of Eve learning the secret. Hence, this strategy change will increase her expected payoff, contradicting the equilibrium condition. □

It follows from Theorem 1 that Alice's equilibrium strategy $\langle a_i \rangle$ may have some employees with whom she shares the secret with certainty, but for all other employees, her secret-sharing distribution is only constrained by a smoothness constraint on the quantities $\mathrm{MaxUE}(\mathcal{T}_i, a_i)$. Furthermore, these quantities do not depend on Eve's strategy, a fact on which we will rely when computing an equilibrium.

From Theorem 1, we also have that:

Corollary 1. *In any Nash equilibrium,*

- *Alice is either secure, that is, Eve has no strategy against her with a positive payoff, or she shares the secret with every employee with a non-zero probability. Formally, either $\mathrm{MaxUE}(\mathcal{T}_i, a_i) = 0$ for every employee i, or $a_i > 0$ for every employee i.*
- *The employees with whom Alice shares the secret with certainty are at most as likely to be targeted by Eve as the other employees, with whom Alice is less likely to share the secret.*

It is interesting to compare the first point of the above corollary with Lemma 3. The former says that Alice shares the secret with every employee with a non-zero probability (when she cannot be secure), while Lemma 3 says that

Alice never shares the secret with an employee if there are at least k employees that have lower probabilities of being targeted and successfully bribed. Since an equilibrium strategy is necessarily a best response, it has to satisfy both constraints. This implies that, in an equilibrium, Eve equalizes the probability of targeting and successfully bribing over the set of employees that maximize her payoff.

Eve's Strategy in an Equilibrium. In this section, we build on the characterization of Alice's equilibrium strategies presented in Theorem 1 to characterize Eve's equilibrium strategies. In the previous paragraph, we discussed how Eve equalizes the probability of targeting and successfully bribing over the set of employees that maximize her payoff.

This notion is made formal in the following theorem:

Theorem 2. *In any Nash equilibrium, if $a_i, a_j < 1$, then $e_i \cdot \Pr[T_i \leq B_i] = e_j \cdot \Pr[T_j \leq B_j]$.*

Proof. Let $\langle a_i \rangle, (\langle e_i \rangle, \langle B_i \rangle)$ be Alice's and Eve's mixed strategies and assume that this strategy profile is a Nash equilibrium. For the sake of contradiction, suppose that $\langle e_i \cdot \Pr[T_i \leq B_i] \rangle$ is non-uniform over the set of employees with whom Alice does not always share the secret. Let I_{max} be the set of employees i for which $e_i \cdot \Pr[T_i \leq B_i]$ is maximal.

First, assume that $k \leq N - |I_{max}|$. Then, Alice's best response never shares the secret with the employees in I_{max}, that is, $a_i = 0$ for all $i \in I_{max}$, as there are k strictly better employees (as stated in Lemma 1). Consequently, we have $e_i = 0$ for every $i \in I_{max}$ as Eve' strategy also has to be a best response. But this implies that $e_i \cdot \Pr[T_i \leq B_i] = 0$ for every i such that $a_i < 1$, which contradicts that $\langle e_i \cdot \Pr[T_i \leq B_i] \rangle$ is non-uniform. Thus, it has to hold that $k > N - |I_{max}|$.

From $k > N - |I_{max}|$, we have that Alice's best response always shares the secret with every employee i for which $e_i \cdot \Pr[T_i \leq B_i]$ is not maximal (as stated in Lemma 1). Consequently, the only employees i for which $a_i < 1$ holds are the employees in I_{max}. But this contradicts that $\langle e_i \cdot \Pr[T_i \leq B_i] \rangle$ is non-uniform since all employees in I_{max} have the same maximal $e_i \cdot \Pr[T_i \leq B_i]$. □

Finding an Equilibrium Based on Theorems 1 and 2, we can formulate the following algorithm for finding an equilibrium of the game:

1. Find an equilibrium strategy $\langle a_i^* \rangle$ for Alice:
   We have to find an $\langle a_i^* \rangle$ that satisfies the constraints of Theorem 1. This can be done, for example, using any multidimensional numerical optimization method (e.g., the Nelder-Mead algorithm[15]) by using the sum of the amounts by which each constraining equality is violated as the objective function. Since we have from Lemma 2 that every MaxUE$(\mathcal{T}_i, a_i)$ is increasing and uniformly continuous in a_i, there always exists a solution $\langle a_i^* \rangle$ satisfying the constraints of Theorem 1. Note that, since MaxUE$(\mathcal{T}_i, a_i)$ is not strictly increasing, the solution might not be unique.

2. Find an equilibrium strategy $(\langle e_i^* \rangle, \langle \mathcal{B} \rangle)$ for Eve:
   We have to find $(\langle e_i^* \rangle, \langle \mathcal{B} \rangle)$ that satisfies both Lemma 3 and Theorem 2.
   Let $MaxUE^* = \max_i MaxUE(\mathcal{T}_i, a_i^*)$ and let I^* be the set of employees for
   whom the maximum is attained. If $MaxUE^* = 0$, then there is no strategy
   with positive payoff for Eve, so let $B_i^* \equiv 0$ for every i (and $\langle e^* \rangle$ can be
   arbitrary). Otherwise:
   (a) For every $i \notin I^*$, let $e_i^* = 0$.
   (b) For every $i \in I^*$, let B_i^* always take some arbitrary but fixed bribe value
       from $\text{ArgMaxBE}(\mathcal{T}_i, a_i^*)$, and let

$$e_i^* = \frac{\frac{1}{\Pr[T_i \leq B_i^*]}}{\sum_j \frac{1}{\Pr[T_j \leq B_j^*]}}. \tag{12}$$

It can be verified easily that $\langle a_i^* \rangle$ also satisfies Lemma 1. Thus, $\langle a_i^* \rangle$ and
$(\langle e_i^* \rangle, \langle \mathcal{B}_i \rangle)$ form an equilibrium.

5   Special Case: Uniform Distributions on Trustworthiness

In this section, we assume that the trustworthiness level of each employee i is
generated by a uniform random variable $T_i \sim \mathcal{U}(l_i, h_i)$, $0 < l_i < h_i < S$. In other
words, we assume that employee i never reveals the secret for a bribe less than
l_i, always reveals it for a bribe more than or equal to h_i, and the probability of
revealing it increases linearly between l_i and h_i. Note that we allow a different
distribution, i.e., different l_i and h_i, for each employee.

We begin our analysis by computing Eve's optimal bribe values for a given
mixed strategy $\langle a_i \rangle$ of Alice.

Lemma 4. *Eve's optimal bribe values are*

$$\text{ArgMaxBE}(\mathcal{T}_i, a_i) = \begin{cases} \{0\} & \text{if } a_i < \frac{h_i}{S} \\ \{0, h_i\} & \text{if } a_i = \frac{h_i}{S} \\ \{h_i\} & \text{otherwise.} \end{cases} \tag{13}$$

The proof is available in the online version on the authors' websites.

For uniform trustworthiness level distributions, the equilibria of the game can
be characterized as follows:

Theorem 3. *If the trustworthiness level of each employee is generated according
to a uniform distribution $\mathcal{U}(l_i, h_i)$, $0 < l_i < h_i < S$, the equilibria of the game
can be characterized as follows:*

- *If $k < \frac{\sum_i h_i}{S}$, then Alice is perfectly secure: in any equilibrium, $a_i \leq \frac{h_i}{S}$ for
  every i, Eve never bribes any of the employees, and both players' payoffs are
  zero.*
- *If $k = \frac{\sum_i h_i}{S}$, then in any equilibrium of the game, $a_i = \frac{h_i}{S}$ for every i, and
  Eve's payoff is zero.*

– If $k > \frac{\sum_i h_i}{S}$, then in any equilibrium of the game, $a_i > \frac{h_i}{S}$ and $B_i \equiv h_i$ for every i, and Eve's payoff is strictly positive while Alice's payoff is strictly negative.

Proof. Let $\langle a_i \rangle, (\langle e_i \rangle, \langle \mathcal{B}_i \rangle)$ be Alice's and Eve's mixed strategies and assume that this strategy profile is a Nash equilibrium. We prove each case separately:

– $k < \frac{\sum_i h_i}{S}$: For the sake of contradiction, suppose that $a_i > \frac{h_i}{S}$ for some i. Then, there has to be a j such that $a_j < \frac{h_i}{S}$, otherwise $\sum_i a_i = k < \frac{\sum_i h_i}{S}$ would not hold. Consequently, $\mathrm{MaxUE}(\mathcal{T}_i, a_i) > \mathrm{MaxUE}(\mathcal{T}_j, a_j)$ and, from Lemma 3, we have that $e_j = 0$. Furthermore, from Theorems 1 and 2, we also have that $e_i > 0$. Therefore, Alice can increase her payoff by decreasing a_i and increasing a_j, which contradicts the equilibrium condition. Thus, $a_i \leq \frac{h_i}{S}$ has to hold for every i.

Now, for the sake of contradiction, suppose that Eve targets and bribes employee i non-zero probability, that is, $e_i > 0$ and $B_i \not\equiv 0$. Since Eve's strategy has to be a best response, we have that $a_i \geq \frac{h_i}{S}$. Consequently, there has to exist some j satisfying $a_j < \frac{h_i}{S}$. From Lemma 3, we have that $e_j = 0$. Therefore, Alice can increase her payoff by decreasing a_i and increasing a_j, which contradicts the equilibrium condition. Thus, Eve never bribes any of the employees, and it follows immediately that both players' payoffs are zero.

– $k = \frac{\sum_i h_i}{S}$: For the sake of contradiction, suppose that $a_i > \frac{h_i}{S}$ for some i, which implies that there has to be a j such that $a_j < \frac{h_i}{S}$. Then, we can show that this leads to a contradiction using the same argument as in the first paragraph of the previous case. Thus, $a_i = \frac{h_i}{S}$ for every i. The rest follows readily from Lemma 4.

– $k > \frac{\sum_i h_i}{S}$: First, it is easy to see that, for any strategy $\langle a_i \rangle$, there has to be at least one i such that $a_i > \frac{h_i}{S}$, which implies $\mathrm{MaxUE}(\mathcal{T}_i, a_i) > 0$. By using the strategy $e_i = 1$ and some constant bribe value from $\mathrm{ArgMaxBE}(\mathcal{T}_i, a_i)$, Eve can achieve a positive payoff. Consequently, for every strategy $\langle a_i \rangle$, Eve's best response payoff has to be strictly positive. It follows immediately that, in any equilibrium, Eve's payoff is strictly positive while Alice's payoff is strictly negative.

Now, for the sake of contradiction, assume that $a_i \leq \frac{h_i}{S}$ for some i, which implies $\mathrm{MaxUE}(\mathcal{T}_i, a_i) = 0$. Then, we have that $e_i = 0$ from Lemma 3. Therefore, Alice can increase her payoff (i.e., decrease her loss) by increasing a_i and decreasing every non-zero component of her strategy, which contradicts the equilibrium condition. Thus, $a_i > \frac{h_i}{S}$ has to hold for every i.

Second, assume indirectly that, for some $\langle a_i \rangle$ and e that form an equilibrium and some i, $a_i < \frac{h_i}{S}$. If $e_i = 0$, then Alice would be able to increase her payoff (i.e., decrease her loss) by simultaneously increasing a_i and decreasing some $a_j > \frac{h_j}{S}$, which would contradict the assumption that $\langle a_i \rangle$ and e form an equilibrium. On the other hand, if $e_i > 0$, then Eve would be able to increase her payoff by simultaneously decreasing e_i and increasing e_j where j is such that $a_j > \frac{h_j}{S}$, which would also lead to a contradiction. Therefore, we have that $a_i \geq \frac{h_i}{S}$ for every i in any equilibrium. Finally, $B_i \equiv h_i$ follows readily from Lemma 4. $\qquad\square$

6 Numerical Illustrations

In this section, we provide numerical illustrations for the results derived in the previous section. Thus, throughout this section, we model the trustworthiness levels of the employees as independent uniform random variables T_i with parameters l_i and h_i.

Figure 1 shows both players' equilibrium payoffs as functions of the number of employees k that have to know the secret. First, when k is less than $\frac{\sum_i h_i}{S}$, Alice can choose a secure strategy such that bribing is infeasible for Eve. Thus, both players' payoffs are zero. Second, when k is larger than $\frac{\sum_i h_i}{S}$, but it is low enough such that $a_i < 1$ for each employee i, Alice distributes $k - \frac{\sum_i h_i}{S}$ evenly among the employees' probabilities. Thus, the probability of compromise and, hence, Alice's loss and Eve's payoff increase linearly with k. It is interesting to note that, while Eve's payoff is a continuous function of k, there is a big drop in Alice's payoff at the point where she can no longer play a secure strategy. This phenomena is caused by the non-zero sum property of our game. Finally, when k is large enough such that Alice assigns probability 1 to some employees, Eve's payoff increases super-linearly, while Alice's loss increases non-monotonically. Although Alice's non-monotonically increasing loss might seem surprising at first, it can be explained easily: as the secret is shared with more and more employees who are more easily bribed (i.e., have lower h_i), Eve can decrease her bribing costs by targeting these employees. This might decrease her success probability, but only by a value that is less than the decrease in her bribing

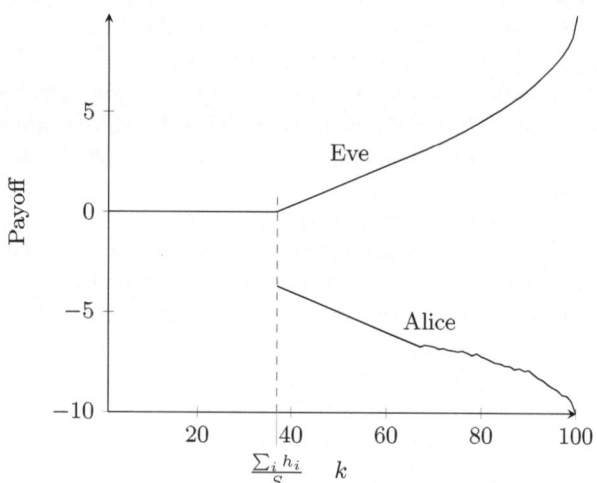

Fig. 1. The players' equilibrium payoffs as functions of the number of employees k that have to know the secret. The total number of employees is $N = 100$, the value of the secret is assumed to be $S = 10$, and the trustworthiness level of each employee i is assumed to be a random variable of the distribution $\mathcal{U}(l_i, h_i)$. For this example, each h_i is drawn from the set $(0, 7)$ uniformly at random.

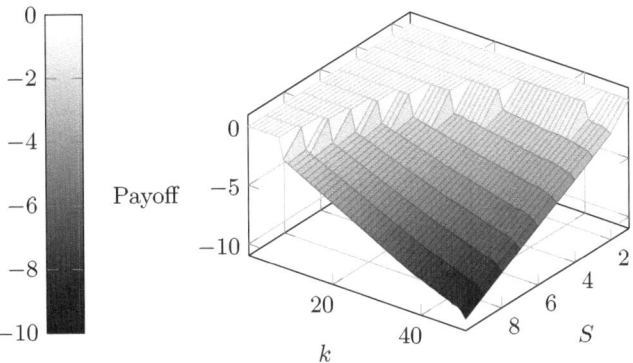

Fig. 2. Alice's equilibrium payoff for all combinations of $1 \leq k \leq 50$ and $1 \leq S \leq 10$. The parameters for this figure were generated in the same way as for Figure 1, but with $N = 50$.

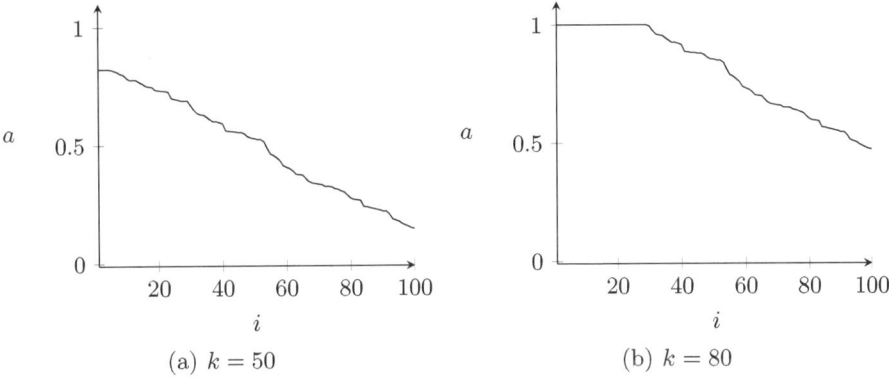

(a) $k = 50$ (b) $k = 80$

Fig. 3. Alice's equilibrium strategies for (a) $k = 50$ and (b) 80. The total number of employees is 100, the value of the secret is assumed to be $S = 10$, the trustworthiness level of each employee i is assumed to be a random variable of the distribution $\mathcal{U}(l_i, h_i)$, and the employees are sorted in decreasing order based on their h_i values. For this example, each h_i is drawn from the set $(0, 7)$ uniformly at random.

costs. Consequently, sometimes Alice is better off if she shares the secret with more employees than she has to.

Figure 2 shows Alice's payoff (darker values indicate a higher loss) for a wide spectrum of parameter combinations of k and S. The figure clearly shows that, for lower values of S, the area where Alice can play a secure strategy (white plain) is greater than the area for higher values of S. Note that, for most values of S, we can identify the same three regions for k as in the previous figure: for $k < \frac{\sum_i h_i}{S}$, Alice's loss is zero; for $k > \frac{\sum_i h_i}{S}$, Alice's loss first increases linearly with k, but for larger values of k, Alice's loss increases non-monotonically.

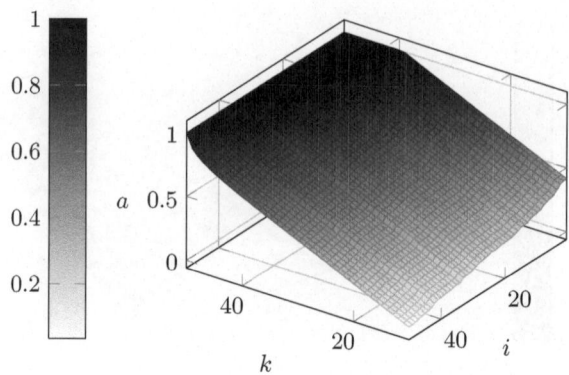

Fig. 4. Alice's equilibrium strategies for $\frac{\sum_i h_i}{S} < k \leq 50$. The parameters for this figure were generated in the same way as for Figure 3, but with $N = 50$. Again, the employees are sorted in decreasing order based on their h_i values.

As expected, the worst case for Alice is when the number of employees k that have to know the secret is large and the value S of the secret is high.

Figure 3 shows Alice's equilibrium strategies for two different values of k. Figure 3(a) shows a case where k is small enough such that Alice does not assign probability 1 to any of her employees, while Figure 3(b) depicts a case where several employees get to know the secret with certainty. Figure 4 shows her equilibrium strategies for $N = 50$ and $\frac{\sum_i h_i}{S} \leq k \leq 50$. The figure clearly shows that, for all values of k, a_i is a monotonically increasing function of h_i, which can be explained by Theorem 1. Furthermore, the figure also confirms our analytical result that no a_i can be 0.

7   Discussion and Concluding Remarks

In this paper, we introduce a game-theoretic model for studying the decision making of a project manager who wants to maximize the security of an organization's intellectual property. Motivated in part by known behavioral methods of assessing trustworthiness [14], we assume that both the project manager and her adversary know the distribution of a random variable representing the trustworthiness of each employee. Finally, we assume that both players are able to estimate the value of the organization's intellectual property [4].

As a result of our analysis, we find that a project manager should select every employee with a non-zero probability, unless there is a secure strategy, where an adversary has no incentives to attack at all. This contradicts the naïve assumption that, to achieve maximal security, only the most trustworthy employees should be selected. The explanation for this is the following: selecting the team members deterministically always gives the adversary the knowledge of which employees to target for bribing. So, by randomizing her strategy, the project manager minimizes the information available to the adversary for planning her attack. It is an even more surprising result that, in an equilibrium, the adversary is at most as likely to target employees that certainly know the secret as those employees that know the secret with a probability less than 1. Again, this contradicts the naïve assumption that an adversary will try to bribe the employees that are the most likely to know the secret.

For the special case of uniform distributions on trustworthiness levels, we find that the game has two distinct outcomes: either the number of team members is small enough, such that the project manager has a perfectly secure strategy, or the security of the secret depends solely on the randomness of selecting the employee with whom it is shared.[1] In the former case, the adversary has no incentives to attack and, consequently, never learns the secret. In the latter case, the adversary always attacks and always bribes the targeted employee with the minimal amount that is never below the employee's trustworthiness level. Thus, if the adversary targeted an employee that actually knows the secret, then it is certainly revealed. The project manager's only possible defense in this case is to randomize the selection of employees.

There are multiple possible directions for future work. First, a limitation of the model is the restriction on the adversary, which constrains her to target only a single employee at a time. This simplification can be motivated by the adversary's incentive to keep her operation covert and, thus, to minimize the number of bribing attempts. However, it would be worthwhile to study the trade-off between the adversary's increased risk of being discovered and the increased probability of learning the secret when she targets multiple employees. As another direction, we want to study our model with specific distributions over trustworthiness levels. In this paper, we provide results for the uniform distribution, which can be well-motivated in practice; however, there are other distributions that can be justified from practical observations: e. g., the beta distribution.

Acknowledgements. We gratefully acknowledge the support of the Penn State Institute for Cyber-Science. The first author would like to thank the Campus Hungary Program for supporting his research visit. The third author would like to thank the Office of Naval Research (ONR) for supporting his research visit under Visiting Scientists Grant N62909-13-1-V029.

References

1. Anderson, R.: Security engineering - A guide to building dependable distributed systems, 2nd edn. Wiley (2008)
2. Anderson, R., Barton, C., Böhme, R., Clayton, R., van Eeten, M., Levi, M., Moore, T., Savage, S.: Measuring the cost of cybercrime. In: WEIS (2012)
3. Band, S., Cappelli, D., Fischer, L., Moore, A., Shaw, E., Trzeciak, R.: Comparing insider IT sabotage and espionage: A model-based analysis. Technical Report CMU/SEI-2006-TR-026, Carnegie Mellon University (2006)

---

[1]Note that the probability that an exact equality occurs is negligible in practice.

4. Bontis, N.: Assessing knowledge assets: A review of the models used to measure intellectual capital. International Journal of Management Reviews 3(1), 41–60 (2001)
5. Colwill, C.: Human factors in information security: The insider threat – Who can you trust these days? Information Security Technical Report 14(4), 186–196 (2009)
6. Corporate Trust (Business Risk & Crisis Mgmt. GmbH). Studie: Industriespionage 2012 - Aktuelle Risiken für die deutsche Wirtschaft durch Cyberwar (2012)
7. D'Arcy, J., Hovav, A., Galletta, D.: User awareness of security countermeasures and its impact on information systems misuse: A deterrence approach. Information Systems Research 20(1), 79–98 (2009)
8. FBI. The insider threat (April 2013), http://www.fbi.gov/about-us/investigate/counterintelligence/insider_threat_brochure
9. Federal Bureau of Investigation. Economic espionage, http://www.fbi.gov/about-us/investigate/counterintelligence/economic-espionage
10. Finn, P.: Chinese citizen sentenced in military data-theft case. Washington Post (March 2013)
11. Johnson, B., Schöttle, P., Böhme, R.: Where to hide the bits? In: Grossklags, J., Walrand, J. (eds.) GameSec 2012. LNCS, vol. 7638, pp. 1–17. Springer, Heidelberg (2012)
12. Liu, D., Wang, X.F., Jean Camp, L.: Game theoretic modeling and analysis of insider threats. International Journal of Critical Infrastructure Protection 1, 75–80 (2008)
13. Moore, A., Cappelli, D., Caron, T., Shaw, E., Spooner, D., Trzeciak, R.: A preliminary model of insider theft of intellectual property. Journal of Wireless Mobile Networks, Ubiquitous Computing, and Dependable Applications 2(1), 28–49 (2011)
14. Munshi, A., Dell, P., Armstrong, H.: Insider threat behavior factors: A comparison of theory with reported incidents. In: IEEE HICSS 2012, pp. 2402–2411 (2012)
15. Nelder, J., Mead, R.: A simplex method for function minimization. Computer Journal 7, 308–313 (1965)
16. Randazzo, M., Keeney, M., Kowalski, E., Cappelli, D., Moore, A.: Insider threat study: Illicit cyber activity in the banking and finance sector. Technical Report CMU/SEI-2004-TR-021, Carnegie Mellon University (June 2005)
17. Ronde, T.: Trade secrets and information sharing. Journal of Economics and Management Strategy 10, 391–417 (2001)
18. Saltzer, J., Schroeder, M.: The protection of information in computer systems. Proceedings of the IEEE 63(9), 1278–1308 (1975)
19. Sandhu, R., Samarati, P.: Access control: Principles and practice. IEEE Communications Magazine 32, 40–48 (1994)

Automated Security Proofs for Almost-Universal Hash for MAC Verification*

Martin Gagné[1], Pascal Lafourcade[2], and Yassine Lakhnech[2]

[1] Department of Computer Science, Saarland University, Germany
[2] Université Grenoble 1, CNRS, VERIMAG, France

Abstract. Message authentication codes (MACs) are an essential primitive in cryptography. They are used to ensure the integrity and authenticity of a message, and can also be used as a building block for larger schemes, such as chosen-ciphertext secure encryption, or identity-based encryption. MACs are often built in two steps: first, the 'front end' of the MAC produces a short digest of the long message, then the 'back end' provides a mixing step to make the output of the MAC unpredictable for an attacker. Our verification method follows this structure. We develop a Hoare logic for proving that the front end of the MAC is an almost-universal hash function. The programming language used to specify these functions is fairly expressive and can be used to describe many block-cipher and compression function-based MACs. We implemented this method into a prototype that can automatically prove the security of almost-universal hash functions. This prototype can prove the security of the front-end of many CBC-based MACs (DMAC, ECBC, FCBC and XCBC to name only a few), PMAC and HMAC. We then provide a list of options for the back end of the MAC, each consisting of only two or three instructions, each of which can be composed with an almost-universal hash function to obtain a secure MAC.

1 Introduction

Message authentication codes (MACs) are among the most common primitives in symmetric key cryptography. They ensure the integrity and provenance of a message, and they can be used, in conjunction with chosen-plaintext (CPA) secure encryption, to obtain chosen-ciphertext (CCA) secure encryption. Given the importance of this primitive, it is important that their proofs of security be the object of close scrutiny. The study of the security of MACs is, of course, not a new field. Bellare et al. [5] were the first to prove the security of CBC-MAC for fixed-length inputs. Following this work, a myriad of new MACs secure for variable-length inputs were proposed ([4,7,8,9,17]). None of these protocols' proofs have been verified by any means other than human scrutiny. Automated proofs can provide additional assurance of the correctness of these security proofs by providing an independent proof of complex schemes. This paper presents a method for automatically proving the security of MACs based on block ciphers and hash functions.

Contributions: To analyze the security of MACs, we first decompose the MAC algorithms into two parts: a 'front-end', whose work is to compress long input messages

---

* This work was partially supported by ANR project ProSe and Minalogic project SHIVA.

J. Crampton, S. Jajodia, and K. Mayes (Eds.): ESORICS 2013, LNCS 8134, pp. 291–308, 2013.
© Springer-Verlag Berlin Heidelberg 2013

into small digests, and a 'back-end', usually a mixing step, which obfuscates the output of the front-end. We present a Hoare logic to prove that the front-ends of block-cipher based and hash based MACs are almost-universal hash functions in the ideal cipher model and random oracle model respectively. We then make a list of operations which, when composed with an almost-universal hash function, yield a secure MAC. We can then attest the security of MACs by first proving the security of the front end using our logic, and then by manually verifying that the back end of the MAC belongs to our list.

Our result differs significantly from previous works that used Hoare logic to generate proofs of cryptographic protocols (such as [12,15]) because those results proved the security of encryption schemes. Proving the security of MACs proved to be singularly more challenging: the security of encryption schemes could be simply proven by showing that the ciphertext is indistinguishable from a random value, whereas the unforgeability property required of MACs cannot, to our knowledge, be captured by their predicates. As a result, we have to consider the simultaneous execution of the program, define a dedicated semantics to capture these executions, and introduce appropriated predicates that keep track of equality and inequality of values between the two executions.

In contrast to the previous results that only deal with schemes that had fixed-length inputs, we are able to analyze for-loops, which allows us to prove the security of protocols that can take arbitrary strings as an input. We describe two heuristics that can be used to discover stable loop invariants and apply them to one example. These heuristics successfully find stable invariants for all the hash functions analyzed in this paper.

Finally, we implemented our method into a prototype [14] that can be used to verify the security of the front-end of several well-known MACs, such as HMAC [4], DMAC [17], ECBC, FCBC and XCBC [8] and PMAC [9], and could be used to verify the security of other hash functions based on the same primitives. We also give a predicate filter that enables us to discard unnecessary predicates, which speeds up our implementation and facilitates the discovery of loop invariants. Our prototype goes through the programs from beginning to end, instead of the more common backward approach, to avoid an exponential blowout in the number of possibilities to examine, due to the many choices of rules that can cause certain predicates caused by the presence of the logical or connector in our Hoare logic.

Related Work: The idea of using Hoare logic to automatically produce proofs of security for cryptographic protocols is not new. Courant et al. [12] presented a Hoare logic to prove the security of asymmetric encryption schemes in the random oracle model. A Hoare logic was also used by Gagné et al. [15] to verify proofs of security of block cipher modes of encryption. Also worth mentioning is the paper by Corin and Den Hartog [11], which presented a Hoare-style proof system for game-based cryptographic proofs.

Fournet et al. [13] developed a framework for modular code-based cryptographic verification. However, their approach considers interfaces for MACs. In a way, our work is complementary to theirs, as our result, coupled with theirs, could enable a more complete verification of systems.

In [1], the authors introduce a general logic for proving the security of cryptographic primitives. This framework can easily be extended using external results, such as [12], to add to its power. Our result could also be added to this framework to further extend it.

Other tools, such as Cryptoverif [10] and EasyCrypt [3,2], can be used to verify the security of cryptographic schemes, but they are not as convenient as our method for proving the security of MACs. Cryptoverif does not support loop constructs, which are an important part of our result, and is generally used for proving the security of higher level protocols, assuming the security of primitives such as MACs. As for Easycrypt, it relies on a game-based approach and requires human assistance to enter the sequence of games. Our result is complementary to these approaches. Integrating our method to these tools would enable a more complete analysis of cryptographic protocols and remove the need for human assistance when analysing MACs.

Outline: In Section 2, we introduce cryptographic background. The following section introduces our grammar, semantics and assertion language. In Section 4, we present our Hoare logic and method for proving the security of almost-universal hash functions, and we discuss our implementation of this logic and treatment of loops in Section 5. We then obtain a secure MAC by combining these with one of the back-end options described in Section 6. Finally, we conclude in Section 7.

2   Cryptographic Background

In this section, we introduce a few notational conventions, and we recall a few cryptographic concepts.

Notation and Conventions
We assume that all variables range over domains whose cardinality is exponential in the security parameter η and that all programs have length polynomial in η. We say that a function $f : \mathbb{N} \to \mathbb{R}$ is *negligible* if, for any polynomial p, there exists a positive integer n_0 such that for all $n \geq n_0$, $f(n) \leq \frac{1}{|p(n)|}$.

For a probability distribution $\mathcal{D}$, we denote by $x \xleftarrow{\$} \mathcal{D}$ the operation of sampling a value x according to distribution $\mathcal{D}$. If S is a finite set, we denote by $x \xleftarrow{\$} S$ the operation of sampling x uniformly at random among the values in S.

MAC Security
A message authentication code ensures the authenticity of a message m by computing a small tag τ, which is sent together with the message to the intended receiver. Upon receiving the message and the tag, the receiver recomputes the tag τ' using the message and his own copy of the key, and he accepts the message as authentic if $\tau = \tau'$. More formally:

Definition 1 (MAC). *A message authentication code is a triple of polynomial-time algorithms (K, MAC, V), where $K(1^\eta)$ takes a security parameter 1^η and outputs a secret key sk, $MAC(sk, m)$ takes a secret key and a message m, and outputs a tag, and $V(sk, m, tag)$ takes a secret key sk, a message m and a tag, and outputs a bit: 1 for a correct tag, 0 otherwise.*

We say that a MAC is secure, or *unforgeable* if it is impossible to compute a new valid message-tag pair for anybody who does not know the secret key, even when given access to oracles that can compute and verify the MACs. This way, when one receives a valid message-tag pair, he can be certain that the message was sent by someone who possesses a copy of his secret key.

Definition 2 (Unforgeability [5]). *A MAC* (K, Mac, V) *is* unforgeable under a chosen-message attack *(UNF-CMA) if for every polynomial-time algorithm* $\mathcal{A}$ *that has oracle access to the MAC and verification algorithm and whose output message* m^* *is different from any message it sent to the* Mac *oracle, the following probability is negligible*

$$Pr[sk \overset{\$}{\leftarrow} K(1^\eta); (m^*, tag^*) \overset{\$}{\leftarrow} \mathcal{A}^{Mac(sk, \cdot), V(sk, \cdot, \cdot)} : V(sk, m^*, tag^*) = 1]$$

A standard method for constructing MACs is to apply a pseudo-random function, or some other form of 'mixing' step, to the output of an almost-universal hash function [18,19]. We assume that a MAC is constructed in this way.

Definition 3 (Almost-Universal Hash). *A family of functions* $\mathcal{H} = \{h_i\}$ *indexed with key* $i \in \{0,1\}^n$ *is a* family of almost-universal hash functions *if for any two distinct strings* M *and* M', $Pr_{h_i \in \mathcal{H}}[h_i(M) = h_i(M')]$ *is negligible, where the probability is taken over the choice of* h_i *in* $\mathcal{H}$.

It is much easier to work with this definition than with the unforgeability definition because of the absence of an adaptive adversary, and the collision probability is taken over all possible choices of key.

Block Cipher Security

Many MAC constructions are based on block cipher, so we quickly recall the definition of block ciphers and their security definition.

A block cipher is a *family of permutations* $\mathcal{E} : \{0,1\}^{K(\eta)} \times \{0,1\}^\eta \to \{0,1\}^\eta$ indexed with a key $k \in \{0,1\}^{K(\eta)}$ where $K(\eta)$ is a polynomial. A block cipher is *secure* if, for a randomly sampled key, the block cipher is indistinguishable from a permutation sampled at random from the set of all permutations of $\{0,1\}^\eta$. However, since random permutations of $\{0,1\}^\eta$ and random functions from $\{0,1\}^\eta$ to $\{0,1\}^\eta$ are statistically close, and that random functions are often more convenient for proof purposes, it is common to assume that secure block ciphers are pseudo-random functions.

Definition 4 (Pseudo-Random Functions). *Let* $P : \{0,1\}^{K(\eta)} \times \{0,1\}^\eta \to \{0,1\}^\eta$ *be a family of functions and let* $\mathcal{A}$ *be an algorithm that takes an oracle and returns a bit. The prf-advantage of* $\mathcal{A}$ *is defined as follows.*

$$Adv_{\mathcal{A},P}^{prf} = \left| Pr[k \overset{\$}{\leftarrow} \{0,1\}^{K(\eta)}; \mathcal{A}^{P(k, \cdot)} = 1] - Pr[R \overset{\$}{\leftarrow} \Phi_\eta; \mathcal{A}^{R(\cdot)} = 1] \right|$$

where Φ_η *is the set of all functions from* $\{0,1\}^\eta$ *to* $\{0,1\}^\eta$. *We say that* P *is a family of pseudo-random functions if for every polynomial-time adversary* $\mathcal{A}$, $Adv_{\mathcal{A},P}^{prf}$ *is a negligible function in* η.

Since all the schemes in this paper require only one key for the block cipher, to simplify the notation, we write only $\mathcal{E}(m)$ instead of $\mathcal{E}(k, m)$, but it is understood that a key was selected at the initialization of the scheme, and remains the same throughout.

Random Oracle Model

For MACs that make use of a hash function, we assume that the hash function behaves like a random oracle. That is, we assume that the hash function is picked at random among all possible functions from the given domain and range, and that every algorithm participating in the scheme, including all adversaries, has oracle access to this random function. This is a fairly common assumption to provide a heuristic argument for the security of cryptographic protocols [6].

Indistinguishable Distributions

Given two distribution ensembles $X = \{X_\eta\}_{\eta \in \mathbb{N}}$ and $X' = \{X'_\eta\}_{\eta \in \mathbb{N}}$, an algorithm $\mathcal{A}$ and $\eta \in \mathbb{N}$, we define the *advantage* of $\mathcal{A}$ in distinguishing X_η from X'_η as the following quantity:

$$\mathsf{Adv}(\mathcal{A}, \eta, X, X') = \left| \mathsf{Pr}[x \overset{\$}{\leftarrow} X_\eta : \mathcal{A}(x) = 1] - \mathsf{Pr}[x \overset{\$}{\leftarrow} X'_\eta : \mathcal{A}(x) = 1] \right|.$$

We say that X and X' are *indistinguishable*, denoted by $X \sim X'$, if $\mathsf{Adv}(\mathcal{A}, \eta, X, X')$ is negligible as a function of η for every probabilistic polynomial-time algorithm $\mathcal{A}$.

3 Model

In this section, we introduce the grammar for the programs describing almost-universal hash function. We present the semantics of each commands, and introduce the assertion language that will be used in for our Hoare logic.

3.1 Grammar

We consider the language defined by the BNF grammar below, where p and q are positive integers.

$$\mathsf{cmd} ::= x := \mathcal{E}(y) \mid x := \mathcal{H}(y) \mid x := y \mid x := y \oplus z \mid x := y\|z \mid x := \rho(i, y)$$
$$\mid \mathsf{for}\ l = p\ \mathsf{to}\ q\ \mathsf{do} : [\mathsf{cmd}_l] \mid \mathsf{cmd}_1 ; \mathsf{cmd}_2$$

We refer to individual instructions as *commands* and to lists of commands as *programs*. Each command has the following effect:

- $x := \mathcal{E}(y)$ denotes application of the block cipher $\mathcal{E}$ to the value of y and assigning the result to x.
- $x := \mathcal{H}(y)$ denotes the application of the hash function $\mathcal{H}$ to the value of y and assigning the result to x.
- $x := y$ denotes the assignment to x of the values of y.
- $x := y \oplus z$ denotes the assignment to x of the xor or the values of y and z.
- $x := y\|z$ denotes the assignment to x of the concatenation of the values of y and z.
- $x := \rho(i, y)$ denotes the computation of the function ρ on input i (an integer) and the value of y and assigning the result to x.
- $c_1 ; c_2$ is the sequential composition of c_1 and c_2.

- for $l = p$ to q do: $[\text{cmd}_l]$ denotes the successive execution of $\text{cmd}_p; \text{cmd}_{p+1}; \ldots;$ cmd_q when $p \leq q$. If $p > q$, the command has no effect.

The function ρ is used to process the *tweak* in a common construction for *tweakable block ciphers* [16]. A fixed-input-length almost-universal function is often sufficient, but exact implementations vary from one scheme to the next, and we want to allow for the possibility of functions that have additional properties. When a scheme uses a function ρ, the properties of the function ρ required for the proof will be added to the initial conditions of the verification procedure using the predicates of Section 3.3. We do not any other assumptions about ρ other than it is a function with fixed output length.

Definition 5 (Generic Hash Function). *A generic hash function $Hash$ on message blocks $m_1, \ldots, m_n$ with output c_n, is represented by a tuple $(\mathcal{F}_{\mathcal{E}}, \mathcal{F}_{\mathcal{H}}, Hash(m_1 \| \ldots \| m_n, c_n)$: **var** x; cmd), where $\mathcal{F}_{\mathcal{E}}$ is a family of pseudorandom permutations (usually a block cipher), $\mathcal{F}_{\mathcal{H}}$ is a family of cryptographic hash functions, and $Hash(m_1 \| \ldots \| m_n, c_n)$: **var** x; cmd is the program of the hash function, where x is the set of all the variables in the program that are neither input variables m_i, output variable c_n, or the special variable k (used to hold a secret key), and the program cmd is in the language described by our grammar.*

The secret key sk of the generic hash is a combination of the value of the special variable k and the choice of the block cipher $\mathcal{E}$ in the family $\mathcal{F}_{\mathcal{E}}$.

We assume that, prior to executing the MAC, the message has been padded using some unambiguous padding scheme, so that all the message blocks $m_1, \ldots, m_n$ are of equal and appropriate length for the scheme, usually the input length of the block cipher. We also assume that each variable in the program cmd is assigned at most once, as it is clear that any program obtained from our language can be transformed into an equivalent program with this property, and that the input variables $m_1, \ldots, m_n$ never appear on the left side of any command since these variables already hold a value before the execution of the program. For simplicity of exposition, we henceforth assume that all the programs in this paper satisfy these assumptions.

We present to the right the program for $Hash_{CBC}$, the hash function that is used as a running example in this paper. We give the program for other hash functions that can be verified with our method in the full version of this paper [14].

$$Hash_{CBC}(m_1 \| \ldots \| m_n, c_n) :$$
$$\textbf{var } i, z_2, \ldots, z_n, c_1, \ldots, c_{n-1};$$
$$c_1 := \mathcal{E}(m_1);$$
$$\textbf{for } i = 2 \textbf{ to } n \textbf{ do:}$$
$$[z_i := c_{i-1} \oplus m_i; c_i := \mathcal{E}(z_i)]$$

3.2 Semantics

In our analysis, we consider the execution of a program on two inputs simultaneously. These simultaneous executions will enable us to keep track of the probability of equality and inequality of strings between the two executions, thereby allowing us to prove that the function is almost-universal.

Each command is a function that takes a configuration and outputs a configurations. A *configuration* γ is a tuple $(S, S', \mathcal{E}, \mathcal{H}, \mathcal{L}_{\mathcal{E}}, \mathcal{L}_{\mathcal{H}})$ where S and S' are states, $\mathcal{E}$ is a block cipher, $\mathcal{H}$ is a hash function (that will be modeled as a random oracle), and $\mathcal{L}_\mathcal{E}$ and $\mathcal{L}_\mathcal{H}$ are sets of strings.

A *state* is a function $S : \mathsf{Var} \to \{0,1\}^* \cup \bot$, where Var is the full set of variables in the program, that assigns bitstrings to variables (the symbol $\bot$ is used to indicate that no value has been assigned to the variable yet). A configuration contains two states, one for each execution of the program.

The set $\mathcal{L}_\mathcal{E}$ records the values for which the functions $\mathcal{E}$ was computed. The set is common for both executions of the program. Every time a command of the type $x := \mathcal{E}(y)$ is executed in the program, we add $S(y)$ and $S'(y)$ to $\mathcal{L}_\mathcal{E}$ if they are not already present. We define $\mathcal{L}_\mathcal{H}$ for the hash function $\mathcal{H}$ similarly.

Let Γ denote the set of configurations and $\mathrm{DIST}(\Gamma)$ the set of distributions on configurations. The semantics is given below, where $S\{x \mapsto v\}$ denotes the state which assigns the value v to the variable x, and behaves like S for all other variables and $\circ$ denotes function composition. The semantic function $\mathsf{cmd} : \Gamma \to \Gamma$ of commands can be lifted in the usual way to a function $\mathsf{cmd}^* : \mathrm{DIST}(\Gamma) \to \mathrm{DIST}(\Gamma)$ by point-wise application of cmd. By abuse of notation we also denote the lifted semantics by $[\![\mathsf{cmd}]\!]$.

$$
\begin{aligned}
&[\![x := \mathcal{E}(y)]\!](S, S', \mathcal{E}, \mathcal{H}, \mathcal{L}_\mathcal{E}, \mathcal{L}_\mathcal{H}) = \\
&\quad (S\{x \mapsto \mathcal{E}(S(y))\}, S'\{x \mapsto \mathcal{E}(S'(y))\}, \mathcal{E}, \mathcal{H}, \mathcal{L}_\mathcal{E} \cup \{S(y), S'(y)\}, \mathcal{L}_\mathcal{H}) \\
&[\![x := \mathcal{H}(y)]\!](S, S', \mathcal{E}, \mathcal{H}, \mathcal{L}_\mathcal{E}, \mathcal{L}_\mathcal{H}) = \\
&\quad (S\{x \mapsto \mathcal{H}(S(y))\}, S'\{x \mapsto \mathcal{H}(S'(y))\}, \mathcal{E}, \mathcal{H}, \mathcal{L}_\mathcal{E}, \mathcal{L}_\mathcal{H} \cup \{S(y), S'(y)\}) \\
&[\![x := y]\!](S, S', \mathcal{E}, \mathcal{H}, \mathcal{L}_\mathcal{E}, \mathcal{L}_\mathcal{H}) = (S\{x \mapsto S(y)\}, S'\{x \mapsto S'(y)\}, \mathcal{E}, \mathcal{H}, \mathcal{L}_\mathcal{E}, \mathcal{L}_\mathcal{H}) \\
&[\![x := y \oplus z]\!](S, S', \mathcal{E}, \mathcal{H}, \mathcal{L}_\mathcal{E}, \mathcal{L}_\mathcal{H}) = \\
&\quad (S\{x \mapsto S(y) \oplus S(z)\}, S'\{x \mapsto S'(y) \oplus S'(z)\}, \mathcal{E}, \mathcal{H}, \mathcal{L}_\mathcal{E}, \mathcal{L}_\mathcal{H}) \\
&[\![x := y||z]\!](S, S', \mathcal{E}, \mathcal{H}, \mathcal{L}_\mathcal{E}, \mathcal{L}_\mathcal{H}) = \\
&\quad (S\{x \mapsto S(y)||S(z)\}, S'\{x \mapsto S'(y)||S'(z)\}, \mathcal{E}, \mathcal{H}, \mathcal{L}_\mathcal{E}, \mathcal{L}_\mathcal{H}) \\
&[\![x := \rho(i,y)]\!](S, S', \mathcal{E}, \mathcal{H}, \mathcal{L}_\mathcal{E}, \mathcal{L}_\mathcal{H}) = \\
&\quad (S\{x \mapsto \rho(i, S(y))\}, S'\{x \mapsto \rho(i, S'(y))\}, \mathcal{E}, \mathcal{H}, \mathcal{L}_\mathcal{E}, \mathcal{L}_\mathcal{H}) \\
&[\![\text{for } l = p \text{ to } q \text{ do: } [\mathsf{cmd}_l]]\!]\gamma = \begin{cases} [\![\mathsf{cmd}_q]\!] \circ [\![\mathsf{cmd}_{q-1}]\!] \circ \ldots \circ [\![\mathsf{cmd}_p]\!]\gamma & \text{if } p \le q \\ \gamma & \text{otherwise} \end{cases} \\
&[\![c_1; c_2]\!] = [\![c_2]\!] \circ [\![c_1]\!]
\end{aligned}
$$

The set of initial distributions $\mathrm{DIST}_0(\mathbb{H})$, where $\mathbb{H} = (\mathcal{F}_\mathcal{E}, \mathcal{F}_\mathcal{H}, Hash(m_1 || \ldots || m_n, c_n) : \mathbf{var}\ x; \mathsf{cmd})$ is a generic hash, contains all the following distributions:

$$
\begin{aligned}
\mathcal{D}_0^{(M,M')} = [\mathcal{E} &\xleftarrow{\$} \mathcal{F}_\mathcal{E}(1^\eta); \mathcal{H} \xleftarrow{\$} \mathcal{F}_\mathcal{H}(1^\eta); u \xleftarrow{\$} \{0,1\}^\eta : \\
&(S\{k \mapsto u, m_1 || \ldots || m_n \mapsto M\}, S'\{k \mapsto u, m_1 || \ldots || m_n \mapsto M'\}, \mathcal{E}, \mathcal{H}, \emptyset, \emptyset)]
\end{aligned}
$$

where M and M' are any two n block messages and k is a variable holding a secret string needed in some MACs (among our examples, $Hash_{PMAC}$ and $Hash_{HMAC}$ need it). Note that $\mathcal{F}_\mathcal{E}$, $\mathcal{F}_\mathcal{H}$, the domain Var of the states and the length n of the input messages are defined in $\mathbb{H}$. These distributions capture the initial situation of Definition 3 where the variables m_i contain the blocks of M and M' in S and S' respectively.

The set $\mathrm{DIST}(\mathbb{H})$ is obtained by executing a program on one of the initial distributions. It contains all the distributions of the form $[\![\mathsf{cmd}]\!]X_0$, where $X_0 \in \mathrm{DIST}_0(\mathbb{H})$ and cmd is a program.

A notational convention. It is easy to see that commands never modify $\mathcal{E}$ or $\mathcal{H}$. Therefore, we can, without ambiguity, write $(\hat{S}, \hat{S}', \mathcal{L}'_{\mathcal{E}}, \mathcal{L}'_{\mathcal{H}}) \overset{\$}{\leftarrow} [\![c]\!](S, S', \mathcal{L}_{\mathcal{E}}, \mathcal{L}_{\mathcal{H}})$ instead of $(\hat{S}, \hat{S}', \mathcal{E}, \mathcal{H}, \mathcal{L}'_{\mathcal{E}}, \mathcal{L}'_{\mathcal{H}}) \overset{\$}{\leftarrow} [\![c]\!](S, S', \mathcal{E}, \mathcal{H}, \mathcal{L}_{\mathcal{E}}, \mathcal{L}_{\mathcal{H}})$.

3.3   Assertion Language

Like [15], our assertion languages deals with block ciphers, so it stands to reason that some of our predicates will be similar to theirs. However, the definition of all the predicates has to be adapted to our new semantics with two simultaneous executions. We also need additional predicates to describe equality or inequality of strings between the two executions, that will allow us to capture the definition of almost-universal hash functions. We first give an intuitive description of our predicates, then we define them all formally.

Empty: means that the probability that $\mathcal{L}_{\mathcal{E}}$ contains an element is negligible.

Eq(x, y): means that the probability that $S(x) \neq S'(y)$ is negligible.

Uneq(x, y): means that the probability that $S(x) = S'(y)$ is negligible.

E$(\mathcal{E}; x; V)$: means that the probability that the value of x is either in $\mathcal{L}_{\mathcal{E}}$ or equal to that of a variable in V is negligible.

H$(\mathcal{H}; x; V)$: means that the probability that the value of x is either in $\mathcal{L}_{\mathcal{H}}$ or equal to that of a variable in V is negligible.

Ind$(x; V; V')$: means that no adversary has non-negligible probability to distinguish whether he is given results of computations performed using the value of x or a random value, when he is given the values of the variables in V and the values of the variables in V' from the parallel execution. In addition to variables in Var, the set V can contain special symbols $\ell_{\mathcal{E}}$ or $\ell_{\mathcal{H}}$. When the symbol $\ell_{\mathcal{E}}$ is present, it means that, in addition to the other variables in V, the distinguisher is also given the values in $\mathcal{L}_{\mathcal{E}}$, similarly for $\ell_{\mathcal{H}}$.

Our Hoare logic is based on statements from the following language.

$$\varphi ::= \varphi \wedge \varphi \mid \varphi \vee \varphi \mid \psi$$
$$\psi ::= \mathsf{Ind}(x; W; V') \mid \mathsf{Eq}(x, y) \mid \mathsf{Uneq}(x, y) \mid \mathsf{Empty} \mid \mathsf{E}(\mathcal{E}; x; V) \mid \mathsf{H}(\mathcal{H}; x; V)$$

where $x, y \in$ Var and $V, V' \subseteq$ Var, and $W \subseteq \mathsf{Var} \cup \{\ell_{\mathcal{E}}, \ell_{\mathcal{H}}\}$. We refer to the statements produced by this grammar as *formulas*.

We introduce a few notational shortcuts that will help in formally defining our predicates. For any set $V \subseteq$ Var, we denote by $S(V)$ the multiset resulting from the application of S on each variable in V. Also, for a set $W \subseteq \mathsf{Var} \cup \{\ell_{\mathcal{E}}\}$ with $\ell_{\mathcal{E}} \in W$, we use $S(W)$ as a shorthand for $S(W \setminus \{\ell_{\mathcal{E}}\}) \cup \mathcal{L}_{\mathcal{E}}$, and similarly for $\ell_{\mathcal{H}}$. For a set $V \subseteq \mathsf{Var} \cup \{\ell_{\mathcal{E}}, \ell_{\mathcal{H}}\}$ and an element $x \in \mathsf{Var} \cup \{\ell_{\mathcal{E}}, \ell_{\mathcal{H}}\}$, we write V, x as a shorthand for $V \cup \{x\}$ and $V - x$ as a shorthand for $V \setminus \{x\}$.

We define that a distribution X satisfies φ, denoted $X \models \varphi$ as follows:

- $X \models \varphi \wedge \varphi'$ iff $X \models \varphi$ and $X \models \varphi'$
- $X \models \varphi \vee \varphi'$ iff $X \models \varphi$ or $X \models \varphi'$
- $X \models \mathsf{Empty}$ iff $\Pr[(S, S', \mathcal{L}_{\mathcal{E}}, \mathcal{L}_{\mathcal{H}}) \overset{\$}{\leftarrow} X : \mathcal{L}_{\mathcal{E}} \neq \emptyset]$ is negligible

- $X \models \mathsf{Eq}(x, y)$ iff $\Pr[(S, S', \mathcal{L}_\mathcal{E}, \mathcal{L}_\mathcal{H}) \xleftarrow{\$} X : S(x) \neq S'(y)]$ is negligible
- $X \models \mathsf{Uneq}(x, y)$ iff $\Pr[(S, S', \mathcal{L}_\mathcal{E}, \mathcal{L}_\mathcal{H}) \xleftarrow{\$} X : S(x) = S'(y)]$ is negligible
- $X \models \mathsf{E}(\mathcal{E}; x; V)$ iff $\Pr[(S, S', \mathcal{L}_\mathcal{E}, \mathcal{L}_\mathcal{H}) \xleftarrow{\$} X : \{S(x), S'(x)\} \cap (\mathcal{L}_\mathcal{E} \cup S(V - x) \cup S'(V - x)) \neq \emptyset]$ is negligible[1]
- $X \models \mathsf{H}(\mathcal{H}; x; V)$ iff $\Pr[(S, S', \mathcal{L}_\mathcal{E}, \mathcal{L}_\mathcal{H}) \xleftarrow{\$} X : \{S(x), S'(x)\} \cap (\mathcal{L}_\mathcal{H} \cup S(V - x) \cup S'(V - x)) \neq \emptyset]$ is negligible
- $X \models \mathsf{Ind}(x; V; V')$ iff the two following formulas hold:

$$[(S, S', \mathcal{L}_\mathcal{E}, \mathcal{L}_\mathcal{H}) \xleftarrow{\$} X : (S(x), S(V - x) \cup S'(V'))] \sim$$
$$[(S, S', \mathcal{L}_\mathcal{E}, \mathcal{L}_\mathcal{H}) \xleftarrow{\$} X; u \xleftarrow{\$} \mathcal{U} : (u, S(V - x) \cup S'(V'))]$$

$$[(S, S', \mathcal{L}_\mathcal{E}, \mathcal{L}_\mathcal{H}) \xleftarrow{\$} X : (S'(x), S'(V - x) \cup S(V'))] \sim$$
$$[(S, S', \mathcal{L}_\mathcal{E}, \mathcal{L}_\mathcal{H}) \xleftarrow{\$} X; u \xleftarrow{\$} \mathcal{U} : (u, S'(V - x) \cup S(V'))]$$

We now present a few lemmas that show useful relations and properties of our predicates. In all these lemmas, it is assumed that $\mathbb{H}$ is any generic hash. The proof of these lemmas is in the full version of this paper [14].

Lemma 1. *The following relations are true for any sets V_1, V_2, V_3, V_4 and variables x, y with $x \neq y$*

1. $\mathsf{Ind}(x; V_1; V_2) \Rightarrow \mathsf{Ind}(x; V_3; V_4)$ *if $V_3 \subseteq V_1$ and $V_4 \subseteq V_2$*
2. $\mathsf{H}(\mathcal{H}; x; V_1) \Rightarrow \mathsf{H}(\mathcal{H}; x; V_2)$ *if $V_2 \subseteq V_1$*
3. $\mathsf{E}(\mathcal{E}; x; V_1) \Rightarrow \mathsf{E}(\mathcal{E}; x; V_2)$ *if $V_2 \subseteq V_1$*
4. $\mathsf{Ind}(x; V_1, \ell_\mathcal{H}; \emptyset) \Rightarrow \mathsf{H}(\mathcal{H}; x; V_1)$
5. $\mathsf{Ind}(x; V_1, \ell_\mathcal{E}; \emptyset) \Rightarrow \mathsf{E}(\mathcal{E}; x; V_1)$
6. $\mathsf{Ind}(x; \emptyset; \{y\}) \Rightarrow \mathsf{Uneq}(x, y) \wedge \mathsf{Uneq}(y, x)$

Note that lines 4, 5 and 6 are particularly helpful because the predicate Ind is much easier to propagate than the other predicates.

We also show that, as a consequence of our definition of $\mathrm{DIST}(\mathbb{H})$, we can always infer the following predicates on the message blocks. This lemma is useful for proving the rules corresponding to commands that introduce a new message block.

Lemma 2. *Let $X \in \mathrm{DIST}(\mathbb{H})$. Then for any integer i, $1 \leq i \leq n$, $X \models \mathsf{Eq}(m_i, m_i)$ $\vee \mathsf{Uneq}(m_i, m_i)$.*

The following formalizes the intuition that if a value can be computed in polynomial time from other values available, then adding this value does not give the adversary any useful information. In general, we say that an expression e is *constructible* from values in a set V if e can be computed in polynomial time from V. But for the purpose of the following lemma, it is sufficient to define constructible expressions as only single variables x, as well as $x \oplus y$ and $x \| y$ for any variables x and y.

---

[1] Since the variable x is removed from the set V when taking the probability, we always have $X \models \mathsf{E}(\mathcal{E}; x; V)$ iff $X \models \mathsf{E}(\mathcal{E}; x; V, x)$. This is to remove the trivial case that $\{S(x), S'(x)\} \cap (\mathcal{L}_\mathcal{E} \cup \{S(x), S'(x)\}) = \emptyset$ never holds, and to simplify the notation. The same is also used for predicates $\mathsf{H}(\mathcal{H}; x; V)$ and $\mathsf{Ind}(x; V; V')$.

Lemma 3. *For any any* $X \in \text{DIST}(\mathbb{H})$, *any sets of variables* V, *any expression* e *constructible from* V, *and any variable* x, z *such that* $z \notin \{x\} \cup \text{Var}(e)$ *if* $X \models \text{Ind}(z; V; V')$ *then* $[\![x := e]\!](X) \models \text{Ind}(z; V, x; V')$. *We emphasize that here we use the notation* $\text{Var}(e)$ *(in its usual sense), that is to say, the variable* z *does not appear at all in* e. *Similarly, if* $X \models \text{Ind}(z; V'; V)$, *then* $[\![x := e]\!](X) \models \text{Ind}(z; V'; V, x)$.

The following, which is useful for proving some of the rules dealing with the concatenation commands, shows that the value of any given variable always have the same length in each execution.

Lemma 4. *For any distribution* $X \in \text{DIST}(\mathbb{H})$, *any program* cmd *produced by our grammar any* $(S, S', \mathcal{E}, \mathcal{H}, \mathcal{L}_\mathcal{E}, \mathcal{L}_\mathcal{H}) \xleftarrow{\$} [\![cmd]\!]X$ *and any variable* $v \in \text{Var}$, $|S(v)| = |S'(v)|$.

4   Proving Almost-Universal Hash

Our main contribution is a Hoare logic for proving that a program is an almost-universal hash function. We require that the program be written in a way so that, on input $m_1 \| \ldots \| m_n$, the program must assign values to variables $c_1, \ldots, c_n$ in such a way that the variable c_1 contains the output of the function on input m_1, the variable c_2 contains the output of the function on input $m_1 \| m_2$ and so on. We model the security of an almost-universal hash function using our predicates as follows.

Proposition 1. *Let* $\mathbb{H} = (\mathcal{F}_\mathcal{E}, \mathcal{F}_\mathcal{H}, Hash(m_1 \| \ldots \| m_n, c_n) : \textbf{var } x; cmd)$ *be a generic hash function on* n-*block messages. Then,* $\mathbb{H}$ *is an almost-universal hash function if, for every positive integer* n, $UNIV(n)$ *holds in the distribution obtained by executing the program on any distribution in* $\text{DIST}_0(\mathbb{H})$, *where*

$$UNIV(n) = \left(\bigwedge\nolimits_{i=1}^{n-1} \text{Uneq}(c_n, c_i) \wedge \bigwedge\nolimits_{i=1}^{n} \text{Eq}(m_i, m_i) \right) \vee \bigwedge\nolimits_{i=1}^{n} \text{Uneq}(c_n, c_i)$$

The proof of this proposition is in the full version of this paper [14].

Hoare Logic Rules

We present a set of rules of the form $\{\varphi\}$cmd$\{\varphi'\}$, meaning that execution of command cmd in any distribution in $\text{DIST}(\mathbb{H})$ that satisfies φ leads to a distribution that satisfies φ'. Using Hoare logic terminology, this means that the triple $\{\varphi\}$cmd$\{\varphi'\}$ is valid.

Since the predicates $\text{Eq}(m_i, m_i)$ are useful only if the whole prefix of the two messages up to the ith block are equal, so that keeping track of the equality or inequality of the message blocks after the first point at which the messages are different is unnecessary. For this reason, when we design our rules, we never produce the predicates $\text{Uneq}(m_i, m_i)$ even when they would be correct.

We group rules together according to their corresponding commands. In all the rules, unless indicated otherwise, we assume that $t \notin \{x, y, z\}$ and $x \notin \{y, z\}$. . In addition, for all rules involving the predicate Ind, we assume that $\ell_\mathcal{E}$ and $\ell_\mathcal{H}$ can be among the elements in the set V. Since some of the rules (for example, rule (G5)) are valid only under certain slightly complex conditions, we use square brackets in the statement of some conditions to remove any ambiguity about their meaning. The proofs of soundness of our rules are given in the full version of this paper [14].

We first introduce a few general rules for consequence, sequential composition, conjunction and disjunction. Let $\phi_1, \phi_2, \phi_3, \phi_4$ be any four formulas in our logic, and let cmd, cmd$_1$, cmd$_2$ be any three commands. These rules are standard, and their proof are omitted.

(Csq) if $\phi_1 \Rightarrow \phi_2$, $\phi_3 \Rightarrow \phi_4$ and $\{\phi_2\}$cmd$\{\phi_3\}$, then $\{\phi_1\}$cmd$\{\phi_4\}$
(Seq) if $\{\phi_1\}$cmd$_1\{\phi_2\}$ and $\{\phi_2\}$cmd$_2\{\phi_3\}$, then $\{\phi_1\}$cmd$_1$; cmd$_2\{\phi_3\}$
(Conj) if $\{\phi_1\}$cmd$\{\phi_2\}$ and $\{\phi_3\}$cmd$\{\phi_4\}$, then $\{\phi_1 \wedge \phi_3\}$cmd$\{\phi_2 \wedge \phi_4\}$
(Disj) if $\{\phi_1\}$cmd$\{\phi_2\}$ and $\{\phi_3\}$cmd$\{\phi_4\}$, then $\{\phi_1 \vee \phi_3\}$cmd$\{\phi_2 \vee \phi_4\}$

Initialization:
We find that the following predicates holds in any distribution $X \in \text{DIST}_0(\mathbb{H})$.

(Init) $\{\text{Ind}(k; \text{Var}, \ell_{\mathcal{E}}, \ell_{\mathcal{H}}; \text{Var} - k) \wedge \text{Eq}(k, k) \wedge \text{Empty}\}$

We recall that k is a special variable holding a secret key. It is sampled at random before executing the program and is the same in both executions, so it is indistinguishable from a random value given any other value.

Generic preservation rules:
Rules (G1) to (G6) show how predicates are preserved by most of the commands when the predicates concern a variable other than that being operated on. For all these rules, we assume that t and t' can be y or z and cmd is either $x := \rho(i, y)$, $x := y$, $x := y \| z$, $x := y \oplus z$, $x := \mathcal{E}(y)$, or $x := \mathcal{H}(y)$.

(G1) $\{\text{Eq}(t, t')\}$ cmd $\{\text{Eq}(t, t')\}$ even if $t = y$ or $t = z$
(G2) $\{\text{Uneq}(t, t')\}$ cmd $\{\text{Uneq}(t, t')\}$ even if $t = y$ or $t = z$
(G3) $\{\text{E}(\mathcal{E}; t; V)\}$ cmd $\{\text{E}(\mathcal{E}; t; V)\}$ provided $x \notin V$ and cmd is not $x := \mathcal{E}(y)$
(G4) $\{\text{H}(\mathcal{H}; t; V)\}$ cmd $\{\text{H}(\mathcal{H}; t; V)\}$ provided $x \notin V$ and cmd is not $x := \mathcal{H}(y)$
(G5) $\{\text{Ind}(t; V; V')\}$ cmd $\{\text{Ind}(t; V; V')\}$ provided [cmd is not $x := \mathcal{E}(y)$ or $x := \mathcal{H}(y)$], $[x \notin V$ unless x is constructible from $V - t]$ and $[x \notin V'$ unless x is constructible from $V' - t]$
(G6) $\{\text{Empty}\}$ cmd $\{\text{Empty}\}$ provided cmd is not $x := \mathcal{E}(y)$

We note that, for rules (G3) to (G6), the straightforward preservation rule does not apply when the command is either of the form $x := \mathcal{E}(y)$ or $x := \mathcal{H}(y)$, because some predicates may no longer hold if the block cipher or the random oracle is computed more than once on any given point. Therefore, the preservation of these predicates for the block cipher and hash commands will have to be handled separately in rules (B4) to (B6) and (H3) to (H5). For rule (G5), in general, we say that the value of a variable x is *constructible* from the values of variables in V if there exists a deterministic polynomial-time algorithm that can compute the value of x from the values in V. In this case, it means that the variables in the right-hand side of cmd are all in V.

Function ρ:

(P1) $\{\text{Eq}(y, y)\}$ $x := \rho(i, y)$ $\{\text{Eq}(x, x)\}$ for integer i

Since the details of the function ρ are not known in advance, we can infer only one rule, that ρ preserves equality, because it is a deterministic function.

Assignment:

Rules (A1) to (A8), for the assignment, are all straightforward, and follow simply from the simple fact that after the command, the value of x is equal to the value of y.

(A1) $\{true\}\ x := m_i\ \{(\mathsf{Eq}(m_i, m_i) \wedge \mathsf{Eq}(x, x)) \vee \mathsf{Uneq}(x, x)\}$

(A2) $\{\mathsf{Eq}(y, y)\}\ x := y\ \{\mathsf{Eq}(x, x)\}$

(A3) $\{\mathsf{Uneq}(y, y)\}\ x := y\ \{\mathsf{Uneq}(x, x)\}$

(A4) $\{\mathsf{Ind}(y; V; V')\}\ x := y\ \{\mathsf{Ind}(x; V; V')\}$ if $x \notin V'$ unless $y \in V'$ and $y \notin V$

(A5) $\{\mathsf{E}(\mathcal{E}; y; V)\}\ x := y\ \{\mathsf{E}(\mathcal{E}; x; V) \wedge \mathsf{E}(\mathcal{E}; y; V)\}$ if $y \notin V$

(A6) $\{\mathsf{H}(\mathcal{H}; y; V)\}\ x := y\ \{\mathsf{H}(\mathcal{H}; x; V) \wedge \mathsf{H}(\mathcal{H}; y; V)\}$ if $y \notin V$

(A7) $\{\mathsf{E}(\mathcal{E}; t; V, y)\}\ x := y\ \{\mathsf{E}(\mathcal{E}; t; V, x, y)\}$

(A8) $\{\mathsf{H}(\mathcal{H}; t; V, y)\}\ x := y\ \{\mathsf{H}(\mathcal{H}; t; V, x, y)\}$

Concatenation:

Rules (C1) to (C6) propagate the predicates for the concatenation command.

(C1) $\{\mathsf{Eq}(y, y)\}\ x := y \| m_i\ \{(\mathsf{Eq}(m_i, m_i) \wedge \mathsf{Eq}(x, x)) \vee \mathsf{Uneq}(x, x)\}$

(C2) $\{\mathsf{Eq}(y, y) \wedge \mathsf{Eq}(z, z)\}\ x := y \| z\ \{\mathsf{Eq}(x, x)\}$

(C3) $\{\mathsf{Uneq}(y, y)\}\ x := y \| z\ \{\mathsf{Uneq}(x, x)\}$

(C4) $\{\mathsf{Ind}(y; V, y, z; V') \wedge \mathsf{Ind}(z; V, y, z; V')\}\ x := y \| z\ \{\mathsf{Ind}(x; V, x; V')\}$ provided $[y \neq z]$, $[x, y, z \notin V]$ and $[x \notin V'$ unless $y, z \in V']$

(C5) $\{\mathsf{Ind}(y; V, \ell_{\mathcal{E}}; V)\}\ x := y \| z\ \{\mathsf{E}(\mathcal{E}; x; V)\}$

(C6) $\{\mathsf{Ind}(y; V, \ell_{\mathcal{H}}; V)\}\ x := y \| z\ \{\mathsf{H}(\mathcal{H}; x; V)\}$

The most important rule for the concatenation is (C4), which states that the concatenation of two random strings results in a random string. Note that it is important for this rule that $y \neq z$, otherwise the string x consists of a string twice repeated, which can be distinguished easily from a random value. The condition $x \notin V'$ unless $y, z \in V'$ is similar to rule (G5), and follows from the constructibility of x from y and z. Rules (C5) and (C6) state that if a string is indistinguishable from a random value given all the values in the set of queries to the block cipher (or the hash function), then clearly it cannot be a prefix of one of the strings $\mathcal{L}_{\mathcal{E}}$. For rules (C1), (C3), (C5) and (C6), the roles of y and z, or y and m_i in the case of (C1), can be exchanged.

Xor operator:

Rules (X1) to (X4) describe the effect of the Xor operation.

(X1) $\{\mathsf{Eq}(y, y)\}\ x := y \oplus m_i\ \{(\mathsf{Eq}(m_i, m_i) \wedge \mathsf{Eq}(x, x)) \vee \mathsf{Uneq}(x, x)\}$

(X2) $\{\mathsf{Ind}(y; V, y, z; V')\}\ x := y \oplus z\ \{\mathsf{Ind}(x; V, x, z; V')\}$ provided $[y \neq z]$, $[y \notin V]$ and $[x \notin V'$ unless $y, z \in V']$

(X3) $\{\mathsf{Eq}(y, y) \wedge \mathsf{Eq}(z, z)\}\ x := y \oplus z\ \{\mathsf{Eq}(x, x)\}$

(X4) $\{\mathsf{Eq}(y, y) \wedge \mathsf{Uneq}(z, z)\}\ x := y \oplus z\ \{\mathsf{Uneq}(x, x)\}$

Rules (X2) is reminiscent of a one-time-pad encryption: if a value z is xor-ed with a random-looking value y, than the result is similarly random-looking provided the value of y is not given. Again, the condition $x \notin V'$ unless $y, z \in V'$ is similar to rule (G5), and follows from the constructibility of x from y and z. The other rules are propagation of the Eq and Uneq predicates. Due to the commutativity of the xor, the role of y and z, or y and m_i in the case of (X1), can be exchanged in all the rules above.

Block cipher:

Since block ciphers are modeled as random functions, that is, functions picked at random among all functions from $\{0, 1\}^\eta$ to $\{0, 1\}^\eta$, the output of the function for a point on which the block cipher has never been computed is indistinguishable from a random value.

(B1) $\{\mathsf{Empty}\}\ x := \mathcal{E}(m_i)\ \{(\mathsf{Uneq}(x,x) \wedge \mathsf{Ind}(x; \mathsf{Var}, \ell_\mathcal{E}, \ell_\mathcal{H}; \mathsf{Var})) \vee$
$(\mathsf{Eq}(m_i, m_i) \wedge \mathsf{Eq}(x,x) \wedge \mathsf{Ind}(x; \mathsf{Var}, \ell_\mathcal{E}, \ell_\mathcal{H}; \mathsf{Var} - x))\}$

(B2) $\{\mathsf{E}(\mathcal{E}; y; \emptyset) \wedge \mathsf{Uneq}(y,y)\}\ x := \mathcal{E}(y)\ \{\mathsf{Ind}(x; \mathsf{Var}, \ell_\mathcal{E}, \ell_\mathcal{H}; \mathsf{Var})\}$

(B3) $\{\mathsf{E}(\mathcal{E}; y; \emptyset) \wedge \mathsf{Eq}(y,y)\}\ x := \mathcal{E}(y)\ \{\mathsf{Ind}(x; \mathsf{Var}, \ell_\mathcal{E}, \ell_\mathcal{H}; \mathsf{Var} - x) \wedge \mathsf{Eq}(x,x)\}$

(B4) $\{\mathsf{E}(\mathcal{E}; y; \emptyset) \wedge \mathsf{Ind}(t; V; V')\}\ x := \mathcal{E}(y)\ \{\mathsf{Ind}(t; V, x; V', x)\}$ even if $t = y$, provided $\ell_\mathcal{E} \notin V$

(B5) $\{\mathsf{E}(\mathcal{E}; y; \emptyset) \wedge \mathsf{Ind}(t; V, \ell_\mathcal{E}, y; V', y)\}\ x := \mathcal{E}(y)\ \{\mathsf{Ind}(t; V, \ell_\mathcal{E}, x, y; V', x, y)\}$

(B6) $\{\mathsf{E}(\mathcal{E}; y; \emptyset) \wedge \mathsf{E}(\mathcal{E}; t; V, y)\}\ x := \mathcal{E}(y)\ \{\mathsf{E}(\mathcal{E}; t; V, y)\}$

This is expressed in rules (B1) to (B3), and also used in the proof of many other rules. Note that, when executing $x := \mathcal{E}(y)$ on a new value, if the values of y from the two executions are equal, then of course the values of x will be equal afterwards. However, if the values of y are not the same in the two executions, then the values of x will be indistinguishable from two *independent* random values afterwards.

Since the querying of a block cipher twice at any point is undesirable, we always require the predicate E as a precondition. We also have rules similar to (B2) to (B6), with the predicate $\mathsf{E}(\mathcal{E}; y; \emptyset)$ replaced by the predicate Empty, since both imply that the value of y is not in $\mathcal{L}_\mathcal{E}$.

Hash Function:

We note that the distinguishing adversary, described in Section 2, does not have access to the random oracle. This is sufficient for our purpose since our goal is only to prove inequality of strings, not their indistinguishability from random strings. As a result, the rules for the hash function are essentially the same as those for the block cipher.

(H1) $\{\mathsf{H}(\mathcal{H}; y; \emptyset) \wedge \mathsf{Uneq}(y,y)\}\ x := \mathcal{H}(y)\ \{\mathsf{Ind}(x; \mathsf{Var}, \ell_\mathcal{E}, \ell_\mathcal{H}; \mathsf{Var})\}$

(H2) $\{\mathsf{H}(\mathcal{H}; y; \emptyset) \wedge \mathsf{Eq}(y,y)\}\ x := \mathcal{H}(y)\ \{\mathsf{Ind}(x; \mathsf{Var}, \ell_\mathcal{H}; \mathsf{Var} - x) \wedge \mathsf{Eq}(x,x)\}$

(H3) $\{\mathsf{H}(\mathcal{H}; y; \emptyset) \wedge \mathsf{Ind}(t; V; V')\}\ x := \mathcal{H}(y)\ \{\mathsf{Ind}(t; V, x; V', x)\}$ even if $t = y$, provided $\ell_\mathcal{H} \notin V$

(H4) $\{\mathsf{H}(\mathcal{H}; y; \emptyset) \wedge \mathsf{Ind}(t; V, \ell_\mathcal{H}, y; V', y)\}\ x := \mathcal{H}(y)\ \{\mathsf{Ind}(t; V, \ell_\mathcal{H}, x, y; V', x, y)\}$

(H5) $\{\mathsf{H}(\mathcal{H}; t; V, y)\}\ x := \mathcal{H}(y)\ \{\mathsf{H}(\mathcal{H}; t; V, y)\}$

For loop:

(F1) $\{\psi(p-1)\}$ for $l = p$ to q do: $[\mathsf{cmd}_l]\ \{\psi(q)\}$ provided
$\{\psi(l-1)\}\ \mathsf{cmd}_l\ \{\psi(l)\}$ for $p \leq l \leq q$

The rule for the For loop simply states that if an indexed formula $\psi(i)$ is preserved through one iteration of the loop, then it is preserved through the entire loop. We discuss methods for finding such a formula in Section 5.

Combining our logic with Proposition 1, we obtain the following theorem.

Theorem 1. *Let* $(\mathcal{F}_\mathcal{E}, \mathcal{F}_\mathcal{H}, Hash(m_1 \| \ldots \| m_n, c_n))$: **var** x; *cmd*) *describe the program to compute a hash function* $Hash$ *on an* n *block message. Then,* $Hash$ *is an almost-universal hash function if, for every positive integer* n, $\{init\}\ cmd\ \{UNIV(n)\}$.

The theorem is the consequence of Proposition 1 and of the soundness of our Hoare logic. We then say that a sequence of formulas $[\phi_0, \ldots, \phi_n]$ is a proof that a program $[\mathsf{cmd}_1, \ldots, \mathsf{cmd}_n]$ computes an almost-universal hash function if $\phi_0 = true$, $\phi_n \Rightarrow UNIV(n)$ and for all i, $1 \leq n$, $\{\phi_{i-1}\}\ \mathsf{cmd}_i\ \{\phi_i\}$ holds.

5   Implementation

We chose to go forward through the program, instead of the more common approach of going backward from the end, after implementing both methods. Going backward through the program can require exploring multiple combinations of choices that all need to be explores when many rules can lead to the necessary predicate. The presence of the logical-or connector in our logic often resulted in an exponential number of possibilities at each step. As a result, our prototype for the forward method was able to find proofs much faster than an implementation of the backwards method.

We start at the beginning of the program and, at each command, apply every possible rule. Once done, we test if the predicate $UNIV(n)$ holds at the end of the program. One downside of this forward approach is that the application of every possible rule can be very time consuming because the formulas tend to grow after each command, which leads to more and more rules being applied at every step. For this reason, we need a way to filter out unneeded predicates, so that execution time remains reasonable.

5.1   Predicate Filter

We say that ϕ is a *predicate on* x if ϕ is either $\mathsf{Eq}(x,y)$, $\mathsf{Uneq}(x,y)$, $\mathsf{E}(\mathcal{E};x;V)$, $\mathsf{H}(\mathcal{H};x;V)$ or $\mathsf{Ind}(x;V_1,V_2)$ (for some $y \in \mathsf{Var}$ and $V_1, V_2 \subseteq \mathsf{Var}$). We say that a predicate ϕ on variable x is *obsolete for program* p if x does not appear anywhere in p and if $\neg(\phi \Rightarrow \mathsf{Uneq}(c_n, c_i))$ and $\neg(\phi \Rightarrow \mathsf{Eq}(m_i, m_i))$ for any i, $1 \leq i \leq n$.[2] The following theorem shows that once a predicate is obsolete, it can be discarded.

Theorem 2. *If there exists a proof $[\phi_0, \ldots, \phi_n]$ that a program $p = [cmd_1, \ldots, cmd_n]$ computes an almost-universal hash function, then there also exists a proof $[\phi'_0, \ldots, \phi'_n]$ that p computes an almost-universal hash function where for each i, $\phi_i \Rightarrow \phi'_i$ and each ϕ'_i does not contain any obsolete predicates for $[cmd_{i+1}, \ldots, cmd_n]$.*

The theorem is a consequence of the fact that, in our logic, the rules for creating a predicate on x following the execution of command $x := e$ only have as preconditions predicates on the variables in e. As a result, we can always filter out obsolete predicates after processing each command.

Also, we note that the only commands that can make a predicate $\mathsf{Eq}(m_i, m_i)$ appear are those of the form $x := e$ in which m_i appears in e. As a result, if we find that, for some integer l, the predicate $\mathsf{Eq}(m_l, m_l)$ is not present in one of the conjunctions of the current formula (after transforming the formula in disjunctive normal form) and that the variable m_l is no longer present in the rest of the program, then there is no longer any chance that it will satisfy the conjunction with $\bigwedge_{j=1}^{n} \mathsf{Eq}(m_j, m_j)$ from $UNIV(n)$. Therefore, we can also safely filter out all other predicates of the form $\mathsf{Eq}(m_i, m_i)$ from that conjunction.

We also add a *heuristic filter* to speed up the execution of our method. We make the hypothesis that the predicate $\mathsf{Ind}(c_n; V; \{c_1, \ldots, c_{n-1}\})$ will be present at the end of the program, which is the case for all our examples, so that we can filter out $\mathsf{Ind}(c_i; V; V')$

---

[2] Here, p will usually be the rest of the program after the program point at which the predicate ϕ holds.

if $i < n$ and c_i is no longer present in the remainder of the program. In addition to speeding up the program, filtering out these predicates greatly simplifies the construction of loop invariants discussed in the next section. If we fail to produce a proof while using the heuristic filter, we simply attempt again to find a proof without it.

5.2 Finding Loop Invariants

The programs describing the almost-universal hash function usually contains for loops. It is therefore necessary to have an automatic procedure to detect the formula $\psi(i)$ that allows us to apply rule (F1). We now show a heuristic that can be used to construct such an invariant, and illustrate how it works by applying them to $Hash_{CBC}$, described in Section 3.1. One could easily verify that it also works on $Hash_{CBC'}, Hash_{HMAC}$ and $Hash_{PMAC}$.

Once we hit a command "for $l = p$ to q do: $[\mathsf{cmd}_l]$", we express the formula that holds before the loop is executed in the form $\varphi(p-1)$. The classical method for finding a stable invariant consists in processing the instructions cmd_l contained in the loop to find the formula $\psi(l)$ such that $\{\varphi(l-1)\} \mathsf{cmd}_l \{\psi(l)\}$. If $\psi(l) \Rightarrow \varphi(l)$, then we have found a formula such that $\{\varphi(l-1)\} \mathsf{cmd}_l \{\varphi(l)\}$ and we can apply rule $(F1)$.

Unfortunately, for most loops, this simple process either does not yield a stable invariant, or gives a stable invariant too weak to produce a proof. We need a heuristic to construct stronger stable invariants. The heuristic we describe here is inspired from widening methods in abstract interpretation. We start with formula $\varphi(l-1)$, and process the program of the loop once to find formula $\psi_1(l)$ such that $\{\varphi(l-1)\} \mathsf{cmd}_l$ $\{\psi_1(l)\}$. Then, we repeat this starting with formula $\psi_1(l-1)$ to find formula $\psi_2(l)$ such that $\{\psi_1(l-1)\} \mathsf{cmd}_l \{\psi_2(l)\}$. The idea is then to inspect formulas $\varphi(l), \psi_1(l)$ and $\psi_2(l)$ for patterns that can be extrapolated. For example, we can try to identify a predicate $\gamma(l)$ such that: (i) $\gamma(l)$ appears in $\varphi(l)$, (ii) $\gamma(l-1) \wedge \gamma(l)$ appears in $\psi_1(l)$, (iii) $\gamma(l-2) \wedge \gamma(l-1) \wedge \gamma(l)$ appears in $\psi_2(l)$. We then use a new starting formula $\varphi'(l)$ which is just like $\varphi(l)$, except that the occurrence of $\gamma(l)$ in $\varphi(l)$ is replaced by $\bigwedge_{j=p-1}^{j=l} \gamma(j)$ in $\varphi'(l)$. Note that, by construction, $\varphi(p-1)$ is equal to $\varphi'(p-1)$, so we know that $\varphi'(p-1)$ is satisfied at the beginning of the loop.[3]

Example: We now apply this method to $Hash_{CBC}$. After processing command $c_1 := \mathcal{E}(m_1)$, we obtain the formula $\varphi(1) = (\mathsf{Ind}(c_1; \mathsf{Var}, \ell_{\mathcal{E}}; \mathsf{Var} - c_1) \wedge \mathsf{Eq}(m_1, m_1) \wedge \mathsf{Eq}(c_1, c_1)) \vee \mathsf{Ind}(c_1)$. Parameterizing this in terms of l, we obtain

$$\varphi(l) = (\mathsf{Eq}(m_l, m_l) \wedge \mathsf{Eq}(c_l, c_l) \wedge \mathsf{Ind}(c_l; \mathsf{Var}, \ell_{\mathcal{E}}; \mathsf{Var} - c_l)) \vee \mathsf{Ind}(c_l)$$

We recall that the two instructions in the loop of $Hash_{CBC}$ are the following: $z_i := c_{i-1} \oplus m_i$; $c_i := \mathcal{E}(z_i)$. After processing the program of the loop on $\varphi(l-1)$, we obtain the following.

$$\psi_1(l) = (\mathsf{Eq}(m_{l-1}, m_{l-1}) \wedge \mathsf{Eq}(m_l, m_l) \wedge \mathsf{Eq}(c_l, c_l) \wedge \mathsf{Ind}(c_l; \mathsf{Var}, \ell_{\mathcal{E}}; \mathsf{Var} - c_l))$$
$$\vee \mathsf{Ind}(c_l)$$

---

[3] We can similarly try to find patterns that appear only after the first iteration of the loop, that is, $\gamma(l)$ appears in $\psi_1(l)$ and $\gamma(l-1) \wedge \gamma(l)$ appears in $\psi_2(l)$, in which case $\bigwedge_{j=p}^{j=l} \gamma(j)$ is added in $\varphi'(l)$.

We get this by applying rules (G1), (X1) and (X2) for the first command and rules (G1), (B2) and (B3) for the second command. Note that $\psi_1(l) \Rightarrow \varphi(l)$, so we could use $\varphi(l)$ to apply rule (F1), but this would not yield a proof of $Hash_{CBC}$. We repeat the same process with $\psi_1(l-1)$ to obtain

$$\psi_2(l) = (\mathsf{Eq}(m_{l-2}, m_{l-2}) \wedge \mathsf{Eq}(m_{l-1}, m_{l-1}) \wedge \mathsf{Eq}(m_l, m_l) \wedge$$
$$\mathsf{Eq}(c_l, c_l) \wedge \mathsf{Ind}(c_l; \mathsf{Var}, \ell_\mathcal{E}; \mathsf{Var} - c_l)) \vee \mathsf{Ind}(c_l).$$

This requires applying the same rules as before, but rule (G1) more often applied for each command. We find $\gamma(l) = \mathsf{Eq}(m_l, m_l)$ and use

$$\varphi'(l) = \left(\left(\bigwedge_{i=1}^{l} \mathsf{Eq}(m_i, m_i) \right) \wedge \mathsf{Eq}(c_l, c_l) \wedge \mathsf{Ind}(c_l; \mathsf{Var}, \ell_\mathcal{E}; \mathsf{Var} - c_l) \right) \vee \mathsf{Ind}(c_l)$$

as our next attempt at finding a stable invariant. We find that $\varphi'(l)$ is a stable invariant for the loop. So we apply the rule (F1) to obtain that $\varphi'(n)$ holds at the end of the program, and we easily find that $\varphi'(n) \Rightarrow UNIV(n)$ for all positive integer n, thereby proving that $Hash_{CBC}$ computes an almost-universal hash function.

5.3 Prototype

We programmed an OCaml prototype of our method for proving that the front end of MACs are almost-universal hash functions. The program requires about 2000 lines of code, and can successfully produce proofs of security for all the examples discussed in this paper in less than one second on a personal workstation. Our prototype is available on [14].

6 Proving MAC Security

As mentioned in Section 2, we prove the security of MACs in two steps: first we show that the 'compressing' part of the MAC is an almost-universal hash function family, and then we show that the last section of the MAC, when applied to an almost-universal hash function, results in a secure MAC. The following shows how a secure MAC can be constructed from an almost-universal hash function. The proof can be found in [4,8,9], so we do not repeat them here.

Theorem 3. *Let $\mathcal{H} = \{h_i\}_{i \in \{0,1\}^\eta}$ and $\mathcal{H}' = \{h_i\}_{i \in \{0,1\}^\eta}$ be families of almost-universal hash function, $\mathcal{F_E}$ be a family of block ciphers and $\mathcal{G}$ be a random oracle. If $h \xleftarrow{\$} \mathcal{H}$, $h_\mathcal{E} \xleftarrow{\$} \mathcal{H}'$, $\mathcal{E}, \mathcal{E}_1, \mathcal{E}_2 \xleftarrow{\$} \mathcal{F_E}$, $\mathcal{G}$ is sampled at random from all functions with the appropriate domain and range and $k, k_1, k_2 \xleftarrow{\$} \{0,1\}^\eta$, then the following hold:*

- $MAC_1(m) = \mathcal{E}(h_i(m))$ *is a secure MAC with key* $sk = (i, k_\mathcal{E})$.[4]
- $MAC_2(m) = \mathcal{G}(k\|h_i(m))$ *is a secure MAC with key* $sk = (i, k)$.
- $MAC_3(m) =$
  $$\begin{cases} \mathcal{E}_1(h_i(m')) \text{ where } m' = pad(m) \text{ if } m\text{'s length is not a multiple of } \eta \\ \mathcal{E}_2(h_i(m)) \text{ if } m\text{'s length is a multiple of } \eta \end{cases}$$
  is a secure MAC with key $sk = (i, k_{\mathcal{E}_1}, k_{\mathcal{E}_2})$.

---

[4] Here, $k_\mathcal{E}$ denotes the secret key associated with block cipher $\mathcal{E}$.

– $MAC_4(m) =$
$$\begin{cases} \mathcal{E}(h_\mathcal{E}(m') \oplus k_1) \text{ where } m' = pad(m) \text{ if } m\text{'s length is not a multiple of } \eta \\ \mathcal{E}(h_\mathcal{E}(m) \oplus k_2) \text{ if } m\text{'s length is a multiple of } \eta \end{cases}$$
is a secure MAC with key $sk = (k_\mathcal{E}, k_1, k_2)$

Combining $Hash_{CBC}$ with MAC_1 and MAC_3 yields the message authentication codes DMAC and ECBC respectively, using $Hash_{CBC'}$ with MAC_3 and MAC_4 yields FCBC and XCBC, combining $Hash_{PMAC}$ and MAC_4 yields a four key construction of PMAC and using $Hash_{HMAC}$ with MAC_2 yields HMAC.

7 Conclusion

We presented a Hoare logic that can be used to automatically prove the security of constructions for almost-universal hash functions based on block ciphers and compression functions modeled as random oracles. We can then obtain a secure MAC by combining with a few operations, such as those presented in Section 6. Our method can be used to prove the security of DMAC, ECBC, FCBC, XCBC, a two-key variant of HMAC and a four-key variant of PMAC. Since the final step of the proof for the MACs is not integrated in the logic, we cannot prove the one key variants of HMAC or PMAC, nor can we prove CMAC or OMAC, which are one-key variants of XCBC. It is however relatively simple to derive the security of these one-key schemes by hand once the security of the multiple key variants has been proven. It remains an open problem to integrate this step into the logic.

It should be possible to extend our logic to prove exact reduction bounds for the security of the ϵ-universal hash function. This could be done by keeping track of exact security for each predicate to obtain a bound on the final invariant. We are also working on integrating our tool for verifying the security of MACs with the tool for verifying the security of encryption modes of operation of [15], to get a general tool for producing security proofs of symmetric modes of operation.

References

1. Barthe, G., Daubignard, M., Kapron, B., Lakhnech, Y.: Computational indistinguishability logic. In: Proceedings of the 17th ACM Conference on Computer and Communications Security, CCS 2010, pp. 375–386. ACM (2010)
2. Barthe, G., Grégoire, B., Heraud, S., Béguelin, S.Z.: Computer-aided security proofs for the working cryptographer. In: Rogaway, P. (ed.) CRYPTO 2011. LNCS, vol. 6841, pp. 71–90. Springer, Heidelberg (2011)
3. Barthe, G., Grégoire, B., Lakhnech, Y., Zanella Béguelin, S.: Beyond provable security verifiable IND-CCA security of OAEP. In: Kiayias, A. (ed.) CT-RSA 2011. LNCS, vol. 6558, pp. 180–196. Springer, Heidelberg (2011)
4. Bellare, M., Canetti, R., Krawczyk, H.: Keying hash functions for message authentication. In: Koblitz, N. (ed.) CRYPTO 1996. LNCS, vol. 1109, pp. 1–15. Springer, Heidelberg (1996)
5. Bellare, M., Kilian, J., Rogaway, P.: The security of cipher block chaining. In: Desmedt, Y.G. (ed.) CRYPTO 1994. LNCS, vol. 839, pp. 341–358. Springer, Heidelberg (1994)

6. Bellare, M., Rogaway, P.: Random oracles are practical: a paradigm for designing efficient protocols. In: CCS 1993: Proceedings of the 1st ACM Conference on Computer and Communications Security, pp. 62–73. ACM, New York (1993)
7. Black, J., Halevi, S., Krawczyk, H., Krovetz, T., Rogaway, P.: UMAC: Fast and secure message authentication. In: Wiener, M. (ed.) CRYPTO 1999. LNCS, vol. 1666, pp. 216–233. Springer, Heidelberg (1999)
8. Black, J., Rogaway, P.: CBC MACs for arbitrary-length messages:The three-key constructions. In: Bellare, M. (ed.) CRYPTO 2000. LNCS, vol. 1880, pp. 197–215. Springer, Heidelberg (2000)
9. Black, J., Rogaway, P.: A block-cipher mode of operation for parallelizable message authentication. In: Knudsen, L.R. (ed.) EUROCRYPT 2002. LNCS, vol. 2332, pp. 384–397. Springer, Heidelberg (2002)
10. Blanchet, B., Pointcheval, D.: Automated security proofs with sequences of games. In: Dwork, C. (ed.) CRYPTO 2006. LNCS, vol. 4117, pp. 537–554. Springer, Heidelberg (2006)
11. Corin, R., den Hartog, J.: A probabilistic hoare-style logic for game-based cryptographic proofs. In: Bugliesi, M., Preneel, B., Sassone, V., Wegener, I. (eds.) ICALP 2006, Part II. LNCS, vol. 4052, pp. 252–263. Springer, Heidelberg (2006)
12. Courant, J., Daubignard, M., Ene, C., Lafourcade, P., Lahknech, Y.: Towards automated proofs for asymmetric encryption schemes in the random oracle model. In: Proceedings of the 15th ACM Conference on Computer and Communications Security, CCS 2008, Alexandria, USA (October 2008)
13. Fournet, C., Kohlweiss, M., Strub, P.: Modular code-based cryptographic verification. In: Chen, Y., Danezis, G., Shmatikov, V. (eds.) ACM-CCS 2011, pp. 341–350. ACM (2011)
14. Gagné, M., Lafourcade, P., Lahknech, Y.: Full paper and OCaml implementation of our method. Computer Science Department, Saarland University, Germany (June 2013), http://www.infsec.cs.uni-saarland.de/ gagne/ macChecker/macChecker.html
15. Gagné, M., Lafourcade, P., Lahknech, Y., Safavi-Naini, R.: Automated security proof for symmetric encryption modes. In: Datta, A. (ed.) ASIAN 2009. LNCS, vol. 5913, pp. 39–53. Springer, Heidelberg (2009)
16. Liskov, M., Rivest, R.L., Wagner, D.: Tweakable block ciphers. In: Yung, M. (ed.) CRYPTO 2002. LNCS, vol. 2442, pp. 31–46. Springer, Heidelberg (2002)
17. Petrank, E., Rackoff, C.: Cbc mac for real-time data sources. Journal of Cryptology 13, 315–338 (1997)
18. Wegman, M., Carter, J.L.: Universal classes of hash functions. Journal of Computer and System Sciences 18(2), 143–154 (1919)
19. Wegman, M., Carter, J.L.: New hash functions and their use in authentication and set equality. Journal of Computer and System Sciences 22(3), 265–279 (1981)

Bounded Memory Protocols
and Progressing Collaborative Systems

Max Kanovich[1], Tajana Ban Kirigin[2], Vivek Nigam[3], and Andre Scedrov[4]

[1] Queen Mary, University of London, UK
mik@dcs.qmul.ac.uk
[2] University of Rijeka, HR
bank@math.uniri.hr
[3] Federal University of Paraíba, João Pessoa, Brazil
vivek@ci.ufpb.br
[4] University of Pennsylvania, Philadelphia, USA
scedrov@math.upenn.edu

Abstract. It is well-known that the Dolev-Yao adversary is a powerful adversary. Besides acting as the network, intercepting, sending, and composing messages, he can remember as much information as he needs. That is, his memory is unbounded. We recently proposed a weaker Dolev-Yao like adversary, which also acts as the network, but whose memory is bounded. We showed that this Bounded Memory Dolev-Yao adversary, when given enough memory, can carry out many existing protocol anomalies. In particular, the known anomalies arise for *bounded memory protocols*, where there is only a bounded number of concurrent sessions and the honest participants of the protocol cannot remember an unbounded number of facts nor an unbounded number of nonces at a time. This led us to the question of whether it is possible to infer an upper-bound on the memory required by the Dolev-Yao adversary to carry out an anomaly from the memory restrictions of the bounded protocol. This paper answers this question negatively (Theorem 2). The second contribution of this paper is the formalization of Progressing Collaborative Systems that may create fresh values, such as nonces. In this setting there is no unbounded adversary, although bounded memory adversaries may be present. We prove the NP-completeness of the reachability problem for Progressing Collaborative Systems that may create fresh values.

1 Introduction

In the symbolic verification of protocol security, one considers a powerful adversary model now usually referred to as the Dolev-Yao adversary, which arose from positions taken by Needham and Schroeder [18] and a model presented by Dolev and Yao [7]. Not only can the Dolev-Yao adversary act as the network, intercepting, sending and composing messages, but he can also remember as much information as he needs. The goal in protocol verification is to demonstrate that such a powerful adversary cannot discover some secret information, when using some protocol(s). Clearly, if it is shown that such a powerful adversary cannot discover the secret symbolically, then weaker adversaries will also not be able to discover the secret.

J. Crampton, S. Jajodia, and K. Mayes (Eds.): ESORICS 2013, LNCS 8134, pp. 309–326, 2013.

In [11], we proposed a Bounded Memory Dolev-Yao adversary, which is very similar to the Dolev-Yao adversary. He also acts as the network, intercepting, sending and composing messages, but differently from the Dolev-Yao adversary, he can remember only a bounded number of facts at a given time. So, in order for him to learn some new information, such as a nonce, he might have to forget some information he previously learned. Clearly, our Bounded Memory Dolev-Yao adversary is weaker than the Dolev-Yao adversary, as the former's memory is bounded, while the latter's is not.

However, despite being weaker, we demonstrated in [11] that many known anomalies can also be carried out by our Bounded Memory Dolev-Yao adversary. We also noticed that the protocols for which we could replay the anomaly with our bounded memory adversary were all *bounded memory protocols*, where one considers that the memory of the system is bounded. That is, in concurrent runs the honest participants of the protocol also cannot remember an unbounded number of facts nor an unbounded number of nonces at a time. This led us to the question of whether it is possible to infer an upper bound on the memory of the Dolev-Yao adversary with respect to the memory restrictions of bounded memory protocols, that is, of the memory used by the participants.

This paper answers this question negatively. That is, it is not possible to determine an upper bound on the memory of the Dolev-Yao adversary even if the memory of the protocol is bounded. From our main result (Theorem 2), we can infer that the Standard Dolev-Yao intruder cannot be constructively approximated by an infinite sequence of increasing memory Bounded Memory Intruders. We show this negative result by proposing a novel undecidability proof for the secrecy problem with the Dolev-Yao adversary. Our undecidability result strengthens the one given in [3,8], confirming the hardness of protocol verification. In particular, we show that the secrecy problem is "very undecidable:" the secrecy problem is undecidable *even for bounded memory protocols* and thus a bound on the memory of the Dolev-Yao adversary is not computable from a bound on the memory used by a protocol. This is accomplished by a novel encoding of Turing machines by means of memory bounded protocols.

The second contribution of this paper is the formalization of Progressing Collaborative Systems that may create fresh values. We are in particular interested in Collaborative Systems [16] that occur in a closed room, where no other agent can enter and where all agents have bounded memory. We ignore concerns about an outside intruder, although inside adversaries may be present, but have bounded memory. We introduced the notion of progressing in [12] inspired by protocols, namely, by the fact that a protocol session is always progressing. That is, once one step of a protocol session is taken, the same step is no longer repeated. Administrative systems normally also have this progressing nature: once an item in an activity to-do list is checked, that activity is not repeated.

However, in [12], we limited ourselves to systems that did not create fresh values, such as nonces. Combining the progressing condition with the creation of fresh values turned out to be surprisingly challenging because of a subtle interaction between the two features. We discuss this in detail in Section 4. This paper extends the formalization of Progressing in [12] to systems that may create fresh values, based on the machinery introduced in [11]. We also prove that the reachability problem for Progressing Systems that may create fresh values in NP-complete.

This paper is structured as follows:

- Section 2 reviews the specification of bounded memory protocols, the Dolev-Yao Adversary, and of Bounded Memory Adversaries. It also reviews some of the complexity results for the secrecy problem;
- Section 3 contains the secrecy undecidability proof with memory bounded protocols. This is a novel, stronger undecidability proof, which allows us to infer that it is not possible to determine an upper bound on the memory of the Dolev-Yao adversary from the memory bound of the protocol;
- Section 4 contains the formalization of Progressing Collaborative System that may create nonces. We argue that its precise formalization is only meaningful when bounding the memory of the participants of the system. We also prove the NP-completeness of the reachability problem;
- Finally in Sections 5 and 6 we comment on related work and conclude by pointing out to future work.

2   Bounded Memory Protocols and Adversaries

We formalize bounded memory protocol theories and adversary theories by means of multiset rewrite rules, similarly as in [3,8]. A set of rewrite rules, or a theory, was proposed in [3,8] for modeling protocols and the standard Dolev-Yao intruder with unbounded memory. In order to carefully compare our complexity results, we closely follow this approach and adapt the theories from [3,8] to formalize bounded memory protocols and Bounded Memory Adversaries.

Assume fixed a sorted first-order alphabet consisting of constant symbols, $c_1, c_2, \ldots$, function symbols, $f_1, f_2, \ldots$, and predicate symbols, $P_1, P_2, \ldots$ all with specific sorts (or types). The multi-sorted terms over the signature are expressions formed by applying functions to arguments of the correct sort. A *fact* is a ground, atomic formula over multi-sorted terms. Facts have the form $P(t_1, \ldots, t_n)$ where P is an n-ary predicate symbol, where $t_1, \ldots, t_n$ are terms, each with its own sort.

The *size of a fact* is the total number of term and predicate symbols it contains. We count one for each predicate, function, constant, and variable symbols. We use $|F|$ to denote the size of a fact F. For example, $|P(x, c)| = 3$, and $|P(f(z, x, n), z)| = 6$. We will normally assume in this paper an upper bound on the size of facts, as in [3,8,16].

A *state*, or *configuration* of the system is a finite multiset of grounded facts, *i.e.*, facts that do not contain variables. Configurations, intuitively, specify the state of the world and are modified by actions. In general, an action is a multiset rewrite rule of the following form:

$$X_1, \ldots, X_n \longrightarrow \exists \boldsymbol{x}.Y_1, \ldots, Y_m \tag{1}$$

where the X_is and Y_js are facts. The collection $X_1, \ldots, X_n$ is called the pre-condition of the rule, while $Y_1, \ldots, Y_m$ is called post-condition. We assume that all free variables are universally quantified. By applying the action for a ground substitution (σ), the pre-condition applied to this substitution $(X_1\sigma, \ldots, X_n\sigma)$ is replaced with the post-condition applied to the same substitution $(Y_1\sigma, \ldots, Y_m\sigma)$. In this process, the existentially quantified variables (x) appearing in the post-condition are replaced by fresh constants, also called nonces in protocol security literature. The rest of the configuration remains untouched. Thus, we can apply the action $P(x), Q(y) \to_A \exists z.R(x, z), Q(y)$ to the global configuration $V, P(t), Q(s)$ to get the global configuration $V, R(t, c), Q(s)$, where the constant c is new.

Given a multiset rewrite system R, one is often interested in the *reachability problem*: Is there a sequence of (0 or more) rules from R which transforms configuration W into Z? If this is the case then we say that Z is reachable from W using R.

Balanced Actions and Empty Facts. An important condition for formalizing bounded protocols is that of *balanced actions*. Balanced actions were introduced in the context of collaborative systems [16]. We classify an action as *balanced* if the number of facts in its pre-condition is the same as the number of facts in its post-condition. That is, $n = m$ in Equation 1. If we restrict all actions in a system to be balanced, then the size of all configurations in a run remains the same as in the initial configuration. Since we assume facts to have a bounded size, the use of balanced actions imposes a bound on the storage capacity of the agents, *i.e.*, balanced systems have constant memory. Creating a new fact by means of a balanced action amounts to inserting that fact into the resulting configuration by replacing a fact appearing in the enabling configuration. In other words the memory of the system is only updated. No new memory space is created.

In order to support the creation of new facts in balanced systems, we use *empty facts*, written $P(*)$. Intuitively, an empty fact denotes an available memory slot that could be filled by some new information. Here $*$ is not a constant, but just used for illustrative purposes. By using empty facts, one can transform unbalanced systems into balanced systems simply by adding enough empty facts to the pre-condition or the post-condition of each rule with so that it becomes balanced. The obtained balanced system can be considered as equivalent to the original, unbalanced one, provided there is no bound on the size of configurations.

2.1 Bounded Memory Protocols

A bounded memory protocol, formally defined below, only contains balanced actions [11]. This means that the number of facts known by the participants at a given time is bounded. Bounding the memory available for protocol sessions also intuitively bounds the number of concurrent protocol sessions. This is because for each protocol session, one needs some free memory slots to remember, for instance, the internal states of the agents involved in the session. However, this does not mean that there may not be an unbounded number of protocol sessions in a trace. Once a protocol session is completed, the memory slots it required can be re-used to initiate a new protocol session.

This is different to the well-founded protocol theories in [3,8] where the rules are not necessarily balanced and where all protocol sessions are created at the beginning of the trace before any protocol session starts executing. In well-founded protocol theories, an unbounded number of protocol sessions can run concurrently and therefore participants are allowed to remember an unbounded number of facts.

Definition 1. *A theory $\mathcal{A}$ is a* balanced role theory *if there is a finite list of predicate names called the* role states $S_0, S_1, \ldots, S_m$ *for some m, such that every rule $L \to \exists t.R$ in $\mathcal{A}$ is balanced and there is exactly one occurrence of a state predicate in L, say S_i, and exactly one occurrence of a state predicate in R, say S_j, such that $i < j$. We call the first role state, S_0,* initial role state, *and the last role state S_m* final role state. *Only rules with final role states can have an empty fact in the post-condition.*

Defining roles in this way, ensures that each application of a rule in $\mathcal{A}$ advances the state forward. Each instance of a role can only result in a finite number of steps in a trace. The request on empty facts formalizes the fact that one of the participants, either the initiator or the responder, sends the "last" protocol message. In [11], one can find several examples of protocols specified as balanced role theories.

In order to allow an unbounded number of protocol sessions in a trace, we allow protocol roles to be created at any time with the of cost of consuming empty facts $P(*)$. At the same time, we allow protocol sessions that have been completed to be forgotten. Once a final role state has been reached, it can be deleted, creating new empty facts $P(*)$ in the process. These empty facts can then be used to create new protocol roles starting hence a new protocol session. Such theories are called role regeneration theories.

Definition 2. *If $\mathcal{A}_1, \ldots, \mathcal{A}_k$ are balanced role theories, a* role regeneration theory *is a set of rules that either have the form*

$$Q_1(\boldsymbol{x}_1) \cdots Q_n(\boldsymbol{x}_n)P(*) \to Q_1(\boldsymbol{x}_1) \cdots Q_n(\boldsymbol{x}_n)S_0(\boldsymbol{x}),$$

where $Q_1(\boldsymbol{x}_1) \ldots Q_n(\boldsymbol{x}_n)$ is a finite list of facts not involving any role states, and S_0 is the initial role state for one of theories $\mathcal{A}_1, \ldots, \mathcal{A}_k$, or the form

$$S_m \to P(*),$$

where S_m is the final state for one of theories $\mathcal{A}_1, \ldots, \mathcal{A}_k$.

This definition is a central difference to the setting in [3,8]. In [3,8] one assumed that all protocol sessions are initialized at the beginning of the trace, that is, all protocol sessions run concurrently. This means that there is no bound on the memory of the (honest) participants since they need to remember that they participate in a possibly unbounded number of protocol sessions. Under the definition above, on the other hand, this is no longer the case as the explicit use of balanced actions in role theories and role regeneration theories allows us to bound the memory of the participants, including the number of concurrent protocols in the system, without bounding the total number of sessions in a trace.

Definition 3. *A pair $(\mathcal{P}, H)$ is a* bounded memory protocol theory *if H is a finite set of facts (called* initial set*), and $\mathcal{P} = \mathcal{R} \uplus \mathcal{A}_1 \uplus \cdots \uplus \mathcal{A}_n$ is a protocol theory where $\mathcal{R}$ is a role regeneration theory involving only facts from H and the initial and final roles states of $\mathcal{A}_1, \ldots, \mathcal{A}_n$, and $\mathcal{A}_1, \ldots, \mathcal{A}_n$ are balanced role theories. For role theories $\mathcal{A}_i$ and $\mathcal{A}_j$, with $i \neq j$, no role state predicate that occurs in $\mathcal{A}_i$ can occur in $\mathcal{A}_j$.*

Intuitively, a bounded memory protocol theory specifies a particular scenario to be model-checked involving some given protocol(s). Besides empty facts, $P(*)$, the finite initial set of facts contains all the facts with the information necessary to start protocol sessions, for instance, shared and private keys, the names of the participants of the network, as well as any compromised keys. Here, for simplicity, we assume only symmetric keys, although other types of keys can be also formalized.

2.2 Standard Dolev-Yao and Bounded Memory Dolev-Yao Adversaries

The powerful adversary proposed by Dolev-Yao [7] acts as the network, that is, all messages communicated are sent through the adversary. He hears everything and learns messages modulo encryption. More precisely, he is capable of intercepting any message sent by a protocol participant and then store the received information, decompose it and decrypt with the keys he possesses. He cannot, however, decrypt messages for which he does not have the correct key. Moreover, he can also create fresh values, encrypt, compose messages from the information he has learned. One of his major strengths is that he can remember as much information as he wants, *i.e.*, his memory is unbounded.

Figure 1a. depicts the rules of such an adversary. The I/O rules specify the fact that the adversary acts as the network receiving all messages sent (N_S) and sending all messages that are received (N_R). The remaining rules are straightforward, specifying when the adversary may decompose and compose messages. Notice that contrary to the formalization of the bounded memory protocols, the actions specifying the Dolev-Yao adversary are not all balanced. In particular, the adversary may always learn new facts, such as in the actions DECS and GEN, where the adversary learns the contents of an encrypted message and creates a nonce.

In [11], we proposed a Bounded Memory Dolev-Yao adversary, which has many capabilities of the Dolev-Yao adversary. He can intercept, send and compose messages, create nonces, etc. But differently from the Dolev-Yao adversary, he can remember only a bounded number of facts of a bounded size, at any given time. This is formally imposed by the balanced adversary theory presented in Figure 1b. In order for him to store some new information, such as a nonce, he might have to forget some information he previously learned. This is specified by additional memory maintenance rule.

2.3 Complexity Results for the Secrecy Problem

In an interaction of malicious adversaries with honest participants, one is interested in *secrecy problem*, namely, in determining whether the adversary can discover a secret s. Formally it is an instance of the reachability problem: Is it the case that a configuration containing $M(s)$, where s is a secret originally owned by an honest participant can be reached from an initial configuration?

Undecidability of the Secrecy Problem. It is known for some time that the secrecy problem is undecidable in general [3,8]. The undecidability proof in [3,8] proceeds by encoding the existential Horn implication problem, which is also proved to be undecidable. However, in that work, one used *well-founded protocol theories*, where the memory of the protocol is unbounded. For instance, in *well-founded protocol theories*,

I/O Rules:

REC : $N_S(x) \to M(x)$

SND : $M(x) \to N_R(x)$

Decomposition Rules:

DCMP : $M(\langle x, y \rangle) \to M(x) \, M(y)$

DECS : $M(k) \, M(enc(k,x)) \to$
$\qquad\qquad M(k) \, M(enc(k,x)) \, M(x)$

Composition Rules:

COMP : $M(x) \, M(y) \to M(\langle x, y \rangle)$

USE : $M(x) \to M(x) \, M(x)$

ENCS : $M(k) \, M(x) \to$
$\qquad\qquad M(k) \, M(enc(k,x))$

GEN : $\to \exists n. M(n)$

I/O Rules:

REC: $N_S(x) \to M(x)$

SND: $M(x) \to N_R(x)$

Decomposition Rules:

DCMP: $M(\langle x, y \rangle) \, P(*) \to M(x) \, M(y)$

DEC: $M(k) \, M(enc(k,x)) \, P(*)$
$\qquad\qquad \to M(k) M(x) \, M(enc(k,x))$

Composition Rules:

COMP: $M(x) \, M(y) \to M(\langle x, y \rangle) \, P(*)$

USE: $M(x) P(*) \to M(x) M(x)$

ENC: $M(k) M(x) \to M(k) \, M(enc(k,x))$

GEN: $P(*) \to \exists n. M(n)$

Memory maintenance rule:

DELM: $M(x) \to P(*)$

(a) a. Theory for the Standard Dolev-Yao Adversary

(b) b. Bounded Memory Dolev-Yao Adversary Theory

Fig. 1. Theories for the Standard and the Bounded Memory Adversaries

it is allowed for an unbounded number of concurrent protocol sessions to run at the same time. In fact, all the protocol sessions in a trace are initialized at the beginning before any session starts. This implies that the participants of the system may remember an unbounded number of facts, namely, the facts containing the information of the protocols in which they are participating in.

In Section 3, we strengthen the result in [3,8], by showing that the secrecy problem is undecidable *even if the memory of the protocol is bounded.* This is accomplished by a novel encoding of Turing machines by means of memory bounded protocols.

PSPACE-completeness of the Secrecy problem for the Bounded Memory Dolev-Yao Adversary. Besides proposing the Bounded Memory Dolev-Yao Adversary and demonstrating that he can carry out known anomalies when given enough memory, we proved in [11] that the secrecy problem when assuming the Bounded Memory Dolev-Yao Adversary is PSPACE-complete. The key insight for this result was showing how to handle the fact that a trace may have an exponential number of nonces, which seems to preclude PSPACE membership. We circumvent the problem of requiring too many fresh values in a trace by reusing obsolete constants instead of creating new values.

The argument goes roughly like this: we assume a balanced system that consists of a number of honest participants and a Bounded Memory Dolev-Yao Adversary and an upper bound on the size of all facts. Since all actions of the system are balanced, including those specifying the adversary (see Figure 1b), the number of facts in any configuration remains the same as in the initial configuration, namely m. Moreover, as we assume an upper bound on the size of facts, namely k, then any configuration in a trace has at most mk symbols. We can then fix a priori a polynomial number of nonce names, namely, $2mk$ names, so that whenever one needs a fresh nonce, one can find a name in this set of $2mk$ names that is fresh to the participants. It may well be the case that some name in this set of nonce names is used many times in a trace. However, for the participants at that point of the trace, the name used seems fresh as no participant can remember it.

This idea will be key for our proposal of Progressing systems with nonce generation in Section 4.

3 Protocol Security Is Very Undecidable: A Bound on the Adversary Cannot Be Inferred from a Bound on a Protocol

We now detail the sound and faithful encoding of Turing machines using bounded memory protocols. We show that an attack on the given protocol by *an unbounded, standard Dolev-Yao intruder* is possible if and only if the encoded Turing machine terminates. From that we infer the undecidability of a Dolev-Yao attack *even for bounded memory protocols*. Notice that our result works even if we assume a (large enough) bound on the size of facts, *e.g.*, a bound a bit greater than 30.

3.1 Encoding of Turing Machine Tapes

Without loss of generality, let $\mathcal{M}$ be a Turing machine such that

(i) $\mathcal{M}$ has only one tape, which is one-way unbounded to the right. The leftmost cell (numbered by 0) contains the marker \$ unerased;

(ii) The initial 3-cell configuration is of the following form, where B stands for the blank symbol:

$$\boxed{\$} \;\boxed{\langle q_1, B \rangle}\; \boxed{B} \tag{2}$$

We write $\boxed{\langle q, \xi \rangle}$ to denote that the corresponding cell contains the symbol ξ and is scanned by $\mathcal{M}$ in its state q.

(iii) We assume that all instructions are "move" instructions. The head of $\mathcal{M}$ cannot move to the leftmost cell marked with \$.

(iv) Finally, $\mathcal{M}$ has only one *accepting* state, q_0.

Encoding of the Tape In our encoding, we need two honest participants only, Alice and Bob. Assume they share a symmetric key K, not known to any other participant. We will encode the tape cells separately as follows:

(a) An unscanned cell that contains symbol ξ_0 is encoded by a term encrypted with the key K

$$E_K(\langle t_0, \xi_0, e_0, t_1 \rangle),$$

where t_0 and t_1 are nonces, and $e_0 = 1$ if the cell is the last cell in a configuration.

(b) The cell that contains symbol ξ and is scanned by $\mathcal{M}$ in state q is also encoded by a term encrypted with the key K

$$E_K(\langle t_1, \langle q, \xi \rangle, 0, t_2 \rangle)$$

where t_1 and t_2 are nonces.

Motivation: The nonces t_0 and t_1 in the terms encoding the tape cell are used for two purposes:

(a) Firstly, t_0 and t_1 serve as "timestamps" of a visit made by $\mathcal{M}$ in the cell. Whenever $\mathcal{M}$ re-visits this cell, the previous term is updated with fresh nonces indicating a new visit;

(b) Secondly, as t_0 and t_1 are unique, they are used to uniquely link cells that are adjacent to each other.

For example, the initial configuration, Equation (2), with three cells is encoded by using the sequence of nonces t_0, t_1, t_2, t_3 as shown below:

$$\langle E_K(\langle t_0, \$, 0, t_1\rangle), E_K(\langle t_1, \langle q_1, B\rangle, 0, t_2\rangle), E_K(\langle t_2, B, 1, t_3\rangle)\rangle$$

Notice the role of the nonces t_0, t_1, t_2, t_3. For instance, the nonce t_1 is used to correctly encode the fact that the cell $\langle q_1, B\rangle$ is to the right of the cell with the mark $\$$.

3.2 Encoding Turing Machine's Actions as a Bounded Memory Protocol

Given a Turing machine $\mathcal{M}$ and the encoding of tapes discussed above, we encode its actions by means of bounded memory protocol called $\mathcal{P}_\mathcal{M}$. We describe the role of Alice (initiator) and Bob (responder):

Alice's Role Assume that Alice is the initiator and her initial state is:

$$\langle E_K(\langle t_0, \$, 0, t_1\rangle), E_K(\langle t_1, \langle q, B\rangle, 0, t_2\rangle), E_K(\langle t_2, B, 1, t_3\rangle), E_K(\langle t_4, B, 1, t_5\rangle)\rangle$$

The protocol starts by Alice updating all nonces t_i to t_i', and sending the following updated message to Bob. At this point, she does not need to remember the previous terms using the nonces t_i. Notice that the last term does not share nonces with the first three. It will be used for extending the tape.

$$\langle E_K(\langle t_0', \$, 0, t_1'\rangle), E_K(\langle t_1', \langle q, B\rangle, 0, t_2'\rangle), E_K(\langle t_2', B, 1, t_3'\rangle), E_K(\langle t_4', B, 1, t_5'\rangle)\rangle$$

That is she erases her memory and is ready to store new facts. In particular, she is waiting for a message from Bob of the form:

$$\langle E_K(\langle t_0, \alpha_0, 0, t_1\rangle), E_K(\langle \tilde{t}_1, \alpha_1, 0, \tilde{t}_2\rangle), E_K(\langle t_2, \alpha_2, e_2, t_3\rangle), E_K(\langle t_4, B, 1, t_5\rangle)\rangle$$

By verifying its integrity with $(t_1 = \tilde{t}_1)$ and $(\tilde{t}_2 = t_2)$, Alice assumes that there is no intrusion in the channel. If some α_i is of the form $\langle q_0, \xi\rangle$, then Alice sends openly a *secret* to Bob, otherwise, Alice sends a neutral message.

Bob's role The role of Bob is to transform the message received with the help of an instruction from the given Turing machine $\mathcal{M}$. Bob is expecting to receive a message (presumably from Alice) of the form:

$$\langle E_K(\langle t_0, \xi_0, 0, t_1\rangle), E_K(\langle \tilde{t}_1, \langle q, \xi\rangle, 0, \tilde{t}_2\rangle), E_K(\langle t_2, \xi_2, e_2, t_3\rangle), E_K(\langle t_4, B, 1, t_5\rangle)\rangle$$

Bob verifies its integrity by $(t_1 = \tilde{t}_1)$ and $(\tilde{t}_2 = t_2)$, and follows one of three cases:

(1)   (Extending the tape) For $e_2 = 1$, Bob *updates* nonces t_i to t'_i, and sends the following updated message to Alice, which provides a new last cell in the chain of four cells

$$\langle E_K(\langle t_0, \xi_0, 0, t'_1 \rangle), E_K(\langle t'_1, \langle q, \xi \rangle, 0, t'_2 \rangle), E_K(\langle t'_2, \xi_2, 0, t'_3 \rangle), E_K(\langle t'_3, B, 1, t'_4 \rangle) \rangle$$

(2)   (Moving the Head of the Machine to the Right) For an $\mathcal{M}$'s instruction of the form $q\xi \rightarrow q'\eta R$, denoting: *"if in state q looking at symbol ξ, replace it by η, move the tape head one cell to the right, and go into state q'"*, Bob *updates* some nonces t_i to t'_i, and sends the following updated message to Alice

$$\langle E_K(\langle t_0, \xi_0, 0, t'_1 \rangle), E_K(\langle t'_1, \eta, 0, t'_2 \rangle), E_K(\langle t'_2, \langle q', \xi_2 \rangle, 0, t_3 \rangle), E_K(\langle t_4, B, 1, t_5 \rangle) \rangle$$

(3)   (Moving the Head of the Machine to the Left) For an $\mathcal{M}$'s instruction of the form $q\xi \rightarrow q'\eta L$, denoting: *"if in state q looking at symbol ξ, replace it by η, move the tape head one cell to the left, and go into state q'"*, Bob *updates* some nonces t_i to t'_i, and sends the following updated message to Alice

$$\langle E_K(\langle t_0, \langle q', \xi_0 \rangle, 0, t'_1 \rangle), E_K(\langle t'_1, \eta, 0, t'_2 \rangle), E_K(\langle t'_2, \xi_2, 0, t_3 \rangle), E_K(\langle t_4, B, 1, t_5 \rangle) \rangle$$

Remark 1. Both Alice and Bob can input and output only messages of the form

$$\langle E_K(\langle t_0, \alpha_0, 0, t_1 \rangle), E_K(\langle t_1, \alpha_1, 0, t_2 \rangle), E_K(\langle t_2, \alpha_2, e_2, t_3 \rangle), E_K(\langle t_4, B, 1, t_5 \rangle) \rangle$$

where the first three components represent the chain of three cells, and the fourth component refers to the last cell in a configuration.

Remark 2. The above protocol is balanced. It can be formalized by a bounded memory protocol see [13]. In particular, only terms of height fixed in advance are used. Nonces are only updated, that is, the old nonces are replaced by new nonces. Therefore, Alice and Bob can forget the old nonces. In fact, Alice and Bob are finite automata, which are allowed to *update nonces* only.

3.3 A Man-in-the-Middle Attack by Mallory

Notice that, according to Remark 1, by active eavesdropping Mallory can accumulate terms of the form

$$E_K(\langle t_1, \alpha_1, e_1, t_2 \rangle) \tag{3}$$

if and only if they are components of outputs generated by Alice or by Bob. We now discuss the following attack on the protocol above:

(1)   For the first run, Mallory intercepts the initial message from Alice, stores it, and resends it to Bob. While Bob responds, Mallory intercepts the message from Bob, stores it, and resends it to Alice.

(2)   For each of the next runs, Mallory first intercepts the initial message from Alice. Taking non-deterministically terms of the form (3) from his memory, Mallory then composes a message of the form:

$$\langle E_K(\langle t_0, \alpha_0, 0, t_1 \rangle), E_K(\langle \tilde{t}_1, \alpha_1, 0, \tilde{t}_2 \rangle), E_K(\langle t_2, \alpha_2, e_2, t_3 \rangle), E_K(\langle t_4, B, 1, t_5 \rangle) \rangle$$

and sends it to Bob. If Bob accepts this message and responds with a transformed one as described in the protocol, then Mallory intercepts this new message from Bob, stores it, and resends it to Alice.

The following lemma shows a certain chain-like structure of the terms accumulated by the adversary. These chain-like structure are specified by the use of nonces and each chain corresponds to reachable configurations of the Machine $\mathcal{M}$.

Lemma 1. *Suppose that a term of the form $E_K(\langle t, \langle q, \xi \rangle, 0, t' \rangle)$ appears in the intruder memory by active eavesdropping. Then there is a unique sequence of nonces $t_0, t_1, \ldots, t_{n+2}$ and a chain of terms from the adversary's memory*

$$E_K(\langle t_0, \$, 0, t_1 \rangle), \ E_K(\langle t_1, x_1, 0, t_2 \rangle), \ldots. \ E_K(\langle t_{j-1}, x_{j-1}, 0, t_j \rangle),$$
$$E_K(\langle t_j, \langle q, x_j \rangle, 0, t_{j+1} \rangle), \ E_K(\langle t_{j+1}, x_{j+1}, 0, t_{j+2} \rangle), \ldots, \ E_K(\langle t_n, x_n, 0, t_{n+1} \rangle),$$
$$E_K(\langle t_{n+1}, B, 1, t_{n+2} \rangle)$$

such that

(a) *$t_j = t$, $x_j = \xi$, and $t_{j+1} = t'$,*
(b) *$\mathcal{M}$ leads from the empty initial configuration to the configuration where the string $x_1 x_2 .. x_j .. x_n$, is written in cells 1, 2,...,j,...,n on the tape*

$	x_1	x_2	$\cdot$	$\cdot$	x_j	$\cdot$	$\cdot$	x_n	$\cdots$

and the j-th cell is scanned by $\mathcal{M}$ in state q.

Proof. By induction on the number of actions performed by Bob to outcome a message one of the components of which is $E_K(\langle t, \langle q, \xi \rangle, 0, t' \rangle)$. ∎

Theorem 1. *There is a Dolev-Yao attack on the above protocol if and only if the machine $\mathcal{M}$ terminates on the empty input.*

Proof. We sketch the proof of both directions of the proof.

(a) The direction from a terminating computation to an attack is straightforward by induction on the length of the computation.
(b) The inverse direction is quite tricky. In the case of a successful attack, a term of the form $E_K(\langle \tilde{t}_1, \langle q_0, \xi \rangle, 0, \tilde{t}_2 \rangle)$, must appear in the adversary's memory. Then by Lemma 1, $\mathcal{M}$ leads from the empty initial configuration to a final configuration where a cell is scanned in state q_0. ∎

Notice that in all attacks above the attacker in fact does not need to create/update fresh nonces, but simply intercept, decompose, compose and copy messages.

Corollary 1. *The existence of a Dolev-Yao attack is undecidable even for bounded memory protocols, $\mathcal{P}_{\mathcal{M}}$, where Alice and Bob are finite automata whom are allowed to update nonces only, all actions by Alice and Bob are balanced, and only terms of height fixed in advance are used by Alice, Bob, and an adversary (even if the actions of the adversary are limited to decompose, compose, and copy).*

Proof. Given a non-recursive recursively enumerable set S, and a sequence of Turing machines $\mathcal{M}_n$ such that $\mathcal{M}_n$ terminates on the empty input iff $n \in S$, it suffices to consider the corresponding bounded memory protocols $\mathcal{P}_{\mathcal{M}_n}$. ∎

Thus an upper bound on the memory of the Dolev-Yao adversary is not computable from a bound on the memory used by a protocol. Based on peculiarities of our encoding described in Section 3.2, we can express such a phenomenon in quantitative terms.

Theorem 2. *Whatever a total recursive function h we take, we can construct a recursive sequence of bounded memory protocols $\mathcal{Q}_n$ so that*

(a) *For any n, there is a Dolev-Yao attack on the bounded memory protocol $\mathcal{Q}_n$.*
(b) *However, for any n starting from some n_0, any Dolev-Yao adversary the size of whose memory is bounded by $h(n)$ is not capable of detecting an attack on the bounded memory protocol $\mathcal{Q}_n$.*

Proof Sketch. Given a total recursive recursive function f, as $\mathcal{Q}_n$ we take the bounded memory protocol $\mathcal{P}_{M_n}$ described in Section 3.2, where M_n is a Turing machine terminating on the empty input with the value $f(n)$.

Roughly, according to Theorem 1, Mallory, whose memory size is bounded by $h(n)$, can play at most $2^{O(h(n))}$ steps. It suffices, therefore, to take the function f such that its time complexity is $\Omega(2^{2^{h(n)}})$. ∎

The Theorem above implies that the Standard Dolev-Yao intruder cannot be constructively approximated by an infinite sequence of increasing memory Bounded Memory Intruders.

4   Progressing Collaborative Systems with Fresh Values

We introduced the notion of progressing in [12] in the context of Collaborative Systems where agents interact in a closed-room setting, and no outside intruder is present. Nevertheless, there may be adversaries inside the system. We are in particular interested in systems where all agents have bounded memory, even the inside adversaries. Collaborative systems can be modelled with multiset rewriting, for instance the multiset rewriting rules for the bounded memory intruder that may be present in the system is shown in Figure 1b.

Progressing is inspired by the nature of security protocols, as well as many administrative and business processes. Namely, once one step of a protocol session is taken, the same step is not repeated. Similarly, whenever one initiates some administrative task, one receives a "to-do" list with the activities or tasks that have to be performed or achieved. Once an item on the list has been "checked", one does not need to return to this item anymore. When all the items have been checked, the process ends. Such a process is always advancing and it is completed within a bounded number of transactions. Additionally, such processes often manipulate a bounded number of values. Consider, for example, the simple process where a bank customer needs a new PIN number: The bank will assign the customer a new PIN number, which is often a four digit number and hence bounded. Even when a customer is allowed to chose a PIN number or some password, it has to satisfy some conditions, e.g., all its characters must be alphanumeric and, in practice, the password is bounded since users are never able to use an unbounded password due to buffer sizes, etc. Consequently, protocols and administrative processes have a polynomial number of steps with respect to the given inputs (or size of the planning problem). In other words they can be considered as *efficient*. That is, one does not need to perform an exponential number of actions to conclude such processes.

To formally capture this intuition, we defined Progressing in [12] as follows: A sequence of actions is *progressing* if *an instance* of an action appears at most once. Here no nonces were allowed, and an instance of an action is obtained by a substitution which replaces all variables appearing in the pre- and post-condition of the action with constants. Assuming a finite signature, *i.e.* a finite number of constant symbols, there is a finite number of instances of any action. This notion of progressing reflects the requirement that progressing processes are efficient, as one needs to consider only traces of polynomial length to check whether a process can be completed or not. For instance, the Towers of Hanoi problem has no progressing plans, since any solution is of exponential length, which implies that one and the same action is necessarily used an exponential number of times. In [12] we show that the progressing reachability problem for systems that do not create nonces is NP-complete.

In administrative systems, it is often the case that one needs to generate fresh values. For instance, whenever a new administrative process is initiated, one creates a fresh identifier different to the identifiers of all the existing processes. In this way, one does not mix up the actions needed for different processes. In [11], we provide further illustrative examples for the need of fresh values in administrative processes.

However, extending this notion of progressing to systems that can create nonces turned out to be quite challenging. The problem arises from the fact that if we allow actions to create fresh values, one may capture processes which require an exponential number of actions, that is, processes that cannot be efficiently carried out. Let us try to extend *naively* the progressing definition above to the case when actions may create nonces as follows: A sequence of actions that may create fresh values is progressing if an instance of an action, with the same constants and the same nonces, appears at most once. Unfortunately, such a definition of progressing is not satisfactory. When a nonce is created, it is fresh, meaning that it hasn't appeared in the system as yet. Consequently, every application of an action that creates a nonce is a new instance of that action. For instance, we can adapt the encoding of the Towers of Hanoi, so that for each move creates a new nonce. Thus each action is a different instance, because a different nonce is used and created. Therefore, the Towers of Hanoi would be according to the naive definition above progressing, which is clearly not what we want.

Therefore, in order to extend the notion of progressing to the case where actions may create nonces, we shouldn't allow unbounded nonce generation. Instead we need to somehow limit the use of nonces, but how many nonces is enough? This question is answered for the case when systems are balanced. As discussed in Section 2.3, for the case of *balanced systems*: one can simulate any plan that uses an unbounded number of nonces by fixing a priori a polynomial number of nonce names [11] with respect to the number of facts in the initial configuration (m) and the upper-bound on the size of facts (k). In the following sections, we formalize these intuitions.

4.1 Balanced Progressing with Fresh Values

We extend the notion of progressing for balanced systems that can create fresh values. Central to our notion will be the definition of when two instances of actions are equivalent (Definition 4). Consider for example the following two instances of an action, where the t_is are terms and n_js are nonce names which do not appear in the alphabet of the language:

$$X_1(t_1)X_2(t_2, t_3, n_1)X_3(n_1, n_2) \rightarrow \exists x. X_4(t_1)X_2(t_2, x, n_3)X_5(n_1, n_3),$$
$$X_1(t_1)X_2(t_2, t_3, n_4)X_3(n_4, n_5) \rightarrow \exists x. X_4(t_1)X_2(t_2, x, n_6)X_5(n_4, n_6).$$

These instances only differ in the nonce names used: the same fresh value, n_3 in the former instance and n_6 in the latter, appear in same facts exactly at the same places, and similarly, for the pairs of nonces (n_1, n_4), and (n_2, n_5). Inspired by a similar notion in λ-calculus [4], and α-equivalence among configurations in [11], we regard instances of actions that differ only in the nonce's names used, as equivalent.

Definition 4. *Two* instances *of an action, r_1 and r_2, are* equivalent *if there is a bijection σ that maps the set of all nonce names appearing in one instance to the set of all nonce names appearing in the other instance, such that $r_1\sigma = r_2$.*

The two instances given above are equivalent because of the following bijection $\{(n_1, n_4), (n_2, n_5), (n_3, n_6)\}$. It is easy to show that the above relation among instances of actions is indeed an equivalence relation.

Definition 5. *Given a balanced multiset rewrite system R, an initial configuration W and a polynomial $f(m, k)$, we say that a sequence of actions is* progressing *if it contains at most $f(m, k)$ equivalent instances of any action, where m is the number of facts in the configuration W and k is the upper bound on size of facts.*

Progressing reachability problem has a solution if for a given multiset rewrite system R and configurations W and Z, there is a *progressing* sequence of actions from R which transforms configuration W into Z.

Notice that our new notion of progressing extends progressing from [12], as they coincide when systems do not allow fresh values. We will, therefore, be able to compare our complexity results.

Furthermore, as per Definition 5, not every computation could be considered as progressing. Here a nonce name may only be used by the same action a polynomial number of times in a computation. Hence, not every reachability problem that has a solution will have a progressing solution. This is formalized by the the polynomial f, reflecting that the process is efficient. For example, in any solution of Towers of Hanoi puzzle, one and the same nonce name has to be updated an exponential number of times by the only action from the representation of this puzzle in [11]. Therefore this problem has no progressing solution as per our Definition 5, as expected.

Notice that, if nonces are allowed, we only conceive progressing in balanced systems, while progressing with no nonces is clear for any in any multiset rewriting system, even the unbalanced ones. This is because nonce update from [11] was only possible in balanced systems.

4.2   Complexity Results for Progressing Systems with Fresh Values

We now investigate the progressing reachability problem when actions can create fresh values.

Theorem 3. *Given a multiset rewrite system R with only balanced actions that can create fresh values, an initial and a final configurations, an upper-bound, k, on the size of facts, an alphabet with a finite number of constant and function symbols, and a polynomial f with two parameters, the progressing reachability problem is NP-complete.*

Proof. We infer the NP lower bound from the encoding of the 3-SAT problem from [12], which is well-known to be NP-complete [6].

For the NP upper bound, Assume given an initial configuration with m facts and a polynomial f with two parameters. Moreover, let n be the number of rules in R, d is the number of constant and function symbols, k the upper bound on the size of facts and l the upper bound on the number of different variables appearing in a rule in R. Here we assume k and l to be much smaller than d and m.

Following [11], we can assume that all nonces are used from a $2mk$ set of nonce names, that is fixed a priori. Hence, the number of constants in the system is $d+2mk$. As actions are applied, instead of fresh values being created, nonces are updated. Obsolete nonce names are picked from the fixed set of $2mk$ nonce names. They are, therefore, different form any nonce in the configuration and can be considered fresh.

Since the size of facts is bounded, we do not need to consider terms that have a size greater than k. Therefore we need to consider at most $(d + 2mk)^k$ terms. Since in progressing traces, one is allowed to use only a polynomial number of instances of a rule, the length of traces is bounded by

$$f(m, k) \times n \times \left((d + 2mk)^k\right)^l = f(m, k) \times n \times (d + 2mk)^{kl}.$$

The above bound is therefore polynomial in the size of the configurations, number of rules and symbols.

Assume that W is the initial configuration and Z is the goal configuration that is the configuration one wants to reach. Also assume that one can check in polynomial time whether a configuration is the final one or not. We show below that there is a polynomial-time deterministic algorithm that checks for valid computations.

We show that we can check in polynomial time, where a plan solves the progressing problem. Let S_i be the configuration at step i, so $S_0 = W$, Q_i be the multiset of pairs, $\langle r, \sigma \rangle$, of rules and substitutions used before step i, so $Q_0 = \emptyset$.

1. Check if $Z \subseteq S_{i-1}$, then ACCEPT; otherwise continue;
2. Guess an action $r_i : X_i \to Y_i$, and a substitution σ_i;
3. Check if $X_i\sigma_i \in S_{i-1}$, then continue; otherwise FAIL;
4. Check if the multiplicity of $\langle r_i, \sigma_i \rangle$ in Q_{i-1} is greater than $f(m, k)$, then FAIL; otherwise continue;
5. $S_i = S_{i-1} \cup \{Y\sigma_i\} \setminus \{X\sigma_i\}$;
6. $Q_i = Q_{i-1} \cup \{\langle r_i, \sigma_i \rangle\}$;
7. Increment i.

Since the size of facts is bounded, all steps are done in polynomial time. The only step that may not be apparent is step 4. However, the set Q_i is bounded by the length of the computation. Therefore, the reachability problem is in NP. □

Although we prove the NP-completeness above for the reachability problem, the result above can be easily be extended to the other compliance problems detailed in [14]. Finally, for our NP-completeness result, we need to assume a bound on the size of facts. This condition normally appears in the specification of administrative processes, where only tokens are used and no function symbols [15]. However, we are currently investigating ways to relax this condition, following [20].

5 Related Work

This paper strengthens the undecidability proof given in [3,8]. In particular, the proof in [3,8] uses an encoding with well-founded protocols theories, whereas our proof uses an encoding with bounded memory protocols. While in bounded memory protocols the memory of the honest participants is bounded, in well-founded protocols it is possible for the honest participants to have an unbounded memory. This is in fact the case in the undecidability proof given in [3,8]. The proof relies on an unbounded number of protocol sessions. Moreover, all these protocols sessions are created before any sessions starts executing, hence participants require an unbounded memory to remember in which protocol sessions they are participating. On the other hand, in our proof, Alice and Bob participate in one protocol session at a time. Whenever one is finished, they can re-use their memory to participate in the subsequent protocol session. This difference is crucial, as with our proof, we can infer that there is no way to compute an upper bound on the memory of the adversary from the memory bounds of the participants, demonstrating further the hardness of the secrecy problem.

Our NP upper bound for the progressing reachability problem in Theorem 3 is different from the NP upper bound obtained [1,20] in the context of protocol security. In their models, the progressing condition is incorporated syntactically into the rules of the theories. Specifically, they use role predicates of the form A_i contain an index i denoting the stage in the protocol. The NP-completeness result in [1,20] is obtained by further restricting systems to have only a bounded number of roles. We, on the other hand, bound the number of instances of actions that can appear in a plan. It would be interesting, however, to check whether our assumption on the existence of an upper-bound on the size of facts could be relaxed as in [20].

Harrison *et al.* present a formal approach to access control [10] and faithfully encode a Turing machine in their system. However, in contrast to our encoding, they use a non-commutative matrix to encode the sequential, non-commutative tape of a Turing machine. In their proofs, the non-commutative nature of the encoding plays an important role. We, on the other hand, encode Turing machine tapes by using commutative multisets. Specifically, they show that if no restrictions are imposed to the systems, the reachability problem is undecidable.

Much work on reachability related problems has been done within the Petri nets community, see *e.g.*, [9]. Specifically, we are interested in the *coverability problem* which is closely related to the reachability problem in multiset rewrite systems. To the best of our knowledge, no work that captures exactly the balanced condition nor the progressing with nonce creation has yet been proposed. In these cases, it does not seem possible to provide direct, *faithful* reductions between our systems and Petri nets.

6   Conclusions

This paper showed that the memory of the adversary cannot be inferred from the memory bounds of the participants (Theorem 2). This is accomplished by proposing a novel undecidability proof by encoding Turing machines by means of bounded memory protocols. This result confirms the hardness of protocol security. It answers negatively an open problem left in [11]. Our second contribution was the formalization of progressing for balanced systems that can create fresh values. We believe that this fragment will provide foundations for a useful class of systems, namely for systems such as administrative processes where the same instance of an action should not be performed an exponential number of times. Finally, we proved the NP-completeness of the Progressing reachability problem.

There are many directions to investigate from here. For instance, it would be interesting to check whether one can adapt the encoding of the Horn implication problem given in [3,8] to use bounded memory protocols, instead of well-founded ones. Another direction is whether one can improve the NP-completeness proof by relaxing the assumption on the upper-bound of facts. This was possible in the context of protocol security as shown in [20].

Together with Carolyn Talcott, we are investigating the use of the computational tool Maude [5] for the specification and model-checking of regulated processes, such as administrative processes [15]. In particular, we are investigating whether our NP-completeness proof can improve Maude's performance in model-checking Progressing systems.

Another direction that we are currently investigating is to extend our model with real times. In particular, systems that can create fresh values and mention real times are of great interest to protocol security. For instance, many distance authentication protocols [17,2] rely on timing measures. Thus extending our model with real times and determining decidable fragments, *e.g.*, balanced systems, is of great interest for the verification of such protocols. We are also currently implementing these protocols in Maude.

Acknowledgments. We thank Elie Bursztein, Iliano Cervesato, Patrick Lincoln, Joshua Guttman, Catherine Meadows, Dale Miller, John Mitchell, Paul Rowe, and Carolyn Talcott for helpful discussions. This material is based upon work supported by the MURI program under AFOSR Grant No: FA9550-08-1-0352 and upon work supported by the MURI program under AFOSR Grant No. FA9550-11-1-0137. Additional support for Scedrov from NSF Grant CNS-0830949 and from ONR grant N00014-11-1-0555. Nigam was partially supported by the Alexander von Humboldt Foundation and CNPq. Kanovich was partially supported by the EPSRC.

References

1. Amadio, R.M., Lugiez, D., Vanackère, V.: On the symbolic reduction of processes with cryptographic functions. Theor. Comput. Sci. 290(1), 695–740 (2003)
2. Brands, S., Chaum, D.: Distance bounding protocols. In: Helleseth, T. (ed.) EUROCRYPT 1993. LNCS, vol. 765, pp. 344–359. Springer, Heidelberg (1994)
3. Cervesato, I., Durgin, N.A., Lincoln, P., Mitchell, J.C., Scedrov, A.: A Meta-Notation for Protocol Analysis. In: CSFW, pp. 55–69 (1999)
4. Church, A.: A formulation of the simple theory of types. J. Symbolic Logic 5, 56–68 (1940)
5. Clavel, M., Durán, F., Eker, S., Lincoln, P., Martí-Oliet, N., Meseguer, J., Talcott, C.: All About Maude. LNCS, vol. 4350. Springer, Heidelberg (2007)
6. Cook, S.A.: The complexity of theorem-proving procedures. In: STOC (1971)
7. Dolev, D., Yao, A.: On the security of public key protocols. IEEE Transactions on Information Theory 29(2), 198–208 (1983)
8. Durgin, N.A., Lincoln, P., Mitchell, J.C., Scedrov, A.: Multiset rewriting and the complexity of bounded security protocols. Journal of Computer Security 12(2), 247–311 (2004)
9. Esparza, J., Nielsen, M.: Decidability issues for Petri nets - a survey. Bulletin of the EATCS 52, 244–262 (1994)
10. Harrison, M.A., Ruzzo, W.L., Ullman, J.D.: On protection in operating systems. In: SOSP (1975)
11. Kanovich, M., Kirigin, T.B., Nigam, V., Scedrov, A.: Bounded memory Dolev-Yao adversaries in collaborative systems. Inf. Comput. Accepted for Publication. An extended abstract appeared in: Degano, P., Etalle, S., Guttman, J. (eds.) FAST 2010. LNCS, vol. 6561, pp. 18–33. Springer, Heidelberg (2011)
12. Kanovich, M., Kirigin, T.B., Nigam, V., Scedrov, A.: Progressing collaborative systems. In: FCS-PrivMod (2010)
13. Kanovich, M., Kirigin, T.B., Nigam, V., Scedrov, A.: Bounded Memory Protocols and Progressing Collaborative Systems (Technical Report), http://www.nigam.info/docs/fcs13-tr.pdf
14. Kanovich, M., Rowe, P., Scedrov, A.: Policy compliance in collaborative systems. In: CSF (2009)
15. Kanovich, M.I., Kirigin, T.B., Nigam, V., Scedrov, A., Talcott, C.L., Perovic, R.: A rewriting framework for activities subject to regulations. In: RTA (2012)
16. Kanovich, M.I., Rowe, P., Scedrov, A.: Collaborative planning with confidentiality. J. Autom. Reasoning 46(3-4), 389–421 (2011)
17. Meadows, C., Poovendran, R., Pavlovic, D., Chang, L., Syverson, P.F.: Distance bounding protocols: Authentication logic analysis and collusion attacks. In: Advances in Information Security (2007)
18. Needham, R.M., Schroeder, M.D.: Using encryption for authentication in large networks of computers. Commun. ACM 21(12), 993–999 (1978)
19. Nigam, V., Kirigin, T.B., Scedrov, A., Talcott, C.L., Kanovich, M.I., Perovic, R.: Towards an automated assistant for clinical investigations. In: IHI (2012)
20. Rusinowitch, M., Turuani, M.: Protocol insecurity with a finite number of sessions and composed keys is NP-complete. Theor. Comput. Sci. 299(1-3), 451–475 (2003)

Universally Composable Key-Management

Steve Kremer[1], Robert Künnemann[2], and Graham Steel[2]

[1] LORIA & INRIA Nancy – Grand-Est, France
[2] INRIA Paris – Rocquencourt, France

Abstract. We present the first universally composable key-management functionality, formalized in the GNUC framework by Hofheinz and Shoup. It allows the enforcement of a wide range of security policies and can be extended by diverse key usage operations with no need to repeat the security proof. We illustrate its use by proving an implementation of a security token secure with respect to arbitrary key-usage operations and explore a proof technique that allows the storage of cryptographic keys externally, a novel development in simulation-based security frameworks.

1   Introduction

Security critical applications often store keys on dedicated hardware security modules (HSM) or key-management servers to separate highly sensitive cryptographic operations from more vulnerable parts of the network. Access to such devices is given to protocol parties by the means of *Security APIs*, e.g., the RSA PKCS#11 standard [1], IBM's CCA [2] and the trusted platform module (TPM) [3] API, all of which protect keys by providing an API that allows to address keys only indirectly, via pointers which are called *handles*. Recent work has tried to define appropriate security notions for APIs in terms of cryptographic games [4,5]. This approach has two major disadvantages: first, it is not clear how the security notion will compose with other protocols implemented by the API. Second, it is difficult to see whether a definition covers the attack model completely, since the game may be tailored to a specific API. Since security APIs are foremost used as building blocks in other protocols, composability is crucial. In this work, we adapt the more general approach to API security of Kremer et al. [5] to a framework that allows for composition.

Composability can be proven in frameworks for simulation-based security, such as GNUC [6], a deviation of the Universal Composability (UC) framework [7]. The requirements of a protocol are formalized by abstraction: an *ideal functionality* computes the protocol's inputs and outputs securely, while a 'secure' protocol is one that emulates the ideal functionality. Simulation-based security naturally models the composition of the API with other protocols, so that proofs of security can be performed in a modular fashion. We decided to use the GNUC model because it avoids shortcomings of the original UC framework which have been pointed out over the years.

Contributions. We present, to the best of our knowledge, the first composable definition of secure key-management in the form of a key-management functionality $\mathcal{F}_{KM}$. It assures that keys are transferred correctly from one security token to another, that the global security policy is respected (even though the keys are distributed on several

J. Crampton, S. Jajodia, and K. Mayes (Eds.): ESORICS 2013, LNCS 8134, pp. 327–344, 2013.
ⓒ Springer-Verlag Berlin Heidelberg 2013

tokens) and that operations which use keys are computed correctly. The latter is achieved by describing operations unrelated to key-management by so-called key-usage functionalities. $\mathcal{F}_{KM}$ is parametric in the policy and the set of key-usage functionalities, which can be arbitrary. This facilitates revision of API designs, because changes to operations that are not part of the key-management or the addition of new functions do not affect the emulation proof. To achieve this extensibility, we investigate what exactly a "key" means in simulation-based security. Common functionalities in such settings do not allow two parties to share the same key. In fact, they do not have a concept of keys, but a concept of "the owner of a functionality" instead. The actual key is kept in the internal state of a functionality, used for computation, but never output. Dealing with key-management, we need the capability to export and import keys and we propose an abstraction of the concept of keys, that we call *credentials*. The owner of a credential can not only compute a cryptographic operation, but he can also delegate this capacity by transmitting the credential. We think this concept is of independent interest, and as a further contribution, subsequently introduce a general proof method that allows the substitution of credentials by actual keys when instantiating a functionality.

Limitations. Our key-management functionality is currently tightly coupled with the employment of a deterministic, symmetric authenticated encryption scheme that is secure against key-dependant messages for key export and import. While practitioners indeed favour deterministic key-encryption in protocol design and standardization efforts (see, e. g., RFC 3394), it restricts the analysis to security devices providing this kind of encryption. We have not yet covered asymmetric encryption of keys in $\mathcal{F}_{KM}$ (but we cover asymmetric encryption of user-supplied data), although $\mathcal{F}_{KM}$ could be extended to support this. Second, adaptive corruption of parties, or of keys that produce an encryption, provokes the well-known commitment problem [8], so we place limitations on the types of corruptions that the environment may produce.

Related Work. Building on the work of Longley and Rigby [9] and Bond and Anderson [10] on API attacks, several recent papers have investigated the security of APIs on the logical level adapting symbolic techniques for protocol analysis [11,12,13], finding many new attacks. As discussed before, recent work on appropriate security notions for APIs in terms of cryptographic games [4,5] lacks composability. Some aspects of the ideal functionality $\mathcal{F}_{crypto}$ by Küsters et al. [14] are similar to our key-management functionality in that they both provide cryptographic primitives to a number of users and enjoy composability. However, the $\mathcal{F}_{crypto}$ approach aims at abstracting a specified set of cryptographic operations on client machines to make the analysis of protocols in the simulation-based security models easier, and addresses neither key-management nor policies. A full version of this paper with complete proofs is available at [15].

2   Background: GNUC

Hofheinz and Shoup [6] recently proposed the GNUC ("GNUC is Not UC") framework as an attempt to address several known shortcomings in UC. These shortcomings are also addressed to a greater or lesser extent by other altenative frameworks [16,17]: we chose GNUC because it is similar in spirit to the original UC yet rigorous and well documented. We now give a short introduction to GNUC and refer the reader to [6] for additional details.

2.1   Machines and Interaction

In GNUC a protocol π is modeled as a library of programs, that is, a function from protocol names to code. This code will be executed by interactive Turing machines. There are two distinguished machines, the environment and the adversary, that π does not define code for. All other machines are called *protocol machines*. Protocol machines can be divided into two subclasses: *regular* and *ideal*. They come to life when they are called by the environment and are addressed using machine ids. A machine id <pid,sid> contains two parts: the party id pid, which is of the form <reg, *basePID*> for regular protocol machines and <ideal> for ideal protocol machines, and the session id sid. Session ids are structured as pathnames of the form $< \alpha_1, \ldots, \alpha_k >$. The last component α_k specifies which protocol is run with which protocol parameters. A machine can come to life by being called by the environment or by a subroutine call. In this case, the session id of the caller has to be a prefix of the session id of the subroutine. Two protocol machines, regular or ideal, are *peers* if they have the same session id. Programs have to declare which other programs they will call as subroutines, defining a static call graph which must be acyclic and have a program r with in-degree 0 – then we say that the protocol is rooted at r.

GNUC imposes the following communication constraints on a regular protocol machine M: it can only send messages to the adversary, to its ideal peer (i. e., a machine with party id <ideal> and the same session id), its subroutines and its caller. As a consequence, regular protocol machines cannot talk directly to regular peers , but via the adversary, modelling an insecure network, or via the ideal peer, who can communicate with all regular protocol parties and the adversary.

The code of the machines is described by a sequence of steps similarly to [6, § 12]. Each step is a block of the form name [conditions]: P. The label name identifies the step. The logical expression [conditions] is a *guard* that must be satisfied to trigger a step. We omit the guard when it is true. A step name in the guard expression evaluates to true if the corresponding step has been triggered at some previous point. P is the code (whose semantics we expect to be clear) to be executed whenever the guard evaluates to true. In particular P may contain *accept-clauses* that describe the form of the message that can be input. The accept clause, too, might have logical conditions that must be satisfied in order to continue the execution of the step. Any message not triggering any step is processed by sending an error message to A.

2.2   Defining Security via Ideal Functionalities

As in other universal composability frameworks, the security of a protocol is specified by a so-called *ideal functionality*, which acts as a third party and is trusted by all participants. Formally, an ideal functionality is a protocol that defines just one protocol name, say r. The behavior defined for this protocol name depends on the type of machine: all regular protocol machines act as "dummy parties" and forward messages received by their caller (which might be the environment) to their ideal peer. The ideal protocol machine interacts with the regular parties and the adversary: using the inputs of the parties, the ideal functionality defines a secure way of computing anything the protocol shall compute, explicitly computing the data that is allowed to leak to the attacker.

For instance, an authenticated channel is specified as a functionality that takes a message from Alice and sends it to the attacker, exposing its content to the network, but only accepting a message from the attacker (the network) if it is the same message Alice sent in the first place.

Now we can define a second protocol, which is rooted at r, and does not necessarily define any behaviour for the ideal party, but for the regular protocol machines. The role of the environment Z is to distinguish whether it is interacting with the ideal system (dummy users interacting with an ideal functionality) or the real system (users executing a protocol). We say that a protocol π *emulates* a functionality $\mathcal{F}$ if for all attackers interacting with π, there exists an attacker, the simulator Sim, interacting with $\mathcal{F}$, such that no environment can distinguish between interacting with the attacker and the real protocol π, or the simulation of this attack (generated by Sim) and $\mathcal{F}$. It is actually not necessary to quantify over all possible adversaries: the most powerful adversary is the so-called dummy attacker A_D that merely acts as a relay forwarding all messages between the environment and the protocol [6, Theorem 5].

Let Z be a program defining an environment, i. e., a program that satisfies the communication constraints that apply to the environment (e. g., it sends messages only to regular protocol machines or to the adversary). Let A be a program that satisfies the constraints that apply to the adversary (e. g., it sends messages only to protocol machines (ideal or regular) it previously received a message from). The protocol π together with A and Z defines a structured system of interactive Turing machines (formally defined in [6, § 4]) denoted $[\pi, A, Z]$. The execution of the system on external input 1^η is a randomized process that terminates if Z decides to stop running the protocol and output a string in Σ^*. The random variable $\mathrm{Exec}[\pi, A, Z](\eta)$ describes the output of Z at the end of this process (or $\mathrm{Exec}[\pi, A, Z](\eta) = \bot$ if it does not terminate). Let $\mathrm{Exec}[\pi, A, Z]$ denote the family of random variables $\{\mathrm{Exec}[\pi, A, Z](\eta)\}_{\eta=1}^{\infty}$. An environment Z is well-behaved if the data-flow from Z to the regular protocol participants and the adversary is limited by a polynomial in the security parameter η. We say that Z *is rooted at* r, if it only invokes machines with the same session identifier referring to the protocol name r. We do not define the notion of a *poly-time protocol* and a bounded adversary here due to space constraints and refer the reader to the definition in [6, § 6].

Definition 1 (emulation w.r.t. the dummy adversary). *Let π and π' be poly-time protocols rooted at r. We say that π' emulates π if there exists an adversary Sim that is bounded for π, such that for every well-behaved environment Z rooted at r, we have*

$$\mathrm{Exec}[\pi, Sim, Z] \approx \mathrm{Exec}[\pi', A_D, Z].$$

where $\approx$ is the usual notion of computational indistinguishability.

3 An Ideal Key Management Functionality and Its Implementation

The network we want to show secure has the following structure: a set of users which takes input from the environment, each of which is connected to his security token. Each security tokens is a network entity, just like the users, but has a secure channel to the user it belongs to. Cryptographic keys are stored on the token, but are not given directly to the user – instead, at creation of a key, the user (and thus the environment) receives a handle to the key.

We consider such a network secure if it emulates a network in which the users are communicating with a single entity, the key-management functionality $\mathcal{F}_{\mathrm{KM}}$, instead of their respective security token. It gives the users access to its operations via handles, too, and is designed to model the "ideal" way of performing key-management. To show the security of the operations that have nothing to do with key-management, it accesses several other functionalities which model the security of the respective operations. This allows us to have a definition that is applicable to many different cases.

In this section we motivate and define our ideal functionality for key management. We explain first its architecture, then our concept of key usage functionalities which cover all the usual cryptographic operations we might want to perform with our managed keys. We then describe our notion of security policies for key management, and finally give an implementation of such a functionality.

3.1   Architecture

Policies. The goal of key-management is to preserve some kind of *policy* on a global level. Our policies express two kinds of requirements: usage policies of the form "key A can only be used for tasks X and Y", and dependency policies of the form "the security of key A may depend on the security of keys B and C". The difficulty lies in enforcing this policy globally when key-management involves a number of distributed security tokens that can communicate only via an untrusted network. Our ideal key-management functionality considers a distributed set of security tokens as a single trusted third party. It makes sure that every use of a key is compliant with the (global) policy. Therefore, if a set of well-designed security tokens with a sound local policy emulates the ideal key-management functionality, they can never reach a state where a key is used for an operation that is contrary to the policy. The functionality associates some meta-data, an *attribute*, to each key. This attribute defines the key's role, and thus its uses. Existing industrial standards [1] and recent academic proposals [4,5] are similar in this respect.

Sharing Secrets. A key created on one security token is *a priori* only available to users that have access to this token (since it is hidden from the user). Many cryptographic protocols require that the participants share some key, so in order to be able to run a protocol between two users of different security tokens, we need to be able to "transfer" keys between devices without revealing them. There are several ways to do this, e. g., using semantically secure symmetric or asymmetric encryption, but we will opt for the simplest, key-wrapping (the encryption of one key by another). While it is possible to define key-management with a more conceptual view of "transferring keys" and allow the implementation to decide for an option, we think that since key-wrapping is relevant in practice (it is defined in RFC 3394), the choice for this option allows us to define the key-management in a more comprehensible way.

Secure Setup. The use of key-wrapping requires some initial shared secret values to be available before keys can be transferred. We model the setup in the following way: a subset of users, *Room*, is assumed to be in a secure environment during a limited setup-phase. Afterwards, the only secure channel is between a user U_i, and his security token ST_i. The intruder can access all other channels, and corrupt any party at any time, as well as corrupt keys, i. e., learn the value of the key stored inside the security token. This models the real world situation where tokens can be initialised securely but then may be lost or subject to, e. g., side channel attacks once deployed in the field.

Operations required. These requirements give a set of operations that key-management demands: creating keys, changing their attributes, transferring keys and secure setup. We argue that a reasonable definition of secure key-management has to provide at least those operations. Furthermore, a user must be able to use the keys for cryptographic operations, e. g., generate a digital signature. This allows the following classification: the first group of operations defines *key-management*, the second *key-usage*. While key-management operations, for example `wrap`, might operate on two keys of possibly different types, key-usage operations are restricted to calling an operation on a single key and user-supplied data.

3.2 Key-Usage (KU) Functionalities

We now define an abstract notion of a functionality making use of a key which we call a key usage (KU) functionality. For every KU operation, $\mathcal{F}_{KM}$ calls the corresponding KU functionality, receives the response and outputs it to the user. We define $\mathcal{F}_{KM}$ for arbitrary KU operations, and consider a security token secure, with respect to the implemented KU functionalities, if it emulates the ideal functionality $\mathcal{F}_{KM}$ parametrized by those KU functionalities. This allows us to provide an implementation for secure key-management independent of which KU functionalities are used.

Credentials. Many existing functionalities, e. g., [7], bind the roles of the parties, e. g., signer and verifier, to a machine ID. In implementations, however, the privilege to perform an operation is linked to the knowledge of a key rather than a machine ID. While for most applications this is not really a restriction, it is for *key*-management. The privilege to perform an operation of a KU functionality must be transferable as some piece of information, which however cannot be the actual key: a signing functionality, for example, that exposes its keys to the environment is not realizable. Our solution is to generate a key, but only send out a *credential*, which is a hard-to-guess pointer that refers to this key. We actually use the key generation algorithm to generate credentials. As opposed to the real world, where security tokens map handles to keys, and compute the results based on the keys, in the ideal world, $\mathcal{F}_{KM}$ maps handles to credentials, and uses those credentials to address KU functionalities, which compute the results. The implementation of a KU functionality maps credentials to cryptographic keys (see Definition 2). While credentials are part of the $\mathcal{F}_{KM}$ and the KU-functionality, they are merely devices used for abstracting keys. They are used in the proofs, but disappear in the reference implementation presented in Section 3.4.

Our approach imposes assumptions on the KU functionalities, as they need to be implementable in a key-manageable way.

Definition 2 (key-manageable implementation). *A key-manageable implementation $\hat{I}$ is defined by (i) a set of commands Cmds that can be partitioned into private and public commands, as well as key-(and credential-)generation, i. e., $\mathcal{C} = \mathcal{C}^{priv} \uplus \mathcal{C}^{pub} \uplus \{\texttt{new}\}$, and (ii) a set of PPT algorithms implementing those commands, $\{impl_C\}_{C \in \mathcal{C}}$, such that for the key-generation algorithm $impl_{\texttt{new}}$ it holds that*

- *for all k, $\Pr[k' = k | (k', public) \leftarrow impl_{\texttt{new}}(1^\eta)]$ is negligible in η, and,*
- *$\Pr[|k_1| \neq |k_2| | (k_1, p_1) \leftarrow impl_{\texttt{new}}(1^\eta); (k_2, p_2) \leftarrow impl_{\texttt{new}}(1^\eta)]$ is negligible in η.*

$\hat{I}$ is a protocol in the sense of [6, §5], i. e., a run-time library that defines only one protocol name. The session parameter encodes a machine id P. When called on this machine, the code below is executed. If called on any other machine no message is accepted. From now on in our code we follow the convention that the response to a query $(\text{Command}, \texttt{sid}, \ldots)$ is always of the form $(\text{Command}^\bullet, \texttt{sid}, \ldots)$, or $\perp$. The variable L holds a set of pairs and is initially empty.

---

new: accept `<new>` from parentId;
$\quad (key, public) \leftarrow impl_{\texttt{new}}(1^\eta); (credential, \_) \leftarrow impl_{\texttt{new}}(1^\eta);$
$\quad L \leftarrow L \cup \{(credential, key)\};$ send `<new`$^\bullet$`,` $credential, public$`>` to parentId
command: accept `<`$C, credential, m$`>` from parentId;
$\quad$ if $(credential, key) \in L$ for some key send `<`$C^\bullet, impl_C(key, m)$`>` to parentId
public_command: accept `<`$C, public, m$`>` from parentId;
$\quad$ send `<`$C^\bullet, impl_C(public, m)$`>` to parentId
corrupt: accept `<`$corrupt, credential$`>` from parentId;
$\quad$ if $(credential, key) \in L$ for some key send `<corrupt`$^\bullet$`,` key`>` to parentId
inject: accept `<inject,`k`>` from parentId;
$\quad (c, $`<ignore>`$) \leftarrow impl_{\texttt{new}}(1^\eta); L \leftarrow L \cup \{(c, k)\};$ send `<inject`$^\bullet$`,`c`>` to parentId

---

The definition requires that each command C can be implemented by an algorithm $impl_C$. If C is private $impl_C$ takes the key as an argument. Otherwise it only takes public data (typically the public part of some key, and some user data) as arguments. In other words, an implementation $\hat{I}$ emulating $\mathcal{F}$ is, once a key is created, stateless w.r.t. queries concerning this key. The calls $\langle\texttt{corrupt}\rangle$ and $\langle\texttt{inject}\rangle$ are necessary for cases where the adversary learns a key, or is able to insert dishonestly generated key-material.

Definition 3 (key-manageable functionality). *A poly-time functionality $\mathcal{F}$ (to be precise, an ideal protocol [6, § 8.2]) is key-manageable iff it is poly-time, and there is a set of commands $\mathcal{C}$ and implementations, i. e., PPT algorithms $\texttt{Impl}_\mathcal{F} = \{impl_C\}_{C \in \mathcal{C}}$, defining a key-manageable implementation $\hat{I}$ (also poly-time) which emulates $\mathcal{F}$.*

3.3 Policies

Since all credentials on different security tokens in the network are abstracted to a central storage, $\mathcal{F}_{\text{KM}}$ can implement a global policy. Every credential in $\mathcal{F}_{\text{KM}}$ is associated to an attribute from a set of attributes A and to the KU functionality it belongs to (which we will call its type). Keys that are used for key-wrapping are marked with the type KW.

Definition 4 (Policy). *Given the KU functionalities $\mathcal{F}_i$, $i \in \{1, \ldots, l\}$ and corresponding sets of commands $\mathcal{C}_i$, a policy is a quaternary relation $\Pi \subset \{\mathcal{F}_1, \ldots, \mathcal{F}_l, \text{KW}\} \times \bigcup_{i \in \{1, \ldots, l\}} \mathcal{C}_i^{priv} \cup \{\texttt{new}, \texttt{wrap}, \texttt{unwrap}, \texttt{attribute\_change}\} \times A \times A$.*

$\mathcal{F}_{\mathrm{KM}}$ is parametrized by a policy Π. If $(\mathcal{F}, C, a, a') \in \Pi$ and if

- $C = \mathtt{new}$, then $\mathcal{F}_{\mathrm{KM}}$ allows the creation of a new key for the functionality $\mathcal{F}$ with attribute a.
- $\mathcal{F} = \mathcal{F}_i$ and $C \in \mathcal{C}_i^{priv}$, then $\mathcal{F}_{\mathrm{KM}}$ will permit sending the command C to $\mathcal{F}$, if the key is of type $\mathcal{F}$ and has the attribute a.
- $\mathcal{F} = \mathtt{KW}$ and $C = \mathtt{wrap}$, then $\mathcal{F}_{\mathrm{KM}}$ allows the wrapping of a key with attribute a' using a wrapping key with attribute a.
- $\mathcal{F} = \mathtt{KW}$ and $C = \mathtt{unwrap}$, then $\mathcal{F}_{\mathrm{KM}}$ allows to unwrapping a wrap with attribute a' using a wrapping key with attribute a.
- if $C = \mathtt{attribute\_change}$, then $\mathcal{F}_{\mathrm{KM}}$ allows the changing of a key's attribute from a to a'.

Note that a' is only relevant for the commands $\mathtt{wrap}$, $\mathtt{unwrap}$ and $\mathtt{attribute\_change}$. Because of the last command, a key can have different attributes set for different users of $\mathcal{F}_{\mathrm{KM}}$, corresponding to different security tokens in the real word.

Example 1. To illustrate the definition of policy consider the case of a single KU functionality for encryption $\mathcal{F}_{\mathrm{enc}}$. The set of attributes A is $\{0, 1\}$: intuitively a key with attribute 1 is allowed for wrapping and a key with attribute 0 for encryption. The following table describes a policy that allows wrapping keys to wrap encryption keys, but not other wrapping keys, and allows encryption keys to perform encryption on user-data, but nothing else – even decryption is disallowed. The policy Π consists of the following 4-tuples $(\mathcal{F}, \mathrm{Cmd}, \mathrm{attr}_1, \mathrm{attr}_2)$ defined in Figure 1.

$\mathcal{F}$	Cmd	attr_1	attr_2
KW	new	1	*
$\mathcal{F}_{\mathrm{enc}}$	new	0	*
KW	wrap	1	0
KW	unwrap	1	0
$\mathcal{F}_{\mathrm{enc}}$	enc	0	*

Fig. 1. Security policy

3.4 The Key-Management Functionality and Reference Implementation

We are now in a position to give a full definition of $\mathcal{F}_{\mathrm{KM}}$ together with an implementation. We give a description of $\mathcal{F}_{\mathrm{KM}}$ in the Listings 2 to 7. For book-keeping purposes $\mathcal{F}_{\mathrm{KM}}$ maintains a set $\mathcal{K}_{\mathrm{cor}}$ of corrupted keys and a wrapping graph $\mathcal{W}$ whose vertices are the credentials. An edge (c_1, c_2) is created whenever (the key corresponding to) c_1 is used to wrap (the key corresponding to) c_2.

Structure. $\mathcal{F}_{\mathrm{KM}}$ acts as a proxy service to the KU functionalities. It is possible to create keys, which means that $\mathcal{F}_{\mathrm{KM}}$ asks the KU functionality for the credentials and stores them, but outputs only a *handle* referring to the key. This handle can be the position of the key in memory, or a running number – we just assume that there is a way to draw them such that they are unique. When a command $C \in \mathcal{C}_i^{priv}$ is called with a handle and a message, $\mathcal{F}_{\mathrm{KM}}$ substitutes the handle with the associated credential, and forwards the output to $\mathcal{F}_i$. The response from $\mathcal{F}_i$ is forwarded unaltered. All queries are checked against the policy. The environment may corrupt parties connected to security tokens, as well as individual keys.

Definition 5 (Parameters to a security token network). *We summarize the parameters of a security token Network as two tuples, $(\mathcal{U}, \mathcal{U}^{\mathrm{ext}}, \mathcal{ST}, Room)$ and $(\overline{\mathcal{F}}, \overline{\mathcal{C}}, \Pi)$.*

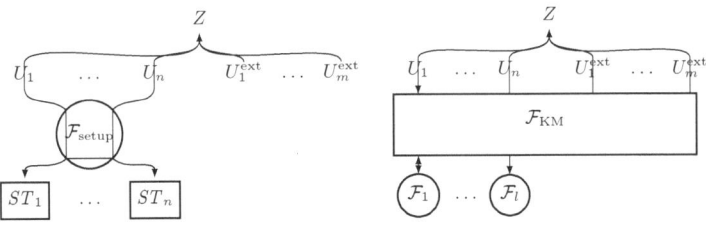

(a) Distributed security tokens in the network   (b) An idealized functionality $\mathcal{F}_{\mathrm{KM}}$ in the same network

Fig. 2. Distributed security tokens in the network (left-hand side) and idealized functionality $\mathcal{F}_{\mathrm{KM}}$ in the same network (right-hand side).

The first tuple defines network parameters: $\mathcal{U} = \{U_1, \ldots, U_n\}$ *are the party IDs of the users connected to a security token and* $\mathcal{U}^{\mathrm{ext}} = \{U_1^{\mathrm{ext}}, \ldots, U_m^{\mathrm{ext}}\}$ *are the party IDs of external users, i.e., users that do not have access to a security token.* $ST = \{ST_1, \ldots, ST_n\}$ *are the party IDs of the security tokens accessed by* $U_1, \ldots, U_n$. *Room* $\subset \mathcal{U}$. *The second tuple defines* key-usage parameters: $\overline{\mathcal{F}} = \{\mathcal{F}_1, \ldots, \mathcal{F}_l\}$, $\overline{\mathcal{C}} = \{\mathcal{C}_1, \ldots, \mathcal{C}_l\}$ *are key-manageable functionalities with corresponding sets of commands. Note that* $\mathrm{KW} \notin \{\mathcal{F}_1, \ldots, \mathcal{F}_l\}$, *and that each* $\mathcal{C}_i \in \overline{\mathcal{C}}$ *is partitioned into the private* $\mathcal{C}_i^{priv}$ *and public commands* $\mathcal{C}_i^{pub}$, *as well as the singleton set consisting of* new. Π *is a policy for* $\overline{\mathcal{F}}$ *(cf. Definition 4) and a membership test on* Π *can be performed efficiently.*

Network setup. Figure 2 shows the network of distributed users and security tokens on the left, and their abstraction $\mathcal{F}_{\mathrm{KM}}$ on the right. There are two kinds of users: $U_1, \ldots, U_n =: \mathcal{U}$, each of whom has access to exactly one security token ST_i, and external users $U_1^{\mathrm{ext}}, \ldots, U_m^{\mathrm{ext}} =: \mathcal{U}^{\mathrm{ext}}$, who cannot access any security token. The security token ST_i can only be controlled via the user U_i. The functionality $\mathcal{F}_{\mathrm{setup}}$ in the real world captures our setup assumptions, which need to be achieved using physical means. Among other things, $\mathcal{F}_{\mathrm{setup}}$ assures a secure channel between each pair (U_i, ST_i). The necessity of this channel follows from the fact that a) GNUC forbids direct communication between two regular protocol machines (indirect communication via A is used to model an insecure channel) and b) $U_1, \ldots, U_n$ can be corrupted by the environment, while $ST_1, \ldots, ST_n$ are incorruptible, since security tokens are designed to be better protected against physical attacks, as well as worms, viruses etc. Although we assume that the attacker cannot gain full control of the device (party corruption), he might obtain or inject keys in our model (key corruption).

ST_i makes subroutine calls to the functionality $\mathcal{F}_{\mathrm{setup}}$ which subsumes our setup assumptions. $\mathcal{F}_{\mathrm{setup}}$ provides two things: 1. a secure channel between each pair U_i and ST_i, 2. a secure channel between some pairs ST_i and ST_j during the *setup phase* (see below). ST_i receives commands from a machine $U_i \in \mathcal{U}$, which is formally defined in the full version [15], and relays arbitrary commands sent by the environment via $\mathcal{F}_{\mathrm{setup}}$. The environment cannot talk directly to ST_i, but the attacker can send queries on behalf of any corrupted user, given that the user has been corrupted previously (by the environment).

Setup phase. The setup is implemented by the functionality $\mathcal{F}_{\text{setup}}$, defined in Appendix A in the full version of this paper [15]. All users in *Room* are allowed to share keys during the setup phase. This secure channel *between two security tokens ST* is only used during the setup phase. Once the setup phase is finished, the expression setup_finished evaluates to true and the functionality enters the run phase. During the run phase, $\mathcal{F}_{\text{setup}}$ provides only a secure channel between a user U_i, which takes commands from the environment, and his security token ST_i.

Implementation. The implementation ST is inspired by [5] and is parametric on the KU parameters $\overline{\mathcal{F}}, \overline{\mathcal{C}}, \Pi$ and the implementation functions $\overline{\text{Impl}} := \{\text{Impl}_\mathcal{F}\}_{\mathcal{F} \in \overline{\mathcal{F}}}$. It is composable in the following sense: if a device performs the key-management according to our implementation, it does not matter how many, and which functionalities it enables access to, as long as those functionalities provide the amount of security the designer aims to achieve (cf. Corollary 1). In Section 5, we show how to instantiate those KU functionalities to fully instantiate a "secure" security token, and how $\mathcal{F}_{\text{KM}}$ facilitates analysis of this configuration.

Executing commands in $\mathcal{C}^{priv}$. If the policy Π permits execution of a command $C \in \mathcal{C}^{priv}$, $\mathcal{F}_{\text{KM}}$ calls the corresponding functionality as a sub-protocol, substituting the handle by the corresponding credential. Similarly, ST_i uses the corresponding key to compute the output of the implementation function $impl_C$ of the command C (Listings 3.4 and 1). Note that the security token communicates with its respective user via $\mathcal{F}_{\text{setup}}$, which forwards messages between ST_i and U_i, serving as a secret channel.

```
command[finish_setup]: accept <C ∈ C_i^priv,h,m> from U ∈ U;
if Store[U,h]=<F_i,a,c> and <F_i,C,a,*>∈ Π and F_i ≠ KW
    call F_i with <C,c,m>; accept <C•,r> from F_i; send <C•,r> to U
```

```
command[finish_setup]: accept <C ∈ C_i'^priv,h,m> from F_setup;
if Store[U_i,h] =<F_i',a,k> and <F_i',C,a,*>∈ Π and F_i' ≠ KW
    send <C•,impl_C(k,m)> to F_setup
```

Listing 1. Executing command C on a handle h with data m ($\mathcal{F}_{\text{KM}}$ above, ST_i below).

Creating keys. A user can create keys of type $\mathcal{F}$ and attribute a using the command <new, $\mathcal{F}$, a>. In $\mathcal{F}_{\text{KM}}$, the functionality $\mathcal{F}$ is asked for a new credential and some public information. The credential is stored with the meta-data at a freshly chosen position h in the store. Similarly, ST stores an actual key, instead of a credential. Both $\mathcal{F}_{\text{KM}}$ and ST output the handle h and the public information given by $\mathcal{F}$, or produced by the key-generation algorithm. $\mathcal{F}_{\text{KM}}$ treats wrapping keys differently: it calls the key-generation function for KW. It is possible to change the attributes of a key in future, if the policy permits (Listing 5).

```
new[ready]: accept <new,F,a> from U ∈ U;
if <F,new,a,*> ∈ Π
    if F =KW then (c, public) ← impl_new^KW (1^η)
    else call F with <new>; accept <new•,c,public> from F
    if c ∈ K ∪ K_cor then send <error> to A
    else create h; Store[U,h] ← <F,a,c>; K := K ∪ {c}; send <new•,h,public> to U
```

```
new[ready]: accept <new,F,a> from ℱ_setup;
    if <F,new,a,*> ∈ Π
        (k, public) ← impl^F_new(1^η); create h; Store[U_i, h] ← <F,a,k>;
        send <new^•,h,public> to ℱ_setup
```

Listing 2. Creating keys of type $\mathcal{F}$, and attribute a ($\mathcal{F}_{\mathrm{KM}}$ above, ST_i below).

Wrapping and Unwrapping. The commands that are important for key-management are handled by $\mathcal{F}_{\mathrm{KM}}$ itself. To transfer a key from one security token to another in the real world, the environment instructs, for instance, U_1 to ask for a key to be *wrapped* (see Listing 3). A wrapping of a key is the encryption of a key with another key, the wrapping key. The wrapping key must of course be on both security tokens prior to that. U_1 will receive the wrap from ST_1 and forward it to the environment, which in turn instructs U_2 to unwrap the data it just received from U_1. The implementation ST_i just verifies if the wrapping confirms the policy, and then produces a wrapping of c_2 under c_1, with additionally authenticated information: the type and the attribute of the key, plus a user-chosen identifier that is bound to a wrapping in order to identify which key was wrapped. This could, e. g., be a key digest provided by the KU functionality the key belongs to. The definition of $\mathcal{F}_{\mathrm{KM}}$ is parametric in the algorithms wrap, unwrap and $impl_{new}$ used to produce the wrapping. When a handle to a credential c is corrupted, the variable $key[c]$ stores the corresponding key, c.f. Listing 6. We use $\$^l$ to denote a bitstring of length l drawn from a uniform distribution.

```
wrap[finish_setup]: accept <wrap,h_1,h_2,id> from U ∈ 𝒰;
if Store[U, h_1]=<KW,a_1,c_1> and Store[U, h_2]=<F,a_2,c_2> and <KW,wrap,a_1,a_2>∈ Π
    if ∃w.<c_2,<F,a_2,id>,w>∈encs[c_1]
        send <wrap^•,w> to U
    else
        𝒲 ← 𝒲 ∪ {(c_1, c_2)};
        if c_1 ∈ 𝒦_cor
            for all c_3 reachable from c_2 in 𝒲 corrupt c_3;
            w ← wrap^<F_2,a_2,id>(c_1, key[c_2])
        else
            w ← wrap^<F_2,a_2,id>(c_1, $^|c_2|)
        encs[c_1] ← encs[c_1] ∪{ <c_2,<F_2,a_2,id>,w>}; send <wrap^•,w> to U
```

```
wrap[finish_setup]: accept <wrap,h_1,h_2,id> from ℱ_setup;
    if Store[U_i, h_1]=<KW,a_1,k_1> and Store[U_i, h_2]=<F_2,a_2,k_2>
        and <KW,wrap,a_1,a_2>∈ Π
    w ← wrap^<F_2,a_2,id>(k_1, k_2); send <wrap^•,w> to ℱ_setup
```

Listing 3. Wrapping key h_2 under key h_1 with additional information id ($\mathcal{F}_{\mathrm{KM}}$ above, ST_i below).

When a wrapped key is unwrapped using an uncorrupted key, $\mathcal{F}_{\mathrm{KM}}$ checks if the wrapping was produced before, using the same identifier. Furthermore, $\mathcal{F}_{\mathrm{KM}}$ checks if the given attribute and types are correct. If this is the case, it creates another entry in Store, i.e., a new handle h' for the user U pointing to the *correct* credentials, type and attribute type of the key. This way, $\mathcal{F}_{KM}$ can guarantee the consistency of its database for uncorrupted keys, see the following Theorem 1. If the key used to unwrap is corrupted, this guarantee cannot be given, but the resulting entry in the store is marked corrupted. It is possible to inject keys by unwrapping a key that was wrapped *outside the device*. Such keys could be generated dishonestly by the adversary, that is, not using their respective key-generation function. In this keys, the $\langle$ inject $\rangle$ call imports cryptographic value of the key onto the KU functionality, which generates a new credential for this value.

```
unwrap[finish_setup]: accept <unwrap,h₁,w,a₂,F₂,id> from U ∈ 𝒰;
  if Store[U, h₁]=<KW,a₁,c₁> and <KW,unwrap,a₁,a₂>∈ Π,F₂ ∈ F̄
    if c₁ ∈ 𝒦cor
        c₂ ← unwrap<F₂,a₂,id>(c₁, w);
        if c₂ ≠ ⊥ and c₂ ∉ 𝒦
          if F₂ =KW
              create h₂; Store[U, h₂]←<F₂,a₂,c₂>; key[c₂] ← c₂; 𝒦cor ←𝒦cor ∪ {c₂}
          else
              call F₂ with <inject,c₂>; accept <inject•,c′>;
              if c′ ∉ 𝒦 ∪ 𝒦cor
                create h₂;
                Store[U, h₂] ← <F₂,a₂,c′>; key[c′] ← c₂; 𝒦cor ← 𝒦cor ∪ {c′};
          send <unwrap•,h> to U
        else if c₂ ≠ ⊥ ∧ c₂ ∈ 𝒦 ∧ c₂ ∈ 𝒦cor
              create h₂; Store[U, h₂] ← <F₂,a₂,c₂>; send <unwrap•,h> to U
        else  // (c₂ = ⊥ ∨ c₂ ∈ 𝒦 \ 𝒦cor)
              send <error> to A
    else if ( c₁ ∉ 𝒦cor and ∃!c₂.<c₂,<F₂,a₂,id>,w>∈encs[c₁])
      create h₂; Store[U, h₂] ← <F₂,a₂,c₂>; send <unwrap•,h₂> to U
```

```
unwrap[finish_setup]: accept <unwrap,h₁,w,a₂,F₂,id> from Fsetup
  if Store[Uᵢ, h₁]=<KW,a₁,k₁> and F₂ ∈ F̄ and <KW,unwrap,a₁,a₂>∈ Π
      and k₂ = unwrap<F₂,a₂,id>(k₁, w) ≠ ⊥
  create h₂; Store[U, h₂] ← <F₂,a₂,k₂>; send <unwrap•,h₂> to Fsetup
```

Listing 4. Unwrapping w created with attribute a_2, F_2 and id using the key h_1. $\exists! x.p(x)$ denotes that there exists exactly one x such that $p(x)$ holds ($\mathcal{F}_{KM}$ above, ST_i below).

There is an improvement that became apparent during the emulation proof (see Section 4). When unwrapping with a corrupted key, $\mathcal{F}_{KM}$ checks the attribute to be assigned to the (imported) key against the policy, instead of accepting that a corrupted wrapping-key might import any wrapping the attacker generated. This prevents, e.g., a corrupted wrapping-key of low security from *creating* a high-security wrapping-key by unwrapping dishonestly produced wrappings. This detail enforces a stronger implementation than the one in [5]: ST validates the attribute given with a wrapping, enforcing that it is sound according to the policy, instead of blindly trusting the authenticity of the wrapping mechanism. Hence our implementation is more robust.

Changing attributes of keys. The attributes associated with a key with handle h can be updated using the command <attr_change,h,a′>.

```
attr_change[finish_setup]: accept <attr_change,h,a'> from U ∈ 𝒰;
if  Store[U,h]=<F,a,c> and<F,attr_change,a,a'>∈ Π
     Store[U,h]=<F,a',c>; send <attr_change•> to U
```

```
attr_change[finish_setup]: accept <attr_change,h,a'> from ℱ_setup;
if  Store[U_i,h]=<F,a,k> and <F,attr_change,a,a'>∈ Π
     Store[U_i,h]=<F,a',k>; send <attr_change•> to ℱ_setup
```

Listing 5. Changing the attribute of h to a' ($\mathcal{F}_{\mathrm{KM}}$ above, ST_i below).

Corruption. Since keys might be used to wrap other keys, we would like to know how the loss of a key to the adversary affects the security of other keys. When an environment "corrupts a key" in $\mathcal{F}_{\mathrm{KM}}$, the adversary learns the credentials to access the functionalities. Since corruption can occur indirectly, via the wrapping command, too, we factored this out into Listing 6. ST implements this corruption by outputting the actual key to the adversary.

```
procedure for corrupting a credential c:
```
```
𝒦_cor ← 𝒦_cor ∪ {c}
for any Store[U,h] =< F, a, c >
    if  F = KW
         key[c] ← c; send <corrupt•,h,c> to A
    else
         call F with <corrupt,c>; accept <corrupt•,k> from F
         key[c] ← k; send <corrupt•,h,k> to A
```

Listing 6. Corruption procedure used in steps `corrupt` and `wrap`

```
corrupt[finish_setup]: accept <corrupt,h> from U ∈ 𝒰;
    if  Store[U,h] =< F, a, c >
         for all c' reachable from c in 𝒲 corrupt c'
```

```
corrupt[finish_setup]: accept <corrupt,h> from ℱ_setup;
    if  Store[U_i,h] =< F, a, k > send <corrupt•,h,k> to A
```

Listing 7. Corrupting h ($\mathcal{F}_{\mathrm{KM}}$ above, ST_i below).

Public key operations. Some cryptographic operations (e. g., digital signatures) allow users without access to a security token to perform certain operations (e. g., signature verification). Those commands do not require knowledge of the credential (in $\mathcal{F}_{\mathrm{KM}}$), or the secret part of the key (in ST). They can be computed using publicly available information. In the case where participants in a high-level protocol make use of, e. g., signature verification, but nothing else, the protocol can be implemented without requiring those parties to have their own security tokens. Note that $\mathcal{F}_{\mathrm{KM}}$ relays this call to the underlying KU functionality unaltered, and independent of its store and policy (see Figure 8). The implementation ST_i does not implement this step, since U_i, U_i^{ext} compute $impl_C(public, m)$ themselves.

```
public_command: accept <C,public,m> from U ∈ U ∪ Uᵉˣᵗ;
    if C ∈ C_{i,pub}
        call F_i with <C,public,m>; accept <C•,r> from F_i; send <C•,r> to U
```

Listing 8. Computing the public commands C using *public* and m ($\mathcal{F}_{\mathrm{KM}}$, note that ST_i does not implement this step).

Before we give the formal definition of $\mathcal{F}_{\mathrm{KM}}$, note that $\mathcal{F}_{\mathrm{KM}}$ is not an ideal protocol in the sense of [6, § 8.2], since not every regular protocol machine runs the dummy party protocol – the party <reg, $\mathcal{F}_i$> relays the communication with the KU functionalities.

Definition 6 ($\mathcal{F}_{\mathrm{KM}}$). *Given the KU parameters* $\overline{\mathcal{F}}, \overline{\mathcal{C}}, \Pi,$ *and polytime algorithms* wrap, unwrap *and* impl$_{new}$, *let the ideal protocols* $\mathcal{F}_{p+1}, \dots, \mathcal{F}_l$ *be rooted at* prot-$\mathcal{F}_{p+1}$, $\dots,$prot-$\mathcal{F}_l$. *In addition to those protocols names,* $\mathcal{F}_{\mathrm{KM}}$ *defines the protocol name* prot-fkm. *For* prot-fkm, *the protocol defines the following behaviour: a regular protocol machine with machine id* <<reg, $\mathcal{F}_i$>, sid> *for* $\mathcal{F}_i \in \{\mathcal{F}_1, \dots, \mathcal{F}_l\}$ *runs the following code:*

```
ready: accept <ready> from parentId
    send <ready> to <ideal,sid> (= F_KM)
relay_to: accept <m> from <ideal,sid> (= F_KM)
    send <m> to <<reg,F_i>,<sid,<prot−F_i,<>>> (= F_i)
relay_from: accept <m> from <<reg,F_i>,<sid,<prot−F_i,<>>>
    send <m> to <ideal,sid> (= F_KM)
```

The ideal party runs the logic for $\mathcal{F}_{\mathrm{KM}}$ *described in Listings 2 to 7.*

Remark 1: Credentials for different KU functionalities are distinct. It is nonetheless possible to encrypt and decrypt arbitrary credentials using <wrap> and <unwrap>. Suppose a designer wants to prove a Security API secure which uses shared keys for different operations. One way or another, she would need to prove that those roles do not interfere. For this case, we suggest providing a functionality that combines the two KU functionalities, and proving that the implementation of the two operations combined emulates the combined functionality. It is possible to assign different attributes to keys of the same KU functionality, and thus restrict their use to certain commands, effectively providing different roles for credentials to the same KU functionality. This can be done by specifying two attributes for the two roles and defining a policy that restricts which operation is permitted for a key of each attribute.

Remark 2: Many commonly used functionalities are not *caller-independent*, often the access to critical functions is restricted to a network party that is encoded in the session identifier. However, we think that it is possible to construct caller-independent functionalities for many functionalities, if the implementation relies on keys but is otherwise stateless. A general technique for transforming such functionalities into key-manageable functionalities that preserves existing proofs is work in progress.

Properties. In order to identify some properties we get from the design of $\mathcal{F}_{\mathrm{KM}}$, we introduce the notion of an attribute policy graph:

Definition 7. *We define a family of* attribute policy graphs $(\mathcal{A}_{\Pi,\mathcal{F}})$, *one for each KU functionality* $\mathcal{F}$ *and one for key-wrapping (in which case* $\mathcal{F} =$ KW) *as follows: a is* *a node in* $\mathcal{A}_{\Pi,\mathcal{F}}$ *if* $(\mathcal{F}, C, a, a') \in \Pi$ *for some* C, a', *and additionally marked* new *if* $(\mathcal{F}, \text{new}, a, a') \in \Pi$. *An edge* (a, a') *is in* $\mathcal{A}_{\Pi,\mathcal{F}}$ *whenever* $(\mathcal{F}, \text{attribute\_change}, a, a') \in \Pi$.

Example 2. For the policy Π described in Example 1, the attribute policy graph $\mathcal{A}_{\Pi,\text{KW}}$ contains one node 1 connected to itself and marked new. Similarly, the attribute policy graph $\mathcal{A}_{\Pi,\mathcal{F}_{\text{enc}}}$ contains one node 0 connected to itself and marked new.

The following theorem shows that *(i)* the set of attributes an uncorrupted key can have in $\mathcal{F}_{\text{KM}}$ is determined by the attribute policy graph, *(ii)* second, there are exactly three ways to corrupt a key, and *(iii)* KU-functionalities receive the corrupt message only if a key is corrupted. The proof of these claims can be found in the full version [15].

Theorem 1 (Properties of $\mathcal{F}_{\text{KM}}$). *Every instance of* $\mathcal{F}_{\text{KM}}$ *with parameters* $\overline{\mathcal{F}}, \overline{\mathcal{C}}, \Pi$ *and session parameters* $\mathcal{U}, \mathcal{U}^{\text{ext}}, \mathcal{ST}, Room$ *has the following properties:*

(1) *At any step of an execution of* $[\mathcal{F}_{\text{KM}}, A_D, Z]$, *the following holds for* $\mathcal{F}_{\text{KM}}$: *for all* $\text{Store}[U, h] = \langle \mathcal{F}, a, c \rangle$ *such that* $c \notin \mathcal{K}_{\text{cor}}$, *there is a node* a' *marked* new *in the attribute policy graph* $\mathcal{A}_{\Pi,\mathcal{F}}$ *such that* a *is reachable from* a' *in* $\mathcal{A}_{\Pi,\mathcal{F}}$ *and there was a step* new *where* $\text{Store}[U', h'] = \langle \mathcal{F}, a', c \rangle$ *was added.*

(2) *At any step of an execution of* $[\mathcal{F}_{\text{KM}}, A_D, Z]$, *the following holds for* $\mathcal{F}_{\text{KM}}$: *all* $c \in \mathcal{K}_{\text{cor}}$ *were either*

  (a) directly corrupted: *there was a* corrupt *triggered by a query* $\langle \text{corrupt}, \text{h} \rangle$ *from* U *while* $\text{Store}[U, h] = \langle \mathcal{F}, a, c \rangle$, *or indirectly, that is,*

  (b) corrupted via wrapping: *there is* $c' \in \mathcal{K}_{\text{cor}}$ *such that at some point the* wrap *step was triggered by a message* $\langle \text{ wrap}, h', h, id \rangle$ *from* U *while* $\text{Store}[U, h'] = \langle \text{KW}, a', c' \rangle$, $\text{Store}[U, h] = \langle \mathcal{F}, a, c \rangle$, *or*

  (c) corrupted via unwrapping (injected): *there is* $c' \in \mathcal{K}_{\text{cor}}$ *such that at some point the* unwrap *step was triggered by a message* $\langle \text{ unwrap}, h', w, a, F, id \rangle$ *from* U *while* $\text{Store}[U, h'] = \langle \text{KW}, a', c' \rangle$ *and* $c = \text{unwrap}_{c'}^{\langle F, a, id \rangle}(w)$ *for some* a, F *and* id.

(3) *At any step of an execution of* $[\mathcal{F}_{\text{KM}}, A_D, Z]$, *the following holds: whenever an ideal machine* $\mathcal{F}_i = \langle \text{ideal}, \langle \text{sid}, \langle \mathcal{F}_i, F \rangle \rangle \rangle$, $F = \langle \langle \text{reg}, \mathcal{F} \rangle, \langle \text{sid} \rangle \rangle$, *accepts the message* $\langle \text{corrupt}, c \rangle$ *for some* c *such that* $\mathcal{F}_{\text{KM}}$ *in session* sid *has an entry* $\text{Store}[U, \; h] = <\mathcal{F}_i, a, c>$, *then* $c \in \mathcal{K}_{\text{cor}}$ *in* $\mathcal{F}_{\text{KM}}$.

4 Proof Overview

We show that, for arbitrary KU parameters $\overline{\mathcal{F}}, \overline{\mathcal{C}}, \Pi$, the network $\pi_{\overline{\mathcal{F}}, \overline{\mathcal{C}}, \Pi, \overline{\text{Impl}}}$, consisting of the set of users $\mathcal{U}$ connected to security tokens $\mathcal{ST}$, the set of external users $\mathcal{U}^{\text{ext}}$ and the functionality $\mathcal{F}_{\text{setup}}$, emulates the key-management functionality $\mathcal{F}_{\text{KM}}$. We will only give a proof sketch here, the complete proof can be found in the full version [15].

Let $\pi_{\overline{\mathcal{F}}, \overline{\mathcal{C}}, \Pi, \overline{\text{Impl}}}$ (in the following: π) denote the network consisting of the programs $\pi(\text{prot-fkm})$ and $\pi(\text{prot-fsetup})$. $\pi(\text{prot-fkm})$ defines the behaviours for users in $\mathcal{U}, \mathcal{U}^{\text{ext}}$ and $\mathcal{ST}$. Parties in $\mathcal{U} \cup \mathcal{U}^{\text{ext}}$ will act according to the convention on machine corruption defined in [6, § 8.1], while parties in $\mathcal{ST}$ will ignore corruption requests (security tokens are assumed to be incorruptible). $\pi(\texttt{prot-fkm})$ is *totally regular*, that is, for other machines, in particular ideal machines, it responds to any message with an error message to the adversary. The protocol π is a $\mathcal{F}_{\text{setup}}$-hybrid protocol.

The proof proceeds as follows: making use of the composition theorem, the last functionality $\mathcal{F}_l$ in $\mathcal{F}_{\text{KM}}$ can be substituted by its key-manageable implementation $\hat{I}_L$. Then, $\mathcal{F}_{\text{KM}}$ can simulate $\hat{I}$ instead of calling it. Let $\mathcal{F}_{\text{KM}}\{\mathcal{F}_l/\hat{I}_l\}$ be the resulting functionality. In the next step, calls to this simulation are substituted by calls to the functions used in $\hat{I}$, $impl_C$ for each $C \in \mathcal{C}_l$. The resulting, partially implemented functionality $\mathcal{F}_{\text{KM}}\{\mathcal{F}_l/\texttt{Impl}_{\mathcal{F}_l}\}$ saves keys rather than credentials (for $\mathcal{F}_l$). We repeat the previous steps until $\mathcal{F}_{\text{KM}}$ does not call any KU functionalities anymore, i. e., we have $\mathcal{F}_{\text{KM}}\{\mathcal{F}_1/\texttt{Impl}_{\mathcal{F}_1}, \ldots, \mathcal{F}_n/\texttt{Impl}_{\mathcal{F}_n}\}$. Then we show that the network of distributed token π emulates the monolithic block $\mathcal{F}_{\text{KM}}\{\mathcal{F}_1/\texttt{Impl}_{\mathcal{F}_1}, \ldots, \mathcal{F}_n/\texttt{Impl}_{\mathcal{F}_n}\}$ that does not call KU functionalities anymore, using a reduction to the security of the key-wrapping scheme. This last step requires restricting the set of environments to those which guarantee that keys are not corrupted after they have been used to wrap. The notion of a *guaranteeing environment*, and the predicate *corrupt-before-wrap* are formally defined in Appendix D [15]. The main result follows from the transitivity of emulation and two lemmas describing the steps we just mentioned.

Corollary 1. *Let $\overline{\mathcal{F}}, \overline{\mathcal{C}}, \Pi$ be KU parameters such that all $F \in \overline{\mathcal{F}}$ are key-manageable. Let $\texttt{Impl}_{\mathcal{F}_i}$ be the functions defining the key-manageable implementation $\hat{I}_i$ of $\mathcal{F}_i$. If $KW = (impl_{\text{new}}^{\text{KW}}, \textsf{wrap}, \textsf{unwrap})$ is a secure and correct key-wrapping scheme(See Definition 12 in Appendix D [15]), then $\pi_{\overline{\mathcal{F}}, \overline{\mathcal{C}}, \Pi, \overline{\texttt{Impl}}}$ emulates $\mathcal{F}_{\text{KM}}$ for environments that guarantee* corrupt-before-wrap.

5   Realizing Key-Usage Functionalities for a Static Key-Hierarchy

To demonstrate the use of Corollary 1, we equip the security token with the functionalities $\mathcal{F}_1 = \mathcal{F}_{\text{Rand}}$ and $\mathcal{F}_2 = \mathcal{F}_{\text{SIG}}$ described below. The resulting security token $ST^{\mathcal{F}_{\text{Rand}}, \mathcal{F}_{\text{SIG}}}$ is able to encrypt keys and random values and sign user-supplied data. It is not able to sign keys, as this task is part of the key-management. The first functionality, $\mathcal{F}_{\text{Rand}}$, is unusual, but demonstrates what can be done within the design of $\mathcal{F}_{\text{KM}}$, as well as it's limitations. It models how random values can be stored as keys, with equality tests and corruption, which means here that the adversary learns the value of the random value. Since our framework requires a strict division between key-management and usage, they can be transmitted (using wrap) and compared, but not appear elsewhere, since other KU functionalities shall not use them. We define $\mathcal{F}_{\text{Rand}}$ as follows:

new: accept $<$new$>$ from parentId $(=:p)$;
$\qquad c \leftarrow \{0,1\}^\eta$; $L \leftarrow L \cup \{(c,0)\}$; send $<$new$^\bullet$,c,$>$ to p
command: accept $<$equal,c,$n>$ from p;
$\qquad$ if $(c,k) \in L$ for some k
$\qquad\qquad$ if $k \notin \mathcal{K}_{\text{cor}}$ send $<$equal$^\bullet$,false$>$ to p
$\qquad\qquad$ else if $n = k$ send $<$equal$^\bullet$,true$>$ to p
corrupt: accept $<$corrupt,$c>$ from p;
$\qquad$ if $(c,0) \in L$
$\qquad\qquad k \leftarrow \{0,1\}^\eta$; $L \leftarrow (L \setminus \{(c,0)\}) \cup \{(c,k)\}$; $\mathcal{K}_{\text{cor}} = \mathcal{K}_{\text{cor}} \cup \{k\}$;

send $<$corrupt$^\bullet, k>$ to A

inject: accept $<$inject,$n>$ from P;
    $(c,<$ignore$>) \leftarrow \{0,1\}^\eta$; $\mathcal{K}_{\text{cor}} \leftarrow \mathcal{K}_{\text{cor}} \cup \{n\}$; $L \leftarrow L \cup \{(c,n)\}$;
    send $<$inject$^\bullet,c>$ to parentId

The two functions $impl_{\text{new}}$ and $impl_{\text{equal}}$ give the key-manageable implementation: $impl_{\text{new}}$ on input 1^η gives output $(n, \_)$ for $n \leftarrow \{0,1\}^\eta$; $impl_{\text{equal}}$ on input n, n' gives output $n = n'$.

Due to space restrictions, the signature functionality $\mathcal{F}_{\text{SIG}}$ is presented in the full version [15]. In the following, we will consider $\mathcal{F}_{\text{KM}}$ for the parameters $\overline{\mathcal{F}} = \{\mathcal{F}_{\text{Rand}}, \mathcal{F}_{\text{SIG}}\}$, $\overline{\mathcal{C}} = \{\{$ equal$\}, \{$sign, verify$\}\}$ and a static key-hierarchy Π, which

$\mathcal{F}$	Cmd	attr$_1$	attr$_2$
KW	new	> 0	$*$
$\neq$ KW	new	0	$*$
$*$	attribute_change	a	a
KW	wrap	> 0	attr$_1 >$ attr$_2$
KW	unwrap	> 0	attr$_1 >$ attr$_2$
$\mathcal{F}_i$	$C \in \mathcal{C}^{priv}$	0	$*$

is defined as the relation that consists of all 4-tuples $(\mathcal{F}, \text{Cmd}, \text{attr}_1, \text{attr}_2)$ such that the conditions in one of the lines in the following table holds. Theorem 1 allows immediately to conclude some useful properties on this instantiation of $\mathcal{F}_{\text{KM}}$: from *(1)* we conclude that all keys with $c \notin \mathcal{K}_{\text{cor}}$ have the attribute they were created with. This also means that the same credential has the same attribute, no matter which user accesses it. From *(2)*, we can see that for each corrupted credential $c \in \mathcal{K}_{\text{cor}}$, there was either a query $<$ corrupt, h $>$, where Store$[U, h] =< \mathcal{F}, a, c >$, or there exists Store$[U, h'] =<$ KW$, a', c' >$, Store$[U, h] =< \mathcal{F}, a, c >$ and a query $<$wrap, $h', h, id>$ was emitted, for $c' \in \mathcal{K}_{\text{cor}}$, or an unwrap query $<$unwrap, $h', w, a, F, id>$ for a $c \in \mathcal{K}_{\text{cor}}$ was emitted. By the definition of the strict key-hierarchy policy, in the latter two cases we have that $a' > a$. It follows that, for any credential c for $\mathcal{F}$, such that Store$[U, h] =< \mathcal{F}, a, c >$ for some U, h and $a, c \notin \mathcal{K}_{\text{cor}}$, as long as every corruption query $<$ corrupt, h$^* >$ at U was addressed to a different key of lower or equal rank key, i. e., Store$[U, h^*] =<$ KW$, a^*, c^* >$, $c^* \neq c$ and $a^* \leq a$. By *(3)*, those credentials have not been corrupted in their respective functionality, i. e., it has never received a message $<$corrupt, $c>$.

6 Conclusions and Outlook

We have presented a provably secure framework for key management in the GNUC model. In further work, we are currently developing a technique for transforming functionalities that use keys but are not key-manageable into key-manageable functionalities in the sense of Definition 2. This way, existing proofs could be used to develop a secure implementation of cryptographic primitives in a plug-and-play manner. Investigating the restrictions of this approach could teach us more about the modelling of keys in simulation-based security.

Acknowledgments. This work has been partially supported by the European Research Council under the European Union's Seventh Framework Programme (FP7/2007-2013) / ERC grant agreement n° 258865, project ProSecure, and by the Direction Générale de l'Armement, contact no 11810242, Secure Interfaces. The authors thank the anonymous reviewers as well as R. Küsters and M. Tuengerthal for their helpful comments.

References

1. RSA Security Inc.: PKCS #11: Cryptographic Token Interface Standard v2.20 (June 2004)
2. IBM: CCA Basic Services Reference and Guide (October 2006),
   http://www-03.ibm.com/security/cryptocards/pdfs/bs327.pdf
3. Trusted Computing Group: TPM Specification version 1.2. Parts 1–3, revision 103 (2007),
   http://www.trustedcomputinggroup.org/
   resources/tpm_main_specification
4. Cachin, C., Chandran, N.: A secure cryptographic token interface. In: Proc. 22th IEEE Computer Security Foundation Symposium, CSF 2009, pp. 141–153. IEEE Comp. Soc. Press (2009)
5. Kremer, S., Steel, G., Warinschi, B.: Security for key management interfaces. In: Proc. 24th IEEE Computer Security Foundations Symposium, CSF 2011, pp. 66–82. IEEE Comp. Soc. Press (2011)
6. Hofheinz, D., Shoup, V.: GNUC: A new universal composability framework. Cryptology ePrint Archive, Report 2011/303 (2011), http://eprint.iacr.org/
7. Canetti, R.: Universally composable signature, certification, and authentication. In: Proc. 17th IEEE workshop on Computer Security Foundations, CSFW 2004, pp. 219–233. IEEE Computer Society (2004)
8. Hofheinz, D.: Possibility and impossibility results for selective decommitments. J. Cryptology 24(3), 470–516 (2011)
9. Longley, D., Rigby, S.: An automatic search for security flaws in key management schemes. Computers and Security 11(1), 75–89 (1992)
10. Bond, M., Anderson, R.: API level attacks on embedded systems. IEEE Computer Magazine, 67–75 (October 2001)
11. Bortolozzo, M., Centenaro, M., Focardi, R., Steel, G.: Attacking and fixing PKCS#11 security tokens. In: Proc. 17th ACM Conference on Computer and Communications Security, CCS 2010, Chicago, Illinois, USA, pp. 260–269. ACM Press (October 2010)
12. Cortier, V., Keighren, G., Steel, G.: Automatic analysis of the security of XOR-based key management schemes. In: Grumberg, O., Huth, M. (eds.) TACAS 2007. LNCS, vol. 4424, pp. 538–552. Springer, Heidelberg (2007)
13. Delaune, S., Kremer, S., Steel, G.: Formal analysis of PKCS#11 and proprietary extensions. Journal of Computer Security 18(6), 1211–1245 (2010)
14. Küsters, R., Tuengerthal, M.: Ideal Key Derivation and Encryption in Simulation-Based Security. In: Kiayias, A. (ed.) CT-RSA 2011. LNCS, vol. 6558, pp. 161–179. Springer, Heidelberg (2011)
15. Kremer, S., Künnemann, R., Steel, G.: Universally composable key-management (2012), http://eprint.iacr.org/2012/189
16. Küsters, R.: Simulation-Based Security with Inexhaustible Interactive Turing Machines. In: Proc. 19th IEEE Computer Security Foundations Workshop, CSFW 2006, pp. 309–320. IEEE Comp. Soc. Press (2006)
17. Maurer, U., Renner, R.: Abstract cryptography. In: Proc. 2nd Symposium in Innovations in Computer Science, ICS 2011, pp. 1–21. Tsinghua University Press (2011)

A Cryptographic Analysis of OPACITY
(Extended Abstract)

Özgür Dagdelen, Marc Fischlin, Tommaso Gagliardoni,
Giorgia Azzurra Marson, Arno Mittelbach, and Cristina Onete

Darmstadt University of Technology, Germany
www.cryptoplexity.de

Abstract. We take a closer look at the Open Protocol for Access Control, Identification, and Ticketing with privacY (OPACITY). This Diffie–Hellman-based protocol is supposed to provide a secure and privacy-friendly key establishment for contactless environments. It is promoted by the US Department of Defense and meanwhile available in several standards such as ISO/IEC 24727-6 and ANSI 504-1. To the best of our knowledge, so far no detailed cryptographic analysis has been publicly available. Thus, we investigate in how far the common security properties for authenticated key exchange and impersonation resistance, as well as privacy-related properties like untraceability and deniability, are met.

OPACITY is not a single protocol but, in fact, a suite consisting of two protocols, one called Zero-Key Management (ZKM) and the other one named Fully Secrecy (FS). Our results indicate that the ZKM version does not achieve even very basic security guarantees. The FS protocol, on the other hand, provides a decent level of security for key establishment. Yet, our results show that the persistent-binding steps, for re-establishing previous connections, conflict with fundamental privacy properties.

1 Introduction

OPACITY is short for the Open Protocol for Access Control, Identification, and Ticketing with privacY. It is basically a Diffie–Hellman-based protocol to establish secure channels in contactless environments. According to Eric Le Saint of the company ActivIdentity, co-inventor in the patent application [47], the development has been sponsored by the US Department of Defense [48]. The inventors have declared the contributions to OPACITY to be a statutory invention with the United States Patent and Trademark Office, essentially allowing royalty-free and public usage of the contribution. The protocol has been registered as an ISO/IEC 24727-6 authentication protocol [27] and is specified in the draft ANSI 504-1 national standard (GICS) [24]. Informal yet outdated descriptions are available through the homepage of the Smart Card Alliance [3].[1]

---

[1] We stress that none of the authors of the present paper has been involved in the development of OPACITY, or is employed by ActivIdentity, or is supported by a non-academic governmental agency for conducting this research.

J. Crampton, S. Jajodia, and K. Mayes (Eds.): ESORICS 2013, LNCS 8134, pp. 345–362, 2013.
© Springer-Verlag Berlin Heidelberg 2013

1.1 Security Assessment of OPACITY

As Eric Le Saint emphasizes in his description of OPACITY [48], "This protocol
was designed expressly to remove the usage restrictions on contactless transactions while still delivering high performance security and privacy." Surprisingly,
we are not aware of any profound and public cryptographic analysis of the protocol, including clear claims about security and privacy goals. The best effort,
in terms of the Smart Card Alliance, seems to be compliance with standards [3]:

> "The protocol strictly follows U.S. government and international stan-
> dards. It has been assessed for compliance with the NIST standard for key
> establishment protocols (SP 800-56A). As a consequence, further protocol
> design reviews are unnecessary prior to FIPS 140-2 security certification."

It is of course not the case —and we do not think that the Smart Card
Alliance statement suggests so— that compliance with SP 800-56A, or certification according to FIPS 140-2, instantaneously gives strong cryptographic
security guarantees. The NIST document SP 800-56A [41] only provides useful but, nonetheless, high-level *recommendations* for key-establishment schemes
based on the discrete logarithm problem, and specifies some schemes from ANSI
X9. To the best of our knowledge, it has not been shown formally yet under
which conditions protocols complying with SP 800-56A are also cryptographically secure (in whatever sense). This is particularly true as OPACITY supports
renegotiation techniques and also states privacy enhancement as an additional
goal. Neither property is discussed in SP 800-56A.

Similarly, even if OPACITY was FIPS 140-2 certified and thus checked by an
accredited authority, this does not necessarily imply strong security guarantees
either. An obvious testimony to this argument are the easy attacks on FIPS
140-2 level 2 certified USB memory tokens where access was always granted for
a fixed string, independently of the password [17,18]. Certification according to
FIPS 140-2, and this is acknowledged in the standard, only intends "to maintain
the security provided by a cryptographic module" in the utilized environment;
the "operator of a cryptographic module is responsible for ensuring that the
security provided by the module is sufficient." (see [39]).

Hence, we believe that OPACITY deserves a closer cryptographic look. Clearly,
there are many practical protocols which lack such an analysis, or have at least
not been scrutinized publicly. What makes OPACITY a worthwhile object for a
cryptographic analysis is:

– OPACITY is standardized and may thus be deployed extensively in the near
  future. This is all the more true as it is a general purpose protocol, suitable,
  for instance, for use in access control for buildings, but also for ticketing in
  transport systems [48].
– OPACITY does not seem to be deployed broadly yet. It is our firm belief
  that protocols should be rigorously analyzed *before* they are actually utilized,
  in order to prevent damage caused by weaknesses discovered after deployment. Furthermore, patching a popular protocol in use is often intricate and
  progresses slowly (see the example of MD5-based certificates [51]).

– OPACITY still has a decent level of abstract description complexity. While nonetheless being quite complex underneath, especially taking into account different execution modes such as renegotiation steps (called persistent binding for OPACITY), this should be contrasted with similar protocols like SSL/TLS where conducting cryptographic proofs is tedious; such works often focus on particular parts or (modified) versions of the protocol [22,38,45,29].

Another point, which we initially thought speaks for OPACITY, is the availability of an open source implementation on Source Forge [43]. Unfortunately, as later confirmed by the developers of OPACITY [49], this implementation seems to refer to an outdated version. The differences were sufficiently large to determine us not to investigate the source code on how the cryptographic concepts are realized; nonetheless, we occasionally consulted the source code in order to extrapolate, in case some specification details were missing.

1.2 Our Results

OPACITY is a family of Diffie-Hellman key-exchange protocols based on Elliptic Curve Cryptography. It comes in two versions, called Zero-Key Management (O-ZKM) and Full Secrecy (O-FS). The first name is due to the fact that the terminal does not need to maintain registered public keys. As such, the parties in the O-ZKM protocol run a Diffie–Hellman based key-exchange protocol using an ephemeral key on the terminal's side and a static (presumably on-card generated) key for the card. The experienced reader may immediately spot the weakness in this approach: since the terminal only uses ephemeral keys, anyone can in principle impersonate the terminal and successfully initiate a communication with the card. Jumping ahead, we note that we can neither achieve a weaker notion of one-way authenticated key exchange [23] with this protocol. Before we go into further details of the security of the protocols, let us point out that the second protocol, O-FS, uses long-term keys on both sides and runs two nested Diffie–Hellman protocols, each one with the static key of the parties and an ephemeral key from the other party. This at least rules out obvious impersonation attacks.

Targeted security properties. Obviously, OPACITY aims at establishing a secure channel between the parties and to provide some form of entity authentication, especially impersonation resistance against malicious cards. Yet, at the same time, OPACITY also seems to target privacy properties. There seems to be a general and rough agreement what we expect from a "secure" key-exchange protocol, despite technical differences in the actual models [5,14]. We opted for the common Bellare-Rogaway (BR) model for key exchange but we also consider key-compromise impersonation resistance and leakage of ephemeral secrets in the related eCK model [34] in the full version [16].[2] We note that cryptographic analysis of similar key exchange protocols, such as for NIST's KEA [4,35,32] or

---

[2] Let us mention here that the protocols cannot be proven secure in the eCK model.

for the ANSI X9.63 specified UM protocols [4,37] cannot be transferred to OPA-CITY, as these protocols differ in security-relevant details and do not support renegotiation (and do not touch privacy issues); we comment on the differences in Section 3.3.

The privacy requirements for OPACITY are, however, less clear than the ones for key secrecy. This is all the more true as they are never specified in the accompanying documents. An earlier version of the OPACITY protocol description [50] mentions the following two goals for the O-FS protocol:

- "The OPACITY protocol does not divulge any data that allows the correlation of two protocol executions with same ICC [card] during an OPACITY session."
- "The OPACITY protocol does not divulge any identifier associated to a particular ICC or card holder during an OPACITY session."

The first requirement resembles the well-known notion of *untraceability* for protocols. We thus adopt the framework of Ouafi and Phan [44] which can be seen as a "BR-like" definition of the Juels and Weiss model [30] matching our approach for the key-agreement part. We do not explore stronger (simulation-based) models like the one in [36] as the protocols fail to provide security even in these more basic models.

The second desirable privacy property seems to be weaker in that it allows linkability in principle, but tries to hide the card's or the card holder's identity. We therefore introduce a notion called *identity hiding* which also follows the BR attack model, but instead of preventing the adversary from distinguishing between two cards —as for untraceability— we only guarantee that one cannot deduce the card's certificate (i.e., its identity). Note that, some authors such as [23], use the term identity hiding to denote the fact that the peer does not learn the partner's identity before the execution ends; our notion here coincides with this idea for the OPACITY protocols.

Basically, identity hiding as defined here is similar to recognizing a person without knowing the person's name. By contrast, untraceability is similar to not being able to tell that a particular person has been seen twice (this is independent of a person's name). Clearly, identity hiding gives weaker anonymity guarantees than untraceability or anonymity of credential systems [9,15]. Even direct anonymous attestation [10] or cross-domain anonymity as in the case of the German identity card [6] support linkability only within specified domains but are otherwise untraceable. Hence, the notion of identity hiding should be taken with caution.

Another desirable privacy property for OPACITY may be *deniability* [21], that is, the inability to use transcripts of communications as proofs towards third parties. Although not explicitly listed as a goal, it may be advantageous for a multi-purpose card protocol like OPACITY. There are different approaches and levels of deniability [8,20,19,23]; in light of what OPACITY can achieve we focus on a very basic level protecting only against abuse of transcripts between honest parties (denoted *outsider deniability* here).

Table 1. Security properties of the OPACITY protocol

	OPACITY-ZKM	OPACITY-FS
BR key secrecy	(only passive and if modified)	✓
+ forward secrecy	—	(only weak)
Impersonation Resistance	(only cards)	(only cards)
Untraceability	—	(only w/o persistent binding)
Identity Hiding	—	✓
(Outsider) Deniability	(only w/o persistent binding)	(only w/o persistent binding)

Finally, the goal of the OPACITY protocols is to establish a key which is subsequently used to secure communication between the card and the terminal. As such, one is of course interested in the security of the secure messaging protocol of OPACITY as well as in the overall composition of the key-agreement protocol and the secure messaging. Here, we rely on recent results for the secure composition of BR-secure key-exchange protocols [12,11]. We next discuss and illustrate exactly which security levels are achieved by OPACITY.

Achieved security properties. Our results are summarized in Table 1. The protocol O-ZKM cannot achieve BR-security against malicious terminals. Even for passive adversaries (merely observing executions between honest parties) the protocol is not secure; it *does* fulfill BR-security *only* after a slight modification of the protocol. The O-FS protocol achieves BR-security under the Gap Diffie–Hellman assumption [42] in the random-oracle model, assuming that the underlying cryptographic primitives are secure.[3] As for impersonation resistance, since the terminal does not authenticate towards the card, we can only hope to achieve security against malicious cards. This is met for both protocols given that the underlying message authentication scheme is secure.

As far as privacy is concerned, we show that neither protocol achieves untraceability nor even a weakened form of untracebility. For O-ZKM this is quite clear, as parts of the card's certificate are sent in clear. For O-FS the certificate is encrypted, yet we show that it is easy to desynchronize the cards' states and hence, due to persistent binding, to mount privacy attacks via desynchronization attacks. If, on the other hand, we only consider O-FS without renegotiation (and thus without any accumulated state), untraceability is met. Note that this is not the case for O-ZKM, that is, even without persistent binding (i.e., renegotiation) O-ZKM is traceable. For identity hiding, we can show that it is met by O-FS but not by O-ZKM.[4]

Concerning (outsider) deniability, we again only give a conditional result: OPACITY without persistent binding can be proved (outsider) deniable both

---

[3] This apparently innocent assumption about the security of the primitives has a hidden layer underneath. OPACITY is not fully specified in the standards and operates in some arguably doubtful modes, so this assumption must be taken with caution. We comment on this later.

[4] Note that O-ZKM contains steps which indicate that some form of identity hiding was aimed for: parts of the identity are only sent encrypted. Nevertheless an easy attack exists which we present in the full version [16].

for O-FS and O-ZKM. Persistent binding does, however, allow for simple attacks in many of the existing models for deniability, as well as, in our rather weak model of outsider deniability. Furthermore, persistent binding opens the door to physical attacks, for example, by simply comparing the state of the physical registers containing the persistent binding information of a terminal and card, one could extract high-confidence proofs that the card and terminal have been partnered in at least a single session.

An extended abstract. This version is an extended abstract of our results. Due to space restrictions we had to sacrifice some details. The interested reader is kindly referred to the full version of this work [16] for more details.

2   Security Model

2.1   Key Secrecy (Authenticated Key Exchange)

We analyze OPACITY with respect to key secrecy in the real-or-random security model by Bellare and Rogaway [5]. Roughly speaking, an adversary should not be able to tell apart a genuine session key from a key uniformly sampled from the key space. The security model defines so-called sessions, describes an attack model, and shows a winning condition for an adversary.

Our model (described in detail in the full version) follows the one in [5] closely. The adversary controls the network and can interact with the parties —(instances of) terminals or cards— through Execute and Send queries: the former is used to run the protocol between an honest terminal and an honest card, and the latter enables the adversary to send protocol messages to honest parties. We assume that the adversary can choose whether an honest terminal should request to reconnect via persistent binding or not (in the protocol this can be done quite easily by an active adversary which can alter or add appropriate bits to the terminal's first message —see the protocol description in Section 3). As usual, the adversary can test sessions (via a Test oracle), ask to reveal session keys, and, for forward-secure versions, corrupt parties (thus receiving the party's long-term secret key and state, i.e., the information stored for persistent binding and, for strong corruption, also the party's random coins and ephemeral secrets). For key secrecy it suffices to consider a single Test-query [1], in which the adversary receives either the true session key or a random key, depending on a random bit b. We also assume that the adversary can register any chosen public key on behalf of corrupted parties, possibly even keys already registered by honest parties, and receive certificates for such keys from the (trusted) certification authority. We assume that identities in certificates are unique.

We specify intended partners by partner id's pid and sessions by session id's sid (defined according to the protocol description). Two sessions are *partnered* if they have both accepted and output the same session id. We assume that untampered executions between honest parties generate the same sid and the same session key. The adversary can only test sessions in which she cannot trivially deduce the session key. A crucial notion for this security definition is that of *freshness*. Informally, an instance P_i is *fresh* (with respect to authenticated key-exchange —AKE— security), iff: (i) the adversary has not asked to reveal the key of that instance, nor of a partnered instance; (ii) the adversary has made no corruption queries, and (iii) neither P_i nor the intended partner pid output by P_i is adversarially controlled (in particular, their secret keys were not registered by the adversary). For the study of forward secrecy we need to adapt the notion of freshness to allow corruptions under certain restrictions. We refer to the full version for an introduction to forward secrecy and an analysis of OPACITY with respect to it.

Eventually, the adversary $\mathcal{A}$ outputs a guess b' for the secret bit b used in the Test-oracle. The adversary is *successful* iff: $b = b'$, and the instance P_i in the Test-oracle is fresh. We are interested in the advantage of the adversary over the simple guessing probability of $1/2$. We usually consider security relative to the adversary's parameters, such as its running time t, the number q_e of initiated executions of protocol instances of Π, and, modeling the key derivation function as a random oracle, the number q_h of random oracle queries of the adversary. For some of the security notions we also make the number of Test queries explicit through a parameter q_t.

Definition 1 (Key Secrecy). *We call a protocol Π, running for security parameter λ, (t, q_e, q_h, ϵ)-secure if no algorithm running in time t, invoking q_e instances of Π and making at most q_h queries to the random oracle can win the above experiment with probability greater than $\frac{1}{2} + \epsilon$. We call the value $\left| \Pr[\mathcal{A} \text{ wins}] - \frac{1}{2} \right|$ the advantage of the algorithm $\mathcal{A}$, and we denote the maximum over all (t, q_e, q_h)-bounded $\mathcal{A}$ by $\mathbf{Adv}_{\Pi}^{ake}(t, q_e, q_h)$.*

The BR model is a strong security model providing confidentiality of agreed session keys and their authenticity (i.e., at most one partner shares the derived keys). Furthermore, one can also show forward secrecy by adjusting the freshness notion. However, as LaMacchia et al. [34] pointed out, certain attacks, such as key-compromise impersonation and leakage of ephemeral secrets, are not covered by the BR model. We discuss these properties and analyze the OPACITY protocols with respect to them in the full version.

2.2   Impersonation Resistance

The notion of authenticated key exchange ensures that only the intended partner can compute the session key (i.e. an adversary that is not partnered with a specific partner in some session, cannot compute that session's key). For some application scenarios, however, we may also need that the terminal can be sure of the card's identity. This could be guaranteed by subsequent use of the computed session keys, but this is application-dependent. Impersonation resistance, as defined here, gives instead direct guarantees and is closer to the security of identification schemes. We give a strong definition based on the BR framework, which includes common properties like passive and active security for identification schemes. Still, note that we only consider impersonation by malicious cards to a terminal (and not that of malicious terminals to a card).

The attack model for impersonation resistance resembles AKE, but this time there are no Test-queries. The adversary's goal is to impersonate an honest card, without using trivial Man-in-the-Middle relaying attacks or making the terminal accept a card which has not been issued (resp. certified) by the certification authority $\mathcal{CA}$. More formally, the terminal must accept in some session sid for partner id pid, such that (a) pid is not adversarially controlled, and (b) there is no accepting card session for honest card pid with the same sid (including also the case that party pid has not been registered with a public key). If this happens we say that the adversary wins.

Definition 2 (Impersonation Resistance). *We call a protocol Π, running for security parameter λ, (t, q_e, q_h, ϵ)-impersonation resistant if no algorithm running in time t, invoking q_e instances of Π and making at most q_h queries to the random oracle can win the above experiment with probability greater than ϵ. We call the value $\Pr[\mathcal{A} \text{ wins}]$ the advantage of the algorithm $\mathcal{A}$, and we denote the maximum over all (t, q_e, q_h)-bounded $\mathcal{A}$ by $\mathbf{Adv}_{\Pi}^{ir}(t, q_e, q_h)$.*

2.3 Privacy for Key Exchange

Privacy in cryptography comes in many different flavors. The OPACITY documentation does not clarify exactly which properties the protocol is aiming for. We consider two reasonable notions, untraceability and identity hiding, and discuss the latter below. Due to space restrictions, the analysis of OPACITY in terms of untraceability is deferred to the full version, where we also define deniability for KE and show that, for OPACITY, it does imply untraceability in the restricted case where the renegotiation mode is not used.

Identity Hiding. Intuitively, an adversary against untraceability should not be able to link two sessions run by the same card. A weaker notion, called *identity hiding*, only stipulates that an adversary is unable to know *which* card authenticates (though she may know that she has seen this card authenticate before). Thus, untraceability hides both the identity (i.e., the certificate) of the card and its history (e.g., its state). By contrast, identity hiding only hides the certificate.

We use the identical security model as for key exchange, but with one exception: we assume a special card $\mathcal{C}^*$ exists, for which two certified key-pairs $(\mathsf{sk}_0^*, \mathsf{pk}_0^*, \mathsf{cert}_0^*)$, $(\mathsf{sk}_1^*, \mathsf{pk}_1^*, \mathsf{cert}_1^*)$ are generated under (potentially different) identities. The adversary is initially given the certificates and public keys of all honest parties except for $\mathcal{C}^*$, together with the assignment of the keys and certificates to the cards. The adversary also receives the two pairs $(\mathsf{pk}_0^*, \mathsf{cert}_0^*)$, $(\mathsf{pk}_1^*, \mathsf{cert}_1^*)$. At the start of the game, a bit b is flipped and $\mathcal{C}^*$ is instantiated with $(\mathsf{sk}_b^*, \mathsf{pk}_b^*, \mathsf{cert}_b^*)$. When the Test oracle is queried, it returns the handle for card $\mathcal{C}^*$, allowing the adversary to access this card by using all the previous oracles, apart from Corrupt. The adversary must predict the bit b, i.e. it must learn whether card $\mathcal{C}^*$ is associated with the left or right key pair. The only restriction is that the partner id pid output in any of the Test sessions is always an identity of an honest terminal (if the terminal is malicious the adversary trivially decrypts the encrypted certificate). Furthermore, no Corrupt queries must be issued to terminals.

Note that in this model the adversary cannot choose the target key pairs adaptively (having received a list of valid certificates). However, our approach is equivalent (up to a factor equal to the square of the number of the certificates) with a model using adaptive selection.

Definition 3 (Identity Hiding). *We call a protocol Π, running for security parameter λ, $(t, q_e, q_t, q_h, \epsilon)$-identity-hiding if no algorithm $\mathcal{A}$ running in time t, invoking q_e instances of Π, including q_t Test-sessions, and making at most q_h queries to the random oracle, can win in the above experiment with probability greater than $\frac{1}{2} + \epsilon$. We call the value $\left| \Pr[\mathcal{A} \text{ wins}] - \frac{1}{2} \right|$ the advantage of the algorithm $\mathcal{A}$, and we denote the maximum over all (t, q_e, q_t, q_h)-bounded $\mathcal{A}$ by* $\mathbf{Adv}_{\Pi}^{id\text{-}hide}(t, q_e, q_t, q_h)$.

3 The OPACITY Protocols

The OPACITY suite contains two key-exchange protocols, one called *OPACITY with Zero-Key Management* (O-ZKM), the other *OPACITY with Full Secrecy* (O-FS). Both protocols allow a terminal $\mathcal{T}$ and a card $\mathcal{C}$ to agree upon session keys $\mathsf{sk_{MAC}}, \mathsf{sk_{Enc}}, \mathsf{sk_{RMAC}}$ (for command authentication, encryption, and response authentication). Note, however, that though subsumed under the same protocol suite, the two protocols are nonetheless quite different, the main difference being that O-ZKM has only one-sided authentication, i.e., the card authenticates to the terminal but not vice versa. Due to space restrictions, in this extended abstract we only present a slightly simplified version of O-FS (see Figure 1); both O-ZKM and the complete O-FS are discussed in detail in the full version. The theorems presented in this extended abstract apply, however, to the full O-FS-protocol. We discuss related protocols in Section 3.3.

3.1 Protocol Descriptions

Both protocols (O-ZKM and -FS) consist of two rounds, the first one initialized by the terminal. Our description closely follows the original formulation in the standards. We make, however, minor changes in notation so as to simplify the diagram and improve legibility. We also change some variable names to be more compliant to standard cryptographic descriptions of protocols. We give a shortened description of the O-FS protocol, without renegotiation, in Figure 1.

From a bird's-eye view the O-FS protocol works as follows. Both the terminal and the card hold a certified key pair $(\mathsf{pk}_{\mathcal{T}}, \mathsf{sk}_{\mathcal{T}})$ and $(\mathsf{pk}_{\mathcal{C}}, \mathsf{sk}_{\mathcal{C}})$, respectively. The protocol works over a suitable elliptic curve $\mathscr{E}$; as such, secret keys are the discrete logarithms of the corresponding public keys (for some generator G). Both parties also generate an ephemeral key pair for each session, denoted by $(\mathsf{epk}_{\mathcal{T}}, \mathsf{esk}_{\mathcal{T}})$ and $(\mathsf{epk}_{\mathcal{C}}, \mathsf{esk}_{\mathcal{C}})$. The terminal first transmits its public keys $\mathsf{pk}_{\mathcal{T}}$ (encapsulated in the certificate) and $\mathsf{epk}_{\mathcal{T}}$, together with a control byte $\mathsf{CB}_{\mathcal{T}}$ for specifying different modes and for indicating a renegotiation request. The first Diffie-Hellman key is computed via the static key $\mathsf{pk}_{\mathcal{T}}$ of the terminal and the

Terminal $\mathcal{T}(\text{cert}_\mathcal{T}, \text{pk}_\mathcal{T}, \text{sk}_\mathcal{T}, \text{pk}_{\mathcal{CA}})$ **Card** $\mathcal{C}(\text{cert}_\mathcal{C}, \text{pk}_\mathcal{C}, \text{sk}_\mathcal{C}, \text{pk}_{\mathcal{CA}})$

1 $(\text{esk}_\mathcal{T}, \text{epk}_\mathcal{T}) \leftarrow \text{KeyGen}(1^\lambda)$

$\xrightarrow{\quad \text{cert}_\mathcal{T}, \text{epk}_\mathcal{T}, \text{CB}_\mathcal{T} \quad}$

$\xleftarrow{\quad \text{OpaqueData, authcrypt, CB}_\mathcal{C}, \text{otID} \quad}$

17 $\text{epk}_\mathcal{C} := \text{otID}$	if $C.\text{vrf}(\text{cert}_\mathcal{T}, \text{pk}_{\mathcal{CA}}) = 0$ abort 2
18 validate $\text{epk}_\mathcal{C}$ belongs to domain of $\mathscr{E}$	extract $\text{ID}_\mathcal{T}, \text{pk}_\mathcal{T}$ from $\text{cert}_\mathcal{T}$ 3
19 $Z_1 \leftarrow \mathcal{DH}_\mathscr{E}(\text{sk}_\mathcal{T}, \text{epk}_\mathcal{C})$	initialize control byte $\text{CB}_\mathcal{C}$ 4
20 $(k_1, k_2) \leftarrow \text{KDF}(Z_1, \text{len}, \text{info}(\text{ID}_\mathcal{T}, \text{epk}_\mathcal{C}))$	
21 $\text{cert}_\mathcal{C} \leftarrow \text{AES}_{k_1}^{-1}(\text{OpaqueData})$	validate $\text{pk}_\mathcal{T}$ belongs to domain of $\mathscr{E}$ 5
22 if $C.\text{vrf}(\text{cert}_\mathcal{C}, \text{pk}_{\mathcal{CA}}) = 0$ abort	$(\text{esk}_\mathcal{C}, \text{epk}_\mathcal{C}) \leftarrow \text{KeyGen}(1^\lambda)$ 6
23 extract $\text{pk}_\mathcal{C}$ from $\text{cert}_\mathcal{C}$	$Z_1 \leftarrow \mathcal{DH}_\mathscr{E}(\text{esk}_\mathcal{C}, \text{pk}_\mathcal{T})$ 7
24 delete temporary keys Z_1, k_1	$(k_1, k_2) \leftarrow \text{KDF}(Z_1, \text{len}, \text{info}(\text{ID}_\mathcal{T}, \text{epk}_\mathcal{C}))$ 8
25 $Z \leftarrow \mathcal{DH}_\mathscr{E}(\text{esk}_\mathcal{T}, \text{pk}_\mathcal{C})$	$\text{OpaqueData} \leftarrow \text{AES}_{k_1}(\text{cert}_\mathcal{C})$ 9
	$\text{otID} := \text{epk}_\mathcal{C}$ 10
	$Z \leftarrow \mathcal{DH}_\mathscr{E}(\text{sk}_\mathcal{C}, \text{epk}_\mathcal{T})$ 11
	delete temporary keys Z_1, k_1 12

26 $(\text{sk}_\text{cfrm}, \text{sk}_\text{MAC}, \text{sk}_\text{Enc}, \text{sk}_\text{RMAC}, \text{nextOtID}, \text{nextZ})$
  $\leftarrow \text{KDF}(Z, \text{len}, \text{info}($
    $\text{ID}_\mathcal{T}, \text{otID}_{|1..8}, \text{epk}_\mathcal{T}{}_{|1..16}, k_2$
  $))$

13 $(\text{sk}_\text{cfrm}, \text{sk}_\text{MAC}, \text{sk}_\text{Enc}, \text{sk}_\text{RMAC}, \text{nextOtID}, \text{nextZ})$
  $\leftarrow \text{KDF}(Z, \text{len}, \text{info}($
    $\text{ID}_\mathcal{T}, \text{otID}_{|1..8}, \text{epk}_\mathcal{T}{}_{|1..16}, k_2$
  $))$

27 delete keys $Z, k_2, \text{esk}_\mathcal{T}, \text{epk}_\mathcal{T}$
  check authcrypt $=$

14 delete temporary keys $Z, k_2, \text{esk}_\mathcal{C}, \text{epk}_\mathcal{C}$

28 $\text{CMAC}_{\text{sk}_\text{cfrm}}($
    $\text{"KC\_1\_V"} \| \text{otID}_{|1..8} \| \text{ID}_\mathcal{T} \| \text{epk}_\mathcal{T}{}_{|1..16}$
  $)$

15 authcrypt $\leftarrow \text{CMAC}_{\text{sk}_\text{cfrm}}($
    $\text{"KC\_1\_V"} \| \text{otID}_{|1..8} \| \text{ID}_\mathcal{T} \| \text{epk}_\mathcal{T}{}_{|1..16}$
  $)$

29 delete sk_cfrm

16 delete sk_cfrm

Fig. 1. The shaded parts describe OPACITY with Full Secrecy without persistent binding. The complete protocol, as well as a line by line description is provided in the full version. The unshaded lines should give a high-level overview of the underlying Diffie-Hellman key exchange.

card's ephemeral key. Analogously, the second Diffie-Hellman key is derived from the terminal's ephemeral key $\text{epk}_\mathcal{T}$ and the card's long-term key $\text{pk}_\mathcal{C}$. Both keys are then used in a cascade of two key-derivation steps to derive the session keys. The card replies with its encrypted certificate (for privacy reasons), a MAC for authentication, a control byte for renegotiation, and its ephemeral public key. Assuming both parties are honest, the terminal can decrypt and validate the card's certificate, validate the MAC, and compute the session keys, too. We give the full protocol and its line-by-line description in the full version.

3.2 Preliminaries

Certificates. OPACITY uses certificates in the card verifiable certificate format (CVC) which is standardized as part of ISO 7816 — Part 8 [26] (to fully formalize our analysis, we define certification schemes in the full version of the paper). Apart from the owner's public key and an identifier for the certification authority, certificates contain application-specific data which can be used to identify the card holder. In OPACITY, this 128-bit field is called GUID and identifies the holder of the card. O-ZKM encrypts GUID using AES and the derived session key. O-FS, on the other hand, encrypts the entire certificate under an intermediate key. The (outdated) source code uses AES in CBC mode with the constant 0-vector as initialization vector. In O-FS, since the key is derived freshly upon every invocation and only used for a single encryption, this should not pose a security threat. For O-ZKM, on the other hand, the session key is used; this might compromise security.

Other functionalities used by protocols. The protocols use a key-derivation function KDF as specified in NIST SP 800-56A (§5.8.1) [41], CMAC for message authentication as specified in NIST SP 800-38B [40] (CMAC is also used as PRF in the key-derivation function) and AES-128 (no mode specified). As hash function, SHA-256 or SHA-512 are deployed. In the analysis below we model KDF through a random oracle. The injective function info is defined according to NIST SP 800-56A and prepares the input to the key-derivation function (it can be thought of the length-encoded concatenation of its input). The input to info, and therefore to the key-derivation function, contains the terminal's identity $\mathsf{ID}_\mathcal{T}$ (not specified in detail, but we assume that this value is globally unique and also determines the terminal's certificate $\mathsf{cert}_\mathcal{T}$ uniquely) and usually parts of the ephemeral keys $\mathsf{otID} = \mathsf{epk}_\mathcal{C}$ and $\mathsf{epk}_\mathcal{T}$, like the leftmost 8 or 16 bytes, $\mathsf{otID}|_{1..8}$ and $\mathsf{epk}_\mathcal{T}|_{1..16}$, respectively.

Security parameters. OPACITY specifies 6 parameter sets describing the length of keys and nonces, block-ciphers, and hash functions. The standard set CS2 recommends to use SHA-256 as hash function, AES-128 for encryption and MACs, and ECDH-256 for static and ephemeral keys. Nonces are 16 bytes long. By contrast, the "very strong security" setting (CS6) uses SHA-512, AES-256, ECDH-512, and 32-byte nonces. In the first case it is claimed that the resulting channel strength is 128 bits, and for CS6 the channel strength is supposedly 256.

Persistent binding. Both protocols can be run in a renegotiation mode which gives a slight performance increase if card and terminal have already successfully exchanged keys. This mode, called *persistent binding*, requires both parties to store intermediate secret values. For lack of space, we refer to the full version for a complete description of the persistent binding as well as to the analysis of the security properties in regard to this mode.

3.3   Related DH Key-Agreement Protocols

We only discuss Diffie-Hellman-based key exchange protocols which are very similar in structure to OPACITY, i.e., pairwise mix static and ephemeral Diffie-Hellman keys of the partners. These are NSA's Key Exchange Algorithm (KEA) and its variants variant KEA+ [35] and KEA+C [32]. Another closely related approach are the schemes described by ANSI X9.63 called "Unified Model" (UM) key-agreement protocols. The UM protocols have been analyzed cryptographically in [37].

Although sharing a similar skeleton —a DH key-agreement protocol using both static and ephemeral keys— the analyses of KEA, UM and their variants [35,32,37] can only serve as a very vague starting point for OPACITY; the protocols differ in numerous security-relevant details. One distinctive property of our analysis here is also that we investigate low-level details more explicitly. Considering such details makes the evaluation more delicate and complex but, on the other hand, gives a more concrete perception of the (in)security of the actual protocol. This, in particular, also concerns the renegotiation step in OPACITY which is neither supported by KEA nor by UM. Our analysis for OPACITY also needs to take additional privacy properties into account. Hence, even if OPACITY resembles the other schemes, the existing analyses provide rather weak implications for OPACITY's overall security (if any at all).

4   Security Analysis of O-FS

The concrete security parameters proposed for O-FS can be found in Section 3; however, for the sake of generality, our analysis features abstract parameters, e.g. instead of the concrete bit size of the proposed curve $\mathcal{E}$, defined on the field $\mathcal{K}$, we write $\#\mathcal{E}(\mathcal{K})$ (this is, in fact, the size of a prime-order subgroup of points). Thus, our analysis formally bounds the success probability of adversaries for *any* proposed set of parameters.

We note that the protocol itself is not perfectly correct in the sense that two honest parties may not derive the same session keys, namely, if renegotiation identifies the wrong previous connection. However, the likelihood of this event, as we detail in the full version, is in the order of $q_e^2 \cdot 2^{-128}$ for q_e executions for the recommended parameters, such that we may simply neglect such mismatches in our analysis. Nonetheless, it would be preferable to specify the behavior for this case clearly in the protocol description.

4.1   Security Assumptions

We prove O-FS secure under the elliptic curve *Gap Diffie–Hellman* (GDH) assumption [42] (by default we assume *all* hard problems are on elliptic curves, omitting to state this explicitly). Informally, the GDH assumption states that the CDH problem remains hard even when given access to an oracle $\mathsf{DDH}(\cdot, \cdot, \cdot)$, which tells whether three group elements form a Diffie–Hellman tuple or not. More formally, let $\langle G \rangle$ be an (additive) group of prime order q and generator $G \in \mathcal{E}$. The GDH problem is (t, Q, ϵ)-hard in $\langle G \rangle$ if any algorithm $\mathcal{A}$ running in time t and making at most Q queries to DDH can, on input $\langle G \rangle, G, sG, tG$, for random s, t, computes stG with probability at most ϵ. We write $\mathbf{Adv}^{\mathrm{GDH}}(t, Q)$ for (a bound on) the probability of any (t, Q)-bounded $\mathcal{A}$ solving the GDH problem.

We use standard cryptographic notation for the other involved primitives. The certification scheme $\mathsf{Cert} = (\mathsf{C.kgen}, \mathsf{C.sign}, \mathsf{C.vrf})$ is modeled as a signature scheme where the signer is a certification authority $(\mathcal{CA})$; $\mathbf{Adv}_{\mathsf{Cert}}^{\mathrm{forge}}(t, Q)$ denotes the maximal probability of forging a fresh certificate within t steps and after requesting at most Q certificates. We use $\mathbf{Adv}_{\mathrm{AES}}^{\mathrm{IND\text{-}CPA}}(t, Q)$ to denote the maximal probability of distinguishing AES ciphertexts (in CBC mode) within t steps for at most Q challenge ciphertexts (see the remark in Section 3.2 about the actual encryption mode), and $\mathbf{Adv}^{forge}_{CMAC}(t, Q)$ for the maximal probability of forging a CMAC in t steps after seeing at most Q MACs. Finally, the key-derivation function (KDF) is modeled as a random oracle.

4.2 Key Secrecy and Impersonation Resistance

For the key-secrecy proof we consider sessions as indicated in Section 2, such that the session id sid for O-FS is set as $\mathsf{sid} = (\mathsf{otID}|_{1..8}, \mathsf{ID}_{\mathcal{T}}, \mathsf{epk}_{\mathcal{T}}|_{1..16})$; the partner id pid is set to the identity $\mathsf{ID}_{\mathcal{T}}$ on the card's side resp. to GUID on the terminal's side. We observe that session id's are usually preferred to comprise the entire communication transcript. The reason is that, roughly, the more information contained in sid, the "tighter" the binding of session keys to specific executions. In this sense, our formally more loose (but, according to the protocol, presumably inevitable) choice for sid's here ties executions to partners, identified via parts of the public keys and the ephemeral keys. Indeed, one easy enhancement for the protocol would be to include the card's certificate in the key-derivation step, or at least its entire public key.

The next theorem shows that O-FS is secure as a key agreement protocol, i.e., O-FS provides key secrecy.

Theorem 1 (Key Secrecy of O-FS). *In the random-oracle model,*

$$\mathbf{Adv}^{ake}_{\Pi_{OFS}}(t, q_e, q_h) \leq \mathbf{Adv}^{forge}_{Cert}(t, q_e) + \frac{3q_e(2q_e + q_h)}{2^{\min\{\ell_{k_2}, \ell_Z\}}}$$
$$+ 2q_e^2 \cdot \mathbf{Adv}^{GDH}(t + O(\lambda \cdot q_e \log q_e), 2q_e + q_h)$$

where λ denotes the security parameter, t the running time of adversary $\mathcal{A}$, and q_e (resp. q_h) the number of executions (resp. queries to the random oracle), and ℓ_{k_2} and ℓ_Z denote the bit lengths of values k_2 resp. Z.

Note that key secrecy does not rely on the security of the authenticated encryption (which only enters the impersonation resistance proof), nor the secrecy of the certificate (which is only used for privacy). At the same time neither step does harm to key secrecy.

Impersonation Resistance. In this section we show that O-FS achieves impersonation resistance. Recall that this means that a malicious card cannot make an honest terminal accept, unless it is a pure relay attack and there is a card session with the same sid.

Theorem 2 (Impersonation Resistance of O-FS). *In the random-oracle model,*

$$\mathbf{Adv}^{ir}_{\Pi_{OFS}}(t, q_e, q_h) \leq 2q_e \cdot \mathbf{Adv}^{forge}_{CMAC}(t + O(\lambda \cdot q_e \log q_e), 0)$$
$$+ 4q_e \cdot \mathbf{Adv}^{ake}_{\Pi_{OFS}}(t, q_e, q_h)$$

where λ denotes the security parameter, t the running time of adversary $\mathcal{A}$, and q_e (resp. q_h) the number of executions (resp. queries to the random oracle).

The proof follows (almost) directly from the key secrecy proof, noting that in order to be able to impersonate one would need to compute a MAC for the secure key sk_{cfrm}.

4.3   Privacy

Though O-FS does not attain untraceability, it does, nevertheless, provide identity hiding. This holds as long as we assume that the unspecified mode of encryption of $cert_C$ with AES is secure (see our remark in Section 3.2).

Theorem 3 (Identity-Hiding in O-FS). *In the random-oracle model,*

$$\mathbf{Adv}_{\Pi_{OFS}}^{id\text{-}hide}(t, q_e, q_t, q_h) \leq \frac{1}{2} + \mathbf{Adv}_{Cert}^{forge}(t, q_e) + \frac{2q_t(2q_t + q_h)}{2^{\ell_{k_2}}}$$
$$+ q_e^2 \cdot \mathbf{Adv}^{GDH}(t + O(\lambda \cdot q_e \log q_e), 2q_e + q_h)$$
$$+ \frac{q_e q_t}{\#\mathscr{E}(\mathcal{K})} + q_t \cdot \mathbf{Adv}_{AES}^{IND\text{-}CPA}(t + O(q_t)) .$$

where λ denotes the security parameter, t the running time of the adversary, and q_e (resp. q_t, q_h) the number of executions (resp. Test-sessions and queries to the random oracle).

5   Security of the Channel Protocol

Here we discuss briefly the security of the secure messaging (used both in ZKM and FS) and of the composition of the channel with the key agreement step.

Secure Messaging. Once the keys are generated the parties use them to secure the communication. The description [24] proposes two modes, one for command and response MACs without confidentiality (using keys sk_{MAC} and sk_{RMAC}, respectively), and the other one for encrypted data transfer under the key sk_{Enc} used by both parties. If only authenticity is required, then the data is secured according to ISO 7816-4 [25]; in case encryption is used the protocol basically follows the encrypt-then-MAC approach, first encrypting the payload.

Alarmingly, according to the standard [24], the terminal can ask the card via the control byte to only create a single key $sk_{Enc} = sk_{RMAC} = sk_{MAC}$, operating in a special mode (ONE_SK). Sharing the key among different primitives usually needs a cautionary treatment. It remains unclear why OPACITY implements this mode, but it does not seem to be recommendable from a pure security perspective. In what follows we assume that independent keys are used instead.

Encryption for the encrypt-then-MAC approach in the secure messaging is not further specified in [24]. The (outdated) implementation relies on AES encryption with a prepended, fixed-length session counter. For authentication the parties first pad the message (or ciphertext) according to ISO 7816-4, basically prepending a MAC chaining value of 16 bytes before computing an AES-based CMAC [7,28] according to SP 800-38B [40]. We omit a formal analysis of secure messaging which, except for the single-key mode, follows the common cryptographic approaches. It would be nonetheless interesting to provide such an analysis, taking into account recent attacks and models for such steps [31,2,45,46]. However, it is beyond our scope here.

Composition. Clearly, a secure key-exchange protocol and secure messaging on their own may not be enough to ensure the security of the composed protocol. Several approaches exist to bridge this gap, ranging from monolithic analysis of the composed protocol, to general-purpose compositional frameworks like Canetti's Universal Composition (UC) model [13]. The latter has been successfully applied to analyze and construct securely composable key-exchange protocols [14]. However, security of key exchange in the UC model (and comparable simulation-based frameworks [33]) already imposes strong requirements on the protocols which are hard to meet.

Since we analyzed O-FS in the game-based BR-model we can apply the recent result by Brzuska et al. [12] to conclude overall channel security of the key agreement combined with secure messaging. This holds as long as O-FS provides a property called public session matching [12], which we discuss in the full version to be true. Since we do not recommend to use O-ZKM we do not address the question for this protocol.

6 Conclusion

Our analysis reveals that, from a cryptographic point of view, O-FS achieves a decent level of key secrecy, but has clear restrictions on privacy guarantees. For one, privacy could be improved by also encrypting the card's control byte CB_C for persistent binding, hiding the fact if the card has been used in connection with that terminal before. Whereas the situation for O-FS is arguable, we do not recommend O-ZKM for deployment. This is due to its rather weak security guarantees for (terminal) authentication and the weaker form of identity hiding.

Our analysis also shows common problems in making precise security claims about real protocols. Like with every cryptographic (or scientific) model we have to abstract out some details. This can be an impediment in particular in view of the fact that the protocol can operate in various modes, e.g., for compatibility reasons. This complexity is the cryptographer's enemy, discussing all possibilities is often beyond a reasonable approach. However, omitting some of these modes is dangerous, as they often admit back doors for attackers. There are some *potential* back doors for OPACITY as well, e.g., the single-key mode ONE_SK for secure messaging. This is magnified by the fact that OPACITY is not fully specified with respect to all relevant details (e.g., which encryption mode is used for OpaqueData). Also, the binding of sessions to their keys is rather loose as merely a partial transcript of the execution enters the key derivation resp. message authentication. In this sense, it should be understood that our (partly positive) cryptographic analysis has its inherent limitations.

Acknowledgments. We thank the anonymous reviewers for comments. Marc Fischlin was supported by a Heisenberg grant Fi 940/3-1 of the German Research Foundation (DFG). This work was supported by CASED (www.cased.de) and by EC SPRIDE.

References

1. Abdalla, M., Fouque, P.-A., Pointcheval, D.: Password-based authenticated key exchange in the three-party setting. In: Vaudenay, S. (ed.) PKC 2005. LNCS, vol. 3386, pp. 65–84. Springer, Heidelberg (2005)
2. Albrecht, M.R., Paterson, K.G., Watson, G.J.: Plaintext recovery attacks against SSH. In: 2009 IEEE Symposium on Security and Privacy, pp. 16–26. IEEE Computer Society Press (May 2009)
3. Smart Card Alliance: Industry technical contributions: Opacity (April 2013), http://www.smartcardalliance.org/pages/ smart-cards-contributions-opacity
4. ANSI X9-63-199X – Public key cryptography for the financial services industry: Key agreement and key transport using elliptic curve cryptography (1999)
5. Bellare, M., Rogaway, P.: Entity authentication and key distribution. In: Stinson, D.R. (ed.) CRYPTO 1993. LNCS, vol. 773, pp. 232–249. Springer, Heidelberg (1994)
6. Bender, J., Dagdelen, Ö., Fischlin, M., Kügler, D.: Domain-specific pseudonymous signatures for the german identity card. In: Gollmann, D., Freiling, F.C. (eds.) ISC 2012. LNCS, vol. 7483, pp. 104–119. Springer, Heidelberg (2012)
7. Black, J., Rogaway, P.: CBC MACs for arbitrary-length messages: The three-key constructions. Journal of Cryptology 18(2), 111–131 (2005)
8. Boyd, C., Mao, W., Paterson, K.G.: Deniable authenticated key establishment for internet protocols. In: Security Protocols Workshop, pp. 255–271 (2003)
9. Brands, S.: Rethinking Public Key Infrastructures and Digital Certificates; Building in Privacy. The MIT Press (2000)
10. Brickell, E.F., Camenisch, J., Chen, L.: Direct anonymous attestation. In: Atluri, V., Pfitzmann, B., McDaniel, P. (eds.) ACM CCS 2004, pp. 132–145. ACM Press (October 2004)
11. Brzuska, C., Fischlin, M., Smart, N., Warinschi, B., Williams, S.: Less is more: Relaxed yet composable security notions for key exchange. Cryptology ePrint Archive, Report 2012/242 (2012), http://eprint.iacr.org/
12. Brzuska, C., Fischlin, M., Warinschi, B., Williams, S.C.: Composability of Bellare-Rogaway key exchange protocols. In: Chen, Y., Danezis, G., Shmatikov, V. (eds.) ACM CCS 2011, pp. 51–62. ACM Press (October 2011)
13. Canetti, R.: Universally composable security: A new paradigm for cryptographic protocols. In: 42nd FOCS, pp. 136–145. IEEE Computer Society Press (October 2001)
14. Canetti, R., Krawczyk, H.: Analysis of key-exchange protocols and their use for building secure channels. In: Pfitzmann, B. (ed.) EUROCRYPT 2001. LNCS, vol. 2045, pp. 453–474. Springer, Heidelberg (2001)
15. Chaum, D.: Security without identification: transaction systems to make big brother obsolete. Commun. ACM 28 (October 1985)
16. Dagdelen, Ö., Fischlin, M., Gagliardoni, T., Marson, G.A., Mittelbach, A., Onete, C.: A cryptographic analysis of OPACITY. Cryptology ePrint Archive, Report 2013/234 (2013), http://eprint.iacr.org/

17. Deeg, M., Eichelmann, C., Schreiber, S.: Programmed insecurity — SySS cracks yet another usb flash drive, http://www.syss.de/fileadmin/ressources/040_veroeffentlichungen/dokumente/SySS_Cracks_Yet_Another_USB_Flash_Drive.pdf

18. Deeg, M., Schreiber, S.: Cryptographically secure? SySS cracks a usb flash drive, https://www.syss.de/fileadmin/ressources/040_veroeffentlichungen/dokumente/SySS_Cracks_SanDisk_USB_Flash_Drive.pdf

19. Di Raimondo, M., Gennaro, R.: New approaches for deniable authentication. Journal of Cryptology 22(4), 572–615 (2009)

20. Dodis, Y., Katz, J., Smith, A., Walfish, S.: Composability and on-line deniability of authentication. In: Reingold, O. (ed.) TCC 2009. LNCS, vol. 5444, pp. 146–162. Springer, Heidelberg (2009)

21. Dwork, C., Naor, M., Sahai, A.: Concurrent zero-knowledge. J. ACM 51(6), 851–898 (2004)

22. Gajek, S., Manulis, M., Pereira, O., Sadeghi, A.-R., Schwenk, J.: Universally composable security analysis of TLS. In: Baek, J., Bao, F., Chen, K., Lai, X. (eds.) ProvSec 2008. LNCS, vol. 5324, pp. 313–327. Springer, Heidelberg (2008)

23. Goldberg, I., Stebila, D., Ustaoglu, B.: Anonymity and one-way authentication in key exchange protocols. Des. Codes Cryptography 67(2), 245–269 (2013)

24. INCITS: 504-1, Information Technology - generic identity command set part 1: Card application command set

25. ISO/IEC: Identification cards - Integrated circuit(s) cards with contacts - Part 4: Organization, security and commands for interchange. Tech. Rep. ISO/IEC 7816-4, International Organization for Standardization, Geneva, Switzerland (2005)

26. ISO/IEC: Identification cards - Integrated circuit(s) cards with contacts - Part 8: Security related interindustry commands. Tech. Rep. ISO/IEC 7816-8, International Organization for Standardization, Geneva, Switzerland (2009)

27. ISO/IEC: Identification Cards – Integrated Circuit Cards Programming Interface – Part 6: Registration procedures for the authentication protocols for interoperability. Tech. Rep. ISO/IEC FDIS 24727-6, International Organization for Standardization, Geneva, Switzerland (2009)

28. Iwata, T., Kurosawa, K.: OMAC: One-key CBC MAC. In: Johansson, T. (ed.) FSE 2003. LNCS, vol. 2887, pp. 129–153. Springer, Heidelberg (2003)

29. Jager, T., Kohlar, F., Schäge, S., Schwenk, J.: On the security of TLS-DHE in the standard model. In: Safavi-Naini, R., Canetti, R. (eds.) CRYPTO 2012. LNCS, vol. 7417, pp. 273–293. Springer, Heidelberg (2012)

30. Juels, A., Weis, S.A.: Defining strong privacy for RFID. Cryptology ePrint Archive, Report 2006/137 (2006), http://eprint.iacr.org/

31. Krawczyk, H.: The order of encryption and authentication for protecting communications (or: How secure is SSL?). In: Kilian, J. (ed.) CRYPTO 2001. LNCS, vol. 2139, pp. 310–331. Springer, Heidelberg (2001)

32. Kudla, C., Paterson, K.G.: Modular security proofs for key agreement protocols. In: Roy, B. (ed.) ASIACRYPT 2005. LNCS, vol. 3788, pp. 549–565. Springer, Heidelberg (2005)

33. Küsters, R., Tuengerthal, M.: Composition theorems without pre-established session identifiers. In: Chen, Y., Danezis, G., Shmatikov, V. (eds.) ACM CCS 2011, pp. 41–50. ACM Press (October 2011)

34. LaMacchia, B.A., Lauter, K., Mityagin, A.: Stronger security of authenticated key exchange. In: Susilo, W., Liu, J.K., Mu, Y. (eds.) ProvSec 2007. LNCS, vol. 4784, pp. 1–16. Springer, Heidelberg (2007)

35. Lauter, K., Mityagin, A.: Security analysis of KEA authenticated key exchange protocol. In: Yung, M., Dodis, Y., Kiayias, A., Malkin, T. (eds.) PKC 2006. LNCS, vol. 3958, pp. 378–394. Springer, Heidelberg (2006)

36. Le, T.V., Burmester, M., de Medeiros, B.: Universally composable and forward-secure RFID authentication and authenticated key exchange. In: Bao, F., Miller, S. (eds.) ASIACCS 2007, pp. 242–252. ACM Press (March 2007)

37. Menezes, A., Ustaoglu, B.: Security arguments for the UM key agreement protocol in the NIST SP 800-56A standard. In: Abe, M., Gligor, V. (eds.) ASIACCS 2008, pp. 261–270. ACM Press (March 2008)

38. Morrissey, P., Smart, N.P., Warinschi, B.: The TLS handshake protocol: A modular analysis. Journal of Cryptology 23(2), 187–223 (2010)

39. NIST: Security Requirements for Cryptographic Modules. Tech. Rep. FIPS 140-2, National Institute of Standards and Technology (2002)

40. NIST: Recommendation for Block Cipher Modes of Operation: The CMAC Mode for Authentication. Tech. Rep. SP 800-38B, National Institute of Standards and Technology (2007)

41. NIST: Recommendation for Pair-Wise Key Establishment Schemes Using Discrete Logarithm Cryptography. Tech. Rep. SP800-56A, National Institute of Standards and Technology (2007)

42. Okamoto, T., Pointcheval, D.: The gap-problems: A new class of problems for the security of cryptographic schemes. In: Kim, K.-c. (ed.) PKC 2001. LNCS, vol. 1992, pp. 104–118. Springer, Heidelberg (2001)

43. OPACITY: Reference Implementation - sourceforge.net/projects/opacity/

44. Ouafi, K., Phan, R.C.-W.: Privacy of recent RFID authentication protocols. In: Chen, L., Mu, Y., Susilo, W. (eds.) ISPEC 2008. LNCS, vol. 4991, pp. 263–277. Springer, Heidelberg (2008)

45. Paterson, K.G., Ristenpart, T., Shrimpton, T.: Tag size does matter: Attacks and proofs for the TLS record protocol. In: Lee, D.H., Wang, X. (eds.) ASIACRYPT 2011. LNCS, vol. 7073, pp. 372–389. Springer, Heidelberg (2011)

46. Paterson, K.G., Watson, G.J.: Authenticated-encryption with padding: A formal security treatment. In: Naccache, D. (ed.) Cryphtography and Security: From Theory to Applications. LNCS, vol. 6805, pp. 83–107. Springer, Heidelberg (2012)

47. Saint, E.L., Fedronic, D.L.J.: Open protocol for authentication and key establishment with privacy (July 2010)

48. Saint, E.L.: Opacity - the new open protocol of choice (August 2012), http://www.itsecurityhub.eu/2012/08/opacity-the-new-open-protocol-of-choice/

49. Saint, E.L.: Personal communication (July 2012)

50. Saint, E.L., Fedronic, D., Liu, S.: Open protocol for access control identification and ticketing with privacy (July 2011), http://www.smartcardalliance.org/resources/pdf/OPACITY_Protocol_3.7.pdf

51. Stevens, M., Sotirov, A., Appelbaum, J., Lenstra, A., Molnar, D., Osvik, D.A., de Weger, B.: Short chosen-prefix collisions for MD5 and the creation of a rogue CA certificate. In: Halevi, S. (ed.) CRYPTO 2009. LNCS, vol. 5677, pp. 55–69. Springer, Heidelberg (2009)

Symbolic Probabilistic Analysis of Off-Line Guessing

Bruno Conchinha[1], David Basin[1], and Carlos Caleiro[2]

[1] Institute of Information Security, ETH Zurich, Switzerland
[2] SQIG - Instituto de Telecomunicações, Department of Mathematics,
IST, TU Lisbon, Portugal

Abstract. We introduce a probabilistic framework for the automated analysis of security protocols. Our framework provides a general method for expressing properties of cryptographic primitives, modeling an attacker more powerful than conventional Dolev-Yao attackers. It allows modeling equational properties of cryptographic primitives as well as property statements about their weaknesses, e.g. primitives leaking partial information about messages or the use of weak random generation algorithms. These properties can be used to automatically find attacks and estimate their success probability. Existing symbolic methods can neither model such properties nor find such attacks. We show that the probability estimates we obtain are negligibly different from those yielded by a generalized random oracle model based on sampling terms into bitstrings while respecting the stipulated properties of cryptographic primitives.

As case studies, we use a prototype implementation of our framework to model non-trivial properties of RSA encryption and automatically estimate the probability of off-line guessing attacks on the EKE protocol.

Keywords: Probability, Off-line Guessing, Equational Theories, Random Oracle Model.

1 Introduction

Cryptographic protocols play an important role in securing distributed computation and it is crucial that they work correctly. Symbolic verification approaches are usually based on the *Dolev-Yao model*: messages are represented by terms in a term algebra, cryptography is assumed to be perfect, and properties of cryptographic operators are formalized equationally [1]. This strong abstraction eases analysis and numerous successful verification tools rely on it [2, 3]. However, it may not accurately represent an attacker's capabilities. As a consequence, broad classes of attacks that rely on weaknesses of cryptographic primitives fall outside the scope of such methods. In contrast, proving security by reasoning directly about bitstrings, as in *computational approaches* [4, 5], yields stronger security guarantees. However, it requires long, error-prone, hand-written proofs to establish the security of given protocols using specific cryptographic primitives.

Much research has been devoted to bridging the gap between these two methods [6]. Below we discuss existing approaches in greater detail.

J. Crampton, S. Jajodia, and K. Mayes (Eds.): ESORICS 2013, LNCS 8134, pp. 363–380, 2013.
© Springer-Verlag Berlin Heidelberg 2013

Related work. There are two main lines of research that aim to bridge the gap between symbolic and computational models: (1) obtaining computational soundness results for symbolic methods, and (2) developing techniques that reason directly with computational models.

The first line of research, developing computational soundness results, was initiated with Abadi and Rogaway's seminal paper [7]. They investigated assumptions under which security against a Dolev-Yao attacker (easier to verify) implies computational security (much stronger). Many such results are now known, e.g. [8–10]. However, such results require strong assumptions on the security of cryptographic primitives. Moreover, messages must be tagged so that their structure is known to any observer, and extending the results to new primitives often involves re-doing most of the work.

The second line of research aims to automate computational security proofs, by formulating security properties in terms of games and obtaining a sequence of security-preserving transformations between such games. Such methods have been implemented by tools like CryptoVerif [11], CertiCrypt [12], and Easy-Crypt [13]. When successful, these tools can prove protocols computationally correct and provide upper bounds on the probability of an attack. [14,15] propose another approach: an automatable, symbolic framework in which it is possible to express security properties of cryptographic primitives and use them to prove computational protocol security.

A limitation of all of the above approaches is that they can only be used to prove security. Failure to obtain a security proof does not imply that an attack exists. Therefore, their usefulness remains limited when cryptographic primitives are too weak to meet the assumptions of their methods.

Our applications in this paper focus on off-line guessing attacks. Given the pervasive use of weak human-picked passwords, off-line guessing attacks are a major concern in security protocol analysis and have been the subject of much research. Symbolic [16,17] and computational approaches [18] have been used, and computational soundness results [19,20] relate the two. However, off-line guessing attacks remain a real threat to protocol security. Password-cracking software is freely available on the Internet, and is remarkably successful [21]. Furthermore, such attacks often rely on weaknesses of cryptographic primitives outside the scope of existing automated methods [22,23].

Contributions. We present a fundamentally new approach to strengthening the security guarantees provided by automated methods. Our approach is in a sense dual to current research that aims to bridge the gap between symbolic and computational models: Rather than assuming strong security properties of cryptographic primitives and using them to prove security, we explicitly describe weaknesses of cryptographic primitives and random number generation algorithms and use them to find attacks.

We propose a probabilistic framework for security protocol analysis in which properties of cryptographic primitives can be specified. Besides equational properties, our framework allows us to express security relevant properties of random number generation algorithms and relations between the input and the output of

cryptographic primitives. For instance, it can model a random number generation algorithm that generates bitstrings representing primes of a certain length,
a hash function that leaks partial information about the original message, or
a cryptosystem whose valid public keys have some recognizable structure. The
specified properties can then be used to find attacks and to estimate their success
probability. Such properties cannot be modeled by existing symbolic methods
and often lead to attacks on real-world implementations.

We model cryptographic functions using a generalized random oracle model.
Given a specification of the cryptographic primitives used and their properties,
symbolic terms are sampled to bitstrings in a way that ensures that the specification properties are always satisfied, but otherwise functions behave as random
oracles. Under reasonable assumptions on the specification, we can define such
generalized random oracles and prove that they yield valid probability measures.
Moreover, we show that probabilities in this model can be effectively computed,
and we provide a prototype implementation that calculates these probabilities.
We believe that this model is interesting in its own right. It is a non-trivial generalization of the standard model of random oracle for hash functions, and it
captures the intuitive idea that cryptographic primitives satisfy stated properties, which can be exploited by an attacker, but otherwise behave ideally.

We illustrate the usefulness of our framework by representing the redundancy
of RSA keys and using this to model and estimate the success probability of
off-line guessing attacks on variants of the EKE protocol [22]. Although these
attacks are well-known, their analysis was previously outside the scope of symbolic methods. Potential further applications of our approach include reasoning
about differential cryptanalysis or side-channel attacks [24], as well as short-
string authentication and distance-bounding protocols.

Outline. In Section 2 we describe our framework's syntax and semantics. In Section 3 we introduce our generalized random oracle model and show that it yields
a computable probability measure. In Section 4 we show how our framework can
be used to find off-line guessing attacks. In Section 5 we draw conclusions and
discuss future work. Our technical report [25] provides full proofs of all results.

2   Definitions

In this section we introduce the syntax and semantics of our framework.

2.1   Setup Specification

Term algebra. A *signature* $\Sigma = \biguplus_{n \in \mathbb{N}} \Sigma_n$ is a set of function symbols, where Σ_i
contains the symbols of arity i. Given a set G of generators, we define $T_\Sigma(G)$ as
the smallest set such that $G \subseteq T_\Sigma(G)$, and if $f \in \Sigma_n$ and $t_1, \ldots, t_n \in T_\Sigma(G)$,
then $f(t_1, \ldots, t_n) \in T_\Sigma(G)$. If $c \in \Sigma_0$, we write c instead of $c()$. Unless otherwise
stated, we will consider $G = \emptyset$ and write T_Σ instead of $T_\Sigma(\emptyset)$. We define the
head of a term $t = f(t_1, \ldots, t_n)$ by $head(t) = f$. The set $sub(t)$ of *subterms* of a

term t is defined as usual. The set $psub(t)$ of *proper subterms* of t is $psub(t) = sub(t) \setminus \{t\}$. If $f \colon A \to B$ and $A' \subseteq A$, we write $f[A']$ for the set $\{f(a) \mid a \in A'\}$.

Given a signature Σ, an *equational theory* $\approx$ is a congruence relation on T_Σ. We write $t \approx t'$ instead of $(t, t') \in \approx$. We consider an equational theory $\approx_R$ obtained from a subterm convergent rewriting system R, as in [26].

Property statements. We assume fixed a set $\mathcal{T}$ of *types*. Given a signature Σ, a *property statement* is a tuple $(f, T_1, \ldots, T_n, T)$, written $f[T_1, \ldots, T_n] \subseteq T$, where $f \in \Sigma_n$ and $T_1, \ldots, T_n, T \in \mathcal{T}$. Property statements represent properties of function symbols by expressing relations between their inputs and outputs. If $ps = (f[T_1, \ldots, T_n] \subseteq T)$, we define the *head symbol* of ps by $head(ps) = f$, $dom(ps) = T_1 \times \ldots \times T_n$ and $ran(ps) = T$.

Given a set PS of property statements and $f \in \Sigma$, we denote by PS_f the set of property statements in PS whose head symbol is f. Note that, in general, we may have more than one property statement associated to each function symbol. We write $f[T_1, \ldots, T_n] \subseteq_{PS} T$ instead of $(f[T_1, \ldots, T_n] \subseteq T) \in PS$.

Syntax. The syntax of our setup is defined by a four-tuple $\langle \Sigma, \approx_R, \mathcal{T}, PS \rangle$, where Σ is a signature, $\approx_R$ is an equational theory on T_Σ defined by a convergent rewriting system R, $\mathcal{T}$ is a set of types, and PS is a set of property statements.

We require that Σ_0 is infinite and that $\Sigma \setminus \Sigma_0$ is finite. Symbols in Σ_0 represent either cryptographically relevant constants (e.g., the constant bitstring 0) or random data generated by agents or the attacker.

Interpretation functions. Let $\mathcal{B} = \{0, 1\}$. A *type interpretation function* is a function $[\![\cdot]\!] \colon \mathcal{T} \to \mathcal{P}(\mathcal{B}^*)$ associating each type $T \in \mathcal{T}$ to a finite and non-empty set $[\![T]\!]$. We extend $[\![\cdot]\!]$ to tuples by defining $[\![T_1 \times \ldots \times T_n]\!] = [\![T_1]\!] \times \ldots \times [\![T_n]\!]$.

A *setup specification* is a pair $\mathcal{S} = \langle S, [\![\cdot]\!]\rangle$, where $S = \langle \Sigma, \approx_R, \mathcal{T}, PS \rangle$ defines the setup's syntax as in the above paragraph and $[\![\cdot]\!]$ is a type interpretation function which consistently defines the behavior of all function symbols: that is, $PS_f \neq \emptyset$ for all $f \in \Sigma$ and, whenever $ps_1, ps_2 \in PS_f$, we have $[\![dom(ps_1)]\!] \cap [\![dom(ps_2)]\!] = \emptyset$. For $c \in \Sigma_0$, this implies that there is a single $T \in \mathcal{T}$ such that $c \subseteq_{PS} T$. We denote this unique type T by $type(c)$.

We assume that functions are undefined unless otherwise specified by a property statement: That is, if $f \in \Sigma_n$ and there is no $ps \in PS_f$ such that $(b_1, \ldots, b_n) \in [\![dom(ps)]\!]$, then the function represented by f is undefined on the input $(b_1, \ldots, b_n)$. In light of this, we set the *domain of definability* of f to be $dom_\mathcal{S}(f) = \biguplus_{ps \in PS_f} [\![dom(ps)]\!]$. Note that $\emptyset \subset dom_\mathcal{S}(f) \subseteq (\mathcal{B}^*)^n$ for all $f \in \Sigma_n$.

Example 1. We specify a simple yet realistic setup that includes: a hash function h that maps any bitstring to a bitstring of length 256; a pairing function $\langle \cdot, \cdot \rangle$ that, given any pair of bitstrings, returns their labeled concatenation; and a symmetric encryption scheme $\{\!|\cdot|\!\}.$ that uses a block cipher together with some reversible padding technique. The corresponding signature $\Sigma^{\mathcal{DY}}$ is given by $\Sigma^{\mathcal{DY}} = \Sigma_0^{\mathcal{DY}} \cup \Sigma_1^{\mathcal{DY}} \cup \Sigma_2^{\mathcal{DY}}$, where $\Sigma_0^{\mathcal{DY}}$ is a countably infinite set of constant symbols, $\Sigma_1^{\mathcal{DY}} = \{h, \pi_1, \pi_2\}$ and $\Sigma_2^{\mathcal{DY}} = \left\{\{\!|\cdot|\!\}., \{\!|\cdot|\!\}.^{-1}, \langle \cdot, \cdot \rangle\right\}$.

Standard equational properties of these primitives are represented by the rewriting system $R_{\mathcal{DY}}$ containing the rules $\pi_1(\langle x,y\rangle) \to x$, $\pi_2(\langle x,y\rangle) \to y$, and $\left\{\left|\left\{|x|\right\}_y\right|\right\}_y^{-1} \to x$. It is simple to check that this rewriting system is convergent.

The types we will consider and their interpretations under $[\![\cdot]\!]$ are as follows. Weak (e.g., human-chosen) passwords are represented by the type pw. We model these passwords as 256-bit bitstrings sampled from a small set: thus, $[\![\mathsf{pw}]\!] \subset \mathcal{B}^{256}$ and $|[\![\mathsf{pw}]\!]| = 2^{24}$. Symmetric keys are represented by the type sym_key, with $[\![\mathsf{sym\_key}]\!] = \mathcal{B}^{256}$; text represents one block of plaintext, with $[\![\mathsf{text}]\!] = \mathcal{B}^{256}$. Furthermore, for each $n,m \in \mathbb{N}$, we consider the following types: $T_{\mathcal{B}^n}$, with $[\![T_{\mathcal{B}^n}]\!] = \mathcal{B}^n$; $T_{\mathcal{B}^{(n,m)}}$, with $[\![T_{\mathcal{B}^{(n,m)}}]\!] = \mathcal{B}^{(n,m)} = \bigcup_{i=n}^{m} \mathcal{B}^i$; and $T_{\mathcal{B}^{n\#m}}$, with $[\![T_{\mathcal{B}^{n\#m}}]\!] = \mathcal{B}^{n\#m} \subseteq \mathcal{B}^{n+m+\lceil \log(n+m)\rceil}$, representing the set of labeled concatenations of two bitstrings of size n and m.

We define PS as the set that contains all property statements of the form $h[T_{\mathcal{B}^n}] \subseteq T_{\mathcal{B}^{256}}$, $\pi_1[T_{\mathcal{B}^{n\#m}}] \subseteq T_{\mathcal{B}^n}$, $\pi_2[T_{\mathcal{B}^{n\#m}}] \subseteq T_{\mathcal{B}^m}$, $\langle T_{\mathcal{B}^n}, T_{\mathcal{B}^m}\rangle \subseteq T_{\mathcal{B}^{n\#m}}$, $\{|T_{\mathcal{B}^{(256n+1,256(n+1))}}|\}_{T_{\mathcal{B}^{256}}} \subseteq T_{\mathcal{B}^{256(n+1)}}$ or $\{|T_{\mathcal{B}^{(256n+1,256(n+1))}}|\}_{T_{\mathcal{B}^{256}}}^{-1} \subseteq T_{\mathcal{B}^{(256n+1,256(n+1))}}$, for $n,m \in \mathbb{N}$. Note that all functions are modeled as undefined on all arguments that fall outside the domains of these property statements. For example, the encryption of any term is undefined unless the key is a 256-bit bitstring.

Example 2. We use our framework to formalize RSA encryption, taking into account properties of the key generation algorithm. An RSA public key is a pair (n,e), where $n = p \cdot q$ is the modulus (with p and q being large primes, typically of around 512 bits), and the exponent e is coprime to $\varphi(n) = (p-1)(q-1)$. The private key d is the multiplicative inverse of e modulo $\varphi(n)$.

We extend the setup specification of Example 1. We add to the signature the following five primitives: the unary functions mod, expn, and inv, representing the extraction of the modulus, the exponent, and the exponent's multiplicative inverse, respectively, from an RSA public-private key pair; a binary function $\{\cdot\}_\cdot^{-1}$, representing the RSA decryption function; and a ternary function $\{\cdot\}_{\cdot,\cdot}$, representing RSA encryption. The only rewriting rule that we must add to model RSA encryption is $\left\{\{m\}_{\mathsf{mod}(k),\mathsf{expn}(k)}\right\}_{\mathsf{inv}(k)}^{-1} \to m$, where m and k are variables.

The additional types that we will use to model properties of these functions and their interpretations are as follows: random represents the random values used to generate an RSA public-private key pair, including two 512-bit prime numbers and the 1024-bit exponent, with $[\![\mathsf{random}]\!] \subseteq \mathcal{B}^{2048}$; prodprime represents the product of two 512-bit prime numbers, so that $[\![\mathsf{prodprime}]\!] \subseteq \mathcal{B}^{1024}$, and, by the prime number theorem, $|[\![\mathsf{prodprime}]\!]| \approx (2^{512}/\log(2^{512}))^2 \approx 2^{1009}$; odd represents 1024-bit odd numbers, with $[\![\mathsf{odd}]\!] \subseteq \mathcal{B}^{1024}$ and $|[\![\mathsf{odd}]\!]| = 2^{1023}$.

The additional property statements we include are the following: mod[random] $\subseteq$ prodprime, because the modulo of an RSA public key is the product of two primes; expn[random] $\subseteq$ odd, because the exponent of an RSA public key is always odd; inv[random] $\subseteq T_{\mathcal{B}^{1024}}$, because an RSA private key is a 1024-bit bitstring (note that we do not allow extracting modulus, exponents, or inverses from anything other than a valid value for generating an RSA key pair);

$\{T_{\mathcal{B}^{1024}}\}_{\text{prodprime,odd}} \subseteq T_{\mathcal{B}^{1024}}$; and $\{T_{\mathcal{B}^{1024}}\}^{-1}_{T_{\mathcal{B}^{1024}}} \subseteq T_{\mathcal{B}^{1024}}$. The last two properties state that encrypting any 1024-bit plaintext with a valid RSA public key yields a 1024-bit bitstring, and that RSA decryption takes a ciphertext and a private key which are both 1024-bit bitstrings and outputs a 1024-bit plaintext. Note that encryption is undefined if the plaintext is not a 1024-bit bitstring, the modulus is not the product of two primes, or the exponent is even.

One limitation of our method is that, although it is simple to express relations between the input and output of a cryptographic primitive, more complex relations between terms are harder to model. For example, modeling the fact that the $\varphi(n)$ and e are coprime would require modeling the public key as a single term. An attacker could then extract the modulus and the exponent from such a key, and it can build such a key from a modulus and an exponent. The simpler model we present here illustrates the expressiveness of our framework and is sufficient to model the attacks in our case studies.

2.2   Semantics

Let us fix a setup specification $\mathcal{S} = \langle\langle \Sigma, \approx_R, \mathcal{T}, PS \rangle, [\![\cdot]\!]\rangle$.

Term assignments. Let $\mathcal{B}^*_\bot = \mathcal{B}^* \cup \{\bot\}$. A term assignment is a function $\omega : T_\Sigma \to \mathcal{B}^*_\bot$ associating a bitstring to each symbolic term. Let Ω be the set of all term assignments. We say that $\omega \in \Omega$ *satisfies* $\approx_R$, and write $\omega \models \approx_R$, if, whenever $t \approx_R t'$, either $\omega(t) = \omega(t')$, or $\omega(t) = \bot$, or $\omega(t') = \bot$. We say that ω satisfies a property statement ps (under $[\![\cdot]\!]$), and write $\omega \models_{[\![\cdot]\!]} ps$ if, whenever $(\omega(t_1), \ldots, \omega(t_n)) \in [\![dom(ps)]\!]$, then $\omega(f(t_1, \ldots, t_n)) \in [\![ran(ps)]\!]$, and whenever $(\omega(t_1), \ldots, \omega(t_n)) \notin [\![dom(ps)]\!]$ for all $ps \in PS_f$, then $\omega(f(t_1, \ldots, t_n)) = \bot$. We say that ω satisfies PS (under $[\![\cdot]\!]$), and write $\omega \models_{[\![\cdot]\!]} PS$, if $\omega \models_{[\![\cdot]\!]} ps$ for all $ps \in PS$. We say that ω satisfies $\mathcal{S}$, and write $\omega \models \mathcal{S}$, when $\omega \models \approx_R$ and $\omega \models_{[\![\cdot]\!]} PS$. We denote by $\Omega_\mathcal{S}$ the set of all $\omega \in \Omega$ which satisfy $\mathcal{S}$.

Example 3. Functions ω that satisfy our equational theory may be such that $\omega(t) = \bot$ and $\omega(t') \neq \bot$ for terms t and t' such that $t \approx_R t'$. To see why this is allowed, recall from Example 1 that $\{\!|\cdot|\!\}^{-1}_\cdot$ represents a symmetric encryption algorithm in which valid keys always have 256 bits. Let $t, k \in \Sigma_0$, with $type(t) = \mathsf{text}$, and $t' = \{\!|\{\!|t|\!\}_k|\!\}^{-1}_k$. We have $t \approx_R t'$. If ω represents a possible real-world assignment (of terms to bitstrings), we have $\omega(t) \neq \bot$ (since t represents a bitstring freshly sampled from $\mathcal{B}^{256}$). Moreover, if $\omega(k)$ is not a 256-bit bitstring, then $\omega(t') = \bot$ since our encryption and decryption functions are only defined for 256-bit keys. Therefore, $\omega(\{\!|\{\!|t|\!\}_k|\!\}^{-1}_k) = \bot$.

Probabilistic models. Since valid, real-world protocol execution traces are finite, we are interested in events that depend on finitely many terms. For each finite set of terms $K \subseteq T_\Sigma$, let Λ_K be the set of functions $\lambda : K \to \mathcal{P}(\mathcal{B}^*_\bot)$ and, for each $\lambda \in \Lambda_K$, let Ω_λ be the set of all $\omega \in \Omega$ such that $\omega(t) \in \lambda(t)$ for all $t \in K$. Let $\Lambda = \bigcup_{K \in \mathcal{P}_{\text{fin}}(T_\Sigma)} \Lambda_K$ and $\Omega_\Lambda = \{\Omega_\lambda \mid \lambda \in \Lambda\}$, where $\mathcal{P}_{\text{fin}}(X)$ is the set of *finite* subsets of X. Note that Ω_Λ is the set of subsets of Ω whose specification depends on only the instantiation of finitely many terms. Thus, we want our probability measure to be defined in the σ-algebra generated by Ω_Λ. Let $\mathcal{F}$ be this σ-algebra; we say that $\mathcal{F}$ is the σ-algebra of *finitely generated events*.

We consider probability spaces $(\Omega, \mathcal{F}, \mu)$, where Ω and $\mathcal{F}$ are as defined above and $\mu \colon \mathcal{F} \to [0, 1]$ is a probability measure. Note that Ω and $\mathcal{F}$ are fixed for a given $\mathcal{S}$; it is μ that we are interested in studying. If $t \in T_\Sigma$, we write $\widehat{t} \colon \Omega \to \mathcal{B}_\perp^*$ to denote the random variable on Ω defined by $\widehat{t}(\omega) = \omega(t)$. We adopt standard (abuses of) notation from probability theory. If $C(b_1, \ldots, b_n)$ is a condition whose satisfaction depends on the bitstring values $b_1, \ldots, b_n$, we write $P_\mu[C(\widehat{t_1}, \ldots, \widehat{t_n})]$ for $\mu(\{\omega \in \Omega \mid C(\widehat{t_1}(\omega), \ldots, \widehat{t_n}(\omega))\})$, provided that $\{\omega \in \Omega \mid C(\widehat{t_1}(\omega), \ldots, \widehat{t_n}(\omega))\} \in \mathcal{F}$. If $\Omega \in \mathcal{F}$, we write $P_\mu[\Omega]$ instead of $\mu(\Omega)$. We say μ *satisfies* the equational theory $\approx_R$ if $\mu(\{\omega \mid \omega \models \approx_R\}) = 1$, and we write $\mu \models \approx_R$ to denote this fact. Analogously, we define the satisfaction of PS (under $[\![\cdot]\!]$) by μ, $\mu \models_{[\![\cdot]\!]} PS$, by $\mu(\{\omega \mid \omega \models_{[\![\cdot]\!]} PS\}) = 1$. We say that μ *satisfies*, or is a *model* of, the setup specification $\mathcal{S}$, written $\mu \models \mathcal{S}$, if $\mu \models \approx_R$ and $\mu \models_{[\![\cdot]\!]} PS$. Note that μ is a model of $\mathcal{S}$ if and only if $\mu(\Omega_\mathcal{S}) = 1$.

3   A Generalized Random Oracle Model

In this section we propose an algorithm for sampling the random variables associated with symbolic terms. Our algorithm interprets functions as random oracles subject to satisfying our setup specification $\mathcal{S} = \langle \langle \Sigma, \approx_R, \mathcal{T}, PS \rangle, [\![\cdot]\!] \rangle$.

3.1   Tentative Term Sampling in the ROM

Term sampling. Suppose that $K \subset T_\Sigma$ is a finite set of terms and P is a partition of K. We define $\approx_P$ to be the smallest congruence relation on T_Σ such that $\approx_R \subseteq \approx_P$ and $t \approx_P t'$ whenever there is $p \in P$ such that $t, t' \in p$. Note that $\approx_P$ may be coarser than both $K/\approx_R$ and P: For example, if there are $a, b \in \Sigma_0$ and $p \in P$ such that $a, b \in p$, then $\{\!\{\{\!\{M\}\!\}_a\}\!\}_b^{-1} \approx_P M$. However, $\{\!\{\{\!\{M\}\!\}_a\}\!\}_b^{-1} \not\approx_R M$ and there is not necessarily a $p \in P$ such that $M, \{\!\{\{\!\{M\}\!\}_a\}\!\}_b^{-1} \in p$.

The sampling algorithm below builds a function ψ_{ROM} mapping a finite set of terms to $\mathcal{B}_\perp^*$. We denote by $P(\psi_{ROM})$ the partition of $dom(\psi_{ROM})$ given by $P(\psi_{ROM}) = \{\psi_{ROM}^{-1}(b) \mid b \in ran(\psi_{ROM})\}$. The algorithm is probabilistic: at various steps, it samples a random bitstring from a finite subset of $\mathcal{B}_\perp^*$. We assume that this sampling is always done with uniform probability distribution. We also assume fixed some total order $\prec$ on the set of terms such that, if $t \in psub(t')$, then $t \prec t'$. We say that such an order is *subterm-compatible*.

Algorithm 1 (Tentative Term Sampling Algorithm)
Input: *a finite set of terms $K \subseteq T_\Sigma$.*
Output: *a function $\psi_{ROM} \colon sub[K] \to \mathcal{B}_\perp^*$.*

1: $\psi_{ROM} \leftarrow \emptyset$
2: let $t_1, \ldots, t_k$ be such that $t_1 \prec \ldots \prec t_k$ and $sub[K] = \{t_1, \ldots, t_k\}$
3: **for** i **from** 1 **to** k

4:      let $t_i = f(t'_1, \ldots, t'_n)$
5:      **if** $(\psi_{ROM}(t'_1), \ldots \psi_{ROM}(t'_n)) \notin dom_S(f)$
6:          $\psi_{ROM}(t_i) \leftarrow \bot$
7:          **continue**
8:      let ps be the unique $ps \in PS_f$ s.t. $(\psi_{ROM}(t'_1), \ldots, \psi_{ROM}(t'_n)) \in [\![dom(ps)]\!]$
9:      **if** $\exists t' \in dom(\psi_{ROM}). \ t_i \approx_{P(\psi_{ROM})} t'$ **and** $\psi_{ROM}(t') \neq \bot$
10:         $\psi_{ROM}(t_i) \leftarrow \psi_{ROM}(t')$
11:         **continue**
12:     randomly sample b from $[\![ran(ps)]\!]$
13:     $\psi_{ROM}(t_i) \leftarrow b$
14: **return** ψ_{ROM}

Algorithm 1 samples terms in order (lines 2–3), by interpreting each function symbol as a random oracle with uniform probability distribution (lines 12–13), and respecting the equational theory in case an equal term has already been sampled (lines 9–10), as long as its argument values (previously sampled) form a tuple in its domain of definability (lines 5–6).

We remark that this procedure is only used to define our probability distribution μ: in general, it may not be feasible to decide membership of the sets $[\![dom(ps)]\!]$ or to sample from $[\![ran(ps)]\!]$. In [25] we describe our algorithm for computing μ.

Problems with the tentative term sampling algorithm. We show that Algorithm 1 does not necessarily yield a probability measure over $\mathcal{F}$ as desired.

Given a finite set $K \subseteq T_\Sigma$ and a subterm-compatible order $\prec$, Algorithm 1 is a probabilistic algorithm, and thus outputs functions $\psi \colon sub[K] \to \mathcal{B}^*_\bot$ with some probability distribution. We would therefore like to define a model μ of $\mathcal{S}$ by defining $\mu(\Omega_\lambda)$ for each generator Ω_λ of $\mathcal{F}$ as the probability that executing Algorithm 1 on input $dom(\lambda)$ yields as output a function ψ_{ROM} such that, for each $t \in dom(\lambda)$, $\psi_{ROM}(t) \in \lambda(t)$.

Unfortunately, the next example shows that this is not well-defined in general. Concretely, we show that there are terms t and t' such that, letting $\lambda_b = \{t \mapsto b, a \mapsto b\}$ for each $b \in \mathcal{B}^*_\bot$, the probability of the set $\bigcup_{b \in \mathcal{B}^*_\bot} \Omega_{\lambda_b}$ depends on the input set K and the order relation $\prec$ considered.

Example 4. Suppose that $a, b, k \in \Sigma_0$ are such that $type(a) = T_{\mathcal{B}^{1024}}$, $type(b) = T_{\mathcal{B}^{1024}}$ and $type(k) = \mathsf{random}$. Consider executing Algorithm 1 on the set $\{t\}$, with $t = \left\{ \{a\}_{mod(k), expn(k)} \right\}^{-1}_b$. Algorithm 1 outputs a function $\psi \colon sub(t) \to \mathcal{B}^*_\bot$. Let us consider the probability that $\psi(t) = \psi(a)$. It is simple to check that both $\psi(t)$ and $\psi(a)$ are sampled by Algorithm 1 with uniform probability distribution from $\mathcal{B}^{1024}$. Therefore, the probability that $\psi(t) = \psi(a)$ is 2^{-1024}.

Now, consider executing Algorithm 1 on the set $\{t, inv(k)\}$. If $t \prec inv(k)$, then the execution of Algorithm 1 will be exactly the same until $\psi(s)$ is sampled for all terms $s \in sub(t)$, and $\psi(inv(k))$ is only sampled afterwards. Therefore, $\psi(s)$ is sampled according to the same probability distribution for all $s \in sub(t)$, and the probability that $\psi(t) = \psi(a)$ is still 2^{-1024}. However, if $inv(k) \prec b$, we have a probability of 2^{-1024} that $\psi(b) = \psi(\mathsf{inv}(k))$. If $\psi(b) = \psi(\mathsf{inv}(k))$, then we have $\psi(t) = \psi(a)$ with probability 1. Otherwise, $\psi(t)$ and $\psi(a)$ will still be sampled from $\mathcal{B}^{1024}$ with uniform probability distribution, and the probability that they are sampled to the same value is again 2^{-1024}. In this case, we conclude that $P[\psi(a) = \psi(t)] = 2^{-1024} \cdot (2 - 2^{-1024}) \neq 2^{-1024}$. Thus, the probability that $\psi(t) = \psi(a)$ depends on both the input set K and the order $\prec$.

Despite the example above, the following result shows that, given a fixed finite set of terms K and a subterm-compatible order $\prec$, Algorithm 1 does yield a probability distribution on the σ-algebra $\mathcal{F}_K$ generated by the set $\{\Omega_\lambda \mid \lambda \in \Lambda_K\}$. We remark that $\mathcal{F}_K$ is the σ-algebra of events that depend only on the instantiation of terms in the set K.

Theorem 2. *There is a unique probability distribution $\mu^{K,\prec} \colon \mathcal{F}_{sub[K]} \to [0,1]$ such that, for each $\lambda \in \Lambda_K$, $\mu^{K,\prec}(\Omega_\lambda)$ is the probability that executing Algorithm 1 on input K and using the order $\prec$ yields a function ψ_{ROM} such that, for each $t \in K$, $\psi_{\mathrm{ROM}}(t) \in \lambda(t)$.*

3.2   Revised Term Sampling in the ROM

To avoid problems like the one illustrated by Example 4 we need two additional hypotheses on the setup specification $\mathcal{S}$. We will explicitly distinguish a set of weak function symbols and consider a revised algorithm that uses this distinction. This revised algorithm is equivalent to Algorithm 1 when all functions are treated as weak. We show that, under these hypotheses, we can define a probability measure from this new sampling algorithm, while also simplifying the calculation of probabilities.

Weak terms. We assume fixed a set $\Sigma^W \subseteq \Sigma$ of *weak function symbols*. We say that a term $t \in T_\Sigma$ is *weak* if $\mathsf{head}(t) \in \Sigma^W$, and denote by T^W the set of weak terms. Intuitively, weak function symbols are those that represent functions whose outputs are sampled from "small" sets, and a probabilistic model must therefore take into account the possibility of collisions between them. By contrast, non-weak function symbols are those that represent functions whose outputs are sampled from large enough sets, so that ignoring the possibility of collisions changes our probability estimates only negligibly. Theorem 4, stated below, formalizes this idea.

Example 5. In our running example, we consider the set of weak function symbols $\Sigma^W = \{\mathsf{h}\} \cup \{a \in \Sigma_0 \mid a \subseteq_{PS} \mathsf{pw}\}$. That is, a term is weak if it is a hash or if it is derived from a humanly-chosen password. Note that the probability of a collision in a hash function is in fact rather low, and indeed the security of many protocols relies on hash functions being collision-resistant. However, modeling hash functions as weak increases the accuracy of our model while still allowing us to define a consistent probability distribution.

Term sampling revisited. If K and K' are sets of terms and P is a partition of K, we let $P|_{K'} = \{p \cap K' \mid p \in P\}$. Note that $P|_{K'}$ is a partition of $K \cap K'$. We denote by $W(\psi_{ROM})$ the partition $P(\psi_{ROM})|_{T^W}$.

Our revised term sampling algorithm, targeted at solving the anomaly described in Example 4, is the same as Algorithm 1 with the exception that we replace the condition $t_i \approx_{P(\psi_{ROM})} t'$ by $t_i \approx_{W(\psi_{ROM})} t'$ in line 9. Note that this revised sampling algorithm does not necessarily respect congruences, i.e., we may have $\psi_{ROM}(t) = \psi_{ROM}(t')$ and $\psi_{ROM}(f(t)) \neq \psi_{ROM}(f(t'))$. However, this only happens if either t or t' is not weak, in which case the collision $\psi_{ROM}(t) = \psi_{ROM}(t')$ only occurs with negligible probability.

This revised algorithm yields a probability distribution on $\mathcal{F}$ provided that the setup specification $\mathcal{S}$ satisfies two reasonable conditions, described below.

Disjointness. The first condition we require on the specification $\mathcal{S}$ is that weak function symbols do not occur in the rewriting system R.

Intuitively, this disjointness condition implies that the equality of terms depends only on the equalities between their weak subterms. Thus, sampling terms in a different order does not affect any equalities because terms are sampled only after all their subterms are sampled. This condition excludes cases like that described in Example 4: because $\mathsf{inv} \notin \Sigma^W$, even if $\psi_{ROM}(b) = \psi_{ROM}(\mathsf{inv}(k))$, we never have $\left\{ \{a\}_{\mathsf{mod}(k),\mathsf{expn}(k)} \right\}_b^{-1} \approx_{W(\psi_{ROM})} a$. The key idea is that equalities between non-weak terms may be disregarded, as they occur only with negligible probability. Ignoring equalities between non-weak terms, besides allowing us to consistently define a probability measure, also simplifies the calculation of probabilities. In [25] we present a simple algorithm for deciding $\approx_P$ (that is, given terms t and t', decide whether $t \approx_P t'$), and thus to perform the test in Line 9 of Algorithm 1 and its revised version.

Compatibility. The second condition we require on our setup is *compatibility*. Let K be a finite set of terms and P be a partition of K. Recall the definition of $\approx_P$ given in Section 3. We say that P is $\approx_R$-*closed* if, for all $t, t' \in K$, whenever $t \approx_P t'$ there is $p \in P$ such that $t, t' \in p$; equivalently, P is $\approx_R$-closed if $\approx_P|_{K \times K} = \{(t, t') \mid$ there exists $p \in P$ such that $t, t' \in p\}$. We are interested in partitions of weak terms. Thus, given a finite set K, we denote by $\mathcal{P}_R^W(K)$ the set of $\approx_R$-closed partitions of $sub[K] \cap T^W$.

A *selection function for* K is a function $\iota: sub[K] \to PS \cup \{\bot\}$ such that, for each $t \in sub[K]$, either $\iota(t) = \bot$ or $head(\iota(t)) = head(t)$. Given $\omega \in \Omega$, we say that ω *satisfies* ι if, for all $t = f(t_1, \ldots, t_n) \in sub[K]$, either $(\omega(t_1), \ldots, \omega(t_n)) \in [\![dom(\iota(t))]\!]$ and $\omega(t) \in [\![ran(\iota(t))]\!]$, or $(\omega(t_1), \ldots, \omega(t_n)) \notin dom_{\mathcal{S}}(f)$ and $\iota(t) = \omega(t) = \bot$. We denote by $I(K)$ the set of selection functions for K, and by $I_{\mathcal{S}}(K) \subseteq I(K)$ the set of selection functions ι for K such that there is $\omega \in \Omega$ that satisfies ι. In [25] we show that, given a finite set of terms K, $I_{\mathcal{S}}(K)$ is a finite and computable set.

If K is a finite set of terms, a selection function for K determines which property statement applies to each term in $sub[K]$: Indeed, if $\omega \in \Omega$ satisfies

PS, there exists exactly one selection function $\iota \in I(K)$ satisfied by ω, which associates each term $f(t_1, \ldots, t_n)$ to the unique property statement $ps \in PS_f$ such that $(\omega(t_1), \ldots, \omega(t_n)) \in [\![dom(ps)]\!]$, or $\bot$ if no such ps exists.

The compatibility condition is that, if K is a finite set of terms, $t \in sub[K]$, $P \in \mathcal{P}_R^W(K)$, $\iota \in I_S(K)$, and $\iota(t) \neq \bot$, then there is $t' \in sub(t)$ such that $t \approx_{P|_{psub(t)}} t'$ and, whenever $t'' \in sub[K]$ and $t \approx_{P|_{psub(t)}} t''$, either $\iota(t'') = \bot$ or $[\![ran(\iota(t'))]\!] \subseteq [\![ran(\iota(t''))]\!]$. Intuitively, this condition requires the equational theory $\approx_R$ and the property statements in PS to be compatible. It is a basic requirement that should be satisfied by any meaningful setup specification. The following example illustrates this.

Example 6 (Incompatibility between $\approx_R$ and PS). Consider a rewriting system R containing the symmetric decryption rewrite rule $\left\{\!\left| \{\!| x |\!\}_y \right|\!\right\}_y^{-1} \to x$ and the property statements $\{\!| T_{\mathcal{B}^{256}} |\!\}_{T_{\mathcal{B}^{256}}}^{-1} \subseteq T_{\mathcal{B}^{128}}$, $\{\!| T_{\mathcal{B}^{256}} |\!\}_{T_{\mathcal{B}^{256}}}^{-1} \subseteq T_{\mathcal{B}^{256}}$. Let $t' = \{\!| \{\!| t |\!\}_k |\!\}_k^{-1}$, where $t, k \in \Sigma_0$ and $type(t) = type(k) = T_{\mathcal{B}^{256}}$. In this case, we have $\iota(t) = T_{\mathcal{B}^{256}}$ and $\iota(t') = T_{\mathcal{B}^{128}}$ for all selection functions $\iota \in I_S(\{t, t'\})$. We have $t \approx_R t'$, $[\![ran(\iota(t))]\!] = T_{\mathcal{B}^{256}}$, and $[\![ran(\iota(t'))]\!] = T_{\mathcal{B}^{128}}$. Because $\mathcal{B}^{128} \cap \mathcal{B}^{256} = \emptyset$, it follows that there is no $\omega \in \Omega$ that satisfies $\approx_R$ and PS. Note that, having $\{\!| T_{\mathcal{B}^{256}} |\!\}_{T_{\mathcal{B}^{256}}}^{-1} \subseteq T_{\mathcal{B}^{256}}$ instead of $\{\!| T_{\mathcal{B}^{256}} |\!\}_{T_{\mathcal{B}^{256}}}^{-1} \subseteq T_{\mathcal{B}^{128}}$, we could have $type(t) = B$ for any non-empty set $B \subseteq \mathcal{B}^{256}$ without violating our compatibility condition.

Example 7. With the choice of Σ^W given in Example 5, our running example (from Examples 1—3) satisfies the disjointness and compatibility conditions.

Probability measure. Under the disjointness and compatibility conditions, the revised sampling algorithm yields a probability measure μ_{ROM}. For each total subterm-compatible order $\prec$ and each $\lambda \in \Lambda$, let $\mu^{\prec}(\lambda)$ be the probability that executing the revised version of Algorithm 1 on input $dom(\lambda)$ using the order $\prec$ yields a function $\psi_{ROM}: sub[K] \to \mathcal{B}_\bot^*$ such that $\psi_{ROM}(t) \in \lambda(t)$ for all $t \in K$.

Theorem 3. *Suppose that the disjointness and compatibility conditions are satisfied by S and Σ^W, and let $\prec$ and $\prec'$ be two subterm-compatible orders. If $\lambda, \lambda' \in \Lambda$ are such that $\Omega_\lambda = \Omega_{\lambda'}$, we have $\mu^{\prec}(\lambda) = \mu^{\prec'}(\lambda')$. There exists a unique extension μ_{ROM} of $\mu^{\prec}$ to $\mathcal{F}$ that is a probability measure, and $\mu_{ROM}(\Omega_S) = 1$.*

Theorem 3 implies that μ_{ROM} is well-defined, as it does not depend on the choice of the order $\prec$, and that it is a model of S.

3.3   Comparing Probability Measures

We describe the relationship between the probability measures $\mu^{K,\prec}$ described in Theorem 2 and the probability measure μ_{ROM} described in Theorem 3.

For each $f \in \Sigma$, let $L_f = \min_{ps \in PS_f} |[\![ran(ps)]\!]|$ and $L = \min_{f \in \Sigma \setminus \Sigma^W} L_f$. Note that, if non-weak terms are always sampled from "large" sets of bitstrings whenever they are defined, then L is large as well. Intuitively, Theorem 4 shows that, in this case, $\mu^{K,\prec}$ and μ_{ROM} coincide except on a set whose probability is "small". More precisely, fixed K, the probability of this set is $\mathcal{O}(1/L)$.

Theorem 4. *For any finite set of terms K, there exists a set $\Omega(K)$ such that, for any subterm-compatible order $\prec$:*

(1) for any $\lambda \in \Lambda_K$, $\mu^{K,\prec}(\Omega_\lambda \cap \Omega(K)) = \mu_{ROM}(\Omega_\lambda \cap \Omega(K))$;
(2) there exists a polynomial function p such that

$$\mu^{K,\prec}(\mathbf{\Omega} \setminus \Omega(K)) = \mu_{ROM}(\mathbf{\Omega} \setminus \Omega(K)) \leq |sub[K]|^2 \cdot |I_S(K)| \cdot (1/L).$$

Note that the statement of Theorem 4 is stronger than merely bounding the difference in the probability of sets in Ω_Λ. For example, Theorem 4 implies that the probability of two terms being sampled to the same bitstring as measured by $\mu^{K,\prec}$ and μ_{ROM} also differs by at most $|sub[K]|^2 \cdot |I_S(K)| \cdot (1/L)$.

Asymptotic interpretation. Suppose that, for each $\eta \in \mathbb{N}$, $\llbracket \cdot \rrbracket_\eta$ is a type interpretation function and $\mathcal{S}_\eta = \langle \langle \Sigma, \approx_R, \mathcal{T}, PS \rangle, \llbracket \cdot \rrbracket_\eta \rangle$ is a setup specification which, together with a set Σ^W of weak function symbols, satisfies the disjointness and compatibility conditions. Assume further that $1/L_\eta$ is negligible as a function of η, where $L_{f,\eta} = \min_{ps \in PS_f} \llbracket ran(ps) \rrbracket_\eta$ and $L_\eta = \min_{f \in \Sigma \setminus \Sigma^W} L_{f,\eta}$ for each $\eta \in \mathbb{N}$. Note that this condition is equivalent to requiring, for each function symbol $f \in \Sigma \setminus \Sigma^W$ and each $ps \in PS_f$, that $1/\left| \llbracket ran(ps) \rrbracket_\eta \right|$ is negligible as a function of η. Intuitively, this condition requires that non-weak terms, when defined, are always mapped to bitstrings sampled from large enough sets.

Let $\mu_\eta^{K,\prec}$ (respectively, $\mu_{ROM,\eta}$) be the probability measure given by Theorem 2 (respectively, Theorem 3) when Algorithm 1 (respectively, the revised version of algorithm 1) is executed using the interpretation function $\llbracket \cdot \rrbracket_\eta$. Then, the following is a corollary of Theorem 4.

Corollary 1. *Let K be a finite set of terms, and suppose that $\left| I_{\mathcal{S}_\eta}(K) \right|$ grows polynomially as a function of η. For any finite set of terms K, there exists a set $\Omega(K)$ such that, for any subterm-compatible order $\prec$:*

(1) for any $\lambda \in \Lambda_K$, $\mu_\eta^{K,\prec}(\Omega_\lambda \cap \Omega(K)) = \mu_{ROM,\eta}(\Omega_\lambda \cap \Omega(K))$;
(2) $\mu_\eta^{K,\prec}(\mathbf{\Omega} \setminus \Omega(K)) = \mu_{ROM,\eta}(\mathbf{\Omega} \setminus \Omega(K))$, and both quantities are negligible as functions of η.

Comparison with the random oracle and ideal cipher models. Algorithm 1 exactly matches the random oracle model for hash functions. Its only difference with respect to the ideal-cipher model for symmetric encryption is that two different bitstrings may be encrypted to the same ciphertext under the same key. However, if the range of the encryption function is large enough (i.e., larger than any polynomial function of the security parameter), then the probability of such a collision is negligible for any (finite) input set. In light of Corollary 1, we thus conclude that the probability measure μ_{ROM} differs only negligibly from the probabilities yielded by the random oracle and the ideal cipher models.

3.4   Computing Probabilities

In [25] we present an equivalent, algebraic definition of the probability measure μ_{ROM} which reduces the problem of computing probabilities of the form $P_{\mu_{ROM}}[t_1 \in B_1, \ldots, t_n \in B_n, t'_1 = t''_1, \ldots, t'_{n'} = t''_{n''}]$ (with $B_1, \ldots, B_n \subseteq \mathcal{B}^*_\perp$) to computing the sizes of intersections of sets in $\{B_1, \ldots, B_n\} \cup [\![\mathcal{T}]\!]$. A full specification of the interpretations of types is not necessary.

Our prototype implementation computes probabilities of this form for the cryptographic primitives and respective properties considered in our running example. The user may, however, need to specify the sizes of intersections of the sets of bitstrings $B_1, \ldots, B_n$ with the specified property types.

Let $T = \{t_1, \ldots, t_n, t'_1, t''_1, \ldots, t'_{n'}, t'_{n''}\}$. Since we must consider $\approx_R$-closed partitions of $T^W_\Sigma \cap sub[T]$, the complexity of the computation is exponential in $|T^W_\Sigma \cap sub[T]|$. However, for the specification considered in our running example, if T contains no subterms of the form $\pi_i(t)$ for $i \in \{1, 2\}$ and t such that $head(t) \neq \langle \cdot, \cdot \rangle$, the complexity is linear in the number of non-weak subterms of T.

4   Off-Line Guessing

Let s be a term representing a bitstring in $B \subset \mathcal{B}^*$ that is intended to be secret. If an attacker can feasibly enumerate all bitstrings in B, he may try to rule out the possibility that s represents each such bitstring. The attacker's ultimate aim is to exclude all but one bitstring in B and thereby learn the secret s even if it may not be directly deduced by constructing terms and reasoning equationally. When the attacker does not need to interact with other agents to verify his guess, this is called an *off-line guessing attack*. In this section we describe how properties of cryptographic primitives described by $\mathcal{S}$ can be used to find and estimate the success probability of non-trivial off-line guessing attacks.

4.1   Attacker Model

We will assume fixed an infinite set $\mathcal{N} \subseteq \Sigma_0$ such that $\Sigma_0 \setminus \mathcal{N}$ is finite. Symbols in $\mathcal{N}$ represent random data generated by the agents, whereas symbols in $\Sigma_0 \setminus \mathcal{N}$ represent cryptographically relevant constants (such as the bitstring 0). We also assume fixed a countably infinite set $\mathcal{V}$ of *variables*, disjoint from Σ.

We represent an attacker's knowledge by a frame [27], i.e., a pair $(\tilde{n}, \sigma)$, written $\nu\tilde{n}.\sigma$, where $\tilde{n} \subseteq \mathcal{N}$ is a finite set of names and $\sigma : \mathcal{V} \rightarrowtail T_\Sigma$ is a substitution. Given a frame $\phi = \nu\tilde{n}.\sigma$, we define $T_\phi = T_{\Sigma \setminus \tilde{n}}(dom(\sigma))$. We say that terms in T_ϕ are ϕ-*recipes* as they represent the ways in which an attacker can build terms.

Suppose that an attacker whose knowledge is represented by a frame $\phi = \nu\tilde{n}.\sigma$ attempts an off-line guessing attack of a secret s. We require that the set of bitstrings tried by the attacker is $[\![type(w)]\!]$ for some $w \in \mathcal{N}$ that does not occur in either $\tilde{n}$ or σ, and we model the attacker's guess by w. Letting $x \notin dom(\sigma)$ be a fresh variable, we consider the frames $\phi_s = \nu\tilde{n}_w.\sigma_s$ and $\phi_w = \nu\tilde{n}_w.\sigma_w$, where $\tilde{n}_w = \tilde{n} \cup \{w\}$, $\sigma_s = \sigma \cup \{x \mapsto s\}$, and $\sigma_w = \sigma \cup \{x \mapsto w\}$. Here, ϕ_s represents the attacker's knowledge using the right guess, while ϕ_w represents his knowledge when his guess is wrong.

Guess verifiers. We consider two ways in which an attacker can verify whether his guess w is correct. First, he can use his guess to construct a pair of terms (t, t') that are equal under $\approx_R$ if $w = s$, but different if $w \neq s$. This is equivalent to ϕ_w and ϕ_s not being statically equivalent, and is the usual definition of security against off-line guessing used in symbolic methods [16, 20, 27]. Second, he can use his guess to construct a term t whose corresponding bitstring satisfies some given property if $w = s$, and not necessarily otherwise.

Given a term t and $p \in \mathbb{N}^*$, we denote the *subterm of t at position p* by $t|_p$, where $t|_\epsilon = t$ and, for $t = f(t_1, \ldots, t_n)$, $t|_{i.p} = t_i|_p$ for $i \in \{1, \ldots, n\}$, where $i.p$ denotes the sequence of integers obtained by prepending i to the sequence p. The set $eqv(\phi, t)$ of *equational verifiers* of a term t (under ϕ) is the set of pairs (t, t') such that $t, t' \in T_{\phi_s}$, $t\sigma_s \approx_R t'\sigma_s$, $t\sigma_w \not\approx_R t'\sigma_w$, and there is no $p \in \mathbb{N}^* \setminus \{\epsilon\}$ such that these conditions hold for the pair $(t|_p, t'|_p)$. These are the pairs of recipes that an attacker may use to validate his guess using the first strategy.

To model the second attacking strategy, we will consider a set $\mathcal{TT}$ of *test types* that model the attacker's ability to test whether a bitstring is in a given set. The set $tv(\phi, t)$ of *type verifiers* of t (under ϕ) is the set of pairs (t, TT) such that $t \in T_{\phi_s}$, $T \in \mathcal{TT}$, $P_{\mu_{ROM}}[\widehat{t\sigma_s} \in [\![TT]\!]] = 1$, $P_{\mu_{ROM}}[\widehat{t\sigma_w} \in [\![TT]\!]] \neq 1$, and there are no $p \in \mathbb{N}^* \setminus \{\epsilon\}$, $TT' \in \mathcal{TT}$ such that these conditions hold for $(t|_p, TT')$. Note that to model a realistic attacker one must choose test types such that $[\![T]\!]$ is efficiently decidable for all $T \in \mathcal{TT}$.

Example 8. We will consider the test types odd, with $[\![odd]\!]$ corresponding to the set of 1024-bit bitstrings that represent an odd number, so that $|[\![odd]\!]| = 2^{1023}$, and nspf, with $[\![nspf]\!]$ corresponding to the set of 1024-bit bitstrings representing numbers with no prime factors smaller than 10^6. We have $|[\![nspf]\!]| \approx \prod_{p \in P_{10^6}} (p - 1)/p \approx 1/24$, where P_i represents the set of prime factors smaller than i. These test types are used to model off-line guessing attacks in Section 4.2.

Our requirements on the sub-positions of verifiers prevent us from having infinite sets of spurious verifiers. For instance, let $h^0(t) = t$ and $h^{n+1}(t) = h(h^n(t))$ for each $n \in \mathbb{N}$, and let (t, t') be an equational verifier. Without this requirement, all pairs $(h^i(t), h^i(t'))$ for $i \in \mathbb{N}$ would be verifiers as well. However, if an attacker tests the pair $(t\sigma_w, t'\sigma_w)$, he cannot obtain more information by testing the pairs $(h^i(t)\sigma_w, h^i(t')\sigma_w)$, for $i > 0$.

In [25] we describe an algorithm for computing equational and type verifiers for any signature Σ and any convergent rewriting system R.

4.2   Off-Line Guessing Examples on EKE

The EKE (Encrypted Key Exchange) protocol, proposed in [22], is designed to allow two parties to exchange authenticated information using a weak symmetric key. The authors show that naive versions of the protocol, while possibly symbolically secure, are nevertheless subject to off-line guessing attacks when implemented using RSA public keys. These examples illustrate that such attacks can result from implementation details that, while often trivial, are outside the scope of traditional symbolic methods.

We now show how our methods can be used to model and estimate the success probability of two such off-line guessing attacks. In both cases it is sufficient to consider the first step of the protocol. Probability calculations in this section rely on the setup specification of our running example and are performed automatically by our prototype implementation in less than one second.

Example 9. In the first step of this version of the protocol, an agent A samples a bitstring from $[\![\mathsf{random}]\!]$ represented by a term $r \in \Sigma_0$ such that $type(r) = \mathsf{random}$, and uses it to compute an RSA public key $\langle \mathsf{mod}(r), \mathsf{expn}(r) \rangle$. Then, A (symmetrically) encrypts this public key with a password s shared between A and the intended recipient B. To keep our analysis simple, we assume that the participants encrypt the modulus and the exponent separately and send them over the network as a pair of encryptions (instead of the encryption of the pair). Thus, this first message is represented by the term $\langle \{\!|\mathsf{mod}(r)|\!\}_s, \{\!|\mathsf{expn}(r)|\!\}_s \rangle$. See [22] for a full description of the protocol and its variants.

After observing this message in the network, the attacker's knowledge is given by $\phi = \nu \tilde{n}.\sigma$, where $\sigma = \{x_1 \mapsto \langle \{\!|\mathsf{mod}(r)|\!\}_s, \{\!|\mathsf{expn}(r)|\!\}_s \rangle\}$ and $\tilde{n} = \{r\}$. The relevant frames for the analysis of off-line guessing are $\phi_s = \nu \tilde{n}_w.\sigma_s$ and $\phi_w = \nu \tilde{n}_w.\sigma_w$, where $\tilde{n}_w = \tilde{n} \cup \{w\}$, $\sigma_s = \sigma \cup \{x_2 \mapsto s\}$, and $\sigma_w = \sigma \cup \{x_2 \mapsto w\}$.

There are no equational verifiers: $eqv(\phi, s) = \emptyset$. However, while it may be infeasible to check whether the modulus is the product of two primes, an attacker can use his guess w to decrypt the pair sent by A and test whether the result is a 1024-bit modulus without small prime factors and an odd exponent e. Thus,

$$tv(\phi, s) = \left\{ (\{\!|\pi_1(x_1)|\!\}_{x_2}^{-1}, \mathsf{nspf}), (\{\!|\pi_2(x_1)|\!\}_{x_2}^{-1}, \mathsf{odd}) \right\}.$$

We have $\widehat{\pi_1(x_1)\sigma_w} \in \mathcal{B}^{1024}$. Thus, $\{\!|\widehat{\pi_1(x_1)}|\!\}_{x_2}^{-1} \sigma_w$ is sampled from $\mathcal{B}^{(769,1024)}$, and the probability that $\{\!|\widehat{\pi_1(x_1)}|\!\}_{x_2}^{-1}$ has 1024 bits is $|\mathcal{B}^{1024}| / |\mathcal{B}^{(769,1024)}| = 2^{1024} / \left| \sum_{i=769}^{1024} 2^i \right| \approx 1/2$. The probability that a 1024-bits bitstring is in $[\![\mathsf{nspf}]\!]$ is approximately $1/24$, and the probability that $\{\!|\pi_2(x_1)|\!\}_{x_2}^{-1}$ is odd is $1/2$. Therefore, each wrong guess satisfies the two type verifiers with probability

$$P_\mu \left[\{\!|\widehat{\pi_1(x_1)}|\!\}_{x_2}^{-1} \sigma_w \in [\![\mathsf{nspf}]\!], \{\!|\widehat{\pi_2(x_1)}|\!\}_{x_2}^{-1} \sigma_w \in [\![\mathsf{odd}]\!] \right] \approx \frac{1}{2} \cdot \frac{1}{24} \cdot \frac{1}{2} = \frac{1}{96}.$$

Since there are $2^{24} - 1$ wrong guesses, we estimate the probability of success of this off-line guessing attack as described above to be $\frac{1}{1+(2^{24}-1)/96} \approx 2^{-17.5}$, corresponding to the probability of picking the right guess from those which satisfy the equational and type verifiers.

Example 10. Consider the same setup as in Example 9, except that only the exponent of the RSA public key is encrypted in the first message. The authors of EKE note that the protocol is still vulnerable to off-line guessing attacks: Since the exponent of an RSA key is always odd, one can decrypt each encryption of a public key with each guess. For the right guess, decrypting each encryption will yield an odd exponent. The probability that a wrong guess achieves this decreases exponentially with the number of encryptions available to the attacker [22].

To formalize this in our setting, we let $\phi = \nu\tilde{n}.\sigma$ be the frame representing the attacker's knowledge, where $\sigma = \{x_i \mapsto \langle \mathsf{mod}(r_i), \{\!|\mathsf{expn}(r_i)|\!\}_s \rangle \mid i \in \{1, \ldots, n\}\}$ and $\tilde{n} = \{r_1, \ldots, r_n, s\}$. The frames ϕ_s and ϕ_w used are as expected: $\phi_s = \nu\tilde{n}_w.\sigma_s$ and $\phi_w = \nu\tilde{n}_w.\sigma_w$, where $\tilde{n}_w = \tilde{n} \cup \{w\}$, $\sigma_s = \sigma \cup \{x_{n+1} \mapsto s\}$, and $\sigma_w = \sigma \cup \{x_{n+1} \mapsto w\}$. As before, there are no equational verifiers: $eqv(\phi, s) = \emptyset$. The set of type verifiers is given by $tv(\phi, s) = \left\{ (\{\!|\pi_2(x_i)|\!\}_{x_{n+1}}^{-1}, \mathsf{odd}) \mid i \in \{1, \ldots, n\} \right\}$. As in Example 9, we obtain $1/(1 + (2^{24} - 1)/2^{n+1}) = 2^{n+1}/(2^{n+1} + 2^{24} - 1)$ as an estimate for the success probability of this off-line guessing attack.

We remark that when assessing the threat level of off-line guessing attacks one must consider not only the probability of success, but also the computational effort involved, i.e., the number of guesses that must be verified. In the attacks modeled by our method, this number is approximated by $G * p$, where G is the size of the space of guesses to be tried and p is the probability that a random guess satisfies all verifiers. This corresponds to the expected number of guesses that an attacker must try before finding one that satisfies all verifiers.

5   Conclusion

We presented a symbolic and automatable probabilistic framework for security protocol analysis. Our framework allows one to express properties of cryptographic primitives which are outside the scope of Dolev-Yao models, thereby modeling a stronger attacker. We illustrated its usefulness by modeling non-trivial properties of RSA and using them to analyze off-line guessing attacks on the EKE protocol which cannot be modeled by existing symbolic methods.

We have proposed a probability distribution based on interpreting functions as random oracles subject to satisfying the properties of cryptographic primitives described in our setup. This is a non-trivial generalization of the random oracle model. By using this probability distribution, we can (automatically) reason about an attack's success probability. In [28] we provide a prototype implementation of our methods, which computes probabilities in our formalization of a Dolev-Yao attacker using RSA asymmetric encryption and terminates in less than one second for all the examples presented in the paper.

More generally, our approach can be used to analyze a broad range of attacks and weaknesses of cryptographic primitives that could not previously be analyzed by symbolic models. These include some forms of cryptanalysis (such as differential cryptanalysis to AES, DES or hash functions, as in [29]) and side-channel attacks [24]. Short-string authentication, used in device pairing protocols, and distance-bounding protocols relying on rapid-bit exchange, are ill-suited for analysis with existing symbolic methods as their analysis is intrinsically probabilistic. However, they are amenable to analysis using our framework.

As future work, we plan to integrate this approach with a symbolic protocol model-checker capable of generating protocol execution traces and the probabilistic queries relevant for deciding whether a trace allows an attack. In the case of off-line guessing, this amounts to computing the sets of equational and type verifiers, a task closely related to that of deciding static equivalence. Since our probabilistic analysis can be performed automatically (as illustrated by our prototype), this allows our analysis to be fully automated. We expect that such an approach will allow us to find numerous new protocol attacks relying on properties of the cryptographic primitives used.

Acknowledgments. The authors would like to thank Luís Alexandre Pereira, Pedro Adão, Benedikt Schmidt, Mohammad Torabi Dashti and Srdjan Marinovic for helpful discussions and feedback, as well as the anonymous reviewers for insightful comments and suggestions. Bruno Conchinha is a recipient of the Google Europe Fellowship in Computer Security, and this research is supported in part by this Google Fellowship. He also acknowledges the support of the FCT PhD grant SFRH/BD/44204/2008. Carlos Caleiro acknowledges the support of the project GeTFun EU FP7 PIRSES-GA-2012-318986, and the FEDER/FCT projects PEst-OE/EEI/LA0008/2013, ComFormCrypt PTDC/EIA-CCO/113033/2009 and UTAustin/MAT/0057/2008 AMDSC of IST.

References

1. Cortier, V., Delaune, S., Lafourcade, P.: A survey of algebraic properties used in cryptographic protocols. J. Comput. Secur. 14, 1–43 (2006)
2. Blanchet, B.: An efficient cryptographic protocol verifier based on Prolog rules. In: Proc. of the 14th IEEE Workshop on Computer Security Foundations, CSFW 2001, pp. 82–96. IEEE Computer Society, Washington, DC (2001)
3. Schmidt, B., Meier, S., Cremers, C.J.F., Basin, D.A.: Automated analysis of Diffie-Hellman protocols and advanced security properties. In: Chong, S. (ed.) CSF, pp. 78–94. IEEE (2012)
4. Goldwasser, S., Micali, S.: Probabilistic encryption. J. Comput. Syst. Sci. 28(2), 270–299 (1984)
5. Bellare, M., Rogaway, P.: Entity authentication and key distribution. In: Stinson, D.R. (ed.) CRYPTO 1993. LNCS, vol. 773, pp. 232–249. Springer, Heidelberg (1994)
6. Blanchet, B.: Security protocol verification: Symbolic and computational models. In: Degano, Guttman (eds.) [30], pp. 3–29
7. Abadi, M., Rogaway, P.: Reconciling two views of cryptography (the computational soundness of formal encryption). J. Cryptology 20(3), 395 (2007)
8. Backes, M., Malik, A., Unruh, D.: Computational soundness without protocol restrictions. In: Yu, T., Danezis, G., Gligor, V.D. (eds.) ACM Conference on Computer and Communications Security, pp. 699–711. ACM (2012)
9. Backes, M., Pfitzmann, B., Waidner, M.: A composable cryptographic library with nested operations. In: Jajodia, S., Atluri, V., Jaeger, T. (eds.) ACM Conference on Computer and Communications Security, pp. 220–230. ACM (2003)
10. Comon-Lundh, H., Cortier, V.: Computational soundness of observational equivalence. In: Ning, P., Syverson, P.F., Jha, S. (eds.) ACM Conference on Computer and Communications Security, pp. 109–118. ACM (2008)
11. Blanchet, B.: A computationally sound mechanized prover for security protocols. IEEE Trans. Dependable Sec. Comput. 5(4), 193–207 (2008)

12. Barthe, G., Grégoire, B., Béguelin, S.Z.: Formal certification of code-based cryptographic proofs. In: Shao, Z., Pierce, B.C. (eds.) POPL, pp. 90–101. ACM (2009)

13. Barthe, G., Crespo, J.M., Grégoire, B., Kunz, C., Zanella Béguelin, S.: Computer-aided cryptographic proofs. In: Beringer, L., Felty, A. (eds.) ITP 2012. LNCS, vol. 7406, pp. 11–27. Springer, Heidelberg (2012)

14. Bana, G., Comon-Lundh, H.: Towards unconditional soundness: Computationally complete symbolic attacker. In: Degano, Guttman (eds.) [30], pp. 189–208

15. Comon-Lundh, H., Cortier, V., Scerri, G.: Tractable inference systems: An extension with a deducibility predicate. In: Bonacina, M.P. (ed.) CADE 2013. LNCS, vol. 7898, pp. 91–108. Springer, Heidelberg (2013)

16. Baudet, M.: Deciding security of protocols against off-line guessing attacks. In: Proceedings of the 12th ACM Conference on Computer and Communications Security, CCS 2005, pp. 16–25. ACM, New York (2005)

17. Corin, R., Doumen, J., Etalle, S.: Analysing password protocol security against off-line dictionary attacks. Electron. Notes Theor. Comput. Sci. 121, 47–63 (2005)

18. Halevi, S., Krawczyk, H.: Public-key cryptography and password protocols. ACM Trans. Inf. Syst. Secur. 2(3), 230–268 (1999)

19. Abadi, M., Warinschi, B.: Password-based encryption analyzed. In: Caires, L., Italiano, G.F., Monteiro, L., Palamidessi, C., Yung, M. (eds.) ICALP 2005. LNCS, vol. 3580, pp. 664–676. Springer, Heidelberg (2005)

20. Abadi, M., Baudet, M., Warinschi, B.: Guessing attacks and the computational soundness of static equivalence. Journal of Computer Security, 909–968 (December 2010)

21. Sectools.org: Top 125 network security tools (January 2013), http://sectools.org/tag/crackers/

22. Bellovin, S.M., Merritt, M.: Encrypted Key Exchange: Password-based protocols secure against dictionary attacks. In: IEEE Symposium on Research in Security and Privacy, pp. 72–84 (1992)

23. Munilla, J., Peinado, A.: Off-line password-guessing attack to Peyravian-Jeffries's remote user authentication protocol. Computer Communications 30(1), 52–54 (2006)

24. Köpf, B., Basin, D.A.: An information-theoretic model for adaptive side-channel attacks. In: CCS 2007, pp. 286–296. ACM (2007)

25. (2013), http://www.infsec.ethz.ch/people/brunoco/infsec/people/brunoco/esorics13_tech.pdf

26. Abadi, M., Cortier, V.: Deciding knowledge in security protocols under equational theories. Theor. Comput. Sci. 367, 2–32 (2006)

27. Abadi, M., Fournet, C.: Mobile values, new names, and secure communication. In: POPL 2001, pp. 104–115. ACM, New York (2001)

28. (2013), http://www.infsec.ethz.ch/people/brunoco/prob_rsa.tar.gz

29. Montalto, B., Caleiro, C.: Modeling and reasoning about an attacker with cryptanalytical capabilities. ENTCS 253(3), 143–165 (2009)

30. Degano, P., Guttman, J.D. (eds.): POST 2012. LNCS, vol. 7215. Springer, Heidelberg (2012)

ASICS: Authenticated Key Exchange Security Incorporating Certification Systems

Colin Boyd[1], Cas Cremers[2], Michèle Feltz[2], Kenneth G. Paterson[3], Bertram Poettering[3], and Douglas Stebila[1]

[1] Queensland University of Technology, Brisbane, Australia
[2] Institute of Information Security, ETH Zurich, Switzerland
[3] Royal Holloway, University of London, Egham, United Kingdom

Abstract. Most security models for authenticated key exchange (AKE) do not explicitly model the associated *certification system*, which includes the certification authority (CA) and its behaviour. However, there are several well-known and realistic attacks on AKE protocols which exploit various forms of malicious key registration and which therefore lie outside the scope of these models. We provide the first systematic analysis of *AKE security incorporating certification systems* (ASICS). We define a family of security models that, in addition to allowing different sets of standard AKE adversary queries, also permit the adversary to register arbitrary bitstrings as keys. For this model family we prove generic results that enable the design and verification of protocols that achieve security even if some keys have been produced maliciously. Our approach is applicable to a wide range of models and protocols; as a concrete illustration of its power, we apply it to the CMQV protocol in the natural strengthening of the eCK model to the ASICS setting.

Keywords: authenticated key exchange (AKE), unknown key share (UKS) attacks, certification authority (CA), invalid public keys, PKI.

1 Introduction

After public key encryption and digital signatures, authenticated key establishment (AKE) is perhaps the most important public key primitive. From a real-world perspective, AKE protocols relying on public key techniques are widely deployed in systems that are used every day by billions of users, including systems such as TLS, IPsec, SSH, and various single sign-on systems. From a theoretical perspective, formal, cryptographically sound modelling for AKE protocols began in the symmetric setting with the seminal work of Bellare and Rogaway [4], and was later extended to the public key setting [6]. Since then, there has been a large body of work in this tradition, and many additions and modifications have been proposed. The most prominent current models in this tradition [3, 12, 25, 33] strengthen or add to the required security properties, cover different protocol classes, and strengthen adversary powers.

Despite intensive study over two decades, important elements of AKE protocols have not been sufficiently modelled, preventing our deeper understanding

J. Crampton, S. Jajodia, and K. Mayes (Eds.): ESORICS 2013, LNCS 8134, pp. 381–399, 2013.
© Springer-Verlag Berlin Heidelberg 2013

of this important primitive and limiting its applicability to real-world protocols. Specifically, the public key infrastructure (PKI) needed to support the authenticity of public keys in AKE, and the interactions between the certification authority (CA), honest parties, and the adversary, are rarely modelled. Rather, with exceptions as noted below, in typical AKE models and proofs it is assumed that all public keys are honestly generated and authentically distributed at the start of the security game, and that there is a single key per party; certificates are excluded from the model. The adversary can corrupt parties, learning all their secrets, but has limited ability to register malicious keys. Roughly speaking, this modelling approach corresponds to an ideal CA, who zealously generates perfect key pairs and securely distributes them to the correct parties.

However, CAs in the real world simply do not operate in such rigorous ways. They have differing strengths of procedures for checking claimed identities[1], so malicious parties might in some cases get arbitrary public keys certified against identifiers of their choice. The most egregious examples involve CAs who, either willingly, under coercion, or as a result of security compromises, have issued certificates for keys and identifiers that they should not have.[2] CAs following best-practices may require that a user requesting a certificate submit a certificate signing request to the CA. This involves the user self-signing the data that is to be certified. Various standards [1,2,32] include other approaches to providing *proofs of possession*. However, even these basic tests of private key ownership are not mentioned in industry guidelines issued by the CA/Browser Forum [10, 11]. Furthermore, these procedures all fall short of the proofs of knowledge [31] required to match what is assumed in typical AKE models. Thus, an attacker may be able to register another party's public key under his own identifier, or register a malformed key which then interacts with properly generated keys in an unfortunate way.

Critically, there are realistic attacks on AKE protocols which cannot be captured by AKE security models that omit CA and PKI aspects:

- Kaliski's *unknown key share* (UKS) attack [22] on early versions of MQV exploits the ability of the adversary to dynamically register a public key (which is valid and for which the adversary *does* know the secret key).
- The UKS attack on KEA described by Lauter and Mityagin [26, p. 380] exploits the adversary's ability to re-register some party's static public key as his own public key.
- Blake-Wilson and Menezes [8] introduced the *duplicate-signature key selection* (DSKS) attack on signature schemes: after observing a user's signature

---

[1] For example, issuance of Extended Validation (EV) certificates requires stronger identity-checking requirements than non-EV certificates, see https://www.cabforum.org/certificates.html for more details.

[2] In June and July 2011, Dutch CA DigiNotar was hacked [18], with the intruder taking control of all 8 of the CA's signing servers; at least 531 rogue certificates were then issued. In August 2011, TURKTRUST CA [17] issued special certificates with wildcard signing capabilities, allowing impersonation of any domain in the Internet. This was discovered, by coincidence, only 18 months later.

σ on a message m, the adversary E is able to compute a signature key pair $(\mathsf{sk}_E, \mathsf{vk}_E)$ (or sometimes just a verification key vk_E) such that σ is also E's signature on the message m. Now, for example, if the Station-to-Station (STS) protocol is implemented using a signature scheme that is vulnerable to DSKS attacks, and the adversary can register arbitrary public keys with the CA, then the protocol is vulnerable to an online UKS attack [8].

- In Lim and Lee small subgroup attacks [27], the adversary extracts information about a party's long-term secret key. Some of these attacks require registering invalid public keys with the CA before engaging in protocol runs with honest participants. Of particular note are the Lim–Lee-style attacks of Menezes and Ustaoglu [29] on the HMQV protocol [23].

We claim that to date there has been no *systematic* treatment in the literature of the behaviour of CAs with respect to public keys and identifiers chosen by the adversary. Our paper sets out to rectify this situation, providing a comprehensive and self-contained treatment of these features, as well as establishing generic results to make protocols resilient against such attacks.

Contributions. Our paper has three main contributions.

First, we present in Section 2 a framework for reasoning about the security of AKE protocols with respect to various CA key registration procedures. This framework allows us to capture several attacks based on adversarial key registration, including UKS attacks, small-subgroup attacks, attacks that occur when the CA does not check if public keys are registered twice, and attacks that occur when multiple public keys can be registered per identifier.

Second, we provide in Section 3 a generic approach to achieve strong security guarantees against adversaries that can register arbitrary public keys for certain types of protocols. In particular, we show how to transform Diffie–Hellman type AKE protocols that are secure in a model where only honest key registration is allowed into protocols that are secure even when adversaries can register arbitrary valid or invalid public keys. In such cases, security is still guaranteed for all sessions (that were considered *clean* or *fresh* in the base model) except those in which the peer's public key is valid but registered by the adversary.

Third, we demonstrate in Section 4 how our methodology can be used to establish strong security guarantees, even when the adversary can register arbitrary public keys, for concrete protocols such as CMQV, NAXOS, and UP, using CMQV as a running example. We provide in Section 5 recommendations for the design of protocols that are secure in our models.

Related Work. The original computational model for key exchange of Bellare and Rogaway [4] has a long-lived key generator, which is used to initialise all parties' keys at the start of the game. This is a standard part of most computational models today. However, in common with several later models [12, 21, 24], the adversary cannot influence long-term keys: only honestly generated keys are considered. Starting with the 1995 model of Bellare and Rogaway [5] it was recognised that the adversary may be able to choose long-term keys for certain parties, whether public keys or symmetric keys. It is possible to identify three different methods that have been used to model such an adversary capability.

1. The adversary can replace long-term keys by providing them as an input to a corrupt query. This was the method used originally by Bellare and Rogaway [5] and was subsequently used in the public key setting by others [7,30].
2. The adversary is allowed to generate arbitrary keys for corrupted parties at any time during the protocol run [23].
3. An additional query is added specifically to set up a user with a new key chosen by the adversary [14,20,35]. This query is typically called establishparty and takes as input the user name and its long-term public key.

These methods allow the models to capture the Kaliski attack [22], which requires the adversary to register a new public key after certain protocol messages have been obtained. However, none of these currently used methods has the generality of our model and, in particular, all of them omit the following realistic features:

- registration of multiple public keys per user;
- flexible checking by certification authorities via a verification procedure;
- adversarial choice of public keys per session.

Special mention should also be made of the model of Shoup [33]. Unlike most popular AKE models today, it uses a simulatability definition of security comparing ideal and real world views. Security is defined to mean that for any real world adversary there is an ideal world adversary (benign by definition) such that the transcripts of the two are computationally indistinguishable. Real-world adversaries have the ability to assign users to public key certificates. Shoup's model has not been widely used and the examples in [33] are not fully worked through. Furthermore, the model cannot represent an adversary who obtains only ephemeral secret keys without knowing the long-term key of the same user and therefore cannot capture security properties common in more modern models.

Other works [13, 19] have considered the security of non-interactive key exchange (NIKE) in settings where the adversary can register arbitrary public keys, analogously to our ASICS setting for interactive key exchange. It is an interesting open problem to examine how the security models and constructions for NIKE [13, 19] can be built upon to achieve security in the ASICS setting.

Critically, all of the approaches mentioned above have only been used to establish results for a handful of specific protocols. In contrast, we establish *generic results* that facilitate the design and verification of AKE protocols, and that can be applied to a large class of protocols.

2   ASICS Model Family

In this section we define a parameterized AKE security model that allows for explicit modelling of the certification of public keys. Prominent AKE security frameworks can be instantiated in this family of models, as well as extensions that allow dynamic adversarial registration of arbitrary bitstrings as public keys.

Generally speaking, from a user's point of view, participation in key exchange encompasses three consecutive phases: First, users set up their individual key pairs; more precisely, each user invokes a randomized algorithm KeyGen that outputs a fresh secret-key/public-key pair $(\mathsf{sk}, \mathsf{pk})$. Second, users contact a certification authority (CA) to get their keys certified: each user provides the CA with its identifier $\hat{P}$ and its public key pk, and obtains a certificate C that binds the identifier to the key. After completing these setup steps, in the third phase, users can engage in interactive sessions with other users to establish shared keys. To do so, they usually require knowledge of their own key pair $(\mathsf{sk}, \mathsf{pk})$, their identifier $\hat{P}$, and the corresponding certificate C. In addition to that, protocols may require a priori knowledge of (a subset of) the peer's public key pk', peer's identifier $\hat{Q}$, and peer's certificate C'. As we will see, our execution model is general enough to cover all these settings. To ease notation, we assume that public key pk and identifier $\hat{P}$ can be readily derived from any certificate C; we use notation $C.\mathsf{pk} = \mathsf{pk}$ and $C.\mathsf{id} = \hat{P}$ correspondingly.

Our work enables the modeling of different degrees of rigour in the checks of consistency and ownership of public keys pk presented to the CA. On the one hand, CAs could be pedantic with such verifications (e.g., require a proof of knowledge of the secret key corresponding to pk); on the other hand, CAs could also just accept any given bitstring pk as valid and issue a certificate on it. The ability to precisely assess the security of key establishment in the face of different CA behaviours is a key contribution of our new model family.

Definition 1. *An* ASICS *protocol* Π *consists of a set of domain parameters, a key generation algorithm* KeyGen, *a public key verification procedure* VP, *and the protocol description* π *that describes how key exchange protocol messages are generated and responded to as well as how the session key is derived.*

We denote by VP the specific *verification procedure* on public keys and identifiers that a considered CA deploys. As different checks on pk and $\hat{P}$ might require different levels of interaction between the registering user and the CA, we model it as a procedure, as opposed to a function. We require that VP is efficient and has binary output. Furthermore, we require that the CA issues the requested certificate only if VP outputs value 1; all certification requests where VP outputs value 0 are rejected. Note that, for simplicity, we only consider non-interactive verification procedures (i.e., two-message registration protocols) between the user and the CA. A more general treatment covering interactive verification procedures as well would introduce additional complexities to our framework.

Specific key exchange protocols might be insecure for one (liberal) instantiation of VP, and be secure for another (stricter) one. Note that CAs that do not perform any check on pk and $\hat{P}$ are modelled by a verification procedure VP that always outputs 1. A verification procedure that performs few checks may output 1 for at least all $\mathsf{pk} \in \mathbf{PK}$, where $\mathbf{PK}$ denotes the set of possible public keys output by KeyGen. Precisely, if the inputs of algorithm KeyGen are security parameter 1^k and randomness $r \in_R \{0,1\}^k$, then we define

$$\mathbf{PK} = \big\{ \mathsf{pk} \mid \text{there exists } r \in \{0,1\}^k \text{ such that } \mathsf{KeyGen}(1^k; r) = (\,\cdot\,, \mathsf{pk}) \big\} \ .$$

A verification procedure with high assurance may require a zero-knowledge argument that the requester knows the secret key corresponding to the public key, and even that the key was generated verifiably at random. Note that we allow VP to keep an internal state between invocations; our model hence covers possible implementations of CAs that reject certification requests with public keys that have already been registered (e.g., for a different identifier).

2.1   Security Model

At a high level, our model stipulates users that generate one or more keys, obtain certificates for these keys from a CA, and use keys and certificates to run (potentially concurrent) sessions of the key agreement protocol. Similar to other security models, the adversary controls all communication in these sessions, corrupts users at will to obtain their secret keys, and arbitrarily reveals established session keys. Innovative is the adversary's additional ability to steer the registration process with the CA: it can obtain from the CA valid certificates for public keys and identifiers of its choosing (as long as VP evaluates to 1), and provides users with such certificates.

To keep our model simple and comprehensible, we abstract away any forgeability issues of certificates and assume the following ideal functionality: no certificate will be considered valid unless it has been issued by the CA. We model this by letting the challenger keep a list $\mathcal{C}$ of all CA-issued certificates and by equipping users with a *certificate verification oracle* $\mathcal{O}_{CV}$ that checks membership in that list; concretely, we assume that $\mathcal{O}_{CV}(C) = 1 \Leftrightarrow C \in \mathcal{C}$. Of course, in concrete implementations, this oracle is replaced by an explicit local verification routine; for instance, if certification is implemented via a signature scheme, this will include its verification procedure.

Sessions and Session State. Users, once they have created their keys and obtained corresponding certificates, can execute protocol sessions. Within a user, each such session is uniquely identified by a pair $s = (C, i)$, where C denotes the certificate used by the user (by himself) in that session, and i is a counter. The user maintains session-specific variables as indicated in Table 1. Some session variables are fixed upon session creation, whereas others can be assigned or updated during protocol execution. Some, such as pcert, status, and key, are considered to be outputs of the key establishment and might be used in higher-level protocols or applications. A session s has *accepted* if $s_{\text{status}} = \text{accepted}$.

Adversarial Queries. The adversary interacts with users by issuing queries. The adversary can direct users to establish long-term key pairs and certificates (kgen, hregister), to initiate protocol sessions (create), and to respond to protocol messages (send). The adversary may be able to learn long-term keys (corrupt), session-specific randomness (randomness), or session keys (session-key) from users. The adversary can also maliciously obtain certificates from the CA (pkregister, npkregister).

Table 1. Elements of session state

acert	certificate of the actor (the user running this session)
pcert	certificate of this session's peer
role	taken role; either $\mathcal{I}$ (initiator) or $\mathcal{R}$ (responder)
sent	concatenation of all messages sent in this session
rcvd	concatenation of all messages received in this session
status	session status; either `active`, `accepted`, or `rejected`
key	key in $\{0,1\}^k$ established in this session
rand	randomness used in this session
data	any additional protocol-specific data

Table 2. Overview of query sets. Additionally, there is a test-session query.

$$\mathcal{Q}_N = \{\mathsf{kgen}, \mathsf{hregister}, \mathsf{create}, \mathsf{send}\} \qquad \text{(Normal protocol behaviour)}$$
$$\mathcal{Q}_S = \{\mathsf{corrupt}, \mathsf{randomness}, \mathsf{session\text{-}key}\} \ \text{(corruption of Secrets)}$$
$$\mathcal{Q}_R = \{\mathsf{pkregister}, \mathsf{npkregister}\} \qquad \text{(adversarial key Registration)}$$

The queries in set $\mathcal{Q}_N = \{\mathsf{kgen}, \mathsf{hregister}, \mathsf{create}, \mathsf{send}\}$, defined as follows, model normal operation of the protocol; they are required in any security model. Initially, the auxiliary variables $\mathcal{HK}$, $\mathcal{C}$, $\mathcal{C}_h$, $\mathcal{C}_{\mathsf{pk}}$, and $\mathcal{C}_{\mathsf{npk}}$ are set to $\emptyset$.

- kgen () By running algorithm KeyGen, a fresh key pair $(\mathsf{sk}, \mathsf{pk})$ is generated. Public key pk is returned to the adversary; secret key sk is stored for processing potential later queries corresponding to pk. The public key is added to the set of honestly generated keys: $\mathcal{HK} \leftarrow \mathcal{HK} \cup \{\mathsf{pk}\}$.
- hregister($\mathsf{pk}, \hat{P}$) The query requires that $\mathsf{pk} \in \mathcal{HK}$ and that VP outputs 1 on input pk^3 and $\hat{P}$; otherwise, it returns $\bot$. The public key pk is registered at the CA for the identifier $\hat{P}$. The resulting certificate C is added to the global set of certificates and to the set of honestly generated certificates: $\mathcal{C} \leftarrow \mathcal{C} \cup \{C\}$ and $\mathcal{C}_h \leftarrow \mathcal{C}_h \cup \{C\}$. The query returns C.
- create $(s = (C, i), r, [C'])$ The query requires that $C \in \mathcal{C}_h$, that a session with counter i for certificate C does not already exist, and that $r \in \{\mathcal{I}, \mathcal{R}\}$; otherwise, it returns $\bot$. A new session s is created for the user with public key $C.\mathsf{pk}$ and identifier $C.\mathsf{id}$. Session variables are initialized as

$$\left(s_{\mathsf{acert}}, s_{\mathsf{pcert}}, s_{\mathsf{role}}, s_{\mathsf{sent}}, s_{\mathsf{rcvd}}, s_{\mathsf{status}}, s_{\mathsf{key}}\right) \leftarrow \left(C, \bot, r, \epsilon, \epsilon, \mathsf{active}, \bot\right).$$

If the optional certificate C' is provided, we set $s_{\mathsf{pcert}} \leftarrow C'$. In addition, a string in $\{0,1\}^k$ is sampled uniformly at random and assigned to s_{rand}; we assume that all randomness required during the execution of session s is deterministically derived from s_{rand}. The user also runs the initialization procedure for the key exchange protocol, which may further initialize its own (internal) state variable s_{data} and optionally generate a message M. If M was generated, set $s_{\mathsf{sent}} \leftarrow M$, and return M. Otherwise, return $\bot$.

---

[3] Reasonable implementations of VP output 1 on all keys $\mathsf{pk} \in \mathcal{HK}$, because $\mathcal{HK} \subseteq$ **PK**.

– send (s, M) The query requires that session s exists and that $s_{\text{status}} =$ active; otherwise, it returns $\perp$. The user continues the protocol execution for this session with incoming message M, which may optionally generate a response message M'. Next, s_{rcvd} is set to $(s_{\text{rcvd}} \parallel M)$ and, if M' is output, s_{sent} is set to $(s_{\text{sent}} \parallel M')$. The protocol execution may (re-)assign values to s_{status} and s_{key}, and to the session's internal state variable s_{data}. Also, if the value s_{pcert} was not provided to the create query, then protocol execution may assign a value to s_{pcert}. If M' was generated, return M'; otherwise return $\perp$.

The queries in set $\mathcal{Q}_S = \{\text{corrupt}, \text{randomness}, \text{session-key}\}$ model the corruption of a user's secrets. Similar queries are found in other standard AKE models [4,12].

– corrupt (pk) The query requires $\text{pk} \in \mathcal{HK}$; otherwise, it returns $\perp$. This query returns the secret key sk corresponding to public key pk.

– randomness (s) The query requires that session s exist; otherwise, it returns $\perp$. The query returns the randomness s_{rand}. This is similar to the ephemeral key reveal query in the eCK model [25].

– session-key (s) The query requires that session s exist and that $s_{\text{status}} =$ accepted; otherwise, it returns $\perp$. The query returns the session key s_{key}.

The hregister query introduced above only allows registration of keys $\text{pk} \in \mathcal{HK}$, i.e., keys held by honest users. In contrast, the adversary can obtain certificates on *arbitrary* (valid) public keys using the following pkregister query. Going even further, the npkregister query allows registration of objects that are not even public keys (always assuming that VP outputs 1 on the candidate object). These queries will allow modelling Kaliski's attack on MQV [22] and small subgroup attacks [27], amongst others. We emphasize that the queries in set $\mathcal{Q}_R = \{\text{pkregister}, \text{npkregister}\}$ have no counterparts in standard definitions of key exchange security.

– pkregister$(\text{pk}, \hat{P})$ The query requires that $\text{pk} \in \mathbf{PK}$ and that VP outputs 1 on input pk and $\hat{P}$; otherwise, it returns $\perp$. The public key pk is registered at the CA for identifier $\hat{P}$. The resulting certificate C is added to the global set of certificates and to the set of certificates generated through pkregister query: $\mathcal{C} \leftarrow \mathcal{C} \cup \{C\}$ and $\mathcal{C}_{\text{pk}} \leftarrow \mathcal{C}_{\text{pk}} \cup \{C\}$. The query returns C.

– npkregister$(\text{pk}, \hat{P})$ The query requires that $\text{pk} \notin \mathbf{PK}$ and that VP outputs 1 on input pk and $\hat{P}$; otherwise, it returns $\perp$. The public key pk is registered at the CA for the identifier $\hat{P}$. The resulting certificate C is added to the global set of certificates and to the set of certificates generated through npkregister query: $\mathcal{C} \leftarrow \mathcal{C} \cup \{C\}$ and $\mathcal{C}_{\text{npk}} \leftarrow \mathcal{C}_{\text{npk}} \cup \{C\}$. The query returns C.

2.2   Security Experiment

Using the above queries, we define a parameterized family of AKE security models. As is common in BR-style AKE models, we must restrict query usage so that the adversary cannot trivially win the security experiment. The conditions under which queries are disallowed are expressed by a *freshness* condition, which typically uses a *matching* condition to formalize intended partner sessions.

Definition 2 (Matching, freshness, ASICS model). *Let Π be an ASICS protocol. A matching condition M for Π is a binary relation on the set of sessions of Π. Let Q be a set of queries such that $\mathcal{Q}_N \subseteq Q \subseteq \mathcal{Q}_N \cup \mathcal{Q}_S \cup \mathcal{Q}_R$. A freshness condition F for (Π, Q) is a predicate (usually depending on a matching condition M) that takes a session of Π and a sequence of queries (including arguments and results) of a security experiment over queries in Q. We call $X = (M, Q, F)$ an ASICS model for Π.*

Definition 3 gives two possible matching conditions. We will later give examples of freshness conditions, in Example 1 on the following page and in Section 4.

The intricacies of matching definitions in AKE protocols are explored in detail by Cremers [15]. Two issues are important here. First, there is a strong connection between the information used in a matching definition and the information used to compute the session key. Second, some protocols like the two-message versions of MQV and HMQV allow sessions to compute the same key even if they perform the same role, whereas other protocols such as NAXOS require the sessions that compute the same key to perform different roles. In the remainder of the paper we will use one of the definitions below, depending on the type of protocol.

Definition 3 (M1-matching, M2-matching). *Let s and s' denote two sessions of an ASICS protocol. We say that session s' M1-matches (or is M1-matching) session s if $s_{\text{status}} = s'_{\text{status}} = \texttt{accepted}$ and*

$$(s_{\text{acert}}.\textsf{pk}, s_{\text{acert}}.\textsf{id}, s_{\text{pcert}}.\textsf{pk}, s_{\text{pcert}}.\textsf{id}, s_{\text{sent}}, s_{\text{rcvd}})$$
$$= (s'_{\text{pcert}}.\textsf{pk}, s'_{\text{pcert}}.\textsf{id}, s'_{\text{acert}}.\textsf{pk}, s'_{\text{acert}}.\textsf{id}, s'_{\text{rcvd}}, s'_{\text{sent}})$$

Similarly, we say that session s' M2-matches (or is M2-matching) session s if s' M1-matches session s and $s_{\text{role}} \neq s'_{\text{role}}$.

The goal of the adversary is to distinguish the session key of a fresh session from a completely random string. This is modelled through an additional query:

- test-session (s) This query requires that session s exists and that $s_{\text{status}} = \texttt{accepted}$; otherwise, it returns $\perp$. A bit b is chosen at random. If $b = 1$, then s_{key} is returned. If $b = 0$, a random element of $\{0, 1\}^k$ is returned.

Definition 4 (ASICS$_X$ experiment). *Let Π be an ASICS protocol and $X = (M, Q, F)$ be an ASICS model. We define experiment ASICS$_X$, between an adversary E and a challenger who implements all users and the CA, as follows:*

1. *The experiment is initialized with domain parameters for security parameter k.*
2. *The adversary E can perform any sequence of queries from Q.*
3. *At some point in the experiment, E issues a test-session query for a session s that has accepted and satisfies F at the time the query is issued.*
4. *The adversary may continue with queries from Q, under the condition that the test session must continue to satisfy F.*
5. *Finally, E outputs a bit b' as E's guess for b.*

Definition 5 (ASICS$_X$ **advantage**). *The adversary E wins the security experiment if it correctly outputs the bit b chosen in the* test-session *query. The* ASICS$_X$-advantage *of E is defined as* $\mathrm{Adv}_{\Pi,E}^{\mathsf{ASICS}_X}(k) = |2\Pr(b = b') - 1|$.

Definition 6 (ASICS **security**). *Let Π be an ASICS protocol and $X = (M, Q, F)$ be an ASICS model. Π is said to be* secure in ASICS model X *if, for all PPT adversaries E, it holds that*

1. *if two users successfully accept in M-matching sessions, then they both compute the same session key, and*

2. *E has no more than a negligible advantage in winning the* ASICS$_X$ *experiment; that is, there exists a negligible function* negl *in the security parameter k such that* $\mathrm{Adv}_{\Pi,E}^{\mathsf{ASICS}_X}(k) \leq \mathrm{negl}(k)$.

Remark 1 (Implicit authentication). Note that the ASICS security definition, like eCK-style security definitions, only provides implicit peer authentication, meaning that the key could only be known by the peer, not explicit authentication that the peer actually was active in the session.

Example 1. Let us consider the following ASICS model as a concrete example. Let $X = (\mathsf{M1}, Q, F)$ be the ASICS model given by $Q = Q_N \cup \{\mathsf{session\text{-}key}\} \cup Q_R$ and F defined as follows. Given a sequence of queries and a session s, F holds if:

- no session-key(s) query has been issued, and
- for all sessions s' such that s' M1-matches s, no query session-key(s') has been issued, and
- no query pkregister$(s_{\mathrm{pcert}}.\mathsf{pk}, s_{\mathrm{pcert}}.\mathsf{id})$ has been issued.

The model X is an extension of a BR-like model with a CA that allows registration of arbitrary keys. If a protocol is secure in X, then it is secure even if the adversary can register arbitrary bitstrings as public keys, as long as the specific peer key used in the test session is not an adversary-generated valid public key.

2.3   Capturing Attacks

We illustrate how several attacks exploiting the adversary's ability to register valid or invalid public keys can be captured in ASICS models.

Kaliski's online UKS attack against MQV [22]. Kaliski's attack against MQV can be captured in an ASICS model where the adversary can register a specific valid public key with his own identifier via a pkregister query. As the adversary knows the secret key corresponding to the registered public key, the attack cannot be prevented by VP requiring a proof-of-possession of the secret key.

UKS attack against KEA based on public-key re-registration [26, p. 380]. Suppose that public key pk has been honestly registered at the CA for some user with identifier $\hat{P}$ via the query hregister$(\mathsf{pk}, \hat{P})$. In this UKS attack on the KEA protocol, the adversary re-registers the public key pk under his own identifier $\hat{L} \neq \hat{P}$ by issuing the query pkregister$(\mathsf{pk}, \hat{L})$. The attack is prevented if VP checks for uniqueness of the public key and outputs 0 when the public key was certified before (as observed in [26, p. 381]). Note that the UKS attack can also be prevented by making the session key derivation depend on users' identifiers.

UKS attack against KEA+ based on impersonation attack. Lauter and Mityagin [26] produced the KEA+ protocol from the KEA protocol and Protocol 4 in [6] by incorporating the identifiers of the user and its peer in the session key computation to prevent UKS attacks; however, a similar but previously unreported UKS attack still works on the KEA+ protocol. This UKS attack involves a type of impersonation attack [34, p. 3]: it requires the adversary to successfully impersonate a user to the CA who then issues a certificate containing the user's identifier, but the adversary's valid public key. We stress that the attack does not arise when only one public key per identifier can be registered. See the full version of this paper [9] for a more detailed description of the attack.

Online UKS attack on STS-MAC based on duplicate-signature key selection (DSKS) [8]. Suppose that the signature scheme employed in the STS-MAC protocol is vulnerable to DSKS attacks. The UKS attack on STS-MAC [8, p. 160] exploits the ability of the adversary to register a valid public key pk under his own identifier during the run of the protocol. More precisely, the adversary first intercepts a user's message containing a signature σ on message m. He then issues a query pkregister(pk, $\hat{L}$) such that σ is also a valid signature on m under pk. The query associates pk with the adversary's identifier $\hat{L}$. Since the adversary knows the secret key corresponding to pk, he obtains a certificate from the CA even if VP requires a proof-of-possession. Countermeasures to such UKS attacks via modification of the protocol are available [8].

Lim–Lee style attack against HMQV with DSA domain parameters, without validation of ephemeral public keys [28]. Let $G = \langle g \rangle$ denote a q-order subgroup of $\mathbb{Z}_p^*$, where q and p are prime and $(p-1)/q$ is smooth. The attack on two-pass HMQV [28, p. 5] can be captured in an ASICS model where the adversary is given access to the queries in the set $Q = \mathcal{Q}_N \cup (\mathcal{Q}_S \setminus \{\text{corrupt}\}) \cup (\mathcal{Q}_R \setminus \{\text{pkregister}\})$. In particular, the adversary can register invalid public keys via the npkregister query. This attack can be prevented by countermeasures such as requiring VP to include a group membership test on the public key submitted for certification, or by including group membership tests on both ephemeral and long-term public keys during protocol execution. Small-subgroup attacks may also exist in other settings, for instance in groups over elliptic curves.

3 Achieving ASICS Security

We provide a modular approach to obtain provable ASICS security for certain types of protocols. We first show in Theorem 1 how a result from Kudla and Paterson [24, Theorem 2] can be adapted to incorporate adversarial registration of valid public keys. Then, in Theorem 2, we indicate how to transform protocols to achieve security in the presence of adversaries that can register arbitrary invalid public keys. We start by defining an adapted version of *strong partnering* [24].

Definition 7 (Strong partnering). *Let Π be an ASICS protocol, and let $X = (M, Q, F)$ be an ASICS model. We say that Π has* strong partnering *in the* ASICS$_X$ *experiment if no PPT adversary, when attacking Π in the* ASICS$_X$ *experiment, can establish two sessions s and s' of protocol Π holding the same session key without being M-matching, with more than negligible probability in the security parameter k.*

Given an ASICS model $X = (M, Q, F)$, we denote by cNR-X ("computational No-Reveals" for session keys, following [24]) the reduced *computational* ASICS$_X$ experiment which is similar to the ASICS$_X$ experiment except that the adversary (a) is not allowed to issue session-key and test-session queries, (b) must pick a session that has accepted and satisfies F at the end of its execution, and (c) output the session key for this session. See Kudla and Paterson [24] for a more detailed description of reduced games.

Definition 8 (cNR-X security). *Let Π be an ASICS protocol and $X = (M, Q, F)$ be an ASICS model. Π is said to be* cNR-X-secure *if, for all PPT adversaries E, it holds that*

1. *if two users successfully accept in M-matching sessions, then they both compute the same session key, and*
2. *E has no more than a negligible advantage in winning the* cNR-X *experiment; that is, there exists a negligible function* negl *in the security parameter k such that* $\mathrm{Adv}_{\Pi,E}^{\mathrm{cNR}\text{-}X}(k) \leq \mathrm{negl}(k)$, *where* $\mathrm{Adv}_{\Pi,E}^{\mathrm{cNR}\text{-}X}(k)$ *is defined as the probability that E outputs (s, s_{key}) for a session s that has accepted and satisfies F.*

Our first theorem deals with the security of DH-type ASICS protocols, which are a generalization of DH-type AKE protocols of Cremers and Feltz [16] to include certificates and to explicitly identify session strings. This class of protocols includes the most prominent modern two-message AKE protocols.

Definition 9 (DH-type ASICS protocol). *A* DH-type ASICS protocol *is an ASICS protocol of the following form, specified by functions $f_\mathcal{I}, f_\mathcal{R}, F_\mathcal{I}, F_\mathcal{R}, H$:*

- *Domain parameters (G, g, q), where $G = \langle g \rangle$ is a group of prime order q generated by g.*
- KeyGen(): *Choose $a \in_R [0, q-1]$. Set $A \leftarrow g^a$. Return secret key* sk $= a$ *and public key* pk $= A$.
- VP$(x, \hat{P}) = 1$ *for all x and all $\hat{P}$ (i.e., the CAs do not perform any checks).*
- *The specification of how users respond to* create *and* send *queries as well as how the session key is computed, namely as the hash H of some string which we call the session string, is given in Figure 1.*

Theorem 1. *Let $X = (M, Q, F)$ be an ASICS model with $\mathcal{Q}_N \subseteq Q \subseteq \mathcal{Q}_N \cup \mathcal{Q}_S$. Let $Y = (M, Q', F')$ be the ASICS model where $Q' = Q \cup \{\mathsf{pkregister}\}$ and F' is defined as follows. A session s is said to satisfy F' if it satisfies F and no*

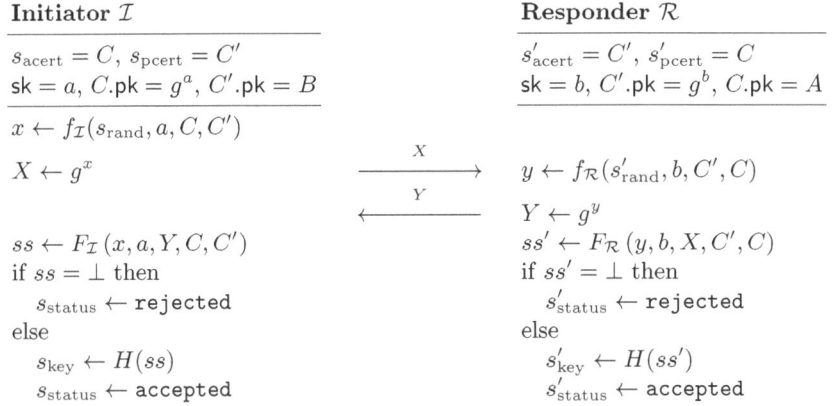

Fig. 1. Messages for generic DH-type ASICS protocol

$\mathsf{pkregister}(s_{\mathrm{pcert}}.\mathsf{pk}, s_{\mathrm{pcert}}.\mathsf{id})$ *query has been issued. Let Π be a DH-type ASICS protocol. Suppose that*

- *Π has strong partnering in the ASICS_Y experiment,*
- *cNR-X security of the related protocol π (defined in the same way as Π except that the session key generated in π is the session string of Π (i.e., $s_{\mathrm{key}}^{\pi} = ss^{\Pi}$)) is probabilistic polynomial-time reducible to the hardness of the computational problem of some relation ϕ,*
- *the session string decisional problem in the ASICS_Y experiment for Π is polynomial-time reducible to the decisional problem of ϕ, and*
- *there is a polynomial-time algorithm that decides whether an arbitrary bit-string is an element of G,*

then the security of Π in ASICS model Y is probabilistic polynomial-time reducible to the hardness of the gap problem of ϕ, if H is modelled as a random oracle.

In the cNR-X experiment of Theorem 1 the queries session-key and pkregister are not allowed, whereas in ASICS_Y both queries are allowed. Theorem 1 states that for any DH-type protocol Π, under certain conditions, it holds that security of the related protocol π in a reduced model (in which public keys can only be honestly registered) implies security of Π in the stronger non-reduced model that additionally captures adversarial registration of valid public keys.

The following theorem, which is applicable to a wider range of protocols than Theorem 1 (e.g., to three-message protocols such as UM [30] or HMQV-C [23]), allows us to achieve security against adversaries that can obtain certificates from the CA for invalid public keys by transforming the protocol to include a group membership test on the peer's public key. In contrast to Theorem 1, no additional requirement is imposed on the freshness condition of model Y.

Theorem 2. *Let $X = (M, Q, F)$ be an ASICS model with $\mathcal{Q}_N \subseteq Q \subseteq \mathcal{Q}_N \cup \mathcal{Q}_S \cup (\mathcal{Q}_R \setminus \{\mathsf{npkregister}\})$.*

Let Π be an ASICS protocol where the domain parameters (G, g, q), the key generation algorithm KeyGen and the verification procedure VP are as in Definition 9.

Let $f(\Pi)$ denote the ASICS protocol derived from Π by adding the following protocol step for each role of the protocol. Upon creation with (or, via send, receipt of) the certificate C' to be used for the peer of session s, the user running session s checks whether the public key C'.pk belongs to the group G before continuing the execution of the protocol. In case the check fails, the protocol execution is aborted and s_{status} is set to rejected.

Suppose that protocol Π is secure in ASICS model X and that there is a polynomial-time algorithm that decides whether an arbitrary bitstring is an element of G. Then the transformed protocol $f(\Pi)$ is secure in ASICS model $Y = (M, Q \cup \{\text{npkregister}\}, F)$.

Combining both theorems, we obtain the following result.

Corollary 1. *Let Π be a DH-type ASICS protocol. Let $X = (M, Q, F)$ and $Y = (M, Q', F')$ be defined as in Theorem 1, and let the conditions of Theorem 1 hold with respect to protocol Π. Let $f(\Pi)$ denote the protocol derived from Π as specified in Theorem 2. Then the transformed protocol $f(\Pi)$ is secure in ASICS model $Z = (M, Q'', F')$, where $Q'' = Q' \cup \{\text{npkregister}\}$, if H is modelled as a random oracle.*

Applying Corollary 1 to a concrete DH-type ASICS protocol that satisfies all the preconditions, we obtain a protocol that is secure in an ASICS model in which (a) sessions (including the test session) may use a certificate for the peer that resulted from an npkregister query, and (b) the certificate of the test session's peer was not the result of a pkregister query. The reader is referred to the full version of this paper [9] for detailed proofs of the above statements.

4   Applications

To illustrate the power of our generic approach, we examine in this section how to apply our technique to Ustaoglu's CMQV protocol [35]. CMQV is a modern DH-type protocol that is comparable in efficiency to HMQV, but enjoys a simpler security proof in the eCK model.

Our results allow us to analyse CMQV in a model that does not include session-key, pkregister, and npkregister queries, which simplifies the overall proof. We verify that CMQV meets the preconditions of Corollary 1, and conclude that a variant of CMQV with group membership test on the peer's public key is ASICS-secure in an eCK-like model. Similarly, our generic approach can be applied to other DH-type candidates such as NAXOS [25] and UP [36].

CMQV [35] was originally proven secure in the eCK model, where there is only one public key per identifier. In the ASICS setting, there is no such unique mapping between user identifiers and public keys. Hence, to be able to prove CMQV secure in the ASICS model, we need to include the public keys of the users in the session string to ensure that they have the same view of these keys when deriving the session key.

CMQV as a DH-type ASICS protocol. Two-pass CMQV can be stated as a DH-type ASICS protocol, by instantiating Definition 9 with the following functions. Let $\mathcal{H}_1 : \{0,1\}^k \times \mathbb{Z}_q^* \to \mathbb{Z}_q^*$, $\mathcal{H}_2 : \{0,1\}^* \to \mathbb{Z}_q$, and $H : \{0,1\}^* \to \{0,1\}^k$ be hash functions. We define $f_\mathcal{I}, f_\mathcal{R}, F_\mathcal{I}, F_\mathcal{R}$ as:

$$f_\mathcal{I}(r, a, C, C') = \mathcal{H}_1(r, a)$$

$$F_\mathcal{I}(x, a, Y, C, C') = \begin{cases} \bot & \text{, if } Y \notin G \setminus \{1\} \\ ((YB^e)^{x+da} \parallel g^x \parallel Y \parallel C.\text{id} \parallel A \parallel C'.\text{id} \parallel B) & \text{, if } Y \in G \setminus \{1\} \end{cases}$$

$$f_\mathcal{R}(r, b, C', C) = \mathcal{H}_1(r, b)$$

$$F_\mathcal{R}(y, b, X, C', C) = \begin{cases} \bot & \text{, if } X \notin G \setminus \{1\} \\ ((XA^d)^{y+eb} \parallel X \parallel g^y \parallel C.\text{id} \parallel A \parallel C'.\text{id} \parallel B) & \text{, if } X \in G \setminus \{1\}, \end{cases}$$

where $d = \mathcal{H}_2(X \parallel C.\text{id} \parallel C'.\text{id})$, $e = \mathcal{H}_2(Y \parallel C.\text{id} \parallel C'.\text{id})$, $A = C.\text{pk}$, $B = C'.\text{pk}$; $\parallel$ denotes tagged concatenation to avoid ambiguity with variable-length strings.

We now show, using Corollary 1, that the resulting DH-type CMQV protocol is a secure ASICS protocol in an ASICS model with leakage queries corresponding to the eCK model.

ASICS model for eCK-like leakage. Define the ASICS model eCK $= (\text{M2}, Q, F)$ for eCK-like leakage [25] as follows. Let $Q = \mathcal{Q}_N \cup \mathcal{Q}_S$. Let F be the condition that a session s satisfies F if, for all sessions s' such that s' M2-matches s, none of the following conditions hold:

- a session-key(s) query has been issued;
- if s' exists:
  - a session-key(s') query has been issued;
  - both corrupt$(s_{\text{acert}}.\text{pk})$ and randomness(s) queries have been issued;
  - both corrupt$(s'_{\text{acert}}.\text{pk})$ and randomness(s') queries have been issued;
- if s' does not exist:
  - both corrupt$(s_{\text{acert}}.\text{pk})$ and randomness(s) queries have been issued;
  - a corrupt$(s_{\text{pcert}}.\text{pk})$ query has been issued.

Theorem 3. *Let $f(\text{CMQV})$ be the DH-type ASICS protocol derived from the CMQV protocol defined above, as specified in Theorem 2. If $\mathcal{H}_1, \mathcal{H}_2$ and H are modelled as random oracles, G is a group where the gap Diffie–Hellman assumption holds and membership in G is decidable in polynomial time, then $f(\text{CMQV})$ is secure in ASICS model $Z = (\text{M2}, \mathcal{Q}_N \cup \mathcal{Q}_S \cup \mathcal{Q}_R, F')$, where a session s is said to satisfy F' if it satisfies the freshness condition F from the eCK model and no pkregister$(s_{\text{pcert}}.\text{pk}, s_{\text{pcert}}.\text{id})$ query has been issued.*

Proof (Sketch). We can readily show that CMQV satisfies the preconditions of Corollary 1 under the above formulation of the eCK model as an ASICS model:

1. *Strong partnering.* It is straightforward to see that CMQV has strong partnering in the ASICS$_{\text{eCK}'}$ game (where eCK' is derived from eCK as described in Theorem 1): since the session key in CMQV is computed via a random

oracle, the probability that two sessions derive the same session key without using the same session string input to the random oracle is negligible.

2. cNR-eCK-*security of the session string variant of CMQV.* This can be shown by an adaptation of Ustaoglu's original proof of CMQV. In large part, the main proof can be followed. However, a few simplifications can be made because the simulation need not answer session-key queries (so preventing key replication attacks and simulating sessions where the public key is a challenge value are easier).

3. *Hardness of the session string decision problem.* It can be easily seen that this is polynomial-time reducible to the decisional problem for Diffie–Hellman triples (U, V, W) by noting that the first component of the CMQV session string σ is equal to $g^{(y+eb)(x+da)} = g^{xy} g^{ady} g^{bex} g^{abde}$; the DDH values (U, V) can be injected into either (X, Y), (A, Y), (B, X), or (A, B), with W inserted into the corresponding part of σ, yielding a polynomial-time reduction.

Detailed proofs of each of the above claims can be found in the full version [9].

5   Lessons Learned and Recommendations

As we started our systematic investigation we assumed that certification authorities would need to perform some minimal checks on public keys to obtain secure KE protocols. Perhaps surprisingly, nearly all of the effort can be shifted to the protocols; and modern protocols often perform sufficient checks. In particular, our results provide formal foundations for some of the protocol-specific observations of Menezes and Ustaoglu [29]: checking that short- and long-term public keys are in the key space (i.e., in group G for DH-type protocols) is not superfluous.

Based on these observations, and given M public keys, N users may need to perform on the order of $M \times N$ such checks in total, even when caching the results. Reasoning purely about the overall amount of computation time used, one could consider moving the burden to the CAs. If the CAs only create certificates after a successful check, the CAs would only perform on the order of M checks in total. Depending on the deployment scenario, this might be a preferable alternative.

Similarly, CAs do not necessarily need to check uniqueness of public keys. As long as the key derivation involves the identifiers in an appropriate way, UKS attacks such as the one on KEA can be prevented. Even if public keys are associated with multiple identifiers, secrecy of the corresponding private key is sufficient to enable ASICS security for the honest user.

In general, our results further justify using as much information as possible in the key derivation function (KDF). This helps with establishing formal security proofs and it is also a prudent engineering principle. In particular, we recommend that in settings where users may have multiple long-term public keys, the input to the KDF should not only include the identifiers and the message transcript, but also the specific public keys used in the session.

We hope our work can serve as a foundation for the development of a range of protocols specifically designed to incorporate certification systems, offering different tradeoffs between efficiency and trust assumptions of the involved parties.

Acknowledgements. C.B. and D.S. are supported by Australian Research Council (ARC) Discovery Project DP130104304. C.C. and M.F. are supported by ETH Research Grant ETH-30 09-3. K.G.P. and B.P. are supported by a EPSRC Leadership Fellowship EP/H005455/1.

References

1. Adams, C., Farrell, S., Kause, T., Mononen, T.: Internet X.509 Public Key Infrastructure Certificate Management Protocol (CMP). RFC 4210 (Proposed Standard) (September 2005), http://www.ietf.org/rfc/rfc4210.txt, updated by RFC 6712
2. Barker, E., Barker, W., Burr, W., Polk, W., Smid, M.: Recommendation for key management — Part 1: General. NIST Special Publication (March 2007), http://csrc.nist.gov/publications/nistpubs/800-57/sp800-57-Part1-revised2_Mar08-2007.pdf
3. Bellare, M., Pointcheval, D., Rogaway, P.: Authenticated key exchange secure against dictionary attacks. In: Preneel, B. (ed.) EUROCRYPT 2000. LNCS, vol. 1807, pp. 139–155. Springer, Heidelberg (2000)
4. Bellare, M., Rogaway, P.: Entity authentication and key distribution. In: Stinson, D.R. (ed.) CRYPTO 1993. LNCS, vol. 773, pp. 232–249. Springer, Heidelberg (1994)
5. Bellare, M., Rogaway, P.: Provably secure session key distribution: The three party case. In: 27th ACM STOC, pp. 57–66. ACM Press (1995)
6. Blake-Wilson, S., Johnson, D., Menezes, A.: Key agreement protocols and their security analysis. In: Darnell, M.J. (ed.) Cryptography and Coding 1997. LNCS, vol. 1355, pp. 30–45. Springer, Heidelberg (1997)
7. Blake-Wilson, S., Menezes, A.: Entity authentication and authenticated key transport protocols employing asymmetric techniques. In: Christianson, B., Crispo, B., Lomas, M., Roe, M. (eds.) Security Protocols 1997. LNCS, vol. 1361, pp. 137–158. Springer, Heidelberg (1998)
8. Blake-Wilson, S., Menezes, A.: Unknown key-share attacks on the station-to-station (STS) protocol. In: Imai, H., Zheng, Y. (eds.) PKC 1999. LNCS, vol. 1560, pp. 154–170. Springer, Heidelberg (1999)
9. Boyd, C., Cremers, C., Feltz, M., Paterson, K.G., Poettering, B., Stebila, D.: ASICS: Authenticated key exchange security incorporating certification sytems. Cryptology ePrint Archive, Report 2013/398 (2013), http://eprint.iacr.org/
10. CA/Browser Forum: Baseline requirements for the issuance and management of publicly-trusted certificates, v1.1 (2011), https://cabforum.org/Baseline_Requirements_V1_1.pdf
11. CA/Browser Forum: Guidelines for the issuance and management of extended validation certificates, v1.4 (2012), https://cabforum.org/Guidelines_v1_4.pdf
12. Canetti, R., Krawczyk, H.: Analysis of key-exchange protocols and their use for building secure channels. In: Pfitzmann, B. (ed.) EUROCRYPT 2001. LNCS, vol. 2045, pp. 453–474. Springer, Heidelberg (2001)

13. Cash, D., Kiltz, E., Shoup, V.: The twin Diffie-Hellman problem and applications. In: Smart, N.P. (ed.) EUROCRYPT 2008. LNCS, vol. 4965, pp. 127–145. Springer, Heidelberg (2008)

14. Chatterjee, S., Menezes, A., Ustaoglu, B.: Combined security analysis of the one- and three-pass Unified Model key agreement protocols. In: Gong, G., Gupta, K.C. (eds.) INDOCRYPT 2010. LNCS, vol. 6498, pp. 49–68. Springer, Heidelberg (2010)

15. Cremers, C.: Examining indistinguishability-based security models for key exchange protocols: the case of CK, CK-HMQV, and eCK. In: Cheung, B.S.N., Hui, L.C.K., Sandhu, R.S., Wong, D.S. (eds.) ASIACCS 2011, pp. 80–91. ACM Press (2011)

16. Cremers, C., Feltz, M.: Beyond eCK: Perfect forward secrecy under actor compromise and ephemeral-key reveal. In: Foresti, S., Yung, M., Martinelli, F. (eds.) ESORICS 2012. LNCS, vol. 7459, pp. 734–751. Springer, Heidelberg (2012)

17. Ducklin, P.: The TURKTRUST SSL certificate fiasco — what really happened, and what happens next? (January 2013),
http://nakedsecurity.sophos.com/2013/01/08/the-turktrust-ssl-certificate-fiasco-what-happened-and-what-happens-next/

18. FOX IT: Black Tulip: Report of the investigation into the DigiNotar Certificate Authority breach (2012),
http://www.rijksoverheid.nl/bestanden/documenten-en-publicaties/rapporten/2012/08/13/black-tulip-update/black-tulip-update.pdf

19. Freire, E.S.V., Hofheinz, D., Kiltz, E., Paterson, K.G.: Non-interactive key exchange. In: Kurosawa, K., Hanaoka, G. (eds.) PKC 2013. LNCS, vol. 7778, pp. 254–271. Springer, Heidelberg (2013)

20. Goldberg, I., Stebila, D., Ustaoglu, B.: Anonymity and one-way authentication in key exchange protocols. Designs, Codes and Cryptography 67(2), 245–269 (2013)

21. Jeong, I.R., Katz, J., Lee, D.-H.: One-round protocols for two-party authenticated key exchange. In: Jakobsson, M., Yung, M., Zhou, J. (eds.) ACNS 2004. LNCS, vol. 3089, pp. 220–232. Springer, Heidelberg (2004)

22. Kaliski, B.S.: An unknown key-share attack on the MQV key agreement protocol. ACM Transactions on Information and System Security (TISSEC) 4, 275–288 (2001)

23. Krawczyk, H.: HMQV: A high-performance secure Diffie-Hellman protocol. In: Shoup, V. (ed.) CRYPTO 2005. LNCS, vol. 3621, pp. 546–566. Springer, Heidelberg (2005)

24. Kudla, C., Paterson, K.G.: Modular security proofs for key agreement protocols. In: Roy, B. (ed.) ASIACRYPT 2005. LNCS, vol. 3788, pp. 549–565. Springer, Heidelberg (2005)

25. LaMacchia, B.A., Lauter, K., Mityagin, A.: Stronger security of authenticated key exchange. In: Susilo, W., Liu, J.K., Mu, Y. (eds.) ProvSec 2007. LNCS, vol. 4784, pp. 1–16. Springer, Heidelberg (2007)

26. Lauter, K., Mityagin, A.: Security analysis of KEA authenticated key exchange protocol. In: Yung, M., Dodis, Y., Kiayias, A., Malkin, T. (eds.) PKC 2006. LNCS, vol. 3958, pp. 378–394. Springer, Heidelberg (2006)

27. Lim, C.H., Lee, P.J.: A key recovery attack on discrete log-based schemes using a prime order subgroup. In: Kaliski Jr., B.S. (ed.) CRYPTO 1997. LNCS, vol. 1294, pp. 249–263. Springer, Heidelberg (1997)

28. Menezes, A.: Another look at HMQV. Cryptology ePrint Archive, Report 2005/205 (2005), http://eprint.iacr.org/

29. Menezes, A., Ustaoglu, B.: On the importance of public-key validation in the MQV and HMQV key agreement protocols. In: Barua, R., Lange, T. (eds.) INDOCRYPT 2006. LNCS, vol. 4329, pp. 133–147. Springer, Heidelberg (2006)

30. Menezes, A., Ustaoglu, B.: Security arguments for the UM key agreement protocol in the NIST SP 800-56A standard. In: Abe, M., Gligor, V. (eds.) ASIACCS 2008, pp. 261–270. ACM Press (2008)

31. Ristenpart, T., Yilek, S.: The power of proofs-of-possession: Securing multiparty signatures against rogue-key attacks. In: Naor, M. (ed.) EUROCRYPT 2007. LNCS, vol. 4515, pp. 228–245. Springer, Heidelberg (2007)

32. Schaad, J.: Internet X.509 Public Key Infrastructure Certificate Request Message Format (CRMF). RFC 4211 (Proposed Standard) (September 2005),
http://www.ietf.org/rfc/rfc4211.txt

33. Shoup, V.: On formal methods for secure key exchange (version 4) (November 1999), revision of IBM Research Report RZ 3120 (April 1999),
http://www.shoup.net/papers/skey.pdf

34. Turner, P., Polk, W., Barker, E.: ITL Bulletin for July 2012: Preparing for and responding to certification authority compromise and fraudulent certificate issuance (2012),
http://csrc.nist.gov/publications/nistbul/july-2012_itl-bulletin.pdf
(accessed March 12, 2013)

35. Ustaoglu, B.: Obtaining a secure and efficient key agreement protocol from (H)MQV and NAXOS. Designs, Codes and Cryptography 46(3), 329–342 (2008)

36. Ustaoglu, B.: Comparing SessionStateReveal and EphemeralKeyReveal for Diffie-Hellman protocols. In: Pieprzyk, J., Zhang, F. (eds.) ProvSec 2009. LNCS, vol. 5848, pp. 183–197. Springer, Heidelberg (2009)

Efficient Privacy-Enhanced Familiarity-Based Recommender System

Arjan Jeckmans, Andreas Peter, and Pieter Hartel

Distributed and Embedded Security Group, University of Twente
{a.j.p.jeckmans,a.peter,pieter.hartel}@utwente.nl

Abstract. Recommender systems can help users to find interesting content, often based on similarity with other users. However, studies have shown that in some cases familiarity gives comparable results to similarity. Using familiarity has the added bonus of increasing privacy between users and utilizing a smaller dataset. In this paper, we propose an efficient privacy-enhanced recommender system that is based on familiarity. It is built on top of any given social network (without changing its behaviour) that already has information about the social relations between users. Using secure multi-party computation techniques and somewhat homomorphic encryption the privacy of the users can be ensured, assuming honest-but-curious participants. Two different solutions are given, one where all users are online, and another where most users are offline. Initial results on a prototype and a dataset of 50 familiar users and 1000 items show a recommendation time of four minutes for the solution with online users and of five minutes for the solution with offline users.

1 Introduction

Recommender systems can help users to find interesting content, for example a movie to watch, or books to buy. These recommender systems often rely on a large database of information from a lot of different users. With such a database the systems then recommend content based on similarity (agreement in rating behaviour) between users. However, studies [11,12,17,25] have shown that for taste related domains, such as movies and books, familiarity (social closeness between users) gives comparable accuracy to using similarity. Familiarity captures how well users know each other (and thus their preferences). Using familiarity instead of similarity removes the information need from unknown users, thus increasing privacy between users. Since no information from unknown users is needed, a recommender system based on familiarity also works on a smaller dataset, leading to a higher efficiency. In this paper we focus on the generation of recommendations using only familiarity. We leave as future work, a recommender system that combines both similarity and familiarity.

As a pre-requisite for a familiarity-based recommender system, a familiarity network needs to be known to the recommendation provider. Since this familiarity information is already present in online social networks, we can leverage these networks to provide recommendations. Our aim is to build a recommendation

J. Crampton, S. Jajodia, and K. Mayes (Eds.): ESORICS 2013, LNCS 8134, pp. 400–417, 2013.

system on top of existing social networks (utilizing the familiarity relationship that is present), while preventing the social network from learning the users' taste preferences (not giving the social network any information that it does not have already).

While the general tastes (and possibly some specific tastes) of friends are known, the exact details of a friend's complete taste are usually not known. Revealing a specific taste to friends can be embarrassing [21] as it does not conform to the group norm, or to the societal norm as a whole. For example, if all friends of a person dislike 'The Hunger Games', but that person loves the book, if the friends find out this could be embarrassing. As such, the privacy of the user with regards to their taste needs to be protected from both friends (specific taste) and the online social network (general and specific taste).

To ensure the privacy of the users, we make use of secure multi-party computation and a somewhat homomorphic encryption scheme. The motivation for a somewhat homomorphic encryption scheme (we use [4]) is: 1) it allows us to do a (bounded) number of additions and at least one multiplication on encrypted data, and 2) the message space is pre-determined by public parameters and is the same across keypairs. The latter property allows for blinding values under one key and unblinding under another.

In constructing our solution, next to privacy, we focus on the efficiency of the solution. Our contribution is the following: First, we look at the privacy that the weighted average recommendation formula can give to the user and friends. We observe that weighted average based on user supplied weights does not provide enough privacy. Based on this, we propose an adjusted formula that offers more privacy. Second, utilizing this adjusted formula, we construct a protocol that computes the recommendation for a user, when all his friends are online. However, users are not guaranteed to be online in a social network. Third, as users can be offline, we also construct a protocol where the users friends are offline, and the user works together with the social network server to compute the recommendations. Not having to wait for all friends to have been online to do their part in the protocol increases the efficiency of the solution. Both protocols are secure, assuming honest-but-curious participants.

In this paper, we will use books as our running example for recommendations. The paper is structured as follows: Section 2 details the state of the art and related work. Section 3 gives the problem specification and details the adjusted recommendation formula. Section 4 outlines the cryptographic primitives that are used. Section 5 details the solution with online friends and the solution with offline friends. Section 6 analyzes the solutions, both in terms of privacy and efficiency. And Section 7 gives concluding remarks with regard to the solutions.

2   Related Work

In this section, we show related work in privacy protecting recommender systems that protect privacy through the use of cryptography and multi-party computation. In 2002, Canny [5] proposed using additive homomorphic encryption to privately compute intermediate values of the collaborative filtering process. These intermediate values are made public and used in singular value decomposition and factor analysis, which leads to recommendations. However, the presented approach suffers from a heavy computational and communication overhead. Moreover, due to the nature of the used recommender system (singular value decomposition), users cannot input their familiarity information.

Hoens et al. [14] designed a privacy preserving recommender system for social networks that computes the weighted average rating for items. It gathers input from friends and friends of friends and onwards by first defining a group of users involved in the computation. Then a threshold homomorphic cryptosystem is set up. This cryptosystem, together with multi-party computation, is used to compute the weighted average. The weights are defined by the user for his friends, and by the friends for the friends of friends, and so on. Privacy is achieved through both cryptographic protocols as well as anonymity through multiple participants. The downsides of this solution are the requirement that users are online, the setup of a big group in advance, and the heavy computational load in the order of hours. Hoens et al. [15] designed a private recommender system for doctors, where patient ratings are aggregated. In this scenario, there is not a predefined group of patients and no weights are given to individual ratings or patients. Hoens et al. offer two solutions, one based on anonymized ratings, and one based on cryptography and multi-party computation. Again, the timing of the solution based on cryptography is in the order of hours.

Basu et al. [2] proposed a privacy preserving version of the slope one predictor, using a threshold additive homomorphic cryptosystem. In their scenario, different parties hold different parts of the data. In a social network setting, this means that each friend holds his own data. The parties pre-compute the deviation and cardinality matrices under encryption and make the cardinality matrix public. Then the prediction for a single item can be computed under encryption and all parties collaborate to decrypt the result. Their timing information, in the order of seconds, is based on a prediction for a single user and single book. This is after pre-computation in the order of hours. There is no support for offline users, nor for familiarity due to the way predictions are computed.

Erkin et al. [9] proposed a collaborative filtering algorithm based on additive homomorphic cryptosystems. This algorithm requires a second semi-trusted server to allow for users to be offline. However, in practical scenarios such a server is usually not available. The protocol of Erkin et al. does not give weights to the ratings. Runtime is in the order of minutes for a dataset of 1000 items and several thousand (variable) users.

Jeckmans et al. [16] proposed to use collaborative servers as a way to allow for offline users. A user can choose a trusted server, that will preserve the privacy on his behalf. The trusted server knows the user's ratings and thus the user has no privacy from this server. This trusted server can then collaborate with another server to increase the accuracy of the recommendations, without losing the privacy of its users. However, this is not a desirable solution for every scenario. In such a distributed setting, it becomes difficult for users to give weights to friends, when friends are on different servers. The runtime of the protocol is in the order of minutes, and does not involve any user interaction, including the user for which the prediction is made.

3 The Problem Specification

We consider the following problem scenario: With an online social network as a basis, how can users use/share the taste information from/with their friends, without leading to undesired disclosure of specific tastes. The following subsections go into more detail about the entities and their relationship, the suggested method of using the taste information, and what undesired disclosure is.

3.1 Architecture

The system consists of three entities:

- the user, for whom a prediction has to be generated,
- the online social network, also denoted as the server, acting as a gateway to access the user's friends and assisting in the prediction computation, and
- the friends of the user, giving their opinions as input for the book predictions.

Because of the nature of online social networks, not all friends will be online when the request for book scores is made. Because the user is unlikely to want to wait until all friends have come online, the online social network acts as an intermediate for the user's friends (while not learning information about the friends' preferences). As such, we distinguish two scenarios; book recommendation when the user's friends are all online, and book recommendation when the user's friends are all offline. It is also possible that some friends of the user are online, while some are offline. For simplicity we take this third scenario to be equal to book recommendation when the user's friends are all offline.

3.2 Recommendation Formula

Before predictions can be made, the familiarity between users has to be captured. Towards this end, the user can score his friends on their familiarity (social closeness) and the expected overlap in reading habits. Scoring a friend essentially gives that friend a weight that determines how heavy his opinion counts towards a specific book recommendation. Based on the friends' ratings for books and the weight for each friend, the recommender system predicts a score for each book. This helps the user to select the next book to read.

A book prediction is denoted by $p_{u,b}$, for user $u, 1 \leq u \leq U$, of book $b, 1 \leq b \leq B$, where U is the total number of users and B is the total number of books. The recommendation formula is as follows:

$$p_{u,b} = \frac{\sum_{f=1}^{F_u} q_{f,b} \cdot r_{f,b} \cdot w_{u,f}}{\sum_{f=1}^{F_u} q_{f,b} \cdot w_{u,f}}, \tag{1}$$

where F_u is the number of friends of a user u, $q_{f,b}$ is 1 if friend f rated book b and 0 otherwise, $r_{f,b}$ the rating of friend f for book b, and $w_{u,f}$ the weight given by the user u to friend f. The indication, $q_{f,b}$, if a book b has been rated a friend f is either 0 or 1, $q_{f,b} \in \{0,1\}$. The range of the prediction, $p_{u,b}$, is equal to the range of the ratings given to a book, $r_{f,b}$. For example, this range can be between 0 and 5 for a 0 to 5 star rating system. The weight given to a friend, $w_{u,f}$, can be in the range between 0 and 1 excluding 0, as 0 would indicate no friendship. This formula has been used in previous research in similarity-based [13], familiarity-based [11] and trust-based recommendation systems [26].

However, when looking at the inherent privacy this formula can give us, we notice two things:

1. Due to the fact that the user u learns the predictions $p_{u,b}$ and determines the weights $w_{u,f}$, with two prediction requests the user can learn which books are rated by one friend, i.e. learn $q_{f,b}$. This is accomplished by changing the weight $w_{u,f}$ for that specific friend. For example, suppose that the user has three friends who have rated two books. The first friend rated the first book with a 5, the second friend rated both books with a 4, and the third friend rated the second book with a 3. When the user request a prediction with all weights set to 1, he will receive a prediction of 4.5 for the first book and 3.5 for the second book. Next, the user requests a prediction with the weights of the first and second friend set to 1, and the weight of the third friend set to 0.5. He will receive a prediction of 4.5 for the first book and 3.67 for the second book, thus he learns that the third friend rated the second book. Given enough runs, the user can learn $q_{f,b}$ for all his friends.

2. Because the user knows $p_{u,b}$, $w_{u,f}$, and $q_{f,b}$, the only unknown values are that of $r_{f,b}$. Given enough runs, the user can also compute $r_{f,b}$ and completely breach the privacy of his friends.

Consequently, when using this formula, we cannot achieve privacy at all. Intuitively, the user has too much control, and the friends have no input beyond their fixed ratings. This asymmetry in the formula leads to an asymmetrical relationship between the user and his friends. As stated by Carley and Krackhardt [6], friendship is not necessarily symmetric, but tends in the direction of symmetry. In general, long strong friendships are symmetric, and newly forged friendships are not symmetric. As such, we aim to bring symmetry to the recommendation formula and balance out the power in the relationship between the user and his friends.

Since the weight from the user to his friends is asymmetrical, we propose to make the weight, and thus the formula, symmetrical. This is accomplished by taking the average of the weight from the user to his friend and the weight from the friend to the user. This results in the following formula:

$$p_{u,b} = \frac{\sum_{f=1}^{F_u} q_{f,b} \cdot r_{f,b} \cdot \left(\frac{w_{u,f}+w_{f,u}}{2}\right)}{\sum_{f=1}^{F_u} q_{f,b} \cdot \left(\frac{w_{u,f}+w_{f,u}}{2}\right)}, \tag{2}$$

where $w_{f,u}$ is the weight given by friend f to user u, with range between 0 and 1 excluding 0. Note that this also requires a bi-directional relationship between the friends. When looking back to the two points made before in light of this adjusted formula, we can say:

1. Since the user can still change the weights that are given to his friends $w_{u,f}$, the user can influence the averaged weight, $\frac{w_{u,f}+w_{f,u}}{2}$. Based on the changed weights and change in predictions, the user can still determine $q_{f,b}$ as before.
2. When the user knows $p_{u,b}$, $w_{u,f}$, and $q_{f,b}$, the values for $r_{f,b}$ and $w_{f,u}$ remain unknown. The fact that both the upper and lower part of the prediction formula remain unknown greatly increases the difficulty of breaching privacy.

To prevent the user from learning $q_{f,b}$, the user's influence on the weight can be removed. However, then this recommender system would lose the user's control and reduce the value of the predictions. Instead, we refer to profile aggregation methods [24], methods that add random ratings [8,20], or methods that add randomness to the output [22]. These solutions can be applied *independent* of our solution and will not be addressed in this paper.

Note that the impact on accuracy of this adjusted formula has not been determined. As this paper focusses on privacy and efficiency, and a suitable dataset to test accuracy could not be found, we leave this as future work.

3.3 Security Model

Both the user and his friends are considered to be honest-but-curious; they will follow the protocol but try to learn the taste of their friends. More specifically, the user u will try to learn $r_{f,b}$ and $w_{f,u}$, while the friends of u will try to learn $w_{u,f}$.

We also assume that the social network server is honest-but-curious; the server will follow the protocol, while trying to learn the tastes of users. The server will try to learn $q_{f,b}$, $r_{f,b}$, $w_{u,f}$, $w_{f,u}$, and $p_{u,b}$. We assume that the users do not collude with the server, as they do not want to impact the privacy of their friends too much.

4   Cryptographic Primitives

To build our solutions, we make use of the cryptographic primitives described in this section. The primitives of additive secret sharing and proxy re-encryption are only used in the solution with offline friends.

4.1   Somewhat Homomorphic Encryption

To protect information during the protocol, we use the somewhat homomorphic encryption scheme of Brakerski and Vaikuntanathan [4]. Specifically, we use that this somewhat homomorphic encryption scheme allows both addition and multiplication of the encrypted messages (though a limited, but configurable amount), and the fact that the message space is the same across multiple key pairs (given the same public parameters).

In the setup phase of the encryption system, the public parameters are chosen. Among others, these are: the message space (which equals $\mathbb{Z}_t$ for some prime number t), the encrypted messages (which are represented in the ring $R_q = \mathbb{Z}_q[x]/\langle f(x) \rangle$ of polynomials over $\mathbb{Z}_q$ for some prime number q, where the polynomial $f(x)$ is cyclotomic and of degree n), and the degree D of allowed homomorphism (which indicates the amount of multiplications that can occur under encryption). The choice of the ring R_q in relation to the prime t and degree of homomorphism D defines the security of the encryption system.

Each party can, based on these public parameters, create a key pair consisting of the secret key SK and the public key PK. The secret key is randomly chosen and the public key is based on the secret key and some randomness. The public key of user u is denoted by PK_u. Given an encryption of m under the public key PK_u, denoted by $[m]_u$, the following homomorphic properties hold (until the error overflows, typically when the degree D has been reached): $[m_1]_u + m_2 = [m_1 + m_2]_u$, $[m_1]_u + [m_2]_u = [m_1 + m_2]_u$, $[m_1]_u \cdot m_2 = [m_1 \cdot m_2]_u$, $[m_1]_u \cdot [m_2]_u = [m_1 \cdot m_2]_u$.

This scheme is semantically secure under the polynomial learning with errors assumption. For more details, we refer to the work of Brakerski and Vaikuntanathan [4].

4.2   Encrypted Division

Because the homomorphic encryption system can only encrypt integers, and thus only operate on integers, division of encrypted values is not straightforward. For example $[5]/[2] \neq [2.5]$ as $[2.5]$ cannot be represented as such. Given that the message space $\mathbb{Z}_t$ is known and the range of the predictions $p_{u,b}$ is also known and significantly smaller, a lookup table can be constructed (and precomputed) to quickly translate the integers after division into the actual fractions they represent. The lookup table looks like this: given two integers x and y, with $\gcd(x, y) = 1$ and x/y as a possible result for $p_{u,b}$, the index is $x \cdot y^{-1} \mod t$ and the resulting value x/y. For integers x' and y' with $\gcd(x', y') \neq 1$, the division result is the same as for $x = x'/\gcd(x', y')$ and $y = y'/\gcd(x', y')$. We denote the set of possible integers for x, X, the set of possible integers for y, Y, and the range of possible predictions $p_{u,b}$, P. The lookup table then has size $|\{x/y \mid \gcd(x,y) = 1, x/y \in P, x \in X, y \in Y\}|$. The size of the lookup table is upper bounded by the size of the message space $\mathbb{Z}_t$. As such, division can happen under encryption and after decryption a table lookup retrieves the actual result.

4.3   Additive Secret Sharing

An alternate method to protect information from multiple parties, while still providing operations on that information, is additive secret sharing [10]. Unlike encryption, where only the party with the key can decrypt it, anybody with enough shares can extract the information. Distribution of the shares prevents extraction of the information, but still allows us to run a protocol to use the information. When a party has a value x that it wants to protect, it creates a random value $r \in_R \mathbb{Z}_k$, where k is a security parameter. The party then creates $s = x - r$. It can give r to a second party, and s to a third. Together the second and third party can reconstruct x by $x = r + s$.

It is also possible to secret share a vector of values, X, of length n. The secret sharing algorithm is then applied to each element of X individually, resulting in the two vectors R and S, both of length n. When combined the vectors R and S sum up to the vector X, $x_i = r_i + s_i$, where $1 \leq i \leq n$.

4.4   Proxy Re-encryption

To share information between two users of the social network without a direct connection, we use proxy re-encryption [3]. Proxy re-encryption allows us to send a (secret) message from one user to his friends through the social network. In proxy re-encryption, based on the keys of two users a re-encryption key can be derived. This re-encryption key is then given to the proxy (the social network server). When given a message encrypted under the key of one user, using the re-encryption key the proxy can translate the message, to a message encrypted under the key of the second user. This way an offline user can store his information on the social network encrypted under his own key. When a friend requires access to that information, the server can translate the information to be encrypted under the key of the friend (provided a re-encryption key has been setup). The friend can then decrypt and use the information left by the offline user.

We require that the re-encryption scheme is unidirectional.In a unidirectional scheme the users do not have to share their private keys to create a re-encryption key. To create a re-encryption key from the user to a friend, only the user's private key and the friend's public key are needed. We further require that the re-encryption scheme is one-hop only, so that only friends of the user can read his information. Some examples of schemes that satisfy these requirements are: Ateniese et al. [1], Libert and Vergnaud [18], and Chow et al. [7]. The proxy re-encryption scheme can be chosen independent of our protocol and is only used to give the friends' information to the user beforehand.

5   Proposed Solutions

In this section we provide the details of the protocols to compute the book recommendations. A protocol is given when all friends are online, and a protocol is given when all friends are offline. For convenience, we make some small cosmetic alterations to the prediction formula 2. *We set the value of $r_{f,b}$ to 0 when $q_{f,b} = 0$, thus $r_{f,b}$ becomes equal to $q_{f,b} \cdot r_{f,b}$. We also divide $w_{u,f}$ and $w_{f,u}$ by 2 before running the protocols (without renaming), remove the need to divide by 2 during the protocol.*

User u	Server	Friends F_u
(PK_u, SK_u)	(PK_u)	(PK_u)
$(w_{u,f}, 1 \leq f \leq F_u)$		$(R_f, Q_f, w_{f,u})$

$\forall f : 1 \leq f \leq F_u$

1. $[w_{u,f}]_u$

$$\xrightarrow{[w_{u,f}]_u}$$

$$[w_{u,f} + w_{f,u}]_u = [w_{u,f}]_u + w_{f,u}$$

$\forall b : 1 \leq b \leq B$

2.
$$[n_{f,b}]_u = [w_{u,f} + w_{f,u}]_u \cdot r_{f,b}$$
$$\xleftarrow{[n_{f,b}]_u}$$

$$[n_b]_u = \sum_{f=1}^{F_u} [n_{f,b}]_u$$

3.
$$[d_{f,b}]_u = [w_{u,f} + w_{f,u}]_u \cdot q_{f,b}$$
$$\xleftarrow{[d_{f,b}]_u}$$

$$[d_b]_u = \sum_{f=1}^{F_u} [d_{f,b}]_u$$

4.
$$\xi_b \in_r \mathbb{Z}_t^*$$
$$[d_b \cdot \xi_b]_u = [d_b]_u \cdot \xi_b$$
$$\xleftarrow{[d_b \cdot \xi_b]_u}$$

$d_b \cdot \xi_b$

$d_b^{-1} \cdot \xi_b^{-1}$

$[d_b^{-1} \cdot \xi_b^{-1}]_u$

$$\xrightarrow{[d_b^{-1} \cdot \xi_b^{-1}]_u}$$

$$[d_b^{-1}]_u = [d_b^{-1} \cdot \xi_b^{-1}]_u \cdot \xi_b$$
$$[p_{u,b}]_u = [n_b]_u \cdot [d_b^{-1}]_u$$
$$\xleftarrow{[p_{u,b}]_u}$$

5. $p_{u,b}$

Fig. 1. Book Recommendation Protocol with Online Friends

5.1 Solution with Online Friends

Fig. 1 shows the recommendation protocol for user u with online friends. We assume that, before the protocol is run, the user u has set up his keys for the somewhat homomorphic encryption scheme, $\{PK_u, SK_u\}$, and distributed the public key. The protocol works as follows:

1. Each friend f of the user u computes their weight $w_{u,f} + w_{f,u}$. To do this, the user u encrypts $w_{u,f}$ for each friend under his own key, and sends $[w_{u,f}]_u$ to the corresponding friend f. The friends compute $[w_{u,f} + w_{f,u}]_u = [w_{u,f}]_u + w_{f,u}$.

2. Given the encrypted weight, each friend computes the impact of his ratings, $(w_{u,f} + w_{f,u}) \cdot r_{f,b}$, for each book. Recall that $r_{f,b} = 0$, when the book is unrated. The friends compute $[n_{f,b}]_u = [w_{u,f} + w_{f,u}]_u \cdot r_{f,b}$, and send

$[n_{f,b}]_u$ to the server. The server sums the values received by the friends into $[n_b]_u = \sum_{f=1}^{F_u} [n_{f,b}]_u$ for each book.

3. In similar fashion, the normalization factor d_b is computed. The friends compute $[d_{f,b}]_u = [w_{u,f} + w_{f,u}]_u \cdot q_{f,b}$, and send $[d_{f,b}]_u$ to the server. The server sums the values received by the friends into $[d_b]_u = \sum_{f=1}^{F_u} [d_{f,b}]_u$ for each book.

4. To compute the predictions $p_{u,b}$, a division has to be performed. Towards this end, the server selects random values ξ_b from the multiplicative domain of the message space $\mathbb{Z}_t^*$ and blinds d_b multiplicatively for each book, $[d_b \cdot \xi_b]_u = [d_b]_u \cdot \xi_b$. The resulting values $[d_b \cdot \xi_b]_u$ are sent to the user u. The user u decrypts to $d_b \cdot \xi_b$ and computes the inverse, $d_b^{-1} \cdot \xi_b^{-1}$, for each book. These inverses are encrypted again under the users key, $[d_b^{-1} \cdot \xi_b^{-1}]_u$, and sent to the server. The server removes the blinding by multiplying with the random values ξ_b again, $[d_b^{-1}]_u = [d_b^{-1} \cdot \xi_b^{-1}]_u \cdot \xi_b$. The server then divides n_b by d_b for each book to determine the predictions, $[p_{u,b}]_u = [n_b]_u \cdot [d_b^{-1}]_u$. The encrypted predictions are then sent to the user u.

5. The user u decrypts the received predictions and uses the precomputed division lookup table to determine the actual predictions.

5.2 Solution with Offline Friends

Usage of Secret Sharing and Proxy Re-encryption. Each friend f of the user secret shares the rating vector R_f and weight $w_{f,u}$. The rating vector R_f is split into the vectors S_f and T_f following the secret sharing method. Similarly, the weight $w_{f,u}$ is split into $x_{f,u}$ and $y_{f,u}$. As the secrets will be reconstructed under encryption, we set the security parameter k of the secret sharing scheme equal to the message space t of the homomorphic encryption system. The friend stores S_f and $x_{f,u}$ on the server. The vectors T_f and Q_f as well as the value $y_{f,u}$ will be distributed to the user u using proxy re-encryption. Therefore, these values are stored under encryption at the server and the re-encryption key to the user u is computed and also stored on the server.

Protocol. Fig. 2 shows the recommendation protocol for user u with offline friends. We assume that, before the protocol is run, the required secrets T_f, Q_f, $y_{f,u}, 1 \leq f \leq F_u$ have been distributed and that both the user u and the server have set up their keys for the somewhat homomorphic encryption scheme, $\{PK_u, SK_u\}$ and $\{PK_s, SK_s\}$ respectively, and exchanged public keys. The protocol works as follows:

1. Both user u and the server compute the weight, $w_{u,f} + w_{f,u}$, for each friend under one another's public key. The weight is computed by $w_{u,f} + w_{f,u} = w_{u,f} + y_{f,u} + x_{f,u}$, where u holds $w_{u,f}$ and $y_{f,u}$, and the server holds $x_{f,u}$. The user u computes $[w_{u,f} + y_{f,u}]_u$ and sends this to the server, while the server computes and sends $[x_{f,u}]_s$. This allows the user to compute $[w_{u,f} + w_{f,u}]_s$ and the server to compute $[w_{u,f} + w_{f,u}]_u$.

User u	Server
(PK_u, SK_u, PK_s)	(PK_u, PK_s, SK_s)
$(T_f, Q_f, w_{u,f}, y_{f,u}, 1 \le f \le F_u)$	$(S_f, x_{f,u}, 1 \le f \le F_u)$

$$\forall f : 1 \le f \le F_u$$

1. $[w_{u,f} + y_{f,u}]_u$ $\qquad\qquad\qquad\qquad\qquad\qquad\qquad\qquad$ $[x_{f,u}]_s$

$$\xrightarrow{\quad [w_{u,f}+y_{f,u}]_u \quad}$$
$$\xleftarrow{\quad [x_{f,u}]_s \quad}$$

$[w_{u,f} + w_{f,u}]_s = [x_{f,u}]_s + (w_{u,f} + y_{f,u})$ $\qquad$ $[w_{u,f} + w_{f,u}]_u = [w_{u,f} + y_{f,u}]_u + x_{f,u}$

$$\forall b : 1 \le b \le B$$

2. $[z_b]_s = \sum_{f=1}^{F_u}[w_{u,f} + w_{f,u}]_s \cdot t_{f,b}$ $\qquad\qquad\qquad$ $[a_b]_u = \sum_{f=1}^{F_u}[w_{u,f} + w_{f,u}]_u \cdot s_{f,b}$

$\xi_{1,b} \in_r \mathbb{Z}_t$

$[z_b + \xi_{1,b}]_s = [z_b]_s + \xi_{1,b}$

$[-\xi_{1,b}]_u$

$$\xrightarrow{\quad [z_b+\xi_{1,b}]_s, [-\xi_{1,b}]_u \quad}$$

3. $[d_b]_s = \sum_{f=1}^{F_u}[w_{u,f} + w_{f,u}]_s \cdot q_{f,b}$ $\qquad\qquad\qquad\qquad\qquad$ $z_b + \xi_{1,b}$

$\xi_{2,b} \in_r \mathbb{Z}_t^*$ $\qquad\qquad\qquad\qquad\qquad\qquad\qquad\qquad\qquad\qquad$ $[z_b]_u = [-\xi_{1,b}]_u + (z_b + \xi_{1,b})$

$[d_b \cdot \xi_{2,b}]_s = [d_b]_s \cdot \xi_{2,b}$ $\qquad\qquad\qquad\qquad\qquad\qquad\qquad\quad$ $[n_b]_u = [z_b]_u + [a_b]_u$

$[\xi_{2,b}]_u$

$$\xrightarrow{\quad [d_b \cdot \xi_{2,b}]_s, [\xi_{2,b}]_u \quad}$$

4. $\qquad\qquad\qquad\qquad\qquad\qquad\qquad\qquad\qquad\qquad\qquad\qquad$ $d_b \cdot \xi_{2,b}$

$\qquad\qquad\qquad\qquad\qquad\qquad\qquad\qquad\qquad\qquad\qquad\qquad\quad$ $d_b^{-1} \cdot \xi_{2,b}^{-1}$

$\qquad\qquad\qquad\qquad\qquad\qquad\qquad\qquad\qquad$ $[d_b^{-1}]_u = [\xi_{2,b}]_u \cdot (d_b^{-1} \cdot \xi_{2,b}^{-1})$

$\qquad\qquad\qquad\qquad\qquad\qquad\qquad\qquad\qquad\quad$ $[p_{u,b}]_u = [n_b]_u \cdot [d_b^{-1}]_u$

$$\xleftarrow{\quad [p_{u,b}]_u \quad}$$

5. $p_{u,b}$

Fig. 2. Book Recommendation Protocol with Offline Friends

2. Given the encrypted weights, both the user u and the server can compute the impact of the secret shared ratings $r_{f,b} = t_{f,b} + s_{f,b}$ for each book. The user u computes $[z_b]_s = \sum_{f=1}^{F_u}[w_{u,f} + w_{f,u}]_s \cdot t_{f,b}$ and the server computes $[a_b]_u = \sum_{f=1}^{F_u}[w_{u,f} + w_{f,u}]_u \cdot s_{f,b}$. Together, this sums up (ignoring encryption for a moment) to $z_b + a_b = \sum_{f=1}^{F_u}(w_{u,f} + w_{f,u}) \cdot (t_{f,b} + s_{f,b}) = \sum_{f=1}^{F_u}(w_{u,f} + w_{f,u}) \cdot r_{f,b} = n_b$. The user u selects random values $\xi_{1,b}$ from the domain of message space $\mathbb{Z}_t$ and uses them to blind $[z_b]_s$. The resulting encryptions, $[z_b + \xi_{1,b}]_s$, and the encryptions to remove the blinding, $[-\xi_{1,b}]_u$, are sent to the server. Note that the server can only remove the blinding using encryptions under the user's public key.

3. The user u computes the combined weight to normalize the prediction using $[d_b]_s = \sum_{f=1}^{F_u}[w_{u,f} + w_{f,u}]_s \cdot q_{f,b}$ for each book. These are blinded multiplicatively with random values $\xi_{2,b}$, taken from the multiplicative domain

of the message space $\mathbb{Z}_t^*$. The resulting encryptions, $[d_b \cdot \xi_{2,b}]_s$, and encryptions to remove the blinding after inversion, $[\xi_{2,b}]_u$, are sent to the server. Meanwhile, the server removes the blinding values $\xi_{1,b}$ and reconstructs $[n_b]_u = [z_b]_u + [a_b]_u$.

4. The server decrypts the received encryptions, $d_b \cdot \xi_{2,b}$, and inverts them, resulting in $d_b^{-1} \cdot \xi_{2,b}^{-1}$. Under the public key of u, the blinding values $\xi_{2,b}$ are removed, resulting in the encryptions $[d_b^{-1}]_u$. The server divides n_b by d_b under the public key of u, $[p_{u,b}]_u = [n_b]_u \cdot [d_b^{-1}]_u$, for each book. The resulting encrypted predictions $[p_{u,b}]_u$ are sent to the user u.

5. The user u decrypts the received predictions and uses the precomputed division lookup table to determine the actual predictions.

6   Analysis of the Solutions

In this section, we first look at the privacy that the two protocols offer in relation to the security model. Then we look at the complexity (computational and communicational) of the protocols. Finally, we look at the performance (runtime) of the protocols with different sized datasets.

6.1   Privacy

Recall from the security model that all parties are honest-but-curious. The user u will try to learn $r_{f,b}$ and $w_{f,u}$. Friends will try to learn $w_{u,f}$. The server will try to learn $q_{f,b}$, $r_{f,b}$, $w_{u,f}$, $w_{f,u}$, and $p_{u,b}$. Given that the parties are honest-but-curious, each party should not be able to distinguish between a protocol execution and a simulation of the protocol based only on the party's input and output. However, only the user u has an output in the protocol. As such, for the server and friends, each message they receive should be indistinguishable from random messages. For the user, messages may depend on the output $p_{u,b}$.

Online Friends. In this protocol, the user's friends only see encrypted values, encrypted under the key of the user u. Given that the homomorphic encryption scheme is semantically secure [4], the encrypted values are indistinguishable from encryptions of random messages. As the friends also get no output from the protocol, the protocol can easily be simulated and the friends learn nothing from the protocol.

The server also only sees encrypted values. As the homomorphic encryption scheme is semantically secure, the encrypted values are indistinguishable from encryptions of random messages. The server receives no output from the protocol, and the protocol can easily be simulated. Thus the server learns nothing from running the protocol.

After the user encrypts and sends $w_{u,f}$, the user only receives $d_b \cdot \xi_b$ and $p_{u,b}$ for all books. As $p_{u,b}$ is the output of the prediction formula 2, the user should always learn this and does not constitute a breach of privacy. The other value, d_b, is randomized multiplicatively over the full multiplicative domain by ξ_b, and is thus indistinguishable from a value chosen at random from the domain. Because this can also be easily simulated, the privacy of d_b is preserved. The only exception to this is when $d_b = 0$, in this case $d_b \cdot \xi_b$ is also equal to 0. This only happens when none of the users friends have given a rating for b, i.e. $q_{f,b} = 0$ for $1 \le f \le F_u$. This situation is deemed acceptable as $q_{f,b}$ is not required to be private. By setting $d_b^{-1} \cdot \xi_b^{-1}$ to 0, the protocol can continue without the server learning anything, resulting in the prediction $p_{u,b} = 0$.

Offline Friends. In the protocol with offline friends, the privacy of the user towards his friends is not in danger, as they are not involved in the protocol. In the other direction, each friend shares some information with both the user and the server. The user receives through the proxy re-encryption T_f, Q_f, and $y_{f,u}$, and the server receives S_f and $x_{f,u}$. Except for Q_f, all these values are additive secret shares and hence indistinguishable from random values [10]. This means that these values can be used as inputs to the protocol. Given that the proxy re-encryption scheme is secure, and Q_f is not required to be private from the user u, the privacy of each friend is not breached.

During the protocol, next to encrypted values, the user only receives $p_{u,b}$. As the homomorphic encryption scheme is semantically secure, the encrypted values are indistinguishable from encryptions of random messages. These messages can thus be simulated. Furthermore, the user receives $p_{u,b}$, as intended, as output of the prediction function. Thus from the user's perspective the protocol can be completely simulated.

Next to encrypted values, which are indistinguishable from encryptions of random values, the server only receives $z_b + \xi_{1,b}$ and $d_b \cdot \xi_{2,b}$. The value of z_b is protected by additive blinding, using $\xi_{1,b}$, and thus indistinguishable from a random value and possible to simulate. For d_b, as in the protocol with online friends, multiplicative blinding, using $\xi_{2,b}$, is used. Thus d_b is indistinguishable from a random value and can be simulated. Only in the case that $d_b = 0$, will the server learn something about $q_{f,b}$, which is a violation of the privacy of the user's friends. This can be avoided by setting $[d_b \cdot \xi_{2,b}]_s$ to $[\xi_{2,b}]_s$ and $[\xi_{2,b}]_u$ to $[0]_u$ when $d_b = 0$. This is only the case when $q_{f,b} = 0$, for $1 \le f \le F_u$, which the user knows. The server will receive $\xi_{2,b}$ instead of 0, which is a random value, and be unable to decrypt $[0]_u$ as it is protected by the user's key. The resulting prediction $p_{u,b}$ will then still be 0.

6.2   Complexity

Table 1 shows the complexity of the computational (comp) and communicational (comm) costs of each step in the protocol with online friends. The costs are given in big-O notation and for each party. The first step shows a complexity related to the number of friends for the user u, and constant for each friend. The second and third step, where the friends contribution is calculated, shows a complexity in the order of number of books for each friend, and in the order of both the number of books and friends for the server. These steps have the largest complexity. The fourth step shows a complexity in the order of number of books for both the user and the server. The final step shows a complexity on the order of the number of books for the user. All steps together it seems that the server has the most work to do.

Table 1. Complexity of the protocol with online friends, F_u is the number of friends and B the number of books

step	User u comp	comm	Server comp	comm	Friend comp	comm
1.	$O(F_u)$	$O(F_u)$			$O(1)$	$O(1)$
2.			$O(BF_u)$	$O(BF_u)$	$O(B)$	$O(B)$
3.			$O(BF_u)$	$O(BF_u)$	$O(B)$	$O(B)$
4.	$O(B)$	$O(B)$	$O(B)$	$O(B)$		
5.	$O(B)$					

Table 2 shows the complexity of the protocol with offline friends. The notation is the same as the previous table. The first step shows a complexity in the order of number of friends for both the user u and the server. The second step shows a complexity related to both the number of books and number of friends for both the user and the server. This step has the greatest complexity in the protocol. The third step shows a complexity in the order of number of books and number of friends for the user, and a complexity in the order of number of books for the server. The fourth step shows a complexity in the order of the number of books. The final step shows a complexity in the order of number of books for the user.

Table 2. Complexity of the protocol with offline friends, F_u is the number of friends and B the number of books

step	User u comp	comm	Server comp	comm	Friend comp	comm
1.	$O(F_u)$	$O(F_u)$	$O(F_u)$	$O(F_u)$		
2.	$O(BF_u)$	$O(B)$	$O(BF_u)$	$O(B)$		
3.	$O(BF_u)$	$O(B)$	$O(B)$	$O(B)$		
4.		$O(B)$	$O(B)$	$O(B)$		
5.	$O(B)$					

The complexity of the homomorphic operations on the ciphertexts depends mainly on the degree of the used polynomials n. However, n also has an impact on the ring R_q and thus on the security of the encryption scheme. As such, there exist a trade-off between the complexity (and efficiency) of the individual homomorphic operations and the security offered to the user. In the performance section, we shall come back to this trade-off.

6.3   Performance

To analyze the performance of the two protocols, an implementation of the somewhat homomorphic encryption scheme has been made in C++ based on the FLINT library. Based on this implementation a prototype program of the protocols has been constructed. The prototype is single threaded and computes the different steps for each party sequentially on the same machine. As such, network latency is not taken into account. All tests are carried out on an Intel Xeon at 3GHz, with 2GB of RAM. As input data, a synthetic dataset has been constructed, as there are no publicly available datasets that have explicit fine-grained familiarity values. Some datasets have friendship links, but only as a binary value. The synthetic dataset consists of either 50, 100, or 200 friends that have each rated 25 books. The total number of books is either 500, 1000, or 2000. Note that it is not possible for 50 friends to rate 2000 books, with only 25 ratings per friend (denoted with n/a). This gives us performance information for different numbers to observe how the solutions scale. A rating is a score between 1 and 100, and the weights between users, after division by 2, is between 1 and 50.

We set the parameters of the somewhat homomorphic encryption scheme to the following, based on the suggestions of Naehrig et al. [23]. The message space t is set to 5000011, to allow for protocol runs with a maximum of 500 friends. For n we take 4096, resulting in a q of 84 bits and a logarithm of the attacker runtime of 255 for the decoding attack [19]. Successfully running the decoding attack breaks the security of the encryption scheme, therefore Naehrig et al. [23] suggest an attacker runtime for the decoding attack of at least 128, giving an equivalent of 128 bits security, or an attack complexity of 2^{128}. Table 3 shows the runtime performance of the prototype implementation with these parameters.

Table 3. Runtime of the prototype with attacker runtime logarithm of 255

online	books		
friends	500	1000	2000
50	113s	236s	n/a
100	149s	309s	706s
200	222s	456s	988s

offline	books		
friends	500	1000	2000
50	132s	282s	n/a
100	182s	387s	1021s
200	282s	588s	1477s

As can be seen from the table, the prototype for the protocol with online friends requires just under 2 minutes for the smallest dataset and over 16 minutes for the largest dataset. As expected, the prototype for the protocol with offline friends is slower. This prototype takes a little over 2 minutes for the smallest dataset and over 24 minutes for the largest dataset. This protocol has the benefit that friends need not be online, but requires more time to protect the information of those friends. When looking at the running times for the different datasets, we see a linear trend with respect to the number of books and a sub linear trend with respect to the number of friends. When looking at the protocol complexity, this is to be expected. Most operations have to be done per book and not per friend, but computing the impact of each friend on each book is linear in both (and the slowest step in the protocols).

We can lower the security of the somewhat homomorphic encryption scheme in order to gain a speed increase of the protocols. This lowered security implies that it is easier, but still very difficult, to break the semantic security of the encryption scheme and recover encrypted messages. Should encrypted messages be recovered, privacy is lost. Towards this end, we take for n 2048, resulting in a q of 83 bits and a logarithm of the attacker runtime of 75. Table 4 shows the runtime performance with these parameters offering lowered security, but more speed.

Table 4. Runtime of the prototype with attacker runtime logarithm of 75

online friends	books 500	1000	2000	offline friends	books 500	1000	2000
50	50s	102s	n/a	50	59s	120s	n/a
100	68s	137s	287s	100	85s	170s	442s
200	104s	209s	441s	200	134s	267s	617s

From the table we can see that these parameters result in runtimes that are more than 2 times faster than the more secure parameters. As expected, the running time relations between the different datasets remains the same. The desired level of security has a large impact on the running time of the protocols, but it does not change the basic properties of the protocols.

7 Conclusion

In this paper, we proposed an efficient privacy-enhanced familiarity-based recommender system. We proposed an adjusted recommendation formula that provides more privacy than weighted average with user supplied weights. Furthermore, two different protocols have been given, one where all friends of the user are online, and another where friends are offline. In both cases, a bi-directional friendship is assumed. The privacy of these protocols has been analyzed, and two edge cases have been found and fixed. The protocols achieve privacy in the honest-but-curious model.

We have implemented the somewhat homomorphic encryption scheme of Brakerski and Vaikuntanathan [4]. Based on this implementation, a prototype of the two protocols has been built and the efficiency of them has been analyzed. The prototype is limited to a single machine and single thread, and does not show the impact of latency. The prototype shows a runtime in the order of minutes with a linear trend with regards to scaling of the input set. This is a significant improvement over the work of Hoens et al. [14], the previous privacy-enhanced recommender systems with user supplied weights, which also assumed honest-but-curious participants and ran in the order of hours. Furthermore, not all users need to be online at some or all stages of the protocol, which is required by most related work. When we compare our work to the work of Erkin et al. [9], which assumes honest-but-curious participants and allows for offline users, we can see the difference in slowdown of the protocol when going from online to offline. The slowdown caused by our protocol is less than 1.5 times, while the slowdown of Erkin et al. is more than 6 times.

For future work, we would like to see if the efficiency of the protocols can be improved further. Furthermore, given our implementation, we would like to see the influence of somewhat homomorphic encryption, as opposed to additive homomorphic encryption, on similar problems.

Acknowledgement. This work is partially funded by the THeCS project as part of the Dutch national program COMMIT.

References

1. Ateniese, G., Fu, K., Green, M., Hohenberger, S.: Improved proxy re-encryption schemes with applications to secure distributed storage. ACM Transactions on Information and System Security 9(1), 1–30 (2006)
2. Basu, A., Vaidya, J., Kikuchi, H.: Efficient privacy-preserving collaborative filtering based on the weighted slope one predictor. Journal of Internet Services and Information Security (JISIS) 1(4), 26–46 (2011)
3. Blaze, M., Bleumer, G., Strauss, M.: Divertible protocols and atomic proxy cryptography. In: Nyberg, K. (ed.) EUROCRYPT 1998. LNCS, vol. 1403, pp. 127–144. Springer, Heidelberg (1998)
4. Brakerski, Z., Vaikuntanathan, V.: Fully homomorphic encryption from ring-LWE and security for key dependent messages. In: Rogaway, P. (ed.) CRYPTO 2011. LNCS, vol. 6841, pp. 505–524. Springer, Heidelberg (2011)
5. Canny, J.F.: Collaborative filtering with privacy. In: IEEE Symposium on Security and Privacy, pp. 45–57 (2002)
6. Carley, K.M., Krackhardt, D.: Cognitive inconsistencies and non-symmetric friendship. Social Networks 18(1), 1–27 (1996)
7. Chow, S.S.M., Weng, J., Yang, Y., Deng, R.H.: Efficient unidirectional proxy re-encryption. In: Bernstein, D.J., Lange, T. (eds.) AFRICACRYPT 2010. LNCS, vol. 6055, pp. 316–332. Springer, Heidelberg (2010)
8. Dokoohaki, N., Kaleli, C., Polat, H., Matskin, M.: Achieving optimal privacy in trust-aware social recommender systems. In: Bolc, L., Makowski, M., Wierzbicki, A. (eds.) SocInfo 2010. LNCS, vol. 6430, pp. 62–79. Springer, Heidelberg (2010)
9. Erkin, Z., Veugen, T., Toft, T., Lagendijk, R.L.: Generating private recommendations efficiently using homomorphic encryption and data packing. IEEE Transactions on Information Forensics and Security 7(3), 1053–1066 (2012)
10. Goldreich, O.: Foundations of cryptography: a primer. Foundations and Trends in Theoretical Computer Science 1, 1–116 (2005)
11. Groh, G., Ehmig, C.: Recommendations in taste related domains: Collaborative filtering vs. social filtering. In: Proc. ACM Group 2007, pp. 127–136 (2007)
12. Guy, I., Zwerdling, N., Carmel, D., Ronen, I., Uziel, E., Yogev, S., Ofek-Koifman, S.: Personalized recommendation of social software items based on social relations. In: Proceedings of the Third ACM Conference on Recommender Systems, RecSys 2009, pp. 53–60. ACM, New York (2009)

13. Herlocker, J.L., Konstan, J.A., Borchers, A., Riedl, J.: An algorithmic framework for performing collaborative filtering. In: Proceedings of the 22nd Annual International ACM SIGIR Conference on Research and Development in Information Retrieval, pp. 230–237 (1999)
14. Hoens, T., Blanton, M., Chawla, N.: A private and reliable recommendation system for social networks. In: 2010 IEEE Second International Conference on Social Computing, SocialCom, pp. 816–825 (August 2010)
15. Hoens, T.R., Blanton, M., Chawla, N.V.: Reliable medical recommendation systems with patient privacy. In: Proceedings of the 1st ACM International Health Informatics Symposium, IHI 2010, pp. 173–182. ACM, New York (2010)
16. Jeckmans, A., Tang, Q., Hartel, P.: Privacy-preserving collaborative filtering based on horizontally partitioned dataset. In: 2012 International Conference on Collaboration Technologies and Systems, CTS, pp. 439–446 (May 2012)
17. Lerman, K.: Social networks and social information filtering on digg. Computing Research Repository (CoRR), abs/cs/0612046:1–8 (2006)
18. Libert, B., Vergnaud, D.: Unidirectional chosen-ciphertext secure proxy re-encryption. In: Cramer, R. (ed.) PKC 2008. LNCS, vol. 4939, pp. 360–379. Springer, Heidelberg (2008)
19. Lindner, R., Peikert, C.: Better key sizes (and attacks) for LWE-based encryption. In: Kiayias, A. (ed.) CT-RSA 2011. LNCS, vol. 6558, pp. 319–339. Springer, Heidelberg (2011)
20. Machanavajjhala, A., Korolova, A., Sarma, A.D.: Personalized social recommendations: accurate or private. Proceedings of the VLDB Endowment 4(7), 440–450 (2011)
21. Masthoff, J., Gatt, A.: In pursuit of satisfaction and the prevention of embarrassment: affective state in group recommender systems. User Modeling and User-Adapted Interaction 16, 281–319 (2006)
22. McSherry, F., Mironov, I.: Differentially private recommender systems: building privacy into the netflix prize contenders. In: Proceedings of the 15th ACM SIGKDD International Conference on Knowledge Discovery and Data Mining, pp. 627–636 (2009)
23. Naehrig, M., Lauter, K., Vaikuntanathan, V.: Can homomorphic encryption be practical? In: Proceedings of the 3rd ACM Workshop on Cloud Computing Security Workshop, CCSW 2011, pp. 113–124. ACM, New York (2011)
24. Shokri, R., Pedarsani, P., Theodorakopoulos, G., Hubaux, J.-P.: Preserving privacy in collaborative filtering through distributed aggregation of offline profiles. In: Proceedings of the Third ACM Conference on Recommender Systems, RecSys 2009, pp. 157–164. ACM, New York (2009)
25. Sinha, R., Swearingen, K.: Comparing recommendations made by online systems and friends. In: Proceedings of the DELOS-NSF Workshop on Personalization and Recommender Systems in Digital Libraries (2001)
26. Victor, P., Cock, M., Cornelis, C.: Trust and recommendations. In: Ricci, F., Rokach, L., Shapira, B., Kantor, P.B. (eds.) Recommender Systems Handbook, pp. 645–675. Springer US (2011)

Privacy-Preserving User Data Oriented Services for Groups with Dynamic Participation

Dmitry Kononchuk, Zekeriya Erkin,
Jan C.A. van der Lubbe, and Reginald L. Lagendijk

Information Security and Privacy Lab
Department of Intelligent Systems
Delft University of Technology
2628 CD, Delft, The Netherlands
{d.kononchuk,z.erkin,j.c.a.vanderlubbe,r.l.lagendijk}@tudelft.nl

Abstract. In recent years, services that process user-generated data have become increasingly popular due to the spreading of social technologies in online applications. The data being processed by these services are mostly considered sensitive personal information, which raises privacy concerns. Hence, privacy related problems have been addressed by the research community and privacy-preserving solutions based on cryptography, like [1–5], have been proposed. Unfortunately, the existing solutions consider static settings, where the computation is executed only once for a fixed number of users, while in practice applications have a dynamic environment, where users come and leave between the executions. In this work we show that user-data oriented services, which are privacy-preserving in static settings, leak information in dynamic environments. We then present building blocks to be used in the design of privacy-preserving cryptographic protocols for dynamic settings. We also present realizations of our ideas in two different attacker models, namely semi-honest and malicious.

Keywords: Privacy, user-data oriented services, secure multi-party computation, threshold homomorphic encryption.

1   Introduction

In the past decade, online social networks and personalized e-commerce applications have become very popular as they offer customized services to people. To provide customization and personalization the data collected from many users need to be processed by a service. One of the typical example of such user-data oriented services are so-called recommender systems [6], which aim to generate personal recommendations for a particular person from the likings of other similar users by computing similarity scores based on profile information or user preferences. Other examples of user-data oriented service that can be named here are reputation systems [7], collective decision making [8] and social classification [9].

Although user-data oriented services proved themselves to be very useful in online services, as they increase the user satisfaction and business profit at the

J. Crampton, S. Jajodia, and K. Mayes (Eds.): ESORICS 2013, LNCS 8134, pp. 418–442, 2013.

same time. But the benefits come with a number of privacy risks since such services heavily depend on the data collected from the users, which is considered private in many cases, for example in case of services for medical domain. The user data can be re-purposed, transferred to third parties, sold or lost by the service provider. In either case, the privacy of the users will be damaged and the consequences will be unpredictable.

To overcome the above mentioned privacy problem, different measures including laws and organizational means have been deployed. These measures are also supported by the scientific solutions, which aim to guarantee the privacy of user data, like data perturbation [10] and data anonymization [11]. The recent idea in the field is to employ secure multiparty computations techniques [12], which allow service providers to process user data through interactive protocols without disclosing their content. This approach has been applied to a wide range of applications including recommender systems [1–3], collaborative filtering [4] and data clustering [5].

Unfortunately, the existing solutions only consider a *static* environment, where the number of users involved in the group service does not change in time. Even though these solutions provide provable privacy protection in static settings, their sequential invocation with changing number of users leaks information, damaging the purpose of the privacy-preserving protocol. As almost all of the popular online services have a *dynamic* setting with constantly joining and leaving users, we consider the privacy-preserving protocols that do not cope with the threats of dynamic execution limited to be used in practice. Therefore, in this paper we aim to provide a solution for privacy-preserving group services in a dynamic setting based on cryptographic tools.

The groups with dynamic participation have drawn attention in the cryptographic community, especially to solve the problem of key management [13, 14]. There is also prior work in data publishing to protect the privacy of users in case of continuous publishing of data of dynamic user groups [15–17]. Nevertheless, to the best of our knowledge, there has been no previous work addressing dynamic settings for user-data oriented services.

In this paper we focus on dynamic settings for user-data oriented services: we define the notion of privacy in this setting and propose novel tools to provide privacy protection to the users of such services. To achieve this, we propose to select a random sub-group of users and compute the services based on the data from this random group, while keeping the group secret. We introduce three different strategies to select this random sub-group, each suitable for a different group service scenario, and present the protocols implementing each strategy in two attacker models, namely semi-honest and malicious. For each protocol we sketch a proof of its correctness and analyze the protocol with respect to number of rounds, communication and computational complexities. Our protocols use homomorphic encryption and zero-knowledge proofs, and are designed to be executed in a constant number of interactive rounds and to be efficient in terms of computational complexity.

The rest of this paper is structured as follows. In Section 2 we formalize the notion of user-data oriented services privacy-preserving in dynamic environment and introduce a method for providing privacy in dynamic setting we use further. In Section 4 we describe the cryptographic protocols in two different security models, while Section 3 contains the cryptographic primitives used for these protocols. In Section 5 we provide an analysis on the complexity of the proposed protocols and some discussion on possible optimizations, and we conclude this paper in Section 6.

2   Proposed Solution

In this section we define user-data oriented services (from now on group services), the notion of privacy in a dynamic setting and propose a method to provide privacy protection to the users of such services.

2.1   Definitions

In our settings, a *user* represents a party that holds a private input — value selected from predefined field $\mathbb{F}$. All users are numbered and denoted as U_i, their private data is denoted as $d_i \in \mathbb{F}$. We assume that the the upper bound of the number of users in the system is N. All other parties that provide computation resources for a group service are called *service parties*. We denote one of such parties as $\mathcal{A}$.

Definition 1 (Group service). *A group service is the system that consists of:*

- *a set of users $\{U_{i \leq N}\}$, each of them holding corresponding private input $d_i \in \mathbb{F}$;*
- *a predefined number of service parties, including $\mathcal{A}$;*
- *a predefined function $f \colon \bigcup_{k=1}^{N} \mathbb{F}^k \to \mathbb{G}$, which is symmetric, i.e. for any permutation π and values $a_1, \ldots, a_M \in \mathbb{F}$, $M \leq N$: $f(a_1, \ldots, a_M) = f(\pi(a_1, \ldots, a_M))$.*

A group service run (execution) is an invocation of the predefined multiparty computation protocol (MPC) that involves a subset of M users $\{U_{i_j}\} \subseteq \{U_{i \leq N}\}$, named participating (or involved) users, and all service parties. During an execution of MPC the result $r = f(d_{i_1}, \ldots, d_{i_M}) \in \mathbb{G}$ is computed and outputted to $\mathcal{A}$.

Described group service is called *privacy-preserving in a static setting*, if after its execution party $\mathcal{A}$ learns only the value of r, and other parties do not learn any information about r and d_i. The notion of dynamic settings is formalized as follows:

Definition 2 (Group service (t, M)-dynamic execution). *A group service with users $\{U_{i \leq N}\}$ is executed (t, M)-dynamically when:*

- there exists a fixed subset of users $\mathcal{U}^D \subset \{U_{i \leq N}\}$ $|\mathcal{U}^D| = M$, named dynamic users, remaining users $\overline{\mathcal{U}^D} = \{U_{i \leq N}\} \setminus \mathcal{U}^D$ are named static ones;
- there exists subsets $\mathcal{U}_1, \ldots, \mathcal{U}_t \subset \mathcal{U}^D$ defining dynamic user participation, such that $\bigcup_{j=1}^{t} \mathcal{U}_j = \mathcal{U}^D$ and $\forall U_i \in \mathcal{U}^D \exists k \in [1, t]: U_i \notin \mathcal{U}_k$;
- the group service is executed t times, computing results $r_1, \ldots, r_t$;
- on a k-th group service execution only the users from $\overline{\mathcal{U}^D} \bigcup \mathcal{U}_k$ are participating.

Clearly, (t, M)-dynamic execution of the privacy-preserving protocols designed for a static setting reveals $\mathcal{A}$ information on the private data of the dynamic users, as this information can be inferred from $\mathcal{A}$'s observations $(\mathcal{U}_1, r_1), \ldots, (\mathcal{U}_t, r_t)$. We define the scenario, when $\mathcal{A}$ exploit such information leakage, as the *new group attack*. This attack can be illustrated on the following example: assume that $\mathcal{U}_1 \setminus \mathcal{U}_2 = U_3$, then by comparing r_1 and r_2 $\mathcal{A}$ can reveal information on d_3 (or even disclose the value of d_3).

To eliminate such an information leakage, we define a upper-bound on the amount of information on dynamic users' private values that $\mathcal{A}$ can infer from $r_1, \ldots, r_t$ and $\mathcal{U}_1, \ldots, \mathcal{U}_t$ available to it. More formally, for each $U_i \in \mathcal{U}^D$ we give a lower-bound for the value of entropy $H_i = H(d_i \mid (\mathcal{U}_1, r_1), \ldots, (\mathcal{U}_t, r_t))$.

Values of H_i cannot be restricted with absolute values, independent from f, as the quantity of information, which $\mathcal{A}$ can deduce from received computation results, strongly depends on properties of f used in a specific group service. For example, if f computes an average of its arguments, then $\mathcal{A}$ can learn the exact values of private input of dynamic users (for some configuration of $\mathcal{U}_1, \ldots, \mathcal{U}_t$). In case f computes just the number of its arguments, $\mathcal{A}$ cannot infer any information about d_i from received r_k.

To restrict the values of H_i in general cases, but using the properties of a specific f, two strategies can be used:

1. using the entropy of $\mathcal{A}$'s prediction of private users' input in a static case;
2. using the entropy of $\mathcal{A}$'s prediction of private data of non-dynamic users in a dynamic case.

The first approach is too strict for practice, therefore in this work we use the second one and define the privacy in the context of a dynamic group service execution as follows:

Definition 3 (Privacy-preserving (t, M)-dynamic execution). *A (t, M)-dynamic execution of a group service with users $\{U_{i \leq N}\}$ and dynamic users $\mathcal{U}^D \subset \{U_{i \leq N}\}$ is called privacy-preserving, when after this execution the following conditions hold:*

- *Party $\mathcal{A}$ learns only the values of r_k and other parties do not learn any information about r_k and d_i.*
- *Party $\mathcal{A}$ can deduce less (or equal) amount of information on the private inputs of dynamic users as on static ones: $\forall U_i \in \mathcal{U}^D \exists U_j \in \overline{\mathcal{U}^D}: H_i \leq H_j$.*

Group service is called *privacy-preserving in a (t, M)-dynamic setting*, if any (t, M)-dynamic execution of a such group service is privacy-preserving.

2.2   Group Masking Method

Based on the previous definitions, we propose a general method, in which a group service is made privacy-preserving in (t, M)-dynamic setting and secured against the new group attack. The method is based on the idea of blurring the difference between dynamic and static users. We achieve this by adding similar random behaviour to both types of users. More formally the method is as follows:

Method (Group masking). Assume, that the group service with users $\{U_{i \leq N}\}$ is executed (t, M)-dynamically and sets $\mathcal{U}_1, \ldots, \mathcal{U}_t \subset \mathcal{U}^D \subset \{U_{i \leq N}\}$ define the dynamic user participation in group service runs. On the k-th run, the set $\widetilde{\mathcal{U}}_k \subseteq \overline{\mathcal{U}^D} \bigcup \mathcal{U}_k$, named *included users*, is randomly selected in a way that it is kept hidden from $\mathcal{A}$. The result r_k is computed as $r_k = f(\{d_i \mid U_i \in \widetilde{\mathcal{U}}_k\})$.

It is clear that group masking reduces the amount of information that $\mathcal{A}$ can deduce about users' private input during the dynamic execution, as it hides from $\mathcal{A}$ which users are participating in the computations. Next, we check whether and in what conditions this method hides enough information to guarantee the dynamic privacy-protection.

Note that as the function f is symmetric, then for any $x, y, z \in \mathbb{F}$ the following two observations hold:

$$H(x \mid r = f(x, y)) = H(y \mid r = f(x, y)) , \tag{1}$$
$$H(x \mid r_1 = f(x, y, z), r_2 = f(z)) = H(y \mid r_1 = f(x, y, z), r_2 = f(z)) . \tag{2}$$

Consequently, if $\widetilde{\mathcal{U}}_1, \ldots, \widetilde{\mathcal{U}}_t$ are generated in a such way that an intersection and a symmetric difference of any number of $\widetilde{\mathcal{U}}_k$ contain at least as many static users as dynamic ones, then the method above guarantees that a group service execution is privacy-preserving.

As far as the specific values of $\widetilde{\mathcal{U}}_k$ are hidden from $\mathcal{A}$, we can relax the condition above and state the following criteria: a group service dynamic execution is privacy-preserving, when an intersection and a symmetric difference of any number of $\widetilde{\mathcal{U}}_k$ contains on average more static users than dynamic ones. Next, we check what conditions should be met to satisfy this criteria.

Let us consider the case, when all $\widetilde{\mathcal{U}}_k$ generated by the group masking method are independent and uniform, in the sense of included users, i.e. on k-th group service execution all involved users (both static and dynamic) have a same probability to be included in $\widetilde{\mathcal{U}}_k$.

Let $\widetilde{\mathcal{U}}_k$ and $\widetilde{\mathcal{U}}_l$ be two sets of included users, both uniform in the sense above. As the sets are uniform, then the probabilities $p = P(U_i \in \widetilde{\mathcal{U}}_k \mid U_i \in \overline{\mathcal{U}^D} \bigcup \mathcal{U}_k)$ and $q = P(U_i \in \widetilde{\mathcal{U}}_l \mid U_i \in \overline{\mathcal{U}^D} \bigcup \mathcal{U}_l)$ are defined. Without loss of generality we assume that $p \geq q$.

Consider the intersection and the symmetric difference of $\widetilde{\mathcal{U}}_k$ and $\widetilde{\mathcal{U}}_l$. It is clear that on average the following statements hold:

$$\left|\left(\widetilde{\mathcal{U}}_k \bigcap \widetilde{\mathcal{U}}_l\right) \bigcap \overline{\mathcal{U}^D}\right| - \left|\left(\widetilde{\mathcal{U}}_k \bigcap \widetilde{\mathcal{U}}_l\right) \bigcap \mathcal{U}^D\right| = pq\left(N - M - \left|\mathcal{U}_k \bigcap \mathcal{U}_l\right|\right), \quad (3)$$

$$\left|\left(\widetilde{\mathcal{U}}_k \triangle \widetilde{\mathcal{U}}_l\right) \bigcap \overline{\mathcal{U}^D}\right| - \left|\left(\widetilde{\mathcal{U}}_k \triangle \widetilde{\mathcal{U}}_l\right) \bigcap \mathcal{U}^D\right| = (p + q - 2pq)\left(N - M - \left|\mathcal{U}_k \bigcap \mathcal{U}_l\right|\right)$$
$$- p\left|\mathcal{U}_k \setminus \mathcal{U}_l\right| - q\left|\mathcal{U}_l \setminus \mathcal{U}_k\right|. \quad (4)$$

Note that as $|\mathcal{U}_k \bigcap \mathcal{U}_l| \leq M$, $|\mathcal{U}_k \bigcap \mathcal{U}_l| + |\mathcal{U}_k \setminus \mathcal{U}_l| + |\mathcal{U}_l \setminus \mathcal{U}_k| \leq M$ and $q \leq p$, then the minimums of Equations (3) and (4) are reached when $|\mathcal{U}_k \bigcap \mathcal{U}_l| = M$. And these minimums are non-negative iff $N \geq 2M$, i.e. when the majority of the users are static.

Consequently, when the majority of the users are static Equations (3) and (4) are non-negative. That is, the intersection and the symmetric difference of any two randomly selected (independent and uniform in the sense of included users) $\widetilde{\mathcal{U}}_k$ and $\widetilde{\mathcal{U}}_l$ contains on average more (or equal) static users than dynamic ones. It is clear that then the same property holds for any number of sets $\widetilde{\mathcal{U}}_k$.

To sum up, if the majority of the users are static, then the group service dynamic execution protected using uniformly and independently selected group masks is privacy-preserving. Next in this work we will target only the settings with majority of the static users.

Note that in real-world group services, for example in aforementioned recommender systems, the utility of computed results depends on the number of users involved in the computation. Hence, applying the group masking method in practice may cause the quality degradation of group service results, due to decreasing the number of users involved in each group service execution. To eliminate such quality fall-of we additionally restrict generated $\widetilde{\mathcal{U}}_k$ by introducing lower-bound of the number of included users:

$$\forall k \in [1, t]: \left|\widetilde{\mathcal{U}}_k\right| \geq Q\left(\left|\overline{\mathcal{U}^D} \bigcup \mathcal{U}_k\right|\right), \quad (5)$$

where function $Q(x)$ specifies the minimum number of parties (from x available), which should participate in a group service execution to compute a result with the level of utility sufficient compared to what can be achieved by involving all x parties. We assume that Q is publicly known, but we will not specify it, because its exact value is defined by a concrete group service and a concrete application.

2.3   Approaches to Select Included Users

As it was stated in Section 2.2, in the settings, where the majority of the users are static, all subsets $\widetilde{\mathcal{U}}_k$ can be selected independently and uniformly, in the sense of included users. Hence, generating of $\widetilde{\mathcal{U}}_k$ can be done without knowing which users are static and which are dynamic, and which users, except involved in k-th execution, exist in the system. So, for the sake of simplicity, we can assume that a group service is executed only once, and that all existing N users are employed during that execution.

A group service execution using group masking method processes as follows: a random subgroup $\mathcal{U} \subset \{U_{i \leq N}\}$ is selected, and then result r is computed as $r = f(\{d_i \mid U_i \in \mathcal{U}\})$ and outputted privately to $\mathcal{A}$. Generating the subgroup $\mathcal{U}$ is equivalent to generating a vector $e \in \{0, 1\}^N$, such that $e_i = 1$ iff $U_i \in \mathcal{U}$. Such a vector e is named a *group mask*.

To apply the group masking method in practice we propose three different approaches for generating a group mask:

Approach 1. Vector e is generated uniformly randomly, such that it contains exactly m ones, where $m \geq Q(N)$ is publicly known.

Approach 2. Each value e_i is generated independently, such that $P(e_i{=}1) = p$, where p is publicly known and satisfies $P(\sum_{i=1}^{N} e_i \geq Q(N)) \approx 1$[1].

Approach 3. Vector e is generated in two steps: (i) uniformly random $m \in_R [Q(N), N]$ is generated; (ii) e is selected uniformly randomly, such that it contains exactly m ones. In this approach, not only the value of e but also the value of m should be hidden from $\mathcal{A}$.

Note that for e generated according to Approach 1, the probability $P(e_i{=}1) = m/N$ and the value $\sum_{i=1}^{N} e_i = m$ are known, while for e generated according to Approach 2, only the probability $P(e_i{=}1) = p$ is known. For a vector generated according to Approach 3 only the lower bound of $P(e_i{=}1)$ is known: $P(e_i{=}1) \geq Q(N)/N$, which is exactly equal to what we can be estimated based on limitation from Equation (5). Hence, we can claim that Approach 3 generates group masks e, such that a priori knowledge about e is minimum. Approach 2 leaks more information on e than Approach 3, and Approach 1 leaks more than Approach 2.

As Approaches 1 and 2 generate group masks with the higher a priori knowledge about the result, this approaches provide more information to potential attackers than Approach 3 and thus they are less secure. Nevertheless, Approaches 1 and 2 have their own advantages, which make them preferable in certain scenarios: Approach 2 can be implemented much more efficiently then Approaches 1 and 3, and thus it introduces a tradeoff between complexity and privacy. Approach 1 has one advantage over other two approaches — it generate group masks with pre-defined number of involved users, which is important for a certain applications, where the values of parameters, say threshold, depend on the amount of data processed or the amount of user participated.

3   Preliminaries

In this section we briefly introduce the cryptographic primitives employed throughout the paper, namely threshold homomorphic encryption and non-interactive zero-knowledge proofs.

---

[1] For example, due to de Moivre–Laplace theorem and the fact that $\Phi(-4) \approx 0$, p satisfying the following inequation is suitable: $Np + 1 - Q(N) - 4\sqrt{Np(1-p)} \geq 0$.

3.1 Threshold Homomorphic Encryption

For our protocols we rely on homomorphic encryption that allows users to process private data without disclosing them. We use its threshold version to make the processing secure even in the case when all except one users are colluding.

A cryptosystem is called additively homomorphic when there exist an operation $\otimes$ such that applying $\otimes$ to encryptions of two messages, say x and y, produces the cyphertext which decryption yields the sum of these messages:

$$D(E(x) \otimes E(y)) = x + y \,, \tag{6}$$

where E and D represent the encryption and decryption functions. The public-key cryptosystem is called K-out-of-N threshold, when contributions from any K (from in total N) users are required to compute the decryption of a given cyphertext.

In this paper we use the threshold Paillier cryptosystem either with a trusted dealer [18] or without it [19]. Both cryptosystems have the same properties, so we will not distinguish them further.

In the threshold Paillier cryptosystem the public key of the form $pk = (n, g, \theta)$ is used. Here n is the RSA modulus, computed as a product of two random safe primes $2p' + 1$ and $2q' + 1$; g is the generator of the field $\mathbb{Z}_{n^2}^*$ such that $g = (n + 1)^a \cdot b^n \bmod n^2$ for random $a, b \in \mathbb{Z}_n^*$; and $\theta = a\beta\eta \bmod n$, where β is randomly chosen from $\mathbb{Z}_n$ and $\eta = p'q'$. The corresponding private key is $sk = \beta\eta$. This key is shared between all users using the Shamir's K-out-of-N secret sharing scheme [20]: each U_i receive $sk_i = f(i) \bmod n\eta$, where f is a random polynomial in $\mathbb{Z}_{n\eta}$ of degree $K - 1$, whose first coefficient is sk.

To encrypt a message $x \in \mathbb{Z}_n$ with the public key $pk = (n, g, \theta)$, $E(x, r)$ is computed with a randomly chosen $r \in \mathbb{Z}_n^*$:

$$E(x, r) = g^x r^n \bmod n^2 \,, \tag{7}$$

where $\Delta = N!$ is publicly known and precomputed.

To perform a threshold K-out-of-N decryption of a cyphertext $c \in \mathbb{Z}_{n^2}^*$ contribution of the users from the set $\mathbb{S}$ of size K is necessary. Each contributing $U_i \in \mathbb{S}$ computes a partial decryption of c:

$$D_i(c) = c^{2\Delta sk_i} \bmod n^2 \,. \tag{8}$$

Partial decryptions are then passed to a party (parties), which would like to receive a decrypted plaintext, and combined as follows:

$$D(c) = L\left(\prod_{U_i \in \mathbb{S}} D_i(c)^{2\mu_i} \bmod n^2\right) \cdot \frac{1}{4\Delta^2\theta} \bmod n \,,$$
$$\text{where } L(x) = \frac{x - 1}{n}, \quad \mu_i = \Delta \cdot \prod_{\substack{U_j \in \mathbb{S} \\ j \neq i}} \frac{j}{j - i} \,. \tag{9}$$

To secure the decryption protocol against malicious private key share holders, the zero-knowledge proofs are used: each user, submitting its partial decryption

$D_i(c)$ should also submit a proof to show that this value was computed correctly, i.e. a proof of correct decryption. These proofs rely on the verification keys VK and $VK_{i=1,\ldots,N}$, which should be generated and distributed together with the public key during the initialization stage. The key VK is a randomly chosen quadratic residue in $\mathbb{Z}_{n^2}^*$ and each VK_i is computed as $VK_i = VK^{\Delta sk_i} \bmod n^2$. Afterwards a user can prove that $D_i(c)$ was computed correctly by proving that $\log_{VK^\Delta} VK_i = \log_{c^{4\Delta}} D_i(c)^2$. We refer the reader to the work [18] for further details.

Note that if all users behave in a semi-honest fashion, then the decryption protocol can be simplified to achieve lower computational complexity: each partial decryption is computed as $D_i(c) = c^{4\mu_i \Delta sk_i} \bmod n^2$ and the combining function is computed as $D(c) = L(\prod_{U_i \in \mathbb{S}} D_i(c) \bmod n^2)/(4\Delta^2 \theta) \bmod n$.

It is clear that this encryption function E has the following properties:

$$E(x, r_x) \cdot E(y, r_y) = E(x + y, r_x r_y) \quad \bmod n^2 , \tag{10}$$

$$E(x, r)^c = E(xc, r^c) \qquad \bmod n^2 , \tag{11}$$

$$E(x, r_1) \cdot r_2^n = E(x, r_1 r_2) \qquad \bmod n^2 . \tag{12}$$

Hence E is homomorphic with respect to addition and multiplication by a constant. Moreover, due to the property (12), any party that knows the public key can build a cyphertext equivalent to the given one. This operation is denoted as rerandomization: $\text{Rand}(c) = c \cdot r^n \bmod n^2$.

The threshold Paillier encryption is semantically secure under the decisional composite residuosity assumption in the random oracle model. We refer the reader to the works [18, 21] for further information on encryption properties.

In this work all operations over plaintext values will be performed over $\mathbb{Z}_n$, for encrypted values over $\mathbb{Z}_{n^2}^*$, and for randomness over $\mathbb{Z}_n^*$. That is, the field used for each operation can be easily determined by the context, and thus we will omit writing $\bmod n$ and $\bmod n^2$ for simplifying the notation. Also we use the notation $[\![x]\!]$ to denote an encryption $E(x, r)$. omitting the randomness for simplicity.

3.2   Zero-Knowledge Proofs

Zero-knowledge (ZK) proofs are the protocols between two parties: the prover and the verifier, during which the prover tries to convince the verifier that a given statement is true, without leaking any information other than the veracity of that statement. A lot of ZK proofs have been proposed recently, an overview of the current development can be found in [22].

In case when a common random string is available to prover and verifier, the existing ZK proof protocol can be made non-interactive using the method by [23]. One of the advantages of resulting non-interactive zero-knowledge (NIZK) proofs is that they can be used not only in a two-party settings, but in a multiparty settings with one prover and many verifiers.

For our protocols, we employ a few NIZK proofs: (i) proof of correct decryption $\Pi_{CD}([\![x]\!], d, i)$, which shows that $d = D_i([\![x]\!])$, based on ZK proof introduced

[18]; (ii) proof of correct multiplication $\Pi_{CM}(\llbracket x \rrbracket, \llbracket y \rrbracket, \llbracket z \rrbracket)$, which shows that $z = xy$, based on the proof introduced in [24]; (iii) and NIZK proof of knowledge of a plaintext, which is chosen from in a given set, $\Pi_{PK}(\llbracket x \rrbracket, \mathbb{S})$, which shows that $x \in \mathbb{S}$, based on the general technique presented in [22].

4   Protocols

In this section we describe how the Approaches 1–3 introduced in Section 2 can be employed to protect an existing group service against the new group attack and to provide a privacy of user data in the dynamic settings.

The group service we consider computes the sum of the users' private data. More precisely, for users $U_1, \ldots, U_N$, each holding corresponding private value d_i, this group service evaluates

$$r = f(d_1, \ldots, d_N) = \sum_{i=1}^{N} d_i \tag{13}$$

and outputs the result privately to $\mathcal{A}$. The group masking method is applied to this group service by modifying its function f to the following:

$$r = f(d_1, \ldots, d_N) = \sum_{i=1}^{N} d_i e_i , \tag{14}$$

where e is a group mask, which is generated according to Approaches 1–3 and is kept hidden from $\mathcal{A}$ and all parties that can collude with $\mathcal{A}$.

We describe the protocols implementing the considered group service and its versions that provide protection against the new group attack in the two security settings:

A. Semi-honest settings, where all parties follow the protocol steps correctly, but can collect the observation during the protocol execution in attempt to obtain any information about private values of other parties.
B. Malicious settings, where all parties can additionally deviate from the protocol.

In both settings parties can collude either to disclose the private data of other (non-colluding with them) parties or to corrupt the computation result. We assume that the number of users participating in each coalition is upper bounded, i.e. that there exists a predefined number $K \leq N$ such, that each coalition involve at most $K - 1$ users and any number of service parties.

For each of these settings we provide four protocols: reference implementation of the considered group service without using the group masking method and three protocols for the group service protected with a group mask generated according to Approaches 1–3. Presented protocols are referenced as **Protocol $\mathcal{P}_1^A$**, where "A" denotes the target security settings and "1" denotes used approach for generating a group mask (0 denotes the protocol without group masking).

In the following protocols the first K users carry the major part of the computations, therefore for simplifying further notation we assume, that in each operation by default only that users are involved, i.e. "all users" should be read as "users $U_{i \leq K}$". Note that at least one of these users is not colluding with others.

We assume that the Paillier K-out-of-N threshold encryption scheme has already been set up: its private key has been shared between all users (each user receives share sk_i) and its public key pk and verification keys VK and $VK_{i=1,...,N}$ are known to all parties. In the following protocols all encryptions are done using pk.

The described protocols work over channels of two types: broadcasted to $U_{i \leq N}$ and point-to-point between $\mathcal{A}$ and U_i. Protocols are designed under the assumption that each party has access to the random oracle and to the common random string. The protocols widely use the well-known subprotocols for threshold Paillier cryptosystem, like secure multiplication [25] and unbound fan-in multiplication subprotocols [25, 26].

4.1   Protocols for Semi-honest Setting

In this section we describe the protocols, which are secure in the semi-honest settings, where parties can form a coalitions involving at most $K - 1$ users and any number of service parties. Following protocols preserve the users' privacy by hiding their data from all other users and party $\mathcal{A}$, and $\mathcal{A}$'s privacy by hiding the computation result from all users. We protect the protocols from the new group attack by using group masking, where a group mask should be kept hidden from all parties (as all parties can collude with $\mathcal{A}$).

Reference Protocol. First, we describe the protocol for reference group service implementation, which just outputs the sum of all users data to $\mathcal{A}$ without using group masking. The protocol is described in Protocol $\mathcal{P}_0^A$.

Input: Each $U_{i \leq N}$ holds his private value d_i.
Output: Party $\mathcal{A}$ receives $r = \sum_{i=1}^{N} d_i$.

1. Each $U_{i \leq N}$ broadcasts $[\![d_i]\!]$.
2. Each user computes $[\![r]\!] = \left[\!\left[\sum_{i=1}^{N} d_i\right]\!\right] = \prod_{i=1}^{N} [\![d_i]\!]$.
3. All users jointly run decryption of $[\![r]\!]$ and open r to $\mathcal{A}$.

Protocol $\mathcal{P}_0^A$. *GS without group masking, semi-honest setting.*

Security and privacy properties of Protocol $\mathcal{P}_0^A$ can be verified as follows. On Steps 1–2 users receive and process only encrypted data. No information can be extracted from it as the K-out-of-N threshold Paillier cryptosystem is known to be semantically secure against $K - 1$ colluding private key holders. On Step 3 all users do partial decryption of $[\![r]\!]$ and $\mathcal{A}$ (and all colluding users) gets access to both computation result r and its partial decryptions $D_i([\![r]\!])$. Values $D_i([\![r]\!])$ do not leak any information about sk_i as it was shown in [18], and the value r is a private output of $\mathcal{A}$ and thus is allowed to be learned by $\mathcal{A}$ and colluding users. Hence, no information about private values is leaked during one protocol execution. However, as the protocol does not use the group masking, it fails to protect the privacy in the dynamic settings.

Protocol with Group Masking Using Approach 1. Next, we present the protocol, which can cope with the new group attack. This protocol uses the proposed group masking method, where the mask is generated according to Approach 1.

Approach 1 requires the group mask e to have the following property: $e \in_R \{0,1\}^N$ and exactly m its components are equal to 1. To generate such vector we use the multiple-try method, which process as follows: (i) users generate t vectors $\beta_j \in_R \{0,1\}^N$ in parallel such, that $\forall l \in [1,N]: P(\beta_{.,l}=1) = m/N$; (ii) users select as e the first β_j, such that its elements sum $b_j = \sum_{l=1}^N \beta_{j,l}$ is equal to m.

Multiple-try method is applicable for generating a vector e as the rate of suitable candidates β_j, i.e. vectors satisfying $\sum_{l=1}^N \beta_{j,l} = m$, is fixed:

$$S = P\left(\sum_{l=1}^N \beta_{j,l}=m\right) = \binom{N}{m}\frac{m^m(N-m)^{N-m}}{N^N} \approx \sqrt{\frac{N}{2\pi m(N-m)}} \ . \quad (15)$$

Consequently, by executing the sufficient numbers of tries t, we can guarantee that the method will fail, i.e. will not generate e, only with negligible probability $2^{-\kappa}$, where κ denotes the statistical security parameter (usually is chosen around 80).

In practice, we can note that $S \geq 1/\sqrt{2\pi m}$, and though we can use the following estimation of the value t: $t = \lceil \kappa\sqrt{2\pi m}\ln 2 \rceil \approx \lceil 1.74\kappa\sqrt{m} \rceil$.

To perform described multiple-try approach in privacy-preserving manner, we should generate each vector β_j jointly random, i.e. in a such way that K users contribute to it and any subgroup of users together cannot infer, which of candidates for β_j are more likely.

Jointly-random generation of vector $\beta \in_R \{0,1\}^N$ is performed in the following way: (i) each U_i independently generate vector $\alpha_i \in_R \{0,1\}^N$; (ii) generated vectors are composed into β using exclusive OR (XOR) as $\beta = \alpha_1 \oplus \ldots \oplus \alpha_K$, where XOR combination is computed bitwise by employing the *unbounded fan-in XOR subprotocol* [25]. Obviously, if XOR subprotocol is secure, then even $K - 1$ colluding users can not extract any information about β.

The following formula holds for β_l as a XOR-combination of K equally distributed random values $\alpha_{i,l}$ (see [27] for construction):

$$P(\beta_l=1) = \frac{1}{2} - \frac{1}{2}(1 - 2P(\alpha_{.,l}=1))^K \ . \quad (16)$$

Consequently, to satisfy the property $\forall l \in [1, N]: P(\beta_l{=}1) = m/N$, each α_i should be generated following the next element distribution:

$$q = P(\alpha_{i,}{=}1) = \frac{1}{2} - \frac{1}{2}\sqrt[K]{1 - 2m/N} . \tag{17}$$

Note that the formula above is inapplicable in cases when $m > N/2$ and K is even. For that cases we suggest to increment the value of K, i.e. to involve one more user into the procedure of generation of β.

Protocol for Approach 2, which is based on the described tools, primitives from Section 3 and aforementioned subprotocols, is given in Protocol $\mathcal{P}_1^A$. Security and privacy of the protocol rely on the security properties of the underlying cryptographic primitives. Note that opening of values b_j on Step 3 does not leak any information about e, as $m = \sum_{i=1}^{N} e_i$ is a priori knowledge.

Input: Each $U_{i \leq N}$ holds his private value d_i.
Output: Party $\mathcal{A}$ receives $r = \sum_{i=1}^{N} d_i e_i$.

1. Each U_i generates t random $\alpha_{i,j} \in_R \{0,1\}^N$ such, that: $\forall l \in [1, N], \forall j \in [1, t]: P(\alpha_{i,j,l}{=}1) = q$.
2. Users jointly run the unbounded fan-in XOR subprotocol tN times in parallel, computing for each $j \in [1, t]$, $l \in [1, N]$ value $[\![\beta_{j,l}]\!] = [\![\oplus_{i=1}^{K} \alpha_{i,j,l}]\!]$.
3. Users locally compute $[\![b_j]\!] = \left[\!\left[\sum_{l=1}^{N} \beta_{j,l}\right]\!\right] = \prod_{l=1}^{N} [\![\beta_{j,l}]\!]$, and jointly run t decryptions in parallel to open values b_j to U_1.
4. U_1 selects minimum j, such that $b_j = m$, and broadcasts $[\![e]\!] = [\![\beta_j]\!]$. This step fails with probability $2^{-\kappa}$.
5. Each $U_{i \leq N}$ computes $[\![d_i e_i]\!] = [\![e_i]\!]^{d_i}$ and broadcasts the result.
6. Users locally compute $[\![r]\!] = \left[\!\left[\sum_{i=1}^{N} d_i e_i\right]\!\right] = \prod_{i=1}^{N} [\![d_i e_i]\!]$, and jointly run decryption to open r to $\mathcal{A}$.

Protocol $\mathcal{P}_1^A$. *GS with 1-st group masking, semi-honest setting.*

Protocol with Group Masking Using Approach 2. Protocol $\mathcal{P}_1^A$ can be simplified to achieve relaxed requirements of Approach 2, where only the probability of user participation is fixed, but not the total amount of participating users.

Resulting protocol is presented in Protocol $\mathcal{P}_2^A$. This protocol utilizes less computational resources and discloses less information about generated e than Protocol $\mathcal{P}_1^A$, but is not applicable for several kinds of group services (see Section 2 for examples).

The security of Protocol $\mathcal{P}_2^A$ can be verified in a same way as for the previous protocol. The correctness of generated e, i.e. the fact that it follows the distribution stated in Approach 2 $P(e_i{=}1) = p$, can be easily verified using Equation (16).

Input: Each $U_{i \leq N}$ holds his private value d_i.
Output: Party $\mathcal{A}$ receives $r = \sum_{i=1}^{N} d_i e_i$.

1. Each U_i generates $\alpha_i \in_R \{0,1\}^N$ such, that:

$$\forall j \in [1, N] : P(\alpha_{i,j}{=}1) = \frac{1}{2} - \frac{1}{2}\sqrt[K]{1 - 2p} \ .$$

2. Users jointly run the unbounded fan-in XOR subprotocol N times in parallel, computing for each $j \in [1, N]$ value $[\![e_j]\!] = [\![\oplus_{i=1}^{K} \alpha_{i,j}]\!]$.
3. Each $U_{i \leq N}$ computes $[\![d_i e_i]\!] = [\![e_i]\!]^{d_i}$ and broadcasts the result.
4. Users locally compute $[\![r]\!] = [\![\sum_{i=1}^{N} d_i e_i]\!] = \prod_{i=1}^{N} [\![d_i e_i]\!]$, and jointly run decryption to open r to $\mathcal{A}$.

Protocol $\mathcal{P}_2^A$. *GS with 2-nd group masking, semi-honest setting.*

Protocol with Group Masking Using Approach 3. Now we present the protocol that uses Approach 3 for generating a group mask. Approach 3, compared to Approaches 1 and 2, generates masks with minimum constraints, and hence discloses less information to potential attackers.

Approach 3 requires the group mask e to have the following property: $e \in_R \{0,1\}^N$ and $\sum_{i=1}^{N} e_i$ is uniformly random in $[Q(N), N]$. To generate such e, three steps are executed: (i) uniformly random $r \in_R [0, N - Q(N)]$ is jointly generated (next $N - Q(N)$ is denoted as σ for notation simplicity); (ii) r is converted to $v \in \{0,1\}^\sigma$, which contains exactly r ones; (iii) v is supplemented by $Q(N)$ ones and permuted to produce e.

To implement the described protocol steps we need to present two additional protocols: *secure unary conversion* and *jointly random shuffling*.

Secure unary conversion. This protocol transforms encrypted integer $[\![r]\!]$, which is from the interval $[0, \sigma]$, to encrypted vector $[\![v]\!] : v \in \{0,1\}^\sigma$ of the following form:

$$v = (\underbrace{1, \ldots, 1}_{r}, \overbrace{0, \ldots, 0}^{\sigma - r}) \ .$$

We implement this protocol using Lagrange polynomial interpolation. Indeed, each vector element v_i can be computed using the function $v_i(x) = (x \overset{?}{\leq} i)$ as $v_i = v_i(r)$. Admitted region of $v_i(x)$ is $\mathbb{Z}_{\sigma+1}$, and hence, $v_i(x)$ can be evaluated in all possible $\sigma + 1$ points and then represented as a Lagrange polynomial:

$$v_i(x) = \sum_{j=0}^{\sigma} v_i(j) \prod_{\substack{l=0 \\ l \neq j}}^{\sigma} \frac{x - l}{j - l} = \sum_{j=0}^{\sigma} \alpha_{i,j} x^j \ . \tag{18}$$

Using the observation above, we can describe the secure unary conversion protocol. First, all users jointly run the *prefix multiplication subprotocol* [25, 26] to compute $([\![r^2]\!], \ldots, [\![r^\sigma]\!])$ from $[\![r]\!]$. And then, each user locally computes for all $i \in [1, \sigma]$ $[\![v_i]\!] = [\![v_i(r)]\!] = [\![\alpha_{i,0}]\!] \prod_{j=1}^{\sigma} [\![r^j]\!]^{\alpha_{i,j}}$ using the same randomness for encrypting $[\![\alpha_{i,0}]\!]$. The common random string can be used as the source of such randomness.

The protocol is, obviously, secure, as all computations are done over encrypted data and the prefix multiplication subprotocol is secure.

Jointly random shuffling. This protocol generates a jointly random permutation π, applies it to a given vector and rerandomizes the result. This subprotocol is based on matrix representations of permutations.

Matrix form of permutation $\pi = \begin{pmatrix} 1\,2\,3\,4\,5 \\ 3\,5\,2\,4\,1 \end{pmatrix}$ is the following full-range matrix $P(\pi)$:

$$P(\pi) = \begin{pmatrix} 0\,0\,1\,0\,0 \\ 0\,0\,0\,0\,1 \\ 0\,1\,0\,0\,0 \\ 0\,0\,0\,1\,0 \\ 1\,0\,0\,0\,0 \end{pmatrix}. \tag{19}$$

Applying a permutation to a vector and composing two permutations in the matrix form are performed using left-multiplication: $\pi(v)^T = P(\pi) \cdot v^T$ and $P(\pi_2 \circ \pi_1) = P(\pi_1) \cdot P(\pi_2)$. Moreover, if a permutation matrix and a source vector are both encrypted, then applying the *secure matrix multiplication subprotocol* [25] to them produces rerandomized shuffle, i.e. $[\![P(\pi) \cdot v^T]\!] = \text{Rand}\,(\pi([\![v]\!]))^T$.

Now we can describe the jointly random shuffling protocol. This protocol uses t-speedup method, which aims to decrease computational complexity of the protocol in t times by executing t additional rounds. For simplicity we assume $t \mid K$. The protocol is as follows:

1. Each user generates random permutation π_i.
2. Each group of t users builds an aggregate permutation by sequential combining permutation matrices $P(\pi_i), \ldots, P(\pi_{i+t})$: U_j receives $[\![P_{i,j-1}]\!]$ from the previous user in a group (U_i sets $[\![P_{i,i-1}]\!] = [\![E]\!]$), permutes matrix elements according to $P(\pi_j)$, rerandomizes the resulting $[\![P_{i,j}]\!]$ and broadcasts it.
3. All $[\![P_i]\!]$ are combined using the *unbound fan-in matrix multiplication subprotocol* [25, 26]. Resulting permutation matrix $P(\pi)$ then applied to the given vector using the secure matrix multiplication.

We can use unbounded fan-in matrices multiplication subprotocol in the protocol above only in case, when the matrix size/field size ratio is negligible: $N/n \leq 2^{-\kappa}$. As in practice $\kappa = 80$ and n is at least 1024 bit long (according to recommendation of [28]), the protocol is applicable for the settings with $N \leq 2^{944}$ users, which is quite mild restriction.

The protocol is secure, because all underlying cryptographic primitives are known to be secure and the following observations hold. For any coalition $\mathbb{A}$ there is at least one group of users $U_i, \ldots, U_{i+t}$, which involves U_{i+k} such that $U_{i+k} \notin \mathbb{A}$. It is clear, that due to the rerandomization used by U_{i+k} on Step 2 of the protocol, coalition cannot learn the value of $P_{i,i+k}$ even in case it knows the value $P_{i,i+k-1}$. Hence, $P_{i,i+k}$ is uniformly random and unknown to users from $\mathbb{A}$, and consequently these users cannot select $\pi_{i+k+1}, \ldots, \pi_{i+t}$ in a such that resulting $P_i = P_{i,i+k} \cdot P(\pi_{i+k+1}) \cdot \ldots \cdot P(\pi_{i+t})$ will not be random. And thus, coalition $\mathbb{A}$ (and any other) cannot reveal a combined permutation of at least one group, and consequently, the combined permutation π. Also, this permutation cannot be traced by comparing the source and the permuted vectors, because the permuted vector is rerandomized due to the properties of encrypted permutation matrix.

In the following protocol we use $t = 6$ as a tradeoff between round and computational complexities: doubling the number of rounds gives a six-time gain in the amount of computations. For simplicity we assume $K = 0 \mod 6$.

By combining two described protocols we can obtain the protocol, which implements Approach 3 for group mask generation. We present the protocol in Protocol $\mathcal{P}_3^A$. The protocol is secure, because all underlying subprotocols and cryptographic primitives are secure. The protocols' Steps 1–3 and Steps 4–7 should be executed in parallel to reduce an overall round complexity and execution time.

Input: Each $U_{i \leq N}$ holds his private value d_i.
Output: Party $\mathcal{A}$ receives $r = \sum_{i=1}^{N} d_i e_i$.

1. Users jointly run the *bounded random number generation subprotocol* [29] and produce $[\![r]\!] : r \in \mathbb{Z}_{\sigma+1}$.
2. Users jointly run the prefix multiplication subprotocol and compute $([\![r^2]\!], \ldots, [\![r^\sigma]\!])$ from $[\![r]\!]$.
3. U_1 builds and broadcasts vector $[\![v]\!]$:

$$[\![v_i]\!] = \begin{cases} [\![\alpha_{i,0}]\!] \cdot \prod_{j=1}^{\sigma} [\![r^j]\!]^{\alpha_{i,j}} & \text{if } i \in [1, \sigma], \\ [\![1]\!] & \text{if } i \in [\sigma+1, N]. \end{cases}$$

4. Each U_i generates random N-dimensional permutation π_i, and builds $P(\pi_i)$.
5. Each $U_{i=1 \mod 6}$ sends $[\![P_i]\!] = [\![P(\pi_i)]\!]$ to U_{i+1}.
6. For $k \in [2, 6]$ one by one: $U_{i=k \mod 6}$ receives $[\![P_{i-1}]\!]$ from U_{i-1}, computes $[\![P_i]\!] = [\![P_{i-1} \cdot P(\pi_i)]\!] = [\![P_{i-1}]\!]^{P(\pi_i)}$, rerandomizes the result and broadcasts it.
7. Users jointly run the unbound fan-in matrix multiplication subprotocol, computing combined permutation matrix $[\![P(\pi)]\!] = [\![\prod_{i=K}^{1} P_i]\!]$.
8. Users jointly run the secure matrix multiplication subprotocol and compute $[\![e]\!] = [\![P(\pi) \cdot v^T]\!]^T$.
9. Each $U_{i \leq N}$ computes $[\![d_i e_i]\!] = [\![e_i]\!]^{d_i}$ and broadcasts the result.
10. Users locally compute $[\![r]\!] = [\![\sum_{i=1}^{N} d_i e_i]\!] = \prod_{i=1}^{N} [\![d_i e_i]\!]$, and jointly run decryption to open r to $\mathcal{A}$.

Protocol $\mathcal{P}_3^A$. *GS with 3-rd group masking, semi-honest setting.*

4.2   Protocols for Malicious Setting

In this section we describe the protocols, which are secure in the malicious setting, where each party can violate the protocol and can participate in a coalition involving at most $K - 1$ user. Hence, in this settings we have one additional security requirement to thus stated in Section 4.1: the correctness of all computations done locally by parties should be publicly verified.

We use non-interactive zero-knowledge proofs for verifying correctness of local operations. When one party sends a proof, all receivers should verify its correctness. We also suppose that on each step of the protocols each party performs basic consistency checks for each processed values: validating that plaintext indeed lays in $\mathbb{Z}_n$, randomness in $\mathbb{Z}_n^*$, and cypertext in $\mathbb{Z}_{n^2}^*$. We omit these checks in the protocol descriptions.

We assume that in the case of detecting a protocol violation, the party aborts. Note that in the following protocols all data received by the users is sent through the broadcast channel. Hence, malicious parties cannot cause two honest users to receive different data. And consequently, if any honest user aborts due to a protocol violation, others will abort simultaneously. Note that if $\mathcal{A}$ is malicious, it can refuse to check the validity of data received from users, and thus an undetected protocol violation can occur. But as $\mathcal{A}$ receives data only on the last step of Protocols $\mathcal{P}_0^B$–$\mathcal{P}_3^B$, such violation cannot harm the privacy of the users.

Reference Protocol. Similarly to the previous settings, in the malicious settings we first present the protocol for reference group service implementation without using the group masking. The protocol is described in Protocol $\mathcal{P}_0^B$.

Input: Each $U_{i \leq N}$ holds his private value d_i.
Output: Party $\mathcal{A}$ receives $r = \sum_{i=1}^{N} d_i$.

1. Each $U_{i \leq N}$ broadcasts $[\![d_i]\!]$ together with $\Pi_{PK}([\![d_i]\!], \mathbb{F})$.
2. Each user computes $[\![r]\!] = \left[\!\left[\sum_{i=1}^{N} d_i\right]\!\right] = \prod_{i=1}^{N} [\![d_i]\!]$.
3. Each U_i runs partial decryption of $[\![r]\!]$ and sends resulting $D_i([\![r]\!])$ together with $\Pi_{CD}([\![r]\!], D_i([\![r]\!]), i)$ to $\mathcal{A}$. User U_1 additionally sends the value $[\![r]\!]$ to $\mathcal{A}$.

Protocol $\mathcal{P}_0^B$. *GS without group masking, malicious setting.*

Note that the additional transmission by U_1 on Step 2 is unavoidable, as for the verification of the proof $\Pi_{CD}([\![r]\!], D_i([\![r]\!]), i)$ submitted by U_i, $\mathcal{A}$ should known the value of all parameters, including $[\![r]\!]$.

Security, privacy and correctness of Protocol $\mathcal{P}_0^B$ can be verified as follows. On Step 1 no information about d_i can leak, because K-out-of-N threshold Paillier cryptosystem is semantically secure even against $K - 1$ colluding private key holders, and Π_{PK} is zero-knowledge. Broadcasted encryption $[\![d_i]\!]$ is proven to be formed correctly by $\Pi_{PK}([\![d_i]\!], \mathbb{F})$. On Step 2, all computations are done over encrypted data and thus are secure. Correctness of these computations are checked by $\mathcal{A}$ on Step 3: if value $[\![r]\!]$ computed by U_i is not equal to $[\![r]\!]$ available to $\mathcal{A}$, then $\mathcal{A}$ detects incorrectness of $\Pi_{CD}([\![r]\!], D_i([\![r]\!]), i)$. On Step 3, $\mathcal{A}$ learns $D_i([\![r]\!])$ and $\Pi_{CD}([\![r]\!], D_i([\![r]\!]), i)$, which reveals nothing about U_i's secret key due to security of threshold Paillier encryption and zero-knowledge of Π_{CD}. Correctness of the executed partial decryptions are verified by Π_{CD}. Hence, the protocol is secure and privacy-preserving in the malicious static setting.

Protocol with Group Masking Using Approach 1. Approach 1 requires the value e to have the following properties: $e \in_R \{0,1\}^N$ and exactly m its components are equal to 1.

To generate such e, we use an approach based on permutations. Users take the predefined vector

$$v = (\underbrace{1, \ldots, 1}_{m}, \overbrace{0, \ldots, 0}^{N-m})$$

and randomly permute it to produce e: $e = \pi(v)$. The permutation is done using the jointly random shuffling protocol introduced in Section 4.1.

The jointly random shuffling protocol should be adjusted to remain being secure in the malicious settings. We require each U_i publishing $[\![P(\pi_i)]\!]$ to provide NIZK proof of $P(\pi_i)$ correctness, named Π_{PMC}, which is described below. Furthermore, we prefer not to use t-speedup method, as it requires to employ complicated and computational intensive NIZK proofs of correctness of local rerandomized permutations of $N \times N$ matrices.

Recalling the example of permutation matrix in Equation (19), one can note that a permutation matrix is a zero-one matrix containing exactly one 1 in each column and row. As in practice $N < n$, this condition can be formalized for any permutation matrix $P(\pi_i)$, which elements are denoted by p_{kl}, as follows: $\forall k, l \in [1, N] p_{kl} \in \{0, 1\}$ and $\forall k \in [1, N] \sum_{l=1}^{N} p_{kl} = \sum_{l=1}^{N} p_{lk} = 1$. The feasibility of the first of these properties can be proved using existing technique introduced in [30] and denoted $\Pi_{BZO}([\![p_{11}]\!], \ldots, [\![p_{NN}]\!])$. To construct the proof for the second property note: if $\sum_{l=1}^{N} p_{kl} = 1$, then $\prod_{l=1}^{N} [\![p_{kl}]\!] = \left[\!\left[\sum_{l=1}^{N} p_{kl}\right]\!\right] = E(1, r_k) = gr_k^N \mod N^2 = c_k$ and only the user, who built an encryptions $[\![p_{kl}]\!] = E(p_{kl}, r_{kl})$, knows the value of $r_k = \prod_{l=1}^{N} r_{kl}$. This user can prove his knowledge by proving the knowledge of N-th root of $(c_k/g) = r_k^N \mod N^2$ using $\Pi_{RK}(\prod_{l=1}^{N} [\![p_{kl}]\!], N)$ introduced in [31].

To sum up, U_i can prove that $[\![P(\pi_i)]\!]$ is formed correctly using one invocation of Π_{BZO} and $2N$ invocations of Π_{RK}, all of which can be done in parallel and non-interactively. We denote this proof as $\Pi_{PMC}([\![P(\pi_i)]\!])$. It is straightforward that Π_{PMC} is zero-knowledge. The resulting protocol using this primitive is described in Protocol $\mathcal{P}_1^B$.

Security, privacy and correctness of Protocol $\mathcal{P}_1^B$ can be verified as follows. Correctness of $P(\pi_i)$ broadcasted on Step 1 is verified by Π_{PMC}, its privacy is

Input: Each $U_{i \leq N}$ holds his private value d_i.
Output: Party $\mathcal{A}$ receives $r = \sum_{i=1}^{N} d_i$.

1. Each U_i generates random N-dimensional permutation π_i, builds $P(\pi_i)$ and broadcasts its encryption $[\![P(\pi_i)]\!]$ together with $\Pi_{PMC}([\![P(\pi_i)]\!])$.
2. Users jointly run the unbound fan-in matrix multiplication subprotocol, computing combined permutation matrix $[\![P(\pi)]\!] = [\![\prod_{i=K}^{1} P(\pi_i)]\!]$.
3. Each $U_{i \leq N}$ locally multiplies $[\![P(\pi)]\!]$ with plaintext $v^T = (1, \ldots, 1, \overbrace{0, \ldots, 0}^{N-m})^T$ and

   $\underbrace{}_{m}$

   obtains $[\![e]\!]^T$.
4. Each $U_{i \leq N}$ computes $[\![d_i e_i]\!] = [\![e_i]\!]^{d_i}$ and broadcasts $[\![d_i]\!], [\![d_i e_i]\!], \Pi_{PK}([\![d_i]\!], \mathbb{F})$ and $\Pi_{CM}([\![d_i]\!], [\![e_i]\!], [\![d_i e_i]\!])$.
5. Each user computes $[\![r]\!] = [\![\sum_{i=1}^{N} d_i e_i]\!] = \prod_{i=1}^{N} [\![d_i e_i]\!]$.
6. Each U_i runs partial decryption of $[\![r]\!]$ and sends resulting $D_i([\![r]\!])$ together with $\Pi_{CD}([\![r]\!], D_i([\![r]\!]), i)$ to $\mathcal{A}$. U_1 additionally sends the value $[\![r]\!]$ to $\mathcal{A}$.

Protocol $\mathcal{P}_1^B$. *GS with 1-st group masking, malicious setting.*

preserved as Π_{PMC} is zero-knowledge and threshold Paillier encryption is semantically secure. Computations on Step 2 are secure, privacy-preserving and correct due to the corresponding properties of the unbound fan-in matrix multiplication subprotocol. Computations on Step 3 obviously do not leak any data. Their correctness is verified on Step 4: if U_i computes the different value of $[\![e_i]\!]$ than honest U_j, then U_j will not accept $\Pi_{CM}([\![d_i]\!], [\![e_i]\!], [\![d_i e_i]\!])$ as valid. Correctness of $[\![d_i e_i]\!]$ computed on Step 4 is verified using $\Pi_{CM}([\![d_i]\!], [\![e_i]\!], [\![d_i e_i]\!])$, the fact that used $[\![d_i]\!]$ is well-formed — by $\Pi_{PK}([\![d_i]\!], \mathbb{F})$.

Step-by-step verification of security, privacy and correctness of the other steps of the protocol is skipped here, as it can be done similarity to Protocol $\mathcal{P}_0^B$.

Protocol with Group Masking Using Approach 2. Approach 2 requires value e to have the following properties: $e \in_R \{0, 1\}^N$ and for all $i \in [1, N]$ $P(e_i=1) = p$.

To generate e_i with respect to the distribution above, we use the following technique: (i) users jointly generate N uniformly random $r_i \in [0, 2^k - 1]$; (ii) each e_i is computed as $e_i = r_i \overset{?}{<} \lceil 2^k p \rceil$. The value of k is publicly known and should be selected in a such way that relative error $\lceil 2^k p \rceil / (2^k p) - 1$ is negligible.

As r_i is a random number from $[0, 2^k - 1]$, it can be generated as k independent bits by employing the *random bit generation subprotocol* [29]. The comparison $(r_i \overset{?}{<} \lceil 2^k p \rceil)$ can be done using the *bitwise less-than subprotocol* from [32], which compares bit-decomposed number with publicly known constant. To use this subprotocol we should additionally restrict the value of k: $k < \log n - \log K - \kappa - 1$. In practice $\kappa = 80$ and n is 1024 bit length, and thus this restriction is satisfied when $k \leq 943 - \log N$.

The protocol based on the described technique and aforementioned subprotocols is given in Protocol $\mathcal{P}_2^B$. Its security, privacy and correctness are based on the corresponding properties of underlying cryptographic primitives and can be verified in the same way as for the previous protocols.

Input: Each $U_{i \leq N}$ holds his private value d_i.
Output: Party $\mathcal{A}$ receives $r = \sum_{i=1}^{N} d_i$.

1. Users jointly run the random bit generation subprotocol kN times in parallel and produce $[\![b_{1,0}]\!], \ldots, [\![b_{N,k-1}]\!]$, where each $b_{i,j} \in \{0,1\}$.
2. Users jointly run the bitwise less-than subprotocol N times in parallel, computing for each $i \in [1, N]$ value $[\![e_i]\!] = \left[\!\left[b_{i,k-1} \ldots b_{i,0} \overset{?}{<} \lceil 2^k p \rceil \right]\!\right]$.
3. Each $U_{i \leq N}$ computes $[\![d_i e_i]\!] = [\![e_i]\!]^{d_i}$ and broadcasts $[\![d_i]\!], [\![d_i e_i]\!], \Pi_{PK}([\![d_i]\!], \mathbb{F})$ and $\Pi_{CM}([\![d_i]\!], [\![e_i]\!], [\![d_i e_i]\!])$.
4. Each user computes $[\![r]\!] = \left[\!\left[\sum_{i=1}^{N} d_i e_i\right]\!\right] = \prod_{i=1}^{N} [\![d_i e_i]\!]$.
5. Each U_i runs partial decryption of $[\![r]\!]$ and sends resulting $D_i([\![r]\!])$ together with $\Pi_{CD}([\![r]\!], D_i([\![r]\!]), i)$ to $\mathcal{A}$. U_1 additionally sends the value $[\![r]\!]$ to $\mathcal{A}$.

Protocol $\mathcal{P}_2^B$. *GS with 2-nd group masking, malicious setting.*

Protocol with Group Masking Using Approach 3. Approach 3 requires value e to have the following properties: $e \in_R \{0,1\}^N$ and $\sum_{i=1}^{N} e_i$ is uniformly random in $[P(N), N]$.

To generate such e we use the same approach as in Protocol $\mathcal{P}_3^A$: (i) generate vector v with uniformly random number (greater or equal to $Q(N)$) of ones, using secure unary conversion subprotocol; (ii) shuffle v to produce e.

The protocol based on the described technique is stated in Protocol $\mathcal{P}_3^B$. Note that Steps 1–4 and Steps 5–6 can be executed in parallel to reduce an overall round complexity and execution time. We leave it to the reader to verify the security, privacy and correctness of the protocol.

5   Complexity Analysis

In this section we give the complexity of the protocols introduced in Section 4. We focus on three aspects of the performance of the protocols: number of interactive rounds executed, amount of data transferred through the network and the computational complexity of local operations executed by the parties.

The most computational intensive local operations are exponentiations in the cyphertext domain. In practice, the complexity of other operations can be considered as negligible comparing to exponentiation of a cyphertext, and thus, can be omitted from consideration while estimating the total local workload.

For the sake of simplicity, here we give only the asymptotic approximation for the number of executed exponentiations and transferred bits. Also we do not

---

Input: Each $U_{i \leq N}$ holds his private value d_i.
Output: Party $\mathcal{A}$ receives $r = \sum_{i=1}^{N} d_i$.

1. Users jointly run the bounded random value generation subprotocol and produce $[\![r]\!] : r \in \mathbb{Z}_{\sigma+1}$.
2. Users jointly run the prefix multiplication subprotocol, computing $([\![r^2]\!], \ldots, [\![r^\sigma]\!])$ from $[\![r]\!]$.
3. Each user computes vector $[\![w]\!]$:

$$\forall i \in [1, \sigma] \colon \ [\![w_i]\!] = [\![\alpha_{i,0}]\!] \cdot \prod_{j=1}^{\sigma} \left[\!\left[r^j\right]\!\right]^{\alpha_{i,j}}$$

   using common randomness for encrypting $[\![\alpha_{i,0}]\!]$.
4. Users set value $[\![v]\!]$:

$$[\![v]\!] = (\underbrace{[\![1]\!], \ldots, [\![1]\!]}_{P(N)}) \| [\![w]\!]$$

   using common randomness for encrypting $[\![1]\!]$.
5. Each U_i generates random N-dimensional permutation π_i, builds $P(\pi_i)$ and broadcasts its encryption $[\![P(\pi_i)]\!]$ together with $\Pi_{PMC}([\![P(\pi_i)]\!])$.
6. Users jointly run the unbound fan-in matrix multiplication subprotocol, computing combined permutation matrix $[\![P(\pi)]\!] = \left[\!\left[\prod_{i=K}^{1} P(\pi_1)\right]\!\right]$.
7. Users jointly run the secure matrix multiplication subprotocol and compute $[\![e]\!] = \left[\!\left[P(\pi) \cdot v^T\right]\!\right]^T$.
8. Each $U_{i \leq N}$ computes $[\![d_i e_i]\!] = [\![e_i]\!]^{d_i}$ and broadcasts $[\![d_i]\!], [\![d_i e_i]\!], \Pi_{PK}([\![d_i]\!], \mathbb{F})$ and $\Pi_{CM}([\![d_i]\!], [\![e_i]\!], [\![d_i e_i]\!])$.
9. Each user computes $[\![r]\!] = \left[\!\left[\sum_{i=1}^{N} d_i e_i\right]\!\right] = \prod_{i=1}^{N} [\![d_i e_i]\!]$.
10. Each U_i runs partial decryption of $[\![r]\!]$ and sends resulting $D_i([\![r]\!])$ together with $\Pi_{CD}([\![r]\!], D_i([\![r]\!]), i)$ to $\mathcal{A}$. U_1 additionally sends the value $[\![r]\!]$ to $\mathcal{A}$.

Protocol $\mathcal{P}_3^B$. *GS with 3-rd group masking, malicious setting.*

consider the workload and bandwidth that is required to create, transfer and verify the NIZK proofs employed through the protocols for the malicious setting, but consider only the number of invocations of these proofs.

The number of interactive rounds, executed exponentiations in the field $\mathbb{Z}_{n^2}^*$ and number of bits transferred through the network during an execution of Protocols $\mathcal{P}_0^A$–$\mathcal{P}_3^B$ are presented in Table 1. The number of invocations of different NIZK proofs during an execution of Protocols $\mathcal{P}_0^B$–$\mathcal{P}_3^B$ are presented in Table 2.

5.1 Possible Optimizations

The presented protocols are constant-round, i.e. the number of interactive rounds executed during each protocol run is constant and does not depend neither on system configuration nor on input data. This property is significant as in practice the round complexity affect on the overall system performance is crucial,

Table 1. Complexity of the protocols

	Number of rounds	Number of exponentiations	Number of bits transferred
Protocol $\mathcal{P}_0^A$	2	$O\left(N\right)$	$O\left(N\right)$
Protocol $\mathcal{P}_1^A$	10	$O\left(K^2 N \kappa \sqrt{m}\right)$	$O\left(K^2 N \kappa \sqrt{m}\right)$
Protocol $\mathcal{P}_2^A$	8	$O\left(K^2 N\right)$	$O\left(K^2 N\right)$
Protocol $\mathcal{P}_3^A$	22	$O\left(K^2 N^3\right)$	$O\left(K^2 N^2\right)$
Protocol $\mathcal{P}_0^B$	2	$O\left(N\right)$	$O\left(N\right)$
Protocol $\mathcal{P}_1^B$	9	$O\left(K^3 N^3\right)$	$O\left(K^2 N^2\right)$
Protocol $\mathcal{P}_2^B$	12	$O\left(K^2 N k\right)$	$O\left(K N k\right)$
Protocol $\mathcal{P}_3^B$	21	$O\left(K^3 N^3\right)$	$O\left(K^2 N^2\right)$

Table 2. Number of invocations of NIZK proofs in the protocols

	Π_{CD}	Π_{CM}	Π_{PK}	Π_{PMC}
Protocol $\mathcal{P}_0^B$	$O\left(K\right)$	0	$O\left(N\right)$	0
Protocol $\mathcal{P}_1^B$	$O\left(K^2 N^2\right)$	$O\left(K^2 N^3\right)$	$O\left(N\right)$	$O\left(K\right)$
Protocol $\mathcal{P}_2^B$	$O\left(K N k\right)$	$O\left(K N k\right)$	$O\left(K N\right)$	0
Protocol $\mathcal{P}_3^B$	$O\left(K^2 N^2\right)$	$O\left(K^2 N^3\right)$	$O\left(N + K \kappa\right)$	$O\left(K\right)$

and thus, proposed protocols can be used for settings with many users, with higher value of K and other parameters. Nevertheless, for the settings where only few users are involved, or where the security settings are relaxed (in terms that maximum number of user involved in each coalition $K - 1$ is smaller), protocols with lower communicational and computational complexities can be used: linear or logarithmic-round protocols.

For example, unbounded fan-in XOR subprotocol can be executed in $O\left(\log K\right)$ rounds, using the logarithmic-depth arithmetic circuits. Shuffling subprotocol can be executed in $O\left(K\right)$ rounds using mixnets [33].

Also note that presented protocols are designed for the general case of $K \leq N$, while for the settings with higher restrictions on maximum number of colluding users the more efficient solutions can be proposed. For example, when $K \leq N/2$, i.e. when there is no coalition involving the majority of the users, protocols based on the Shamir secret sharing [20] can be used.

Other possible approach for optimisations, is to reduce the users' workload by passing their duties to the separate service parties. It can be done, for example, by introducing service parties $\mathcal{B}_1, \ldots, \mathcal{B}_K$ such, that no more than $K - 1$ of them are colluding. It is clear, that in this settings Protocols $\mathcal{P}_0^A$–$\mathcal{P}_3^B$ can be carried by these service parties, while users only need to once pass their encrypted private data.

6   Conclusion

In this paper we propose a method to provide protection of user data processed by a group service in dynamic scenarios, which are more realistic than static ones for a wide range of applications. This method is realized using a set of cryptographic protocols, which are designed with performance in mind, offering the powerful privacy-protection tool for group services in two mostly addressed security settings. The protocols are shown to be correct, secure and privacy-preserving. The complexity analysis with respect to the versions in two attacker models clearly shows the advantages and disadvantages of the protocols in terms of computational and communication costs, and the level of privacy protection. Our protocols can be further used as building blocks for implementing privacy-preserving group services in a dynamic setting.

Acknowledgements. We would like to thank Sebastiaan de Hoogh for suggesting the t-speedup method for the shuffling subprotocol in Protocol $\mathcal{P}_3^A$. This publication was supported by the Dutch national program COMMIT.

References

1. McSherry, F., Mironov, I.: Differentially Private Recommender Systems: Building Privacy into the Netflix Prize Contenders. In: Elder IV, J.F., Fogelman-Soulié, F., Flach, P.A., Zaki, M.J. (eds.) KDD, pp. 627–636. ACM (2009)
2. Beye, M., Erkin, Z., Lagendijk, R.: Efficient privacy preserving K-means clustering in a three-party setting. In: IEEE International Workshop on Information Forensics and Security, WIFS, pp. 1–6. IEEE (2011)
3. Erkin, Z., Veugen, T., Toft, T., Lagendijk, R.: Generating Private Recommendations Efficiently Using Homomorphic Encryption and Data Packing. IEEE Transactions on Information Forensics and Security 7, 1053–1066 (2012)
4. Canny, J.: Collaborative filtering with privacy. In: IEEE Symposium on Security and Privacy, pp. 45–57. IEEE, IEEE Computer Society (2002)
5. Jagannathan, G., Pillaipakkamnatt, K., Wright, R.: A new privacy-preserving distributed k-clustering algorithm. In: Proceedings of the Sixth SIAM International Conference on Data Mining, pp. 492–496 (2006)
6. Resnick, P., Varian, H.R.: Recommender Systems - Introduction to the Special Section. Commun. ACM 40, 56–58 (1997)
7. Resnick, P., Kuwabara, K., Zeckhauser, R., Friedman, E.: Reputation systems. Commun. ACM 43, 45–48 (2000)
8. Kacprzyk, J.: Group decision making with a fuzzy linguistic majority. Fuzzy Sets and Systems 18, 105–118 (1986)
9. Mathes, A.: Folksonomies – cooperative classification and communication through shared metadata. Computer Mediated Communication 47 (2004)
10. Kargupta, H., Datta, S., Wang, Q., Sivakumar, K.: On the Privacy Preserving Properties of Random Data Perturbation Techniques. In: ICDM, pp. 99–106. IEEE Computer Society (2003)

11. Zhou, B., Pei, J., Luk, W.S.: A brief survey on anonymization techniques for privacy preserving publishing of social network data. SIGKDD Explorations 10, 12–22 (2008)

12. Yao, A.C.: Protocols for secure computations. In: Proceedings of the 23rd Annual IEEE Symposium on Foundations of Computer Science, pp. 160–164. IEEE Computer Society, Washington, DC (1982)

13. Steiner, M., Tsudik, G., Waidner, M.: CLIQUES: a new approach to group key agreement. In: Papazoglou, M.P., Takizawa, M., Kramer, B., Chanson, S. (eds.) ICDCS, pp. 380–387 (1998)

14. Wu, S., Chen, K.: An Efficient Key-Management Scheme for Hierarchical Access Control in E-Medicine System. Journal of Medical Systems 36, 2325–2337 (2012)

15. Xiao, X., Tao, Y.: M-invariance: towards privacy preserving re-publication of dynamic datasets. In: Proceedings of the 2007 ACM SIGMOD International Conference on Management of Data, pp. 689–700. ACM (2007)

16. Bu, Y., Fu, A.W.C., Wong, R.C.W., Chen, L., Li, J.: Privacy preserving serial data publishing by role composition. PVLDB 1, 845–856 (2008)

17. Bhagat, S., Cormode, G., Krishnamurthy, B., Divesh, S.: Prediction promotes privacy in dynamic social networks. In: Proceedings of the 3rd Conference on Online Social Networks, WOSN 2010, p. 6. USENIX Association, Berkeley (2010)

18. Fouque, P.-A., Poupard, G., Stern, J.: Sharing decryption in the context of voting or lotteries. In: Frankel, Y. (ed.) FC 2000. LNCS, vol. 1962, pp. 90–104. Springer, Heidelberg (2001)

19. Nishide, T., Sakurai, K.: Distributed Paillier Cryptosystem without Trusted Dealer. In: Chung, Y., Yung, M. (eds.) WISA 2010. LNCS, vol. 6513, pp. 44–60. Springer, Heidelberg (2011)

20. Shamir, A.: How to Share a Secret. Commun. ACM 22, 612–613 (1979)

21. Paillier, P.: Public-Key Cryptosystems Based on Composite Degree Residuosity Classes. In: Stern, J. (ed.) EUROCRYPT 1999. LNCS, vol. 1592, pp. 223–238. Springer, Heidelberg (1999)

22. Hazay, C., Lindell, Y.: Sigma Protocols and Efficient Zero-Knowledge. In: Efficient Secure Two-Party Protocols. Information Security and Cryptography, pp. 147–175. Springer, Heidelberg (2010)

23. Blum, M., Feldman, P., Micali, S.: Non-Interactive Zero-Knowledge and Its Applications (Extended Abstract). In: Simon, J. (ed.) STOC, pp. 103–112. ACM (1988)

24. Cramer, R., Damgård, I., Nielsen, J.B.: Multiparty Computation from Threshold Homomorphic Encryption. Cryptology ePrint Archive, Report 2000/055 (2000), http://eprint.iacr.org/2000/055

25. Cramer, R., Damgård, I., Nielsen, J.B.: Multiparty Computation from Threshold Homomorphic Encryption. In: Pfitzmann, B. (ed.) EUROCRYPT 2001. LNCS, vol. 2045, pp. 280–299. Springer, Heidelberg (2001)

26. Bar-Ilan, J., Beaver, D.: Non-cryptographic fault-tolerant computing in constant number of rounds of interaction. In: Proceedings of the Eighth Annual ACM Symposium on Principles of Distributed Computing, pp. 201–209. ACM (1989)

27. Davies, R.: Exclusive OR (XOR) and hardware random number generators (2002), http://www.robertnz.net/

28. Barker, E., Barker, W., Burr, W., Polk, W., Smid, M.: Recommendation for key management–part 1: General (revision 3). NIST special publication 800-57 (2012)

29. Damgård, I., Fitzi, M., Kiltz, E., Nielsen, J.B., Toft, T.: Unconditionally Secure Constant-Rounds Multi-party Computation for Equality, Comparison, Bits and Exponentiation. In: Halevi, S., Rabin, T. (eds.) TCC 2006. LNCS, vol. 3876, pp. 285–304. Springer, Heidelberg (2006)

30. Peng, K., Bao, F.: Efficient Vote Validity Check in Homomorphic Electronic Voting. In: Lee, P.J., Cheon, J.H. (eds.) ICISC 2008. LNCS, vol. 5461, pp. 202–217. Springer, Heidelberg (2009)
31. Guillou, L.C., Quisquater, J.-J.: A "Paradoxical" identity-based signature scheme resulting from zero-knowledge. In: Goldwasser, S. (ed.) CRYPTO 1988. LNCS, vol. 403, pp. 216–231. Springer, Heidelberg (1990)
32. Catrina, O., de Hoogh, S.: Improved Primitives for Secure Multiparty Integer Computation. In: Garay, J.A., De Prisco, R. (eds.) SCN 2010. LNCS, vol. 6280, pp. 182–199. Springer, Heidelberg (2010)
33. Chaum, D.: Untraceable Electronic Mail, Return Addresses, and Digital Pseudonyms. Commun. ACM 24, 84–88 (1981)

Privacy-Preserving Matching
of Community-Contributed Content

Mishari Almishari[1,*], Paolo Gasti[2], Gene Tsudik[3], and Ekin Oguz[3]

[1] King Saud University
[2] New York Institute of Technology
[3] University of California, Irvine

Abstract. Popular consumer review sites, such as Yelp and Tripadvisor, are based upon massive amounts of voluntarily contributed content. Sharing of data among different review sites can offer certain benefits, such as more customized service and better-targeted advertisements. However, business, legal and ethical issues prevent review site providers from sharing data in bulk.

This paper investigates how two parties can *privately compare* their review datasets. It presents a technique for two parties to determine which (or how many) users have contributed to both review sites. This is achieved based only upon review content, rather than personally identifying information (PII). The proposed technique relies on extracting certain key features from textual reviews, while the privacy-preserving user matching protocol is built using additively homomorphic encryption and garbled circuit evaluation. Experimental evaluation shows that the proposed technique offers highly accurate results with reasonable performance.

1 Introduction

On-line social networks (OSNs) are a valuable resource for untold masses who rely on them in both personal or professional aspects of everyday life, including: sharing personal content [2,4], broadcasting pithy "news" messages to others with similar interests [7], finding jobs or identifying job candidates [5], planning travel [6], and assessing businesses (stores, restaurants, services) [8] or products [1]. A typical OSN provides the framework wherein volunteers contribute virtually all available content. Within this framework, users generally reveal – often unwittingly – tremendous amounts of personal information, including habits and tastes. This information is very valuable for quickly detecting trends and serving timely targeted advertisements [3].

Community-based review sites form a specific class of OSNs. Well-known examples are yelp.com, tripadvisor.com and amazon.com. On these sites, users read and contribute reviews expressing their opinions on different products, services and businesses. Users can also discover other groups or individuals with

---

* Work performed while at University of California, Irvine.

J. Crampton, S. Jajodia, and K. Mayes (Eds.): ESORICS 2013, LNCS 8134, pp. 443–462, 2013.
© Springer-Verlag Berlin Heidelberg 2013

similar interests. In recent years, such sites have become very popular. For example, yelp.com received 78 million unique monthly visitors, on average, in the second quarter of 2012 [9]. Also, in 2012, yelp.com users have contributed more than 30 million reviews [9].

The most valuable asset of community-based review sites is user-generated content. It is perceived to be unbiased and represents the main reason for attracting multitudes of people to sites like yelp.com or tripadvisor.com. While review sites are happy to let anyone – including casual users without accounts – read individual reviews, they zealously guard *bulk* user content. To this end, they usually employ both technical and legal (e.g., terms of service [10]) measures to prevent bulk access and large-scale content harvesting.

We believe that sharing user-related information across sites could be beneficial to review sites themselves as well as their users. Various sites have access to information concerning different aspects of public and private lives of their users. Knowing which users belong to multiple sites would allow the latter to provide better service or better-targeted ads, e.g., a travel site could highlight gastronomic destinations for users who contributed to a restaurant review site, or a product-oriented site might advertise ski gear for users who reviewed mountain resorts on a travel site.

This paper makes the following contributions:

1. We construct a technique that identifies common users across two review sites by comparing user-generated content, rather than user names or IDs. (In general, IDs are problematic because users tend not to use consistent identifiers across sites. Furthermore, imposing, incentivizing or enforcing consistent identification/naming is very difficult.)
2. We show how to efficiently implement the proposed technique *with privacy*, such that one of the two sites learns *only* which (or how many) users belong to both, while the other learns nothing. Furthermore, this is achieved with a high degree of accuracy.

Previous literature [12,43] shows that sets of anonymous reviews can be linked by merely relying on simple textual features. However, these prior techniques require at least one of the parties to reveal all of its reviews or their compact representation. Our work explores new and more sophisticated textual features, and provides the first privacy-preserving approach for efficiently computing user similarity.

Our work also helps mitigate so-called *review spam* [35], which involves creating fake reviews, with the intent to over-promote or defame a product or a service. Fake reviews appear as if generated by legitimate users and are therefore hard to identify. We anticipate that detection of suspected spammers' accounts would be a useful service. One way to implement this service is as follows: one site with the expertise in detecting spammer accounts accumulates a set of confirmed spammers along with their content. It then runs our protocols with any other site that has a set of its own suspected spammers. As a result, the latter obtains a list of confirmed spammers.

Organization: Related work is summarized in Section 2. Our review matching algorithm (without privacy) is introduced in Section 3. Next, cryptographic preliminaries are discussed in Section 4, followed by our privacy-preserving matching protocols in Sections 5 and 6. Then, protocol performance is assessed in Section 7 and Section 8 concludes the paper. Security analysis can be found in Appendix A.

2   Related Work

Most related work falls into two categories: (1) authorship identification and (2) privacy-preserving protocols. The former offers a number of results showing that authorship linkage based on textual (stylometric) features is feasible and sometimes very effective. The latter yields numerous cryptographic techniques for privately computing certain set operations and similarity measures.

2.1   Authorship Identification and Linkage

Most prior work on this topic deals with free-style text, such as news reports, scripts, novels, essays and diaries. This is motivated by the recent increase in scholastic, academic and regular literary plagiarism.

A number of techniques have been explored to identify common authorship. For example, Narayanan et al. [43] conducted a large-scale author identification study of anonymous blogs using stylometric features. A number of features were extracted and used in training classifiers that recognized authors based on their writing style. A set of $100,000$ blog authors was used to evaluate proposed techniques. Accuracy of up to 80% was obtained.

A more recent result [12] shows how to link reviews authored by the same person. One de-anonymization technique was based on constructing a Naïve Bayesian (NB) model [39] for every user and then mapping each set of anonymous reviews to the corresponding user with the highest probability. The second technique was based on the symmetric Kullback-Leibler (KL) divergence distance function [14]. With KL, the user whose reviews have the shortest distance to anonymous reviews is labeled as the original author. This demonstrates that anonymous review sets (at least, for prolific reviewers) by same author can be linked with very high probability. Moreover, distribution of digram (two-letter) tokens is very effective in determining similarity among review sets.

There have been other interesting authorship analysis studies. Notably, [32] proposed a technique that extracts frequent pattern write-prints that distinguish an author. Accuracy reached 88% using a single anonymous message. The study in [11] explored author identification and similarity detection by using stylistic features, based on Karhunen-Loeve transform to obtain write-prints. Accuracy reached 91% in identifying the author of anonymous text from a set of 100 authors. Results indicate the feasibility of linking bodies of text authored by the same person. A comprehensive survey of authorship identification and attribution studies can be found in [48].

2.2   Privacy-Preserving Protocols

There is extensive literature on secure multi-party computation. Starting from the seminal work on garbled circuit evaluation [51,28], it has been shown that any function can be securely evaluated by representing it as a boolean circuit. Similar results exist for secure evaluation of any function using secret sharing techniques, e.g., [46], or homomorphic encryption, e.g., [20].

Recent results on garbled circuits provide optimizations that reduce computation and communication overheads associated with circuit construction and evaluation. Kolesnikov and Schneider [38] described an optimization that permits XOR gates to be evaluated for free, i.e., without communication normally associated with such gates and without involving any cryptographic functions. This optimization is possible when the hash function used for creating garbled gates is correlation-robust under the definition in [19]. Under similar assumptions, Pinkas et al. [45] provided a mechanism for reducing communication complexity of binary gates by 25%: each gate can be specified by encoding only three outcomes of the gate instead of four. Finally, [37] improved complexity of certain common operations, such as addition, multiplication, and comparison, by reducing the number of non-XOR gates.

In recent years, a number of tools have been developed for automatically creating a secure protocol from its function description written in a high-level language. Examples include Fairplay [41], VIFF [24] and TASTY [31]. However, "custom" optimized protocols for specific applications are often much more efficient than such general techniques.

There are also a number of results in privacy-preserving set operations, e.g., private set intersection (PSI) [27,36,29,30,34,25] and cardinality-only PSI (PSI-CA) [21]. The work in [34] introduced a PSI protocol based on oblivious pseudorandom functions (OPRFs) secure in the malicious model. This protocol incurs linear complexity in size of combined client/server inputs and it is secure under the One-More Gap Diffie-Hellman assumption. In [21], a very efficient, also OPRF-based, PSI-CA protocol is constructed offering linear complexity in the size of server and client inputs. Its security, in the semi-honest model, is based on the DDH assumption.

As mentioned in Section 1, although PSI and PSI-CA offer functionalities similar to those required to determine common authors across multiple review sites, *noisy* nature of features extracted from reviews prevents the use of such tools. Whereas, privacy-preserving protocols in [16] are more relevant to our context of review matching. In particular, [16] shows how to efficiently and privately approximate the computation of Jaccard index [49] using minhash techniques [17]. This approach is effective to compare text in order to detect plagiarism or enforce copyright.

3   Review Matching

Contributors to a review site are referred to, and are known by, their user-names, unique per site. As mentioned in Section 1, relying solely on user-names to determine common users across sites is problematic, since identical user-names on different sites may not correspond to the same user. Conversely, the same person may select distinct user-names on different sites. Similarly, relying on the user's real identity for matching may not be viable, since users may not be willing to disclose any personal information.

Let C (client) and S (server) denote two mutually suspicious review sites. Each site has access to a collection of reviews, partitioned by user. Let $U_C = \{C_1, C_2, \ldots, C_v\}$ denote the set of users that of C, and $U_S = \{S_1, S_2, \ldots, S_w\}$ – the set of users of S. R_{C_i} and R_{S_i} refer to the set of reviews authored by C_i and S_i, respectively. $C's$ goal is to learn privately (i.e., without disclosing the content of reviews associated with its users) one of the following: **Common Users**, denoted as $\Psi = U_C \cap U_S$, or **Number of Common Users** ($|\Psi|$). Notation is summarized in Table 1.

Table 1. Notation

v	Number of users at C	$\hat{\Psi}$	Common users computed by the matching algorithm
w	Number of users at S	er	Error rate
U_C	Users of C	rr	Recall rate
U_S	Users of S	ε	Matching threshold
Ψ	Common users ($U_C \cap U_S$)	mr	matching user approximation error
X_i	Feature vector computed from C_i's reviews	Y_j	feature vector computed from S_j' reviews
C_i	user at C	S_j	user at S
R_{C_i}	set of reviews authored by C_i	R_{S_j}	set of reviews authored by S_j

In this section, we construct a technique for computing Ψ and $|\Psi|$ *without privacy*. We then add privacy features in Sections 5 and 6.

3.1 Matching Process Overview

To find common users, we need to determine similarity between two sets of reviews. We consider C_i and S_j as corresponding to the same user if their corresponding review sets are very similar. One way to assess similarity is to use a distance function. This works as follows: from each user review set, extract a number of features and represent them as a vector. Let $X = feat(\cdot)$ be a feature extraction function that takes as input a set of reviews and returns the associated feature vector X. Let $d = D(\cdot, \cdot)$ be a distance function that takes as input two feature vectors and outputs a value $d \geq 0$. Informally, 0 indicates that two inputs are identical, and the larger the d, the more different they are. We say that two feature vectors X, Y (and their corresponding review sets) are *similar* if $D(X, Y) \leq \varepsilon$, for some value ε.

Each protocol party computes a feature vector per user resulting in a set of feature vectors $\mathcal{X} = \{X_1, \ldots, X_v\}$ for C and $\mathcal{Y} = \{Y_1, \ldots, Y_w\}$ for S, where $X_i = feat(R_{C_i})$, and $Y_i = feat(R_{S_i})$. Let X_i and Y_j be the feature vectors corresponding to reviews of users C_i and S_j, respectively. We approximate *Common Users* and *Number of Common Users* as: **Matching Users**, defined as

$\widehat{\Psi} = \{C_i \in U_C \mid \exists S_j \in U_S \text{ s.t. } D(X_i, Y_j) \leq \varepsilon\}$ and **Number of Matching Users**, defined as $|\widehat{\Psi}|$. Clearly, approximation accuracy depends on specific properties of the features being considered and on the distance function D.

There are several distance functions that have been shown to provide good results on textual documents retrieval, including Cosine, Jaccard, and Euclidean distances [13]. We rely on Euclidean distance. Our experiments (see Section 3.3) confirm that it is a sensible choice for review similarity. Euclidean distance between vectors $X = \{x_1, \ldots, x_\ell\}$ and $Y = \{y_1, \ldots, y_\ell\}$ is defined as:

$$D'(X, Y) = \sqrt{\sum_{i=1}^{\ell}(x_i - y_i)^2}$$

For technical reasons, in the rest of the paper, we consider D to be *squared euclidean distance*, i.e., $D(X, Y) = (D'(X, Y))^2$. We acknowledge that other distance functions may offer different, and possibly better, accuracy results. We leave evaluation of other distance functions to future work.

3.2   Dataset: Training and Testing Settings

To assess accuracy of our review matching technique, we rely on approximately 1 million reviews from $1,997$ users of yelp.com.[1] We define two metrics that capture two performance aspects of review matching process:

1. Recall Ratio (rr) – measures $\widehat{\Psi}$'s coverage of Ψ: $rr = |\widehat{\Psi} \cap \Psi|/|\Psi|$.
2. Error Ratio (er) – measures how often an element not in Ψ is included in $\widehat{\Psi}$:

$$er = \frac{|\{(C_i, S_j) \text{ s.t. } C_i \neq S_j \text{ and } D(X_i, Y_j) \leq \varepsilon\}|}{|\{(C_i, S_j) \text{ s.t. } C_i \neq S_j\}|}$$

We divide users (along with their reviews) into two distinct sets of nearly the same size: Tr and Te, used for training and testing purposes, respectively. We use Tr to determine a set of features and a threshold ε that maximize rr while keeping er low. We then check how these parameters perform over Te. We emphasize that no data from Te is used to select any parameters.

For every user in Tr, we randomly split its reviews into two parts. Let Tr_C and Tr_S represent first and second half of each user's reviews. Based on Tr_C and Tr_S, we build two sets of feature vectors P_C^{Tr} and P_S^{Tr}. We then select ε as follows: First, we compute the distance between all pairs of feature vectors from P_C^{Tr} and P_S^{Tr}. Then, we vary rr from (0%-100%] by selecting different values for ε. For each ε, we measure corresponding er. Finally, we select ε that yields the best trade-off between rr and er.[2]

---

[1] Experiments were performed on the same dataset used in [12].

[2] Ideally, evaluation of our technique would be performed on two or more datasets from different sites, which share a *correctly identified* subset of users. However, we are not aware of the existence of such a dataset. Therefore, we rely on partitioning reviews from each user into two sets.

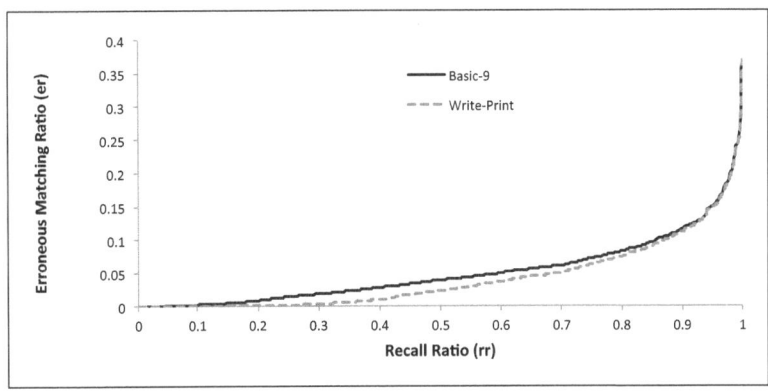

Fig. 1. Error and recall ratio of Write-Print and Basic-9

3.3 Feature Sets

Proper selection of features is crucial for achieving high accuracy. We now assess different feature sets and determine the combination that offers the best performance.

Write-Prints and Basic-9 Features. We first examine two standard feature sets: Basic-9 [18] and Write-Print [11]. The former consists of 9 features that measure different textual characteristics, e.g., number of unique words used in a review set and its ratio to the total number of words. These features have been shown to be effective in identifying authors of anonymous texts [18]. Write-Print is a set of static and dynamic features that fall into five groups: lexical, syntactic, structural, content and idiosyncratic. It is highly effective in identifying authors, as shown in [11]. We use the implementation of both feature sets from JStylo ([42]), a stylometric java-based library.[3]

Figure 1 shows rr and er values on Tr for various ε values, as described in Section 3.2, using either Basic-9 or Write-Print. Results in Figure 1 show that, regardless of ε, features we consider do not allow us to achieve high rr and low er. Thus, we explore different feature sets.

Character n-gram. *n-grams* (n consecutive characters in a text fragment) are a well-known feature that have been extensively used in textual analysis. We experiment with n-gram feature sets for n = 2 (digrams) and n = 3 (trigrams). As shown in [12], digrams are very effective in identifying review authors. N-gram feature vectors for sets of reviews are constructed as follows: each array element labeled with a given n-gram represents frequency of occurrence of this n-gram in a user's review set.

---

[3] JStylo implements a partial set of Write-Print features that amounts to 22 feature categories.

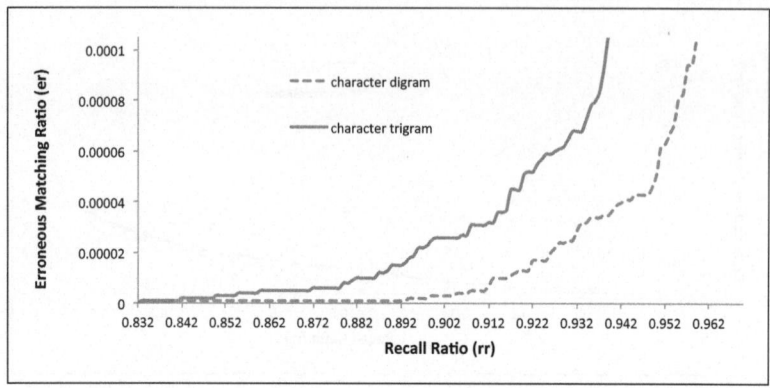

Fig. 2. Error and recall ratio of character digram and trigram

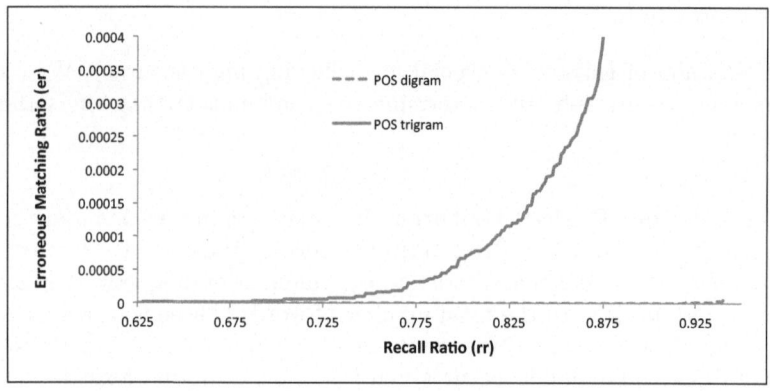

Fig. 3. Error and recall ratio of POS digrams and trigrams

Figure 2 shows rr and er results using digrams and trigrams. Digrams show better performance compared to Write-Prints and Basic-9 features. For example, for $rr = 95\%$, $er = 5.11 \cdot 10^{-5}$ with digrams and $2.01 \cdot 10^{-4}$ with trigrams.

Part-Of-Speech (POS) Tagging. Part-Of-Speech (POS) tagging involves mapping words to parts of speech, e.g., noun or verb. The idea is that different individuals write using distinct grammatical structures and choose different words. We rely on digram and trigram versions of POS tags (2 or 3 consecutive parts of speech tags) and use Stanford POS Maxent Tagger [50] to label each word with one of 45 possible POS tags. We assign weights to POS features similarly to character n-grams.

Figure 3 shows performance results of POS features. Clearly, digrams outperform trigrams: for example, with $rr = 95\%$, the corresponding $er = 7.01 \cdot 10^{-6}$ digrams and $6 \cdot 10^{-3}$ with trigrams.

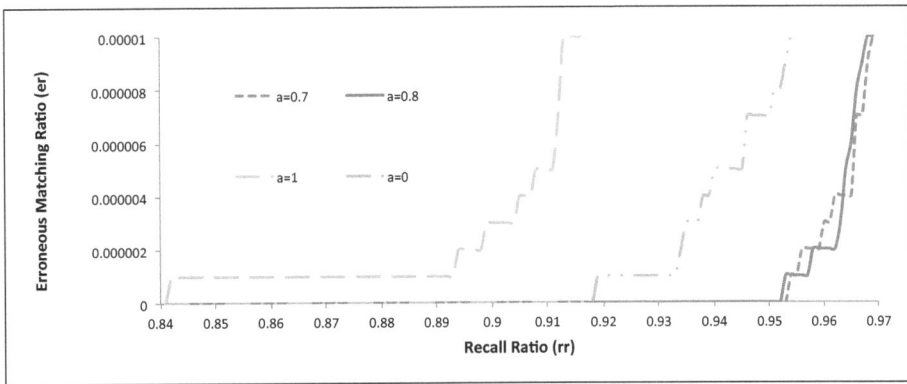

Fig. 4. error and recall ratio of combining character and POS digrams

Combining Character and POS n-grams. Since character and POS digram feature sets offer good performance, we explore ways to combine them to further improve matching accuracy. In particular, we use a simple weighted average technique, i.e.:

$$D_{combined}(X,Y) = (a) \times D_{character\_digram}(X,Y) + (1-a) \times D_{POS\_digram}(X,Y)$$

We vary a from 0 to 1 (in 0.1 increments) to determine impact on rr and er.

With our training dataset, values of a between 0.7 and 0.8 lead to $er < 10^{-5}$. There are two reasons for limiting er this way: (1) $er \approx 10^{-5}$ is relatively high and could lead to poor approximation of Ψ when v, w are very large[4], and (2) for our dataset, there is no a value that gives better performance over the full range of rr.

Figure 4 summarizes the experiments. Combining character and POS digram features yields increased matching accuracy. Since $a = 0.7$ and $a = 0.8$ provide roughly the same performance, we pick $a = 0.7$. We choose ε that yeilds $rr = 95.3\%$ and $er = 0\%$ in Tr. We test selected ε on Te and the results are virtually identical ($rr = 95.5\%$ and $er = 0\%$). Note that, when selecting the threshold, we choose ε such that it maximizes rr, while keeping $er = 0\%$ to reduce inaccuracy of approximating Ψ incurred by larger er values.

When combining character and POS digrams, the resulting feature set size contains $2,701$ features: the former contribute 676 (26^2) and the latter – 2025 (45^2) features. Even both digram types are a subset of Write-Print features, they perform significantly better than the entire Write-Print feature set; see Figure 1.

3.4   Approximation Error

Though er and rr represent good metrics for determining accuracy of matching algorithms, they do not offer easy-to-interpret information for the *number*

---

[4] Note that the number of errors grows proportionally to $v \cdot w$.

of *matching users* algorithm. We therefore define matching user approximation error (mr) as:

$$mr = \frac{abs(|\widehat{\Psi}| - |\Psi|)}{|\Psi|}$$

Since our choice for ε leads to $er = 0\%$, mr mainly depends on rr. Given our accuracy results, $|\widehat{\Psi}| = rr \cdot |\Psi|$. Thus, $mr = 1 - rr$, i.e., $mr < 5\%$. This shows that our review matching technique closely approximates Ψ with $\widehat{\Psi}$.

4   Cryptographic Preliminaries

Security Model. We use the standard model for secure two-party computation in the presence of semi-honest (also known as honest-but-curious) participants. In this model, participants follow prescribed protocol behavior, while trying to learn or infer additional information beyond that obtained during normal protocol execution. A protocol is considered secure in the semi-honest model if the view of protocol execution for each party is computationally indistinguishable from the view simulated using that party's input and output only. This means that protocol execution does not reveal any additional information to participants. A more formal definition is as follows:

Definition 1. *Suppose participants P_1 and P_2 run a protocol π that computes function $f(\text{in}_1, \text{in}_2) = (\text{out}_1, \text{out}_2)$, where in_i and out_i denote P_i's input and output, respectively. Let $\text{VIEW}_\pi(P_i)$ denote P_i's view during the execution of π. It is formed by P_i's input, internal random coin tosses r_i, and messages $m_1, \ldots, m_t$ passed between parties during execution:*

$$\text{VIEW}_\pi(P_i) = (\text{in}_i, r_i, m_1, \ldots, m_t).$$

We say that π is secure in the semi-honest model, if for each P_i, there exists a probabilistic polynomial time simulator S_i such that

$$\{S_i(\text{in}_i, f_i(\text{in}_1, \text{in}_2))\} \equiv \{\text{VIEW}_\pi(P_i), \text{out}_i\},$$

where "$\equiv$" denotes computational indistinguishability.

Homomorphic Encryption. Our protocols require existence of a semantically secure additively homomorphic encryption scheme. In such a scheme, $\text{Enc}(m_1) \cdot \text{Enc}(m_2) = \text{Enc}(m_1 + m_2)$, and, therefore, $\text{Enc}(m)^a = \text{Enc}(a \cdot m)$. While any such scheme (e.g., Paillier [44]) would suffice, the construction by Damgård et al. [23,22] (DGK) is of particular interest here.

DGK was designed to work with small plaintext spaces and has shorter ciphertext size than other similar schemes. A DGK public key consists of: (i) a small (possibly prime) integer u that defines plaintext space, (ii) a k-bit RSA modulus $N = pq$ where p and q are $k/2$-bit primes, such that, if v_p and v_q are t-bit primes, and $uv_p|(p-1)$ and $uv_q|(q-1)$, and (iii) elements $g, h \in \mathbb{Z}_N^*$ such that g has order uv_pv_q and h has order v_pv_q. Given a message $m \in \mathbb{Z}_u$, encryption is performed as: $\text{Enc}(m) = g^m h^r \bmod N$, where $r \leftarrow \{0, 1\}^{2.5t}$.

Homomorphic-Based Comparison. Our protocols rely on privacy-preserving comparison to determine whether the distance between two feature vectors is below a threshold. Such a distance (d) is computed in the encrypted domain by the server, and compared (also in its encrypted form) with threshold ε.

We base our comparison protocol on that of Erkin et al. [26]. It relies on the observation that $d < \varepsilon$ is true iff the l-th bit of $a = 2^l + d - \varepsilon$ is 1 (for $0 <= d, \epsilon < 2^l$). Given $\mathsf{Enc}(d)$, encryption of a is computed by S as $\mathsf{Enc}(a) = \mathsf{Enc}(2^l) \cdot \mathsf{Enc}(d) \cdot \mathsf{Enc}(\varepsilon)^{-1}$. Encryption of the l-th bit of a is then: $\mathsf{Enc}(a_l) = \mathsf{Enc}(2^{-l} \cdot (a - (a \bmod 2^l)))$. Value a is available to S only in encrypted form, and computing $a \bmod 2^l$ in the encrypted domain requires interaction between C and S:

> S "masks" $\mathsf{Enc}(a)$ by selecting a random r and computing $\mathsf{Enc}(\hat{a}) = \mathsf{Enc}(a) \cdot \mathsf{Enc}(r)$. Then, S sends $\mathsf{Enc}(\hat{a})$ to C, who decrypts it and returns the encryption of $c = \hat{a} \bmod 2^l$ to S. Next, S "unmasks" $\mathsf{Enc}(c)$ by computing $\mathsf{Enc}(c) \cdot \mathsf{Enc}(r)^{-1} = \mathsf{Enc}(a \bmod 2^l)$.

5   Privacy-Preserving Computation of Matching List

We now present a protocol for Privacy-Preserving Computation of Matching List (PPCML). It involves two participants: C and S. At the end, C learns the set of users in its input that match those in S's input, while S learns nothing. For simplicity's sake, we represent C's input as a single feature vector, corresponding to one user, while S's input is a set of w feature vectors, from w users. This protocol can be trivially extended to the case where both parties input a *set* of feature vectors.

Weighted Average. As discussed in Section 3.3, we use a weighted average distance function $D_{combined}$ with $a = 0.7$. $D_{combined}$ can be also computed as a square Euclidean distance function between a feature vector for user in C and a user in S. This is done by updating the weights of the feature vector by multiplying all digram feature weights by $\sqrt{a}$, and all POS digram feature weights by $\sqrt{1-a}$.

Scaling. Since our protocol can only process integer vectors, we first need to scale values in feature vectors from the domain $[0,1] \subset \mathbb{R}$ to $[0,10^h] \subset \mathbb{N}$ by multiplying all features by 10^h for some h. Intuitively, larger h allows for better precision. However, the number of bits required to represent values in $[0,10^h]$ – and therefore the cost of our protocol – increases with h. Our experiments showed that $h = 4$ provides a reasonable tradeoff between cost and accuracy. With this scaling, we obtain a scaled ε value that gives exactly the same rr and er as the non-scaled version in both Tr and Te. Moreover, we determined that using $h > 4$ does not improve precision and recall significantly.

Protocol Input:
C: feature vector $X = (x_1, \ldots, x_\ell)$ and key-pair (pk, sk).
S: $\mathcal{Y} = \{Y_1, \ldots, Y_w\}$ where $Y_m = (y_{m,1}, \ldots, y_{m,\ell})$, for $0 < m \le w$ is a feature vector.

Protocol Output:
C: 1, if Euclidean distance between X and any vector in $\mathcal{Y}$ is below ε,[5] and 0
  otherwise.
S: nothing.

Protocol Steps:
1. For $i = 1, \ldots, \ell$, C computes $\{\langle \mathsf{Enc}(x_i), \mathsf{Enc}(x_i^2) \rangle\}$ and sends results to S.
2. For $m = 1, \ldots, w$ and $j = 1, \ldots, \ell$, S computes $\{\mathsf{Enc}(y_{m,j}^2)\}$.
3. For $m = 1, \ldots, w$, S computes encrypted square Euclidean distance between
   X and Y_m as:

$$\mathsf{Enc}(d_m) = \mathsf{Enc}\left(\sum_{i=1}^{\ell}(x_i - y_{m,i})^2\right) = \prod_{i=1}^{\ell}\left(\mathsf{Enc}(x_i^2)\mathsf{Enc}(y_{m,i}^2)\mathsf{Enc}(x_i)^{(-2y_{m,i})}\right)$$

4. For each $m = 1, \ldots, w$, S and C invoke an instance of the privacy-preserving
   comparison protocol [26] to determine whether $d_m < \varepsilon^2$, i.e., S learns $\mathsf{Enc}(\delta_m)$,
   where $\delta_m = 1$ iff $d_m < \varepsilon^2$.
5. S computes $\mathsf{Enc}(\alpha) = \prod_{m=1}^{w} \mathsf{Enc}(\delta_m)$. Note that α represents the number of
   vectors in $\mathcal{Y}$ for which square Euclidean distance from X is less than ε^2.
6. S returns $u = \mathsf{Enc}(\alpha)^r = \mathsf{Enc}(\alpha \cdot r)$, where r is a random element chosen
   uniformly from the message space (except 0).
7. C computes $z = \mathsf{Dec}(u) = \alpha \cdot r$. If $z \neq 0$, C outputs 1; otherwise it outputs 0.

Although there are techniques for computing square roots using secure multi-party computation, e.g., [40], their performance is quite below par for our application. Fortunately, comparison of Euclidean distance with ε can be performed without computing any square roots, by comparing ε with the square of Euclidean distance (see Step 4).

In practice, C's input would contain multiple feature vectors. C can simply run the protocol multiple times – once per input vector. Security of the protocol would be unaffected, except that S would learn the upper bound on the number of vectors in C's input.

In the rest of paper, we use the term PPCML to refer to the combination of (possibly) multiple instance of the protocol above, one per feature vector of C. Security analysis of the protocol sketched out above is provided in Appendix A.

6   Privacy-Preserving Computation of Matching List Size

We now extend PPCML by restricting C's knowledge to the number of users that occur in both C and S, i.e., we obtain Privacy-Preserving Computation of Matching List *Size* (S-PPCML). In this protocol, each party's input is a set of feature vectors. C learns the matching list (set intersection) size while S only learns the upper bound on the number of C's users.

---

[5] The protocol implements $D(X, Y) \overset{?}{<} \varepsilon$ instead of $D(X, Y) \overset{?}{\leq} \varepsilon$ as defined in Section
  3.1. In our setting, $(D(X, Y) \overset{?}{\leq} \varepsilon) = (D(X, Y) \overset{?}{<} \varepsilon')$ for $\varepsilon' = \varepsilon + 1$.

Protocol Input:

C: set of feature vectors $\mathcal{X} = \{X_1, \ldots, X_v\}$, with $X_n = (x_{n,1}, \ldots, x_{n,\ell})$ and key pair (pk, sk).

S: set $\mathcal{Y} = \{Y_1, \ldots, Y_w\}$ where $Y_m = (y_{m,1}, \ldots, y_{m,\ell})$ is a feature vector.

Protocol Output:

C: number of feature vectors $X_n \in \mathcal{X}$ with Euclidean distance less than ε for at least one vector from $\mathcal{Y}$; i.e., $|\widehat{\Psi}|$.

S: nothing.

Protocol Steps:

1. For each $n = 1, \ldots, v$ and $i = 1, \ldots, \ell$, C computes $\{\langle \mathsf{Enc}(x_{n,i}), \mathsf{Enc}(x_{n,i}^2) \rangle\}$ and sends them to S.
2. For each $m = 1, \ldots, w$ and $j = 1, \ldots, \ell$, S computes $\{\mathsf{Enc}(y_{m,j}^2)\}$.
3. For each $n = 1, \ldots, v$ and $m = 1, \ldots, w$, S computes encrypted square Euclidean distance between X_n and Y_m as

$$\mathsf{Enc}(d_{n,m}) = \mathsf{Enc}\left(\sum_{i=1}^{\ell}(x_{n,i} - y_{m,i})^2\right) = \prod_{i=1}^{\ell}\left(\mathsf{Enc}(x_{n,i}^2)\mathsf{Enc}(y_{m,i}^2)\mathsf{Enc}(x_{n,i})^{(-2y_{m,i})}\right)$$

4. For each $n = 1, \ldots, v$ and $m = 1, \ldots, w$, S and C interact in a privacy-preserving manner to compare $\mathsf{Enc}(d_{n,m})$ against ε^2; S learns $\mathsf{Enc}(\delta_{n,m})$, where $\delta_{n,m} = 1$ iff $d_{n,m} < \varepsilon^2$.
5. For each $n = 1, \ldots, v$, S computes $\mathsf{Enc}(\alpha_n) = \prod_{m=1}^{w} \mathsf{Enc}(\delta_{nm})$. Note that α_n represents the number of vectors in $\mathcal{Y}$ that fall within ε of X_n.
6. For each $n = 1, \ldots, v$, S and C interact in a privacy-preserving manner to compare $\mathsf{Enc}(\alpha_n)$ to 0. Let β be the outcome of this comparison – i.e., $(\beta_n = 1)$ iff $(\alpha_n > 0)$; S learns $\mathsf{Enc}(\beta_n)$.
7. S computes $\mathsf{Enc}(\gamma) = \prod_{n=1}^{v} \mathsf{Enc}(\beta_n)$ and sends it to C.
8. C decrypts and outputs γ, which corresponds to the number of users it shares with S.

6.1   Protocol Optimizations: AS-PPCML

We now discuss some optimizations.

Dataset-Dependent Optimizations. The goal of Step 6 in the S-PPCML protocol is to "combine" multiple matches between a single feature vector from C and multiple vectors from S into one. According to our experiments, the value of ε selected in Section 3.3 allows us to keep error rate at 0 (with our dataset) and matching rate at 95% *without* performing Step 6. Therefore, removing this step has virtually no impact on the result of the computation. We refer to this modified version of the protocol as *Approximate* S-PPCML (AS-PPCML).

Garbled Circuits. As shown in [15,47], comparison protocols can be implemented more efficiently using garbled circuits, rather than homomorphic encryption. Therefore, we can easily optimize the S-PPCML protocol by replacing homomorphic-based comparison with one using a garbled circuit.

For each X_n and Y_m from $C's$ and $S's$ inputs, respectively, S computes encrypted Euclidean distance between the two as in our S-PPCML protocol. Then S "obfuscates" the result by multiplying it with a random value $r_{n,m}$. The obfuscated value is returned to C, which inputs it into the comparison circuit. S inputs ε and $r_{n,m}$. The circuit adds $-r_{n,m}$ to C's input in order to "unmask" it, and compares the result with ε. C only learns the outcome of the comparison, while S learns nothing.

We implemented this comparison circuit based on the design of efficient circuits for addition modulo 2^N and comparison described in [37].

Other Optimizations. We perform as much computation as possible in the unencrypted domain. In particular, both S and C compute, in the clear, summation of the squares of all elements in their feature vectors.

6.2 Optimized Protocol

The protocol below includes all the aforementioned optimizations.

– **Protocol Input:** C's input is a set of feature vectors $\mathcal{X} = \{X_1, \ldots, X_v\}$, with $X_n = (x_{n,1}, \ldots, x_{n,\ell})$ and key pair (pk, sk). S's input is $\mathcal{Y} = \{Y_1, \ldots, Y_w\}$ where $Y_m = (y_{m,1}, \ldots, y_{m,\ell})$ is a feature vector.
– **Protocol Output:** C's output is the number of feature vectors $X_n \in \mathcal{X}$ that have square Euclidean distance smaller than ε^2 with at least one vector from $\mathcal{Y}$; i.e., $|\widehat{\Psi}|$.

Protocol steps:

1. For each $n = 1, \ldots, v$ and $i = 1, \ldots, \ell$, C encrypts $\{\langle \mathsf{Enc}(x_{n,i}), \mathsf{Enc}(c_n) = \mathsf{Enc}(\sum_{i=1}^{\ell} x_{n,i}^2) \rangle\}$ and sends results to S.
2. For each $m = 1, \ldots, w$, S computes $\{\mathsf{Enc}(s_m) = \mathsf{Enc}(\sum_{j=1}^{\ell} y_{m,j}^2)\}$.
3. For each $n = 1, \ldots, v$ and $m = 1, \ldots, w$, S computes the encrypted square Euclidean distance between X_n and Y_m as

$$\mathsf{Enc}(d_{n,m}) = \mathsf{Enc}\left(\sum_{i=1}^{\ell}(x_{n,i} - y_{m,i})^2\right) = \mathsf{Enc}(c_n) \cdot \mathsf{Enc}(s_m) \cdot \prod_{i=1}^{\ell}\left(\mathsf{Enc}(x_{n,i})^{(-2y_{m,i})}\right)$$

4. For each $n = 1, \ldots, v$ and $m = 1, \ldots, w$, S randomizes the value computed in the previous step as: $\mathsf{Enc}(\hat{d}_{n,m}) = \mathsf{Enc}(d_{n,m}) \cdot \mathsf{Enc}(r_{n,m})$, where $r_{n,m}$ is uniformly selected from the message space. Then, S shuffles these values and sends them to C.
5. C decrypts all $\{\mathsf{Enc}(\hat{d}_{n,m})\}$; C and S evaluate a garbled circuit over input $\{\mathsf{Enc}(\hat{d}_{n,m})\}$ for C and $\{-r_{n,m}\}, \varepsilon^2$ for S. The circuit implements functionality $(\hat{d}_{n,m} + (-r_{n,m})) < \varepsilon^2$, where addition is performed modulo 2^N for some N.
6. C outputs $\gamma = \sum_{n=1}^{v} \sum_{m=1}^{w} \delta_{n,m}$.

7   Implementation and Performance

In this section we provide implementation details for our protocols, and report on performance measurements. All protocols are implemented in C. Our code is compiled using GCC 4.2 and relies on the GMP library to implement number-theoretic cryptographic operations and on OpenSSL for symmetric cryptography. Tests are run under Ubuntu 8.04 LTS.

Measurements are performed on a machine with two quad-core 2.5 GHz Intel Xeon CPUs and 16 GB memory. In order to provide results comparable with the state of the art, we restrict our code to run on a single CPU core. However, since there is no data dependency in the steps that represent the bulk of the computation, our protocols scale virtually linearly with the number of available cores.

We instantiated DGK with a 1024-bit modulus. We also set the security parameter $t = 160$ and $u = 2^{20}$, since the largest plaintext value in our dataset does not require over 19 bits. Our garbled circuit implementation uses the OT protocol in [33] for transferring keys corresponding to input wires. It reduces OT_L^M to OT_κ^κ. We set the security parameter $\kappa = 80$, $M = 20$ (since we selected $u = 2^{20}$) and $L = 128$ (the symmetric key size)[6]. We assume that the data-independent part of OT is performed by C and S prior to running AS-PPCML. All performance results in this section correspond to the average of 50 runs. Step-3 of the PPCML protocol is optimized by pushing most of the computation to the unencrypted domain: S computes $\sum_i y_{n,i}^2$ and then encrypts the result.

On-Line Computation Complexity
Table 2 illustrates our measurements, where both C and S hold 300 feature vectors (i.e., $v = w = 300$). For C, the total cost is dominated by the homomorphic comparison, while the most expensive step for S is the computation of the Euclidean distance.

Table 2. Breakdown of the server- and client-side on-line computation of our PPCML protocol for $v = w = 300$

Server		Client	
Step-3: Euclidean Distance	518.9 s	Step-4: Comparison	1096.83 s
Step-4: Comparison	125.15 s	Step-7: Decryption	39.11 ms
Step-5: Multiplication	179.4 ms		
Step-6: Exponentiation	7.386 ms		
Total	≈ 10.7 min	Total	≈ 18.3 min

Tables 3 shows the computation cost of our basic S-PPCML protocol, while Table 4 shows the breakdown of the computations of the AS-PPCML Protocol.

---

6 L is dictated by the key size of AES – used to encrypt input wires in the garbled circuit – rather than by security reasons. In fact, using an 80-bit key would provide the desired level of security. However, performance-wise there would be virtually no difference.

Table 3. Breakdown of the server- and client-side on-line computation of our basic S-PPCML protocol for $v = w = 300$

Server		Client	
Step-3: Euclidean Distance	518.9 s	Step-4: Comparison	1096.83 s
Step-4: Comparison	125.15 s	Step-6: Comparison	3.66 s
Step-5: Multiplication	179.4 ms	Step-8: Decryption	0.13 ms
Step-6: Comparison	417.2 ms		
Step-7: Multiplication	0.598 ms		
Total	≈ 10.7 min	Total	≈ 18.3 min

Table 4. Breakdown of the server-side and client-side on-line computation of our AS-PPCML protocol for $v = w = 300$

Server		Client	
Step-3: Euclidean Distance	518.9 s	Step-5-a: Decryptions	11.7 s
Step-4: Randomization	180 ms	Step-5-b: Comparison	11.1 s
Step-7: Comparison	10.8 s		
Total	≈ 8.8 min	Total	22.8 s

The use of a garbled circuit for comparing Euclidean distance with the threshold has a great impact on the performance of the AS-PPCML protocol. In particular, total time is reduced by a 1.2x factor for the server and by a 48x for the client.

On-Line Communication Complexity. The on-line communication cost is proportional to $v \cdot w$. Let $|N|$ indicate the number of bits corresponding to a DGK ciphertext. The following exchanges of information contribute to the total bandwidth (on-line) required by the PPCML protocol:

- The encrypted vectors sent by C to S account for $((2701 + 1) \cdot v) \cdot |N|$ bits.
- The homomorphic-based comparison $- (2 \cdot M + 3) \cdot w \cdot v \cdot |N|$ bits.
- The results sent by S to $C - v \cdot |N|$ bits.

Thus, the on-line data exchanged between C and S amounts to $(2702 \cdot v + (2 \cdot M + 3) \cdot w \cdot v + v) \cdot |N|$ bits. In our setting, this amounts to 572 MB.

Similarly, the on-line communication cost of the S-PPCML protocol is $(2701 \cdot v + (2 \cdot M + 3) \cdot w \cdot v + (2 \cdot M + 3) \cdot v + 1) \cdot |N|$ bits, i.e., 573 MB in our setting.

Finally, the AS-PPCML protocol relies on a garbled circuit for comparison, which incur on-line communication cost of $2 \cdot M \cdot (L + \kappa) \cdot w \cdot v$ bits. Therefore the total cost of the AS-PPCML protocol is $((2702 \cdot v + w \cdot v) \cdot |N| + 2 \cdot M \cdot (L + \kappa) \cdot w \cdot v)$ bits, corresponding to 200 MB in our setting.

8   Conclusion

In this paper we have introduced a set of protocols that implement PPCML and S-PPCML/AS-PPCML functionalities. The first allows two parties representing two user communities – e.g., two review websites – to *privately* determine which users belong to both communities. The second protocol allows the parties to privately compute how many users they have in common. Our protocols compare user-generated content rather than user identifiers, such as user-IDs or IP addresses.

We implement our protocols and measure their performance on commodity hardware. Our results indicate that the overhead introduced by the privacy-preserving computation is relatively small. In particular, two parties which hold 300 users each can determine the number of common users in a matter of minutes.

As for the future work, we plan to optimize our protocols for multi-core CPUs. Parallel implementation of our protocols can provide significant speedup, allowing clusters with hundreds of CPUs to run protocols over sets of millions of users.

References

1. Amazon, http://www.amazon.com
2. Facebook, http://www.facebook.com
3. Facebook Reports Third Quarter 2012 Results,
   http://investor.fb.com/releasedetail.cfm?ReleaseID=715607
4. Google+, https://plus.google.com
5. Linkedin, http://www.linkedin.com
6. TripAdvisor, http://www.tripadvisor.com
7. Twitter, http://www.twitter.com
8. Yelp, http://www.yelp.com
9. Yelp – About Us, http://www.yelp.com/about
10. Yelp – Terms of Service, http://www.yelp.com/static?country=US&p=tos
11. Abbasi, A., Chen, H.: Writeprints: A Stylometric Approach to Identity-Level Identification and Similarity Detection in Cyberspace. ACM Transactions on Information Systems (2008)
12. Almishari, M., Tsudik, G.: Exploring linkability of user reviews. In: Foresti, S., Yung, M., Martinelli, F. (eds.) ESORICS 2012. LNCS, vol. 7459, pp. 307–324. Springer, Heidelberg (2012)
13. Baeza-Yates, R.: Modern Information Retrieval. Addison-Wesley Longman Publishing Co., Inc. (1999)
14. Bishop, C.: Pattern Recognition and Machine Learning. Springer (2006)
15. Blanton, M., Gasti, P.: Secure and efficient protocols for iris and fingerprint identification. In: Atluri, V., Diaz, C. (eds.) ESORICS 2011. LNCS, vol. 6879, pp. 190–209. Springer, Heidelberg (2011)
16. Blundo, C., De Cristofaro, E., Gasti, P.: EsPRESSo: Efficient Privacy-Preserving Evaluation of Sample Set Similarity. In: Di Pietro, R., Herranz, J., Damiani, E., State, R. (eds.) DPM 2012 and SETOP 2012. LNCS, vol. 7731, pp. 89–103. Springer, Heidelberg (2013)
17. Border, A.: On the resemblance and containment of documents. Compression and Complexity of Sequences (1997)
18. Brennan, M., Greenstadt, R.: Practical Attacks Against Authorship Recognition Techniques. In: IAAI (2009)
19. Choi, S.G., Katz, J., Kumaresan, R., Zhou, H.-S.: On the security of the "Free-XOR" technique. In: Cramer, R. (ed.) TCC 2012. LNCS, vol. 7194, pp. 39–53. Springer, Heidelberg (2012)

20. Cramer, R., Damgård, I., Nielsen, J.B.: Multiparty computation from threshold homomorphic encryption. In: Pfitzmann, B. (ed.) EUROCRYPT 2001. LNCS, vol. 2045, pp. 280–300. Springer, Heidelberg (2001)
21. De Cristofaro, E., Gasti, P., Tsudik, G.: Fast and Private Computation of Cardinality of Set Intersection and Union. In: Pieprzyk, J., Sadeghi, A.-R., Manulis, M. (eds.) CANS 2012. LNCS, vol. 7712, pp. 218–231. Springer, Heidelberg (2012)
22. Damgård, I., Geisler, M., Krøigård, M.: A correction to efficient and secure comparison for on-line auctions. Cryptology ePrint Archive, Report 2008/321 (2008)
23. Damgård, I., Geisler, M., Krøigård, M.: Homomorphic encryption and secure comparison. Journal of Applied Cryptology 1(1), 22–31 (2008)
24. Damgård, I., Geisler, M., Krøigaard, M., Nielsen, J.B.: Asynchronous multiparty computation: Theory and implementation. In: Jarecki, S., Tsudik, G. (eds.) PKC 2009. LNCS, vol. 5443, pp. 160–179. Springer, Heidelberg (2009)
25. De Cristofaro, E., Tsudik, G.: Practical private set intersection protocols with linear complexity. In: Sion, R. (ed.) FC 2010. LNCS, vol. 6052, pp. 143–159. Springer, Heidelberg (2010)
26. Erkin, Z., Franz, M., Guajardo, J., Katzenbeisser, S., Lagendijk, I., Toft, T.: Privacy-preserving face recognition. In: Goldberg, I., Atallah, M.J. (eds.) PETS 2009. LNCS, vol. 5672, pp. 235–253. Springer, Heidelberg (2009)
27. Freedman, M.J., Nissim, K., Pinkas, B.: Efficient private matching and set intersection. In: Cachin, C., Camenisch, J.L. (eds.) EUROCRYPT 2004. LNCS, vol. 3027, pp. 1–19. Springer, Heidelberg (2004)
28. Goldreich, O., Micali, S., Wigderson, A.: How to play any mental game or a completeness theorem for protocols with honest majority. In: ACM Symposium on Theory of Computing, STOC, pp. 218–229 (1987)
29. Hazay, C., Lindell, Y.: Efficient protocols for set intersection and pattern matching with security against malicious and covert adversaries. In: Canetti, R. (ed.) TCC 2008. LNCS, vol. 4948, pp. 155–175. Springer, Heidelberg (2008)
30. Hazay, C., Nissim, K.: Efficient Set Operations in the Presence of Malicious Adversaries. In: Nguyen, P.Q., Pointcheval, D. (eds.) PKC 2010. LNCS, vol. 6056, pp. 312–331. Springer, Heidelberg (2010)
31. Henecka, W., Kogl, S., Sadeghi, A.-R., Schneider, T., Wehrenberg, I.: TASTY: Tool for Automating Secure Two-partY computations. In: ACM Conference on Computer and Communications Security, CCS, pp. 451–462 (2010)
32. Iqbal, F., Binsalleeh, H., Fung, B., Debbabi, M.: A unified data mining solution for authorship analysis in anonymous textual communications. In: Information Sciences (INS): Special Issue on Data Mining for Information Security (2011)
33. Ishai, Y., Kilian, J., Nissim, K., Petrank, E.: Extending oblivious transfers efficiently. In: Boneh, D. (ed.) CRYPTO 2003. LNCS, vol. 2729, pp. 145–161. Springer, Heidelberg (2003)
34. Jarecki, S., Liu, X.: Fast secure computation of set intersection. In: Garay, J.A., De Prisco, R. (eds.) SCN 2010. LNCS, vol. 6280, pp. 418–435. Springer, Heidelberg (2010)
35. Jindal, N., Liu, B.: Opinion Spam and Analysis. In: ACM International Conference on Web Search and Data Mining (2008)
36. Kissner, L., Song, D.: Privacy-preserving set operations. In: Shoup, V. (ed.) CRYPTO 2005. LNCS, vol. 3621, pp. 241–257. Springer, Heidelberg (2005)
37. Kolesnikov, V., Sadeghi, A.-R., Schneider, T.: Improved garbled circuit building blocks and applications to auctions and computing minima. In: Garay, J.A., Miyaji, A., Otsuka, A. (eds.) CANS 2009. LNCS, vol. 5888, pp. 1–20. Springer, Heidelberg (2009)

38. Kolesnikov, V., Schneider, T.: Improved garbled circuit: Free XOR gates and applications. In: Aceto, L., Damgård, I., Goldberg, L.A., Halldórsson, M.M., Ingólfsdóttir, A., Walukiewicz, I. (eds.) ICALP 2008, Part II. LNCS, vol. 5126, pp. 486–498. Springer, Heidelberg (2008)

39. Lewis, D.D.: Naive(bayes) at forty:the independence assumption in information retrieval. In: Nédellec, C., Rouveirol, C. (eds.) ECML 1998. LNCS, vol. 1398, pp. 4–15. Springer, Heidelberg (1998)

40. Liedel, M.: Secure distributed computation of the square root and applications. In: Ryan, M.D., Smyth, B., Wang, G. (eds.) ISPEC 2012. LNCS, vol. 7232, pp. 277–288. Springer, Heidelberg (2012)

41. Malkhi, D., Nisan, N., Pinkas, B., Sella, Y.: Fairplay – a secure two-party computation system. In: USENIX Security Symposium, pp. 287–302 (2004)

42. McDonald, A.W.E., Afroz, S., Caliskan, A., Stolerman, A., Greenstadt, R.: Use Fewer Instances of the Letter "i": Toward Writing Style Anonymization. In: Fischer-Hübner, S., Wright, M. (eds.) PETS 2012. LNCS, vol. 7384, pp. 299–318. Springer, Heidelberg (2012)

43. Narayanan, A., Paskov, H., Gong, N., Bethencourt, J., Stefanov, E., Shin, E., Song, D.: On the Feasibility of Internet-Scale Author Identification. In: IEEE Symposium on Security and Privacy (2012)

44. Paillier, P.: Public-key cryptosystems based on composite degree residuosity classes. In: Stern, J. (ed.) EUROCRYPT 1999. LNCS, vol. 1592, pp. 223–238. Springer, Heidelberg (1999)

45. Pinkas, B., Schneider, T., Smart, N.P., Williams, S.C.: Secure two-party computation is practical. In: Matsui, M. (ed.) ASIACRYPT 2009. LNCS, vol. 5912, pp. 250–267. Springer, Heidelberg (2009)

46. Rabin, T., Ben-Or, M.: Verifiable secret sharing and multiparty protocols with honest majority. In: ACM Symposium on Theory of Computing, STOC, pp. 73–85 (1989)

47. Sadeghi, A.-R., Schneider, T., Wehrenberg, I.: Efficient privacy-preserving face recognition. In: Lee, D., Hong, S. (eds.) ICISC 2009. LNCS, vol. 5984, pp. 229–244. Springer, Heidelberg (2010)

48. Stamatatos, E.: A Survey of Modern Authorship Attribution Methods. Journal of the American Society for Information Science and Technology (2009)

49. Tan, P., Steinbach, M., Kumar, V.: Introduction to Data Mining. Addison-Wesley (2005)

50. Toutanova, K., Klein, D., Manning, C., Singer, Y.: Feature-Rich Part-of-Speech Tagging with a Cyclic Dependency Network. In: HLT-NAACL (2003)

51. Yao, A.: How to generate and exchange secrets. In: IEEE Symposium on Foundations of Computer Science, FOCS, pp. 162–167 (1986)

A Security Analysis

Security of the protocol presented in Section 5 is based on that of security assumptions about our building blocks. In particular, we assume that DGK encryption is semantically secure. This was shown in [23,22] under the RSA setting.

We now outline how to simulate the view of C and S using each party's inputs and outputs only. We show that such simulation is indistinguishable from a real execution of the protocol. This allows us to claim that the protocol is secure in the honest-but-curious (HbC) model.

C's input consists of a feature vector and a private key, while its output is a single bit b. Given these values, the simulator constructs messages to C as follows: during the comparison protocol (Step 4) the simulator sends encryptions of random values to C. Since DGK is semantically secure, C cannot detect it. Then, if $b = 0$ the simulator returns to C $u = \mathsf{Enc}(0)$ and $u = \mathsf{Enc}(r)$ (for a random r) otherwise. Since the outcome of decryption is distributed identically to that what C expects, simulation cannot be detected.

S's input is a database consisting of w feature vectors; S has no output. The simulator encrypts two random values per each element of the feature vector and sends them to S. Since DGK is semantically secure, S cannot detect that the message from the simulator represents encryption of random values. During privacy-preserving comparison, the simulator sends encryption of random values to S (Step 4). S, however, cannot decide with any non-negligible probability that these values are indeed random.

An analogous argument extends to the protocols in Section 6. However, security of these protocols relies on two additional assumptions: (1) oblivious transfer used is for garbled circuit evaluation is secure; and (2) garbled circuit evaluation is secure.

Assumption (1) holds if the hash function used to instantiate the oblivious transfer protocol in [33] is either correlation-robust, or modeled as a random oracle. Also, [33] requires the use of a secure pseudorandom generator. With respect to (2), security of garbled circuits with "free-XOR" was proven under the assumption that the hash function is correlation-robust under the definition of [19], or is instantiated as a random oracle.

Ballot Secrecy and Ballot Independence Coincide[*]

Ben Smyth[1] and David Bernhard[2]

[1] INRIA Paris-Rocquencourt, France
[2] University of Bristol, England

Abstract. We study ballot independence for election schemes:
- We formally define ballot independence as a cryptographic game and prove that ballot secrecy implies ballot independence.
- We introduce a notion of controlled malleability and show that it is sufficient for ballot independence. We also show that non-malleable ballots are sufficient, but not necessary, for ballot independence.
- We prove that ballot independence is sufficient for ballot secrecy under practical assumptions.

Our results show that ballot independence is necessary in election schemes satisfying ballot secrecy. Furthermore, our sufficient conditions enable simpler proofs of ballot secrecy.

1 Introduction

Voters should be able to express their free will in elections without fear of retribution; this property is known as privacy. Cryptographic formulations of privacy depend on the specific setting and *ballot secrecy*[1] [2–4] has emerged as a *de facto* standard privacy requirement of election schemes.

- *Ballot secrecy.* A voter's vote is not revealed to anyone.

Ballot secrecy provides privacy in an intimidation-free environment and stronger properties such as *receipt-freeness* and *coercion resistance* [5] provide privacy in environments where intimidation may occur. Bernhard *et al.* [6–8] propose a cryptographic formalisation of ballot secrecy. However, we show that their definition allows election schemes that reveal voters' votes to be proven secure and we strengthen the definition to prevent this issue.

Ballot independence [4,9] is seemingly related to ballot secrecy.

- *Ballot independence.* Observing another voter's interaction with the election system does not allow a voter to cast a meaningfully related vote.

---

[*] The full version of this paper is available as an IACR Cryptology ePrint [1].

[1] The terms *privacy* and *ballot secrecy* occasionally appear as synonyms in the literature and we favour ballot secrecy because it avoids confusion with other privacy notions, such as receipt-freeness and coercion resistance, for example.

J. Crampton, S. Jajodia, and K. Mayes (Eds.): ESORICS 2013, LNCS 8134, pp. 463–480, 2013.

Indeed, Cortier and Smyth [4, 10, 11] attribute a class of ballot secrecy attacks to the absence of ballot independence. However, ballot independence has not been formally defined and its relationship with ballot secrecy is unknown. We provide a definition of ballot independence and show that ballot secrecy and ballot independence coincide in practical settings.

In traditional paper-based elections, physical mechanisms can be used to achieve privacy, for instance, ballots are completed in isolation inside polling booths, placed into locked ballot boxes, and mixed with other ballots before tallying. (See Schneier [12] for a detailed, informal security analysis of Papal elections.) By comparison, the provision of ballot secrecy is more difficult in end-to-end verifiable election schemes, since ballots are posted on publicly readable bulletin boards. Nonetheless, ballot secrecy is a *de facto* standard property of election schemes and, hence, must be satisfied. The aforementioned physical mechanisms also provide an assurance of ballot independence in paper-based elections, however, the motivation for election schemes satisfying ballot independence is unclear, indeed, Bulens, Giry & Pereira [13, §3.2] question whether ballot independence is a desirable property of election schemes and highlight the investigation of voting schemes which allow the submission of related votes whilst preserving ballot secrecy as an interesting research direction. Moreover, in the context of the Helios [14, 15] election scheme, Desmedt & Chaidos [16] present a protocol which allows Bob to cast the same vote as Alice, with Alice's cooperation, and claim that Bob cannot learn Alice's vote. In this paper, we study the relationship between ballot secrecy and ballot independence and show that the two properties coincide in practical settings.

Contribution and Outline. In Section 3 we show that the definition of ballot secrecy by Bernhard *et al.* allows election schemes that reveal voters' votes to be proven secure and we present a stronger definition of ballot secrecy to prevent this issue. In Section 4 we propose a definition of ballot independence and give sufficient conditions to achieve this notion, including a definition of controlled-malleable encryption. In Section 5 we prove that ballot secrecy implies ballot independence, thereby providing an argument to end the ballot independence debate: ballot independence is a necessary property of election schemes (assuming ballot secrecy is required). In addition, we critique (Section 5.1) the results by Desmedt & Chaidos and argue that their security results do not support their claims. In Section 6 we present a practical class of election schemes (which includes Helios) for which ballot secrecy and ballot independence coincide.

Related work. The concept of independence was introduced by Chor *et al.* [17] and studied in the context of election schemes by Gennaro [9]. Cortier and Smyth [4, 10, 11] have discovered attacks on ballot secrecy in several election schemes and considered the relationship to independence [4, Section 7]; their evidence suggests ballot secrecy implies ballot independence in homomorphic voting systems such as Helios. However, Cortier & Smyth did not make any formal claims, because ballot independence had not been formally defined. By comparison, in this paper, we present a formal definition of ballot independence and prove that ballot secrecy implies ballot independence. Bernhard, Pereira & Warinschi [7] show that a non-malleable encryption scheme is sufficient to build an election scheme satisfying ballot secrecy and our work generalises their result.

2   Preliminaries

We adopt standard notation for the application of probabilistic algorithms: if A is a probabilistic algorithm, then $A(x_1, \ldots, x_n; r)$ is the result of running A on input $x_1, \ldots, x_n$ and coins r. We let $y \leftarrow A(x_1, \ldots, x_n)$ denote picking r at random and assigning the output of $A(x_1, \ldots, x_n; r)$ to the variable y. If S is a finite set, then $x \leftarrow S$ assigns a uniformly chosen element of S to x. If α is neither a probabilistic algorithm nor a set, then $x \leftarrow \alpha$ assigns α to x. Vectors are denoted using boldface, for example, $\mathbf{x}$. We extend set membership notation to vectors: we write $x \in \mathbf{x}$ (respectively, $x \notin \mathbf{x}$) if x is an element (respectively, x is not an element) of the vector $\mathbf{x}$.

2.1   Non-malleable Encryption

Let us recall the standard syntax for *asymmetric encryption schemes.*

Definition 1 (Asymmetric encryption scheme). *An asymmetric encryption scheme is a triple of efficient algorithms* (Gen, Enc, Dec) *such that:*

- *The key generation algorithm* Gen *takes a security parameter 1^n as input and outputs a key pair (pk, sk), where pk is a public key and sk is a private key.*
- *The encryption algorithm* Enc *takes a public key pk and message m as input, and outputs a ciphertext c.*
- *The decryption algorithm* Dec *takes a private key sk and ciphertext c as input, and outputs a message m or the special symbol $\bot$ denoting failure.*

Moreover, the scheme must be correct: for all $(pk, sk) \leftarrow$ Gen(1^n), we have for all messages m and ciphertexts $c \leftarrow$ Enc$_{pk}(m)$, that Dec$_{sk}(c) = m$ with overwhelming probability.

Non-malleability [18–20] is a standard computational security model used to evaluate the suitability of encryption schemes. Intuitively, if an encryption scheme satisfies non-malleability, then an adversary is unable to construct a ciphertext *"meaningfully related"* to a challenge ciphertext, thereby capturing the idea that ciphertexts are tamper-proof. Formally, Definition 2 recalls the non-malleability game proposed by Bellare *et al.* [19].

Definition 2 (Non-malleable encryption). *Let $\Pi = $ (Gen, Enc, Dec) be an asymmetric encryption scheme, $\mathcal{A} = (A_1, A_2)$ be an adversary, and*

$$NM\text{-}CPA_{\mathcal{A}, \Pi}(n) := |Succ^{CPA}_{\mathcal{A}, \Pi}(n) - Succ^{CPA}_{\mathcal{A}, \Pi, \$}(n)|$$

where $Succ_{A,\Pi}^{CPA}(n)$ and $Succ_{A,\Pi,\$}^{CPA}(n)$ are defined below, and n is a security parameter.

$$Succ_{A,\Pi}^{CPA}(n) = Pr[(pk, sk) \leftarrow \mathsf{Gen}(1^n); \; (M, s) \leftarrow A_1(pk);$$
$$x \leftarrow M; \; y \leftarrow \mathsf{Enc}_{pk}(x); \; (R, \mathbf{y}) \leftarrow A_2(M, s, y);$$
$$\mathbf{x} \leftarrow \mathsf{Dec}_{sk}(\mathbf{y}) : y \notin \mathbf{y} \wedge \bot \notin \mathbf{x} \wedge R(x, \mathbf{x})]$$

$$Succ_{A,\Pi,\$}^{CPA}(n) = Pr[(pk, sk) \leftarrow \mathsf{Gen}(1^n); \; (M, s) \leftarrow A_1(pk);$$
$$x, x' \leftarrow M; \; y \leftarrow \mathsf{Enc}_{pk}(x); \; (R, \mathbf{y}) \leftarrow A_2(M, s, y);$$
$$\mathbf{x} \leftarrow \mathsf{Dec}_{sk}(\mathbf{y}) : y \notin \mathbf{y} \wedge \bot \notin \mathbf{x} \wedge R(x', \mathbf{x})]$$

In the above games we insist that the message space is valid (that is, $|x| = |x'|$ for any $x, x' \leftarrow M$ given non-zero probability in the message space) and samplable in polynomial time, and the relation R is computable in polynomial time. We say Π satisfies NM-CPA if for all probabilistic polynomial-time adversaries A and security parameters n, there exists a negligible function negl such that $\mathsf{NM\text{-}CPA}_{A,\Pi}(n) \leq \mathsf{negl}(n)$.

3 Election Schemes and Ballot Secrecy

Based upon Bernhard et al. [6–8], we define a syntax for *election schemes* as follows.

Definition 3 (Election scheme). *An* election scheme *is a tuple of efficient algorithms* (Setup, Vote, BB, Tally) *such that:*

- *The* setup algorithm Setup *takes a security parameter 1^n as input and outputs a bulletin board $\mathfrak{bb}$, vote space $\mathfrak{m}$, public key pk, and private key sk, where $\mathfrak{bb}$ is a multiset and $\mathfrak{m}$ is a set.*
- *The* vote algorithm Vote *takes a public key pk and vote $v \in \mathfrak{m}$ as input, and outputs a ballot b.*
- *The* bulletin board algorithm BB *takes a bulletin board $\mathfrak{bb}$ and ballot b as input, where $\mathfrak{bb}$ is a multiset. It outputs $\mathfrak{bb} \cup \{b\}$ if successful (i.e., b is added to $\mathfrak{bb}$) or $\mathfrak{bb}$ to denote failure (i.e., b is not added).*
- *The* tally algorithm Tally *takes a private key sk and bulletin board $\mathfrak{bb}$ as input, where $\mathfrak{bb}$ is a multiset. It outputs a multiset $\mathfrak{v}$ representing the election result if successful or the empty set $\emptyset$ to denote failure, and auxiliary data aux.*

Moreover, the scheme must satisfy the following correctness property: for all parameters $(\mathfrak{bb}_0, \mathfrak{m}, pk, sk) \leftarrow \mathsf{Setup}(1^n)$, votes $v \in \mathfrak{m}$, multisets $\mathfrak{bb}$, ballots $b \leftarrow \mathsf{Vote}_{pk}(v)$, bulletin boards $\mathfrak{bb}' \leftarrow \mathsf{BB}(\mathfrak{bb}, b)$ and tallying data $(\mathfrak{v}, aux) \leftarrow \mathsf{Tally}_{sk}(\mathfrak{bb})$ and $(\mathfrak{v}', aux') \leftarrow \mathsf{Tally}_{sk}(\mathfrak{bb}')$, we have with overwhelming probability that $\mathfrak{bb}' = \mathfrak{bb} \cup \{b\}$ and if $\mathfrak{v} \neq \emptyset$, then $\mathfrak{v}' = \mathfrak{v} \cup \{v\}$ and $|\mathfrak{v}| = |\mathfrak{bb}|$, otherwise, $\mathfrak{v}' = \emptyset$.

In comparison with earlier presentations by Bernhard *et al.*, Definition 3 is stricter, since we explicitly define the bulletin board and election result as multisets. Moreover, the correctness condition, asserting that the election result corresponds to the multiset of votes cast, is new. Although the correctness condition restricts the applicability of our definition – for example, we cannot model schemes with weighted votes nor schemes which only reveal the winning candidate (as opposed to the number of votes for each candidate) – we believe it is useful for simplicity. In addition, there are some minor differences in error handling and we merge some functionality into a single function[2].

We demonstrate the applicability of our definition by recalling the construction (Definition 4) for election schemes proposed by Bernhard *et al.* [6,7]. We stress that more sophisticated schemes can also be captured – for example, Bernhard *et al.* [6–8] model Helios – but the following scheme is sufficient for our purposes.

Definition 4 (Enc2Vote). *Given an asymmetric encryption scheme $\Pi = (\mathsf{Gen}, \mathsf{Enc}, \mathsf{Dec})$, we define the election scheme $\mathsf{Enc2Vote}(\Pi)$ as follows.*

- Setup *takes a security parameter 1^n as input and outputs $(\emptyset, \mathfrak{m}, pk, sk)$, where $(pk, sk) \leftarrow \mathsf{Gen}(1^n)$ and $\mathfrak{m}$ is the encryption scheme's message space.*
- Vote *takes a public key pk and vote $v \in \mathfrak{m}$ as input, and outputs $\mathsf{Enc}_{pk}(v)$.*
- BB *takes a bulletin board $\mathfrak{bb}$ and ballot b as input, where $\mathfrak{bb}$ is a multiset. If $b \in \mathfrak{bb}$, then the algorithm outputs $\mathfrak{bb}$ (denoting failure), otherwise, the algorithm outputs $\mathfrak{bb} \cup \{b\}$.*
- Tally *takes as input a private key sk and a bulletin board $\mathfrak{bb}$, where $\mathfrak{bb}$ is a multiset. It outputs the multiset $\{\mathsf{Dec}_{sk}(b) \mid b \in \mathfrak{bb}\}$ and auxiliary data $\bot$.*

Intuitively, given an asymmetric encryption scheme Π satisfying NM-CPA, the construction $\mathsf{Enc2Vote}(\Pi)$ derives ballot secrecy from Π until tallying and the Tally algorithm maintains ballot secrecy by returning the number of votes for each candidate as an unordered multiset of votes[3].

Ballot Secrecy. Ballot secrecy is a *de facto* standard property of election schemes and, based upon Bernhard *et al.* [6–8], we formalise a cryptographic game for ballot secrecy (Definition 5). We will describe the differences between

---

[2] In essence, the tally algorithm defined by Bernhard *et al.* outputs a tally τ and an additional algorithm is used to compute the election result $\mathfrak{v}$ from τ. We combine the functionality of these two algorithms into a single function but distinguish between the result $\mathfrak{v}$ and auxiliary data *aux*, which is typically used to store signatures of knowledge proving that the election result has been correctly computed from the bulletin board.

[3] Definition 4 rectifies a mistake in the presentation by Bernhard, Pereira & Warinschi [7] which outputs a vector of votes (rather than a multiset) ordered by the time at which each vote was cast and therefore does not provide ballot secrecy, since there is a mapping between the order in which votes were cast and the votes. (Bernhard *et al.* [6] avoid this problem in a similar fashion.)

our formalisation and earlier presentations after our definition. Informally, our game proceeds as follows. First, the challenger executes the setup algorithm to construct a bulletin board bb_0, a vote space m, a public key pk, and a private key sk; the challenger also initialises a bulletin board bb_1 as a copy of bb_0 and selects a random bit β. Secondly, the adversary executes the algorithm A_1. The algorithm A_1 has access to an oracle $\mathcal{O}$ as follows: $\mathcal{O}(v_0, v_1)$ allows the adversary to honestly cast a vote $v_0 \in m$ on bulletin board bb_0 and honestly cast a vote $v_1 \in m$ on bulletin board bb_1, where the votes are cast using ballots constructed by the Vote algorithm; $\mathcal{O}(b)$ allows the adversary to cast a ballot b, where b is constructed by the adversary and might be rejected by the bulletin board; and $\mathcal{O}()$ returns the bulletin board bb_β. Thirdly, the challenger computes the election result v as follows: if the honestly cast votes on the bulletin board bb_0 correspond to the honestly cast votes on the bulletin board bb_1, then the challenger reveals the election result for bb_β, otherwise, the challenger reveals the election result for bb_0, thereby preventing the adversary from trivially revealing β when the honestly cast votes differ. (The distinction between bb_0 and bb_1 is trivial when the honestly cast votes differ, because the adversary can test for the presence of honestly cast votes in the election result.) Formally, we introduce the multisets L_0 and L_1 to record the honestly cast votes on bulletin boards bb_0 and bb_1, and model the correspondence between bulletin boards as an equality test on L_0 and L_1, that is, we compute $(v, aux) \leftarrow \mathsf{Tally}_{sk}(bb_\alpha)$ such that $\alpha = \beta$, if $L_0 = L_1$, and $\alpha = 0$, otherwise. Finally, the adversary executes the algorithm A_2 on the election result v and any state information s provided by A_1. The election scheme satisfies ballot secrecy if the adversary has less than a negligible advantage over guessing the bulletin board she interacted with.

Definition 5 (IND-SEC: Ballot secrecy). *Let* $\Gamma = (\mathsf{Setup}, \mathsf{Vote}, \mathsf{BB}, \mathsf{Tally})$ *be an election scheme,* $\mathcal{A} = (A_1, A_2)$ *be an adversary, and* IND-SEC$_{\mathcal{A},\Gamma}(n)$ *be the quantity defined below, where* n *is the security parameter.*

$$2 \cdot Pr[L_0 \leftarrow \emptyset; L_1 \leftarrow \emptyset; (bb_0, m, pk, sk) \leftarrow \mathsf{Setup}(1^n);\ bb_1 \leftarrow bb_0;\ \beta \leftarrow \{0,1\};$$

$$s \leftarrow A_1^{\mathcal{O}}(m, pk);\ (v, aux) \leftarrow \mathsf{Tally}_{sk}(bb_\alpha) : A_2(bb_\beta, v, aux, s) = \beta] - 1$$

In the above game, L_0 *and* L_1 *are multisets, the oracle* $\mathcal{O}$ *is defined below, and the bit* α *is defined as follows: if* $L_0 = L_1$, *then* $\alpha = \beta$, *otherwise,* $\alpha = 0$.

- $\mathcal{O}(v_0, v_1)$ *executes* $L_0 \leftarrow L_0 \cup \{v_0\}; L_1 \leftarrow L_1 \cup \{v_1\}; b_0 \leftarrow \mathsf{Vote}_{pk}(v_0); b_1 \leftarrow \mathsf{Vote}_{pk}(v_1); bb_0 \leftarrow \mathsf{BB}(bb_0, b_0); bb_1 \leftarrow \mathsf{BB}(bb_1, b_1),$ *if* $v_0, v_1 \in m$.
- $\mathcal{O}(b)$ *assigns* $bb_\beta' \leftarrow bb_\beta$, *executes* $bb_\beta \leftarrow \mathsf{BB}(bb_\beta, b)$ *and if* $bb_\beta \neq bb_\beta'$, *then executes* $bb_{1-\beta} \leftarrow \mathsf{BB}(bb_{1-\beta}, b)$.
- $\mathcal{O}()$ *outputs* bb_β.

We say Γ *satisfies* ballot secrecy *if for all probabilistic polynomial-time adversaries* $\mathcal{A}$ *and security parameters* n, *there exists a negligible function* negl *such that* IND-SEC$_{\mathcal{A},\Gamma}(n) \leq \mathsf{negl}(n)$.

Our game captures a setting where an adversary can cast ballots on behalf of a subset of voters, whom we call dishonest voters, and controls the distribution of votes cast by the remaining voters, whom we call honest voters, but honest voters always cast ballots constructed by the Vote algorithm. Furthermore, at the end of the election, the adversary obtains the election result. Intuitively, if the adversary loses the game, then the adversary is unable to distinguish between the bulletin boards bb_0 and bb_1, hence, the adversary cannot distinguish between an honest ballot $b_0 \in bb_0$ and an honest ballot $b_1 \in bb_1$, therefore, voters' votes cannot be revealed. On the other hand, if the adversary wins the game, then there exists a strategy to distinguish honestly cast ballots. We stress that a unanimous election result will always reveal all voters' votes and we tolerate this factor in our game by challenging the adversary to guess the bit β, rather than the distribution of votes.

Comparing IND-SEC and earlier definitions. In comparison with earlier definitions by Bernhard *et al.* [6–8], Definition 5 permits $\alpha \in \{0, 1\}$, whereas, earlier presentations implicitly[4] insist $\alpha = 0$. It follows that Definition 5 allows the adversary to access auxiliary data generated by tallying bb_β, whereas, earlier definitions only allow the adversary to access the auxiliary data generated by tallying bb_0. Accordingly, earlier definitions implicitly assume that auxiliary data cannot be used to violate ballot secrecy, indeed, this corresponds to the description by Bernhard *et al.* [6, §2.2]: *"[ballot secrecy] is satisfied if an adversary [...] cannot learn anything about the votes of [...] honest voters beyond what can be inferred from the election result."* Unfortunately, however, it is possible that the auxiliary data can reveal voters' votes. For example, a variant of Enc2Vote (Definition 4) could define auxiliary data that maps ballots to decrypted ballots, thereby violating ballot secrecy; indeed, as highlighted in Footnote 3, Bernhard, Pereira & Warinschi [7] provided such a mapping in their variant of Enc2Vote. As discussed, we permit $\alpha \in \{0, 1\}$, rather than $\alpha = 0$, thereby strengthening Definition 5 in comparison with earlier definitions and, thus, overcoming the limitations of previous works.

4 Ballot Independence

Intuitively, if an election scheme satisfies ballot independence, then an adversary is unable to construct a ballot that will be accepted by the election's bulletin board *and* be meaningfully related to a non-adversarial ballot from the bulletin board [4, Section 7.2], thereby capturing the notion that accepted ballots are tamper-proof. Building upon inspiration from non-malleable encryption, we formalise ballot independence as a non-malleability game.

4.1 Non-malleability Game

The concept of non-malleability and first formalisation is due to Dolev, Dwork & Naor [18, 20]. Bellare *et al.* [19] build upon these results to introduce NM-CPA

---

[4] Earlier presentations do not explicitly define a bit α, however, they always tally bb_0 and this implicitly corresponds to $\alpha = 0$ in Definition 5.

(Definition 2) and based upon NM-CPA, we formalise ballot independence (Definition 6) as a pair of cryptographic games: $\mathsf{Succ}^{BB}_{\mathcal{A},\Pi}$ and $\mathsf{Succ}^{BB}_{\mathcal{A},\Pi,\$}$. The first three steps of both games are identical. First, the challenger sets up the keys, vote space, and bulletin board. Secondly, the adversary gets the vote space $\mathfrak{m}$, the public key pk and the board $\mathfrak{bb}$ as input and must return a distribution M on the vote space. The adversary may also read the board and submit ballots of his own. Thirdly, the challenger samples a vote v from M. At this point the two games diverge: in $\mathsf{Succ}^{BB}_{\mathcal{A},\Pi}$, the challenger constructs a ballot $\mathsf{Vote}_{pk}(v)$ and adds it to the bulletin board; whereas, in $\mathsf{Succ}^{BB}_{\mathcal{A},\Pi,\$}$, the challenger samples a second vote v' from M, constructs a ballot $\mathsf{Vote}_{pk}(v')$ and adds it to the bulletin board. Fourthly, the adversary must compute a relation R which is intended to distinguish the election results produced by the two games. Finally, the challenger tallies the election and evaluates the relation R on the vote v and, after removing the challenge vote, the election result. The adversary's advantage is the difference between the probabilities that his relation is satisfied in each game.

Definition 6 (NM-BB: Ballot independence). *Let $\Gamma = (\mathsf{Setup}, \mathsf{Vote}, \mathsf{BB}, \mathsf{Tally})$ be an election scheme, $\mathcal{A} = (A_1, A_2)$ be an adversary, and*

$$\mathsf{NM\text{-}BB}_{\mathcal{A},\Gamma}(n) := |\mathsf{Succ}^{BB}_{\mathcal{A},\Pi}(n) - \mathsf{Succ}^{BB}_{\mathcal{A},\Pi,\$}(n)|$$

where $\mathsf{Succ}^{BB}_{\mathcal{A},\Pi}(n)$ and $\mathsf{Succ}^{BB}_{\mathcal{A},\Pi,\$}(n)$ are defined below, and n is the security parameter.

$$\mathsf{Succ}^{BB}_{\mathcal{A},\Pi}(n) = Pr[(\mathfrak{bb}, \mathfrak{m}, pk, sk) \leftarrow \mathsf{Setup}(1^n);\ (M, s) \leftarrow A_1^{\mathcal{O}}(\mathfrak{m}, pk);$$
$$v \leftarrow M;\ b \leftarrow \mathsf{Vote}_{pk}(v);\ \mathfrak{bb} \leftarrow \mathsf{BB}(\mathfrak{bb}, b);\ R \leftarrow A_2^{\mathcal{O}}(s);$$
$$(\mathfrak{v}, aux) \leftarrow \mathsf{Tally}_{sk}(\mathfrak{bb}) : R(v, \mathfrak{v} \backslash \{v\})]$$

$$\mathsf{Succ}^{BB}_{\mathcal{A},\Pi,\$}(n) = Pr[(\mathfrak{bb}, \mathfrak{m}, pk, sk) \leftarrow \mathsf{Setup}(1^n);\ (M, s) \leftarrow A_1^{\mathcal{O}}(\mathfrak{m}, pk);$$
$$v, v' \leftarrow M;\ b \leftarrow \mathsf{Vote}_{pk}(v');\ \mathfrak{bb} \leftarrow \mathsf{BB}(\mathfrak{bb}, b);\ R \leftarrow A_2^{\mathcal{O}}(s);$$
$$(\mathfrak{v}, aux) \leftarrow \mathsf{Tally}_{sk}(\mathfrak{bb}) : R(v, \mathfrak{v} \backslash \{v'\})]$$

In the above games we let $\mathcal{O}$ be defined as follows: $\mathcal{O}(b)$ executes $\mathfrak{bb} \leftarrow \mathsf{BB}(\mathfrak{bb}, b)$ and $\mathcal{O}()$ outputs $\mathfrak{bb}$. Moreover, we insist the vote space sampling algorithm M and the relation R are computable in polynomial time, and for all $v \leftarrow M$ we have $v \in \mathfrak{m}$. We say Γ satisfies NM-BB (or ballot independence) if for all probabilistic polynomial-time adversaries $\mathcal{A}$ and security parameters n, there exists a negligible function negl such that $\mathsf{NM\text{-}BB}_{\mathcal{A},\Gamma}(n) \leq \mathsf{negl}(n)$.

Intuitively, if an adversary wins the game, then the adversary is able to construct a relation R which holds for a challenge ballot $b \leftarrow \mathsf{Vote}_{pk}(v)$ but fails for $b \leftarrow \mathsf{Vote}_{pk}(v')$. However, we must avoid crediting the adversary for trivial and unavoidable relations which hold iff the challenge vote appears in the election result, hence, we remove the challenge vote from the election result. By contrast, if the adversary can derive a ballot containing the challenge vote and the bulletin board accepts such a ballot, then the adversary can win the game. For example, suppose an election scheme allows the bulletin board to accept duplicate ballots and witness that an adversary can win the game as follows, namely, the adversary selects M as a uniform distribution on $\mathfrak{m}$, calls $\mathcal{O}(b)$ with the challenge ballot b, and defines a relation $R(v, \mathfrak{v})$ that holds iff $v \in \mathfrak{v}$. In this setting, $R(v, \{v\})$ always holds at the end of $\mathsf{Succ}^{\mathrm{BB}}_{\mathcal{A}, \Pi}$, whereas, $R(v, \{v'\})$ holds with probability $1/\mathfrak{m}$ at the end of $\mathsf{Succ}^{\mathrm{BB}}_{\mathcal{A}, \Pi, \$}$, since v' is sampled independently from v. Finally, if an adversary loses the game, then the adversary is unable to construct a suitable relation, hence, there is no ballot which the bulletin board will accept such that the ballot is related to $\mathsf{Vote}_{pk}(v)$ but not $\mathsf{Vote}_{pk}(v')$, therefore, the adversary cannot cast a ballot which is meaningfully related to an honest voter's ballot.

Comparing NM-BB and NM-CPA. The main distinction between the notion of non-malleability (Definition 2) and our definition of ballot independence is: NM-CPA universally quantifies over ciphertexts, whereas, NM-BB quantifies over ballots accepted by the bulletin board. It follows that non-malleability for encryption is intuitively stronger than ballot independence, since non-malleability for encryption insists that the adversary cannot construct ciphertexts meaningfully related to the challenge ciphertext, whereas, ballot independence tolerates meaningfully related ballots, assuming that they are rejected by the bulletin board algorithm BB. For example, suppose an adversary $\mathcal{A}$ includes the challenge ciphertext in the vector $\mathbf{y}$ and observe that this adversary cannot win NM-CPA$_{\mathcal{A}, \Pi}(n)$, due to the constraint $y \notin \mathbf{y}$; by comparison, suppose an adversary $\mathcal{B}$ copies the challenge ballot b and observe that this adversary can win NM-BB$_{\mathcal{B}, \Gamma}(n)$. Nonetheless, for ballot independence, the bulletin board must not contain meaningfully related ballots and, hence, checking for meaningfully related ballots is a prerequisite of the bulletin board algorithm BB.

Non-malleable Ballots are Sufficient. Non-malleability for encryption prevents the adversary from constructing a ciphertext meaningfully related to the challenge ciphertext and, hence, it follows that non-malleable ballots are sufficient for ballot independence. Indeed, we can derive non-malleable ballots in our Enc2Vote construction using encryption schemes satisfying NM-CPA.

Proposition 7. *Given an encryption scheme Π satisfying NM-CPA, the election scheme* Enc2Vote(Π) *satisfies ballot independence.*

In Proposition 7, it is sufficient for the bulletin board algorithm, defined by Enc2Vote(Π), to reject ballots that already appear on the bulletin board since non-malleability prevents the adversary from creating ballots meaningfully related to honest voters' votes (except for exact copies). The proof is essentially the same as that of [7, Theorem 4.2].

4.2   Indistinguishability Game

Our non-malleability game (NM-BB) captures an intuitive notion of ballot independence, however, the definition is relatively complex and security proofs in this setting are relatively difficult. Bellare & Sahai [21] observed similar complexities with definitions of non-malleability for encryption and show that NM-CPA is equivalent to a simpler, indistinguishability-based notion. In a similar direction, we introduce an indisinguishability game IND-BB for ballot independence and, based upon Bellare & Sahai's proof, show that our games NM-BB and IND-BB are equivalent.

We model ballot independence as an indistinguishability game between an adversary and a challenger (Definition 8). Informally, the game proceeds as follows. First, the challenger initialises the bulletin board $\mathfrak{bb}$, defines the vote space $\mathfrak{m}$, and constructs a key pair (pk, sk). Secondly, the adversary executes the algorithm A_1 on the public key pk and vote space $\mathfrak{m}$, and outputs the triple (v_0, v_1, s), where $v_0, v_1 \in \mathfrak{m}$ and s is some state information. Thirdly, the challenger randomly selects a bit β, computes a challenge ballot b, and updates the bulletin board with b. Fourthly, the adversary executes the algorithm A_2 which outputs some state t. Next, the challenger computes the election result $\mathfrak{v}$. Finally, the adversary executes the algorithm A_3 on the input t and $\mathfrak{v} \backslash \{v_\beta\}$. The election scheme satisfies ballot independence if the adversary has less than a negligible advantage over guessing the bit β.

Definition 8 (IND-BB: Ballot independence). *Let $\Gamma = (\mathsf{Setup}, \mathsf{Vote}, \mathsf{BB},$ $\mathsf{Tally})$ be an election scheme, $\mathcal{A} = (A_1, A_2, A_3)$ be an adversary, n be the security parameter and $IND\text{-}BB_{\mathcal{A},\Gamma}(n)$ the cryptographic game defined below.*

$$2 \cdot Pr[(\mathfrak{bb}, \mathfrak{m}, pk, sk) \leftarrow \mathsf{Setup}(1^n);\ (v_0, v_1, s) \leftarrow A_1^{\mathcal{O}}(\mathfrak{m}, pk);\ \beta \leftarrow \{0, 1\};$$
$$b \leftarrow \mathsf{Vote}_{pk}(v_\beta);\ \mathfrak{bb} \leftarrow \mathsf{BB}(\mathfrak{bb}, b);\ t \leftarrow A_2^{\mathcal{O}}(s);\ (\mathfrak{v}, aux) \leftarrow \mathsf{Tally}_{sk}(\mathfrak{bb}):$$
$$A_3(t, \mathfrak{v} \backslash \{v_\beta\}) = \beta] - 1$$

In the above game we let $\mathcal{O}$ be defined as follows:

- *$\mathcal{O}(b)$ executes $\mathfrak{bb} \leftarrow \mathsf{BB}(\mathfrak{bb}, b)$*
- *$\mathcal{O}()$ outputs $\mathfrak{bb}$*

Moreover, we insist that $v_0, v_1 \in \mathfrak{m}$. We say Γ satisfies IND-BB (or ballot independence) if for all probabilistic polynomial-time adversaries $\mathcal{A}$ and security parameters n, there exists a negligible function negl such that $IND\text{-}BB_{\mathcal{A},\Gamma}(n) \leq \mathsf{negl}(n)$.

Intuitively, if an adversary wins the game, then the adversary is able to distinguish between challenge ballots $b \leftarrow \mathsf{Vote}_{pk}(v_0)$ and $b \leftarrow \mathsf{Vote}_{pk}(v_1)$. As per our NM-BB game, we avoid trivial and unavoidable distinctions by removing the challenge vote from the election result.

Our ballot independence games are based on standard security models for encryption: NM-BB is based on non-malleability whereas IND-BB game is based on indistinguishability. Bellare and Sahai [21] have shown that non-malleability is equivalent to a notion of indistinguishability for encryption and we adapt their proof to show that NM-BB and IND-BB are equivalent.

Theorem 9 (NM-BB = IND-BB). *Given an election scheme Γ, we have Γ satisfies NM-BB if and only if Γ satisfies IND-BB.*

Theorem 9 relates the advantage of an adversary casting a vote meaningfully related to an honest voter's vote to an advantage in guessing the honest voter's vote, in a setting where the election result does not contain the honest voter's vote. The proof of Theorem 9 can be found in the full version of our paper [1].

4.3   Controlled Malleability Is Sufficient

Recall that ballot independence tolerates meaningfully related ballots, assuming they are rejected by the bulletin board. It follows intuitively that we can weaken the requirement for an NM-CPA encryption scheme in Proposition 7, assuming we modify Enc2Vote's bulletin board algorithm to reject ballots meaningfully related to existing ballots on the bulletin board. We start with a simple example. Given an encryption scheme satisfying NM-CPA, we can derive a new encryption scheme by prepending a random bit to all ciphertexts and removing this bit before decryption. This new encryption scheme does not satisfy NM-CPA, however, we can derive an election scheme satisfying ballot independence using Enc2Vote if we modify Enc2Vote's bulletin board algorithm as follows: given a bulletin board 𝔟𝔟 and ballot b, reject b if it is identical to any ballot already on 𝔟𝔟 up to the first bit. This example shows that non-malleable ballots are not necessary for ballot independence. Let us now formalise a notion of *controlled malleability*[5], denoted NM-CPA/R (pronounced "NM-CPA modulo R"), which we will show is sufficient for ballot independence.

Definition 10 (Controlled malleability). *Let $\Pi = (\mathsf{Gen}, \mathsf{Enc}, \mathsf{Dec})$ be an asymmetric encryption scheme and R be an efficiently computable equivalence relation on Π's ciphertext space. We say that Π satisfies NM-CPA/R (or controlled malleability) if for all efficient adversaries $\mathcal{A}$ the following probability is negligible*

$$Pr\left[(pk, sk) \leftarrow \mathsf{Gen}(1^n); \beta \leftarrow \{0,1\} \; : \; \mathcal{A}^{\mathsf{chal}_\beta, \mathsf{dec}}(pk) = \beta\right]$$

where the oracles chal *and* dec *are defined as follows and each oracle may be called once, in any order.*

- chal$_\beta$ *takes two messages m_0 and m_1 of equal length as input, computes $c^* \leftarrow \mathsf{Enc}_{pk}(m_\beta)$, and outputs c^*.*
- dec *takes a vector $\mathbf{c}$ of ciphertexts as input. If* chal$_\beta$ *has previously output a ciphertext c^* such that $R(c, c^*)$ holds for some $c \in \mathbf{c}$, then output $\perp$, otherwise, output $\mathsf{Dec}_{sk}(\mathbf{c})$.*

---

[5] The term is taken from Kohlweiss et al. [22] who introduce controlled malleability for zero-knowledge proofs.

Our definition generalises non-malleability for encryption, in particular, NM-CPA = NM-CPA/R, when R is the identity. Moreover, we note that our definition could be adapted to a notion of CCA2/R by allowing arbitrarily many decryption queries. The construction Enc2Vote can be generalised to asymmetric encryption schemes satisfying controlled malleability as follows.

Definition 11 (Enc2Vote/R). *Suppose $\Pi = (\mathsf{Gen}, \mathsf{Enc}, \mathsf{Dec})$ is an asymmetric encryption scheme and R is an efficiently computable equivalence relation on Π's ciphertext space, we define* Enc2Vote/$R(\Pi) = (\mathsf{Setup}, \mathsf{Vote}, \mathsf{BB}, \mathsf{Tally})$ *as follows. Let the* Setup, Vote *and* Tally *algorithms be given by* Enc2Vote(Π). *The* BB *algorithm takes* bb *and* b *as input, where* bb *is a multiset. If there exists* $b' \in$ bb *such that* $R(b, b')$, *then* BB *outputs* bb, *otherwise,* BB *outputs* bb $\cup \{b\}$.

Assuming that the relation R does not relate fresh, honestly generated ciphertexts in Π's ciphertext space to other values (Definition 12), we can ensure that Enc2Vote/$R(\Pi)$ satisfies the correctness condition of election schemes and, hence, Enc2Vote/$R(\Pi)$ is an election scheme satisfying ballot independence by (Proposition 13).

Definition 12 (Sparse relation). *Let $\Pi = (\mathsf{Gen}, \mathsf{Enc}, \mathsf{Dec})$ be an asymmetric encryption scheme and R be an efficiently computable equivalence relation on Π's ciphertext space. We say R is a* sparse *relation if for all $(pk, sk) \leftarrow \mathsf{Gen}$, c and m, we have $c' \leftarrow \mathsf{Enc}(m, pk)$ yields $R(c, c') = 0$ with overwhelming probability.*

Proposition 13. *Suppose Π is an asymmetric encryption scheme and R is an efficiently computable and sparse equivalence relation on Π's ciphertext space such that Π satisfies NM-CPA/R. We have* Enc2Vote/$R(\Pi)$ *satisfies ballot independence.*

The proof of Proposition 13 is similar to the proof of [7, Theorem 4.2].

Design Paradigms and Discussion. We derive the following design paradigms from our results: 1) use non-malleable ballots (Section 4.1), or 2) identify and reject related ballots using controlled malleability. The latter paradigm is particularly useful when ballots contain malleable data such as voter identities or pseudonyms, since we can tolerate malleability and provide provable security. Moreover, it facilitates more realistic models of election schemes in comparison with earlier work, for example, Bernhard *et al.* [6–8] abstractly model Helios ballots as non-malleable ciphertexts, whereas, in practice, Helios ballots embed non-malleable ciphertexts in malleable JavaScript Object Notation (JSON) data structures (this is particularly relevant, since Smyth & Cortier [23, §4.1] have shown that the JSON structures introduces vulnerabilities).

5   Ballot Secrecy Implies Ballot Independence

In this paper, all election schemes satisfy correctness: the bulletin board algorithm BB adds honestly constructed ballots to the bulletin board, the tally algorithm Tally includes honest votes in the election result, and the number of votes in an election result corresponds to the number of ballots (that is, each ballot contains one vote). In this setting, an election scheme satisfying ballot secrecy also satisfies ballot independence.

Theorem 14 (Ballot secrecy implies ballot independence). *Given an election scheme Γ satisfying ballot secrecy, we have Γ satisfies ballot independence.*

Proof (Proof sketch). The proof is by a standard reduction argument: given a successful IND-BB adversary, we construct an adversary against IND-SEC. The single challenge query on (v_0, v_1) becomes a pair of vote queries $\mathsf{Vote}(v_0, v_1)$ and $\mathsf{Vote}(v_1, v_0)$, and oracle queries $\mathcal{O}(b)$ become ballot queries. When we obtain the election outcome from the IND-SEC game, we remove v_0 and v_1 since this is the distribution that the IND-BB adversary expects. Finally, we show that the advantage translates between games.   □

Theorem 14 relates an advantage in guessing an honest voter's vote in a setting where the election result *does not* contain the honest voter's vote to an advantage in the ballot secrecy game where the election result *does* include the honest voter's vote. It follows, by Theorem 9, that an advantage in casting a vote meaningfully related to an honest voter's vote translates into an advantage in guessing an honest voter's vote, hence, we have shown that ballot independence is necessary for ballot secrecy in election schemes defined by Definition 3. The proof of Theorem 14 can be found in the full version of our paper [1].

5.1 Critique of Desmedt and Chaidos's Helios Variant

Intuitively, Theorem 14 contradicts the results by Desmedt & Chaidos [16], who claim to provide a variant of the Helios election scheme which allows Bob to cast the same vote as Alice, with Alice's cooperation, whilst preventing Bob from learning Alice's vote. In their protocol, Bob selects Alice's ballot from the bulletin board and communicates with Alice to generate a new ballot that is guaranteed to contain the same vote as Alice's. Desmedt & Chaidos's security claim is true *before the election result is announced*, since Bob gains no advantage in guessing Alice's vote. However, *after the election result is announced*, the claim is false. We can informally contradict this claim – using results by Cortier & Smyth [4,10,11] – in an election with voters Alice, Bob and Charlie: if Bob casts the same vote as Alice, then Bob can learn Alice's vote by observing the election result and checking which candidate obtained at least two votes (that is, Bob can learn Alice's vote when the election result is not unanimous). We believe the erroneous claim by Desmedt & Chaidos is due to an invalid inference from their computational security result. Indeed, although the result [16, Theorem 1] is correct, their model does not support their claims for real world security: Desmedt & Chaidos consider a passive adversary that cannot observe the election result, whereas, we believe a practical notion of security must consider an *active* adversary who can cast ballots and observe the election result, since this captures the capabilities of an attacker in the real world. Nonetheless, a weaker notion of ballot secrecy may be satisfiable in Desmedt & Chaidos's variant of Helios, assuming Alice never cooperates with the adversary. Clearly, no claims can be made about Bob's knowledge of Alice's vote in this setting. We have shown Desmedt & Chaidos our results and Chaidos agrees with our findings [24].

5.2 Discussion

We have shown that election schemes satisfying ballot secrecy must also satisfy ballot independence. However, we must concede that alternative formalisms of election schemes may permit different results. Indeed, Cortier & Smyth [4, Section 7.1] present a result to the contrary using anonymous channels, which are implicitly excluded from our model. Moreover, our model also excludes settings where the adversary cannot control a majority of voters and places some restrictions on the election result, namely, the election result is captured as a multiset which reveals the number of votes for each candidate. In this setting, an election result can be computed from a partial election result if the votes of the remaining voters are known. This property is implicitly used in our proof of Theorem 14. On the other hand, some practical election schemes do not have this property. For example, consider an election scheme which announces the winning candidate, but does not provide a breakdown of the votes for each candidate [25–28]. It follows that knowledge of a partial election result can only be used to derive the election result if the adversary controls a majority of voters. Similarly, given an election result and knowledge of a minority of votes, a partial election result which excludes the known votes cannot be derived. In this setting, we believe election schemes can satisfy ballot secrecy but not ballot independence, since casting a minority of related ballots is not sufficient to reveal a voter's vote. Formal treatment of this case and consideration of whether such schemes are practical is a possible direction for future work.

6   Sufficient Conditions for Ballot Secrecy

The main distinctions between our ballot secrecy (IND-SEC) and ballot independence (IND-BB) games are as follows.

1. The challenger in our ballot independence game explicitly defines a challenge ballot and adds the ballot to the bulletin board, whereas, the challenger in our ballot secrecy game provides the adversary with an oracle $\mathcal{O}_{\mathcal{B}}(\cdot, \cdot)$.

The two formulations are similar, indeed, the challenger's computation $b \leftarrow \mathsf{Vote}_{pk}(v_\beta)$; $\mathfrak{bb} \leftarrow \mathsf{BB}(\mathfrak{bb}, b)$ is similar to an oracle call $\mathcal{O}_{\mathcal{B}}(v_0, v_1)$. Moreover, a hybrid argument will show that it does not matter if we give the adversary only one challenge ballot or many oracle calls.

2. The adversary in our ballot secrecy game has access to the auxiliary data produced during tallying, but the adversary in our ballot independence game does not.

The second point distinguishes our two games; Theorem 14 shows that ballot secrecy is stronger than independence and Footnote 3 gives a case where it is strictly stronger: the presentation of the Enc2Vote construction by Bernhard, Pereira & Warinschi provides ballot independence, but the auxiliary data maps voters to votes, thereby violating ballot secrecy. Nonetheless, by restricting the adversary's access to auxiliary data we can show that the two games are equivalent (Theorem 15) and, hence, in the absence of auxiliary data, ballot independence is a sufficient condition for ballot secrecy, in particular, Enc2Vote and Enc2Vote/R are constructions for election schemes satisfying ballot secrecy.

Theorem 15 (NM-BB = IND-SEC, without auxiliary data). *Suppose Γ = (Setup, Vote, BB, Tally) is an election scheme such that there exists a constant symbol $\bot$ and for all parameters $(\mathfrak{bb}_0, \mathfrak{m}, pk, sk) \leftarrow \mathsf{Setup}(1^n)$, multisets $\mathfrak{bb}$ and tallying data $(\mathfrak{v}, aux) \leftarrow \mathsf{Tally}_{sk}(\mathfrak{bb})$, we have $aux = \bot$. It follows that Γ satisfies ballot secrecy if and only if Γ satisfies ballot independence.*

A proof of Theorem 15 can be found in the full version of this paper [1]. In essence, the proof uses a standard hybrid argument to show that it is sufficient to consider a variant of the IND-SEC game in which the adversary is restricted to a single oracle call $\mathcal{O}(v_0, v_1)$ and shows that an adversary in this game can be used to construct a successful adversary against IND-BB.

Intuitively, we can generalise Theorem 15 to election schemes in which the auxiliary data can be simulated. Since the auxiliary data output by election schemes typically consists of signatures of knowledge proving that the election result has been correctly computed from the bulletin board, we expect many practical election schemes will satisfy zero-knowledge auxiliary data, indeed, Helios outputs partial ElGamal decryptions [29, 30] and proofs demonstrating knowledge of discrete logarithms [31–33] which can be simulated. In this context, we believe ballot secrecy and ballot independence coincide (Remark 16). Unfortunately, formalising zero-knowledge is a complex issue – in particular, the simulator needs some extra capabilities compared to the election officials (otherwise the officials could publish simulated proofs!) – to which there is no general solution and, hence, there is no general proof of Remark 16. Nonetheless, we believe Remark 16 can be shown to hold for particular formalisations of zero-knowledge, for instance, a proof could be constructed in the programmable random oracle model (the proof would essentially be that of Theorem 15 with the simulator being run at the appropriate point; we briefly comment on this in the proof of Theorem 15) and, hence, a proof of ballot secrecy can be reduced to a proof of ballot independence.

Remark 16 (NM-BB = IND-SEC for zero-knowledge auxiliary data). Given an election scheme Γ satisfying zero-knowledge auxiliary data (informally, zero-knowledge auxiliary data means that the auxiliary data can be simulated given the result), we have Γ satisfies ballot secrecy if and only if Γ satisfies ballot independence.

Remark 16 suggests that ballot independence is a sufficient condition for ballot secrecy in election schemes where auxiliary data can be simulated. Coupled with earlier results [8], this should facilitate a proof of ballot secrecy in Helios. (Bernhard *et al.* [6] provide a proof of ballot secrecy in a variant of Helios which uses the Naor & Yung transformation [34] to derive non-malleable ballots and Bernhard, Pereira & Warinschi [8] prove that Helios satisfies ballot secrecy in the special case of referendums, however, a full proof of ballot secrecy in Helios is not currently known.)

7   Conclusion

We have formalised *ballot independence* in a variant of the model for election schemes proposed by Bernhard *et al.* Our main results are as follows. Ballot secrecy implies ballot independence; the converse holds too if there is no auxiliary data. Moreover, we have argued that ballot independence and ballot secrecy coincide if auxiliary data is "zero knowledge;" since auxiliary data typically consists of zero knowledge proofs, this assumption is realistic and holds for election schemes such as Helios, for instance. Furthermore, we provide some sufficient conditions for ballot independence and, hence, ballot secrecy: we show that non-malleable ballots are sufficient but not necessary for independence and secrecy, and introduce a weaker notion of controlled-malleable encryption which we show is sufficient, moreover, this notion is better suited to modelling the way ballots are handled in practice (for example, by Helios). In addition, we show that the notion of ballot secrecy proposed by Bernhard *et al.* does not capture attacks which rely on auxiliary data and we adopt a stronger definition. Furthermore, we show that the variant of Helios proposed by Desmedt & Chaidos does not satisfy ballot secrecy.

Acknowledgements. We are particularly grateful to Bogdan Warinschi and the anonymous reviewers who read earlier versions of this paper and provided useful guidance. This work has been partly supported by the European Research Council under the European Union's Seventh Framework Programme (FP7/2007-2013) / ERC project *CRYSP* (259639) and by EPSRC via grant EP/H043454/1.

References

1. Smyth, B., Bernhard, D.: Ballot secrecy and ballot independence coincide. Cryptology ePrint Archive, Report 2013/235 (2013)
2. Delaune, S., Kremer, S., Ryan, M.: Coercion-Resistance and Receipt-Freeness in Electronic Voting. In: CSFW 2006: 19th Computer Security Foundations Workshop, pp. 28–42. IEEE Computer Society (2006)
3. Backes, M., Hriţcu, C., Maffei, M.: Automated Verification of Remote Electronic Voting Protocols in the Applied Pi-calculus. In: CSF 2008: 21st Computer Security Foundations Symposium, pp. 195–209. IEEE Computer Society (2008)
4. Cortier, V., Smyth, B.: Attacking and fixing Helios: An analysis of ballot secrecy. Journal of Computer Security 21(1), 89–148 (2013)

5. Delaune, S., Kremer, S., Ryan, M.D.: Verifying privacy-type properties of electronic voting protocols. Journal of Computer Security 17(4), 435–487 (2009)
6. Bernhard, D., Cortier, V., Pereira, O., Smyth, B., Warinschi, B.: Adapting Helios for provable ballot privacy. In: Atluri, V., Diaz, C. (eds.) ESORICS 2011. LNCS, vol. 6879, pp. 335–354. Springer, Heidelberg (2011)
7. Bernhard, D., Pereira, O., Warinschi, B.: On Necessary and Sufficient Conditions for Private Ballot Submission. Cryptology ePrint Archive, Report 2012/236 (version 20120430:154117b) (2012)
8. Bernhard, D., Pereira, O., Warinschi, B.: How Not to Prove Yourself: Pitfalls of the Fiat-Shamir Heuristic and Applications to Helios. In: Wang, X., Sako, K. (eds.) ASIACRYPT 2012. LNCS, vol. 7658, pp. 626–643. Springer, Heidelberg (2012)
9. Gennaro, R.: Achieving independence efficiently and securely. In: PODC 1995: 14th Principles of Distributed Computing Symposium, pp. 130–136. ACM Press (1995)
10. Smyth, B., Cortier, V.: A note on replay attacks that violate privacy in electronic voting schemes. Technical Report RR-7643, INRIA (June 2011) http://hal.inria.fr/inria-00599182/
11. Cortier, V., Smyth, B.: Attacking and fixing Helios: An analysis of ballot secrecy. In: CSF 2011: 24th Computer Security Foundations Symposium, pp. 297–311. IEEE Computer Society (2011)
12. Schneier, B.: Hacking the Papal Election (2013), https://www.schneier.com/blog/archives/2013/02/hacking_the_pap.html
13. Bulens, P., Giry, D., Pereira, O.: Running Mixnet-Based Elections with Helios. In: EVT/WOTE 2011: Electronic Voting Technology Workshop/Workshop on Trustworthy Elections. USENIX Association (2011)
14. Adida, B.: Helios: Web-based Open-Audit Voting. In: USENIX Security 2008: 17th USENIX Security Symposium, pp. 335–348. USENIX Association (2008)
15. Adida, B., Marneffe, O., Pereira, O., Quisquater, J.: Electing a University President Using Open-Audit Voting: Analysis of Real-World Use of Helios. In: EVT/WOTE 2009: Electronic Voting Technology Workshop/Workshop on Trustworthy Elections. USENIX Association (2009)
16. Desmedt, Y., Chaidos, P.: Applying Divertibility to Blind Ballot Copying in the Helios Internet Voting System. In: Foresti, S., Yung, M., Martinelli, F. (eds.) ESORICS 2012. LNCS, vol. 7459, pp. 433–450. Springer, Heidelberg (2012)
17. Chor, B., Goldwasser, S., Micali, S., Awerbuch, B.: Verifiable Secret Sharing and Achieving Simultaneity in the Presence of Faults. In: FOCS 1985: 26th Foundations of Computer Science Symposium, pp. 383–395. IEEE Computer Society (1985)
18. Dolev, D., Dwork, C., Naor, M.: Non-Malleable Cryptography. In: STOC 1991: 23rd Theory of Computing Symposium, pp. 542–552. ACM Press (1991)
19. Bellare, M., Desai, A., Pointcheval, D., Rogaway, P.: Relations Among Notions of Security for Public-Key Encryption Schemes. In: Krawczyk, H. (ed.) CRYPTO 1998. LNCS, vol. 1462, pp. 26–45. Springer, Heidelberg (1998)
20. Dolev, D., Dwork, C., Naor, M.: Nonmalleable Cryptography. Journal on Computing 30(2), 391–437 (2000)
21. Bellare, M., Sahai, A.: Non-malleable Encryption: Equivalence between Two Notions, and an Indistinguishability-Based Characterization. In: Wiener, M. (ed.) CRYPTO 1999. LNCS, vol. 1666, pp. 519–536. Springer, Heidelberg (1999)
22. Chase, M., Kohlweiss, M., Lysyanskaya, A., Meiklejohn, S.: Malleable Proof Systems and Applications. In: Pointcheval, D., Johansson, T. (eds.) EUROCRYPT 2012. LNCS, vol. 7237, pp. 281–300. Springer, Heidelberg (2012)
23. Smyth, B., Cortier, V.: Does Helios ensure ballot secrecy? Cryptology ePrint Archive, Report 2010/625 (version 20101217:132825) (2010)

24. Chaidos, P.: Private email communication (March/April 2013)
25. Benaloh, J., Yung, M.: Distributing the Power of a Government to Enhance the Privacy of Voters. In: PODC 1986: 5th Principles of Distributed Computing Symposium, pp. 52–62. ACM Press (1986)
26. Hevia, A., Kiwi, M.: Electronic Jury Voting Protocols. In: Rajsbaum, S. (ed.) LATIN 2002. LNCS, vol. 2286, pp. 415–429. Springer, Heidelberg (2002)
27. Hevia, A., Kiwi, M.A.: Electronic jury voting protocols. Theoretical Computer Science 321(1), 73–94 (2004)
28. Desmedt, Y., Kurosawa, K.: Electronic Voting: Starting Over? In: Zhou, J., López, J., Deng, R.H., Bao, F. (eds.) ISC 2005. LNCS, vol. 3650, pp. 329–343. Springer, Heidelberg (2005)
29. Pedersen, T.P.: A Threshold Cryptosystem without a Trusted Party. In: Davies, D.W. (ed.) EUROCRYPT 1991. LNCS, vol. 547, pp. 522–526. Springer, Heidelberg (1991)
30. Chaum, D., Pedersen, T.P.: Wallet Databases with Observers. In: Brickell, E.F. (ed.) CRYPTO 1992. LNCS, vol. 740, pp. 89–105. Springer, Heidelberg (1993)
31. Chaum, D., Evertse, J.-H., van de Graaf, J., Peralta, R.: Demonstrating Possession of a Discrete Logarithm Without Revealing It. In: Odlyzko, A.M. (ed.) CRYPTO 1986. LNCS, vol. 263, pp. 200–212. Springer, Heidelberg (1987)
32. Chaum, D., Evertse, J.-H., van de Graaf, J.: An Improved Protocol for Demonstrating Possession of Discrete Logarithms and Some Generalizations. In: Price, W.L., Chaum, D. (eds.) EUROCRYPT 1987. LNCS, vol. 304, pp. 127–141. Springer, Heidelberg (1988)
33. Schnorr, C.-P.: Efficient Identification and Signatures for Smart Cards. In: Brassard, G. (ed.) CRYPTO 1989. LNCS, vol. 435, pp. 239–252. Springer, Heidelberg (1990)
34. Naor, M., Yung, M.: Public-key Cryptosystems Provably Secure against Chosen Ciphertext Attacks. In: STOC 1990: 22nd Theory of Computing Symposium, pp. 427–437. ACM Press (1990)

Election Verifiability or Ballot Privacy: Do We Need to Choose?

Édouard Cuvelier, Olivier Pereira, and Thomas Peters

Université catholique de Louvain
ICTEAM – Crypto Group
1348 Louvain-la-Neuve – Belgium

Abstract. We propose a new encryption primitive, *commitment consistent encryption* (CCE), and instances of this primitive that enable building the first universally verifiable voting schemes with a perfectly private audit trail (PPAT) and practical complexity. That is:

- the audit trail that is published for verifying elections guarantees everlasting privacy, and
- the computational load required from the participants is only increased by a small constant factor compared to traditional voting schemes, and is optimal in the sense of Cramer, Gennaro and Schoenmakers [16].

These properties make it possible to introduce election verifiability in large scale elections as a pure benefit, that is, without loss of privacy compared to a non-verifiable scheme and at a similar level of efficiency.

We propose different approaches for constructing voting schemes with PPAT from CCE, as well as two efficient CCE constructions: one is tailored for elections with a small number of candidates, while the second is suitable for elections with complex ballots.

1 Introduction

Elections enable a set of voters to express their opinion regarding one or more questions, and to build an aggregate outcome from these personal opinions. While very simple elections mechanisms, like hand raising, can be very convenient to organize, various properties are usually required from voting schemes nowadays, which are not guaranteed by a hand raising process.

Vote privacy is probably the most important property that has been added on top of correctness/verifiability (guaranteed by the hand raising process), and became mandatory for public elections in most countries during the 19th century, as a way to prevent coercion and bribery [36].

Elections guaranteeing the privacy of the votes while preserving the correctness of the outcome are unfortunately much harder to organize in a trustworthy way: as usual, correctness and privacy guarantees tend to conflict.

As a result, most voting schemes used today enforce privacy at the expense of the correctness properties: in traditional paper-based scheme, it is most of

J. Crampton, S. Jajodia, and K. Mayes (Eds.): ESORICS 2013, LNCS 8134, pp. 481–498, 2013.

the time impossible for a voter to convince himself that his vote is included in the urns that are tallied (he has to trust election officers on that), and the same happens with the commonly deployed non verifiable electronic voting schemes, which also make it impossible for the voters to verify what is counted by the computers, if there is anything counted at all.

As a way to solve this problem, universally verifiable voting systems were proposed in the seminal works of Benaloh et al. [7, 13], works that have been followed by a considerable body of research during the last 25 years (see [12, 15, 16, 18, 22, 27, 32, 34, 35] for instance). Universally verifiable elections are realized by including in the voting process the production of an audit trail (which can be electronic, made of paper, or both) that makes it possible for voters to check that their vote was recorded properly and that the election outcome is consistent with all the votes submitted by legitimate voters (formal definitions appear in [30, 29] for instance.)

The adoption of universally verifiable technologies is however complicated if the audit trail that is provided in order to guarantee the correctness of an election in turn weakens the privacy of the votes: this raises questions about the relative importance of the correctness improvement resulting from the audit trail versus the potential decrease of privacy that results from that same audit trail, as well as about the consequences of any (even partial) failure with respect to one of these properties. These are sensitive problems, and the balance between these requirements will typically depend on the specifics of each election (stakes, voter population, culture, . . .).

This compromise between correctness and privacy needs to be made in the vast majority of the verifiable voting schemes that have been proposed [7, 16, 18, 22, 27, 34, 35] (we discuss the few exceptions in Section 1.2) including those that have been used in real-world elections. The public audit trail of all those voting systems indeed includes information that could reveal individual votes if a computationally secure cryptosystem is broken, which will eventually happen in a hard to predict future, either because of the increase of power of computing devices, or because of a cryptanalytic breakthrough that can happen at any time.

For instance, Helios [3] publishes encrypted votes, which may eventually reveal those votes if the encryption scheme that is used is broken. This in part motivated the decision of the IACR to only display aliases instead of voter names on their election bulletin board: in case of broken encryption, the election bulletin board would then only reveal the content of encrypted votes but not their author (the voting server is still aware of the link between aliases and voters, though, and these aliases circulate in cleartext emails). Such a procedure however impairs eligibility verifiability, as it becomes infeasible for the voters to verify whether the ballots present on the bulletin board have been submitted by legitimate voters or are the result of ballot stuffing by the organizers [29, 4].

In a similar way, Scantegrity II [11] publishes a Q table containing the confirmation codes that have been unveiled during the voting phase, and, as soon as there are few dozen of voters, the content of this table will determine uniquely the value of the seed used to build the original P table, which in turn reveals the votes corresponding to all voter receipts. This may be enough to defeat the purpose of the introduction of privacy in voting systems, since voters may be coerced just by fear of a future loss of privacy.

1.1 Contributions

We address this problem by proposing a new primitive, commitment consistent encryption (CCE), that can be plugged in voting schemes as a replacement for traditional encryption. The use of this primitive makes it possible to obtain verifiable elections with a perfectly private audit trail (PPAT), that is, an audit trail that preserves the privacy of the votes even when facing a computationally unbounded adversary. As a result, adding a PPAT on top of a traditional voting scheme provides the benefits of universally verifiable voting technologies without interfering with the privacy properties of the original system.

As an important example of application, we investigate the use of CCE for building single-pass [8] voting schemes with PPAT. Single-pass voting schemes support a voting process that executes asynchronously and in a single step, which makes them well-suited for large scale elections: voters just produce their ballot and send it to the authorities. The reception of the ballots and the tally are then orchestrated by a set of authorities, who are also in charge of publishing the election audit trail. The correctness of this audit trail ensures the correctness of the election outcome even if *all* authorities are corrupted. Still, the privacy of the votes relies on the number of corrupted authorities to be lower than a certain threshold.

With this application in mind, we design two efficient CCE encryption schemes. The first of our schemes is additively homomorphic and is particularly suitable for elections based on homomorphic tallying. It is however limited to elections that have a small election outcome space (e.g., elections in which the outcome is simply the sum of votes received by the candidates). Our second scheme is suitable for elections with mixnet-based tallying, in which all ballots are decrypted after shuffling, which allows supporting arbitrary ballot formats. We eventually propose a third scheme that is flexible enough to be used in both contexts but is much less efficient and complicated to use.

Our first two schemes admit simple distributed and threshold key generation procedures: all computations happen in prime order groups and the standard threshold key generation techniques available in such groups apply [24]. This is particularly important, especially in terms of round complexity, as the trustees of an election will often not be able to setup specific software for running key generation: for instance, the Helios voting system used by IACR relies on n-out-of-n distributed key generation just to keep the key generation ceremony simple (traditional threshold key generation would require more than one single round).

These two CCE schemes are also very efficient, making them usable in Java-Script applications like Helios for instance: based on the performance on the JSBN cryptographic library, the preparation of any vote that can be encoded on 256 bits requires less than a second.

Based on these schemes, we obtain the first universally verifiable voting protocols with PPAT and optimal efficiency (in the sense of [16]):

- the ballot size and the voter computational load do not depend on the number of voters nor on the number of authorities and
- the workload of the tallying authorities grows linearly with the number of voters and candidates.

Furthermore, our schemes do not rely on expensive cut-and-choose techniques: the number of exponentiations to be performed is independent of the security parameter.

1.2   Related Works

Very few voting protocols offer a perfectly private audit trail, and they all require either an amount of work by the voters that grows linearly with the number of trustees, or the use of specific communication channels, or are inefficient.

A first class of voting schemes that can offer a PPAT is based on blind signatures [22]. Here, ballots are blindly signed by an authority, then unblinded by the voters who eventually publish their authority signed ballot through an anonymous channel. The vote privacy issue is here taken care of by the anonymous channel and the audit trail only contains anonymous information. Setting up a perfectly anonymous channel can however be very challenging in a large scale election.

A second approach was proposed by Cramer, Franklin, Schoenmakers and Yung [15]. Here, a verifiable secret sharing scheme is used by the voters to distribute the information needed to tally their vote. The shares are then distributed to the authorities either through private channels or protected by encryption. The computational load of the voters then grows linearly with the number of authorities, which motivated the consecutive proposal by Cramer, Gennaro and Schoenmakers of a scheme that offers a computationally private audit trail but a work load for the voters that is independent of the number of authorities [16].

In the same spirit as the work of Cramer et al. [15], Moran and Naor proposed a voting scheme with everlasting privacy [33]. Here again, the privacy of the votes is protected through secret sharing and the complexity of the ballot preparation task grows linearly with the number of authorities.

As far as we know, our solutions are the first to offer a PPAT while being based on the third approach of e-voting, that is, the tallying of threshold encrypted ballots [7, 13, 16, 27]. In a contemporary work, Demirel, van de Graaf and Araújo [20, 19] explore a similar problem and propose a solution based on the combination of Pedersen commitments and Paillier encryption proposed of Moran and Naor [33]. As acknowledged by these authors, this solution is not practical: it relies on cut-and-choose zero-knowledge (ZK) proofs, which makes it slower than ours by approximately 4 orders of magnitude for comparable security levels, and requires the execution of sophisticated MPC protocols for distributed key generation by the trustees.

In terms of modeling, symbolic techniques also have been recently proposed to model everlasting privacy [4].

Two Flavors of Verifiability. Just like privacy, verifiability is a property that comes in computational and perfect flavors. The huge majority of schemes offer the computational variant, typically by relying on zero-knowledge proofs that only are computationally sound. The solutions we propose share this feature.

We believe that the balance between computational and perfect verifiability is however very different of the one we have for privacy. First, to have any impact, an attack on the verifiability must be mounted on-the-fly during the election: a falsified proof of verifiability proposed after 20 years will not convince anyone, while a loss of privacy after 20 years might be a practical concern. Second, the adoption of verifiable protocols is often conditioned by improvements on traditional non-verifiable systems. So, having the possibility to bring verifiability without weakening privacy (by publishing ciphertexts) might be a core decision factor. Similar considerations motivated the design of Scantegrity: its practical adoption is expected to have been facilitated by the absence of need to decrease the usability of the paper ballots [11].

Coercion resistance. The historical motivation for introducing secret ballots was the prevention of bribery or coercion. The schemes we propose address the concern of a voter who fears that the audit data of an election could reveal their vote. This concern is certainly the most ubiquitous and hard to prevent through law enforcement or by voter education: it does not require any visible step by a coercer who just needs to look at available data. We do not focus on specific coercion resistance procedures in our simple application examples, as coercion prevention is a much broader problem than what can be addressed at a protocol level, especially when vote-by-mail is authorized or when nothing prevents bringing camera phones in a voting booth. Our schemes are however compatible with most existing approaches, e.g., revoting as first used in Estonia or coercion detection [25].

Roadmap. The rest of this paper is organized as follows. Section 2 introduces our new encryption primitives, CC and CCVA encryption. Section 3 discusses security properties that these encryption primitives need to satisfy for use in voting applications. Section 4 defines two efficient CCVA schemes and explains how they can be plugged in classical voting schemes. We finally analyse the efficiency of our solutions in Section 5.

2 Commitment Consistent Encryption

We introduce a new encryption primitive, *commitment consistent encryption* (CCE). A CCE primitive is a traditional public key encryption scheme that offers an extra feature: from any CCE ciphertext, it is possible to derive a commitment on the encrypted message, and the private key can also be used to obtain an opening on that commitment. In the context of elections, we expect voters to CC encrypt their vote, which will allow authorities to compute the tally in a traditional way (e.g., by decrypting the homomorphic sum of the ciphertexts). Furthermore, when receiving a CC ciphertext, the authorities can use a

DeriveCom algorithm to derive commitments from CC ciphertexts and post that commitment on the bulletin board. This provides a PPAT if the commitments are perfectly hiding. In order to offer universal verifiability, the authorities can also make use of an Open algorithm that makes it possible to derive openings of commitments on the election tally.

For simplicity, we make our whole treatment in the single-key setting. The extension to the full threshold setting is orthogonal to our concerns and can be made using traditional techniques. In the following, an efficient algorithm runs in PPT, and a negligible function decreases faster than any inverse polynomial. An overwhelming function is close to 1 up to a negligible function.

Definition 1 (CC Encryption). *A commitment consistent encryption scheme Π is a tuple of efficient algorithms* (Gen, Enc, Dec, DeriveCom, Open, Verify) *defined as follow :*

Gen(1^n): *Given a security parameter n, output a triple (pp, pk, sk), respectively the public parameters, the public key and the secret key.*

Enc(pk, m): *Output a ciphertext c which is an encryption using the public key pk of a message m chosen in the plaintext space $\mathcal{M}$ defined by pp.*

Dec(sk, c): *From a ciphertext c, output a message m using the secret key sk.*

DeriveCom(pk, c): *Output a commitment d from a ciphertext c using pk.*

Open(sk, c): *Output an auxiliary value a using the secret key sk. This auxiliary value can be considered as part of an opening for a commitment.*

Verify(pk, d, m, a): *From a message m, a commitment d with respect to key pk and an auxiliary value a, output a bit. This algorithm checks the validity of the opening (m, a) with respect to d and pk.*

It is implicit that pp is given to each algorithm apart from Gen.

Correctness. We expect CCE schemes to satisfy the following correctness properties. For any $(pp, pk, sk) \leftarrow$ Gen(1^n), any message $m \in \mathcal{M}$ and any ciphertext $c \leftarrow$ Enc(pk, m), it holds with overwhelming probability in n that Dec(sk, c) $= m$ and Verify($pk,$ DeriveCom(pk, c), Dec(sk, c), Open(sk, c)) $= 1$. For the sake of simplicity we will often shorten the expression above as Verify(pk, c).

The security properties that we can expect from a CCE scheme and for the derived commitments are the traditional ones and we will discuss later those that are appropriate for our applications.

The CCE definition does not guarantee that it is unfeasible to produce ciphertexts that look just like honestly computed CCE ciphertexts but are not consistent, which might be an issue for verifiable decryption. For instance, an attacker might be able to produce a ciphertext such that the DeriveCom function will provide a commitment that cannot be opened, which might be a problem if some parties are required to provide a decryption. In order to solve this problem, we introduce the concept of validity augmentation (VA) for CCE schemes.

From an operational point of view, a validity augmentation of a CCE scheme adds three algorithms: Expand, Strip and Valid. Expand augments the public key for the needs of the other algorithms. Valid takes an augmented CCE ciphertext c^{va} that contains a CCE ciphertext along with some proofs of validity, and runs a verification procedure on those proofs to make sure that it is possible to extract from the ciphertext a commitment and an encryption of an opening for that commitment. Eventually, Strip removes those proofs to provide some homomorphic properties such as additivity on the encrypted messages.

Definition 2 (Validity augmentation). *A scheme $\Pi^{VA} :=$ (VA.Gen, VA.Enc, VA.Dec, VA.DeriveCom, VA.Open, VA.Verify, Expand, Strip, Valid) is a validity augmentation of the CCE scheme $\Pi :=$ (Gen, Enc, Dec, DeriveCom, Open, Verify) if Π^{VA} is a CCE scheme equipped with three additional efficient algorithms Expand, Strip and Valid that satisfy the following conditions.*

Augmentation. VA.Gen *runs* Gen *to get* (pp, pk, sk) *and outputs an updated triple* $(pp^{va}, pk^{va}, sk^{va}) := (pp, \text{Expand}(pk), sk)$.

Validity. $\text{Valid}(pk^{va}, c^{va}) = 1$ *for every honestly generated ciphertext and keys and, for any PPT adversary $\mathcal{A}$, the following probability is negligible in n:*

$$\Pr\left[\text{Valid}(pk^{va}, c^{va}) = 1 \land \neg\text{Verify}(pk, \text{Strip}(pk^{va}, c^{va})) = 1 \mid c^{va} \leftarrow \mathcal{A}(pp^{va}, pk^{va}); (pp^{va}, pk^{va}, sk^{va}) \leftarrow \text{VA.Gen}(1^n)\right]$$

This condition guarantees that decryption and opening succeed.

Consistency. *The distributions of* $\text{Strip}(pk^{va}, \text{VA.Enc}(pk^{va}, m))$ *and* $\text{Enc}(pk, m)$ *are the same for all m, that is, we can strip a VA ciphertext into a normal one. Furthermore, the decryption, opening and verification of Π^{VA} are consistent with those of Π: for every ciphertext and generated keys, it must hold that* $\text{VA.Dec}(sk^{va}, c^{va}) = \text{Dec}(sk, \text{Strip}(pk^{va}, c^{va}))$, $\text{VA.Open}(sk^{va}, c^{va}) = \text{Open}(sk, \text{Strip}(pk^{va}, c^{va}))$ *and* $\text{VA.Verify}(pk^{va}, c^{va}) = \text{Verify}(pk, \text{Strip}(pk^{va}, c^{va}))$.

We refer to the result of the augmentation of a CCE scheme as a CCVA encryption scheme or simply a CCVAE scheme.

3   Voting with a Perfectly Private Audit Trail

In the spirit of [8], we now propose a "minivoting" scheme, that we use to describe how a validity augmented CCE scheme can be used to submit ballots in an election. We then describe the security guarantees that CCE schemes need to provide for their application in voting with PPAT.

The minivoting scheme we consider follows a classic workflow. First, a setup phase takes place, during which two clean bulletin boards $\boldsymbol{PB}$ and $\boldsymbol{SB}$ are created and elections keys are generated and appropriately published. The board $\boldsymbol{PB}$ contains the public audit trail, while $\boldsymbol{SB}$ is kept secret by the authorities and used to compute the tally. Voters then produce their ballots by encrypting their votes and send these ballots to the election authorities. The ballots are processed by these authorities, and the bulletin boards are updated accordingly. At the end of the voting phase, a tallying protocol is executed and the election outcome is published.

Definition 3 (Minivoting scheme)
Let Π be a CCVA encryption scheme, and let ρ be a result function that takes a set of valid votes and produces the corresponding election outcome. From these, we build a minivoting scheme $\mathsf{Enc2Vote}(\Pi, \rho)$ *as follows.*

$\mathsf{Setup}(1^n)$ *runs the key generation algorithm* Gen *of Π on the same input, obtaining a triple* (pp, pk, sk). *It also initializes a public and a secret bulletin board,* $\boldsymbol{PB}$ *and* $\boldsymbol{SB}$, *to* $\bot$.

$\mathsf{Vote}(pk, v)$ *is executed by voters to prepare their ballot: it encrypts a vote v with pk using Π, obtaining a ballot b.*

$\mathsf{ProcessBallot}(pk, b, \boldsymbol{PB}, \boldsymbol{SB})$ *is executed by the authorities every time a ballot is received. It rejects b if it is already present in* $\boldsymbol{SB}$. *Otherwise, it runs* $\mathsf{Valid}(pk, b)$ *and rejects b if it fails. If all these steps succeed, it appends b on* $\boldsymbol{SB}$ *and* $\mathsf{DeriveCom}(pk, b)$ *on* $\boldsymbol{PB}$.

$\mathsf{Tally}(sk, \boldsymbol{PB}, \boldsymbol{SB})$ *decrypts all ballots on* $\boldsymbol{SB}$, *obtaining a vector of votes* $\boldsymbol{v}$, *and publishes $\rho(\boldsymbol{v})$ on* $\boldsymbol{PB}$.

A minivoting scheme does not require any proof of the validity of the ballots (e.g., that they would encrypt 0 or 1 in an approval voting system), nor publishes any specific information regarding a proof of correctness of the tally, which will be needed for universal verifiability. For modularity, we address these concerns separately: the structure of these proofs of correctness will indeed be dependent of the result function ρ.

We now focus on the privacy of the votes that is offered in such a minivoting scheme, which we capture through the following experiment, slightly adapted from [8] to allow a distinction between the private and public bulletin boards.

The Vote Privacy experiment $\mathsf{VotePriv}^B_{\mathcal{A}, \Pi, \rho}(n)$

1. The challenger picks a bit $\beta \leftarrow \{0, 1\}$ uniformly at random. He also runs the Setup algorithm of the voting scheme on input 1^n and obtains the resulting triple (pp, pk, sk) and empty bulletin boards $\boldsymbol{PB}_\beta$ and $\boldsymbol{SB}_\beta$. He then sends pp, pk to $\mathcal{A}$ and creates two other empty bulletin boards $\boldsymbol{PB}_{1-\beta}$ and $\boldsymbol{SB}_{1-\beta}$. $\mathcal{A}$ is allowed to see the board $\boldsymbol{B}_\beta$, where $\boldsymbol{B}$ is a parameter of the experiment.
2. $\mathcal{A}$ can then perform two types of queries:
   $\mathsf{Vote}(v_0, v_1)$ On such a query, the challenger executes $\mathsf{Vote}(pk, v_i)$, obtaining a ballot b_i, and then runs $\mathsf{ProcessBallot}(pk, b_i, \boldsymbol{SB}_i)$, for $i \in \{0, 1\}$.
   $\mathsf{Ballot}(b)$ On such a query, the challenger executes $\mathsf{ProcessBallot}(pk, b, \boldsymbol{SB}_\beta)$ and, if it succeeds, also runs $\mathsf{ProcessBallot}(pk, b, \boldsymbol{SB}_{1-\beta})$.
3. The challenger computes the tally $t_0 := \mathsf{Tally}(sk, \boldsymbol{SB}_0)$ and appends t_0 on $\boldsymbol{PB}_\beta$ and $\boldsymbol{SB}_\beta$.
4. $\mathcal{A}$ outputs a bit β'. If $\beta = \beta'$ then the output of the experiment is 1 and we say that $\mathcal{A}$ wins.

Definition 4 (Perfectly Private Audit Trail). *A minivoting scheme* $\mathsf{Enc2Vote}(\Pi, \rho)$ *has a* perfectly private audit trail *(PPAT) if, for every adversary* $\mathcal{A}$, $\Pr[\mathsf{VotePriv}^{\boldsymbol{PB}}_{\mathcal{A}, \Pi, \rho}(n) = 1] = \frac{1}{2}$.

Since this definition does not place any bound on the computational power of the adversary, the everlasting privacy of the votes is guaranteed against people who only see the PB board.

In some contexts (e.g., when using groups of unknown order), it is useful to relax the above definition by accepting statistical indistinguishability and tolerating a negligible advantage over $\frac{1}{2}$. Independently of this, the private bulletin board, only seen by the authorities, should provide computational ballot privacy.

Definition 5 (Ballot Privacy [8]). *A minivoting scheme* Enc2Vote(Π, ρ) *has ballot privacy if, for every PPT adversary $\mathcal{A}$, there is a negligible function ϵ such that,* $\Pr[\mathsf{VotePriv}_{\mathcal{A},\Pi,\rho}^{SB}(n) = 1] = \frac{1}{2} + \epsilon(n)$.

Security. The following two theorems define security properties of a CCVAE scheme that guarantee the PPAT and ballot privacy of the corresponding minivoting scheme.

Theorem 1. *Let Π be a CCVA encryption scheme, and let ρ be a result function. If the output of* DeriveCom *is perfectly hiding, then the minivoting scheme* Enc2Vote(Π, ρ) *has a perfectly private audit trail.*

Proof. The view of the adversary is the $\mathsf{VotePriv}_{\mathcal{A},\Pi,\rho}^{PB}$ experiment and this view is independent of β: PB only contains perfectly hiding commitments and then a tally that is always computed from SB_0, which is independent of β. □

Theorem 2 ([9]). *Let Π be an NM-CPA CCVAE scheme, and let ρ be a result function. Then the minivoting scheme* Enc2Vote(Π, ρ) *has ballot privacy.*

The NM-CPA security property [21] is easy to reach from an IND-CPA encryption scheme, as shown in [9]: it is enough to augment each ciphertext with a sigma proof of knowledge of the message and randomness used to build this ciphertext. We observe that this sigma proof not only guarantees the knowledge of the plaintext and randomness, but also that the ciphertext is well-formed. We can then define a validity augmentation in a straightforward way: Expand adds the oracle $\mathcal{H}$ to the public key, Strip removes the sigma proof from the ciphertext, and Valid returns "1" only if the proof is valid. The validity condition holds thanks to the completeness and the soundness of the proof. The consistency of the augmentation is straightforward by inspection of Definition 2.

A first example of CCVAE scheme, called PPATP, based on Paillier encryption and Pedersen commitments following a suggestion by Moran and Naor [33] is available in the full version of this paper [17]. The full version also contains a generalized version of this construction with security proofs.

4 Efficient CCVAE Schemes

This section describes two efficient and usable constructions of CCVAE schemes. The first scheme, PPATS, allows using traditional ballot validity proof techniques and completing the tally through the homomorphic addition of encrypted votes.

The decryption process however involves a stage of exhaustive search of the plaintext (just as the exponential ElGamal scheme used in many applications), which restricts the use of this scheme to elections in which this kind of exhaustive search can be done, e.g., when the outcome is simply a count of the number of votes that each candidate received. The second scheme, PPATC, is tailored for mixnet based tallying procedures: the ciphertexts are not additively homomorphic but the decryption procedure is efficient regardless of the message. In both tally procedures we show explicitly how the process does not affect the PPAT as well as the ballot privacy of voting schemes provided by our CCVAE schemes.

Computational Setting. Our two efficient CCVAE schemes rely on the existence of a bilinear group generator that, on input 1^n, produces a description of bilinear groups $\Lambda_{sxdh} = (q, \mathbb{G}_1, \mathbb{G}_2, \mathbb{G}_T, e, g, h)$ where $\mathbb{G}_1$, $\mathbb{G}_2$ and $\mathbb{G}_T$ are groups of prime order q, with $|q| = n$, e is an efficient and non-degenerating bilinear map $e : \mathbb{G}_1 \times \mathbb{G}_2 \to \mathbb{G}_T$ and g, h are generators of $\mathbb{G}_1$ and $\mathbb{G}_2$ respectively (we refer the reader unfamiliar with those objects to [23]). We expect that these groups are chosen in such a way that there is no known efficient mapping between $\mathbb{G}_1$ and $\mathbb{G}_2$ in either direction. This is necessary, as the security of our schemes relies on the hardness on the DDH problem in both of these groups. This setting, often called the SXDH setting, is usually considered as the choice that offers the highest level of flexibility and performance for high security parameters. Common concrete choices include the use of BLS and BN curves [5, 6].

Note that all our schemes could be adapted easily to the symmetric pairing settings, typically by relying on the hardness of the DLIN problem instead of DDH [10]. The choice we made provides more efficient protocols and also makes it possible to compute in smaller fields for equivalent security levels.

4.1 CCVA Encryption for Elections with Simple Ballots

The PPATS scheme makes use of two compatible homomorphic ingredients: ElGamal encryption and the TC2 perfectly hiding commitment scheme proposed by Abe et al. [1], which is binding in the Λ_{sxdh} setting. The resulting CCE scheme is compatible with sigma protocols, and the definition of a validity augmentation is then simple.

The PPATS *CCVAE scheme:*

VA.Gen$_S(1^n)$: Generate $\Lambda_{sxdh} = (q, \mathbb{G}_1, \mathbb{G}_2, \mathbb{G}_T, e, g, h)$ for $|q| = n$ together with the following additional public random generators $g_1 = g^{x_1}$ in $\mathbb{G}_1$ and $h_1 \in \mathbb{G}_2$. The triple (pp_S, pk_S, sk_S) is defined as $((\Lambda_{sxdh}, h_1), g_1, x_1)$. The augmented key $pk_S^{va} = \mathsf{Expand}(pk_S)$ is computed by adding the description of an efficient hash function $\mathcal{H}$ with range $\mathbb{Z}_q$, resulting in the triple $(pp_S^{va} = pp_S, pk_S^{va}, sk_S^{va} = sk_S)$.

VA.Enc$_S(pk_S^{va}, m \,; r, s)$: Compute the CCE ciphertext $c = \mathsf{Enc}_S(pk_S, m; r, s)$ as $(d, c_1, c_2) = (h^r h_1^m, g^s, g^r g_1^s)$ for random $r, s \in_R \mathbb{Z}_q$ and $m \in \mathbb{Z}_q$. Then compute the validity proof as follows. Compute $c' = (h^u h_1^t, g^v, g^u g_1^v)$ for random t, u, v in $\mathbb{Z}_q$. Then compute $\sigma_{cc} = (\nu_{cc}, z)$ where $\nu_{cc} = \mathcal{H}(pp_S^{va}, pk_S^{va}, c, c')$

and $z = (z_m, z_r, z_s) = (t + \nu_{cc} m, u + \nu_{cc} r, v + \nu_{cc} s)$. Output the ciphertext $c^{\mathsf{va}} = (c, \sigma_{cc})$.

$\mathsf{VA.Dec_S}(sk_\mathsf{S}^{\mathsf{va}}, c^{\mathsf{va}})$: Parse c^{va} as $(d, c_1, c_2, \sigma_{cc})$ and return m, the discrete logarithm of $e(c_1^{x_1}/c_2, h) \cdot e(g, d)$ in basis $e(g, h_1)$.

$\mathsf{VA.DeriveCom_S}(pk_\mathsf{S}^{\mathsf{va}}, c^{\mathsf{va}})$: Parse c^{va} as $(d, c_1, c_2, \sigma_{cc})$ and return d.

$\mathsf{VA.Open_S}(sk_\mathsf{S}^{\mathsf{va}}, c^{\mathsf{va}})$: Parse c^{va} as $(d, c_1, c_2, \sigma_{cc})$, then compute and output the ElGamal decryption $a = c_2/c_1^{x_1}$, i.e., g^r (consisting of the TC2 auxiliary value with respect to d).

$\mathsf{VA.Verify_S}(pk_\mathsf{S}^{\mathsf{va}}, d, m, a)$: Return 1 only if $e(a, h) = e(g, d/h_1^m)$.

$\mathsf{Valid_S}(pk^{\mathsf{va}}, c^{\mathsf{va}})$: Parse c^{va} as $(c, \sigma_{cc}) = (d, c_1, c_2, \nu_{cc}, z)$ and output 1 only if the proof σ_{cc} checks, that is, if $\nu_{cc} = \mathcal{H}(pp_\mathsf{S}^{\mathsf{va}}, pk_\mathsf{S}^{\mathsf{va}}, c, c')$ where $c' = \mathsf{Enc_S}(pk_S, z) \cdot c^{-\nu_{cc}}$ (with componentwise operation).

The algorithm $\mathsf{Strip_S}$ returns c from c^{va} in the obvious way. Applying $\mathsf{Strip_S}$ to PPATS ciphertexts leads to a homomorphic CCE scheme.

Theorem 3. *The* PPATS *scheme is an NM-CPA secure CCVAE scheme in the random oracle model in the Λ_{sxdh} setting.*

Proof (Sketch – See full version for details [17]). We first observe that the soundness of the Valid_S algorithm results from the one of the σ_{cc} proof, which shows that PPATS is a CCVAE scheme. The NM-CPA security of PPATS results from the observation that a PPATS ciphertext is made of a CCE ciphertext c that is IND-CPA secure, augmented with the sigma proof of knowledge of the corresponding plaintext and randomness. □

Proving vote validity. Some voting schemes require the voters to prove the validity of the votes published on $\boldsymbol{PB}$. Such proofs, which must be perfectly ZK to preserve PPAT, can be easily computed here for the Pedersen-like commitments posted on $\boldsymbol{PB}$ using standard techniques [14].

Elections with Homomorphic Tallying from PPATS. We can now use this scheme to build a voting scheme PPATSVote based on $\mathsf{Enc2Vote}(\mathsf{PPATS}, \rho_\mathsf{S})$ but from which we modify the Tally algorithm as follows.

1. *Stripping*: Once the polls are closed, the authorities run $\mathsf{Valid_S}$ and $\mathsf{Strip_S}$ on the CCVAE ciphertexts stored on $\boldsymbol{SB}$, obtaining CCE homomorphic ciphertexts.
2. *Aggregation*: The authorities multiply those ciphertexts, obtaining one resulting CCE ciphertext c.
3. *Decryption*: The authorities compute $v = \mathsf{Dec_S}(sk_\mathsf{S}, c)$ the result of the election. To prove the correctness of the decryption, they also run $\mathsf{Open_S}$ on c, obtaining an auxiliary value a. Finally the authorities append (v, a) on $\boldsymbol{PB}$.

Theorem 4. *The* PPATSVote *scheme offers a PPAT and ballot privacy in the Λ_{sxdh} setting in the random oracle model.*

Proof. The PPATSVote scheme is equivalent to the $\mathsf{Enc2Vote}(\mathsf{PPATS}, \rho_\mathsf{S})$ scheme except that it also discloses the auxiliary value a on $\boldsymbol{PB}$. This value is fully determined by the commitment on the outcome and by the outcome itself, which implies that it does not provide any extra information to an unbounded adversary, and the PPAT property offered by Enc2Vote(PPATS, ρ_S) is then preserved. The trustees having access to $\boldsymbol{SB}$ also see the decryption factors produced by Dec. They are however indistinguishable of random group elements under DDH, as for standard ElGamal decryption, and therefore do not help breaking ballot privacy.   □

Audit Procedure. The audit procedure consists in the following steps:
1. Run all the verification procedures on the commitments displayed on $\boldsymbol{PB}$. If the verification procedure fails for any commitment, abort.
2. Multiply all the commitments, obtaining a commitment on the election outcome.
3. Verify that the announced outcome v and auxiliary value a are indeed an opening of the election outcome commitment. Abort if it is not the case.

The first step guarantees the validity of the votes posted, while the second and last step guarantee that the tally matches the posted votes. The binding property of the commitment scheme guarantees that the only opening that the authorities will ever be able to provide comes from a honest tallying process. We emphasize that this last verification is very efficient: it only requires the verification of an opening of one constant-size commitment—no ZK proof is needed here, contrary to traditional approaches.

As far as eligibility may be concerned, the bulletin board can also associate a name with each commitment recorded on $\boldsymbol{PB}$ without affecting the PPAT. This offers to any observers the possibility to verify that the posted votes have been submitted by valid voters (e.g., by interrogating those voters in case of doubt).

Verifiability/Accountability. Verifiability makes it possible to check whether votes have been recorded and tallied properly. In order to decide what action must be taken if a verification fails, it is sometimes useful to have a stronger property: accountability. This property was highlighted by Küsters et al. [30] and applied to the Bingo voting scheme and then to several variants of the Helios voting system [31].

While plugging the PPATS scheme into Helios would not have any noticeable impact on the verifiability analysis of Helios proposed by Kremer et al. [29], the distinction between the private and public board and between perfect and computational privacy has more impact on the accountability analyses of Küsters et al. [31]. In particular, while the ballot validity test is fully public in Helios, replacing ElGamal encryption with the PPATS scheme adds a step during which authorities could decide to reject a ciphertext because de σ_{cc} proof would be invalid, which could not be verified from the content of $\boldsymbol{PB}$ since neither σ_{cc} nor the corresponding statement appear on that board. As a result, it will not be possible to determine whether the authorities or the voter are cheating without disclosing to a judge information that only offer conditional privacy. Different strategies for improving the accountability in the case of Helios have been explored in [3, 31]. A rigorous cryptographic analysis of verifiability/accountability of a fully-fledged voting system is an open problem (note that all current works on Helios [29, 31] abstracted the cryptographic aspects and, as result, overlooked the recently found attacks on the verifiability of Helios [9]), and is out of our scope.

4.2 CCVA Encryption for Elections with Complex Ballots

The PPATS scheme is appropriate for elections with simple ballots. In some elections, it is however useful to be able to encode complex votes in a single ciphertext. This happens for instance in elections with a very large number of candidates or with complex tallying rules that make the homomorphic aggregation approach impractical, or in elections where arbitrary write-ins need to be supported. For those elections, a tallying approach based on verifiable mixnets is usually adopted, which is the motivation for our definition of the PPATC scheme below. This scheme has an efficiency comparable to the previous one but offers efficient decryption procedures for arbitrary plaintext. The corresponding CCE scheme is however not additively homomorphic any more, but this is not a problem in a mixnet setting since ballots are individually decrypted. ElGamal encryption is a core ingredient of this scheme, together with the Λ_{sxdh}-secure and perfectly hiding commitment scheme of Abe et al [2].

The PPATC *CCVAE scheme:*

VA.Gen$_C(1^n)$: Generate $\Lambda_{sxdh} = (q, \mathbb{G}_1, \mathbb{G}_2, \mathbb{G}_T, e, g, h)$ for $|q| = n$ together with the following additional public rabdom generators $g_1 = g^{x_1}$, $g_2 = g^{x_2}$ in $\mathbb{G}_1$ and $h_1 \in \mathbb{G}_2$. The triple (pp_C, pk_C, sk_C) is defined as $((\Lambda_{sxdh}, h_1), (g_1, g_2), (x_1, x_2))$. The augmented key $pk_C^{va} = \mathsf{Expand}(pk_C)$ is computed by adding to pk_C the description of an efficient hash function $\mathcal{H}$ with range $\mathbb{Z}_q$, resulting in the triple $(pp_C^{va} = pp_C, pk_C^{va}, sk_C^{va} = sk_C)$.

VA.Enc$_C(pk_C^{va}, m; r, r_1, r_2)$: Compute $c = \mathsf{Enc}_C(pk_C, m; r, r_1, r_2)$, the CCE ciphertext $(c_1, c_2, c_3, d_1, d_2) = (g^{r_1}, g^{r_2}, g_1^r g_2^{r_2}, h^r h_1^{r_1}, mg^{r_1})$ for $m \in \mathbb{G}_1$ and random $r, r_1, r_2 \in_R \mathbb{Z}_q$. Then compute the following validity proof. Select random $s, s_1, s_2 \in_R \mathbb{Z}_q$ and compute the elements $c' = (c_1', c_2', c_3', d_1')$ as $(g^{s_1}, g^{s_2}, g_1^s g_2^{s_2}, h^s h_1^{s_1})$. Compute $\nu_{cc} = \mathcal{H}(pp_C^{va}, pk_C^{va}, c, c')$ and then $f = s + \nu_{cc} r$, $f_1 = s_1 + \nu_{cc} r_1$, $f_2 = s_2 + \nu_{cc} r_2$. Set $\sigma_{cc} = (\nu_{cc}, f, f_1, f_2)$. The ciphertext c^{va} is made of (c, σ_{cc}).

VA.Dec$_C(sk_C^{va}, c^{va})$: Parse c^{va} as $(c_1, c_2, c_3, d_1, d_2, \sigma_{cc})$ and return $d_2/c_1^{x_1}$.

VA.DeriveCom$_C(pk_C^{va}, c^{va})$: Parse c^{va} as $(c_1, c_2, c_3, d_1, d_2, \sigma_{cc})$ and return (d_1, d_2).

VA.Open$_C(sk_C^{va}, c^{va})$: Parse c^{va} as $(c_1, c_2, c_3, d_1, d_2, \sigma_{cc})$, and return $a = c_3/c_2^{x_2}$.

VA.Verify$_C(pk_C^{va}, d_1, d_2, m, a)$: Return 1 if $e(g, d_1) = e(a, h)e(d_2/m, h_1)$ and 0 otherwise.

Valid$_C(pk^{va}, c^{va})$: Parse c^{va} as $(c_1, c_2, c_3, d_1, d_2, \nu_{cc}, f, f_1, f_2)$ and test whether all elements of the ciphertext are properly encoded. Compute $c_1' = g^{f_1}/c_1^{\nu_{cc}}$, $c_2' = g^{f_2}/c_2^{\nu_{cc}}$, $c_3' = g_1^f g_2^{f_2}/c_3^{\nu_{cc}}$ and $d_1' = h^f h_1^{f_1}/d_1^{\nu_{cc}}$ and return 1 only if $\nu_{cc} = \mathcal{H}(pp_C^{va}, pk_C^{va}, c_1, c_2, c_3, d_1, d_2, c_1', c_2', c_3', d_1', d_2')$.

The algorithm Strip$_C$ returns c from c^{va} in the obvious way. Applying Strip$_C$ to a PPATC ciphertext leads to a CCE ciphertext that is homomorphic with respect to the curve group law in $\mathbb{G}_1$, which is sufficient for obtaining the randomization properties needed for mixing. The use of the PPATC scheme also requires the existence of an efficient mapping between the votes and $\mathbb{G}_1$. This can be realized easily in most cases. For instance, most pairing friendly curves of the form $y^2 = x^3 + b$ on $\mathbb{F}_q$ have q chosen in such a way that any message y in $\mathbb{Z}_q$ can be mapped on a point $((y^2 - b)^{\frac{1}{3}}, y)$ [6].

Theorem 5. *The* PPATC *scheme is an NM-CPA secure CCVAE scheme in the random oracle model in the Λ_{sxdh} setting.*

The proof is similar to the one of Theorem 3.

A Verifiable Shuffle for Voting Systems with PPAT.

We now would like to shuffle the PPATC ciphertexts and publish openings of the corresponding anonymized commitments. Since our scheme is randomizable, this does not raise any specific concern.

We also need to make the shuffle verifiable, that is, to provide a proof of shuffle, which needs to preserve the information theoretic privacy of $\boldsymbol{PB}$. Various perfect (or statistical) ZK proof of shuffles can be used for that purpose [26, 28, 37]: these guarantee that a simulator can produce a proof of shuffle just from the inputs and output of that shuffle that is indistinguishable from a real proof, even by an unbounded adversary.

In our context, we need to verifiably shuffle, with a single permutation, both the CCE ciphertexts and the extracted commitments to keep track of their concordance. The commitment consistent shuffle approach proposed by Terelius and Wikström [38, 37] seems particularly natural for that purpose. This approach splits the proof of shuffle in two stages. First a perfectly hiding commitment on the permutation matrix used in the shuffle is computed and made public. This is the most computationally intensive part of the protocol and, interestingly, it is independent of the actual values that we need to shuffle and of the randomization factors that will be applied on the ciphertexts. Then, a much cheaper proof is produced that shows that the shuffle performed on the ciphertexts is consistent with the commitment on that permutation matrix. In our case, that proof can be computed both for the PPATC ciphertexts on $\boldsymbol{SB}$ and for the corresponding commitments on $\boldsymbol{PB}$.

We sketch the resulting tallying protocol below.

1. *Stripping*: The authorities run $\mathsf{Valid}_\mathsf{C}$ and $\mathsf{Strip}_\mathsf{C}$ on the ciphertexts stored on $\boldsymbol{SB}$, obtaining a vector $\boldsymbol{v}$ of l ciphertexts and a vector $\boldsymbol{d}$ of commitments.
2. *Permutation Commitment*: The authorities select a random permutation π and compute a commitment u on that permutation, together with a validity proof P_π.
3. *Shuffle*: The authorities select random vectors $\boldsymbol{r}, \boldsymbol{r_1}, \boldsymbol{r_2}$ from $\mathbb{Z}_q^l$ and compute a vector of ciphertexts $\boldsymbol{v}'$ where $v_i' = v_{\pi^{-1}(i)} \cdot \mathsf{Enc}_\mathsf{C}(pk_\mathsf{C}, 1, \boldsymbol{r}_{\pi^{-1}(i)}, \boldsymbol{r_1}_{\pi^{-1}(i)}, \boldsymbol{r_2}_{\pi^{-1}(i)})$ (1 represents the neutral element in $\mathbb{G}_1$). The last two components of $\boldsymbol{v}'$ are posted on $\boldsymbol{PB}$ and denoted $\boldsymbol{d}'$.

4. *Proof of shuffle*: The authorities compute two commitment consistent proofs of shuffle with respect to the committed permutation π: P_v that shows that v' is indeed a shuffle of v and P_d that shows that d' is a shuffle on d. P_v is posted on SB and P_d is posted on PB.

5. *Decryption of openings*: The authorities verify the proofs, then decrypt all the ciphertexts in v' and run Open on these ciphertext in order to obtain the auxiliary values for the corresponding commitment. The plaintexts and auxiliary values are published on PB.

Of course, the three middle stages of this procedure, corresponding to the verifiable shuffling, should be repeated by several independent authorities.

The tally audit procedure for an observer consists in the following stages.

1. Verify the proof of permutation commitment P_π and abort if it fails.
2. Verify the proof of shuffle P_d and abort if it fails.
3. Verify that the authorities published valid openings for the shuffled commitments d' and abort otherwise.

The fact that this whole procedure preserves the PPAT follows from the fact that all the commitments are perfectly hiding and that all the proofs can be made perfect zero-knowledge.

5 Conclusion

We proposed a new cryptographic primitive, CCVA encryption, that enables the systematic design of voting schemes with a perfectly private audit trail. We further proposed CCVA schemes that are suitable for the organization of large-scale elections.

The PPATP scheme mentioned in section 3 and detailed in the full version of the paper [17] is fully generic and can be used with all classical tallying techniques. Its key generation algorithm is fairly sophisticated, though, and this scheme is also quite inefficient compared to our other schemes. We address then two other CCVAE schemes, PPATS and PPATC, that are much more efficient and simple to use though less flexible. They still can be used for the two most widely used vote tallying techniques: homomorphic aggregation and mixnets.

Efficiency measures. Table 1 gives an evaluation of the computational workload that our three schemes require, at comparable security levels, for computing a CCVA ciphertext and a validity proof in the case of a $0/1$ vote (details appear in the full version of the paper [17].)

The first four numbers on each line count the number of exponentiations to be performed in each group – fractional values appear when non-full exponents are used. The last column, giving total costs, results from the following estimations. We associate a unit cost to the multiplication of two 256-bit integers and assume that this cost grows quadratically with the length of the operands. We target a security level equivalent to 2048-bit RSA modulus N. We select $\mathbb{G}_1$ to be taken on $\mathbb{F}_p$ for a 256-bit long prime p and $\mathbb{G}_2$ to be taken on $\mathbb{F}_{p^2}$. The cost of a

Table 1. Ciphertext computation workload

Scheme	$\mathbb{Z}_P^*$	$\mathbb{Z}_{N^2}^*$	$\mathbb{G}_1$	$\mathbb{G}_2$	Total Cost
PPATP (0/1 vote)	5.375	4	0	0	4202496
PPATP (256-bit vote)	3.375	4	0	0	3809280
PPATS (0/1 vote)	0	0	6	6	115200
PPATC (256-bit vote)	0	0	9	4	96000

point addition is evaluated to 16 multiplications in the underlying field, and the cost of a point duplication to 7 multiplications. In order to perform EC point multiplication and modular exponentiation, we consider the simple square and multiply algorithm.

As expected, this table shows very important differences between PPATP and the other two schemes: computing a PPATP ciphertext is roughly 40 times more expensive than computing a PPATC ciphertext. The cost of the PPATS and PPATC schemes is low enough to make it possible to use these schemes even on fairly slow platforms. For instance, considering the computation of a ciphertext in JavaScript in a browser using the JSBN library, which allows computing a point multiplication in a 256-bit prime order group in less than 30ms in the Chrome web browser, the computation of a PPATC ciphertext that can encode a 256-bit vote would take less than a second.

The costs of computing a PPATS and a PPATC ciphertexts are similar. The associated tallying techniques are very different though, being much more complex for PPATC. A mixnet based technique also reveals much more information than a technique based on the homomorphic aggregation of ballots. As a result, we would recommend using the PPATS scheme as long as the ballot format allows it, even if the resulting ballot preparation cost is higher than the one that would be obtained by using PPATC.

Acknowledgements. This research was supported by the WIST Walloon Region project CAMUS, the ARC French community project SCOOP and the ISEC European action grant B-CCENTRE. Édouard Cuvelier is funded by a FRIA grant of the F.R.S.-FNRS. The authors are grateful to the anonymous reviewers for their constructive feedback and they wish to thank Sylvie Baudine for her help in improving the paper.

References

1. Abe, M., Haralambiev, K., Ohkubo, M.: Signing on elements in bilinear groups for modular protocol design. IACR Cryptology ePrint Archive 2010, 133 (2010)
2. Abe, M., Haralambiev, K., Ohkubo, M.: Group to group commitments do not shrink. In: Pointcheval, D., Johansson, T. (eds.) EUROCRYPT 2012. LNCS, vol. 7237, pp. 301–317. Springer, Heidelberg (2012)
3. Adida, B., de Marneffe, O., Pereira, O., Quisquater, J.-J.: Electing a university president using open-audit voting: Analysis of real-world use of Helios. In:

Moran, T., Jefferson, D., Hall, J.L. (eds.) Electronic Voting Technology Workshop/Workshop on Trustworthy Elections. Usenix (August 2009)

4. Arapinis, M., Cortier, V., Kremer, S., Ryan, M.: Practical everlasting privacy. In: Basin, D., Mitchell, J.C. (eds.) POST 2013 (ETAPS 2013). LNCS, vol. 7796, pp. 21–40. Springer, Heidelberg (2013)

5. Barreto, P.S.L.M., Lynn, B., Scott, M.: Constructing elliptic curves with prescribed embedding degrees. In: Cimato, S., Galdi, C., Persiano, G. (eds.) SCN 2002. LNCS, vol. 2576, pp. 257–267. Springer, Heidelberg (2003)

6. Barreto, P.S.L.M., Naehrig, M.: Pairing-friendly elliptic curves of prime order. In: Preneel, B., Tavares, S. (eds.) SAC 2005. LNCS, vol. 3897, pp. 319–331. Springer, Heidelberg (2006)

7. Benaloh, J.: Verifiable Secret-Ballot Elections. PhD thesis, Yale University (1987)

8. Bernhard, D., Cortier, V., Pereira, O., Smyth, B., Warinschi, B.: Adapting Helios for provable ballot privacy. In: Atluri, V., Diaz, C. (eds.) ESORICS 2011. LNCS, vol. 6879, pp. 335–354. Springer, Heidelberg (2011)

9. Bernhard, D., Pereira, O., Warinschi, B.: How not to prove yourself: Pitfalls of the fiat-shamir heuristic and applications to Helios. In: Wang, X., Sako, K. (eds.) ASIACRYPT 2012. LNCS, vol. 7658, pp. 626–643. Springer, Heidelberg (2012)

10. Boneh, D., Boyen, X., Shacham, H.: Short group signatures. In: Franklin, M. (ed.) CRYPTO 2004. LNCS, vol. 3152, pp. 41–55. Springer, Heidelberg (2004)

11. Carback, R., Chaum, D., Clark, J., Conway, J., Essex, A., Herrnson, P.S., Mayberry, T., Popoveniuc, S., Rivest, R.L., Shen, E., Sherman, A.T., Vora, P.L.: Scantegrity II municipal election at Takoma Park: The first E2E binding governmental election with ballot privacy. In: USENIX Security Symposium, pp. 291–306. USENIX Association (2010)

12. Chaum, D., Essex, A., Carback, R., Clark, J., Popoveniuc, S., Sherman, A., Vora, P.L.: Scantegrity: End-to-End voter-verifiable optical-scan voting. IEEE Security and Privacy 6(3), 40–46 (2008)

13. Cohen (Benaloh), J., Fischer, M.: A robust and verifiable cryptographically secure election scheme. In: Proceedings of 26th Symposium on Foundations of Computer Science, Portland, OR, pp. 372–382. IEEE (1985)

14. Cramer, R., Damgård, I., Schoenmakers, B.: Proof of partial knowledge and simplified design of witness hiding protocols. In: Desmedt, Y.G. (ed.) CRYPTO 1994. LNCS, vol. 839, pp. 174–187. Springer, Heidelberg (1994)

15. Cramer, R., Franklin, M., Schoenmakers, B., Yung, M.: Multi-authority secret-ballot elections with linear work. In: Maurer, U.M. (ed.) EUROCRYPT 1996. LNCS, vol. 1070, pp. 72–83. Springer, Heidelberg (1996)

16. Cramer, R., Gennaro, R., Schoenmakers, B.: A secure and optimally efficient multi-authority election scheme. In: Fumy, W. (ed.) EUROCRYPT 1997. LNCS, vol. 1233, pp. 103–118. Springer, Heidelberg (1997)

17. Cuvelier, E., Pereira, O., Peters, T.: Election verifiability or ballot privacy: Do we need to choose? Cryptology ePrint Archive, Report 2013/216 (2013), http://eprint.iacr.org/

18. Damgård, I., Jurik, M.: A generalisation, a simplification and some applications of Paillier's probabilistic public-key system. In: Kim, K. (ed.) PKC 2001. LNCS, vol. 1992, pp. 119–136. Springer, Heidelberg (2001)

19. Demirel, D., van de Graaf, J.: A publicly-verifiable mixnet with everlasting privacy towards observers. Cryptology ePrint Archive, Report 2012/420 (2012), http://eprint.iacr.org/

20. Demirel, D., van de Graaf, J., Araújo, R.: Improving Helios with everlasting privacy towards the public. In: Halderman, A., Pereira, O., eds.: EVT/WOTE 2012. USENIX (2012)

21. Dolev, D., Dwork, C., Naor, M.: Non-malleable cryptography. SIAM Journal on Computing 30(2), 391–437 (2000)

22. Fujioka, A., Okamoto, T., Ohta, K.: A practical secret voting scheme for large scale elections. In: Zheng, Y., Seberry, J. (eds.) AUSCRYPT 1992. LNCS, vol. 718, pp. 244–251. Springer, Heidelberg (1993)

23. Galbraith, S.D., Paterson, K.G., Smart, N.P.: Pairings for cryptographers. Discrete Appl. Math. 156(16) (September 2008)

24. Gennaro, R., Jarecki, S., Krawczyk, H., Rabin, T.: Secure distributed key generation for discrete-log based cryptosystems. J. Cryptology 20(1), 51–83 (2007)

25. Grewal, G.S., Ryan, M., Bursuc, S., Ryan, P.: Caveat coercitor: Coercion-evidence in electronic voting. In: IEEE Security and Privacy Symposium (2013)

26. Groth, J.: A verifiable secret shuffle of homomorphic encryptions. Journal of Cryptology 23(4), 546–579 (2010)

27. Hirt, M., Sako, K.: Efficient receipt-free voting based on homomorphic encryption. In: Preneel, B. (ed.) EUROCRYPT 2000. LNCS, vol. 1807, pp. 539–556. Springer, Heidelberg (2000)

28. Jakobsson, M., Juels, A., Rivest, R.L.: Making mix nets robust for electronic voting by randomized partial checking. In: USENIX Security Symposium, pp. 339–353. USENIX (2002)

29. Kremer, S., Ryan, M., Smyth, B.: Election verifiability in electronic voting protocols. In: Gritzalis, D., Preneel, B., Theoharidou, M. (eds.) ESORICS 2010. LNCS, vol. 6345, pp. 389–404. Springer, Heidelberg (2010)

30. Küsters, R., Truderung, T., Vogt, A.: Accountability: definition and relationship to verifiability. In: CCS 2010, pp. 526–535. ACM (2010)

31. Küsters, R., Truderung, T., Vogt, A.: Clash attacks on the verifiability of e-voting systems. In: IEEE Symposium on Security and Privacy, S&P 2012, pp. 395–409. IEEE Computer Society (2012)

32. Moran, T., Naor, M.: Receipt-free universally-verifiable voting with everlasting privacy. In: Dwork, C. (ed.) CRYPTO 2006. LNCS, vol. 4117, pp. 373–392. Springer, Heidelberg (2006)

33. Moran, T., Naor, M.: Split-ballot voting: Everlasting privacy with distributed trust. ACM Trans. Inf. Syst. Secur. 13(2) (2010)

34. Ryan, P.Y.A., Bismark, D., Heather, J., Schneider, S., Xia, Z.: The Prêt à Voter verifiable election system. IEEE Transactions on Information Forensics and Security 4, 662–673 (2009)

35. Sako, K., Kilian, J.: Receipt-free mix-type voting scheme - a practical solution to the implementation of a voting booth. In: Guillou, L.C., Quisquater, J.-J. (eds.) EUROCRYPT 1995. LNCS, vol. 921, pp. 393–403. Springer, Heidelberg (1995)

36. Saltman, R.G.: The history and politics of voting technology. Palgrave Macmillan (2006)

37. Terelius, B., Wikström, D.: Proofs of restricted shuffles. In: Bernstein, D.J., Lange, T. (eds.) AFRICACRYPT 2010. LNCS, vol. 6055, pp. 100–113. Springer, Heidelberg (2010)

38. Wikström, D.: A commitment-consistent proof of a shuffle. In: Boyd, C., González Nieto, J. (eds.) ACISP 2009. LNCS, vol. 5594, pp. 407–421. Springer, Heidelberg (2009)

Enforcing Privacy in the Presence of Others: Notions, Formalisations and Relations

Naipeng Dong*, Hugo Jonker, and Jun Pang

Faculty of Sciences, Technology and Communication,
University of Luxembourg, Luxembourg

Abstract. Protecting privacy against bribery/coercion is a necessary requirement in electronic services, like e-voting, e-auction and e-health. Domain-specific privacy properties have been proposed to capture this. We generalise these properties as *enforced privacy*: a system enforces a user's privacy even when the user collaborates with the adversary. In addition, we account for the influence of third parties on a user's privacy. Third parties can help to break privacy by collaborating with the adversary, or can help to protect privacy by cooperating with the target user. We propose *independency of privacy* to capture the negative privacy impact that third parties can have, and *coalition privacy* to capture their positive privacy impact. We formally define these privacy notions in the applied pi calculus and build a hierarchy showing their relations.

1 Introduction

Privacy is of great importance to electronic services such as e-voting, e-auction, and e-health. A large amount of research has been done in this area, for example, using statistical methods. In the literature, an important focus is privacy in communication protocols, since most electronic services use the Internet. To capture privacy in protocols, a wide variety of privacy properties have been proposed, such as anonymity, untraceability, quantified privacy, etc. (e.g., see [1–5]). We focus on a subset of such properties – non-quantified (binary) data privacy, i.e., properties that are either satisfied or not (as opposed to providing a quantitative answer).

Classical data privacy assumes that users want to keep their privacy [1, 3, 4]. However, a user may want to reveal information to the adversary due to bribery or coercion. Systems providing electronic services need to protect against such threats (e.g., [6–9]). This was first achieved in voting: a system in which a voter could not undo his privacy after voting (preventing vote selling) [6], and later, a system in which a voter, coerced to communicate continuously with the adversary, cannot undo his privacy [8]. These ideas were lifted to an e-auction system [7] and an e-health system [9]. Following this development of stronger systems, domain-specific formalisations of privacy properties against bribery and coercion were proposed in the literature: receipt-freeness and coercion-resistance

---

* Supported by a grant from the Fonds National de la Recherche (Luxembourg).

J. Crampton, S. Jajodia, and K. Mayes (Eds.): ESORICS 2013, LNCS 8134, pp. 499–516, 2013.
© Springer-Verlag Berlin Heidelberg 2013

in e-voting [10], e-auction [11], and e-health [12]. In order to address these privacy concerns domain-independently, we propose a generic notion of *enforced privacy*: a user's privacy is preserved even if the user collaborates with the adversary by sharing information.

Our notions of (enforced) data privacy focus only on one target user – ignoring the privacy impact of other users. However, a third party may help to break user privacy (*collaboration*), e.g., revealing your vote may enable the adversary to deduce another voter's vote. On the other hand, a third party can help maintain privacy (*coalition*), e.g., a non-coerced voter (who votes as the adversary desires) can swap receipts with a coerced voter, providing the coerced voter "proof" of compliance while being free to vote as he pleases. Accounting for the privacy effect of third parties is particularly necessary in domains where many non-trusted roles are involved. For example, pharmacists in e-health may be able to help reveal prescription behaviour of doctors. In order to ensure doctor prescribing-privacy, an e-health system must prevent this [9, 13]. This requirement has been expressed and formalised in e-health [12] and e-voting [14]. In this paper, we generalise these formalisations as *independency of privacy*: the help of a set of third parties does not enable the adversary to break a target user's privacy. To capture the converse situation – the privacy effect of third parties helping the target user by sharing information with the target user, we propose a new notion of *coalition privacy*: a target user's privacy is preserved with the help of a set of third parties sharing information with the target user. In particular, we use this notion to also capture the situation where third parties are involved but no information is shared between the target user and third parties. In this case, the mere *existence* of the third parties can help to create a situation where privacy is preserved.

In addition to identifying these (new) privacy notions, this paper contributes on formalising them in a new formal framework and formally prove their relations. Cryptographic protocols are well known to be error-prone and formal approaches have shown to be efficient in addressing this problem, e.g., see [15, 16]. Thus, formalising privacy notions is a necessary step to verify the privacy claims of a protocol. Our framework is based on the applied pi calculus as it provides an intuitive way for modelling privacy properties and cryptographic protocols. In addition, it is supported by the ProVerif [17] tool, which allows us to verify many privacy properties automatically [18, 19].

We present a formal framework which allows us to give domain-independent formalisations. We define a standard form of protocols which is able to represent any protocol. To formally define enforced privacy properties and independency of privacy properties, we model *collaboration* between users and the adversary. The collaboration allows us to precisely specify which information is shared and how it is shared, thus provides the necessary flexibility for modelling various types of collaboration. To model coalition privacy properties, we propose the notion of *coalition* in our framework to formally capture the behaviour and shared information among a target user and a set of third parties. In our framework, the foundational property data-privacy, is formalised in a classical way as strong secrecy:

Table 1. Privacy notions

target user collaborates with adversary	third parties			
	all neutral	*some attacking*	*some defending*	*some defending some attacking*
no	priv	ipriv	cpriv	cipriv
yes	epriv	iepriv	cepriv	ciepriv

equivalence of two processes where a variable is instantiated differently [20]. Based on this property, we formalise enforced-privacy, independency-of-privacy and independency-of-enforced-privacy using the formalisation of collaboration. Using the formalisation of coalition, four corresponding coalition privacy properties are formalised. Finally, we formally discuss how the formalised privacy properties are related in a privacy hierarchy. In addition, we show that many existing formalisations are instances of properties in our hierarchy.

2 Privacy Notions

With respect to the classical Dolev-Yao adversary [21][1], we distinguish between two classes of privacy-affecting behaviour: the target user (collaborating with the adversary or not), and the behaviour of third parties. Third parties may be *neutral*, collaborating with the adversary (*attacking*), or collaborating with the target user (*defending*) – thus we also consider the situation where some are attacking and some are defending. A target user who collaborates with the adversary is not under the adversary's direct control, contrary to a compromised user who genuinely shares initial private information with the adversary. A *neutral* third party, like an honest user, follows the protocol specification exactly. Thus, such a third party neither actively helps nor actively harms the target user's privacy. A *defending* third party helps the target user to preserve his privacy. An *attacking* third party communicates with the adversary to break the target user's privacy. Note that we do not consider a third party that attacks and defends the target user simultaneously. Given this classification, a target user will find himself one of the following four situations w.r.t. third parties: 1) all are neutral; 2) some are attacking; 3) some are defending; and 4) some are attacking, some are defending. In the latter three cases, the remaining third parties (if any) are considered neutral. Combining the various behaviours of the third parties with those of the target user gives rise to eight privacy properties (see Tab. 1).

Motivation examples for each property are as follows – data-privacy (priv): the adversary cannot link the contents of an encrypted email to the user; enforced-privacy (epriv): a voter should not be able to prove to a vote-buyer how he

---

[1] Note that the Dolev-Yao adversary is not assumed to fully control authenticated users. Bribed or coerced users cannot be modelled as part of the adversary, as they are not trusted by the adversary. In addition, it is necessary to model which information and how users share the information, especially those obtained from channels hidden from the adversary.

voted; independency-of-privacy (ipriv): in e-health the adversary cannot link a doctor to his prescriptions, despite the help of a pharmacist; independency-of-enforced-privacy (iepriv): the adversary should not be able to link a doctor to his prescriptions (to prevent bribes), even when both the pharmacist and the doctor are helping him; coalition-privacy (cpriv): in location-based services, the user's real location is hidden amongst the locations of the helping users; coalition-enforced-privacy (cepriv): in anonymous routing, a sender remains anonymous if he synchronises with a group of senders, even if he seems to collaborate; coalition-independency-of-privacy (cipriv): the adversary cannot link an RFID chip to its identity, even though some malicious readers are helping the adversary, provided other RFID tags behave exactly as the target one; coalition-independency-of-enforced-privacy (ciepriv): in electronic road pricing, other users may hide a user's route from the adversary, even if the user seems to collaborate and malicious routers relay information on passing cars to the adversary.

The examples above illustrate that similar privacy concerns arise in many different domains – e-voting, e-health, location-based services, RFID, etc. So far, attempts at formalising privacy have usually been domain-specific (e.g., [22, 2, 10, 3, 4, 23, 11, 12, 24]). We advocate a domain-independent approach to privacy, and develop a formal framework to achieve this in Sect. 3.

3   Formal Framework

3.1   The Applied Pi Calculus

The applied pi calculus [25] assumes an infinite set of *names* to model data and communication channels, an infinite set of *variables* and a finite set of *function symbols* each with an associated arity to capture cryptographic primitives. A constant is defined as a function symbol with arity zero. *Terms* are defined as either names, or variables or function symbols applied on other terms to capture communicated messages. We denote the variables in a term N as $\mathsf{Var}(N)$. In addition, the applied pi calculus assumes a set of base types (e.g., the universal type *Data*) and a type system (sort system) for terms generated by the base set. Terms are assumed to be well-typed and syntactic substitutions preserve types. Processes (see Fig. 1) are defined to model protocols. A name is *bound* if it is under restriction. A variable is *bound* by restrictions or inputs. Names and variables are *free* if they are not delimited by restrictions or by inputs. The sets of free names, free variables, bound names and bound variables of a process A are denoted as $\mathsf{fn}(A)$, $\mathsf{fv}(A)$, $\mathsf{bn}(A)$ and $\mathsf{bv}(A)$, respectively. A term is *ground* when it does not contain variables. A process is *closed* if it does not contain free variables. $\{M/x\}$ is a substitution which replaces variable x with term M. A *context* $C[\_]$ is defined as a process with a hole, which may be filled with any process. An evaluation context is a context whose hole is not under a replication, a conditional, an input or an output. Finally, we use $\nu\tilde{n}$ to abbreviate the process generating a list of names (i.e., $\nu\mathrm{n}_1 \cdots \nu\mathrm{n}_n$) and use $\nu\tilde{n}/\mathrm{n}_i$ to abbreviate process $\nu\mathrm{n}_1 \cdots \nu\mathrm{n}_{i-1}.\nu\mathrm{n}_{i+1}.\cdots.\nu\mathrm{n}_n$ (erasing $\nu\mathrm{n}_i$ from process $\nu\tilde{n}$). Several equivalence relations on processes are defined in the applied pi calculus.

$P, Q, R ::=$	plain processes	$A, B, C ::=$	extended processes
0	null process	P	plain process
$P \mid Q$	parallel composition	$A \mid B$	parallel composition
$!P$	replication	$\nu n.A$	name restriction
$\nu n.P$	name restriction	$\nu x.A$	variable restriction
if $M =_E N$ then		$\{M/x\}$	active substitution
P else Q	conditional		
$in(v, x).P$	message input		
$out(v, M).P$	message output		

Fig. 1. Applied pi processes

We mainly use labelled bisimilarity $\approx_\ell$ [25]. Two processes are labelled bisimilar if the adversary cannot distinguish them.

3.2 Well-Formed Protocols

For the simplicity of formalisation, we define a standard form of a protocol, inspired by Arapinis et al. [3], and any protocol can be written in this form.

Definition 1 (well-formed protocols). *A protocol with p roles is well-formed if it is a closed plain process P_w of the form:*

$$P_w = \nu\tilde{c}.(genkey \mid !R_1 \mid \cdots \mid !R_p)$$
$$R_i = \nu id_i.\nu data_i.init_i.!(\nu s_i.\nu sdata_i.sinit_i.main_i) \quad (\forall i \in \{1, \cdots, p\})$$

1. *P_w is canonical [3]: names and variables in the process never appear both bound and free, and each name and variable is bound at most once;*
2. *data is typed, channels are ground, private channels are never sent on any channel;*
3. *$\nu\tilde{c}$, $\nu data_i$ and $\nu sdata_i$ may be null;*
4. *$init_i$ and $sinit_i$ are sequential processes;*
5. *genkey, $init_i$, $sinit_i$ and $main_i$ can be any process (possibly null) such that P_w is a closed plain process.*

In process P_w, $\tilde{c}$ are channel names; *genkey* is a sub-process in which shared data (e.g., keys shared between two roles) are generated and distributed; R_i ($1 \leq i \leq p$) is a role. To distinguish instances taking the same role R_i, each instance is dynamically associated with a distinct identity νid_i; $data_i$ is private data of an instance; $init_i$ models the initialisation of an instance; $(\nu s_i.\nu sdata_i.sinit_i.main_i)$ models a session of an instance. To distinguish sessions of the same instance, each session is dynamically associated to a distinct identity (νs_i); $sdata_i$ is private data of a session; $sinit_i$ models the initialisation of a session; $main_i$ models the behaviour of a session.

Note that this standard form does not limit the type of protocols we consider. A role may include a number of sub-roles so that a user may take more than one part in a protocol. The identities do not have to be used in the process. All of

$\nu\tilde{c}$, νdata$_i$ and νsdata$_i$ may be null and *genkey*, *init*$_i$, *sinit*$_i$ and *main*$_i$ can be any process (possibly null) such that P_w is a closed plain process. Any process can be written in a canonical form by α-conversion [3]. Thus, any protocol can be written as a well-formed protocol.

3.3   Data-Privacy

We formally define the property data-privacy that acts as the foundation upon which other properties are built. To do so, we need to make explicit *which data* is protected. Thus, the property data-privacy always specifies the target data. In process P_w, the target data τ can be expressed as a bound name (complicated target data can be reduced to bound names) which belongs to a role (the target role R_i), i.e., $\tau \in \mathsf{bn}(R_i)$. For the sake of simplicity, we (re)write the role R_i in the form of $R_i = \nu id_i.\nu\tau.\hat{R}_i$, where $\hat{R}_i$ is a plain process which has two variables id_i and τ. By α-conversion we can always transform R_i into the above form.

Intuitively, data-privacy w.r.t. τ of protocol P_w, is the inability of the adversary to link an honest user taking role R_i to his instantiation of the target data τ. An honest user taking role R_i is modelled as process R_i. $\hat{R}_i\{\mathsf{id}/id, t/\tau\}$ denotes an instance of the target user in which the target user instantiates the target data with t where t denotes any data which can be used to replace the target data. The data-privacy can be modelled as strong secrecy [20] of the target data: the adversary cannot distinguish an execution of R_i where $\tau = \mathsf{t}_1$ from an execution where $\tau = \mathsf{t}_2$, for $\mathsf{t}_1 \neq \mathsf{t}_2$.

Definition 2. *A well-formed protocol P_w satisfies data-privacy (priv) w.r.t. data τ ($\tau \in \mathsf{bn}(R_i)$), if $C_{P_w}[\hat{R}_i\{\mathsf{id}/id_i, \mathsf{t}_1/\tau\}] \approx_\ell C_{P_w}[\hat{R}_i\{\mathsf{id}/id_i, \mathsf{t}_2/\tau\}]$.*

In the above definition, id is a constant, t_1 and t_2 are free names. Since $R_i = \nu id_i.\nu\tau.\hat{R}_i$, process $\hat{R}_i\{\mathsf{id}/id_i, \mathsf{t}_1/\tau\}$ is an instance of role R_i where the identity is id and the target data is t_1. The evaluation context $C_{P_w}[\_]$ models neutral third parties. Thus, $C_{P_w}[\hat{R}_i\{\mathsf{id}/id_i, \mathsf{t}_1/\tau\}]$ is an instance of the protocol P_w, similarly for $C_{P_w}[\hat{R}_i\{\mathsf{id}/id_i, \mathsf{t}_2/\tau\}]$. The only difference between these two instances is the instantiation of the target data τ. Thus, this definition captures data-privacy by using the relation $\approx_\ell$: the adversary cannot distinguish a user process with different target data.

3.4   Modelling Collaboration with the Adversary

In order to define enforced privacy properties where the target user collaborates with the adversary and independency privacy properties where a set of third parties collaborate with the adversary, we need to model *collaboration* of users (a target user/third parties) with the adversary.

The process of a set of users is modelled as processes of each user in parallel. Since a user process is modelled as a role in a well-formed protocol and each user process can be any role, the set of users of a protocol P_w is formally defined as a plain process $R_U = R_{u_1} \mid \cdots \mid R_{u_m}$, $\forall i \in \{1, \ldots, m\}$, $R_{u_i} \in \{R_1, \ldots, R_p\}$.

Inspired by the formal definition of coercion in [10], the collaboration between a set of users and the adversary is formalised as a transformation of the process of the set of users. Note that a user may not always share *all* his information, e.g., a bribed user in a social network may reveal his relation with another user, but not his password. A way to express partly information sharing is to specify which terms of a process are shared and how they are shared. Since the process of a set of users is canonical in a well-formed protocol, bound names and variables are different in each user process. Thus, we can express information of a set of users as a set of terms appearing in the process of the set of users. Terms appearing in a plain process R_U are $\mathsf{Term}(R_U)$.

$$
\begin{aligned}
&\mathsf{Term}(0) = \emptyset & &\mathsf{Term}(P \mid Q) = \mathsf{Term}(P) \cup \mathsf{Term}(Q) \\
&\mathsf{Term}(!P) = \mathsf{Term}(P) & &\mathsf{Term}(\nu n.P) = \{n\} \cup \mathsf{Term}(P) \\
&\mathsf{Term}(\mathsf{in}(v,x).P) = \{x\} \cup \mathsf{Term}(P) & &\mathsf{Term}(\mathsf{out}(v,M).P) = \{M\} \cup \mathsf{Term}(P) \\
&\mathsf{Term}(if\ M =_E N\ then\ P\ else\ Q) = \mathsf{Term}(P) \cup \mathsf{Term}(Q)
\end{aligned}
$$

Thus, a collaboration can be specified as a specification defined as follows.

Definition 3 (collaboration specification). *A collaboration specification of a process R_U is a tuple $\langle \Psi, \Phi, c_{out}, c_{in} \rangle$. $\Psi \subseteq \mathsf{Term}(R_U)$ denotes the set of terms sent to the adversary each of which is of base type, $\Phi \subseteq \mathsf{Term}(R_U)$ represents terms to be replaced by information provided by the adversary, c_{out} is a fresh channel for sending information to the adversary, and c_{in} is a fresh channel for reading information from the adversary, i.e., $c_{out}, c_{in} \notin \mathsf{fn}(R_U) \cup \mathsf{bn}(R_U)$.*

Given a plain process R_U and a collaboration specification $\langle \Psi, \Phi, c_{out}, c_{in} \rangle$ of the process, the transformation of R_U is given by $R_U^{\langle \Psi, \Phi, c_{out}, c_{in} \rangle}$.

Definition 4 (collaboration behaviour). *Let R_U be a plain process, and $\langle \Psi, \Phi, c_{out}, c_{in} \rangle$ be a collaboration specification of R_U. Collaboration behaviour of R_U according to $\langle \Psi, \Phi, c_{out}, c_{in} \rangle$ is defined as:*

- $0^{\langle \Psi, \Phi, c_{out}, c_{in} \rangle} \quad \hat{=}\ 0,$
- $(P \mid Q)^{\langle \Psi, \Phi, c_{out}, c_{in} \rangle} \quad \hat{=}\ P^{\langle \Psi, \Phi, c_{out}, c_{in} \rangle} \mid Q^{\langle \Psi, \Phi, c_{out}, c_{in} \rangle},$
- $(!P)^{\langle \Psi, \Phi, c_{out}, c_{in} \rangle} \quad \hat{=}\ !P^{\langle \Psi, \Phi, c_{out}, c_{in} \rangle},$
- $(\nu n.P)^{\langle \Psi, \Phi, c_{out}, c_{in} \rangle} \quad \hat{=}\ \begin{cases} \nu n.\mathsf{out}(c_{out}, n).P^{\langle \Psi, \Phi, c_{out}, c_{in} \rangle} & if\ n \in \Psi, \\ \nu n.P^{\langle \Psi, \Phi, c_{out}, c_{in} \rangle} & otherwise, \end{cases}$
- $(\mathsf{in}(v,x).P)^{\langle \Psi, \Phi, c_{out}, c_{in} \rangle} \quad \hat{=}\ \begin{cases} \mathsf{in}(v,x).\mathsf{out}(c_{out}, x).P^{\langle \Psi, \Phi, c_{out}, c_{in} \rangle} & if\ x \in \Psi, \\ \mathsf{in}(v,x).P^{\langle \Psi, \Phi, c_{out}, c_{in} \rangle} & otherwise, \end{cases}$
- $(\mathsf{out}(v,M).P)^{\langle \Psi, \Phi, c_{out}, c_{in} \rangle} \hat{=} \begin{cases} \mathsf{in}(c_{in}, x).\mathsf{out}(v, x).P^{\langle \Psi, \Phi, c_{out}, c_{in} \rangle}\ if\ M \in \Phi \\ \qquad \wedge c_{in} \neq \bot,\ where\ x\ is\ a\ fresh\ variable, \\ \mathsf{out}(v,M).P^{\langle \Psi, \Phi, c_{out}, c_{in} \rangle} \qquad otherwise, \end{cases}$
- $(if\ M =_E N\ then\ P\ else\ Q)^{\langle \Psi, \Phi, c_{out}, c_{in} \rangle} \hat{=}$
  $\begin{cases} \mathsf{in}(c_{in}, x).if\ x = \mathsf{true}\ then\ P^{\langle \Psi, \Phi, c_{out}, c_{in} \rangle}\ else\ Q^{\langle \Psi, \Phi, c_{out}, c_{in} \rangle}\ if\ c_{in} \neq \bot, \\ \qquad where\ x\ is\ a\ fresh\ variable\ and\ \mathsf{true}\ is\ a\ constant, \\ if\ M =_E N\ then\ P^{\langle \Psi, \Phi, c_{out}, c_{in} \rangle}\ else\ Q^{\langle \Psi, \Phi, c_{out}, c_{in} \rangle} \qquad otherwise. \end{cases}$

Note that we use $c_{in} = \bot$ to denote that the adversary neither prepares information for the coerced users nor controls the conditional evaluations of the users. We only specify user behaviour in a collaboration with the adversary. The adversary's behaviour may be omitted, as in the applied pi calculus the adversary is considered as the environment and does not need to be explicitly modelled. Our approach to reasoning about the adversary's behaviour in a collaboration (e.g., enforcing a voter to cast a particular vote) follows the line of the definition of coercion-resistance in [10]. Namely, a context $C[\_] = \nu c_{out}.\nu c_{in}(\_ \mid Q)$ models a specific way of collaboration of the adversary, where Q models the adversary's behaviour in the context. In this way, we separate the adversary's behaviour of distinguishing two processes, which is modelled by the environment, from the behaviour of collaborating with users which is modelled by the context.

3.5   Modelling User Coalitions

To define coalition privacy properties, we need to formally define a *coalition* between a target user and a set of defending third parties. The notion collaboration from the previous section cannot be adopted directly, as it does not specify the adversary's behaviour, whereas a coalition must specify the behaviour of *all* involved users.

Given a set of users $R_U = R_{u_1} \mid \cdots \mid R_{u_m}$, a coalition of the users specifies communication between (potentially) each pair of users. For every communication, a coalition specification needs to make explicit who the sender and receiver are (unlike collaboration). Similar to the specification of collaboration, a coalition specification makes explicit which data is sent on which channel. To make the behaviour of both communicating parties explicit, we need to specify how the term in a communication is referred to in the receiver's process. A communication in a coalition is specified as a tuple $\langle R_{u_i}, R_{u_j}, M, c, y \rangle$ where $R_{u_i}, R_{u_j} \in \{R_{u_1}, \ldots, R_{u_m}\}$ ($R_{u_i} \neq R_{u_j}$) are the sender and receiver process, respectively; $M \in \mathsf{Term}(R_{u_i})$ is the data sent in the communication; $c \notin \mathsf{fn}(R_U) \cup \mathsf{bn}(R_U)$ is a fresh channel used in the communication; $y \notin \mathsf{fv}(R_U) \cup \mathsf{bv}(R_U)$ is the variable used by the receiver to refer to the term M. A coalition specifies a set of communications of this type (denoted as Θ). For the simplicity of modelling, we assume that for each communication, the coalition uses a distinct channel and distinct variable, i.e., $\forall \langle R_{u_i}, R_{u_j}, M, c, y \rangle \in \Theta$ and $\langle R'_{u_i}, R'_{u_j}, M', c', y' \rangle \in \Theta$ we have $c \neq c' \wedge y \neq y'$.

A coalition specifies a set of terms which are communicated by the originating user process and are replaced in the coalition. In addition, a coalition needs to define how a term is replaced. In a collaboration, the adversary is assumed to be able to compute and prepare this, but in a coalition, no user can compute and prepare information for other users. Thus, this ability has to be explicitly specified in a coalition as a set of substitutions $\Delta = \{\{N/M\} \mid M \in \mathsf{Term}(R_U)\}$. The new term N are calculated from a set of terms $N_1, \ldots, N_n$ which are generated by the user, read in by the original process, or read in from coalition members.

A successful coalition requires that there are no such situations where N cannot be calculated in the user process when M needs to be replaced.

Moreover, in a coalition, we allow the coalition to decide values of conditional evaluations (similar to collaboration, where the adversary decides this). Since no user in a coalition has the ability to specify the values of evaluations, these need to be assigned specifically. In addition, to add more flexibility, we allow a coalition to specify which evaluations are decided by the coalition and which are not. The evaluations of a plain user process R_U is $\mathsf{Eval}(R_U)$. The assignments of evaluations are specified as a set $\Pi \subseteq \{(e, b) \mid e \in \mathsf{Eval}(R_U) \wedge b \in \{\mathsf{true}, \mathsf{false}\}\}$.

$$\mathsf{Eval}(0) = \emptyset \qquad\qquad \mathsf{Eval}(P \mid Q) = \mathsf{Eval}(P) \cup \mathsf{Eval}(Q)$$
$$\mathsf{Eval}(!P) = \mathsf{Eval}(P) \qquad\qquad \mathsf{Eval}(\nu n.P) = \mathsf{Eval}(P)$$
$$\mathsf{Eval}(\mathsf{in}(v, x).P) = \mathsf{Eval}(P) \qquad \mathsf{Eval}(\mathsf{out}(v, M).P) = \mathsf{Eval}(P)$$
$$\mathsf{Eval}(if\ M =_E N\ then\ P\ else\ Q) = \{M =_E N\} \cup \mathsf{Eval}(P) \cup \mathsf{Eval}(Q)$$

Definition 5 (coalition specification). *A coalition[2] of a set of users R_U is specified as a tuple $\langle \Theta, \Delta, \Pi \rangle$ where Θ is a set of communication, Δ is a set of substitutions and Π is an assignment for a set of evaluations.*

With the above setting, given a set of users R_U and a coalition specification $\langle \Theta, \Delta, \Pi \rangle$ on users, the behaviour of a user in the coalition is modelled as a coalition transformation of the user's original process, as defined in Def. 6.

In the definition, process $\mathsf{in}(c_1, y_1').!\mathsf{out}(c_1', y_1') \mid \cdots \mid \mathsf{in}(c_\ell, y_\ell').!\mathsf{out}(c_\ell', y_\ell')$ models the receiving behaviour of process R in the coalition. The coalition specifies which channel is use to receive data. The received data on a channel are referred to as a distinct fresh variable. The received data is sent out over a distinct private channel. The association of channels and variables is modelled in ξ. This sending behaviour is used for the process $R^{\langle \Gamma, \Delta, \Pi \rangle}$ to read the data when it is needed. Process $R^{\langle \Gamma, \Delta, \Pi \rangle}$ models the sending behaviour, substitution of terms, assignments of evaluations. F captures the variables which are in $\{y_1, \ldots, y_\ell\}$ and has not been read in yet.

Definition 6 (coalition behaviour). *Let $R_U = R_{u_1} \mid \cdots \mid R_{u_m}$ be a plain process of a set of users, $\langle \Theta, \Delta, \Pi \rangle$ be a coalition specification of process R_U, $R \in \{R_{u_1}, \cdots, R_{u_m}\}$ be a plain user process, the transformation of the process R in the coalition is given by $R^{\langle \Theta, \Delta, \Pi \rangle}$:*

$$R^{\langle \Theta, \Delta, \Pi \rangle} = \nu \eta.(R^{\langle \Gamma, \Delta, \Pi \rangle} \mid \mathsf{in}(c_1, y_1').!\mathsf{out}(c_1', y_1') \mid \cdots \mid \mathsf{in}(c_\ell, y_\ell').!\mathsf{out}(c_\ell', y_\ell'))$$

where $\Gamma = \{\langle R, R_{u_j}, M, c, y \rangle \mid \langle R, R_{u_j}, M, c, y \rangle \in \Theta\}$, $\eta = \{c_1', \ldots, c_\ell'\}$, c_1', ..., c_ℓ' are fresh, $\{c_1, \ldots, c_\ell\} = \{c \mid \langle R_{u_i}, R, M, c, y \rangle \in \Theta\}$, $y_1', \ldots, y_\ell'$ are fresh variables, $\xi = \{(c_1, y_1', c_1'), \ldots, (c_\ell, y_\ell', c_\ell')\}$ defines the association of channels and variables in process $\mathsf{in}(c_1, y_1').!\mathsf{out}(c_1', y_1') \mid \cdots \mid \mathsf{in}(c_\ell, y_\ell').!\mathsf{out}(c_\ell', y_\ell')$, and $R^{\langle \Gamma, \Delta, \Pi \rangle}$ is given by:

---

[2] This model does not include the coalition strategies in which the target users and defending third parties are able to generate new data, initiate new sessions, establishing new secrets, etc.

- $0_F^{\langle \Gamma, \Delta, \Pi \rangle} \qquad\qquad \hat{=}\ 0,$
- $(P \mid Q)_F^{\langle \Gamma, \Delta, \Pi \rangle} \qquad \hat{=}\ P_F^{\langle \Gamma, \Delta, \Pi \rangle} \mid Q_F^{\langle \Gamma, \Delta, \Pi \rangle},$
- $(!P)_F^{\langle \Gamma, \Delta, \Pi \rangle} \qquad\quad \hat{=}\ !P_F^{\langle \Gamma, \Delta, \Pi \rangle},$

- $(\nu n.P)_F^{\langle \Gamma, \Delta, \Pi \rangle} \qquad \hat{=}$
$$\begin{cases} \nu n.\text{out}(c_1, n).\ \cdots\ .\text{out}(c_\ell, n).P_F^{\langle \Gamma, \Delta, \Pi \rangle} \\ \qquad \text{if } \{c_1, \ldots, c_\ell\} = \{c \mid \langle R, R_{u_j}, n, c, y \rangle \in \Gamma\}, \\ \nu n.P_F^{\langle \Gamma, \Delta, \Pi \rangle} \\ \qquad\qquad\qquad\qquad\qquad\qquad otherwise, \end{cases}$$

- $(\text{in}(v, x).P)_F^{\langle \Gamma, \Delta, \Pi \rangle} \quad \hat{=}$
$$\begin{cases} \text{in}(v, x).\text{out}(c_1, x).\ \cdots\ .\text{out}(c_\ell, x).P_F^{\langle \Gamma, \Delta, \Pi \rangle} \\ \qquad \text{if } \{c_1, \ldots, c_\ell\} = \{c \mid \langle R, R_{u_j}, x, c, y \rangle \in \Gamma\}, \\ \text{in}(v, x).P_F^{\langle \Gamma, \Delta, \Pi \rangle} \\ \qquad\qquad\qquad\qquad\qquad\qquad otherwise, \end{cases}$$

- $(\text{out}(v, M).P)_F^{\langle \Gamma, \Delta, \Pi \rangle} \quad \hat{=}$
$$\begin{cases} \text{in}(c'_1, y_1).\cdots.\text{in}(c'_\ell, y_\ell).\text{out}(v, N).P_{F \setminus \{y_1, \ldots, y_\ell\}}^{\langle \Gamma, \Delta, \Pi \rangle} \\ \qquad \text{if } \{N/M\} \in \Delta, \{y_1, \ldots, y_\ell\} \subseteq F \cup \text{Var}(N), \\ \qquad\qquad\qquad\qquad\qquad\qquad \forall i \in \{1, \ldots, \ell\}, \\ \qquad \langle R_i, R, c_i M, y_i \rangle \in \Theta \wedge (c_i, y'_i, c'_i) \in \xi, \\ \text{out}(v, M).P_F^{\langle \Gamma, \Delta, \Pi \rangle} \\ \qquad\qquad\qquad\qquad\qquad\qquad otherwise, \end{cases}$$

- $(\text{if } M =_E N \text{ then } P \text{ else } Q)_F^{\langle \Gamma, \Delta, \Pi \rangle} \hat{=}$
$$\begin{cases} P_F^{\langle \Gamma, \Delta, \Pi \rangle} & \text{if } (M =_E N, \text{true}) \in \Pi, \\ Q_F^{\langle \Gamma, \Delta, \Pi \rangle} & \text{if } (M =_E N, \text{false}) \in \Pi, \\ \text{if } M =_E N \text{ then } P_F^{\langle \Gamma, \Delta, \Pi \rangle} \text{ else } Q_F^{\langle \Gamma, \Delta, \Pi \rangle} & otherwise. \end{cases}$$

with F initially equals to $\{y_1, \ldots, y_\ell \mid \langle R_{u_i}, R, M, c, y \rangle \in \Theta\}$.

Given a set of users R_U and a coalition specification $\langle \Theta, \Delta, \Pi \rangle$ for them, the coalition is now modelled as $R_U^{\langle \Theta, \Delta, \Pi \rangle} = \nu \Omega.(R_{u_1}^{\langle \Theta, \Delta, \Pi \rangle} \mid \cdots \mid R_{u_m}^{\langle \Theta, \Delta, \Pi \rangle})$ where $\Omega = \{c \mid \langle R_{u_i}, R_{u_j}, M, c, y \rangle \in \Theta\}$.

4 Formalising the Privacy Notions

4.1 Enforced-Privacy

Enforced-privacy is the adversary's unlinkability of a target user to his data even when the user collaborates with the adversary. Different collaborations impact privacy differently, so when we say a protocol satisfies enforced-privacy, it always refers to a specific collaboration specification.

Similar as in receipt-freeness and coercion-resistance [10], when a protocol P_w satisfies enforced-privacy w.r.t. a target data τ (which belongs to role R_i) and a collaboration specification $\langle \Psi, \Phi, c_{out}, c_{in} \rangle$ defined on process $\hat{R}_i$ (where $R_i = \nu \text{id}_i.\nu \tau.\hat{R}_i$), there exists a process P_f for the target user to execute, such that the adversary cannot distinguish between real collaboration with $\tau = t_1$ and fake collaboration (by means of process P_f) with $\tau = t_2$.[3]

---

[3] In the epistemic notion of coercion-resistance, enforced-privacy can be defined as the existence of a *counter-strategy* for the target user to achieve his own goal, but the adversary cannot distinguish it from the target user following the adversary's instructions [26].

Definition 7. *A well-formed protocol P_w satisfies enforced-privacy (epriv) w.r.t. target data τ and collaboration specification $\langle \Psi, \Phi, \mathsf{c}_{out}, \mathsf{c}_{in} \rangle$, if there exists a closed plain process P_f, such that for any context $\mathcal{C}[\_] = \nu \mathsf{c}_{out}.\nu \mathsf{c}_{in}.(\_ \mid Q)$ satisfying $\mathsf{bn}(P_w) \cap \mathsf{fn}(\mathcal{C}[\_]) = \emptyset$ and $C_{P_w}[\mathcal{C}[\hat{R}_i^{\langle \Psi, \Phi, \mathsf{c}_{out}, \mathsf{c}_{in} \rangle}\{id/id_i, t/\tau\}]] \approx_\ell C_{P_w}[\hat{R}_i^{\langle \Psi, \emptyset, \mathsf{c}'_{out}, \perp \rangle}\{id/id_i, \mathsf{t}_1/\tau\}]$, we have*

1. $\mathcal{C}[P_f]^{\backslash(\mathsf{c}'_{out}, \cdot)} \approx_\ell \hat{R}_i\{id/id_i, \mathsf{t}_2/\tau\}$,
2. $C_{P_w}[\mathcal{C}[\hat{R}_i^{\langle \Psi, \Phi, \mathsf{c}_{out}, \mathsf{c}_{in} \rangle}\{id/id_i, t/\tau\}]] \approx_\ell C_{P_w}[\mathcal{C}[P_f]]$,

where $\tau \in \mathsf{bn}(R_i)$, $R_i = \nu id_i.\nu \tau.\hat{R}_i$, $\langle \Psi, \Phi, \mathsf{c}_{out}, \mathsf{c}_{in} \rangle$ is defined on $\hat{R}_i$, t is a free name representing a piece of data, and $\mathcal{C}[P_f]^{\backslash(\mathsf{c}'_{out}, \cdot)} = \nu \mathsf{c}'_{out}.(\mathcal{C}[P_f] \mid !\mathsf{in}(\mathsf{c}'_{out}, x))$.

The process $\hat{R}_i^{\langle \Psi, \Phi, \mathsf{c}_{out}, \mathsf{c}_{in} \rangle}\{id/id_i, t/\tau\}$ models the behaviour of the collaborating target user. The behaviour of the adversary in the collaboration is implicitly modelled as Q in the context $\mathcal{C}[\_] = \nu \mathsf{c}_{out}.\nu \mathsf{c}_{in}.(\_ \mid Q)$. Thus a specific collaboration is modelled as $\mathcal{C}[\hat{R}_i^{\langle \Psi, \Phi, \mathsf{c}_{out}, \mathsf{c}_{in} \rangle}\{id/id_i, t/\tau\}]$. Note that sometimes the target data in the collaboration is not decided by $\{t/\tau\}$, but by the context $\mathcal{C}[\_]$. The target data is actually instantiated by $C_{P_w}[\mathcal{C}[\hat{R}_i^{\langle \Psi, \Phi, \mathsf{c}_{out}, \mathsf{c}_{in} \rangle}\{id/id_i, t/\tau\}]] \approx_\ell C_{P_w}[\hat{R}_i^{\langle \Psi, \emptyset, \mathsf{c}'_{out}, \perp \rangle}\{id/id_i, \mathsf{t}_1/\tau\}]$. The first equivalence shows that even if the context $\mathcal{C}[\_]$ is able to decide the target data, the target user can still actually instantiate the target data with t_2 by executing the process P_f. The second equivalence shows that the adversary cannot distinguish the target user following the collaboration in process $\hat{R}_i^{\langle \Psi, \Phi, \mathsf{c}_{out}, \mathsf{c}_{in} \rangle}\{id/id_i, t/\tau\}$ from executing the process P_f, in the context of the adversary collaboration $\mathcal{C}[\_]$.

4.2 Independency-of-Privacy

Next, we account for attacking third parties. As different sets of third parties may differently influence the target user's privacy, and since different collaboration amongst the same third parties leads to different privacy properties, independency-of-privacy is defined with respect to a set of third parties and a collaboration specification between them and the adversary.

Definition 8 (third parties). *Given a well-formed protocol P_w and an instance of the target user $\hat{R}_i\{id/id, t/\tau\}$, a set of third parties is defined as a set of users $R_U = R_{u_1} \mid \cdots \mid R_{u_m}$ where $\forall i \in \{1, \cdots, m\}, R_{u_i} \neq \hat{R}_i\{id/id, t/\tau\}$. We use R_T to denote a set of attacking third parties and R_D to denote a set of defending third parties.*

The collaboration between a set of attacking third parties R_T and the adversary is expressed as a collaboration specification $\langle \Psi^t, \Phi^t, \mathsf{c}^t_{out}, \mathsf{c}^t_{in} \rangle$ defined on process R_T. The behaviour of the third parties in the collaboration is modelled as $R_T^{\langle \Psi^t, \Phi^t, \mathsf{c}^t_{out}, \mathsf{c}^t_{in} \rangle}$. Inspired by the domain-specific formal definitions, vote-independence [14] in e-voting and independency-of-prescribing-privacy [12] in

e-health, independency-of-privacy is defined as follows: a well-formed proto-
col P_w satisfies independency-of-privacy w.r.t. $(R_T, \langle \Psi^t, \Phi^t, c_{out}^t, c_{in}^t \rangle)$ and $\tau \in$
$bn(R_i)$, if the adversary cannot distinguish the honest target user executing role
R_i with $\tau = t_1$ from the same user with $\tau = t_2$, even when the set of third parties R_T collaborates with the adversary according to collaboration specification
$\langle \Psi^t, \Phi^t, c_{out}^t, c_{in}^t \rangle$.

Definition 9. *A well-formed protocol P_w satisfies independency-of-privacy (ipriv)*
w.r.t. data τ and attacking third parties $(R_T, \langle \Psi^t, \Phi^t, c_{out}^t, c_{in}^t \rangle)$ if

$$C_{P_w}[\hat{R}_i\{id/id_i, t_1/\tau\} \mid R_T^{\langle \Psi^t, \Phi^t, c_{out}^t, c_{in}^t \rangle}] \approx_\ell C_{P_w}[\hat{R}_i\{id/id_i, t_2/\tau\} \mid R_T^{\langle \Psi^t, \Phi^t, c_{out}^t, c_{in}^t \rangle}],$$

where $\langle \Psi^t, \Phi^t, c_{out}^t, c_{in}^t \rangle$ is a collaboration specification of process R_T.

If the equivalence holds, then despite this collaboration, adversary cannot distin-
guish $\hat{R}_i\{id/id_i, t_1/\tau\}$ in which the target user uses $\tau = t_1$ from $\hat{R}_i\{id/id_i, t_2/\tau\}$
in which the target user uses $\tau = t_2$.

4.3   Independency-of-Enforced-Privacy

We define independency-of-enforced-privacy (iepriv) based on epriv in a similar fashion as ipriv. More precisely, iepriv of a protocol P_w is defined w.r.t.
target data $\tau \in bn(R_i)$, a collaboration specification $\langle \Psi, \Phi, c_{out}, c_{in} \rangle$ defined
on process $\hat{R}_i$ with $R_i = \nu id_i.\nu \tau.\hat{R}_i$, and a set of attacking third parties together with a collaboration specification defined on the third parties processes
$(R_T, \langle \Psi^t, \Phi^t, c_{out}^t, c_{in}^t \rangle)$. A well-formed protocol P_w satisfies iepriv w.r.t. τ,
$\langle \Psi, \Phi, c_{out}, c_{in} \rangle$, and $(R_T, \langle \Psi^t, \Phi^t, c_{out}^t, c_{in}^t \rangle)$, if there exists a closed plain process P_f for the target user to execute, such that, despite the help of third parties
R_T according to $\langle \Psi^t, \Phi^t, c_{out}^t, c_{in}^t \rangle$, the adversary cannot distinguish between
the target user collaborating with $\tau = t_1$, and him really using $\tau = t_2$ but
faking collaboration for $\tau = t_1$ by P_f.

Definition 10. *A well-formed protocol P_w satisfies independency-of-enforced-*
privacy (iepriv) w.r.t. τ, $\langle \Psi, \Phi, c_{out}, c_{in} \rangle$, and $(R_T, \langle \Psi^t, \Phi^t, c_{out}^t, c_{in}^t \rangle)$, if there
exists a closed plain process P_f, such that for any $C[\_] = \nu c_{out}.\nu c_{in}.(\_ \mid Q)$
satisfying $bn(P_w) \cap fn(C[\_]) = \emptyset$ and $C_{P_w}[C[\hat{R}_i^{\langle \Psi, \Phi, c_{out}, c_{in} \rangle}\{id/id_i, t/\tau\}] \mid R_T] \approx_\ell$
$C_{P_w}[\hat{R}_i^{\langle \Psi, \emptyset, c'_{out}, \perp \rangle}\{id/id_i, t_1/\tau\} \mid R_T]$, we have

$$1.\ C[P_f]^{\backslash (c'_{out}, \cdot)} \approx_\ell \hat{R}_i\{id/id_i, t_2/\tau\},$$
$$2.\ C_{P_w}[C[\hat{R}_i^{\langle \Psi, \Phi, c_{out}, c_{in} \rangle}\{id/id_i, t/\tau\}] \mid R_T^{\langle \Psi^t, \Phi^t, c_{out}^t, c_{in}^t \rangle}]$$
$$\approx_\ell C_{P_w}[C[P_f] \mid R_T^{\langle \Psi^t, \Phi^t, c_{out}^t, c_{in}^t \rangle}],$$

where $\langle \Psi, \Phi, c_{out}, c_{in} \rangle$ is a collaboration specification for target user process $\hat{R}_i$,
and $\langle \Psi^t, \Phi^t, c_{out}^t, c_{in}^t \rangle$ is a collaboration specification of third party process R_T.

This formalisation adds third parties collaboration $R_T^{\langle \Psi^t, \Phi^t, c_{out}^t, c_{in}^t \rangle}$ to Def. 7.

4.4   Coalition Privacy Properties

Corresponding to each privacy property defined above, we define coalition privacy properties which take into account defending third parties.

Definition 11 (defensive coalition). *Given an instance of the target user $\hat{R}_i\{id/id, t/\tau\}$, a set of defending third parties R_D, and a coalition specification $\langle \Theta, \Delta, \Pi \rangle$ defined on $(\hat{R}_i\{id/id, t/\tau\} \mid R_D)$, the coalition is modelled as $\nu\Omega.(\hat{R}_i\{id/id, t/\tau\} \mid R_D)^{\langle \Theta, \Delta, \Pi \rangle}$, where $\Omega = \{c \mid \langle R_{u_i}, R_{u_j}, M, c, y \rangle \in \Theta\}$. The target user's behaviour in the coalition is $\hat{R}_i\{id/id, t/\tau\}^{\langle \Theta, \Delta, \Pi \rangle} = \nu\eta.((\hat{R}_i\{id/id, t/\tau\})^{\langle \Gamma, \Delta, \Pi \rangle} \mid P_\gamma)$, where η is a set of fresh channels $\{c'_1, \ldots, c'_\ell\}$, $\Gamma = \{\langle \hat{R}_i\{id/id, t/\tau\}, R_{u_j}, M, c, y \rangle \mid \langle \hat{R}_i\{id/id, t/\tau\}, R_{u_j}, M, c, y \rangle \in \Theta\}$, and $P_\gamma = \mathsf{in}(c_1, y'_1).!\mathsf{out}(c'_1, y'_1) \mid \cdots \mid \mathsf{in}(c_\ell, y'_\ell).!\mathsf{out}(c'_\ell, y'_\ell)$ with $\{y'_1, \ldots, y'_\ell\}$ being fresh variables, and $\{(c_1, \ldots, c_\ell\} = \{c \mid \langle R_{u_i}, \hat{R}_i\{id/id, t/\tau\}, M, c, y \rangle \in \Theta\}$. The third parties' behaviour in the coalition is $R_D^{\langle \Theta, \Delta, \Pi \rangle}$.*

Coalition-Privacy. Intuitively, coalition-privacy means that a target user's privacy is preserved due to the cooperation of a set of defending third parties. A well-formed protocol P_w satisfies coalition-privacy w.r.t. $\tau \in \mathsf{bn}(R_i)$ and $(R_D, \langle \Theta, \Delta, \Pi \rangle)$ ($\langle \Theta, \Delta, \Pi \rangle$ is defined on $\hat{R}_i \mid R_D$, where $R_i = \nu id_i.\nu\tau.\hat{R}_i$), if the adversary cannot distinguish an honest user in role R_i using $\tau = \mathsf{t}_1$ from the user actually using $\tau = \mathsf{t}_2$ while helped by a set of defending third parties.

Definition 12. *A well-formed protocol P_w satisfies coalition-privacy (cpriv) w.r.t. data τ and coalition $(R_D, \langle \Theta, \Delta, \Pi \rangle)$ if $C_{P_w}[\hat{R}_i\{id/id_i, \mathsf{t}_1/\tau\} \mid R_D] \approx_\ell C_{P_w}[\nu\Omega.(\hat{R}_i\{id/id_i, \mathsf{t}_2/\tau\} \mid R_D)^{\langle \Theta, \Delta, \Pi \rangle}]$, where $\langle \Theta, \Delta, \Pi \rangle$ is a coalition specification defined on $\hat{R}_i\{id/id_i, \mathsf{t}_2/\tau\} \mid R_D$.*

In the definition, the coalition is modelled as $\nu\Omega.(\hat{R}_i\{id/id_i, \mathsf{t}_2/\tau\} \mid R_D)^{\langle \Theta, \Delta, \Pi \rangle}$, where the target user instantiates the target data with t_2. The equivalence shows that the adversary cannot distinguish the target user instantiating the target data with t_2 in the coalition from the target user instantiating the target data with t_1. In this way, coalition-privacy ensures the target user's privacy when there exists a set of third parties cooperating with him following a pre-defined coalition specification.

Coalition-Enforced-Privacy. Taking into account defending third parties, we define coalition-enforced-privacy based on enforced-privacy. As before, coalition-enforced-privacy specifies a target data τ and a collaboration specification of the target user $\langle \Psi, \Phi, c_{out}, c_{in} \rangle$. As in coalition-privacy, coalition-enforced-privacy specifies a set of defending third parties R_D and a coalition specification $\langle \Theta, \Delta, \Pi \rangle$. In coalition-enforced-privacy, the target user both cooperates with the adversary and defending third parties. Similar to enforced-privacy, we assume that the target user lies to the adversary if possible. We do not assume that the target user lies to the defending third parties, as they help the target user maintain privacy.

Intuitively, coalition-enforced-privacy means that a target user is able to lie to the adversary about his target data when helped by defending third parties – the adversary cannot tell whether the user lied. This property is modelled as the combination of coalition-privacy and enforced-privacy: a protocol P_w satisfies coalition-enforced-privacy w.r.t $\tau \in \mathsf{bn}(R_i), \langle \Psi, \Phi, c_{out}, c_{in} \rangle$ and $(R_D, \langle \Theta, \Delta, \Pi \rangle)$, for $\langle \Psi, \Phi, c_{out}, c_{in} \rangle$ a collaboration specification defined on $\hat{R}_i$ with $R_i = \nu id_i.\nu\tau.\hat{R}_i$, and $\langle \Theta, \Delta, \Pi \rangle$ a coalition specification defined on the target user and R_D, if there exists a process P_f, such that the adversary cannot distinguish between genuine collaboration with $\tau = t_1$ and faking collaboration using P_f with the help of the coalition for $\tau = t_2$.

Definition 13. *A well-formed protocol P_w satisfies coalition-enforced-privacy* (cepriv) *w.r.t. data τ, $\langle \Psi, \Phi, c_{out}, c_{in} \rangle$ and $(R_D, \langle \Theta, \Delta, \Pi \rangle)$, if there exists a closed plain process P_f, such that for any $C[\_] = \nu c_{out}.\nu c_{in}.(\_ \mid Q)$ satisfying $\mathsf{bn}(P_w) \cap \mathsf{fn}(C[\_]) = \emptyset$ and $C_{P_w}[C[\hat{R}_i^{\langle \Psi, \Phi, c_{out}, c_{in} \rangle} \{id/id_i, t/\tau\}] \mid R_D] \approx_\ell C_{P_w}[\hat{R}_i^{\langle \Psi, \emptyset, c'_{out}, \perp \rangle} \{id/id_i, t_1/\tau\} \mid R_D]$, we have*

1. $\nu\Omega.(\nu\eta.(C[P_f]^{\backslash(c'_{out}, \cdot)} \mid P_\gamma) \mid R_D^{\langle \Theta, \Delta, \Pi \rangle}) \approx_\ell \nu\Omega.(\hat{R}_i \{id/id_i, t_2/\tau\} \mid R_D)^{\langle \Theta, \Delta, \Pi \rangle}$,
2. $C_{P_w}[C[\hat{R}_i^{\langle \Psi, \Phi, c_{out}, c_{in} \rangle} \{id/id_i, t/\tau\}] \mid R_D]$
$$\approx_\ell C_{P_w}[\nu\Omega.(\nu\eta.(C[P_f] \mid P_\gamma) \mid R_D^{\langle \Theta, \Delta, \Pi \rangle})],$$

where Ω, η, P_γ are defined in Def. 11, $\langle \Psi, \Phi, c_{out}, c_{in} \rangle$ is defined on $\hat{R}_i$, $\langle \Theta, \Delta, \Pi \rangle$ is a coalition specification defined on $\hat{R}_i \{id/id_i, t_2/\tau\} \mid R_D$.

The collaboration between the target user and the adversary instantiating the target data with t_1 is modelled by $C_{P_w}[C[\hat{R}_i^{\langle \Psi, \Phi, c_{out}, c_{in} \rangle} \{id/id_i, t/\tau\}] \mid R_D] \approx_\ell C_{P_w}[\hat{R}_i^{\langle \Psi, \emptyset, c'_{out}, \perp \rangle} \{id/id_i, t_1/\tau\} \mid R_D]$. The target user's actual behaviour of instantiating the target data with t_2 in process P_f is modelled as the first equivalence. The second equivalence shows that the adversary cannot distinguish the target user following the collaboration with the adversary from the target user lying to the adversary with the help of defending third parties.

Coalition-Independency-of-Privacy. Similarly, we define the privacy notion of coalition-independency-of-privacy with respect to a target data τ, a set of attacking third parties with a collaboration specification $(R_T, \langle \Psi^t, \Phi^t, c_{out}^t, c_{in}^t \rangle)$, and a set of defending third parties R_D with a coalition specification $\langle \Theta, \Delta, \Pi \rangle$. Note that we require that there is no intersection between attacking third parties and defending third parties, i.e., $R_T \cap R_D = \emptyset$, as we assume a third party cannot be both attacking and defending at the same time. A well-formed protocol P_w satisfies coalition-independency-of-privacy w.r.t. τ, $(R_T, \langle \Psi^t, \Phi^t, c_{out}^t, c_{in}^t \rangle)$ and $(R_D, \langle \Theta, \Delta, \Pi \rangle)$, if the adversary, even with the collaboration of a set of attacking third parties, cannot distinguish the target user instantiating $\tau = t_1$ from the target user actually instantiating $\tau = t_2$ in the coalition with the help of defending third parties.

Definition 14. *A well-formed protocol P_w satisfies coalition-independency-of-privacy* (cipriv) *w.r.t. data τ, $(R_T, \langle \Psi^t, \Phi^t, c_{out}^t, c_{in}^t \rangle)$, and $(R_D, \langle \Theta, \Delta, \Pi \rangle)$, if*

$$C_{P_w}[\hat{R}_i \{id/id_i, t_1/\tau\} \mid R_D \mid R_T^{\langle \Psi^t, \Phi^t, c_{out}^t, c_{in}^t \rangle}]$$
$$\approx_\ell C_{P_w}[\nu\Omega.((\hat{R}_i \{id/id_i, t_2/\tau\} \mid R_D)^{\langle \Theta, \Delta, \Pi \rangle}) \mid R_T^{\langle \Psi^t, \Phi^t, c_{out}^t, c_{in}^t \rangle}],$$

where $\langle \Psi^t, \Phi^t, c_{out}^t, c_{in}^t \rangle$ is a collaboration specification of process R_T, $\langle \Theta, \Delta, \Pi \rangle$ is a coalition specification defined on $\hat{R}_i \{id/id_i, t_2/\tau\} \mid R_D$.

Coalition-Independency-of-Enforced-Privacy. Finally, we consider the case combining all situations together: the target user collaborates with the adversary following $\langle \Psi, \Phi, c_{out}, c_{in} \rangle$, a set of attacking third parties R_T collaborate with the adversary following $\langle \Psi^t, \Phi^t, c_{out}^t, c_{in}^t \rangle$, and a set of defending third parties R_D and a coalition $\langle \Theta, \Delta, \Pi \rangle$. We formally define the property as follows.

Definition 15. *A well-formed protocol P_w satisfies coalition-independency-of-enforced-privacy* (ciepriv) *w.r.t.* τ, $\langle \Psi, \Phi, c_{out}, c_{in} \rangle$, $(R_T, \langle \Psi^t, \Phi^t, c_{out}^t, c_{in}^t \rangle)$, $(R_D, \langle \Theta, \Delta, \Pi \rangle)$, *if there exists a closed plain process P_f such that for any context* $C[\_] = \nu c_{out}.\nu c_{in}.(\_ \mid Q)$ *satisfying* $\mathsf{bn}(P_w) \cap \mathsf{fn}(C[\_]) = \emptyset$ *and* $C_{P_w}[C[\hat{R}_i^{\langle \Psi, \Phi, c_{out}, c_{in} \rangle}\{id/id_i, t/\tau\}] \mid R_T \mid R_D] \approx_\ell C_{P_w}[\hat{R}_i^{\langle \Psi, \emptyset, c_{out}', \perp \rangle}\{id/id_i, t_1/\tau\} \mid R_T \mid R_D]$, *we have*

1. $\nu\Omega.(\nu\eta.(C[P_f]^{\backslash(c_{out}', \cdot)} \mid P_\gamma) \mid R_D^{\langle \Theta, \Delta, \Pi \rangle}) \approx_\ell \nu\Omega.((\hat{R}_i\{id/id_i, t_2/\tau\} \mid R_D)^{\langle \Theta, \Delta, \Pi \rangle})$,

2. $C_{P_w}[C[\hat{R}_i^{\langle \Psi, \Phi, c_{out}, c_{in} \rangle}\{id/id_i, t/\tau\}] \mid R_D \mid R_T^{\langle \Psi^t, \Phi^t, c_{out}^t, c_{in}^t \rangle}]$
$\approx_\ell C_{P_w}[\nu\Omega.(\nu\eta.(C[P_f] \mid P_\gamma) \mid R_D^{\langle \Theta, \Delta, \Pi \rangle}) \mid R_T^{\langle \Psi^t, \Phi^t, c_{out}^t, c_{in}^t \rangle}]$,

where Ω, η, P_γ are defined in Def. 11, $\langle \Psi, \Phi, c_{out}, c_{in} \rangle$ is a collaboration specification defined on $\hat{R}_i$, $\langle \Psi^t, \Phi^t, c_{out}^t, c_{in}^t \rangle$ is a collaboration specification defined on R_T, $\langle \Theta, \Delta, \Pi \rangle$ is a coalition specification defined on $\hat{R}_i\{id/id_i, t_2/\tau\} \mid R_D$.

Remark. As certain coalitions may fail to maintain privacy, the coalition privacy properties can be generalised by requiring the existence of a successful coalition. The general version of coalition privacy properties allows us to reason about the existence of a coalition such that a user's privacy is preserved. How to find such a coalition is an interesting topic for studying coalition privacy properties. Each property defined in the above can be instantiated in many different forms by specifying the parameters of the property (such as target data, collaboration, coalition). Furthermore, only the target user is allowed to lie to the adversary – we do not consider lying third parties. Properties, ipriv, iepriv, cipriv and ciepriv, can be extended by allowing third parties to lie. For details, see [27].

5   Relations between the Privacy Notions

We show the relations between the privacy properties in Fig. 2: ρ specifies a collaboration of the target user with the adversary, θ specifies a set of attacking third parties and their collaboration with the adversary, and δ specifies a set of defending third parties and their coalition with the target user.

The left diamond in Fig. 2 shows the relations between privacy properties which do not consider defending third parties while the right diamond shows the relations between privacy properties which consider defending third parties. In the left diamond, $epriv_\rho$ and $ipriv_\theta$ are stronger than priv, meaning that if a protocol satisfies $epriv_\rho$ or $ipriv_\theta$, then the protocol satisfies priv. Intuitively, if the adversary cannot break privacy with the help from the target user (in $epriv_\rho$) or from a set of attacking third parties (in $ipriv_\theta$), the adversary cannot break privacy without any help (in priv). Similarly, if the adversary cannot break privacy with the help from both target user and attacking third parties (in $\mathsf{iepriv}_{\rho,\theta}$), the adversary cannot break privacy with the help from only one of them (in epriv_ρ and ipriv_θ). Thus, $\mathsf{iepriv}_{\rho,\theta}$ is stronger than both enforced-privacy$_\rho$ and ipriv_θ. This is described as Thm. 1. Similar reasoning holds in the right diamond as described in Thm. 2. Each privacy property in the left diamond has a weaker corresponding property in the right diamond, meaning that if a protocol satisfies a privacy property in the left diamond, there exists a coalition such that the property satisfies the corresponding coalition privacy property in the right diamond. Intuitively, if a protocol preserves privacy of a target user without any help from third parties, the protocol can still preserve his privacy with the help from others. This is described as Thm. 3.

Theorem 1. *(1)* $\forall\theta$, $\mathsf{iepriv}_{\rho,\theta}$ $\Longrightarrow \mathsf{epriv}_\rho$, *(2)* $\forall\rho$, $\mathsf{iepriv}_{\rho,\theta}$ $\Longrightarrow$ ipriv_θ, *(3)* $\forall\rho$, epriv_ρ $\Longrightarrow$ priv, *and (4)* $\forall\theta$, ipriv_θ $\Longrightarrow \mathsf{priv}$.

Theorem 2. *(1)* $\forall\theta$, $\mathsf{ciepriv}_{\rho,\theta,\delta}$ $\Longrightarrow \mathsf{cepriv}_{\rho,\delta}$, *(2)* $\forall\rho$, $\mathsf{ciepriv}_{\rho,\theta,\delta}$ $\Longrightarrow \mathsf{cipriv}_{\theta,\delta}$, *(3)* $\forall\rho$, $\mathsf{cepriv}_{\rho,\delta}$ $\Longrightarrow$ cpriv_δ, *and (4)* $\forall\theta$, $\mathsf{cipriv}_{\theta,\delta}$ $\Longrightarrow$ cpriv_δ.

Theorem 3. *(1)* $\mathsf{ciepriv}_{\rho,\theta}$ $\Longrightarrow$ $\exists\delta$, $\mathsf{ciepriv}_{\rho,\theta,\delta}$, *(2)* epriv_ρ $\Longrightarrow$ $\exists\delta,\mathsf{cepriv}_{\rho,\delta}$, *(3)* ipriv_θ $\Longrightarrow$ $\exists\delta$, $\mathsf{cipriv}_{\theta,\delta}$, *and (4)* $\mathsf{priv} \Longrightarrow \exists\delta$, cpriv_δ.

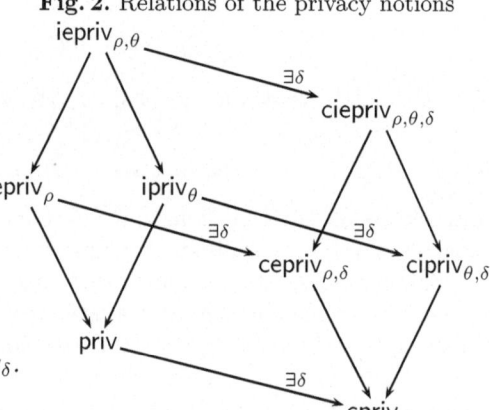

Fig. 2. Relations of the privacy notions

6   Discussion

Privacy notions modelled as strong secrecy can be captured by data-privacy. For instance, anonymity [3] is data-privacy where the target data is a user's identity. Various domain-specific properties, which capture privacy in domains where data-privacy is too strong to be satisfied, can be instantiated by cpriv. For instance, bidding-privacy [11] in sealed-bid e-auctions is defined as the adversary cannot determine a bidder's bidding-price, assuming the existence of a winning bid. This can be instantiated as cpriv where the target data is a bid, the defending third party is the winning bidder and the coalition specification is $\langle\emptyset,\emptyset,\emptyset\rangle$. Vote-privacy [22] is defined as the adversary cannot determine a voter's vote with the existence of a counter-balancing voter. This can be instantiated as cpriv where the target data is a vote, the defending third party is the counter-balancing voter and the coalition specification is $\langle\emptyset,\Delta,\emptyset\rangle$ where Δ specifies how to replace the counter-balancing voter's vote.

Enforced privacy notions like receipt-freeness or coercion-resistance can be captured by either epriv or cepriv. Receipt-freeness [10] in voting can be instantiated by cepriv, where the target data and the coalition are the same as in vote-privacy, and the collaboration specification is $\langle\Psi,\emptyset,\mathsf{c}_{out},\bot\rangle$ where Ψ contains all private terms generated and read-in in the target voter process. Similarly, coercion-resistance [10] in voting is an instance of coalition-enforced-privacy.

The two independency of privacy properties, independency-of-prescribing-privacyand independence-vote-privacy, are instances of cipriv. For example, the property independence-vote-privacy [14] can be considered as an instance of cipriv, where the target data and the coalition are the same as in vote-privacy, the set of attacking third parties is a third voter, and the collaboration specification of the third voter is $\langle \Psi, \Phi, c_{out}, c_{in} \rangle$ where Ψ are all generated and read-in terms and Φ are all communicated terms in the third voter process. For details, see [27].

7   Conclusion and Future Work

In this paper, we have identified (enforced) privacy notions in the presence of third parties. We formalised the collaboration of users, including the target user and attacking third parties, with the adversary and the coalition among users (the target user with defending third parties) in a generic way. The identified privacy notions are formally defined in the applied pi calculus. We presented the relations among the properties as a privacy hierarchy. We also showed that various existing privacy properties in the literature can be instantiated as one of the properties in the hierarchy.

We have already mentioned a few interesting research directions in the paper, for example, how to find a coalition and synthesise strategy for the coalition to satisfy some coalition privacy properties for a protocol, and how to extend our privacy hierarchy to capture situations where a third party is coerced but has a strategy to lie to the adversary. One important future work is to apply our privacy notions to real-world applications such as online social networks.

References

1. Reiter, M.K., Rubin, A.D.: Crowds: Anonymity for web transactions. ACM Transactions on Information and System Security 1(1), 66–92 (1998)
2. van Deursen, T., Mauw, S., Radomirović, S.: Untraceability of RFID protocols. In: Onieva, J.A., Sauveron, D., Chaumette, S., Gollmann, D., Markantonakis, K. (eds.) WISTP 2008. LNCS, vol. 5019, pp. 1–15. Springer, Heidelberg (2008)
3. Arapinis, M., Chothia, T., Ritter, E., Ryan, M.D.: Analysing unlinkability and anonymity using the applied pi calculus. In: Proc. 23rd CSF, pp. 107–121. IEEE (2010)
4. Bohli, J., Pashalidis, A.: Relations among privacy notions. ACM Transactions on Information and System Security 14(1), 4:1–4:24 (2011)
5. Jonker, H.L., Pang, J.: Bulletin boards in voting systems: Modelling and measuring privacy. In: Proc. 6th ARES, pp. 294–300. IEEE (2011)
6. Benaloh, J., Tuinstra, D.: Receipt-free secret-ballot elections (extended abstract). In: Proc. 26th STOC, pp. 544–553. ACM (1994)
7. Abe, M., Suzuki, K.: Receipt-free sealed-bid auction. In: Chan, A.H., Gligor, V.D. (eds.) ISC 2002. LNCS, vol. 2433, pp. 191–199. Springer, Heidelberg (2002)
8. Juels, A., Catalano, D., Jakobsson, M.: Coercion-resistant electronic elections. In: Proc. 4th WPES, pp. 61–70. ACM (2005)

9. De Decker, B., Layouni, M., Vangheluwe, H., Verslype, K.: A privacy-preserving eHealth protocol compliant with the Belgian healthcare system. In: Mjølsnes, S.F., Mauw, S., Katsikas, S.K. (eds.) EuroPKI 2008. LNCS, vol. 5057, pp. 118–133. Springer, Heidelberg (2008)
10. Delaune, S., Kremer, S., Ryan, M.D.: Verifying privacy-type properties of electronic voting protocols. Journal of Computer Security 17(4), 435–487 (2009)
11. Dong, N., Jonker, H., Pang, J.: Analysis of a receipt-free auction protocol in the applied pi calculus. In: Degano, P., Etalle, S., Guttman, J. (eds.) FAST 2010. LNCS, vol. 6561, pp. 223–238. Springer, Heidelberg (2011)
12. Dong, N., Jonker, H., Pang, J.: Formal analysis of privacy in an eHealth protocol. In: Foresti, S., Yung, M., Martinelli, F. (eds.) ESORICS 2012. LNCS, vol. 7459, pp. 325–342. Springer, Heidelberg (2012)
13. Dong, N., Jonker, H., Pang, J.: Challenges in eHealth: From enabling to enforcing privacy. In: Liu, Z., Wassyng, A. (eds.) FHIES 2011. LNCS, vol. 7151, pp. 195–206. Springer, Heidelberg (2012)
14. Dreier, J., Lafourcade, P., Lakhnech, Y.: Vote-independence: A powerful privacy notion for voting protocols. In: Garcia-Alfaro, J., Lafourcade, P. (eds.) FPS 2011. LNCS, vol. 6888, pp. 164–180. Springer, Heidelberg (2012)
15. Lowe, G.: Breaking and fixing the Needham-Schroeder public-key protocol using FDR. In: Margaria, T., Steffen, B. (eds.) TACAS 1996. LNCS, vol. 1055, pp. 147–166. Springer, Heidelberg (1996)
16. Chadha, R., Kremer, S., Scedrov, A.: Formal analysis of multi-party contract signing. In: Proc. 17th CSFW, pp. 266–279. IEEE (2004)
17. Blanchet, B.: An efficient cryptographic protocol verifier based on prolog rules. In: Proc. 14th CSFW, pp. 82–96. IEEE (2001)
18. Blanchet, B., Abadi, M., Fournet, C.: Automated verification of selected equivalences for security protocols. Journal of Logic and Algebraic Programming 75(1), 3–51 (2008)
19. Cheval, V., Blanchet, B.: Proving more observational equivalences with ProVerif. In: Basin, D., Mitchell, J.C. (eds.) POST 2013. LNCS, vol. 7796, pp. 226–246. Springer, Heidelberg (2013)
20. Blanchet, B.: Automatic proof of strong secrecy for security protocols. In: Proc. 25th S&P, pp. 86–100. IEEE (2004)
21. Dolev, D., Yao, A.C.C.: On the security of public key protocols. IEEE Transactions on Information Theory 29(2), 198–207 (1983)
22. Kremer, S., Ryan, M.D.: Analysis of an electronic voting protocol in the applied pi calculus. In: Sagiv, M. (ed.) ESOP 2005. LNCS, vol. 3444, pp. 186–200. Springer, Heidelberg (2005)
23. Dahl, M., Delaune, S., Steel, G.: Formal analysis of privacy for anonymous location based services. In: Mödersheim, S., Palamidessi, C. (eds.) TOSCA 2011. LNCS, vol. 6993, pp. 98–112. Springer, Heidelberg (2012)
24. Dreier, J., Lafourcade, P., Lakhnech, Y.: Defining privacy for weighted votes, single and multi-voter coercion. In: Foresti, S., Yung, M., Martinelli, F. (eds.) ESORICS 2012. LNCS, vol. 7459, pp. 451–468. Springer, Heidelberg (2012)
25. Abadi, M., Fournet, C.: Mobile values, new names, and secure communication. In: Proc. 28th POPL, pp. 104–115. ACM (2001)
26. Küsters, R., Truderung, T.: An epistemic approach to coercion-resistance for electronic voting protocols. In: Proc. 30th S&P, pp. 251–266. IEEE (2009)
27. Dong, N., Jonker, H.L., Pang, J.: Enforcing privacy in the presence of others: Notions, formalisations and relations. Technical report, University of Luxembourg (2013), http://satoss.uni.lu/projects/epriv/

Mining Malware Specifications
through Static Reachability Analysis

Hugo Daniel Macedo and Tayssir Touili

LIAFA, CNRS and Univ. Paris Diderot, France
{macedo,touili}@liafa.univ-paris-diderot.fr

Abstract. The number of malicious software (malware) is growing out of control. Syntactic signature based detection cannot cope with such growth and manual construction of malware signature databases needs to be replaced by computer learning based approaches. Currently, a single modern signature capturing the semantics of a malicious behavior can be used to replace an arbitrarily large number of old-fashioned syntactical signatures. However teaching computers to learn such behaviors is a challenge. Existing work relies on dynamic analysis to extract malicious behaviors, but such technique does not guarantee the coverage of all behaviors. To sidestep this limitation we show how to learn malware signatures using *static* reachability analysis. The idea is to model binary programs using pushdown systems (that can be used to model the stack operations occurring during the binary code execution), use reachability analysis to extract behaviors in the form of trees, and use subtrees that are common among the trees extracted from a training set of malware files as signatures. To detect malware we propose to use a tree automaton to compactly store malicious behavior trees and check if any of the subtrees extracted from the file under analysis is malicious. Experimental data shows that our approach can be used to learn signatures from a training set of malware files and use them to detect a test set of malware that is 10 times the size of the training set.

1 Introduction

Malware (malicious software) is software developed to damage the system that executes it, e.g.: virus, trojans, rootkits, etc. A malware variant performs the same damage as another known malware, but its code, its syntactical representation, is different. Malware can be grouped into families, sets of malware sharing a common trait. Security reports acknowledge a steady increase in the number of new malware. For instance, in 2010 the number of newly unique variants of malware was 286 million [13] and recent numbers confirm the trend [21]. Such numbers challenge current malware detection technology and because variants can be automatically generated the problem tends to get worse. Research confirms the unsuitability of current malware detectors [14,24]. The problem is the low-level of the techniques used.

The basic detection technique is signature matching, it consists in the inspection of the binary code and search for patterns in the form of binary sequences [27]. Such patterns, malware signatures in the jargon and syntactic signatures throughout this paper, are manually introduced in a database by experts. As it is possible to automatically generate an unbounded number of variants, such databases would have to grow arbitrarily, not to mention it takes about two months to manually update them [14].

J. Crampton, S. Jajodia, and K. Mayes (Eds.): ESORICS 2013, LNCS 8134, pp. 517–535, 2013.

An alternative to signature detection is dynamic analysis, which runs malware in a virtual machine. Therefore, it is possible to check the program behavior, for instance to detect calls to system functions or changes in sensitive files, but as the execution duration must be limited in time it is difficult to trigger the malicious behaviors, since these may be hidden behind user interaction or require delays.

To overcome the problems of the previous techniques, a precise notion of malicious behavior was introduced. Such is the outcome of the recent use of model-checking techniques to perform virus detection [3,9,11,16,17,18,26,24,25,22]. Such techniques allow to check the behavior (not the syntax) of the program without executing it. A malicious behavior is a pattern written as a logical formula that specifies at a semantic level how the syntactic instructions in the binary executable perform damage during execution. As the malicious behavior is the same in all the variants of a malware, such patterns can be used as modern (semantic) signatures which can be efficiently stored.

The prime example of a malicious behavior is self-replication [27]. A typical instance of such behavior is a program that copies its own binary representation into another file, as exemplified in the assembly fragment of Fig. 1. The attacker program discovers and stores its file path into a memory address m by calling the *GetModuleFileName* function with 0 as first parameter and m as second parameter. Later such file name is used to infect another file by calling *CopyFile* with m as first parameter. Such malicious behaviors can naturally be defined in terms of system functions calls and data flow relationships.

l_1 : push m
l_2 : mov ebx 0
l_3 : push ebx
l_4 : call *GetModuleFileName*
l_5 : push m
l_6 : call *CopyFile*

Fig. 1. Malware assembly fragment

System functions are the mediators between programs and their environment (user data, network access,...), and as those functions can be given a fixed semantics, and are defined in an Application Programming Interface (**API**), they can be used as a common denominator between programs, i.e. if the syntactical representation of programs is different but both interact in the same way with the environment, the programs are semantically equivalent from an observer perspective.

A *data flow* expresses that a value outputted at a certain time instant of program execution by a function is used as an input by another function at a following instant. For example when a parameter is outputted by a system call and is used as an input of another. Such data flow relations allow us to characterize combined behaviors purported by the related system calls. For instance, in the example of Fig. 1 it is the data flow evidenced by the variable m, defined at the invocation of *GetModuleFileName* and used at the invocation of *CopyFile* that establishes the self-replication behavior.

The malicious behaviors can be described naturally by trees expressing data flows among system calls made at runtime. Due to code branches during execution it is possible to have several flows departing from the same system call, thus a tree structure is particularly suitable to represent malicious behaviors. Plus, as such behaviors are described independently of the functionality of the code that makes the calls, system call data flow based signatures are more robust against code obfuscations. Thus, a remaining challenge is to learn such trees from malware binary executables.

Recent work [2,10,14] shows that we can teach computers to learn malicious behavior specifications. Given a set of malware, the problem of extracting malicious behavior signatures consists in the extraction of the behaviors included in the set and use statistical machinery to choose the ones that are more likely to appear. However the approaches rely on dynamic analysis of executables which do not fully cover all behaviors. To overcome these limitations, in this paper we show how to use static reachability analysis to extract malicious behaviors, thus covering the whole behaviors of a program at once and within a limited time.

Our Approach. We address such challenge in the following way: given the set of known malware binary executables, we extract its malicious behaviors in the form of edge labeled trees with two kinds of nodes. One kind represents the knowledge that a system function is called, the other kind of nodes represents which values were passed as parameters in the call (because some data flows between functions are only malicious when the calls were made with a specific parameter e.g. the 0 passed to *GetModuleFileName* in the self-replication behavior). Tree labels describe either a relation among system calls or the number of the parameter instantiated. For example, the malicious behavior displayed in Fig. 1 can be displayed in the tree shown in Fig. 2. The tree captures the self-replication behavior.

The edge on the left means that the *GetModuleFile-Name* function is called with 0 as first parameter (thus it will output the path to the malware file that called it) while the edge on the right captures the data flow between the two system calls i.e. the second parameter of a call to *GetModuleFileName* is an output and it is

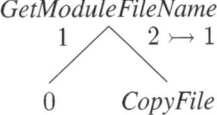

Fig. 2. Self-replication behavior

used as an input in the first parameter of a call to *CopyFile*. Thus, such tree describes the following behavior: *GetModuleFileName* is called with 0 as first parameter and its second parameter will be used as input in the first parameter of a subsequent call to *CopyFile*.

The first step in the tree extraction process is to model the malware binaries, which involves modeling (recursive) procedure calling and return, and parameter passing that are implemented using a stack. For this aim, we model each of the files using a pushdown system (**PDS**), an automaton that mimics the binary code execution as a state transition system. With this model one is able to rigorously define the behavior of the program and use the decidable and efficient state reachability analysis of **PDS**s to calculate all the states and the contents of the stack that can occur during execution. Therefore, if malware performs a system call with certain parameters, the reachability analysis will reveal it even if the call is obfuscated, e.g.: jump to function address. The same happens if the call is made using indirect addressing because the analysis will reveal that during execution the entry point of the system call is reached. Our approach also works against bitwise manipulation of parameters, because we assume the system functions are not changed by the attacker, thus when the executions reaches the entry point of the system function, parameters must not be obfuscated, for instance in the example above even if the value of m is obfuscated, at the entry point of the call the value must be m to purport the self-replication behavior.

From the reachability analysis of each **PDS**, we obtain a multi-automaton (**MA**), a finite automaton encoding the possibly infinite reachable configurations (states and stack contents)[8,12]. As the number of system functions is finite, we cut the finite automaton to represent only the states corresponding to system function entry points and stacks limited to the finite number of parameters passed to the function.

We analyze all data flows using the **MA**s to build trees, written as system call dependency trees (**SCDT**s), representing such flows. The extracted trees correspond to a superset of the data flows present in the malware because the **PDS** model is an overapproximation of the behaviors in the binary program. This means, that when a data flow is found using our approach, there exists an execution path in the model evidencing such data flow, but such execution path may not be possible in the binary program due to approximation errors.

From the trees (**SCDT**s) extracted from the set of known malware binary executables we use a data-mining algorithm to compute the most frequent subtrees. We assume such correspond to malicious behaviors and we will term them malicious system call dependency trees (**MalSCDT**s). The usage of such data-mining algorithm allows to compute behaviors, which we use as signatures that are general and implementation details independent, therefore robust.

To store and recognize **MalSCDT**s we infer an automaton, termed **HELTA**, recognizing trees containing **MalSCDT**s as subtrees. This allows to efficiently store the malware signatures and recognize behaviors if they are hidden inside another behavior. The overview of the learning process from the malware files to the database of semantic signatures is depicted in Figure 3.

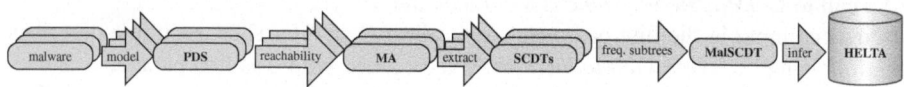

Fig. 3. Learning malicious behaviors

To evaluate the efficiency of the computed malicious behaviors, we show they can be applied to efficiently detect malware. To perform malware detection on a binary executable, we extract trees using the same procedure used in the learning process (described above), but applied to a single file. We check whether the automaton storing malicious behaviors accepts any subtree of the extracted trees (**SCDT**s). If that is the case the executable contains a malicious behavior and is classified as malware. The depiction of such process is shown in Figure 4.

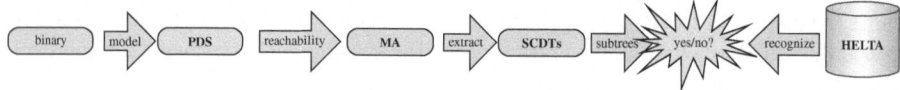

Fig. 4. Malware detection

We implemented a tool that extracts the behaviors and selects the malicious candidates using an algorithm for the frequent subgraph problem[1]. With such tool we were

---

[1] A tree is a special case of a graph.

able to infer some signatures not inferred using previous approaches [2,10,14] because our signatures track calls to functions of the Win32 API instead of calls to the Native API. It is a fact that it is always possible to use the previous approaches to find Native API level signatures equivalent to the ones we infer, therefore we do not claim our tool can express more behaviors, instead we claim that our approach is complementary to such works. It allows to express behaviors at different API levels and to extract more abstract/readable (Win32 API level) signatures.

We obtained promising results, and we were able to detect 983 malware files using the malicious trees inferred from 193 malware files, with a 0% false positive rate (thus showing our approach learns malicious behaviors that do not appear in benign programs). This number of detected malware is larger than the 16 files reported in [10] and in line with the 912 files detected in [14]. Our false positive detection rate is better (5% reported in [2]).

Outline. In Section 2 we show how to model binary executables as **PDS**s. Malware signatures are defined as labeled trees in Section 3. We present an algorithm to infer malware specifications in Section 4, and we show how to use tree automata to perform malware detection in Section 5. Experimental data shows our approach can be used to detect malware as detailed in Section 6. The related work is summarized in Section 7 and in Section 8 we present conclusions and future work.

2   Binary Code Modeling

Malware detection is performed directly in the executable encoding of the software (binary code containing machine instructions and data). By modeling the operational semantics of binary code, we are able to analyze it without relying on execution. This section introduces the modeling framework and how we model executable files.

2.1   Pushdown Systems

A pushdown system (**PDS**) is a triple $\mathcal{P} = (P, \Gamma, \Delta)$ where P is a finite set of control points, Γ is a finite alphabet of stack symbols, and $\Delta \subseteq (P \times \Gamma) \times (P \times \Gamma^*)$ is a finite set of transition rules. A configuration $\langle p, \omega \rangle$ of $\mathcal{P}$ is an element of $P \times \Gamma^*$. We write $\langle p, \gamma \rangle \hookrightarrow \langle q, \omega \rangle$ instead of $((p, \gamma), (q, \omega)) \in \Delta$. The immediate successor relation $\leadsto_{\mathcal{P}} \subseteq (P \times \Gamma^*) \times (P \times \Gamma^*)$ is defined as follows: if $\langle p, \gamma \rangle \hookrightarrow \langle q, \omega \rangle$, then $\langle p, \gamma\omega' \rangle \leadsto_{\mathcal{P}} \langle q, \omega\omega' \rangle$ for every $\omega' \in \Gamma^*$. The reachability relation $\Rightarrow$ is defined as the reflexive and transitive closure of the immediate successor relation.

Given a set of configurations C, $post(C)$ is defined as the set of immediate successors of the elements in C. The reflexive and transitive closure of $post$ is denoted as $post^*(C) = \{c' \in P \times \Gamma^* \mid \exists c \in C, c \Rightarrow c'\}$. Analogously $pre(C)$ is defined as the set of immediate predecessors of elements in C. Its reflexive and transitive closure is denoted as $pre^*(C) = \{c \in P \times \Gamma^* \mid \exists c' \in C, c \Rightarrow c'\}$.

Given a pushdown system $\mathcal{P} = (P, \Gamma, \Delta)$, a $\mathcal{P}$-multi-automaton, $\mathcal{P} - MA$ or **MA** when $\mathcal{P}$ is clear from context, is a tuple $\mathcal{A} = (\Gamma, Q, \delta, P, F)$, where Q is a finite set of states, $\delta \subseteq Q \times \Gamma \times Q$ is a transition relation, $P \subseteq Q$ is the set of initial states corresponding to the control points of $\mathcal{P}$, and $F \subseteq Q$ is a set of final states.

The transition relation for **MA** is the smallest relation $\rightarrow \subseteq Q \times \Gamma^* \times Q$ satisfying:

- $q \xrightarrow{\gamma} q'$ if $(q, \gamma, q') \in \delta$
- $q \xrightarrow{w\gamma} q'$ if $q \xrightarrow{w} q''$ and $q'' \xrightarrow{\gamma} q'$

$\mathcal{A}$ accepts (recognizes) a configuration $\langle p, w \rangle$ if $p \xrightarrow{w} q$ for some $q \in F$. The set of configurations recognized by a **MA** $\mathcal{A}$ is called regular and is designated by $Conf(\mathcal{A})$. The $post^*$ and pre^* of regular configurations can be efficiently computed:

Theorem 1. *[8,12] For a pushdown system $\mathcal{P} = (P, \Gamma, \Delta)$ and **MA** $\mathcal{A}$, there exist MAs $\mathcal{A}_{post^*}$ and $\mathcal{A}_{pre^*}$ recognizing $post^*(Conf(\mathcal{A}))$ and $pre^*(Conf(\mathcal{A}))$ respectively. These can be constructed in polynomial time and space.*

2.2 Modeling Binary Programs with PDSs

We use the approach detailed in [24, Section 2] to model each executable program $\mathbb{P}$. The approach relies on the assumption that there exists an oracle $\mathcal{O}$ computing a **PDS** $\mathcal{P} = (P, \Gamma, \Delta)$ from the binary program, where P corresponds to the control points of the program, Γ corresponds to the approximate set of values pushed to the stack, and Δ models the different instructions of the program. The obtained **PDS** mimics the runs of program $\mathbb{P}$.

In addition to the approach of [24], let **API** be the set of all Application Programming Interface function names available in the program. We assume the oracle $\mathcal{O}$ approximates the set $P_{API} \subseteq P$ of control points of a program that correspond to instruction addresses that at program runtime are translated (dynamically linked) by the operating system into system function entry points, the number of parameters of such functions and the type of each parameter. We consider a simple type system: $\tau ::= in \mid out$ (*in* for input parameter, and *out* for output) containing the atomic value *out* used to denote a parameter that is modified after function execution and *in* to denote the parameter is not changed by the function.

We assume, $\mathcal{O}$ computes a function $\varrho_\lambda : P_{API} \rightarrow$ **API** that identifies program control points corresponding to system calls with an unique function name, a function $\varrho_\tau : P_{API} \times \mathbb{N} \rightarrow 2^\tau$ such that $\varrho_\tau(p, n)$ is the set[2] of possible types of the n-th parameter of the system call that has p as entry point, and a function $\varrho_{ar} : P_{API} \rightarrow \mathbb{N}$ defining the number of parameters for each system call in P_{API} For example, if we consider the program of Fig. 1, we obtain $P_{API} = \{l_g, l_c\}$ since these two points correspond to system call entry points, $\varrho_\lambda(l_g) = GetModuleFileName$ since l_g corresponds to the entry point of the function *GetModuleFileName*. $\varrho_{ar}(l_g) = 3$ since *GetModuleFileName* has three parameters, and $\varrho_\tau(l_g, 2) = \{out\}$ since the second parameter of the *GetModuleFileName* function is defined as an output, and analogously $\varrho_\tau(l_g, 1) = \varrho_\tau(l_g, 3) = \{in\}$, since these correspond to input parameters.

---

[2] The API defines parameters that are both input and output.

3   Malicious Behavior Specifications

As already mentioned, malicious behaviors, data flow relationships between system function calls, will be expressed as trees where nodes represent system functions or parameter values and edges specify the data flow or the number of the parameter to which the value was passed. We will now formally introduce the notion of edge labeled trees.

3.1   Edge Labeled Trees

An unranked alphabet is a finite set $\mathcal{F}$ of symbols. Given an unranked alphabet $\mathcal{F}$, let a set of colors $\mathcal{C}$ be an alphabet of unary symbols and disjoint from $\mathcal{F}$, and $\mathcal{X}$ be a set of variables disjoint from $\mathcal{F}$. The set $\mathcal{T}(\mathcal{F}, \mathcal{C}, \mathcal{X})$ of colored terms over the unranked alphabet $\mathcal{F}$, colors $\mathcal{C}$ and variables $\mathcal{X}$ it is the smallest set of terms such that:

- $\mathcal{F} \subseteq \mathcal{T}(\mathcal{F}, \mathcal{C}, \mathcal{X})$,
- $\mathcal{X} \subseteq \mathcal{T}(\mathcal{F}, \mathcal{C}, \mathcal{X})$, and
- $f(c_1(t_1), \ldots, c_n(t_n)) \in \mathcal{T}(\mathcal{F}, \mathcal{C}, \mathcal{X})$, for $n \geq 1$, $c_i \in \mathcal{C}$, $t_i \in \mathcal{T}(\mathcal{F}, \mathcal{C}, \mathcal{X})$.

If $\mathcal{X} = \emptyset$ then $\mathcal{T}(\mathcal{F}, \mathcal{C}, \mathcal{X})$ is written as $\mathcal{T}(\mathcal{F}, \mathcal{C})$, and its elements are designated as ground terms. Each element of the set of terms can be represented by an edge labeled tree. For example, let $\mathcal{F} = \{f\}$, $\mathcal{C} = \{c_1, c_2\}$, and $\mathcal{X} = \emptyset$. The colored tree $f(c_1(a), c_2(b)) \in \mathcal{T}(\mathcal{F}, \mathcal{C})$ can be represented by the edge labeled tree of Fig. 5.

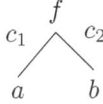

Fig. 5. Example

Let $\mathcal{X}_n$ be a set of n variables. A term $E \in \mathcal{T}(\mathcal{F}, \mathcal{C}, \mathcal{X}_n)$ is called an environment and the expression $E[t_1, \ldots, t_n]$ for $t_1, \ldots, t_n \in \mathcal{T}(\mathcal{F}, \mathcal{C})$ denotes the term in $\mathcal{T}(\mathcal{F}, \mathcal{C})$ obtained from E by replacing the variable x_i by t_i for each $1 \leq i \leq n$.

A subtree t' of a tree t in $\mathcal{T}(\mathcal{L}, \mathcal{C})$, written as $t' \lhd t$, is a term such that there exists an environment E in $\mathcal{T}(\mathcal{L}, \mathcal{C}, \{x\})$ where x appears only once and $t = E[t']$.

The tree $f(c_1(a), c_2(b))$ represents the same behavior as tree $f(c_2(b), c_1(a))$. Thus, to efficiently compare edge labeled trees, and to avoid missing malicious behaviors due to tree representation, we define a canonical representation of edge labeled trees. We assume that $\mathcal{F}$ and $\mathcal{C}$ are totally ordered.

A term is in canonical form if it is a constant (leaf) or if it is a function (tree node) where each argument is in canonical form and arguments are sorted without repetitions by term order.

Let $c \in \mathcal{C}$ and $t \in \mathcal{F}(\mathcal{C}, \mathcal{T})$ such that $\mathcal{F}, \mathcal{C}$, and $\mathcal{T}$ are respectively ordered by $<^{\mathcal{F}}, <^{\mathcal{C}}$, and $<^{\mathcal{T}}$, and t is in canonical form. We assume a subtree insertion operation (**insert_subtree**) where **insert_subtree**$(c(t), t')$ adds $c(t)$ as a child to the root of t' in the correct place to maintain a canonical representation of the tree, overwriting if the subtree $c(t)$ already exists.

3.2   System Call Dependency Trees

We will represent malware behaviors as trees encoding data flow relationships between system function calls. Tree nodes represent either system functions or parameter values.

Edge colors label the characteristics of the data flow between functions, e.g. $2 \rightarrowtail 1$ labeling an edge from function f and f' means that at some point f is called with some value v as second parameter, which is of type *out*, and afterwards f' is called with v as first parameter, which in turn is of type *in*. Moreover, when an edge connects a node labeled with function f and a child node with some value v, meaning the function was called with parameter v, it will be labeled with the number of the parameter, thus to represent a call was made with 0 as first parameter to function f, we add 1 as a label of the edge from node f to node 0.

Definition 1. *Formally, let $\mathcal{F}$ be the set of all system call function names (the union of all possibly **API** function names returned by the oracle of Section 2) and values passed as function parameters (a subset of the union of all Γ sets calculated by the oracle). In addition, let $\mathcal{C}$ be a set of colors containing all the possible parameter numbers and data flows, i.e.: $\mathcal{C} = \{1, \ldots, \max_{f \in API}(\varrho_{ar}(f))\} \cup \{x \rightarrowtail y \mid x, y \in \{1, \ldots, \max_{f \in API}(\varrho_{ar}(f))\}\}$ A System Call Dependency Tree, written as **SCDT**, is defined as a ground term of the set $\mathcal{T}(\mathcal{F}, \mathcal{C})$.*

Example. Let $\mathcal{F} = \{0, GetModuleFileName, CopyFile\}$ and $\mathcal{C} = \{1, 2 \rightarrowtail 1\}$, the behavior of Fig. 2 can be described by $t = GetModuleFileName(1(0), 2 \rightarrowtail 1(CopyFile))$.

4 Mining Malware Specifications

In this section we show how to compute the **SCDT**s corresponding to malware behaviors that we will use as malware specifications. Given a finite set of programs $\mathbb{P}_1, \ldots, \mathbb{P}_q$ known to be malicious in advance we compute **PDS**s $\mathcal{P}_1, \ldots, \mathcal{P}_q$ that model these malicious programs. Then, for each **PDS** $\mathcal{P}_i$ we compute a set of trees $\mathbb{TS}_i$ that contains the data flows represented as **SCDT**s for the program $\mathbb{P}_i$. From the computed set of trees for each program, $\mathbb{TS}_1, \ldots, \mathbb{TS}_q$, we calculate the common subtrees, the ones that are most probable to appear in malware, that we use as malware specifications.

To compute the sets of trees $\mathbb{TS}_i$ we proceed as follows: For each program $\mathbb{P}_i$ modeled as a **PDS** $\mathcal{P}_i$ we compute the finite automaton encoding the set of reachable configurations from the initial state using the reachability analysis algorithm from [12]. As there may be an infinite number of configurations and we are only interested in the configurations whose control points correspond to a system function entry point with some finite number of elements in the stack (only the parameters of the function under consideration are important), we build another automaton recognizing such finite set of configurations. For each of such configurations, understood as possible data flow origins, we repeat the process to calculate the reachable configurations, understood as possible data flow destinations. Then, if a data flow between configurations is found, i.e. the value passed as a parameter to an origin configuration has type *out* and the same value passed as a parameter of type *in* to a destination configuration, we build a **SCDT** with the origin function as root node and an edge to a node corresponding to the destination function.

To calculate the common subtrees we use the algorithm [30] computing frequent subgraph, to compute frequent subtrees.

4.1   System Call Targeted Reachability Analysis

To compute the data flows for a malware pushdown system model $\mathcal{P} = (P, \Gamma, \Delta)$, we first calculate the reachability of $\mathcal{P}$ using the algorithms presented in [12]. From $\mathcal{P}$ we build the (**MA**) automaton $\mathcal{A}$ that recognizes the $post^*(\langle p_i, \epsilon \rangle)$, i.e. the set of reachable configurations from the initial configuration $\langle p_i, \epsilon \rangle$, where p_i is a designated initial control point and ϵ denotes the empty stack.

MA Trimming.   To compute data flows between system call related control points $p_o, p_d \in P_{API}$ with parameter numbers $\varrho_{ar}(p_o) = m$ and $\varrho_{ar}(p_d) = n$ we need to consider only the top $m + 1$ and $n + 1$ elements of the stack reached at control points p_o and p_d because, in assembly, parameters are passed to functions through the stack. Before invoking a function the parameters are pushed in reverse order into the stack, and after the return address is pushed. Thus, if a function receives m parameters, then at its entry point, for instance p_o, the top $m + 1$ elements of the stack correspond to the parameters plus the return address. Thus we only need to consider the top $m + 1$ elements of the stack reached at control point p_o. This is the reason why we can analyze the possibly infinite number of configurations encoded in the reachability resulting finite automaton, we only inspect a finite subset. To abbreviate the algorithm that computes **SCDT** we define such subset of configurations in terms of a new automaton obtained by cutting the **MA** resulting from the reachability analysis.

Definition 2. *Given a **MA** $\mathcal{A}$ recognizing the reachable configurations of a **PDS** $\mathcal{P} = (P, \Gamma, \Delta)$ we define the trim automaton $\mathcal{A}^\dagger$ as the automaton recognizing the configurations in the set: $\{\langle p, w \rangle \in P_{API} \times \Gamma^* \mid |w| = \varrho_{ar}(p) + 1 \wedge \exists w' \in \Gamma^* s.t. \langle p, ww' \rangle$ is accepted by $\mathcal{A}\}$*

Intuitively, we cut the automaton and keep only configurations where control points p correspond to system function entry points, and the stacks are bounded by the number of parameters of the function plus one to take into account the return address. The trim operation will be written as Ψ, thus $\mathcal{A}^\dagger = \Psi(\mathcal{A})$. It is trivial to prove that the $Conf(\mathcal{A}^\dagger)$ is a finite language, in fact the number of configurations corresponding to valid system call function entry point, and its finite number of parameters is at most:
$O(|P_{API}| \cdot |\Gamma| \cdot \max_{p \in P_{API}}(\varrho_{ar}(p)))$.

4.2   Extracting SCDTs

Algorithms 1 and 2 detail our approach to extract behaviors. We assume a maximum tree height $h \in \mathbb{N}$ is given as input. We write $\omega[n]$ to denote the n-th element of some word $\omega \in \Gamma^*$.

The Algorithm 1 iterates over the models $\mathcal{P}_1, \ldots, \mathcal{P}_q$ (line 1). For each it initializes the set of resulting trees to the empty set (line 2) and computes the configurations corresponding to system calls that are reachable from the given initial configuration $\langle p_i, \epsilon \rangle$ (line 3). The initial configuration is built using the binary executable entry point and an empty

---

Algorithm 1. ExtractSCDT

1 **forall the** $\mathcal{P}_i$ **do**
2      $TS_i \longleftarrow \emptyset$;
3      $\mathcal{A}_i^\dagger \longleftarrow \Psi(post^*(\langle p_i, \epsilon \rangle))$;
4   **forall the** $\langle p_o, \omega_o \rangle \in Conf(\mathcal{A}_i^\dagger)$ **do**
5 | $TS_i \longleftarrow TS_i \cup \{\text{BuildSCDT}(\langle p_o, \omega_o \rangle, h)\}$;
6   **end**
7 **end**
8 **return** TS;

stack. Then, for every configuration corresponding to a system call entry point $\langle p_o, \omega_o \rangle$ recognized by the trim automaton (line 4) it calls **BuildSCDT** to build a **SCDT** tree of height at most h with the function of entry point p_o as root (line 5).

The **BuildSCDT** procedure is displayed in Algorithm 2, it is used to recursively build a tree. First, the tree to be returned is initialized to be the origin system call entry point p_o (line 1). When the maximum desired tree height is not reached (line 2), we calculate what are the system calls reached from $\langle p_o, \omega_o \rangle$ (line 3) and check for flows to any system call related configuration $\langle p_d, \omega_d \rangle$ (line 4). If a data flow is found between two configurations (line 5), i.e. there are parameter numbers n and m such that the value passed to system call at control point p_o is the same as the value passed in position m of system call at a control point p_d, and there is in fact a flow (line 6) i.e. the parameter n of the function corresponding to the entry point p_o is of type *out* and the parameter m of the function corresponding to the entry point p_d is of type *in*, we add a new child with label $n \rightarrowtail m$ to the recursively computed tree for the destination system call p_d (line 7).

Algorithm 2. BuildSCDT

---

1 tree $= \varrho_\lambda(p_o)$;
2 **if** $h > 0$ **then**
3      $\mathcal{A}^\dagger \longleftarrow \Psi(post^*(\langle p_o, \omega_o \rangle))$;
4   **forall the** $\langle p_d, \omega_d \rangle \in Conf(\mathcal{A}^\dagger) \setminus \{\langle p_o, \omega_o \rangle\}$ **do**
5   **forall the** (n, m) *s.t.* $1 \leq n \leq \varrho_{ar}(p_o) \wedge 1 \leq m \leq \varrho_{ar}(p_d)$ **do**
6   **if** $w_o[n] = w_d[m] \wedge \varrho_\tau(p_o, n) = out \wedge \varrho_\tau(p_d, m) = in$ **then**
7   tree $\longleftarrow$ **insert_subtree** $(n \rightarrowtail m(\text{BuildSCDT}(\langle p_d, \omega_d \rangle, h-1)), \text{tree})$;
8   **end**
9   **end**
10   **end**
11 **end**
12 **forall the** $n \in \{1, .., \varrho_{ar}(p_o)\}$ **do**
13   tree $\longleftarrow$ **insert_subtree** $(n(w_o[n]), \text{tree})$;
14 **end**
15 **return** tree;

To add the edges representing the values passed as parameters in the call of p_o we iterate over the possible number of parameters of the origin system call entry point (line 12) and add an edge with the number of parameter n and the value passed in the stack $\omega_o[n]$ (line 13). When the maximum desired tree height is reached, the algorithm returns only a tree with p_o as root and the values passed as parameters in the call.

4.3 Computing Malicious Behavior Trees

After extracting **SCDT**s for each of the inputed malware programs, one has to compute which are the ones that correspond to malicious behaviors. The **SCDT**s that correspond to malicious behaviors will be named malicious trees. To choose the malicious trees we compute the most frequent subtrees in the set $\mathbb{TS}$ of trees extracted from the set of malware used to train our detector. For that we need the notion of *support set*, the set of trees containing some given subtree, and the notion of *tree support* that gives the ratio of trees containing the subtree to the whole set of trees.

Given a finite set of trees $\mathbb{TS} \subseteq \mathcal{T}(\mathcal{F}, \mathcal{C})$ and a tree $t \in \mathbb{TS}$, the *support set* of a tree t is defined as $T_t = \{t' \mid t \vartriangleleft t', t' \in \mathbb{TS}\}$. The *tree support* of a tree t in the set $\mathbb{TS}$ is calculated as $sup(t) = \frac{|T_t|}{|\mathbb{TS}|}$. For a fixed threshold k the set of frequent trees of T is the set of trees with *tree support* greater than k.

Definition 3. *For a set of system call dependency trees trees* $\mathbb{TS} \subseteq \mathcal{T}(\mathcal{F},\mathcal{C})$ *and a given threshold* k, *a malicious behavior tree is a tree* $t \in \mathbb{TS}$ *s.t.* $sup(t) \geq k$. *The set of malicious behavior trees will be called* **MalSCDT**.

To compute frequent subtrees we specialize the frequent subgraph algorithm presented in [30] to the case of trees. The algorithm receives a set of trees and a support value $k \in [0,1]$ and outputs all the subtrees with support at least k. The graph algorithm works by defining a lexicographical order among the trees and mapping each to a canonical representation using a code based on the depth-first search tree generated by the traversal. Using such lexicographical order the subtree search space can be efficiently explored avoiding duplicate computations.

5 Malware Detection

We show in this section how the malicious behaviors trees that we computed using our techniques can be used to efficiently detect malware. To decide whether a given program $\mathbb{P}$ is malware or not, we apply again the technique described in Section 4 to compute the **SCDT**s for the program $\mathbb{P}$ being analyzed. Then we check whether such trees correspond to malicious behaviors, i.e. whether such trees contain subtrees that correspond to malicious behaviors.

To efficiently perform this task, we use tree automata. The advantage of using tree automata is that we can build the minimal automaton that recognizes the set of malicious signatures, to obtain a compact and efficient database. Plus, malware detection, using membership in automata, can be done efficiently. However, we need to adapt tree automata to suite malware detection, that is, to de-

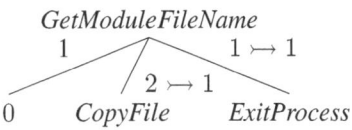

Fig. 6. Behaviors extracted from $\mathbb{P}$

fine automata that can recognize *edge labeled* trees. Furthermore, we cannot use standard tree automata because the trees that can be generated from the program $\mathbb{P}$ to be analyzed may have arbitrary arities (since we do not know a priori the behaviors of $\mathbb{P}$). For example the behavior of the program $\mathbb{P}$ can be described by the tree of Fig. 6 that contains the self-replication malicious behavior of Fig. 2. However, if we use a binary tree automaton $\mathbb{H}$ to recognize the tree of Fig. 2, $\mathbb{H}$ will not recognize the tree of Fig. 6, because $\mathbb{P}$ contains the malicious behaviors and extra behaviors. To overcome this problem we will use unranked tree automata (a.k.a. hedge automata), since the trees that can be obtained by analysing program $\mathbb{P}$ might have arbitrary arity.

In this section, we show how to use hedge automata for malware detection. First, we give the formal definition of hedge automata. Then, we show how we can infer a hedge automaton to recognize malicious behaviors that may be contained in some tree. And we conclude by explaining how to use it to detect malware.

5.1 Tree Automata for Edge Labeled Trees

Definition 4. *An* hedge edge labeled tree automaton *(**HELTA**) over $\mathcal{T}(\mathcal{F}, \mathcal{C})$ is a tuple $\mathbb{H} = (Q^{\mathbb{H}}, \mathcal{F}, \mathcal{C}, \mathcal{A}, \Delta^{\mathbb{H}})$ where $Q^{\mathbb{H}}$ is a finite set of states, $\mathcal{A} \subseteq Q^{\mathbb{H}}$ is the set of final states, and $\Delta^{\mathbb{H}}$ is a finite set of rewriting rules defined as $f(R) \to q$ for $f \in \mathcal{F}, q \in Q^{\mathbb{H}}$, and $R \subseteq \left[\mathcal{C}(Q^{\mathbb{H}}) \right]^*$ is a regular word language over $\mathcal{C}(Q^{\mathbb{H}})$ i.e. the language encoding all the possible children of the tree node f.*

*We define a move relation $\to_{\mathbb{H}}$ between ground terms in $\mathcal{T}(\mathcal{F} \cup Q^{\mathbb{H}}, \mathcal{C})$ as follows: Let $t, t' \in \mathcal{T}(\mathcal{F} \cup Q^{\mathbb{H}}, \mathcal{C})$, the move relation $\to_{\mathbb{H}}$ is defined by: $t \to_{\mathbb{H}} t'$ iff there exists an environment $E \in \mathcal{T}(\mathcal{F} \cup Q^{\mathbb{H}}, \mathcal{C}, \{x\})$, a rule $r = f(R) \to q \in \Delta^{\mathbb{H}}$ such that $t = E[f(c_1(q_1), \ldots, c_n(q_n))]$, and $c_1(q_1) \ldots c_n(q_n) \in R$, and $t' = E[q]$. We write $\overset{*}{\to}_{\mathbb{H}}$ to denote the reflexive and transitive closure of $\to_{\mathbb{H}}$. Given an **HELTA** $\mathbb{H} = (Q^{\mathbb{H}}, \mathcal{F}, \mathcal{C}, \mathcal{A}, \Delta^{\mathbb{H}})$ and an edge labeled tree t, we say that t is accepted by a state q if $t \overset{*}{\to}_{\mathbb{H}} q$, t is accepted by $\mathbb{H}$ if $\exists q \in \mathcal{A}$ s.t. $t \overset{*}{\to}_{\mathbb{H}} q$.*

Intuitively, given an input term t, a run of $\mathbb{H}$ on t according to the move relation $\to_{\mathbb{H}}$ can be done in a bottom-up manner as follows: first, we assign nondeterministically a state q to each leaf labeled with symbol f if there is in $\Delta^{\mathbb{H}}$ a rule of the form $f(R) \to q$ such that $\epsilon \in R$. Then, for each node labeled with a symbol f, and having the terms $c_1(t_1), \ldots, c_1(t_n)$ as children, we must collect the states $q_1, \ldots, q_n$ assigned to all its children, i.e., such that $c_i(t_i) \overset{*}{\to}_{\mathbb{H}} q_i$, for $1 \leq i \leq n$, and then associate a state q to the node itself if there exists in $\Delta^{\mathbb{H}}$ a rule $r = f(R) \to q$ such that $q_1 \ldots q_n \in R$. A term t is accepted if $\mathbb{H}$ reaches the root of t in a final state.

5.2 Inferring Tree Automata from Malicious Behavior Trees

In this section we show how to infer an **HELTA** recognizing trees containing the inferred malicious behaviors. Thus, if t is a malicious behavior, and t' is a behavior of a program $\mathbb{P}$ that is under analysis, such that t' contains the behavior described by t, the automaton must recognize it. As an example assume $t \in$ **MalSCDT** is a tree of the form $f(c_1(a), c_2(b)))$, s.t. $a, b \in \mathcal{F}$ and $E \in \mathcal{T}(\mathcal{F}, \mathcal{C}, \{x\})$ is an environment, then the automaton must recognize trees t' of the form: $E[\mathbf{f}(c_1^1(t_1^1), \ldots, c_{m_1}^1(t_{m_1}^1), \mathbf{c_1}(\mathbf{a}(e_1)), c_1^2(t_1^2), \ldots, c_{m_2}^2(t_{m_2}^2), \mathbf{c_2}(\mathbf{b}(e_2)), c_1^3(t_1^3), \ldots, c_{m_3}^3(t_{m_3}^3))]$ meaning the tree is embedded in other tree, i.e. t is a subtree of t' and it may have extra behaviors $c_i^j(t_i^j)$ and also extra subtrees $e_1, e_2 \in \mathcal{T}(\mathcal{F}, \mathcal{C})$ as child of the leafs a and b.

Let $t \in$ **MalSCDT**, we define the operation $\Omega : $ **MalSCDT** $\to \mathcal{T}(\mathcal{F}, \mathcal{C})$ that transforms a malicious tree into the set of all system call dependency trees containing the malicious behavior t. Ω is defined inductively as:

(1) $\Omega(a) = \{a(t) \mid t \in \mathcal{T}(\mathcal{F}, \mathcal{C})\}$, if $a \in \mathcal{F}$ is a leaf,
(2) $\Omega(f(c_1(t_1), \ldots, c_n(t_n))) = \{f(c_1^1(t_1^1), \ldots, c_{n_1}^1(t_{n_1}^1), c_1(\Omega(t_1)), c_1^2(t_1^2), \ldots, c_{n_2}^2(t_{n_2}^2), \ldots, c_1^n(t_1^n), \ldots, c_{n_n}^n(t_{n_n}^n), c_n(\Omega(t_n)), c_1^{n+1}(t_1^{n+1}), \ldots, c_{n_{n+1}}^{n+1}(t_{n_{n+1}}^{n+1})) \mid c_i^j \in \mathcal{C}$ and $t_i^j \in \mathcal{T}(\mathcal{F}, \mathcal{C})\}$, otherwise.

The first rule asserts that after the leaves of the malicious behavior t there may be other behaviors, while the second asserts that in the nodes of the tree t' there may be extra behaviors, for instance the edge to *ExitProcess* in Fig. 6. Then, if t is a malicious behavior tree, we would like to compute an **HELTA** that recognizes all the trees t' s.t. $\exists t'' \in \Omega(t)$ and $t' = E[t'']$ for an environment $E \in \mathcal{T}(\mathcal{F}, \mathcal{C}, \{x\})$.

Let **MalSCDT** be a finite set of malicious trees, by definition each $t \in$ **MalSCDT** is a term of $\mathcal{T}(\mathcal{F}, \mathcal{C})$. We infer an **HELTA** $\mathbb{H} = (Q^{\mathbb{H}}, \mathcal{F}, \mathcal{C}, \mathcal{A}, \Delta^{\mathbb{H}})$ recognizing trees containing malicious behaviors. Where $Q^{\mathbb{H}} = \{q_t \mid t \lhd t'$ and $t' \in$ **MalSCDT**$\} \cup \{q_t \mid t \in \mathcal{F}\}$ i.e. contains a state for each subtree of the trees to accept, plus a state for each possible symbol of the alphabet that will be reached when a subtree with such symbol as root is not recognized. The final states are defined as the states that correspond to recognizing a malicious tree $\mathcal{A} = \{q_t \mid t \in$ **MalSCDT**$\}$. And $\Delta^{\mathbb{H}}$ is defined by rules:

R1 For all $f \in \mathcal{F}$, $f([\mathcal{C}(Q^{\mathbb{H}})]^*) \to q_f \in \Delta^{\mathbb{H}}$

R2 For all $t = f(c_1(t_1), \dots, c_n(t_n))$ such that $t \lhd t'$ and $t' \in$ **MalSCDT**, $f([\mathcal{C}(Q^{\mathbb{H}})]^*$ $c_1(q_{t_1}) [\mathcal{C}(Q^{\mathbb{H}})]^* \dots [\mathcal{C}(Q^{\mathbb{H}})]^* c_n(q_{t_n}) [\mathcal{C}(Q^{\mathbb{H}})]^*) \to q_{f(c_1(t_1),\dots,c_n(t_n))} \in \Delta^{\mathbb{H}}$

R3 For all final state $q_t \in \mathcal{A}$ and all $f \in \mathcal{F}$, $f([\mathcal{C}(Q^{\mathbb{H}})]^*, q_t, [\mathcal{C}(Q^{\mathbb{H}})]^*) \to q_t \in \Delta^{\mathbb{H}}$

Intuitively, for $f \in \mathcal{F}$, states q_f recognize all the terms whose roots are f. This is ensured by R1. In the rules $[\mathcal{C}(Q^{\mathbb{H}})]^*$ allows to recognize terms t in (1) and $c_i^j(t_i^j)$ in (2). For a subtree t_i of a malicious behavior t in every **MalSCDT**, q_{t_i} recognizes $\Omega(q_{t_i})$. This is ensured by rules R2, which guarantees that a malicious tree containing extra behaviors is recognized. R3 guarantees that a tree containing a malicious behavior as subtree is recognized, i.e. R3 ensures that if t is a malicious behavior and $E \in \mathcal{T}(\mathcal{F}, \mathcal{C}, \{x\})$ is an environment, then q_t recognizes $E[t']$ for every t' in $\Omega(t)$.

In the following we assert that if a tree t' contains a subtree t'' that contains a malicious behavior t, then the inferred automaton will recognize it (even if there are extra behaviors). Proof should follow by induction.

Theorem 2. *Given a term $t \in$ MalSCDT, and $t' \in \mathcal{T}(\mathcal{F}, \mathcal{C})$. If there $\exists t'' \in \Omega(t)$ and an environment $E \in \mathcal{T}(\mathcal{F}, \mathcal{C}, \{x\})$ and $t' = E[t'']$, then $t' \xrightarrow{*}_{\mathbb{H}} q_t$.*

5.3 Malware Detection

The detection phase works as follows. Given a program $\mathbb{P}$ to analyze we build a **PDS** model $\mathcal{P}$ using the approach described in Section 2, then we extract the set of behaviors $\mathbb{TS}$ contained in $\mathbb{P}$ using the approach in Section 4. Then we use the automaton $\mathbb{H}$ to search if any of the trees in $\mathbb{TS}$ can be matched by the automaton. If that is the case the program $\mathbb{P}$ is deemed malware.

Example. Suppose the tree in Fig. 6 was extracted and the tree in Fig. 2 is the only malicious behavior in **MalSCDT**, which in turn is defined using $\mathcal{C} = \{1, 2 \rightarrowtail 1\}$ and $\mathcal{F} = \{0, CopyFile, ExitProcess, GetModuleFileName\}$. We define an automaton $\mathbb{H}$ where the set of states is $Q^{\mathbb{H}} = \{q_0, q_{ExitProcess}, q_{CopyFile}, q_{GetModuleFileName(1(0), 2 \rightarrowtail 1(CopyFile))}\}$, the accepting set is $\mathcal{A} = \{q_{GetModuleFileName(1(0), 2 \rightarrowtail 1(CopyFile))}\}$, and $\Delta^{\mathbb{H}}$ contains rules processing the leaves: $0([\mathcal{C}(Q^{\mathbb{H}})]^*) \to_{\mathbb{H}} q_0$, $ExitProcess([\mathcal{C}(Q^{\mathbb{H}})]^*) \to_{\mathbb{H}} q_{ExitProcess}$, and $CopyFile([\mathcal{C}(Q^{\mathbb{H}})]^*) \to_{\mathbb{H}} q_{CopyFile}$. And a rule $GetModuleFileName([\mathcal{C}(Q^{\mathbb{H}})]^*, 1(q_0), [\mathcal{C}(Q^{\mathbb{H}})]^*, 2 \rightarrowtail 1(q_{CopyFile}), [\mathcal{C}(Q^{\mathbb{H}})]^*) \to_{\mathbb{H}} q_{GetModuleFileName(1(0), 2 \rightarrowtail 1(CopyFile))}$ processing the whole malicious behavior of Fig. 2.

6   Experiments

To evaluate our approach, we implemented a tool prototype that was tested on a dataset of real malware and benign programs. The input dataset of malware contains 1176 malware instances (Virus, Backdoors, Trojans, Worms,...) collected from virus repositories as VX Heavens and a disjoint dataset of 250 benign files collected from a Windows XP fresh operating system installation. We arbitrarily split the malware dataset into a training and test group. The train dataset was used to infer the malicious trees that were used in the detection of the samples of the test group. We were able to detect 983 malware files using the malicious trees inferred from 193 malware files, and show that benign programs are benign, thus a 0% false positive rate.

6.1   Inferring Malicious Behaviors

To infer malicious behaviors, we transformed each of the 193 malware binary files into a **PDS** model using the approach described in Section 2. To implement the oracle $\mathcal{O}$, we use the *PoMMaDe* tool [25] that uses Jakstab [19] and IDA Pro [15]. Jakstab performs static analysis of the binary program. However, it does not allow to extract API functions information, so IDA Pro is used to obtain such information, thus obtaining ϱ_{ar} and ϱ_{λ}. The ϱ_{τ} function was obtained by querying the available information in the MSDN website.

We apply Algorithm 1 to the **PDS** models to extract **SCDT**s for each of the malware instances. The current results were obtained with an h value of 2. In practice, to avoid the overapproximation of malicious trees, in the generation of **SCDT**s for the detection phase we consider the condition in line 6 of Algorithm 2, $w_o[n] = w_d[m]$ true only when we know the value outputted by the oracle is precise.

To compute the **MalSCDT** we encode the extracted **SCDT** as graphs and try to calculate the most frequent subgraphs. We use the gSpan [30] tool for that, it computes frequent subgraph structures using a depth-first tree search over a canonical labeling of graph edges relying on the linear ordering property of the labeling to prune the search space. The tool has been applied in various domains as active chemical compound structure mining and its performance is competitive among other tools [29]. The tool supports only undirected graphs, therefore a mismatch

Table 1. Training dataset

Name	#
Backdoor.Win32.Agent	26
Worm.Win32.AutoRun	13
Email-Worm.Win32.Bagle	19
Email-Worm.Win32.Batzback	4
Backdoor.Win32.Bifrose	46
Backdoor.Win32.Hupigon	5
Email-Worm.Win32.Kelino	7
Trojan-PSW.Win32.LdPinch	13
Email-Worm.Win32.Mydoom	26
Email-Worm.Win32.Nihilit	7
Backdoor.Win32.SdBot	14
Backdoor.Win32.Small	13
Total	193

with the trees (that can be seen as rooted, acyclic direct graphs) used in this work. The mismatch is overcome via a direction tag in the graph labels.

For the 193 files extracted **SCDT**s we have run the gSpan tool with support 0.6%. This is a tunable value for which we chose the one that allows better detection results. With this value we obtained 1026 subtrees (**MalSCDT**s), and best detection results. From the inferred malicious trees output from gSpan, we build a tree automaton recognizing such trees.

The training dataset contains 12 families of malware summarized in Table 1. In average, our tool extracts 7 **SCDT**s in 30 seconds for each malware file. To store the 1026 discovered **MalSCDT**s the automaton file used 24Kb of memory.

6.2   Detecting Malware

Malware detection is reduced to generating **SCDT**s and checking whether they are recognized by the inferred automaton. Thus, to perform detection on an input binary file, we model it as **PDS** using the approach described in Section 2 and extract **SCDT**s using the approach detailed in Section 4.2. If any subtree of the extracted tree is recognized by the automaton recognizing the malicious behaviors, we decide the binary sample is malware. We implemented such procedure in our tool and were able to detect 983 malware samples from 330 different families.

In Table 2 we show the range of malware families and number of samples that our tool detects as malware. In average, our tool extracts 64 **SCDT**s in 2.15 seconds for each file (this value may be largely improved given that runtime efficiency was not a main goal of the prototype design). The discrepancy in the number of trees generated (compared to the training set) is justified by an implementation choice regarding the oracle approximation of the set of values pushed to the stack. In the generation of **SCDT**s for the detection phase we consider the condition in line 6 of Algorithm 2, $w_o[n] = w_d[m]$ true even if the values are approximated. Such cases were discarded in the generation of **SCDT**s in the inference step where it holds only when the oracle outputs precise values. The automaton tree recognition execution time is negligible (< 0.08 secs) in all cases. To check the robustness of the detector, we applied it to a set of 250 benign programs. Our tool was able to classify such programs as benign, obtaining a 0% false positive rate. In 88% of the cases the tool extracts **SCDT**s and at least in 44% of the files there is a call to a function involved in malicious behavior (e.g. *GetModuleFileName*, *ShellExecute,...*), but no tree was recognized as malicious. This value is in line with the values detailed in [10,14] and better than the 5% reported in [2].

7   Related Work

Malicious behaviors have been defined in different ways. The foundational approaches via computable functions [1], based in Kleene's recursion theorem [4,5,6], or the neat definition using MALog [20] capture the essence of such behaviors, but are too abstract to be used in practice or require the full specification of software functionality. Our work is close to the approaches using model checking and temporal logic formulas as malicious behavior specification [24,25]. In such works specifications have to be designed by hand while we are able to learn them automatically. Some of the trees we infer describe malicious behaviors encoded in such formulas.

Regarding semantic signature inference there are the works [10,14] where the extraction of behaviors is based on dynamic analysis of executables. From the execution traces collected, data flow dependencies among system calls are recovered by comparing parameters and type information. The outcome are dependence graphs where the nodes are labeled by system function names and the edges capture the dependencies between the system calls. Another dynamic analysis based approach is the one of [2] where trees, alike ours, express the same kind of data flows between nodes representing system calls. Both approaches are limited by the drawbacks of dynamic analysis. For instance, time limitations, limited system call tracing or an overhead up to $90\times$ slower during execution [23]. Plus, from the dataset made publicly available in [2], we

Table 2. Test dataset name family and number of samples (#) detected

Name	#	Name	#	Name	#	Name	#
Backdoor.Win32.AF	1	Backdoor.Win32.MoonPie	1	Backdoor.Win32.UpRootKit	1	Email-Worm.Win32.Kelino	6
Backdoor.Win32.Afbot	1	Backdoor.Win32.Mowalker	1	Backdoor.Win32.Ursus	1	Email-Worm.Win32.Kergez	1
Backdoor.Win32.Afcore	6	Backdoor.Win32.Mtexer	2	Backdoor.Win32.Utilma	1	Email-Worm.Win32.Kipis	2
Backdoor.Win32.Agent	66	Backdoor.Win32.Mydons	1	Backdoor.Win32.VB	2	Email-Worm.Win32.Kirbster	1
Backdoor.Win32.Agobot	47	Backdoor.Win32.Ncx	1	Backdoor.Win32.VHM	1	Email-Worm.Win32.Klez	9
Backdoor.Win32.Alcodor	1	Backdoor.Win32.NerTe	3	Backdoor.Win32.Vatos	1	Email-Worm.Win32.Lacrow	2
Backdoor.Win32.Antilam	9	Backdoor.Win32.NetControl	2	Backdoor.Win32.Verify	1	Email-Worm.Win32.Lara	1
Backdoor.Win32.Apdoor	6	Backdoor.Win32.NetShadow	1	Backdoor.Win32.WMFA	1	Email-Worm.Win32.Lentin	10
Backdoor.Win32.Assasin	3	Backdoor.Win32.NetSpy	8	Backdoor.Win32.WRT	1	Email-Worm.Win32.Locksky	2
Backdoor.Win32.Asylum	8	Backdoor.Win32.Netbus	2	Backdoor.Win32.WbeCheck	3	Email-Worm.Win32.Lohack	3
Backdoor.Win32.Avstral	2	Backdoor.Win32.Netdex	2	Backdoor.Win32.Webdor	6	Email-Worm.Win32.LovGate	3
Backdoor.Win32.BLA	2	Backdoor.Win32.Netpocalipse	1	Backdoor.Win32.Whisper	1	Email-Worm.Win32.Mescan	1
Backdoor.Win32.BNLite	1	Backdoor.Win32.Neurotic	2	Backdoor.Win32.Wilba	1	Email-Worm.Win32.Mimail	1
Backdoor.Win32.BO2K	6	Backdoor.Win32.Nuclear	3	Backdoor.Win32.Winker	5	Email-Worm.Win32.Miti	1
Backdoor.Win32.Bancodor	1	Backdoor.Win32.Nucledor	2	Backdoor.Win32.WinterLove	7	Email-Worm.Win32.Modnar	1
Backdoor.Win32.Bandok	1	Backdoor.Win32.Nyrobot	1	Backdoor.Win32.Wisdoor	7	Email-Worm.Win32.Mydoom	8
Backdoor.Win32.Banito	4	Backdoor.Win32.Optix	9	Backdoor.Win32.Wollf	4	Email-Worm.Win32.NWWF	1
Backdoor.Win32.Beastdoor	6	Backdoor.Win32.PPCore	1	Backdoor.Win32.XBot	1	Email-Worm.Win32.Navidad	1
Backdoor.Win32.Bifrose	5	Backdoor.Win32.PPdoor	2	Backdoor.Win32.XConsole	1	Email-Worm.Win32.NetSky	2
Backdoor.Win32.BoomRaster	1	Backdoor.Win32.Pacak	1	Backdoor.Win32.XLog	2	Email-Worm.Win32.NetSup	1
Backdoor.Win32.Breplibot	6	Backdoor.Win32.Padodor	5	Backdoor.Win32.Xdoor	2	Email-Worm.Win32.Netav	1
Backdoor.Win32.Bushtrommel	2	Backdoor.Win32.PcClient	12	Backdoor.Win32.Y2KCount	1	Email-Worm.Win32.Newapt	6
Backdoor.Win32.ByShell	1	Backdoor.Win32.PeepViewer	1	Backdoor.Win32.Ythac	1	Email-Worm.Win32.Nihilit	1
Backdoor.Win32.Cabrotor	1	Backdoor.Win32.Peers	2	Backdoor.Win32.Zerg	1	Email-Worm.Win32.Nirky	1
Backdoor.Win32.Cafeini	1	Backdoor.Win32.Penrox	1	Backdoor.Win32.Zombam	1	Email-Worm.Win32.Paroc	1
Backdoor.Win32.Cheng	1	Backdoor.Win32.Pepbot	1	Backdoor.Win32.Zomby	1	Email-Worm.Win32.Parrot	1
Backdoor.Win32.Cigivip	1	Backdoor.Win32.Pingdoor	1	Constructor.Win32.Delf	1	Email-Worm.Win32.Pepex	2
Backdoor.Win32.Cmjspy	8	Backdoor.Win32.Pipes	1	Constructor.Win32.ETVM	2	Email-Worm.Win32.Pikis	2
Backdoor.Win32.Cocoazul	2	Backdoor.Win32.Plunix	1	Constructor.Win32.EvilTool	1	Email-Worm.Win32.Plage	1
Backdoor.Win32.Codbot	4	Backdoor.Win32.Pornu	1	Constructor.Win32.MS04-032	1	Email-Worm.Win32.Plexus	1
Backdoor.Win32.Coldfusion	3	Backdoor.Win32.Probot	1	Constructor.Win32.MS05-009	1	Email-Worm.Win32.Pnguin	1
Backdoor.Win32.CommInet	3	Backdoor.Win32.Proxydor	2	Constructor.Win32.SPL	1	Email-Worm.Win32.Poo	1
Backdoor.Win32.Coredoor	1	Backdoor.Win32.Psychward	5	Constructor.Win32.SS	2	Email-Worm.Win32.Postman	1
Backdoor.Win32.Crunch	1	Backdoor.Win32.Ptakks	1	Constructor.Win32.VCL	1	Email-Worm.Win32.Qizy	1
Backdoor.Win32.DKangel	2	Backdoor.Win32.Puddy	1	DoS.Win32.Aspcode	1	Email-Worm.Win32.Rammer	1
Backdoor.Win32.DRA	4	Backdoor.Win32.R3C	1	DoS.Win32.Ataker	1	Email-Worm.Win32.Rapita	1
Backdoor.Win32.DSNX	3	Backdoor.Win32.RAT	2	DoS.Win32.DStorm	1	Email-Worm.Win32.Rayman	1
Backdoor.Win32.DarkFtp	3	Backdoor.Win32.RDR	1	DoS.Win32.Igemper	1	Email-Worm.Win32.Repah	2
Backdoor.Win32.DarkMoon	1	Backdoor.Win32.Rbot	8	DoS.Win32.SQLStorm	1	Email-Worm.Win32.Ronoper	20
Backdoor.Win32.Delf	31	Backdoor.Win32.Redkod	4	Email-Worm.Win32.Anar	2	Email-Worm.Win32.Roron	23
Backdoor.Win32.Dindang	1	Backdoor.Win32.Revenge	1	Email-Worm.Win32.Android	1	Email-Worm.Win32.Sabak	1
Backdoor.Win32.DragonIrc	1	Backdoor.Win32.Rirc	1	Email-Worm.Win32.Animan	1	Email-Worm.Win32.Savage	2
Backdoor.Win32.Dumador	3	Backdoor.Win32.Robobot	1	Email-Worm.Win32.Anpir	1	Email-Worm.Win32.Scaline	1
Backdoor.Win32.Expir	1	Backdoor.Win32.Ronater	1	Email-Worm.Win32.Ardurk	2	Email-Worm.Win32.Scrambler	1
Backdoor.Win32.HacDef	2	Backdoor.Win32.Rootcip	1	Email-Worm.Win32.Asid	1	Email-Worm.Win32.Seliz	1
Backdoor.Win32.Hackarmy	3	Backdoor.Win32.Roron	1	Email-Worm.Win32.Assarm	1	Email-Worm.Win32.Sharpei	1
Backdoor.Win32.Hupigon	4	Backdoor.Win32.RtKit	4	Email-Worm.Win32.Atak	1	Email-Worm.Win32.Silly	1
Backdoor.Win32.IRCBot	6	Backdoor.Win32.Ruledor	4	Email-Worm.Win32.Avron	2	Email-Worm.Win32.Sircam	1
Backdoor.Win32.Ierk	1	Backdoor.Win32.SPing	3	Email-Worm.Win32.Bagle	3	Email-Worm.Win32.Skudex	2
Backdoor.Win32.Jacktron	1	Backdoor.Win32.SatanCrew	1	Email-Worm.Win32.Bagz	5	Email-Worm.Win32.Sonic	4
Backdoor.Win32.Jeemp	1	Backdoor.Win32.Sbot	2	Email-Worm.Win32.Banof	1	Email-Worm.Win32.Stator	1
Backdoor.Win32.Katherdoor	7	Backdoor.Win32.SdBot	63	Email-Worm.Win32.Bater	1	Email-Worm.Win32.Stopin	3
Backdoor.Win32.Katien	2	Backdoor.Win32.Seed	3	Email-Worm.Win32.Batzback	3	Email-Worm.Win32.Sunder	1
Backdoor.Win32.Ketch	4	Backdoor.Win32.Serman	1	Email-Worm.Win32.Blebla	1	Email-Worm.Win32.Svoy	2
Backdoor.Win32.Kidterror	1	Backdoor.Win32.ShBot	1	Email-Worm.Win32.Bumdoc	2	Email-Worm.Win32.Swen	1
Backdoor.Win32.Konik	1	Backdoor.Win32.Shakdos	1	Email-Worm.Win32.Charch	1	Email-Worm.Win32.Tanatos	3
Backdoor.Win32.Krepper	2	Backdoor.Win32.Shox	1	Email-Worm.Win32.Cholera	1	Email-Worm.Win32.Taripox	2
Backdoor.Win32.Labrus	1	Backdoor.Win32.SilverFTP	1	Email-Worm.Win32.Coronex	3	Email-Worm.Win32.Totilix	1
Backdoor.Win32.LanFiltrator	2	Backdoor.Win32.Sinf	1	Email-Worm.Win32.Cult	1	Email-Worm.Win32.Trilissa	4
Backdoor.Win32.LanaFTP	1	Backdoor.Win32.Sinit	4	Email-Worm.Win32.Delf	4	Email-Worm.Win32.Trood	2
Backdoor.Win32.Laocoon	1	Backdoor.Win32.SkyDance	1	Email-Worm.Win32.Desos	1	Email-Worm.Win32.Unis	1
Backdoor.Win32.Latinus	5	Backdoor.Win32.Small	22	Email-Worm.Win32.Donghe	3	Email-Worm.Win32.Urbe	3
Backdoor.Win32.Lemerul	1	Backdoor.Win32.Sporkbot	1	Email-Worm.Win32.Drefir	1	Email-Worm.Win32.Valha	1
Backdoor.Win32.Lesbot	1	Backdoor.Win32.SpyBoter	9	Email-Worm.Win32.Duksten	2	Email-Worm.Win32.Volag	1
Backdoor.Win32.Levelone	2	Backdoor.Win32.Stang	1	Email-Worm.Win32.Dumaru	10	Email-Worm.Win32.Vorgon	2
Backdoor.Win32.Liondoor	1	Backdoor.Win32.Stats	1	Email-Worm.Win32.Energy	1	Email-Worm.Win32.Warezov	1
Backdoor.Win32.Lithium	3	Backdoor.Win32.Stigmador	1	Email-Worm.Win32.Entangle	1	Email-Worm.Win32.Winevar	1
Backdoor.Win32.Litmus	1	Backdoor.Win32.SubSeven	1	Email-Worm.Win32.Epon	1	Email-Worm.Win32.Wozer	1
Backdoor.Win32.LittleBusters	1	Backdoor.Win32.Sumatrix	1	Email-Worm.Win32.Eyeveg	3	Email-Worm.Win32.Xanax	2
Backdoor.Win32.LittleWitch	1	Backdoor.Win32.Suslix	1	Email-Worm.Win32.Fix2001	1	Email-Worm.Win32.Yanz	1
Backdoor.Win32.Livup	1	Backdoor.Win32.Symes	1	Email-Worm.Win32.Frethem	2	Email-Worm.Win32.Yenik	1
Backdoor.Win32.Lixy	1	Backdoor.Win32.Sysinst	1	Email-Worm.Win32.Frubee	1	Email-Worm.Win32.Zircon	4
Backdoor.Win32.Lurker	1	Backdoor.Win32.System33	1	Email-Worm.Win32.GOPworm	1	Exploit.Win32.Agent	3
Backdoor.Win32.Lyusane	1	Backdoor.Win32.Sytr	1	Email-Worm.Win32.Gift	2	Exploit.Win32.AntiRAR	1
Backdoor.Win32.MSNMaker	1	Backdoor.Win32.TDS	3	Email-Worm.Win32.Gismor	1	Exploit.Win32.CAN	1
Backdoor.Win32.MServ	1	Backdoor.Win32.Takit	1	Email-Worm.Win32.Gizer	2	Exploit.Win32.CVE-2006-1359	1
Backdoor.Win32.MainServer	1	Backdoor.Win32.Tasmer	1	Email-Worm.Win32.Gunsan	2	Exploit.Win32.CrobFTP	1
Backdoor.Win32.Matrix	3	Backdoor.Win32.Telemot	1	Email-Worm.Win32.Haltura	1	Exploit.Win32.DCom	3
Backdoor.Win32.Medbot	1	Backdoor.Win32.TheThing	3	Email-Worm.Win32.Hanged	1	Exploit.Win32.DameWare	1
Backdoor.Win32.Mellpon	2	Backdoor.Win32.Thunk	1	Email-Worm.Win32.Happy	1	Net-Worm.Win32.Muma	1
Backdoor.Win32.Metarage	1	Backdoor.Win32.Tonerok	3	Email-Worm.Win32.Ivalid	1	Trojan-PSW.Win32.LdPinch	16
Backdoor.Win32.Mhtserv	1	Backdoor.Win32.URCS	2	Email-Worm.Win32.Jeans	1	Worm.Win32.AutoRun	34
Backdoor.Win32.Micronet	1	Backdoor.Win32.Undernet	1	Email-Worm.Win32.Kadra	1		
Backdoor.Win32.MiniCommander	1	Backdoor.Win32.Unwind	1	Email-Worm.Win32.Keco	3	Total	983

notice the signatures involve only functions from the Native API library. Our approach has the advantage of being API independent, thus the level of analysis may be tuned, plus Win32 API function based signatures should be shorter as each high level function should be translated into a set of calls to the Native API functions.

In [7] the authors propose to learn behaviors of binary files by extracting program control-flow graphs using dynamic analysis. Such graphs contain assembly instructions that correspond to control flow information e.g. jmp, but that introduces more possibilities to circumvent such signatures by rewriting the code. From the graphs, trees are computed and the union of all such trees is used to infer an automaton that is used in detection. Our inference does not output all the trees, only the most frequent, improving the learning process and generalizing from the training dataset.

An alternative to semantic signatures are works based on machine learning approaches as [28], which shows that by mining "$n-$grams" (a sequence of n bits), it is possible to distinguish malware from benign program. In our approach, the distinguishing features (malicious behaviors) can be seen as traces of program execution, thus having a meaning that can be more easily understood.

8   Conclusion

In this work, we have shown how to combine *static* reachability analysis techniques to infer malware semantic signatures in the form of malicious trees, which describe the data flows among system calls. Our experiments show that the approach can be used to automatically infer specifications of malicious behaviors and detect several malware samples from an a priori given smaller set of malware. We were able to detect 983 malware files using the malicious trees inferred from 193 malware files, and applied the detector to 250 benign files obtaining a 0% false positive rate.

As future work we envisage the improvement of the binary modeling techniques, for example enriching the function parameter type system to allow better approximations. The usage of more advanced mining techniques, e.g. structural leap mining used in [14], can be used to improve the learning approach. In another direction, given the relation between modal formulas and tree models a comparison between our approach and the approach in [24] concerning expressiveness and complexity is envisaged. Finally, a complexity study with respect to the depth of the trees extraction (parameter h in Algorithm 1) and size of the **HELTA** would be another alternative direction.

Summing up, the reachability analysis of **PDS** models of executables can play a major role in the malware specification inference domain. The ability to precisely analyze stack behavior enables the extraction of executables system call data flows and overcomes typical obfuscated calls to such routines.

References

1. Adleman, L.M.: An abstract theory of computer viruses. In: Goldwasser, S. (ed.) CRYPTO 1988. LNCS, vol. 403, pp. 354–374. Springer, Heidelberg (1990)
2. Babić, D., Reynaud, D., Song, D.: Malware analysis with tree automata inference. In: Gopalakrishnan, G., Qadeer, S. (eds.) CAV 2011. LNCS, vol. 6806, pp. 116–131. Springer, Heidelberg (2011)

3. Bergeron, J., Debbabi, M., Erhioui, M.M., Ktari, B.: Static analysis of binary code to isolate malicious behaviors. In: WETICE, pp. 184–189. IEEE Computer Society (1999)
4. Bonfante, G., Kaczmarek, M., Marion, J.-Y.: Toward an Abstract Computer Virology (2005)
5. Bonfante, G., Kaczmarek, M., Marion, J.-Y.: On Abstract Computer Virology from a Recursion Theoretic Perspective. Journal in Computer Virology 1, 45–54 (2006)
6. Bonfante, G., Kaczmarek, M., Marion, J.-Y.: A Classification of Viruses Through Recursion Theorems (2007)
7. Bonfante, G., Kaczmarek, M., Marion, J.-Y.: Architecture of a morphological malware detector. Journal in Computer Virology 5, 263–270 (2009)
8. Bouajjani, A., Esparza, J., Maler, O.: Reachability analysis of pushdown automata: Application to model-checking. In: Mazurkiewicz, A., Winkowski, J. (eds.) CONCUR 1997. LNCS, vol. 1243, pp. 135–150. Springer, Heidelberg (1997)
9. Christodorescu, M., Jha, S.: Static analysis of executables to detect malicious patterns. In: Proceedings of the 12th Conf. on USENIX Security Symposium (2003)
10. Christodorescu, M., Jha, S., Kruegel, C.: Mining specifications of malicious behavior. In: Proceedings of the 1st India Software Engineering Conference, ISEC 2008, pp. 5–14 (2008)
11. Christodorescu, M., Jha, S., Seshia, S.A., Song, D.X., Bryant, R.E.: Semantics-aware malware detection. In: IEEE Symposium on Security and Privacy, pp. 32–46 (2005)
12. Esparza, J., Hansel, D., Rossmanith, P., Schwoon, S.: Efficient algorithms for model checking pushdown systems. In: Emerson, E.A., Sistla, A.P. (eds.) CAV 2000. LNCS, vol. 1855, pp. 232–247. Springer, Heidelberg (2000)
13. Fossi, M., Egan, G., Haley, K., Johnson, E., Mack, T., Adams, T., Blackbird, J., Low, M., Mazurek, D., McKinney, D., et al.: Symantec internet security threat report trends for 2010
14. Fredrikson, M., Jha, S., Christodorescu, M., Sailer, R., Yan, X.: Synthesizing near-optimal malware specifications from suspicious behaviors. IEEE S. Security and Privacy (2010)
15. Hex-Rays, S.: Ida pro (2011)
16. Holzer, A., Kinder, J., Veith, H.: Using verification technology to specify and detect malware. In: Moreno Díaz, R., Pichler, F., Quesada Arencibia, A. (eds.) EUROCAST 2007. LNCS, vol. 4739, pp. 497–504. Springer, Heidelberg (2007)
17. Kinder, J., Katzenbeisser, S., Schallhart, C., Veith, H.: Detecting malicious code by model checking. In: Julisch, K., Kruegel, C. (eds.) DIMVA 2005. LNCS, vol. 3548, pp. 174–187. Springer, Heidelberg (2005)
18. Kinder, J., Katzenbeisser, S., Schallhart, C., Veith, H.: Proactive Detection of Computer Worms Using Model Checking. IEEE Trans. on Dependable and Secure Computing (2010)
19. Kinder, J., Veith, H.: Jakstab: A static analysis platform for binaries. In: Gupta, A., Malik, S. (eds.) CAV 2008. LNCS, vol. 5123, pp. 423–427. Springer, Heidelberg (2008)
20. Kramer, S., Bradfield, J.C.: A general definition of malware. Journal in Computer Virology 6(2), 105–114 (2010)
21. McAfee. McAfee threats report: Third quarter 2012. Technical report, McAfee (2012)
22. Singh, P., Lakhotia, A.: Static verification of worm and virus behavior in binary executables using model checking. In: Information Assurance Workshop, pp. 298–300 (2003)
23. Skaletsky, A., Devor, T., Chachmon, N., Cohn, R.S., Hazelwood, K.M., Vladimirov, V., Bach, M.: Dynamic program analysis of Microsoft Windows applications. In: ISPASS (2010)
24. Song, F., Touili, T.: Efficient malware detection using model-checking. In: Giannakopoulou, D., Méry, D. (eds.) FM 2012. LNCS, vol. 7436, pp. 418–433. Springer, Heidelberg (2012)
25. Song, F., Touili, T.: Pushdown model checking for malware detection. In: Flanagan, C., König, B. (eds.) TACAS 2012. LNCS, vol. 7214, pp. 110–125. Springer, Heidelberg (2012)

26. Song, F., Touili, T.: LTL model-checking for malware detection. In: Piterman, N., Smolka, S.A. (eds.) TACAS 2013. LNCS, vol. 7795, pp. 416–431. Springer, Heidelberg (2013)
27. Szor, P.: The Art of Computer Virus Research and Defense. Addison-Wesley Pro. (2005)
28. Tahan, G., Rokach, L., Shahar, Y.: Mal-id: Automatic malware detection using common segment analysis and meta-features. Journal of Machine Learning Research 1, 1–48 (2012)
29. Wörlein, M., Meinl, T., Fischer, I., Philippsen, M.: A quantitative comparison of the subgraph miners MoFa, gSpan, FFSM, and Gaston. In: Jorge, A.M., Torgo, L., Brazdil, P.B., Camacho, R., Gama, J. (eds.) PKDD 2005. LNCS (LNAI), vol. 3721, pp. 392–403. Springer, Heidelberg (2005)
30. Yan, X., Han, J.: gSpan: Graph-based substructure pattern mining. In: ICDM (2002)

Patrol: Revealing Zero-Day Attack Paths through Network-Wide System Object Dependencies

Jun Dai, Xiaoyan Sun, and Peng Liu

College of Information Sciences and Technology,
Pennsylvania State University, University Park, PA 16802
{jqd5187,xzs5052,pliu}@ist.psu.edu

Abstract. Identifying attack paths in enterprise network is strategically necessary and critical for security defense. However, there has been insufficient efforts in studying how to identify an attack path that goes through unknown security holes. In this paper, we define such attack paths as *zero-day attack paths*, and propose a prototype system named Patrol to identify them at runtime. Using system calls, Patrol builds a *network-wide system object dependency graph* that captures dependency relations between OS objects, and identifies *suspicious intrusion propagation paths* in it as candidate zero-day attack paths through forward and backward tracking from intrusion symptoms. Patrol further identifies highly suspicious candidates among these paths, by recognizing indicators of unknown vulnerability exploitations along the paths through rule-based checking. Our evaluation shows that Patrol can work accurately and effectively at runtime with an acceptable performance overhead.

1 Introduction

1.1 Zero-Day Attack Paths

When deploying enterprise network security defense, it is important to consider multi-step attacks. Given that today's network is usually under basic protection from security deployments like firewall and IDS, it's not easy for attackers to directly break into their final target. Instead, determined attackers patiently compromise other intermediate hosts as stepping-stones. That is, attackers often have to go through an *attack path* before they achieve their goal. An attack path is a sequence of vulnerability exploits on compromised hosts. It's necessary and critical to find the attack paths hidden in the network.

Suppose that a host is compromised by a local or remote exploit. If this exploit is enabled by a known vulnerability, it's not zero-day. If this

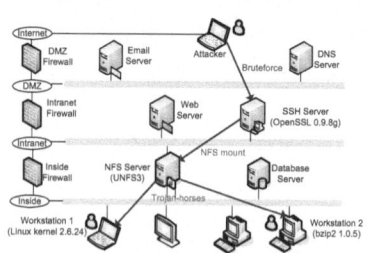

Fig. 1. An example attack scenario

J. Crampton, S. Jajodia, and K. Mayes (Eds.): ESORICS 2013, LNCS 8134, pp. 536–555, 2013.

exploit is enabled by an unknown vulnerability, it is zero-day. If an attack path includes one or more zero-day exploits, it is a *zero-day attack path*.

Fig. 1 illustrates an example attack scenario including three steps. Step 1, a brute-force key guessing attack is used to exploit *CVE-2008-0166* on *SSH Server* to gain root privilege. Step 2, the export table on *NFS Server* is inappropriately configured to allow any user to share files through a public directory (*/exports*), so two crafted trojan-horses are uploaded to this directory. The trojan-horses contain exploit code of *CVE-2009-2692* and *CVE-2011-4089*. Step 3, once a trojan-horse file is mounted and installed by an innocent user like *Workstation 1* or *2*, arbitrary code is executed to create a hidden channel. Hence, two attack paths exist: *p1{CVE-2008-0166, NFS misconfiguration, CVE-2009-2692}* and *p2{CVE-2008-0166, NFS misconfiguration, CVE-2011-4089}*. Let's assume the time now is *August 1, 2009*, then *CVE-2008-0166* becomes the only known vulnerability. If the attackers are still able to exploit all the vulnerabilities in this scenario, then *p1* and *p2* both become zero-day attack paths.

Zero-day exploit problem is so important and challenging. Zero-day attack path problem is beyond zero-day exploit problem. This paper aims to take the first steps to address the zero-day attack path problem.

1.2 Possible Solutions

The literature is explored for possible solutions of zero-day attack path problem. However, we find that no existing technique can well address this problem due to the unknown nature of zero-day attack path.

Attack graph [1–3]. By considering vulnerabilities in combination (not merely in isolation), attack graph can generate attack paths that show exploit sequences to specific attack goals. But, this notion has been primarily applied to model causality dependencies among known vulnerabilities. Unknown vulnerabilities are not captured and zero-day attack paths will accordingly be missing in attack graph. Notable exceptions are recent research [4] [5], which have pioneered the attack graph based analysis and modeling of zero-day vulnerabilities. However, a solution to identify zero-day attack paths at runtime is further expected.

Penetration test [6–8]. This solution uses real exploits to reveal some speculated attack paths. It requires huge knowledge and operation input from human intelligence. Hence, the cost is usually too expensive. Besides, the attack paths in their discovery are largely known ones, because it's very difficult to exploit unknown vulnerabilities in penetration tests.

Alert correlation [9] [10]. This solution correlates isolated alerts to form potential attack paths. Although it has potentials to be automatic and inexpensive, it may induce high false rates. The false rates are twofold: 1) The correlation itself is inaccurate because it attempts to integrate possibly different contexts into a unified "story"; 2) The alerts that the correlation largely depends on genetically inherit false rates from security sensors like IDS. When the two folds of false rates are combined together, the accuracy of the whole solution gets worse.

Techniques to detect zero-day exploits may help the identification of zero-day attack path, such as anomaly detection [11–18] and specification-based detection

[19] [20]. By profiling normal behavior and detecting deviations, these techniques are capable of detecting novel exploits. However, they are hard to cope with false positives. Besides, the identification of novel exploits doesn't mean the identification of zero-day attack paths. As pointed above, IDS alert correlation needs to be involved and thus introduces one more fold of false rates.

1.3   Key Insights and Our Approach

This paper leverages a different strategy to identify the zero-day attack paths. Instead of first collecting vulnerabilities or alerts and then correlating them into paths, we first try to build a superset graph and identify the suspicious intrusion propagation paths hidden in it as candidate zero-day attack paths, and then recognize the highly suspicious candidates among these paths. Interested readers can refer to Fig. 2 for an example of a superset graph (Fig. 2a) and the suspicious intrusion propagation paths (Fig. 2b) hidden in it.

We make this decision for four *key insights*: 1) As the only way for programs to interact with OS, system calls are found hard-to-avoid and attack neutral; 2) We find that a network-wide superset graph can be generated from system calls, and zero-day attack paths are showing themselves in it. This graph is also attack neutral. It exists no matter whether any vulnerability is exploited or not; 3) The superset graph is inherently a set of paths. We find a way to get its appropriate subsets as candidate zero-day attack paths. These paths actually and naturally correlate vulnerability exploitations, different from the logical correlation in attack graph; 4) The candidate zero-day attack paths expose unknown vulnerability exploitations along them, and thus can orientate us to recognize such exploitations. With these paths serving as network-wide attack context, the accuracy and performance of detecting unknown vulnerability exploitations can be better than the detection with only isolated per-host context.

The following summarizes our main contributions:

1. We propose to build a *network-wide system object dependency graph* (SODG) as the superset graph. Built from system calls, an SODG is made up of OS objects like processes/files/sockets (nodes) and dependency relations between them (edges). It neutrally captures the occurrence of vulnerability exploits.
2. We propose to identify *suspicious intrusion propagation paths* (SIPPs) in the network-wide SODG as candidate zero-day attack paths. The SIPPs actually and naturally correlate known/unknown vulnerability exploitations. We further coin the concepts of vulnerability shadow and shadow indicator to help recognize the highly suspicious candidates among the SIPPs.
3. We implemented a prototype system, called *Patrol*, which can work accurately and effectively at runtime with an acceptable performance overhead.

2   Models and Assumptions

We assume a network consists of Unix-like operating systems, in which system objects can be mainly classified into processes, files and sockets. We propose to

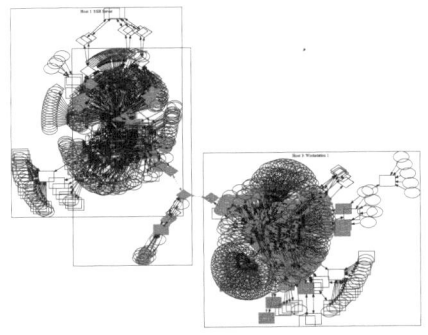
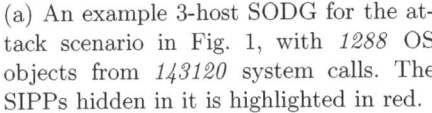
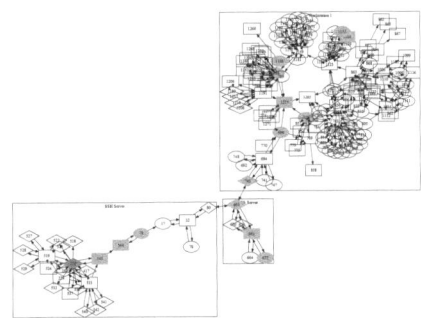

(a) An example 3-host SODG for the attack scenario in Fig. 1, with *1288* OS objects from *143120* system calls. The SIPPs hidden in it is highlighted in red.

(b) The red colored SIPPs hidden in (a), with *175* OS objects. The trigger node is highlighted in red and other verified malicious nodes in grey.

Fig. 2. This figure is to show what the SODG and SIPPs are like. A box contains a per-host SODG, in which a rectangle denotes a process, a diamond denotes a socket, and an ellipse denotes a file. *They look unreadable because of the fine granularity at OS-level and the scale of network. Readers are not expected to understand the details.* A main merit of Patrol is that it can dig out SIPPs from the network-wide SODG.

build a network-wide system object dependency graph (SODG) using system call traces. Since a system call is designed to be the only way to get service from OS in modern operating systems, attackers have to talk to the system via system calls. Therefore, although unknown exploits could not be seen by us, they can be seen by SODG. Fig. 2a gives an example of a 3-host SODG.

To build a network-wide SODG, we first need to construct the SODG for each host, namely per-host SODG. As in Definition 1, a per-host SODG is a directed graph made up of OS objects (nodes) and dependency relations (directed edges) between them. System calls are parsed to generate these nodes and edges. There are several types of dependency relations. For example, system call *read* infers that a process depends on a file (denoted as *file→process*), while *write* determines that a file depends on a process (*process→file*). Table 1 gives the dependency rules to help generate dependency relations from system calls. *start* and *end* respectively denote the timestamp at which a system call is invoked and returned.

Definition 1. *per-host System Object Dependency Graph*
If the system call trace for the i-*th* host is denoted as Σ_i, then the per-host SODG for the host is a directed graph $G(V_i, E_i)$, where:

- V_i is the set of nodes, and initialized to empty set $\varnothing$;
- E_i is the set of directed edges, and initialized to empty set $\varnothing$;
- If a system call $syscall \in \Sigma_i$, and *dep* is the dependency relation parsed from *syscall* according to dependency rules in Table 1, where $dep \in \{(src \rightarrow sink), (src \leftarrow sink), (src \leftrightarrow sink)\}$, *src* and *sink* are OS objects (mainly a process,

Table 1. System call dependency rules

Dependency	Events	System calls
process→file	process modifies file	write, pwrite64, rename, mkdir, linkat, link, symlinkat, symlink, fchmodat, fchmod, chmod, fchownat, mount
file→process	process uses but does not modify file	stat64, lstat64, fstat64, open, read, pread64, execve, mmap2, mprotect, linkat, link, symlinkat, symlink
process↔file	process uses and modifies file	open, rename, mount, mmap2, mprotect
process→process	process creation or termination	vfork, fork, kill
process↔process	process creation	clone
process→socket	process writes socket	write, pwrite64
socket→process	process checks or reads socket	fstat64, read, pread64
process↔socket	process writes socket	mount, connect, accept, bind, sendto, send, sendmsg, recvfrom, recv, recvmsg
socket↔socket	process reads or writes socket	connect, accept, sendto, sendmsg, recvfrom, recvmsg

file or socket), then $V_i = V_i \cup \{src, sink\}$, $E_i = E_i \cup \{dep\}$. dep inherits timestamps $start$ and end from $syscall$;

– If $(a \rightarrow b) \in E_i$ and $(b \rightarrow c) \in E_i$, then c transitively depends on a.

As shown in Definition 2, the network-wide SODG is constructed by recursively concatenating the per-host SODGs. If and only if at least one directed edge exists between two nodes from two different SODGs, these two SODGs can be concatenated together (by the $\cup$ operation in Cantor set theory).

Definition 2. *network-wide System Object Dependency Graph*
If the per-host SODG for the i-*th* host is denoted as $G(V_i, E_i)$, then the network-wide SODG can be denoted as $\cup G(V_i, E_i)$, where:

– $\cup G(V_2, E_2) = G(V_1, E_1) \cup G(V_2, E_2) = G(\cup V_2, \cup E_2)$, iff $\exists obj_1 \in V_1$, $obj_2 \in V_2$ and $dep_{1,2} \in \cup E_2$, where $dep_{1,2} \in \{obj_1 \leftarrow obj_2, obj_1 \rightarrow obj_2, obj_1 \leftrightarrow obj_2\}$. $\cup V_2$ denotes $V_1 \cup V_2$, and $\cup E_2$ denotes $E_1 \cup E_2$;
– $\cup G(V_i, E_i) = \{\cup G(V_{i-1}, E_{i-1})\} \cup G(V_i, E_i) = G(\cup V_i, \cup E_i)$, iff $\exists obj_{i-1} \in \cup V_{i-1}$, $obj_i \in V_i$ and $dep_{i-1,i} \in \cup E_i$, where $dep_{i-1,i} \in \{obj_{i-1} \leftarrow obj_i, obj_{i-1} \rightarrow obj_i, obj_{i-1} \leftrightarrow obj_i\}$. $\cup V_i$ denotes $V_1 \cup \cdots \cup V_i$, and $\cup E_i$ denotes $E_1 \cup \cdots \cup E_i$.

The network-wide SODG is inherently a set of paths. A zero-day attack path will be one of them if it exists. Hence, we propose to identify suspicious intrusion propagation paths (SIPPs) in the network-wide SODG as candidate zero-day attack paths.

As in Definition 3, the SIPPs are a subgraph of the network-wide SODG, of which the OS objects are all "suspicious": given a trigger node tn, they either have affected tn through direct or transitive dependency relations before $lat(tn)$, or have been affected by tn after $eat(tn)$. Trigger nodes refer to SODG objects that are involved in the alerts from existing security sensors, such as Snort [21], Tripwire [22], or our system itself.[1] We assume trigger nodes can be noticed by administrators. The SIPPs inherently reveal the attacker's trace at OS level.

---

[1] To reduce dependency on efficiency of security monitoring tools, Patrol implements another mode: heavy mode, in which Patrol feeds itself with its own alerts as seeds.

Fig. 2b gives an example of the SIPPs hidden in the 3-host SODG, using the SSH socket (node *225*) noticed from the Snort alert "SSH potential brute force attack" as the trigger node.

Definition 3. *Suspicious Intrusion Propagation Paths* (SIPPs)
If the network-wide SODG is denoted as $\cup G(V_i, E_i)$, where $G(V_i, E_i)$ denotes the per-host SODG for the i-*th* host, then the SIPPs are a subgraph of $\cup G(V_i, E_i)$, denoted as $G(V', E')$, where:

- V' is the set of nodes, and $V' \subset \cup V_i$;
- E' is the set of directed edges, and $E' \subset \cup E_i$;
- V' is initialized to include *trigger nodes* only;
- For $\forall obj' \in V'$, if $\exists obj \in \cup V_i$ where $(obj \rightarrow obj') \in \cup E_i$ and $start(obj \rightarrow obj') \leq lat(obj')$, then $V' = V' \cup \{obj\}$ and $E' = E' \cup \{(obj \rightarrow obj')\}$. $lat(obj')$ maintains the *latest access time* to obj' by edges in E';
- For $\forall obj' \in V'$, if $\exists obj \in \cup V_i$ where $(obj' \rightarrow obj) \in \cup E_i$ and $end(obj' \rightarrow obj) \geq eat(obj')$, then $V' = V' \cup \{obj\}$ and $E' = E' \cup \{(obj' \rightarrow obj)\}$. $eat(obj')$ maintains the *earliest access time* to obj' by edges in E'.

A network-wide SODG can be unmanageably complex. A main merit of Patrol is that it can dig out SIPPs from the network-wide SODG. The size of the identified SIPPs is much smaller (see Table 4 in Appendix for the statistics of the 3-host SODG and SIPPs in Fig 2). The SIPPs will include almost all the zero-day attack paths. The only possible way for a zero-day attack path to escape SIPPs is that it includes only zero-day exploits on all compromised hosts. This is very rare and unlikely, because it's almost impossible for attackers to exploit only zero-day vulnerabilities along the path. Therefore, a zero-day attack path will be a path in SIPPs if it exists. Section 3.5 will propose a method to help recognize highly suspicious candidate zero-day attack paths among the SIPPs.

3   System Design

3.1   System Overview

Fig. 3 shows the overview of our system. It consists of four components:
System call auditing and filtering. We first perform system call auditing on each host, and then send the system call traces from individual hosts to the analysis machine after filtering (according to filtering rules). Among the four components, only system call auditing and filtering is on the fly. The other three are performed off-line, to reduce overhead imposed on individual hosts.
SODG graph generation. To construct a network-wide SODG, two steps are needed: per-host SODG generation and inter-host SODG generation. First, the collected system call logs are parsed based on dependency rules to build per-host SODGs. Then, per-host SODGs are concatenated into a network-wide SODG.
SIPPs identification. To dig out the SIPPs "hidden" inside the network-wide SODG, trigger nodes are used as seeds to track the forward and backward OS

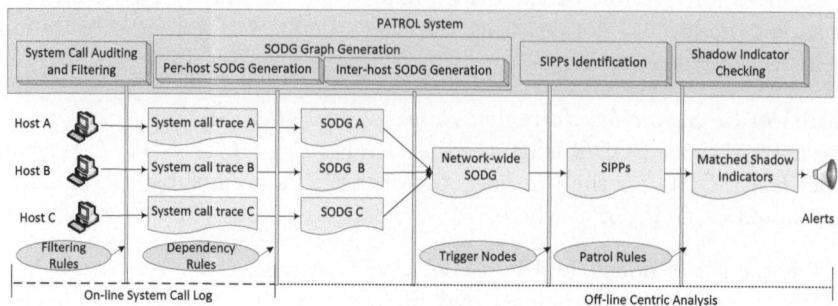

Fig. 3. System overview of Patrol

dependencies across the boundaries of individual hosts. These dependencies identify the nodes and edges of SIPPs.

Shadow indicator checking. To help identify highly suspicious candidate zero-day attack paths among the SIPPs, we also perform shadow indicator checking, which is a new technique that we will present in Section 3.5.

3.2   System Call Auditing and Filtering

Several requirements are expected for system call auditing: 1) System call auditing should be done against all running processes, rather than against specific processes. It's hard to pre-determine which process to audit, so process-specific system call auditing could miss important system calls that carry critical intrusion information. 2) System call auditing should be network-wide, meaning that: first, all hosts of the network should be audited; second, the socket communications between hosts should be captured. Network-wide system call auditing is the basis for identifying suspicious paths across hosts. 3) Sufficient OS-aware information should be preserved for accurate OS object identification. Due to the reuse of process ID and file descriptor numbers, it's inaccurate to identify system processes and files solely by their IDs or descriptor numbers. 4) The time that a system call is invoked and returned should be recorded. Time information can later help determine whether a system call is involved in intrusion propagation.

Considering unfiltered data would cause more bandwidth/CPU costs on data transfer and analysis, system calls are filtered before being sent to the analysis machine. Some filtering rules are applied to prune system calls which involve OS objects that are either highly redundant or possibly innocent. This is called *filtering preprocessing*, which can boost the speed of graph generation and reduce the complexity of resulted graphs. For example, we currently perform pruning for the following objects: 1) The dynamic linked library files like *libc.so.** and *libm.so.**. They are loaded every time an executable is run, and thus cause a lot of redundancy; 2) Dummy objects like *stdin/stdout* and */dev/null*; 3) Objects about pseudo-terminal master and slave (*/dev/ptmx* and */dev/pts*); 4) Log relevant objects like *syslogd* and */var/log/**; 5) Objects relevant with system maintenance (*apt-get* and *apt-config*). More filtering rules could be specified to prune more system calls, gaining better speed boosting. However, it also takes more risk filtering out objects involved in vulnerability exploitations. Due to this tradeoff, filtering rules for preprocessing are enabled as options.

After filtering, system call traces are sent to the analysis machine. Considering accumulative data may cause bigger latency on data transfer and analysis, we set a parameter called *time window* to tune the frequency of sending system call logs. It is the periodic time span during which system calls are logged.

3.3 SODG Generation and Concatenation

System calls from individual hosts are used to construct per-host SODGs. A per-host SODG can be constructed by first parsing system calls into OS objects (process/file/socket) and dependency relations between them. OS objects then become SODG nodes and dependency relations become SODG edges. Dependency rules are proposed and used in related works [23–25] to help determine dependency relation types according to specific system calls. Table 1 lists the dependency rules used in Patrol. In addition to dependency rules, system call arguments also contribute to the parsing. They are used to uniquely recognize and name SODG nodes, and help infer the edge direction between them. For example, system call "*sys_open, start:470880, end:494338, pid:6707, pname:scp, pathname:/mnt/trojan, inode:9453574*" from our trace is transformed to $(6707, scp) \leftarrow (/mnt/trojan, 9453574)$, where *pid* and *pname* are used to recognize the process, and *pathname* and *inode* are used to identify the file.

Hosts communicate with each other, hence a per-host SODG may have directed edges to or from other per-host SODGs. This insight can be leveraged to build the network-wide SODG by concatenating per-host SODGs. If and only if there exists at least one directed edge between two nodes from two different per-host SODGs, these two SODGs can be concatenated together. Such edges can serve as the glue for concatenation. We find that directed edges between per-host SODGs are usually caused by socket-based communications. A local program can communicate with a remote program through message passing, which can be captured by system call *socketcall*. Hence, two per-host SODGs can be concatenated together by identifying and pairing socket objects. For example, system call "*sys_accept, start:681154, end:681162, pid:4935, pname:sshd, srcaddr:172.18.34.10, srcport:36036, sinkaddr:192.168.101.5, sinkport:22*" results in a directed edge $(172.18.34.10, 36036) \rightarrow (192.168.101.5, 22)$, where a socket object is denoted as a tuple $(ip, port)$. This edge can be used to concatenate the per-host SODGs of *172.18.34.10* and *192.168.101.5*. The network-wide SODG is constructed by recursively concatenating the per-host SODGs. First, two per-host SODGs can be concatenated into a 2-host SODG. Then, the 3rd per-host SODG can be glued to the 2-host SODG, the 4th per-host SODG glued to the 3-host SODG, and so on. The algorithm goes on recursively and ends when no edge exists between any per-host SODG and the resulted network-wide SODG.

3.4   SIPPs Identification

SIPPs identification is designed to dig out SIPPs from the network-wide SODG. A benefit of the network-wide SODG is that intra-host forward and backward dependency tracking can be extended across the boundaries of individual hosts. Using trigger nodes as seeds, such inter-host dependency tracking identifies all network SODG objects that have direct or transitive dependency relations to or from trigger nodes, i.e. SIPPs by Definition 3. Hence, the SIPPs identification begins with the recognition of trigger nodes. Trigger nodes could be files that are deleted, added, or modified in unexpected ways, and processes that behave in an unusual or malicious manner, such as conducting abnormal port scanning, or making disallowed system calls. They are usually raised by security sensors like Snort, Tripwire, etc., and noticed by administrators.

Trigger nodes are not necessarily the start of an intrusion. For example, what an IDS detects could be later manifestation of the start. In that case, Patrol will use trigger nodes to first perform backward tracking to find the intrusion start, and then use the start to perform forward tracking. Basically, backward dependency tracking is used to identify all the SODG objects that have directly or transitively affected trigger nodes, and forward tracking is to identify objects that have been affected by trigger nodes. In patrol, backward and forward dependency tracking are both implemented based on breadth-first search (BFS) algorithm [26], as depicted in Definition 3. In simple words, the SIPPs is initialized to include only trigger nodes, and then BFS is recursively invoked to add new nodes and edges from the network-wide SODG. For each object obj' in SIPPs, the latest and earliest access time are respectively maintained in $lat(obj')$ and $eat(obj')$. In backward tracking, if obj' depends on another object obj in SODG, and the timestamp $start$ of this dependency relation is earlier than $lat(obj')$, it means that obj has affected obj'. So, obj and the dependency relation should be added into SIPPs. Similarly, in forward tracking, if another object obj in SODG depends on obj', and the timestamp end of this dependency relation is later than $eat(obj')$, it means that obj has been affected by obj' and should be added into SIPPs together with the dependency relation.

3.5   Shadow Indicator Checking

The SIPPs could still be complex. To further identify highly suspicious candidate zero-day attack paths among the SIPPs, we propose the concepts of vulnerability shadow and shadow indicator. These concepts are based on the observation that vulnerabilities share some features. CWE [27] enumerates 693 common weaknesses, and CAPEC [28] classifies 400 common attack patterns. These common features could exist in vulnerabilities found in a long time span, and even in some future unknown vulnerabilities.

The concept of vulnerability shadow is much in the same spirit. But instead of directly characterizing vulnerabilities, we propose to characterize *exploitations* of them at the OS level. This is because, due to the existence of shared features, exploitations of some vulnerabilities often result in similar characteristics

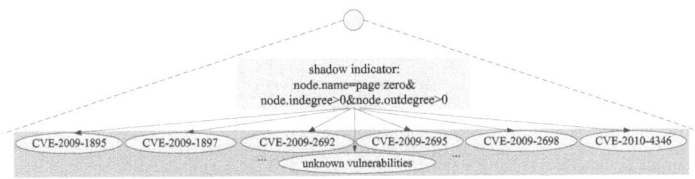

Fig. 4. A vulnerability shadow example: *bypassing mmap_min_addr*

in SODG. The insight here is that, the characteristics extracted from previous exploitations of known vulnerabilities can be applied to detect the exploitation of unknown vulnerabilities. We leverage this insight as follows: we define such common characteristics as an indicator function, which is used to indicate membership of elements in set theory, and use this function to build a set. The resulted set is a set of known and unknown vulnerabilities, whose exploitations all have the common characteristics. Such a set is named *vulnerability shadow*, and its set indicator function is called *shadow indicator*.

Definition 4. *Vulnerability Shadow* and *Shadow Indicator*
A vulnerability shadow is a Cantor set denoted as $S = \{v | p(SODG(v))\}$, where:
- v is a known or unknown vulnerability, whose exploitation is part of the SODG represented as $SODG(v)$;
- p, the shadow indicator for S, is a boolean-valued set indicator function: $SODG(v) \rightarrow \{$true, false$\}$. p can be a conjunction of several predicates, in a form like $p = p_1 \& p_2 \& \cdots \& p_n$ (n is a natural number), where for $\forall 1 \leq i \leq n$, p_i is predicating an attribute of a node or edge in $SODG(v)$, and $\&$ stands for AND operation in logic (p is true, iff p_i is true for $\forall 1 \leq i \leq n$);
- $v \in S$, iff $p(SODG(v)) = true$.

Fig. 4 shows an example vulnerability shadow *bypassing mmap_min_addr*, with *node.name=page_zero&node.indegree>0&node.outdegree>0* as its shadow indicator.[2] This indicator was first observed in exploiting CVE-2009-1895 and CVE-2009-1897, and then can be used to recognize the exploitations of CVE-2009-2692, CVE-2009-2695, CVE-2009-2698, etc. A very intriguing implication of vulnerability shadow is that, unknown vulnerabilities that do not have a CVE ID yet could exist in this shadow, if and only if their exploitations can make the shadow indicator become true.

Shadow indicators imply occurrence of an exploitation and should not appear in legitimate paths. In addition to the trigger node, if other shadow indicators appear on a path in SIPPs, the path is very likely to be an attack path. If

---

[2] The kernel variable *mmap_min_addr* is tunable to specify the minimum virtual address that a process is allowed to *mmap*. *Bypassing mmap_min_addr* makes a violation to map user-land *page zero*, which can be triggered later by null pointer dereference to gain privileges. Page zero is parsed from *mmap2(null, 4096, *, *, *)=0* or *mprotect(0, 4096, *)=0*, where * is the wildcard.

no alerts from vulnerability scanners or traditional IDS can be associated with any of these indicators, this path is reported as a highly suspicious candidate zero-day attack path. Rule-based checking is employed to recognize the shadow indicators in SIPPs. As Snort rules are developed for Snort to capture attack signature at packet level, Patrol rules are invented for Patrol to capture shadow indicators at OS level. A Patrol rule is like this: *indicator indicator_object (function: indicator_function; msg: "vulnerability_shadow_name")*.

Each rule specifies the object to check upon in *indicator_object*. If no object is specified, "any" is used to check on every object. Each rule contains the indicator function in *indicator_function*. The function specifies unexpected attribute values of the nodes or edges in SIPPs. A message will display the name of the vulnerability shadow when the function returns true. The following gives the Patrol rule for checking the shadow indicator of bypsssing mmap_min_addr: *indicator page_zero (function: indegree>0&outdegree>0; msg: "bypassing mmap_min_addr")*.

The attributes used to specify *indicator_function* include graph attributes and system call attributes. The graph attributes like *indegree* (a node's inward edge number) and *outdegree* (outward edge number) allow us to characterize exploitations from the perspective of graph. In addition to graph attributes, system call attributes such as *syscall* (system call name), *argument* (arguments) and *rtn* (return value) can also be taken into consideration. Patrol maintains association between graph edges and corresponding system calls. Hence, system calls can be revisited for inspection of its arguments and return values. For example, the following Patrol rule is used to detect symlink inconsistency: *indicator any (function: outdegree=0&∃(syscall=linkat&rtn=0); msg: "symlink inconsistency between request and creation")*.[3]

4   Implementation

The system design is implemented into a prototype named Patrol, through approximately 5493 lines of code, which include about 2411 lines of C code for a loadable kernel module auditing 39 system calls, and 3082 lines of gawk code for data analysis which produces dot-compatible [29] output for graph visualization.

System Call Auditing and OS-Aware Reconstruction. Patrol hooks system calls via a loadable kernel module, which can audit all running processes. Interested system calls are audited, including those encapsulated in system call *socketcall*, such as *sys_accept*, *sys_sendto*, etc. In the module, codes are inserted to each system call to 1) record its arguments and return values; 2) refer OS kernel data structures, retrieving process descriptor from *task_struct* and file descriptor from *files_struct*. The OS-aware information such as process descriptors, absolute file paths and inode numbers are preserved for accurate OS object identification. The timestamps *start* and *end* respectively record the time that the

---

[3] If a symbolic link created is inconsistent with the one requested, an attacker can exploit race condition to make arbitrary code executed as the requested link is referenced. Because *linkat* has other alternatives like *symlinkat*, *link*, and *symlink*, this rule has several siblings.

system call is invoked and returned. The resulted kernel module supports Linux kernel versions 2.6.24 through 2.6.32.

Graph Representation and Edge Aggregation. We represent our graphs with an adjacency matrix (*Map*) because during SODG generation and SIPPs identification we need to quickly look up if there is already an existing edge connecting two nodes. With adjacency matrix, the query takes only $O(1)$ time, while with other data structures it may take $O(|v|)$ or $O(|e|)$ time, where $|v|$ and $|e|$ are respectively the number of nodes and edges in a graph. For each pair of SODG nodes (*srcObj* and *sinkObj*), there could be a large number of edges between them. The edges are caused by different system calls or the same system call with different timestamps. Our implementation aggregates them into a single one, maintaining the matrix cell (*Map[srcObj, sinkObj]*) to count the number of edges, and a timestamp list (*tMap[srcObj, sinkObj]*) to associate this aggregated edge with different timestamps.

Light Mode and Heavy Mode. To reduce dependency on efficiency of the traditional security sensors, Patrol implements another mode: heavy mode, in which Patrol feeds itself with its own alerts as seeds. In light mode, Patrol gets fed with trigger nodes, identifies SIPPs, and continues with rule-based checking against SIPPs to detect if shadow indicators exist. In heavy mode, it doesn't use any trigger nodes from other tools. Instead, it directly matches shadow indicators against the whole network-wide SODG. If any shadow indicators are matched, they are then used as trigger nodes to initiate the light-mode running. That is, a heavy mode can be run to replace the role of security sensors, but it also causes heavier workload. For example, the heavy mode can detect the brute-force attack exploiting CVE-2008-0166 in seconds after the SODG is built, without relying on any Snort alert. This paper focuses on illustration of light mode.

5 Evaluation

5.1 Experimental Setup

The ideal environment to evaluate Patrol is a real-world enterprise network. However, accesses to production kernels are tightly controlled by policy. We therefore built a web-shop test-bed for evaluation. Fig. 1 illustrates the test-bed network, which is set up with firewalls, Nessus [30], Oval [31], Snort, Wireshark [32], Ntop [33] and Tripwire. The hosts are typically deployed with Dell PowerEdge T310 with two 2.53GHz Intel(R) Xeon(R) X3440 quad-core processor and 4GB of RAM running 32-bit Linux 2.6.24 through 2.6.32.

We implemented the attack scenario in Fig. 1. In order to produce zero-day attack paths, the attacks have to exploit unknown vulnerabilities. However, a typical zero-day attack can remain undisclosed for 312 days on average [34]. Due to such lack of zero-day resources, we emulate unknown vulnerabilities by using published vulnerabilities. Our strategy is to tune the "time" back to a history date and assume vulnerabilities published after that date are still unknown.

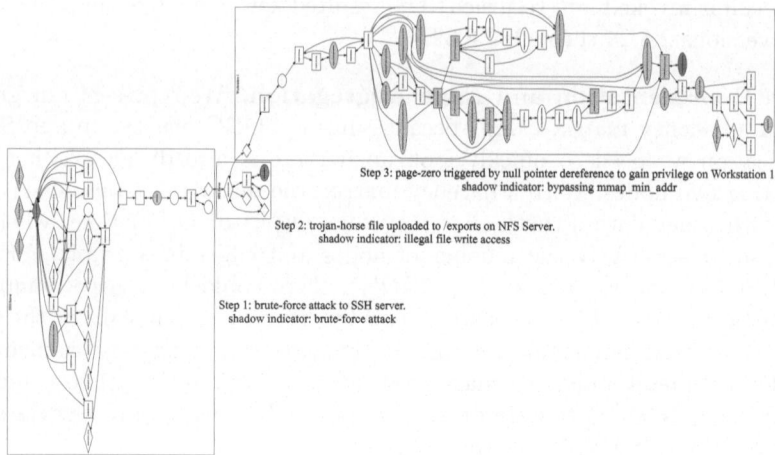

Step 3: page-zero triggered by null pointer dereference to gain privilege on Workstation 1.
shadow indicator: bypassing mmap_min_addr

Step 2: trojan-horse file uploaded to /exports on NFS Server.
shadow indicator: illegal file write access

Step 1: brute-force attack to SSH server.
shadow indicator: brute-force attack

Fig. 5. The zero-day attack path *p1* dug out from the SIPPs (Fig. 2b) by Patrol, capturing the 3-step attack in the attack scenario. The identified shadow indictors are highlighted in red color. The grey nodes are proved to be malicious during verification.

Such emulation enables us to evaluate the correctness of our approach, because 1) timelines can be maintained for vulnerability shadows to make sure that no specific knowledge of the emulated vulnerabilities is needed; 2) the exploit code and other information about the emulated vulnerabilities can be available for verification. This paper assumes that the time is tuned to August 1, 2009, so that CVE-2008-0166 becomes the only known vulnerability in the attack scenario.

5.2   Correctness

Of all the vulnerabilities in the attack scenario, only the exploit of CVE-2008-0166 triggered an alert "SSH potential brute force attack" from Snort. Hence, both of the zero-day attack paths *p1* and *p2* in the attack scenario were missing. In contrast, using the SSH socket (node *225* in the figures) noticed from the Snort

alert as the trigger node, Patrol successfully identified both *p1* and *p2* at the OS level. Fig. 5 and Fig. 7 respectively illustrate *p1*[4] and *p2*. Since *p2* and *p1* share the same Step 1 and Step 2, Fig. 7 only shows the Step 3 of *p2*.

We verified the correctness of *p1* and *p2*, by comparing the nodes and edges on them with the

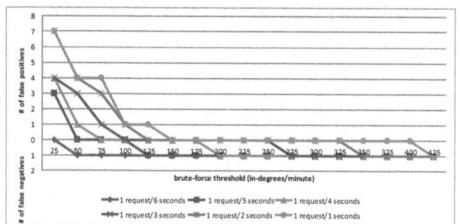

Fig. 6. False positives and negatives of shadow indicator checking for brute-force attack

---

[4] There were hundreds of socket communications coming from different ports of the same malicious IP (*192.168.202.2*) to node *225*. For simplicity, only three of them are illustrated.

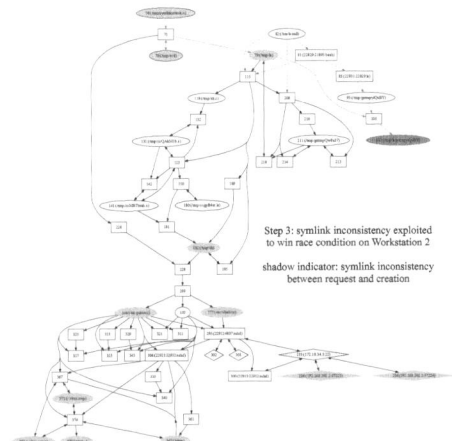

Fig. 7. Step 3 of the zero-day attack path *p2* identified by Patrol. The red and green dotted lines respectively denote the execution of the attack processes and innocent processes. The red lines replaced the requested symlink */tmp/ls* (*79*) with malicious code */tmp/evil* (*78*), which was later referenced by the the innocent process *ls* (*115*). The identified shadow indictor is highlighted in red color. The grey nodes are proved to be malicious during verification.

intrusion knowledge extracted from the exploit code, the CVE entries in NVD [35] and the documentation of corresponding vulnerable applications. We marked the nodes in Fig. 5 and Fig. 7 with grey color if they were verified to be malicious. It shows that Patrol correctly captured the malicious objects interacting with each other to accomplish the intrusion break-in and propagation.

We also evaluated the false positives of the shadow indicator checking on the two identified paths. For this, we kept Patrol running intensively for 72 hours against a variety of applications and services in the test-bed. It turns out that the false positive rate of shadow indicator checking is indicator-specific. For example, the indicator checking for *bypassing mmap_min_addr* and *symlink inconsistency* got 0 false positives, while the indicator checking for *brute-force attack* had false positives varying with the setup of a parameter and the workload of the host. The brute-force shadow indicator ($node.indegree > threshold_{bruteforce}$) uses $threshold_{bruteforce}$ to specify the maximum in-degree per minute allowed for a SODG node. Fig. 6 illustrates the impact of $threshold_{bruteforce}$ on false positives and negatives for SSH Server. As the threshold increases, the false positives first decrease and then stay at 0 until the false negative appears. As the request speed increases, the false positives increase and a bigger threshold is needed.

Furthermore, the above false positives can be tolerated by Patrol to some extent. For example, for brute-force shadow indicator checking, the false alarmed objects include: 1) DNS related process (avahi-daemon) or sockets (port 53 or 5353); 2) uninitialized sockets (port 0); 3) dynamic linked library files. However, none of them were on the same SIPPs with other shadow indicators. Hence, with the help of SIPPs, most of the false positives could be eliminated.

5.3   Efficiency

Time window size and filtering preprocessing are two important factors impacting the efficiency of Patrol data analysis. Time window is the periodic time span

Table 2. Statistics for time window based tests on data analysis

time window size (mins)	5	15	25	35	45	55
# of syscalls in filtered log	17550	52649	87748	122848	157947	193047
time overhead of SODG generation (s)	44.94	108.88	278.52	601.93	1097.33	1836.47
# of objects in SODG	526	1425	2326	3227	4101	4977
time overhead of SIPPs identification (s)	0.91	7.54	22.75	48.79	76.75	107.02
# of objects on SIPPs	374	1094	1811	2519	3209	3903
time overhead of indicator checking (s)	0.004	7.033	18.149	31.159	60.932	76.497
total overhead (s)	52.26	142.30	350.90	726.58	1291.95	2089.31
syscall generation speed (KB/s)	1.02	1.027	1.034	1.033	1.032	1.034
data analysis speed (KB/s)	5.839	6.498	4.418	2.985	2.157	1.634
storage size (raw)(MB)	2.731	8.189	13.65	19.107	24.568	30.026
storage size (compressed)(MB)	0.298	0.903	1.514	2.118	2.722	3.333

during which system calls are collected and analyzed. All the evaluation results in this subsection use the arithmetic mean averaging over 10 runs of tests.

Impact of Time Window Size. We set the time window size to values from 5 mins to 55 mins. Table 2 illustrates the statistics of Patrol data analysis for SSH server. To get overhead under heavy workload, requests were loaded to SSH Server at the speed of 1 request per 5 seconds. Data analysis spends time mainly on SODG generation, SIPPs identification and shadow indicator checking. Fig. 8 plots the time overheads. The results show that SODG generation dominates the time overhead, and its computation cost increases approximately quadratic with the time window size. The time overheads of SIPPs identification and shadow indicator checking tend to be linear and relatively much smaller. Fig. 9 shows that the speed of Patrol data analysis is maximized when time window size is *15 mins*. This speed is far beyond the system call generation. We also noticed that the caused latency is about *2.37 mins*, and the storage requirement is about *0.085 GB/day*. Today's hard disk is large enough to accommodate this substantial amount of log traffic. Considering the test is done in quite request-intensive workload, both the time and storage overheads are reasonable. We therefore determine the time window size for the test-bed network to be 15 mins.

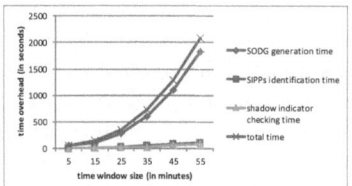

Fig. 8. Time overhead of Patrol data analysis varying with time window size

Fig. 9. Patrol data analysis speed vs. system call generation speed

The above results are theoretically supported. SODG generation checks each existing object to avoid duplication before adding new objects. Hence, the computational complexity of SODG generation can be $O(|v|^2)$. The SIPPs identification is using the BFS algorithm, thus its time complexity is $O(|v| + |e|)$ [26],

Table 3. Comparison results between filtered and unfiltered data analysis

	SSH Server		NFS Server		Workstation 1	
filtered/unfiltered	filtered	unfiltered	filtered	unfiltered	filtered	unfiltered
# of syscalls in log	22249	82133	11761	14944	21722	46043
time overhead on SODG(s)	58.38	1812.966	42.286	48.447	51.012	101.138
# of objects	650	15960	34	210	604	1007
# of processes	230	273	7	121	106	138
# of files	248	15515	17	79	473	844
# of sockets	171	171	10	10	23	23
# of dependencies	18697	97805	11813	15056	19649	43712

where $|v|$ and $|e|$ are respectively the number of nodes and edges in SODG. The shadow indicator checking checks each object and dependency of SIPPs in worst case, therefore its complexity is also $O(|v'| + |e'|)$, where $|v'|$ and $|e'|$ are respectively the number of nodes and edges in SIPPs.

Impact of Filtering Preprocessing. Table 3 summarizes the SODG generation time with filtering enabled and disabled respectively. The results show that unfiltered data costs more time than filtered data. The worst case overhead is the unfiltered SODG generation for SSH Server. It spent about half an hour. The large overhead is mainly because the algorithm checks each existing object to avoid duplication before adding new objects. When the system object number reaches very high, such as *15960* in this case, the time cost rises very quickly. We also noticed that among these objects, the number of files is extremely large as *15515*. The filtered SODG generation costs less than one minute because a large number of these files are effectively pruned by filtering rules.

5.4 Performance Overhead

We use LMBench [36] to measure the performance impact of Patrol on individual core kernel system calls. The outputs show that the addon overhead of most modified system calls in Patrol is within 10%. Some of them are even working with negligible overhead, such as *sys_read* and *sys_write*. The worst case overhead is 52.7% for *sys_stat* and 175% for *sys_fstat*. These results are to be expected, because of the relatively small amount of work done in each call compared to the work of recording OS-aware object information. For example, 175% is larger than 52.7% because of the smaller denominator, but in both cases the imposed overhead was equally 0.3-0.4 microseconds. The common case is much better.

We use UnixBench to measure the slow-down of the whole system that orchestrates the above individual system calls together. The outputs show that the performance overhead of Patrol is 20.8% for the whole system, with larger overhead to I/O-intensive applications than CPU-intensive applications. We also use kernel decompression and kernel compilation to measure the system performance of Patrol in intensive workload. The results show that the two workloads impose 15.93% overhead and 20.34% overhead on the system.

5.5 Scalability

Regarding the scalability, let's consider the main overhead imposed on bandwidth, SODG generation and SIPPs identification for an enterprise network equipped with 10000 hosts, 10 GB/s network bandwidth and a HPC cluster of 640 processor cores (20 processors with 32 cores per processor).

With converging traffic from hosts to the cluster, the bandwidth cost will be about 10000 times the system call generation speed for each host. Taking the speed 1.027 KB/s from Table 2, the *bandwidth overhead* is about 10.029 MB/s which only occupies less than 1% of total bandwidth.

The SODG generation costs time mainly on per-host SODG generation which is a parallelizable task ($\alpha=0$ in Equation 1). Given the data collected in 1 time window, the *SODG generation time* for 10000 hosts is estimated to be 28.35 minutes according to the following Gustafson's law, taking single-host SODG generation overhead as 108.88 seconds from Table 2.

$$\frac{t_1}{t_p} = p - \alpha(p - 1) = \alpha + p(1 - \alpha) \tag{1}$$

where p is the number of processors for parallel computing, α is the fraction of running time a program spends on non-parallelizable parts, t_1 is the execution time of the sequential algorithm, and t_p is the execution time with maximum speed-up under parallelization of the program.

SIPPs identification from a trigger node is non-parallelizable ($\alpha=1$) due to the sequential nature of dependency tracking. Hence, the SIPPs identification time increases linearly with the host-length of SIPPs (l). Its maximum can be estimated by constructing service dependency transitive closure ("host A can reach host B through one or more service dependencies") in enterprise network. Let's suppose $l=100$, and the *SIPPs identification time* will be about 12.57 minutes, taking time overhead of single-host SIPPs identification as 7.54 seconds from Table 2. SIPPs identification from different trigger nodes and branching in SIPPs identification can be done in parallel. As long as the number of trigger nodes and branches don't exceed p, SIPPs identification can be easily handled within 12.57 minutes. We make conservative estimation by $\alpha=1$, hence the efficiency for parallel computing can be better in reality than estimated.

6   Related Work

Patrol draws inspirations from previous research such as system call-based intrusion detection and system object dependency tracking.

System calls are used in pioneer works by Forrest et al. [11] and Lee et al. [12] for intrusion detection. System call-based IDS mainly leverages statistical properties of system call sequence [13] [14] and system call arguments [16] [17]. Bhatkar et al. further takes into account the temporal properties involving arguments of different system calls [18]. Instead of providing individual intrusion alerts, the aim of Patrol is to identify zero-day attack paths through network-wide dependencies parsed from system calls. These paths provide network-wide attack context, and help detect unknown vulnerability exploitations.

System object dependency tracking is first proposed by King et al. [23] to automatically identify sequences of intrusion steps. The follow-up works [37] [38] further propose to integrate system object dependency tracking and alert correlation techniques. Given a large number of existing IDS alerts, these works target on identifying their correlations. In contrast, Patrol takes an inverse strategy to first identify SIPPs hidden in the network-wide SODG, and then recognize unknown vulnerability exploitations on these paths.

7   Discussion and Conclusion

In addition to the promising potentials, the current version of Patrol may face challenges such as 1) If an attack path goes through a victim machine hosting kernel mode service like nfs-kernel-server, Patrol may lose trace halfway since it relies on system call interface; 2) If an attack is a long-term attack, Patrol may successfully capture its intrusion propagation paths at different time spans, but fail to correlate them.

In conclusion, this paper identifies the problem of zero-day attack paths in practical network defense. This paper proposes a prototype system named Patrol. By building a network-wide system object dependency graph, identifying suspicious intrusion propagation paths in it, and recognizing shadow indicators on these paths, Patrol can dig out the zero-day attack paths at runtime.

Acknowledgments. We want to thank the anonymous reviewers for their valuable and helpful comments. This work was supported by ARO W911NF-09-1-0525 (MURI), NSF CNS-0905131, AFOSR W911NF1210055, and ARO MURI project "Adversarial and Uncertain Reasoning for Adaptive Cyber Defense: Building the Scientific Foundation".

References

1. Sheyner, O., Haines, J., Jha, S.: Automated generation and analysis of attack graphs. IEEE Oakland (2002)
2. Jajodia, S., Noel, S., O'Berry, B.: Topological analysis of network attack vulnerability. Managing Cyber Threats: Issues, Approaches and Challanges (2003)
3. Ou, X., Govindavajhala, S., Appel, A.W.: MulVAL: A logic-based network security analyzer. In: USENIX Security (2005)
4. Wang, L., Jajodia, S., Singhal, A., Cheng, P., Noel, S.: k-Zero day safety: A network security metric for measuring the risk of unknown vulnerabilities. In: TDSC (2013)
5. Albanese, M., Jajodia, S., Singhal, A., Wang, L.: An efficient approach to assessing the risk of zero-day vulnerabilities. In: SECRYPT (2013)
6. Long, J.: Google Hacking for Penetration Testers. Syngress (2007)
7. McClure, S.: Hacking Exposed: Network Security Secrets and Solutions. McGraw-Hill (2009)
8. Network Penetration Testing. MosaicSecurity.com.
https://mosaicsecurity.com/categories

9. Debar, H., Wespi, A.: Aggregation and correlation of intrusion-detection alerts. In: Lee, W., Mé, L., Wespi, A. (eds.) RAID 2001. LNCS, vol. 2212, pp. 85–103. Springer, Heidelberg (2001)
10. Valdes, A., Skinner, K.: Probabilistic alert correlation. In: Lee, W., Mé, L., Wespi, A. (eds.) RAID 2001. LNCS, vol. 2212, pp. 54–68. Springer, Heidelberg (2001)
11. Forrest, S., Hofmeyr, S.A., Somayaji, A., Longstaff, T.A.: A sense of self for unix processes. IEEE Oakland (1996)
12. Lee, W., Stolfo, S.J., Chan, P.K.: Learning patterns from unix process execution traces for intrusion detection. In: AI Approaches to Fraud Detection and Risk Management (1997)
13. Kosoresow, A.P., Hofmeyer, S.A.: Intrusion detection via system call traces. IEEE Software (1997)
14. Hofmeyr, S.A., Forrest, S., Somayaji, A.: Intrusion detection using sequences of system calls. Journal of Computer Security (1998)
15. Wagner, D., Dean, D.: Intrusion Detection via Static Analysis. IEEE Oakland (2001)
16. Kruegel, C., Mutz, D., Valeur, F., Vigna, G.: On the detection of anomalous system call arguments. In: Snekkenes, E., Gollmann, D. (eds.) ESORICS 2003. LNCS, vol. 2808, pp. 326–343. Springer, Heidelberg (2003)
17. Tandon, G., Chan, P.: Learning rules from system call arguments and sequences for anomaly detection. In: ICDM DMSEC (2003)
18. Bhatkar, S., Chaturvedi, A., Sekar, R.: Dataflow anomaly detection. IEEE Oakland (2006)
19. Sekar, R., Gupta, A., Frullo, J., Shanbhag, T.: Specification-based Anomaly Detection: A New Approach for Detecting Network Intrusions. In: ACM CCS (2002)
20. Ko, C., Ruschitzka, M., Levitt, K.: Execution Monitoring of Security-Critical Programs in Distributed Systems: A Specification-Based Approach. IEEE Oakland (1997)
21. Snort. Sourcefire, Inc., http://www.snort.org
22. Tripwire. Tripwire, Inc., http://www.tripwire.com
23. King, S.T., Chen, P.M.: Backtracking intrusions. In: ACM SOSP (2003)
24. Xiong, X., Jia, X., Liu, P.: Shelf: Preserving business continuity and availability in an intrusion recovery system. In: ACSAC (2009)
25. Goel, A., Po, K., Farhadi, K., Li, Z., de Lara, E.: The taser intrusion recovery system. In: ACM SOSP (2005)
26. Knuth, D.E.: The Art Of Computer Programming (1997)
27. CWE. MITRE, http://cwe.mitre.org
28. CAPEC. MITRE, http://capec.mitre.org
29. Graphviz, http://www.graphviz.org
30. Nessus. Tenable Network Security, http://www.tenable.com
31. Oval. MITRE, http://oval.mitre.org
32. Wireshark. Wireshark Foundation, http://www.wireshark.org
33. Ntop, http://www.ntop.org
34. Bilge, L., Dumitras, T.: An Empirical Study of Zero-Day Attacks In The Real World. In: ACM CCS (2012)
35. NVD. MITRE, http://nvd.nist.gov
36. McVoy, L.W., Staelin, C.: lmbench: Portable Tools for Performance Analysis. In: USENIX (1996)
37. King, S.T., Mao, Z.M., Lucchetti, D.G., Chen, P.M.: Enriching intrusion alerts through multi-host causality. In: NDSS (2005)
38. Zhai, Y., Ning, P., Xu, J.: Integrating IDS alert correlation and OS-Level dependency tracking. In: IEEE Intelligence and Security Informatics (2006)

Appendix

Table 4. Statistics for the 3-host SODG and SIPPs in Fig 2

metrics	SSH Server	NFS Server	Workstation 1
time window size (in minutes)	15	15	15
# of syscalls in unfiltered log	82133	14944	46043
# of syscalls in filtered log	22249	11761	21722
growth rate of compressed syscall log (GB/day)	0.126	0.019	0.065
# of objects in graph	650	34	604
# of processes in graph	230	7	106
# of files in graph	248	17	473
# of sockets in graph	171	10	23
# of dependencies in graph	18697	11813	19649
# of inter-host dependencies from last host in graph	50	11	1
# of inter-host dependencies to next host in graph	1	11	0
average indegree/outdegree in graph	29	347	33
max indegree in graph	8640	8478	12909
object index of max indegree in graph	543	661	1123
max outdegree in graph	9908	8294	12784
object index of max outdegree in graph	225	663	1153
# of objects in SIPPs	26	6	143
# of processes in SIPPs	8	1	62
# of files in SIPPs	3	2	75
# of sockets in SIPPs	15	3	5
# of dependencies in SIPPs	8905	11664	4059
# of inter-host dependencies from last host in SIPPs	14	1	1
# of inter-host dependencies to next host in SIPPs	1	8	0
average indegree/outdegree in SIPPs	343	1944	28
max indegree in SIPPs	8581	8442	410
object index of max indegree in SIPPs	543	661	808
max outdegree in SIPPs	8686	8280	2373
object index of max outdegree in SIPPs	225	663	783

Measuring and Detecting Malware Downloads in Live Network Traffic

Phani Vadrevu[1], Babak Rahbarinia[1], Roberto Perdisci[1,2],
Kang Li[1], and Manos Antonakakis[3]

[1] Dept. of Computer Science, University of Georgia, Athens, GA, USA
[2] School of Computer Science, Georgia Institute of Technology, Atlanta, GA, USA
[3] Damballa, Inc.
{vadrevu,babak,perdisci,kangli}@cs.uga.edu, manos@damballa.com

Abstract. In this paper, we present AMICO, a novel system for measuring and detecting malware downloads in live web traffic. AMICO learns to distinguish between malware and benign file downloads from the *download behavior* of the network users themselves. Given a labeled dataset of past benign and malware file downloads, AMICO learns a *provenance classifier* that can accurately detect future malware downloads based on information about where the downloads originated from. The main intuition is that to avoid current countermeasures, malware campaigns need to use an "agile" distribution infrastructure, e.g., frequently changing the domains and/or IPs of the malware download servers. We engineer a number of statistical features that aim to capture these fundamental characteristics of malware distribution campaigns.

We have deployed AMICO at the edge of a large academic network for almost nine months, where we continuously witness hundreds of new malware downloads per week, including many *zero-days*. We show that AMICO is able to accurately detect malware downloads with up to 90% true positives at a false positives rate of 0.1% and can detect zero-day malware downloads, thus providing an effective way to complement current malware detection tools.

1   Introduction

Drive-by downloads and social engineering attacks have become one of the most prevalent ways through which machines are compromised with malicious software, or *malware* [10, 17, 19]. As a consequence, by simply browsing the Web, users (or their browsers) may be either forced or lured to download and run malware samples, effectively relinquishing control of their machines to the attackers.

Users often rely on host-based anti-virus software (AVs) to protect themselves from malware infections. However, it is known that AVs are only partially effective due to the sophisticated code polymorphism techniques adopted by malware authors, and are not capable of protecting users from the latest threats [13]. To compensate for this detection gap, modern browsers make use of URL blacklists, such as Google Safe Browsing [8] (GSB). Essentially, GSB maintains a large list

J. Crampton, S. Jajodia, and K. Mayes (Eds.): ESORICS 2013, LNCS 8134, pp. 556–573, 2013.
© Springer-Verlag Berlin Heidelberg 2013

of domain names and URLs that are known to be related to malware downloads. Therefore, every time the user visits a URL, before the browser fetches the URL content, the GSB API is queried. If the URL is blacklisted, the browser stops loading the URL's content and the user will be notified, thus preventing a possible malware download. Unfortunately, by nature, static blacklists such as GSB also lag behind the threat, and suffer from a non-negligible number of false negatives, as we show in Section 4.6.

In this paper, we present AMICO[1], a novel system for measuring and detecting malware downloads in live web traffic using *download provenance* information (see Figure 1). Every time a network user downloads an executable file (we limit ourselves to Windows executables, in the current implementation), AMICO performs an on-the-fly reconstruction of the download from the network traffic, and copies the file to a download history database. In addition, the database stores information regarding *who* (i.e., what and how many machines) downloaded the file and *where* the download came from. By leveraging the (partial) ground truth provided by existing AV tools, we can label some of these downloads as either malware or benign. Using these labeled download events collected during an initial training period, AMICO learns the *provenance characteristics* of past malware and benign executable files from the *download behavior* of the network users themselves. This allows us to build a statistical classifier that, given a new file download and its related provenance information, is able to accurately classify whether the downloaded file is likely to be malicious or not. Unlike traditional AV products, AMICO does not rely on searching for signs of malicious code in the content of the downloaded files. Furthermore, the classification is performed independently of whether third-party detection results may exist about the new downloads, and can therefore be used to *complement existing malware defense* techniques (see Section 3 for details).

The intuitions that motivate us to leverage provenance information for detecting malware downloads are as follows. To avoid signature-based AV detection, malware authors make heavy use of code polymorphism. Therefore, victim machines infected with the same malware may in fact have downloaded different "variants" of the same malware file. Consequently, a given malware file may be downloaded by only few machines. On the other hand, benign executable files are fairly "stable", and change only when a new release version is available. Therefore, benign files may be downloaded, in time, by several different clients.

Furthermore, to avoid static blacklists, malware distribution sites need to frequently relocate. For example, the attacker may register a large set of domain names that point to the distribution site. This allows for "advertising" the malware downloads (e.g., though email spam, drive-by download exploit servers, etc.) from frequently changing domains. Similarly, the IP address of the malware distribution server may periodically change (although more slowly, compared to the domain changes). On the other hand, benign executable files are typically hosted at professionally-operated service providers with a fairly stable domain

---

[1] <u>A</u>ccurate <u>M</u>alware <u>I</u>dentification via <u>C</u>lassification of live network traffic <u>O</u>bservations.

name and network infrastructure. Even when the benign files are distributed via content delivery networks (CDNs), both the domain name (especially the second-level domain) and the IP address or BGP prefix of the distribution server may be fairly stable, especially with respect to download requests originating from the same local network. This causes malware downloads to have a download source "footprint" that is noticeably different from benign downloads.

Once deployed, for each new executable file download event AMICO measures a number of provenance features specifically engineering to capture the above observations, and is able to accurately classify the downloads into benign or malicious. Notice also that while our current implementation of AMICO is designed to monitor the traffic from the edge of a network, nothing prevents us from deploying AMICO "within" a web proxy (e.g., using the ICAP protocol (RFC 3507)). This may be particularly useful in enterprise network environments, which typically already deploy a web proxy, and often perform SSL man-in-the-middle[2] to enable fine-grained inspection of encrypted traffic. This would allow AMICO to also observe possible file downloads over HTTPS, further increasing its coverage.

In summary, we make the following contributions:

- We present AMICO, a novel system that aims to efficiently measure and detect malware downloads in live network traffic. In contrast to static blacklists, AMICO builds a provenance classifier that can dynamically and accurately detect malware samples based on the download behavior of the network users.
- We have deployed AMICO at the edge of a large academic network serving tens of thousands of users for almost nine months. Our measurements show that, in spite of the widespread use of malware URL blacklists in modern browsers, we continuously witness hundreds of new malware downloads per week, including many zero-days. Surprisingly, a non-negligible number of malware downloads originate from even the most popular websites.
- We perform an extensive evaluation of AMICO's malware detection capabilities. The experimental results show that our provenance classifier is able to accurately detect malware downloads with up to 90% true positives at a false positives rate of 0.1%.

2   Related Work

Malware Detection: Oberheide et al. [13] highlight the limitations of signature-based AV tools, and propose a new system called CloudAV that leverages a combination of AV tools to improve malware detection coverage. Some researchers have proposed to improve the detection of malware file content using statistical machine learning techniques [9, 14, 15], rather than signature matching. Others have focused on measuring specific types of malware distribution tactics, such as rogue AV campaigns and pay-per-install (PPI) operations, or on measuring and

---

[2] For example, http://crypto.stanford.edu/ssl-mitm/

detecting drive-by malware downloads [5–7, 10, 16, 17, 21]. Our work is different, because we do not focus on the file content or drive-by downloads. Rather, AMICO aims to detect malware downloads in general by inspecting network traffic in real-time, and by leveraging download provenance information.

Domain Reputation: A number of systems that aim to detect malicious, low-reputation domain names have been proposed [2, 3]. These systems are able to detect malicious domains in general (e.g., spam domains, phishing sites, malware download sites, etc.), with particular emphasis on malware command-and-control (C&C) domains. Our work is different, because we specifically aim to detect malware file downloads. We correlate many different features that go beyond domain names and the IP addresses they resolve to, such as the file download features, URL features, and download request features. Furthermore, in Section 4.3 we show that domain reputation systems by themselves are not sufficient to accurately detect malware downloads.

Google CAMP: CAMP [18] detects malware domains based on a reputation score computed over a number properties of the download source (e.g., the domain name of the download server, the server IP, etc.). Although, AMICO and CAMP share similar goals, our AMICO system differs in many important aspects from CAMP. First of all, AMICO is *browser agnostic*, whereas CAMP is built within Google Chrome, and can only monitor downloads from Chrome users[3]. More importantly, CAMP is a *closed-source service*: all download information and decision rules are "owned" by Google, and a network administrator has no easy way to gain a complete picture about executable file downloads happening in his/her network. On the other hand, AMICO was designed to exactly fulfill this network admins' need, by offering *network-wide information about what clients in the monitored traffic are downloading malware files and from where*. This enables the administrators to promptly respond to security incidents and limit potential damage to other network assets. Furthermore, unlike in CAMP, by deploying AMICO the information about what machines may be infected will not leave the local network. This may be particularly important in highly sensitive enterprise or government networks, where shipping information such as visited URLs, downloaded files, and potential malware infections to a third-party may pose risks to the reputation of the institutions that operates the network.

AMICO and CAMP also differ with respect to their technical approach. For example, we measure several statistical features that are not used in CAMP, and empoly a different, machine-learning-based approach.

3   System Description

In this section, we discuss the internals of our system. AMICO consists of three main components, shown in Figure 1: (1) the *download reconstruction* module, (2) the *download history* database, and (3) the *provenance classifier*. In the following, we provide details on how these components work.

---

[3] It appears that Microsoft may also have built a similar proprietary system specific to IE9 [12], although we were not able to find its technical details.

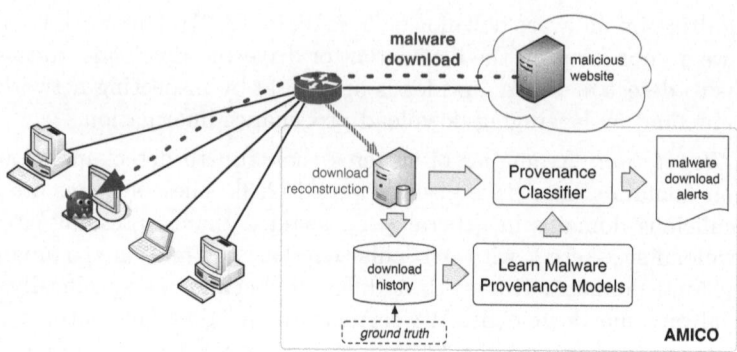

Fig. 1. AMICO System Overview

3.1 Reconstruction of Executable Files

The *download reconstruction* module aims to inspect all web traffic, and extract a copy of Microsoft Windows executable files that are being downloaded by the network users. To this end, AMICO monitors all traffic at the edge of a network, and performs efficient real-time TCP flow reconstruction using a custom-built multi-threaded software component. As TCP flows are being reconstructed, a traffic identification module keeps track of all HTTP flows, and discards the remaining non-HTTP traffic. HTTP request-response pairs are reconstructed on-the-fly, and the responses are inspected to determine whether they carry a portable executable (PE) file [11]. Every time a PE file is detected, AMICO copies the reconstructed response on persistent memory, along with the related HTTP request and some additional information, such as source and destination IPs and ports, and a timestamp. Sensitive information, such as source IP addresses, cookies, and certain HTTP headers, are either anonymized or removed outright, in accordance with policies set forth by our Institutional Review Board.

3.2 Download History Database

The *download history* database stores all information gathered by the download reconstruction module. In our current implementation, as soon as a downloaded file is stored, AMICO computes the SHA1 hash of the file and automatically queries VirusTotal (VT) [1], to determine whether the file had ever been scanned before and was found to be malicious by any AV. This is done merely for convenience, to avoid acquiring and running multiple local AV scanners.

It is important to notice that the information obtained from the AVs is necessary to build the ground truth used to label *past* download events and train the provenance classifier, as discussed in Section 3.3. However, to this end AMICO only submits the hash of downloaded files to VT, and does not need to submit the URL and `Referer` of the download events, which may be considered as more sensitive by the network administrator.

Notice also that if submitting the file hashes to a third-party services such as VT still represents a concern, the network administrator can "conceal" the origin of the file hashes by submitting them through a proxy located in a separate network. In alternative, submitting the file hashes can be avoided completely by scanning the downloaded files locally, using multiple different AV products. In this latter configuration, AMICO would prevent any leakage of information from the monitored network to third-parties.

3.3 Provenance Classifier

The provenance classifier aims to complement AV-based malware detection, by identifying malicious file downloads based on *how the file was downloaded*, rather than how the file "looks". To this end, we extract a number of provenance features that aim to capture the following facts: Has any of the network users ever downloaded the same file in the past? Has any executable file been downloaded from this domain name, server IP address, BGP prefix, etc.? If so, were the previously downloaded files malicious (or at least suspicious)?

We first give a description of the detection features used by AMICO, and then describe how the provenance classifier can be trained and deployed.

Provenance Features. Let e be an executable file download event occurred at time t_e. Also, let F_e be the downloaded file, $Host_e$ be the domain name associated with the HTTP request for the file, URL_e be the URL of the request (i.e., the file path, file name, query string, etc.), and $ServIP_e$ be the IP address of the server from which the file was downloaded. We translate each such event into a *feature vector* $\vec{v}_e$ as follows. We first consider only *past* download events, namely events occurred at any time $t < t_e$, and measure the following main groups of features (a complete list of features is given in Appendix):

- **Past file downloads**: We measure four different features as follows: the number of times that the file F_e was downloaded in the past (we use the file's SHA1 to compute this more efficiently); the (estimated) number of distinct clients that downloaded that file; how many days ago was F_e downloaded for the first time; and how many times per day (in average) the client machines in the monitored network downloaded the same file F_e.
  Intuition: Many benign executable files are downloaded, in time, by several different clients. Also, their hash is typically very "stable" and only changes after a new version release. On the other hand, due to heavy polymorphism applied by malware developers to evade signature-based AV detection, the hash of a given malware will change frequently. Consequently, the same malware file will typically be downloaded by only few victims.
- **Domain features**: Let d_e be the domain name related to the download request, and let $2LD(d_e)$ be its effective second-level domain[4]. Overall, we

---

[4] For example, 2LD(www.bbc.co.uk) = bbc.co.uk. To compute the effective 2LDs we use the Mozilla public suffix list (`publicsuffix.org`) augmented with a large list of second-level domains related to dynamic-DNS providers.

measure a set of twenty-four features, twelve of which are related to past download events from d_e, and another twelve related to past downloads from any domain under $2LD(d_e)$ (i.e., any domain that matches $*.2LD(d_e)$). For example, we measure how many confirmed malware samples had been previously downloaded from d_e; the number of confirmed benign files from the same domain; the ratio between malware and benign downloads; the total number of executable downloads from d_e (including the "unknown" files that cannot be labeled either way), the average number of AV labels for the confirmed malware samples (i.e., how many different AVs flagged the file as malware), etc. We measure similar features for $2LD(d_e)$.

Intuition: To avoid static blacklists, attackers often register many different domain names that can be used to "advertise" the malware downloads. Each malware download domain is typically used for a short amount of time before it is replaced with a new one, and may therefore serve only a small number of malware downloads to a few victims. On the other hand, benign executable files are typically hosted at professionally-run service providers, and their server's domain names (or their second-level domains) are usually very stable, serving the same benign files to potentially many clients. Our domain features attempt to capture such intuitions.

- **Server IP features**: In a way similar to the *domain features*, we measure twenty-four different features, twelve of which are related to the $ServIP_e$ and another twelve to its BGP prefix, $BGP(ServIP_e)$. For example, we measure how many confirmed malware samples had been previously downloaded from $ServIP_e$; the number of confirmed benign files from the same IP; the ratio between malware and benign downloads; etc. We repeat the same measurements for $BGP(ServIP_e)$.

Intuition: While malware samples are heavily polymorphic, the network infrastructure used to distribute different variants of the same malware is usually somewhat more stable. This is particularly true for the server IP from which the downloads originated. In fact, while the attackers have a good level of flexibility regarding registering new domain names to be used for malware distribution, it is more difficult to change IP addresses with high frequency. Therefore, we may see more than one malware download from the same server IP, or the same BGP prefix.

- **URL features**: Given the URL_e related to the download, we only consider its path, file, and query string (i.e., we don't consider the domain name as being part of the URL). From URL_e we measure six different features. For example, we measure the number of total past file downloads that share the same URL, the number of confirmed distinct files downloaded form that URL, and the number of confirmed malware samples. Because URLs may change frequently, especially if they contain name-value pairs in the query string, we also measure similar features related to the *URL structure*. For example, one way to derive the URL structure is to replace all alphanumeric characters with wildcards, keeping special characters such as '/', '.', '?', '=', '&', ':', ';',etc. We can then measure the total number of past downloads that share the same URL structure, the number of confirmed malware, etc.

Intuition: The intuition here is that, unlike for benign downloads, malware URLs may change frequently to avoid blacklists. Furthermore, we noticed several malware distribution campaigns that advertise many different download URLs with a similar "anomalous" structure, compared to URLs used in benign file downloads. Therefore, if the current download's URL_e has the same structure as URLs used in several past malware download, we should increase the likelihood that URL_e is also related to a malware download. Our URL features attempt to capture these observations.

– **Download request features**: In addition to the features described above, which *look into the past*, we measure five different features that *look at the present* single download event e. We check whether the header of the HTTP request that initiated the download contained a valid domain name in the Host field, and whether a Referer URL was or not present. Also, we consider the file extension (if any) extracted from the URL_e as a feature, and we measure the total length of the URL and the "depth" for the URL path (e.g., /a/b/c/d.exe has a depth of four).

   Intuition: These features are justified by the fact that we empirically observed many cases in which malware download requests do not carry any Referer string, or may report an IP address in the Host filed, instead of a domain. Also, the URLs for malware downloads often "look" visually different from the URLs related to benign downloads (e.g., the URL may have a .gif or .jpg extension, although it serves an executable file). The download request features attempt to capture these observations.

It is worth noting that none of the features (or groups of features) described above are sufficient by themselves to accurately distinguish between malware-related and benign file downloads. However, as we show in Section 4, each group provides a meaningful contribution. Furthermore, in combination they yield high classification accuracy. In Section 4, we also show that the overall accuracy does not heavily depend on one single group of features. In turn, this makes AMICO more robust to evasion, because an attacker would need to evade different types of features at the same time, as discussed more in details in Section 5. In addition, evading some groups of features such as the server IP and domain features, may require the attacker to make heavy changes to her malware distribution infrastructure, thus causing the attacker to incur a significant cost.

Training and Deploying the Classifier. To build the provenance classifier, so that AMICO can automatically distinguish between benign and malware downloads, we take a supervised learning approach. That is, we first collect a set of *labeled* executable file download events, and use this initial *training set* to learn the malware provenance models, as shown in Figure 1. The process used to label the download events is described in Section 4.2.

The training phase proceeds in two high-level steps. We first monitor the network traffic for a period of time T_f (one month, in our experiments), and record a "bootstrap" set of download events. Essentially, the information collected during T_f allows us to measure our detection features over new download events (i.e., events that occur after T_f). After this initial T_f period, we are ready to collect new downloads and compute the feature vectors necessary for training the provenance classifier. To this end, we collect new download events for an additional period of time T_{train} (two months, in our experiments). For each new download event e at time t_e, we compute the related features using information about all downloads observed until $t < t_e$. We label the download events gathered during T_{train} for which ground truth is available (see Section 3.2), and use their feature vectors to train the *provenance classifier*.

Once the classifier is trained, any new executable file downloaded after $(T_f + T_{train})$ can be translated into a feature vector and classified by AMICO into either *malware* or *benign* using the provenance classifier. Specifically, for each new download event e, the classifier will output a *malware score*, $s(e)$. If the score $s(e)$ is greater than a given threshold, AMICO labels the downloaded file as *malware*, and raises an alert (e.g., notifies the network administrator). The detection threshold can be chosen during training to produce the desired trade-off between true and false positives. In Section 4 we show that AMICO can achieve high true positives even at very low false positive rates.

It is important to notice that for each download event e observed at time t_e, we extract its features by *looking back at past downloads and their related past ground truth*. Namely, we only consider information about downloads observed at any time $t < t_e$. To classify the new event e, we rely solely on the output of the provenance classifier, and do not use any information from external sources about e itself. Specifically, we do not consider any information that may be obtained from VirusTotal or GSB about e. In Section 4.6, we show that AMICO can in fact complement popular AV- or blacklist-based malware defense tools, because it can detect many malware downloads missed by third-party systems.

4   Evaluation

4.1   Implementation and Deployment

We implemented AMICO using different languages. We custom-built the download reconstruction module in C, to achieve high efficiency. Preliminary performance experiments show that one single instance of the reconstruction module can sustain over 300Mbps of traffic on commodity hardware. However, a machine with a multi-core CPU can run multiple instances independently on different network interfaces. For example, in our experiments, we run two instances of the reconstruction module that receive traffic from two different traffic mirroring sources on the same machine. We are currently monitoring over 600Mbps of traffic (during peak time) from the campus-wide WiFi network of our entire academic institution. The datasets and experiments we discuss below are derived from approximately nine months of traffic, from July 2012 to March 2013.

The components of AMICO used to store the download events, extract the detection features, and collect the ground truth, are written in Python. To build the provenance classifier we use the *Random Forest* algorithm [4] implemented in Weka [20], because it can be trained very efficiently and performs competitively compared to more complex algorithms. Our prototype implementation

of AMICO is available under open-source license at http://www.cs.uga.edu/
~perdisci/amico/.

4.2   Experimental Setup

Measuring the Detection Features. To measure the detection features used
by AMICO, we follow the definitions given in Section 3.3. It is worth remembering that some features measure things such as the number of malware, benign,
and total samples downloaded *in the past* from a given domain name or server
IP address, for example. To label past download events we proceed as follows.
During deployment, for each file download captured by AMICO, we compute its
SHA1 hash, and immediately submit the hash to VirusTotal (VT). If VT returns
"unknown" as an answer, i.e., nobody has ever submitted a file with that hash
before, we mark the downloaded file as *unknown to VT*. It is worth remembering
here that, as we discussed in Section 3.2, if submitting the file hashes to a third-
party system such as VT was a concern, we could simply scan the downloaded
files *locally* using multiple different AVs. In our current prototype, we chose to
rely on VT mainly because it made our system deployment easier.

Every file analyzed by VT is scanned with more than 40 different AV products.
However, we noticed that some of the AV scanners produced a non-negligible
number of false positives (e.g., marking some well known benign executable files
as malware). We noticed this was especially true for less well-known AV products.
Therefore, we decided to consider a "trusted" subset of nine AV products[5] that
are very well known, and cover a large AV market share. Given this set of trusted
AVs, we use the following labeling rules on VT's results:

Labeling Rules
1) if the SHA1 of the file was not present in VT, label the file as *unknown
to VT*, otherwise
2) label the file as *malware* if two or more "trusted" AVs flagged the file
as malware;
3) label the file as *benign* if none of the AVs (either trusted or non-
trusted) flagged the file as malware;
4) label the file as *suspicious* in all other cases.

Notice that when measuring the features from a new download event e observed at time t_e, we only use the labels obtained from VT's output over *past*
download events, i.e., at any time $t < t_e$. In other words, we do not use any
third-party information (from AVs or blacklists) related to e itself.

Establishing the Ground Truth. To evaluate the results of our deployment
of AMICO, we need to collect *clean*, reliable ground truth that contains as little
noise as possible. To achieve this goal, we proceed as follows. If a download was
labeled as *unknown to VT*, we submit the file ourselves to VT (we only submit
samples that pass a number of privacy-preservation criteria). For each sample

---

[5] Avast, AVG, McAfee, F-Secure, Kaspersky, Sophos, Microsoft, TrendMicro, and Symantec.

that was either already present in VT or submitted by us, after one month time we send a "re-scan" request to VT, so that the same file is scanned again by all AVs. The intuition is that it may take some time for AV companies to build signatures for new malware samples [13]. Therefore, even though a malware may be missed by the AVs at the time of submission, after one month it is likely that the AV companies may have developed the necessary detection signatures (we did observe several of such AV label changes during our study).

It is important to notice that the one-month VT re-scan procedure described earlier is used only for the purpose of collecting the ground truth "externally" to AMICO, to enable a more reliable evaluation of our system's accuracy. The re-scan information is not used for the purpose of measuring the statistical features used by the provenance classifier.

Cross-Validation Dataset (CVD). To collect the dataset of labeled downloads for cross-validation (see Section 4.4), we proceeded as follows. We first collected one month (T_f) of "bootstrap" download events, to enable the measurement of the detection features for future downloads. We then collected new download events and computed the related feature vectors for the remaining eight months. To label these feature vectors, we used the ground truth obtained as explained above. Overall, we obtained 55,396 *benign*, and 4,928 *malware* feature vectors (the *suspicious* samples are excluded from the cross-validation).

Training Dataset (TRD). Besides cross-validation tests, we also performed an evaluation of a real-world deployment of AMICO (see Section 4.5). To this end, we followed the guidelines discussed in Section 3.3. Like for **CVD**, we first collected one month (T_f) of initial download events. Then, we further collected new download events and the related feature vectors for the following two months (T_{train}), and we used these two-month data as a training dataset for the provenance classifier. To label the feature vectors in the training dataset, we used the ground truth gathered as explained earlier. Overall, the training data contained 16,074 *benign*, and 1,273 *malware* feature vectors.

Test Dataset (TSD). The test dataset consists of all download events collected after the first three months $(T_f + T_{train})$ necessary to gather the "bootstrap" download events and the training data. Essentially, this dataset consists of the last six months of download observations. Overall, the test dataset contained 39,322 *benign*, and 3,655 *malware* feature vectors.

4.3   Live Traffic Measurements

In this section we report a number of measurements on the traffic observed during the last six months of our deployment of AMICO. Notice that here we discuss findings related only to the *download reconstruction* module and *download history* database. We defer the evaluation of the provenance classifier (and the entire AMICO system) to Sections 4.4 and 4.5.

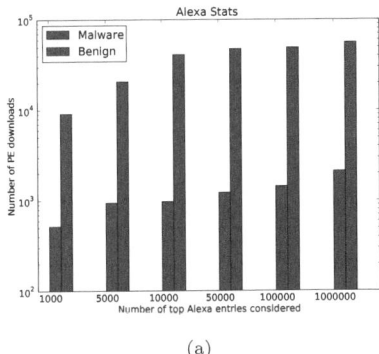
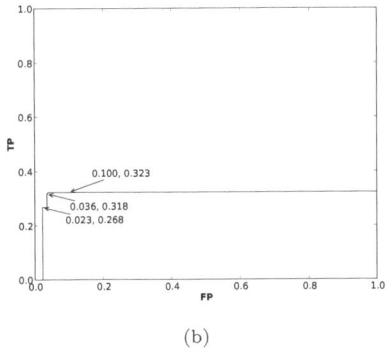

(a)   (b)

Fig. 2. Downloads from top Alexa domains (a); Detection results using Notos (b)

During deployment, our sensors observed web traffic from several thousands distinct source IP addresses per day within our network. Table 1 reports a number of statistics about the reconstructed download events. To label the downloads we applied the "clean" ground truth labeling rules discussed in Section 4.2. Overall, we observed an average of 24 confirmed malware downloads per day, 67 daily suspicious downloads, and 253 daily benign downloads.

Table 1. Overall live network download statistics for executable files

	Malware		Suspicious		Benign	
	Total	Daily Avg.	Total	Daily Avg.	Total	Daily Avg
Download events	5,326	24	15,665	67	59,988	253
Distinct files	1,893	12	2,879	38	5,849	112
Distinct domains	849	10	1,009	27	1,338	43
Distinct server IPs	1,009	6	2,186	41	2,776	59

Figure 2(a) reports the number of confirmed malware and benign downloads that we observed from the top 1,000, 5,000, 10,000, 100,000, and 1M most popular domains[6], according to Alexa (`alexa.com`). Surprisingly, we found that about 18% of all confirmed malware downloads originated from the top 10,000 domains, and we also observed 518 malware downloads originating from the top 1,000 domains. After investigating, we noticed that these malware samples were downloaded from websites related to software distribution, file sharing, and cloud services (e.g. `softonic.com`, `hotfile.com`, `amazonaws.com`, `cloudfront.net`, etc.). Furthermore, we found that 40% of the domains from which benign downloads originated were "unpopular" sites outside of the top 1M rank. These two facts make it difficult to implement a purely whitelist-based approach to preventing malware downloads, because such an approach would likely cause a non-negligible number of false positives and false negatives.

The above results may also have an impact on domain reputation systems. Therefore, we performed experiments to verify if dynamic domain reputation

---

[6] The list of domains we consider reports second-level domains.

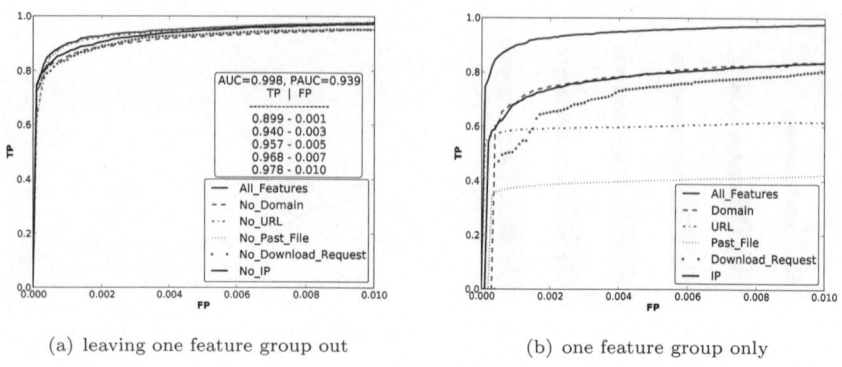

(a) leaving one feature group out   (b) one feature group only

Fig. 3. 10-fold cross-validation results (FPs in [0,1%])

systems, in particular Notos [2], would be sufficient to block malware downloads. To this end, we fed all (domain name, server IP) pairs related to the malware downloads observed by AMICO. We then queried Notos to obtain a reputation score for each such pair. By varying a detection threshold over Notos' scores, we obtained the ROC curve in Figure 2(b) (notice that the FP rate is in [0,1]). As we can see, Notos has a relatively low detection rate for malware download domains. The reason why the ROC in Figure 2(b) is flat, is because many samples were "rejected" by Notos and assigned a score of zero, because Notos did not have enough information to compute a reliable score. We believe this is due to the fact that the reputation system is "biased" towards accurately detecting malware command-and-control (C&C) domains, rather than malware download servers. It is also worth noting that the version of Notos we used was trained on domain reputation information from a different network environment, and this may be another cause for the relatively low detection rate.

From the above discussion we can extrapolate two important observations: (1) using only domain name information to detect malware downloads may not be sufficient; and (2) training on the traffic specific to the deployment environment may yield better detection results. This further motivates the approach taken by AMICO, which *learns many different types of features related to the download behavior of the users in the monitored live network.*

4.4 Cross-Validation

To evaluate AMICO's malware detection accuracy, we perform 10-fold cross-validation tests using the entire **CVD** data (see Section 4.2). Figure 3(a) shows the ROC curve we obtained by using all features, as well as the ROC curves obtained by removing one of the feature groups described in Section 3.3 at a time. Note that we only plot the *partial* ROC for false positive rates ranging from 0 to 1%, to highlight the classifier performance at low false positives. The small table embedded in Figure 3(a) provides the trade-off between the true positive

(TP) rate and false positive (FP) rate for some selected operation points on the "all features" ROC. It also reports the normalized area under the ROC and partial ROC curves (AUC and PAUC). As we can see, we can achieve a TP rate close to 98% at 1% FP rate. Furthermore, when we tune the detection threshold to achieve a FP rate of 0.1%, the classifier still yields an TP rate close to 90%, using all features. In addition, from Figure 3(a) we can see that the provenance classifier is not overly reliant on a single group of features.

Figure 3(b) shows the results obtained using only one group of features at the time. As we can see, each feature group gives a meaningful contribution to accurately detecting malware downloads, with the server IP and domain features providing the largest single contributions.

4.5 Train-Test Experiments

In this section, we discuss experiments performed to demonstrate the accuracy of AMICO in a real-world deployment setting. To this end we train the provenance classifier over the **TRD** dataset, and test it on the remaining **TSD** dataset. Figure 4 reports the ROC curve computed by using a provenance classifier built with all available features, as well as ROC curves related to separate tests in which we eliminate one group of features at a time. Like for the cross-validation results, we see that AMICO can achieve more than 90% TP rate for an FP rate $\leq 1\%$. Also, we can see that no one particular feature group is critical to obtaining good classification results.

Table 2 highlights the classification results for new malware downloads characterized by a never-before-seen file (*unseen SHA1*), and/or domain (*unseen domain*), and/or server IP (*unseen sever IP*). The "correct" column reports the number of correctly classified malware downloads. The detection threshold is set so to keep the overall FP rate (measured on benign **TSD** downloads) below 1%. As we can see, even when AMICO observes a completely new file from a new source (domain or server IP), it can still accurately classify the download event.

4.6 New Findings

In this section we discuss how AMICO can successfully complement existing malware detection approaches, such as AV scanners and static URL blacklists. All results discussed below consider a configuration of AMICO's detection threshold that yields an FP rate $\leq 1\%$.

1) Malware "unknown" to VT: Of the 3,655 confirmed *malware* downloads in the test dataset **TSD** (see Section 4.2), 1,031 malware samples were initially *unknown to VT*. That is, the first time we submitted the file's SHA1 to VT, the file was not present in VT's database. Of these, AMICO correctly classified 974 (94.5%) as malware at the time of download.

2) Zero-day malware: We also found 187 malware downloads for which all nine "trusted" AV scanners in VT initially classified the file as benign (i.e., no AV label was attributed to the files, the first time they were scanned), and then were labeled as malware after the one-month re-scan (see Section 4.2).

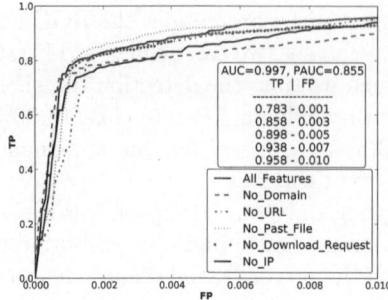

Fig. 4. Performance of Provenance Classifier on all test instances (FPs in [0,1%])

Table 2. Detection of "unseen" malware downloads (FP=1%)

Unseen Feature	Correct %
SHA1	90% (895/994)
Domain	85% (360/422)
Server IP	93% (1139/1222)
SHA1 & Domain	85% (328/386)
SHA1 & Domain & Server IP	85% (295/346)

Therefore, we regard these file downloads as *zero-days*. Of these 187 zero-day malware downloads, AMICO classified correctly 147 (78.6%).

3) Static blacklists: For each download event observed by AMICO, we queried GSB at the time of the download to see if the domain name or URL associated to the download was present in the blacklist (we query GSB only for the purpose of enabling a comparison between our system and URL blacklists). Surprisingly, we found that out of the 3,655 malicious downloads, at the time of download GSB failed to detect 3,562 (97.5%). We believe this apparently high false negative rate is likely due to the fact that many potential malware downloads are already blocked by GSB, and therefore cannot be observed in the network traffic. However, many malware downloads that evade GSB's static blacklist are observable in the traffic, and can be captured by AMICO. Of the 3,562 malware downloads missed by GSB, AMICO correctly detected 3,412 (95.8%).

5 Limitations

Our current implementation of AMICO focuses on inspecting HTTP traffic, because we mainly target malware downloads that happen via the browser. To evade AMICO, malware developers may attempt to propagate their malware samples over HTTPS, thus "hiding" the executable files from AMICO's reconstruction module. However, it is worth noting that switching to HTTPS may have some drawbacks for the attacker. For example, because the domain names associated with the malware distribution servers have to change frequently, to avoid static blacklists, for each new domain the attacker would have to purchase a signed SSL certificate from a certificate authority (CA), thus incurring a non-negligible cost. In alternative, the attacker may use self-signed certificates. However, in this case the browser will typically alert the user of a potential security problem, thus possibly scaring away a large fraction of potential victims. Furthermore, AMICO could be deployed "within" a web proxy that performs SSL man-in-the-middle.

It may be possible for sophisticated exploit code to force the browser to download an encrypted PE file, which can then be decrypted before the original malware file is executed. This scenario is analogous to detecting malware updates initiated from an infected machine, in which the method for downloading the files can be (almost) freely chosen by the already running malware instance. We therefore consider this scenario outside the scope of this paper. Notice that this limitation also affects any in-browser detection system, such as Google CAMP [18], because reporting the file downloads to CAMP could be disabled by the browser exploit code.

An attacker may also attempt to evade the statistical features measured by AMICO. However, while the attacker may be able to evade a few single features, most of AMICO's features are engineered to capture the fundamental characteristics of current evasive behavior of malware download campaigns. Namely, we attempt to capture those characteristics of malware downloads that the attackers already uses to evade existing detection tools, for example by frequently changing domain names, URLs, or the network infrastructure that supports the malware download operations. Therefore, evading the majority of AMICO's features would likely force malware campaigns back into a more "stable" malware distribution infrastructure, which may in turn be more easily blocked by static blacklists, for example. Therefore, we believe AMICO provides a robust complement to existing detection techniques, forcing attackers to incur a significant cost to try to evade both AMICO and current detection tools at the same time.

6   Conclusion

We presented AMICO, a novel system for accurately measuring and detecting malware downloads in live network traffic using *download provenance* information. To this end, AMICO uses a number of statistical features purposely engineering to capture the fundamental characteristics of malware distribution campaigns. We showed that AMICO is able to accurately detect malware downloads with up to 90% true positives at a false positives rate of 0.1%, including many zero-day malware, thus complementing current malware detection tools.

Acknowledgments. This work would not have been possible without the help of Christopher Workman, Jesse Bowling, Charles Leggett, and Alexander Merck, who assisted us throughout the deployment of AMICO on our campus network. We also thank the anonymous reviewers for their helpful comments. This material is based in part upon work supported by the National Science Foundation under Grants No. CNS-1149051 and OCI-1127195. Any opinions, findings, and conclusions or recommendations expressed in this material are those of the authors and do not necessarily reflect the views of the National Science Foundation.

References

1. Virustotal, https://www.virustotal.com
2. Antonakakis, M., Perdisci, R., Dagon, D., Lee, W., Feamster, N.: Building a dynamic reputation system for dns. In: Proceedings of the 19th USENIX Conference on Security, USENIX Security 2010 (2010)

3. Bilge, L., Kirda, E., Kruegel, C., Balduzzi, M.: Exposure: Finding malicious domains using passive dns analysis. In: Proceedings of Annual Network and Distributed System Security Symposium, NDSS (2011)
4. Breiman, L.: Random forests. Mach. Learn. 45(1), 5–32 (2001)
5. Caballero, J., Grier, C., Kreibich, C., Paxson, V.: Measuring pay-per-install: the commoditization of malware distribution. In: Proceedings of the 20th USENIX Conference on Security, SEC 2011 (2011)
6. Cova, M., Leita, C., Thonnard, O., Keromytis, A.D., Dacier, M.: An analysis of rogue AV campaigns. In: Jha, S., Sommer, R., Kreibich, C. (eds.) RAID 2010. LNCS, vol. 6307, pp. 442–463. Springer, Heidelberg (2010)
7. Curtsinger, C., Livshits, B., Zorn, B., Seifert, C.: Zozzle: fast and precise in-browser javascript malware detection. In: Proceedings of the 20th USENIX Conference on Security, SEC 2011 (2011)
8. Google. Google safe browsing API,
   https://developers.google.com/safe-browsing/
9. Zico Kolter, J., Maloof, M.A.: Learning to detect and classify malicious executables in the wild. J. Mach. Learn. Res. 7, 2721–2744 (2006)
10. Lu, L., Yegneswaran, V., Porras, P., Lee, W.: Blade: an attack-agnostic approach for preventing drive-by malware infections. In: Proceedings of the 17th ACM Conference on Computer and Communications Security, CCS 2010 (2010)
11. Microsoft. Microsoft PE and COFF specification,
    http://msdn.microsoft.com/library/windows/hardware/gg463125
12. Microsoft. Smartscreen application reputation - building reputation,
    http://blogs.msdn.com/b/ie/archive/2011/03/22/
    smartscreen-174-application-reputation-building-reputation.aspx
13. Oberheide, J., Cooke, E., Jahanian, F.: Cloudav: N-version antivirus in the network cloud. In: Proceedings of the 17th Conference on Security Symposium, SS 2008 (2008)
14. Perdisci, R., Lanzi, A., Lee, W.: Classification of packed executables for accurate computer virus detection. Pattern Recogn. Lett. 29(14), 1941–1946 (2008)
15. Perdisci, R., Lanzi, A., Lee, W.: Mcboost: Boosting scalability in malware collection and analysis using statistical classification of executables. In: Proceedings of the 2008 Annual Computer Security Applications Conference, ACSAC 2008, pp. 301–310 (2008)
16. Provos, N., Mavrommatis, P., Rajab, M.A., Monrose, F.: All your iframes point to us. In: Proceedings of the 17th Conference on Security Symposium, SS 2008 (2008)
17. Provos, N., McNamee, D., Mavrommatis, P., Wang, K., Modadugu, N.: The ghost in the browser analysis of web-based malware. In: Proceedings of the First Conference on First Workshop on Hot Topics in Understanding Botnets, HotBots 2007, p. 4. USENIX Association, Berkeley (2007)
18. Rajab, M.A., Ballard, L., Lutz, N., Mavrommatis, P., Provos, N.: CAMP: Content-agnostic malware protection. In: Proceedings of Annual Network and Distributed System Security Symposium, NDSS (February 2013)
19. Townsend, K.: R&d: The art of social engineering. Infosecurity 7(4), 32–35 (2010)
20. Weka. Weka 3: Data mining software in java, www.cs.waikato.ac.nz/ml/weka/
21. Zhang, J., Seifert, C., Stokes, J.W., Lee, W.: Arrow: Generating signatures to detect drive-by downloads. In: Proceedings of the 20th International Conference on World Wide Web, WWW 2011(2011)

A List of Features

(a) Domain Features

domain_malware_downloads	integer
domain_suspicious_downloads	integer
domain_benign_downloads	integer
domain_total_downloads	integer
domain_malware_ratio	real
domain_suspicious_ratio	real
domain_benign_ratio	real
domain_avg_av_labels	real
domain_avg_trusted_labels	real
domain_unknown_hashes	integer
domain_total_hashes	integer
domain_unknown_hash_ratio	real
2ld_malware_downloads	integer
2ld_suspicious_downloads	integer
2ld_benign_downloads	integer
2ld_total_downloads	integer
2ld_malware_ratio	real
2ld_suspicious_ratio	real
2ld_benign_ratio	real
2ld_avg_av_labels	real
2ld_avg_trusted_labels	real
2ld_unknown_hashes	integer
2ld_total_hashes	integer
2ld_unknown_hash_ratio	real

(b) Server IP Features

server_ip_malware_downloads	integer
server_ip_suspicious_downloads	integer
server_ip_benign_downloads	integer
server_ip_total_downloads	integer
server_ip_malware_ratio	real
server_ip_suspicious_ratio	real
server_ip_benign_ratio	real
server_ip_avg_av_labels	real
server_ip_avg_trusted_labels	real
server_ip_unknown_hashes	integer
server_ip_total_hashes	integer
server_ip_unknown_hash_ratio	real
bgp_malware_downloads	integer
bgp_suspicious_downloads	integer
bgp_benign_downloads	integer
bgp_total_downloads	integer
bgp_malware_ratio	real
bgp_suspicious_ratio	real
bgp_benign_ratio	real
bgp_avg_av_labels	real
bgp_avg_trusted_labels	real
bgp_unknown_hashes	integer
bgp_total_hashes	integer
bgp_unknown_hash_ratio	real

(c) Past File Downloads

hash_life_time	integer
num_dumps_with_same_hash	integer
hash_daily_dump_rate_per_client	real
estimated_clients_with_same_hash	integer

(d) Download Request Features

referer_exists	integer
host_name_exists	integer
extension_class	string
url_length	integer
directory_depth	integer

(e) URL Features

url_malware_downloads	integer
url_total_downloads	integer
url_distinct_sha1s	integer
url_struct_malware_downloads	integer
url_struct_total_downloads	integer
url_struct_distinct_sha1s	integer

Automated Certification
of Authorisation Policy Resistance[*]

Andreas Griesmayer[1] and Charles Morisset[2]

[1] ARM, Cambridge, UK
`andreas.griesmayer@arm.com`
[2] Center for Cybercrime and Computer Security,
School of Computing Science, Newcastle University, UK
`charles.morisset@ncl.ac.uk`

Abstract. Attribute-based Access Control (ABAC) extends traditional Access Control by considering an access request as a set of pairs *attribute name-value*, making it particularly useful in the context of open and distributed systems, where security relevant information can be collected from different sources. However, ABAC enables *attribute hiding attacks*, allowing an attacker to gain some access by withholding information.

In this paper, we first introduce the notion of policy *resistance* to attribute hiding attacks. We then propose the tool ATRAP (Automatic Term Rewriting for Authorisation Policies), based on the recent formal ABAC language PTaCL, which first automatically searches for resistance counter-examples using Maude, and then automatically searches for an Isabelle proof of resistance. We illustrate our approach with two simple examples of policies and propose an evaluation of ATRAP performances.

Keywords: Attribute-based Access Control, Monotonicity, Attribute hiding, Model Checking, Proof assistant.

1 Introduction

An authorisation policy for a security mechanism is a document describing which user requests are authorised and which ones are denied. Many languages exist in the literature to define policies, most of them considering a request as a triple subject-object-mode. Recent approaches [23,22,10] consider more expressive requests, consisting of a set of pairs of attribute name and attribute values, thus defining the model known as Attribute Based Access Control (ABAC).

A major feature of ABAC is its ability to gather attribute information from different sources. This is essential in open and distributed systems, which indeed often lack a central security point providing all required information. In order to make a security decision, such systems need to combine information from different sources including the user herself (e.g., personal identification), the

---

[*] Work partially supported by the International Exchange Scheme of the Royal Society and conducted in part at Imperial College London where A. Griesmayer was supported by the Marie Curie Fellowship "DiVerMAS" (FP7-PEOPLE-252184).

J. Crampton, S. Jajodia, and K. Mayes (Eds.): ESORICS 2013, LNCS 8134, pp. 574–591, 2013.

environment (e.g., date or location), the data requested (e.g., relationship with other objects) and other users (e.g., availability of higher-ranked users).

Delegating the retrieval of security relevant information clearly brings more flexibility in open systems, but also raises the problem of information withholding, malicious or not. Tschantz and Krishnamurthi introduce in [24] the notion of safety, such that a policy is safe when "incomplete requests should only result in a grant of access if the complete one would have". More recently, Crampton and Morisset identify in [10] the notion of an *attribute hiding attack*, where a user hides some attribute values in order to get access to a resource she would be denied otherwise.

As a running example to illustrate our research problem, consider a fictional organisation, sponsored by both Austria and France, where documents can be submitted and reviewed. The organisation has a simple conflict-of-interest policy stating that a document cannot be reviewed by someone with the same nationality as the submitter. The implementation of such a policy might lead to attribute hiding attacks: Consider a policy for a document submitted by an Austrian member that states that it cannot be accessed by another Austrian member; If an Austrian attacker is able to hide her nationality, for instance by corrupting the corresponding data, then she could access the document. Such an attack is particularly relevant when a user can have multiple nationalities.

In this paper, we focus on the behaviour of authorisation policies when facing attribute hiding attacks. More precisely, we introduce the notion of *resistance*: a policy is resistant when every query obtained by adding information to an allowed query is also allowed. This definition generates the following research questions:

1. Is it possible to automatically detect whether a policy is resistant or not?
2. If a policy is not resistant, can we exhibit a counter-example?
3. If a policy is resistant, can we construct a formal proof of it?

The main contribution of this paper is to positively answer these questions, at least in a partial way. In order to do so, we present the tool ATRAP (Automated Term Rewriting for Authorisation Policies), which combines the term-rewriting tool Maude [8] and the proof assistant Isabelle/Isar [20,25] to analyse the resistance of PTaCL policies. The core of the tool is written in Java and handles the communication between Maude and Isabelle by generating the respective inputs and interpreting their results. ATRAP is capable of generating counter-examples for non resistant policies, and of building an Isabelle proof for resistant policies. Although ATRAP is sound, i.e., all counter-examples and proofs generated are indeed correct, ATRAP is not (yet) complete, as it may fail in some cases to find a counter-example in a reasonable amount of time or to build a proof.

The rest of the paper is structured as follows: in Section 2. we present the language PTaCL and introduce its evaluation in Maude. In Section 3. we define the notion of policy resistance and show how this property can be verified in practice. In Section 4. we describe our approach to find a counter-example of resistance, and in Section 5. we present how a *proof* of resistance can be automatically generated, after which we conclude and present future work in Section 6.

Related Work

The notion of resistance introduced in this paper is related to that of safety given in [24], which roughly states that the evaluation of a request should be "lower" than that of a request with strictly more information. This notion is close to that of (weak)-monotonicity [10]. As shown in Section 3, a (weakly) monotonic policy is also resistant, while the converse does not always hold.

There exist several approaches using model-checking to analyse access control policies [15,27]. For instance, SMT solving can be used to check whether a given request can eventually be granted with a particular role in Administrative-RBAC policies [1,2]. Similarly, XACML policies can be automatically compared using a SAT solver [16]. To the best of our knowledge, we are the first to automatically analyse the resistance of policy, and also to allow for the generation of a structured proof.

The automation of ATRAP relies on term-rewriting, which has already been considered for the formalisation of access control [3,11], leading to the analysis of rewrite-based policies [18]. In particular, Bertolissi and Uttha propose in [4] to relate the properties of a rewrite system, such as totality or consistency, with those of an access control policy encoded in this system. This approach allow them to use the rewrite system CiME to generate proof certificates for these properties in the proof assistant CoQ. We follow a similar objective here, in that we generate proof certificates using a rewrite system, however we focus on the notion of resistance, which is not a property of the rewrite system itself, but of the policy.

ATRAP relies on the encoding of PTaCL in Isabelle, mentioned in [10], in order to generate a proof of resistance. Brucker et al. present in [6] an encoding of an access control model into HOL, in the context of healthcare policies. Finally, it is worth mentioning that some of the techniques used in ATRAP are inspired by previous work [13], where the basic idea of using term-rewriting to generate proofs is used in the context of program refinement.

2   PTaCL

XACML 3.0 [22] is an OASIS standard for representing authorisation policies, and given an access request, its complete request evaluation cycle can be summarised as follows: (i) the request is submitted to the Policy Enforcement Point (PEP); (ii) the PEP forwards the request to the Context Handler (CH); (iii) the CH collects all attributes necessary to the evaluation of the request; (iv) the CH forwards the complete request to the Policy Decision Point (PDP); (v) the PDP evaluates the complete request and returns the corresponding decision to the CH, which returns it to the PEP.

PTaCL [10] formalises the evaluation of the request by the PDP, which considers each request as complete, or more precisely, cannot make a distinction between incomplete and complete requests. In other words, if the CH is unable to collect some attributes, and forwards an incomplete request to the PDP, this request is evaluated in the same way than a complete one.

$$
\begin{array}{c|ccc}
\sqcap & 1 & 0 & \bot \\
\hline
1 & 1 & 0 & \bot \\
0 & 0 & 0 & \bot \\
\bot & \bot & \bot & \bot
\end{array}
\qquad
\begin{array}{c|ccc}
\sqcup & 1 & 0 & \bot \\
\hline
1 & 1 & 1 & \bot \\
0 & 1 & 0 & \bot \\
\bot & \bot & \bot & \bot
\end{array}
\qquad
\begin{array}{c|ccc}
\tilde{\sqcap} & 1 & 0 & \bot \\
\hline
1 & 1 & 0 & \bot \\
0 & 0 & 0 & 0 \\
\bot & \bot & 0 & \bot
\end{array}
\qquad
\begin{array}{c|ccc}
\tilde{\sqcup} & 1 & 0 & \bot \\
\hline
1 & 1 & 1 & 1 \\
0 & 1 & 0 & \bot \\
\bot & 1 & \bot & \bot
\end{array}
\qquad
\begin{array}{c|cc}
X & \neg X & \sim X \\
\hline
1 & 0 & 1 \\
0 & 1 & 0 \\
\bot & \bot & 0
\end{array}
$$

(a) Weak operators $\qquad\qquad$ (b) Strong operators $\qquad$ (c) Unary

Fig. 1. Binary and unary operators on the target decision set $\{1, 0, \bot\}$

We present in this section the language PTaCL through the description of an illustrative example. We introduce the different definitions required for the understanding of this example, and refer to [10] for further details about the language. We take as example the one given in the introduction, where the access to a document is based on the nationality of the requester.

2.1 3-valued Logic

The 3-valued logic extends the traditional Boolean logic $\{1, 0\}$, where 1 represents *true* and 0 represents *false*, by considering an additional value $\bot$ [19]. The usual Boolean operators, such as the conjunction, disjunction, negation, etc, can be extended to the set $\{1, 0, \bot\}$, as shown in Fig. 1. The weak operators consider the value $\bot$ as absorbing, while the strong ones "resolve" $\bot$ as much as possible.

The logic $\{1, 0, \bot, \tilde{\sqcup}, \sim, \neg\}$ is proven in [10] to be functionally complete, using a result from Jobe [17], which means that any logical operator can be built from these operators and constants. In the following, we sometimes use the set $\{1, 0, \bot, \tilde{\sqcap}, \sim, \neg\}$, since $x \mathbin{\tilde{\sqcap}} y = \neg(\neg x \mathbin{\tilde{\sqcup}} \neg y)$. In addition, we use the three valued logic both to represent the result of target evaluation and the result of policy composition. In order to avoid any confusion, we use $\{1_T, 0_T, \bot_T\}$ for the former, and $\{1_P, 0_P, \bot_P\}$ for the latter, whose meaning will be given in due course.

2.2 Target and Policy

Following recent work [23,22], PTaCL is attribute-based, meaning that a request is modeled as a set of attribute name-value pairs. Our running example uses an attribute **nat**, whose value can be either FR or AT. For instance, the request $\{(\mathbf{nat}, \mathsf{FR})\}$ represents a request made by a French national.

In addition, PTaCL is target-based [5,7,9,21,22,26], meaning that an access control policy contains a target that specifies the requests to which the policy is applicable, and a body (either a single decision or another policy) describing how applicable requests should be evaluated.

In its simplest form, an *atomic target* is a pair (n, v), where n is an attribute name and v is an attribute value. For instance, the target $(\mathbf{nat}, \mathsf{FR})$ evaluates to 1_T (match) if the request contains $(\mathbf{nat}, \mathsf{FR})$, to 0_T (no-match) if it contains $(\mathbf{nat}, \mathsf{AT})$, but not $(\mathbf{nat}, \mathsf{FR})$, and to $\bot_T$ (indeterminate) if it does not contain any value for the attribute **nat**. In other words, PTaCL can distinguish between a non-matching value for an attribute and a missing attribute. More formally,

Table 1. PTaCL evaluation

	t_1	p_1	t_2	p_2
$\emptyset$	$\perp_T$	$\{1_P, 0_P\}$	$\perp_T$	$\{1_P, 0_P\}$
$\{(\mathbf{nat}, \mathsf{FR})\}$	0_T	$\{1_P\}$	1_T	$\{1_P\}$
$\{(\mathbf{nat}, \mathsf{AT})\}$	1_T	$\{0_P\}$	0_T	$\{0_P\}$
$\{(\mathbf{nat}, \mathsf{FR}), (\mathbf{nat}, \mathsf{AT})\}$	1_T	$\{0_P\}$	1_T	$\{1_P\}$

the semantics of an atomic target (n, v) for a request $q = \{(n_1, v_1), \cdots, (n_k, v_k)\}$ is given as:

$$[\![(n, v)]\!](q) = \begin{cases} 1_T & \text{if } (n, v') \in q \text{ and } v = v', \\ \perp_T & \text{if } (n, v') \notin q, \\ 0_T & \text{otherwise.} \end{cases}$$

More complex targets can be built using the logical operators not_T, for the negation of a target, opt_T, for the optional target (i.e., transform $\perp_T$ into 0_T) and and_P, for the strong conjunction of targets, interpreted by $\neg$, $\sim$ and $\sqcap$, respectively. Since this set of operators is functionally complete ($\sqcap$ can be built from $\tilde{\sqcup}$ and $\neg$ [10]), any other logical combination can be achieved with them.

Finally, an *authorisation policy* can be defined as single decision, i.e., either 1_P (allow) or 0_P (deny), a targeted policy (t, p), where t is a target, or a logical composition of two policies, using the operators not_P for the negation of a policy, dbd_P for the deny-by-default of a policy, or and_P for the conjunction of two policies, interpreted by $\neg$, $\sim$ and $\tilde{\sqcap}$, respectively. Here again, these three operators suffice to build any other logical operator. Given an access request, the evaluation of a policy returns the set of all possible decisions. The logical operators are therefore extended in a point-wise way, and the evaluation of a targeted policy (t, p) for a request q is given by:

$$[\![(t, p)]\!]_P(q) = \begin{cases} [\![p]\!]_P(q) & \text{if } [\![t]\!]_T(q) = 1_T, \\ \{\perp_P\} & \text{if } [\![t]\!]_T(q) = 0_T, \\ \{\perp_P\} \cup [\![p]\!]_P(q) & \text{otherwise.} \end{cases}$$

where $\perp_P$ represents the not-applicable decision. For instance, the policy p_1 that explicitly denies any access to Austrian citizens and otherwise allows the access can be defined as:

```
t1 :: (Tatom "nat" "AT")
p1 : Pnot (Pdbd (Pnot (Ptar t1 (Patom Zero))))
```

We adopt a declarative syntax, where the double-colon is used for target definition, and a single-colon for policy definition. In the above, the target `t1` is defined as the atomic target $(\mathbf{nat}, \mathsf{AT})$ with the keyword `Tatom`, `Patom Zero` represents the atomic policy that always returns 0_P (whereas `One` represents the decision 1_P), `Ptar t1 (Patom Zero)` is the above policy guarded by the target `t1`, and thus evaluates to: $\{0_P\}$ if `t1` evaluates to 1_T; to $\{\perp_P\}$ if `t1` evaluates to 0_T; and to $\{0_P, \perp_P\}$

if t1 evaluates to $\perp_T$. Furthermore, Pnot and Pdpd defines the negation and deny-by-default operators, and therefore the constructor Pnot (Pdbd (Pnot x)) acts as an allow-by-default operator, i.e., transforms $\perp_P$ to 1_P. Similarly, the policy p_2 that explicitly authorises any access to French citizens and otherwise denies the access can be defined as:

```
t2 :: (Tatom "nat" "FR")
p2 : Pdbd (Ptar t2 (Patom One))
```

The evaluation of p_1 and p_2 for four different requests is given in Table 1. Note that the evaluation might return more than one decision, which can be interpreted as an inconclusive decision. In XACML, such decisions are defined by the Indeterminate decision. The way an inconclusive decision is concretely interpreted by the PEP is left to the implementer, and might vary from a risk-advert approach (e.g., any inconclusive decision is interpreted as 0_P) to a risk-prone approach (e.g., if 1_P is a possible decision, then the PEP allows the request).

2.3 Maude Evaluation

ATRAP uses the term rewriting system Maude [8] to model PTaCL and dynamically generate and evaluate requests for a given policy. The syntax for the PTaCL terms in Maude closely resembles the syntax given above. Based on this formalisation, we define *equations* and *rewrite rules* to manipulate the syntax tree based on pattern matching.

To evaluate a request, we model the operators for *targets*, *policies* and the three valued logic used in PTaCL. The definition of an operator starts with the keyword op, followed by a pattern that allows parameters at positions marked with "_" (underline), and the signature of the operator after a ":" (colon), where the list on the left hand side of -> defines the parameters, and the right hand side the result type. The definition is completed by a "." (full stop). To exemplify the notation we give the definitions for decisions and policy operations:

```
op ALLOW : -> decision .
op DENY : -> decision .
op BOT : -> decision .

op Patom _ : decision  -> policy .
op Pnot _ : policy -> policy .
op Pdbd _ : policy -> policy .
op Pand _ _ : policy policy -> policy .
```

The first three lines give parameter-free operators to define the decisions for 1_P (ALLOW), 0_P (DENY) and $\perp_P$ (BOT) respectively. The decisions are prefixed with the keyword Patom to form a basic policy, and combined with Pnot, Pdbd and Pand to form more complex expressions. Similar operators exist for the targets, where the basic element Tatom holds a key-value pair for the attributes. While these operators capture the structure of the policies, operators can also be associated with equations to modify them or evaluate requests. Equations correspond to operators and are defined using the keyword eq. When one of the patterns on the left of the = matches, it is replaced by the pattern on the right hand side.

```
op dbd _ : decision  -> decision .
eq dbd DENY = DENY .
eq dbd ALLOW = ALLOW .
eq dbd BOT = DENY .

op strongand _ _ : decision  decision  -> decision [assoc comm] .
eq strongand ALLOW d = d .
eq strongand DENY d = DENY .
eq strongand d d = d .
```

While the *deny-by-default* operator dbd has only one parameter and replaces possible BOT values by DENY, the equations can also contain variables which match all possible patterns for the respective type. The keywords assoc and comm declare that the operator for strongand is associative and commutative respectively, which is considered by Maude in pattern matching (e.g., we only need strongand ALLOW d and can omit strongand d ALLOW). Note that while in general associative-commutative rewriting is NP complete, Maude supports effective algorithms for handling the equational rewriting steps for typical patterns in time proportional to the logarithm of the term size [12]. The definitions for equations are evaluated from top to bottom. That is, for the equations above, eq strongand d d = d is only considered if both of the parameters are BOT. In addition to the policies, we define *requests* as sets of (key =? value) pairs and an operation peval that evaluates a request on a given policy.

ATRAP uses this formalisation in three ways: to evaluate a request against a policy, to compute a counter-example demonstrating that a policy is not resistant, and to search for a proof tree that shows the resistance of a policy.

3 Policy Resistance

To introduce the notion of policy resistance, consider the evaluation of the request $\{(\mathbf{nat}, \mathsf{FR}), (\mathbf{nat}, \mathsf{AT})\}$ with the policy p_1, as given in Table 1: this request, corresponding to a user with both French and Austrian citizenships, is initially denied; however, if the attribute $(\mathbf{nat}, \mathsf{AT})$ is "removed", then the request becomes allowed.

In general, several reasons can explain the absence of an attribute in a request, such as an error during the transmission of the attributes, the expiration of the attribute certificate, the non-existence of this attribute, etc. In particular, an attribute might be withheld intentionally (e.g., a user does not want to disclose her address for privacy reasons), by mistake (e.g., a user is not aware of the fact that it should be disclosed) or maliciously (e.g., a user wants to hide some "negative" information).

In the latter case, the omission of an attribute can be seen as an *attribute hiding attack* [10] from a user, trying to gain a better answer by hiding some information. A policy is resistant when it is able to resist to such attacks:

Definition 1. *A policy p is resistant if, and only if, for any requests q and q',
if $q' \subseteq q$ and if $[\![p]\!](q') = \{1_P\}$, then $[\![p]\!](q) = \{1_P\}$.*

In other words, if a request q is not allowed, then any sub-request $q' \subseteq q$ is also
not allowed. For instance, we can observe that the policy p_1 is not resistant,
while the policy p_2 is.

There are many ways to prove that a policy p is resistant, the most straightforward one being to exhaustively check any pair of requests q, q' such that
$q' \subseteq q$. We describe an implementation of this approach in Section 4 using
Maude, together with the notion of a normal form for requests, allowing us to
reduce the set of requests to check.

In some cases, we can also use the *structure* of the policy to prove its resistance. For instance, the policy Ptar t (Patom Zero) clearly evaluates, for any
request, either to $\{0_P\}$ or to $\{0_P, \bot\}$, regardless of the definition of t, and is
therefore trivially resistant. Generalising this example, we can observe (and formally prove) that if a policy cannot return 1_P, then it is resistant. Furthermore:

- if p cannot return 1_P, then Ptar t p cannot return 1_P, for any t;
- if p cannot return 1_P, then Pdbd p cannot return 1_P;
- if p cannot return 1_P, then Pand p p1 and Pand p1 p cannot return 1_P;
- if p cannot return 1_P, then Pnot p cannot return 0_P;
- if p cannot return 0_P, then Pnot p cannot return 1_P;
- if p cannot return 0_P, then Ptar t p cannot return 0_P.

In other words, it might be possible to prove that a policy is resistant simply
by inspecting its structure, without checking each possible pair of requests. As
another example, a policy without any target clearly evaluates identically for
any request (since all requests are equally applicable), and therefore is resistant.

In addition, the notion of weak-monotonicity is introduced in [10], such that,
intuitively speaking, a target is weakly monotonic if removing information from
a request lowers the evaluation of the target.

Definition 2. *A target t is* weakly monotonic *if for all requests q and for every
$q' \subseteq q$, $[\![t]\!](q') \preccurlyeq [\![t]\!](q)$, where $\preccurlyeq$ is the reflexive closure of $\bot_T \prec 0_T \prec 1_T$. A
policy p is weakly monotonic if and only if every target in p is weakly monotonic.*

Any atomic target (n, v) is weakly-monotonic, and the operators opt_T and
and_T preserve the weak-monotonicity [10]. In other words, any policy whose
targets are built without the operator not_T is weakly monotonic. Moreover, as a
direct result from Theorem 6 of [10] (which is recalled in [14]), we have:

- If p is weakly monotonic and built without dbd$_P$, then it is resistant;
- If p is weakly monotonic and built without not$_P$, then it is resistant;

Finally, the notion of resistance can be proved in a compositional way:

- If p is resistant, then Pdbd p is resistant;
- If p1 and p2 are resistant, then Pand p1 p2 is resistant.

These rules make it possible to prove the resistance of a conjunctive policy in a different way for each sub-policy. Clearly, all the rules presented in this section are only implications, and a policy might be resistant even though it does not satisfy any of them. We show in Section 5 how ATRAP can use these rules, together with their encoding in Isabelle and Maude, to automatically build a proof of resistance.

Remark 1. A (strongly) monotonic policy, as defined in [10] is also trivially resistant. However, in order to prove the (strong) monotonicity of an atomic target, attributes must be assumed to be *compact*, i.e., either all the values of an attribute are given, or none are. For instance, the compactness of the attribute **nat** would mean that a user can either hide all of her nationalities, or none of them, but cannot only hide one. Hence, proving resistance using (strong) monotonicity requires the assumption of compactness from the environment, whereas we aim here at generating *complete* proofs, i.e., without assumption. The integration of such assumptions when all other strategies have failed is left for future work.

4   Search for Non-resistance

We use the PTaCL encoding in Maude to automatically search for possible counter-examples to resistance. A naive approach for a policy p would simply consist in checking any two requests q and q', such that $q' \subseteq q$ and $[\![p]\!](q') = \{1_P\}$, in order to ensure that $[\![p]\!](q) = \{1_P\}$. However, the set of all possible requests can potentially be very large. For instance, in our previous example, focusing only on the **nat** attribute, the United Nations Organisation currently counts 193 members[1], meaning there are 193 pairs $(\mathbf{nat}, v)$ possible, and thus $\mathbf{card}(\mathcal{Q}) = 2^{193}$.

In order to simplify the search, we first introduce the *normal form* of a request for a given policy. We then describe our correct and complete search for counter-examples in Maude, and finally we present some experimental results.

4.1   Normal Form of Requests

Intuitively speaking, the evaluation of a request against a policy mostly depends on whether the request contains the atomic targets present in the policy: given an attribute n, all pairs (n, v) that do not explicitly appear in the policy are evaluated in the same way. For instance, consider the policy p_1: it is clear that the pairs $(\mathbf{nat}, \mathsf{FR})$, $(\mathbf{nat}, \mathsf{DE})$ or $(\mathbf{nat}, \mathsf{UK})$ are evaluated similarly.

Hence, given a policy p, we write $\mathcal{A}(p)$ for the set of atomic targets appearing in p. For instance, $\mathcal{A}(p_1) = \{(\mathbf{nat}, \mathsf{AT})\}$ and $\mathcal{A}(p_2) = \{(\mathbf{nat}, \mathsf{FR})\}$. Given an attribute n and a policy, we write $fv(p, n)$ for a fresh value of n with respect to p, i.e., a value such that $(n, fv(p, n)) \notin \mathcal{A}(p)$. If p explicitly mentions all possible values for n, we define $fv(p, n)$ to return a random value for n. Finally, the normal form of a request q for a policy p is given by keeping all pairs (n, v) that appear both in q and $\mathcal{A}(p)$, and replacing any (n, v) in q that does not appear in $\mathcal{A}(p)$ by $(n, fv(p, n))$. More formally:

---

[1] http://www.un.org/depts/dhl/unms/whatisms.shtml#states

Definition 3. *The normal form of a request q is given by:*

$$\mathsf{nf}_p(q) = (q \cap \mathcal{A}(p)) \cup \{(n, fv(p, n)) \mid \exists v \ (n, v) \notin \mathcal{A}(p) \wedge (n, v) \in q\}$$

Given a set of requests $\mathcal{Q}$ and a policy p, we write $\mathsf{NF}_p(\mathcal{Q}) = \{\mathsf{nf}_p(q) \mid q \in \mathcal{Q}\}$. In the following, we omit the subscript when p is clear from context. For instance, the set of requests in normal form for the policy p_1 is given by:

$$\mathsf{NF}_{p_1}(\mathcal{Q}) = \{\emptyset, \{(\mathbf{nat}, \mathsf{AT})\}, \{(\mathbf{nat}, \mathsf{NV})\}, \{(\mathbf{nat}, \mathsf{NV}), (\mathbf{nat}, \mathsf{AT})\}\}$$

where NV represents the fresh value for the attribute $\mathbf{nat}$, i.e., $\mathsf{NV} = fv(p_1, \mathbf{nat})$.

This notion of normal is consistent both with policy evaluation and request inclusion (the proofs can be found in [14]).

Proposition 1. *For any policy p and any request q, $[\![p]\!](q) = [\![p]\!](\mathsf{nf}(q))$.*

Proposition 2. *Given any requests q and q', if $q' \subseteq q$, then $\mathsf{nf}(q') \subseteq \mathsf{nf}(q)$.*

Remark 2. The simplicity of the normal form comes from the fact that PTaCL does not allow for complex atomic targets, such as the comparison of attribute values. For instance, one cannot directly write the atomic target stating that $\mathbf{age}$ must be lower than 18, and must instead generate the disjunction of all atomic target for $\mathbf{age}$ between 0 and 18. Note however that, as long as attributes have a finite domain, all possible targets can be defined, hence PTaCL can be seen here as a low-level language, designed for policy analysis. The design of richer atomic targets is planned for future work.

4.2   Search for Counter-Examples

As a consequence of Proposition 1 and Proposition 2, the resistance of a policy can be decided only by looking at the set of requests in normal form.

Proposition 3. *A policy p is resistant if, and only if, given q and q' in $\mathsf{NF}_p(\mathcal{Q})$, if $q' \subseteq q$ and if $[\![p]\!](q') = \{1_P\}$, then $[\![p]\!](q) = \{1_P\}$.*

In other words, we can restrict our attention to $\mathsf{NF}_p(\mathcal{Q})$, whose size is bounded by $2^{|\mathcal{A}(p)|+n}$, where n stands for the number of attributes, instead of $\mathcal{Q}$, whose size is 2^N, where N is the number of all possible attribute name-values pairs. Finally, it is worth observing that, in order for a policy p to be resistant, it is enough to check, for any allowed request q, whether removing any pair attribute value changes the decision. More formally:

Proposition 4. *A policy p is resistant if, and only if, for any request q such that $[\![p]\!](q) \neq \{1_P\}$, if $[\![p]\!](q \setminus \{(n, v)\}) \neq \{1_P\}$, for any attribute n and any value v.*

Combining Propositions 4 and 3, we conclude that to find a counter-example to resistance, we only need to check all pairs (q, q'), where $q, q' \in \mathsf{NF}_p(\mathcal{Q})$ and $q = q' \cup \{(n, v)\}$. Proposition 4 allows us to reduce the number of comparisons needed for the search for counter-examples from an upper bound of $2^{|\mathcal{A}(p)|+n} \times 2^{|\mathcal{A}(p)|+n}$ (comparison of all subsets) to $2^{|\mathcal{A}(p)|+n} \times (|\mathcal{A}(p)| + n)$, i.e., where each subset needs to be checked against at most $|\mathcal{A}(p)| + n$ direct subsets.

The seach for counter-examples is performed by generating and evaluating the largest possible request $q_m = \mathcal{A}(p) \cup \{(n, fv(n)) \mid (n, v) \in \mathcal{A}(p)\}$, and systematically removing attributes to see if a reduction of a request (hiding of an attribute) can lead to an increase of access in the policy. This manipulation of requests is performed using *rewrite rules*, which are defined similarly to equations, but in contrast to them are not evaluated deterministically, i.e., may be executed whenever the left hand side pattern matches.

The Maude command for the search has the following form:

```
search  sres ( bldevallist  ( policy  Requests  Defs  DecsList ))  =>* error ( x: DecsList ).
```

where policy is the ID of a top level policy to check, the set Requests is the maximal request in normal form, and Defs are the policy definitions. The operator bldevallist repeatedly removes attribues from the request, evaluates it with respect to the policy, and stores the result in DecsList. The operator sres traverses the list and searches for pairs that violate resistance, in which case the violating request pair is wrapped into an error operator. Removing an element from the set Request is nondeterministic, and thus may generate different lists of decisions. The maude command search systematically explores all the possible outcomes and returns those that match the search command, resp. can be rewritten to an error label. For instance, when analysing the policy p_1, ATRAP outputs:

```
Counter-example #1
["nat" =? "new_value"]:                    [ALLOW]
["nat" =? "AT", "nat" =? "new_value"]:  [DENY]
```

4.3   Experimental Results

We experiment the search for counter-examples by randomly generating some policies, and executing the search for each policy. We write $P\langle m, n, k, l, r \rangle$ for a set of r random policies, such that m stands for the maximal height of each policy, n for the maximal width of each target, k for the number of attributes and l for the number of values for each attribute.

Figure 2 represents the execution time (on 2 GHz Intel core i7 with 8GB of RAM) for the search of counter-examples for each $p \in P\langle 4, 4, 4, 4, 300 \rangle$, indexed by $\mathcal{A}(p)$ and with a logarithmic scale for the execution time. Over the 300 policies, 252 are resistant, and this ratio of 0.85 is consistent with other experiments, and seems to be independent of the policy dimensions. Note that the times shown in this Figure are for complete searches, i.e., searches finding *all* possible counter-examples. Hence, the time required to analyse a policy is the same whether the policy is resistant or not. As expected from the theoretical analysis of the previous section, the search for counter is exponential in the size of $\mathcal{A}(p)$.

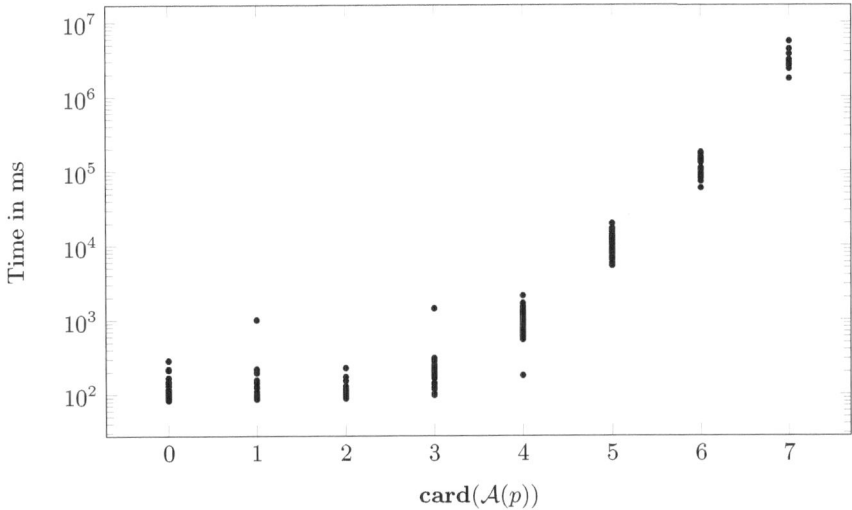

Fig. 2. Automatic search for counter-examples for $P\langle 4, 4, 4, 4, 300\rangle$

5 Certification of Resistance

If no counter-example is found, ATRAP tries to build a proof of resistance of the policy, following a proof-obligation discharge approach, where Maude is used to automatically generate a proof that can be checked in Isabelle [20,25]. To reach this goal, ATRAP encodes the policy and the deduction mechanism in rewrite logic and calls Maude to perform a search for the proof. The result is parsed into Java classes and mapped into a corresponding proof in Isabelle, which is then called to validate the proof. It is worth mentioning that the encoding in Maude of the deduction mechanism is independent to the counter-examples search described in the previous section, although both techniques share the encoding of PTaCL.

Our approach revolves around two main entities: proof obligation and proof technique. A *proof obligation* corresponds to a goal, i.e., to a property that we want to prove. The top-level goal is a proof of resistance, which in turn may require further sub-goals like weak-monotonicity to form a complete proof tree. A *proof technique* describes a method to discharge a proof obligation, using some rules described in Section 3.

Rather than encoding the proofs manually in Isabelle, we use Maude to search for viable proof trees that are then encoded and checked in Isabelle. To facilitate this goal, each proof obligation and technique have corresponding facets in Maude, Isabelle and Java. In Maude, the facet of a proof obligation is represented as an operator (e.g., isResistant) that takes a policy or target ID and a proof technique. In Java this is implemented in form of public classes, which have a field statement corresponding to the Isabelle definition of the proof obligation. For instance, the field statement of the class ResistanceProof is equal to resistant p q1 q, where p is the name of the policy over which this class is defined and where q and q1 are the universally quantified variables representing the variables q and q' of Definition 1. The Isabelle facet of a proof obligation is then a definition over either a target or a policy. For instance, the definition of resistance in Isabelle is given as:

definition resistant :: " policy ⇒ request ⇒ request ⇒ bool" **where**
" resistant p q1 q ≡ (set q1)⊆(set q) → peval p q1 = {One} → peval p q = {One}"

The Maude facet of a proof technique is an operator defined over policies and/or targets. For instance, let r_1 be the rule stating that a policy is resistant if it is weakly-monotonic and without the notP operator. Note that for technical reasons, we also need to impose that a policy is well-formed, i.e., each atomic policy is either 1P or 0P, and not ⊥P. This rule is represented in Maude as the operator ResWFWMWNProof. A proof technique is implemented in Java as a class local to that corresponding to the proof obligation. For instance, in order to define the rule r_1, the class ResistanceProof comes with a local class WeakMonotonicityWithoutNotWF. This class is defined with three fields: WellFormedProof, WithoutNotProof, WeakMonotonicPolicyProof, each being a public class. In other words, in order to use the rule r_1, one must first exhibit a proof that the policy is well-formed, a proof that it is built without the notP constructor, and a proof that it is weakly-monotonic. Finally, this structure is mapped to Isabelle, where the proof technique for a proof obligation is a proven lemma whose goal is that proof obligation. For instance, the lemma corresponding to rule r_1 is defined in Isabelle as[2]:

lemma weak_monotonic_without_not_resistant :
" well_formed_policy p ⇒ weak_pmonotonic p q1 q ⇒ policy_without_not p
    ⇒ resistant p q1 q"

To generate the proof tree, each rule of Section 3 is modelled in Maude in a basic, compositional form. Starting from the initial goal of proving resistance of a policy p, the proof generation then follows the structure of the policy to generate new proof obligations for sub-proofs according to the components and properties of p.

While binary operators like Pand trigger sub-proofs for both operands, the proof generation is also guided by properties and preconditions of the lemma to apply. To show, e.g., resistance using the rule r_1, we need to establish well-formedness, weak-monotonicity, and check that the policy does not use notP. Well-formedness and use of notP can easily be checked by Maude doing a syntactic check. Only if both conditions are fulfilled, a proof for weak monotonicity is instantiated. When all conditions for a proof are fulfilled, the *proof obligation* is replaced by a description of the actual proof. For instance, the rewrite rule corresponding to the rule r_1 is given as:

```
genproof( isResistant (p, noproof),
          isWF(p, pr1), isWN(p, pr2), isWM(p, pr3),pis | defs )
=> genproof(isResistant(p, ResWFWMWNProof(p)),
          isWF(p, pr1), isWN(p, pr2), isWM(p, pr3), pis | defs)
```

---

[2] All ATRAP lemmas are available at http://www.morisset.eu/atrap/.

```
theory p2 imports atrap begin
  definition t2 ::  target where "t2 = (Tatom ''nat''  ''FR'')"
  definition pone :: policy where "pone = Patom One"
  definition pt :: policy where "pt = Ptar t2 pone"
  definition p2 :: policy where "p2 = Pdbd pt"


lemma "resistant p2 q1 q" proof −
  have wf: " well_formed_policy  p2"
    by (simp add: p2_def pt_def pone_def t2_def)
  have without_not: " policy_without_not  p2"
    by (simp add: p2_def pt_def pone_def t2_def)
  have weak_monotonic: "weak_pmonotonic p2 q1 q" proof −
    have wm_p: "weak_pmonotonic pt q1 q" proof −
      have wm_p: "weak_pmonotonic pone q1 q" by (simp add: pone_def)
      have wm_t: "weak_tmonotonic t2 q1 q"
        by (simp add: tatom_weak_monotonic t2_def)
      from wm_p wm_t show ?thesis by (simp add:pt_def) qed
    from wm_p show ?thesis by (simp add:p2_def) qed
  from wf without_not weak_monotonic show ?thesis
    by ( insert  weak_monotonic_without_not_resistant  [of p2 q1 q], simp)
qed
```

Fig. 3. Generated Isabelle Proof

where noproof indicates that the proof obligation was not fulfilled yet, and pr1, pr2, and pr3 are previously generated subproofs. The variables pis and defs hold the available sub-proofs and policy definitions respectively. This approach also allows for manual intervention by the user by supplying the generation mechanism by external information about the system or predefining proof obligations with their respective techniques.

Running Example. The policy p_2 is automatically proven to be resistant by ATRAP, which executes the following Maude command (where the policy pt is introduced as an intermediary step):

rew genproof(isResistant (P "p2", noproof) | (T "t2"::(Tatom "nat" "FR"),
   P "pone"=Patom ALLOW, P "pt"=Ptar T "t2" P "pone", P "p2"=Pdbd P "pt")).

This proof-obligation is automatically discharged using the rules described above, and the following proof-obligation is returned:

isResistant (P "p2", ResWFWMWNProof(P "p2")), isWF(P "p2",WFBFProof(P "p2")),
isWN(P "p2", WNBFProof(P "p2")), isWM(P "p2", WMPdbd(P "p2",P "pt")),
isWM(P "pt", WMwithPtar(P "pt",T "t2",P "pone")),
isWM(T "t2" ,WMwithTAtom(T "t2")), isWM(P "pone", WMwithPAtom(P "pone")))

Informally, this proof can be read as follows: p2 is resistant, since it is well-formed, weakly-monotonic and without-not; p2 is well-formed which can checked by "brute-force", i.e., by checking the definition of p2; p2 is without the not_P operator, which can also be checked by "brute-force"; p2 is weakly-monotonic, since it is the deny-by-default of the weakly-monotonic policy pt; pt is weakly-monotonic, since it is the composition of the weakly-monotonic target t2 and of the weakly-monotonic policy pone; t2 is weakly-monotonic, since it is atomic; and pone is weakly-monotonic since it is atomic.

ATRAP parses this Maude proof-obligation, and using the Java mechanism described above, the following Isabelle theory is automatically generated. This theory is built on the logic atrap.thy, which includes the definition of the three-valued logic, the definition of PTaCL, and the lemmas corresponding to the different rules described in Section 3.

Fig. 3 presents the generated proof for the running example. For the sake of compactness, we do not go through Isabelle/Isar's syntax, but intuitively, the structure of the proof follows the informal description given above, and the tactics used are limited to the simplification tactic (which unfolds the definition of the entities involved in the proof), and the insertion of existing lemmas. It is worth observing that the generated proof is human readable, and is structurally very close to the corresponding mathematical proof. We believe this aspect to be particularly important as a security designer is not necessarily an expert in proof techniques, and ATRAP provides a high-level proof, without having to rely blindly on a verification tool.

5.1   Experimental Results

We now evaluate the performance of ATRAP for the generation of resistance proof. The complexity of the proof generation mostly depends on the number of constructors of a policy p, which we refer to by $size(p)$, since the number of applicable rules directly depends on that number. Figure 4 shows some evaluation times for $P\langle 8, 3, 3, 3, 500\rangle$, where the y axis is logarithmic. As expected, the complexity of the proof search is exponential in $size(p)$, making the proof search most of the time faster than the search for counter-examples (the few exceptions to that rule come from policies p with large sizes, but small $\mathcal{A}(p)$, i.e., policies where a same target is repeated a large number of times).

However, although usually faster than the counter-examples search, the accuracy of the proof generation decreases with $size(p)$. For instance, writing T_n for $P\langle n, n, 2, 2, 1000\rangle$, for T_1, we generated the proof for all of the 957 resistant policies, this ratio falls to $905/920 \approx 0.98$ for T_2, to $762/883 \approx 0.86$ for T_3, to $659/864 \approx 0.76$ for T_4, to $558/852 \approx 0.66$ for T_5, to $503/861 \approx 0.58$ for T_6, etc.

Theses results, together with those of Section 4.3, should be seen as a validation of the ATRAP approach, rather than a "real-world" characterisation of policy resistance. Indeed, the policies analysed are randomly generated, and therefore the samples do not necessarily represent policies defined in a concrete context. In particular, it is not necessarily the case that about 85% of the policies enforced in existing information systems are resistant. Similarly, even though the accuracy of the proof search decreases with the number of constructors used, a very large policy whose targets consist only of conjunctions of atomic targets, and using only the operator and$_P$, could be easily proved resistant.

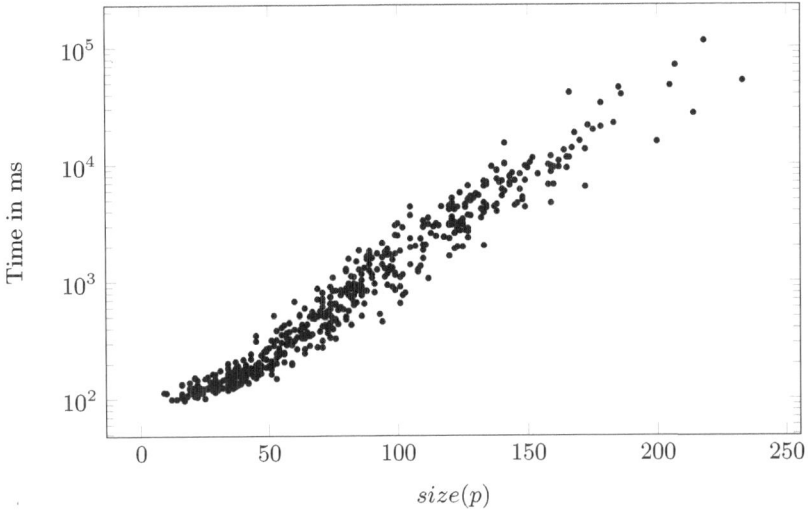

Fig. 4. Automatic search for proof for $P\langle 8, 3, 3, 3, 500\rangle$

6   Conclusion - Future Work

This paper presents the tool ATRAP, which, given a PTaCL policy, is capable of positively answer the three questions stated in the Introduction, i.e., can automatically detect the resistance of a policy by exhibiting a counter-example when it is not resistant, and, in some cases, by generating an Isabelle proof when it is. The different mechanisms are illustrated with two simple policies.

Using Proposition 3, we are able to limit the number of requests to evaluate when searching a counter-example, while maintaining the correctness and completeness of the approach. We have also implemented a collection of proof techniques allowing to prove efficiently the resistance of a policy, although large policies might fail to be proven automatically. However, the rules presented in Section 3 can also be seen as a policy construction guide, since a policy built using only those rules is resistant, by construction.

An interesting lead to explore for future work is to increase the interactivity between the search for counter-examples and the proof generation, by leveraging the different complexity of each approach. More precisely, we should take advantage of Maude to rewrite a policy to an equivalent one, such that the latter policy could be proven to be resistant more easily. This leads to the question of the existence of a normal form for policies, such that one could build a complete collection of resistance rules, i.e., if a policy in normal form is resistant, then there exists a set of structural proofs to prove it. At this stage, this remains as an open question.

We however believe that one of the strengths of our approach is its flexibility, and rules can be incrementally added. In order to so, one needs to provide the corresponding rule in Maude, together with Isabelle lemma and the Java class linking the two. Clearly, an interesting future work would consist in formalising this extendability, by having an explicit, abstract notion of rule, with multiple facets, i.e., one facet for Maude, one for Isabelle, one for Java. We could also extend our approach to other properties of access control policies, for instance by relying on the underlying properties of the rewrite system [4].

Another relevant problem is the one of fixing a policy, in order to transform a non-resistant policy into a resistant one. This problem raises the question of policy "closeness", i.e., given a non-resistant policy, it is not enough to create a resistant one, we also need to ensure that the new policy is close enough to the original one. It is worth noting that ATRAP can generate partial proof of resistance, i.e., even if the whole policy is not resistant, it might identify some sub-policies that are, which might be helpful to fix a given policy.

Finally, as we mentioned, the current version of PTaCL can be seen as a low level language, and it would therefore be worth interfacing a "higher" level language with PTaCL, in order to analyse more complex policies, for instance include relational targets. XACML 3.0 would be a good candidate for such an extension, since both languages are attribute and target-based. In general, we plan to release ATRAP as an open-source software, and to generally optimise the searches for counter-examples and proofs. In this regard, it would be worth looking at parallel/distributed computation, since the evaluation of each pair of requests $(q, q \setminus \{(n, v)\}$ can be performed independently.

Acknowledgements. The authors would like to thank Jason Crampton for valuable discussions about PTaCL and policy resistance.

References

1. Alberti, F., Armando, A., Ranise, S.: Efficient symbolic automated analysis of administrative attribute-based rbac-policies. In: Proceedings of the 6th ACM ASI-ACCS 2011, pp. 165–175. ACM, New York (2011)
2. Armando, A., Ranise, S.: Scalable automated symbolic analysis of administrative role-based access control policies by smt solving. Journal of Computer Security 20(4), 309–352 (2012)
3. Barker, S., Fernández, M.: Term rewriting for access control. In: Damiani, E., Liu, P. (eds.) Data and Applications Security 2006. LNCS, vol. 4127, pp. 179–193. Springer, Heidelberg (2006)
4. Bertolissi, C., Uttha, W.: Automated analysis of rule-based access control policies. In: Proceedings of the 7th Workshop on Programming Languages Meets Program Verification, PLPV 2013, pp. 47–56. ACM, New York (2013)
5. Bonatti, P., De Capitani Di Vimercati, S., Samarati, P.: An algebra for composing access control policies 5(1), 1–35 (2002)
6. Brucker, A.D., Brügger, L., Kearney, P., Wolff, B.: An approach to modular and testable security models of real-world health-care applications. In: Proceedings of ACM SACMAT 2011, pp. 133–142. ACM, New York (2011)
7. Bruns, G., Huth, M.: Access control via Belnap logic: Intuitive, expressive, and analyzable policy composition. ACM Transactions on Information and System Security 14(1), 9 (2011)

8. Clavel, M., Durán, F., Eker, S., Lincoln, P., Martí-Oliet, N., Meseguer, J., Talcott, C.: All About Maude. LNCS, vol. 4350. Springer, Heidelberg (2007)

9. Crampton, J., Huth, M.: An authorization framework resilient to policy evaluation failures. In: Gritzalis, D., Preneel, B., Theoharidou, M. (eds.) ESORICS 2010. LNCS, vol. 6345, pp. 472–487. Springer, Heidelberg (2010)

10. Crampton, J., Morisset, C.: PTaCL: A language for attribute-based access control in open systems. In: Degano, P., Guttman, J.D. (eds.) POST 2012. LNCS, vol. 7215, pp. 390–409. Springer, Heidelberg (2012)

11. Dougherty, D.J., Kirchner, C., Kirchner, H., Santana de Oliveira, A.: Modular access control via strategic rewriting. In: Biskup, J., López, J. (eds.) ESORICS 2007. LNCS, vol. 4734, pp. 578–593. Springer, Heidelberg (2007)

12. Eker, S.: Associative-commutative rewriting on large terms. In: Nieuwenhuis, R. (ed.) RTA 2003. LNCS, vol. 2706, pp. 14–29. Springer, Heidelberg (2003)

13. Griesmayer, A., Liu, Z., Morisset, C., Wang, S.: A framework for automated and certified refinement steps. Innov. Syst. Softw. Eng. 9(1), 3–16 (2013)

14. Griesmayer, A., Morisset, C.: Automated certification of authorisation policy resistance. CoRR, abs/1306.4624 (2013), http://arxiv.org/abs/1306.4624

15. Guelev, D.P., Ryan, M., Schobbens, P.-Y.: Model-checking access control policies. In: Zhang, K., Zheng, Y. (eds.) ISC 2004. LNCS, vol. 3225, pp. 219–230. Springer, Heidelberg (2004)

16. Hughes, G., Bultan, T.: Automated verification of access control policies using a sat solver. Int. J. Softw. Tools Technol. Transf. 10(6), 503–520 (2008)

17. Jobe, W.: Functional completeness and canonical forms in many-valued logics. Journal of Symbolic Logic 27(4), 409–422 (1962)

18. Kirchner, C., Kirchner, H., Santana de Oliveira, A.: Analysis of rewrite-based access control policies. Electron. Notes Theor. Comput. Sci. 234, 55–75 (2009)

19. Kleene, S.: Introduction to Metamathematics. D. Van Nostrand, Princeton (1950)

20. Nipkow, T., Paulson, L.C., Wenzel, M.T.: Isabelle/HOL. LNCS, vol. 2283. Springer, Heidelberg (2002)

21. OASIS. eXtensible Access Control Markup Language (XACML) Version 2.0. Committee Specification (2005)

22. OASIS. eXtensible Access Control Markup Language (XACML) Version 3.0. Committee Specification 01 (2010)

23. Rao, P., Lin, D., Bertino, E., Li, N., Lobo, J.: An algebra for fine-grained integration of XACML policies. In: Proceedings of the 14th ACM Symposium on Access Control Models and Technologies, pp. 63–72. ACM, New York (2009)

24. Tschantz, M., Krishnamurthi, S.: Towards reasonability properties for access-control policy languages. In: Ferraiolo, D., Ray, I. (eds.) 11th ACM Symposium on Access Control Models and Technologies, Proceedings, SACMAT 2006, pp. 160–169. ACM (2006)

25. Wenzel, M.: The isabelle/isar reference manual (2007)

26. Wijesekera, D., Jajodia, S.: A propositional policy algebra for access control 6(2), 286–235 (2003)

27. Zhang, N., Ryan, M., Guelev, D.P.: Synthesising verified access control systems through model checking. J. Comput. Secur. 16(1), 1–61 (2008)

Fine-Grained Access Control System Based on Outsourced Attribute-Based Encryption

Jin Li[1], Xiaofeng Chen[2], Jingwei Li[3], Chunfu Jia[3],
Jianfeng Ma[4], and Wenjing Lou[5]

[1] School of Computer Science and Educational Software,
Guangzhou University, P.R. China
jinli71@gmail.com
[2] State Key Laboratory of Integrated Service Networks,
Xidian University, P.R. China
xfchen@xidian.edu.cn
[3] College of Information Technical Science,
Nankai University, P.R. China
lijw@mail.nankai.edu.cn, cfjia@nankai.edu.cn
[4] School of Computer Science and Technology,
Xidian University, P.R. China
jfma@mail.xidian.edu.cn
[5] Department of Computer Science,
Virginia Polytechnic Institute and State University, USA
wjlou@vt.edu

Abstract. As cloud computing becomes prevalent, more and more sensitive data is being centralized into the cloud for sharing, which brings forth new challenges for outsourced data security and privacy. Attribute-based encryption (ABE) is a promising cryptographic primitive, which has been widely applied to design fine-grained access control system recently. However, ABE is being criticized for its high scheme overhead as the computational cost grows with the complexity of the access formula. This disadvantage becomes more serious for mobile devices because they have constrained computing resources.

Aiming at tackling the challenge above, we present a generic and efficient solution to implement attribute-based access control system by introducing secure outsourcing techniques into ABE. More precisely, two cloud service providers (CSPs), namely key generation-cloud service provider (KG-CSP) and decryption-cloud service provider (D-CSP) are introduced to perform the outsourced key-issuing and decryption on behalf of attribute authority and users respectively. In order to outsource heavy computation to both CSPs without private information leakage, we formulize an underlying primitive called outsourced ABE (OABE) and propose several constructions with outsourced decryption and key-issuing. Finally, extensive experiment demonstrates that with the help of KG-CSP and D-CSP, efficient key-issuing and decryption are achieved in our constructions.

J. Crampton, S. Jajodia, and K. Mayes (Eds.): ESORICS 2013, LNCS 8134, pp. 592–609, 2013.

1 Introduction

Cloud computing is an emerging computing paradigm in which IT resources and capacities are provided as services over the Internet while hiding platform and implementation details. Promising as it is, this paradigm also brings forth new challenges for data security and privacy when users outsource sensitive data for sharing on cloud servers, which are likely outside of the same trusted domain of data owners.

Data access control has been evolving in the past thirty years and various techniques have been developed to effectively implement fine-grained access control [20], which allows flexibility in specifying differential access rights of individual users. However, traditional access control systems are mostly designed for in-house services and depend greatly on the system itself to enforce authorization policies. Thus, they cannot be applied in cloud computing because users and cloud servers are no longer in the same trusted domain. For the purpose of helping the data owner impose access control over data stored on untrusted cloud servers, a feasible consideration would be encrypting data through certain cryptographic primitives but disclosing decryption keys only to authorized users. One critical issue of this branch of approaches is how to achieve the desired security goals without introducing high complexity of key management and data encryption. Existing work resolve this issue either by introducing a per file access control list (ACL) for fine-grained access control, or by categorizing files into several filegroups for efficiency. As the system scales, however, the ACL-based scheme would introduce an extremely high complexity which could be proportional to the number of system users. The filegroup-based scheme, on the other hand, is just able to provide coarse-grained access control of data.

Aiming at providing fine-grained access control over encrypted data, a novel public key primitive namely attribute-based encryption (ABE) [23] is introduced in the cryptographic community, which enables public key-based one-to-many encryption. In ABE system, users' keys and ciphertexts are labeled with sets of descriptive attributes and access policies respectively, and a particular key can decrypt a ciphertext only if the associated attributes and policy are matched.

Though ABE is a promising primitive to design fine-grained access control system in cloud computing, there are several challenges remained in the application of ABE.

- One of the main drawbacks of ABE is that the computational cost in decryption phase grows with the number of attributes specified in the access policy. The drawback appears more serious for resource-constrained users such as mobile devices and sensors. Therefore, one challenge is *how to reduce the decryption complexity of ABE such that it can be applied to fine-grained access control for users with resource-constrained devices.*
- Beyond decryption, generating user's private key in existing ABE schemes also requires a great quantity of modular exponentiations. Furthermore, the revocation of any single user in existing ABE requires key-update at authority for remaining users who share his/her attributes. All of these heavy tasks

centralized at authority side would make it become the efficiency bottleneck in the whole access control system. Therefore, another challenge is *how to reduce the key-issuing complexity of ABE such that scalable access control can be supported.*

1.1 Contribution Overview

Aiming at tackling the challenges described above, we propose a generic construction of attribute-based access control system under an interesting architecture, in which two cloud service providers (CSPs) namely key generation-cloud service provider (KG-CSP) and decryption-cloud service provider (D-CSP) are involved to perform the outsourced heavy tasks for users' key issuing and file access. With the help of the CSPs, the computational complexity at both user and attribute authority sides is reduced. Furthermore, since only small computation is required at authority side for single user's private key update, the proposed system is able to efficiently support user revocation.

The challenge issue in the proposed system is how to outsource the heavy computation to the CSPs as much as possible but without private information leakage. Our solution is introducing an underlying primitive namely outsourced ABE (OABE), which allows expensive tasks to be securely outsourced to CSPs to relieve computation overhead at local. We provide several OABE constructions with outsourced key-issuing and decryption. As far as we know, this work is the first attempt considering outsourcing key-issuing and decryption in ABE simultaneously. Our first construction requires only constant computation (nearly two single-based exponentiations) at attribute authority during key-issuing besides efficient decryption. Our second construction provides access control in a fine-grained manner but remains the same efficiency as previous constructions.

1.2 Organization

The rest of this paper is organized as follows. In Section 2, we present the architecture and adversary model for attribute-based access control system. In Section 3, an efficient access control system based on OABE is described. In Section 4, we propose a basic OABE construction with outsourced decryption for access control. Several OABE constructions with outsourced key-issuing and decryption for improved access control are presented in Section 5. In Section 6, an extensive experimental result is provided for demonstrating the efficiency of our main OABE construction. In Section 7, the previous work related to ours is surveyed. Finally, we draw conclusion in Section 8.

2 Attribute-Based Access Control System Model

In this section, we describe the architecture for the attribute-based access control system and define its security model.

2.1   Introduction of Attribute-Based Encryption

ABE has been widely applied to impose fine-grained access control on encrypted data recently. There are two kinds of ABE having been proposed: key-policy attribute-based encryption (KP-ABE) and ciphertext-policy attribute-based encryption (CP-ABE). In KP-ABE, each ciphertext is labeled by the encryptor with a set of descriptive attributes. Each private key is associated with an access structure that specifies which type of ciphertexts the key can decrypt. Whereas, in CP-ABE, the access structure is specified in ciphertext by encryptor and each private key is associated with a set of attributes. Without loss of generality, we are able to denote (I_{enc}, I_{key}) as the input to encryption and key generation of ABE. Accordingly, in CP-ABE scheme, $(I_{enc}, I_{key}) = (\mathbb{A}, \omega)$ while that is $(\omega, \mathbb{A})$ in KP-ABE, where ω and $\mathbb{A}$ denotes an attribute set and an access structure, respectively. In ABE, there are two entities: the attribute authority and users. The attribute authority is in charge of the issue of attribute private key to users requesting them. In more detail, the definition of four algorithms in ABE is given as follows.

- Setup(λ) : The setup algorithm takes as input – a security parameter λ. It outputs (PK, MK), where PK denotes the public key and MK denotes the master key of the attribute authority.
- KeyGen(I_{key}, MK) : The key extraction algorithm takes as input – a user's access structure (resp. attribute set) I_{key} and the attribute authority's master key MK. It outputs the user's private key SK.
- Encrypt(M, I_{enc}) : The encryption algorithm takes as input – a message M and the attribute set (resp. access structure) I_{enc}. It outputs the ciphertext CT with access policy I_{enc}.
- Decrypt(CT, SK) : The decryption algorithm takes as input – a ciphertext CT which was assumed to be encrypted under the attribute set (resp. access structure) I_{enc} and the private key SK for access structure (resp. attribute set) I_{key}. It outputs the message M if $\gamma(I_{key}, I_{enc}) = 1$ and the error symbol $\perp$ otherwise, where the predicate γ is predefined.

2.2   Architecture for the Attribute-Based Access Control System

As shown in Fig. 1, the architecture for the attribute-based access control system consists of the following entities:

- *Attribute Authority (AA)*. This is a key authority for the attribute set. It is in charge of issuing, revoking, and updating attribute keys for users.
- *Data Owner*. This is a user who owns data files and wishes to outsource them into the external storage server provided by a CSP. It is responsible for defining and enforcing an attribute set (resp. access policy) on its own files.
- *User*. This is an entity who wants to access an outsourced file. If the user owns an access privilege of an encrypted file, and is not revoked, he/she will be able to obtain the file.

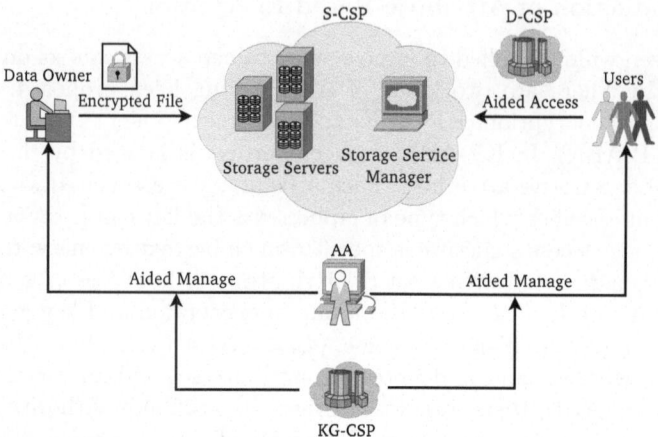

Fig. 1. Architecture for Attribute-based Access Control System

- *Storage-Cloud Service Provider (S-CSP).* This is an entity that provides a data storage outsourcing service. In this paper, we assume that S-CSP is always online and has abundant storage capacity and computation power.
- *Key Generation-Cloud Service Provider (KG-CSP).* This is an entity that provides an outsourcing computing service for AA through undertaking the expensive tasks delegated by AA.
- *Decryption-Cloud Service Provider (D-CSP).* This is an entity that provides an outsourcing computing service through performing partial decryption on ciphertext.

We give an overview of the attribute-based access control system as follows.

- **System Setup.** Public parameter and master key are initialized for the system and AA keeps the master key as secret information.
- **New User Grant.** When a new user wants to join the system, with the aid of KG-CSP, AA issues an attribute private key to him/her based on his/her attributes .
- **New File Creation.** When a data owner wants to outsource and share a file with some users, he/she encrypts the file to be uploaded under a specified attribute set (resp. access policy).
- **File Access.** When a user wants to access an outsourced file, he/she downloads ciphertext from S-CSP and decrypts it with the help of D-CSP.
- **User Revocation.** When there is a user to be revoked, AA updates "affected" users' private keys with the help of KG-CSP, while the "affected" ciphertexts having been stored on S-CSP will be updated as well.

2.3   Adversary Model and Security Requirements

We assume that S-CSP, D-CSP and KG-CSP are honest but curious. More precisely, they will follow our proposed protocols, but try to find out as much secret information as possible based on their possessions. Furthermore, D-CSP is allowed to collude with curious users and S-CSP. Thus, two types of adversaries are considered in our access control system: i) users colluding with D-CSP and S-CSP; ii) semi-trusted KG-CSP, which is not allowed to collude with users.

The security requirement considered in this paper is *semantic security of data*, which is defined as follows: Unauthorized users (that is, the two types of adversaries defined above) without appropriate access structure (resp. attributes) matching the attributes (resp. policy) embedded in ciphertext should be prevented from accessing the underlying plaintext.

3   OABE-Based Access Control System

In this section, we provide a generic construction of the attribute-based access control system. Its security analysis is presented as well.

3.1   Building Block: OABE

Based on the system model provided in Section 2, we attempt to define an underlying primitive namely OABE with outsourced key-issuing and decryption for realizing our access control system. Notice that the definitions of **Setup** and **Encrypt** in OABE are identical to traditional ABE shown in Section 2.1, we only show the definitions of *outsourced key-issuing protocol* and *outsourced decryption protocol*.

Outsourced Key-Issuing Protocol. Three entities including users, AA and KG-CSP are involved in this protocol. Upon receiving a key-issuing request from a user, AA firstly sends an outsourcing key (denoted as OK) to KG-CSP and receives a private key component (denoted as SK_1) for the user. The other component SK_2 is computed locally by AA. At a high level, the protocol is described as follows.

$$\text{User} \underset{SK}{\overset{\text{request}}{\rightleftarrows}} \text{AA} \underset{SK_1}{\overset{OK}{\rightleftarrows}} \text{KG-CSP}$$

The outsourced key-issuing protocol consists of the following three polynomial-time algorithms.

- O-KeyGen-PreProc(I_{key}, MK) : The preprocessing algorithm run by AA takes as input – the access structure (resp. attribute set) I_{key} for a user, the master key MK. It outputs the key pair (OK, AK) where OK denotes the outsourcing key for KG-CSP and AK denotes the secret key for AA to compute the other component of private key.

- O-KeyGen-Outsource(I_{key}, OK) : The outsourced algorithm run by KG-CSP takes as input – the access structure (resp. attribute set) I_{key} and the outsourcing key OK. It outputs the private key component SK_1.
- O-KeyGen-PostProc(AK, SK_1) : The postprocessing algorithm run by AA takes as input – the secret key AK and the private key SK_1. It outputs $SK = (SK_1, SK_2)$ as the user's private key.

Outsourced Decryption Protocol. Two entities including users and D-CSP are involved in this protocol. More precisely, upon receiving the ciphertext CT, the user delivers SK_1 along with CT to D-CSP and receives a partially decrypted ciphertext CT'. Finally, the message is completely computed by the user with SK. At a high level, it can be described as follows.

- O-Decrypt-Outsource(CT, SK_1) : The outsourced algorithm run by D-CSP takes as input – a ciphertext CT assumed to be encrypted under the attribute set (resp. access structure) I_{enc} and the private key component SK_1 for access structure (resp. attribute set) I_{key}. It outputs the partially decrypted ciphertext CT' if $\gamma(I_{\text{key}}, I_{\text{enc}}) = 1$, otherwise outputs $\perp$.
- O-Decrypt-Dec(CT', SK) : The complete decryption algorithm run by the user takes as input – the partially decrypted ciphertext CT' and the private key SK. It outputs a message M.

Security Model

Two types of adversaries are classified as in Section 2.3:

- *Type-I Adversary.* It is defined as a curious user colluding with D-CSP. Such an adversary is allowed to ask for all the SK_1 and the private keys SK of dishonest users. The goal of this adversary is to obtain useful information from ciphertext not intended for him/her. Notice that Type-I adversary cannot get outsourcing key OK for any user.
- *Type-II Adversary.* It is defined as a curious KG-CSP. Such an adversary owns outsourcing keys OK for all users in the system and tries to extract any useful information from ciphertext.

Having the intuition above, we are able to follow the replayable chosen-ciphertext attack (RCCA) security given in [15] and define it for both type-I and type-II adversaries in our OABE. The security definition is similar to the previous work [15], where the only difference is that an additional security game is defined to simulate the type-II adversary with the outsourcing keys of all users.

Definition 1 (RCCA Security). *An OABE scheme with outsourced key-issuing and decryption is secure against replayable chosen-ciphertext attack if all polynomial-time adversaries have at most a negligible advantage in the RCCA security games for both type-I and type-II adversaries.*

3.2 Generic Construction of OABE-Based Access Control System

System Setup. Choose a security parameter 1^λ and run the algorithm $\mathsf{Setup}(1^\lambda)$ of OABE to obtain the public parameter PK and the master key MK. The public parameter is then published, while the master key is kept by AA as a secret.

New File Creation. Whenever a data owner wants to create and upload a file $\mathcal{F}$ to S-CSP, he/she firstly defines an attribute set (resp. access structure) I_{enc} for this file. Then, the owner randomly picks a symmetric key K from the key space and encrypts the file $\mathcal{F}$ with K using standard symmetric key algorithm such as AES to obtain the ciphertext $CT_{\mathcal{F}}$. Later on, he/she runs the algorithm $\mathsf{Encrypt}(I_{\mathrm{enc}}, K)$ of OABE to generate the ciphertext CT_K which is an encryption of the symmetric key with respect to I_{enc}. Finally, the data owner uploads the ciphertext $(CT_{\mathcal{F}}, CT_K)$ to S-CSP.

New User Grant. Assuming a user wants to join the system, he/she needs to be issued a private key on his/her access structure (resp. attribute set) I_{key} from AA who then runs the outsourced key-issuing protocol. In concrete, AA outsources the operation of key-issuing by running the algorithm of O-KeyGen-PreProc(I_{key}, MK) to obtain an outsourcing key OK. Using OK, KG-CSP runs O-KeyGen-Outsource(I_{key}, OK) to generate a private key component SK_1. Finally, AA generates the other private key component SK_2 and assigns $SK = (SK_1, SK_2)$ to the user.

File Access. Suppose a user wants to access and retrieve files of his/her interests. He/She firstly downloads the ciphertext $(CT_{\mathcal{F}}, CT_K)$. To decrypt the ciphertext while relieving the local computation overhead, the user runs the outsourced decryption protocol with D-CSP by sending CT_K and the private key component SK_1. If the user's I_{key} in SK_1 matches I_{enc} embedded in CT_K, D-CSP is able to successfully compute and return the partially decrypted ciphertext CT_K'. Upon receiving CT_K', the user performs complete decryption to get the symmetric key K, with which he/she decrypts and retrieves the file $\mathcal{F}$.

User Revocation. Whenever there is a user to be revoked, a public parameter update technique in [24] is utilized. Specifically, AA determines a minimal set of attributes according to the user's I_{key} and updates the corresponding components in PK and MK. Then, AA updates private keys $SK = (SK_1', SK_2)$ for all the "affected" users by running the outsourced key-issuing protocol with KG-CSP. Additionally, to update "affected" ciphertexts having been stored in S-CSP, a re-encrypting key is generated by AA to be sent to S-CSP. S-CSP uses such a key to update the "affected" ciphertexts with the latest version of PK. Notice that the main computation at AA side is updating private keys for "affected" users. Utilizing the outsourced key-issuing protocol, such complexity is minimized.

Security Analysis

Theorem 1. *The generic construction of access control system is semantically-secure if the underlying hybrid encryption satisfies RCCA security.*

Proof. The security will be analyzed based on the security model of access control system given in 2.3. More specifically, two types of adversaries will be considered here, that is, type-I and type-II adversaries. For each type adversary, we show how to construct a simulator to break the hybrid encryption at a high level.

Since the file is encrypted with a hybrid encryption as $(CT_\mathcal{F}, CT_K)$, to get any information about $\mathcal{F}$, the adversary should decrypt CT_K to retrieve the symmetric key K. However such a key is protected by OABE. Thus, in the above generic construction, a hybrid encryption has been utilized to encrypt the file. As we know, the above hybrid encryption scheme could achieve RCCA security if the following two conditions satisfy [9], that is, i) the OABE scheme is RCCA secure and ii) the symmetric key encryption scheme is CCA secure. Thus, data confidentiality can be reduced to the confidentiality security of the underlying OABE and symmetric key encryption [9]. Moreover, the privacy of OABE ciphertext on S-CSP against outside users without I_{key} can be trivially guaranteed because its security definition inherits that in traditional ABE. Another attack on data confidentiality is launched by KG-CSP. Such an attack is modeled as type-II adversary by introducing an oracle $\mathcal{O}_{OK}(\cdot)$ in the corresponding security game of OABE. Specifically, we allow such an adversary to ask for outsourcing keys OK for all the users, but it is not allowed to get any secret key of users. Curious users can collude with both D-CSP and S-CSP to launch attack, which is modeled as type-I adversary in the definition of OABE. Therefore, the security of the attribute-based access control system is reduced to that of underlying OABE and symmetric encryption.

In the following sections, we take our focus on OABE and attempt to provide secure OABE construction for attribute-based access control system.

4   Basic OABE Construction with Outsourced Decryption

4.1   Access Structure

Definition 2 (Access Structure). *Let* $\{P_1, \ldots, P_n\}$ *be a set of parties. A collection* $\mathbb{A} \subseteq 2^{\{P_1, \ldots, P_n\}}$ *is monotone if* $\forall B, C$: *if* $B \in \mathbb{A}$ *and* $B \subseteq C$ *then* $C \in \mathbb{A}$. *An access structure (resp. monotone access structure) is a collection (resp. monotone collection)* $\mathbb{A}$ *of non-empty subsets of* $\{P_1, \ldots, P_n\}$. *The sets in* $\mathbb{A}$ *are called authorized sets.*

Denote ω and $\mathbb{A}$ as an attribute set and access structure, respectively. We define a predicate $\gamma(\omega, \mathbb{A})$ as follows

$$\gamma(\omega, \mathbb{A}) = \begin{cases} 1 \text{ if } \omega \in \mathbb{A} \\ 0 \text{ otherwise} \end{cases}$$

In this paper, the role of the party is taken by attributes. Thus, the access structure $\mathbb{A}$ contains the authorized sets of attributes. Specifically, the access structure represented by tree can be supported in this paper.

Let $\mathcal{T}$ be an access tree, in which each interior node is a threshold gate (i.e. AND gate or OR gate) while the leaves are associated with attributes. A user is able to decrypt a ciphertext with a given key if and only if there is an assignment of attributes from the private key to leaf nodes of the tree such that the tree is satisfied.

4.2 Basic Mathematical Tools

We introduce two basic mathematical tools that will be used in the following constructions.

Definition 3 (Bilinear Map). *Let $\mathbb{G}$ and $\mathbb{G}_T$ be cyclic groups of prime order q, writing the group action multiplicatively. g is a generator of $\mathbb{G}$. Let $e : \mathbb{G} \times \mathbb{G} \to \mathbb{G}_T$ be an efficient map with the following properties:*

- *Bilinearity: $e(g_1^a, g_2^b) = e(g_1, g_2)^{ab}$ for all $g_1, g_2 \in \mathbb{G}$, and $a, b \in_R \mathbb{Z}_q$;*
- *Non-degeneracy: There exists $g_1, g_2 \in \mathbb{G}$ such that $e(g_1, g_2) \neq 1$, in other words, the map does not send all pairs in $\mathbb{G} \times \mathbb{G}$ to the identity in $\mathbb{G}_T$.*

Definition 4 (DBDH assumption). *The decision Bilinear Diffie-Hellman (DBDH) assumption is that, given g, g^x, g^y, $g^z \in \mathbb{G}$ for unknown random values $x, y, z \in_R \mathbb{Z}_q$, and $T \in_R \mathbb{G}_T$, it is difficult to decide if $T = e(g, g)^{xyz}$ for a probabilistic polynomial algorithm.*

4.3 Proposed Construction

We only consider to outsource the decryption computation of ABE and propose a basic OABE construction with outsourced decryption. In another word, the KG-CSP will not be involved. For simplicity, this basic construction only considers to support for access structure described as $\mathbb{A} = \{\omega \subseteq \mathcal{U} : |\omega \cap \omega^*| \geq d\}$ where $\mathcal{U}$ is the attribute universe, ω and ω^* are attribute sets and d is a predefined threshold value. Actually, it can be easily extended to an OABE supporting access structure represented by tree as shown in Section 5.2.

Before providing the construction, we define the Lagrange coefficient $\Delta_{i,S}$ for $i \in \mathbb{Z}_p$ and a set S of elements in $\mathbb{Z}_p$ as $\Delta_{i,S} = \prod_{j \in S, j \neq i} \frac{x-j}{i-j}$.

Setup Phase

- Setup(λ) : Define a bilinear group $\mathbb{G}$ of prime order p with a generator g and a bilinear map $e : \mathbb{G} \times \mathbb{G} \to \mathbb{G}_T$. Next, define the attributes in universe $\mathcal{U}$ as elements in $\mathbb{Z}_p$. For simplicity let $n = |\mathcal{U}|$ and the first n elements in $\mathbb{Z}_p$ (i.e. $1, 2, \ldots, n \bmod p$) can be taken to be the universe. Select $x \in_R \mathbb{Z}_p$ and set $g_1 = g^x$. Pick $g_2, h, h_1, \ldots, h_n \in_R \mathbb{G}$. Output the public parameter $PK = (g, g_1, g_2, h, h_1, \ldots, h_n)$ and the master key $MK = x$ which is kept secret by AA.

Key-Issuing Phase. A hybrid policy $\mathcal{P} = \mathcal{P}_\theta \wedge \mathcal{P}_\omega$ is utilized in the key-issuing phase, where $\wedge$ is an AND gate connecting two sub-policies $\mathcal{P}_\omega$ and $\mathcal{P}_\theta$. More precisely, a default attribute θ is appended with each user's attribute set and the master key x is randomly split into x_1 and x_2 for each user to generate private key components on $\mathcal{P}_\omega$ and $\mathcal{P}_\theta$ respectively.

The key generation algorithm is described as follows.

- KeyGen(ω, MK) : Upon receiving a private key request on attribute set ω, the authority selects $x_1 \in_R \mathbb{Z}_p$ and sets $x_2 = x - x_1 \bmod p$. Furthermore, select a $(d-1)$-degree polynomial $q(\cdot)$ such that $q(0) = x_1$. Then, for each $i \in \omega$, choose $r_i \in_R \mathbb{Z}_p$, and compute $d_{i0} = g_2^{q(i)}(g_1 h_i)^{r_i}$ and $d_{i1} = g^{r_i}$. For the default attribute θ, compute $d_{\theta 0} = g_2^{x_2}(g_1 h)^{r_\theta}$ and $d_{\theta 1} = g^{r_\theta}$ by choosing $r_\theta \in_R \mathbb{Z}_p$. The private key is $SK = (SK_1, SK_2)$ where $SK_1 = \{d_{i0}, d_{i1}\}_{i \in \omega}$ and $SK_2 = \{d_{\theta 0}, d_{\theta 1}\}$.

Encryption Phase. Based on the logical split of user's attribute private key, the default attribute θ should be embeded in each ciphertext to make the decryption successful. The encryption algorithm works as follows.

- Encrypt(M, ω') : To encrypt a message M with respect to an attribute set ω', select $s \in_R \mathbb{Z}_p$ and compute $C_0 = Me(g_1, g_2)^s$, $C_1 = g^s$, $E_\theta = (g_1 h)^s$ and $E_i = (g_1 h_i)^s$ for each $i \in \omega'$. Finally, output the ciphertext $CT = (\omega' \cup \{\theta\}, C_0, C_1, \{E_i\}_{i \in \omega' \cup \{\theta\}})$.

Outsourced Decryption Phase. The outsourced decryption consists of the following two algorithms.

- O-Decrypt-Outsource(CT, SK_1) : Suppose that a ciphertext CT is encrypted with an attribute set ω'. After receiving the private key component SK_1 for attribute set ω sent from a user, D-CSP continutes to compute the partially decrypted ciphertext CT': after selecting $S \subseteq \omega' \cap \omega$ with $|S| = d$, it computes $\dfrac{\prod_{i \in S} e(C_1, d_{i0})^{\Delta_{i,S}(0)}}{\prod_{i \in S} e(d_{i1}, E_i)^{\Delta_{i,S}(0)}} = e(g, g_2)^{sx_1}$. Fianlly, the partially decrypted ciphertext CT' is obtained as $CT' = (C_0, C_1, E_\theta, e(g, g_2)^{sx_1})$.

- O-Decrypt-Dec(CT', SK) : Upon receiving CT' from D-CSP, the user completely decrypts the ciphertext and gets a message M as $M = \dfrac{e(d_{\theta 1}, E_\theta)C_0}{e(g, g_2)^{sx_1}e(C_1, d_{\theta 0})}$.

4.4 Security Analysis

The main challenge in our construction is to prevent attacks from the collusion between users and D-CSP. However, such collusion is resistant due to the random split on master key x for each user. More precisely, if two different users call for their private keys, AA will choose two random splits (x_1, x_2) and (x_1', x_2') such that $x_1 + x_2 = x \bmod p$ and $x_1' + x_2' = x \bmod p$. Note that x_1 and x_1' are used to generate the private key component SK_1 and SK_1' respectively, while SK_2 and SK_2' are separately generated from x_2 and x_2'. In this sense, the ciphertext can be correctly decrypted only when SK_1 matches SK_2. Therefore, even if a group of curious users collude with D-CSP to obtain all SK_1, they cannot forge a valid private key for themselves to perform decryption successfully out of their scopes.

Since basic outsoured decryption is supported, we only need to consider the security against type-I adversary. Then, we have the following security result.

Theorem 2. *The basic OABE scheme with outsourced decryption is secure against chosen-plaintext attack in selective model under DBDH assumption.*

Proof. Assume there exists an adversary $\mathcal{A}$ breaks the proposed scheme, we can build a simulator $\mathcal{S}$ that uses $\mathcal{A}$ as a sub-algorithm to solve the DBDH problem (X, Y, Z, T) as follows. The simulator $\mathcal{S}$ runs $\mathcal{A}$ and receives a challenge attribute set ω^* from $\mathcal{A}$. $\mathcal{S}$ sets $g_1 = X, g_2 = Y$ and $h = g_1^{-1}g^{-\alpha}$ where $\alpha \in_R \mathbb{Z}_p$. For $i \in \omega^*$, it selects $\alpha_i \in_R \mathbb{Z}_p$ and sets $h_i = g_1^{-1}g^{\alpha_i}$. For $i \notin \omega^*$, it selects $\alpha_i \in_R \mathbb{Z}_p$ and sets $h_i = g^{\alpha_i}$. Finally, $\mathcal{S}$ sends the public parameter $PK = (g, g_1, g_2, h, h_1, \ldots, h_n)$ to $\mathcal{A}$, where n is the number of attributes in universe. $\mathcal{A}$ is provided two types of oracles as follows:

i) Upon receiving the private key component SK_1 request on ω, $\mathcal{S}$ checks whether the entry $(\omega, \cdot, SK_1)$ exists in T. If so return SK_1; otherwise, if $|\omega \cap \omega^*| < d$, $\mathcal{S}$ picks $x_2 \in_R \mathbb{Z}_p$ and defines three sets Γ, Γ' and S, where $\Gamma = \omega \cap \omega^*, |\Gamma'| = d - 1, \Gamma \subseteq \Gamma' \subseteq \omega$ and $S = \Gamma' \cup \{0\}$. Then, for each $i \in \Gamma'$, compute $d_{i0} = g_2^{\tau_i}(g_1 h_i)^{r_i}$ and $d_{i1} = g^{r_i}$ where $\tau_i, r_i \in_R \mathbb{Z}_p$. For each $i \in \omega \backslash \Gamma'$, set $r_i = -y\Delta_{0,S}(i) + r_i'$ by choosing $r_i' \in_R \mathbb{Z}_p$. Finally, compute $d_{i0} = g_2^{\sum_{j \in \Gamma'} \Delta_{j,S}(i)\tau_j - (x_2 + \alpha_i)\Delta_{0,S}(i)}(g_1 h_i)^{r_i'}$ and $d_{i1} = g_2^{-\Delta_{0,S}(i)}g^{r_i'}$. Otherwise (i.e. $|\omega \cap \omega^*| \geq d$), $\mathcal{S}$ picks $x_1 \in_R \mathbb{Z}_p$ and randomly selects a $(d-1)$-degree polynomial $q(\cdot)$ with $q(0) = x_1$. Then, for each attribute $i \in \omega$, $d_{i0} = g_2^{q(i)}(g_1 h_i)^{r_i}$ and $d_{i1} = g^{r_i}$ where $r_i \in_R \mathbb{Z}_p$.

ii) Upon receiving a private key request on ω with $|\omega \cap \omega^*| < d$, $\mathcal{S}$ checks whether the entry $(\omega, SK, \cdot)$ exists in T. If so return SK; otherwise if the value x_2 for such entry has not been selected, $\mathcal{S}$ picks $x_2 \in_R \mathbb{Z}_p$ and the remaining simulation is similar to the first case (i.e. $|\omega \cap \omega^*| < d$) to obtain SK_1, and compute $SK_2 = (d_{\theta 0} = g_2^{x_2}(g_1 h)^{r_\theta}, d_{\theta 1} = g^{r_\theta})$, where $r_\theta \in_R \mathbb{Z}_p$. Finally, after adding (ω, SK, SK_1) into T, $\mathcal{S}$ returns $SK = (SK_1, SK_2)$.

Two challenge messages M_0 and M_1 are chosen by $\mathcal{A}$. The simulator $\mathcal{S}$ flips a fair binary coin ν and generates the ciphertext of M_ν as $CT^* = (\omega^* \cup \{\theta\}, M_\nu T, g^z, g^{-z\alpha}, \{g^{z\alpha_i}\}_{i \in \omega^*})$. Note that: i) If $\mu = 0$, then $T = e(g, g)^{xyz}$. Let $s = z$ and we have $C_0 = M_\nu T = M_\nu e(g, g)^{xyz} = M_\nu e(g_1, g_2)^z, C_1 = g^z, E_\theta = g^{-z\alpha} = (g_1 g_1^{-1} g^{-\alpha})^z = (g_1 h)^z$ and $E_i = g^{z\alpha_i} = (g_1 g_1^{-1} g^{\alpha_i})^z = (g_1 h_i)^z$ for $i \in \omega^*$. Therefore, the ciphertext is a random encryption of the message M_ν under the attribute set ω^*.

The above querying phase is repeated with the restriction that $\mathcal{A}$ cannot issue a private key request on ω with $\gamma_d(\omega, \omega^*) = 1$.

$\mathcal{A}$ outputs a guess ν' of ν. If $\nu' = \nu$, $\mathcal{S}$ outputs $\mu' = 0$ to indicate that it was given a DBDH-tuple; otherwise, it outputs $\mu' = 1$ to indicate it was given a random 4-tuple.

5   Improved OABE Construction for Efficient Access Control System

In this section, based on the basic OABE, we further propose two OABE constructions supporting outsourced key-issuing and fine-grained access control.

5.1   OABE Construction with Outsourced Key-Issuing

Notice that in our basic construction, any adversary possessing either SK_1 or SK_2 cannot extract any useful information from the ciphertext. Thus, we are able to outsource the operation of generating SK_1 to KG-CSP but remain computing SK_2 at AA. Considering on this, we propose an OABE construction with outsourced key-issuing and decryption. Since the other phases are identical to our basic construction, we only provide the outsourced key-issuing protocol as follows.

- O-KeyGen-PreProc(ω, MK) : The preprocessing algorithm in outsourced key-issuing protocol is run by AA. It picks $x_1 \in_R \mathbb{Z}_q$ and sets $x_2 = x - x_1 \bmod q$. Finally, output (OK, AK) where $OK = x_1$ and $AK = x_2$.
- O-KeyGen-Outsource(ω, OK) : The outsourcing algorithm is run by KG-CSP. It randomly selects a $(d-1)$-degree polynomial $q(\cdot)$ with $q(0) = x_1$, and computes $SK_1 = (\{d_{i0}, d_{i1}\}_{i\in\omega})$ where $d_{i0} = g_2^{q(i)}(g_1h_i)^{r_i}, d_{i1} = g^{r_i}$ and $r_i \in_R \mathbb{Z}_p$.
- O-KeyGen-PostProc(SK_1, AK) : The postprocessing algorithm is run by AA. It computes $SK_2 = (d_{\theta 0}, d_{\theta 1})$ where $d_{\theta 0} = g_2^{x_2}(g_1h)^{r_\theta}, d_{\theta 1} = g^{r_\theta}$ and $r_\theta \in_R \mathbb{Z}_p$. Finally output $SK = (SK_1, SK_2)$.

We have shown that the proposed construction is resistant to the type-I adversary in Section 4.4. Therefore, it is only needed to prove its security under the attack launched by the type-II adversary. Intuitively, in order to decrypt ciphertext, the adversary has to recover $e(g_1, g_2)^s$. The adversary could utilize Lagrange interpolation on SK_1 and $C_1 = g^s$ from ciphertext to recover the desired value. This will result in $e(g, g_2)^{sx_1}$ but blinded by $e(g, g_2)^{sx_2}$ which cannot be removed unless the other component of private key SK_2 is used.

Thus, we can get the following security result based on the analysis above.

Theorem 3. *The proposed OABE construction with outsourced key-issuing and decryption is secure against chosen-plaintext attack launched by type-II adversary.*

5.2   OABE Construction for Fine-Grained Access Control

Though we describe our outsourcing key-issuing technique in the threshold ABE, it can be easily extended to be applied to the access tree-based KP-ABE scheme [14] to enable fine-grained access control.

The idea behind this extension is to build a hybrid tree $\mathcal{T}$ as shown in Fig. 2, where $\wedge$ and $\vee$ denote AND and OR gates respectively, and A_i denotes the attribute.

To facilitate working with the access tree, we define a few notations and functions as follows.

- num_x is the number of children of an interior node x. Therefore, if assuming y is the child of node x, we could denote $\mathsf{index}(y)$ as such number associated with the node y.
- k_x is the threshold value of an interior node x, specifically, when $k_x = 1$, the threshold gate at x is OR gate and when $k_x = num_x$, that is an AND gate.
- The function $\mathsf{parent}(x)$ returns the parent of the node x in the tree. $\mathsf{attr}(x)$ returns the attribute associated with the leaf node x.

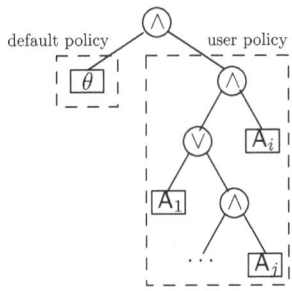

default policy   user policy

Fig. 2. Hybrid Tree Policy

Suppose the access tree specified by user is denoted as $\mathcal{T}_U$. Assuming the parameters have been assigned as the setup algorithm in Section 4.3, we provide the outsourced key-issuing protocol for access tree-based KP-ABE scheme as follows.

- O-KeyGen-PreProc($\mathcal{T}_U, MK$) : Randomly pick a one-degree polynomial $q_R(\cdot)$ with $q_R(0) = x$. Set $x_1 = q_R(1)$ and $x_2 = q_R(2)$. Finally output $OK = x_1$ and $AK = x_2$.
- O-KeyGen-Outsource($\mathcal{T}_U, OK$) : Firstly, choose a $(k_x - 1)$-degree polynomial $q_x(\cdot)$ for each node x (including leaves) in the tree $\mathcal{T}_U$ in a top-down manner. We note that the polynomial $q_x(\cdot)$ is chosen with the restriction that $q_x(0) = x_1$ if x is the root node in $\mathcal{T}_U$, otherwise $q_x(0) = q_{\mathsf{parent}(x)}(\mathsf{index}(x))$. Let Y_U be the set of leaf nodes in $\mathcal{T}_U$, then the private key component SK_1 is set to be $(\{g_2^{q_y(0)}(g_1 h_{\mathsf{attr}(y)})^{r_y}, g^{r_y}\})$.
- O-KeyGen-PostProc(AK, SK_1) : After generating the private key component $SK_2 = (\{g_2^{x_2}(g_1 h)^{r_\theta}, g^{r_\theta}\})$ where $r_\theta \in_R \mathbb{Z}_p$, AA outputs the private key $SK = (SK_1, SK_2)$.

6   Performance Evaluation

As shown in Fig. 3, we provide a thorough experimental evaluation of the construction proposed in Section 5.1. Our experiment is simulated with the pairing-based cryptography (PBC) library [19] on a Linux machine with Intel Core 2 processor running at 2.40 GHz and 2G memory.

Our analysis is in terms of four phases in the construction. In Fig. 3(a) and Fig. 3(c), it is not surprising to see that as with existing ABE scheme [23], the computational cost in setup and encryption grows linearly with the number of attributes. In our outsourced construction, during the outsourced key-issuing phase the computation at AA just includes three exponentiations in $\mathbb{G}$, while that at U during the outsourced decryption phase just includes three bilinear pairings and one exponentiation in $\mathbb{G}_T$. The time cost for the both outsourced phases are reflected respectively in Fig. 3(b) and Fig. 3(d). Compared with the other OABE schemes such as [15,25], the computational cost at user side in the decryption algorithm is almost the same with ours. However, their work cannot support outsourced key-issuing because they used the blinding technique during user key-issuing.

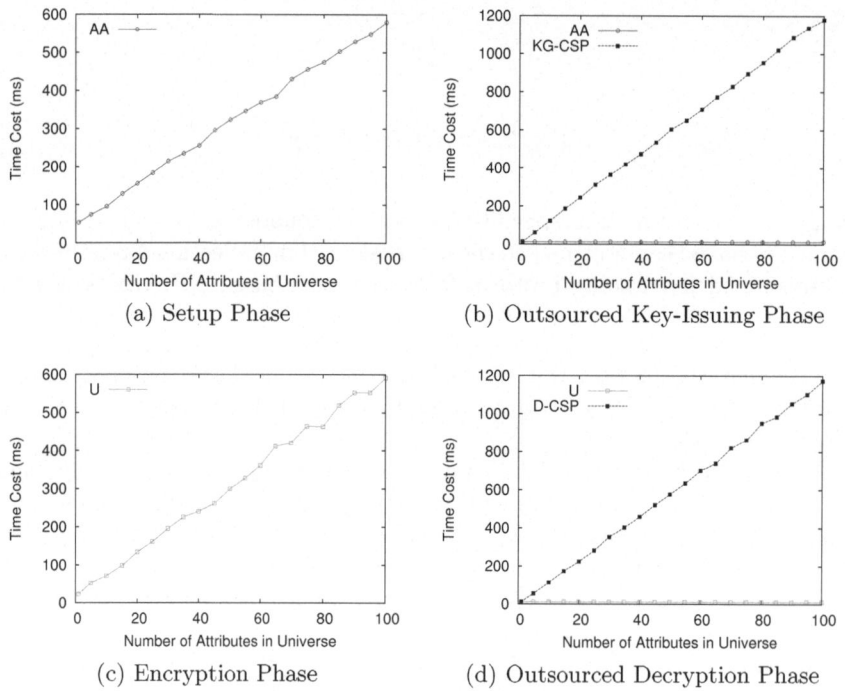

(a) Setup Phase

(b) Outsourced Key-Issuing Phase

(c) Encryption Phase

(d) Outsourced Decryption Phase

Fig. 3. Performance Evaluation

7   Related Work

Attribute-Based Encryption. The notion of ABE, which was introduced as fuzzy identity-based encryption in [23], was firstly dealt with by Goyal et al. [14]. Two different and complementary notions of ABE were defined as KP-ABE and CP-ABE. A construction of KP-ABE was provided in the same paper [14], while the first CP-APE construction supporting tree-based access structure in generic group model is presented by Bethencourt et al. [4].

Subsequently, a number of variants of ABE schemes have been proposed since its introduction. They range from extending its functionality to proposing schemes with stronger security proofs. Such as ABE schemes supporting for any kinds of access structures [21], ABE with multi-authorities [5], etc.

Recently, a novel paradigm for ABE was provided [15,25,18]. In [15], Green et al. considered to outsource the decryption of ABE to eliminate the overhead at user side, while an outsourced ABE with outsourced encryption and decryption was presented in [25][18]. We point out that the outsourcing decryption technique in [15,25] is to blind user's attribute private key by running a number of exponentiations. But such key blinded operation is eliminated in our construction in Section 4.3 through introducing a default attribute (actually, our technique provides a feasible way to realize the "piecewise key generation" property recently introduced in [22]). Moreover, it seems that all of the previous work lacks of the consideration on the reducing overhead computation at attribute authority. In another word, these work cannot support outsourced key-issuing due to the blinding technique used in the key generation algorithm.

Outsourcing Computation To reduce the load at local, it always desires to deliver expensive computational tasks outside. Actually, how to securely outsource different kinds of expensive computations has drawn much attention from theoretical computer science community [2,3,1,7]. But they are not suitable for reliving ABE computational overhead at user or authority side. To achieve this goal, the traditional approach is to utilize server-aided techniques [17,16,6]. However, previous work is oriented to accelerating the speed of exponentiation using untrusted servers. Directly utilizing these techniques in ABE will not work efficiently. Another approach might be to leverage recent general outsourcing technique or delegating computation [13,11,10,8,12] based on fully homomorphic encryption or interactive proof system. However, Gentry [12] has shown that even for weak security parameters on "bootstrapping" operation of the homomorphic encryption, it would take at least 30 seconds on a high performance machine. Therefore, even if the privacy of the input and output can be preserved by utilizing these general techniques, the computational overhead is still huge and impractical.

8   Conclusion

In this paper, we propose an efficient attribute-based access control system in cloud computing. In our system, two CSPs namely KG-CSP and D-CSP are introduced as employees to finish the outsourced heavy tasks for user management and file access respectively. The overhead at both users and attribute authority sides is thus being minimized. A challenging issue in the proposed system is how to outsource the computational task to CSPs without any private information leakage. To deal with this issue, we formulize an underlying primitive namely OABE and provide several OABE constructions with outsourced key-issuing and decryption. Finally, through extensive experiments, it demonstrates that our OABE construction achieves efficient key-issuing and decryption at AA and user sides respectively.

Acknowledgement. We are grateful to the anonymous referees for their invaluable suggestions. This work is supported by the National Natural Science Foundation of China (Nos. 61100224, 61272455 and 61272423), the National Key Basic Research Program of China (2013CB834204) and the Specialized Research Fund for the Doctoral Program of Higher Education of China (20100031110030). Besides, Lou's work was supported by US National Science Foundation under grant CNS-1155988.

References

1. Atallah, M.J., Frikken, K.B.: Securely outsourcing linear algebra computations. In: Proceedings of the 5th ACM Symposium on Information, Computer and Communications Security, ASIACCS 2010, pp. 48–59. ACM, New York (2010)
2. Atallah, M.J., Pantazopoulos, K., Rice, J.R., Spafford, E.E.: Secure outsourcing of scientific computations. In: Zelkowitz, M.V. (ed.) Trends in Software Engineering, Advances in Computers, vol. 54, pp. 215–272. Elsevier (2002)
3. Benjamin, D., Atallah, M.J.: Private and cheating-free outsourcing of algebraic computations. In: Proceedings of the 2008 Sixth Annual Conference on Privacy, Security and Trust, PST 2008, pp. 240–245. IEEE Computer Society, Washington, DC (2008)
4. Bethencourt, J., Sahai, A., Waters, B.: Ciphertext-policy attribute-based encryption. In: IEEE Symposium on Security and Privacy 2007, pp. 321–334 (May 2007)
5. Chase, M., Chow, S.S.: Improving privacy and security in multi-authority attribute-based encryption. In: Proceedings of the 16th ACM Conference on Computer and Communications Security, pp. 121–130. ACM, New York (2009)
6. Chen, X., Li, J., Ma, J., Tang, Q., Lou, W.: New algorithms for secure outsourcing of modular exponentiations. In: Foresti, S., Yung, M., Martinelli, F. (eds.) ESORICS 2012. LNCS, vol. 7459, pp. 541–556. Springer, Heidelberg (2012)
7. Chen, X., Li, J., Susilo, W.: Efficient fair conditional payments for outsourcing computations. IEEE Transactions on Information Forensics and Security 7(6), 1687–1694 (2012)
8. Chung, K.-M., Kalai, Y.T., Liu, F.-H., Raz, R.: Memory delegation. In: Rogaway, P. (ed.) CRYPTO 2011. LNCS, vol. 6841, pp. 151–168. Springer, Heidelberg (2011)
9. Fujisaki, E., Okamoto, T.: Secure integration of asymmetric and symmetric encryption schemes. In: Wiener, M. (ed.) CRYPTO 1999. LNCS, vol. 1666, pp. 537–554. Springer, Heidelberg (1999)
10. Gennaro, R., Gentry, C., Parno, B.: Non-interactive verifiable computing: Outsourcing computation to untrusted workers. In: Rabin, T. (ed.) CRYPTO 2010. LNCS, vol. 6223, pp. 465–482. Springer, Heidelberg (2010)

11. Gentry, C.: Fully homomorphic encryption using ideal lattices. In: Proceedings of the 41st Annual ACM Symposium on Theory of Computing, STOC 2009, pp. 169–178. ACM, New York (2009)
12. Gentry, C., Halevi, S.: Implementing gentry's fully-homomorphic encryption scheme. In: Paterson, K.G. (ed.) EUROCRYPT 2011. LNCS, vol. 6632, pp. 129–148. Springer, Heidelberg (2011)
13. Goldwasser, S., Kalai, Y.T., Rothblum, G.N.: Delegating computation: interactive proofs for muggles. In: Proceedings of the 40th Annual ACM Symposium on Theory of Computing, STOC 2008, pp. 113–122. ACM, New York (2008)
14. Goyal, V., Pandey, O., Sahai, A., Waters, B.: Attribute-based encryption for fine-grained access control of encrypted data. In: Proceedings of the 13th ACM Conference on Computer and Communications Security, pp. 89–98 (2006)
15. Green, M., Hohenberger, S., Waters, B.: Outsourcing the decryption of abe ciphertexts. In: Proceedings of the 20th USENIX conference on Security, SEC 2011, p. 34. USENIX Association, Berkeley (2011)
16. Hohenberger, S., Lysyanskaya, A.: How to securely outsource cryptographic computations. In: Kilian, J. (ed.) TCC 2005. LNCS, vol. 3378, pp. 264–282. Springer, Heidelberg (2005)
17. Jakobsson, M., Wetzel, S.: Secure server-aided signature generation. In: Kim, K. (ed.) PKC 2001. LNCS, vol. 1992, pp. 383–401. Springer, Heidelberg (2001)
18. Li, J., Jia, C., Li, J., Chen, X.: Outsourcing encryption of attribute-based encryption with mapreduce. In: Chim, T.W., Yuen, T.H. (eds.) ICICS 2012. LNCS, vol. 7618, pp. 191–201. Springer, Heidelberg (2012)
19. Lynn, B.: The pairing-based cryptography library,
http://crypto.stanford.edu/pbc/
20. McDaniel, P., Prakash, A.: Methods and limitations of security policy reconciliation. ACM Trans. Inf. Syst. Secur. 9(3), 259–291 (2006)
21. Ostrovsky, R., Sahai, A., Waters, B.: Attribute-based encryption with non-monotonic access structures. In: Proceedings of the 14th ACM Conference on Computer and Communications Security, CCS 2007, pp. 195–203. ACM, New York (2007)
22. Sahai, A., Seyalioglu, H., Waters, B.: Dynamic credentials and ciphertext delegation for attribute-based encryption. In: Safavi-Naini, R., Canetti, R. (eds.) CRYPTO 2012. LNCS, vol. 7417, pp. 199–217. Springer, Heidelberg (2012)
23. Sahai, A., Waters, B.: Fuzzy identity-based encryption. In: Cramer, R. (ed.) EUROCRYPT 2005. LNCS, vol. 3494, pp. 457–473. Springer, Heidelberg (2005)
24. Yu, S., Wang, C., Ren, K., Lou, W.: Achieving secure, scalable, and fine-grained data access control in cloud computing. In: Proceedings of the 29th Conference on Information Communications, INFOCOM 2010, pp. 534–542. IEEE Press, Piscataway (2010)
25. Zhou, Z., Huang, D.: Efficient and secure data storage operations for mobile cloud computing. Cryptology ePrint Archive, Report 2011/185 (2011)

Purpose Restrictions on Information Use*

Michael Carl Tschantz[1,**], Anupam Datta[2], and Jeannette M. Wing[3,**]

[1] University of California, Berkeley
mct@berkeley.edu
[2] Carnegie Mellon University
danupam@cmu.edu
[3] Microsoft Research
wing@microsoft.com

Abstract. Privacy policies in sectors as diverse as Web services, finance and healthcare often place restrictions on the purposes for which a governed entity may use personal information. Thus, automated methods for enforcing privacy policies require a semantics of *purpose restrictions* to determine whether a governed agent *used information* for a purpose. We provide such a semantics using a formalism based on planning. We model planning using Partially Observable Markov Decision Processes (POMDPs), which supports an explicit model of information. We argue that information use is for a purpose if and only if the information is used while planning to optimize the satisfaction of that purpose under the POMDP model. We determine information use by simulating ignorance of the information prohibited by the purpose restriction, which we relate to noninterference. We use this semantics to develop a sound audit algorithm to automate the enforcement of purpose restrictions.

1 Introduction

Purpose is a key concept for privacy policies. Some policies limit the use of certain information to an explicit list of purposes. The privacy policy of The Bank of America states, "Employees are authorized to access Customer Information for business purposes only." [1]. The HIPAA Privacy Rule requires that healthcare providers in the U.S. use protected health information about a patient with that patient's authorization or only for a fixed list of allowed purposes, such as treatment and billing [2]. Other policies prohibit using certain information for a purpose. For example, Yahoo!'s privacy policy states "Yahoo!'s practice on Yahoo! Mail Classic is not to use the content of messages stored in your Yahoo! Mail account for marketing purposes." [3].

---

* This research was supported by the U.S. Army Research Office grants DAAD19-02-1-0389 and W911NF-09-1-0273 to CyLab, by the National Science Foundation (NSF) grants CCF0424422 and CNS1064688, and by the U.S. Department of Health and Human Services grant HHS 90TR0003/01. The views and conclusions contained in this document are those of the authors and should not be interpreted as representing the official policies, either expressed or implied, of any sponsoring institution, the U.S. government or any other entity.
** The authors conducted most of this work while at Carnegie Mellon University.

J. Crampton, S. Jajodia, and K. Mayes (Eds.): ESORICS 2013, LNCS 8134, pp. 610–627, 2013.
© Springer-Verlag Berlin Heidelberg 2013

Each of these examples presents a constraint on the purposes for which the organization may use information. We call these constraints *purpose restrictions*.

Let us consider a purpose restriction in detail. As a simplification of the Yahoo! example, consider an advertising network attempting to determine which advertisement to show for marketing to a visitor of a website (such as an email website). To improve its public image and to satisfy government regulations, the network adopts a privacy policy containing a restriction prohibiting the use of the visitor's gender for the purpose of marketing.

The network has access to a database of information about potential visitors, which includes their gender. Since some advertisements are more effective, on average, for some demographics than others, using this information is in the network's interest. However, the purpose restriction prohibits the use of gender for selecting advertisements since it is a form of marketing. Since tension exists between selecting the most effective ad and obeying the purpose restriction, internal compliance officers and government regulators should audit the network to determine whether it has complied with the privacy policy.

However, the auditors may find manually auditing the network difficult and error prone leading them to desire automated tools to aid them. Indeed, the difficulty of manually auditing purpose restrictions has led to commercial software for this task (e.g., [4]). However, their approaches have been ad hoc.

Our goal is to place purpose restrictions governing information use on a formal footing and to automate their enforcement. In the above example, intuitively, the auditor must determine what information the network used while planning which ads to show to a user. In general, determining whether the purpose restriction was obeyed involves determining facts about how the audited agent (a person, organization, or computer system) planned its actions. In particular, philosophical inquiry [5] and an empirical study [6] show that the behavior of an audited agent is for a purpose when the agent chooses that behavior while planning to satisfy the purpose. Our prior work has used a formal model of planning to automate the auditing of purpose restrictions that limit visible actions to certain purposes [6].

We build upon that work to provide formal semantics and algorithms for purpose restrictions limiting *information uses*, whose occurrence the auditor cannot directly observe. For example, while the ad network is prohibited from using the visitor's gender, it may access the database to use other information even if the database returns the gender as part of a larger record. Thus, our model must elucidate whether the network *used* the gender component of the accessed information.

To provide auditing algorithms, we need a formal model of planning. Fortunately, research in artificial intelligence has provided a variety of formal models of planning. To select an appropriate model for auditing, we examine the key features of our motivating example of the ad network. First, it shows that purposes are not just goals to be achieved since the purpose of marketing is quantitative: marketing can be satisfied to varying degrees and more can always be done. Second, the example shows that outcomes can be probabilistic since the network does not know what ad will be best for each visitor but does have statistical information about various demographics. Lastly, the policy is governing the use of information. Thus, our model needs an explicit model of information.

The first two features suggest using Markov Decision Processes (MDPs), which we have successfully used in an auditing algorithm for purpose restrictions on observable actions [6]. However, needing an explicit model of information requires us to use an extension of MDPs, Partially Observable Markov Decision Processes (POMDPs), which make the ability of the planning agent to observe its environment and collect information explicit. We use a POMDP to model the agent's environment where the purpose in question defines the reward function of the POMDP. The explicitness of observations (inputs) in the POMDP model allows us to go beyond standard research on planning to provide a semantics of *information use* by considering how the agent would plan if some observations were conflated to ignore information of interest.

In more detail, we quotient the POMDP's space of observations to express information use. Intuitively, to use information is to see a distinction, and to not use information corresponds to ignoring this distinction. Thus, we quotient by an equivalence relation that treats two observations as indistinguishable if they differ only by information whose use is prohibited by a purpose restriction. For example, the ad network promising not to use gender should quotient its observations by an equivalence relation that treats the genders as equivalent. By conflating observations that differ only by gender, the network will ignore gender, simulating ignorance of it. Such quotienting is defined for POMDPs since observations probabilistically constrain the space of possible current states of the agent's environment, and quotienting just decreases the constraint's accuracy.

We use our quotienting operation to provide two different definitions of what it means for an agent to obey a purpose restriction involving information use. The first requires that the agent uses the quotiented POMDP to select its behavior. We call this definition *cognitive* since it refers to the agent's cognitive process of selecting behavior. Since the auditor cannot examine the agent's cognitive processes and might only care about their external consequences, we offer a second weaker definition that depends upon the agent's observable behavior. The *behaviorist* definition only requires that the agent's behaviors be consistent with using the quotiented POMDP. It does not depend upon whether the agent actually used that POMDP or a different process to select its behavior.

We use the behaviorist definition as the basis of an auditing algorithm that compares the behaviors of an agent to each of the behaviors that is acceptable under our notion of simulated ignorance. Despite comparing to multiple behaviors, our algorithm only needs to optimize the quotiented POMDP once. For the behaviorist definition, we prove that the algorithm is sound (Theorem 1) and is complete when the POMDP can be optimized exactly (Theorem 2).

To show that our semantics is strong enough, we compare it to *noninterference*, a prior formalization of information use for automata [7]. This definition examines how an input to an automaton affects the automaton's output. Our approach is similar but uses POMDPs instead of automata. We relate the two models by defining how an automaton can implement a strategy for a quotiented

POMDP, which allows us to prove that the cognitive definition implies a form of noninterference (Theorem 3). On the other hand, we show that an agent can obey the behaviorist definition while still exhibiting interference. However, interestingly, such interference cannot further the restricted purpose showing that the behaviorist definition is strong enough to prevent interference *for that purpose*.

Since an action's purpose can depend upon how it fits into a chain of actions, we focus on post-hoc auditing. Nevertheless, other enforcement mechanisms can employ our semantics. Despite focusing on privacy policies, our semantics and algorithm may aid the enforcement of other policies restricting the use of information to only certain purposes, such as those governing intellectual property.

Contributions and Outline. We start by reviewing related work and POMDPs (Sections 2 and 3). Our first contribution is definitional: we use our quotienting characterization of information use to provide both the cognitive and behaviorist definitions of complying with a purpose restriction on information use (Section 4). Our second contribution is our auditing algorithm accompanied by theorems of soundness and a qualified form of completeness (Section 5). Our final contribution is relating our formalization to noninterference with a theorem showing that the cognitive definition implies noninterference (Sections 6). We end with conclusions (Sections 7). All proofs are in a related technical report [8].

2   Prior Work

Information Flow Analysis. Research on information flow analysis led to noninterference [7], a formalization of information flow, or use. However, prior methods of detecting noninterference have typically required access to the program running the system in question. These analyses either used the program for directly analyzing its code (see [9] for a survey), for running an instrumented version of the system (e.g., [10–13]), or for simulating multiple executions of the system (e.g., [14–16]). Traditionally, the requirement of access to the program has not been problematic since the analysis has been motivated as a tool for software engineers securing a program that they have designed.

However, in our setting of enforcing purpose restrictions, such access is not always possible since the analyzed system can be a person who could be adversarial and whose behavior the auditor can only observe. On the other hand, the auditor has information about the purposes that the system should be pursuing. Since the system is a purpose-driven agent, the auditor can understand its behavior in terms of a POMDP model of its environment. Thus, while prior work provides a definition of information use, it does not provide appropriate models or methods for determining whether it occurs in our setting.

Enforcing Purpose Restrictions. Most prior work on using formal methods for enforcing purpose restrictions has focused on when observable actions achieve a purpose [17–24]. That is, they define an action as being for a purpose if that action (possibly as part of a chain of actions) results in that purpose being achieved. Our work differs from these works in two ways.

First, we define an action as being for a purpose when that action is part of a plan for maximizing the satisfaction of that purpose. Our definition differs by treating purposes as rewards that can be satisfied to varying degrees and by focusing on the plans rather than outcomes, which allows an action to be for a purpose even if it probabilistically fails to improve it. The semantics of purpose we use follows from informal philosophical inquiry [5] and our prior work using Markov Decision Processes to formalize purpose restrictions for actions [6]. Jafari et al. offer an alternative view of planning and purposes in which a purpose is high-level action related to low-level actions by a plan [25]. Our views are complementary in that theirs picks up where ours leaves off: Our model of planning can justify the plans that their model accepts as given while their model allows for reasoning about the relationships among purposes with a logic.

Second, we consider information use. While the aforementioned works address restrictions on information *access*, they do not have a model of information *use*, such as noninterference [7]. In particular, we extend our prior work [6] to model how the agent uses information while selecting actions with a POMDP. We show that if the agent does not use the information under our model, then noninterference holds. While Martinelli et al. have used POMDPs for enforcing quantitative access controls, we differ by using POMDPs to model information use itself instead of for modeling policies governing information use treated as observable actions [26]. Hayati and Abadi provide a type system for tracking information flow in programs with purpose restrictions in mind [27]. However, their work presupposes that the programmer can determine the purpose of a function and provides no formal guidance for making this determination.

Minimal disclosure requires that the amount of information granted should be as little as possible while still achieving the purpose behind the grant. This differs from purpose restrictions, which do not require the amount of information used to be minimal and often involve purposes that are never fully achieved (e.g., more marketing is always possible). Thus, unlike works on minimal disclosure [28, 29], we model purposes as being satisfied to varying degrees. Furthermore, we model probabilistic failures of the agent's plan, which allows us to identify when information use is for a purpose despite not increasing the purpose's satisfaction.

Planning. Since our formal definition is in terms of planning, automating auditing depends upon automated *plan recognition* [30]. We build upon works that use models of planning to recognize plans (e.g., [31–34]). The most related work has provided methods of determining when a sequence of actions are for a purpose (or "goal" in their nomenclature) given a POMDP model of the environment [34]. Our algorithm for auditing is similar to their algorithm. However, whereas their algorithm attempts to determine the probability that a sequence of actions are for a purpose, we are concerned with whether a use of information could be for a purpose. Thus, we must first develop a formalism for information use. We must also concern ourselves with the soundness of our algorithm rather than its accuracy in terms of a predicted probability. Additionally, we use traditional POMDPs to model purposes that are never fully satisfied instead of the goal POMDPs used in their work.

3   Modeling Purpose-Driven Agents

We review the Partially Observable Markov Decision Process (POMDP) model and then show how to model the above motivating example as one. We start with an agent, such as a person, organization, or artificially intelligent computer, that attempts to maximize the satisfaction of a purpose. The agent uses a POMDP to plan its actions. The POMDP models the agent's environment and how its actions affects the environment's state and the satisfaction of the purpose. The agent selects a plan that optimizes the expected total discounted reward (degree of purpose satisfaction) under the POMDP. This plan corresponds to the program running the audited system.

POMDPs. To define POMDPs, let $\mathsf{Dist}(X)$ denote the space of all distributions over the set X and let $\mathbb{R}$ be the set of real numbers. A POMDP is a tuple $\langle \mathcal{Q}, \mathcal{A}, \tau, \rho, \mathcal{O}, \nu, \gamma \rangle$ where

- $\mathcal{Q}$ is a finite state space representing the states of the agent's environment;
- $\mathcal{A}$, a finite set of actions;
- $\tau : \mathcal{Q} \times \mathcal{A} \to \mathsf{Dist}(\mathcal{Q})$, a transition function from a state and an action to a distribution over states representing the possible outcomes of the action;
- $\rho : \mathcal{Q} \times \mathcal{A} \to \mathbb{R}$, a reward function measuring the immediate impact on the satisfaction of the purpose when the agent takes the given action in the given state;
- $\mathcal{O}$, a finite observation space containing any observations the agent may perceive while performing actions;
- $\nu : \mathcal{A} \times \mathcal{Q} \to \mathsf{Dist}(\mathcal{O})$, a distribution over observations given an action and the state resulting from performing that action; and
- γ, a discount factor such that $0 \leq \gamma < 1$.

We say that a POMDP *models a purpose* if ρ measures the degree to which the purpose is satisfied. To select actions for that purpose, the agent should select those that maximizes its expected total discounted reward, $\mathbb{E}\left[\sum_{i=0}^{\infty} \gamma^i u_i\right]$ where i represents time and u_i, the reward from the agent's ith action.

This goal is complicated by the agent not knowing *a priori* which of the possible states of the POMDP is the current state of its environment. Rather it holds beliefs about which state is the current state. In particular, the agent assigns a probability to each state q according to how likely the agent believes that the current state is the state q. A *belief state* β captures these beliefs as a distribution over states of $\mathcal{Q}$ (i.e., $\beta \in \mathsf{Dist}(\mathcal{Q})$). An agent updates its belief state as it performs actions and makes observations. When an agent takes the action a and makes the observation o starting with the beliefs β, the agent develops the new beliefs β' where $\beta'(q')$ is the probability that q' is the next state.

We define $\mathsf{up}_m(\beta, a, o)$ to equal the updated beliefs β'. β' assigns to the state q' the probability $\beta'(q') = \Pr[\mathrm{Q}'{=}q'|\mathrm{O}{=}o, \mathrm{A}{=}a, \mathrm{B}{=}\beta]$ where Q' is a random variable over next states, $\mathrm{B}{=}\beta$ identifies the agent's current belief state as β, $\mathrm{A}{=}a$ identifies the agent's current action as a, and $\mathrm{O}{=}o$ identifies the observation the agent makes while performing action a as o. We may reduce $\mathsf{up}_m(\beta, a, o)$ to the following formula in terms of the POMDP model:

$$\mathsf{up}_m(\beta, a, o)(q') = \frac{\nu(a, q')(o) \sum_{q \in \mathcal{Q}} \beta(q) * \tau(q, a)(q')}{\sum_{q' \in \mathcal{Q}} \nu(a, q')(o) \sum_{q \in \mathcal{Q}} \beta(q) * \tau(q, a)(q')}$$

To maximize its expected total discounted reward, the agent does not need to track its history of actions and observations independently of its beliefs as such beliefs are a sufficient statistic. Thus, the agent need only consider for each possible belief β it can have, what action it would perform. That is, the agent can plan by selecting a *strategy*: a function from the space of beliefs $\mathsf{Dist}(\mathcal{Q})$ to the space of actions $\mathcal{A}$. (We use the word "strategy" instead of the more common "policy" to avoid confusion with privacy policies.)

The goal of the agent is find the optimal strategy. By the Bellman equation [35], the expected value of a belief state β under a strategy σ is

$$V_m(\sigma, \beta) = \mathrm{R}_m(\beta, \sigma(\beta)) + \gamma \sum_{o \in \mathcal{O}} \mathrm{N}_m(\beta, \sigma(\beta))(o) * V_m(\sigma, \mathsf{up}_m(\beta, \sigma(\beta), o)) \quad (1)$$

where R_m and N_m are ρ and ν raised to work over beliefs: $\mathrm{R}_m(\beta, a) = \sum_{q \in \mathcal{Q}} \beta(q) * \rho(q, a)$ and $\mathrm{N}_m(\beta, a)(o) = \sum_{q, q' \in \mathcal{Q}} \beta(q) * \tau(q, a)(q') * \nu(a, q')(o)$. A strategy σ is optimal if it maximizes V_m for all belief states, that is, if for all β, $V_m(\sigma, \beta)$ is equal to $V_m^*(\beta) = \max_{\sigma'} V_m(\sigma', \beta)$. Prior work has provided algorithms for finding optimal strategies by reducing the problem to one of finding an optimal strategy for a related Markov Decision Process (MDP) that uses these belief states as its state space (e.g., [36]). (For a survey, see [37].)

Example. We can formalize the motivating example provided in Section 1 as a POMDP m_{ex}. Here, we provide an overview that is sufficient for understanding the rest of the paper; [8] provides additional details.

For simplicity, we assume that the only information relevant to advertising is the gender of the visitor. Thus, the state space $\mathcal{Q}$ is determined by three factors: the visitor's gender, the gender (if any) recorded in the database, and what advertisement (if any) the network has shown to the visitor.

Also for simplicity, we assume that the network is choosing among three advertisements. We use the action space $\mathcal{A} = \{\mathsf{lookup}, \mathsf{ad}_1, \mathsf{ad}_2, \mathsf{ad}_3\}$. The actions ad_1, ad_2, and ad_3 correspond to the network showing the visitor one of the three possible advertisements while lookup corresponds to the network looking up information on the visitor. We presume ad_1 is the best for females and the worst for males, ad_3 is the best for males and the worst for females, and ad_2 strikes a middle ground. In particular, we use $\rho(q, \mathsf{ad}_1) = 9$ for a state q in which the visitor is a female and has not yet seen an ad. The reward 9 could refer to a measure of the click through rate or the average preference assigned to the ad by females during market research. If the visitor were instead a male, the reward would be 3. For ad_3, the rewards are reversed with 3 for females and 9 for males. For ad_2, the reward is 7 for both genders. The action lookup or showing a second ad produces reward of zero. We use a discounting factor of $\gamma = 0.9$.

The function τ shows how actions change the environment's state while ν shows how observations accompany these actions. τ enforces that showing an ad changes the state into one in which showing a second ad produces no further rewards. It also specifies that performing lookup does not change the state of the environment. On the other hand, ν shows that lookup can change the state of the agent's knowledge. In particular, it shows that performing lookup produces an observation $\langle d, \alpha \rangle$. The observation reveals that the database holds data d about the visitor's gender and α about what if any ad the visitor has seen. Thus, the observation space is $\mathcal{O} = \{f, m, \perp\} \times \{ad_1, ad_2, ad_3, \varnothing\}$ with f for the database showing a female, m for a male, $\perp$ for no gender entry, ad_i for the visitor having seen ad_i, and $\varnothing$ for the visitor having not seen an ad.

How the network will behave depends upon the network's initial beliefs β_{ex1}. We presume that the network believes its database's entries to be correct, that it has not shown an advertisement to the visitor yet, and that visitors are equally likely to be female or male. Under these assumptions, the optimal plan for the network is to first check whether the database contains information about the visitor. If the database records that the visitor is a female, then the network shows her ad_1. If it records a male, the network shows ad_3. If the database does not contain the visitor's gender (holds $\perp$), then the network shows ad_2. The optimal plan is not constrained as to what the agent does after showing the advertisement as it does not affect the reward. (In [8], we discuss using the idea of *non-redundancy* to eliminate this artifact.)

This optimal plan characterizes the form of the set of optimal strategies. The set contains multiple optimal strategies since the network is unconstrained in the actions it performs after showing the advertisement. The optimal strategies must also specify how the network would behave under other possible beliefs it could have had. For example, if the network believed that all visitors are females regardless of what its database records, then it would always show ad_1 without first checking its database.

Intuitively, using any of these optimal strategies would violate the privacy policy prohibiting using gender for marketing. The reason is that the network selected which advertisement to show using the database's information about the visitor's gender.

We expect the network constrained to obeying the policy will show ad_2 to all visitors (presuming approximately equal numbers of female and male visitors). Our reasoning is that the network must plan as though it does not know and cannot learn the visitor's gender. In this state of simulated ignorance, the best plan the network can select is the middle ground of ad_2. The next section formalizes this planning under simulated ignorance.

4   Constraining POMDPs for Information Use

We now provide a formal characterization of how an agent pursuing a purpose should behave when prohibited from using a class of information. Recall the intuition that using information is using a distinction and that not using it corresponds to ignoring the distinction. We use this idea to model sensitive information with an equivalence relation $\equiv$. We set $o_1 \equiv o_2$ for any two observations o_1 and o_2 that differ only by sensitive information.

From $\equiv$ and a POMDP m, we construct a POMDP $m/\equiv$ that ignores the prohibited information. For each equivalence class of $\equiv$, $m/\equiv$ will conflate its members by treating every observation in it as indistinguishable from one another. To ignore these distinctions, on observing o, the agent updates its belief state as though it has seen some element of $\equiv[o]$ but is unsure of which one where $\equiv[o]$ is the equivalence class that holds the observation o.

To make this formal, we define a quotient POMDP $m/\equiv$ that uses a quotiented space of observations. Let $\mathcal{O}/\equiv$ be the set of equivalence classes of $\mathcal{O}$ under $\equiv$. Let $\nu/\equiv$ give the probability of seeing any observation of an equivalence class: $\nu/\equiv(a, q')(O) = \sum_{o \in O} \nu(a, q')(o)$ where O is an equivalence class in $\mathcal{O}/\equiv$. Given $m = \langle \mathcal{Q}, \mathcal{A}, \tau, \rho, \mathcal{O}, \nu, \gamma \rangle$, let $m/\equiv$ be $\langle \mathcal{Q}, \mathcal{A}, \tau, \rho, \mathcal{O}/\equiv, \nu/\equiv, \gamma \rangle$.

Proposition 1. *For all POMDPs m and equivalences $\equiv$, $m/\equiv$ is a POMDP.*

Example. Returning to the example POMDP of Section 3, the policy governing the network states that the network will not use the database's entry about the visitor's gender for determining the advertisement to show the visitor. The auditor must decide how to formally model this restriction. One way would be to define $\equiv_{ex}$ such that for all g and g' in $\{f, m, \perp\}$, and α in $\{ad_1, ad_2, ad_3, \varnothing\}$, $\langle g, \alpha \rangle \equiv_{ex} \langle g', \alpha \rangle$, conflating the gender for all observations. Under this requirement, $m_{ex}/\equiv_{ex}$ will be such that the optimal strategy will be determined solely by the network's initial beliefs and performing the action lookup will be of no benefit. Any optimal strategy for $m_{ex}/\equiv_{ex}$ will call for performing ad_2 from the initial beliefs β_{ex1} discussed above.

Alternatively, the auditor might conclude that the policy only forces the network to ignore whether the database records the visitor as a female or male and not whether the database contains this information. In this case, the auditor would use a different equivalence $\equiv'_{ex}$ such that $\langle f, \alpha \rangle \equiv'_{ex} \langle m, \alpha \rangle$ but $\langle f, \alpha \rangle \not\equiv'_{ex} \langle \perp, \alpha \rangle \not\equiv'_{ex} \langle m, \alpha \rangle$ for all α. Under the initial beliefs β_{ex1}, the network would behave identically under $\equiv_{ex}$ and $\equiv'_{ex}$. However, if the network's beliefs were such that it is much more likely to not know a female's gender than a male's, then it might choose to show ad_1 instead of ad_2 in the case of observing $\langle \perp, \varnothing \rangle$.

The next proposition proves that we constructed the POMDP $m/\equiv$ so that beliefs are updated as if the agent only learns that some element of an equivalence class of observations was observed but not which one. That is, we prove that the updated belief $\mathsf{up}_{m/\equiv}(\beta, a, \equiv[o])(q')$ is equal to the probability that the next environmental state is q' given the distribution β over possible last states, that the last action was a, and that the observation was a member of $\equiv[o]$. Recall that Q' is a random variable over the next state while O, A, and B identify the last observation, action, and belief state, respectively.

Proposition 2. *For all POMDPs m, equivalences $\equiv$, beliefs β, actions a, observations o, and states q', $\mathsf{up}_{m/\equiv}(\beta, a, \equiv[o])(q') = \Pr[Q'{=}q' \mid O \in \equiv[o], A{=}a, B{=}\beta]$.*

Propositions 1 and 2 show that $m/\equiv$ is a POMDP that ignores the distinctions among observations that only differ by sensitive information. They justify the following definition, which explains how a purpose-driven agent should act when prohibited from using certain information. They show that it correctly prevents the use of the prohibited information. The definition's appeal to optimizing a POMDP is justified by our prior work showing that an action is for a purpose when that action is selected as part of a plan optimizing the satisfaction of that purpose [6]. We extend this result to information by concluding that information used to select an action is used for that action's purpose.

Definition 1 (Cognitive). *An agent obeys the purpose restriction to perform actions for the purpose modeled by the POMDP m without using the information modeled by $\equiv$ iff the agent selects an strategy by optimizing $m/\equiv$.*

We call the above definition *cognitive* since it refers to the strategy selected by the agent as part of a cognitive process that the auditor cannot measure. Rather, the auditor can only view the agent's external behavior and visible aspects of the environment. That is, the auditor can only view the agent's actions and observations, which we refer to collectively as the agent's *execution*.

We can formalize the agent's execution using a function exe. Even when the agent uses the POMDP $m/\equiv$ with observation space $\mathcal{O}/\equiv$ to select a strategy, the actual observations the agent makes lie in $\mathcal{O}$, complicating exe. We recursively define $\mathsf{exe}(m, \equiv, \sigma, \beta_1, \boldsymbol{o})$ to be the agent's execution that arises from it employing a strategy σ observing a sequence of observations $\boldsymbol{o} = [o_1, \ldots o_n]$ in $\mathcal{O}^*$ starting with beliefs β_1 for a POMDP $m/\equiv$. For the empty sequence $[]$ of observations, $\mathsf{exe}(m, \equiv, \sigma, \beta, []) = [\sigma(\beta)]$ since the agent can only make one action before needing to wait for the next observation and updating its beliefs. For nonempty sequences $o{:}\boldsymbol{o}$, it is equal to $\sigma(\beta){:}o{:}\mathsf{exe}(m, \equiv, \sigma, \mathsf{up}_{m/\equiv}(\beta, \sigma(\beta), \equiv[o]), \boldsymbol{o})$ where $x{:}y$ denotes prepending element x to the sequence y.

A single execution $\boldsymbol{e}$ can be consistent with both an optimal strategy for $m/\equiv$ and a strategy that is not optimal for $m/\equiv$. Consider for example, the execution $\boldsymbol{e} = [\mathsf{ad}_2] = \mathsf{exe}(m_{\mathsf{ex}}, \equiv_{\mathsf{ex}}, \sigma, \beta_{\mathsf{ex}}, [])$ that arises from an optimal strategy σ for $m_{\mathsf{ex}}/\equiv_{\mathsf{ex}}$. This execution can also arise from the agent planning for a different purpose, such as maximizing kickbacks for showing certain ads, provided that ad_2 also just so happens to maximize that purpose. Since the auditor only observes the execution $\boldsymbol{e}$ and not the cognitive process that selected the action ad_2, the auditor cannot know by which process the agent selected the ad. Thus, the auditor cannot determine from an execution that an agent obeyed a purpose restriction under Definition 1.

Some auditors may find this fundamental limitation immaterial since such an agent's actions are still consistent with an allowed strategy. Since the actual reasons behind the agent selecting those actions do not affect the environment, an auditor might not find concerning an agent doing the right actions for the wrong reasons. To capture this more consequentialist view of compliance, we provide a weaker definition that focuses on only the agent's execution.

Definition 2 (Behaviorist). *An agent performing execution* e *obeys the purpose restriction to perform actions for the purpose modeled by the POMDP* m *and initial beliefs* β_1 *without using the information modeled by the equivalence relation* $\equiv$ *given the observations* o *iff* $e = \mathsf{exe}(m, \equiv, \sigma, \beta_1, o)$ *for some* σ *that is an optimal strategy of* $m/\equiv$.

5 Auditing Algorithm

Under the behaviorist definition, to determine whether an agent obeyed a prohibition against using certain information for a purpose pursued by the agent, the auditor can compare the agent's behaviors to the appropriate strategies. The auditor records the agent's execution in a log ℓ that shows the actions and observations of the agent. For example, databases for electronic medical records log many of the actions and observations of healthcare providers. The auditor may then compare the recorded behavior to that dictated by Definition 2, i.e., to the optimal strategies for the quotient POMDP modeling the purpose while ignoring disallowed information.

Given our formal model, we can automate the comparison of the agent's behavior to the allowable behavior. We use an algorithm AUDIT that takes as inputs a POMDP m, an equivalence relation $\equiv$, and a log $\ell = [a_1, o_1, a_2, o_2, \ldots, a_n, o_n]$ such that the audited agent is operating in the environment m under a policy prohibiting information as described by $\equiv$ and took action a_i followed by observation o_i for all $i \leq n$. For simplicity, we assume that ℓ records all relevant actions and observations. AUDIT returns whether the agent's behavior, as recorded in ℓ, is inconsistent with optimizing the POMDP $m/\equiv$.

AUDIT operates by first constructing the quotient POMDP $m/\equiv$ from m and $\equiv$. Next, similar to a prior algorithm [34], for each i, AUDIT checks whether performing the recorded action a_i in the current belief state β_i is optimal under $m/\equiv$. The algorithm constructs these belief states from the observations and initial belief state β_1. Due to the complexity of solving POMDPs [38], we use an approximation algorithm to solve for the value of performing a_i in β_i (denoted $Q^*_{m/\equiv}(\beta_i, a_i)$) and the optimal value $V^*_{m/\equiv}(\beta_i)$. Unlike prior work, for soundness, we require an approximation algorithm SOLVEPOMDP that produces both lower bounds $\mathsf{V}^*_{\text{low}}$ and upper bounds V^*_{up} on $V^*_{m/\equiv}(\beta_i)$. Many such algorithms exist (e.g., [39–42]). For each β_i and a_i in ℓ, AUDIT checks whether these bounds show that $Q^*_{m/\equiv}(\beta_i, a_i)$ is strictly less than $V^*_{m/\equiv}(\beta_i)$. If so, then the action a_i is sub-optimal for β_i and AUDIT returns true. Pseudo-code for AUDIT follows:

AUDIT($\langle \mathcal{Q}, \mathcal{A}, \tau, \rho, \mathcal{O}, \nu, \gamma \rangle, \equiv, \beta_1, [a_1, o_1, a_2, o_2, \ldots, a_n, o_n]$):
01     $m' = \langle \mathcal{Q}, \mathcal{A}, \tau, \rho, \mathcal{O}/\equiv, \nu/\equiv, \gamma \rangle$
02     $\langle \mathsf{V}^*_{\text{low}}, \mathsf{V}^*_{\text{up}} \rangle := \text{SOLVEPOMDP}(m')$
03   for ($i := 1$; $i \leq n$; i++):
04   if ($\mathsf{Q}^*_{\text{up}}(\mathsf{V}^*_{\text{up}}, \beta_i, a_i) < \mathsf{V}^*_{\text{low}}(\beta_i)$):
05   return true
06          $\beta_{i+1} := \mathsf{up}_{m/\equiv}(\beta_i, a_i, \equiv[o_i])$;
07   return false

where $Q^*_{up}(V^*_{up}, \beta, a)$ is a function that uses V^*_{up} to return an upper bound on $Q^*_{m/\equiv}(\beta, a)$. $Q^*_{up}(V^*_{up}, \beta, a)$ equals:

$$R_m(\beta, a) + \gamma \sum_{O \in \mathcal{O}/\equiv} N_m(\beta, a))(O) * V^*_{up}(up_{m'}(\beta, \sigma(\beta), O))$$

Theorem 1 (Soundness). *If* AUDIT *returns true, then the agent did not follow an optimal strategy for* $m/\equiv$, *violating both Definitions 1 and 2.*

Thus, if AUDIT returns true, either the agent optimized some other purpose, used information it should not have, used a different POMDP model of its environment, or failed to correctly optimize the POMDP. Each of these possibilities should concern the auditor and is worthy of further investigation.

If the algorithm returns false, then the auditor cannot find the agent's behavior inconsistent with an optimal strategy and should spend his time auditing other agents. However, AUDIT is incomplete and such a finding does not mean that the agent surely performed its actions for the purpose without using the prohibited information. For the cognitive definition, incompleteness is unavoidable since the definition depends upon cognitive constructs that the auditor cannot measure. For example, recall that the network could display the execution $e = [ad_2]$ either from performing the allowed optimization or by performing some disallowed optimization that also results in the action ad_2 being optimal.

For the behaviorist definition, incompleteness results since a better approximation might actually show that $Q^*_{m/\equiv}(\beta_i, a_i) < V^*_{m/\equiv}(\beta_i)$ for some i. In principle this source is avoidable by using an exact POMDP solver instead of an approximate one. However, the exact solution to some POMDPs is undecidable [43]. Nevertheless, we can prove that this inability is the only source of incompleteness.

Theorem 2 (Qualified Completeness). *If* Audit *using an oracle to exactly solve POMDPs returns false, then the agent obeyed the purpose restriction according to the behaviorist definition (Definition 2).*

Other Purpose Restrictions. AUDIT is specialized for determining whether or not the audited agent performed its actions for a purpose without using some prohibited information. While such a question is relevant to an internal compliance officer auditing employees, it does not correspond to the purpose restrictions found in outward-facing privacy policies.

One type of restriction found in such policies is the *not-for* restriction prohibiting information from being used for a purpose. For example, Yahoo! promised to *not* use contents of emails *for* marketing. This restriction is similar to the condition checked by AUDIT, but is weaker in that audited agent may obey it either (1) by performing actions for that purpose without using that information (which AUDIT checks) or (2) by not performing actions for that purpose.

A second type is the *only-for* restriction, which limits the agent to using a class of information only for a purpose. For example, HIPAA requires that medical records are used *only for* certain purposes such as treatment. It is also weak in that the agent can obey it either (1) by performing actions for the purpose (which AUDIT checks using equality for $\equiv$ to allow the agent to use the information) or (2) by not using the information in question while performing actions for some other purpose.

For both of these types, our algorithm can handle the first option (1) for compliance. However, for both these types, the second option (2) for compliance involves an open-ended space of possible alternative purposes that could have motivated the agent's actions. In some cases (e.g., healthcare), this space may be small enough to check each alternative (e.g., treatment, billing, research, training) with AUDIT. In other cases, the auditor might have the authority to compel the agent to explain what its purpose was. In either of these cases, the auditor could use AUDIT to explore these alternative purposes.

Modeling. AUDIT requires a POMDP that models how various actions affect the purpose in question. Future work could ease the process of model construction using techniques from reinforcement learning, such as SARSA [44], that automatically construct models from observing the behavior of multiple agents.

In some cases, the auditor might be able to compel the agent to provide the POMDP used. In this case, AUDIT would check whether the agent's story is consistent with its actions.

6   Relationship with Noninterference

We have provided a definition of information use in terms of a POMDP. Prior work provides the *noninterference* definition of information use for automata [7]. In this section, we show that our definition implies a form of noninterference. In particular, we show that agents using strategies optimizing $m/\equiv$ has noninterference for $\equiv$, which suggests that our definition is sufficiently strong to rule out information use. We start by reviewing automata and noninterference.

Automaton Model of Systems. The agent using the POMDP to select a strategy can implement that strategy as a *control system* or *controller* (e.g., [45]). We follow Goguen and Meseguer's work and model systems as deterministic automata [7]. However, since we do not analyze the internal structure of systems (it is unavailable to the auditor), our approach can be applied to other models. We limit our discussion to deterministic systems since there are many competing generalizations of noninterference to the nondeterministic setting (e.g., [46–48]), but the main competitors collapse into standard noninterference in the deterministic case [49].

A system automaton $s = \langle t, r \rangle$ consists of a labeled transition system (LTS) t and a current state r. An LTS $t = \langle \mathcal{R}, \mathcal{O}, \mathcal{A}, \mathsf{next}, \mathsf{act} \rangle$ describes the automaton's behavior where $\mathcal{R}$ is a set of states; $\mathcal{O}$, a set of observations (inputs); $\mathcal{A}$, a set of actions (outputs); $\mathsf{next} : \mathcal{R} \times \mathcal{O} \to \mathcal{R}$ is a transition function; and $\mathsf{act} : \mathcal{R} \to \mathcal{A}$ is a function identifying the action that the automation selects given its current state. The current state $r \in \mathcal{R}$ changes as the system makes observations and takes actions.

As with POMDPs, an execution of a system s modeled as an automaton corresponds to an interleaving of observations from the environment and actions taken by the system. Let $\mathsf{exe}(s, \boldsymbol{o})$ denote the execution of s on a sequence $\boldsymbol{o}$ of observations. As for POMDPs, we define exe for systems recursively: $\mathsf{exe}(\langle t, r\rangle, []) = [\mathsf{act}(r)]$ and $\mathsf{exe}(\langle t, r\rangle, o{:}\boldsymbol{o}) = \mathsf{act}(r){:}o{:}\mathsf{exe}(\langle r, \mathsf{next}(r, o)\rangle, \boldsymbol{o})$ where $t = \langle \mathcal{R}, \mathcal{O}, \mathcal{A}, \mathsf{next}, \mathsf{act}\rangle$.

Noninterference. Recall that we set $o_1 \equiv o_2$ for any two observations o_1 and o_2 that differ only by sensitive information. To not use the sensitive information, the system s should treat such related observations identically.

To formalize this notion, we raise $\equiv$ to work over sequences of observations and actions (i.e., executions and sequences of observations). For such sequences $\boldsymbol{x}$ and $\boldsymbol{y}$ in $(\mathcal{O} \cup \mathcal{A})^*$, $\boldsymbol{x} \equiv \boldsymbol{y}$ iff they are of the same length and for each pair of elements x and y at the same position in $\boldsymbol{x}$ and $\boldsymbol{y}$, respectively, $x \equiv y$ where $\equiv$ is treated as equality when comparing actions.

Definition 3. *A system s has* noninterference *for $\equiv$ iff for all observation sequences $\boldsymbol{o}_1$ and $\boldsymbol{o}_2$ in $\mathcal{O}^*$, $\boldsymbol{o}_1 \equiv \boldsymbol{o}_2$ implies that $\mathsf{exe}(s, \boldsymbol{o}_1) \equiv \mathsf{exe}(s, \boldsymbol{o}_2)$.*

Our definition corresponds to the form of noninterference enforced by most type systems for information flow. (See [9] for a survey.) Unlike Goguen and Meseguer's definition, ours does not require the system's behavior to remain unchanged regardless of whether or not it receives sensitive information. Rather, the system's behavior may change upon receiving sensitive information, but this change must be the same regardless of the value of the sensitive information. (See [50] for a discussion.)

Relationship. We now characterize the relationship between our quotienting definition of information use and noninterference. We do so by considering a control system s operating in an environment modeled by a POMDP m. We require that s and m share the same sets of actions $\mathcal{A}$ and observations $\mathcal{O}$. However, the state spaces $\mathcal{R}$ of s and $\mathcal{Q}$ of m differ with $\mathcal{R}$ representing the internal states of the system and $\mathcal{Q}$ representing the external states of the environment.

We relate systems and strategies by saying that a system s *implements* a strategy σ for $m/\equiv$ and beliefs β_1 iff for all $\boldsymbol{o}$ in $\mathcal{O}^*$, $\mathsf{exe}(s, \boldsymbol{o}) = \mathsf{exe}(m, \equiv, \sigma, \beta_1, \boldsymbol{o})$. We denote the set of such implementing systems as $\mathsf{Imp}(m, \equiv, \sigma, \beta_1)$. This definition allows us to formalize the intuition that agents using strategies optimizing $m/\equiv$ has noninterference for $\equiv$. In fact, systems implementing any strategy for $m/\equiv$ has noninterference since any such implementation respects $\equiv$.

Theorem 3. *For all systems q, POMDPs m, initial beliefs β_1, strategies σ, and equivalences $\equiv$, if s is in $\mathsf{Imp}(m, \equiv, \sigma, \beta_1)$, then s has noninterference for $\equiv$.*

Agents obeying a purpose restriction under the cognitive definition (Definition 1) will employ a system in $\mathsf{Imp}(m, \equiv, \sigma, \beta_1)$. Thus, Theorem 3 shows that the cognitive definition is sufficiently strong to rule out information use.

Information Use for Other Purposes. The situation is subtler for the weaker behaviorist definition (Definition 2) and the algorithm AUDIT based upon it. Systems exist that will pass AUDIT and satisfy the behaviorist definition despite having interference by using the protected information for some purpose other than the restricted one. The key is that there could be more than one optimal strategy for a POMDP and that the agent may use the choice among optimal strategies to communicate information. The behavior of such a system will be consistent with whichever optimal strategy it selects, satisfying the behaviorist definition and AUDIT. However, such a system will not actually implement any strategy for the quotiented POMDP $m/\equiv$ since it distinguishes between observations conflated by $\equiv$.

For example, consider modifying the motivating example found in Section 3 in two ways to make the POMDP m'_{ex}. First, let ad_2 come in two versions, ad_2^a and ad_2^b, which are otherwise the same as the original ad_2. Second, change the POMDP so that the network must perform the action lookup before showing any ads. The agent can optimize $m'_{ex}/\equiv$ by either using a strategy σ^a or σ^b. Under σ^a, starting from the initial beliefs β_{ex1} discussed above, the network will first perform lookup and then show ad_2^a. Under σ^b, it will show ad_2^b after lookup.

The network's ability to choose between σ^a and σ^b can result in interference. In particular, the network might not implement either of them and instead delay the choice between ad_2^a and ad_2^b until after the observation from lookup informs it of the visitor's gender. The network could then use ad_2^a for a female and ad_2^b for a male. While such a system would use the information and have interference, it obeys the behaviorist definition with its actions consistent with either σ^a or σ^b.

Since such systems use the prohibited information to choose between *optimal* strategies, doing so does not actually increase its satisfaction of the purpose. Thus, this information use is not intuitively for that purpose and the agent must be motivated by some other purpose. Thus, the behaviorist definition does not allow the agent to use the information for the purpose prohibited by the restriction, but rather allows the agent to use the information for other purposes.

The auditor might want to prevent such interference since it violates the cognitive definition. The modifications to the example illustrate two ways that the auditor can do so if he has sufficient control over the agent's environment. The first is to ensure that only a single strategy is optimal. The second is to make sure that the agent can avoid learning the protected information (such as by performing the action lookup) and that learning it incurs a cost. When learning information is optional and costly, the agent will only be able to learn it if doing so increases its total reward, and not just to select among optimal strategies that do not depend upon using that information. A third possible modification is to require the agent to perform an action committing it to a single strategy before it can learn the protected information.

In some cases an auditor can detect such information flows without modifying the POMDP. For example, intuitively, we would expect the ad network to handle more than one visitor. The auditor could compare the network's behavior when given a female to that when given a male. A difference in treatment indicates that the network is not consistently implementing either of the optimal strategies.

7   Conclusion

We use planning to create the first formal semantics for determining when information is used for a purpose. We have provided an auditing algorithm based on our formalism. We have discussed applying our algorithm to the problem of enforcing purpose restrictions found in privacy policies.

Our methods have applications beyond enforcing purpose restrictions. For example, due to privacy concerns, much interest exists in determining how third-party data collection agencies use the information they collect. (See [51] for a survey.) Despite being a question of information flow, program analyses are inapplicable since the programs are unavailable, as in our setting. Unlike our setting, these agencies typically do not subject themselves to purpose restrictions. Nevertheless, their desire for profit implicitly restrains their behavior in a manner similar to a purpose restriction. Thus, our semantics and algorithm provide a starting point for investigating such agencies.

Acknowledgments. We appreciate discussions with Lorrie Faith Cranor, Joseph Y. Halpern, and Manuela M. Veloso on this work. We thank Amit Datta, Dilsun Kaynar, and Divya Sharma for many helpful comments on this paper.

References

1. Bank of America Corp.: Bank of America privacy policy for consumers (2005)
2. Office for Civil Rights: Summary of the HIPAA privacy rule. OCR Privacy Brief, U.S. Department of Health and Human Services (2003)
3. Yahoo!: Privacy policy: Yahoo Mail (2013)
4. FairWarning: Privacy breach detection for healthcare. White Paper (2010)
5. Taylor, R.: Action and Purpose. Prentice-Hall (1966)
6. Tschantz, M.C., Datta, A., Wing, J.M.: Formalizing and enforcing purpose restrictions in privacy policies. In: 2012 IEEE Symp. on Security and Privacy, pp. 176–190 (2012)
7. Goguen, J.A., Meseguer, J.: Security policies and security models. In: IEEE Symp. on Security and Privacy, pp. 11–20 (1982)
8. Tschantz, M.C., Datta, A., Wing, J.M.: Purpose restrictions on information use. Technical Report CMU-CyLab-13-005 and CMU-CS-13-116, Carnegie Mellon University (June 2013)
9. Sabelfeld, A., Myers, A.C.: Language-based information-flow security. IEEE Journal on Selected Areas in Communications 21(1), 5–19 (2003)
10. Vachharajani, N., Bridges, M.J., Chang, J., Rangan, R., Ottoni, G., Blome, J.A., Reis, G.A., Vachharajani, M., August, D.I.: RIFLE: An architectural framework for user-centric information-flow security. In: 37th Annual IEEE/ACM Intl. Symp. on Microarchitecture, pp. 243–254 (2004)
11. Newsome, J., Song, D.X.: Dynamic taint analysis for automatic detection, analysis, and signature generation of exploits on commodity software. In: Network and Distributed System Security Symp. The Internet Society (2005)
12. Venkatakrishnan, V.N., Xu, W., DuVarney, D.C., Sekar, R.: Provably correct run-time enforcement of non-interference properties. In: Ning, P., Qing, S., Li, N. (eds.) ICICS 2006. LNCS, vol. 4307, pp. 332–351. Springer, Heidelberg (2006)

13. McCamant, S., Ernst, M.D.: A simulation-based proof technique for dynamic information flow. In: 2007 Wksp. on Programming Languages and Analysis for Security, pp. 41–46. ACM (2007)

14. Yumerefendi, A.R., Mickle, B., Cox, L.P.: Tightlip: keeping applications from spilling the beans. In: 4th USENIX Conf. on Networked Systems Design and Implementation, p. 12 (2007)

15. Capizzi, R., Longo, A., Venkatakrishnan, V.N., Sistla, A.P.: Preventing information leaks through shadow executions. In: 2008 Annual Computer Security Applications Conf., pp. 322–331. IEEE Computer Society (2008)

16. Devriese, D., Piessens, F.: Noninterference through secure multi-execution. In: 2010 IEEE Symp. on Security and Privacy, pp. 109–124 (2010)

17. Agrawal, R., Kiernan, J., Srikant, R., Xu, Y.: Hippocratic databases. In: VLDB 2002: 28th Intl. Conf. on Very Large Data Bases, pp. 143–154. VLDB Endowment (2002)

18. Byun, J.W., Bertino, E., Li, N.: Purpose based access control of complex data for privacy protection. In: SACMAT 2005: Tenth ACM Symp. on Access Control Models and Technologies, pp. 102–110 (2005)

19. Al-Fedaghi, S.S.: Beyond purpose-based privacy access control. In: Eighteenth Australasian Database Conf., pp. 23–32. Australian Computer Society, Inc. (2007)

20. Byun, J.W., Li, N.: Purpose based access control for privacy protection in relational database systems. The VLDB Journal 17(4), 603–619 (2008)

21. Peng, H., Gu, J., Ye, X.: Dynamic purpose-based access control. In: Intl. Symp. on Parallel and Distributed Processing with Applications, pp. 695–700. IEEE Computer Society (2008)

22. Jafari, M., Safavi-Naini, R., Sheppard, N.P.: Enforcing purpose of use via workflows. In: WPES 2009: 8th ACM Wksp. on Privacy in the Electronic Society, pp. 113–116 (2009)

23. Ni, Q., Bertino, E., Lobo, J., Brodie, C., Karat, C.M., Karat, J., Trombetta, A.: Privacy-aware role-based access control. ACM Trans. Inf. Syst. Secur. 13, 24:1–24:31 (2010)

24. Enamul Kabir, M., Wang, H., Bertino, E.: A conditional purpose-based access control model with dynamic roles. Expert Syst. Appl. 38, 1482–1489 (2011)

25. Jafari, M., Fong, P.W., Safavi-Naini, R., Barker, K., Sheppard, N.P.: Towards defining semantic foundations for purpose-based privacy policies. In: First ACM Conf. on Data and Application Security and Privacy, pp. 213–224 (2011)

26. Martinelli, F., Morisset, C.: Quantitative access control with partially-observable markov decision processes. In: Second ACM Conf. on Data and Application Security and Privacy, pp. 169–180 (2012)

27. Hayati, K., Abadi, M.: Language-based enforcement of privacy policies. In: Martin, D., Serjantov, A. (eds.) PET 2004. LNCS, vol. 3424, pp. 302–313. Springer, Heidelberg (2005)

28. Massacci, F., Mylopoulos, J., Zannone, N.: Hierarchical Hippocratic databases with minimal disclosure for virtual organizations. The VLDB Journal 15(4), 370–387 (2006)

29. Barth, A., Mitchell, J., Datta, A., Sundaram, S.: Privacy and utility in business processes. In: CSF 2007: 20th IEEE Computer Security Foundations Symp., pp. 279–294 (2007)

30. Schmidt, C., Sridharan, N., Goodson, J.: The plan recognition problem: An intersection of psychology and artificial intelligence. Artificial Intelligence 11(1-2), 45–83 (1978)

31. Baker, C.L., Tenenbaum, J.B., Saxe, R.R.: Bayesian models of human action understanding. In: Advances in Neural Information Processing Systems 18, pp. 99–106. MIT Press (2006)

32. Baker, C.L., Saxe, R., Tenenbaum, J.B.: Action understanding as inverse planning. Cognition 113(3), 329–349 (2009)

33. Ramírez, M., Geffner, H.: Plan recognition as planning. In: 21st International Joint Conf. on Artificial Intelligence, pp. 1778–1783 (2009)

34. Ramírez, M., Geffner, H.: Goal recognition over POMDPs: Inferring the intention of a POMDP agent. In: 22nd International Joint Conf. on Artificial Intelligence, pp. 2009–2014. IJCAI/AAAI (2011)

35. Bellman, R.: On the theory of dynamic programming. National Academy of Sciences 38, 716–719 (1952)

36. Sondik, E.J.: The optimal control of partially observable Markov processes. PhD thesis, Stanford University (1971)

37. Monahan, G.E.: A survey of partially observable Markov decision processes: Theory, models, and algorithms. Management Science 28(1), 1–16 (1982)

38. Papadimitriou, C., Tsitsiklis, J.N.: The complexity of Markov decision processes. Math. Oper. Res. 12, 441–450 (1987)

39. Zhou, R., Hansen, E.A.: An improved grid-based approximation algorithm for POMDPs. In: 17th International Joint Conf. on Artificial Intelligence, vol. 1, pp. 707–714. Morgan Kaufmann (2001)

40. Smith, T., Simmons, R.: Point-based POMDP algorithms: Improved analysis and implementation. In: Conf. on Uncertainty in Artificial Intelligence (July 2005)

41. Kurniawati, H., Hsu, D., Lee, W.S.: SARSOP: Efficient point-based POMDP planning by approximating optimally reachable belief spaces. In: Proc. Robotics: Science and Systems (2008)

42. Poupart, P., Kim, K.E., Kim, D.: Closing the gap: Improved bounds on optimal POMDP solutions. In: Intl. Conf. on Automated Planning and Scheduling. AAAI (2011)

43. Madani, O.: Complexity Results for Infinite-Horizon Markov Decision Processes. PhD thesis, University of Washington (2000)

44. Rummery, G.A., Niranjan, M.: On-line Q-learning using connectionist systems. Technical Report CUEF/F-INFENG/TR 166, Cambridge University Engineering Department (1994)

45. Kaelbling, L.P., Littman, M.L., Cassandra, A.R.: Planning and acting in partially observable stochastic domains. Artif. Intell. 101, 99–134 (1998)

46. McCullough, D.: Noninterference and the composability of security properties. In: IEEE Symp. on Security and Privacy, pp. 177–186 (1988)

47. Wittbold, J.T., Johnson, D.M.: Information flow in nondeterministic systems. In: IEEE Symp. on Security and Privacy, pp. 144–161 (1990)

48. McLean, J.: A general theory of composition for trace sets closed under selective interleaving functions. In: 1994 IEEE Symp. on Security and Privacy, p. 79 (1994)

49. Clark, D., Hunt, S.: Non-interference for deterministic interactive programs. In: Degano, P., Guttman, J., Martinelli, F. (eds.) FAST 2008. LNCS, vol. 5491, pp. 50–66. Springer, Heidelberg (2009)

50. Tschantz, M.C., Wing, J.M.: Extracting conditional confidentiality policies. In: Sixth IEEE Intl. Conferences on Software Engineering and Formal Methods (2008)

51. Mayer, J.R., Mitchell, J.C.: Third-party web tracking: Policy and technology. In: IEEE Symp. on Security and Privacy, pp. 413–427 (2012)

Distributed Shuffling for Preserving Access Confidentiality

Sabrina De Capitani di Vimercati[1], Sara Foresti[1], Stefano Paraboschi[2],
Gerardo Pelosi[3], and Pierangela Samarati[1]

[1] Università degli Studi di Milano, 26013 Crema, Italy
firstname.lastname@unimi.it
[2] Università degli Studi di Bergamo, 24044 Dalmine, Italy
parabosc@unibg.it
[3] Politecnico di Milano, 20133 Milan, Italy
gerardo.pelosi@polimi.it

Abstract. The shuffle index has been recently proposed for organizing and accessing data in outsourcing scenarios while protecting the confidentiality of the data as well as of the accesses to them. In this paper, we extend the shuffle index to the use of multiple servers for storing data, introducing a new protection technique (shadow) and enriching the original ones by operating in a distributed scenario. Our distributed shuffle index produces a significant increase in the protection of the system, with no additional costs.

1 Introduction

Recent years have witnessed an over increasing reliance on external services for data storage and management, towards the emerging cloud scenario, characterized by a rich and diverse availability of providers offering storage and computational functionalities. Together with data management functionality, the research and industrial communities have been investigating different solutions to ensure confidentiality of data whose management is outsourced to the cloud [8]. Complementing data confidentiality, more recent approaches have also considered protection of *access* and *pattern confidentiality*, which require to maintain confidential to the server storing the data the fact that a given access aims at a specific target or that two accesses aim at the same target. Among these approaches, the *shuffle index* [5] organizes data in a hierarchical encrypted data structure and provides access and pattern confidentiality by obfuscating accesses and dynamically changing the allocation of data to physical blocks, so to break the correspondence between data and locations where they are stored. Such a dynamic allocation prevents the server observing sequences of accesses from withdrawing inferences which could compromise pattern confidentiality and even break data confidentiality. The advantages of the shuffle index are the ability to support equality and range predicates in data retrieval, and the limited performance overhead compared with other access protection solutions [7].

J. Crampton, S. Jajodia, and K. Mayes (Eds.): ESORICS 2013, LNCS 8134, pp. 628–645, 2013.

The availability of different providers for data outsourcing can help in providing protection in cloud scenarios and has been investigated in some proposals, adopting, for example, data fragmentation and slicing at different servers (e.g., [3, 16]). The intuition is that relying on multiple servers (in contrast to a single one) for managing data or providing services naturally increases protection, since it diminishes the knowledge and visibility that each server has on the data and on accesses to them, and enjoys diversity of risks.

In this paper, we extend the shuffle index to operate with multiple servers for storing and accessing data. Every data access entails accessing the servers and shuffling data dynamically changing their allocation even across servers. Since retrieval of the targeted data may entail traversing the hierarchical structure across servers (i.e., a parent might be stored at one server and a children at another), we introduce a *shadowing* technique that ensures protection of this path information by making observations by each server as if the server was the only one involved in the access. The distribution of the shuffle index increases protection for data and accesses, quickly destroying knowledge that servers might have and effectively preventing the servers from acquiring knowledge by observing sequences of accesses. Such increased protection comes without impact on the system performance.

The remainder of the paper is organized as follows. Section 2 recalls the basic concepts of the shuffle index on which we build. Section 3 extends the index organization to the adoption of multiple servers. Section 4 introduces shadows and extends the original protection techniques (covers, cache, and shuffling) to operate with them. Section 5 describes access execution. Section 6 discusses the protection offered by our approach illustrating how distributing the shuffle index provides greater confidentiality guarantees while not impacting performance. Section 7 illustrates related work. Section 8 concludes the paper.

2   Basic Concepts

A shuffle index [5] organizes the outsourced data as an abstract *unchained B+-tree* $\mathcal{T}^a(\mathcal{N}^a)$ (i.e., leaves are not connected in a linked list) with fan out F defined over a candidate key K, with actual data stored in the leaves of the tree. Each internal node of the index is a pair $n^a = \langle values, children \rangle \in \mathcal{N}^a$, where *values* is a list of q values with $\lceil \frac{F}{2} \rceil - 1 \leq q \leq F - 1$ (the lower-bound does not apply to the root) ordered from the smallest to the greatest, and *children* is a list of $q + 1$ children. The first child of a node is the root of the subtree with all values $v < values[1]$; the i-th child is the root of the subtree storing the values v such that $values[i - 1] \leq v < values[i]$, $i = 2, \ldots, q$; the last child is the root of the subtree with all values $v \geq values[q]$. Leaf nodes are pairs $n^a = \langle values, tuples \rangle \in \mathcal{N}^a$, where *tuples* represents the tuples with index value in *values*. Figure 1(a) illustrates an example of unchained B+-tree with fan out 3. For simplicity, we refer to the content of a node with a label (e.g., a), instead of explicitly reporting the values it represents.

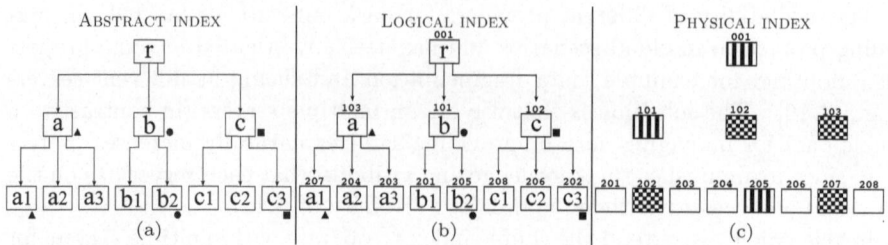

Fig. 1. An example of abstract (a), logical (b), and physical (c) shuffle index
Legend: ■ target, • node in cache, ▲ cover; blocks read and written: chessboard filling, blocks written: lines filling

At the *logical level*, nodes are allocated to logical addresses that work as logical *identifiers*. Given an abstract unchained B+-tree $\mathcal{T}^a(\mathcal{N}^a)$, its logical representation $\mathcal{T}$ is a triple $(\mathcal{N}, \mathcal{ID}, \phi)$, with $\mathcal{N}$ a set of logical nodes, $\mathcal{ID}$ a set of logical identifiers, and $\phi : \mathcal{N}^a \rightarrow \mathcal{ID}$ a bijective function that associates a logical identifier with each abstract node. Note that the possible order among identifiers does not necessarily correspond to the order in which nodes appear in the value-ordered abstract representation. Each non-leaf abstract node $n^a = \langle values, children \rangle$ in $\mathcal{N}^a$ is represented by a logical node $n = \langle id, vals, ptrs \rangle$ in $\mathcal{N}$, with $id = \phi(n^a)$, $vals = values$, and $ptrs[j] = \phi(children[j])$, $j = 0, \ldots, q$. In fact, pointers to the children of the nodes in the abstract unchained B+-tree are translated, at the logical level, into the identifiers of the corresponding child nodes. Analogously, each abstract leaf node $n^a = \langle values, tuples \rangle$ in $\mathcal{N}^a$ translates into a logical node $n = \langle id, vals, t \rangle$ that includes tuples $t = tuples$ instead of pointers to children. Figure 1(b) illustrates an example of logical representation of the abstract index in Figure 1(a). Logical identifiers are reported on the top of each node and, for easy reference, their first digit denotes its level in the tree.

At the *physical level*, logical identifiers are mapped to physical addresses and the shuffle index is represented by a set of disk *blocks* storing the nodes in the tree. Every node is encrypted by first prefixing it with a random salt and then applying symmetric encryption in CBC mode. Formally, each non-leaf node $\langle id, vals, ptrs \rangle \in \mathcal{N}$ (leaf node $\langle id, vals, t \rangle \in \mathcal{N}$, resp.) is stored at block $\langle id, b \rangle$, where $b = E_k(salt \| id \| vals \| ptrs)$ ($b = E_k(salt \| id \| vals \| t)$, resp.), with E a symmetric encryption function, k the encryption key, and $salt$ a nonce generated for each encryption. Figure 1(c) illustrates the physical representation of the logical index in Figure 1(b), which corresponds to the view of the server.

The retrieval of the leaf block containing the tuple corresponding to a given index value (target value) requires an iterative process. Starting from the root of the tree and ending at a leaf, the client reads from the server the block in the path to the target, and decrypts the block for retrieving the address of the child to be read at the next step. To protect the fact that different accesses may aim at the same content, this iterative process is extended by:

– performing, in addition to the target search, other fake *cover searches*, guaranteeing indistinguishability of target and cover searches and operating on

disjoint paths of the tree (retrieving, at every level of the tree, $num\_cover+1$ blocks at the same time);
- maintaining a set of num_cache nodes in a local *cache* for each level of the tree, but level 0;
- mixing (*shuffling*) the content of all retrieved blocks as well as those maintained in cache, and overwriting them accordingly on the server.

Cover searches protect the confidentiality of accesses by introducing uncertainty on the leaf block target of the access (any of the accessed leaves could store the searched value). The cache makes searches repeated within a short time interval not recognizable as such. In fact, if the target of an access is in cache, the corresponding block is not read from the server (the target is substituted by an additional cover). Shuffling destroys the correspondence between nodes and the physical blocks where they are stored. (Note that at every reallocation, a node is encrypted with a different random salt.) Repeated accesses to the same block do not then imply repeated accesses to the same node. As an example of access to the shuffle index in Figure 1, consider a search for $c3$ that adopts $a1$ as cover, and assume that the cache contains the path to $b2$. The access visits the tree level by level. The client has the root r in cache, downloads and decrypts blocks 102 and 103 from the server, shuffles and encrypts nodes a, b, and c (e.g., allocating a to 102, b to 101, and c to 103), and overwrites blocks 101, 102, and 103 at the server. At the leaf level, the client downloads and decrypts blocks 202 and 207, shuffles and encrypts nodes $a1$, $b2$, and $c3$, and overwrites blocks 202, 205, and 207 at the server. Figure 1(c) illustrates the observations on the access at the server in terms of blocks read and/or written. Note that the root (being in cache) is only written. The server cannot detect which among the accessed leaves is the target of the access and how the content of blocks has been shuffled.

3   Distributed Shuffle Index

In a *distributed shuffle index*, the data owner exploits more than one server for storing and managing data, enjoying then increased protection of data, access, and pattern confidentiality by dynamically changing the allocation of the nodes also across the servers. For simplicity, we illustrate our distributed shuffle index assuming the use of *two* servers, with the note that the approach can be easily extended to the consideration of an arbitrary number of servers. For simplicity of notation and clarity of the figures, we denote our servers by $\mathcal{S}_G$ and $\mathcal{S}_Y$, coloring nodes stored at them with *Green* and *Yellow*, respectively (in b/w printouts, Green is the darker color).

The consideration of more than one server for the allocation of an abstract index and for accesses to it requires revising the shuffle index structure discussed in Section 2 with the following extensions.

- *Abstract level.* The root r^a of a distributed shuffle index is extended to have twice the capacity as the other nodes. Hence, for an index with fan out F, the root can contain up to $2F-1$ values (in contrast to the original $F-1$). In the translation to the logical level, the abstract root $r^a = \langle values, children \rangle$ will be interpreted as two abstract root nodes, r_0^a and r_1^a, each storing around half of the values and children in r^a. Formally, $r_0^a = \langle values_0, children_0 \rangle$ and $r_1^a = \langle values_1, children_1 \rangle$ with $values_0 = values[1, \ldots, \lceil q/2 \rceil]$, $values_1 = values[\lceil q/2 \rceil + 2, \ldots, q]$, $children_0 = children[0, \ldots, \lceil q/2 \rceil]$, and $children_1 = children[\lceil q/2 \rceil + 1, \ldots, q]$, where q is the number of index values in the abstract root. (Note that $values[\lceil q/2 \rceil + 1]$ disappears since it is no more needed for the index.) The set $\mathcal{N}^a$ of abstract nodes therefore becomes $\mathcal{N}^a = \mathcal{N}^a \setminus \{r^a\} \cup \{r_0^a, r_1^a\}$.

- *Logical level.* The logical identifiers of a distributed shuffle index must take into consideration logical identifiers (which translate to physical addresses) at the two servers. We then distinguish, in the set $\mathcal{ID}$ of logical identifiers, two different subsets: $\mathcal{ID}_G$, corresponding to addresses at server $\mathcal{S}_G$, and $\mathcal{ID}_Y$, corresponding to addresses at server $\mathcal{S}_Y$, with $\mathcal{ID}_G \cup \mathcal{ID}_Y = \mathcal{ID}$. The result of function ϕ over an abstract node, determining the logical identifier of the node, therefore determines also the server at which the abstract node is stored. Function ϕ guarantees the natural requirement to store r_0^a and r_1^a at different servers. Formally, $\phi(r_0^a) \in \mathcal{ID}_X$ and $\phi(r_1^a) \in \mathcal{ID}_Z$, with $X, Z \in \{Y, G\}$ and $X \neq Z$. In the following, given a node n in the set $\mathcal{N}$ of logical nodes, we will use $\sigma(n.id)$ to denote the server at which the node is stored. Formally, given $n = \langle id, vals, ptrs \rangle$, with $id = \phi(n^a)$, $id \in \mathcal{ID}_G \Longrightarrow \sigma(n.id) = \mathcal{S}_G$; $id \in \mathcal{ID}_Y \Longrightarrow \sigma(n.id) = \mathcal{S}_Y$.

- *Physical level.* It works like in the original shuffle index, storing (according to allocation function ϕ defined at the logical level) nodes at each server in encrypted form as described in Section 2.

Figure 2 illustrates an example of abstract, logical, and physical distributed shuffle index. For simplicity and easy reference, logical identifiers start with a letter denoting the server where the corresponding block is stored (G for $\mathcal{S}_G$ and Y for $\mathcal{S}_Y$) and nodes stored at server $\mathcal{S}_G$ and $\mathcal{S}_Y$ are color-coded (*Green* and *Yellow*). In the following, without loss of generality, we assume that the physical address of a block corresponds to the logical identifier of the node it stores. Also, we use the term *node* to refer to an abstract content and *block* to refer to a specific memory slot in the logical/physical structure. When either terms can be used, we will use node/block interchangeably.

4   Shadows, Covers, Cache, and Shuffling

The shuffle index entails two types of protections. The first involves obfuscating the fact that the access aims at a specific block. The second is the shuffling, which changes the allocation of nodes so to dynamically modify the node/block correspondence. Both these types of protection, provided by cover searches, caching, and shuffling in the original proposal, are complemented in the distributed shuffle index with the consideration of *shadows*. In this section, we introduce shadows and extend cover searches, cache, and shuffling to operate with them.

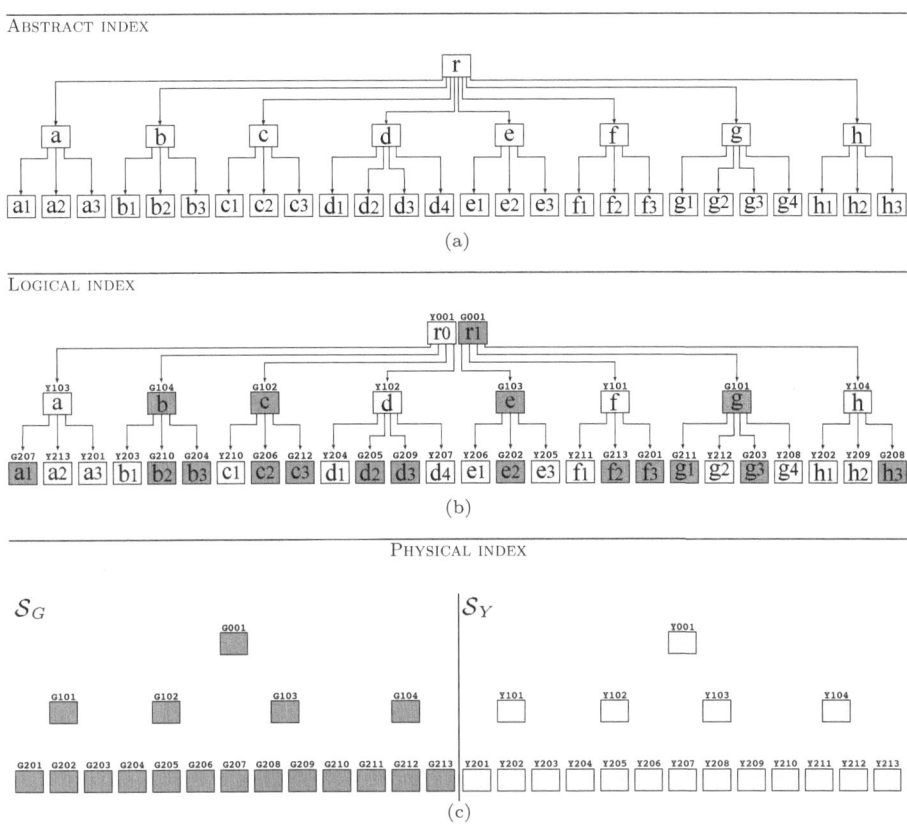

Fig. 2. An example of abstract (a), logical (b), and physical (c) shuffle index, distributed over two servers

4.1   Shadows

Retrieval of a target key value in a distributed shuffle index entails traversing the index starting from the root ancestor of the target and following, at every node, the pointer to the child in the path to the leaf possibly containing the target value. Such a path can naturally involve nodes stored at any of the servers. For instance, with reference to the shuffle index in Figure 2 a search for target value $e3$ involves access to blocks (G001/Y001;G103;Y205), with G001 and G103 stored at $\mathcal{S}_G$, and Y001 and Y205 stored at $\mathcal{S}_Y$. (For simplicity, we assume both roots to be always accessed.) Like in the original shuffle index proposal, we assume each server, which initially knows only the number of blocks it stores, to potentially have knowledge of the height of the shuffle index and of the level of the node stored at each of its blocks (which can be acquired by observing the iterations in the accesses). Combined with such knowledge, discontinuity of accesses with respect to levels (e.g., for $\mathcal{S}_Y$) could leak information to the servers. To avoid such a leakage, in our approach, every time we need to access a block at one of the servers, we will also access another block, which we call *shadow*, at the other server. With shadows, each server will observe accesses to blocks as if it was the only one storing the data structure and involved in the access. With respect to this aspect, any block at the other server at the same level as the block for which it works as shadow would do. The choice of the shadow for a block during a given access, however, needs to take into account the fact that the shuffle index changes allocation of nodes at every access. Re-allocating a node n requires changing in its parent the pointer to n, to refer to the block where it has been moved. Therefore, the nodes involved in an access should always form a sub-tree. In other words, a shadow at a given level should be child of a node that is available for the access (i.e., read in the path to the target or to a cover, or available in cache).

A convenient way to ensure this requirement is to use, as shadow of a node for a given access, one of its siblings stored at the other server. For each node n, we call *far siblings* of n the children of the same parent (i.e., n's siblings) stored at a server different from the one where n is stored. We denote with $FS(n)$ the nodes having such properties at a given time with respect to a node n, as formally defined in the following.

Definition 1 (Far siblings and shadow). *Let* $\mathcal{T}(\mathcal{N}, \mathcal{ID}_G, \mathcal{ID}_Y, \phi)$ *be a logical index, and n be a non-root node in $\mathcal{N}$. The* far siblings *of node n, denoted $FS(n)$, are defined as* $FS(n) = \{n_i \in \mathcal{N} : \text{parent}(n_i) = \text{parent}(n) \text{ and } \sigma(n_i.id) \neq \sigma(n.id)\}$. *As particular cases,* $FS(r_0) = \{r_1\}$ *and* $FS(r_1) = \{r_0\}$.
The shadow *of a node for a given access is one of its far siblings selected for the specific access.*

For instance, with reference to the shuffle index in Figure 2(b), $FS(e) = \{f, h\}$, and $FS(e3)=\{e2\}$. Assuming to choose h and $e2$ as shadows for e and $e3$, respectively, the search for key value $e3$ will translate into accessing blocks (G001;G103;G202) at $\mathcal{S}_G$ and blocks (Y001;Y104;Y205) at $\mathcal{S}_Y$.

Note that the far siblings relationship is dynamic as every re-allocation of nodes, which will operate across servers, changes it. Also, the shadow relationship is dynamic as, at any given access to a node, any of its far siblings can be dynamically selected to serve as shadow. Although in principle nodes can be randomly allocated to servers, distributing allocation uniformly provides better protection and has the advantage that the set $FS(n)$ of a node n can never be empty. We then require uniform distribution between the two servers among the children of each node (storing half of the node's children at one server and half at the other). The allocation function ϕ must enforce a balanced allocation of nodes' children to the servers, satisfying the following property.

Property 1 (Balanced allocation). Let $\mathcal{T}(\mathcal{N}, \mathcal{ID}_G, \mathcal{ID}_Y, \phi)$ be a logical index. $\mathcal{T}$ satisfies the *balanced allocation* property iff:

1. $\sigma(r_0.id) \neq \sigma(r_1.id)$ (i.e., the two roots are stored at a different server);
2. $\forall \langle id, vals, ptrs \rangle \in \mathcal{N}: |\text{card}(ptrs_G) - \text{card}(ptrs_Y)| \leq 1$,
   with $ptrs_G = \{id_i \in ptrs: id_i \in \mathcal{ID}_G\}$ and $ptrs_Y = \{id_i \in ptrs: id_i \in \mathcal{ID}_Y\}$.

The first condition in the property states that the two roots are stored at different servers. The second condition states that, for each node, half of its children are stored at server $\mathcal{S}_G$ and the other half at server $\mathcal{S}_Y$. Property 1 guarantees that every node n, child of a node with k children, has at least $\left\lfloor \frac{k}{2} \right\rfloor$ far siblings. It is easy to see that the distributed shuffle index in Figure 2 obeys to the balanced allocation property.

4.2 Covers

As in the original proposal, cover searches are fake searches executed in parallel with the search for the target value to the aim of hiding the target request within a group of other requests. The fact that the shuffle index is distributed has two effects with respect to covers: one is the extension of the definition of cover search, the other is the application of shadows to covers.

As in [5], the only constraint on covers chosen for an access is that they actually act as such, that is, they should be indistinguishable from actual searches, and their paths should not intersect or intersect the path to the target. The first aspect is already guaranteed from [5], the latter aspect simply requires extending the definition of cover searches to the consideration of the fact that the root is split, and therefore the constraint that paths of the covers have only the root in common translates into requiring that their paths have nothing in common but - possibly - any of the roots, as formally stated by the following definition.

Definition 2 (Cover searches). *Let* $\mathcal{T}(\mathcal{N}, \mathcal{ID}_G, \mathcal{ID}_Y, \phi)$ *be a logical index built on candidate key* K *with domain* $\mathcal{D}$, *and* v_0 *be a value in* $\mathcal{D}$. *A set* $\{v_1, \ldots, v_{num\_cover}\} \subseteq \mathcal{D}$ *is a set of cover searches for* v_0 *iff* $\forall path_i, path_j \in \{path_0, \ldots, path_{num\_cover}\}$, $i \neq j$: $(path_i \cap path_j) \setminus \{r_0, r_1\} = \emptyset$, *where* $path_i$ *is the set of nodes in the path from* r_0 *or* r_1 *to the leaf where* v_i *is possibly stored.*

Note that the nodes in the paths to covers can be indifferently stored at one of the two servers. This does not create any problem in our approach. In fact, just like the target, covers will also be shadowed and for every node to be accessed in the path to a cover at a server, one of its far siblings will be accessed at the other server. In particular, for each level in the shuffle index, if a node n_c in the path to a cover is actually stored at a different server from the node n_t in the path to the target, n_c will act as a protection of n_t's shadow and n_c's shadow will act as a protection for n_t, respectively, at the two servers. The application of shadows to nodes in the path to covers nicely provides a symmetric behavior at the two servers, regardless of where these nodes are stored. In fact, a server will observe access to *num_cover + 1* different blocks for each level, but level 0.

As an example, consider the distributed shuffle index in Figure 2(b), and a search for *e3* (path $(r_1;e;e3)$), using *a2* as cover (path $(r_0;a;a2)$). Assuming to choose, in the set of its far siblings, h as shadow for e, c for a, $e2$ for $e3$, and *a1* for *a2*, the accessed blocks are (G001;G102,G103;G202,G207) at $\mathcal{S}_G$ and (Y001;Y103,Y104;Y205,Y213) at $\mathcal{S}_Y$.

4.3 Cache

Caching works essentially like in the original proposal, maintaining a copy of the last *num_cache* target searches (where for each target search all nodes in the path to the target leaf are maintained). In addition to the actual targets, in our distributed scenario, we also store, in association with every node n in the path to the target, the node n' that acted as n's shadow last time n was accessed.

Formally, the cache of a distributed shuffle index is defined as follows.

Definition 3 (Cache). *Let* $\mathcal{T}(\mathcal{N}, \mathcal{ID}_G, \mathcal{ID}_Y, \phi)$ *be a logical index with height* h. *A cache of size* num_cache *for* $\mathcal{T}$ *is a layered structure of* $h{+}1$ *sets* $Cache_0, \ldots, Cache_h$ *of pairs of nodes where:*

1. *$Cache_0$ contains pair $\langle r_i, r_j \rangle$ with $i, j \in \{0, 1\}$ and $i \neq j$;*
2. *$Cache_l$, $l = 1, \ldots, h$, contains num_cache pairs of nodes $\langle n_i, n_j \rangle$ s.t. n_i and n_j belong to the l-th level of $\mathcal{T}$, with n_i and n_j far siblings one of the other (cache balancing);*
3. *$\forall \langle n_i, n_j \rangle \in Cache_l$, $l = 1, \ldots, h$, the node parent of n_i and n_j in the shuffle index belongs to $Cache_{l-1}$ (path continuity).*

Note how the path continuity requirement (Condition 3 in the definition), requesting that the parent of a cached node be also in cache and here extended to the consideration of shadows, does not impose any complication to the approach. As a matter of fact, the choice of the shadows among the far siblings of target nodes included in the cache nicely guarantees that their parent (being a target) is already in the cache by construction.

A nice advantage of including shadows in cache is that $Cache_l$, $l = 1, \ldots, h$, contains $2num\_cache$ nodes, half of which are stored at $\mathcal{S}_G$ and the others are stored at $\mathcal{S}_Y$. This will provide a symmetric behavior of the access at the two servers, with each of them operating with a view as if it was the only one involved in the access (see Section 5). After the search illustrated in Section 4.2 for value $e3$ over the distributed shuffle index in Figure 2(b), the cache includes the nodes in the path to $e3$ and their shadows (i.e., $\langle r_1, r_0 \rangle$, $\langle e, h \rangle$, and $\langle e3, e2 \rangle$).

4.4 Shuffling

Shuffling aims at destroying the one-to-one correspondence between blocks and nodes stored in them. The idea is to randomly re-allocate all nodes available in an access (i.e., accessed as targets, covers, shadows or in cache) so to break the otherwise static relationship between nodes and blocks where they are stored. Shuffling is formally defined as follows.

Definition 4 (Shuffling). *Given a set $ID \subseteq \mathcal{ID}_G \cup \mathcal{ID}_Y$ of logical identifiers, a shuffling, denoted by π, over ID is a random permutation $\pi: ID \to ID$.*

The effect of a shuffling $\pi: ID \to ID$ over shuffle index $\mathcal{T}(\mathcal{N}, \mathcal{ID}_G, \mathcal{ID}_Y, \phi)$ is that the corresponding abstract index remains unchanged while the allocation of some nodes (and the pointers to them in their parents) is changed. More precisely, each node $\langle id, vals, ptrs \rangle$ is updated as follows: $id=\pi(id)$ if $id \in ID$, it remains unchanged otherwise; and $\forall i = 0, \ldots, q$ with q the number of values in $vals$, $ptrs[i]=\pi(ptrs[i])$ if $ptrs[i] \in ID$, it remains unchanged otherwise.

Like in the original (non-distributed) shuffle index, shuffling is performed only within levels and not cross-levels, due to complications that would otherwise arise for updating pointers to children.

Also, in our distributed shuffle index, where nodes (accessed because in the paths to the target or to a cover, or present in cache) are always accompanied by a shadow, we need to ensure that shuffling does not compromise the balanced allocation of the index. We then require the shuffling to ensure balancing, as captured by the following property.

Property 2 (Balanced shuffling). Let $\mathcal{T}(\mathcal{N}, \mathcal{ID}_G, \mathcal{ID}_Y, \phi)$ be a logical index, and $\mathcal{P} = \{\langle n_1, n_1' \rangle, \ldots, \langle n_m, n_m' \rangle\}$ be a set of pairs of nodes in $\mathcal{N}$ s.t. $\forall \langle n_i, n_i' \rangle \in \mathcal{P}$, $\sigma(n_i.id) \neq \sigma(n_i'.id)$. A shuffling π over $ID_{\mathcal{P}}=\{id : \exists \langle n_i, n_i' \rangle \in \mathcal{P}$ with $id=n_i.id$ or $id=n_i'.id\}$ is *balanced* iff $\forall \langle n_i, n_i' \rangle \in \mathcal{P}$, $\sigma(\pi(n_i.id)) \neq \sigma(\pi(n_i'.id))$.

Balanced shuffling essentially guarantees that pairs of nodes provided as input and stored at different servers before the shuffling remain stored at different servers after the shuffling. Since we operate shuffling on pairs of nodes that are far siblings one of the other, balanced shuffling ensures that these pairs of nodes will remain as such after the shuffling (indeed, shuffling does not change the 'being child of' relationship over the abstract index). Note that this does not mean that the two nodes in a pair can only be swapped one with the other as shuffling can actually change the blocks to which they are allocated; the only constraint is that the two nodes do not end up being stored at the same server. It is then easy to see that a balanced shuffling guarantees that the shuffling does not compromise the balanced allocation of the shuffle index (Property 1).

We realize a balanced shuffling by: *i)* randomly shuffling the nodes allocated at each of the two servers separately; and *ii)* possibly swapping the allocation of a node and its shadow. The random shuffling (step *i)*) does not move nodes from $\mathcal{S}_G$ to $\mathcal{S}_Y$ or vice versa. The controlled swapping (step *ii)*) operates between pairs of nodes stored at the two servers: whenever a node allocated at $\mathcal{S}_G$ is moved to $\mathcal{S}_Y$, its shadow (which by definition is at $\mathcal{S}_Y$) is moved from $\mathcal{S}_Y$ to $\mathcal{S}_G$, and vice versa. More precisely, our shuffling works as follows.

- Consider a logical index $\mathcal{T}(\mathcal{N}, \mathcal{ID}_G, \mathcal{ID}_Y, \phi)$, a set $\mathcal{P} = \{\langle n_1, n_1' \rangle, \ldots, \langle n_m, n_m' \rangle\}$ of pairs of nodes in $\mathcal{N}$, and the set $ID_{\mathcal{P}}=\{id : \exists \langle n_i, n_i' \rangle \in \mathcal{P}$ with $id=n_i.id$ or $id=n_i'.id\}$ of their identifiers.
- Define an *intra-server shuffling* over $ID_{\mathcal{P}}$, $\pi_1 : ID_{\mathcal{P}} \rightarrow ID_{\mathcal{P}}$, such that $\forall id \in ID_{\mathcal{P}}$, $\sigma(\pi_1(id)) = \sigma(id)$.
- Randomly select a subset S of pairs of nodes in $\mathcal{P}$ for *inter-server swapping*.
- Return π over $ID_{\mathcal{P}}$ such that $\forall \langle n_i, n_i' \rangle \in \mathcal{P}$:

  - if $\langle n_i, n_i' \rangle \in S \implies \pi(n_i.id) = \pi_1(n_i'.id)$ and $\pi(n_i'.id) = \pi_1(n_i.id)$;
  - if $\langle n_i, n_i' \rangle \notin S \implies \pi(n_i.id) = \pi_1(n_i.id)$ and $\pi(n_i'.id) = \pi_1(n_i'.id)$.

Note that, while guaranteeing balancing, our shuffling can move a node to any block on which the shuffling is operating (either at the same or at a different server). This provides for a fast degradation of the correspondences between nodes and blocks, ensuring the protection of access and pattern confidentiality (see Section 6).

As an example, consider the shuffle index in Figure 2(b), reported in Figure 3(a) for the reader's convenience, and the set $\mathcal{P} = \{\langle r_0,r_1\rangle;\ \langle e,h\rangle,\ \langle a,c\rangle,\ \langle b,d\rangle;\ \langle e3,e2\rangle,\ \langle a2,a1\rangle,\ \langle b1,b2\rangle\}$ of pairs of nodes accessed by the search for value $e3$ illustrated above. Figures 3(b) and (c) illustrate an example of intra-server shuffling π_1 over $ID_\mathcal{P}$ and of inter-server swapping, with $S=\{\langle r_0,r_1\rangle;\ \langle a,c\rangle,\langle e,h\rangle;\langle a1,a2\rangle\}$, respectively. It is easy to see that the resulting shuffling π satisfies the balancing property (e.g., $\sigma(r_0.id)=\mathcal{S}_G$ and $\sigma(r_1.id)=\mathcal{S}_Y$). Figure 3(d) illustrates the shuffle index after the shuffling.

5   Access Execution

The application of shadows, covers, cache, and shuffling when performing an access works in combination to ensure two kinds of protection: *i)* obfuscating the fact that the access aims at a specific block (shadows, covers, and cache); and *ii)* changing the allocation of nodes so to dynamically modify the node/block correspondence and therefore provide protection for future accesses. Access execution with our protection techniques works as follows.

Given a search for a target value v, we first choose a set of *num_cover*+1 cover searches for v (Definition 2), where the additional one is to be used if a node in the path to v is in cache. For each level l of the distributed shuffle index, we identify the blocks in the paths to covers and target and choose a shadow (Definition 1) for each of them. Like covers, shadows are chosen in such a way to ensure block diversity, meaning that they should not appear in the paths to the target and to covers, and should not be stored in $Cache_l$. Intuitively, block diversity guarantees that all the techniques play a role in providing protection as they will not end up clashing over the same blocks.

Enforcement of block diversity also on shadows, and application of shadows to both the target and cover searches, as well as availability of shadows in cache, provide a nice symmetric behavior of the access at the two servers, with each of them observing *num_cover + 1* reads and *num_cover + num_cache + 1* writes for each level of the shuffle index (but level 0). In other words, each server will observe a pattern of (read/write) accesses to blocks as if it was the only server storing the data and managing the access. Note that this does not cause any performance overhead with respect to the single server solution while enjoying significant higher protection (see Section 6).

For instance, consider the shuffle index in Figure 3(a). Figure 4 illustrates, step by step, a search for value $e3$ that adopts $a2$ as cover and that assumes that the local cache has size one and contains the path to $b1$ (e.g., $\langle r_0,r_1\rangle$, $\langle b,d\rangle$ and $\langle b1,b2\rangle$, with d and $b2$ the shadows for b and $b1$ chosen in a previous search). Among its far siblings, h is chosen as shadow for e, c for a, $e2$ for

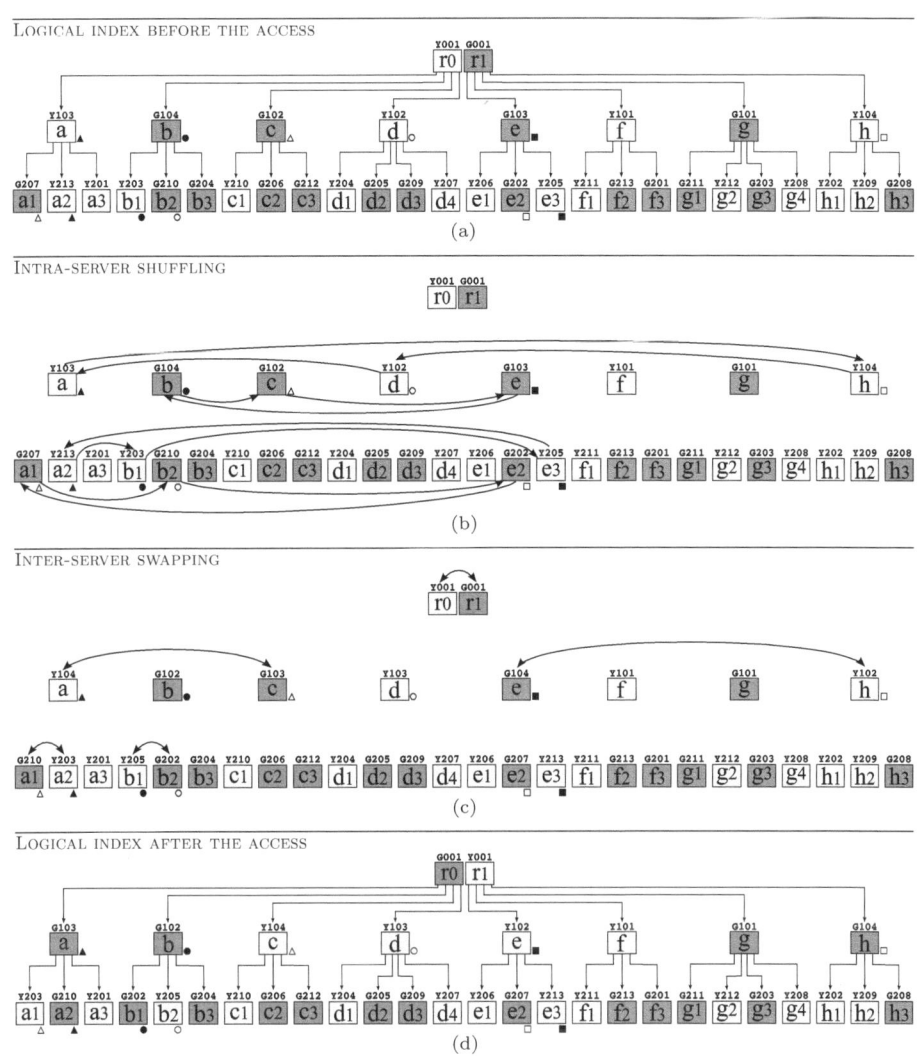

Fig. 3. Evolution of the shuffle index for our running example
Legend: ■ target and □ its shadow; ● node in cache and ○ its shadow; ▲ cover and △ its shadow

e3, and *a1* for *a2*. The columns of the table represent: the visited level of the shuffle index (*l*); the content of the cache (*Cache$_l$* in *Retrieved nodes*) and the nodes read from the servers (*Read* in *Retrieved nodes*); the balanced shuffling (*shuffle*); the nodes in the cache (*Cache$_l$* in *Shuffled nodes*) and read (*Non_Cached* in *Shuffled nodes*) after the shuffling; the nodes written on the server that are also kept in cache (*Cache$_{l-1}$* in *Written nodes*) or that are only stored at the server (*Non_Cached_P* in *Shuffled nodes*). Note that column

l	Retrieved nodes		Shuffle	Shuffled nodes		Written nodes	
	$Cache_l$	Read		$Cache_l$	Non_Cached	$Cache_{l-1}$	Non_Cached_P
0	Y001 r0 [Y103,G104,G102,Y102] G001 r1 [G103,Y101,G101,Y104]		Y001→G001 G001→Y001	G001 r0 [Y103,G104,G102,Y102] Y001 r1 [G103,Y101,G101,Y104]			
1	G104 b • [Y203,G210,G204,-] Y102 d ∘ [Y204,G205,G209,Y207]	G103 e ■ [Y206,G202,Y205,-] Y104 h □ [Y202,Y209,Y208,-] Y103 a ▲ [G207,Y213,Y201,-] G102 c △ [Y210,G206,G212,-]	G104→G102 Y102→Y103 G103→Y102 Y104→G104 Y103→G103 G102→Y104	G102 b • [Y203,G210,G204,-] Y103 d ∘ [Y204,G205,G209,Y207]	Y102 e ■ [Y206,G202,Y205,-] G104 h □ [Y202,Y209,Y208,-] G103 a ▲ [G207,Y213,Y201,-] Y104 c △ [Y210,G206,G212,-]	Y001 r1 [Y102,Y101,G101,G104] G001 r0 [G103,G102,Y104,Y103]	
2	Y203 b1 • G210 b2 ∘	Y205 e3 ■ G202 e2 □ Y213 a2 ▲ G207 a1 △	Y203→G202 G210→Y205 Y205→Y213 G202→G207 Y213→G210 G207→Y203	G202 b1 • Y205 b2 ∘	Y213 e3 ■ G207 e2 □ G210 a2 ▲ Y203 a1 △	Y102 e ■ [Y206,G207,Y213,-] G104 h □ [Y202,Y209,G208,-] Y213 e3 ■ G207 e2 □	G102 b • [G202,Y205,G204,-] Y103 d ∘ [Y204,G205,G209,Y207] G103 a ▲ [Y203,G210,Y201,-] Y104 c △ [Y210,G206,G212,-] G202 b1 • Y205 b2 ∘ G210 a2 ▲ Y203 a1 △

Fig. 4. An example of access to the distributed shuffle index in Figure 2 searching for $e3$, with $a2$ as cover

Legend: ■ target and □ its shadow; • node in cache and ∘ its shadow; ▲ cover and △ its shadow

$Cache_{l-1}$ in *Written nodes* represents the status of the local cache at the end of the access. The evolution of the shuffle index for the search in Figure 4 is illustrated in Figure 3.

Figure 5 shows the observations of the servers in terms of blocks read and written by the access in Figure 4. The different blocks read provide confusion to each of the server with respect to which is the target of the access (as a matter of fact, the observations of a server might even not include the target but its shadow); the different blocks written provide confusion over what is stored in the blocks after the access (as a matter of fact, even the set of nodes stored at each server might have changed), thus practically destroying any possibility for the servers to correlate observations over different access requests (see Section 6).

6   Discussion and Evaluation of the Approach

We discuss the protection guarantees and the performance of our distributed shuffle index, in particular comparing it with the original proposal [5] adopting a single server.

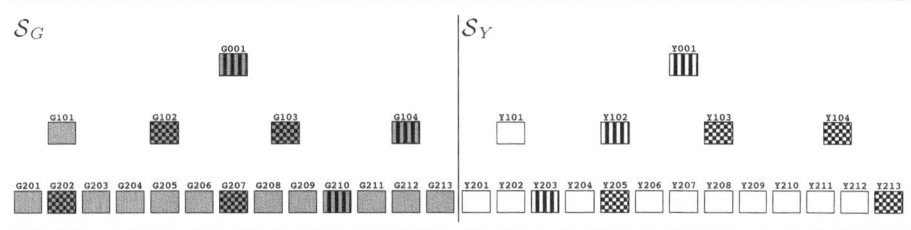

Fig. 5. Observations by each server of read/written blocks in our running example
Legend: blocks read and written: chessboard filling, blocks written: lines filling

Protection. Like in [5], we focus the analysis on leaf nodes, which are more exposed than the internal ones. Indeed, internal nodes are clearly involved in shuffling operations more often than leaf nodes. Also, while in the analysis we assume the servers not to collude, we note that a possible collusion can cause a slight decrease of protection but does not cause critical breaches because the distributed shuffle index would remain protected as in the case of a shuffle index employing $2num\_cover + 1$ covers and a double cache size. We start by noting that access confidentiality naturally increases with the use of two servers. In fact, even if no cover was to be applied, the server could have just a 50% confidence that its observations refer to blocks in the path to a target as they could just refer to their shadows. Shadows provide then a natural increase to the protection when covers are applied. The fact that shuffling operates across servers also provides a natural protection since, again, every node has 50% probability of remaining on the same server after a shuffling is applied. (Note that encryption with a different salt at every re-allocation prevents servers from making any inference on the shuffling performed.)

To study the protection offered by shuffling, we model the knowledge of a server on the fact that a node n is stored at a given block id as a probability value $\mathcal{P}(n, id)$, expressing the confidence in such a knowledge, with $\mathcal{P}(n, id) = 1$ corresponding to certainty and $\mathcal{P}(n, id) = \frac{1}{|\mathcal{N}'|}$, with $\mathcal{N}'$ the set of leaf nodes in $\mathcal{N}$, corresponding to complete absence of knowledge. We assume the worst starting case where a server knows the exact correspondence between nodes and blocks (i.e., $\mathcal{P}(n, id) = 1$ when n is allocated at block id, $\mathcal{P}(n, id) = 0$ otherwise) and evaluate the knowledge degradation of the server due to the shuffling performed at every access.

Let $ID'_G \subseteq \mathcal{ID}_G$ and $ID'_Y \subseteq \mathcal{ID}_Y$ be the sets of identifiers of the m leaf blocks accessed at servers $\mathcal{S}_G$ and $\mathcal{S}_Y$, respectively. Consider also a leaf node $n \in \mathcal{N}$ and suppose that server $\mathcal{S}_G$ knows that n is stored at one of the m accessed blocks (the same discussion applies to server $\mathcal{S}_Y$). After the access, two cases can occur: *i)* n is still stored at server $\mathcal{S}_G$, or *ii)* n has been moved to server $\mathcal{S}_Y$. In the first case, for all $id_G \in ID'_G$, we have that $\mathcal{P}(n, id_G) = \sum_{id_G \in ID'_G} \frac{\mathcal{P}(n, id_G)}{2m}$ since there is a 50% chance for node n to remain at server $\mathcal{S}_G$ and there are m possible blocks where the node can be stored. In the second case, node n can be moved to any of the m blocks accessed at server $\mathcal{S}_Y$. However, server $\mathcal{S}_G$

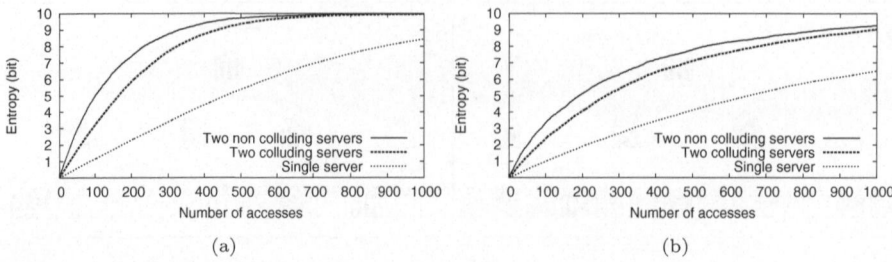

Fig. 6. Evolution of the entropy for values of γ equal to 0.5 (a) and 0.25 (b). Every access request directed to a server has $num\_cover=3$ and $num\_cache=1$

does not know which are the m leaf blocks accessed at server $\mathcal{S}_Y$. Then, for all $id_Y \in \mathcal{ID}_Y$ we have that $P(n, id_Y) = \dfrac{1 - \sum_{id_G \in \mathcal{ID}_G} P(n, id_G)}{|\mathcal{ID}_Y|}$.

We performed a set of experiments for studying the degradation of the knowledge of a server at the aggregate level. These experiments evaluate the entropy of the server knowledge under different configurations (i.e., varying the number of covers and the size of the cache) with different access profiles, where access profiles have been simulated by randomly generating sequences of accesses following a self-similar[1] probability distribution with skewness γ in the range [0.25, 0.5]. We then evaluated the increase of entropy at the increase of the number of accesses for three scenarios where: *1)* the shuffle index is distributed over two servers; *2)* the shuffle index is distributed over two servers but the two servers collude; *3)* the shuffle index is stored at a single server. Note that the second scenario has a double role, representing two different cases: *2.1)* when the two servers collude (exchanging all the knowledge they have on the initial allocation as well as the knowledge on every subsequent observation); *2.2)* when a single server is applied but with the use of $2num\_cover + 1$ covers and with a cache of size $2num\_cache$. Figure 6 illustrates the experimental results using 3 covers and a cache with size 1 for every access request directed to a server, considering a logical shuffle index with 1000 leaves, skewness γ equal to 0.5 and 0.25, and varying the number of accesses. (Experiments with different configurations presented a similar behavior.) As it is visible in the figures, in the scenario where the shuffle index is distributed over two servers (scenario 1, solid line), the entropy increases much faster than in the scenario of a single server subject to a similar workload (scenario 3, dotted line). The dashed line, reporting the entropy evolution in case of collusion (scenario 2), with respect to the other two lines tells us that: *i)* collusion among servers implies a slower knowledge degradation (as the servers combine their knowledge), but does not cause confidentiality breaches (since entropy remains high); *ii)* the use of two servers, even when such servers collude, enjoys a faster entropy increase and hence, protection guarantees, over the case when a single server is used but with the application of $2num\_cover + 1$ covers and with a double size of the cache.

---

[1] Given a domain of cardinality d, a self-similar distribution with skewness γ provides a probability equal to $1-\gamma$ of choosing one of the first γd domain values.

System Performance. The performance of the distributed shuffle index is based on the response time experienced by the client when submitting an access request. Among the different factors contributing to the response time, in our experimental evaluation, we observed that the latency of the network is the factor with the greatest impact in a large-bandwidth WAN scenario (which is the most interesting and natural environment for data outsourcing applications [5,6]).

To assess the system performance, we considered a data set of 2 GiB stored in the leaves of a shuffle index with 3 levels with nodes of 8 KiB. To properly configure the network environment, we adopted a professional-grade tool suite (i.e., Traffic Control and Network Emulation, for Linux systems) and we chose a representative WAN configuration suitable for interactive traffic, with LAN-like bandwidth and round-trip time modeled as a normal distribution with mean of 100 ms and standard deviation of 2.5 ms. Then, we compared the average response time in two different scenarios: *i)* our distributed shuffle index where each request accesses m leaf blocks at each of the two servers; and *ii)* the original (non-distributed) shuffle index where each request accesses $2m$ leaf blocks. The experiments considered a variety of configurations, with different values for m. The average response time in the distributed scenario is approximately 5% lower than the one obtained in the original scenario. As an example, fixing $m = 3$, the average response time is 380 ms in the distributed scenario and 405 ms in the original one. Our experiments also show that, in both the original and distributed scenario, the costs of adopting one additional cover search (cache element, respectively) is 1.18% (0.6%, respectively) of the average response time.

7   Related Work

Previous related works proposed different indexing techniques for the evaluation of queries over encrypted data (e.g., [4,13,14,18–20]). These solutions however aim at protecting data confidentiality only. Traditional approaches for protecting access and pattern confidentiality are based on PIR protocols (e.g., [2,10]), which however suffer from high computation and communication costs and do not provide content confidentiality. More efficient PIR solutions rely on the presence of different copies of the data stored at different servers (e.g., [1]), and are based on the assumption that servers do not communicate with each-other.

The first approach that protects data, access, and pattern confidentiality has been illustrated in [22] and combines the pyramid-shaped hierarchy layout of the Oblivious RAM (ORAM) data structure [11] with Bloom filters. Even if this proposal adopts an enhanced reordering technique between adjacent levels of the ORAM to provide a limited amortized cost of accesses, the response time of queries submitted during the reordering of the bottom level of the structure remains linear in the database size. Different approaches try to mitigate the cost of these accesses, for instance by limiting shuffling to fetched records (e.g., [9]); guaranteeing a constant number of interactions between the data owner and the server, independently from the number of levels in the ORAM (e.g., [21]); introducing the support for concurrent accesses by multiple clients (e.g., [12]).

ORAM has been recently extended to the distributed scenario [16], but its privacy guarantees rely on the presence of non-communicating servers.

The line of works most related to our is represented by solutions that provide data, access, and pattern confidentiality by exploiting dynamic data allocation, which destroys the otherwise static relationship between disk blocks and the information they store (e.g., [5, 6, 15, 23]). The first approach adopting dynamic data allocation has been introduced in [15] and is based on a B-tree index structure. This proposal however does not guarantee pattern confidentiality. Similarly to the shuffle index [5], the proposal in [23] adopts cover searches, repeated searches, and shuffling protection techniques to provide access and pattern confidentiality. This solution is less flexible than the shuffle index, as it does not have an underlying index structure and the number of cover searches is fixed. Our solution provides higher protection guarantees than the proposals above, since we operate in a distributed scenario. Also, with respect to distributed PIR and distributed ORAM approaches, we remove the limiting assumption that the storing servers cannot communicate.

8 Conclusions

We extended the shuffle index to the consideration of multiple servers. Our approach is based on distributing the index structure over two servers, and on the use of shadows for providing to each server a view as if it was the only server storing the data. The distributed index enjoys an increased protection with respect to the use of a single server while not impacting performance.

Acknowledgements. This work was supported in part by the EC within the 7FP under grant agreement 257129 (PoSecCo), by the Italian Ministry of Research within PRIN project "GenData 2020" (2010RTFWBH), and by Google, under the Google Research Award program.

References

1. Cachin, C., Micali, S., Stadler, M.: Computationally private information retrieval with polylogarithmic communication. In: Stern, J. (ed.) EUROCRYPT 1999. LNCS, vol. 1592, pp. 402–414. Springer, Heidelberg (1999)
2. Chor, B., Kushilevitz, E., Goldreich, O., Sudan, M.: Private information retrieval. Journal of the ACM 45(6), 965–981 (1998)
3. Ciriani, V., De Capitani di Vimercati, S., Foresti, S., Jajodia, S., Paraboschi, S., Samarati, P.: Combining fragmentation and encryption to protect privacy in data storage. ACM TISSEC 13(3), 22:1–22:33 (2010)
4. Damiani, E., De Capitani Vimercati, S., Jajodia, S., Paraboschi, S., Samarati, P.: Balancing confidentiality and efficiency in untrusted relational DBMSs. In: Proc. of CCS 2003, Washington, DC (October 2003)
5. De Capitani di Vimercati, S., Foresti, S., Paraboschi, S., Pelosi, G., Samarati, P.: Efficient and private access to outsourced data. In: Proc. of ICDCS 2011, Minneapolis, MN (June 2011)

6. De Capitani di Vimercati, S., Foresti, S., Paraboschi, S., Pelosi, G., Samarati, P.: Supporting concurrency in private data outsourcing. In: Atluri, V., Diaz, C. (eds.) ESORICS 2011. LNCS, vol. 6879, pp. 648–664. Springer, Heidelberg (2011)

7. De Capitani di Vimercati, S., Foresti, S., Samarati, P.: Managing and accessing data in the cloud: Privacy risks and approaches. In: Proc. of CRiSIS 2012, Cork, Ireland (October 2012)

8. De Capitani di Vimercati, S., Foresti, S., Samarati, P.: Selective and fine-grained access to data in the cloud. In: Jajodia, S., Kant, K., Samarati, P., Swarup, V., Wang, C. (eds.) Secure Cloud Computing. Springer (2013)

9. Ding, X., Yang, Y., Deng, R.: Database access pattern protection without full-shuffles. IEEE TIFS 6(1), 189–201 (2011)

10. Gasarch, W.: A survey on private information retrieval. Bulletin of the EATCS 82, 72–107 (2004)

11. Goldreich, O., Ostrovsky, R.: Software protection and simulation on Oblivious RAMs. Journal of the ACM 43(3), 431–473 (1996)

12. Goodrich, M., Mitzenmacher, M., Ohrimenko, O., Tamassia, R.: Privacy-preserving group data access via stateless Oblivious RAM simulation. In: Proc. of SODA 2012, Kyoto, Japan (January 2012)

13. Hacigümüs, H., Iyer, B., Mehrotra, S., Li, C.: Executing SQL over encrypted data in the database-service-provider model. In: Proc. of SIGMOD 2002, Madison, WI (June 2002)

14. Hore, B., Mehrotra, S., Canim, M., Kantarcioglu, M.: Secure multidimensional range queries over outsourced data. The VLDB Journal 21, 333–358 (2012)

15. Lin, P., Candan, K.S.: Hiding traversal of tree structured data from untrusted data stores. In: Proc. of WOSIS 2004, Porto, Portugal (April 2004)

16. Lu, S., Ostrovsky, R.: Distributed Oblivious RAM for secure two-party computation. In: Sahai, A. (ed.) TCC 2013. LNCS, vol. 7785, pp. 377–396. Springer, Heidelberg (2013)

17. Murugesan, M., Jiang, W., Clifton, C., Si, L., Vaidya, J.: Efficient privacy-preserving similar document detection. VLDBJ 19(4), 457–475 (2010)

18. Samarati, P., De Capitani di Vimercati, S.: Data protection in outsourcing scenarios: Issues and directions. In: Proc. of ASIACCS 2010, Beijing, China (April 2010)

19. Wang, C., Cao, N., Ren, K., Lou, W.: Enabling secure and efficient ranked keyword search over outsourced cloud data. IEEE TPDS 23(8), 1467–1479 (2012)

20. Wang, H., Lakshmanan, L.V.: Efficient secure query evaluation over encrypted XML databases. In: Proc. of VLDB 2006, Seoul, Korea (September 2006)

21. Williams, P., Sion, R.: Single round access privacy on outsourced storage. In: Proc. of CCS 2012, Raleigh, NC (October 2012)

22. Williams, P., Sion, R., Carbunar, B.: Building castles out of mud: Practical access pattern privacy and correctness on untrusted storage. In: Proc. of CCS 2008, Alexandria, VA (October 2008)

23. Yang, K., Zhang, J., Zhang, W., Qiao, D.: A light-weight solution to preservation of access pattern privacy in un-trusted clouds. In: Atluri, V., Diaz, C. (eds.) ESORICS 2011. LNCS, vol. 6879, pp. 528–547. Springer, Heidelberg (2011)

Range Extension Attacks on Contactless Smart Cards

Yossef Oren, Dvir Schirman, and Avishai Wool

Cryptography and Network Security Lab, School of Electrical Engineering
Tel-Aviv University, Ramat Aviv 69978, Israel
{yos@eng,dvirschi@post}.tau.ac.il, yash@acm.org

Abstract. The security of many near-field RFID systems such as credit cards, access control, e-passports, and e-voting, relies on the assumption that the tag holder is in close proximity to the reader. This assumption should be reasonable due to the fact that the nominal operation range of the RFID tag is only few centimeters. In this work we demonstrate a range extension setup which breaks this proximity assumption. Our system allows full communications with a near-field RFID reader from a range of 115cm – two orders of magnitude greater than nominal range – and uses power that can be supplied by a car battery. The added flexibility offered to an attacker by this range extension significantly improves the effectiveness and practicality of relay attacks on real-world systems.

Keywords: RFID, Contactless smart card, ISO/IEC 14443, Relay attack.

1 Introduction

1.1 Background

Over the last few years, radio frequency identification (RFID) and near field communication (NFC) technologies have become increasingly popular. They are used in applications which benefit from the ease of use, the increased data rate, and computational abilities offered by RFID technologies compared to traditional technologies like magnetic stripe or bar-code. There are in general two categories of passively-powered RFID tags: (a) **UHF tags** compliant with ISO/IEC 18000 which operate at a range of few meters and are mainly used for marking products or components, and (b) **HF tags** compliant with ISO/IEC 14443 which operate at a range of few centimeters and are used in a variety of security-sensitive applications such as payment cards, access control, e-passports, national ID-cards, and e-voting. In both categories tags are generally low cost devices which communicate with a more powerful **reader** over a wireless medium. This work focuses on physical layer security issues of ISO/IEC 14443 HF tags, which are also commonly referred to as **contactless smart cards**.

All of the applications mentioned above require security controls, whether to defend the user's privacy, to prevent unauthorized access, or to keep the user's

J. Crampton, S. Jajodia, and K. Mayes (Eds.): ESORICS 2013, LNCS 8134, pp. 646–663, 2013.
© Springer-Verlag Berlin Heidelberg 2013

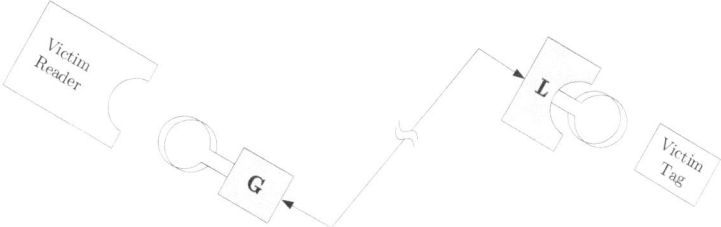

Fig. 1. An RFID channel under a relay attack. Device L is the leech, while device G is the ghost.

money safe. Most RFID applications deal with security issues through secure protocols and cryptography, but they also rely on the **assumption of proximity** between the tag and the reader as a security feature. In older technologies, like magnetic stripe credit cards or contact-based smart cards, the assumption of proximity was guaranteed due to the contact-based interface between the card and the reader. Near field RFID standards like ISO/IEC 14443 are also perceived to guarantee proximity since the nominal operation range for communication between a tag and a reader is only few centimeters. Therefore, most contactless smart card secure protocols inherently assume that the tag holder stands right in front of the reader.

1.2 Related Work

In [3] Desmedt et al. presented a generic way to defeat protocols with a assumption of proximity called the **mafia fraud attack**, or the **relay attack**. Previous works have already noted the relevance of relay attacks to the contactless smart card scenario [15] and have demonstrated that relays can be practically built and used to attack such systems [7,6,30,14,28]. As illustrated in Figure 1, a relay is established by placing two special communication devices (called the "ghost" and the "leech") between the victim reader and the victim tag. The ghost and the leech communicate via a long-range channel such as a wireless connection. The leech transmits any packets sent by the victim reader to the victim tag, receives the victim tag's responses, and sends them back to the ghost, which finally forwards them to the victim reader. Since the ghost and the leech are built and controlled by the attacker, they do not have to comply to any standard. This allows the communication ranges between leech and tag and between ghost and reader to be increased, beyond the nominal standards, improving the effectiveness of the relay attack. The work of [16] showed how to build a low-cost, extended-range RFID leech device. In [8] extended range eavesdropping and skimming attacks are described.

Despite the fact that relay attacks have been a known threat for several years, and that building a relay system is well within the budget of even a moderately-funded attacker, there is a surprising lack of reports on relay attacks occurring on real-world contactless smart card systems [2]. One possible explanation is the high risk incurred by the attacker: while the victim tag can be accessed with relatively low risk (for example, by following the victim and placing a skimmer near his back pocket), the victim reader is generally located in a high-security location such as a store counter or a border crossing, and is protected by additional security measures such as security cameras or guards.

1.3   Contributions

In this work we present a design for a modified ghost device which dramatically increases the range of the ghost-reader communication channel. The main novelty of our design is the use of two different antennas and RF front ends: One for the reader-to-ghost receive path, and one for the ghost-to-reader transmit path. Since our modifications are completely in the analog domain, they are not expected to increase the processing delay of the relay or otherwise interfere with the RFID protocol.

We experimentally verify the effectiveness of our modified ghost device in a series of experiments. In our experiments we show an effective reader-to-ghost range of 140cm, an effective ghost-to-reader range of 115cm, and therefore, a full bi-directional range of 115cm. These ranges are two orders of magnitude greater than the nominal tag-to-reader range. Most significantly, our device can be built with a moderate-to-low budget and uses power that can be supplied by a car battery.

We also study the implications of the improved ghost device on the security of several contactless RFID scenarios. Specifically, the extended range can increase the severity of relay attacks by allowing the attacker to move away from the victim reader, possibly even to the next room or to a nearby car. Beyond posing a significant threat to the security of contactless smart card applications, we also show how the range extension setup can also be used for legitimate purposes – e.g., to allow handicapped persons to use their RFID tag from a distance.

Document Structure

This paper is organized as follows. The next section gives a brief background of contactless smart card standards and describes relay attacks. Section 3 presents the design of our range extension system. Section 4 presents the experimental results. Section 5 discusses possible attack scenarios and legitimate uses for our setup. Finally, section 5.3 summarizes the implications of our work.

2   The ISO/IEC 14443 Standard

Most close range RFID applications are based on the ISO/IEC 14443 standard. This standard specifies the operation method and parameters for proximity-coupling smart cards. The nominal operation range for this standard is 5-10 cm. The standard calls the RFID reader a Proximity Coupling Device (PCD), so we will use the terms reader and PCD interchangeably. The tag is called a

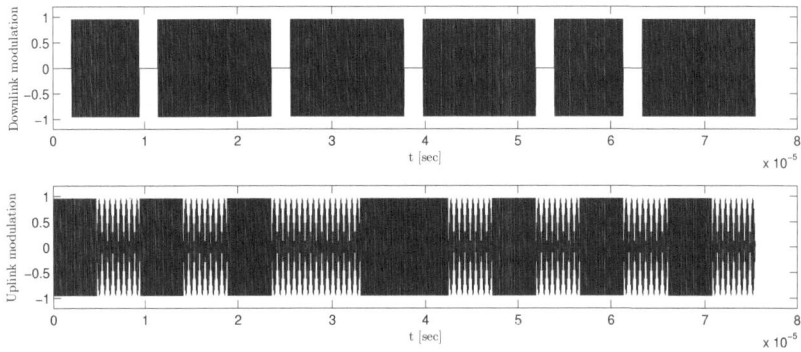

Fig. 2. Example communication signals for ISO/IEC14443-2 type A. Top: Downlink modulation, Bottom: Uplink modulation

Proximity Integrated Circuit Card (PICC), so we will use the terms tag and PICC interchangeably.

The standard consists of 4 parts: part 1 covers the physical characteristics of the PICC [10]; part 2 specifies the characteristics of the fields to be provided for power and bi-directional communication between the PCD and the PICC [12]; part 3 defines the routines for the initialization of the PICC as well as an anti-collision routine for multiple PICCs [13]; part 4 specifies a half-duplex block transmission protocol featuring the special needs of a contactless environment and defines the activation and deactivation sequence of the protocol [11]. Note that the higher parts of the standard are intended to be used in conjunction with the lower parts.

The standard defines two types of tags, type A and type B. The two types differ in modulation techniques, initialization protocols, and transmission protocols. Our work focuses on type A, hence the following sections will describe only type A properties.

The parts of the standard that are relevant to the design of our range extension setup, are parts 2,3, and 4, we highlight their relevant features here.

2.1   ISO/IEC 14443 Part 2: Radio Frequency Power and Signal Interface

This part defines the physical layer interface between the PCD and the PICC. the PICC (tag) is passive – it has no source of power, and draws all its energy from the reader's transmission signal. The communication is based on inductive coupling between an active reader and a passive tag. We will refer to the channel from the reader to the tag as the **downlink** channel, and the channel from the tag to the reader as the **uplink** channel.

According to the standard the carrier frequency of the reader is $f_c = 13.56 \, MHz$. The operating magnetic field produced by the reader should lie within the range of 1.5 A/m rms to 7.5 A/m rms. And, the bit rate during initialization part is defined as $f_c/128 \approx 106\ kbits/S$.

Downlink Modulation: The communication from the reader to the tag uses Amplitude Shift Keying (ASK) with modulation depth of 100%. The transmitted bits are coded with modified Miller coding as shown in Figure 2 (top). In order to guarantee a continuous power supply to the passive tag, the length of the blanking intervals is only 2-3 μs.

Uplink Modulation: Since the tag has no independent power source, it transmits its signal by means of load modulation of a sub-carrier at $f_{sc} = f_c/16 \approx 847\ kHz$. This modulation is physically carried out by switching a load inside the PICC on and off.

The transmitted bits are Manchester coded and modulated by on/off keying of the sub-carrier (i.e., the sub-carrier is ASK 100% modulated by the Manchester coded bits) – see Figure 2 (bottom).

2.2   ISO/IEC 14443 Timing Parameters

The ISO/IEC 14443 standard defines two critical timing parameters called the Frame Delay Time (FDT), which defines the maximal time delay during the initialization protocol [13], and Frame waiting time (FWT) which defines the maximal time delay during the transmission protocol [11]. Both of these parameters define the time delay allowed from the end of a PCD's frame transmission to the start of the PICC's response reception. These parameters are set to about 90μs during initialization of the protocol (FDT), and to about 300μs-5s (FWT).

After the initialization protocol is completed, if a PICC requires a longer calculation time, it can ask for additional time through sending a WTX request [11], which can extend the FWT up to its maximal value of about 5 seconds. The WTX request can be sent multiple times in order to achieve longer calculation times.

One of the practical limitations that relay attacks face is the issue of timing. Without careful attention, the relay can introduce delays into the communication channel, which may break the protocols: As mentioned above, the initialization protocol has strict delay constraints, while during the transmission protocol longer delays can be established, but not without actively interfering in the activation protocol.

3   Ghost System Design

Our goal in this work is to demonstrate an extended-range ghost device – i.e., a device that can pretend to be a tag to a legitimate reader. Unlike a real tag our ghost device is an active device that has a power source.

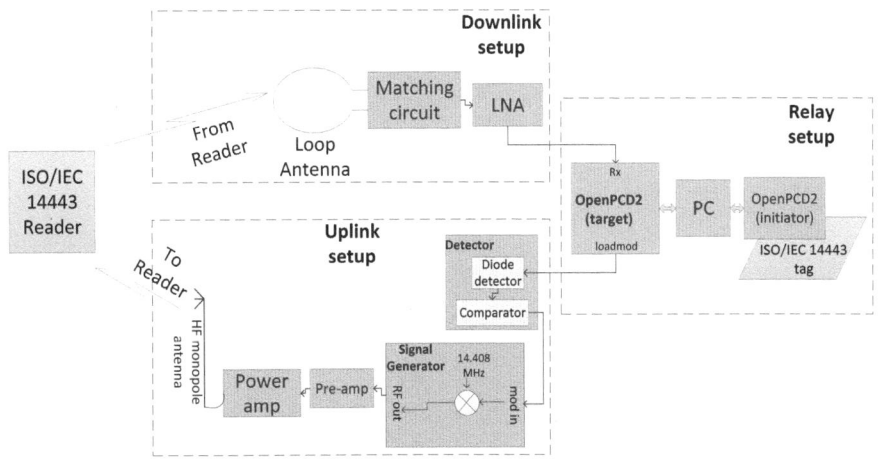

Fig. 3. Block diagram of full range extension system

We made the following design decisions when creating our ghost device: (1) We use two separate antennas, one for the downlink, and one for the uplink. The downlink reception antenna is a large loop antenna which allows greater sensitivity and therefore, can receive the signal from a greater range. For the uplink transmission we use the close range magnetic field emitted from an HF monopole antenna. (2) We use active load modulation for the uplink, to overcome the nominal range limitations of the magnetic coupling. (3) We perform a relay of protocol level 4, while implementing protocol level 3 independently in front of the reader and the tag, to overcome the strict timing requirements of the initialization protocol at level 3.

The system can be divided into three independent building blocks: downlink, uplink, and relay. In the following sections these three building blocks are described. The system is designed to be mounted on a car, and to get its power from a standard car battery. A block diagram of our design can be seen in Figure 3.

We tested our ghost using a relay infrastructure. We used standard unmodified hardware for the leech device, while making all the required changes for range extension only on the ghost device.

3.1 Downlink Channel Design

The relay setup is based on two OpenPCD2 [17] boards. OpenPCD2 is a RFID/NFC open source development board based on NXP's PN532 chip [22]. Thus, the control logic for the Ghost device is based on one of the openPCD2 devices (see figure fig:Diagram).

Our extended range downlink is based on connecting a large loop antenna to the antenna ports of the PN532 (on the OpenPCD2 board). We used a 39 cm copper tube loop antenna built for a previous leech project in our lab [16].

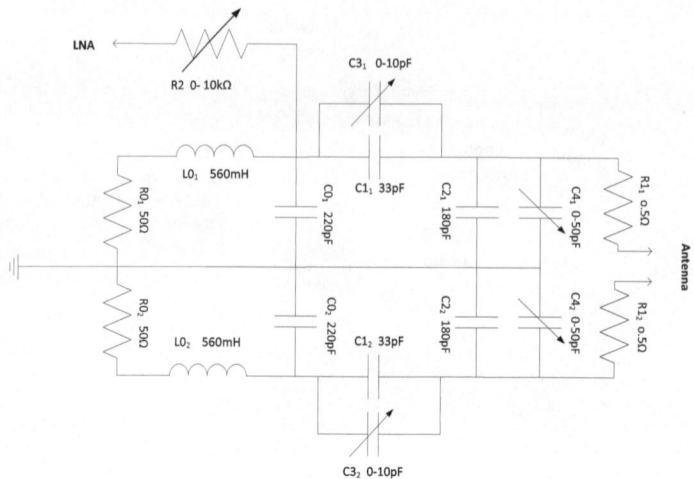

Fig. 4. Downlink antenna matching circuit. The fixed components values are roughly tuned for our antenna, the variable components are used for fine tuning.

The antenna is connected via a matching circuit through a low noise amplifier (ZFL-500LN [18]) to the Rx port of the PN532.

Matching the Antenna: In order to transfer maximum power from the antenna to the PN532's input an impedance matching circuit is needed. The circuit was designed according to NXP's application note [21]: First measuring the antenna impedance, then calculating appropriate values for the tuning capacitors and resistors. The Q resistor (R1) value was chosen to achieve a quality factor of 25 as recommended by NXP. Since we use the antenna only for reception, the Tx1 and Tx2 ports of the PN532 chip were not connected to the matching circuit, and instead 50Ω resistors ($R0_{1,2}$) were added. The matching circuit scheme can be seen in Figure 4.

The matching circuit was first tuned by transmitting a 13.56 MHz carrier wave signal from a signal generator through another loop antenna, and measuring the amplitude at the Rx output with a scope, while the circuit is connected to the OpenPCD2 board. The variable capacitors were tuned for the maximum amplitude value. Finally, the matching was verified using a network analyzer by measuring the S_{11} value of the matching circuit and the antenna (i.e., the input return loss of the antenna).

3.2   Uplink Channel Design

A key idea behind the uplink is to replace the load modulation technique with an **active** modulation technique and transmit the signal through a power amplifier and a mobile monopole HF antenna.

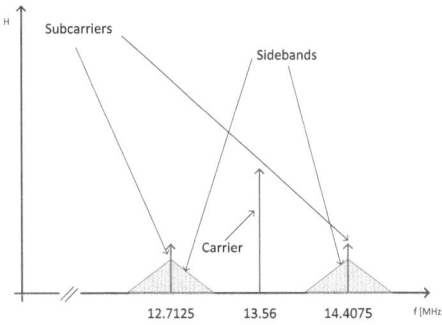

Fig. 5. Spectral image of ISO/IEC 14443 communication

Active Load Modulation. is a technique introduced by Finkenzeller et al. in [4,5]. This technique uses active circuitry which produces the same spectral image as ISO/IEC 14443 type A load modulation, causing the reader to observe the transmitted signal as if it was a standard load modulated signal. Active load modulation operates in the following way:

As described in Section 2.1 the uplink transmission channel of ISO/IEC 14443-2 is based on an ASK modulation of a sub-carrier. When looking at the spectral image of this modulation the result is two sidebands centered at $f_{1,2} = f_c \pm f_{sc}$, and each band functions as carrier for the Manchester coded bits (see Figure 5). According to [5] a typical ISO/IEC 14443 compliant reader evaluates only the upper side band, hence the relevant part of the spectral image is the upper sideband centered at $f_{USB} = f_c + f_{sc} = 13.56 + \frac{13.56}{16} = 14.4075\ MHz$. Therefore, In order to emulate the load modulation signal we can directly modulate the Manchester coded bit stream using an ASK 100% modulation of a 14.4075 MHz carrier signal.

Doing so, with an active powered transmitter, allows us to bypass the need for near-field magnetic coupling, and achieve transmission ranges that are 2 orders of magnitude greater than the nominal range.

The Transmitting Antenna: Nominal RFID communication is based on magnetic coupling between two loop antennas. As explained in [5] an effort to increase the range of an active transmitting signal requires either to dramatically increase the current injected to the antenna, or to increase the area of the loop (which also introduces more noise). An alternative approach is to use the field generated by an HF monopole antenna. Monopole antennas are designed for electric field (plane wave) transmission rather than magnetic coupling. However, the antenna still produces a magnetic field in the near field region. Moreover, there may be a coupling between the electric field produced by the monopole antenna to the reader's circuit, which also contributes to the range extension.

There are several advantages of using a monopole antenna for this setup. First, since it usually looks like a simple pole it is easier to hide, which helps in disguising an attack setup. Second, there is a variety of commercial antennas in the ham radio market which are designed for the desired frequency range. And third, we hypothesize that the uplink range will be longer, and the power consumption will be reduced in comparison to our 39cm loop antenna.

In order to choose the appropriate antenna we conducted a preliminary jamming experiment (see section 4.2). We got the best jamming range with a military broadband helically wound antenna, NVIS-HF1-BC. The considerations for choosing the uplink antenna are further described in [23].

Implementation: In order to produce an active load modulation signal from the PN532 chip we made use of a little-used output pin named LOAD_MOD. This pin is meant to be connected to an external load, and therefore carries the modulated sub-carrier signal. The OpenPCD2 board does not make use of the LOAD_MOD pin, and the regular libnfc code does not instruct the PN532 to activate the pin. Thus, we needed to solder a connector directly into the pin and modify the libnfc code to activate it.

For our setup we needed to work with the digital Manchester coded bit stream rather than the modulated sub-carrier signal. Therefore, we built a simple detector circuit consisting of a diode detector and a comparator which extracts the bit stream from the modulated sub-carrier signal. We used the extracted bit stream to modulate a 14.4075 MHz carrier. Note that for our experiments we produced the modulated signal by entering the bit stream into a signal generator (Agilent N9310A). The signal generator can be easily replaced by a simple circuit containing an oscillator and a mixer.

Since our signal generator's output power reaches only up to 15 dBm, we needed to amplify the signal. We used a Mini-Circuits ZHL-32A [19] amplifier which serves as a pre-amplifier, and a RM-Italy KL400 [26] (a ham radio amplifier) which serves as a power amplifier. The amplifier output is connected to our uplink antenna described above.

The KL400 amplifier is a mobile amplifier intended to be used in a car mounted setup. It requires a $12V_{DC}$ power supply, and when working at full power it uses up to 24A, which can be supplied from a standard car battery.

3.3 Relay Setup

Since our focus was the construction of the ghost system and not the relay itself, we implemented the relay part of the attack inside a single PC. For the leech device we used an unmodified OpenPCD2 board. The ghost antennas are connected to a second OpenPCD2 board. The OpenPCD2 boards run a libnfc compatible firmware and are both connected to a PC running Linux Fedora 17 with libnfc [1].

We make use of one of the programs in libnfc, called nfc-relay-picc, which is a relay application built for boards using the PN532 chip. nfc-relay-picc was designed to overcome the timing issues discussed in Section 2.2, which limit the effectiveness of relay attacks. The program operates in the following way:

- One device is selected as initiator (a leech in our terminology), and the other device is selected as target (a ghost in our terminology).
- The leech is placed in front of a victim tag, emulating a reader. It performs the initialization and activation protocols defined in the standard, towards the tag (further description of these protocols can be found in [13,11]).
- The tag credentials are acquired by the leech and relayed to the ghost device.
- The ghost emulates a tag with the data acquired from the original tag and waits for a reader to activate it.
- When the ghost is activated by the victim reader, it performs the initialization and activation protocols directly with the reader, using the victim tag's credentials acquired earlier, thus overcoming the very strict delay constraints of the anticollision level 3 protocol.
- While a transmission protocol is established between the ghost and the reader, a parallel transmission is established between the leech and the tag.
- After both transmission protocols are established, each APDU (level 4) frame from the reader is relayed through the ghost→PC→leech relay to the tag, and vice versa.
- In order to overcome timing issues during the transmission itself, the ghost sends WTX requests each time the FWT period is about to expire.

Note that in itself the nfc-relay-picc program and the OpenPCD2 boards are designed to operate within the nominal range of 5-10cm.

To use this program with our uplink setup we had to slightly change the libnfc source, in order to enable an output of the modulated sub-carrier signal out of the LOAD_MOD pin of the PN532 chip.

4   Experiments and Results

In this section we describe the experiments done to test our setup, including preliminary experiments to validate our assumptions, and measurements of the final setup. All of the experiments described below were done with a TI MF S4100 Reader [9] acting as the victim reader, and a ISO/IEC 14443 type A sample tag which was provided inside the OpenPCD2 package as the victim tag. The MF reader was selected since it generates read requests at a high rate (more than 10 times per second). In addition, the TI reader's controller software emits a loud beep when it receives an answer from the tag.

4.1   Reader-to-Ghost (Downlink) Range Estimation

Our first experiment was to measure the reception range of our downlink copper tube loop antenna in isolation. For this purpose we connected the antenna and the matching circuit to a simple detector circuit consisting of a diode detector and a comparator, connected the detector's output of a scope, and measured the received pulses. In order to estimate the reception performance we used the following metric:

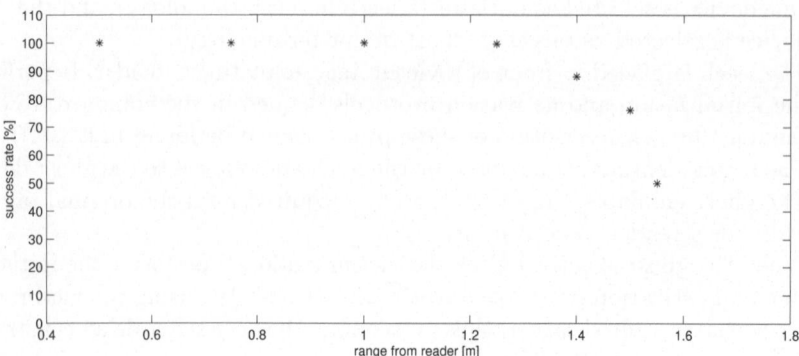

Fig. 6. Downlink performance as a function of the distance from the reader

- A reference measurement was taken at a close range, measuring the reception of few repeated REQA frames.
- For each measurement the number of positive pulses was counted.
- For each measurement, we define an error rate metric as the normalized difference between the number of pulses in this measurement and in the reference measurement.

Figure 6 present the results of the experiment. We observed good downlink reception up to a range of 140cm, followed by a dramatic drop in quality within less than 20 cm. A similar experiment was done using a spectrum analyzer with an analog output as the detector, and we observed a reception range of about 350cm. However, we believe that our detector's 140cm range predicts the expected results more accurately, since the ghost's PN532 chip needs to receive the messages error-free in order to decode them.

Based on [25] we believe that a greater downlink range may well be possible. However, we must note that the ghost range is bounded by both the uplink and the downlink ranges.

4.2 Ghost-to-Reader (Uplink) Range Estimation

An isolated estimation of the uplink performance was a more challenging task, since transmission from the tag to the reader occurs only after a successful reception of a reader's frame by the tag (i.e., a working downlink channel is required). Hence, in order to test the performance of the RF part of the uplink channel (signal generator, amplifier, and antenna) we conducted a jamming experiment. The basic principle of the jamming setup is to use the same setup as the uplink channel, only without modulation, in order to transmit a continuous wave signal at the upper side band frequency (14.4075 MHz, recall Figure 5). By transmitting a powerful signal towards the reader at the same frequency as the tag's transmission, we block the tag's response and jam the communication between the reader and the tag.

Table 1. Jamming experiment results

Antenna	Full jamming range [cm]	Partial jamming range [cm]
39 cm loop	95	125
Hustler	110	165
Helically wound	200	230

We assume that since in the jamming case the signal should only interfere with a legitimate signal, and not transmit any information, jamming should be an easier task than uplink transmission. Therefore, by measuring the jamming range we obtain an upper bound on the achievable uplink range.

Another objective of the jamming experiment was to determine which antenna is the best for the uplink channel.We tested the following three antennas:

a.   39cm copper tube loop antenna (the one used for the downlink setup)
b.   New-Tronics Hustler: MO-4 (mast) + RM-20-S (resonator), which is designed for the 14–14.35MHz ham radio band [20] (See [29, §6-29])
c.   Broadband vertical helically wound antenna: NVIS-HF1-BC (See [29, §6-37])

Note that in the jamming experiment the KL400 power amplifier was not used, and the signal was amplified only with the Mini-Circuits pre-amplifier. Furthermore, since no information was transmitted, we did not need to worry about distortion, and the amplifier was operated with 15dBm input power, above its 1dB compression point. The results of the jamming experiments are summarized in Table 1. Jamming was identified using an ISO14443A compliant tag placed next to the reader. Using TI's demo software the computer beeps every time a tag is recognized. We distinguish between two jamming types: full jamming is defined when no beep is heard from the reader for more than 10 seconds, while partial jamming is defined when 1-2 beeps per second are heard, but still significantly fewer beeps than with no jamming signal at all (5-10 beeps per second).

We notice that the helically wound antenna gives the best jamming range, and therefore, it was chosen for use in the uplink channel. The jamming experiment is described in further details in [23].

4.3   Full Range Extension Experiment

After estimating the achievable ranges of the different building blocks in isolation, we constructed a full range extension device (ghost). All the range extension experiments were done with the helically wound antenna chosen during the jamming experiments as the uplink antenna, and the 39cm copper tube loop antenna as the downlink antenna.

A successful downlink can be observed by watching the PN532 response to a reader's frame, which is manifested in a signal on the LOAD_MOD pin. As a diagnostic tool, a scope was used to monitor the LOAD_MOD output, in order to identify a successful downlink. The measured downlink range is **120cm** – two orders of magnitude greater than the nominal range, and enough in many cases for an attacker to move far enough from the victim reader to avoid capture.

On the other hand, uplink measurements were more complex, since the uplink channel was found to be very sensitive to the surrounding environment and cable orientation. A successful uplink was identified by hearing the TI reader's demo software beep for a successful read of a tag. So, a successful uplink also meant a successful range extended relay. Our first attempts with measuring uplink ranges produced suspiciously high ranges. We discovered that the high range was due to an unwanted coupling effect as noticed by [30]. In our initial setup a coaxial cable was passing between the uplink setup and the reader (not connected to any of them), serving as a waveguide for the uplink signal.

We then decided to move our setup outside of the building in order to work in a clear and robust environment. The first measurements were held with only the Mini-Circuit's 25dB pre-amplifier which has an output-1dB-compression-point of 29dBm (~800mW). In practice, we noticed that at output levels of above 25dBm (~300 mW) the performance of the uplink channel was severely degraded. We believe that this is the result of noise created by operating the amplifier close to its compression point. Therefore, all the measurements were done using a 0dBm power at the output of the signal generator.

At first, the experiment was held with the monopole antenna alone, and we achieved only a 35cm uplink range. We believe that this is due to the fact that monopole antennas need to be placed over a proper ground plane for optimal performance. Since the wave length of our uplink signal is ~20m a true ground plane is impractical. Instead, we assumed a car mounted setup, in which the car itself can serve as a ground plane. To emulate a private car's dimensions we used a $1m^2$ tin plate as a ground plane. With the antenna bolted onto the tin plate and using only the pre-amplifier we managed to get an uplink range of 85cm. We noticed that this setup is very sensitive to the orientation of the antenna cable regarding the tin plate – with different cable orientations the maximal uplink range varied between 45cm to 85cm. We further noticed that the best uplink ranges were achieved when the antenna was facing the side of the victim reader and not its front. A possible explanation is that when the uplink antenna was placed in front of the reader, it was jamming the downlink antenna from receiving the reader's signal, and therefore preventing a full relay.

At last, after establishing a good setup for the uplink antenna, we added the power amplifier into the transmission chain. Since our pre-amplifier can only produce up to 300mW without distorting the signal, yet the RM-Italy KL400 amplifier's input power must be at least 1W, we had to bypass an internal relay inside the amplifier's circuit in order to let the amplifier open for transmission with lower input power. During our experiments we set the KL400 only up to its 2nd power level (out of 6 possible levels) due to radiation hazard concerns (both for the equipment, and for our safety). Later we measured the output power of the modified KL400 amplifier set to its 2nd level and found out the output power of our system was about 7W.

Table 2. Range extension results

Antenna setup	Amplifier	Full bidirectional range [cm]
no ground plane	pre-amplifier ($P_{out} = 300mW$)	35
$1m^2$ ground plane	pre-amplifier ($P_{out} = 300mW$)	85
$1m^2$ ground plane	pre-amplifier + power amplifier ($P_{out} = 7W$)	115

After all modifications, the measured uplink range including the power amplifier was **115cm**, which is almost the same as our measured downlink range, and again enough for an adversary to mount his attack from the next room. The results of the different uplink setups are summarized in Table 2. The final setup including the tin plate and the power amplifier can be seen in Figure 7.

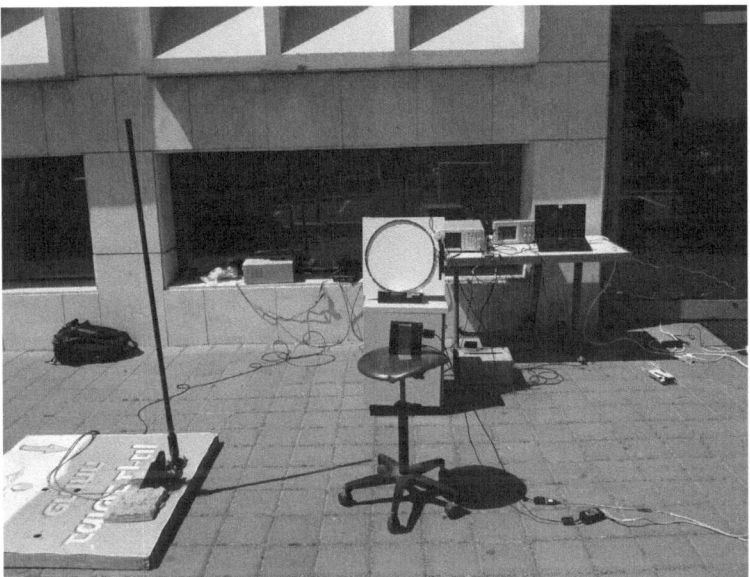

Fig. 7. The full range extension setup outside our building. The victim reader is located on the lab stool in the middle of the picture. The uplink antenna on its ground plane is on the left. The downlink loop antenna is behind the reader. The victim tag is on the table in the back, next to the laptop running the relay software.

5   Discussion and Conclusions

The range extension setup described in this work has significant implications on the security of close range RFID systems. The same setup can also be used for legitimate purposes, in order to enhance RFID capabilities. In this section we briefly introduce two attack scenarios and some legitimate use examples for this setup.

5.1   Attack Scenarios

E-voting. The work of [24] presents a set of physical attacks on Israel's proposed e-voting system which uses ISO/IEC 14443 tags as voting ballots. Using a relay setup an attacker can mount a **ballot sniffing attack** (which allows him to learn at any time which votes were already cast into the ballot box), a **single dissident attack** (which can undetectably suppress the votes for any amount of voters), and finally a **ballot stuffing attack** (which gives the adversary complete control over previously cast votes).

Using a nominal-range relay the attacks mentioned in [24] are limited since the adversary must be in a range of 5-10 cm from the target ballots, which places him inside the ballot station's room, and in front of the election committee members. However, if the relay setup is enhanced with a range extension setup the attacks can be mounted from a distance, possibly even from outside the room, which allows the attacker to mount the attack without being detected.

Access Control. One of the most common application of close range RFID is for access control into restricted areas. Using personal RFID tags only authorized personnel can enter a restricted area.

Using a relay setup an adversary can use a victim worker's identity while he is away from the restricted door, and the tag lies in his pocket, to open the door. However, using a nominal relay setup, this attack scenario is limited, since when the attacker approaches the door holding his ghost device instead of a regular tag he can be easily spotted by the other workers who walk by. Alternatively, if the attacker mounts a range extension setup in a distance from the door (possibly even behind a wall), he can cause the door to open while an accomplice walks towards the door and waves a decoy blank tag in front of the reader. Since the accomplice does not carry any special hardware other than a decoy tag, the risk incurred by the attacker is drastically lowered.

An interesting twist on this attack would be combination of an RFID zapper [27] and an extended-range ghost. An RFID zapper is a low-cost device which can completely disable a victim tag by applying a high-energy electromagnetic pulse to its RF input. If an attacker first zaps a victim's tag, then applies an extended-range ghost attack to the reader just as the victim attempts to use his (now disabled) tag, it will give any human observers the impression that one tag is used, while effectively activating a different tag. This forces an innocent user to be an accomplice to the relay attack described above.

5.2   Legitimate Uses for Range Extension

Besides breaking the close range assumption, and violating the system's security, the range extension setup can be used for legitimate purposes.

For example, a handicapped person sitting in a wheel chair might find it hard to use RFID tags, since most of the readers are placed out of his reach. By mounting a range extension setup onto the wheel chair, the user will now find it possible to enter through doors with RFID access control, or pay for public transportation without asking for help.

As another example, nowadays many parking lots have RFID tags for subscribers. Many drivers find it hard to reach the RFID reader through the car's window. By mounting a range extension setup onto his car, the driver can enter into the parking lot without the effort of reaching the reader at the entrance of the parking lot.

5.3   Conclusions

In this work we presented a range extension setup for contactless smart cards. The setup can be mounted on any car, and powered by a regular car battery. The entire setup costs about \$2,000. The uplink antenna constitutes most of the sum, and can be replaced by a cheaper model for cost reduction.

Using this setup the close range assumption of ISO/IEC 14443 applications is broken, since the tag does not have to be placed 5-10cm from the reader, but can be at a distance of over 1m. Moreover, the more severe implication of this attack is in combination with the known relay attack. While one of the drawbacks of a regular relay attack is that the attacker can be seen operating a device right next to the reader or the tag, using our range extended ghost together with a range extended leech presented at [16] the attacker can conceal his devices, and in the case of the range extended ghost might even place his device in the next room.

The attacks mentioned above operate at the physical layer of the standard, and therefore, are difficult to defend against by a protocol based solution. Designers of close range RFID applications like: credit cards, e-passports, access control, and e-voting should take into consideration the threats introduced by extending the nominal operation range of ISO/IEC 14443 tags.

References

1. libnfc website (2013), http://nfc-tools.org/index.php?title=Main_Page
2. APACS. APACS response to BBC watchdog and chip and PIN. Press realese (February 2007),
   http://www.chipandpin.co.uk/media/documents/
   APACSresponsetoWatchdogandchipandPIN-06.02.07.pdf
3. Desmedt, Y., Goutier, C., Bengio, S.: Special uses and abuses of the Fiat-Shamir passport protocol. In: Pomerance, C. (ed.) CRYPTO 1987. LNCS, vol. 293, pp. 21–39. Springer, Heidelberg (1988)
4. Finkenzeller, K.: Battery powered tags for ISO/IEC 14443, actively emulating load modulation. In: 7th European Workshop on Smart Objects: Systems, Technologies and Applications (RFID SysTech) (May 2011)
5. Finkenzeller, K., Pfeiffer, F., Biebl, E.: Range Extension of an ISO/IEC 14443 type A RFID System with Actively Emulating Load Modulation. In: 7th European Workshop on Smart Objects: Systems, Technologies and Applications (RFID SysTech) (May 2011)

6. Francis, L., Hancke, G., Mayes, K., Markantonakis, K.: Practical NFC peer-to-peer relay attack using mobile phones. In: Ors Yalcin, S.B. (ed.) RFIDSec 2010. LNCS, vol. 6370, pp. 35–49. Springer, Heidelberg (2010)
7. Hancke, G.P.: Practical attacks on proximity identification systems (short paper). In: SP 2006: Proceedings of the 2006 IEEE Symposium on Security and Privacy, Oakland, CA, pp. 328–333. IEEE Computer Society (2006)
8. Hancke, G.P.: Practical eavesdropping and skimming attacks on high-frequency RFID tokens. Journal of Computer Security 19(2), 259–288 (2011)
9. Texas Instruments. Multi function reader series 4000 (March 2005),
   http://www.ti.com/rfid/docs/manuals/pdfSpecs/RF-MFR-RNLK-00.pdf
10. International Organization for Standardization, Geneva. ISO/IEC 14443-1 Identification cards – Contactless integrated circuit cards – Proximity cards – Part 1: Physical characteristics (2008)
11. International Organization for Standardization, Geneva. ISO/IEC 14443-4 Identification cards – Contactless integrated circuit cards – Proximity cards – Part 4: Transmission protocol (2008)
12. International Organization for Standardization, Geneva. ISO/IEC 14443-2 Identification cards – Contactless integrated circuit cards – Proximity cards – Part 2: Radio frequency power and signal interface (2010)
13. International Organization for Standardization, Geneva. ISO/IEC 14443-3 Identification cards – Contactless integrated circuit cards – Proximity cards – Part 3: Initialization and anticollision (2011)
14. Issovits, W., Hutter, M.: Weaknesses of the ISO/IEC 14443 protocol regarding relay attacks. In: 2011 IEEE International Conference on RFID-Technologies and Applications (RFID-TA), pp. 335–342. IEEE (2011)
15. Kfir, Z., Wool, A.: Picking virtual pockets using relay attacks on contactless smartcards. In: International Conference on Security and Privacy for Emerging Areas in Communications Networks, Los Alamitos, CA, USA, pp. 47–58. IEEE Computer Society (2005)
16. Kirschenbaum, I., Wool, A.: How to build a low-cost, extended-range RFID skimmer. In: Proceedings of the 15th USENIX Security Symposium, Vancouver, B.C., Canada. USENIX Association (2006)
17. Bit Manufaktur. OpenPCD2 (2012),
   http://www.openpcd.org/OpenPCD_2_RFID_Reader_for_13.56MHz
18. Mini-Circuits. ZFL-500LN low noise amplifier,
   http://www.minicircuits.com/pdfs/ZFL-500LN.pdf
19. Mini-Circuits. ZHL-32A coaxial amplifier (August 2009),
   http://www.minicircuits.com/pdfs/ZHL-32A.pdf
20. New-Tronics. mobile HF hustler antenna (October 2008),
   http://www.new-tronics.com/main/html/mobile__hf.html
21. NXP. AN1425 - RF Amplifier for NXP Contactless NFC Reader ICs (August 2011),
   http://www.nxp.com/download/grouping/10529/application_note
22. NXP. PN532 - Near Field Communication (NFC) controller (September 2012),
   http://www.nxp.com/documents/short_data_sheet/PN532_C1_SDS.pdf
23. Oren, Y., Schirman, D., Wool, A.: RFID jamming and attacks on Israeli e-voting. In: ITG-Fachbericht-Smart SysTech 2012 (2012)
24. Oren, Y., Wool, A.: RFID-Based electronic voting: What could possibly go wrong? In: International IEEE Conference on RFID, Orlando, USA, pp. 118–125 (2010)
25. Pfeiffer, F., Finkenzeller, K., Biebl, E.: Theoretical limits of ISO/IEC 14443 type A RFID eavesdropping attacks. In: ITG-Fachbericht-Smart SysTech 2010 (2012)

26. RM-Italy. KL400 Linear Amplifier (2005),
    `http://www.rmitaly.com/scheda.asp?IDGr=1&cat=0&tipo=96`
27. Runge, T.: Schriftliche arbeit jugend forscht: Der RFID-Zapper (February 2007)
    (in German), `http://rfidzapper.dyndns.org/RFID-ZAPPER.pdf`
28. Sportiello, L., Ciardulli, A.: Long distance relay attack. RFIDSec (July 2013)
29. Straw, R.D.: The ARRL antenna book: The Ultimate Reference for Amateur Radio
    Antennas. Amer Radio Relay League (2003)
30. Thevenon, P.-H., Savry, O., Tedjini, S., Malherbi-Martins, R.: Attacks on the HF
    physical layer of contactless and RFID systems. In: Current Trends and Challenges
    in RFID (2011)

CellFlood: Attacking Tor Onion Routers on the Cheap

Marco Valerio Barbera[1], Vasileios P. Kemerlis[2],
Vasilis Pappas[2], and Angelos D. Keromytis[2]

[1] Sapienza University, Rome, Italy
`barbera@di.uniroma1.it`
[2] Columbia University, NY, USA
`{vpk,vpappas,angelos}@cs.columbia.edu`

Abstract. In this paper, we introduce a new Denial-of-Service attack against Tor Onion Routers and we study its feasibility and implications. In particular, we exploit a design flaw in the way Tor software builds virtual circuits and demonstrate that an attacker needs only a fraction of the resources required by a network DoS attack for achieving similar damage. We evaluate the effects of our attack on real Tor routers and we propose an estimation methodology for assessing the resources needed to attack any publicly accessible Tor node. Finally, we present the design and implementation of an effective solution to the problem that relies on cryptographic client puzzles, and we present results from its performance and effectiveness evaluation.

Keywords: Tor network, DoS, client puzzles.

1 Introduction

To date, the Tor network [5], one of the most widely used anonymizing systems, consists of more than 3000 Onion Routers that serve daily over 400000 users [25]. Tor helps people all around the world circumvent censorships imposed by oppressive governments, anonymously report abuses of civil rights, and support the freedom of speech and information [28]. It is therefore easy to understand why its security and anonymity properties have attracted a lot of attention over the past years. On the one hand, the community of people and volunteers grown around the Tor network are interested in keeping it secure and operational for its users. On the other hand, however, oppressive governments and organizations may be interested in finding ways to identify people who use it or hinder others from utilizing its services [26].

Being a distributed system operated by volunteers, the anonymity of Tor users is vulnerable to attacks where a set of malicious routers, controlled by an adversary, join the network with the aim of gaining control of user circuits. The Tor network is specifically designed and continuously updated to address these types of threats, but another option available to the adversary would be that of putting a network DoS attack into place with the aim of making it impossible, or very hard, for users to communicate with Tor routers and Tor routers with each other [2]. Such an attack could be used to either significantly

J. Crampton, S. Jajodia, and K. Mayes (Eds.): ESORICS 2013, LNCS 8134, pp. 664–681, 2013.

degrade the users' perceived quality of service, which would discourage them from using Tor, or to affect the topology of the Tor network in a way that favours traffic flowing through malicious routers, thus increasing the power of the adversary. A network DoS would not require a deep knowledge of the Tor network internals and could be performed by using well known, pre-existing, off-the-shelf methods [29]. Clearly, since such an attack is orthogonal to those that the Tor network was designed to address, we cannot expect Tor to be resilient to it.

Nevertheless, the protocols used by clients to setup circuits through the Tor network are *vulnerable to a simple attack that would allow an adversary to achieve an effect similar to that of a network DoS, but with just a fraction of its bandwidth resources.* In this paper, we present this attack, named *CellFlood* , and provide an experimental evaluation of it both in a controlled environment and on the real Tor network. Our results, and our estimations based on measurements from a real Tor router, show that CellFlood is not only effective, but also cheap enough to make a feasible alternative to more sophisticated attacks to the Tor network that have been presented in the past. As a way to mitigate the effect of this attack, we propose to use a *client puzzle*-based technique that would allow Tor routers under attack to keep their ability to provide service to honest clients. The main contributions of our work are the following.

- We study CellFlood, a new DoS attack against Onion Routers that significantly impacts their ability to serve circuit creation requests. As opposed to a straightforward network DoS attack, which produces a very large number of lightweight service requests, our attack uses few "heavy" circuit creation requests that can be quickly generated by the attacker on the cheap, but require long processing from the victim. For instance, to halve the processing capability of our least powerful routers, this attack requires only 178 Kb/s, which is the 0.2% of the resources needed for a network DoS attack that matches the maximum Tor data rate supported by the router. For our newest routers, depending on the amount of resources (*i.e.,* CPU cores) they dedicate to serve Tor requests, the attack can require between 2.5 Mb/s (1 core) and 40 Mb/s (16 cores), which is between 1.0% and the 16.0% of the resources needed for an equivalent network DoS.
- We conducted an extensive evaluation regarding the feasibility of the attack both in a controlled environment as well as on the real Tor network. Our findings demonstrate that the attack is effective under different configuration parameters.
- We introduce a lightweight estimation technique for the resilience of a remote, non-cooperative Onion Router to the attack. Our estimates show that, to halve the processing capability of 48 among the most used Onion Routers of the Tor network, CellFlood would require between 2.6 and 9.76 Mb/s per router.
- We discuss the design, implementation, and effectiveness of a mitigation scheme based on client puzzles. Our improved version of the protocol allows routers under attack to easily impose a cap on the attacking host(s), thus preserving their ability to process honest client requests. At the same time, our tests confirm that our protocol has a small impact on the quality of the service perceived by Tor users, even in extreme scenarios.

2 Background

Tor is a distributed overlay network of Onion Routers (ORs), or just routers for brevity, which allows users to get anonymous access to websites and other network services (*e.g.,* SSH, IRC, SMTP, DNS, VNC). Tor decouples clients from the endpoints they aim at connecting to by means of multi-hop paths named *circuits*. Each circuit typically consists of three routers that forward user data from source to destination (and vice versa) in an encrypted way. Data flow through Tor in 512-byte packets, called *cells*, which are routed using "Onion Routing" [11]. When sending data, a Tor client fills the payload of a RELAY_DATA cell, and encrypts it iteratively with a different symmetric key (*session key*) for each hop on the circuit. Upon receiving a cell, an OR removes ("peels off") one layer of encryption, with the session key previously negotiated with the client, and forwards the result to the next hop on the circuit (or the final destination).

The negotiation of a session key with each router in a circuit is performed in steps. At each step, the client sends a RELAY_EXTEND cell to the latest router OR_i that the circuit has been extended to. The cell wraps an *onionskin*, indicated as $E(g^x)$, where g^x is the first half of a Diffie-Hellman exchange, and E denotes encryption with the *onion key* of the next router OR_{i+1} in the circuit. The onion key is a public 1024-bit RSA key the client previously downloaded from a set of trusted Tor authorities. Upon receiving the RELAY_EXTEND cell, OR_i extracts the onionskin and sends it to OR_{i+1} in the payload of a CREATE cell. OR_{i+1} uses its private onion key to decrypt g^x, computes the second half g^y of the handshake, a hash of g^{xy}, and sends everything back to OR_i in the payload of a CREATED cell. Finally, OR_i forwards the CREATED cell to the client by encapsulating it into a RELAY_EXTENDED cell.

The procedure to negotiate a session key with the router at the first hop of a circuit is slightly different. Firstly, since there is no other OR between the client and the entry router, the client must put the onionskin directly in the payload of a CREATE cell (instead of using a RELAY_EXTEND cell). Secondly, most of the times a more lightweight procedure is used that does not involve a Diffie-Hellman exchange, nor public key cryptography. This is because, by default, a Tor client keeps an authenticated and secure TLS connection with a set of three *guard nodes* from which all the circuits are initiated [31]. When using a guard node as the first hop of a circuit, the client and the router exchange the random data used to setup the session key in the payload of a CREATE_FAST and CREATED_FAST cell, without any further encryption (TLS is sufficient).

3 The CellFlood Attack

Whenever a Tor client extends a circuit, it generates an onionskin using the public onion key of the target router. Likewise, the target router processes it using its private onion key. This operational model makes the processing of onionskins from routers a more expensive than that of generating them. For instance, as we experimentally verified, doing 1024-bit private key operations on a modern high-end server is $\sim$ 20 times slower than doing 1024-bit public key operations [22], which translates into the time to process a CREATE cell being 4 times bigger than that of generating it. This imbalance can be exploited by malicious clients to consume, with relatively small effort, all the computational resources of an OR by means of a continuous stream of CREATE cells. To make matters worse, an attacker does not even have to create a different onionskin for each CREATE cell, as all the cells may contain the same onionskin.

Due to the architecture of Tor software, flooding a Tor router with an excessive number of CREATE requests does not necessarily disrupt the router's ability to forward RELAY_DATA cells. Indeed, Tor delegates the processing of onionskins to a pool of one or more threads (processes), called *CPU Workers*; this allows the main thread (process) to keep up with the more critical work on the RELAY_DATA cells, while the CPU workers perform the expensive and delay-tolerant tasks in the background. Nonetheless, a router that receives CREATE cells at a rate higher from what its CPU workers can process collectively will eventually start discarding them by replying with DESTROY cells. As a consequence, an OR that is under attack is going to discard onionskins produced by honest clients too, which in turn will eventually stop selecting that OR for their circuits. Thus, if CellFlood is performed strategically, on a selected set of important ORs, it may result in overloading the surviving part of Tor (*e.g.,* by overwhelming the unaffected routers with an excessive number or circuits), as well as favouring circuits passing through certain routers, which may well be compromised or controlled by attackers [2] (*i.e.,* similar to the *link-cutting* attack described by Bellovin and Gansner [1]), thus degrading the anonymity of the Tor network as a whole.

According to our experiments, even routers running on recent hardware can only process a limited amount of CREATE cells per second (*i.e.,* a few Mbit/s), which makes them potentially vulnerable to CellFlood. On the other hand, Tor routers can process data to be relayed at a much higher speed, in the order of tens of hundreds of Mbit/s. *Hence, an attacker that is interested in excluding a router or a set of routers from the Tor network will be better off using a stream of CREATE cells, rather than a simpler, but more expensive (in terms of computational resources), DoS attack at the network level.*

3.1 Feasibility Study

Controlled Experiments. To study the effect of CellFlood on an OR, we first performed experiments on a controlled environment. In particular, we investigated the capacity of a router, under different attack loads, to process benign CREATE cells that carry onionskins produced by honest clients. Specifically, given the rate R_t cells/s at which legitimate CREATE cells reach the victim router, and rate R_a cells/s at which the attacker sends its bogus CREATE cells, we estimate the final rate $R_x \leq R_t$ of benign cells that can be processed by the router. To launch an attack, we built a custom Tor client that can establish a TLS connection to any victim router in the Tor network and start sending through it a continuous stream of CREATE requests at a specified rate, keeping count of the percentage of requests that get processed. An important aspect of CellFlood is that generating the malicious stream of CREATE cells does not involve any cryptographically heavy operation; all cells have exactly the same onionskin in their payload and differ only on the cell header field storing the id of the circuit to be created.

Our testbed consisted of four hosts connected together through an isolated 100 Mbit/s network. A *Victim* host (armed with a 2.66GHz Core 2 Duo CPU) played the role of the victim OR in a private Tor network. According to our benchmarks, when idle, a single core of *Victim* has a processing *capacity* (C) of ~ 550 CREATE cells/s (~ 2.1 Mbit/s).

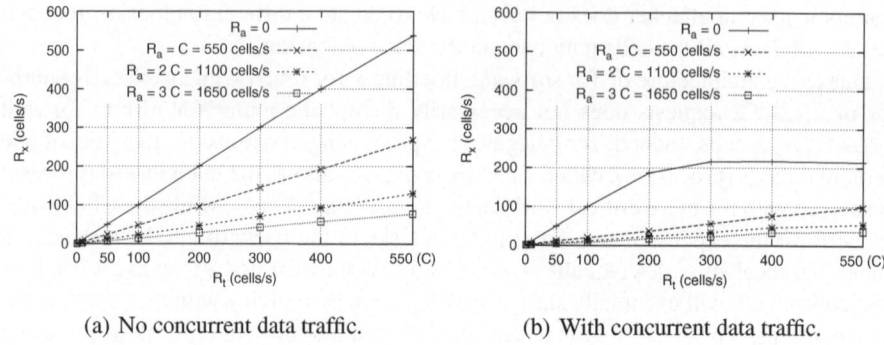

(a) No concurrent data traffic.   (b) With concurrent data traffic.

Fig. 1. The effect of CellFlood on a Tor Onion Router. R_t denotes the rate of benign cells, R_a is the rate of bogus cells, and R_x shows the cells/s actually processed.

On the other hand, *Victim* can sustain a stream of data cells up to ~ 250 Mbit/s, which shows the magnitude of the advantage an attacker may have in flooding an OR router with CREATE cells. The *Attacker* and *Client0* hosts, running on exactly the same hardware (featuring a 3GHz Pentium 4 CPU), are used to generate two concurrent cell streams: one with bogus CREATE cells and another with benign. Finally, *Client1* (also armed with a 2.66GHz Core 2 Duo CPU), was used to generate a flow of random data to be forwarded by the victim router. For our experiments, we used Tor v0.2.2.35 with all options set to their default setting; the size of the pending CREATE cells queue (MaxOnionsPending) and the maximum number of CPU workers (NumCPUs) had their default values, 100 and 1, respectively.

Figure 1(a) shows the results obtained when *Victim* processes streams of CREATE cells, one from *Attacker*, the other from *Client0*, in absence of any concurrent data stream. Each line in the plot shows how the final rate R_x of accepted client requests varies according to R_t, given a fixed rate of R_a. We varied R_a between C (*i.e.,* 550 cells/sec), $2C$, and $3C$, which corresponds to 2.1, 4.2, and 6.3 Mbit/s of cell traffic. As the figure shows, when there is no attack (topmost line in the plot) all benign onion-skins get processed. When the attacker rate R_a matches the capacity C, the number of requests successfully processed drops by approximately a factor of 2, whereas with $R_a = 2C$ and $R_a = 3C$, the drop factor is ~ 4 and ~ 8, respectively.

Next, we evaluated CellFlood under a more realistic scenario, where the victim router processed a stream of RELAY_DATA cells coming from *Client1* at the maximum speed allowed by the network, along with the stream of CREATE cells. We also configured the victim router to limit its relay bandwidth to 5 MB/s (*i.e.,* 40 Mbit/s), by setting the BandwidthRate and BandwidthBusrst options, accordingly—this setting is commonly used by Tor routers running on high speed networks for keeping the Tor bandwidth capped. As Fig 1(b) shows, in absence of an attack (topmost line of the plot) the capacity C of the relay dropped to ~ 250 cells/s (~ 0.9 Mbit/s), as opposed to the 550 cells/s that was the original capacity. This is because the stream of CREATE cells now competes with the stream of RELAY_DATA cells. Nevertheless, the other lines of the plot confirm that CellFlood remains highly successful and has similar effects.

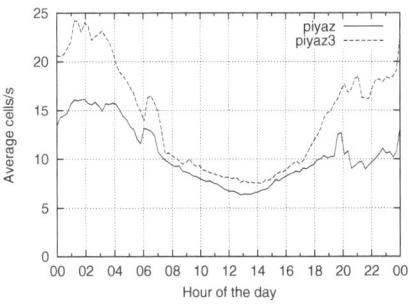
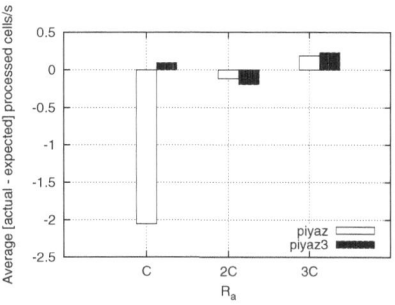

Fig. 2. Daily average of CREATE cells/s received by Onion Routers *Piyaz* and *Piyaz3*

Fig. 3. The accuracy of CellFlood when attacking Tor Onion Routers in the wild

Experiments in the Wild. To assess the effectiveness of CellFlood on public Tor nodes, which are subject to delay, packet loss, *etc.*, we used two ORs under our control that were actively participating to the Tor network. The first, nicknamed *Piyaz* was running on a Xen virtual machine with two virtual 3.06GHz cores, each with a capacity C of 78 cells/s ($\sim$ 0.30 Mbit/s). The other router, nicknamed *Piyaz3*, was a Xeon server with 2.67GHz cores, each with a capacity of 658 cells/s ($\sim$ 2.5 Mbit/s). At the time of the experiments, both *Piyaz* and *Piyaz3* had the fast, stable, and guard flags on, which are given by the Tor authorities to relays with bandwidth and uptime above a certain threshold, so as to provide Tor clients with a hint regarding which routers are the most reliable ones. During our experiments, both ORs were processing an amount of data traffic that varied between 16 and 32 MB/s. Figure 2 shows how the rate of CREATE cells/s received by the two routers varies, on average, throughout the day. Both ORs show a similar trend; they receive a higher rate of CREATE cells/s at night.

To diversify our tests, we decided to run the CellFlood attack on our routers once every hour, for 2 minutes at a time. Each day, for 3 days, we used a different rate of cells for our attack (*i.e.*, C, $2C$, and $3C$), so as to check whether our results was consistent with those we got from the controlled experiment. The concurrent data traffic that the routers were handling during our tests was always lower than the maximum they were able to process, so we expected our results to be consistent to those shown in Fig. 1(b). Specifically, we expected R_x to be close to $\frac{1}{2}R_t$ for $R_a = C$, $\frac{1}{4}R_t$ for $R_a = 2C$, and $\frac{1}{8}R_t$ for $R_a = 3C$. Our findings are shown in Fig. 3. Each bar represents the average difference between the value of R_x measured during the attack and the value of R_x that we were expecting. The difference was always negligible: when *Piyaz* used as a victim, the difference was $\leq$ 2 cells/s on average, whereas when *Piyaz3* was the victim, the difference was even smaller, always $\leq$ 0.2 cells/s on average.

4   Global-Scale CellFlood

The experiments presented in Sect. 3.1 indicate that an attacker can disrupt the ability of an OR to respond to circuit creation requests, with only a fraction of the bandwidth needed to perform a network DoS of comparable impact. The next step of our study is to quantify to which extent this is true for core Tor routers. Because of lack of publicly available data regarding the hardware resources of Tor ORs, we remotely measured the capacity of real nodes by means of a custom estimation tool. In the remainder of this section, we will describe the tool and present the results of our estimations.

4.1   Remote Estimation Procedure

We are interested in studying the maximum rate of CREATE cells a remote Tor router, not under our control, can process (denoted as C in Sect. 3). This problem is somewhat related to that of estimating the bandwidth capacity of a non-cooperative remote host, for which a number of packet-pair techniques have been proposed in the past [21]. However, these techniques do not fit our purpose. The CREATE cells are processed in parallel by multiple CPU workers, and therefore, we have no guarantee that their replies will be received in order. Hence, we opted for a simpler technique that involves flooding the remote router for a short period of time (*e.g.,* one minute) with a train of valid CREATE cells, sent at the maximum speed allowed by the network, and counting the percentage F of requests the router was able to process. A value of F less than 1 implies that the router was able to process cells at a smaller rate $R' = R \times F < R$ (recall that R is the rate at which the client sends the CREATE cells train), which is a lower bound of the capacity C we try to estimate—this is because during a measurement the OR may receive CREATE cells from other clients as well. Thus, by knowing R and F, we can compute R' and use it as an approximation of C. The percentage F can be easily obtained by counting the number of requests replied with a CREATED cell over the total number of cells sent, as the number of cells the remote router was not able to process are replied with a DESTROY cell[1]. The rate R is simply the number of cells per second at which our client was flooding the target router.

   To validate the accuracy of our remote estimation procedure we performed a preliminary test on a small set of 12 ORs that were participating to the Tor network at the time. Thanks to active support from their administrators, we were able to get very accurate estimations regarding the *actual* capacity C of these routers, which could then use as the ground truth for the results obtained through remote estimations. The capacity C was estimated based on: *(i)* the number S of 1024-bit private key operations reported by the OpenSSL speed utility, *(ii)* the maximum number of concurrent CPU workers the router is allowed to spawn, and *(iii)* the number of CPU cores available. Specifically, by assuming a linear relation between S and the number N of CREATE cells a CPU worker can process per second, it is possible to compute the value N_A of a machine A as $N_A = \frac{S_A N_B}{S_B}$, by just knowing two reference values, S_B and N_B, computed on any other machine B. If the number of CPU cores is at least equal to the maximum number of CPU workers Tor is allowed to spawn, the capacity C of a router A can be then computed as N_A multiplied by the number of CPU workers. Tests performed on a heterogeneous set of machines in our laboratory confirmed that this local estimation technique works within a level of accuracy that is sufficient for our purposes: in all cases, the absolute error in our local estimations was less than 20 cells/s (*i.e.,* $\sim$ 80 Kbit/s), while, on average, the error was about 10 cells/s (*i.e.,* $\sim$ 40 Kbit/s).

---

[1] Error code: END_CIRC_REASON_INTERNAL .

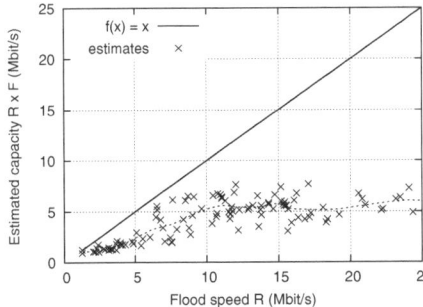
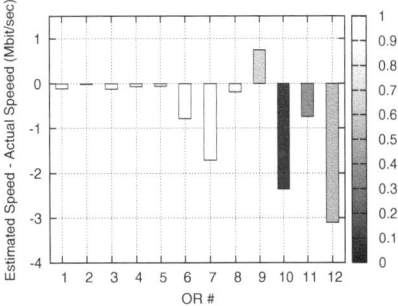

Fig. 4. Example result from the remote capacity estimation. The router was probed every 2 hours, for 60 seconds, over a period of 11 days.

Fig. 5. Accuracy of the remote capacity estimation procedure. The shade represents the confidence of the measurement (lighter shade correspond to higher confidence).

With the results of our local estimation at hand, we remotely estimated the capacity of the routers in the test set during a timespan of 11 days. The estimation of the capacity of a router is the result of 126 measurements (one every 2 hours) each lasting 60 seconds. Each measurement produces a pair of values (R, F), where R is the speed at which the cells were reaching the router and the product $R \times F$ is the estimated capacity. Figure 4 shows the measurements relative to a router in the test set. Each point in the plot represents a measurement, and the line $f(x) = x$ is where the points relative to the measurement that did not hit the capacity of the router would lie. The figure shows a clear trend: as the the rate R increases, the value $R \times F$ starts following roughly the $f(x) = 7$ line, meaning that the measurements hit the capacity of the router and forced it to discard some cells.

For each router our measurements yielded two values: the maximum estimated capacity, and a confidence metric for the accuracy of the estimation. The former is given by the point $\max_i (R_i, F_i)$—i.e., the measurement that maximizes the estimated capacity $R_i \times F_i$. The latter is the value $1.0 - F_i$, that is, the percentage of cells the router was not able to process during the measurement that produced the highest estimated capacity. The intuition behind this choice is that, the higher the percentage $1.0 - F_i$ of cells the router was forced to discard, the more certain we can be about the rate R_i having exceeded the capacity of the router—i.e., the value $R_i \times F_i$ is a good approximation of the capacity. Although the confidence metric gets values in the interval $[0, 1]$, values close are 1 are not common. For instance, a confidence of 0.9 would mean that the rate R was ten times bigger than the capacity of the router, which can presumably happen only when the capacity of the router is very low. We thus deem confidence values of at least 0.5 as high, since they are produced by measurements where the rate R was at least twice as the capacity.

Figure 5 shows the aggregate results of the estimations that we performed on the 12 ORs. Each bar represents the difference between the remotely and locally estimated capacity of a given router. The shade of the columns represents the confidence metric described above. The lighter the shade, the higher the confidence. As the picture shows,

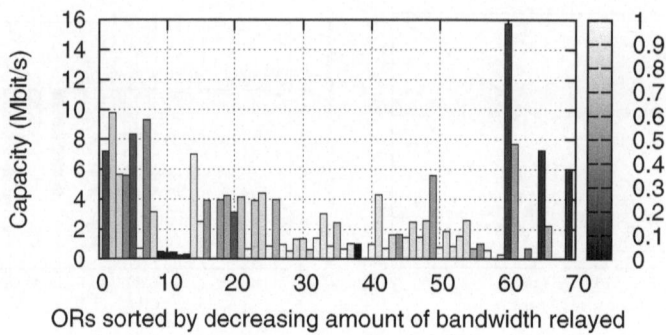

Fig. 6. Estimated capacity C for the 78 Tor Onion Routers

in almost all the cases our remote estimation technique gives a lower bound of the actual capacity of the routers (*i.e.*, the columns have negative values). This is normal, since the routers were probably receiving a concurrent flow of CREATE cells during our measurements. The only case were we overestimated the capacity was for router number 9. However, this is acceptable for the type of study we are doing (*i.e.*, the router is computationally "weaker" from what we think).

4.2   Estimating the Effects of CellFlood on Tor

We ran our remote estimation tool on a set of 78 routers selected according to both the amount of time they had been part of the network (at least 2 months) and the amount of data they were relaying, as it was reported in [27]. This allowed us to get a snapshot of the routers that were part of the "core" of Tor, that is, the set of ORs on which the network was depending on in order to provide a good and reliable service to its users. At the time of the experiment (May 2012), these routers were responsible for the $\sim 50\%$ of the total traffic flowing through the Tor network. As with the tests of Sect. 4.1, we ran our remote estimation tool every 2 hours for 11 days, with each measurement lasting 60 seconds. Results are shown in Fig. 6. The height of each bar in the plot represents the estimated capacity C of a router, whereas the shade represents the confidence of the measurement (*i.e.*, the lighter the bar, the higher the confidence). For some of the routers, especially those in the range 14–59, we measured low C values (around 2 and 4 Mbit/s) with high confidence (above 0.5). On the other hand, the measurements of the capacity of the topmost 8 routers yielded higher values (4 to 10 Mbit/s), but for two of them the confidence was rather low (less than 0.4). The measurements of the 5 routers in the range 9–13 yielded very low capacity (less than 1 Mbit/s) but a confidence level very close to 0, meaning that there was never enough bandwidth between them and our measuring machines to give an accurate estimation. The router number 60 was the one with highest capacity (close to 16 Mbit/s), plus, the confidence of the measurement was close to 0.1, so we can expect the actual capacity of that router to be even higher. In general, our confidence values were high (*i.e.*, at least 0.5) for 48 routers, which were relaying for 22% (*i.e.*, 2.8 Gbit/s) of the total amount of data flowing through the Tor network at that time. Considering our findings in Sect. 3.1, these values are low enough to open the possibility for an attacker to cause a significant disruption to specific routers or to the Tor network as a whole with relatively small bandwidth resources. For instance, the total bandwidth needed in order to flood those 48 routers whose capacity was measured with high confidence would just be around 116 Mbit/s. Even in the pessimistic case where our estimation gave only the 50% of the actual values (which, given our high confidence values, is unlikely) the total bandwidth needed by an adversary to clog them would just be 232 Mbit/s.

5 Client Puzzles to the Rescue

As a countermeasure to the CellFlood attack we propose a solution based on *client puzzles*. With client puzzles, a server under attack commits the resources needed to satisfy a given request (*i.e.,* processing an onionskin) only after the client has performed some computationally intensive work, usually in the form of solving a cryptographic problem. This adds a computational constraint to the attacking host(s), thus reducing the power of the adversary. Client puzzles are a good fit for Tor for several reasons. First, each router can defend itself against a CellFlood attack without cooperating with other ORs. This is consistent with the trust model of Tor, where any router can turn out to be malicious. Second, client puzzles are not affected from how the attack is orchestrated. That is, whether coming directly from a router or a client, or indirectly, through another router by encapsulating onionskins into RELAY_EXTEND cells (instead of CREATE cells). Third, the topology of the network will be preserved, as routers under attack will not be forced to close any active connections in the hope of stopping the attack. Finally, the difficulty of client puzzles can be adjusted according to the strength of the attack, thus making the solution effective even in the case of a global-scale CellFlood.

Figure 7 shows how the client puzzle protocol works when establishing a session key with the first two hops of a circuit. The procedure for the 3rd (4th, 5th, *etc.*) hop is similar and omitted for brevity. If a CREATE_FAST cell is used for the first hop of the circuit, puzzles will never be issued, as no intensive cryptographic operation is required (see Sect. 2). In the remainder of this section, we will discuss in great detail the design and implementation of our mitigation scheme for CellFlood attacks that is based on client puzzles.

5.1 Building and Solving Puzzles

Our client puzzles are built upon SHA256-based message authentication codes (HMAC). To build a puzzle, the router generates s (a random 64-bit key) and computes the value $X = \text{HMAC}(s, P|H)$, where $P|H$ is a message resulting from the concatenation of the onionskin P contained in the payload of the CREATE cell and the hash H of the router's public *identity key*, which is a long-term public key that establishes the router's identity. Finally, a key s' is generated by setting the least k-bits of s to 0. The puzzle is the triplet (s', k, X) and does not include the HMAC message $P|H$, since P and H are both known to the client. To solve the puzzle, the client has to guess the k unknown bits of s starting from s', by computing, for each tentative s'',

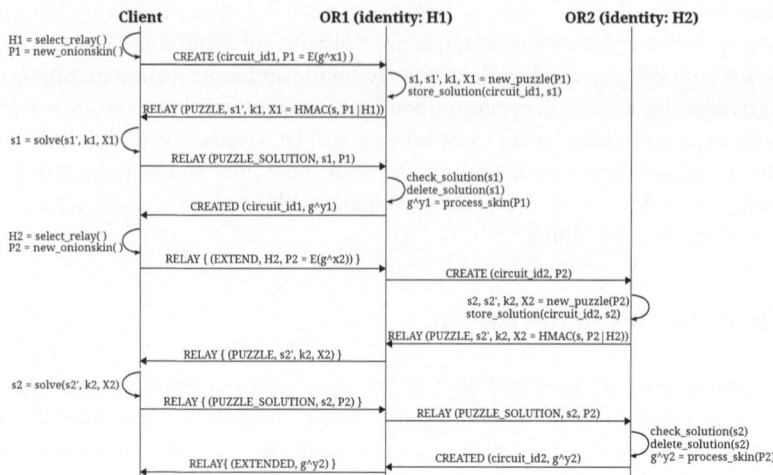

Fig. 7. Client puzzle protocol for mitigating CellFlood attacks (assuming that CREATE_FAST cells are not used and puzzles are send at each hop). '{}' denotes encryption with the session key.

HMAC$(s'', P|H)$ and comparing it against X to check whether $s'' = s$. Since finding a pre-image for SHA256 is computationally infeasible, a puzzle with k unknown bits requires an average of 2^{k-1} tentatives, which grows exponentially with k. This allows the puzzle complexity to be adjusted at will from few milliseconds up to several hours.

5.2 Sending Puzzles and Solutions

As Fig. 7 shows, puzzles and puzzle solutions travel in the payload of RELAY cells with command code PUZZLE and PUZZLE_SOLUTION, respectively. These cells are subsequently encrypted (resp. decrypted) with the session key previously negotiated with any router in the portion of the circuit built thus far. The only router that can read both the puzzle and its solution is the last one, which stands between the client and the router that issued the puzzle. That is, OR_1 in Fig. 7, when the client is extending the circuit to OR_2. What prevents OR_1 to maliciously interfere with the protocol is the fact that the client expects the HMAC message used to generate the puzzle to be $P_2|H_2$. This ensures that the client will refuse to solve any puzzle produced with another pair of P_2 and H_2, and that no other router but OR_2 (with identity H_2) will accept the solution.

Another important detail is that the use of RELAY cells (to send puzzles and puzzle solutions) makes our protocol backwards compatible with the ORs that implement the original Tor protocol, which does not support puzzle messages. These routers will be able to encrypt/decrypt PUZZLE and PUZZLE_SOLUTION cells, similarly to any other RELAY cell. Also, a non puzzle-compatible client that receives a PUZZLE cell will ignore it and try a different OR. This allows for the incremental adoption of our solution, since it does not require all routers and clients to upgrade their software at once.

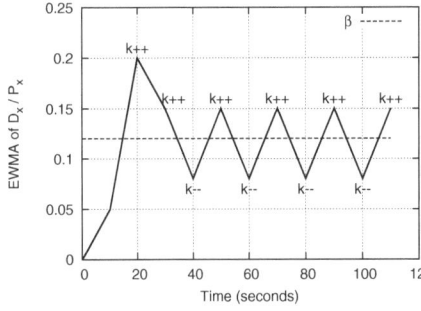

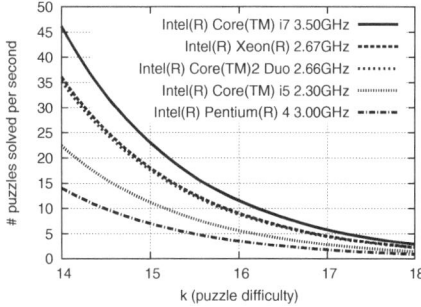

Fig. 8. The change of parameter k when the Onion Router is under attack (Δ_x set to 10s, β set to 0.12)

Fig. 9. Time required to solve puzzles of varying difficulty

5.3 Verifying Solutions

To check whether a puzzle solution is correct, a router compares the received solution s to the one stored when the puzzle was generated (check_solution in Fig. 7). In our implementation, storing a puzzle solution requires 18 bytes of memory (8 for the puzzle solution + 8 for the connection id + 2 for the circuit ID), and it stays in memory until the router receives a reply from the client or a timeout Δ_p expires (delete_solution). The role of the timeout is to prevent an attacker from consuming all the memory of a router, by leaving puzzles unsolved.

Choosing a good value for Δ_p is not hard; even with a Δ_p as big as 2 minutes, an attack of 189 Mbit/s will consume 100 MB of memory. Considering that our measurements have shown that the most important routers of the Tor network can support a stream of CREATE cells of a few Mbit/s (see Sect. 4.1), an attacker that dedicates 189 Mbit/s of bandwidth for clogging *each* router is much more powerful than the model of the adversary we are considering. Also, according to our tests, a timeout of 2 minutes is way more than enough even for slow clients to be able to solve the puzzle on time. Nevertheless, the Δ_p parameter can be adjusted to greater or smaller values depending on the situation. An alternative strategy could be to not store the solution, and give each puzzle an expire time to avoid an adversary reusing the same solution multiple times. Setting the expire time, however, is a complicated task that requires carefully estimating the capacity of the attacker (in terms of bandwidth) and the speed at which honest clients can solve puzzles. A big value will give too much power to the attacker, whereas a small value will discriminate slow honest clients. We believe that our solution strikes a balance between security and performance, as it comes with moderate cost.

5.4 Choosing the Puzzle Difficulty

Two possible approaches can be used here: *(i)* always send puzzles to clients, or *(ii)* send puzzles only when an attack is in place. The first approach is simpler, but most of the time it imposes an unnecessary load on Tor clients. The second one is lightweight, but it involves inferring whether a DoS attack is in place or not. For the latter case, a custom and lightweight approach could be used where each Δ_x seconds the router counts the total number P_x of CREATE cells that it was able to process and the number D_x of those that it had to discard because all the CPU workers were busy. An exponential moving average (EWMA) $\overline{\mu} \in [0, \inf)$ of the fraction D_x/P_x could used to detect when the average percentage of dropped cells reaches a threshold value β. The first time $\overline{\mu}$ becomes bigger than a threshold β, the router starts sending puzzles with a initial difficulty parameter k (*e.g.*, $k = 16$) for Δ_x seconds. At the end of the interval, the router increases or decreases the difficulty k of the puzzle by one bit depending on whether the updated value of $\overline{\mu}$ has become smaller than β or not. This would allow the router to continuously adjust the difficulty parameter k, as shown in Fig. 8. To avoid imposing a too heavy load on an honest client, the maximum puzzle difficulty could be set up to be around 20. The parameter β should be set to very low values (even 0), depending on how likely the router administrator believes his CPU workers will be discarding cells during the normal operation time. Finally, the value of Δ_x is not very critical, but it should be short enough to allow quickly finding the right puzzle difficulty.

5.5   Testing and Evaluation

Puzzle Solution Performance. We studied the time it takes to solve client puzzles on a wide range of machines, which vary from slow, outdated hardware, to brand-new, high-end workstations. Figure 9 shows the speed at which our machines were able to solve puzzles for $k \in [14 - 18]$. As the figure shows, even for a value as small as 17, our fastest host (armed with an Intel Core i7 3.5GHz CPU) can solve just around 6 puzzles per second. It is interesting to notice that for a fixed k, there is no big difference between the performance of different hardware. For instance, our slowest machine (the 3GHz Pentium 4) is slower by a factor of ~ 3.2 with respect to our fastest one. Thus, a router can easily estimate, within a reasonable level of accuracy, what would be the impact of sending a puzzle of a difficulty k to honest clients and attackers alike. According to this data, using a puzzle of difficulty $k = 18$ should be good enough for slowing down an attack performed with today's off-the-shelf hardware. For instance, if the capacity C of a victim router is 300 cells/s, which is lower than that of *Piyaz3*, an attacker should use the equivalent of around ~ 100 cores of our fastest Core i7 3.5GHz machine, to successfully clog the router. On the other hand, the slowest clients should only experience a delay of around 1 second.

Puzzle Generation Performance. To evaluate the load imposed by the client puzzle protocol on ORs, we studied the time it takes for our test machines to read a CREATE cell and generate a puzzle, and the time it takes to read a PUZZLE_SOLUTION cell and verify the solution. The tests machines used were *Victim* and *Client1*, plus the two routers *Piyaz* and *Piyaz3* (see Sect. 3.1). Figure 10 compares the capacity of these machines to process RELAY cells containing data to be forwarded (RELAY_DATA column), to read a CREATE cell and generate the relative puzzle (RELAY PUZZLE column), and to check the solution (RELAY PUZZLE SOLUTION column). For clarity, the capacity is shown in Mbit/s instead of cells/s, knowing that a cell size is 512 bytes. As the figure shows, even our slowest machines, namely *Client1* and *Piyaz*, when idle, can process

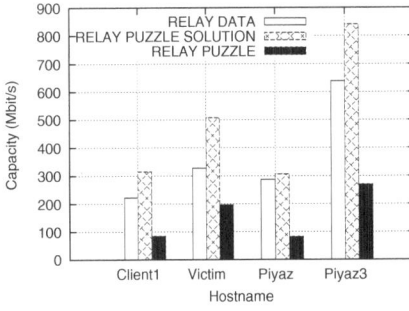
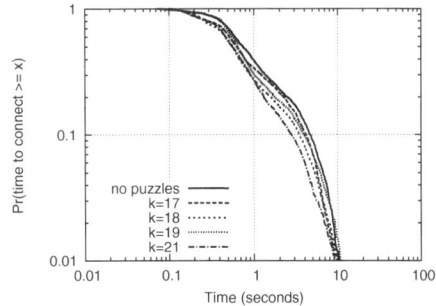

Fig. 10. Time required by different Onion Routers to generate puzzle cells and verify puzzle solutions, compared with the time it takes to process regular RELAY_DATA cells.

Fig. 11. Distribution of time-to-connect when simulating a Tor client solving client puzzles

CREATE cells and generate the relative puzzles at around 90 Mbit/s. For *Victim* and *Piyaz3*, the value is at least 200 Mbit/s. On the other hand, checking whether the puzzle solution is correct is much faster, even faster than processing a RELAY_DATA cell, since it just requires comparing the received solution with the one the router stored in memory. From the security point of view, the values we got for the puzzle generation on *Victim* and *Piyaz3* do not represent an issue. An adversary that floods a router with 200 Mbit/s of data represents a threat anyway. For what concerns the slower machines *Client1* and *Piyaz*, performances can be improved using a SHA1-based HMAC (instead of the SHA256-based HMAC). According to our experiments, this would increase their capacity to generate puzzles up to 230 Mbit/s. To compensate for the higher speed at which clients would be able to solve SHA1 HMAC puzzles, the routers should slightly increase the difficulty k of their puzzles by one or two bits. Obviously, using a different parameter k does not affect the puzzle generation speed in a noticeable way.

Quality of Service. Finally, we considered how the user-perceived quality of service would change in case our puzzle protocol was actually used in the Tor network. To evaluate it, we set up an automatic test where a modified version of the Tor client introduced fake delays in the generation of circuits. This allowed us to simulate both the time delay caused by the transmission of puzzles and puzzle solutions, and the time spent by the client to solve the puzzles. The first type of delay is computed starting from the Δ_1, Δ_2, and Δ_3 intervals of time needed for the RELAY_EXTEND and RELAY_EXTENDED (or CREATE and CREATED) cells to be exchanged between the client and the routers at the first, second, and third hops of the circuits respectively. By adding Δ_i to the circuit creation time, we simulate the exchange of the PUZZLE and PUZZLE_SOLUTION cells between the client and the i-th hop of the circuit. Note that if the client uses a CREATE_FAST cell for the first hop of the circuit, puzzles will not be used and the extra delay Δ_1 will be ignored. The simulation of the time needed to solve each puzzle was based on a parameter telling the difficulty k of the puzzles. Again, this delay is

Table 1. CPU usage when simulating a Tor client solving client puzzles

Difficulty k	Avg. Sol. Time (seconds)	CPU Idle time %	Avg. CPU usage % (when not idle)
0	0	90	3
17	0.5	90	23
18	1.0	87	37
19	2.0	85	52
21	8.0	66	75

added to each hop of the circuit except for the first one, unless the client decided to use a CREATE cell instead of a CREATE_FAST cell.

To automate the test, we implemented a simple HTTP client consecutively fetching 500 random web pages through our Tor client. The client randomly pauses between each request and the next, so as to simulate the time between user's clicks. The length of the pause is drawn from the UNC *think-time* distribution [12]. This distribution is also used by Jansen and Hopper [13] when simulating Tor users activity in their Shadow simulator. In our evaluation, we focused only on the time it takes for the HTTP client to connect to the web server hosting the page, as our client puzzle protocol affects solely the creation of the circuits. Results are shown on Fig. 11 and Table 1. In these experiments we assumed both the best-case scenario when no router asks the client to solve puzzles (*i.e.*, Δ_i is not used), and the worst-case scenario where *all* the routers send puzzle cells in reply to the client's CREATE cells (*i.e.*, both Δ_2 and Δ_3 are always used, whereas Δ_1 is not used in case of a CREATE_FAST cell). In the latter case, the puzzle difficulty parameter k was set to 17, 18, 19 and 21. The results are computed by running 5 independent tests for each value k. The Tor client was running on *Client1*, which is also the oldest machine we had available in our lab.

6   Related Work

Most of the research on Tor has focused on techniques aimed at degrading user's anonymity by means of congestion attacks (Evans *et al.* [7], Murdoch and Danezis [19]), web page fingerprints (Shi and Matsura [23]), observations of the throughput of Tor streams (Mittal *et al.* [16]), or by means of colluding nodes (Fu *et al.* [9], Levine *et al.* [14]). Other attacks study the potential threat of a (semi) *global* adversary (Murdoch and Zieliński [17], Edman and Syverson [6], Chakravarty *et al.* [3]), although this does not fit into Tor's original adversary model. Specific attacks to Tor bridges and Hidden Services have been studied by McLachlan and Hopper [15], and by Murdoch [18], respectively. Borisov *et al.* [2] study a selective DoS attack where Tor routers controlled by an adversary relay only messages of circuits they can fully deanonymize, by controlling the first and the last hop, while disrupting everything else. They show that this type of adversary has a significant advantage over a passive adversary like the one presented by Syverson *et al.* [24]. Danner *et al.* [4] give a countermeasure to this attack that works by probing the network for misbehaving routers. The proposed technique is able to detect all the adversary-controlled routers with $O(n)$ probes, where n is the total number of routers of the Tor network. A DoS-like packet spinning technique is presented by Pappas *et al.* [20]. By increasing the circuit creation latency of the honest routers, they allow an adversary to increase the probability of malicious routers to be selected. As the method presented by Evans *et al.* [7], this attack works by building arbitrary long circuits, which has become harder since Tor v0.2.1.3.

To the best of our knowledge, the only work in literature that is close to ours is the one presented by Fraser *et al.* [8]. Their attack, however, exploits the well known DoS attack against the TLS handshakes, whereas we focus on the circuit creation protocol, which is specific to Tor only. Their solution is based on stateless client puzzles, but they do not evaluate the impact of the time-window parameter telling how long a puzzle solution is valid, which, on the other hand, we believe is critical (more about this in Sect. 5.3). Also, as opposite to us, they do not give an estimation of the vulnerability of the routers currently being part of the Tor network. Finally, their solution might actually make it easier for censoring devices to spot Tor bridges by means of fingerprint attacks (interested readers are referred to the recent study by Winter and Lindskog [30]).

7 Conclusions

In this paper, CellFlood, a DoS attack that exploits a security weakness in the circuit creation protocol of the Onion Routers has been evaluated for the first time. Our results, based on tests in a controlled environment and on an estimation performed on a set of crucial Tor nodes, have confirmed that this attack could be not only possible but also effective, and easier to perform, than a standard network DoS. We have proposed, fully implemented, and evaluated a backward-compatible solution based on a client puzzle protocol that would allow Tor nodes to increase at will the computational resources needed to perform this attack. Our results show that the load imposed to honest clients by our improved protocol would be moderate even in a worst-case scenario.

Acknowledgments. This work was supported by DARPA and the NSF through Contracts FA8650-11-C-7190 and CNS-12-22748, respectively. Any opinions, findings, conclusions or recommendations expressed herein are those of the authors, and do not necessarily reflect those of the US Government, DARPA, or the NSF.

References

1. Bellovin, S.M., Gansner, E.R.: Using link cuts to attack Internet routing. Tech. rep. (2002)
2. Borisov, N., Danezis, G., Mittal, P., Tabriz, P.: Denial of service or denial of security? In: CCS. ACM (2007)
3. Chakravarty, S., Stavrou, A., Keromytis, A.D.: Traffic analysis against low-latency anonymity networks using available bandwidth estimation. In: Gritzalis, D., Preneel, B., Theoharidou, M. (eds.) ESORICS 2010. LNCS, vol. 6345, pp. 249–267. Springer, Heidelberg (2010)
4. Danner, N., Krizanc, D., Liberatore, M.: Detecting denial of service attacks in tor. In: Dingledine, R., Golle, P. (eds.) FC 2009. LNCS, vol. 5628, pp. 273–284. Springer, Heidelberg (2009)
5. Dingledine, R., Mathewson, N., Syverson, P.: Tor: The second-generation onion router. Tech. rep., DTIC Document (2004)

6. Edman, M., Syverson, P.: As-awareness in tor path selection. In: CCS. ACM (2009)
7. Evans, N., Dingledine, R., Grothoff, C.: A practical congestion attack on tor using long paths. In: USENIX Security. USENIX (2009)
8. Fraser, N., Kelly, D., Raines, R., Baldwin, R., Mullins, B.: Using client puzzles to mitigate distributed denial of service attacks in the tor anonymous routing environment. In: ICC. IEEE (2007)
9. Fu, X., Ling, Z., Luo, J., Yu, W., Jia, W., Zhao, W.: One cell is enough to break tor's anonymity. In: Black Hat Technical Security Conference (2009)
10. Goldberg, I., Stebila, D., Ustaoglu, B.: Anonymity and one-way authentication in key exchange protocols. Designs, Codes and Cryptography (2012)
11. Goldschlag, D.M., Reed, M.G., Syverson, P.F.: Hiding routing information. In: Anderson, R. (ed.) IH 1996. LNCS, vol. 1174, pp. 137–150. Springer, Heidelberg (1996)
12. Hernández-Campos, F., Jeffay, K., Smith, F.: Tracking the evolution of web traffic: 1995-2003. In: MASCOTS. IEEE (2003)
13. Jansen, R., Hopper, N.: Shadow: Running tor in a box for accurate and efficient experimentation. Tech. rep., DTIC Document (2011)
14. Levine, B.N., Reiter, M.K., Wang, C.-X., Wright, M.: Timing attacks in low-latency mix systems. In: Juels, A. (ed.) FC 2004. LNCS, vol. 3110, pp. 251–265. Springer, Heidelberg (2004)
15. McLachlan, J., Hopper, N.: On the risks of serving whenever you surf: vulnerabilities in tor's blocking resistance design. In: Workshop on Privacy in the Electronic Society. ACM (2009)
16. Mittal, P., Khurshid, A., Juen, J., Caesar, M., Borisov, N.: Stealthy traffic analysis of low-latency anonymous communication using throughput fingerprinting. In: CCS. ACM (2011)
17. Murdoch, S.J., Zieliński, P.: Sampled traffic analysis by internet-exchange-level adversaries. In: Borisov, N., Golle, P. (eds.) PET 2007. LNCS, vol. 4776, pp. 167–183. Springer, Heidelberg (2007)
18. Murdoch, S.: Hot or not: Revealing hidden services by their clock skew. In: CCS. ACM (2006)
19. Murdoch, S., Danezis, G.: Low-cost traffic analysis of tor. In: Security and Privacy. IEEE (2005)
20. Pappas, V., Athanasopoulos, E., Ioannidis, S., Markatos, E.P.: Compromising anonymity using packet spinning. In: Wu, T.-C., Lei, C.-L., Rijmen, V., Lee, D.-T. (eds.) ISC 2008. LNCS, vol. 5222, pp. 161–174. Springer, Heidelberg (2008)
21. Prasad, R., Dovrolis, C., Murray, M., Claffy, K.: Bandwidth estimation: metrics, measurement techniques, and tools. IEEE Network 17(6) (2003)
22. RSA Laboratories: How fast is the RSA algorithm?, https://www.rsa.com/rsalabs/node.asp?id=2215
23. Shi, Y., Matsuura, K.: Fingerprinting attack on the tor anonymity system. In: Qing, S., Mitchell, C.J., Wang, G. (eds.) ICICS 2009. LNCS, vol. 5927, pp. 425–438. Springer, Heidelberg (2009)
24. Syverson, P., Tsudik, G., Reed, M., Landwehr, C.: Towards an analysis of onion routing security. In: Federrath, H. (ed.) Anonymity 2000. LNCS, vol. 2009, pp. 96–114. Springer, Heidelberg (2001)
25. Tor Project: Tor metrics portal, https://metrics.torproject.org
26. Tor Project: Using tor hidden services for good, https://blog.torproject.org/blog/using-tor-good
27. TorStatus: http://torstatus.blutmagie.de/
28. WikiLeaks: Tor, http://www.wikileaks.org/wiki/WikiLeaks:Tor
29. Wikipedia: Low orbit ion cannon, http://en.wikipedia.org/wiki/Low_Orbit_Ion_Cannon
30. Winter, P., Lindskog, S.: How china is blocking tor. arXiv preprint arXiv:1204.0447 (2012)
31. Wright, M., Adler, M., Levine, B., Shields, C.: Defending anonymous communications against passive logging attacks. In: Security and Privacy. IEEE (2003)

Appendix

A   User-Perceived Quality of Service

In Table 1, the difficulty parameter k of the puzzles is compared to the average time needed to solve a puzzle (second column), to the percentage of time that the CPU was idle during the tests (third column), and to the average CPU usage level when the CPU was *not* idle (last column). From the table it can be observed that, as the difficulty of the puzzle increases, the average CPU idle time decreases and the average CPU usage percentage increases. It is interesting to see that although the time it takes to solve a puzzle is as high as 8 seconds, the average CPU load is only 75%. Figure 11 represents the distribution of the time-to-connect for varying client puzzle difficulty. As the figure shows, there is never a relevant difference in the time it takes for the connection to be established. In other words, the user's perceived quality of service is not affected in a noticeable way, not even in the case of $k = 21$ and all routers requiring the client to solve puzzles before building a circuit. There reason is that the Tor client software maintains a small pool of pre-built circuits that can readily serve new user request. Plus, "dirty" circuits are reused for a certain amount of time before being closed definitively. This design choice has been done in order to deal with any network delay there might be in the creation of circuits. As our experiments have shown, this mechanism is good enough to absorb the extra-delay imposed by client puzzles too.

One last important detail is that of our custom implementation of Tor delegates the solution of the received puzzles to a pool of CPU workers, so as to avoid introducing a delay in the processing of data to/from the Tor network. Using a single CPU worker was sufficient even on the slow machine we used for these tests.

B   Ntor Handshake

Starting with v0.2.4.8-alpha (released in January 2013), Tor supports a new circuit extension handshake protocol, *ntor*, designed by Goldberg *et. al* [10]. Ntor improves upon the original protocol we described in Sect. 2 both in terms of security and speed by using Dan Bernstein's "curve25519" elliptic-curve Diffie-Hellman function. As of June 2013, only about 7% of the routers of the Tor network support the new handshake protocol, although this percentage is destined to grow over time. Preliminary tests performed in our laboratory confirm that, depending on the machine, ntor provides a speed up factor in processing create circuit requests of up to 4x. Nevertheless, as for the original circuit extension handshake protocol, ntor presents an imbalance in the amount of resources needed for client and routers respectively to extend a circuit, which is still exploitable to perform a DoS attack like the one described in this paper.

Nowhere to Hide: Navigating around Privacy in Online Social Networks

Mathias Humbert, Théophile Studer,
Matthias Grossglauser, and Jean-Pierre Hubaux

LCA, EPFL, Lausanne, Switzerland
firstname.lastname@epfl.ch

Abstract. In this paper, we introduce a navigation privacy attack, where an external adversary attempts to find a target user by exploiting publicly visible attributes of intermediate users. If such an attack is successful, it implies that a user cannot hide simply by excluding himself from a central directory or search function. The attack exploits the fact that most attributes (such as place of residence, age, or alma mater) tend to correlate with social proximity, which can be exploited as navigational cues while crawling the network. The problem is exacerbated by privacy policies where a user who keeps his profile private remains nevertheless visible in his friends' "friend lists"; such a user is still vulnerable to our navigation attack. Experiments with Facebook and Google+ show that the majority of users can be found efficiently using our attack, if a small set of attributes are known about the target as side information. Our results suggest that, in an online social network where many users reveal a (even limited) set of attributes, it is nearly impossible for a specific user to "hide in the crowd".

1 Introduction

Over the last few years, online social networks (OSNs) have revolutionized the way people behave and interact with each other over the Internet. OSNs enable the majority of users to not just be passive consumers of the Web, but to become active producers of content, and to be storytellers of their own lives for the first time online. The other side of the coin is that privacy breaches are intrinsically bound to OSNs, and new forms of surveillance and control have emerged with OSNs. Recruiters are now known to look up Facebook profiles of job applicants, and hiring discrimination based on OSNs has become a serious threat [2, 10]. Some employers and colleges even request the Facebook passwords of job applicants and student athletes in order to get full access to their profiles [36]. OSNs have also been exploited by government agencies of authoritarian regimes to infiltrate protesters' social networks. Several Syrian activists have notably reported having been arrested and forced to reveal their Facebook passwords [35]. These practices are only the tip of the iceberg of privacy erosion caused by OSNs.

The first, straightforward method for finding an individual in an online social network is to rely on a central directory, if available. Obviously, a user u trying

J. Crampton, S. Jajodia, and K. Mayes (Eds.): ESORICS 2013, LNCS 8134, pp. 682–699, 2013.

to keep his profile private would opt not to be listed in such a directory or, if this privacy option is not available,[1] make use of a pseudonym. The second method to reach u is to rely on the social links between users and to navigate via these links towards u. This approach works if some of u's friends show their friend lists publicly (thereby exposing u), which is the default setting in most OSNs.

In order to find a hidden user, an attacker could search the whole public social graph. However, such an exhaustive search, despite guaranteeing to find any user in the giant component,[2] would certainly be too expensive for OSNs that contain hundreds of millions users, notably because of the anti-crawling features deployed by virtually all OSNs. To reduce the search cost, the attacker can decide to crawl only a targeted subset of OSN users. In this paper, we evaluate the feasibility of such an attack for *large* networks and ultimately answer the following question: Is it possible to find a target profile by navigating a small fraction of the whole network, by relying on public attributes of queried profiles? Answering this question is crucial for privacy, because reaching the target profile or its neighborhood is *the necessary precondition* for any targeted attack such as the inference of hidden attributes (e.g., political or religious views) through other personal attributes [7, 29], or through friends' public attributes [8, 22, 33].

To the best of our knowledge, this is the first work proposing to find a target profile in an OSN by making use of social links between users. Our *navigation attack* is generic in order to apply to any attribute-enhanced OSN (such as Facebook, Google+, or Twitter). We propose a search algorithm that relies on a space of attributes and distance heuristics based on A^* search [17]. The categories of attributes and their priorities can be adapted to any kind of OSN. Given the OSN visibility, privacy policies, and the users' privacy choices, we show how the attack can be efficiently carried out, by implementing it in the two largest OSNs, Facebook and Google+. For these OSNs, building upon results on navigation and routing in social networks, the attack first relies on geographical attributes only, then making use of additional types of attributes (such education or work) as soon as it reaches the target's city. Our results demonstrate that 66.5% of Facebook users are findable by crawling a median number of users smaller than 400; and 59% of Google+ users are findable by crawling a median number of users small than 300. This shows that it is very difficult to hide in an OSN, however large it is and to prevent targeted attacks and/or to deny the existence of a profile. Moreover, targets' cities are reached in 92% and 93.5% of the cases by crawling a median number of 13 and 8 users, in Facebook and Google+, respectively. This shows the efficiency of geographic navigation in Facebook and Google+. We propose two main explanations for the failed cases. First, the users least likely to be discovered are those who have a small number of friends, or privacy-cautious friends (who do not reveal too much information), or friends whose revealed information is not similar to their own information. Second, users

---

[1] It is the case of Facebook since the end of 2012.

[2] This holds if the search starts from the giant component and the target is in this component too. This is a fair assumption for current OSNs; for example, in Facebook, 99.91% of users belong to the giant component [39].

living in larger cities tend to be harder than others to discover in Facebook. Although the latter reason is inherent to the structure of the OSN and to the limit we impose on the number of crawled users, the former is essentially due to the privacy settings of the targets' friends and the OSN dynamics. Our results show that homophily in social networks [5, 30] does not only allow us to infer hidden attributes of OSN users locally, but also allows us to efficiently navigate toward the target. Note that we do not assume any prior knowledge about the network structure and the users' distribution in the network. Moreover, by starting the navigation from a random user in the network, we consider the worst-case scenario for the attacker and provide a lower-bound on the attack efficiency. It is clear that the use of advanced search filters or source users closer to the target can only further benefit the attacker. We briefly show how this can dramatically reduce the search cost. Finally, we show that simple countermeasures exist and could be implemented upstream by the OSN operators.

2   Related Work and Background

We present here the most closely related work on privacy threats in OSNs, showing how our paper complements existing attacks. We also discuss the background on navigation in social networks.

2.1   Privacy Issues in OSNs

Acquisti and Gross were among the first to mention the potential risks induced by information sharing in OSNs in their seminal papers [1, 13]. They study in detail the Facebook privacy settings and data visibility, and they emphasize the potential threats caused by weak privacy settings (used by most users). In [23] and [24], Krishnamurthy and Wills study what types of information are shared with whom, by default or not, and what kind of privacy settings are available for various pieces of *personally identifiable information*. They show that, among 12 OSNs, 10 publicly reveal social links by default and 1 reveals them always (i.e., without any possibility of changing the settings). 7 reveal by default the user's location and 5 always reveal it. 8 reveal the attended schools by default and 6 the employers. These statistics are relevant for our work as they show what kind of attributes are publicly revealed, and thus can be used for the navigation.

He et al. [18] were among the first to propose inference attacks based on the users' neighborhood. They make use of Bayesian inference and multi-hop inference to predict private attributes based on the friends, and friends of friends of the targeted users. The authors apply their analytical findings to a LiveJournal dataset with hypothetical attributes. In the same vein, Lindamood et al. propose to infer political affiliation (binary attribute: liberal or conservative) based on a modified Naive Bayes classifier [27]. Their results show that simply sanitizing user attributes or links is not enough to prevent inference attacks. Johnson [20] also emphasizes that social links can leak very sensitive information about a specific Facebook user, for instance whether a certain user is homosexual or not.

Zheleva and Getoor [43] propose novel inference attacks based on social links and group memberships, which they apply in four different social networks. Another work on inference of undisclosed attributes proposes to rely on any of the user's public attributes, and on any of the aggregates of his friends' attributes [22]. Finally, Chaabane et al. [7] show how music interests can be used to infer private sensitive attributes of Facebook users. Their approach does not rely on users' social links or group memberships, but only on users' attributes.

Thomas et al. [37] examine how the lack of joint privacy controls can put a user's privacy at risk. Notably, they highlight the inherent interdependent privacy risks due to friends in Facebook, and the fact that a user had no control over his friends' friend lists. They present inference techniques that, based on wall posts and friends, present improvements compared to previous work by relying only on friends to infer private attributes. Yamada et al. [42] also emphasize the impact of conflicting privacy policies on users' privacy. They propose 3 different attacks: friend-list, profile and wall-post recovery attacks. Dey et al. [8] estimate the leakage of age information in Facebook, either by relying on the target's profile directly, or by using information released by the targets' friends.

While these previous papers exploit the notion of homophily to infer hidden attributes of a user from the visible attributes of his neighbors, our work exploits the global structure of visible attributes to navigate efficiently towards a target. While the former is a purely local operation, ours exploits a macroscopic property of the social network. It complements existing work by showing how to efficiently find anyone in an OSN, necessary condition for any targeted inference attack.

Finally, Jain and Kumaraguru propose an integrated system which uses major dimensions of a user identity (profile, content and network) to search and link a user across multiple social networks [19]. Our work notably differs in the method used to search for a user. Our navigation attack does not require the targeted user to be present in multiple OSNs, and does not assume the target profile to be known in one OSN in order to find him in another.

2.2   Navigation in Social Networks

The seminal experiment by Milgram [31] shows that any arbitrarily selected individuals can reach any other person through a short chain of acquaintances. There generally exists a short path from any individual to another, thanks to a few long-range social links. However, knowing that short chains exist does not tell us how arbitrary pairs of strangers are able to find them. Since Milgram's experiment, there have been many theoretical and experimental papers that explain how people can find short paths, and thus navigate, in social networks [26]. Travers and Milgram ask 296 arbitrarily selected individuals in the United States to generate acquaintance chains (using postal mail) to a single target person. Out of the 296 starting chains, 64 reach the target (22% of completion rate) with a mean number of intermediaries between the sources and the target of 5.2 [38]. They also show that chains converge essentially by using geographic information; but once in the target's city, they often circulate before entering the target's circle of acquaintances. Dodds et al. propose a similar social-search experimental approach except that they rely on e-mails instead of classic postal service to reach a target [9]. They show that geography clearly dominates the routing strategies of senders at early stages of the chains and is less frequently used than other characteristics (such as occupation) after the third step.

Liben-Nowell et al. study the role of geography in order to route messages in social networks and provide a theoretical model to explain path discovery [26]. To the best of our knowledge, they are the first to analyze routing in an online social network (LiveJournal). However, they limit themselves to the problem of reaching the target's city. They show that geography remains a crucial factor in online connections and is thus very helpful when trying to reach a target. Lattanzi et al. extend this one-dimensional approach based on geographical proximity to a multidimensional space of interests relying on a model of social networks called "affiliation networks" [25]. In contrast with these contributions, our work studies large OSNs that allow users to finely tune their privacy settings to protect their privacy. Our paper notably shows that privacy policies remain weak and do not protect enough the privacy-cautious users, notably against navigation attacks.

Knowing that acquaintances' and social networks show small-world properties, we now question whether current OSNs do so as well. Mislove et al. already provided a piece of the answer to that question in 2007 [32]. The considered OSNs exhibit power-law degree distributions, a densely connected core of high-degree nodes linking small groups of strongly clustered nodes and, as a result, short path lengths. A crucial step in providing evidence about the small-world characteristics of OSNs has recently been achieved with the publication of two reports by Facebook researchers on the Facebook full social graph [6, 39]. Their dataset of 721 million users shows the main small-world properties: 99.91% users belong to the largest component, the distribution of nodes degree follows a power-law distribution, and the average distance between users equals 4.7, showing that OSNs are even smaller than real-world social networks. We can thus predict that, by relying on users' attributes, most OSNs should also be navigable. However, how to efficiently navigate on them was until now an open question. Furthermore, Facebook reports considered the full social graph, with all social links, whereas the attacker assumed in this work would not have access to all those links. In this paper, we study if the public subgraph induced by the users' privacy settings on their social links is navigable by relying on publicly revealed attributes.

3   Model

OSN Model Online social networks can be described as social links between online users who own a personal profile. Formally, an OSN can be defined as a graph $G = (V, E)$, where the vertex set, V, represents the set of users[3] and E, the edge set, their social links. Each user $u \in V$ is endowed with a set of attributes A_u that is a subset of the set A of the available attributes (gender, birthdate, education, city, ...). OSNs with symmetric social links requiring mutual consent, such

---

[3] In the rest of the paper, we will alternatively write *user*, *node* or *vertex* to refer to a member of the OSN.

as Facebook or LinkedIn, can be modeled as undirected graphs, whereas OSNs with asymmetric social links, such as Twitter or Google+, can be represented as directed graphs.[4]

In most OSNs, users can decide to what extent and with whom they share information by appropriately tuning their privacy settings. For instance, in Facebook users can reveal personal attributes to *friends* only, to *friends of friends*, or to *everyone* in the OSN. The same settings are generally available for their list of social links. $A_u^i = \emptyset$ denotes that a particular attribute A^i is not publicly revealed by user u. Embedding users' privacy settings on their social links into the original social graph G induces a directed public subgraph D, where directed edges are those whose tail vertices have publicly available social links. Formally, $D = (V, E_d)$, with $E_d = \{(u,v)|(u,v) \in E, \Gamma(u) \neq \emptyset\}$, where $\Gamma(u)$ represents the out-neighbors of $u \in D$. Note that we make the conservative assumption that all privacy settings except the public one (e.g., *everyone* in Facebook) are private (e.g., *friends*, *friends of friends*), as we cannot access the information if we are not part of a user's close neighborhood.

Attacker Model. The attacker can be any external curious entity that wants to collect data or infer information about a target t. We assume that the attacker controls at least one node and can thus have access to information publicly visible in the OSN. In order to reach his target, the attacker will search the public subgraph D, relying on all public social links and other public personal attributes (such as place of residence and work, educational affiliations, hobbies, etc.). We assume this attacker to have prior knowledge on the values of a subset A_t' of t's personal attributes, that he will use to navigate towards the target. As the attacker will reach the target through the target's social links (friends, friends of friends, ...), he will also discover at least one friend of the target, which can be useful for friend-based inference attacks [8,33,42]. Finally, note that the attacker we consider in this work is passive, in that he does not subvert any user account or interact with other OSN users, e.g., to create social ties with them.

4 Approach

We present here our navigation attack and algorithm. This attack is generic in order to apply to any attribute-enhanced OSN. We suppose that the attacker cannot rely on any search directory to find the target or to jump towards any user close to the target and that the navigation's starting point is randomly selected. This helps us evaluate the feasibility of a navigation attack in the worst-case scenario, and provide an upper-bound on the number of nodes that need to be crawled before reaching a target in general. In Subsec. 6.2, we nevertheless show how the attacker can take advantage of search filters to quicken the navigation.

In the generic scenario, the attacker navigates from user to user through public social links, until he reaches the target. He makes an informed decision about the

---

[4] Note that Facebook now also allows asymmetric social links, by enabling users to become subscribers of other users.

Algorithm 1. TargetedCrawler

1: $F \leftarrow s$ % Initializing the frontier with the source user
2: $E \leftarrow \varnothing$ % The explored set is initially empty
3: **repeat**
4:     **if** $F = \varnothing$ **then**
5:         Failure
6:     **else**
7:         Select the user $u^* \in F$ with the lowest estimated cost to the target t and remove it from F
8:         $E \leftarrow u^*$
9:         **if** $t \in \Gamma(u^*)$ **then**
10:             Return t's profile and the path from s to t
11:         **else**
12:             **for all** $u \in \Gamma(u^*)$ **do**
13:                 $c_u = d_{\mathrm{hop}}(s, u) + d_{\mathrm{rem}}(u, t)$
14:                 **if** $u \notin F$ AND $u \notin E$ **then**
15:                     $F \leftarrow (u, c_u)$
16:                 **else if** $u \in F$ AND $c_u < c_u^{\mathrm{old}}$ **then**
17:                     $c_u^{\mathrm{old}} = c_u$
18:                     Replace the former parent of u by u^*
19:                 **end if**
20:             **end for**
21:         **end if**
22:     **end if**
23: **until** t reached

---

next user to visit by relying on information publicly revealed by users at each hop towards the target and on his prior knowledge about the target. Whereas in Milgram's experiment every participant in the chain could rely on his own local information about his acquaintances to make a decision about the next user to select, the attacker here relies on global information bounded by the attributes publicly revealed by users on the path. Our navigation attack is represented by Algorithm 1, called TargetedCrawler. This generic algorithm relies on a heuristic model inspired by A^* search [17].

The TargetedCrawler's inputs are (i) the source user s, from which the attacker will start crawling, (ii) the target user t that he has to reach, (iii) a subset of the target's attributes $A'_t \subseteq A_t$ known a priori by the attacker, (iv) the distance functions for each attribute, and (v) the priority of the attributes. The priorities depend essentially on the OSN and on the prior knowledge about the target's attributes. For instance, we will give higher priority to profession or workplace attributes in job-oriented OSNs (such as LinkedIn), to interests in microblogging OSNs (like Twitter), or to geographical attributes for mobile OSNs. The highest- and lowest-priority attributes will be represented as A^1 and A^N, respectively. The algorithm outputs t's profile and the shortest discovered path from s to t.

The total estimated cost c_u (line 13) from the source to the target at some node u on the path is divided into (i) the cost from the source to u, $d_{\mathrm{hop}}(s, u)$

(hop distance), and the estimated remaining cost from u to the target, $d_{\text{rem}}(u, t)$, that is expressed as

$$d_{\text{rem}}(u, t) = \begin{cases} k_h d_h(A_u^h, A_t^h) & \text{if } d_j(A_u^j, A_t^j) = 0 \; \forall j < h \\ k_1 d_1(A_u^1, A_t^1) & \text{otherwise} \end{cases} \tag{1}$$

where $d_h(A_u^h, A_t^h)$ is the distance function between users u and t in the attribute h (attribute with h^{th} priority). The distance functions can be represented by (i) binary values (e.g., 0 or 1 for last names), (ii) real values (e.g., difference for ages, or geographical distance for locations), or (iii) integers based on hierarchical decompositions (e.g., half the tree distance for tree-based hierarchies). k_h is a normalization parameter translating the attribute distance into a hop distance. k_h should decrease with h, as the more attributes we share, the closer to each other we should be. With d_{rem}, the targeted crawler will reach a user sharing the same first-priority attribute as the target before considering the second-priority attribute, then reach a user sharing a second-priority attribute before considering the third-priority attribute, and so on. We conjecture that OSN users share certain categories of attributes more than others (depending on the OSN) and that these attributes affect the way users cluster different OSNs. Thus, in order to increase the search efficiency, we prioritize different categories of attributes depending on the type of OSN.

5 Experiments

As the current largest OSN (1.1 billion users as of March 2013), Facebook is the most representative candidate for evaluating our attack. Moreover, its privacy policies are notoriously designed to encourage public disclosure: the default policy for many important user attributes is *everybody*, i.e., full public visibility.[5] We also implemented our attack in Google+ in order to validate our findings in Facebook. This OSN is now the second largest OSN, after Facebook [40], and shares many privacy features with Facebook. It also reveals the users' social links by default but, contrary to Facebook, allows users to be not searchable by name.

5.1 Implementation in Facebook and Google+

Gathering Source-Target Pairs Before beginning the navigation attack, we had to collect source users from which to start and target users to be reached. To further evaluate the paths' symmetry, we chose to select pairs of users that would act both as source and target. In order to have representative and meaningful results, we wanted to avoid sampling biases as much as possible. Unfortunately, as Facebook and Google+ IDs are encoded over 64 bits, there is a very small probability that a randomly generated ID corresponds to an existing profile.

---

[5] As of this writing, this is the case for the following attributes: current city, hometown, sexual orientation, friend list, relationship status, family, education, work, activities, as well as music, books, movies, and the sports users like.

For this reason, to gather source and target profiles, we decided to sample on the Facebook directory, as in [7]. The Facebook directory[6] has a tree structure, and profiles are sorted in first-name alphabetical order. The first layer of the tree is divided into Latin characters and non-Latin characters. Then, all subsequent layers are divided by alphabetical order into at most 120 subcategories, until the fifth layer, where we can actually select users' profiles. At each layer of the directory tree, we randomly selected one branch, until we reached the last layer, where we randomly selected one profile. Unfortunately for us, Google+ does not provide such a public directory. Thus, we decided to sample source and target users by relying on a random walk method. Our method starts by walking through 50 different profiles in order to reach a random profile in the network [34]. Once we have reached this profile, we select a node with a probability inversely proportional to its (bidirectional) degree, to be added to the source-target set. This probability compensates the random-walk bias towards high-degree nodes [11]. Finally, we only retain profiles with at least two publicly accessible attributes, assuming these to be part of the attacker's prior knowledge.[7] We discuss the representativeness of our target set in Subsection 5.2.

Navigating in Facebook and Google+. Because of the very limited Facebook API, we had to implement our own crawler of users' friend lists. With the standard HTTP request to access the friend list, Facebook provides only the first 60 friends of a user. Then, it dynamically provides the rest of the friends if the Web user scrolls down the friend list's page. While the user is scrolling down, his Web browser actually sends an Ajax request to get the subsequent 60 friends in the friend list. The server replies in about 2 seconds with a JSON (JavaScript Object Notation) object that contains the next 60 friends in the list. We parsed the list of user IDs of each JSON object, as well as the additional piece of information (if any) provided right below each friend's name that would be used for the navigation. We also implemented our own crawler for Google+. We could get both of all outgoing and incoming social links with only two HTTP requests. Both requests returned a JSON object with the social links (names), and some attributes (including location, employer, education) useful for the navigation.

Several lessons can be learned from previous work on navigation in social networks: (i) Geography and occupation are the two most crucial dimensions in choosing the next hop in a chain [21]; (ii) geography tends to dominate in the early stages of routing [9]; (iii) adding non-geographic dimensions once the chain has reached a point geographically close to the target can make the routing more efficient [38, 41]; and (iv) seeking hubs (highly connected users) seems to be effective in some experiments [4, 38] and to have limited effect in others [9]. As Facebook and Google+ share many properties with real social networks, we incorporate these findings into our navigation attack in order to maximize its

---

[6] http://www.facebook.com/directory

[7] This does *not* mean that a target without any publicly available attributes could not be found. We need this information here to replace the prior knowledge the attacker is assumed to have.

efficiency. We select location (*current city* or *hometown*) as the first-priority attribute in Algorithm 1, and education, employer/workplace, and last name as second-priority attributes. We make this choice also because of the OSN structure and design. All aforementioned attributes are those most publicly shared by the Facebook and Google+ users. Location (*current city* or *hometown*), *education* and *work* are publicly revealed by around 35%, 30%, and 25% of the Facebook users, respectively [7, 14]. In Google+, location, education, and employer are publicly shared by 26%, 27%, and 21% of the users, respectively [28]. Moreover, all these attributes are directly available from the social links' JSON objects, thus hindering us from crawling all friends' profiles individually, and thus dramatically decreasing the number of HTTP requests and crawling time.

We propose relying on two different types of distance function to evaluate the similarity between two locations. The first metric is computed as half the tree distance, where the tree is defined by a discrete geographical hierarchy: $d_1(A_u^1, A_t^1)$ is equal to 3, 2, 1, or 0, if user u shares a continent, a country, a region/state or a city, respectively, with the target t. $d_1(A_u^1, A_t^1) = 4$ if u and t are from different continents. The second distance metric relies on the real geographical distances between two locations and $d_1(A_u^1, A_t^1)$ is then defined as

$$d_1(A_u^1, A_t^1) = \max(0, \log(d_{\text{geo}}(u, t)/\alpha)) \qquad (2)$$

where the logarithm is base-10, d_{geo} is the great-circle distance (in km), and α is a normalization constant set to 1 km. We notice that this distance is very close to the discrete-hierarchy distance (first metric). In order to infer detailed geographical information from any location attribute, we relied on GeoNames[8], a Web service with a database containing over 10 million geographical names. More precisely, we used GeoNames (i) to find the region, country and continent associated with a city in the first distance metric and (ii) to compute the distance between two locations in the second metric. k_1 is set to 2 to get a maximal (theoretical) hop distance of around 8.

We give all non-geographical attributes second priority. We make these design choices mainly because we can only access a single attribute in the Facebook users' friend lists (below each friend's name). These structural constraints, imposed by the OSN architecture, lead us to trade off some of Algorithm 1's steps against efficiency. Moreover, we make use of a binary distance function for these second-priority attributes (0 if two attributes match, 1 otherwise) because (i) we believe it is more efficient to directly select users based on whether they share the same attribute with the target once we have reached the same city, and (ii) it is particularly complex to build more elaborate distance functions for last names, employers, high schools or universities. k_2 can be set to any number strictly smaller than 2; we chose $k_2 = 1$.

For simplicity, we verify whether we have reached the target profile by checking his ID or alias, which both uniquely identify users. An attacker who is not supposed to know such identifiers will have to check the target's first and last names that, in addition to the location, should uniquely identify most of the

---

[8] http://www.geonames.org/

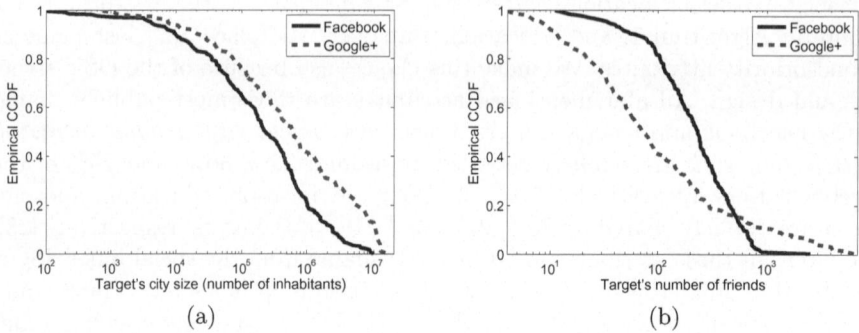

Fig. 1. Empirical complementary cumulative distributions of (a) the targets' city sizes, and (b) the targets' degrees

people. In case there are multiple matching targets, the attacker could, for instance, just check the profile pictures of these few potential targets in order to select the correct target. Facial recognition could be further used to automatize the targets' check for targets making use of pseudonyms.[9]

5.2   Dataset Description

We ran our experiments on Facebook from April to November 2012, not too intensively, with a crawler having a behavior similar to an energetic human user, in order to avoid overloading the system. Despite this, we attempted to reach 200 targets, collecting approximately 393k different friend lists. We also targeted 200 different users in Google+, during Spring 2013, collecting 398k friend lists. For the Google+ crawler, we took similar precautions as for Facebook.

In both Facebook and Google+, we gathered targets in 42 different countries spread over all continents. North America encompasses 33.5% of the targets in Facebook and 44% in Google+, Asia 26% in Facebook and 31% in Google+, Europe 18% and 15%, South America 13.5% and 8%, Africa 7.5% and 1%, and Oceania 1.5% and 1%. The continent distribution is quite close to the actual distribution of users' continents, except for North America that is a bit over-represented with respect to Europe and Asia. USA represents 26% of the targets in Facebook, followed by Indonesia, Brazil, and India, with 9.5%, 8.5%, and 8%, respectively. Almost the same sequence appears in Google+, with USA representing 38% of the targets, India 13%, Brazil 4%, and Indonesia 4%.

Regarding the targets' cities, we can notice in Figure 1(a) that the populations' distributions of Facebook and Google+ follow a similar shape, Google+'s targets living in cities with slightly more inhabitants than Facebook's. The average and the median city populations are equal to 870k and 233k, respectively, in Facebook, and to 2.6M and 440k, respectively, in Google+.

---

[9] Face recognition has been shown to be very accurate and efficient for subject re-identification in OSNs [3].

Table 1. Success rates and numbers of crawled nodes for all continents

Continent	Facebook			Google+		
	% success	# nodes: mean	median	% success	# nodes: mean	median
North America	71.6	1,065	467	67.1	668	272
Asia	51.9	1,061	658	49.2	565	179
Europe	86.1	513	144	53.3	348	72
South America	59.3	1,275	445	56.3	667	628
Africa	60	1,500	1,608	67	805	100
Oceania	66.7	2,270	553	100	92	14

Regarding the targets' degrees (friends' or social links' numbers), we clearly notice a phase transition in the degree distribution (Fig. 1(b)) in Facebook, which is very similar to the one shown in [39]. Moreover, the average target has 291 friends, which is fairly close to the global average that was around 278 in April 2012 according to [16]. The targets' degree distribution is more scattered in Google+, with more targets having degrees smaller than 100 and greater than 1000. The median number of social links is equal to 71, smaller than Facebook, but its average is 424, greater than Facebook. It is hard to link these numbers with other studies, as Google+ is a recent OSN evolving rapidly [28]. The geographical distance between sources and targets is quite uniformly distributed between 450 km (shortest distance) and 18,962 km (longest distance) in Facebook, and between 285 km and 15,814 km in Google+.

6   Results

In this section, we will first exhibit the results of our generic navigation attack, showing its success rate and efficiency. We will also provide some explanations for the failed cases. We will then mention how, by using some search filters, we can drastically reduce the crawling effort.

6.1   General Results

Our objective is *not* to launch a brute-force attack by crawling millions of nodes, which would demand a lot of resources. We rather aim to develop an algorithm that can reach a specific target in the network in a limited amount of time. For this reason, we decided to stop the attack after a certain number of crawled nodes, even if the frontier F is not empty. We choose a limit of 4,000 users, which takes about 14 hours in Facebook (much slower than in Google+). We assume this is the maximum bearable time for an attacker attempting to reach someone in Facebook and, for consistency, we keep the same limit with Google+. Despite this limit, our attack successfully reaches its target in 66.5% of the cases in Facebook, and 59% of the cases in Google+. Using the Clopper-Pearson interval in order to evaluate the confidence interval for this success rate, we find that 95% of the users are reachable with a success rate in the intervals [59.5%, 73%]

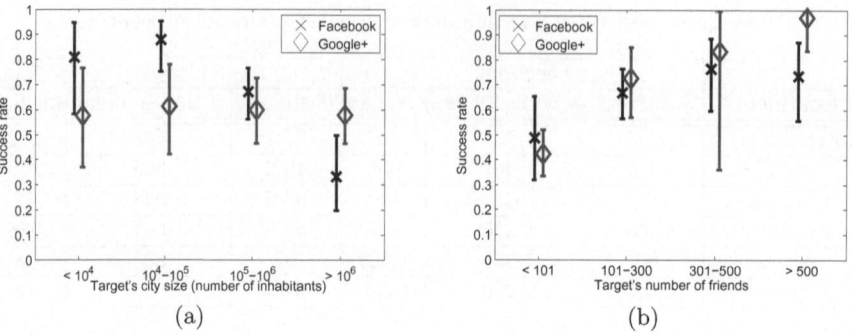

Fig. 2. Success rates (and their 95% confidence intervals) with respect to (a) the target's city size, and (b) his number of friends

and [52%, 66%] for Facebook and Google+, respectively. The Clopper-Pearson interval is an exact method for calculating binomial confidence intervals. It is quite conservative, thus the interval above might be wider than necessary in order to achieve 95% confidence. Table 1 shows the success rates, average and median numbers of crawled nodes, for each continent.

We notice that the North American targets are reached quite successfully in both OSNs, whereas reaching Asian users is more challenging. We also note that European targets are reached very successfully in Facebook but not in Google+. Figure 2 helps us understand these discrepancies. In particular, Figure 2(a) shows that in Facebook the success rate drops with the size of the target's city, but not in Google+. We note in Figure 2(b) that the success rate increases with the target's number of friends, especially in Google+. Lower success rates in Facebook can be explained by comparing the average numbers of inhabitants of the continents. We find that European and North American city populations have averages far below 1M (217k and 449k, respectively), whereas Asia, South America and Africa have average city sizes close to or above 1M (925k, 1.83M, and 2.46M, respectively). This lower success rate is certainly due to the fact that, in large cities, our algorithm has to crawl more nodes in order to cover all the users living in these cities. Our 4,000-node limit is certainly too low for such cities. However, this does not seem to explain the difference in success rates in Google+. This is probably due to the fact that Google+ is more recent and smaller than Facebook, there are less people publicizing the same city, hence fewer people to potentially crawl. The number of friends of the targets seems to have the highest impact on the success rate in Google+. For instance, the median number of friends in Europe is equal to 33, whereas it is equal to 81 in North America. This is certainly due to the young age of Google+, and lower rate of adoption by European users. We must also mention that source users have no effect on the success rate: all crawls successfully navigate out of the source neighborhood, and the large majority of them (92% in Facebook and 93.5% in Google+) reach the target's city.

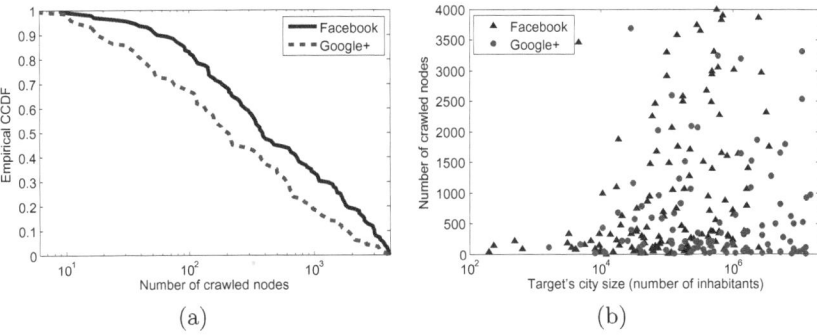

Fig. 3. (a) Empirical CCDF of the number of crawled nodes in successful cases, (b) number of crawled nodes with respect to the target's city size (number of inhabitants)

We evaluate the nodes' efficiency by looking at the number of nodes crawled in our searches. Crawling a node in our experiment means crawling a user's friend list, not his personal profile. On average, 983 and 591 nodes needed to be crawled before a target could be reached, in Facebook and Google+, respectively. Half of the targets were attained in 380 and 291 or fewer nodes in Facebook and Google+, respectively. European targets were especially rapidly reached, after 513 and 348 nodes on average, half of the targets being found after less than 144 and 72 crawled nodes in Facebook and Google+, respectively. We see in Figure 3(b) that the number of crawled nodes is (positively) correlated to the target's city size. This is again due to the fact that more nodes will be seen in larger cities, thus the target is reached after a higher expected number of crawled nodes. Moreover, for all failed and successful cases, on average 44 and 28 nodes had to be crawled before we reached a user in the target's city, and in half of the searches we found a user living in the target's city in less than 13 and 8 crawled nodes, in Facebook and Google+, respectively. This shows that our search algorithm makes use of long-range social links to efficiently reach the target's city, and that the most challenging part of the search is the navigation within the target's city, when we have to narrow down the search using second-priority attributes.

From each subgraph crawled during a successful attack, we reconstructed the shortest discovered path from the source to the target. Figure 4(a) illustrates the distribution of the shortest discovered path lengths. We notice that it goes from 4 to 18 hops in Facebook, with most of shortest paths being between 9 and 11-hops long. This is around twice the distance found in [6] with the knowledge of the full social graph. The shortest paths are between 3 and 11 hops in Google+, most of them being 6 hops long. This result is similar to the diameter obtained in [12], where 90% of the pairs were separated by a distance of 5, 6 or 7 hops.

We show in Figure 4(b) the evolution of the information that displayed by the nodes on the shortest path (SP). It shows that the city is especially useful 3, 2, and 1 hop(s) before the target, for both OSNs. At 4 (and more) hops from the

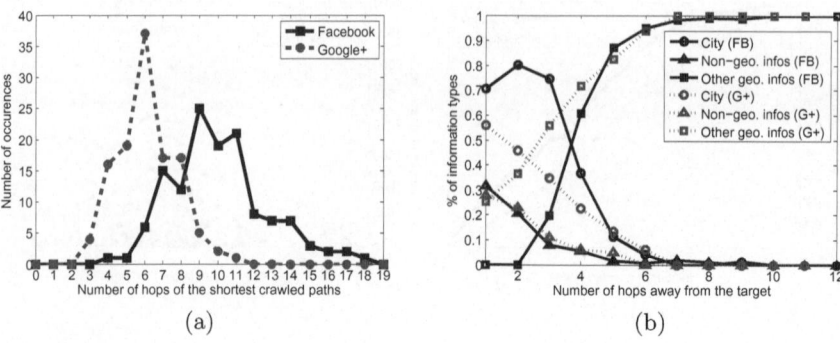

Fig. 4. (a) Histograms of the shortest discovered path lengths within the crawled subgraphs, and (b) evolutions of the information types used to navigate towards the target

target, other (non-local) geographical attributes are used to navigate towards the target. We also note that the crawler starts using other types of attributes (education, work, or last name) 4 hops before the target (certainly once we have reached the target's city) and their influence is increasing while getting closer to the target. At the latest hop before the target, the city is represented in 70% of cases in Facebook and 56% in Google+, non-geographical information representing around 30% of cases in both OSNs. This shows that geographical information remains crucial, but also that other types of information can still be useful when we get close to the target, as it was already mentioned in [38]. Finally, we note that 25% of the targets in Google+ were found from a last hop sharing no similar attributes with the target. These targets were reached from a last user who is geographically close (at a median distance of 32 km) but does not share the same location.

6.2   Jumping towards the Target

Facebook provides an additional feature in order to help people find their acquaintances in the network: It allows users to apply search filters on location, education or workplace. We did not want to rely extensively on this feature for our navigation attack because we wanted to keep it generic and applicable to other OSNs. However, we show here that the attacker can take advantage of Facebook's search filters to facilitate his attack.

We search for the last names and the cities of the targets using the Facebook search filters, and then crawl the friend lists of the users found by the search directory. We search for last names because users sharing same last names are more likely to be relatives, thus to be friends. Our targets can also appear in the users found by the search filters, as we chose targets that are in the Facebook directory for our experiments. Searching for the last names and the cities of our targets, we directly find the targets in 49.5% of the search results. As targets are assumed to not be in the directory, we remove them from the list of users to be crawled. At least 10 users satisfying the search criteria are found in 30% of the filtered searches, and the search requests output no user in 15% of the cases. By crawling only the friend lists of users found by our filtered search, we reach the targets with a success rate of 16.5%.

7   Countermeasures

Countermeasures should logically be developed and implemented by the OSN operators themselves. An obvious solution, already advanced in [37], is to set the visibility policy as the intersection of visibility policies selected by all users involved in the published information. Although it is difficult to force a friend to change his privacy settings on his personal attributes, it is possible to enforce his social links' privacy policy. Choosing the intersection of both users' policies on social links would mean that a user electing to reveal his social links to his friends, or friends of friends only, would automatically enforce non-public social links for his own friends. It would prevent any curious stranger from accessing his profile by using his friends' friend lists. OSN operators could also prevent anyone from publicly showing his social links, as it is the case in LinkedIn. They could at least design non-public default privacy settings on social links. Detailed formal requirements to protect multilateral privacy are presented in [15].

If the OSN operators themselves do not re-design their privacy policies, the users could also take action. The first option is to change the default privacy settings on social links to more restrictive settings. For this option though, users must collectively deviate from the default policy in order for it to be efficient. Finally, if more users decided to hide their personal attributes (such as city, education, ...), the attacker's ability to navigate efficiently in the social graph would decrease, thus reducing the threat presented in this paper.

8   Conclusion

We believe our navigation attack to be the first to rely on social links to find a target's profile. We describe a search algorithm that relies on public attributes of users and distance heuristics, and that discovers 66.5% and 59% of the targeted users, in a median number of crawled nodes smaller than 400 and 300, in Facebook and Google+, respectively. Moreover, the targets' cities are reached in more than 90% of the cases, in a median number of 13 and 8 crawled nodes, respectively, showing the efficiency of geographic navigation in these OSNs. The navigation within the targets' cities, which relies on more attributes, is less efficient and successful. One important reason for the failed cases is the privacy behaviors of the target's friends: the more friends with public attributes and social links, the more likely the target is to be found.

In future work, we plan to propose other search algorithms, especially for once we have reached the target's city. We also plan to apply our navigation attack to other OSNs, and build a theoretical model to support our experimental findings.

Acknowledgements. We would like to thank Abdelberi Chaabane, Mohamed Ali Kaafar, Roger Michoud and Kevin Fahy for their help in the implementation of the crawlers. We are also very grateful to Jens Grossklags for helpful preliminary discussions, as well as Nevena Vratonjic, Igor Bilogrevic and Kévin Huguenin for their feedback.

References

1. Acquisti, A., Gross, R.: Imagined communities: Awareness, information sharing, and privacy on the facebook. In: Danezis, G., Golle, P. (eds.) PET 2006. LNCS, vol. 4258, pp. 36–58. Springer, Heidelberg (2006)
2. Acquisti, A.: An experiment in hiring discrimination via online social networks. Berkeley (April 2012)
3. Acquisti, A., Gross, R., Stutzman, F.: Faces of facebook: Privacy in the age of augmented reality. BlackHat USA (2011)
4. Adamic, L., Lukose, R., Puniyani, A., Huberman, B.: Search in power-law networks. Physical Review E 64 (2001)
5. Aiello, L.M., Barrat, A., Schifanella, R., Cattuto, C., Markines, B., Menczer, F.: Friendship prediction and homophily in social media. ACM Transactions on the Web (TWEB) 6 (2012)
6. Backstrom, L., Boldi, P., Rosa, M., Ugander, J., Vigna, S.: Four degrees of separation. In: Proceedings of the 3rd Annual ACM Web Science Conference (2011)
7. Chaabane, A., Acs, G., Kaafar, M.: You are what you like! Information leakage through users' interests. In: NDSS (2012)
8. Dey, R., Tang, C., Ross, K., Saxena, N.: Estimating age privacy leakage in online social networks. In: INFOCOM (2012)
9. Dodds, P., Muhamad, R., Watts, D.: An experimental study of search in global social networks. Science 301, 827–829 (2003)
10. Finder, A.: For some, online persona undermines a résumé. The NY Times (2006)
11. Gjoka, M., Kurant, M., Butts, C.T., Markopoulou, A.: A walk in Facebook: Uniform sampling of users in online social networks. Tech. rep., UC Irvine (2011)
12. Gong, N.Z., Xu, W., Huang, L., Mittal, P., Stefanov, E., Sekar, V., Song, D.: Evolution of social-attribute networks: measurements, modeling, and implications using Google+. In: IMC (2012)
13. Gross, R., Acquisti, A.: Information revelation and privacy in online social networks. In: WPES (2005)
14. Gundecha, P., Barbier, G., Liu, H.: Exploiting vulnerability to secure user privacy on a social networking site. In: KDD (2011)
15. Gurses, S.: Multilateral privacy requirements analysis in online social network services. Ph.D. thesis, KU Leuven (2010)
16. Hachman, M.: Facebook now totals 901 million users, profits slip (April 2012), http://www.pcmag.com/article2/0,2817,2403410,00.asp
17. Hart, P., Nilsson, N., Raphael, B.: A formal basis for the heuristic determination of minimum cost paths. IEEE Transactions on Systems Science and Cybernetics 4, 100–107 (1968)
18. He, J., Chu, W.W., Liu, Z(V.): Inferring privacy information from social networks. In: Mehrotra, S., Zeng, D.D., Chen, H., Thuraisingham, B., Wang, F.-Y. (eds.) ISI 2006. LNCS, vol. 3975, pp. 154–165. Springer, Heidelberg (2006)
19. Jain, P., Kumaraguru, P.: Finding nemo: Searching and resolving identities of users across online social networks. arXiv preprint arXiv:1212.6147 (2012)

20. Johnson, C.: Project Gaydar: An MIT experiment raises new questions about on-line privacy. Boston Globe (2009)
21. Killworth, P., Bernard, H.: The reversal small-world experiment. Social Networks 1, 159–192 (1979)
22. Kótyuk, G., Buttyán, L.: A machine learning based approach for predicting undis-closed attributes in social networks. In: SESOC (2012)
23. Krishnamurthy, B., Wills, C.: Characterizing privacy in online social networks. In: WOSN (2008)
24. Krishnamurthy, B., Wills, C.: On the leakage of personally identifiable information via online social networks. In: WOSN (2009)
25. Lattanzi, S., Panconesi, A., Sivakumar, D.: Milgram-routing in social networks. In: Proceedings of the 20th International Conference on World Wide Web (2011)
26. Liben-Nowell, D., Novak, J., Kumar, R., Raghavan, P., Tomkins, A.: Geographic routing in social networks. Proceedings of the National Academy of Sciences of the United States of America 102 (2005)
27. Lindamood, J., Heatherly, R., Kantarcioglu, M., Thuraisingham, B.: Inferring pri-vate information using social network data. In: WWW (2009)
28. Magno, G., Comarela, G., Saez-Trumper, D., Cha, M., Almeida, V.: New kid on the block: Exploring the Google+ social graph. In: IMC (2012)
29. Mao, H., Shuai, X., Kapadia, A.: Loose tweets: an analysis of privacy leaks on twitter. In: WPES (2011)
30. McPherson, M., Smith-Lovin, L., Cook, J.M.: Birds of a feather: Homophily in social networks. Annual Review of Sociology, 415–444 (2001)
31. Milgram, S.: The small world problem. Psychology Today 2, 60–67 (1967)
32. Mislove, A., Marcon, M., Gummadi, K., Druschel, P., Bhattacharjee, B.: Measure-ment and analysis of online social networks. In: IMC (2007)
33. Mislove, A., Viswanath, B., Gummadi, K., Druschel, P.: You are who you know: inferring user profiles in online social networks. In: WSDM (2010)
34. Mohaisen, A., Yun, A., Kim, Y.: Measuring the mixing time of social graphs. In: IMC (2010)
35. Preston, J.: Seeking to disrupt protesters, Syria cracks down on social media. (May 2011), http://www.nytimes.com/2011/05/23/world/middleeast/23facebook.html?_r=1
36. Sullivan, B.: Govt. agencies, colleges demand applicants' facebook passwords (2012), http://redtape.msnbc.msn.com/_news/2012/03/06/10585353-govt-agencies-colleges-demand-applicants-facebook-passwords?chromedomain=usnews
37. Thomas, K., Grier, C., Nicol, D.M.: unFriendly: Multi-party privacy risks in social networks. In: Atallah, M.J., Hopper, N.J. (eds.) PETS 2010. LNCS, vol. 6205, pp. 236–252. Springer, Heidelberg (2010)
38. Travers, J., Milgram, S.: An experimental study of the small world problem. So-ciometry, 425–443 (1969)
39. Ugander, J., Karrer, B., Backstrom, L., Marlow, C.: The anatomy of the Facebook social graph. Tech. rep. (2011)
40. Watkins, T.: Suddenly, Google Plus is outpacing Twitter to become the world's sec-ond largest social netwo. Business Insider (2013), http://www.businessinsider.com/google-plus-is-outpacing-twitter-2013-5
41. Watts, D., Dodds, P., Newman, M.: Identity and search in social networks. Sci-ence 296, 1302–1305 (2002)
42. Yamada, A., Kim, T., Perrig, A.: Exploiting privacy policy conflicts in online social networks. Tech. rep. (2012)
43. Zheleva, E., Getoor, L.: To join or not to join: the illusion of privacy in social networks with mixed public and private user profiles. In: WWW (2009)

Current Events: Identifying Webpages
by Tapping the Electrical Outlet

Shane S. Clark[1], Hossen Mustafa[2], Benjamin Ransford[3],
Jacob Sorber[4], Kevin Fu[5], and Wenyuan Xu[2,6,*]

[1] University of Massachusetts Amherst
[2] University of South Carolina
[3] University of Washington
[4] Clemson University
[5] University of Michigan
[6] Zhejiang University

Abstract. Computers plugged into power outlets leak identifiable information by drawing variable amounts of power when performing different tasks. This work examines the extent to which this side channel leaks private information about web browsing to an observer taking measurements at the power outlet. Using direct measurements of AC power consumption with an instrumented outlet, we construct a classifier that correctly identifies unlabeled power traces of webpage activity from a set of 51 candidates with 99% precision and 99% recall. The classifier rejects samples of 441 pages outside the corpus with a false-positive rate of less than 2%. It is also robust to a number of variations in webpage loading conditions, including encryption. When trained on power traces from two computers loading the same webpage, the classifier correctly labels further traces of that webpage from either computer. We identify several reasons for this consistently recognizable power consumption, including system calls, and propose countermeasures to limit the leakage of private information. Characterizing the AC power side channel may help lead to practical countermeasures that protect user privacy from an untrustworthy power infrastructure.

1 Introduction

Computer users commonly assume that software mechanisms, such as in-browser encryption, protect their private information. Research on side channels has challenged this assumption by showing that computer components such as the CPU [18] and the keyboard [32] can leak private information. Along the same lines, this paper examines the feasibility of inferring private information from a general-purpose computer's AC power consumption, despite significant additive noise from the power grid [6].

Past work has exploited AC power side channels for information leakage, but at the level of an entire household [24] or a device with a constrained state space [8,6]. For example, a television that is dedicated to displaying videos produces relatively consistent power consumption over multiple plays of the same video. Given a small number of candidate videos, it is possible to identify which of them is playing [8]. A general-purpose

---

* Corresponding author.

J. Crampton, S. Jajodia, and K. Mayes (Eds.): ESORICS 2013, LNCS 8134, pp. 700–717, 2013.

computer, on the other hand, exhibits a tremendous state space because of its practically unconstrained operation. Executing the same computing task at different times may result in different power consumption patterns because of different background tasks or I/O workloads (e.g., network activity). Nevertheless, we find that system-wide traces of AC power consumption leak enough information about the operation of a general-purpose computer to identify the webpage that the computer is loading (out of a set of known pages). Because browsers use a diverse subset of the available hardware components, our results suggest that this technique may generalize to other computing workloads.

Several factors work to our advantage. Web browsers increasingly take advantage of hardware to improve the user's experience (by, e.g., executing native code [35]), resulting in resource consumption that scales with the webpage's complexity. Another factor is that modern computers and operating systems aggressively try to reduce power consumption [30], resulting in energy-proportional computing in which the power consumption tightly fits the workload [6]. Both of these factors increase the system's dynamic range, which in turn increases the information available in power traces.

There are also challenges to the task of identifying webpages from AC power consumption. The fundamental challenge is separating interesting activity from baseline power consumption, which a computer's power supply aggregates. Other challenges stem from the dynamic nature of the Internet and modern websites. The round trip time for fetching webpages may change over time; many websites include scripts that run long after the page loads, and many customize content for each visitor.

This paper's contribution is an attack on privacy that identifies specific web-browsing activities via an AC power side channel. We characterize and measure this side channel by designing methods to extract patterns of power consumption as a computer loads a webpage. These patterns, which are obscure in the time domain but more apparent in the frequency domain, act as power signatures that allow an eavesdropper to determine which webpage is being loaded. Additionally, these power signatures are robust against a variety of changes to the computing environment, including background processes, changes in network location, or the use of a VPN. Because most of the identifiable information occurs at under 10 kHz in the frequency domain, capturing and exfiltrating power measurements is within reason for a simple embedded device that could fit discreetly inside a power outlet.

Using a covertly modified electrical outlet to record power consumption, we trained and tested a classifier with over 100 hours of traces representing more than 13,000 page loads from a set of 51 webpages from sites representing over 30% of global page views. Given a power trace with 51 possible labels, the classifier identified the correct match from the training set with 99% precision (resistance to false positives) and 99% recall (resistance to false negatives). Given an unlabeled trace from one of 441 webpages *not* in the training set, the classifier's false positive rate is less than 2%. In some cases, the classifier succumbs to overfitting when trained on traces from a single computer, confusing other consistent power activity for browsing activity. However, when trained on traces from two computers, the classifier identifies the common patterns that are due to browser activity and can correctly label unseen traces from either computer.

This work conceptually bridges the gap between previous work on circuit-level direct-current (DC) power analysis [18] and coarser-grained, household-level activity recognition via AC power measurements [12,26,11]. This paper also proposes several hardware and software countermeasures to minimize information leakage.

Threat Model. Focusing on the AC power side channel, this paper considers an attacker with physical access to a power outlet the victim might use. Possible easy targets include outlets in coffee shops and airports. A simple modification to a power outlet enables discreet data recording. Because most users implicitly trust power outlets, an attacker may gain easy, *persistent* access to a victim's power-consumption patterns.

2   Background and Challenges

This section distinguishes AC power measurements from DC power measurements, which have been studied extensively in literature about side channels [18,4]. It breaks down the power budget of a computer and discusses how the actions of a web browser influence power consumption. Finally, it explains some of the challenges inherent in our attempts to classify AC power traces.

2.1   AC versus DC Power Traces

DC power measurements explored in previous research involve tracing individual components' power consumption on a circuit board. Such techniques require access to internal hardware elements and are overly intrusive from the viewpoint of our threat model. An attacker conforming to our threat model seeks a power-analysis technique that is relatively nonintrusive and does not involve opening or modifying the victim's computer. Every computer operates on power drawn from a power grid. A laptop user may avoid drawing power from the grid by relying on the battery, but this is a temporary solution. Monitoring AC power consumption affords a *system-wide* view of the computer's activity, although individual activities may be difficult to identify because all components' signals are added together.

Challenge: Noise.   Both the "upstream" (e.g., household) circuit and the power supply itself introduce noise onto the power line. Since this noise is omnipresent, we make no attempts to remove it, unlike previous work [8]; instead, we provide noisy inputs to classifiers and rely on the presence of a non-noise signal to influence classification. Eschewing filtering also simplifies the hardware we use to gather traces.

Challenge: Periodicity.   Whereas DC signals often feature prominent level shifts and other artifacts that are amenable to time-domain analysis, the *alternating* nature of AC current essentially convolves sets of sinusoids, making time-domain analysis difficult. We therefore perform analysis in the frequency domain. Before classification, we transform traces into the frequency domain (Figure 1b) using the Fourier transform. In addition to making certain signals easier to identify (e.g., 60 Hz utility power in the U.S.), this approach enables meaningful comparisons despite misaligned traces, or traces of different lengths, and the additive nature of the SMPS's power consumption preserves frequency information from individual components' power consumption.

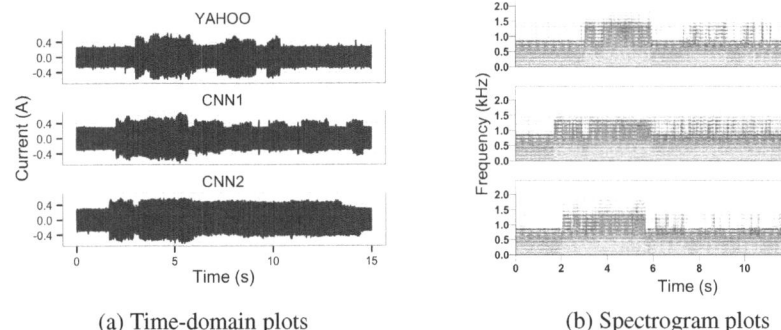

(a) Time-domain plots   (b) Spectrogram plots

Fig. 1. Time- and frequency-domain plots of several power traces as a MacBook loads two different pages. In the frequency domain, brighter colors represent more energy at a given frequency. Despite the lack of obviously characteristic information in the time domain, the classifier correctly identifies all of the above traces.

2.2   Tracking Hardware Components' Power Consumption

To develop intuition about what kinds of tasks are likely to induce identifiable activity patterns on the power line, we measured the power consumption of a laptop (MacBook-1, Appendix A) under a variety of workloads designed to stress individual subsystems. We used a P3 Kill A Watt power monitor [25] to measure power consumption. Table 1 summarizes the results, which suggest that the MacBook's CPU and GPU dominate power consumption under load. The network interfaces and solid-state storage draw comparatively little power.

Prior side-channel work has leveraged network characteristics such as packet timings [28] or lengths [33,34] to classify webpages according to their network traffic. A reasonable question to ask is whether network classifiers are likely to apply to the problem of webpage identification. We tapped the activity LED of a network switch port to capture a representation of a computer's network traffic while also tracing the

Table 1. MacBook power consumption under various types of load. Numbers beginning with + are relative to the baseline of 8 W.

Condition	Power (W) vs. Baseline
Baseline (idle, screen off)	8
One core at 100%	+7
Two cores at 100%	+11
GPU at 100%	+11
Wired network saturated	+2
Wireless network saturated	+3
File copy, SSD to SSD	+6
Screen at maximum brightness	+6

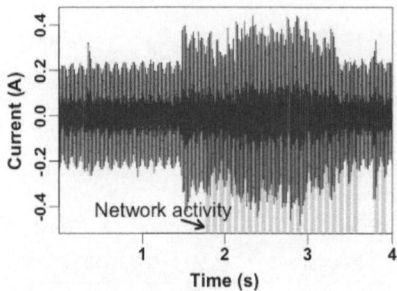
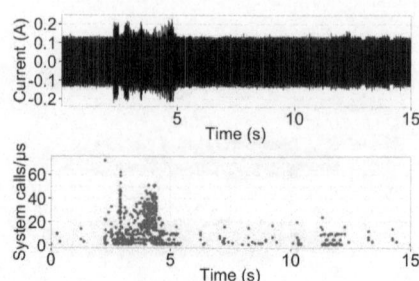

(a) The network activity is correlated with high current consumption, but is not the only cause. Spikes before and after network activity show that local computation dominates the consumption.

(b) The system call activity (as measured by DTrace) is also correlated with high current consumption, and our results suggest that systems exercised by system calls are a major cause of consumption.

Fig. 2. Time-domain plots as a MacBook loads webpages. Both network activity and system calls appear to correlate with energy consumption.

computer's AC power line. Figure 2a shows an example from our tests. The computer consumes power performing other tasks before the network interface actually begins to send and receive packets. Furthermore, the AC power provides insight into client scripts and rendering loads unavailable in a network trace.

Power consumption appears to be more strongly correlated with system calls than with network activity as shown by Figure 2b. Tracking the number of system calls initiated by the browser process with DTrace captures memory allocation and disk I/O in addition to network activity, enabling monitoring of all of the components we have identified as major power consumers.

3   Approach: Supervised Learning Classifier

To distinguish among webpages, we adopt a supervised learning approach, in which we train a classifier on labeled AC power traces and then attempt to match unlabeled traces. An AC power trace contains artifacts of every powered computer component, each of which may have its own clock rate or power signature, and each of which processes information differently. We assume that disentangling these signals (multicore CPU, multicore video card, multiple drives, etc.) from a single AC power trace is intractable with current techniques, and instead focus on coarser-grained, *system-level* questions, such as which popular webpage the user is loading. Because it is prohibitively difficult to build a generative model of how computing tasks will map to power consumption— a discriminative modeling approach is more appropriate. Our supervised-learning approach fits this requirement; it requires only a labeled training set and learns its own model of how feature values map to class labels. Specifically, we train *support vector machines* (SVMs) using the open-source library libsvm [5].

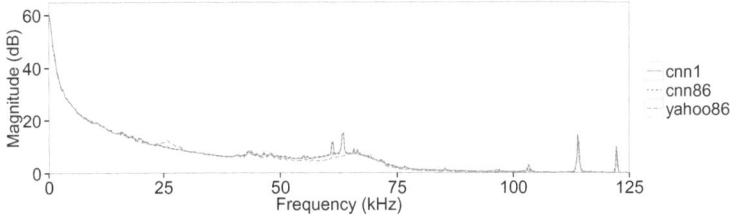

Fig. 3. Plots of three of our Fourier transform feature vectors. While the pages are difficult to separate visually in the time domain, the two cnn.com samples are indistinguishable to the eye in the frequency domain, whereas yahoo.com diverges around 25 and 65 kHz.

3.1   Feature Selection

Classification requires extracting feature vectors on which to train a classifier. A naïve classifier might simply consider the *length* feature of a sample in the time domain, defined as the length of time for which power consumption remains above a predetermined threshold. However, background tasks add confounding noise in the time domain, which may obscure the true endpoints of a specific task, and tasks often include periods of both high and low power consumption. Mean, minimum, and maximum power are equally unsuitable choices for similar reasons. A more robust approach is to classify traces based on features from the frequency domain.

We transform traces into the frequency domain by first calculating the spectrogram using rectangular sliding windows 1000 samples wide with 50% overlap. We then collapse the spectrogram into a single Fourier transform by summing over all of the time steps. As a base set of features for classification, we divide the Fourier transform of each power trace into 500 segments, each 250 Hz wide, starting at 0–250 Hz and ending at 124.75–125 kHz, half the 250 kHz sample rate at which we recorded traces. This process yields 500 features, each of which represents the power present within one 250 Hz slice of spectrum over the duration of the trace.

As described in Section 2.1, classifying in the frequency domain allows meaningful comparisons between misaligned traces or traces of different lengths. Using the output directly from the Fourier transform as a feature vector is a simple approach and yields excellent results. It is also straightforward to visualize differences in the Fourier transform, as shown in Figure 3. Plotting the feature vector reveals consistent features between the two traces of cnn.com and recognizable differences between a trace of yahoo.com and the cnn.com traces, which are not obvious in the time domain.

3.2   Classification

We train a binary classifier for each page in our corpus. After training all 51 SVMs, we use each of them to classify test samples. A test sample is an *unlabeled* 500-dimensional feature vector, obtained in the same way as the training samples, that is *not* in the training set. Each SVM determines whether the test sample was an instance of the webpage it was trained to recognize. In the interest of simplicity, we do not implement a multi-class labeling solution in which all 51 SVMs collectively generate a single output, but there are a variety of well-studied techniques for this purpose and libsvm implements several of them [15].

There are three notable details of the training process. First, we linearly normalize feature values across all samples. This prevents features with large values (e.g., the low frequency elements) from dominating features with smaller values. Second, we use standard 10-fold cross-validation to avoid overfitting at training time. By repeatedly splitting the training set and retraining each time, the classifier avoids the possibility of biases in a small number of training examples producing a biased model. Finally, we use a radial basis function (RBF) kernel, as recommended by the authors of libsvm [5].

4   Methods and Metrics

To cover a diverse set of webpages representing typical Internet traffic, we chose 48 webpages drawn from Alexa's list of the top $1,000,000$ websites [2], discarding duplicates and adult websites. By Alexa's estimates, these top 48 websites represent over 30% of global page views. We added the top Google result for "cheap Viagra" as an example of a potentially embarrassing (or malicious) page. To include a page that loads with negligible latency, we added two authors' department's home pages, a < 1 ms round trip from one of our measurement points, bringing the number of webpages in our training set to 51.

The Alexa rankings list *websites*, but it is more meaningful to collect traces of individual *webpages*. Each of our traces represents an automated load of the front page of one of the 51 websites. To record realistic power traces of user browsing, we used a custom Chrome extension (see §4.1) to collect at least 90 consecutive traces of each page. For webpages that require users to log in before displaying useful information, we logged in as the first or second author. We believe that our choice to consider front pages is reasonable because users are likely to visit the front page of a given website and then follow links to other pages. The notable exceptions to this tendency are bookmarked pages and direct links from other people or sites.

Evaluation Metrics.   Because our classifier uses standard machine-learning techniques, we use standard metrics from machine learning to evaluate its performance. In the following definitions, *tp* and *tn* refer to true positives and true negatives (correct labelings), and *fp* and *fn* refer to false positives and false negatives (incorrect labelings).

Precision, $tp/(tp+fp)$, is the fraction of positively labeled examples whose labels are correct. It measures the classifier's ability to exclude negative examples.
Recall, $tp/(tp+fn)$, is the fraction of all the examples that *should* have been positively labeled that *are* correctly positively labeled. It measures the classifier's ability to identify positive examples.

We present experimental results in terms of *precision* and *recall* because the standard *accuracy* metric is often misleading. In most of our experiments, the number of negative examples is roughly 50 times the number of positive examples because, for each webpage, there are more traces of *other* webpages in the testing set than there are of that webpage. Because of this disparity between positive and negative examples, the classifier could achieve greater than 98% accuracy by simply classifying all examples as negative. A perfect classifier would achieve 100% accuracy, 100% precision, and 100% recall. For any imperfect classifier, there is a tradeoff between precision and recall.

4.1   Experimental Setup

This section describes the experimental setup we used to capture AC power traces.[1]

> **Safety note:** This paper is not a complete manual for electrical safety. Measuring "hot" terminals is potentially fatally dangerous and should be conducted only under qualified supervision. Do not try this in a non-laboratory setting.

Using an instrumented outlet (described next), we measured the power consumption of two Apple MacBook computers, a Lenovo T410 laptop, and a Dell Vostro desktop PC, all running different operating system versions. (For detailed hardware and software specifications, see Appendix A.) To approximate the environments of typical users, we used a stock installation of each operating system. In particular, we allowed default background processes to run. Experiments with the two MacBook computers were carried out approximately one year apart using similar but non-identical instrumented outlets.

To record each workload's power signature, we monitored electrical current between the power supply and an instrumented outlet. A modern AC outlet has three terminals: *hot*, *neutral*, and *ground*. To measure a power supply's instantaneous current on the hot–neutral circuit, we placed a 0.1 Ω *sense resistor* (part #13FR100E-ND) in series with one terminal of a standard outlet. We attached an Agilent U2356A data acquisition unit (DAQ) to the terminals of the sense resistor. The DAQ samples the voltage across its probes and sends the data via USB to another PC (not the computer being measured). We recorded 16-bit samples at a rate of 250 kHz to capture workload artifacts occurring at up to 125 kHz.

Finally, we developed a Chrome extension to automate the repeated loading of a target webpage. The extension repeatedly: opens a new window, pauses, loads the page, pauses again, and finally closes the window. For webpages that did not require user credentials, the script opened browser windows in a *private browsing* mode to purge the browser environment of confounding data. To compare webpage identifiability across browsers, we also used the iMacros extension for Firefox [1] to mimic our Chrome extension. We recorded continuously with the DAQ while running experiments. A script with knowledge of the browser extensions' timings chopped the DAQ's output into separate trace files to be used with our classifier. While the majority of the webpages we profiled show no changes within the measurement period, there are notable exceptions. A number of high-turnover webpages including cnn.com, cnet.com, and reddit.com underwent content changes during our measurements.

---

[1] We use the terms *power trace*, *voltage trace*, and *current trace* interchangeably. What we actually record is a *voltage trace* that maps trivially to current ($I_{sense} = V_{sense}/R_{sense}$, with R_{sense} constant) and therefore power ($P = I_{sense}V_{RMS}$, with V_{RMS} a constant 120 volts (RMS) in North America).

5   Evaluation

This section summarizes our experimental results over a wide range of conditions. While there are a limitless number of questions to ask about how well a classifier works under different conditions, we have distilled them down to the following six questions regarding causality and intuition:

- How effectively can the SVM classifier differentiate webpages from one another? (Section 5.1)
- How robust is the classifier in the presence of content distribution services, anonymity services, encryption, and caching, as well as changes in network location, type, or interface? (Section 5.2)
- How is classifier performance affected by changes in operating system or hardware? (Section 5.3)
- How does the classifier's performance change when the test traces include background activities? (Section 5.4)
- How does sampling rate affect classification? (Section 5.5)
- How well does the classifier exclude samples of pages outside the corpus? (Section 5.6)

We find that our classifier can differentiate webpages with high precision and recall rates (each averaging 99%) and that it is robust against many of the variations we tested, including the use of a VPN, and changes in the location or network interface. It is not robust against changes of machine or operating system. Where our classifier performs poorly, we find in most cases that increasing the diversity of the training set improves its performance along all metrics. The total number of power traces we tested across all experiments was 13, 110, chronicling over 100 hours of 250 kHz trace recordings.

5.1   Page Differentiation

Our SVM classifier effectively differentiates among the 51 popular webpages we tested. As a baseline, we varied only the webpage under test and held all other variables constant. These other variables include machine under test, network location, network interface, operating system, and web browser. By varying only the webpage under test, we minimize differences that are not actually the result of variation among webpages.

We gathered all of the data for this experiment twice, using slightly different Mac-Books and instrumented outlets built to the same specifications in different locations. Here we present the results of combining the two data sets into a single corpus. After gathering $\sim$90 traces for each of the 51 webpages on each of the MacBooks (for a total of $\sim$180 traces), we used the experimental protocol described in Section 3.2 to label each trace. Each SVM labels a trace as either matching or not matching the page for which it was trained. The total size of the corpus for this experiment was 9, 240 traces. We used half of these traces for training and the remaining traces for testing. With $\sim$90 training examples per label, the SVM classifier achieves an average 99% precision and 99% recall over all webpages in the data set.

The classifier's performance varied among the tested webpages. The precision and recall were both 100% for 18 of the 51 webpages. The lowest precision for any page was

93% for `skype.com` and the lowest recall for any page was 88% for `slashdot.org`. A plausible explanation for the classifier's relatively poor performance on `skype.com` is that the front page underwent a significant design change between the capture of our two data sets, which we confirmed by inspecting snapshots from the Internet Archive Wayback Machine [16]. The poor recall for `slashdot.org` could be explained by the high turnover of the front page or inconsistent load times. `godaddy.com`, which uses a commercial content distribution service, also yielded lower recall results.

5.2 Diverse Browsing Conditions

We varied the conditions under which our browser operated and found that the SVM classifier is robust against local network connection type, use of cache, VPN encryption, and the passage of time for most webpages. It is not robust against the use of a caching content-distribution network (CDN) such as Coral [10].

Our training and testing setup was as follows. We repeated this process for three webpages: one simple page (`google.com`) and two complex pages (`cnn.com` and `cnet.com`). For each page, we gathered the following sets of traces on one of our MacBooks:

- **Time:** Traces gathered a month later, to test how fresh the training set must be.
- **Cache:** Traces recorded with a warm browser cache, to test whether the classifier depends on specific network traffic patterns.
- **VPN:** Traces recorded while connected to a VPN concentrator a 1.5 ms round trip away (essentially measuring only cryptographic overhead), to test whether encrypting normal traffic would be an effective countermeasure.
- **WiFi:** Traces recorded while connected to our lab network wirelessly instead of via wired Ethernet, to test whether the training phase overfits the SVMs to "clean" low-latency wired traffic.
- **CDN:** Traces recorded with web traffic passing through the Coral CDN, to test whether a caching proxy sufficiently disguises traffic.

To test each one of these sets, we trained an SVM on all of the *other* sets using only samples from the same MacBook. For example, to study whether the SVM could correctly label traces in the *WiFi* set, we trained the SVM on the *Time, Cache, VPN,* and *CDN* sets in addition to the *Base* set of samples. In contrast to training only on the *Base* set, this training approach avoids overfitting the SVM to that set. After training the classifier, we instructed it to classify the traces in the test set.

The only condition that hurt performance, for two of the three webpages, was the use of the Coral CDN. For `cnn.com`, the classifier incorrectly labeled all traces from the *Coral* set as negatives; for `google.com`, the classifier incorrectly labeled 45 of 50 traces as negatives, resulting in a 10% recall rate. The classifier's poor performance on Coralized pages illustrates that, while the network interface's power consumption may not uniquely determine how a trace is classified, the network interface may still alter the timing of characteristic consumption patterns for *downstream* devices such as the CPU and GPU that act on its outputs. Coralizing `cnet.com` likely made little difference in its classifiability because `cnet.com` is already distributed via a commercial CDN.

The classifier's performance on traces from the *VPN* set deserve special attention. It suggests that encryption and decryption, at least as implemented by our MacBook's

PPTP VPN, have little effect on power-trace classification—i.e., the SVM classifier is robust against VPN encryption. Our MacBook's processor does not include hardware support for the AES-NI instruction set, which is designed to improve AES performance [27]. With AES-NI support, performance and energy efficiency should both be improved, reducing the encryption and decryption impact even further.

Network Location. The Coral results suggest that changes in latency or throughput alter packet arrival times enough to thwart the classifier. To test this hypothesis, we created two static pages that do not have any running scripts or asynchronous content and gathered traces of one MacBook loading each page in different locations. One location had a residential connection and the other a university research network connection. We then trained on all pages in the corpus, including samples of the static pages using only one of the two locations. We tested on samples from the untrained location.

When trained on the residential connection and tested on the university connection, the classifier's precision and recall were 100% and 73% respectively. This result shows that the training did not lead to any false negatives for other pages, but was not able to identify all samples. When we reversed the training and testing locations, the precision and recall were both 100%. This experiment demonstrates that it is not always necessary to use or simulate a potential victim's connection to train an effective classifier, but that the network connection's impact is determined largely by page content.

Tor. Based on the classifier's reduced performance when using Coral, we evaluated Tor [7] configured as a local SOCKS proxy. While Coral introduces higher latencies and less consistent throughput, Tor adds additional complications. Not only does the Tor network add latency and reduce throughput, but Tor includes encryption and decryption operations and the exit node changes unpredictably, which can change the language or content of some pages. We gathered 91 traces of MacBook-1 loading `google.com` and tested them against an SVM trained on samples from all of the other browsing conditions. Tor proved to be a very effective countermeasure, with only 2 of the 91 Tor samples correctly identified, yielding 2% recall.

5.3   Operating System and Machine Diversity

Operating System. Training on traces from a single operating system limits the classifier's effectiveness to that operating system. However, training on traces from two operating systems allows the classifier to correctly identify both OSes. To test this behavior, we gathered traces of `google.com` and `cnn.com` using Windows 7 and Linux (Ubuntu 10.04) on the desktop PC. For both sets of traces, we used the same versions of the Chrome browser and our custom Chrome extension for test automation. When trained only on examples from one operating system, the classifier failed to correctly label traces from the other. The only exception was a single trace of `cnn.com` loaded from Linux, which the classifier identified correctly despite the having been trained only on examples from Windows 7. When we rearranged the input sets so that each contained an equal number of traces from each OS, then trained on one of these mixed sets, the classifier *correctly labeled* all unlabeled traces from the other mixed set.

Differences among OSes include system timers, drivers, memory management, GUI characteristics, and performance tuning. All of these differences may play roles in differentiating power-consumption patterns. The above result suggests that a prospective attacker should collect traces under as many different operating systems as possible.

Machine Diversity. When we varied both machine *and* operating system, the SVM classifier failed to correctly label any traces. We trained an SVM on the MacBook (running Mac OS 10.7.3) with 50 webpages and tested on the Lenovo laptop (running Windows 7) for 5 webpages (google.com, cnn.com, espn.com, live.com, and youtube.com). Then switched the roles and trained and tested again. For all webpages, the SVM failed to correctly label traces from one machine when trained only on examples from the other. The precision and recall never exceeded 10%.

Training on examples from *both* machines allowed the SVM to classify traces from both machines accurately: 98.4% precision and 98.2% recall on average for the 5 webpages. This result suggests that, as in the operating system experiment, the problem lies in the lack of training diversity. In the future, we intend to test this hypothesis by training an SVM on a small, but diverse, set of machines and then testing traces from machines that are not represented in the training set.

5.4   Background Activities

Noting the tendency of users to browse multiple webpages at the same time and running background processes, we measured the classifier's sensitivity to background noise. We randomly chose one of the 51 webpages in our training set—live.com —and loaded it with combinations of background processes. We collected traces for live.com on a MacBook when a combination of the following 4 processes were running: gmail.com, iTunes radio, pandora.com, and a word processor. We collected traces for 8 combinations in total, e.g., only gmail.com; gmail.com, pandora.com, and word processor together, etc. We trained the SVM with examples for all 51 webpages without any background process and tested it using the background examples. In all cases, the classifier was able to classify live.com accurately with 100% precision and 100% recall.

Even though we only tested one webpage and a small set of background processes, the result suggests that the classifier can be robust against combinations of background processes. A possible explanation for the classifier's robustness is that the background processes do not saturate the CPU load and have little effect on the GPU load because they are literally in the background and do not draw to the screen. Quantifying the limits of this robustness will require further investigation.

5.5   Sampling Rate Differentiation

Decreasing the sampling rate at which an instrumented outlet records voltage would allow for tracing and exfiltration using simple, low-cost hardware. To understand how robust the classifier is to changes in sampling rate, we repeated the set of page differentiation tests, but simulated lower sampling rates by restricting the set of input features to those representing lower-frequency components. Figure 4 compares the results with the original sampling rate against results with simulated lower sampling rates. Each reduction in sampling rate is by a factor of two.

Reducing the sampling rate by a factor of more than 30 (from 250 kHz to 7.8 kHz) incurs only a 9% reduction in average precision and recall. These results show that the

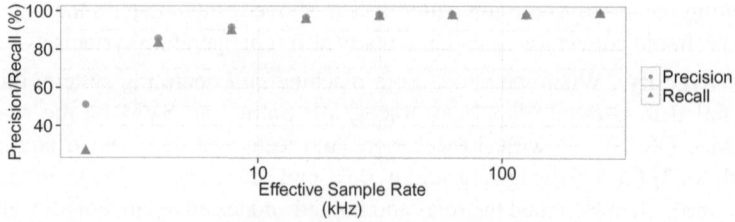

Fig. 4. The average precision and recall across all 51 pages with exponentially increasing sample rate. The classifier's performance decreases with sampling rate, but the precision and recall do not drop below 90% until the sampling rate is less than 4 kHz.

lower frequency bands alone contain enough information to accurately classify webpages. An attacker could likely produce a compact and inexpensive measurement device capable of mounting successful attacks.

5.6   Exclusion of Unknown Pages

Our classifier reliably identifies pages appearing in the training set, but a practical attack would require the classifier to reject pages *not* appearing in the training set as well. With training and testing sets that resembled each other, a classifier could perform equally well in the previous experiments whether it learned to cluster positive or negative examples. To test the hypothesis that the SVMs learned to cluster only *negative* examples during training, we tested them with a set of previously unseen webpage samples that were not in the training set.

We gathered one trace from each of 441 webpages randomly selected from a list of 1 million popular pages published by Alexa [2], making sure to remove pages that were already in the training set. We then tested all 441 pages against all 51 trained SVMs and measured their false-positive rates. The total false positive rate over all classifiers was 1.6%, leading us to reject the above hypothesis and conclude that the SVMs correctly learned to cluster positive examples.

6   Countermeasures to Limit Information Leakage

This section sketches several countermeasures to mitigate the threats described in Section 1. Hardware and software countermeasures both present inherent tradeoffs. Hardware mechanisms that increase design complexity or cost may not find traction with high-volume manufacturers. Software countermeasures that increase computational work may vitiate energy-efficiency measures. Altering workloads to disguise activity may negatively affect usability or user satisfaction. Effective yet usable countermeasures remain an open problem.

Software Countermeasure: Delays and Throttling.   The classifier's poor performance with traces gathered using Coral or Tor suggests that delays complicate classification. Tor in particular is a very effective countermeasure according to our experiments. For users unable or unwilling to use Tor, it may be possible to leverage similar changes in activity patterns. A defensive idea from Song et al. [28] is to introduce random delays in the time domain, which will cause changes in the frequency domain that may confuse our classifier. The problem with random delays, as Song et al. point out, is that different instances of the same private signal, with different random delays added to each, give an attacker enough information to learn the true timing of the signal by simply averaging the delays. The same problem afflicts the defensive strategy of randomizing the order in which the browser loads page elements.

Hardware Countermeasure: Current Filtering. Filtering circuitry that damps current fluctuations could prevent workload-dependent information from leaking onto the AC power line. SMPSes internally implement low-pass filters to remove high-frequency noise and meet government EMI standards [9]. Our experiments reveal that, for the SMPSes we tested, the frequencies useful for classification are below the internal filter's cutoff. A more aggressive low-pass filter or a high-pass filter could remove additional information, but would likely increase the cost and physical size of an SMPS. Our sampling rate experiments show that the classifier is effective until the maximum observable frequency drops below 4 kHz, so much more filtering would likely be required.

7   Related Work

AC Power Event Recognition. This work focuses on classifying run-time events on the order of seconds on a general-purpose computer, in contrast to previous work that measured on–off transitions at a large granularity from a household vantage point. Research on recognizing activity by measuring AC power goes back to at least 1989, when Hart proposed *nonintrusive load monitoring* (NILM) to map changes in total household power consumption to appliance activations [12,13]. Hart also recognized the potential for abuse of NILM techniques. Recently, Gupta et al. proposed ElectriSense, a system that uses a single-point monitor to detect electromagnetic interference (EMI) generated by consumer electronics' switched-mode power supplies [26,11]. Both NILM and ElectriSense effectively capture and identify *on* and *off* events at the device level, but neither aims to infer the internal states of integrated commodity devices such as personal computers, as our work does.

Enev et al. refined the ElectriSense concept by studying the correlation of EMI with video signals being played on modern high-definition televisions [8]. They classified signals (video segments) more than 15 minutes long. In comparison, we focus on classifying signals containing shorter periods of activity and monitor comparatively complex general-purpose hardware. Our sensing apparatus is also somewhat simpler, relying on a single sense resistor and no hardware filtering.

Our prior work has argued that ever-increasing energy proportionality has positive and negative consequences for security and privacy and presented preliminary webpage classification results with a smaller corpus [6]. This work instead focuses specifically on attacks against user privacy and presents a much more in-depth empirical analysis.

Network Traffic Analysis. Past work has, like ours, exploited side channels to learn sensitive information from traffic that may be encrypted. From previous work we borrow the intuition that webpages induce characteristic activity patterns that are robust against encryption and the passage of time. Several researchers have trained classifiers on encrypted or obfuscated web traffic and observed that they could match webpages against their training set using only packet-length information [14,22,23,29]. Our classifier uses AC power traces as input rather than network traces, and so observes a noisier, aggregate side channel.

Parasitic Modulation. Our work focuses on leakage via a wired channel, unlike many past works that focus on leakage via parasitic modulation. Looking at CRT monitors, van Eck published the first unclassified side channel analysis work, demonstrating that the screen image could be reconstructed remotely using a TV receiver and tuned oscillators [31]. Kuhn further analyzed leakage from CRT and LCD monitors based on parasitic modulation [19,20,21]. Vuagnoux and Pasini also investigated leakage via parasitic modulation, though they targeted keyboards rather than monitors and detached their laptop power supplies to avoid interference [32]. Barisani and Bianco independently demonstrated keystroke recovery for PS/2 keyboards by attaching a resistor to the AC power cable, as in our work. They focus only on information from the keyboard and rely on the observation of high-speed switching specified by the PS/2 protocol [3].

DC Power Analysis. Our methods are *not* designed to find key material, unlike past work studying DC circuits that required pin-level access to components or detailed knowledge of the circuits under test. Kocher et al. summarize much of the abundant research on timing and power side channels [17,18]. The most straightforward of these attacks measures a small portion of the complete system and uses domain knowledge to infer the information being processed. This type of attack requires physical access to the system, knowledge of the cryptosystem under attack, and thousands of accurate measurements of the same process.

8   Extensions and Future Work

Alternative Tracing Methods. In our experiments, we physically connect probes to an AC circuit to trace electrical activity. An ancillary goal of this work is to demonstrate that it is possible to covertly modify a power outlet, so physical contact with the computer's power cord is a reasonable expectation under our threat model. However, less-invasive methods exist to measure the current along the power cable. In particular, a *Hall effect sensor*, which measures current via the magnetic field around a wire, could provide a way to trace power consumption if modifying the outlet is infeasible. Such an eavesdropper could easily be removed when not in use. We have not tested our classifier against traces captured with a Hall effect sensor, but we have confirmed that Hall effect sensors matching our sense resistor's sensitivity exist.

Another possibility is indirect measurement similar to that of Enev et al. [8]: connecting measurement equipment in parallel with the victim on the same electrical circuit but on a different outlet. We expect classification performance to decline because of the higher noise floor, but measurements might reveal that traces from outside the victim's outlet are *qualitatively* good enough for an attacker to use.

Adding Classification Features. The current SVM classifier relies solely on a coarse-grained Fourier transform to learn unique webpage features. There are many promising extensions to the feature space that could improve classification performance. One simple extension would be to increase the resolution of the Fourier transforms used to train and test the classifier. Doing so would increase the dimensionality of the feature space, and possibly the classifier's ability to distinguish among webpages.

An extension that takes advantage of SMPS load characteristics would be to simultaneously sample both voltage and current. As Section A discusses, SMPSes are nonlinear loads that pull the voltage and current waveforms out of phase in a way that is related to the workload. The changing relationship between the voltage and current waveforms over time may reveal more information about the state of the system that is orthogonal to raw current consumption.

Detecting Other Activities.   As we have emphasized in this work, computers are complex, general-purpose devices. The space of possible actions that a user might take is vast. While we have focused on web activity in order to address a well-defined, tractable problem, future work could address a broad range of other activities. Tasks as simple as counting keystrokes, regardless of whether different keys can be recognized, may reveal sensitive information. Song et al. have demonstrated that counting keystrokes can reduce the search space for brute-force password cracking by a factor of 50 [28].

9   Conclusions

This work demonstrates that a computer's AC power consumption reveals sensitive information about computing tasks, specifically the webpage that the computer is loading. We designed methods for webpage identification that extract power consumption signatures that are obscure in the time domain but more apparent in the frequency domain. With a data set of over 13,000 power traces of 51 popular webpages, our trained classifier can correctly label unseen traces with 99% precision and 99% recall. The power trace signatures are robust against several variations including the use of an encrypting VPN, background processes, changes in network location, or even the use of a different computer. This is the first paper that quantifies the degree to which information about browsing activity leaks via the AC power supply. We believe it represents an early step in understanding this side channel. The increasing dynamic range of hardware power consumption will lead to further information leakage. Open research problems include the design and evaluation of countermeasures to mitigate the privacy risks of using untrusted power infrastructure.

Acknowledgments. We thank the members of the SPQR group and Erik Learned-Miller for discussions and feedback on drafts. This material is based upon work supported by the National Science Foundation under Grant No. GEO-1124657, CNS-0845671, CNS-0923313, CNS-1331652, and S121000000211. This publication was made possible by Cooperative Agreement No. 90TR0003/01 from the Department of Health and Human Services. Its contents are solely the responsibility of the authors and do not necessarily represent the official views of the National Science Foundation or HHS.

References

1. iMacros for Firefox (loaded September 2011),
   http://www.iopus.com/imacros/firefox/
2. Alexa Internet, Inc. Top 1,000,000 sites (updated daily) (loaded February 12, 2012),
   http://s3.amazonaws.com/alexa-static/top-1m.csv.zip
3. Barisani, A., Bianco, D.: Sniffing keystrokes with lasers/voltmeters. CanSecWest (March 2009), Presentation slides
4. Becker, G.T., Strobel, D., Paar, C., Burleson, W.: Detecting software theft in embedded systems: A side-channel approach. IEEE Transactions on Information Forensics and Security 7(4) (August 2012)
5. Chang, C.-C., Lin, C.-J.: LIBSVM: A library for support vector machines. ACM Transactions on Intelligent Systems and Technology 2 (2011)
6. Clark, S.S., Ransford, B., Fu, K.: Potentia est scientia: Security and privacy implications of energy-proportional computing. In: HotSec 2012 (August 2012)
7. Dingledine, R., Mathewson, N., Syverson, P.: Tor: The second-generation onion router. In: USENIX Security Symposium (August 2004)
8. Enev, M., Gupta, S., Kohno, T., Patel, S.: Televisions, video privacy, and powerline electromagnetic interference. In: ACM Conference on Computer and Communications Security (CCS) (October 2011)
9. Federal Communications Commission. Code of Federal Regulations, Title 47, Part 15, Sections 101–103 (October 2010)
10. Freedman, M.J., Freudenthal, E., Mazières, D.: Democratizing content publication with Coral. In: USENIX/ACM Symposium on Networked Systems Design and Implementation (NSDI) (March 2004)
11. Gupta, S., Reynolds, M.S., Patel, S.N.: ElectriSense: Single-point sensing using EMI for electrical event detection and classification in the home. In: International Conference on Ubiquitous Computing (UbiComp) (September 2010)
12. Hart, G.W.: Residential energy monitoring and computerized surveillance via utility power flows. IEEE Technology and Society Magazine (June 1989)
13. Hart, G.W.: Nonintrusive appliance load monitoring. Proceedings of the IEEE 80(12) (1992)
14. Hintz, A.: Fingerprinting websites using traffic analysis. In: Dingledine, R., Syverson, P.F. (eds.) PET 2002. LNCS, vol. 2482, pp. 171–178. Springer, Heidelberg (2003)
15. Hsu, C.-W.: Multi-label classification, http://www.csie.ntu.edu.tw/~cjlin/
   #multi_label_classification
16. Internet Archive. Internet archive wayback machine (loaded March 2013),
   http://archive.org/web/web.php
17. Kocher, P.C.: Timing attacks on implementations of diffie-hellman, RSA, DSS, and other systems. In: Koblitz, N. (ed.) CRYPTO 1996. LNCS, vol. 1109, pp. 104–113. Springer, Heidelberg (1996)
18. Kocher, P., Jaffe, J., Jun, B.: Differential power analysis. In: Wiener, M. (ed.) CRYPTO 1999. LNCS, vol. 1666, pp. 388–397. Springer, Heidelberg (1999)
19. Kuhn, M.G.: Electromagnetic eavesdropping risks of flat-panel displays. In: Martin, D., Serjantov, A. (eds.) PET 2004. LNCS, vol. 3424, pp. 88–107. Springer, Heidelberg (2005)
20. Kuhn, M.G.: Security limits for compromising emanations. In: Rao, J.R., Sunar, B. (eds.) CHES 2005. LNCS, vol. 3659, pp. 265–279. Springer, Heidelberg (2005)
21. Kuhn, M.G., Anderson, R.J.: Soft tempest: Hidden data transmission using electromagnetic emanations. In: Aucsmith, D. (ed.) IH 1998. LNCS, vol. 1525, pp. 124–142. Springer, Heidelberg (1998)
22. Liberatore, M., Levine, B.N.: Inferring the source of encrypted HTTP connections. In: ACM Conference on Computer and Communications Security (CCS) (October 2006)

23. Lu, L., Chang, E.-C., Chan, M.C.: Website fingerprinting and identification using ordered feature sequences. In: Gritzalis, D., Preneel, B., Theoharidou, M. (eds.) ESORICS 2010. LNCS, vol. 6345, pp. 199–214. Springer, Heidelberg (2010)
24. Molina-Markham, A., Shenoy, P., Fu, K., Cecchet, E., Irwin, D.: Private memoirs of a smart meter. In: ACM Workshop on Embedded Sensing Systems for Energy-Efficiency in Buildings (BuildSys) (November 2010)
25. P3 International. P3 — Kill A Watt (loaded February 13, 2012), http://www.p3international.com/products/special/P4400/P4400-CE.html
26. Patel, S.N., Robertson, T., Kientz, J.A., Reynolds, M.S., Abowd, G.D.: At the flick of a switch: Detecting and classifying unique electrical events on the residential power line (Nominated for the best paper award). In: Krumm, J., Abowd, G.D., Seneviratne, A., Strang, T. (eds.) UbiComp 2007. LNCS, vol. 4717, pp. 271–288. Springer, Heidelberg (2007)
27. Rott, J.: Intel Advanced Encryption Standard instructions (AES-NI) (February 2012), http://software.intel.com/en-us/articles/intel-advanced-encryption-standard-instructions-aes-ni
28. Song, D.X., Wagner, D., Tian, X.: Timing analysis of keystrokes and timing attacks on SSH. In: USENIX Security Symposium (August 2001)
29. Sun, Q., et al.: Statistical identification of encrypted web browsing traffic. In: IEEE Symposium on Security and Privacy (May 2002)
30. United States Environmental Protection Agency. ENERGY STAR program requirements for computers (July 2009), http://www.energystar.gov/ia/partners/prod_development/revisions/downloads/computer/Version5.0_Computer_Spec.pdf
31. van Eck, W.: Electromagnetic radiation from video display units: An eavesdropping risk? Computers & Security 4(4) (December 1985)
32. Vuagnoux, M., Pasini, S.: Compromising electromagnetic emanations of wired and wireless keyboards. In: USENIX Security Symposium (August 2009)
33. White, A.M., Matthews, A.R., Snow, K.Z., Monrose, F.: Phonotactic reconstruction of encrypted VoIP conversations: Hookt on Fon-iks. In: IEEE Symposium on Security and Privacy (May 2011)
34. Wright, C.V., Ballard, L., Monrose, F., Masson, G.M.: Language identification of encrypted VoIP traffic: Alejandra y Roberto or Alice and Bob? In: USENIX Security Symposium (August 2007)
35. Yee, B., Sehr, D., Dardyk, G., Chen, B., Muth, R., Ormandy, T., Okasaka, S., Narula, N., Fullagar, N.: Native Client: A sandbox for portable, untrusted x86 native code. In: IEEE Symposium on Security and Privacy (May 2009)

A   Hardware Specifications

MacBook-1: 2008 model, dual-core Intel Core 2 Duo processor, 4 GB of RAM, Intel GMA X3100 GPU, 80 GB Corsair SATA II MLC solid-state drive, and Mac OS 10.6.8. We removed the battery from MacBook-1 during all experiments.

MacBook-2: 2008 model, dual-core Intel Core 2 Duo processor, 4 GB of RAM, Intel GMA X3100 GPU, 320 GB SATA magnetic drive, and Mac OS 10.7.3. The battery remained in MacBook-2 during all experiments.

Dell Vostro desktop PC: quad-core Intel Core i5 processor, 4 GB of RAM, AMD Radeon 6450 GPU, and 250 GB SATA magnetic drive. We tested the desktop PC under Windows 7 and Ubuntu 10.04.

Lenovo T410 Laptop: Intel Core i5 processor, 4 GB of RAM, 300 GB SATA magnetic drive, and Windows 7 OS. The battery remained in the laptop during all experiments.

Eliminating Cache-Based Timing Attacks
with Instruction-Based Scheduling

Deian Stefan[1], Pablo Buiras[2], Edward Z. Yang[1], Amit Levy[1], David Terei[1],
Alejandro Russo[2], and David Mazières[1]

[1] Stanford University
[2] Chalmers University of Technology

Abstract. Information flow control allows untrusted code to access sensitive and trustworthy information without leaking this information. However, the presence of covert channels subverts this security mechanism, allowing processes to communicate information in violation of IFC policies. In this paper, we show that concurrent deterministic IFC systems that use time-based scheduling are vulnerable to a cache-based internal timing channel. We demonstrate this vulnerability with a concrete attack on Hails, one particular IFC web framework. To eliminate this internal timing channel, we implement instruction-based scheduling, a new kind of scheduler that is indifferent to timing perturbations from underlying hardware components, such as the cache, TLB, and CPU buses. We show this scheduler is secure against cache-based internal timing attacks for applications using a single CPU. To show the feasibility of instruction-based scheduling, we have implemented a version of Hails that uses the CPU retired-instruction counters available on commodity Intel and AMD hardware. We show that instruction-based scheduling does not impose significant performance penalties. Additionally, we formally prove that our modifications to Hails' underlying IFC system preserve non-interference in the presence of caches.

1 Introduction

The rise of extensible web applications, like the Facebook Platform, is spurring interest in information flow control (IFC) [27, 35]. Popular platforms like Facebook give approved apps full access to users' sensitive data, including the ability to violate security policies set by users. In contrast, IFC allows websites to run untrusted, third-party apps that operate on sensitive user data [11, 21], ensuring they abide by security policies in a mandatory fashion.

Recently, Hails [11], a web-platform framework built atop the LIO IFC system [39, 40], has been used to implement websites that integrate third-party untrusted apps. For example, the code-hosting website GitStar.com built with Hails uses untrusted apps to deliver core features, including a code viewer and wiki. GitStar relies on LIO's IFC mechanism to enforce robust privacy policies on user data and code.

LIO, like other IFC systems, ensures that untrusted code does not write data that may have been influenced by sensitive sources to public sinks. For example, an untrusted address-book app is allowed to compute over Alice's friends list and display a stylized version of the list to Alice, but it cannot leak any information about her friends to arbitrary end-points. The flexibility of IFC makes it particularly suitable for the web, where access control lists often prove either too permissive or too restrictive.

J. Crampton, S. Jajodia, and K. Mayes (Eds.): ESORICS 2013, LNCS 8134, pp. 718–735, 2013.

However, a key limitation of IFC is the presence of *covert channels*, i.e., "channels" not intended for communication that nevertheless allow code to subvert security policies and share information [22]. A great deal of research has identified and analyzed covert channels [25]. In this work, we focus on the *internal timing covert channel*, which occurs when sensitive data is used to manipulate the timing behavior of threads so that other threads can observe the order in which shared public resources are used [38, 44]. Though we do not believe our solution to the internal timing covert channel affects (either positively or negatively) other timing channels, such as the external timing covert channel, which is derived from measuring external events [1, 5, 12] (e.g., wall-clock), addressing these channels is beyond our present scope.

LIO eliminates the internal timing covert channel by restricting how programmers write code. Programmers are required to explicitly decouple computations that manipulate sensitive data from those that can write to public resources, eliminating covert channels *by construction*. However, decoupling only works when *all* shared resources are modeled. LIO only considers shared resources that are expressible by the programming language, e.g., shared-variables, file descriptors, semaphores, channels, etc. Implicit operating system and hardware state can still be exploited to alter the timing behavior of threads, and thus leak information. Reexamining LIO, we found that the underlying CPU cache can be used to introduce an internal timing covert channel that leaks sensitive data. A trivial attack can leak data at 0.75 bits/s and, despite the low bandwidth, we were able to leak all the collaborators on a private GitStar.com project in less than a minute.

Several countermeasures to cache-based attacks have previously been considered, primarily in the context of cryptosystems following the work of Kocher [18] (see Section 8). Unfortunately, many of the techniques are not designed for IFC scenarios. For example, modifying an algorithm implementation, as in the case of AES [7], does not naturally generalize to arbitrary untrusted code. Similarly, flushing or disabling the cache when switching protection domains, as suggested in [6, 49], is prohibitively expensive in systems like Hails, where context switches occur hundreds of times per second. Finally, relying on specialized hardware, such as partitioned caches [29], which isolate the effects of one partition from code using a different partition, restricts the deployability and scalability of the solution; partitioned caches are not readily available and often cannot be partitioned to an arbitrary security lattice.

This paper describes a countermeasure for cache-based attacks when execution is confined to a single CPU. Our method generalizes to arbitrary code, imposes minimal performance overhead, scales to an arbitrary security lattice, and leverages hardware features already present in modern CPUs. Specifically, we present an instruction-based scheduler that eliminates internal timing channels in concurrent programs that time-slice a single CPU and contend for the same cache, TLB, bus, and other hardware facilities. We implement the scheduler for the LIO IFC system and demonstrate that, under realistic restrictions, our scheduler eliminates such attacks in Hails web applications.

Our contributions are as follows.

▶ We implement a cache-based internal timing attack for LIO.
▶ We close the cache-based covert channel by scheduling user-level threads on a single CPU core based on the number of instructions they execute (as opposed to the

amount of time they execute). Our scheduler can be used to implement other concurrent IFC systems which implicitly assume instruction-level scheduling (e.g., [13, 14, 32, 38, 46]).

▶ We implement our instruction-based scheduler as part of the Glasgow Haskell Compiler (GHC) runtime system, atop which LIO and Hails are built. We use CPU performance counters, prevalent on most modern CPUs, to pre-empt threads according to the number of retired instructions. The measured impact on performance, when compared to time-based scheduling, is negligible.

We believe these techniques to be applicable to operating systems that enforce IFC, including [20, 26, 47], though at a higher cost in performance for application code that is highly optimized for locality (see Section 5).

▶ We augment the LIO [40] semantics to model the cache and formally prove that instruction-based scheduling removes leaks due to caches.

The paper is organized as follows. Section 2 discusses cache-based attacks and existing countermeasures. In Section 3 presents our instruction-based scheduling solution. Section 4 describes our modifications to GHC's runtime, while Section 5 analyses their performance impact. Formal guarantees and discussions of our approach are detailed in Sections 6 and 7. We describe related work in Section 8 and conclude in Section 9.

2   Cache Attacks and Countermeasures

The severity of information leakage attacks through the CPU hardware cache has been widely considered by the cryptographic community (e.g. [28, 31]). Unlike crypto work, where attackers extract sensitive information through the execution of a fixed crypto algorithm, we consider a scenario in which the attacker provides arbitrary code in a concurrent IFC system. In our scenario, the adversary is a developer that implements a Hails app that interfaces with user-sensitive data using LIO libraries.

We found that, knowing only the cache size of the underlying CPU, we can easily build an app that exploits the shared cache to carry out an internal timing attack that leaks sensitive data at 0.75 bits/s. Several IFC systems, including [13, 14, 32, 38, 40, 46], model internal timing attacks and address them by ensuring that the outcome of a race to a public resource does not depend on secret data. Unfortunately, these systems only account for resources explicitly modeled at the programming language level and not underlying OS or hardware state, such as the CPU cache or TLB. Hence, even though the semantics of these systems rely on instruction-based scheduling (usually to simplify expressing reduction rules), real-world implementations use time-based scheduling for which the formal guarantees do not hold. The instruction-based scheduler proposed in this work can be used to make the assumptions of such concurrent IFC systems match the situation in practice. In the remainder of this section, we show the internal timing attack that leverages the hardware cache. We also discuss several existing countermeasures that could be employed by Hails.

2.1   Example Cache Attack

We mount an internal timing attack by influencing the scheduling behavior of threads through the cache. Consider the code shown in Figure 1. The attack leaks the secret

| 1. | `lowArray := new Array[M];` |
| 2. | `fillArray(lowArray)` |

1. `if secret`	1. `for i in [1..n]`	1. `for i in [1..n+m]`
2. `then highArray := new Array[M]`	2. `skip`	2. `skip`
3. `fillArray(highArray)`	3. `readArray(lowArray)`	3. `outputLow(0)`
4. `else skip`	4. `outputLow(1)`	
thread 1	thread 2	thread 3

Fig. 1. A simple cache attack

boolean value `secret` in thread 1 by affecting when thread 2 writes to the public channel relative to thread 3.

The program starts (lines 1–2) by creating and initializing a public array `lowArray` whose size M corresponds to the cache size; `fillArray` simply sets every element of the array to 0 (this will place the array in the cache). The program then spawns three threads that run concurrently. Assuming a round-robin time-based scheduler, the execution of the attack proceeds as illustrated in Figure 2, where `secret` is set to true (top) and false (bottom), respectively.

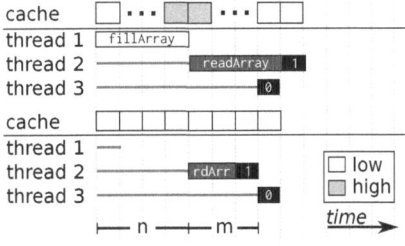

Fig. 2. Execution of the cache attack with `secret` true (top) and false (bottom)

▶ Depending on the secret value `secret`, thread 1 either performs a no-operation (`skip` on line 4), leaving the cache intact, or evicts `lowArray` from the cache (lines 2–3) by creating and initializing a new (non-public) array `highArray`.

▶ We assume that thread 1 takes less than n steps to complete its execution—a number that can be determined experimentally; in Figure 2, n is four. Hence, to allow all the effects on the cache due to thread 1 to settle, thread 2 delays its computation by n steps (lines 1–2). Subsequently, the thread reads every element of the public array `lowArray` (line 3), and finally writes 1 to a public output channel (line 4). Crucial to carrying out the attack, the duration of thread 2's reads (line 3) depends on the state of the cache: if the cache was modified by thread 1, i.e., `secret` is true, thread 2 needs to wait for all the public data to be retrieved from memory (as opposed to the cache) before producing an output. This requires evicting `highArray` from the cache and fetching `lowArray`, a process that takes a non-negligible amount of time. However, if the cache was not touched by thread 1, i.e., `secret` is false, thread 2 will get few cache misses and thus produce its output with no delay.

▶ We assume that thread 2 takes less than m, where m<n, steps to complete reading `lowArray` (line 3) when the reads hit the cache, i.e., `lowArray` was not replaced by `highArray`. Like n, this metric can be determined experimentally; in Figure 2, m is three. Using this, thread 3 simply delays its computation by n+m steps (lines 1–2) and then writes 0 to a public output channel (line 3). The role of thread 3 is solely to

serve as a baseline for thread 2's output: producing its output before thread 2 when the latter is filling the cache, i.e., secret is true; conversely, it produces an output after thread 2 if thread 1 did not touch the cache, i.e., secret is false.

We remark that the race between thread 2 and thread 3 to write to a shared public channel, influenced by the cache state, is precisely what facilitates the attack. We described how to leak a single bit, but the attack can easily be magnified by wrapping it in a loop. Note also that we have assumed the attacker has complete control of the cache—i.e., the cache is not affected by other code running in parallel. However, the attack is still plausible under weaker assumptions so long as the attacker deals with the additional noise, as exemplified by the timing attacks on AES [28].

2.2 Existing Countermeasures

The internal timing attack arises as a result of cache effects influencing thread-scheduling behavior. Hence, one series of countermeasures addresses the problem through low-level CPU features that provide better control of the cache.

Flushing the cache.   Naively, we can flush the cache on every context switch. In the context of Figure 1, this guarantees that, when thread 2 executes the readArray instruction, its duration is not affected by thread 1 evicting lowArray from the cache—the cache will *always* be flushed on a context switch, hence thread 3 will always write to the output channel first.

No-fill cache mode.   Several architectures, including Intel's Xeon and Pentium 4, support a cache *no-fill* mode [15]. In this mode, read/write hits access the cache; misses, however, read from and write to memory directly, leaving the cache unchanged. As considered by Zhang et al. [49], we can execute all threads that operate on non-public data in this mode. This approach guarantees that sensitive data cannot affect the cache. Unfortunately, threads operating on non-public data and relying on the cache will suffer from performance degradation.

Partitioned cache.   Another approach is to partition the cache according to the number of security levels, as suggested in [49]. Using this architecture, a thread computing on secret data only accesses the secret partition, while a thread computing on public data only access the public one. This approach effectively corresponds to giving each differently-labeled thread access to its own cache and, as a result, the scheduling behavior of public threads cannot be affected by evicting data from the cache.

Unfortunately, none of the aforementioned solutions can be used in systems built with Hails (e.g., GitStar). Flushing the cache is prohibitively expensive for preemptive systems that perform a context switch hundreds of times per second—the impact on performance would gravely reduce usability. The no-fill mode solution is well suited for systems wherein the majority of the threads operate on public data. In such cases, only threads operating on sensitive data will incur a performance penalty. However, in the context of Hails, the solution is only slightly less expensive than flushing the cache. Hails threads handle HTTP requests that operate on individual (non-public) user data, hence most threads will not be using the cache. Another consequence of threads handling differently-labeled data is that partitioned caches can only be used in a limited way (see Section 8). Specifically, to address internal timing attacks, it is required that we

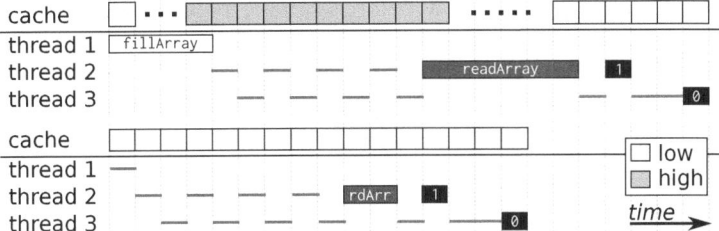

Fig. 3. Execution of cache attack program of Figure 1 with `secret` set to true (top) and false (bottom). In both executions, we highlight that the threads execute one "instruction" at a time in a round-robin fashion. The concurrent threads take the same amount of time to complete execution as in Figure 2. However, since we use instructions to context switch threads, the interleaving between thread 2 or 3 is not influenced by the actions in thread 1, and thus the internal timing attack does not arise—the threads' output order cannot encode sensitive data.

partition the cache according to the number of security levels in the lattice. Given that most existing approaches can only partition caches up to 16-ways at the OS level [24], and fewer at the hardware level, an alternative scalable approach is necessary. Moreover, neither flushing nor partitioning the cache can handle timing perturbations arising from other pieces of hardware such as the TLB, buses, etc.

3   Instruction-Based Scheduling

As the example in Figure 2 shows, races to acquire public resources are affected by the cache state, which in turn might be affected by secret values. It is important to highlight that the number of instructions executed in a given quantum of time might vary depending on the state of the cache. It is precisely this variability that reintroduces dangerous races into systems. However, the actual set of instructions executed is not affected by the cache. Hence, we propose scheduling threads according to the number of instructions they execute, rather than the amount of time they consume. The point at which a thread produces an output (or any other visible operation) is determined according to the number of instructions it has executed, a measurement unaffected by the amount of time it takes to perform a read/write from memory.

Consider the code in Figure 1 executing atop an instruction-based scheduler. An illustration of this is shown in Figure 3. For simplicity of exposition, the instruction granularity is at the level of commands (`skip`, `readArray`, etc.) and therefore context switches are triggered after one command gets executed. (In Section 4, we describe a more practical and realistic instruction-based scheduler.) Observe that the amount of time it takes to execute an instruction has not changed from the time-based scheduler of Figure 2. For example, `readArray` still takes 6 units of time when `secret` is true, and 2 when it is false. Unlike Figure 2, however, the interleaving between thread 2 and thread 3 did not change depending on the state of the cache (which did change according to `secret`). Therefore, a race to write to the public channel between thread 2 and thread 3 cannot be caused by the secret, through the cache. The second thread always executes $n+1 = 5$ instructions before writing 1 to the public channel, while the third thread always executes $n+m+1 = 8$ instructions before writing 0.

Our proposed countermeasure, the implementation of which is detailed in Section 4, eliminates the cache-based internal timing attacks without sacrificing scalability and with a minor performance impact. With instruction-based scheduling, we do not require flushing of the cache. In this manner, applications can safely utilize the cache to retain most of their performance without giving up system security, and unlike current partitioned caches, we can scale up to consider arbitrarily complex lattices.

4   Implementation

We implemented an instruction-based scheduler for LIO. In this section, we describe this implementation and detail some key design features we believe to be useful when modifying concurrent IFC systems to address cache-based timing attacks.

4.1   LIO and Haskell

LIO is a Haskell library that exposes concurrency to programmers in the form of "green," lightweight threads. Each LIO thread is a *native* Haskell thread that has an associated security level (label) which is used to track and control the flow of information to/from the thread. LIO relies on Haskell libraries for creating new threads and the runtime system for managing them.

In general, M lightweight Haskell threads may concurrently execute on N OS threads. (It is common, however, for multiple Haskell threads to execute on a single OS thread, i.e., $M : 1$ mapping.) The Haskell runtime, as implemented by the GHC system, uses a round-robin scheduler to context switch between concurrently executing threads. Specifically, the scheduler is invoked whenever a thread blocks/terminates or a timer signal alarm is received. The timer is used to guarantee that the scheduler is periodically executed, allowing the runtime to implement preemptive scheduling.

4.2   Instruction-Based Scheduler

As previously mentioned, timing-based schedulers render systems, such as LIO, vulnerable to cache-based internal timing attacks. We implement our instruction-based scheduler as a drop-in replacement for the existing GHC scheduler, using the number of retired instructions to trigger a context switch.

Specifically, we use performance monitoring units (PMUs) present in almost all recent Intel [15] and AMD [3] CPUs. PMUs expose hardware performance counters that are typically used by developers to optimize code—they provide metrics such as the number of cache misses, instructions executed per cycle, branch mispredictions, etc. Importantly, PMUs also provide a means for counting the number of retired instructions.

Using the perfmon2 [9] Linux monitoring interface and helper user-level library libpfm4, we modified the GHC runtime to configure the underlying PMU to count the number of retired instructions the Haskell process is executing. Specifically, with perfmon2 we set a data performance counter register to $2^{64} - n$, which the CPU increments upon retiring an instruction.[1] Once the counter overflows, i.e., n instructions have been retired, perfmon2 is sent a hardware interrupt. In our implementation, we configured perfmon2 to handle the interrupt by delivering a signal to the GHC runtime.

If threads share no resources, upon receiving a signal, the executing Haskell thread can immediately save its state and jump to the scheduler. However, preempting a thread which is operating on a shared memory space can be dangerous, as the thread may have left memory in an inconsistent state. (This is the case for many language runtimes, not solely GHC's.) To avoid this, GHC produces code that contains *safe points* where threads may yield. Hence, a signal does not cause an immediate preemption. Instead, the signal handler simply sets a flag indicating the arrival of a signal; at the next safe point, the thread "cooperatively" yields to the scheduler.

To ensure liveness, we must guarantee that given any point in execution, a safe point is reached in n instructions. Though GHC already inserts many safe points as a means of invoking the garbage collector (via the scheduler), tight loops that do not perform any allocation are known to hang execution [10]. Addressing this eight-year old bug, which would otherwise be a security concern in LIO, we modified the compiler to insert safe points on function entry points. This modification, integrated in the mainline GHC, has almost no effect on performance and only a 7% bloat in average binary size.

4.3 Handling IO

Threads yield at safe points in their execution paths as a result of a retired instruction signal. However, there are circumstances in which threads would like to explicitly yield prior to the reception of a retired instruction signal. In particular, when a thread performs a blocking operation, it immediately yields to the scheduler, registering itself to wake up when the operation completes. Thus, any IO action is a yield which allows the thread to give up the rest of its scheduling quantum.

While yields are not intrinsically unsafe, it is not safe to allow the leftover scheduling quantum to be passed on to the next thread. Thus, after running any asynchronous IO action, the runtime must reset the retired instruction counter. Hence, whenever a thread enters the scheduler loop due to being blocked, we reset the retired instruction counter.

5   Performance Evaluation

We evaluated the performance of instruction-based scheduling against existing time-based approaches using the nofib benchmark suite [30]. nofib is the standard benchmarking suite used for measuring the performance of Haskell implementations.

In our experimental setup, we used the latest development version of GHC (the Git master branch as of November 6, 2012). The measurements were taken on the same hardware as Hails [11]: a machine with two dual-core Intel Xeon E5620 (2.4GHz) processors, and 48GB of RAM.

---

[1] Though the bit-width of the hardware counters vary (they are typically 40-bits wide) perfmon2 internally manages a 64-bit counter.

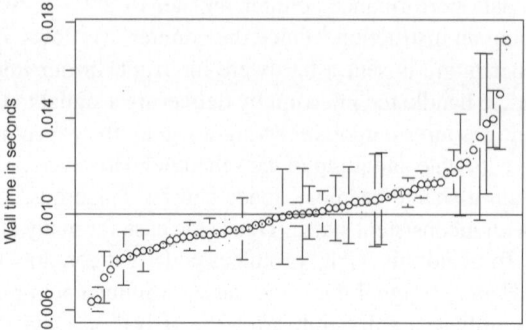

Fig. 4. Mean time between timer signal and retired-instruction signal. Each point represents a program from nofib, which have been sorted on the *x*-axis by their mean time.

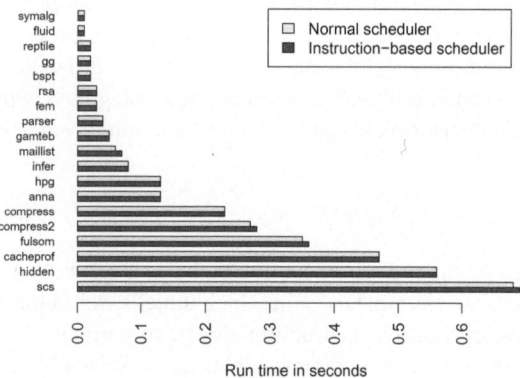

Fig. 5. Change to run time from instruction-based scheduling

We first needed to find an instruction budget—number of instructions to retire before triggering the scheduler. We found a poorly chosen instruction budget could increase runtime by 100%. To determine a good parameter, we measured the mean time between retired-instruction signals with an initially guessed instruction budget parameter. We then adjusted the parameter so the median test program had a 10 millisecond mean time-slice (the default quantum size in vanilla GHC with time-based scheduling) and verified our final choice by re-running the measurements. For our specific setup, an instruction budget of approximately 37,100,000 retired-instructions corresponded to a 10 millisecond time quantum. We plot the mean and standard deviation across all nofib applications with the final tuning parameter in Figure 4. We found that most programs receive a signal within 2 milliseconds of when they would have normally received the signal using the standard time-based scheduler. While the instruction budget parameter will vary across machines, it is relatively simple to bootstrap this parameter by performing these measurements at startup and tuning the budget accordingly.

Next, we compared the performance of Haskell's timer-based scheduler with our instruction-based scheduler. We used a subset of the nofib benchmark suite called the real benchmark, which consists of "real world programs", as opposed to synthetic benchmarks (however, results for the whole nofib suite are comparable). Figure 5 shows the run time of these programs with both scheduling approaches. With an optimized instruction budget parameter, instruction-based scheduling has no impact to the runtime of the majority of nofib applications and results in only a very slight increase in runtime for others (about 1%).

This result may seem surprising: instruction-based scheduling purposely punishes threads with good data locality, so one might expect a more substantial performance impact. We hypothesize that this is the case due to two reasons. First, with preemptive scheduling, we are already inducing cache misses when we switch from running one thread to another—instruction-based scheduling only perturbs when these preempts occur, and as seen in Figure 4, these perturbations are very minor. Second, modern L2 caches are quite large, meaning that hardware is more forgiving of poor data locality—an effect that has been measured in the behavior of stock lazy functional programs [2].

6   Cache-Aware Semantics

In this section we recall relevant design aspects of LIO [40] and extend the original formalization to consider how caches affect the timing behavior of programs. Importantly, we formalize instruction-based scheduling and show how it removes cache-based internal timing covert channels.

6.1   LIO Overview

At a high level, LIO provides the LIO monad, which is used in place of IO. Wrapping standard Haskell libraries, LIO exports a collection of functions that untrusted code may use to access the filesystem, network, shared variables, etc. Unlike the standard libraries, which usually return IO actions, these functions return actions in the LIO monad, thus allowing LIO to perform label checks before executing a potentially unsafe action.

Internally, the LIO monad keeps track of a *current label*, L_{cur}. The current label is effectively a ceiling over the labels of all data that the current computation may depend on. This label eliminates the need to label individual definitions and bindings: symbols in scope are (conceptually) labeled with L_{cur}.[2] Hence, when a computation C, with current label L_C, observes an object labeled L_O, C's label is raised to the least upper bound or *join* of the two labels, written $L_C \sqcup L_O$. Importantly the current label governs where the current computation can write, what labels may be used when creating new channels or threads, etc. For example, after reading O, the computation should not be able to write to a channel K if L_C is more restricting than L_K—this would potentially leak sensitive information (about O) into a less sensitive channel.

Note that an LIO computation can only execute a sub-computation on sensitive data by either raising its current label or forking a new thread in which to execute this sub-computation. In the former case, raising the current label prevents writing to less sensitive endpoints. In the latter case, to observe the result (or timing and termination behavior) of the sub-computation the thread must wait for the forked thread to finish, which

---

[2] As described in [39], LIO does, however, allow programmers to heterogeneously label data they consider sensitive.

(STEP)
$$\frac{\{\Sigma, \langle \sigma, e \rangle\}_\zeta \longrightarrow_k \{\Sigma', \langle \sigma', e' \rangle\}_{\zeta'} \qquad q > 0}{\{\Sigma, \zeta, q, \langle \sigma, e \rangle \lhd t_s\} \hookrightarrow \{\Sigma', \zeta', q - k, \langle \sigma', e' \rangle \lhd t_s\}}$$

(PREEMPT)
$$\frac{q \leq 0}{\{\Sigma, \zeta, q, t \lhd t_s\} \hookrightarrow \{\Sigma, \zeta, q_i, t_s \rhd t\}}$$

Fig. 6. Semantics for threadpools under round-robin time-based scheduling

first raises the current label. A consequence of this design is that differently-labeled computations are decoupled, which, as mentioned in Section 1, is key to eliminating the internal timing covert channel.

In the next subsection, we will outline the semantics for a cache-aware, time-based scheduler where the cache attack described in Section 2 is possible. Moreover, we show that we can easily adapt this semantics to model the new LIO instruction-based scheduler. Interested readers may refer to the extended version of the paper, which can be found online at [41].

6.2 Cache-Aware Semantics

We model the underlying CPU cache as an abstract memory shared among all running threads, which we will denote with the symbol ζ. Every step of the sequential execution relation will affect ζ according to the current instruction being executed, the runtime environment, and the existing state of the cache. As in [40], each LIO thread has a thread-local runtime environment σ, which contains the current label $\sigma.\text{lbl}$. The global environment Σ, common to all threads, holds references to shared resources.

In addition, we explicitly model the number of machine cycles taken by a single execution step as a result of the cache. Specifically, the transition $\zeta \rightarrow_k^{(\Sigma,\sigma,e)} \zeta'$ captures the parameters that influence the cache (Σ, σ, and e) as well as the number of cycles k it takes for the cache to be updated.

A *cache-aware* evaluation step is obtained by merging the reduction rule of LIO with our formalization of CPU cache as given below:

$$\frac{\{\Sigma, \langle \sigma, e \rangle\} \xrightarrow{\gamma} \{\Sigma', \langle \sigma', e' \rangle\} \qquad \zeta \rightarrow_k^{(\Sigma,\sigma,e)} \zeta' \qquad k \geq 1}{\{\Sigma, \langle \sigma, e \rangle\}_\zeta \xrightarrow{\gamma}_k \{\Sigma', \langle \sigma', e' \rangle\}_{\zeta'}}$$

We read $\{\Sigma, \langle \sigma, e \rangle\}_\zeta \xrightarrow{\gamma}_k \{\Sigma', \langle \sigma', e' \rangle\}_{\zeta'}$ as "the configuration $\{\Sigma, \langle \sigma, e \rangle\}$ reduces to $\{\Sigma', \langle \sigma', e' \rangle\}$ in one step, but k machine cycles, producing event γ and modifying the cache from ζ to ζ'." As in LIO [40], the relation $\{\Sigma, \langle \sigma, e \rangle\} \xrightarrow{\gamma} \{\Sigma', \langle \sigma', e' \rangle\}$ represents a single execution step from thread expression e, under the run-time environments Σ and σ, to thread expression e' and run-time environments Σ' and σ'. Events are used to communicate information between the threads and the scheduler, e.g., when spawning new threads.

Figure 6 shows the most important rules of our time-based scheduler in the presence of cache effects. We elide the rest of the rules for brevity. The relation $\hookrightarrow$ represents a single evaluation step for the program threadpool, in contrast with $\longrightarrow$ which is only for a single thread. Configurations are of the form $\{\Sigma, \zeta, q, t_s\}$, where q is the number of cycles available in the current time slice and t_s is a queue of thread configurations of the form $\langle \sigma, e \rangle$. We use a standard deque-like interface with operations $\lhd$ and $\rhd$ for front and back insertion, respectively, i.e., $\langle \sigma, e \rangle \lhd t_s$ denotes a threadpool in which the first thread is $\langle \sigma, e \rangle$ while $t_s \rhd \langle \sigma, e \rangle$ indicates that $\langle \sigma, e \rangle$ is the last one.

As in LIO, threads are scheduled in a round-robin fashion. Our scheduler relies on the number of cycles that each step takes; we respectively write q_i and q as the initial and remaining number of cycles assigned to a thread in each quantum. In rule (STEP), the number of cycles k that the current instruction takes is reflected in the scheduling quantum. Consequently, threads that compute on data that is not present in the cache will take more cycles, i.e., have a higher k, so they will run "slower" because they are allowed to perform fewer reduction steps in the remaining time slice. In practice, this permits attacks, such as that in Figure 1, where the interleaving of the threads can be affected by sensitive data. Rule (PREEMPT) is used when the thread has exhausted its cycle budget, triggering a context switch by moving the current thread to the end of the queue.

We can adapt this semantics to reflect the behavior of the new instruction-based scheduler. To this end, we replace the number of cycles q with an instruction budget; we write b_i for the initial instruction budget and b for the current budget. Crucially, we change rule (STEP) into rule (STEP-CA), given by

$$
(\text{STEP-CA})
$$
$$
\frac{\{\Sigma, \langle \sigma, e \rangle\}_{\zeta} \longrightarrow_k \{\Sigma', \langle \sigma', e' \rangle\}_{\zeta'} \qquad b > 0}{\{\Sigma, \zeta, b, \langle \sigma, e \rangle \lhd t_s\} \hookrightarrow \{\Sigma', \zeta', b-1, \langle \sigma', e' \rangle \lhd t_s\}}.
$$

Rule (STEP-CA) executes a sequential instruction in the current thread, provided the instruction budget is not empty ($b > 0$), and updates the cache accordingly ($\{\Sigma, \langle \sigma, e \rangle\}_{\zeta} \longrightarrow_k \{\Sigma', \langle \sigma', e' \rangle\}_{\zeta'}$). It is important to remark that the effects of the underlying cache ζ, as indicated by k, are intentionally ignored by the scheduler. This subtle detail captures the essence of removing the cache-based internal timing channel. (Our formalization of a time-based scheduler does not ignore k and thus is vulnerable.) Similarly, rule (PREEMPT) turns into rule (PREEMPT-CA), where q and q_i are respectively replaced with b and b_i to reflect the fact that there is an instruction budget instead of a cycle count. The rest of the rules can be adapted in a straightforward manner. Our rules have the invariant that the instruction budget gets decremented by one when a thread executes one instruction.

By changing the cache-aware semantics in this way, we obtain a generalized semantics for LIO. In fact, the previous semantics for LIO [40], is a special case, with $b_i = 1$, i.e., the threads perform only one reduction step before a context-switch happens. In addition, it is easy to extend our previous termination-sensitive non-interference result to the instruction-based semantics. The security guarantees of our approach are stated below.

Theorem 1 (Termination-sensitive non-interference). *Given a program function f, an attacker that observes data at level L, and a pair of inputs e_1 and e_2 indistinguishable to the attacker, then for every reduction sequence starting from $f(e_1)$ there is a corresponding reduction sequence starting from $f(e_2)$ such that both sequences reach indistinguishable configurations.*

Proof Sketch: Our proof relies on the *term erasure technique* as used in [23, 34, 39], and follows in a similar fashion to that of [40]. We refer the interested reader to the extended version of the paper for details [41].

7   Limitations

This section discusses some limitations of our current implementation, the significance of these limitations, and how the limitations can be addressed.

Nondeterminism in the hardware counters.   While the retired-instruction counter should be deterministic, in most hardware implementations there is some degree of nondeterminism. For example, on most x86 processors the instruction counter adds an extra instruction every time a hardware interrupt occurs [45]. This anomaly could be exploited to affect the behavior of an instruction-based scheduler, causing it to trigger a signal early. However, this is only a problem if a high thread is able to cause a large number of hardware interrupts in the underlying operating system. In the Hails framework, attackers can trigger interrupts by forcing a server to frequently receive HTTP responses, i.e., trigger a hardware interrupt from the network interface card. Hails, however, provides mechanisms to mitigate the effects of external events, using the techniques of [4, 48], that can reduce the frequency of such operations. Nevertheless, the feasibility of such attacks is not directly clear and left as future work.

Scheduler and garbage collector instruction counts.   For performance reasons, we do not reset the retired-instruction counter prior to re-entering user code. This means that instruction counts include the instructions executed from when the previous thread received the signal, to when the previous thread yields, to when the next thread is scheduled. While this suggests that thread are not completely isolated, we think that this interaction is extremely difficult to exploit. This is because the number of instructions it takes for the scheduler to schedule a new thread is essentially fixed, and the "time to yield" for any code is highly dependent on the compiler, which we assume is not under the control of an adversary.

Parallelism.   Unfortunately, we cannot simply run instruction-based scheduling on multiple cores. Threads running in parallel will be able to race to public resources. Under normal conditions, such races can be still influenced by the state of the (L3) cache. Some parallelism is, however, possible. For instance, we can extend the instruction-based scheduler to parallelize regions of code that do not share state or have side effects (e.g., synchronization operations or writes to channels). To this end, when a thread wishes to perform a side effect, it is required that all the other threads lagging behind (as per retired-instruction count) first complete the execution of their side effects. Hence, an implementation would rely on a synchronization barrier whenever a side-effecting computation is executed; at the barrier, the execution of all the side effects is done in a pre-determined order. Although we believe that this "optimization" is viable, we have not implemented it, since it requires major modifications to the GHC runtime system and the performance gains due to parallelism requiring such strict synchronization barriers are not clear. We leave this investigation to future work.

Even without built-in parallelism, we believe that instruction-based scheduling represents a viable and deployable solution when considering modern web applications and data-centers. In particular, when an application is distributed over multiple machines, these machines do not share a processor cache and thus can safely run the application concurrently. Attacks which involve making these two machines access shared external resources can be mitigated in the same fashion as external timing attacks [4, 40, 48, 49]. Load-balancing an application in this manner is already a well-established technique for deploying applications.

8   Related Work

Impact of cache on cryptosystems.   Kocher [18] was one of the first to consider the security implications of memory access-time in implementations of cryptographic primitives and systems. Since then, several attacks (e.g., [28, 31]) against popular systems have successfully extracted secret keys by using the cache as a covert channel. As a countermeasure, several authors propose partitioning the cache (e.g., [29]). Until recently, partitioned caches have been of limited application in dynamic information flow control systems due to the small number of partitions available. The recent Vantage cache partition scheme of Sanchez and Kozyrakis [37], however, offers tens to hundreds of configurable partitions and high performance. As hardware is not yet available with Vantage, it is hard to evaluate its effectiveness for our problem domain. However, we expect it to be mostly complimentary to our instruction-based scheduler. Specifically, a partitioned cache can be used to safely run threads in parallel, each group of threads using instruction-based schedulers. Other countermeasures (e.g., [28]) are primarily implementation-specific, and, while applicable to cryptographic primitives, they do not easily generalize to arbitrary code.

Language-based information-flow security.   Several works (e.g., [13]) consider systems that satisfy *possibilistic non-interference* [38], which states that a concurrent program is secure iff the possible observable events do not depend on sensitive data. An alternative notion, *probabilistic non-interference*, considers a concurrent program secure iff the probability distribution over observable events is not affected by sensitive data [44]. Zdancewic and Myers introduce *observational low-determinism* [46], which intuitively states that the observable behavior of concurrent systems must be deterministic. After this seminal work, several authors improve on each other's definitions on low-determinism (e.g., [14]). Other IFC systems rely on deterministic semantics and a determined class of runtime schedulers (e.g., [32]).

The lines of work mentioned above assume that the execution of a single step is performed in a single unit of time, corresponding to an instruction, and show that races to publicly-observable events cannot be influenced by secret data. Unfortunately, the presence of the cache breaks the correspondence between an instruction and a single unit of time, making cache attacks viable. Instruction-based scheduling could be seen as a necessary component in making the previous concurrent IFC approaches practical.

Agat [1] presents a code transformation for sequential programs such that both code paths of a branch have the same memory access pattern. This eliminates timing covert channels, even those relying on the cache. This transformation has been adapted by several authors (e.g., [36]). This approach, however, focuses on avoiding attacks relying on the data cache, while leaving the instruction cache unattended.

Russo and Sabelfeld [33] consider non-interference for concurrent systems under co-operative and deterministic scheduling. An implementation of such a system was presented by Tsai et al. in [42]. This approach eliminates internal timing leaks, including those relying on the cache, by restricting the use of yields. Cooperative schedulers are intrinsically vulnerable to attacks that use termination as a covert channel. In contrast, our solution is able to safely preempt non-terminating computations while guaranteeing termination-sensitive non-interference.

Secure multi-execution [8] preserves confidentiality of data by executing the same sequential program several times, one for each security level. In this scenario, the cache-based covert channel can only be removed in specific configurations [16]. Zhang et al. [49] provide a method to mitigate external events when their timing behavior could be affected by the underlying hardware. This solution is directly applicable to our system when considering external events. Similar to our work, they consider an abstract model of the hardware machine state which includes a description of time. However, their semantics focus on sequential programs, wherein attacks due to the cache arise in the form of externally visible events.

Hedin and Sands [12] present a type-system for preventing external timing attacks for bytecode. Their semantics is augmented to incorporate history, which enables the modeling of cache effects. We proceed in a similar manner when extending the original LIO semantics [40] to consider caches.

System security.   In order to achieve strong isolation, Barthe et al. [6] present a model of virtualization which flushes the cache upon switching between guest operating systems. Different from our scenario, flushing the cache in such scenarios is common and does not impact the already-costly context-switch.

Allowing some information leakage, Köpft et al. [19] combines abstract interpretation and quantitative information-flow to analyze leakage bounds for cache attacks. Kim et al. [17] propose StealthMem, a system level protection against cache attacks. Stealth-Mem allows programs to allocate memory which does not get evicted from the cache. In fact, this approach could be seen as a software-level partition of the cache. StealthMem is capable of enforcing confidentiality for a stronger attacker model than ours, i.e., they consider programs with access to wall-clock and perhaps running on multi-cores. As other works on partition caches, StealthMem does not scale to scenarios with arbitrarily complex security lattices.

Performance monitoring counters.   The use of PMUs for tasks other than performance monitoring is a relatively recent one. Vogl and Ekert [43] also use PMUs, but for monitoring applications running within a virtual machine, allowing instruction level monitoring of all or specific instructions. While the mechanism is the same, our goals are different: we merely seek to replace interrupts generated by a clock-based timer with interrupts generated by hardware counters; their work introduces new interrupts that trigger vmexits. This causes a considerable slowdown, while we achieve no major performance impact.

9 Conclusion

Cache-based internal timing attacks constitute a practical set of attacks. We present instruction-based scheduling as a solution to remove such attacks. Different from simply flushing the cache on a context switch or partitioning the cache, this new class of schedulers also removes timing perturbations introduced by other components of the underlying hardware (e.g., the TLB, CPU buses, etc.). To demonstrate the applicability of our solution, we implemented a scheduler using the CPU retired-instruction counters available on commodity Intel and AMD hardware. We integrated the scheduler into the Hails IFC web framework, replacing the timing-based scheduler. This integration was, in part, possible because of the scheduler's negligible performance impact and, in part, due to our formal guarantees. Specifically, by generalizing previous results, we proved that instruction-based scheduling for LIO preserves confidentiality and integrity of data, i.e., termination-sensitive non-interference. Finally, we remark that our design, implementation, and proof are not limited to LIO; we believe that instruction-based scheduling is applicable to other concurrent deterministic IFC systems where cache-based timing attacks could be a concern.

Acknowledgments. We would like to thank David Sands for useful comments. This work was funded by DARPA CRASH under contract #N66001-10-2-4088, by multiple gifts from Google, and by the Swedish research agency VR, STINT, and the Barbro Osher foundation. Deian Stefan is supported by the DoD through the NDSEG Fellowship Program.

References

[1] Agat, J.: Transforming out timing leaks. In: Proc. ACM Symp. on Principles of Programming Languages, pp. 40–53 (January 2000)

[2] Ahmad, A., DeYoung, H.: Cache performance of lazy functional programs on current hardware. Technical report, CMU (December 2009)

[3] AMD. BIOS and kernel developer's guide for AMD family 11h processors (July 2008)

[4] Askarov, A., Zhang, D., Myers, A.C.: Predictive black-box mitigation of timing channels. In: Proc. of the 17th ACM CCS, ACM (2010)

[5] Barthe, G., Rezk, T., Warnier, M.: Preventing timing leaks through transactional branching instructions. Electron. Notes Theor. Comput. Sci. 153 (May 2006)

[6] Barthe, G., Betarte, G., Campo, J., Luna, C.: Cache-leakage resilient OS isolation in an idealized model of virtualization. In: 2012 IEEE 25th Computer Security Foundations Symposium (CSF). IEEE Computer Society (June 2012)

[7] Bonneau, J., Mironov, I.: Cache-collision timing attacks against AES. In: Goubin, L., Matsui, M. (eds.) CHES 2006. LNCS, vol. 4249, pp. 201–215. Springer, Heidelberg (2006)

[8] Devriese, D., Piessens, F.: Noninterference through secure multi-execution. In: Proc. of the 2010 IEEE Symposium on Security and Privacy, SP 2010. IEEE Computer Society (2010)

[9] Eranian, S.: Perfmon2: a flexible performance monitoring interface for Linux. In: Proc. of the 2006 Ottawa Linux Symposium, pp. 269–288. Citeseer (2006)

[10] GHC. Infinite loops can hang Concurrent Haskell (2005),
http://hackage.haskell.org/trac/ghc/ticket/367

[11] Giffin, D.B., Levy, A., Stefan, D., Terei, D., Mazières, D., Mitchell, J., Russo, A.: Hails: Protecting data privacy in untrusted web applications. In: Proc. of the 10th Symposium on Operating Systems Design and Implementation (October 2012)

[12] Hedin, D., Sands, D.: Timing aware information flow security for a JavaCard-like bytecode. Elec. Notes Theor. Comput. Sci. 141 (2005)

[13] Honda, K., Vasconcelos, V.T., Yoshida, N.: Secure information flow as typed process behaviour. In: Smolka, G. (ed.) ESOP 2000. LNCS, vol. 1782, pp. 180–199. Springer, Heidelberg (2000)

[14] Huisman, M., Worah, P., Sunesen, K.: A temporal logic characterisation of observational determinism. In: Proc. IEEE Computer Sec. Foundations Workshop (July 2006)

[15] Intel. Intel 64 and IA-32 architectures software developer's manual (August 2012)

[16] Kashyap, V., Wiedermann, B., Hardekopf, B.: Timing- and termination-sensitive secure information flow: Exploring a new approach. In: Proc. of IEEE Symposium on Sec. and Privacy. IEEE (2011)

[17] Kim, T., Peinado, M., Mainar-Ruiz, G.: STEALTHMEM: system-level protection against cache-based side channel attacks in the cloud. In: Proceedings of the 21st USENIX Conference on Security Symposium, Security 2012. USENIX Association (2012)

[18] Kocher, P.C.: Timing attacks on implementations of Diffie-Hellman, RSA, DSS, and other systems. In: Koblitz, N. (ed.) CRYPTO 1996. LNCS, vol. 1109, pp. 104–113. Springer, Heidelberg (1996)

[19] Köpf, B., Mauborgne, L., Ochoa, M.: Automatic quantification of cache side-channels. In: Madhusudan, P., Seshia, S.A. (eds.) CAV 2012. LNCS, vol. 7358, pp. 564–580. Springer, Heidelberg (2012)

[20] Krohn, M., Yip, A., Brodsky, M., Cliffer, N., Kaashoek, M.F., Kohler, E., Morris, R.: Information flow control for standard OS abstractions. In: Proc. of the 21st Symp. on Operating Systems Principles (October 2007a)

[21] Krohn, M., Yip, A., Brodsky, M., Morris, R., Walfish, M.: A World Wide Web Without Walls. In: 6th ACM Workshop on Hot Topics in Networking (Hotnets) (November 2007b)

[22] Lampson, B.W.: A note on the confinement problem. Communications of the ACM 16(10), 613–615 (1973)

[23] Li, P., Zdancewic, S.: Arrows for secure information flow. Theoretical Computer Science 411(19), 1974–1994 (2010)

[24] Lin, J., Lu, Q., Ding, X., Zhang, Z., Zhang, X., Sadayappan, P.: Gaining insights into multicore cache partitioning: Bridging the gap between simulation and real systems. In: Proc. of the Intl. Symposium on High Performance Computer Architecture. IEEE (2008)

[25] Millen, J.: 20 years of covert channel modeling and analysis. In: IEEE Symp. on Security and Privacy (1999)

[26] Murray, T., Matichuk, D., Brassil, M., Gammie, P., Bourke, T., Seefried, S., Lewis, C., Gao, X., Klein, G.: sel4: from general purpose to a proof of information flow enforcement. In: Proceedings of the 34th IEEE Symp. on Security and Privacy (2013)

[27] Myers, A.C., Liskov, B.: A decentralized model for information flow control. In: Proc. of the 16th ACM Symp. on Operating Systems Principles, pp. 129–142 (1997)

[28] Osvik, D.A., Shamir, A., Tromer, E.: Cache attacks and countermeasures: the case of AES. In: Pointcheval, D. (ed.) CT-RSA 2006. LNCS, vol. 3860, pp. 1–20. Springer, Heidelberg (2006)

[29] Page, D.: Partitioned cache architecture as a side-channel defence mechanism. IACR Cryptology ePrint Archive 2005 (2005)

[30] Partain, W.: The nofib benchmark suite of Haskell programs. In: Proceedings of the 1992 Glasgow Workshop on Functional Programming (1992)

[31] Percival, C.: Cache missing for fun and profit. In: Proc. of BSDCan 2005 (2005)

[32] Russo, A., Sabelfeld, A.: Securing interaction between threads and the scheduler. In: Proc. IEEE Computer Sec. Foundations Workshop, pp. 177–189 (July 2006a)

[33] Russo, A., Sabelfeld, A.: Security for multithreaded programs under cooperative scheduling. In: Virbitskaite, I., Voronkov, A. (eds.) PSI 2006. LNCS, vol. 4378, pp. 474–480. Springer, Heidelberg (2007)

[34] Russo, A., Claessen, K., Hughes, J.: A library for light-weight information-flow security in Haskell. In: Proc. ACM SIGPLAN Symposium on Haskell, pp. 13–24. ACM Press (September 2008)

[35] Sabelfeld, A., Myers, A.C.: Language-based information-flow security. IEEE Journal on Selected Areas in Communications 21(1) (January 2003)

[36] Sabelfeld, A., Sands, D.: Probabilistic noninterference for multi-threaded programs. In: Proc. IEEE Computer Sec. Foundations Workshop, pp. 200–214 (July 2000)

[37] Sanchez, D., Kozyrakis, C.: Vantage: Scalable and efficient fine-grain cache partitioning. In: International Symposium on Computer Architecture. ACM IEEE (2011)

[38] Smith, G., Volpano, D.: Secure information flow in a multi-threaded imperative language. In: Proc. ACM Symp. on Principles of Programming Languages, pp. 355–364 (January 1998)

[39] Stefan, D., Russo, A., Mitchell, J.C., Mazières, D.: Flexible dynamic information flow control in Haskell. In: Haskell Symposium. ACM SIGPLAN (September 2011)

[40] Stefan, D., Russo, A., Buiras, P., Levy, A., Mitchell, J.C., Mazières, D.: Addressing covert termination and timing channels in concurrent information flow systems. In: Proc. of the 17th ACM SIGPLAN International Conference on Functional Programming (September 2012)

[41] Stefan, D., Buiras, P., Yang, E., Levy, A., Terei, D., Russo, A., Mazières, D.: Eliminating cache-based timing attacks with instruction-based scheduling: Extended version (2013), http://www.cse.chalmers.se/~buiras/esorics2013_extended.pdf

[42] Tsai, T.C., Russo, A., Hughes, J.: A library for secure multi-threaded information flow in Haskell. In: Proc. IEEE Computer Sec. Foundations Symposium (July 2007)

[43] Vogl, S., Eckert, C.: Using Hardware Performance Events for Instruction-Level Monitoring on the x86 Architecture. In: Proceedings of the 2012 European Workshop on System Security EuroSec 2012 (2012)

[44] Volpano, D., Smith, G.: Probabilistic noninterference in a concurrent language. J. Computer Security 7(2-3) (November 1999)

[45] Weaver, V.M., McKee, S.A.: Can hardware performance counters be trusted? Workload Characterization 08 (2008), http://ieeexplore.ieee.org/xpls/abs_all.jsp?arnumber=4636099

[46] Zdancewic, S., Myers, A.C.: Observational determinism for concurrent program security. In: Proc. IEEE Computer Sec. Foundations Workshop, pp. 29–43 (June 2003)

[47] Zeldovich, N., Boyd-Wickizer, S., Kohler, E., Mazières, D.: Making information flow explicit in HiStar. In: Proc. of the 7th Symp. on Operating Systems Design and Implementation, Seattle, WA, pp. 263–278 (November 2006)

[48] Zhang, D., Askarov, A., Myers, A.C.: Predictive mitigation of timing channels in interactive systems. In: Proc. of the 18th ACM CCS. ACM (2011)

[49] Zhang, D., Askarov, A., Myers, A.C.: Language-based control and mitigation of timing channels. In: Proc. of PLDI. ACM (2012)

Data-Confined HTML5 Applications

Devdatta Akhawe[1], Frank Li[1], Warren He[1], Prateek Saxena[2], and Dawn Song[1]

[1] University of California, Berkeley, Berkeley, CA, USA
[2] National University of Singapore, Singapore

Abstract. Rich client-side applications written in HTML5 proliferate on diverse platforms, access sensitive data, and need to maintain *data-confinement invariants*. Applications currently enforce these invariants using implicit, ad-hoc mechanisms. We propose a new primitive called a *data-confined sandbox* or DCS. A DCS enables complete mediation of communication channels with a small TCB. Our primitive extends currently standardized primitives and has negligible performance overhead and a modest compatibility cost. We retrofit our design on four real-world HTML5 applications and demonstrate that a small amount of effort enables strong data-confinement guarantees.

1 Introduction

Rich client-side applications written in HTML, CSS, and JS—including browser extensions, packaged browser applications (Chrome Apps) [17], Windows 8 Metro applications [32], and applications in newer browser operating systems (B2G [33], Chrome OS [18])—are fast proliferating on diverse computing platforms. These "HTML5" applications run with access to sensitive user data, such as browsing history, personal and social data, and financial documents, as well as capability bearing tokens that grant access to these data. A recent study of 5,943 Google Chrome browser extensions revealed that 58% required access to the user's browsing history, and 35% requested permissions to the user's data on all websites [10].

Applications handling sensitive data need the ability to *verifiably confine* data to specific principals and to prevent it from leaking to malicious actors. On one hand, the developers want an easy, high-assurance way to confine sensitive data; on the other, platform vendors and security auditors want to verify sensitive data confinement. For example, consider LastPass, a real-world HTML5-based password manager with close to a million users[1]. By design, LastPass only stores an encrypted version of the user's data in the cloud and decrypts it at the client side with the user's master password. It is critical that the decrypted user data (i.e., the clear-text password database) never leave the client. We term this requirement a *data-confinement invariant*. Data-confinement invariants are fundamental security specifications that limit the flow of sensitive data to a trusted set of security principals. These data-confinement invariants are not

---

[1] https://www.lastpass.com

J. Crampton, S. Jajodia, and K. Mayes (Eds.): ESORICS 2013, LNCS 8134, pp. 736–754, 2013.

explicitly stated in today's HTML5 applications but are implicitly necessary to preserve their privacy and security guarantees.

We observe two hurdles that hinder practical, high-assurance data confinement in existing client-side HTML5 applications. First, mechanisms to specify and enforce data-confinement invariants are absent in HTML5 platforms as a result, they remain hidden in application designs; raising the TCB. Second, client-side HTML5 applications have numerous channels to communicate with distrusting principals, and no unified monitoring interface like the OS system call interface exists. Due to the number of channels available to HTML5 applications, attackers can violate data confinement invariants even in the absence of code injection vulnerabilities [45,26]. As we explain in Section 3.2, previous research proposals do not offer complete mediation, or have an unacceptably large TCB and compatibility cost.

We introduce the data-confined sandbox (or DCS), a novel security primitive for client-side HTML5 applications. A data-confined sandbox is a unit of execution, such as code executing in an `iframe`, the creator of which explicitly controls all the data imported and exported by the DCS. Our design provides the creator of a DCS a secure reference monitor to interpose on all communications, privileged API accesses, and input/output data exchanges originating from the DCS.

Data-confined sandboxes are a fundamental primitive to enable a data-centric security architecture for emerging HTML5 applications. By moving much of the application code handling sensitive data to data-confined sandboxes, we can enable applications that have better resilience to privacy violating attacks and that are easy to audit by security analysts.

Contributions. We make the following main contributions:

- We introduce the concept of data confinement for client-side HTML5 applications that handle sensitive data (Section 2).
- We identify the limitations of current security primitives in the HTML5 platform that make them insufficient for implementing data-confinement invariants (Section 3.2).
- We design and implement a data-confined sandbox, a novel mechanism in web browsers that provides complete mediation on all explicit data communication channels (Section 4) and discuss how to implement such a new primitive without affecting the security invariants maintained by the HTML5 platform (Section 4.3).
- We demonstrate the practicality of our approach by modifying four applications that handle sensitive data to provide strong data confinement guarantees (Section 6). All our code and case studies are publicly available online [13].

2   Data Confinement in HTML5 Applications

Data confinement is a data-centric property, which limits the flow of sensitive data to an explicitly allowed set of security principals. In this section, we present example data-confinement invariants from real-world applications. Our focus is on modern HTML5 applications that handle sensitive data or tokens with complex client-side logic leading to a large client-side TCB.

2.1 Password Managers

Password managers organize a user's credentials across the web in a centralized store. Consider LastPass, a popular password manager that stores encrypted credential data in the cloud. LastPass decrypts the password database only at the client side (in a 'vault') with a user provided master password. A number of data-confinement invariants are implicit in the design of LastPass.

- First, the user's master password should never be sent to *any* web server (including LastPass servers).
- Second, the password database should only be sent back to the LastPass servers after encryption.
- Third, the decrypted password database on the client-side should not leak to *any* web site.
- Finally, only individual decrypted passwords should be sent only to their corresponding websites: e.g., the credentials for facebook.com should only be used on facebook.com.

2.2 Client-Side SSO Implementations

Single sign-on (SSO) mechanisms have emerged on the web to manage users' online identities. These mechanisms rely on confining secret tokens to an allowed set of principals. Consider Mozilla's recent SSO mechanism called BrowserID. It has the following data-confinement invariants implicit in its design:

- It aims to share authorization tokens only with specific participants in one run of the protocol.
- Similar to the 'vault' in LastPass, BrowserID provides an interface for managing credentials in a user 'home page.' This home page data should not leak to external websites.
- The user's BrowserID credentials (master password) should never be leaked to a third party: only the authorization credentials should be shared with the intended web principals involved in the particular instance of the protocol flow.

Other SSO mechanisms, like Facebook Connect, often process capability-bearing tokens (such as OAuth tokens). Implementation weaknesses and logic flaws can violate these invariants, as researchers demonstrated in 2010 [24,3], 2011 [43], and 2012 [41].

2.3   Electronic Medical Record Applications

Electronic medical record (EMR) applications provide a central interface for patient data, scheduling, clinical decisions, and billing. Strict compliance regulations, such as HIPAA, require data confinement for these applications, with financial and reputational penalties for violations. OpenEMR is the most popular open-source EMR application [38] and has a strict confinement requirement: an instance of OpenEMR should not leak user data to *any* principal other than hospital servers.

Note the dual requirements in this application: first, OpenEMR's developers want to ensure data confinement to their application; second, hospitals need to verify that OpenEMR is not leaking patient data to any external servers. In the current design, it is difficult for hospitals to verify this: any vulnerability in the client-side software can allow data disclosure.

2.4   Web Interfaces for Sensitive Databases

Web-based database administration interfaces are popular today, because they are easy to use. PhpMyAdmin is one such popular interface with thousands of downloads each week [34]. The following data-confinement invariants are implicit in its design:

- Data received from the database server is not sent to any website.
- User inputs (new values to store) are only sent to the database server's data insertion endpoint.

Currently, a code injection vulnerability in the client-side interface can enable attackers to steal the entire database, as the interface executes with the database user's privileges. Moreover, the application is large and not easily auditable to ensure data-confinement invariants.

Prevalence of Data Confinement. The discussion above only provides exemplars: *any* application handling sensitive data typically has a confinement invariant. Due to space constraints, we have made our analysis of the twenty most popular Google Chrome extensions available online [13]. All applications handling sensitive data (sixteen applications in total) maintained an invariant implicitly.[2] The trusted code base for these extensions varied from 7.5KB to 1.24MB. Sensitive data available to the extensions vary from access to the user's browsing history to the user's social media login credentials.

3   Problem Formulation

Given the prevalence of data confinement in HTML5 applications, we aim to support secure data confinement in HTML5 applications. Due to the increasingly sensitive nature of data handled by modern HTML5 applications, a key

---

[2] The remaining four extensions dealt mainly with the website style and appearance and did not access sensitive data.

requirement is *high assurance*: small TCB, complete mediation. Further, for ease of adoption, we aim for a mechanism with minimal compatibility costs.

The idea of such high assurance mechanisms is not new, with Saltzer and Schroeder laying it down as a fundamental requirement for secure systems [39]. Our focus is on developing a high assurance mechanism for HTML5 applications. We first discuss the challenges in achieving high assurance data confinement in HTML5 applications, followed by a discussion on why current and proposed primitives do not satisfy all our goals. We discuss our design in Section 4.

3.1   HTML5 and Data Confinement: Challenges

A number of idiosyncrasies of the HTML5 platform make practical data confinement with a small TCB difficult. First, the HTML5 platform lacks mechanisms to explicitly state data-confinement invariants—current ad-hoc mechanisms do not separate policy and enforcement mechanism. Due to the coarse-grained nature of the same origin policy, enforcing these invariants on current HTML5 platforms increases the TCB to the whole application.

Achieving a small TCB is particularly important on the HTML5 platform. The JavaScript language and the DOM interface make modular reasoning about individual components difficult. All code runs with ambient access to the DOM, cookies, localStorage, and the network. Further, techniques like prototype hijacking can violate encapsulation assumptions and allow attackers to leak private variables in other modules. The DOM API makes confinement difficult to ensure even in the absence of code injection vulnerabilities [45,26].

Achieving complete mediation on the HTML5 platform is also difficult. The HTML5 platform has a large number of data disclosure channels, as by design it aims to ease cross-origin resource loading and communication. We categorize these channels as:

- **Network channels**. HTML5 applications can make network requests via HTML elements like img, form, script, and video, as well as JavaScript and DOM APIs like XMLHttpRequest and window.open. Furthermore, CSS stylesheets can issue network requests by referencing images, fonts, and other stylesheets.
- **Client-side cross-origin channels**. Web browsers support a number of channels for client-side cross-origin communication. This includes exceptions to the same-origin policy in JavaScript such as the window.location object. Initially, mashups used these cross-origin communication mechanisms for fragment ID messaging (via the location.hash property) between cross-origin windows. Current mashups rely on newer channels like postMessage, which are also a mechanism for data leaks.
- **Storage Channels**. Another source of data exfiltration are storage channels like localStorage, cookies, and so on. These channels do not cause network requests or communicate with another client-side channel as above; instead, they allow code to exfiltrate data to other code that will run in the future in the same origin (or, in case of cookies, even other related origins). Browsers tie storage channels to the origin of an application.

Given the wide number of channels available for inadvertent data disclosure, we observe that no unified interface exists for ensuring confinement of fine-grained code elements in the HTML5 platform. This is in contrast to system call interposition in commodity operating systems that provides complete mediation. For example, mediation of data communication channels using system call sandboxing techniques is well-studied for modern binary applications [30,19,36]. Previous work also developed techniques to automate identification and isolation of subcomponents that process sensitive data [30,7]. Our work shares these design principles, but targets HTML5 applications.

3.2   Insufficiency of Existing Mechanisms

None of the primitives available in today's HTML5 platform achieve complete mediation with a small TCB. Browser-supported primitives, such as Content Security Policy (CSP), block some network channels but not all. Current mechanisms in web browsers aim for integrity, not confinement. For example, even the most restrictive CSP policy cannot block data leaks through anchor tags and `window.open`. Similarly, our previous work on privilege separation of HTML5 applications does not provide any confinement guarantees [4]. An unprivileged child can leak data by making a request for an image or including a CSS style from a remote host.

Table 1. Comparison of current solutions for data confinement

System Name	Complete Mediation	Compatibility Cost	Small TCB
HSTS	No: HTTPS pages only	Low	Yes
CSP	No: anchors and `window.open`	High: disables eval	Yes
JS Static Analysis	No: no CSS & DOM	High: disables eval	No
JS IRMs (Cajole, Conscript)	No: no CSS & DOM	High: disables eval	Yes
JSand	No: no CSS	High: SES	No
Treehouse	Yes	High: code change	No
sandbox with Temp. Origins	No: all network channels	Low	Yes
Data-confined sandboxes	**Yes**	**Low**	**Yes**

Recent work on information flow and non-interference show promise for ensuring fine-grained data-confinement in JavaScript; unfortunately, these techniques currently have high overhead for modern applications [11]. IBEX proposed writing extensions in a high-level language (FINE) in a language amenable to deep analysis to ensure conformance with specific policies [23]. In contrast, our work does not require significant changes to web applications. Further, as we explain below, these approaches also have a large TCB.

Another approach to interpose on all data communication channels is to do static analysis of the application source code [14,16,31]. Static analysis systems cannot reason about dynamic constructs such as `eval`, which are used pervasively by existing applications [37] and modern JavaScript libraries [1]. As a result, such mechanisms have a high compatibility cost. When combined with rewriting techniques, such as cajoling [16], JS analysis techniques can achieve complete mediation on client-side cross-frame channels; but still do not provide complete mediation over DOM and CSS channels.

JSand [2] introduced a client-side method of sandboxing third-party JavaScript libraries. It does so by encapsulating all Javscript objects in a wrapper that mediates property accesses and assignments, via an application-defined policy. This approach does not protect against scriptless attacks such as those using CSS. Additionally, it relies on the use of Secure EcmaScript 5 (SES), which is not compatible for some JavaScript libraries. JSand does provide a support layer to improve compatibility with legacy JavaScript code, but this is a partial transformation and involves a high performance overhead.

Treehouse uses new primitives, like web workers and EcmaScript5 sealed objects, in the HTML5 platform to ensure better interposition [27]. Treehouse proposes to execute individual components in web workers at the client side. One concern with the Treehouse approach is that web workers also run with some ambient privileges: e.g., workers have access to XMLHttpRequest, synchronous file APIs, script imports, and spawning new workers, which attackers can use to leak data. Treehouse relies on the seal/unseal features of ES5 to prevent access to these APIs, but this mechanism requires intrusive changes to existing applications and has a high compatibility cost.

Perhaps the most important limitation of *all* primitives not directly supported by browsers is their large TCB. For example, in the case of Treehouse, application code (running in workers) cannot have direct access to the DOM, since that would break all security guarantees. Instead, application code executes on a virtual DOM in the worker that the parent code copies over to the main web page. As a result, the security of these mechanisms depends on the correctness of the monitor/browser model (e.g., the parent's client side monitor in Treehouse).

Since the DOM, HTML, CSS, and JS are so deeply intertwined in a modern HTML5 platform, such a client side monitor is essentially replicating the core logic of the browser, leading to a massive increase in the TCB. Further, Treehouse implements this complex logic in JavaScript. Corresponding issues plague static analysis systems, new language mechanisms like IBEX, and code rewriting systems like Caja—all of them assume a model of the HTML5 platform to implement their analysis/rewriting logic.

While implementing a model of HTML5 for analysis and monitoring is difficult, the approaches discussed above suffer from another fundamental limitation: they work on a model of HTML5, not the real HTML5 standard implemented in the platform (browser). Any mismatch between the browser and the model can lead to a vulnerability, as observed (repeatedly) for Caja [20,22,21,15] and AdSafe [31,35].

3.3   Threat Model

We focus on *explicit* data communication channels in the HTML5 platform core, as defined above. Ensuring comprehensive mediation on explicit data channels is an important first step in achieving data-confined HTML5 applications. Our proposed primitive does not protect against covert and side channels (such as shared browser caches [28] and timing channels [6]) or self exfiltration channels [9], which are a subject of ongoing research. These channels are important. However, we point out that popular isolation mechanisms on existing systems also do not protect against these [46,8,44]. We believe explicit channels cover a large space of attacks, and we plan to investigate extending our techniques to covert channels in the future.

In addition to focusing on explicit channels, our primitive only targets the core HTML5 platform; our ideas extend to add-ons/plugins, however we exclude them from our present implementation. We defend against the standard web attacker model, in which the attacker cannot tamper with or observe network traffic for other web origins and cannot subvert the integrity of the HTML5 platform itself [3].

4   The Data Confined Sandbox

To draw a parallel with binary applications, current mechanisms for confining HTML5 applications are analogous to analyzing the machine code *before* it executes to decide whether it violates any guarantees. We argued above that such mechanisms cannot provide high assurance. Instead, taking a systems view of the problem of data confinement, we argue for an `strace`-like high assurance monitor for the HTML5 platform.

We call our primitive the data confined sandbox, or DCS (Section 4.1). Our key contribution is identifying that the shrewd design of the DCS primitive provides high assurance with minimal compatibility concerns (Section 4.2). Introducing any new primitive on the HTML5 platform brings up security concerns. A primitive like DCS that provides monitoring capabilities to arbitrary code is particularly fraught. We discuss how we ensure that we do not introduce new vulnerabilities due to our primitive in Section 4.3.

4.1   Design of DCS

Figure 1 presents the architecture of an application using the DCS design. Our design extends our previous work on privilege separation [4]. Our key contribution is identifying how to extend the ideas of privilege separation to provide complete mediation on the HTML5 platform. We first recap privilege separated HTML5 applications and then discuss the DCS design.

Modern HTML5 platforms allow applications to run arbitrary code (specified via a `data:/blob:` URI) in a temporary, unprivileged origin [4]. Privilege separated HTML5 applications run most application code in an arbitrary number of unprivileged iframes (children). A small privileged parent iframe, with access to full privileges of the web origin, provides access to privileged APIs, such as cookie access and platform APIs like camera access. Unprivileged children communicate with the parent through a tightly controlled `postMessage` channel (dotted arrows in Figure 1).

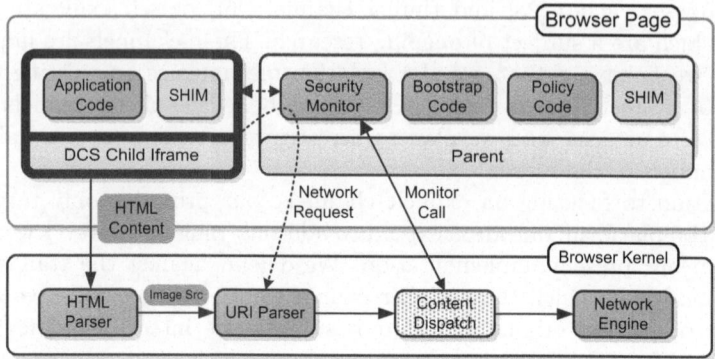

Fig. 1. High-level design of an application running in a DCS. The only component that runs privileged is the parent. The children run in data-confined sandboxes, with no ambient privileges and all communication channels monitored by the parent.

The parent can enforce policies on the requests it receives over this postMessage channel from its unprivileged children [4]. The parent uses its privileged interfaces to fulfill approved requests, such as authenticated XMLHttpRequest calls (curved dotted arrow in Figure 1). To increase assurance, the parent code enforces a number of security invariants such as disabling all dynamic code evaluation, allowing only a text interface with the children, and setting appropriate MIME types for static code downloaded by the bootstrap code.

Though this privilege separation architecture provides integrity, it does *not* provide data confinement. Any compromised child can make arbitrary requests on the network through the numerous data disclosure channels outlined earlier. We propose a new primitive, the *data-confined sandbox* or DCS, that enforces confinement of data in the child. Our primitive relies on the browser to ensure confinement. Similar to privilege separation, applications only need to switch to using the DCS and write an appropriate policy.

Consider the browser kernel in Figure 1. Any content that a DCS child requests the browser to display passes through the HTML/JS/CSS parser. If the browser encounters a URI that it needs to load, it invokes the URI parser, which then invokes the content dispatch logic in the browser. We modify this code for DCS children to call a security monitor that the parent defines (solid arrow in Figure 1). The security monitor in the parent is transparent to the child. The browser's call to the parent also includes the unique id identifying the child iframe and details about the request. From there, the security monitor can decide whether to grant the request or not.

Example. Consider the 'vault' for the LastPass web application. In our redesign, when the user navigates to the LastPass application, the server returns bootstrap code (the parent) that downloads the original application code and executes it in a data-confined sandbox (the child). The code in the DCS starts executing and makes network requests to include all the complex UI, DOM, and encryption libraries. Finally, the LastPass child code in the DCS makes a request for the encrypted password database and decrypts it with the user provided password.

The parent security monitor can enforce a simple policy such as only allowing network requests to `http://lastpass.com`. Alternatively, the parent can enforce stateful policies: e.g., the monitor function could only allow resource loads (i.e., scripts, images, styles) until the DCS child loads the encrypted password database. After loading the encrypted database, the security monitor disallows all future network requests.

4.2   Achieving High Assurance

Recall our goals of complete mediation, small TCB, and backwards compatibility. We discuss how our DCS design achieves all of them.

Complete Mediation. As discussed Section 3, HTML5 applications only have three channels for data leakage: storage channels tied to the origin, network channels, and client-side cross-origin channels. Since all application code runs in children of temporary origins that only exist for the duration of the application's execution, the application code does not have access to any (storage) channel tied to the origin (e.g., cookies, localStorage).

In a DCS, except for a blessed `postMessage` channel to the parent, the browser disables all client-side communication channels. This includes cross-origin communication channels like `postMessage` and cross-origin window properties (like `location.hash`). The `postMessage` channel is the *only* client-side cross-origin channel available to the data-confined child, and the browser guarantees that the channel only connects to the parent. The `postMessage` channel allows the parent to proxy privileged APIs for the child. Further, the `postMessage` channel also allows the parent to provide a channel to proxy `postMessages` to other client-side `iframes`—our design only enforces complete mediation by the parent.

HTML5 applications can request network resources via markup like scripts, images, links, anchors, and forms and JavaScript APIs like `XMLHttpRequest`. In our design, the children can continue to make these network requests; the DCS transparently interposes on all these network channels. The parent defines a 'monitor' function that the browser executes before dispatching a network request. If the function returns false, the browser will not make the network request.

We rely on an external monitor (i.e., one running in the parent) over an inline one. This ensures that the monitor does not share any state with the unprivileged child, making it easier to reason about its runtime integrity and correctness. As we discuss in Section 5, the security monitor is not hard to implement—most browsers already have an internal API for controlling network access, which they expose to internal browser code as well as popular extensions such as AdBlock and NoScript.

Small TCB. The TCB in any data confinement mechanism includes the policy code and the enforcement code. In our design, this includes the monitor code in the parent as well as our browser modifications to ensure complete mediation for the parent monitor. Relying on the browser allows us to create a data confinement design with a small enforcement code, as evidenced by our 214 line implementation described in Section 5. This small enforcement TCB allows for easier validation and auditing.

Compatibility. Our design for network request mediation is discretionary, as compared to client-side channels that we block outright. An alternative design is to disallow all network requests too, and only permit network access via the postMessage channel between the parent and child. Such a design has a significantly higher compatibility cost. HTML5 applications pervasively employ network channels. In contrast, the use of client-side channels is rare—for example, Wang et al. report that cross-origin window.location read and writes occur in less than 0.1% of pages [40]. Therefore, we find that it is acceptable to disable cross-origin client-side channels and force the child to use the blessed postMessage channel to the parent to access these.

4.3   Security Considerations

Our design of the DCS primitive is careful not to introduce new security vulnerabilities in the browser. We do not want to allow an arbitrary website to learn information or execute actions that it could not already learn or execute. The security policy of the current web platform is the same-origin policy. The introduction of the DCS should not violate any of the existing same-origin policy invariants baked into the platform. We enforce this goal with the following two invariants:

- *Invariant 1*: The parent should *only* be able to monitor application code that it could already monitor on the current web platform (albeit, through more fragile mechanisms).
- *Invariant 2*: The parent should not be able to infer anything about a resource requested by a DCS that is not already possible on the current web platform.

We explain how our design enforces the above invariants. First, in our design, a data-confined sandbox can only apply to iframes with a data: URI source, not to arbitrary URIs. Therefore, a malicious site cannot monitor arbitrary web pages. In an iframe with a data: URI source, the creator of the iframe (the parent) specifies the source code that executes. This code is under complete control of the parent anyways. The parent can parse the data: URI source for static requests and redefine the DOM APIs to monitor dynamic requests [25]. Thus, even in the absence of our primitive, the parent can already monitor any requests a data: URI iframe makes.

To ensure Invariant 2, we only call the security monitor for the *first* request made for a particular resource. As we noted above, the parent can already monitor this request. Future requests (e.g., redirects) are not in the control of the parent, and we do not call the security monitor for them. While this can cause security issues (particularly, if the parent whitelists an open-redirect), allowing the parent to monitor redirects would cause critical vulnerabilities.

For example, consider a page at `http://socialnetwork.com/home` that redirects to `http://socialnetwork.com/username`. Consider a DCS child created by `attacker.com` parent. If this child creates an iframe with source `http://socialnetwork.com/home`, our modified browser calls the security monitor with this URI before dispatching the request. However, to ensure Invariant 2, the browser does *not* call the security monitor with the redirect URI (i.e., `http://socialnetwork.com/username`). Further, since the iframe is now executing in the security context of `http://socialnetwork.com/`, Invariant 1 ensures that any image or script loads made by the `socialnetwork.com` iframe do not call the security monitor.

5   Implementation

We implemented support for data-confined sandboxes in the Firefox browser. Our modified browser and our case studies (Section 6) are all available online [13]. Our implementation is fewer than 214 lines of code, with only 60 lines being the core functionality. The low implementation cost substantiates our intuition that the monitoring facility is best provided by the browser. Since major browsers already support temporary origins, we only need to add support for mediating client-side and network channels of a DCS child.

First, we restrict cross-origin client-side channels to a blessed postMessage channel. As a fundamental security invariant, the same-origin policy restricts cross-origin JavaScript access to a restrictive white-list of properties. In Firefox, this whitelist is present in `js/xpconnect/wrappers/AccessCheck.cpp`. We modified the `IsPermitted` function to block all cross-origin accesses, except for the blessed `postMessage` channel.

The `NSIContentPolicy` interface is a standard Firefox API used to monitor network requests. Popular security and privacy extensions, such as NoScript, AdBlock, and RequestPolicy, rely on this API, as do security features such as CSP and mixed content blocking. We register a listener to forward requests for monitored DCS children to the parent's security monitor function. We do *not* implement a new mediation infrastructure—any bypass of our mediation infrastructure would also be a critical vulnerability in the Firefox browser, allowing bypass of all the features and extensions discussed above.

Applications can mark an `iframe` as a DCS using the `dcfsandbox` attribute, similar to the `iframe sandbox` attribute. An `iframe` that has this attribute only supports a `data:` or `blob:` URIs for its `src` attribute. Such a DCS `iframe` implements all the restrictions that a `sandboxed iframe` supports, but provides a complete mediation interface to the parent as described above.

To measure the overhead of calling the parent's monitor code, we measured the increase in latency caused by a simple monitor that allows all requests. We measured the time required for script loads from a web server running on the local machine and found that the load time increased from 16.73ms to 16.74ms.

This increase is statistically insignificant, and pales in comparison to the typical latencies of 100ms observed on the web.

Due to the semantics of network requests in HTML5, the monitor function runs synchronously: a long running monitor function could freeze the child. The ability to cause stability problems via long running synchronous tasks is already a problem in browsers and is not an artifact stemming from our design.

6   Case Studies

We retrofit our application architecture to four web applications to demonstrate the practicality of our approach. We focus on open-source software for our case studies, since that allows us to share our results freely online [13]. Table 2 summarizes all our case studies. Similar to previous work, we use TCB size instead of lines of code as a metric due to the prevalence of JavaScript minification.

We find that we needed minimal changes (at most 184 lines of code) to port existing applications to our design, mirroring our previous experience with privilege separation. In this section, we focus on the policies we implemented for each application; the accompanying technical report provides full details of our experience porting these applications to run under a DCS [5],

Table 2. List of our case studies, as well as the individual components and policies

Application	Initial TCB	New TCB	Lines Changed	Component	Confinement Policy	Other Policies
Clipperz	1.4MB	6.3KB	67	Vault UI	Only to Clipperz server & Direct Login Child	None
				Direct Login	Open arbitrary web-sites	CSP Policy disabling dynamic code
BrowserID	206.9KB	5.7KB	184	Management	Only to BrowserID server	None
				Dialog	Only to BrowserID server, secure password input	API requests must match state machine
OpenEMR	149.1KB	6.1KB	51	Patient Information	Whitelist of necessary request signatures	None
SQL Buddy	100KB	2.97KB	11	Admin UI	Only to MySQL server	User confirmation for database writes

6.1   The Clipperz Password Manager

Clipperz is an open-source HTML5 password manager that allows a user to store sensitive data, such as website logins, bank account credentials, and credit card information encrypted in the cloud [12]. Clipperz decrypts it at the client side with the user provided password. Users access their data in a single 'vault' page. Users can also click on 'direct login' links that load a site's login page, fill in the user name/password, and submit the login form. All of Clipperz's code and libraries run in a single security principal, with access to all sensitive data. The Clipperz application uses inline scripts and `data:` URIs extensively. We found that enforcing strong CSP restrictions to protect against XSS breaks the Clipperz application.

```
1   var doneLoading_mainframe = false, doneLoading_secondframe = false;
2   function monitor(params) {
3       if (params.id === "mainframe") { /*Policy for UI child*/
4           if (params.url === base_uri) { /*base_uri is the installation
                  directory*/
5               return true;
6           } else if (params.type == "IMAGE") {
7               return check_img_whitelist(params.url);
8           } else if (params.type == "SCRIPT") {
9               if (!doneLoading_mainframe && params.url === base_uri + "/shim1.
                      js") {
10                  doneLoading_mainframe = true;
11                  return true;
12              } else if (!doneLoading_mainframe) {
13                  return check_script_whitelist(params.url);
14              }
15          }
16      } else if (params.id == "secondframe") { /*Policy for non-UI child*/
17          if (params.url === base_uri) { return true;}
18          else if (params.type == "SCRIPT") {
19              if (!doneLoading_secondframe && params.url === base_uri + "/shim2
                      .js") {
20                  doneLoading_secondframe = true;
21                  return true;
22              } else if (!doneLoading_secondframe) {
23                  return check_script_whitelist(url);
24              }
25          }
26      }
27      return false;}
```

Listing 1.1. A basic policy for Clipperz

Data-Confinement. We modified Clipperz to run in a pair of data-confined sandboxes: one for the UI and another for the non-UI functionality. Our modifications required minimal effort (67 lines changed) and reduced the TCB from 1.4MB to 6.3KB. This new TCB includes 42 lines of policy code.

Invariants. We apply a temporal policy for each sandbox as shown in Listing 1.1. For both sandboxes, the monitor code in our modified Clipperz applications only allows the DCS access to postMessage and a whitelist of images and JavaScript files (lines 7, 13, and 23). We also enforce a temporal policy: we allow network requests only until the sandbox downloads the password database (lines 10 and 20). Once the DCS sandbox downloads the password database, our policy disallows further network access save for navigation to pages like the help page. Relying on a whitelist of network resources means that we can guarantee the secrecy of the user's master password, which is impossible in the current HTML5 platform.

We do not allow the UI code to execute direct logins, since it presents a possible self-exfiltration channel [9]. Instead, it must send a message telling the non-UI component to do a direct login. The non-UI component retrieves the appropriate credentials and completes the direct login process. The non-UI component does not need complex UI code and executes with a restrictive CSP, providing higher assurance.

6.2 The BrowserID SSO Mechanism

BrowserID is a new authentication service by Mozilla. Similar to other single sign-on mechanisms like Facebook Connect and OpenID, BrowserID enables websites (termed Relying Parties) to authenticate a user using Mozilla's centralized service. Users set up a single "master" email/password to sign in to the trusted BrowserID service and can have the service authenticate the user to a Relying Party. Other single sign-on mechanisms share similar designs, and our results are more generally applicable to other single sign-on systems.

BrowserID uses the EJS templating system [29], which loads template files from the server and converts them to code at runtime using `eval`. A number of modern JavaScript templating languages use this technique [1]. The use of `eval` limits the applicability of CSP and static analysis techniques.

Data-Confinement. We modified BrowserID to execute in a data-confined sandbox. We required minimal effort to port BrowserID—the majority of the changes (184 lines) were to switch the EJS library from synchronous XmlHttpRequests to asynchronous requests supported by privilege separated HTML5 applications. Our modifications reduced the TCB from 206.9KB to 5.7KB, which includes 81 lines of policy code.

Invariants. Running BrowserID in a DCS we were able to implement a policy to provide two key guarantees. First, the login and credential managers (management component) do not communicate with any servers other than the BrowserID servers. This allows us to enforce secrecy on the master BrowserID username/password.

Second, the parent ensures that in one instance of the authentication protocol, the DCS executes the whole protocol with the same BrowserID and Relying Party window. Our design guarantees that sensitive tokens are never leaked to parties outside these participants. In the past, single sign-on mechanisms have had implementation bugs that allowed a MITM of an authentication flow [43,41]; our design prevents such bugs.

For further hardening, we implemented a state machine in the security policy based on the intended dialog behavior, which ensures that the dialog (which asks for passwords and other user input) component performs a series of requests consistent with transitions possible in the state machine. This prevents a compromised dialog DCS from making arbitrary requests in the user's session, such as deleting her account.

6.3 The OpenEMR Patient Information Pages

OpenEMR is the most popular open-source electronic medical record system [38]. With support for a variety of records like patients, billing, prescriptions, medical reports amongst others, OpenEMR is a comprehensive and complex web application. Patient records, prescriptions, and medical reports are highly sensitive data, with most jurisdictions having laws regulating their access and distribution, possibly with penalties for inadvertent disclosure.

We focus on the patient information component of the OpenEMR application. OpenEMR accesses the patient details by using a session variable named `pid` (patient id). Once the user sets the patient id, all future requests, such as 'demographic data,' 'notes,' and so on, can only refer to the particular patient. To navigate to another patient, the user uses the search interface to reset the patient id.

Setting the patient id for a particular session just requires a GET request with a `set_pid` parameter. An attacker can accomplish this with any content injection. For example, an attacker could inject a specially crafted image tag that causes a user to make such a request. As a result, after a user loads the image, the OpenEMR server will return medical records for the attacker-specified user. Note that this is not an XSS attack, but a content injection attack.

Data-Confinement. We modified the patient information component to run under a DCS. This required modifications to 51 lines of code and reduced the TCB from 149.1KB to 6.1KB, which includes a 38-line policy.

Invariants. First, the DCS verifiably ensures that sensitive medical data does not leak to untrusted principals. The DCS can also prevent the page from making arbitrary calls to the large, feature-rich application. In our case, we programmed the security policy to allow only a short whitelist of (method, URL) pairs necessary for the page to function. For example, the monitor denies any request with a `set_pid` parameter. This protects against the content injection attack discussed above. This would not be possible with an origin-based whitelist.

6.4   The SQL Buddy Database Administration Interface

SQL Buddy is an open-source web-based application to handle the administration of MySQL databases. It allows database administrators to browse data stored in a MySQL database and to execute SQL queries and manage database users. SQL Buddy does not use any of the client-side communication channels we block in a DCS.   ·

Data-Confinement. We reused previous work on privilege separation of SQL Buddy, which required only 11 lines of change to the 100KB SQL Buddy application. Our data-confined SQL Buddy application has a TCB of 2.97KB, which includes a 124-line policy.

Invariants. By executing SQL Buddy in a DCS, we can enforce strong confinement policies. The application runs in two logical stages. Initially, the policy restricts communication to only static SQL Buddy resources. Our first-stage policy allows the application to load only these whitelisted JavaScript and CSS files. After loading the scripts and stylesheets, the application only accesses the network to load static images and to make `XMLHttpRequests` to a special endpoint.

Our second-stage policy locks down communication to these two channels. The flexibility of the DCS policy interface is key to enforcing a different policy for each stage.

Our policy restricts all explicit communication channels: if the SQL Buddy DCS is compromised, it cannot send data to arbitrary servers. Our design also allows us to enforce finer grained policies. For example, we have the secure parent show confirmation prompt for database writes. This prevents compromised code in the DCS from surreptitiously modifying the database.

7   Related Work

A number of previous works share our goals of improving assurance in web applications. We gave a detailed comparison to closely related works in Section 3.2. Data confinement has been investigated in native binary applications as well [30]. Zalewski [45] and Heidrich et al. [26] point at a number of attacks that violate data-confinement invariants even in the absence of code injection. IceShield demonstrated the efficacy of modern ES5 features to create a tamper-resistant mediation layer for JavaScript in modern browsers [25]; these may be used a basis for implementing data confinement policy checkers in the future.

8   Conclusion

Modern HTML5 applications handle increasingly sensitive personal data, and require strong data-confinement guarantees. However, current approaches to ensure confinement are ad-hoc and do not provide high assurance. We presented a new design for achieving data-confinement that guarantees complete mediation with a small TCB. Our design is practical, has negligible performance overhead, and does not require intrusive changes to the HTML5 platform. We empirically show that our new design can enable data-confinement in a number of applications handling sensitive data and achieve a drastic reduction in TCB. Future work includes investigating and mitigating covert channels.

Acknowledgements. We thank the anonymous reviewers for their valuable feedback. This research is partially supported by research grant R-252-000-495-133 from Ministry of Education, Singapore. This work was supported by Intel through the ISTC for Secure Computing; by the National Science Foundation under grant numbers CCF-0424422, 0842695, and 0831501 CT-L; by the Air Force Office of Scientific Research under MURI awards FA9550-08-1-0352 and FA9550-09-1-0539; by the Office of Naval Research under MURI grant no. N000140911081.

References

1. Chromium Bug Tracker: http://crbug.com/107538
2. Agten, P., Acker, S.V., Brondsema, Y., Phung, P.H., Desmet, L., Piessens, F.: JSand: Complete client-side sandboxing of third-party javascript without browser modifications. In: ACSAC (2012)
3. Akhawe, D., Barth, A., Lam, P., Mitchell, J., Song, D.: Towards a Formal Foundation of Web Security. In: CSF (2010)
4. Akhawe, D., Saxena, P., Song, D.: Privilege Separation in HTML5 Applications. In: USENIX Security (2012)
5. Akhawe, D., Li, F., He, W., Saxena, P., Song, D.: Data-confined html5 applications. Technical Report UCB/EECS-2013-20, EECS Department, University of California, Berkeley (March 2013)
6. Barth, A.: Timing Attacks on CSS Shaders (2011), http://goo.gl/Mos4a
7. Brumley, D., Song, D.: Privtrans: Automatically Partitioning Programs for Privilege Separation. In: USENIX Security (2004)
8. Cabuk, S., Brodley, C.E., Shields, C.: Ip covert timing channels: design and detection. In: CCS (2004)
9. Chen, E., Gorbaty, S., Singhal, A., Jackson, C.: Self-exfiltration: The dangers of browser-enforced information flow control. In: W2SP (2012)
10. Chia, P.H., Yamamoto, Y., Asokan, N.: Is this app safe?: A large scale study on application permissions and risk signals. In: WWW (2012)
11. Chugh, R., Meister, J.A., Jhala, R., Lerner, S.: Staged information flow for JavaScript. In: PLDI (2009)
12. Clipperz: http://www.clipperz.com/
13. Code Release: https://github.com/devd/data-confined-html5-applications
14. Crockford, D.: AdSafe, http://www.adsafe.org/
15. Hayes, G.: Hacking caja part 2,
    http://www.thespanner.co.uk/2012/09/18/hacking-caja-part-2/
16. Google: Caja, http://developers.google.com/caja/
17. Google: Chrome web store, https://chrome.google.com/webstore
18. Google: Chromium os, http://www.chromium.org/chromium-os
19. Google: Seccomp sandbox for linux,
    http://code.google.com/p/seccompsandbox/
20. Google Caja Bug 51:
    http://code.google.com/p/google-caja/issues/detail?id=51
21. Google Caja Bug 1093:
    http://code.google.com/p/google-caja/issues/detail?id=1093
22. Google Caja: http://code.google.com/p/google-caja/issues/detail?id=520
23. Guha, A., Fredrikson, M., Livshits, B., Swamy, N.: Verified security for browser extensions. In: IEEE S&P (2011)
24. Hanna, S., Shin, E., Akhawe, D., Boehm, A., Saxena, P., Song, D.: The emperor's new apis: On the (in) secure usage of new client-side primitives. In: W2SP (2010)
25. Heiderich, M., Frosch, T., Holz, T.: ICESHIELD: Detection and mitigation of malicious websites with a frozen DOM. In: Sommer, R., Balzarotti, D., Maier, G. (eds.) RAID 2011. LNCS, vol. 6961, pp. 281–300. Springer, Heidelberg (2011)
26. Heiderich, M., Niemietz, M., Schuster, F., Holz, T., Schwenk, J.: Scriptless attacks: stealing the pie without touching the sill. In: CCS (2012)
27. Ingram, L., Walfish, M.: Treehouse: Javascript sandboxes to help web developers help themselves. In: USENIX ATC (2012)

28. Jackson, C., Bortz, A., Boneh, D., Mitchell, J.C.: Protecting browser state from web privacy attacks. In: WWW (2006)
29. Jupiter-IT: EJS Javascript Templates, http://embeddedjs.com/
30. Khatiwala, T., Swaminathan, R., Venkatakrishnan, V.: Data Sandboxing: A Technique for Enforcing Confidentiality Policies. In: ACSAC (2006)
31. Maffeis, S., Mitchell, J.C., Taly, A.: Object capabilities and isolation of untrusted web applications. In: IEEE S&P (2010)
32. Microsoft: Metro Apps, http://msdn.microsoft.com/en-us/windows/apps/
33. Mozilla: Boot2gecko, https://wiki.mozilla.org/B2G
34. phpMyAdmin: http://www.phpmyadmin.net/
35. Politz, J.G., Eliopoulos, S.A., Guha, A., Krishnamurthi, S.: ADsafety: type-based verification of javascriptsandboxing. In: USENIX Security (2011)
36. Provos, N.: Improving host security with system call policies. In: Proceedings of the 12th Conference on USENIX Security Symposium, vol. 12, p. 18. USENIX Association, Berkeley (2003)
37. Richards, G., Lebresne, S., Burg, B., Vitek, J.: An analysis of the dynamic behavior of javascript programs. ACM SIGPLAN Notices (2010)
38. Riley, S.: 5 OpenSource EMRs worth reviewing (2011), http://bit.ly/hUa6ll
39. Saltzer, J., Schroeder, M.: The protection of information in computer systems. Proceedings of the IEEE 63(9), 1278–1308 (1975)
40. Singh, K., Moshchuk, A., Wang, H., Lee, W.: On the incoherencies in web browser access control policies. In: IEEE S&P (2010)
41. Sun, S., Hawkey, K., Beznosov, K.: Systematically breaking and fixing openid security: Formal analysis, semi-automated empirical evaluation, and practical countermeasures. Computers & Security (2012)
42. Tizen: https://www.tizen.org/
43. Wang, R., Chen, S., Wang, X.: Signing me onto your accounts through facebook and google: a traffic-guided security study of commercially deployed single-sign-on web services. In: IEEE S&P (2012)
44. Xu, Y., Bailey, M., Jahanian, F., Joshi, K., Hiltunen, M., Schlichting, R.: An exploration of l2 cache covert channels in virtualized environments. In: CCSW (2011)
45. Zalewski, M.: Postcards from the post-xss world, http://lcamtuf.coredump.cx/postxss/
46. Zhang, Y., Juels, A., Reiter, M.K., Ristenpart, T.: Cross-VM side channels and their use to extract private keys. In: CCS (2012)

KQguard: Binary-Centric Defense against Kernel Queue Injection Attacks

Jinpeng Wei[1], Feng Zhu[1], and Calton Pu[2]

[1] Florida International University, Miami, Florida, USA
{weijp,fzhu001}@cs.fiu.edu
[2] Georgia Institute of Technology, Atlanta, Georgia, USA
calton@cc.gatech.edu

Abstract. Kernel callback queues (KQs) are the mechanism of choice for handling events in modern kernels. KQs have been misused by real-world malware to run malicious logic. Current defense mechanisms for kernel code and data integrity have difficulties with kernel queue injection (KQI) attacks, since they work without necessarily changing legitimate kernel code or data. In this paper, we describe the design, implementation, and evaluation of KQguard, an efficient and effective protection mechanism of KQs. KQguard uses static and dynamic analysis of kernel and device drivers to learn the legitimate event handlers. At runtime, KQguard rejects all the unknown KQ requests that cannot be validated. We implement KQguard on the Windows Research Kernel (WRK) and Linux and extensive experimental evaluation shows that KQguard is efficient (up to ~5% overhead) and effective (capable of achieving zero false positives against representative benign workloads after appropriate training and very low false negatives against 125 real-world malware and nine synthetic attacks). KQguard protects 20 KQs in WRK, can accommodate new device drivers, and through dynamic analysis of binary code can support closed source device drivers.

1   Introduction

One of the most time-critical functions of an operating system (OS) kernel is interrupt/event handling, e.g., timer interrupts. In support of asynchronous event handling, multi-threads kernels store the information necessary for handling an event as an element in a kernel callback queue (called KQ for short), specialized for that event type. To avoid interpretation overhead, each element of a KQ contains a callback function pointer to an event handler specialized for that specific event, plus its associated execution context (as input parameters of the event handler function). When an event happens, a kernel thread invokes the specified callback function to handle the event.

KQs are the mechanism of choice for handling events in modern kernels. As concrete examples, we found 20 KQs in the Windows Research Kernel (WRK) and 22 in Linux. In addition to being popular with kernel programmers, KQs also have become a very useful tool for kernel-level malware such as rootkits (Section 5.1 and [5, 24]). For example, the Pushdo spam bot has misused the Registry Operation Notification

J. Crampton, S. Jajodia, and K. Mayes (Eds.): ESORICS 2013, LNCS 8134, pp. 755–774, 2013.
© Springer-Verlag Berlin Heidelberg 2013

Queue of the Windows kernel to monitor, block, or modify legitimate registry operations [10]. This paper includes 125 examples of real-world malware misusing KQs demonstrating these serious current exploits, and nine additional synthetic potential misuses for illustration of future dangers.

The above-mentioned kernel-level malware misuses the KQs to execute malicious logic, by inserting their own requests into the KQs. This kind of manipulation is called *KQ Injection* or simply KQI. Although KQI appears similar to Direct Kernel Object Manipulation (DKOM) [6] or Kernel Object Hooking (KOH) [13], it is more expressive thus powerful than the other two. While DKOM attacks only tamper with non-control data and KOH attacks only tamper with control data, KQI attacks are capable of doing both because the attacker can supply both control data (i.e., the callback function) and/or non-control data (i.e., the parameters). Moreover, KQI is stealthier than DKOM or KOH in terms of invasiveness: DKOM or KOH attacks *modify* legitimate kernel objects so they are invasive, while KQI attacks just *insert* new elements into KQs and do not have to modify any legitimate kernel objects.

Several seminal defenses have been proposed for DKOM and KOH attacks [1, 3, 26, 36]. Unfortunately, they are not directly applicable to KQI attacks either because of their own limitations or the uniqueness of KQIs. For example, CFI [1] is a classic defense against control data attacks, but it cannot address non-control data attacks launched via KQ injection (Section 2.2 provides a concrete example in WRK). Gibraltar [3] infers and enforces *invariant* properties of kernel data structures, so it seems able to cover KQs as one type of kernel data structure. Unfortunately, Gibraltar relies on periodic snapshots of the kernel memory, which makes it possible for a *transient* malicious KQ request to evade detection. Petroni [26] advocates detecting DKOM by checking the integrity of kernel data structures against specifications, however, the specifications are elaborate and need to be manually written by domain experts. Finally, KQI attacks inject *malicious* kernel data, which makes HookSafe [36] an inadequate solution because the latter can only protect the integrity of *legitimate* kernel data. Therefore, new solutions are needed to defend against KQI attacks.

Inspired by the above research, our KQ defense endorses the general idea of using data structure invariants. However, we address the limitation of existing approaches so that our KQ integrity checking covers both persistent and transient attacks. More specifically, our defense intercepts and checks the validity of *every* KQ request to ensure the execution of legitimate event handlers only, by filtering out all untrusted callback requests. In [37], we develop a KQ defense for Linux (called PLCP) that employs static source code analysis to automatically derive specifications of legitimate KQ requests. However, the reliance on source code limits the practical applicability of PLCP in systems such as Windows in which there are a large number of third-party, closed source device drivers that need KQs for their normal operation.

Therefore, in this paper, we build KQguard, an effective defense against KQI attacks that can support closed source device drivers. Specifically, we make the following contributions: (1) we introduce the KQguad mechanism that can distinguish attack

KQ requests from legitimate KQ event handlers, (2) we employ dynamic analysis of the binary code to automatically generate specifications of legitimate KQ requests (called EH-Signatures) in closed source device drivers, (3) we build a static analysis tool that can automatically identify KQs from the source code of a given kernel, (4) we implement the KQguard in WRK [39] and the Linux kernel, (5) our extensive evaluation of KQguard on WRK shows its effectiveness against KQ exploits (125 real-world malware samples and nine synthetic rootkits), detecting all except two of the attacks (very low false negative rate). With appropriate training, we eliminated all false alarms from KQguard for representative workloads. For resource intensive benchmarks, KQguard carries a small performance overhead of up to about 5%.

The rest of the paper is organized as follows. Section 2 summarizes the problem caused by rootkits misusing KQs. Section 3 describes the high level design of KQguard defense by abstracting the KQ facility. Section 4 outlines some implementation details of KQguard for WRK, validating the design. Section 5 presents the results of an experimental evaluation, demonstrating the effectiveness and efficiency of KQguard. Section 6 outlines related work and Section 7 concludes the paper.

2   Problem Analysis: KQ Injection

2.1   Importance of KQ Injection Attacks

Functionally, KQs are kernel queues that support the callback of a programmer-defined event handler, specialized for efficient handling of that particular event. For example, the soft timer queue of the Linux kernel supports scheduling of timed event-handling functions. The requester (e.g., a device driver) specifies an event time and a callback function to be executed at the specified time. When the system timer reaches the specified time, the kernel timer interrupt handler invokes the callback function stored in the soft timer request queue (Fig. 1). More generally and regardless of the specific event semantics among the KQs, their control flow conforms to the same abstract type: For each request in the queue, a kernel thread invokes the callback function specified in the KQ request to handle the event.

Kernel-level rootkits exploit the KQ callback mechanism to execute malicious logic by inserting their own request into a KQ (e.g., by supplying malicious callback function or data in step 1 of Fig. 1). This kind of manipulation, called a *KQ injection* attack, only uses legitimate kernel interface and it does not change legitimate kernel code or statically allocated data structures such as global variables. Therefore, syntactically a KQ injection request is indistinguishable from normal event handlers. Consider the Registry Operation Notification Queue as illustration. Using it in defense, anti-virus software event handlers can detect potential intruder malicious activity on the Windows registry. Using it in KQ injection attack, Pushdo [10] can monitor, block, or modify legitimate registry operations.

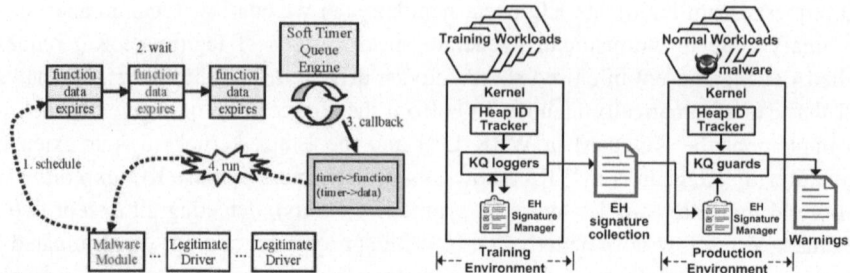

Fig. 1. Life cycle of a timer request in Linux   **Fig. 2.** Overall Architecture of KQguard

Several KQ injection attacks by real world malware have been documented (Table 1 in Section 5.1). Specifically, malware has misused KQs to hide better against discovery [2,18], to carry out covert operations [9,10,27], and to attack security products directly [4]. Further details can be found in our technical report [38]. Undoubtedly, KQ injection attacks represent a clear and present danger to current OS kernels.

2.2   KQ Injection Attack Model

The KQ injection malware listed in Table 1 (Section 5.1) misuse KQs in a straightforward way. They prepare a malicious function in kernel space and use its address as the callback function pointer in a KQ request. We call these *callback-into-malware* attacks. Since their malicious functions must be injected somewhere in the kernel space, callback-into-malware attacks can be detected by runtime kernel code integrity checkers such as SecVisor [29]. Therefore, they are considered the basic level of attack.

Unfortunately, a more sophisticated level of KQ injection attacks, called *callback-into-libc* (in analogy to return-into-libc [32, 35]), create a malicious callback request containing a legitimate callback function but malicious input parameters. When activated, the legitimate callback function may carry out *unintended* actions that are beneficial to the attacker. For example, one legitimate callback function in the asynchronous procedure call (APC) queue of the WRK is `PsExitSpecialApc`, which can cause the currently executing thread to terminate with an exit status code that is specified in the "NormalContext" parameter field of the APC request structure. Therefore, hypothetically an attacker can inject an APC request with `PsExitSpecialApc` as the callback function to force a thread to terminate with a chosen exit status code (set in the "NormalContext" field). This kind of Callback-into-libc attack can be used to shutdown an anti-virus program but make the termination appear normal to an Intrusion Detection System, by setting a misleading exit status code.

Callback-into-libc KQ injection attacks represent an interesting challenge, since they allow an attacker to execute malicious logic without injecting his own code, and the above example shows that such attacks can target non-control data (e.g., the exit status code of a thread). Therefore, they cannot be defeated by approaches that focus on control data (e.g., CFI [1]).

The design of KQguard in Section 3 shows how we can detect both callback-into-malware and callback-into-libc KQ injection attacks.

2.3   Design Requirements of KQ Defense

An effective KQ defense should satisfy four requirements: efficiency, effectiveness, extensibility, and inclusiveness. In this section, we outline the reasons KQguard satisfies these requirements. Some previous techniques may solve specific problems but have difficulties with satisfying all four requirements. We defer a discussion of related work to Section 6.

Efficiency: It is important for KQ defenses to minimize their overhead; KQguard is designed to protect KQs with low overhead, including the time-sensitive ones. *Effectiveness*: KQ defenses should detect all the KQ injection attacks (zero false negatives) and make no mistakes regarding the legitimate event handlers (zero false positives); KQguard is designed to achieve this level of precision and recall by focusing on the recognition of all legitimate event handlers. *Extensibility*: Due to the rapid proliferation of new devices, it is important for KQ defenses to extend their coverage to new device drivers; the KQguard design isolates the knowledge on legitimate event handlers into a table (EH-Signature collection) that is easily extensible. *Inclusiveness*: A practical concern of commercial kernels is the protection of third-party, closed source device drivers; KQguard uses static analysis when source code is available and dynamic analysis to protect the closed source legitimate drivers.

3   Design of KQguard

In this section, we describe the design of KQguard as a general protection mechanism for the KQ abstract type. The concrete implementation is described in Section 4.

3.1   Architecture Overview and Assumptions

The main idea of KQguard is to differentiate legitimate KQ event handlers from malicious KQ injection attacks based on characteristics of *known-good* event handlers. For simplicity of discussion, we call such characteristics *Callback-Signatures*. A Callback-Signature is an effective representation of a KQ event handler (or a KQ request) for checking. One special type of Callback-Signatures is those of the legitimate KQ event handlers, and we call them *EH-Signatures*.

How to specify or discover the EH-Signatures is a practical challenge in the design of KQguard. Since legitimate KQ requests are originated from legitimate kernel or device drivers, in order to specify EH-Signatures we need to study the behavior of the core kernel and legitimate drivers. In an ideal kernel development environment, one could imagine annotating the entire kernel and all device driver code to make KQ requests explicit, e.g., by defining a KQ abstract type. Processing the KQ annotations in the complete source code will give us the exact EH-Signature collection.

Unfortunately, this is not practical because many third-party closed source device drivers are unlikely to share their source code.

Therefore, our design decision is to apply dynamic binary code analysis to automate the process of obtaining a specialized EH-Signature collection that fits the configuration and usage of each system. Specifically, our design uses the architecture shown in Fig. 2. We extend the kernel in a dedicated training environment to log (collect) EH-Signatures of KQ requests that the kernel encounters during the execution of legitimate device drivers. Then we extend the kernel in a production environment to use such learned EH-Signatures to guard against KQ injection attacks, which can be launched by malware installed in the production environment.

By employing dynamic analysis, our design does not require source code of the device drivers, thus it satisfies the inclusiveness requirement. Moreover, by having two kinds of environments, we decouple the collection and the use of EH-Signatures, which allows future legitimate drivers to be supported by KQguard: we can run the new driver in the training environment to collect its EH-Signatures and then add the new EH-Signatures into the signature collection used by the production environment. By using this method, our design satisfies the extensibility requirement.

In order to guarantee that EH-Signatures learned from the training environment is applicable to the production environment, we assume that the training environment and the production environment run the same OS and set of legitimate device drivers.

In order to guarantee that all the Callback-Signatures learned from the training environment represent legitimate KQ requests, we assume that any device driver that is run in the training environment is benign. This assumption may not hold on a consumer system because a normal user may not have the knowledge and capability to tell whether a new driver is benign or not. Therefore, we expect that KQguard is used in a strictly controlled environment (such as military and government) where a knowledgeable system administrator ensures that only benign device drivers are installed in the training environment, by applying standard security practices.

As is typical of any dynamic analysis approach, we assume that a representative and comprehensive workload is available during training to trigger all the legitimate KQ event handlers. Because some legitimate KQ requests may be made only under certain conditions, the workload must be comprehensive so that such KQ requests can be triggered and thus logged. Otherwise, KQguard may raise false alarms.

3.2   Building the EH-Signature Collection

In order to collect EH-Signatures in a training environment, we first instrument the kernel with KQ request logging capability and then run comprehensive workloads to trigger legitimate KQ requests.

3.2.1   Instrumentation of the Kernel to Log EH-Signatures

To collect EH-Signatures, we instrument all places in the kernel where KQ request information is available. Specifically, we extend kernel functions that initialize, insert, or dispatch KQ requests. We extend these functions with a KQ request logging utility, which generates and logs Callback-Signatures from every "raw" KQ request (i.e., with absolute addresses) submitted by the legitimate kernel and device drivers. The details of Callback-Signature generation are non-trivial and deferred to Section 3.5.

In general, the information contained in EH-Signatures is readily available in the kernel, although the precise location of such information may differ from kernel to kernel. It is a matter of identifying the appropriate location to instrument the kernel to extract the necessary information. Section 3.6 describes our non-trivial search for all the locations of these simple changes, in which we employ static source code analysis on the entire kernel. The extensions are applied to the kernel at source code level. The instrumented kernel is then rebuilt for the EH-Signature collection process.

3.2.2   Dynamic Profiling to Collect EH-Signatures

In this step, we run a representative set of benchmark applications using a comprehensive workload on top of the instrumented kernel. During this phase, the kernel extensions described in Section 3.2.1 are triggered by every KQ request.

To avoid false negatives in KQ defense, the training is performed in a clean environment to ensure no malware Callback-Signatures are included. To avoid false positives, the training workload needs to be comprehensive enough to trigger all of the legitimate KQ requests. Our evaluation (Section 5.3) shows a very low false positive rate, indicating the feasibility of the dynamic profiling method. In general, the issue of test coverage for large scale software without source code is a significant challenge and beyond the scope of this paper.

3.3   Validation Using EH-Signature Collection

As shown in the "Production Environment" part of Fig. 2, we modify the dispatcher of every identified KQ to introduce a KQ guard that checks the legitimacy of a pending KQ request before the dispatcher invokes the callback function. To perform the check, the KQ guard first builds the Callback-Signature from a pending request (detailed in Section 3.5), and then matches the Callback-Signature against the EH-Signature Collection. If a match is found, the dispatcher invokes the confirmed event handler. Otherwise, the dispatcher takes necessary actions against the potential threat (e.g., generating a warning message). The details of signature matching are discussed in Section 3.4.

To reduce performance overhead, we cache the results of KQ validation so as to avoid repeatedly checking a KQ request if its Callback-Signature has not changed since the last time it is checked. Specifically, we maintain cryptographic hashes of the "raw" KQ requests (identified by memory location) that pass the validation, so that when the same KQ request (at the recorded memory location) is to be checked again, we recalculate the cryptographic hash and compare it with the stored one. Our profiling study confirms that a significant fraction (~90%) of KQ validation is redundant because the same KQ requests are repeatedly enqueued, dispatched, dequeued, and enqueued again. Therefore, caching the validation results for such repeated KQ requests can reduce performance overhead of KQ defense.

3.4   Specification of the Callback-Signatures

A critical design issue of KQguard is the determination of the set of characteristics in the Callback-Signatures: it must precisely identify the same KQ requests in the training and production environments. On one hand, the set must not include characteristics that can vary between the two environments (e.g., the expiration time in a soft timer request) because otherwise even the same legitimate KQ requests would appear different (false positives); on the other hand, the set must include all the *invariant* characteristics between the two environments because otherwise a malicious KQ request that differs from a legitimate request only in the missing characteristics would also pass the check, resulting in false negatives. For example, the malicious KQ request in Fig. 3.b is allowed by a KQ guard that only checks the shaded fields, although it causes a malicious function bar_two to be invoked; and the malicious KQ request achieves this by tampering with the "action" field of structure se that is not covered by the Callback-Signature. Here when the KQ request is dispatched, foo is invoked with qe.data as its parameter.

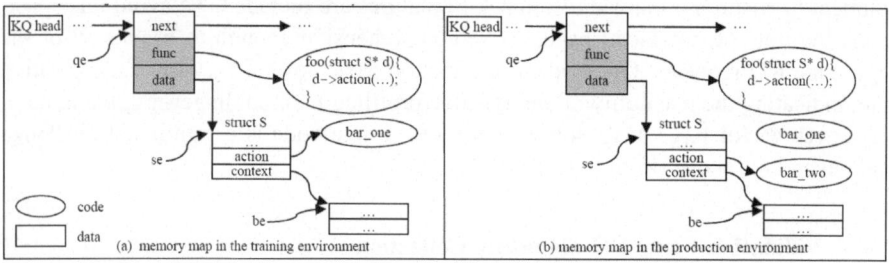

Fig. 3. Illustration of a False Negative Caused by a Callback-Signature that Only Includes the Shaded Fields. The two KQ requests have different executions (i.e., bar_one vs bar_two), but their Callback-Signatures are the same. Here bar_two is a malicious function.

In order to minimize false negatives such as the one demonstrated in Fig. 3, one could include more characteristics (e.g., se.action) into the Callback-Signatures. However, there are some challenges in doing that with closed source device drivers. Specifically, in order to realize that se.action is important, one can get hints from how foo works, but without source code, it is non-trivial to figure out that foo invokes se.action. Another possibility is to use the type information of se (e.g., struct S) to know that its "action" field is a function pointer and such information can be derived from the type of KQ request data fields (e.g., qe.data); unfortunately, this is often not possible because the data fields of KQ requests are often generic pointers (i.e., void *); in that case, one cannot figure out the type of se easily if it resides in a closed source device driver. Therefore, in order to support closed source device drivers, our KQ defense assumes that:

Kernel data reachable from KQ requests (e.g., se.action) can be identified and it has integrity in both the training and the production environments (i.e., changing of this field from bar_one to bar_two is prohibited by some other security measures).

To avoid "reinventing the wheel", we note that techniques such as KOP [7] can correctly locate kernel data such as se.action despite the existence of generic pointers, and techniques such as HookSafe [36] can prevent malware from tampering with invariant function pointers in legitimate kernel data structures, such as se.action. Moreover, both KOP and HookSafe can be used to cover even "deeper" kernel data such as be in Fig. 3. Note that the inclusion of qe.data in the Callback-Signature is very critical because it ensures that if qe can pass the check performed by KQguard, se is a legitimate kernel data structure, and thus its "action" field can be protected by HookSafe (HookSafe is designed to protect only legitimate kernel data structures).

Note that HookSafe cannot be an alternative defense against KQ injection attacks from the top level (e.g., by ensuring that "func" and "data" fields in Fig. 3 are not tampered with) for two reasons. First, not all top-level KQ request data structures are legitimate because malware can allocate and insert its own KQ request data structure. Second, not all top-level legitimate KQ request data structures are invariant (i.e., their values do not change) but HookSafe can only protect invariant kernel data. We have observed multiple cases in the APC queue of the WRK in which top-level legitimate KQ requests change their values during normal execution. For example, IopfComple-teRequest (in WRK\base\ntos\io\iomgr\iosubs.c) inserts an APC request with callback function IopCompleteRequest (in WRK\base\ntos\io\iomgr \internal.c); when this APC request is dispatched (i.e., IopCompleteRequest is invoked), its callback function field is changed to IopUserCompletion before it is inserted back to the APC queue.

To summarize the above discussion, (1) we need to support closed source device drivers, (2) we need a way to defend against KQ injection attacks from the top level, and (3) techniques are available to guard deeper kernel data reachable from KQ requests. Based on these three observations, in this paper we choose a Callback-Signature format that focuses on KQ request level (the top level) characteristics: (callback_function, callback_parameters, insertion_path, allocation). Here callback_function is the callback function pointer stored in a KQ request, callback_parameters represents the relevant parameters stored in it, insertion_path represents how the KQ request is inserted (by which driver? along which code path?), and allocation represents how its memory is allocated (global, heap, or stack? by which driver?).

Each characteristic in our Callback-Signature is important for effective KQ guarding. callback_function is used to protect the kernel against callback-into-malware attacks, and both callback_function and callback_parameters are used to protect the kernel against callback-into-libc attacks (Section 2.2). Furthermore, insertion_path and allocation provide the context of the KQ request and thus can also be very useful. For example, if KQguard only checks callback_function and callback_parameters, malware can insert an *existing* and *legitimate* KQ request object LKQ if it can somehow benefit from the dispatching of LKQ (e.g., resetting a watchdog timer).

To ensure that the signature matching of a KQ request observed during the production use and one observed during the training can guarantee the same *execution*, we need to make sure that the code and static data of the core kernel and legitimate device drivers have integrity in the production environment. We also need to ensure that malware cannot directly attack KQ guards, including their code and the EH-Signature collection. We can leverage a hypervisor (e.g., Xen) to satisfy the above requirements. The idea is to run the modified kernel (with KQ guards) on top of a hypervisor and extend the shadow-based memory management of the hypervisor to write-protect code and static data of the modified kernel [37]. Note that this protection covers KQ guards and the EH-signature collection because they are part of the modified kernel.

3.5   Generation of Callback-Signatures from KQ Requests

In both EH-Signature collection (Section 3.2) and KQ request validation (Section 3.3), Callback-Signatures need to be derived from raw KQ requests. This is called Callback-Signature generation and we discuss the details in this subsection.

3.5.1   Motivation for Delinking

As we discuss in Section 3.4, a Callback-Signature is a tuple (callback_function, callback_parameters, insertion_path, allocation). Since callback_function and callback_parameters correspond to fields in KQ requests (e.g., the "func" field of qe in Fig. 3), it seems that we can simply copy the value of those fields into a Callback-Signature. However, when a Callback-Signature contains a memory reference (e.g., a parameter that points to a heap object), we have to overcome one challenge: namely, what the KQ loggers and the KQ guards can directly observe is an absolute memory address; however, the absolute addresses of the same variable or function can be different in the training and production environments, for example, when they are inside a device driver that is loaded at different starting addresses in the two environments. Therefore, if we use absolute addresses in the Callback-Signatures, there will not be a match for the same callback function, which results in false positives.

In order to resolve this issue, we raise the level of abstraction for memory references in the Callback Signatures so that variations at the absolute address level can be tolerated. For example, we translate a callback function pointer (absolute address) into a unique module ID, plus the offset relative to the starting address of its containing module (usually a device driver, and we treat the core kernel as a special module). Under the assumption that the kernel maintains a uniform mapping of module location to module ID, the pair (module ID, offset) becomes an invariant representation of the callback function pointer independent of where the module is loaded. This kind of translation is called *delinking*.

3.5.2   Details of Delinking

KQguard delinks memory references (i.e., pointers) in different ways depending on the allocation type of the target memory. As Fig. 4 shows, there can be three types of allocations: global variable, heap variable, and local variable.

The pointer to a global variable is translated into (module ID, offset), in the same way as the callback function pointer (Section 3.5.1). There can be two kinds of global variables depending on whether they reside in a device driver inside the kernel or in a

user-level library (e.g., a DLL on Windows). We care about user-level global variables because some KQ parameters reference user-level memory (e.g., the APC
queue on Windows). We regard device drivers and user-level libraries uniformly as
modules and we modify the appropriate kernel functions to keep track of their address
ranges when they are loaded (e.g., PspCreateThread for DLLs).

The pointer to a heap object is translated into a call stack that corresponds to the
code path that originates from a requester (e.g., a device driver) and ends in the allocation of the heap object. We use a call stack rather than the immediate return address
because the immediate return address may not be in the requester's address space
(i.e., it may be in some wrapper function for the heap allocation function and the requester can call a function at the top of the call chain to allocate a heap object). Since
most kernels do not maintain the request call stack for allocated heap objects, we
instrument their heap allocator functions to collect such information, and the instrumentation is called Heap ID Tracker in Fig. 2. Specifically, the Heap ID Tracker traverses the call stack frames backwards until it reaches a return address that falls within the code section of a device driver or it reaches the top of the stack; if no device
driver is found during the traversal, the core kernel is used as the requester; all return
addresses encountered during this traversal are part of the call stack, and each of them
is translated into a (module ID, offset) pair, in the same way as the callback function pointer discussed in Section 3.5.1. Similar to global variables, our delinking supports two types of heap objects: kernel-level and user-level.

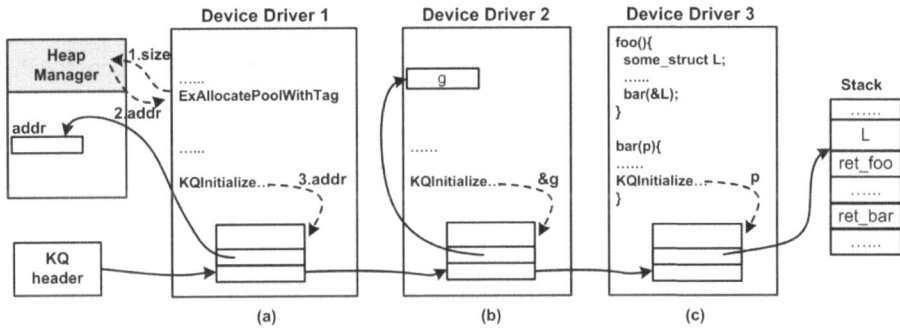

Fig. 4. Illustration of Different Allocation Types of Pointers: (a) Heap Variable, (b) Global
Variable, (c) Local Variable

The pointer to a local variable is translated into a pair (call_stack, l_offset). The
call stack starts in a function where a KQ request is inspected (e.g., in a KQ insertion
function), and it stops in the function that contains the local variable (e.g., L in function foo in Fig. 4.c).Each return address encountered during the traversal is translated
into a (module ID, offset) pair. Finally, l_offset is the relative position of the local
variable in its containing stack frame. For example, if [ebp-8] is used to represent the
local variable, l_offset is 8. We have not observed any pointers to user-level local
variables, so we do not cover the translation for pointers to user-level local variables.

Because the static type of a KQ request data (e.g., the "data" field of a soft timer request structure) is often a generic pointer (i.e., `void *`), we have to detect its actual type at runtime. Given the raw value of a piece of KQ request data, we run a series of tests to decide the suitable delinking for it if it is considered a pointer. First, we test whether the raw value falls within the address range of a loaded driver or a user-level library to decide whether it should be delinked as a pointer to a global variable. If the test fails, we test whether it falls within the address range of an allocated heap object to decide whether it should be delinked as a pointer to a heap variable. If this test also fails, we test whether it falls within the address ranges of the stack frames to see whether it should be delinked as a pointer to a local variable. If this test still fails, we determine the KQ data to be a non-pointer, and no delinking is performed.

3.6   Automated Detection of KQs

Since every KQ can be exploited by malware (part of the attack surface), we need to build the EH-Signatures for all of KQs. But before we can guard a KQ, we must first know its existence. Therefore, we design and implement a KQ discovery tool that automates the process of finding KQs in a kernel by analyzing its source code. Since kernel programmers are not intentionally hiding KQs, they usually follow similar programming patterns that our tool uses effectively:

- A KQ is typically implemented as a linked list or an array. In addition to insert/delete, a KQ has a dispatcher that operates on the corresponding type.

- A KQ dispatcher usually contains a loop to act upon all or a subset of queue elements. For example, `pm_send_all` in Fig. 5 contains the dispatcher loop for the Power Management Notification queue of Linux kernel 2.4.32.

- A KQ dispatcher usually changes the kernel control flow, e.g., invoking a callback function contained in a queue element.

Based on the above analysis, the KQ discovery tool recognizes a KQ in several steps. It starts by detecting a loop that iterates through a candidate data structure.

```
/* linux-2.4.32/kernel/pm.c */                      ......}
int pm_send_all (pm_request_t rqst, void *data)       entry = entry->next;    }
{      ......                                       ......}
 entry = pm_devs.next;                             int    pm_send(struct    pm_dev    *dev,
 while (entry != &pm_devs) {                        pm_request_t rqst, void *data)
  struct pm_dev *dev=list_entry(entry, struct pm_dev, en-  {......
try);                                                  status    =    (*dev->callback)(dev,    rqst,
   if (dev->callback) {                             data);......}
    int status = pm_send(dev, rqst, data);
```

Fig. 5. Details of the Power Management Notification Queue on Linux Kernel 2.4.32

Then it checks whether a queue element is derived and acted upon inside the loop. Next, our tool marks the derived queue element as a *taint* source and performs a flow-sensitive taint propagation through the rest of the loop body; this part is flow-sensitive because it propagates taint into downstream functions through parameters (e.g., `dev` passed from `pm_send_all` to `pm_send` in Fig. 5). During the propagation, our tool checks whether any tainted function pointer is invoked (e.g., `dev->callback` in `pm_send` in Fig. 5), and if that is the case, it reports a candidate KQ. Due to space constraints we omit further details, but the results (e.g., KQs found in WRK) are interesting and discussed in Section 4.

4   Implementations of KQguard

The KQguard design (Section 3) is implemented on the WRK and Linux (kernel version 3.5). Due to space constraint, we only present our implementation on the WRK, which consists of about 3,900 lines of C code and 2,003 lines of Objective Caml code.

Construction of Callback-Signatures in WRK. In order to collect the Callback-Signatures for the 20 KQs in the WRK, we instrument the kernel in two sets of functions. The first set of functions initialize, insert, or dispatch KQs and our instrumentation consists of 600 lines of C code. To support delinking of Callback-Signatures, we instrument the device driver loader function (`IopLoadDriver`) and the thread creation function (`PspCreateThread`), and we also instrument heap allocation or deallocation functions (`ExAllocatePoolWithTag`, `ExFreePool`, `NtAllocateVirtualMemory`, and `NtFreeVirtualMemory`) to keep track of the address ranges of allocated heap memory blocks and the call stack to the heap allocation function. Our instrumentation of the heap allocator / deallocator consists of 800 lines of C code.

Automated Detection of KQs for the WRK. We implement the KQ discovery algorithm (Section 3.6) based on static source code analysis, using the C Intermediate Language (CIL) [22]. Our implementation consists of 2,003 lines of Objective Caml code. We applied the KQ discovery tool to the WRK source code (665,950 lines of C), 20 KQs were detected (seven of them are mentioned in Table 1 and the rest can be found in [38]), and they include all the KQs that we are aware of, which suggests the usefulness of our KQ discovery algorithm. However, whether these 20 KQs cover *all* KQs in the WRK is an interesting and open question.

Callback-Signature Collection Management. We developed a set of utility functions to manage the Callback-Signatures, including the EH-Signatures. These functions support the generation, comparison, insertion, and search of Callback-Signatures. They are implemented in 2,200 lines of C code.

Validation of Callback-Signature in WRK. We instrument the dispatcher of every identified KQ in the WRK in the production environment so that the dispatcher checks the legitimacy of a pending KQ request before invoking the callback function (Section 3.3). Our instrumentation consists of about 300 lines of C code.

5   Evaluation of KQguard in WRK

Due to space constraints, we only report the evaluation results of the WRK implementation of KQguard in this section. We evaluate both the effectiveness and efficiency of KQguard through measurements on production kernels. By effectiveness we mean precision (whether it misidentifies the attacks found, measured in false positives) and recall (whether it misses a real attack, measured in false negatives) of KQguard when identifying KQ injection attacks. By efficiency we mean the overhead introduced by KQguard. In both the training and the production systems used in our evaluation, the hardware is a 2.4 GHz Intel Xeon 8-Core server with 16 GB of RAM, and the operating system is Windows Server 2003 Service Pack 1 running the WRK.

5.1   Real-World KQ Injection Attacks

We start our evaluation of KQguard effectiveness by testing our WRK implementation (Section 4) against real-world KQ injection attacks in Windows OS. Since malware technology keeps advancing, we focus on the most recent and the most influential malware samples that represent the state of the art. Specifically, we chose 125 malware samples from the top 20 malware families [40] and the top 10 botnet families [41]. These samples are known to have KQ injection behaviors.

Overall, our test confirmed that 98 samples inject the APC queue, 34 samples inject the DPC queue, 32 samples inject the load image notification queue, 20 samples inject the process creation/deletion notification queue, four samples inject the file system registration change queue, four samples inject the registry operation notification queue, and two samples inject the system worker thread queue.

Table 1 reports the results of 10 representative spam bot samples. We started with malware with reported KQ injection attacks, which are marked with a "√" with citation. We were able to confirm some of these attacks, shaded in gray. The rows with shaded "√" without citations are confirmed new KQ injection attacks that have not been reported by other sources. For example, Rustock.J injects an APC request with a callback function at address 0xF83FE316, which falls within the address range of a device driver called msliksurserv.sys that is loaded by Rustock.J; this APC request raises an alarm because it does not match any of the EH-Signatures we have collected.

For all the malware that we were able to activate (the Rustock.C sample failed to run in our test environment), we confirmed the reported KQ injection attacks, except for the Duqu attack on load image notification queue and Storm on the APC queue.

Table 1. Known KQ Injection Attacks in Representative Malware

KQ Malware	Timer/ DPC	Worker Thread	Load Image	Create Process	APC	FsRegistration Change	RegistryOp Callback
Rustock.C	√ [2, 18]			√ [27]	√ [27]		
Rustock.J			√	√	√		
Pushdo	√			√ [10]	√	√ [10]	√ [10]
Storm	√		√ [4]		√ [23]		
Srizbi	√				√		
TDSS			√		√	√	
Duqu	√		√ [16]		√		
ZeroAccess	√	√ [11]			√ [11]		√
Koutodoor	√			√			
Pandex					√		
Mebroot	√						

The Rustock samples show that malware designers have significant ability and flexibility in injecting different KQs. Concretely, Rustock.J has stopped using the timer queue, which Rustock.C uses, but Rustock.J started to use the load image notification queue, which Rustock.C does not. This may have happened to Duqu's attack on the same queue, or Duqu does not activate the attack on load image notification queue during our experiment. Overall, our evaluation indicates that KQguard can have a low false negative rate because it detects all except two of the KQ injection attacks by 125 real-world malware samples.

5.2   Protection of All KQs

In addition to real world malware, we create synthetic KQ injection attacks for two reasons. First, nine KQs have maximum queue length of zero during the testing in Section 5.1, suggesting that malware is not actively targeting them for the moment; however, the Rustock evolution shows that malware writers may consider such KQs in the near future, so we should ensure that guards for such KQs work properly. Second, the malware analyzed in Section 5.1 belongs to the callback-into-malware category. Although there have been no reports of callback-into-libc attacks in the wild, it is important to evaluate the effectiveness of KQ-guard for both kinds of attacks. Therefore, for completeness, we developed test Windows device drivers for each of the KQs that have not been called and we have confirmed that our KQ defense can detect all the test drivers, which suggests that our defense is effective against potential and future KQ injection attacks.

5.3   False Alarms

We have experimentally confirmed that it is possible to reduce the false positives of KQ guarding to zero. This is achievable when the training workload is comprehensive enough to produce the full EH-Signature collection.

We first collect EH-Signatures on a training machine with Internet access. We repeatedly log in, run a set of normal workload programs, and log off. In order to trigger all possible code paths that insert KQ requests, we actively do the above for fifteen hours. During this process, we gradually collect more and more EH-Signatures until the set does not grow. At the end of training, we collect 813 EH-Signatures. The set of workload programs include Notepad, Windows Explorer, WinSCP, Internet Explorer, 7-Zip, WordPad, IDA, OllyDbg, CFF Explorer, Sandboxie, and Python.

Next we feed the collected EH-Signatures into a production machine with KQ guarding and use that machine for normal workloads as well as the KQ injection malware evaluation and the performance overhead tests. During such uses, we observe zero false alarms. The normal workload programs include the ones mentioned above as well as others such as Firefox not used in training.

While the experimental result appears encouraging, we avoid making a claim that dynamic analysis can always achieve zero false positives. For example, the APC queue has 733 EH-Signatures, such EH-Signatures have 14 unique callback functions, and the most popular callback function is `IopCompleteRequest`, occurring in 603

EH-Signatures. While these 603 EH-Signatures share the same callback function, their insertion paths originate from 51 device drivers, two DLLs, and the core kernel, so the average number of EH-Signatures per requester (e.g., a device driver) is 11, and the largest number is 45 (from the driver ntfs.sys). This result implies that there can be potentially many code paths within a driver that can prepare and insert an APC request with the same callback function, which may or may not be triggered in our training. Moreover, there are in total 199 device drivers in our evaluation system, but our training only observes a subset of them (e.g., 51 in terms of `IopCompleteRequest`); so some legitimate KQ requests from the remaining drivers may be triggered by events such as inserting a USB device, which we have not tested yet. Fortunately, our experience suggests that it is possible to collect the set of EH-Signatures that fits the configuration and usage of a given system with enough training workloads.

5.4   Performance Overhead

We evaluate the performance overhead of KQguard in two steps: microbenchmarks and macrobenchmarks.

For the first step, we measure the overhead of KQguard validation check and heap object tracking. KQguard validation check matches Callback-Signatures against the EH-Signature Collection, and its overhead consists of matching the four parts of a Callback-Signature. Heap object tracking affects every heap allocation and deallocation operation (e.g., `ExAllocatePoolWithTag` and `ExFreePool`). These heap operations are invoked at a global level, with overhead proportional to the overall system and application use of the heap. Specifically, we measure the total time spent in performing 1,000 KQguard validation checks for the DPC queue and the I/O timer queue, two of the most active KQs. The main result is that global heap object tracking during the experiment dominated the KQguard overhead. Specifically, DPC queue validation consumed 93.7 milliseconds of CPU, while heap object tracking consumed 8,527 milliseconds. These 1,000 DPC callback functions are dispatched over a time span of 250,878 milliseconds (4 minutes 11 seconds). Therefore, the total CPU consumed by our KQguard validation for DPC queue and the supporting heap object tracking is 8,620.7 milliseconds (or about 3.4% of the total elapsed time). The measurements of the I/O timer queue (180 ms for validation, 11,807 ms for heap object tracking, and 345,825 ms total elapsed time) confirm the DPC queue results.

For the second step, Table 2 shows the results of five application level benchmarks that stress one or more system resources, including CPU, memory, disk, and network. Each workload is run multiple times and the average is reported. We can see that in terms of execution time of the selected applications, KQguard incurs modest elapsed time increases, from 2.8% for decompression to 5.6% for directory copy. These elapsed time increases are consistent with the microbenchmark measurements, with higher or lower heap activities as the most probable cause of the variations. We also run the PostMark file system benchmark and the PassMark PerformanceTest bench-mark and see similar overhead (3.9% and 4.9%, respectively).

Table 2. Performance Overhead of KQ Guarding in WRK

Workload	Original (sec)	KQ Guarding (sec)	Slowdown
Super PI [33]	2,108±41	2,213±37	5.0%
Copy directory (1.5 GB)	231±9.0	244±15.9	5.6%
Compress directory (1.5 GB)	1,113±24	1,145±16	2.9%
Decompress directory (1.5 GB)	181±4.1	186±5.1	2.8%
Download file (160 MB)	145±11	151±11	4.1%

6   Related Work

In this section, we survey related work that can potentially solve the KQ injection problem and satisfy the four design requirements: efficiency, effectiveness, extensibility, and inclusiveness (Section 2.3).

SecVisor [29] and NICKLE [28] are designed to preserve kernel code integrity or block the execution of foreign code in the kernel. They can defeat callback-into-malware KQ attacks because such attacks require that malicious functions be injected somewhere in the kernel space. However, they cannot detect callback-into-libc attacks because such attacks do not inject malicious code or modify legitimate kernel code. HookSafe [36] is capable of blocking the execution of malware that modifies legitimate function pointers to force a control transfer to the malicious code. However, HookSafe cannot prevent KQ injection attacks because they do not modify existing and legitimate kernel function pointers but instead supply malicious data in their own memory (i.e., the KQ request data structures). CFI [1] can ensure that control transfers of a program during execution always conform to a predefined control flow graph. Therefore, it can be instantiated into an alternative defense against KQIs that supply malicious control data. However, CFI cannot defeat the type of KQI attacks that supply malicious non-control data because they do not change the control flow. SBCFI [25] can potentially detect a callback-into-malware KQ attack. However, SBCFI is designed for persistent kernel control flow attacks (e.g., it only checks periodically) but KQ injection attacks are transient, so SBCFI may miss many of them. Moreover, SBCFI requires source code so it does not satisfy the inclusiveness requirement. IndexedHooks [19] provides an alternative implementation of CFI for the FreeBSD 8.0 kernel by replacing function addresses with indexes into read-only tables, and it is capable of supporting new device drivers. However, similar to SBCFI, IndexedHooks requires source code so it does not satisfy the inclusiveness requirement. PLCP [37] is a comprehensive defense against KQ injection attacks, capable of defeating both callback-into-malware and callback-into-libc attacks. However, PLCP does not satisfy the inclusiveness requirement due to its reliance on source code.

7   Conclusion

Kernel Queue (KQ) injection attacks are a significant problem. We test 125 real world malware attacks [2,4,10,11,14,16,18,23,27] and nine synthetic attacks to cover 20

KQs in the WRK. It is important for a solution to satisfy four requirements: efficiency (low overhead), effectiveness (precision and recall of attack detection), extensibility (accommodation of new device drivers) and inclusiveness (protection of device drivers with and without source code). Current kernel protection solutions have difficulties with simultaneous satisfaction of all four requirements.

We describe the KQguard approach to defend kernels against KQ injection attacks. The design of KQguard is independent of specific details of the attacks. Consequently, KQguard is able to defend against not only known attacks, but also anticipated future attacks on currently unscathed KQs. We evaluated the WRK implementation of KQguard, demonstrating the effectiveness and efficiency of KQguard by running a number of representative application benchmarks. In effectiveness, KQguard achieves very low false negatives (detecting all but two KQ injection attacks in 125 real world malware and nine synthetic attacks) and zero false positives (no false alarms after a proper training process). In performance, KQguard introduces a small overhead of about 100 microseconds per validation and up to about 5% slowdown for resource-intensive application benchmarks due to heap object tracking.

Acknowledgements.   We thank Chenghuai Lu for sharing his knowledge and experience on real-world malware and Open Malware for sharing their malware samples. We also thank the anonymous reviewers for their useful comments. This research is supported by Centre for Strategic Infocomm Technologies (CSIT), Singapore. The opinions in this paper do not necessarily represent CSIT, Singapore.

References

1. Abadi, M., Budiu, M., Erlingsson, U., Ligatti, J.: Control flow integrity. In: Proceedings of the 12th ACM CCS (2005)
2. Anselmi, D., et al.: Battling the Rustock Threat. Microsoft Security Intelligence Report, Special edn. (January 2010 through May 2011)
3. Baliga, A., Ganapathy, V., Iftode, L.: Automatic inference and enforcement of kernel data structure invariants. In: Proceedings of ACSAC 2008 (2008)
4. Boldewin, F.: Peacomm.C - Cracking the nutshell. Anti Rootkit, (September 2007), http://www.antirootkit.com/articles/eye-of-the-storm-worm/Peacomm-C-Cracking-the-nutshell.html
5. Brumley, D.: Invisible intruders: rootkits in practice. Login: 24 (September 1999)
6. Butler, J.: DKOM (Direct Kernel Object Manipulation), http://www.blackhat.com/presentations/win-usa-04/bh-win-04-butler.pdf
7. Carbone, M., Cui, W., Lu, L., Lee, W., Peinado, M., Jiang, X.: Mapping kernel objects to enable systematic integrity checking. In: Proceedings of ACM CCS 2009 (2009)
8. Castro, M., Costa, M., Harris, T.: Securing Software by Enforcing Dataflow Integrity. In: Proceedings of OSDI 2006 (2006)
9. Chiang, K., Lloyd, L.: A Case Study of the Rustock Rootkit and Spam Bot. In: Proceedings of the First Workshop on Hot Topics in Understanding Botnets, HotBots 2007 (2007)
10. Decker, A., Sancho, D., Kharouni, L., Goncharov, M., McArdle, R.: Pushdo/Cutwail: A Study of the Pushdo/Cutwail Botnet. Trend Micro Technical Report (May 2009)

11. Giuliani, M.: ZeroAccess – an advanced kernel mode rootkit, rev 1.2.,
    `http://www.prevxresearch.com/zeroaccess_analysis.pdf`
12. Hayes, B.: Who Goes There? An Introduction to On-Access Virus Scanning, Part One.
    Symantec Connect Community (2010)
13. Hoglund, G.: Kernel Object Hooking Rootkits (KOH Rootkits) (2006), `http://my.`
    `opera.com/330205811004483jash520/blog/show.dml/314125`
14. Kapoor, A., Mathur, R.: Predicting the future of stealth attacks. In: Virus Bulletin 2011,
    Barcelona (2011)
15. Kaspersky Lab. The Mystery of Duqu: Part One, `http://www.securelist.com/`
    `en/blog/208193182/The_Mystery_of_Duqu_Part_One`
16. Kaspersky Lab. The Mystery of Duqu: Part Five, `http://www.securelist.com/`
    `en/blog/606/The_Mystery_of_Duqu_Part_Five`
17. Kil, C., Sezer, E., Azab, A., Ning, P., Zhang, X.: Remote attestation to dynamic system
    properties: Towards providing complete system integrity evidence. In: Proceedings of the
    International Conference on Dependable Systems and Networks, DSN 2009 (2009)
18. Kwiatek, L., Litawa, S.: Yet another Rustock analysis... Virus Bulletin (August 2008)
19. Li, J., Wang, Z., Bletsch, T., Srinivasan, D., Grace, M., Jiang, X.: Comprehensive and Ef-
    ficient Protection of Kernel Control Data. IEEE Transactions on Information Forensics and
    Security 6(2) (June 2011)
20. Microsoft. Using Timer Objects,
    `http://msdn.microsoft.com/en-us/library/ff565561.aspx`
21. Microsoft. Checked Build of Windows, `http://msdn.microsoft.com/en-`
    `us/library/windows/hardware/ff543457%28v=vs.85%29.aspx`
22. Necula, G.C., McPeak, S., Rahul, S.P., Weimer, W.: CIL: Intermediate language and tools
    for analysis and transformation of C programs. In: Nigel Horspool, R. (ed.) CC 2002.
    LNCS, vol. 2304, pp. 213–228. Springer, Heidelberg (2002)
23. OffensiveComputing. Storm Worm Process Injection from the Windows Kernel,
    `http://offensivecomputing.net/papers/storm-3-9-2008.pdf`
24. Petroni, N., Fraser, T., Molina, J., Arbaugh, W.A.: Copilot—a coprocessor-based kernel
    runtime integrity monitor. In: Proceedings of the 13th USENIX Security Symposium
    (2004)
25. Petroni, N., Hicks, M.: Automated detection of persistent kernel control flow attacks. In:
    Proceedings of ACM CCS 2007 (2007)
26. Petroni, N., Fraser, T., Walters, A., Arbaugh, W.A.: An Architecture for Specification-
    Based Detection of Semantic Integrity Violations in Kernel Dynamic Data. In: Proceed-
    ings of the 15th USENIX Security Symposium (2006)
27. Prakash, C.: What makes the Rustocks tick! In: Proceedings of the 11th Association of an-
    ti-Virus Asia Researchers International Conference, AVAR 2008 (2008)
28. Riley, R., Jiang, X., Xu, D.: Guest-transparent prevention of kernel rootkits with VMM-
    Based memory shadowing. In: Lippmann, R., Kirda, E., Trachtenberg, A. (eds.) RAID
    2008. LNCS, vol. 5230, pp. 1–20. Springer, Heidelberg (2008)
29. Seshadri, A., Luk, M., Qu, N., Perrig, A.: SecVisor: A tiny hypervisor to provide lifetime
    kernel code integrity for commodity OSes. In: Proceedings of ACM SOSP 2007 (2007)
30. Sharif, M., Lee, W., Cui, W., Lanzi, A.: Secure in-VM monitoring using hardware virtua-
    lization. In: Proceedings of ACM CCS 2009 (2009)
31. Smalley, S., Vance, C., Salamon, W.: Implementing SELinux as a Linux Security Module.
    Technical Report. NSA (May 2002)
32. Designer, S.: Bugtraq: Getting around non-executable stack (and fix),
    `http://seclists.org/bugtraq/1997/Aug/63`

33. Super PI, http://www.superpi.net/
34. Symantec Connect Community. W32.Duqu: The Precursor to the Next Stuxnet (October 2011),
    http://www.symantec.com/connect/
    w32_duqu_precursor_next_stuxnet
35. Tran, M., Etheridge, M., Bletsch, T., Jiang, X., Freeh, V., Ning, P.: On the Expressiveness of Return-into-libc Attacks. In: Sommer, R., Balzarotti, D., Maier, G. (eds.) RAID 2011. LNCS, vol. 6961, pp. 121–141. Springer, Heidelberg (2011)
36. Wang, Z., Jiang, X., Cui, W., Ning, P.: Countering kernel rootkits with lightweight hook protection. In: Proceedings of ACM CCS 2009 (2009)
37. Wei, J., Pu, C.: Towards a General Defense against Kernel Queue Hooking Attacks. Elsevier Journal of Computers & Security 31(2), 176–191 (2012)
38. Wei, J., Zhu, F., Pu, C.: KQguard: Protecting Kernel Callback Queues. Florida International University Technical Report, TR-2012-SEC-03-01 (2012),
    http://www.cis.fiu.edu/~weijp/Jinpeng_Homepage_
    files/WRK_Tech_Report_03_12.pdf
39. Windows Research Kernel v1.2., https://www.facultyresourcecenter.com/
    curriculum/pfv.aspx?ID=7366&c1=en-us&c2=0
40. Top 20 Malware Families in 2010, http://blog.fireeye.com/research/
    2010/07/worlds_top_modern_malware.html
41. Top 10 Botnet Families in 2009, https://blog.damballa.com/archives/572

Run-Time Enforcement of Information-Flow Properties on Android
(Extended Abstract)

Limin Jia[1], Jassim Aljuraidan[1], Elli Fragkaki[1], Lujo Bauer[1], Michael Stroucken[1], Kazuhide Fukushima[2], Shinsaku Kiyomoto[2], and Yutaka Miyake[2]

[1] Carnegie Mellon University, Pittsburgh, USA
{liminjia,aljuraidan,elli,lbauer,mxs}@cmu.edu
[2] KDDI R&D Laboratories, Inc., Tokyo, Japan
{ka-fukushima,kiyomoto,miyake}@kddilabs.jp

Abstract. Recent years have seen a dramatic increase in the number and importance of mobile devices. The security properties that these devices provide to their applications, however, are inadequate to protect against many undesired behaviors. A broad class of such behaviors is violations of simple information-flow properties. This paper proposes an enforcement system that permits Android applications to be concisely annotated with information-flow policies, which the system enforces at run time. Information-flow constraints are enforced both between applications and between components within applications, aiding developers in implementing least privilege. We model our enforcement system in detail using a process calculus, and use the model to prove noninterference. Our system and model have a number of useful and novel features, including support for Android's single- and multiple-instance components, floating labels, declassification and endorsement capabilities, and support for legacy applications. We have developed a prototype of our system on Android 4.0.4 and tested it on a Nexus S phone, verifying that it can enforce practically useful policies that can be implemented with minimal modification to off-the-shelf applications.

1 Introduction

Recent years have seen a dramatic increase in the number and importance of smartphones and other mobile devices. The security properties that mobile operating systems provide to their applications, however, are inadequate to protect against many undesired behaviors, contributing to the rapid rise in malware targeting mobile devices [27,20].

To mitigate application misbehavior, mobile OSes like Android rely largely on strong isolation between applications and permission systems that limit communication between applications and access to sensitive APIs. Researchers have investigated these mechanisms, finding them vulnerable to application collusion [32,21], information-flow leaks [32,12], and privilege-escalation attacks [9,13]. Attempts to address these issues have produced tools for detecting information leaks [11,7,17], improvements to permission systems (e.g., [26,24]), as well as other mechanisms for restricting applications' access to data and resources (e.g., [5]).

J. Crampton, S. Jajodia, and K. Mayes (Eds.): ESORICS 2013, LNCS 8134, pp. 775–792, 2013.

Many common misbehaviors that are beyond the reach of Android's permission system are violations of simple information-flow properties. This is because Android's permission system supports only those policies that allow or deny communication or access to sensitive resources based on the (mostly static) permissions of the caller and callee. Once data has been sent from one application to another, the sender has relinquished all control over it.

Recent work on preventing undesired information flows on Android typically focuses on using a specific mechanism to enforce a pre-determined global policy [11,7]. Other works have developed more powerful mechanisms that track control flow and allow finer-grained control over communication and resource accesses [10,5]; these also typically lack a convenient policy language. Although a few formal analyses of Android's security architecture have provided some insight about its limitations [33], works that introduce more powerful mechanisms typically do not formally investigate the properties that those mechanisms exhibit.

This paper fills many of these gaps by proposing a DIFC-style enforcement system for Android that allows convenient, high-level specification of policy and has a well-understood theory, backed by a proof of noninterference. Building on techniques for controlling information flow in operating systems [19,36], our system permits policy to be specified via programmer- or system-defined labels applied to applications or application components. Enforcing information-flow policies at the level of application components is a practically interesting middle ground between process- (e.g., [19]) and instruction-level (e.g., [23]) enforcement, offering finer-grained control than process-level enforcement, but retaining most of its convenience. Labels specify a component's or application's secrecy level, integrity level, and declassification and endorsement capabilities. We also allow floating labels, which specify the minimal policy for a component, but permit multipurpose components (e.g., an editor) to be instantiated with labels derived from their callers (e.g., to prevent them from exfiltrating a caller's secrets).

We develop a detailed model of our enforcement system using a process calculus, using which we prove noninterference. The modeling—and the design of the system—is made particularly challenging by the desire to fully support key features of Android's programming model. Challenging features include single- and multiple-instance components and enforcement at two levels of abstraction—at the level of applications, which are strongly isolated from each other, and at the level of application components, which are not. Our formal analysis reveals that floating labels and the ability of single-instance components to make their labels stricter at run time—features that appear necessary to support practical scenarios—can, if not implemented carefully, easily compromise the noninterference property of the system.

Proving noninterference was also challenging because traditional ways in which information-flow systems are modeled in process calculi do not directly apply to Android: the security level of the channel through which an Android component communicates changes as the system executes. To model this, we enhance pi-calculus with a labeled process, $\ell[P]$, to associate each component with its run-time security level. The labeled process and the techniques for specifying noninterference can be applied to the modeling of other distributed systems, such as web browsers.

The contributions of this paper are the following:

1. We propose the first DIFC-style enforcement system for Android that allows convenient, high-level specification of policy and has a well-understood theory (§3).
2. We develop a faithful process-calculus model of Android's main programming abstractions and our system's enforcement mechanism (§4).
3. We define noninterference for our enforcement system and prove that it holds (§5), in the presence of dynamically changing security levels of components.
4. We implement our system on Android 4.0.4 and test it on a Nexus S phone; through a case study with minimally modified off-the-shelf applications, we show that our system can specify and enforce practically interesting policies (§6).

For space reasons, we omit many details, which appear in our technical report [1].

2   Background and Related Work

In this section we briefly introduce Android and review related work.

Android Overview. Android is a Linux-based OS; applications are written in Java and each executes in a separate Dalvik Virtual Machine (DVM) instance. Applications are composed of *components*, which come in four types: *activities* define a specific user interface (e.g., a dialog window); *services* run in the background and have no user interface; *broadcast receivers* listen for system-wide broadcasts; and *content providers* provide an SQL-like interface for storing data and sharing them between applications.

Activities, services, and broadcast receivers communicate via asynchronous messages called *intents*. If a recipient of an intent is not instantiated, the OS will create a new instance. The recipient of an intent is specified by its class name or by the name of an "action" to which multiple targets can subscribe. Any component can attempt to send a message to any other component. The OS mediates both cross- and intra-application communications via intents. Between applications, intents are the only (non-covert) channel for establishing communication. Components within an application can also communicate in other ways, such as via public static fields. Such communication is not mediated, and can be unreliable because components are short lived—Android can garbage collect all but the currently active component. Hence, although Android's abstractions do not prevent unmediated communication between components, the programming model discourages it. We will often write that a component *calls* another component in lieu of explaining that the communication is via an intent.

Android uses *permissions* to protect components and sensitive APIs: a component or API protected by a permission can be called only by applications that hold this permission. Permissions are strings (e.g., android.permission.INTERNET) defined by the system or declared by applications. Applications acquire permissions only at install time, with the user's consent. Additionally, content providers use *URI permissions* to dynamically grant and revoke access to their records, tables, and databases.

Related Work. We discuss two categories of most closely related work.

Information Flow. Enforcing information-flow policies has been an active area of research. Some develop novel information-flow type systems (cf. [31]) that enforce noninterference properties statically; others use run-time monitoring, or hybrid techniques (e.g., [8,29,22,2,3,16]). These works track information flow at a much finer level of granularity than ours; in contrast, the goals of our design included minimally impacting legacy code and run-time performance on Android.

Our approach is most similar to work on enforcing information-flow policies in operating systems [37,35,19]. There, each process is associated with a label. The components in our system can be viewed as processes in an operating system. However, most of these works do not prove any formal properties of their enforcement mechanisms. Krohn et al. [18] presented one of the first proofs of noninterference for practical DIFC-based operating systems. Our design is inspired by Flume [19], but has many differences. For instance, Flume does not support floating labels. In Android, as we show through examples, floating labels are of practical importance. Because Flume has no floating labels, a stronger noninterference can be proved for it than can be proved for our system: Flume's definition of noninterference is based on a stable failure model, a simulation-based definition. Our definition is trace-based, and does not capture information leaks due to a high process stalling.

A rich body of work has focused on noninterference in process calculi [14,30]. Recently, researchers have re-examined definitions of noninterference for reactive systems [4,28]. In these systems, each component waits in a loop to process input and produce one or more outputs (inputs to other components). These works propose new definitions of noninterference based on the (possibly infinite) streams produced by the system. Our definition of noninterference is weaker, since we only consider finite prefixes of traces. These reactive models are similar to ours, but do not consider shared state between components, and assume the inputs and outputs are the only way to communicate, which is not the case for Android. Further, to model the component-based Android architecture more faithfully, we extend pi-calculus with a label context construct, which also enables formal analysis of our enforcement mechanism in the presence of Android components' ability to change their labels at run time. To our knowledge, such dynamic behavior has rarely been dealt with in the context of process calculus.

Android Security. Android's permission system has been shown inadequate to protect against many attacks, including privilege-escalation attacks [9,13] and information leaks [11,32,6,12]. Closest to the goal of our work are projects such as TaintDroid [11] and AppFence [17], which automatically detect and prevent information leaks. They operate at a much finer granularity than our mechanism, tracking tainting at the level of variables, enforce fixed policies, and have not been formally analyzed.

Formal analyses of Android-related security issues and language-based approaches to solving them have received less attention. Shin et al. [33] developed a formal model to verify functional correctness properties of Android, which revealed a flaw in the permission naming scheme [34]. Our prior work proposed a set of enhancements to Android's permission system designed to enforce information-flow-like policies, for which some correctness properties were also formally proved [15]. The work described in this paper is different in several respects: we build on more well-understood theory of information flow; we support more flexible policies (e.g., in prior work it is not possible to specify that information should not leak to a component unless that component is protected by some permission); we make persistent state more explicit; and we formally model our enforcement system in much greater detail, thus providing much stronger correctness guarantees. The labeled context used in the modeling and the techniques developed for specifying noninterference in this paper can be applied to other systems, and we view the formalism as a main contribution of this paper. In comparison, the proofs in our prior work are customized for that specific system.

3   Enforcing Information-Flow Properties

We next describe a scenario that exemplifies the Android permission system's inability to implement many simple, practical policies (§3.1). We then discuss key aspects of our system and show it can specify (§3.2) and enforce (§3.3) richer policies.

3.1   Motivating Scenario

Suppose a system has the following applications: a *secret-file manager* for managing files such as lists of bank-account numbers; a general-purpose text *editor* and a *viewer* that can modify and display this content; and an *email application*. Because of their sensitive

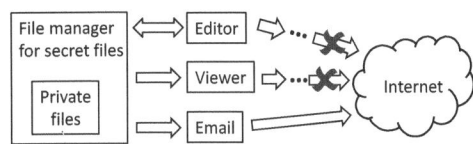

Fig. 1. A simple scenario that cannot be implemented using Android permissions

content, we want to prevent files managed by the secret-file manager from being inadvertently or maliciously sent over the Internet; this should be allowed only if the user explicitly requests it through the file manager. This scenario is shown in Figure 1.

The desired (information-flow) policy is representative of practical scenarios that Android currently does not support. In Android, one might attempt to prevent the editor or viewer from exfiltrating data by installing only viewers and editors that lack the Internet permission; these then could not send out secret data directly, but they could still do so via another application that has the Internet permission (e.g., the email client).

3.2   Key Design Choices

In general, the attacker model we consider is one where an application may try to exfiltrate data or access sensitive resources that it is not permitted to access, including by taking advantage of cooperating or buggy applications.

We now discuss the design of our system and explain how it can specify and enforce our desired example policy. We revisit the example more concretely in §6.

Enforcement Granularity. Traditionally, information-flow properties have been enforced either at instruction level (e.g., [23,16]) or at process level (e.g., [19]). Android's division of applications into components invites the exploration of an interesting middle ground between these two. Android applications are typically divided into a relatively few key components, e.g., an off-the-shelf file manager with which we experimented was comprised of five components. Hence, component-level specification would likely not be drastically more complex than application-level specification. This additional granularity, however, could enable policies to be more flexible and better protect applications (and components) from harm or misuse.

Unfortunately, enforcing purely component-level policies is difficult. The Android programming model strongly encourages the use of components as modules. In fact, the Android runtime may garbage collect any component that is not directly involved in interacting with the user; using Android's narrow interface for communication between components is the only reliable method of cross-component communication. However, neither Android nor Java prevent components *that belong to the same application* from exchanging information without using the Android interfaces, e.g., by directly writing to public static fields. Hence, Android's component-level abstractions are not robust enough to be used as an enforcement boundary; fully mediating interactions between components would require a lower-level enforcement mechanism. Although such enforcement is possible, e.g., with instruction-level information-flow tracking [23], implementation and integration with existing platforms and codebases is difficult and can cause substantial run-time overhead.

We pursue a hybrid approach. We allow policy specification at both component level and application level. Enforcement of component-level policies is best-effort: When programmers adhere to Android's programming conventions for implementing interactions between components, most potential policy violations that are the result of application compromise or common programmer errors will be prevented by the enforcement system. On the other hand, the components of a non-conformant application will be able to circumvent its component-level policy (but not its application-level policy, nor other applications' application- or component-level policy). Thus, component-level policies are a tool to help programmers to better police their own code and implement least privilege, and also act in concert with application-level policy to regulate cross-application interactions at a more fine-grained level. However, application-level policies are enforced strictly because Android provides strong isolation between applications.

Policy Specification via Labels. We use labels to express information-flow policies and track information flows at run time. A *label* is a triple (s, i, δ), where s is a set of *secrecy tags*, i a set of *integrity tags*, and δ a set of *declassification and endorsement capabilities*. For convenience, we also refer to s as a secrecy label and i as an integrity label; and to δ as the set of declassification capabilities, even though δ also includes endorsement capabilities. Labels are initially assigned to applications and components by developers in each application's manifest; we call these *static* labels. At run time, each application and component also has an *effective* label, which is derived by modifying the static label to account for declassification and endorsement. Additionally, secrecy labels s and integrity labels i can be declared as *floating*; we explain this below.

Labels as Sets of Tags. Implementing secrecy and integrity labels as sets of tags was motivated by the desire to help with backward compatibility with standard Android permissions. In Android, any application can declare new permissions at installation time. We similarly allow an application to declare new secrecy and integrity tags, which can then be used as part of its label. The lattice over labels, which is required for enforcement, does not need to be explicitly declared—this would be impractical if different applications declare their own tags. Rather, the lattice is defined by the subset relation between sets of tags. The permissions that legacy applications possess or require of their callers can be mapped to tags and labels. A more detailed discussion can be found in our technical report [1].

Declassification and Endorsement. The declassification capabilities, δ, specify the tags a component or application may remove from s or add to i. We make the declassification capabilities part of the label, because whether a component may declassify or endorse is a part of the security policy. Declaratively specifying declassification policy makes it easier to reason about and aids backward compatibility: declassification (or endorsement) that is permitted by policy can be applied to a legacy application or component automatically by the enforcement system when necessary for a call to succeed.

Returning to the example from §3.1: The secret-file manager application may be labeled with the policy ({FileSecret}, {FileWrite}, {-FileSecret}). Intuitively, the first element of this label conveys that the secret-file manager is tainted with the secret files' secrets (and no other secrets); the second element that the file manager has sufficient integrity to add or change the content of files; and the third element that the file manager is allowed to declassify. The file manager's effective label will initially be the same as this static label. If the file manager exercises its declassification capability -FileSecret, its effective label will become ({}, {FileWrite}, {-FileSecret}).

The complement to declassification and endorsement is *raising* a label. Any component may make its effective secrecy label more restrictive by adding tags to it, and its effective integrity label weaker by removing tags. After a component has finished executing code that required declassification or endorsement, it will typically raise its effective label to the state it was in prior to declassification or endorsement. Components without declassification capabilities can also raise their labels, but this is rarely likely to be useful, since raising a label can be undone only by declassifying or endorsing.

Floating Labels. Some components or applications, e.g., an editor, may have no secrets of their own but may want to be compatible with a wide range of other applications. In such cases, we can mark the secrecy or integrity label as *floating*, e.g., (F{}, F{}, {}), to indicate that the secrecy or integrity element of a component's effective label is inherited from its caller. The inheriting takes place only when a component is instantiated, i.e., when its effective label is first computed. Floating labels serve a very similar purpose to polymorphic labels in Jif [23].

In our example, the editor's static policy is (F{}, F{}, {}). If instantiated by the file manager, the editor's effective secrecy label becomes {FileSecret}, allowing the editor and the file manager to share data, but preventing the editor from calling any applications or APIs that have a secrecy label weaker than {FileSecret}. If the editor also had secrets to protect, we might give it the static label (F{EditorSecret}, F{}, {}). Then, the editor's effective label could be floated to ({EditorSecret, FileSecret}, {}, {}), but any instantiation of the editor would carry an effective secrecy label at least as restrictive as {EditorSecret}. Similarly, when the editor is instantiated by the file manager, its static integrity label F{} would yield an effective integrity label {FileWrite}, permitting the editor to save files, and preventing components without a FileWrite integrity tag from sending data to the editor.

Unlike secrecy and integrity labels, declassification capabilities cannot be changed dynamically; they are sufficiently powerful (and dangerous) that allowing them to be delegated is too likely to yield a poorly understood policy.

3.3   Enforcement Approach and Limitations

We described in §3.2 how to specify rich, practically useful policies in our system; we next outline how they are enforced. The crux of our enforcement system is a reference monitor that intercepts calls between components, which we build on top of Android's activity manager (§6). Much of its responsibility is maintaining the mapping from applications and components (and their instances) to their effective labels. Our formal model (§4) abstracts the bookkeeping responsibilities into a *label manager* and the purely enforcement duties into an *activity manager*. We next discuss how our reference monitor makes enforcement decisions and how our system handles persistent state.

Application- and Component-Level Enforcement.   When two components try to communicate via an intent, our reference monitor permits or denies the call by comparing the caller's and the callee's labels. When the caller and callee are part of the same application, the call is allowed only if the caller's effective secrecy label is a subset of the callee's and the caller's effective integrity label is a superset of the callee's. The comparison is more interesting when the caller and callee are in different applications. Then, a call is allowed if it is consistent with both component-level labels and application-level labels of the caller's and callee's applications.

If the callee component (and application) has a floating (static) label, the callee's effective integrity label is constructed as the union of its static integrity label and effective integrity labels of the caller and the caller's application. The effective secrecy label (and the callee's application's effective labels) is constructed similarly.

Declassification and endorsement change the effective labels of components and applications, and are permitted only when consistent with policy. For programmer convenience, the reference monitor will automatically declassify or endorse a caller component when this is necessary for a call to be permitted. We discuss this further in §6.

From the standpoint of policy enforcement, returns (from a callee to a caller), including those that report errors, are treated just like calls. As a consequence, a return may be prohibited by policy (and prevented) even if a call is allowed.

Much of the functionality of Android applications is accomplished by calling Android and Java APIs, e.g., for accessing files or opening sockets. We assign these APIs labels similarly as we would to components. For instance, sending data to sockets potentially allows information to be leaked to unknown third parties; therefore, we assign a label with an empty set of secrecy tags to the socket interface to prevent components with secrets from calling that API. We treat globally shared state, e.g., individual files, as components, and track their labels at run time.

Persistent State.   Multi-instance components intuitively pose little difficulty for enforcing information-flow policies: each call to such a component generates a fresh instance of the component bereft of any information-flow entanglements with other components.

More interesting are single-instance components, which can be targets for multiple calls from other components, and whose state persists between those calls. Interaction between single-instance components and the ability of components to raise their labels can at first seem to cause problems for information-flow enforcement.

Consider, for example, malicious components A and B that seek to communicate via a colluding single-instance component C. Suppose that A's static secrecy label is {FileSecret} and B's is {}, preventing direct communication from A to B; C's static secrecy label is {}. Component C, upon starting, sends B an intent, then raises its effective label to {FileSecret}. A sends the content of a secret file to C; their labels permit this. If the content of the secret file is "Attack," C exits; otherwise, C continues running. B calls C, then calls C again. If B receives two calls from C, then it learns that A's secret file is "Attack." C can only make the second call to B after exiting, which only happens when A's secret file is "Attack." The information leak arose because C changed its label by exiting. To prevent such scenarios (and to allow us to prove noninterference, which ensures that no similar scenarios remain undiscovered), raising a label must change not only a component's effective label, but also its static label.

Limitations. We do not address communication via covert channels, e.g., timing channels. Recent work has identified ways in which these may be mitigated by language-based techniques [38]; but such techniques are outside the scope of this paper. We also do not address the robustness of Android's abstractions: stronger component-level abstractions would permit robust, instead of best-effort, enforcement of information-flow policies within applications. Improving these abstractions, or complementing them by, e.g., static analysis, could thus bolster the efficacy of our approach.

Many security architectures are vulnerable to user error. On Android, a user can at installation time consent to giving an application more privileges than is wise. Our system does not address this; we design an infrastructure that supports rich, practically useful policies. Because our approach allows developers to better protect their applications, they may have an incentive to use it. However, we do not tackle the problem of preventing the user from making poor choices (e.g., about which applications to trust).

4   Process Calculus Model

We next show a process calculus encoding of Android applications and our enforcement mechanism. The full encoding captures the key features necessary to realistically model Android, such as single- and multi-instance components, persistent state within component instances, and shared state within an application. Many details that we omit for brevity can be found in our technical report [1].

4.1   Labels and Label Operations

Labels express information-flow policies and are used to track flows at run time. A *label* is composed of sets of *tags*. We assume a universe of secrecy tags $\mathcal{S}$ and integrity tags $\mathcal{I}$. Each secrecy tag in $\mathcal{S}$ denotes a specific kind of secret, e.g., contact information. Each integrity tag in $\mathcal{I}$ denotes a capability to access a security-sensitive resource.

Simple labels $\kappa ::= (\sigma, \iota)$ *Process labels* $K ::= (Q(\sigma), Q(\iota), \delta)$ where $Q = C$ or $Q = F$

A simple label κ is a pair of a set of secrecy tags σ drawn from $\mathcal{S}$ and a set of integrity tags ι drawn from $\mathcal{I}$. Simple labels form a lattice $(\mathcal{L}, \sqsubseteq)$, where $\mathcal{L}$ is a set of simple labels and $\sqsubseteq$ is a partial order over simple labels. Intuitively, the more secrecy tags a component has, the more secrets it can gather, and the fewer components it can send intents to. The fewer integrity labels a component has, the less trusted it is, and the fewer other components it can send intents to. Consequently, the partial order over simple labels is defined as follows: $(\sigma_1, \iota_1) \sqsubseteq (\sigma_2, \iota_2)$ iff $\sigma_1 \subseteq \sigma_2$, and $\iota_2 \subseteq \iota_1$

AM Erasure of label	$C(\sigma)^- = \sigma$	$F(\sigma)^- = \top$	$(Q(\sigma), Q(\iota), \delta)^- = ((Q(\sigma))^-, \iota)$
PF Erasure of label	$C(\iota)^* = \iota$	$F(\iota)^* = \top$	$(Q(\sigma), Q(\iota), \delta)^* = (\sigma, (Q(\iota))^*)$
Label Declassify	$(C(\sigma), C(\iota), \delta) \uplus_d \delta_1 =$		
	$(C(\sigma \backslash \{t | (-t) \in \delta_1\}), C(\iota \cup \{t | (+t) \in \delta_1\}), \delta)$		

Fig. 2. Selected label operations

Secrecy and integrity labels are annotated with C for concrete labels or F for floating labels. A process label K is composed of a secrecy label, an integrity label, and a set of declassification capabilities δ. An element in δ is of the form $-t_s$, where $t_s \in \mathcal{S}$, or $+t_i$, where $t_i \in \mathcal{I}$. A component with capability $-t_s$ can remove the tag t_s from its secrecy tags σ; a component that has $+t_i$ can add the tag t_i to its integrity tags ι.

We define operations on labels (Figure 2). An *AM erasure* function K^- is used by the activity manager to reduce process labels to simple labels that can easily be compared. This function removes the declassification capabilities from K, and reduces a floating secrecy label to the top secrecy label. This captures the idea that declassification capabilities are not relevant to label comparison, and that a callee's floating secrecy label will never cause a call to be denied. The *PF* erasure function K^* is used in defining noninterference, and is explained in §5. The declassification operation $K \uplus_d \delta_1$ removes from K the secrecy tags in δ_1, and adds the integrity tags in δ_1.

4.2 Preliminaries

We chose a process calculus as our modeling language because it captures the distributed, message-passing nature of Android's architecture. The Android runtime is the parallel composition of component instances, application instances, and the reference monitor, each modeled as a process.

The syntax of our modeling calculus, defined below, is based on π-calculus. We use $'|'$ for parallel composition, and reserve $|$ for BNF definitions. *aid* denotes an application identifier, and *cid* a component identifier, both drawn from a universe of identifiers. c denotes constant channel names. Specific interfaces provided by an application or component are denoted as $aid \cdot c$ and $aid \cdot cid \cdot c$.

The only major addition is the labeled process $\ell[P]$. Label contexts ℓ include the unique identifiers for applications (*aid*) and components (*cid*), channel names (c) that serve as identifiers for instances, and a pair (ℓ_1, ℓ_2) that represents the label of a component and its application. Bundling a label with a process aids noninterference proofs by making it easier to identify the labels associated with a process.

Names	$a ::= x \mid c \mid aid \cdot c \mid aid \cdot cid \cdot c$	*Proc*	$P ::= \mathbf{0} \mid \operatorname{in} a(x).P \mid \operatorname{in} a(\mathsf{patt}).P$
Label ctx	$\ell ::= aid \mid cid \mid c \mid (\ell_1, \ell_2)$		$\mid \operatorname{out} e_1(e_2).P \mid P_1 + P_2 \mid \nu x.P \mid {!}P$
Expr	$e ::= x \mid a \mid ctr\, e_1 \cdots e_k$		$\mid (P_1 {'|'} P_2) \mid \ell[P] \mid \operatorname{if} e \operatorname{then} P_1 \operatorname{else} P_2$
	$\mid (e_1, \cdots, e_n)$		$\mid \operatorname{case} e \operatorname{of}\{ctr_1 \boldsymbol{x}_1 \Rightarrow P_1 \dots$
			$\mid ctr_n \boldsymbol{x}_n \Rightarrow P_n\}$

We extend the standard definition of a process P with if statements, pattern-matching statements, and a pattern-matched input in $x(\mathsf{patt})$ that accepts only outputs that match with patt. These extensions can be encoded directly in π-calculus, but we add them as primitive constructors to simplify the representation of our model.

$$
\begin{aligned}
\textit{Application} \quad &App(\textit{aid}) &=& \quad \textit{aid}[!(\text{in } \textit{aid}\cdot c_L(c_{AI}).c_{AI}[\textit{AppBody}(\textit{aid}, c_{AI})])] \\
\textit{App body} \quad &\textit{AppBody}(\textit{aid}, c_{AI}) &=& \quad \nu c_{svL}.\nu c_{sv}.\text{out } c_{svL}(s_0).(SV(c_{svL}, c_{sv})\,'|' \\
& & & \quad (c_{AI}, \textit{cid}_1)[CP_1(\textit{aid}, \textit{cid}_1, c_{AI}, c_{sv})]\,'|'\cdots \\
& & & \quad '|'\,(c_{AI}, \textit{cid}_n)[CP_n(\textit{aid}, \textit{cid}_n, c_{AI}, c_{sv})]) \\
\textit{Component} \quad &CP(\textit{aid}, \textit{cid}, c_{AI}, c_{sv}) &=& \quad !(\text{in } \textit{aid}\cdot \textit{cid}\cdot c_{cT}(\_=c_{AI}, I, c_{nI}, c_{lock}, \textit{rt}). \\
& & & \quad (c_{AI}, c_{nI})[...\text{in } c_{nI}(I).\langle \text{out } I(\text{self})\rangle.A(...)]) \\
\textit{Comp body} \quad &A(\textit{cid}, \textit{aid}, I, c_{AI}, \textit{rt}, ...) &::=& \quad ...\mid \text{out } a_m(\text{call}_I, \textit{rt}, \textit{aid}, c_{AI}, \textit{cid}_{ce}, I)\,'|'\,A(...)
\end{aligned}
$$

Fig. 3. Partial encoding of applications and components

4.3 A Model of Android and Our Enforcement Architecture

We model as processes the three main constructs necessary to reason about our enforcement mechanism: application components, the activity manager, and the label manager. The activity manager is the part of the reference monitor that mediates calls and decides whether to allow a call based on the caller's and the callee's labels. The label manager is the part of the reference monitor that keeps track of the labels for each application, component, and application and component instance.

Life-cycles of Applications and Components and Their Label Map. A large part of the modeling effort is spent on ensuring that the process model faithfully reflects the life-cycles of applications and components, which is crucial to capturing information flows through persistent states within or across the life-cycles. The reference monitor maintains a label map Ξ, which reflects these life-cycles.

Android supports single- and multi-instance components. Once created, a single-instance component can receive multiple calls; the instance body shares state across all these calls. A fresh instance of a single-instance component is created only when the previous instance has exited and the component is called again. A component does not share state across its instantiations. For a multi-instance component, a new instance is created on every call to that component. An application is similar to a single-instance component, and all component instances within one application instance share state.

All calls are asynchronous; returning a result is treated as a call from the callee to the caller. When a component instance is processing a call, any additional intents sent to that instance (e.g., new intents sent to a single-instance component, or results being returned to a multi-instance component) are blocked until the processing has finished.

Encoding Applications and Components. A partial encoding of applications and components is shown in Figure 3. We delay explaining the label contexts $\ell[...]$ until §5—they are annotations that facilitate proofs, and have no run-time meaning.

We encode a recursive process using the ! operator. A process $!(\text{in } c(x).P)$ will run a new process P each time a message is sent to c. This models the creation of a run-time instance of an application or a component. In both cases, we call channel c the *launch channel* of P, and say that P is *launched* from c.

An application $App(\textit{aid})$ with ID $\textit{aid}$ is the parallel composition of a shared state SV and components $CP_i(\textit{aid}, \textit{cid}_i, c_{AI}, c_{sv})$. Each application has a designated launch channel $\textit{aid}\cdot c_L$. The channel c_{AI}, passed as an argument to the launch channel, serves as a unique identifier for an application instance. Once an application is launched, it

0     $AM_I = $ in $a_m($call$_I, kA_{cr}, kC_{cr}, rt, aid, c_{AI}, cid_{ce}, I)$.
1     $\nu c.$ out $t_m($lookUp, $cid_{ce}, c)$. in $c(s)$.
2   case s of ...
18 | M$(k_{ce}) \Rightarrow$ if $k_{cr}^- \sqsubseteq k_{ce}^-$
19   then $\nu c_{nI}.\nu c_{lock}.$ out $t_m($upd, $\{ (c_{nI}, (c_{lock}, k_{ce} \vartriangleleft kC_{cr}^-)), ...\})$.
20                $(aid, (c_{AI}, c_{nI}))[$out $aid \cdot aid \cdot c_{cT}(c_{AI}, I, c_{nI}, c_{lock}, rt)]$
21   else $\mathbf{0}$

Fig. 4. Partial encoding of the activity manager

launches the shared state. At this point, the application's components are ready to receive calls, and we call this application instance an *active launched* instance.

A component $CP(aid, cid, c_{AI}, c_{sv})$ is launched from a designated creation channel $aid \cdot cid \cdot c_{cT}$ after a message is received on that channel. The message is a tuple $(\_ = c_{AI}, I, c_{nI}, c_{lock}, rt)$ whose first argument $(\_)$ must match the current application instance (c_{AI}). I is the intent conveyed by the call. c_{nI} is the new intent channel for the component to process multiple calls. c_{lock} is the channel used to signal the reference monitor that this instance has finished processing the current intent and is ready to receive a new one. Finally, rt contains information about whether and on what channel to return a result. A components receives messages on the new intent channel, then proceeds to execute its body (denoted A).

The body of a component is defined in terms of the operations that a component can perform. It is parameterized over several variables, which are free in the body and are bound by outer-layer constructs. A component can use if and case statements, and read or write to the shared state in its application. It can also request from the label manager to change its (and its application's) label, and can call another component by sending a request to the activity manager. All of these operations are encoded using the process calculus. E.g., the call operation is encoded as out $a_m($call$_I, rt, ...)$, where a_m is the designated channel to send requests to the activity manager.

Label Manager and Activity Manager. The label manager T_M maintains the label map Ξ and processes calls to update the mapping through a designated channel t_m.

Android's activity manager mediates all intent-based communication between components, preventing any communication that is prohibited by policy. The top-level process of the activity manager is of the form: $A_M = !(AM_I + AM_E + AM_{EX} + AM_R)$. The activity manager processes four kinds of calls: AM_I processes calls between components within the same application; AM_E processes inter-application calls; AM_{EX} processes exits, and AM_R processes returns.

We show an example of processing calls between components within the same application (Figure 4): When the activity manager receives a request to send intent I to a component cid_{ce}, it asks the label manager for the callee's label. A possible reply is one that indicates that the callee is a multi-instance component (M(k_{ce})). The activity manager allows the call if the caller's label is lower than or equal to the callee's. If the call is permitted, a new callee instance is launched. To do this, the activity manager (1) generates a new-intent channel and a lock channel for the new instance; (2) updates the label mapping to record the label of this new active instance; and (3) sends a message containing the intent to the callee's creation channel.

Overall System. We assume that an initial process init bootstraps the system and launches the label manager with the static label map that reflects the labels of applications and components at install time, and then calls the first process with fixed labels: $S = T_M \mid A_M \mid App_1(aid_1) \mid ... \mid App_n(aid_n) \mid$ init.

5   Noninterference

To show that our system prevents information leakage, we prove a noninterference theorem. We use the simple label κ_L as the label of malicious components. We call components whose labels are not lower than or equal to κ_L *high components*, and others *low components*. Low components are considered potentially controlled by the attacker. We want to show that a system S that contains both high and low components behaves the same as a system composed of only the low components in S.

Choice between Trace and Bisimulation-based Equivalence. Processes P and Q are trace equivalent if for any trace generated by P, Q can generate an equivalent trace, and vice versa. Another commonly-used equivalence, barbed bisimulation, is stronger: it additionally requires those two processes to simulate each other after every τ transition.

Our decision about which notion of process equivalence to use for our noninterference definition is driven by the functionality required of the system so that practically reasonable policies can be implemented. As discussed earlier, floating labels are essential to implement practical applications in Android. However, allowing an application (or single-instance component) to have a floating label weakens our noninterference guarantees: In this case, we cannot hope to have bisimulation-based noninterference (see our technical report [1] for an example).

Rather than disallowing floating labels, we use a weaker, trace-equivalence-based definition of noninterference. This still provides substantial assurance of our system's ability to prevent disallowed information flows: noninterference would not hold if our system allowed: (1) explicit communication between high and low components; or (2) implicit leaks in the reference monitor's implementation, such as branching on data from a high component affecting low components differently depending on the branch.

High and Low Components. Most commonly seen techniques that classify high and low events based on a fixed security level assigned to each channel cannot be directly applied to the Android setting, as the components may declassify, raise, or instantiate their labels at run time. Whether an input (output) is a high or low event depends on the run-time label of the component that performs the input (output). Similarly, whether a component is considered high or low, also depends on its run-time label. This makes the definitions and proofs of noninterference more challenging. To capture such dynamic behavior, we introduce the label contexts of processes, and use the run-time mapping of these labels in the label manager to identify the high and low components in the system. The current label of a process can be computed from its label context and the label map Ξ. For a process with nested label contexts $\ell_1[...\ell_n[P]...]$, the innermost label ℓ_n reflects the current label of process P.

Our mechanism enforces information-flow policies at both component and application level; we consequently define noninterference to demonstrate the effectiveness of the enforcement at both levels. Next, we explain how to use the application ID, the component-level label, and the application-level label to decide whether a process is high or low for our noninterference theorem.

Without loss of generality, we pick one application whose components do not access the shared state of that application, and decide whether each of its components is high or low solely based on each component's label; all other applications, whose components may access the shared applicate state, are treated as high or low at the granularity of an application, based on their application-level labels. We write aid_c to denote the specific application whose components we treat as individual entities and disallow their accesses to the shared state.

Now we can define the procedure of deciding whether a process is high or low. We first define a binary relation $\sqsubseteq_{aid_c}$ between a label context $(aid, (\kappa_1, \kappa_2))$ and a simple label κ. We say that $(aid, (\kappa_1, \kappa_2))$ is lower than or equal to κ relative to aid_c. This relation compares the application-level label (κ_1) to κ_L if the application is not aid_c, and compares the component-level label (κ_2) to κ_L if the application ID is aid_c.

$(aid, (\kappa_1, \kappa_2)) \sqsubseteq_{aid_c} \kappa_L$ iff $\kappa_1 \sqsubseteq \kappa_L$ when $aid \neq aid_c$ and $\kappa_2 \sqsubseteq \kappa_L$ when $aid = aid_c$

Now, given the label map Ξ, let $\Xi\langle c\rangle$ denote the label associated with a channel name c in Ξ. We say that a process of the form $aid[...(c_{AI}, c_{nI})[P]...]$ is a low process with regard to κ_L if $(aid, ((\Xi\langle c_{AI}\rangle)^*, (\Xi\langle c_{nI}\rangle)^*)) \sqsubseteq_{aid_c} \kappa_L$; otherwise, it is a high process. Please see our tech report for a formal definition and additional details [1].

The function K^* (Figure 2) removes the declassification capabilities in K, and reduces floating integrity labels to the lowest integrity label (on the lattice). This is because a call to a component with a floating integrity label may result in a new instance with a low integrity label, a low event observable by the attacker; hence, a floating component should always be considered a low component.

Traces. The actions relevant to our noninterference definitions are intent calls received by an instance, since the only explicit communication between the malicious components (applications) and other parts of the system is via intents. We model intents I as channels. The encoding of components includes a special output action $\langle$out $I(\text{self})\rangle$ right after the component receives a new intent (Figure 3). This outputs to the intent channel the current labels of the component, denoted by self. Traces consist of these outputs (out $I(aid, (kA, kC))$), which contain information about both what the recipient has learned and the security label of the recipient. We call such an action low, if $(aid, (kA, kC)) \sqsubseteq_{aid_c} \kappa_L$, and high otherwise.

We restrict the transition system to force the activity manager's processing of a request—from receiving it to denying, allowing, or delaying the call—to be atomic. Some requests require that a lock be acquired; we assume the activity manager will only process a request if it can grab the lock. This matches reality, since the run-time monitor will process one call at a time, and the run-time monitor's internal transitions are not visible to the outside world. We write a small-step Android-specific transition as $S \xrightarrow{\alpha}_A S'$, and $S \xRightarrow{\tau}_A S'$ to denote zero or multiple τ transitions from S to S'.

Noninterference. We define the projection of traces $t|_{\kappa_L}^{aid_c}$, which removes all high actions from t. The function $\text{projT}(\Xi; \kappa_L; aid_c)$ removes from Ξ mappings from IDs or channel names to high labels. Similarly, $\text{proj}(P, \kappa_L, aid_c, \Xi)$ removes high components, applications, and instances from P. The resulting configuration is the low system that does not contain secrets or sensitive interfaces.

We say that a declassification step is *effective* with regard to κ_L and aid_c if the label of the declassified instance before the step is not lower than or equal to κ_L relative to aid_c, and the label after is. We call a sequence of transitions $\overset{t}{\Longrightarrow}_A$ *valid* if each step preserves the application-level label of aid_c (application aid_c cannot exit the application or raise its application-level label), and if it is not an effective declassification step.

We prove a noninterference theorem, which captures the requirements on both cross-application and intra-application communications. The theorem only concerns traces generated by valid transitions. Declassification can cause the low actions that follow it to differ between the two systems. However, we do allow arbitrary declassification prior to the projection of the high components. A component that declassified will be treated as a low component, and will afterward be denied any secrets unless further declassification occurs elsewhere. Changing aid_c's application-level label interferes with our attempt to view components in aid_c as independent entities.

Theorem 1 (Noninterference)
For all κ_L, for all applications $App(aid_1), \cdots , App(aid_n)$,
given a aid_c ($aid_c = aid_i$), $i = 1 \ldots n$, whose components do not access the shared variable,
let $S = A_M \,|\, T_M \,|\, App(aid_1), \cdots , App(aid_n)$ be the initial system configuration, $S \Longrightarrow_A S'$,
$S' = A_M \,|\, T_M \,|\, \nu c.(T_{MI}(\Xi) \,|\, AC(aid_c) \,|\, S'')$, where $T_{MI}(\Xi)$ is an instance of the tag manager, Ξ is the current label map, and $AC(aid_c)$ is an active launched instance of aid_c,
let $\Xi' = \mathsf{projT}(\Xi; \kappa_L; aid_c)$,
$S_L = A_M \,|\, T_M \,|\, \nu c'.(T_{MI}(\Xi') \,|\, \mathsf{proj}(AC(aid_c) \,|\, S'', \kappa_L, aid_c, \Xi'))$

   1. $\forall t$ s.t. $S' \overset{t}{\Longrightarrow}_A S_1$, and $\overset{t}{\Longrightarrow}_A$ is a sequence of valid transitions, $\exists t'$ s.t. $S_L \overset{t'}{\Longrightarrow}_A S_{L1}$, and $t|_{\kappa_L}^{\sqsubseteq aid_c} = t'|_{\kappa_L}^{\sqsubseteq aid_c}$

   2. $\forall t$ s.t. $S_L \overset{t}{\Longrightarrow}_A S_{L1}$, and $\overset{t}{\Longrightarrow}_A$ is a sequence of valid transitions, $\exists t'$ s.t. $S' \overset{t'}{\Longrightarrow}_A S_1$, and $t|_{\kappa_L}^{\sqsubseteq aid_c} = t'|_{\kappa_L}^{\sqsubseteq aid_c}$

6 Case Study and Implementation

We implemented our system on Android 4.0.4, using techniques similar to those used by other works [5,15]. Here we describe in detail our policy for the example scenario from §3.1, and briefly discuss our implementation.

Motivating Scenario Revisited. The policy of our example from §3.1 prohibits secret files from being leaked on the Internet, but allows them to be manipulated by applications and emailed at the user's behest. Files may be edited, but can be emailed only if the file manager itself calls the email application. We extend the example to also allow files to be emailed if they are first encrypted.

We first show how to implement this policy by assigning application-level labels. The file manager is labeled with ({FileSecret}, {FileWrite}, {-FileSecret}). The editor is labeled with (F{}, F{}, {}), to indicate that its effective secrecy and integrity labels are inherited from its caller, but it has no ability to declassify or endorse. The email application is labeled with ({ReadContacts, ... }, {}, {+Internet, ... }). The "..." signify additional secrecy tags and endorsement capabilities that enable the email application to read user accounts, cause the phone to vibrate, etc. To permit callers with low integrity, tags that permit access to resources (e.g., to vibration functionality) appear as endorsement capabilities rather than integrity tags. The encryption application is labeled with

(F{}, F{}, {-T, +WriteExternalStorage}). It has floating secrecy and integrity labels and can declassify all secrets it acquires, and so it must be trusted to correctly encrypt files and not reveal files without encrypting them. The encryption application also needs the WriteExternalStorage tag to be able to store encrypted data on the SD card.

This choice of labels achieves our desired functionality as follows: When called by the file manager, the editor's label floats to ({FileSecret}, {FileWrite}, {}). The editor cannot declassify FileSecret and so cannot leak the file; because it has FileWrite, it can save the file to secret storage. To email the file, a user invokes the email application via the file manager, which adds the file content to the intent that starts the email application, and removes FileSecret by declassifying before sending the intent. The file can also be released via the encryption application. If invoked by the file manager, the encryption application floats to ({FileSecret}, {FileWrite}, {-T,+WriteExternalStorage}); its capability to declassify any secret (-T) allows it to release data to any application.

We used component-level policy to restrict the file manager's declassification capability to only the component whose task is to send files to other applications. The duties of the components can be inferred from their names. We label the Main activity and the File provider with ({FileSecret}, {FileWrite}, {}) since they need to handle files; the Help and DirectoryInfo activities with ({FileSecret}, {}, {}); the Settings activity with ({FileSecret}, {FileWrite}) because it needs to return a result to the Main activity; and the Send activity with ({FileSecret}, {FileWrite}, {-FileSecret}).

Implementation. Our case study is fully implemented and has been tested on a Nexus S phone. We extended Android's manifest file syntax to support our labels. Run-time enforcement is via extensions to Android's activity manager, which already mediates communication between components. The biggest challenges were in providing more detailed information about callers to the activity manager and capturing low-level actions that it did not mediate; we do this via kernel-level middleware [25]. For backward compatibility, we mapped system-declared permissions to secrecy and integrity tags, and assigned label signatures to Android and Java APIs. Please see our technical report [1] for more detail about the implementation.

As part of booting the phone to the point where it can execute ordinary applications, over 50 built-in applications start running. Our case study used minimally modified off-the-shelf applications: Open Manager 2.1.8, Qute Text Editor 0.1, Android Privacy Guard 1.0.9, Email 2.3.4. Our system's implementation totaled ∼1200 lines of code: ∼650 in the reference monitor, 400 for bookkeeping, 100 for enhancing IPCs, and 50 for syntactic support for labels. We measured overheads on the order of 7.5 ms for the label checks incurred by each call[1]. Performance was sufficiently good for this overhead not to be observable to the user.

7   Conclusion

We propose the first DIFC-style enforcement system for Android that allows convenient, high-level specification of policy and has a well-understood theory. To support Android's programming model the system had to incorporate several features that

---

[1] Even averaging over hundreds of runs, variance between sets of runs was too great to report more precise measurements.

are new to information-flow systems, including multi-level policy specification and enforcement, floating labels, and support for persistent state and single-instance components. Our system strikes a balance between providing strong formal properties (noninterference) and applicability, achieving most of each. A prototype and case study validate the design of our system, and confirm that it can enforce practical policies on a Nexus S phone.

Acknowledgments. This research was supported in part by Department of the Navy grant N000141310156 issued by the Office of Naval Research; by NSF grants 0917047 and 1018211; by a gift from KDDI R&D Laboratories Inc.; and by Kuwait University.

References

1. Aljuraidan, J., Fragkaki, E., Bauer, L., Jia, L., Fukushima, K., Kiyomoto, S., Miyake, Y.: Run-time enforcement of information-flow properties on Android. Technical Report CMU-CyLab-12-015, Carnegie Mellon University (2012)
2. Arden, O., George, M.D., Liu, J., Vikram, K., Askarov, A., Myers, A.C.: Sharing mobile code securely with information flow control. In: Proc. IEEE S&P (2012)
3. Austin, T.H., Flanagan, C.: Multiple facets for dynamic information flow. In: Proc. POPL (2012)
4. Bohannon, A., Pierce, B.C., Sjöberg, V., Weirich, S., Zdancewic, S.: Reactive noninterference. In: Proc. CCS (2009)
5. Bugiel, S., Davi, L., Dmitrienko, A., Fischer, T., Sadeghi, A.R., Shastry, B.: Towards taming privilege-escalation attacks on Android. In: Proc. NDSS (2012)
6. Chaudhuri, A.: Language-based security on Android. In: Proc. PLAS (2009)
7. Chin, E., Felt, A.P., Greenwood, K., Wagner, D.: Analyzing inter-application communication in Android. In: Proc. MobiSys (2011)
8. Chudnov, A., Naumann, D.A.: Information flow monitor inlining. In: Proc. IEEE CSF (2010)
9. Davi, L., Dmitrienko, A., Sadeghi, A.-R., Winandy, M.: Privilege escalation attacks on Android. In: Burmester, M., Tsudik, G., Magliveras, S., Ilić, I. (eds.) ISC 2010. LNCS, vol. 6531, pp. 346–360. Springer, Heidelberg (2011)
10. Dietz, M., Shekhar, S., Pisetsky, Y., Shu, A., Wallach, D.S.: Quire: Lightweight provenance for smart phone operating systems. In: Proc. USENIX Sec. (2011)
11. Enck, W., Gilbert, P., gon Chun, B., Cox, L.P., Jung, J., McDaniel, P., Sheth, A.N.: TaintDroid: An information-flow tracking system for realtime privacy monitoring on smartphones. In: Proc. OSDI (2010)
12. Enck, W., Octeau, D., McDaniel, P., Chaudhuri, S.: A study of Android application security. In: Proc. USENIX Sec. (2011)
13. Felt, A.P., Wang, H., Moshchuk, A., Hanna, S., Chin, E.: Permission re-delegation: Attacks and defenses. In: Proc. USENIX Sec. (2011)
14. Focardi, R., Gorrieri, R.: A classification of security properties for process algebras. J. of Comput. Secur. 3, 5–33 (1994)
15. Fragkaki, E., Bauer, L., Jia, L., Swasey, D.: Modeling and enhancing android's permission system. In: Foresti, S., Yung, M., Martinelli, F. (eds.) ESORICS 2012. LNCS, vol. 7459, pp. 1–18. Springer, Heidelberg (2012)
16. Hedin, D., Sabelfeld, A.: Information-flow security for a core of JavaScript. In: Proc. IEEE CSF (2012)

17. Hornyack, P., Han, S., Jung, J., Schechter, S., Wetherall, D.: These aren't the droids you're looking for: Retrofitting Android to protect data from imperious applications. In: Proc. CCS (2011)
18. Krohn, M., Tromer, E.: Noninterference for a practical DIFC-based operating system. In: Proc. IEEE S&P (2009)
19. Krohn, M., Yip, A., Brodsky, M., Cliffer, N., Kaashoek, M.F., Kohler, E., Morris, R.: Information flow control for standard OS abstractions. In: Proc. SOSP (2007)
20. Loftus, J.: DefCon dings reveal Google product security risks (2011), `http://gizmodo.com/5828478/` (accessed July 10, 2012)
21. Marforio, C., Francillon, A., Čapkun, S.: Application collusion attack on the permission-based security model and its implications for modern smartphone systems. Technical Report 724, ETH Zurich (April 2011)
22. Moore, S., Chong, S.: Static analysis for efficient hybrid information-flow control. In: Proc. IEEE CSF (2011)
23. Myers, A.C.: Practical mostly-static information flow control. In: Proc. POPL (1999)
24. Nauman, M., Khan, S., Zhang, X.: Apex: extending Android permission model and enforcement with user-defined runtime constraints. In: Proc. ASIACCS (2010)
25. NTT Data Corporation: TOMOYO Linux (2012), `http://tomoyo.sourceforge.jp/` (accessed April 10, 2012)
26. Ongtang, M., McLaughlin, S.E., Enck, W., McDaniel, P.D.: Semantically rich application-centric security in Android. In: Proc. ACSAC (2009)
27. Passeri, P.: One year of Android malware (full list) (2011), `http://hackmageddon.com/2011/08/11/one-year-of-android-malware-full-list/` (accessed July 10, 2012)
28. Rafnsson, W., Sabelfeld, A.: Limiting information leakage in event-based communication. In: Proc. PLAS (2011)
29. Russo, A., Sabelfeld, A.: Dynamic vs. static flow-sensitive security analysis. In: Proc. IEEE CSF (2010)
30. Ryan, P.Y.A., Schneider, S.A.: Process algebra and non-interference. J. Comput. Secur. 9(1-2) (2001)
31. Sabelfeld, A., Myers, A.C.: Language-based information-flow security. IEEE Journal Sel. Area. Comm. 21(1), 5–19 (2003)
32. Schlegel, R., Zhang, K., Zhou, X., Intwala, M., Kapadia, A., Wang, X.: Soundcomber: A stealthy and context-aware sound trojan for smartphones. In: Proc. NDSS (2011)
33. Shin, W., Kiyomoto, S., Fukushima, K., Tanaka, T.: A formal model to analyze the permission authorization and enforcement in the Android framework. In: Proc. SocialCom/PASSAT (2010)
34. Shin, W., Kwak, S., Kiyomoto, S., Fukushima, K., Tanaka, T.: A small but non-negligible flaw in the Android permission scheme. In: Proc. POLICY (2010)
35. Yip, A., Wang, X., Zeldovich, N., Kaashoek, M.F.: Improving application security with data flow assertions. In: Proc. SOSP (2009)
36. Zeldovich, N., Boyd-Wickizer, S., Kohler, E., Mazières, D.: Making information flow explicit in HiStar. In: Proc. OSDI (2006)
37. Zeldovich, N., Boyd-Wickizer, S., Mazières, D.: Securing distributed systems with information flow control. In: Proc. NSDI (2008)
38. Zhang, D., Askarov, A., Myers, A.C.: Language-based control and mitigation of timing channels. In: Proc. PLDI (2012)

Author Index